AMERICAN DECADES
PRIMARY SOURCES

1960–1969

AMERICAN DECADES
PRIMARY SOURCES
1960-1969

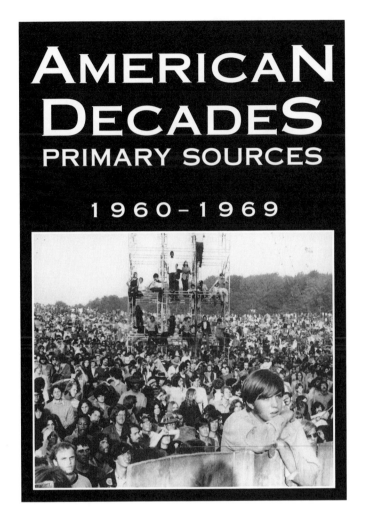

CYNTHIA ROSE, PROJECT EDITOR

GALE®

THOMSON

GALE

Detroit • New York • San Diego • San Francisco • Cleveland • New Haven, Conn. • Waterville, Maine • London • Munich

American Decades Primary Sources, 1960–1969

Project Editor
Cynthia Rose

Editorial
Jason M. Everett, Rachel J. Kain, Pamela A. Dear, Andrew C. Claps, Thomas Carson, Kathleen Droste, Christy Justice, Lynn U. Koch, Michael D. Lesniak, Nancy Matuszak, John F. McCoy, Michael Reade, Rebecca Parks, Mark Mikula, Polly A. Rapp, Mark Springer

Data Capture
Civie A. Green, Beverly Jendrowski, Gwendolyn S. Tucker

Permissions
Margaret Abendroth, Margaret A. Chamberlain, Lori Hines, Jacqueline Key, Mari Masalin-Cooper, William Sampson, Shalice Shah-Caldwell, Kim Smilay, Sheila Spencer, Ann Taylor

Indexing Services
Lynne Maday, John Magee

Imaging and Multimedia
Randy Bassett, Dean Dauphinais, Leitha Etheridge-Sims, Mary K. Grimes, Lezlie Light, Daniel W. Newell, David G. Oblender, Christine O'Bryan, Kelly A. Quin, Luke A. Rademacher, Denay Wilding, Robyn V. Young

Product Design
Michelle DiMercurio

Composition and Electronic Prepress
Evi Seoud

Manufacturing
Rita Wimberley

For permission to use material from this product, submit your request via Web at http://gale-edit.com/permissions, or you may download our Permissions Request form and submit your request by fax or mail to:

Permissions Department
The Gale Group, Inc.
27500 Drake Rd.
Farmington Hills, MI 48331-3535
Permissions Hotline:
248-699-8006 or 800-877-4253, ext. 8006
Fax: 248-699-8074 or 800-762-4058

Cover photographs reproduced by permission of Amalie Rothschild/Bettmann/Corbis (The crowd at the Woodstock music festival, background), Bettmann/Corbis (Dr. Kathryn Clarenbach and Betty Friedan, center; President John F. Kennedy, spine; Olympian Wilma Rudolph, right), and U.S. National Aeronautics and Space Administration (Edward "Buzz" Aldrin, left).

LIBRARY OF CONGRESS CATALOGING-IN-PUBLICATION DATA

American decades primary sources / edited by Cynthia Rose.
　　v. cm.
Includes bibliographical references and index.
Contents: [1] 1900-1909 — [2] 1910-1919 — [3] 1920-1929 — [4] 1930-1939 — [5] 1940-1949 — [6] 1950-1959 — [7] 1960-1969 — [8] 1970-1979 — [9] 1980-1989 — [10] 1990-1999.
　　ISBN 0-7876-6587-8 (set : hardcover : alk. paper) — ISBN 0-7876-6588-6 (v. 1 : hardcover : alk. paper) — ISBN 0-7876-6589-4 (v. 2 : hardcover : alk. paper) — ISBN 0-7876-6590-8 (v. 3 : hardcover : alk. paper) — ISBN 0-7876-6591-6 (v. 4 : hardcover : alk. paper) — ISBN 0-7876-6592-4 (v. 5 : hardcover : alk. paper) — ISBN 0-7876-6593-2 (v. 6 : hardcover : alk. paper) — ISBN 0-7876-6594-0 (v. 7 : hardcover : alk. paper) — ISBN 0-7876-6595-9 (v. 8 : hardcover : alk. paper) — ISBN 0-7876-6596-7 (v. 9 : hardcover : alk. paper) — ISBN 0-7876-6597-5 (v. 10 : hardcover : alk. paper)
　　1. United States—Civilization—20th century—Sources. I. Rose, Cynthia.
E169.1.A471977 2004
973.91—dc21

2002008155

Contents

Entries are arranged in chronological order by date of primary source. For entries with one primary source, the entry title is the primary source title. Entries with more than one primary source have an overall entry title, followed by the titles of the primary sources.

Fashion and Design

Government and Politics

The Media

Medicine and Health

Sports

Advisors and Contributors

Advisors

CARL A. ANTONUCCI, JR. has spent the past ten years as a reference librarian at various colleges and universities. Currently director of library services at Capital Community College, he holds two master's degrees and is a doctoral candidate at Providence College. He particularly enjoys researching Rhode Island political history during the 1960's and 1970's.

KATHY ARSENAULT is the dean of library at the University of South Florida, St. Petersburg's Poynter Library. She holds a master's degree in library science. She has written numerous book reviews for *Library Journal,* and has published articles in such publications as the *Journal of the Florida Medical Association,* and *Collection Management.*

JAMES RETTIG holds two master's degrees. He has written numerous articles and has edited *Distinguished Classics of Reference Publishing* (1992). University librarian at the University of Richmond, he is the recipient of three American Library Association awards: the Isadore Gibert Mudge Citation (1988), the G.K. Hall Award for Library Literature (1993), and the Louis Shores-Oryx Press Award (1995).

HILDA K. WEISBURG is the head library media specialist at Morristown High School Library and specializes in building school library media programs. She has several publications to her credit, including: *The School Librarians Workshop, Puzzles, Patterns, and Problem Solving: Creative Connections to Critical Thinking,* and *Learning, Linking & Critical Thinking: Information Strategies for the K-12 Library Media Curriculum.*

Contributors

EUGENIA F. BELL is a freelance editor and publication manager who holds a bachelor's in philosophy from Pennsylvania State University. She spent four years as an editor of architecture and design books for the Princeton Architectural Press before working for a year as a publications manager for the Walker Art Center in Minneapolis, Minnesota. She is the author of *The Chapel at Ronchamp* (1999).

Chapter: Fashion and Design.

SONIA G. BENSON is a self-employed writer and editor based in San Juan Capistrano, California. Prior to beginning her freelance career, she spent nine years at Gale Research in positions ranging from associate editor to managing editor. She is the author of the *Korean War Reference Library,* and has edited numerous books.

Chapter: Fashion and Design.

TIMOTHY G. BORDEN has contributed to such publications as *History Behind the Headlines, Michigan Historical Review, Polish American Studies,* and *Northwest*

Ohio Quarterly. He also serves as reader/referee of Notre Dame University at Lebanon's *Palma Journal.*
Chapter: Lifestyles and Social Trends.

PETER J. CAPRIOGLIO is a professor emeritus at Middlesex Community College, where he taught social sciences for thirty years prior to his retirement. He has a master's in sociology, and he is currently at work on a book entitled, *The Glory of God's Religions: A Beginner's Guide to Exploring the Beauty of the World's Faiths.*
Chapter: Religion.

PAUL G. CONNORS earned a doctorate in American history from Loyola University in Chicago. He has a strong interest in Great Lakes maritime history, and has contributed the article "Beaver Island Ice Walkers" to *Michigan History.* He has worked for the Michigan Legislative Service Bureau as a research analyst since 1996.
Chapter: Government and Politics. *Essay:* Using Primary Sources. *Chronologies:* Selected World Events Outside the United States; Government and Politics, Sports Chapters. *General Resources:* General, Government and Politics, Sports.

CHRISTOPHER CUMO is a staff writer for *The Adjunct Advocate Magazine.* Formerly an adjunct professor of history at Walsh University, he has written two books, *A History of the Ohio Agricultural Experiment Station, 1882–1997* and *Seeds of Change,* and has contributed to numerous scholarly journals. He holds a doctorate in history from the University of Akron.
Chapters: Medicine and Health, Science and Technology. *Chapter Chronologies and General Resources:* Business and the Economy, Education, Medicine and Health, Science and Technology.

JENNIFER HELLER holds bachelor's degrees in religious studies and English education, as well as a master's in curriculum and instruction, all from the University of Kansas. She has been an adjunct associate professor at Johnson County Community College in Kansas since 1998. She is currently at work on a dissertation on contemporary women's religious literature.
Chapter Chronology and General Resources: Religion.

DAVID M. HOLFORD has worked as an adjunct instructor at Ohio University, Park College, and Columbus State Community College; education curator for the Ohio Historical Society; and held editorial positions at Glencoe/McGraw Hill and Holt, Rinehart, and Winston. He also holds a doctorate in history from Ohio State University. A freelance writer/editor

since 1996, he has published *Herbert Hoover* (1999) and *Abraham Lincoln and the Emancipation Proclamation (2002).*
Chapter Chronologies and General Resources: Lifestyles and Social Trends, The Media.

MILLIE JACKSON is an associate librarian at Grand Valley State University in Allendale, Michigan. She has previously worked as an English teacher and as the special collections librarian at Oklahoma State University. Dr. Jackson's dissertation on ladies's library associations in Michigan won the American Library Association's Phyllis Dain Library History Dissertation Award in 2001.
Chapters: The Arts, Education.

JONATHAN KOLKEY is the author of *The New Right, 1960–1968* and *Germany on the March: A Reinterpretation of War and Domestic Politics Over the Past Two Centuries.* He earned a doctorate in history from UCLA. Currently an instructor at West Los Angeles College, he is at work on *The Decision For War,* a comprehensive historical study of the politics and decision-making process behind war. Dr. Kolkey lives in Playa Del Rey, California.
Chapter: Business and the Economy.

SCOTT A. MERRIMAN currently works as a part-time instructor at the University of Kentucky and is finishing his doctoral dissertation on Espionage and Sedition Acts in the Sixth Court of Appeals. He has contributed to *The History Highway* and *History.edu,* among others. Scott is a resident of Lexington, Kentucky.
Chapter: Law and Justice.

JOSEPH R. PHELAN is a scholar in residence at Strayer University in Washington, D.C. Previously he served as director for the Office of the Bicentennial of the U.S. Constitution at the National Endowment for the Humanities and has taught at the University of Toronto, the Catholic University of America, and the Art Gallery of Ontario.
Chapter: The Media.

LORNA BIDDLE RINEAR is the editor and co-author of *The Complete Idiot's Guide to Women's History.* A Ph.D. candidate at Rutger's University, she holds a bachelor's from Wellesley College and a master's degree from Boston College. She resides in Bellingham, Massachusetts.
Chapter Chronologies and General Resources: The Arts, Fashion and Design.

MARY HERTZ SCARBROUGH earned both her bachelor's in English and German and her J.D. from the University of South Dakota. Prior to becoming a free-lance writer in 1996, she worked as a law clerk in the Federal District Court for the District of South Dakota and as legal counsel for the Immigration and Naturalization Service. She lives in Storm Lake, Iowa.

Chapter Chronology and General Resources: Law and Justice.

WILLIAM J. THOMPSON has been a history instructor at the Community College of Baltimore County, Catonsville, since 1996. He received both his bachelor's and master's degrees in history from the University of Maryland, Baltimore County. He has written for the *Encyclopedia of African American Civil Rights,* the *Washington Post,* and the *Baltimore Sun.*

Chapter: Sports.

ACKNOWLEDGMENTS

Following is a list of the copyright holders who have granted us permission to reproduce material in this volume of American Decades Primary Sources. *Every effort has been made to trace copyright, but if omissions have been made, please let us know.*

Copyrighted material in *American Decades Primary Sources, 1960–1969*, was reproduced from the following periodicals: *American Antiquity: A Quarterly Review of American Archaeology*, v. 33, 1968. Reproduced by permission. — *The Black Scholar*, v. 1, June, 1970. Copyright 1970 by The Black Scholar. Reproduced by permission. — *Dance Magazine*, v. 44, March, 1970. Copyright 1970 by Danad Publishing Company, Inc. Reprinted with the permission of Dance Magazine, Inc. —Don't Mourn, Organize: SDS Guide to Community Organizing, 1968. — *El Grito*, Summer, 1968 for "The Mexican-American and the Church" by Cesar E. Chavez. Reproduced by permission of the author. — *Encounter*, June, 1967 for "A Dialogue" by Marshall McLuhan and Gerald Emanuel Stearn. Reproduced by permission of the Estate of Gerald Emanuel Stearn. — *Harper's Magazine*, v. 220, April, 1960; v. 234, March, 1967. Copyright © 1960, 1967 by Harper's Magazine. Renewed 1988. All rights reserved. Reproduced by permission. — *JAMA*, v. 188, June 29, 1964; v. 193, September, 1965. Reproduced by permission. — *Life*, December 6, 1963. © 1963; October 21, 1966. © 1963, renewed 1991; © 1966 by The Time Inc. Magazine Company. — *Los Angeles Times*, April 4, 1975. Copyright, 1975, Los Angeles Times. Reproduced by permission. — *The Nation*, v. 198, February 10, 1964. © 1964, renewed 1992 The Nation magazine/ The Nation Company, Inc. Reproduced by permission. — *National Geographic*, v. 118, August, 1960. © 1960. Renewed 1988 by National Geographic Society. Reproduced by permission. — *New York Times*,

February 11, 1962; September 2, 1962; January 12, 1964; November 20, 1966; October 20, 1968; January 5, 1969; April 3, 1969; July 21, 1969; January 1, 1971; January 31, 1988. Copyright © 1962, renewed 1990; Copyright © 1962, renewed 1990; Copyright © 1964, renewed 1992; Copyright © 1966; Copyright © 1968; Copyright © 1969; Copyright © 1969; Copyright © 1969; Copyright © 1971; Copyright © 1988 by The New York Times Company. Reproduced by permission. — *New Yorker*, v. 36, October 22, 1960 for "Our Far-Flung Correspondents: Hub Kids Bids Adiue" by John Updike. © 1960 by The New Yorker Magazine, Inc. Renewed 1988. All rights reserved. — *Newsweek*, July 7, 1969; September 26, 2000. © 1969, 2000 Newsweek, Inc. All rights reserved. Reproduced by permission. — *P/A News Report*, v. 46, 1965. — *Ramparts*, v. 2, Christmas, 1963. Reproduced by permission. — *Science*, v. 158, December, 1967. Copyright 1967 by AAAS. Reproduced by permission. — *Scientific American*, v. 203, September, 1960; v. 217, December, 1967. © 1960. Renewed 1988; Copyright © 1967 by Scientific American, Inc. All rights reserved. Reproduced by permission. — *Sports Illustrated*, v. 15, October 2, 1961; April 25, 1966. © 1961, renewed 1989; © 1966 by Time, Inc./ November 28, 1966. Reproduced by permission. — *Time*, v. 93, April 11, 1969. © 1969 Time, Inc. Reproduced by permission. — *TV Guide*, February 1–8, 1964 for "Television and the Feminine Mystique" by Betty Friedan; December 14, 1968 for "Chicago: A Post-Mortem" by Reuven Frank. Reproduced by permission of the respective authors. — *U.S. News & World*

Report, v. 56, April 27, 1964; v. 56, May 25, 1964; v. 60, April 25, 1966; v. 67, November 17, 1969; v. 67, December 18, 1969. Copyright © 1964, renewed 1992; Copyright © 1964, renewed 1992; Copyright © 1966; Copyright © 1969; Copyright © 1969 by U.S. News & World Report, Inc. All rights reserved. Reproduced by permission. — *Washington Post*, January 13, 1969. © 1969 Washington Post Book World Service/Washington Post Writers Group. Reproduced by permission.

Copyrighted material in *American Decades Primary Sources, 1960–1969*, was reproduced from the following books: Abdul-Jabbar, Kareem and Peter Knobler. From *Giant Steps*. Bantam Books, 1983. Copyright © 1983 by Kareem Abdul-Jabbar. All rights reserved. Reproduced by permission of Bantam Books, a division of Random House, Inc. —Aldrin, Buzz and Malcolm McConnell. From *Men From Earth*. Bantam Books, 1989. Copyright © 1989 by Research & Engineering Consultants, Inc. and Malcolm McConnell. All rights reserved. Reproduced by permission of Bantam Books, a division of Random House, Inc. —Ali, Muhammad with Richard Durham. From *The Greatest: My Own Story*. Random House, 1975. Copyright © 1975 by Muhammad Ali, Herbert Muhammad, Richard Durham. All rights reserved. —Auerbach, Arnold Red and Paul Sann. From *Red Auerbach: Winning the Hard Way*. Little, Brown and Company, 1966. Copyright © 1966 by Arnold Red Auerbach Family Trust. All rights reserved. —Bethe, H.A. From *Nobel Lectures, Volume Physics, 1901–1970*. Elsevier Publishing Company, 1970. Copyright © 1970 by The Nobel Foundation. All rights reserved. Reproduced by permission of the author. —Bly, Robert. From *The Light Around the Body*. Harper & Row, Publishers, 1967. Copyright © 1959, 1960, 1961, 1962, 1963, 1964, 1965, 1966, 1967 by Robert Bly. All rights reserved. Reproduced by permission of HarperCollins Publishers. —Boyd, Malcolm. From *Are You Running With Me, Jesus?* Holt, Rinehart and Winston, 1965. Copyright © 1965 by Malcolm Boyd. All rights reserved. Reproduced by permission of the author. —Breslin, Jimmy. From *Can't Anybody Here Play This Game?* Ballantine Books, 1970. Revised Edition. Copyright © 1970 by James Breslin. All rights reserved. Reproduced by permission of the author. —Brown, Helen Gurley. From *Sex and the New Single Girl*. Bernard Geis Associates, 1970. Copyright © 1970 by Helen Gurley Brown. All rights reserved. Reproduced by permission of the author. —Bruner, Jerome S. From *On Knowing: Essays for the Left Hand*. The Belknap Press of Harvard University Press, 1962. Copyright © 1962, renewed 1979 by the President and Fellows of Harvard College. All rights reserved. Reproduced by permission. —Bugliosi, Vincent with Curt Gentry. From *Helter Skelter: The True Story of the Manson Murders*. W.W. Norton & Company, Inc., 1974. Copyright © 1974 by Curt Gentry and Vincent Bugliosi. All rights reserved. Reproduced by permission. —Carols, John with CD Jackson, Jr. From *Why? The Biography of John Carols*. CD Books, 2000. Copyright © 2000 by CD Jackson. All rights reserved. Reproduced by permission of CD Jackson, Jr. —Carson, Rachel. From *Silent Spring*. Houghton Mifflin Company, 1962. Copyright © 1962 by Rachel L. Carson. Renewed 1990, by Roger Christic. All rights reserved. Reproduced by permission. —Cassels, Louis. From *What's the Difference? A Comparison of the Faiths Men Live By*. Doubleday & Company, Inc. 1965. Copyright © 1965 by Doubleday, a division of Random House, Inc. Reproduced by permission of the publisher. —Chall, Jeanne S. From *Learning to Read: The Great Debate*. McGraw-Hill Book Company, 1967. Copyright © 1967 by McGraw Hill, Inc. All rights reserved. —Chamberlain, Wilt and David Shaw. From *Wilt: Just Like Any Other 7-Foot Black Millionaire Who Lives Next Door*. Macmillan Publishing Co., Inc., 1973. Copyright © 1973 by Wilt Chamberlain and David Shaw. All rights reserved. Reproduced by permission of Macmillan Publishing Co, Inc., an imprint of Simon & Schuster Macmillan. —Cleaver, Eldridge. From *Soul on Ice*. Dell Publishing, 1992. Copyright © 1968, 1991 by Eldridge Cleaver. All rights reserved. Reproduced by permission of Dell Publishing, a division of Random House, Inc. —Coles, Robert. From *Children of Crisis: A Study of Courage and Fear*. Little, Brown and Company, 1964. Copyright © 1964, 1965, 1966, 1967 by Robert Coles. Renewed 1992. All rights reserved. Reproduced by permission. —Coon, Carleton S. From *The Origin of Races*. Alfred A. Knopf, 1968. Copyright © 1962 by Carleton S. Coon. All rights reserved. Reproduced by permission of the Estate of Carleton S. Coon. —Cox, Harvey. From *The Secular City*. Macmillan Company, 1965. Copyright © 1965 by Harvey Cox. All rights reserved. Reproduced by permission of the author. —Cronkite, Walter. From *Reporting Vietnam: Part One: American Journalism 1959–1969*. 1998. Copyright © 1968 by CBS and Walter Cronkite. All rights reserved. Reproduced by permission of the author. —Diller, Phyllis. From *Phyllis Diller's Housekeeping Hints*. Doubleday and Company, Inc., 1966. Copyright © 1966 by BAM Productions. All rights reserved. Reproduced by permission. —Diller, Phyllis. From *Phyllis Diller's Marriage Manual*. Doubleday and Company, Inc., 1967. Copyright © 1967 by Phyllis Diller. All rights reserved. Reproduced by permission. —Dylan, Bob. From "Blowin' in the Wind." M. Witmark & Sons, 1962. Copyright © 1962 by M. Witmark & Sons. Renewed 1990 by Robert Dylan. All rights reserved. Reproduced by permission. —Erikson, Erik H. From *Identity Youth and Crisis*. W.W. Norton & Company, Inc., 1968. Copyright © 1968 by W.W. Norton & Company, Inc. Austen Riggs Monograph No. 7. All rights reserved. Reproduced by permission. —Evers, Medgar and William Peters. From *For Us, the Living*. Doubleday & Company, Inc., 1967. Copyright © 1967 by Myrlie B. Evers and William Peters. All rights reserved. Reproduced by permission of the author and Curtis Brown, Ltd. —Friedan, Betty. From *The Feminine Mystique*. W.W. Norton & Company, Inc., 1963. Copyright © 1963, renewed 1991 by Betty Friedan. All rights reserved. Reproduced by permission. —From "The Black Berets," in *The Red Smith Reader*. Edited by Dave Anderson, Vintage Books, 1983. Copyright © 1968 by Publishers-Hall Syndicate. All rights reserved. Reproduced by permission of Random House, Inc. —Ginzberg, Eli and Alice M. Yohalem. From *Educated American Women: Self-Portraits*. Columbia University Press, 1966. Copyright © 1966 Columbia University Press, New York. All rights reserved. Republished with permission of the Columbia University Press, 562 W. 113th St., New York, NY 10025. —Gioglio, Gerald R. From *Days of Decision: An Oral History of Conscientious Objectors in the Military During the Vietnam War*. The Broken Rifle Press, 1989. Copyright © 1989 by Gerald R. Gioglio. All rights reserved. Reproduced by permission. —Glenn, John with Nick Taylor. From *John Glenn: A Memoir*. Bantam Books, 1999. Copyright © 1999 by John Glenn. All rights reserved. Reproduced in the world by permission of Bantam Books, a division of Random House, Inc. Reproduced in the U.K. by permission of Jankow & Nesbitt Associates. —Goldwater, Barry M. From *The Conscience of a Conservative*. A MacFadden Capitol Hill Book, 1960. Copyright © 1960 by Victor Publishing Company, Inc. All rights reserved. Reproduced by permission. —Goodman, Paul. From *The Community of Scholars*. Random House, 1962. Copyright © 1962 by Paul Goodman. Renewed 1990 by Sally Goodman. All rights reserved. Reproduced by permission of the Literary Estate of Paul Goodman. —Graham, Billy. From *World Aflame*. Doubleday, 1965. Copyright © 1965 by Billy Graham Evangelistic Association. All rights reserved. Reproduced by permission of the author. —Hawkins, Alex. From *My Story:(And I'm Sticking To It)*. Algonquin Books, 1989. Copyright © 1989 by C. Alex Hawkins. All rights reserved. Reproduced by permission. —Heller, Joseph. From *Catch-22*. Simon & Schuster, 1955. Copyright © 1955, 1961 by Joseph Heller. Copyright renewed © 1989 by Joseph Heller. All rights reserved. Reproduced by permission of Simon & Schuster, an imprint of Simon & Schuster Macmillan. —Hewitt, Don. From *Tell Me A Story: Fifty Years and 60 Minutes in Television*. Public Affairs, 2001. Copyright © 2001 by Don Hewitt. All rights reserved. Reproduced by permission. —Jacobs, Jane. From *The Death and Life of Great American Cities*. Vintage Books, A Division of Random House, 1961. Copyright © 1961, renewed 1989 by Jane Jacobs. All

rights reserved. Reproduced by permission of Random House, Inc. —Jones, LeRoi. From *Two Plays by LeRoi Jones: "Dutchman" and "The Slave."* William Morrow and Company, 1964. Copyright © 1964 by LeRoi Jones. All rights reserved. Reproduced by permission of HarperCollins Publishers. —Kennedy, Robert F. From Conclusion to *The Enemy Within*. Harper & Row, Publishers, 1960. Copyright © 1960 by Robert F. Kennedy. Renewed 1988 by Ethel Kennedy. All rights reserved. Reproduced by permission of HarperCollins Inc. —King, Martin Luther, Jr. From *Strength to Love*. Harper & Row, 1963. Copyright © 1963, renewed 1981 by Coretta Scott King. All rights reserved. Reproduced by arrangement with The Heirs to the Estate of Martin Luther King, Jr., c/o Writers House Inc. as agent for the proprietor. —Kohl, Herbert. From *36 Children*. The New American Library, 1967. Copyright © 1967 by Herbert Kohl. All rights reserved. Reproduced in the world by permission of The New American Library, a division of Penguin Putnam Inc. Reproduced in the UK by permission of Lescher & Lescher Ltd. —Kozol, Jonathan. From *Death at an Early Age: The Destruction of the Hearts and Minds of Negro Children in the Boston Public Schools*. Houghton Mifflin Company, 1967. Copyright © 1967 by Jonathan Kozol. All rights reserved. Reproduced by permission of the author. —Kramer, Jerry. From *Instant Replay: The Green Bay Diary of Jerry Kramer*. Edited by Dick Schaap. The New American Library, 1969. Copyright © 1968 by Jerry Kramer and Dick Schaap. All rights reserved. Reproduced by permission of Sterling Lord Literistic, Inc. —Kuhn, Thomas S. From *The Structure of Scientific Revolutions, Volume II, No. 1*. The University of Chicago Press, 1962. Copyright © 1962, 1970 by The University of Chicago. Renewed by Thomas S. Kuhn. All rights reserved. Reproduced by permission. —Kunen, James Simon. From *The Strawberry Statement—Notes of a College Revolutionary*. Random House, 1968. Copyright © 1968 by James S. Kunen. All rights reserved. Reprinted by permission of Sterling Lord Literistic, Inc. —Lee, Harper. From *To Kill a Mockingbird*. Harper Collins Publishers, 1960. Copyright © 1960 by Harper Lee, copyright © renewed 1988. All rights reserved. Reproduced in the world by permission of HarperCollins Publishers. Reproduced in the UK and British Commonwealth by permission of Aitken & Stone Ltd. —Lennon, John and Paul McCartney. From "A Hard Day's Night." Copyright © 1964 by Northern Songs Limited. All rights reserved. Reproduced by permission. —Lombardi, Vince with W.C. Heinz. From *Run to Daylight*. Grosset & Dunlap, 1967. Copyright © 1963 by Vincent Lombardi, W.C. Heinz and Robert Riger. All rights reserved. Reproduced by permission of Grosset & Dunlap, a division of Penguin Putnam Inc. —Makower, Joel. From *Woodstock: The Oral History*. Tilden Press, 1989. Copyright © 1989 by Tilden

Press Inc. All rights reserved. Reproduced by permission. —Maris, Roger and Jim Ogle. From *Roger Maris at Bat*. Duell, Sloan and Pearce, 1962. Copyright © 1962 by Roger Maris. Renewed 1990 by Patricia and Kevin J. Maris. All rights reserved. —Meredith, James. From *Three Years in Mississippi*. Indiana University Press, 1966. Copyright © 1966 by James H. Meredith. All rights reserved. Reproduced by permission of the author. —Momaday, N. Scott. From *House Made at Dawn*. Harper & Row, Publishers, 1966. Copyright © 1966, 1967, 1968 by N. Scott Momaday. All rights reserved. Reproduced by permission of HarperCollins Publishers. —Murray, Donald M. From *A Writer Teaches Writing: A Practical Method of Teaching Composition*. Houghton Mifflin Company, 1968. Copyright © 1968 by Donald M. Murray. All rights reserved. Reproduced by permission of the author. —Nader, Ralph. From Preface to *Unsafe at Any Speed: The Designed-In Dangers of the American Automobile*. Grossman Publishers, 1965. Copyright © 1965 by Ralph Nader. All rights reserved. Reproduced by permission of Grossman Publishers, a division of Penguin Putnam Inc. —Namath, Joe Willie with Dick Schaap. From *I Can't Wait Until Tomorrow. . .'Cause I Get Better-Looking Every Day*. Random House, 1969. Copyright © 1969 by Random House, Inc. All rights reserved. Reproduced by permission of Random House, Inc. —Nicklaus, Jack with Ken Bowden. From *My Story*. Simon & Schuster, 1997. Copyright © 1997 by Jack Nicklaus. All rights reserved. Reproduced by permission of Simon & Schuster Macmillan. —Palmer, Arnold with James Dodson. From *A Golfer's Life*. Ballantine Books, 1999. Copyright © 1999 by Arnold Palmer Enterprises, Inc. All rights reserved. Reproduced by permission of Ballantine Books, a division of Random House, Inc. —Pluto, Terry. From *Tall Tales: The Glory Years of the NBA, in the Words of the Men Who Played, Coached, and Built Pro Basketball*. Simon & Schuster, 1992. Copyright © 1992 by Terry Pluto. All rights reserved. Reproduced by permission of the author. —Rudolph, Wilma. From *Wilma*. Edited by Martin Ralbovsky. New American Library, 1977. Copyright © 1977 by Bud Greenspan. All rights reserved. Reproduced by permission of New American Library, a division of Penguin Putnam Inc. —Schlafly, Phyllis. From *The Power of the Positive Woman*. A Jove/HBJ Book, 1977. Copyright © 1977 by Phyllis Schlafly. All rights reserved. Reproduced by permission of A Jove/HBH Book, a division of Penguin Putnam Inc. —Schwarz, Karen. From *What You Can Do for Your Country: An Oral History of the Peace Corps*. William Morrow and Company, Inc., 1991. Copyright © 1991 by Karen Schwarz. All rights reserved. Reproduced by permission of author and her agent Robin Straus Agency, Inc. NY. —Seaver, Tom and Dick Schaap. From *The Perfect Game: Tom Seaver and the Mets*. E.P. Dutton & Co., Inc., 1970. Copyright © 1970 by Tom Seaver and Dick Schaap. All rights reserved. Reproduced by permission of E.P. Dutton & Co., a division of Penguin Putnam Inc. —Sexton, Anne. From *All My Pretty Ones*. Houghton Mifflin Company, 1961. Copyright © 1961, 1962 by Anne Sexton. Copyright © 1961 by Harper & Brothers. Renewed 1990 by Linda G. Sexton. All rights reserved. Reproduced by permission. —Susann, Jacqueline. From *Valley of the Dolls*. Grove Press, 1966. Copyright © 1966 by Tiger, LLC. All rights reserved. Reproduced by permission. —Thompson, Hunter S. From *Fear and Loathing in Las Vegas: A Savage Journey to the Heart of the American Dream*. Warner Books, 1971. Copyright © 1971 by Hunter S. Thompson. All rights reserved. Reproduced by permission. —Unitas, Johnny and Ed Fitzgerald. From *Pro Quarterback: My Own Story*. Simon and Schuster, 1965. Copyright © 1965 by Johnny Unitas and Ed Fitzgerald. All rights reserved. Reproduced in the U.S., Philippines and Canada by permission of Simon & Schuster Macmillan. Reproduced in the rest of the world and electronic by permission of Sterling Lord Literistic, Inc. —Vonnegut, Kurt. From *Slaughterhouse-Five or The Children's Crusade: A Duty-Dance with Death*. Delta, 1969. Copyright © 1969 by Kurt Vonnegut, Jr. All rights reserved. Reproduced in the world by permission of Dell Publishing, a division of Random House, Inc. In the U.K. by permission of the author. —Whitcomb, John C. and Henry M. Morris. From *The Genesis Flood: The Biblical Record and Its Scientific Implications*. P&R Publishing, 1961. Copyright © 1961 by Presbyterian and Reformed Publishing Company. All rights reserved. Reproduced by permission. —Williams, Ted with John Underwood. From *My Turn At Bat: The Story of My Life*. Simon and Schuster, 1969. Copyright © 1969 by Ted Williams and John Underwood. All rights reserved. Reproduced in the U.S. it's dependencies, the Philippines and Canada by permission of Simon & Schuster Macmillan. Reproduced in the rest of the world by JCA Literary Agency. —Winant, Fran. From *Out of the Closets: Voices of Gay Liberation*. Edited by Karla Jay and Allen Young. A Douglas Book, 1972. Copyright © 1971 by Fran Winant. All rights reserved. Reproduced by permission of the author. —Wooden, John with Jack Tobin. From *They Call Me Coach*. Contemporary Books, 1988. Copyright © 1988 by John Wooden and Jack Tobin. All rights reserved.

Copyrighted material in *American Decades Primary Sources, 1960–1969*, was reproduced from the following web sites: Chavez, Cesar E., "Prayer of the Farm Workers' Struggle." Online at: http://www.sfsu.edu/cecipp/cesar_chavez/prayer.htm. Reproduced by permission of the author. —Chavez, Cesar E., "We Shall Overcome." Online at: http://www.sfsu.edu/cecipp/cesar_chavez/venceremos.htm. Reproduced by permission of the author. —King,

Martin Luther, Jr. "Eulogy for the Martyred Children," September 18, 1963. http://www.mlkonline.com. Reproduced by arrangement with The Heirs to the Estate of Martin Luther King, Jr., c/o Writers House Inc. as agent for the proprietor. —King, Martin Luther, Jr. "Letter From Birmingham Jail," April 16, 1963. Online at: http:// www.mlkonline.com/jail.html. Reproduced by arrangement with The Heirs to the Estate of Martin Luther King, Jr., c/o Writers House Inc. as agent for the proprietor. — King, Martin Luther, Jr. "The American Dream." http://www.stanford.edu/group/King/sermons/65704_The _American_Dream.html. Copyright 1963 Dr. Martin Luther King Jr., copyright renewed 1991 Coretta Scott King. Reproduced by arrangement with The Heirs to the Estate of Martin Luther King, Jr., c/o Writers House Inc. as agent for the proprietor.

ABOUT THE SET

American Decades Primary Sources is a ten-volume collection of more than two thousand primary sources on twentieth-century American history and culture. Each volume comprises about two hundred primary sources in 160–170 entries. Primary sources are enhanced by informative context, with illustrative images and sidebars—many of which are primary sources in their own right—adding perspective and a deeper understanding of both the primary sources and the milieu from which they originated.

Designed for students and teachers at the high school and undergraduate levels, as well as researchers and history buffs, *American Decades Primary Sources* meets the growing demand for primary source material.

Conceived as both a stand-alone reference and a companion to the popular *American Decades* set, *American Decades Primary Sources* is organized in the same subject-specific chapters for compatibility and ease of use.

Primary Sources

To provide fresh insights into the key events and figures of the century, thirty historians and four advisors selected unique primary sources far beyond the typical speeches, government documents, and literary works. Screenplays, scrapbooks, sports box scores, patent applications, college course outlines, military codes of conduct, environmental sculptures, and CD liner notes are but a sampling of the more than seventy-five types of primary sources included.

Diversity is shown not only in the wide range of primary source types, but in the range of subjects and opinions, and the frequent combination of primary sources in entries. Multiple perspectives in religious, political, artistic, and scientific thought demonstrate the commitment of *American Decades Primary Sources* to diversity, in addition to the inclusion of considerable content displaying ethnic, racial, and gender diversity. *American Decades Primary Sources* presents a variety of perspectives on issues and events, encouraging the reader to consider subjects more fully and critically.

American Decades Primary Sources' innovative approach often presents related primary sources in an entry. The primary sources act as contextual material for each other—creating a unique opportunity to understand each and its place in history, as well as their relation to one another. These may be point-counterpoint arguments, a variety of diverse opinions, or direct responses to another primary source. One example is President Franklin Delano Roosevelt's letter to clergy at the height of the Great Depression, with responses by a diverse group of religious leaders from across the country.

Multiple primary sources created by particularly significant individuals—Dr. Martin Luther King, Jr., for example—reside in *American Decades Primary Sources*. Multiple primary sources on particularly significant subjects are often presented in more than one chapter of a volume, or in more than one decade, providing opportunities to see the significance and impact of an event or figure from many angles and historical perspectives. For example, seven primary sources on the controversial Scopes "monkey" trial are found in five chapters of the

1920s volume. Primary sources on evolutionary theory may be found in earlier and later volumes, allowing the reader to see and analyze the development of thought across time.

Entry Organization

Contextual material uses standardized rubrics that will soon become familiar to the reader, making the entries more accessible and allowing for easy comparison. Introduction and Significance essays—brief and focused—cover the historical background, contributing factors, importance, and impact of the primary source, encouraging the reader to think critically—not only about the primary source, but also about the way history is constructed. Key Facts and a Synopsis provide quick access and recognition of the primary sources, and the Further Resources are a stepping-stone to additional study.

Additional Features

Subject chronologies and thorough tables of contents (listing titles, authors, and dates) begin each chapter. The main table of contents assembles this information conveniently at the front of the book. An essay on using primary sources, a chronology of selected events outside the United States during the twentieth century, substantial general and subject resources, and primary source-type and general indexes enrich *American Decades Primary Sources*.

The ten volumes of *American Decades Primary Sources* provide a vast array of primary sources integrated with supporting content and user-friendly features.

This value-laden set gives the reader an unparalleled opportunity to travel into the past, to relive important events, to encounter key figures, and to gain a deep and full understanding of America in the twentieth century.

Acknowledgments

A number of people contributed to the successful completion of this project. The editor wishes to acknowledge them with thanks: Eugenia Bradley, Luann Brennan, Neva Carter, Katrina Coach, Pamela S. Dear, Nikita L. Greene, Madeline Harris, Alesia James, Cynthia Jones, Pamela M. Kalte, Arlene Ann Kevonian, Frances L. Monroe, Charles B. Montney, Katherine H. Nemeh, James E. Person, Tyra Y. Phillips, Elizabeth Pilette, Noah Schusterbauer, Andrew Specht, Susan Strickland, Karissa Walker, Tracey Watson, and Jennifer M. York.

Contact Us

The editors of *American Decades Primary Sources* welcome your comments, suggestions, and questions. Please direct all correspondence to:

Editor, *American Decades Primary Sources*
The Gale Group, Inc.
27500 Drake Road
Farmington Hills, MI 48331–3535
(800) 877–4253

For email inquiries, please visit the Gale website at www.gale.com, and click on the Contact Us tab.

ABOUT THE VOLUME

The 1960s was an active decade in the United States—politically, militarily, socially, and popularly. The 1960s saw the world come to the brink of nuclear war as the United States and Soviet Union faced off in the Cuban Missile Crisis, and U.S. advisors and troops were sent to Vietnam to combat communist forces wanting to take over that country. President John F. Kennedy was assassinated as he campaigned in Texas for reelection, plunging the nation into stunned mourning. Martin Luther King Jr. gave his inspiring "I Have a Dream" speech at the March on Washington, and the Civil Rights Act became law, but King himself was assassinated. The public demonstrated in support of civil rights and against the military draft, sometimes resulting in riots and violence. While the 1960s contained the upheaval of violence and change, is also saw the colorful burst of tie dye, the first airing of *Sesame Street,* the wild popularity of the Beatles, and the first man to walk on the moon. The following documents are just a sampling of the offerings available in this volume.

Highlights of Primary Sources, 1960–1969

- Lyrics to "Blowin' in the Wind," by Bob Dylan, and flyer for the March on Washington to protest the Vietnam War, where Peter, Paul, and Mary performed the song

- *Unsafe at Any Speed,* by consumer advocate Ralph Nader

- *As the Seed Is Sown,* report on Head Start program

- Tie Dye clothing

- Codes of conduct for use by troops in Vietnam: "Nine Rules," "The Enemy in Your Hands," and "Guidance for Commanders in Vietnam"

- "Prayer of the Farm Workers' Struggle," by César Chávez

- "Vast Wasteland" speech delivered by FCC Chairman Newton Minow to the National Association of Broadcasters, May 1961

- First Surgeon General's report on Smoking and Health, 1964

- *Humanae Vitae:* Encyclical of Pope Paul VI on the Regulation of Birth

- Dr. Martin Luther King Jr.'s letter from a Birmingham jail

- Photograph of a bootprint on the surface of the Moon from the *Apollo 11* lunar landing

- *Roger Maris At Bat,* excerpt from Maris's 1962 autobiography detailing his chasing Ruth's home run record the year before

- *Chicago Trial Testimony,* by Allen Ginsberg

Volume Structure and Content

Front matter

- Table of Contents—lists primary sources, authors, and dates of origin, by chapter and chronologically within chapters.

- About the Set, About the Volume, About the Entry essays—guide the reader through the set and promote ease of use.

- Highlights of Primary Sources—a quick look at a dozen or so primary sources gives the reader a feel for the decade and the volume's contents.

- Using Primary Sources—provides a crash course in reading and interpreting primary sources.

- Chronology of Selected World Events Outside the United States—lends additional context in which to place the decade's primary sources.

Chapters:

- The Arts
- Business and the Economy
- Education
- Fashion and Design
- Government and Politics
- Law and Justice
- Lifestyles and Social Trends
- The Media
- Medicine and Health
- Religion
- Science and Technology
- Sports

Chapter structure

- Chapter table of contents—lists primary sources, authors, and dates of origin chronologically, showing each source's place in the decade.

- Chapter chronology—highlights the decade's important events in the chapter's subject.

- Primary sources—displays sources surrounded by contextual material.

Back matter

- General Resources—promotes further inquiry with books, periodicals, websites, and audio and visual media, all organized into general and subject-specific sections.

- General Index—provides comprehensive access to primary sources, people, events, and subjects, and cross-referencing to enhance comparison and analysis.

- Primary Source Type Index—locates primary sources by category, giving readers an opportunity to easily analyze sources across genres.

About the Entry

The primary source is the centerpiece and main focus of each entry in *American Decades Primary Sources.* In keeping with the philosophy that much of the benefit from using primary sources derives from the reader's own process of inquiry, the contextual material surrounding each entry provides access and ease of use, as well as giving the reader a springboard for delving into the primary source. Rubrics identify each section and enable the reader to navigate entries with ease.

Entry structure

- Key Facts—essential information pertaining to the primary source, including full title, author, source type, source citation, and notes about the author.

- Introduction—historical background and contributing factors for the primary source.

- Significance—importance and impact of the primary source, at the time and since.

- Primary Source—in text, text facsimile, or image format; full or excerpted.

- Synopsis—encapsulated introduction to the primary source.

- Further Resources—books, periodicals, websites, and audio and visual material.

Navigating an Entry

Entry elements are numbered and reproduced here, with an explanation of the data contained in these elements explained immediately thereafter according to the corresponding numeral.

Primary Source/Entry Title, Primary Source Type

•1• | "Ego"
•2• | Magazine article

•1• **PRIMARY SOURCE/ENTRY TITLE** The entry title is the primary source title for entries with one primary source. Entry titles appear as catchwords at the top outer margin of each page.

•2• **PRIMARY SOURCE TYPE** The type of primary source is listed just below the title. When assigning source types, great weight was given to how the author of the primary source categorized it. If a primary source comprised more than one type—for example, an article about art in the United States that included paintings, or a scientific essay that included graphs and photographs—each primary source type included in the entry appears below the title.

Composite Entry Title

•3• | Debate Over *The Birth of a Nation*

•1• "Capitalizing Race Hatred"
•2• Editorial

•1• **"Reply to the *New York Globe*"**

•2• Letter

•3• **COMPOSITE ENTRY TITLE** An overarching entry title is used for entries with more than one primary source, with the primary source titles and types below.

Key Facts

•4• **By:** Norman Mailer

•5• **Date:** March 19, 1971

•6• **Source:** Mailer, Norman. "Ego." *Life* 70, March 19, 1971, 30, 32–36.

•7• **About the Author:** Norman Mailer (1923–) was born in Long Branch, New Jersey. After graduating from Harvard and military service in World War II (1939–1945), Mailer began writing, publishing his first book, the best-selling novel *The Naked and the Dead,* in 1948. Mailer has written over thirty books, including novels, plays, political commentary, and essay collections, as well as numerous magazine articles. He won the Pulitzer Prize in 1969 and 1979. ■

•4• **AUTHOR OR ORIGINATOR** The name of the author or originator of the primary source begins the Key Facts section.

•5• **DATE OF ORIGIN** The date of origin of the primary source appears in this field, and may differ from the date of publication in the source citation below it; for example, speeches are often given before they are published.

•6• **SOURCE CITATION** The source citation is a full bibliographic citation, giving original publication data as well as reprint and/or online availability (usually both the deep-link and home-page URLs).

•7• **ABOUT THE AUTHOR** A brief bio of the author or originator of the primary source gives birth and death dates and a quick overview of the person's life. This rubric has been customized in some cases. If the primary source is the autobiography of an artist, the term "author" appears; however, if the primary source is a work of art, the term "artist" is used, showing the person's direct relationship to the primary source. Terms like "inventor" and "designer" are used similarly. For primary sources created by a group, "organization" may have been used instead of "author." If an author is anonymous or unknown, a brief "About the Publication" sketch may appear.

Introduction and Significance Essays

•8• **Introduction**

. . . As images from the Vietnam War (1964–1975) flashed onto television screens across the United States in the late 1960s, however, some reporters took a more active role in questioning the pronouncements of public officials. The broad cul-

tural changes of the 1960s, including a sweeping suspicion of authority figures by younger people, also encouraged a more restive spirit in the reporting corps. By the end of the decade, the phrase "Gonzo Journalism" was coined to describe the new breed of reporter: young, rebellious, and unafraid to get personally involved in the story at hand. . . .

•8• **INTRODUCTION** The introduction is a brief essay on the contributing factors and historical context of the primary source. Intended to promote understanding and jump-start the reader's curiosity, this section may also describe an artist's approach, the nature of a scientific problem, or the struggles of a sports figure. If more than one primary source is included in the entry, the introduction and significance address each one, and often the relationship between them.

•9• **Significance**

Critics of the new style of journalism maintained that the emphasis on personalities and celebrity did not necessarily lead to better reporting. As political reporting seemed to focus more on personalities and images and less on substantive issues, some observers feared that the American public was ill-served by the new style of journalism. Others argued that the media had also encouraged political apathy among the public by superficial reporting. . . .

•9• **SIGNIFICANCE** The significance discusses the importance and impact of the primary source. This section may touch on how it was regarded at the time and since, its place in history, any awards given, related developments, and so on.

Primary Source Header, Synopsis, Primary Source

•10• **Primary Source**

The Boys on the Bus [excerpt]

•11• **SYNOPSIS:** A boisterous account of Senator George McGovern's ultimately unsuccessful 1972 presidential bid, Crouse's work popularized the term "pack journalism," describing the herd mentality that gripped reporters focusing endlessly on the same topic. In later years, political advisors would become more adept at "spinning" news stories to their candidates' advantage, but the essential dynamics of pack journalism remain in place.

•12• The feverish atmosphere was halfway between a high school bus trip to Washington and a gambler's jet junket to Las Vegas, where small-time Mafiosi were lured into betting away their restaurants. There was giddy camaraderie mixed with fear and low-grade hysteria. To file a story late, or to make one glaring factual error, was to chance losing everything—one's job, one's expense account, one's drinking buddies, one's mad-dash existence, and the methedrine buzz that comes from knowing stories that the public would not know for hours and secrets that the public would never know. Therefore reporters channeled their gambling instincts into late-night poker games and private bets on the outcome of the elections. When it came to writing a story, they were as cautious as diamond-cutters. . . .

•10• **PRIMARY SOURCE HEADER** The primary source header signals the beginning of the primary source, and "[excerpt]" is attached if the source does not appear in full.

•11• **SYNOPSIS** The synopsis gives a brief overview of the primary source.

•12• **PRIMARY SOURCE** The primary source may appear excerpted or in full, and may appear as text, text facsimile (photographic reproduction of the original text), image, or graphic display (such as a table, chart, or graph).

Text Primary Sources

The majority of primary sources are reproduced as plain text. The font and leading of the primary sources are distinct from that of the context—to provide a visual clue to the change, as well as to facilitate ease of reading. Often, the original formatting of the text was preserved in order to more accurately represent the original (screenplays, for example). In order to respect the integrity of the primary sources, content some readers may consider sensitive was retained where it was deemed to be integral to the source. Text facsimile formatting was used sparingly and where the original provided additional value (for example, Aaron Copland's typing and handwritten notes on "Notes for a Cowboy Ballet").

Narrative Break

•13•   I told him I'd rest and then fix him something to eat when he got home. I could hear someone enter his office then, and Medgar laughed at something that was said. "I've got to go, honey. See you tonight. I love you." "All right," I said. "Take care." Those were our last words to each other.

■ ■ ■

Medgar had told me that President Kennedy was speaking on civil rights that night, and I made a mental note of the time. We ate alone, the children and I. It had become a habit now to set only four places for supper. Medgar's chair stared at us, and the children, who had heard

about the President's address to the nation, planned to watch it with me. There was something on later that they all wanted to see, and they begged to be allowed to wait up for Medgar to return home. School was out, and I knew that Van would fall asleep anyway, so I agreed.

•13• **NARRATIVE BREAK** A narrative break appears where there is a significant amount of elided material, beyond what ellipses would indicate (for example, excerpts from a nonfiction work's introduction and second chapter, or sections of dialogue from two acts of a play).

Image Primary Sources

Primary source images (whether photographs, text facsimiles, or graphic displays) are bordered with a distinctive double rule. The Primary Source header and Synopsis appear under the image, with the image reduced in size to accommodate the synopsis. For multipart images, the synopsis appears only under the first part of the image; subsequent parts have brief captions.

•14• "Art: U.S. Scene": *The Tornado* by John Steuart Curry (2 OF 4)

•14• **PRIMARY SOURCE IMAGE HEADER** The primary source image header assists the reader in tracking the images in a series. Also, the primary source header listed here indicates a primary source with both text and image components. The text of the *Time* magazine article "Art: U.S. Scene," appears with four of the paintings from the article. Under each painting, the title of the article appears first, followed by a colon, then the title of the painting. The header for the text component has a similar structure, with the term "magazine article" after the colon. Inclusion of images or graphic elements from primary sources, and their designation in the entry as main primary sources, is discretionary.

Further Resources

•15• **Further Resources**

BOOKS
Dixon, Phil. *The Negro Baseball Leagues, 1867–1955: A Photographic History.* Mattituck, N.Y.: Amereon House, 1992.

PERIODICALS
"Steven Spielberg: The Director Says It's Good-Bye to Spaceships and Hello to Relationships." *American Film* 13, no. 8, June 1988, 12–16.

WEBSITES
Architecture and Interior Design for 20th Century America, 1935–1955. American Memory digital primary source collection, Library of Congress. Available online at http://memory.loc.gov/ammem/gschtml/gotthome

.html; website home page: http://memory.loc.gov/ammem/ammemhome.html (accessed March 27, 2003).

AUDIO AND VISUAL MEDIA

E.T.: The Extra-Terrestrial. Original release, 1982, Universal. Directed by Steven Spielberg. Widescreen Collector's Edition DVD, 2002, Universal Studios.

•**15•** **FURTHER RESOURCES** A brief list of resources provides a stepping stone to further study. If it's known that a resource contains additional primary source material specifically related to the entry, a brief note in italics appears at the end of the citation. For websites, both the deep link and home page usually appear.

USING PRIMARY SOURCES

The philosopher R.G. Collingwood once said, "Every new generation must rewrite history in its own way." What Collingwood meant is that new events alter our perceptions of the past and necessitate that each generation interpret the past in a different light. For example, since September 11, 2001, and the "War on Terrorism," the collapse of the Soviet Union seemingly is no longer as historically important as the rise of Islamic fundamentalism, which was once only a minor concern. Seen from this viewpoint, history is not a rigid set of boring facts, but a fascinating, ever-changing field of study. Much of this fascination rests on the fact that historical interpretation is based on the reading of primary sources. To historians and students alike, primary sources are ambiguous objects because their underlying meanings are often not crystal clear. To learn a primary document's meaning(s), students must identify its main subject and recreate the historical context in which the document was created. In addition, students must compare the document with other primary sources from the same historical time and place. Further, students must cross-examine the primary source by asking of it a series of probing investigative questions.

To properly analyze a primary source, it is important that students become "active" rather than "casual" readers. As in reading a chemistry or algebra textbook, historical documents require students to analyze them carefully and extract specific information. In other words, history requires students to read "beyond the text" and focus on what the primary source tells us about the per-

son or group and the era in which they lived. Unlike chemistry and algebra, however, historical primary sources have the additional benefit of being part of a larger, interesting story full of drama, suspense, and hidden agendas. In order to detect and identify key historical themes, students need to keep in mind a set of questions. For example, Who created the primary source? Why did the person create it? What is the subject? What problem is being addressed? Who was the intended audience? How was the primary source received and how was it used? What are the most important characteristics of this person or group for understanding the primary source? For example, what were the authors' biases? What was their social class? Their race? Their gender? Their occupation? Once these questions have been answered reasonably, the primary source can be used as a piece of historical evidence to interpret history.

In each *American Decades Primary Sources* volume, students will study examples of the following categories of primary sources:

- Firsthand accounts of historic events by witnesses and participants. This category includes diary entries, letters, newspaper articles, oral-history interviews, memoirs, and legal testimony.

- Documents representing the official views of the nation's leaders or of their political opponents. These include court decisions, policy statements, political speeches, party platforms, petitions, legislative debates, press releases, and federal and state laws.

- Government statistics and reports on such topics as birth, employment, marriage, death, and taxation.

- Advertisers' images and jingles. Although designed to persuade consumers to purchase commodities or to adopt specific attitudes, advertisements can also be valuable sources of information about popular beliefs and concerns.

- Works of art, including paintings, symphonies, play scripts, photographs, murals, novels, and poems.

- The products of mass culture: cartoons, comic books, movies, radio scripts, and popular songs.

- Material artifacts. These are everyday objects that survived from the period in question. Examples include household appliances and furnishings, recipes, and clothing.

- Secondary sources. In some cases, secondary sources may be treated as primary sources. For example, from 1836 to 1920, public schools across America purchased 122 million copies of a series of textbooks called the McGuffey Reader. Although current textbooks have more instructional value, the Reader is an invaluable primary source. It provides important insights into the unifying morals and cultural values that shaped the worldview of several generations of Americans, who differed in ethnicity, race, class, and religion.

Each of the above-mentioned categories of primary sources reveals different types of historical information. A politician's diary, memoirs, or collection of letters, for example, often provide students with the politicians' unguarded, private thoughts and emotions concerning daily life and public events. Though these documents may be a truer reflection of the person's character and aspirations, students must keep in mind that when people write about themselves, they tend to put themselves at the center of the historical event or cast themselves in the best possible light. On the other hand, the politician's public speeches may be more cautious, less controversial, and limited to advancing his or her political party's goals or platform.

Like personal diaries, advertisements reveal other types of historical information. What information does the WAVES poster on this page reveal?

John Phillip Faller, a prolific commercial artist known for his *Saturday Evening Post* covers, designed this recruitment poster in 1944. It was one of over three hundred posters he produced for the U.S. Navy while enrolled in that service during World War II. The purpose of the poster was to encourage women to enlist in the WAVES (Women Accepted for Volunteer Emergency Service), a women's auxiliary to the Navy established in

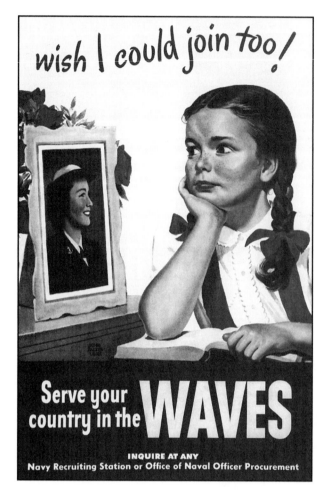

1942. It depicts a schoolgirl gazing admiringly at a photograph of a proud, happy WAVE (perhaps an older sister), thus portraying the military service as an appropriate and admirable aspiration for women during wartime. However, what type of military service? Does the poster encourage women to enlist in military combat like World War II male recruitment posters? Does it reflect gender bias? What does this poster reveal about how the military and society in general feel about women in the military? Does the poster reflect current military and societal attitudes toward women in the military? How many women joined the WAVES? What type of duties did they perform?

Like personal diaries, photographs reveal other types of historical information. What information does the next photograph reveal?

Today, we take electricity for granted. However, in 1935, although 90 percent of city dwellers in America had electricity, only 10 percent of rural Americans did. Private utility companies refused to string electric lines

THE LIBRARY OF CONGRESS.

to isolated farms, arguing that the endeavor was too expensive and that most farmers were too poor to afford it anyway. As part of the Second New Deal, President Franklin Delano Roosevelt issued an executive order creating the Rural Electrification Administration (REA). The REA lent money at low interest rates to utility companies to bring electricity to rural America. By 1950, 90 percent of rural America had electricity. This photograph depicts a 1930s tenant farmer's house in Greene County, Georgia. Specifically, it shows a brand-new electric meter on the wall. The picture presents a host of questions: What was rural life like without electricity? How did electricity impact the lives of rural Americans, particularly rural Georgians? How many rural Georgians did not have electricity in the 1930s? Did Georgia have more electricity-connected farms than other Southern states? What was the poverty rate in rural Georgia, particularly among rural African Americans? Did rural electricity help lift farmers out of poverty?

Like personal diaries, official documents reveal other types of historical information. What information does the next document, a memo, reveal?

From the perspective of the early twenty-first century, in a democratic society, integration of the armed services seems to have been inevitable. For much of American history, however, African Americans were prevented from joining the military, and when they did enlist they were segregated into black units. In 1940, of the nearly 170,000-man Navy, only 4,007, or 2.3 percent, were African American personnel. The vast majority of these men worked in the mess halls as stewards—or, as labeled by the black press, "seagoing bellhops." In this official document, the chairman of the General Board refers to compliance with a directive that would enlist African Americans into positions of "unlimited general service." Who issued the directive? What was the motivation behind the new directive? Who were the members of the General Board? How much authority did they wield? Why did the Navy restrict African Americans to the "messman branch"? Notice the use of the term "colored race." Why was this term used and what did it imply? What did the board conclude? When did the Navy become integrated? Who was primarily responsible for integrating the Navy?

CONFIDENTIAL

DOD Dir. 5200.10, June 29, 1960
RND by *RB* date *Oct 5 1961*

DOWNGRADED AT 3 YEAR INTERVALS;
DECLASSIFIED AFTER 12 YEARS
DOD DIR 5200.10 NARS-NT

G.B. No. 421
(Serial No. 201)
SECRET

Feb 3, 1942

From: Chairman General Board.
To: Secretary of the Navy.

Subject: Enlistment of men of colored race to other than
               Messman branch.

Ref: (a) SecNav let. (SC)P14-4/MM (03200A)/Gen of
             Jan 16, 1942.

       1.   The General Board, complying with the directive
contained in reference (a), has given careful attention to the
problem of enlisting in the Navy, men of the colored race
in other than the messman branch.

       2.   The General Board has endeavored to examine the
problem placed before it in a realistic manner.

A.   Should negroes be enlisted for **unlimited** general service?

       (a) Enlistment for general service implies that the
individual may be sent anywhere, - to any ship or station where
he is needed. Men on board ship live in particularly close
association; in their messes, one man sits beside another; their
hammocks or bunks are close together; in their common tasks they
work side by side; and in particular tasks such as those of a
gun's crew, they form a closely knit, highly coordinated team.
How many white men would choose, of their own accord, that their
closest associates in sleeping quarters, at mess, and in a gun's
crew should be of another race? How many would accept such
conditions, if required to do so, without resentment and just
as a matter of course? The General Board believes that the
answer is "Few, if any," and further believes that if the issue were
forced, there would be a lowering of contentment, teamwork
and discipline in the service.

       (b) One of the tennets of the recruiting service
is that each recruit for general service is potentially a leading
petty officer. It is true that some men never do become petty
officers, and that when recruiting white men, it is not possible
to establish which will be found worthy of and secure promotion
and which will not. If negroes are recruited for general service,
it can be said at once that few will obtain advancement to petty
officers. With every desire to be fair, officers and leading
petty officers in general will not recommend negroes for promotion
to positions of authority over white men.

DOWNGRADED AND
DECLASSIFIED

- 1 -

CONFIDENTIAL

The General Board is convinced that the enlistment of negroes for unlimited general service is unadvisable.

B.   Should negroes be enlisted in general service but detailed in special ratings or for special ships or units?

    (a) The ratings now in use in the naval service cover every phase of naval activity, and no new ratings are deemed necessary merely to promote the enlistment of negroes.

    (b) At first thought, it might appear that assignment of negroes to certain vessels, and in particular to small vessels of the patrol type, would be feasible. In this connection, the following table is of interest:

Type of Ship	Total Crew	Men in Pay Grades 1 to 4	Men in Pay Grades 5 to 7 (Non-rated)
Battleship	1892	666	1226
Light Cruiser (10,000 ton)	988	365	623
Destroyer (1630 ton)	206	109	97
Submarine	54	47	7
Patrol Boat (180 foot)	55	36	19
Patrol Boat (110 foot)	20	15	5

NOTE: Pay grades 1 to 4 include Chief Petty Officers and Petty Officers, 1st, 2nd and 3rd Class; also Firemen, 1st Class and a few other ratings requiring length of service and experience equal to that required for qualification of Petty Officers, 3rd class. Pay grades 5 to 7 include all other non-rated men and recruits.

There are no negro officers and so few negro petty officers in the Navy at present that any vessels to which negroes might be assigned must have white officers and white petty officers. Examination of the table shows the small number of men in other than petty officer ratings that might be assigned to patrol vessels and indicates to the General Board that such assignments would not be happy ones. The assignment of negroes to the larger ships, where well over one-half of the crews are non-rated men, with mixture of whites and negroes, would inevitably lead to discontent on the part of one or the other, resulting in clashes and lowering of the efficiency of the vessels and of the Navy.

- 2 -

The material collected in these volumes of *American Decades Primary Sources* are significant because they will introduce students to a wide variety of historical sources that were created by those who participated in or witnessed the historical event. These primary sources not only vividly describe historical events, but also reveal the subjective perceptions and biases of their authors. Students should read these documents "actively," and with the contextual assistance of the introductory material, history will become relevant and entertaining.

—Paul G. Connors

CHRONOLOGY OF SELECTED WORLD EVENTS OUTSIDE THE UNITED STATES, 1960–1969

1960

- On January 1, Soviet premier Nikita Khrushchev states in a New Year's toast that the Soviet Union might disarm unilaterally if it fails to reach an arms agreement with the West.

- On January 3, the Moscow State Symphony becomes the first Soviet orchestra to play in the United States.

- On January 8, West Berlin students demonstrate against outbreaks of neo-Nazism and anti-Semitism.

- On January 12, Soviet police expose a black-market rock 'n' roll ring that produces phonograph records on X-ray plates.

- On January 19, the United States and Japan sign a treaty of mutual cooperation and security.

- On January 23, the bathyscaphe *Trieste,* a joint U.S.-French venture, plunges almost seven miles to the deepest part of Pacific Ocean.

- On January 24, Pope John XXIII presides over the first diocesan ecclesiastical council in Rome.

- On February 1, in Algeria a revolt by European immigrants collapses.

- On February 5, anti-Communist demonstrators disrupt the Soviet Exhibition in Havana.

- On February 7, archaeologists discover ancient biblical scrolls in a cave one thousand feet above the Dead Sea.

- On February 8, France becomes the world's fourth nuclear power after detonating an atomic bomb in the Sahara Desert in Africa.

- On February 18, the Winter Olympics begin in Squaw Valley, California.

- On February 19, despite appeals by anti-U.S. Chileans, several hundred thousand flock to welcome President Dwight Eisenhower to Santiago.

- On March 1, earthquakes, a tidal wave, and fires level the Moroccan resort city of Agadir, killing nearly twelve thousand and leaving almost everyone homeless.

- On March 14, in New York, Israeli premier David Ben-Gurion and West German chancellor Konrad Adenauer meet for the first time to discuss German-Israeli relations.

- On March 18, the Shanghai People's Court sentences Roman Catholic bishop James Edward Walsh, a U.S. citizen, to twenty years in prison for leading Chinese priests to spy against Communist China.

- On March 21, Cuban soldiers shoot down an American private plane and capture its pilot and copilot, whom they suspect of attempting to rescue Cuban political prisoners.

- On March 21, South African police fire on twenty thousand antiapartheid demonstrators, killing fifty-six.

- On April 9, a white man shoots and wounds South African white supremacist prime minister Hendrik Verwoerd in Johannesburg.

- On April 26, South Korea's National Assembly demands President Syngman Rhee's resignation after a student protest against government election policies.

- On May 5, Soviet premier Nikita Khrushchev presents evidence to the Supreme Soviet that Soviet forces shot down an American U-2 spy plane over the Soviet Union and captured its pilot, Gary Powers.

- On May 7, twenty-three-year-old Mikhail Tol of Soviet Latvia becomes the youngest world chess champion in the twentieth century after defeating Mikhail Botvinnick in two months of matches in Moscow.

- On May 7, the Paris summit between Soviet premier Nikita Khrushchev and U.S. president Dwight D. Eisenhower breaks down.

- On May 11, France launches the SS *France,* the world's longest passenger liner, at Saint Nazaire, France.

- On May 20, *La Dolce Vita,* by Italian director Federico Fellini, wins the award for best film at the Cannes Film Festival.

- On May 23, the Israeli government announces its detention of former Nazi SS Colonel Adolf Eichmann.

- On May 27, a military coup overthrows Turkish dictator Adnan Menderes.

- On June 1, British composer Benjamin Britten premieres the opera *A Midsummer Night's Dream* at Jubilee Hall in Aldeburgh, England.

- On June 9, Typhoon Mary, packing 135 mph winds, hits Hong Kong, killing many and leaving 120,000 homeless.

- On June 13, a Rome court announces the annulment of actress Ingrid Bergman's marriage to Roberto Rossellini.

- On June 16, President Eisenhower agrees, at the request of Japanese officials, to postpone his visit to Japan due to anti-American riots.

- On June 20, U.S. boxer Floyd Patterson defeats Ingemar Johansson of Sweden to reclaim the world heavyweight boxing title.

- On June 20, Algerian rebels agree to peace talks in Paris after nearly six years of war.

- On June 30, King Baudouin I of Belgium grants the Republic of Congo in Africa independence.

- On July 1, British Somaliland and the U.N. trust territory of Somalia merge to form the Republic of Somalia in Africa.

- On July 11, Kremlin officials announce that the Soviet Union has shot down an American RB-47 reconnaissance jet after it violated Soviet airspace.

- On July 14, the U.N. Security Council authorizes Secretary General Dag Hammarskjöld to send U.N. troops to the Republic of the Congo to restore peace to the emerging nation plagued by civil war.

- On July 21, fifty-nine-year-old Francis Chichester wins the transatlantic solo race aboard his sloop *Gypsy Moth* in a record forty days.

- On July 24, Marshal Andrei A. Grechko succeeds Ivan S. Konev as supreme commander of Warsaw Pact forces.

- On July 27, the United States, Great Britain, and the Soviet Union agree at the Geneva test-ban talks to bar atmospheric tests as well as all underground detonations of more than 4.75 on the Richter scale.

- On July 29, Dr. Andre Danjon, director of the Paris Observatory, reports that the day has lengthened by one-tenth of a second because three solar eruptions in July 1959 slowed the earth's rotation.

- In August, Harvard University physicists confirm Albert Einstein's Special Theory of Relativity.

- On August 3, an English translation of *The Last Temptation of Christ,* by Greek novelist Nikos Kazantzakis, is pub-lished in New York. Religious conservatives condemn the novel for implying a sexual relationship between Jesus and Mary Magdelan.

- On August 6, Bangu of Brazil defeats Kilmarnock of Scotland 2-0 in New York to win the American Challenge Cup in the International Soccer League's first title playoff.

- On September 11, the Rome Summer Olympics end, with Soviet athletes winning the most medals.

- On September 19, Soviet premier Nikita Khrushchev and Cuban leader Fidel Castro arrive in New York City under police security for the convening of the U.N. General Assembly.

- On October 5, Jean Anouilh premiers the play *Becket* in New York City.

- On October 10, a cyclone and a tidal wave kill five thousand people in East Pakistan along the Bay of Bengal.

- On October 12, Soviet premier Nikita Khrushchev pounds his desk with his shoe to protest a speech at the United Nations by a Philippine delegate against Soviet colonialism in Eastern Europe.

- On October 21, Britain announces its first nuclear submarine, the *Dreadnought.*

- On October 28, the Swedish Royal Academy awards no Nobel Peace Prize for the seventeenth time since 1901.

- On November 2, a London court rules, in the first test of Great Britain's new obscenity laws, that D.H. Lawrence's *Lady Chatterley's Lover* is not obscene.

- On November 7, the Soviet team wins the Olympic chess tournament in Leipzig, East Germany, with the United States second.

- On December 1, Congolese troops arrest Congolese premier Patrice Lumumba, whom political enemies accuse of inciting rebellion.

- On December 12, British biologist and writer Peter Brian Medawar receives the Nobel Prize in physiology or medicine.

- On December 13, former Deputy Premier Antoine Gizenga forms a new government in the Congo.

1961

- Thieves steal Spanish painter Francisco Goya's portrait of the duke of Wellington from the National Gallery in London.

- In January, British physicist Sir John Cockcroft wins the 1961 Atoms for Peace Award.

- In January, French voters endorse plans for Algerian self-determination.

- On January 2, Soviets begin exchanging old rubles for new at a rate of ten old to one new ruble.

- On January 3, the United States severs diplomatic ties with Cuba.

- On January 31, Israeli Prime Minister David Ben-Gurion resigns.

- In March, the Soviet Union launches a spacecraft carrying a dog into orbit around Earth.

- On April 12, Soviet cosmonaut Yuri Gagarin becomes the first man to orbit Earth.

- From April 17 to April 20, Fidel Castro's forces repulse an invasion of Cuban exiles backed by the United States at Cuba's Bay of Pigs.

- On April 26, the French army puts down a revolt in Algiers, Algeria.

- In June, Arthur Ramsey becomes the one hundredth archbishop of Canterbury.

- In June, France suspends peace negotiations with Algerian nationalists.

- In June, oil-rich Kuwait becomes independent of Britain.

- On June 30, the U.S. government abandons its efforts to exchange U.S. bulldozers for Cuban exiles captured during the Bay of Pigs invasion.

- In July, British troops enter Kuwait to counter an Iraqi threat of invasion.

- In July, General Park Chung Hee becomes chairman of South Korea's military junta.

- On August 13, the Soviet Union closes the border between East and West Berlin.

- From August 15 to August 17, East Germany constructs the Berlin Wall to separate East and West Berlin.

- On October 23, the Soviet Union detonates a bomb of between thirty and fifty megatons, the largest explosion to date.

- From October 26 to October 28, U.S. and Soviet tanks face off at the border between East and West Berlin.

- On November 3, U Thant of Burma becomes secretary-general of the United Nations.

- On November 12, West Germany announces it will pay each of the seventy-three Polish women used in Nazi experiments up to ten thousand dollars.

- On December 10, Rolf Edberg, Swedish ambassador to Norway, accepts the Nobel Peace Prize for the late Dag Hammarskjold.

- On December 11, an Israeli court convicts Adolf Eichmann for his role in the deaths of six million Jews during World War II.

1962

- Russian novelist Aleksandr Solzhenitsyn publishes *One Day in the Life of Ivan Denisovich,* a grim novel of life in exile in Siberia.

- British novelist Anthony Burgess publishes *A Clockwork Orange.*

- On January 4, Begum Liaquat Ali Khan, Pakistani ambassador to Italy, wins the first International Gimbel Award for her role in the emancipation of Pakistani women.

- On January 7, President Bung Sukarno of Indonesia escapes an assassination attempt when a grenade explodes behind his car, killing three bystanders.

- On January 18, North Vietnam announces that the Vietnam People's Revolutionary Party will govern communist territory in the south.

- On February 3, the U.S. Congress bans trade between the United States and Cuba.

- On February 10, U.S. and Soviet officials exchange U-2 pilot Gary Powers and Soviet spy Rudolf Abel at the border between East and West Germany.

- On February 20, the Israeli Knesset votes to maintain military rule over Arabs in Israeli-occupied lands.

- On February 27, South Vietnamese Air Force officers flying U.S. planes bomb the presidential palace in Saigon, South Vietnam.

- On March 7, the British Royal College of Physicians concludes that cigarette smoking causes lung cancer.

- On March 12, the British Ministries of Health and Education launch a program to warn the public about the dangers of smoking.

- On March 14, the United States and Soviet Union join fifteen nations in Geneva, Switzerland, for disarmament talks.

- On March 18, France and the Algerian provisional government sign a truce ending nearly seven years of Algerian rebellion against French rule in Algeria.

- On March 22, British anthropologist Louis S.B. Leakey announces his 1961 discovery of the remains of a 14-million-year-old humanlike creature.

- On March 28, a bloodless military coup ousts President Arturo Frondizi of Argentina.

- On April 7, a military court in Havana, Cuba, sentences 1,179 prisoners of the 1961 Bay of Pigs invasion to thirty years in prison.

- On April 8, French voters approve the Algerian peace agreement in a national referendum.

- On April 10, a two-sided Pablo Picasso painting, *Death of a Harlequin* and *Woman Sitting in a Garden,* is purchased in London for $224,000, a record for a painting by a living artist.

- In May, U.S. and Soviet tanks pull back from a confrontation at the border between East and West Berlin.

- On May 17, Swedish boxer Ingemar Johansson knocks out Wales fighter Dick Richardson in the eighth round in Göteburg, Sweden, to win the European heavyweight boxing championship.

- On May 31, Israel executes Nazi war criminal Adolf Eichmann.

- On June 3, a New York–bound Air France jet chartered by members of the Atlanta Art Association crashes after takeoff from Orly International Air Field in Paris.

- On June 3, three thousand government troops crush an uprising by five hundred marines at Venezuelan naval headquarters in Puerto Cabello.

- On June 7, the Secret Army Organization in Algeria increases terrorist bombings against the Muslim-led Algerian provisional government.

- On June 17, Brazil defeats Czechoslovakia, 3-1, to defend its World Cup soccer title in Santiago, Chile.

- On June 30, the Vatican censures Catholic priest Pierre Teilhard de Chardin's *The Phenomenon of Man,* a book in which the late French priest attempted to reconcile church teachings and evolution.

- On July 1, nearly all physicians in Saskatchewan, Canada, go on strike to protest the new health-care plan modeled after the British National Health Service.

- On July 4, British yachtsman Francis Chichester sets a transatlantic solo voyage record of thirty-three days aboard the *Gypsy Moth III*.

- On July 10, American Telephone and Telegraph's *Telstar*, the first privately owned satellite, relays television images from the United States to Europe.

- On July 18, a military junta overthrows the Peruvian government in a bloodless coup.

- On July 30, Eastern and Western European countries dispute Berlin air rights.

- On August 14, violence between East and West Berliners continues along the Berlin Wall.

- On August 21, Soviet cosmonauts contradict Western reports that their two spaceships docked when they tell reporters that the spaceships had not come within three miles of each other.

- On September 28, a Canadian satellite, the first from a country other than the United States or the Soviet Union, launches into orbit from California.

- On October 8, the U.S. Defense Department reports that forty-six American soldiers have died in South Vietnam.

- On October 20, Indian and Chinese troops clash at the border between India and Tibet.

- On October 22, President John F. Kennedy announces a naval blockade against Cuba in response to evidence that the Soviets are constructing missile installations on the island and shipping weapons there.

- On October 23, Dick Tiger of Nigeria scores a fifteen-round decision over Gene Fullmer in San Francisco to win boxing's world middleweight championship.

- On October 24, the United States begins its quarantine on arms shipments to Cuba.

- On October 28, Soviet premier Nikita Khrushchev announces the withdrawal of all Soviet missiles from Cuba in response to Kennedy's October 27 pledge not to invade Cuba.

- On November 20, the United States ends its quarantine of Cuba after the Soviets agree to remove all their bombers from the island.

- On November 21, the Soviet Union ends its military alert in the aftermath of the Cuban missile crisis.

- On November 25, candidates loyal to President Charles de Gaulle win National Assembly elections, the first time in modern French history that a single party controls Parliament.

- On November 30, U Thant wins a four-year term as secretary-general of the United Nations.

- In December, a team of English surgeons transplants a dead man's kidney into a living patient at the Leeds General Infirmary.

- On December 11, U.S. chemist James D. Watson and his British colleagues Francis Crick and Maurice Wilkins share the Nobel Prize in physiology or medicine for the discovery of the structure of deoxyribonucleic acid (DNA).

- On December 20, the Dominican Republic holds its first free elections in thirty-eight years.

- On December 24, Cuba exchanges 1,113 prisoners from the Bay of Pigs invasion for $53 million of medicine and baby food from the U.S.-based Cuban Families Committee.

- On December 31, North Vietnamese leader Ho Chi Minh vows to outlast American aid to South Vietnam and wage war for ten years if necessary.

1963

- On January 25, North and South Korea announce that they will field a joint team for the 1964 Olympic Games in Tokyo, Japan.

- On January 29, France blocks Great Britain's application to join the European Economic Community.

- On February 5, the Canadian Parliament removes the conservative Canadian government headed by John Diefenbaker in a no-confidence vote over Canadian defense policies.

- On February 7, the executive board of the International Olympic Committee bars Indonesia from the Olympics for refusing to allow Israeli and Nationalist Chinese participation in the 1962 Asian Games in Jakarta, Indonesia.

- On February 8, anti-communist air force officers overthrow Iraqi premier Abdul Karim Dassim and execute him the next day.

- On February 22, Norwegian explorer Helge Ingstad reports the discovery of Nordic artifacts in Newfoundland dating about 1000 C.E.

- On March 9, U.S. officials say their use of chemical defoliants do not harm humans and animals in response to a Chinese accusation that the chemicals kill South Vietnamese civilians, livestock, and crops.

- On March 21, an eruption of the Agung volcano on the island of Bali kills some fifteen hundred people.

- On March 27, delegates to the Union of Writers Conference in Moscow denounce Russian poet Yevgeny Yevtushenko for having allowed Western publication of his *Precocious Autobiography*.

- On April 2, a Soviet fighter plane fires on a private twin-engine plane flying an air corridor to West Berlin in violation of international law.

- On April 15, tens of thousands protest nuclear weapons at a peace rally in Hyde Park, London.

- On April 17, Canadian prime minister Diefenbaker resigns after the opposition Liberal Party gains a majority in Parliament.

- On April 22, Liberal Party leader Lester Pearson becomes Canada's new prime minister.

- On May 1, Soviet premier Nikita Khrushchev salutes Cuban Premier Fidel Castro at a May Day celebration in Moscow.

- On May 22, the North Atlantic Treaty Organization (NATO) approves a nuclear alliance.

- On May 27, voters elect Jomo Kenyatta the first African prime minister of Kenya.

- On May 31, Pope John XXIII receives last rites and dies on June 3 at age eighty-one.

- On June 5, British war secretary John Profumo resigns after admitting that he lied to Parliament about his relationship with Christine Keeler, who had ties to the Soviet Union.

- On June 16, Valentina V. Tereshkova, a Soviet cosmonaut, becomes the first woman in space.

- On June 16, Prime Minister David Ben-Gurion of Israel resigns.

- On June 21, the College of the Cardinals elects Giovanni Battista Cardinal Montoni Pope. He takes the name Paul VI.

- On June 26, President John F. Kennedy proclaims "Ich bin ein Berliner." (I too am a Berliner) in pledging U.S. support of West Germany against communism.

- On June 27, President John F. Kennedy appoints Henry Cabot Lodge U.S. ambassador to South Vietnam.

- On July 20, U.S., British, and Soviet negotiators draft a nuclear test-ban treaty.

- On July 24, Cuba takes over the U.S. embassy in Havana after the U.S. freezes Cuban accounts in U.S. banks.

- On July 30, after disappearing in Beirut, Lebanon, British journalist H.A.R. Philby takes refuge in the Soviet Union.

- On August 8, a masked gang escapes with more than $5 million from a mail train near London.

- On August 30, Washington and Moscow open an emergence hotline for instant communication between U.S. and Soviet leaders.

- On September 15, the British create the country of Malaysia.

- On October 7, a hurricane kills five thousand people in Haiti and leaves one hundred thousand homeless.

- From November 12 to November 16, Soviet police detain Professor Frederick C. Barghoorn, chair of the Soviet studies department at Yale University, on charges of espionage.

- On December 9, Zanzibar and Pemba become independent of Britain.

- On December 11, Kenya becomes independent of Britain.

1964

- INTELSAT is formed as an international venture in which countries share the cost of developing and launching communications satellites.

- On January 4, Pope Paul VI tours the Holy Land and meets with Patriarch Benedictos of Jerusalem in the first meeting between the heads of the Roman Catholic and Eastern Orthodox churches in five hundred years.

- On March 26, Defense Secretary Robert S. McNamara warns that U.S. forces will remain in South Vietnam until communists end efforts to take over the South.

- On May 27, Prime Minister Jawaharlal Nehru of India, who held that office since its independence in 1948, dies at age seventy-four.

- On May 29, Quebec members of the Canadian Parliament accept Prime Minister Lester Pearson's proposal for a new flag with a maple-leaf design after rejecting his recommendation to keep the Union Jack.

- In June, British anthropologist Louis S.B. Leakey announces his discovery of *Homo habilis*.

- On June 12, a court sentences eight South African anti-apartheid leaders, including Nelson Mandela, to life in prison.

- On September 14, Pope Paul VI opens the third session of the Ecumenical Council, Vatican II, in Saint Peter's Basilica in Rome.

- In October, the Swedish Royal Academy awards the Nobel Prize in literature to French philosopher, novelist, and dramatist Jean Paul Sartre. Sartre refuses the award.

- In October, physicists James W. Cronin and Val Fitch assert that time can move toward the future or past.

- On October 5, fifty-seven East Germans escape to West Berlin by tunnel.

- On October 9, the Summer Olympics begin in Tokyo.

- On October 12, the Soviet Union launches the first space flight with more than one cosmonaut.

- On October 15, Leonid Brezhnev replaces Nikita Khrushchev as premier of the Soviet Union.

- On October 15, Harold Wilson, leader of the Labour Party, becomes prime minister of Britain.

- On October 16, China detonates its first nuclear bomb in a test.

- On October 23, the republic of Zambia, formerly the British protectorate Northern Rhodesia, becomes independent.

- On November 2, Saudi Arabian religious and political authorities dethrone the sick King Saud and crown his half brother, Crown Prince Faisal.

1965

- The Arecibo Observatory in Puerto Rico shows that Venus rotates in the opposite direction from the other planets.

- Goya's portrait of the duke of Wellington, which was stolen in 1961, is returned to London's National Gallery.

- On January 4, in his State of the Union address, President Lyndon Johnson of the United States invites an exchange of Soviet and U.S. television broadcasts.

- On January 14, the two Irish prime ministers meet for the first time since Ireland's 1922 partition.

- On January 19, the United States claims that a recent Soviet underground nuclear test may violate the test-ban treaty between the two nations.

- On January 21, Indonesia withdraws from the United Nations.

- On January 24, fashion reports indicate that European designers have turned to plastics in creating new household items.

- On January 30, the United States agrees to widen cultural ties with the Soviet Union.

- On February 1, troops loyal to the Laos government repel a coup attempt by army officers.

- On February 8, the Soviet Union pledges antiaircraft systems to North Vietnam following President Lyndon Johnson's authorization of U.S. aircraft to bomb North Vietnam in "Operation Rolling Thunder."

- On February 12, twenty-one protesters die in riots in southern India.

- On February 19, U.N. secretary-general U Thant says that a financial crisis at the United Nations will force the organization to seek additional funds for 1965.

- On February 20, the United Nations announces it will try to help India lower its birth rate.

- On February 23, Syria hangs naturalized U.S. citizen Farhan Attassi for spying.

- On February 24, U.S. officials admit that U.S. military advisers are leading combat troops in the Vietnam War.

- On February 24, U.N. secretary-general U Thant urges the United States to withdraw its troops from South Vietnam and to stop bombing both North and South Vietnam.

- On February 26, Indonesia seizes rubber estates in which U.S. banks had invested, outraging U.S. financiers.

- On February 27, China opens its borders to visits by Japanese citizens.

- On March 1, the Russian film *The Overcoat* opens in New York City.

- On March 3, Great Britain announces cuts in defense spending.

- On March 4, two thousand students attack the U.S. embassy in Moscow.

- On March 14, Israel and West Germany agree to talks aimed at establishing diplomatic relations between the two countries.

- On March 17, French philosopher, novelist, and dramatist Jean-Paul Sartre cancels a U.S. lecture tour to protest the American war in Vietnam.

- On March 18, cosmonaut Aleksei Leonev walks ten minutes in space.

- On March 29, a bomb explosion at the U.S. embassy in Saigon, capital of South Vietnam, kills six.

- On April 3, the United States accuses the Soviet Union of harassing U.S. ships at sea.

- On April 4, East German guards prohibit West Berlin mayor Willy Brandt from driving to Berlin from West Germany.

- On April 8, the Vatican names Cardinal Konig as its envoy to atheists.

- On April 25, U.S. officials confirm for the first time that North Vietnamese troops are fighting in South Vietnam.

- On April 28, President Lyndon Johnson announces that 405 U.S. marines have landed in the Dominican Republic to protect and evacuate American citizens.

- On May 13, Israel and West Germany establish diplomatic relations.

- On May 22, a cease-fire suspends fighting in the Dominican Republic.

- On May 24, satellite television links art buyers in New York and London.

- On June 5, U.S. officials acknowledge that U.S. troops are fighting in South Vietnam, rather than merely protecting U.S. air bases as President Lyndon Johnson had promised.

- On June 7, guerrillas murder U.S. consul Allison Wanamaker in Argentina.

- On June 18, Air Force officer Nguyen Cao Ky becomes South Vietnamese premier.

- On June 28, six nations join in opening the Comsat telephone system.

- On July 6, France withdraws its delegate from the Common Market.

- On July 15, U.S. spacecraft *Mariner 4* sends back to Earth the first photos of Mars taken from space.

- On July 20, the British House of Lords bans the death penalty for criminals convicted of murder.

- On August 5, Greek premier George Athansiadas-Novas resigns as thousands of backers of former prime minister George Papandreou continue to protest.

- On September 1, India and Pakistan clash over Kashmir.

- On September 10, the Vatican exonerates the Jews of responsibility in the death of Jesus.

- On September 17, Stephanos Stephanopoulos becomes prime minister of Greece.

- From September 21 to September 22, India and Pakistan accept a U.N.-sponsored cease-fire in Kashmir.

- On October 14, Paul Cézanne's *Maisons a l'Estaque* sets an auction record for impressionist art.

- On October 15, Soviet writer Mikhail Sholokhov wins the Nobel Prize in literature.

- On October 25, the United Nations Children's Fund wins the Nobel Peace Prize.

- From October 28 to November 14, the U.S. Army and North Vietnamese Army (NVA) clash in the Ia Drang Valley in South Vietnam, one of the few traditional battles of the war.

- On November 12, Philippine senator Ferdinand Marcos wins his country's presidential election.

- On November 24, Soviet officials sentence U.S. tourist Newcomb Mott to eighteen months in prison for crossing the Soviet border without authorization.

- On November 27, the Vatican recovers stolen manuscripts by Italian poets Petrarch and Torquato Tasso.

- On November 30, France urges the United States to leave Vietnam.

- On December 10, *The New York Times* reports that South Vietnamese troops have withdrawn from combat to leave U.S. marines and soldiers to do the fighting.

- On December 19, five international teams of scientists report having identified evidence of the explosion that created the universe 15 billion years ago. Scientists call this explosion the Big Bang.

- On December 19, President Charles de Gaulle wins 54.7 percent of the vote in the French presidential elections.

- On December 20, General William Westmoreland, commander of U.S. troops in South Vietnam, authorizes troops to pursue enemy troops into Cambodia.

- On December 21, the Soviet Union pledges to increase aid to North Vietnam to counter the ferocity of U.S. attacks.

- On December 25, Mexico begins a televised literacy program.

- On December 27, a gas rig collapses in the North Sea, killing thirteen.

- On December 30, Ferdinand Marcos begins his presidency in the Philippines.

1966

- China publishes a book of quotations of Chairman Mao Tse-tung.

- On January 19, voters elect Indira Gandhi, daughter of former prime minister Jawaharlal Nehru, prime minister of India.

- On February 3, an unmanned Soviet craft, *Luna 9,* makes the first soft landing on the Moon.

- On February 17, France launches its first satellite into orbit around Earth.

- On March 1, in the first contact with another planet, a Soviet spacecraft crashes onto the surface of Venus.

- On March 12, France announces that it will withdraw from NATO.

- On March 23, the archbishop of Canterbury, the Most Reverend Arthur Michael Ramsey, meets with Pope Paul VI in Rome.

- On April 3, the Soviet Union's *Luna 10* becomes the first man-made object to orbit the Moon.

- In May, China executes thousands of people it suspects of disloyalty in the Great Proletarian Cultural Revolution.

- On May 10, the Guatemalan Congress elects Mendez Montenegro president in a runoff election.

- On May 13, China accuses the United States of violating its airspace and shooting down a Chinese military training plane.

- On May 30, two Buddhist monks burn themselves to death in protest over government policies in South Vietnam.

- On June 6, the government press criticizes army official Lo Juiching for the first time in Communist Chinese history.

- On June 15, Syrians and Israelis fight a three-hour sea and air battle in and over the Sea of Galilee.

- On June 19, South Vietnamese troops end Buddhist resistance in Hue, the ancient Imperial city and symbol of Vietnamese independence.

- On June 28, a three-man military junta led by Lt. General Juan Carlos Ongania ousts Argentine President Arturo Illia.

- On June 29, Prime Minister Harold Wilson of Britain publicly criticizes U.S. bombing of Vietnam.

- On June 30, the United States begins to withdraw troops from France.

- On July 1, the United States begins to withdraw troops from the Dominican Republic.

- On July 1, President Joseph Mobutu of the Congo orders officials to change the European names of the Congo's cities to African names.

- On July 4, in Belfast, Northern Ireland, a thirty-pound concrete block is dropped on the roof of a car containing Queen Elizabeth II and Prince Philip; no one is injured.

- On July 9, Egyptian President Gamal Nasser declares that Arab countries will never accept Israel as their neighbor.

- On July 11, the Soviet Union announces its athletes will not participate in the eighth annual U.S.-Soviet track meet to protest U.S. policy in Vietnam.

- On July 14, Welsh nationalists for the first time win a seat in the British House of Commons.

- On July 16, Chinese officials report that Chairman Mao Tse-tung recently swam fifteen kilometers in an hour and five minutes in the Yangtze River.

- On July 18, the International Court of Justice dismisses a lawsuit challenging South Africa's right to govern South-West Africa.

- On July 19, Argentina and Great Britain open talks on the future of the Falkland Islands.

- On August 12, North Korea asserts independence from both Chinese and Soviet influence and declares it will follow its own path.

- On August 13, a parade of ten thousand East German soldiers marks the fifth anniversary of the construction of the Berlin Wall.

- On August 17, North Korea aligns itself with the Soviet Union after accusing China of "Trotskyism."

- On August 20, a survey reports that a majority of Roman Catholics use some form of artificial birth control.

- On August 24, Pro-Mao Chinese youths called Red Guards further the Cultural Revolution by breaking into private homes to destroy all items they deem Western.

- On August 30, North Vietnam and China sign an aid agreement.

- On September 1, President Charles de Gaulle of France urges the United States to withdraw from Vietnam in a speech in Cambodia.

- On September 6, an assassin stabs South African prime minister Hendrik Verwoerd to death during a session of Parliament.

- On September 6, Syria announces it has crushed a coup by Baath Party founder Michel Aflak.

- On September 14, new South African prime minister B.J. Vorster pledges to continue apartheid, a policy whereby the white minority oppressed the black majority.

- On September 19, the last American troops leave the Dominican Republic.

- On October 20, Israeli writer Shmuel Agnon wins the Nobel Prize in literature.

- On October 22, the U.S. delegation opposes United Nations sanctions against South Africa on the grounds that they would be counterproductive.

- On October 23, the International Cancer Congress convenes in Tokyo.

- In November, archeologists Clifford Evans and Betty J. Maggers assert that pottery from South America from 3000 B.C.E. was influenced by the Japanese, suggesting contact between South America and Japan at that time.
- On November 1, North Korean troops kill eight U.S. soldiers in the demilitarized zone between North and South Korea in violation of the 1953 armistice.
- On November 24, U.S. scientists ask Pope Paul VI to end the Church's opposition to birth control.
- On November 29, the United Nations votes, 57-47, not to admit China.
- In December, Dr. Audouin Dollfus of France's Meudon Observatory discovers a tenth moon of the planet Saturn.
- On December 1, the West German Parliament elects Kurt-Georg Kiesinger chancellor.
- On December 2, the United Nations ratifies the first international treaty governing the exploration of space.
- On December 21, a Soviet court sentences an American tourist to three years in a labor camp for having sold U.S. dollars on the black market.
- On December 26, the European Economic Community denies Spain membership on the grounds that it is not a democracy.

1967

- On January 4, Pope Paul VI bans unorthodox liturgies such as jazz masses.
- On January 5, British dramatist Harold Pinter premieres the play *The Homecoming* in New York.
- On January 16, Lynden Oscar Pindling becomes the first black prime minister of the Bahama Islands.
- On January 20, Cuba executes Enrique Gonzalez Rodriguez for acting as an agent for the U.S. Central Intelligence Agency.
- On January 20, Pope Paul VI confers with Soviet president Nikolai Podgorny in the first meeting between a Roman Catholic pontiff and a Communist head of state.
- On January 31, Romania becomes the first Eastern Bloc country to recognize West Germany.
- On February 3, Prime Minister Lester Pearson announces the creation of a government commission on the status of women in Canadian society.
- On February 13, Canada denies entry to U.S. psychiatrist and LSD proponent Timothy Leary.
- On February 21, Mao Tse-tung orders Red Guards to cease political activity.
- On March 1, Marshall McLuhan publishes *The Medium Is the Message.*
- On March 5, Colonel Fidel Sanchez Hernandez wins the presidential election in El Salvador.
- On March 6, Svetlana Stalina, only daughter of the late Joseph Stalin, asks for U.S. asylum at the U.S. embassy in New Delhi, India.
- On March 15, Artur Da Costa e Silva becomes president of Brazil.

- On April 15, the Soviets announce that they will allow 390 state farms to sell crops and livestock for profit.
- On April 20, René Ribiere and Gaston Deferre, two French politicians, fight a duel after a heated argument in the French Assembly; neither man is hurt.
- On April 21, the army overthrows the interim government of Premier Panayotis Kanellopoulos of Greece.
- On April 24, Greek authorities ban miniskirts for girls and long hair for boys.
- On April 25, Swaziland, a former British colony, becomes a self-governing British protectorate.
- On April 26, Eugene Blake, general secretary of the World Council of Churches, urges the United States to stop bombing North Vietnam.
- On May 19, U.S. B-52s bomb downtown Hanoi.
- In June, physicists Steven Weinberg and Sheldon Glashow independently propose electroweak unification, stating that it should be possible to unify the four basic forces of physics into one grand theory.
- On June 5, Israel defeats Syria, Jordan, and the United Arab Republic in the Six Day War.
- On June 17, China detonates its first hydrogen bomb.
- From June 23 to June 25, U.S. president Lyndon Johnson and Soviet premier Aleksey Kosygin discuss arms control, Vietnam, and the Middle East in Glassboro, New Jersey.
- On June 26, U.S. and Panamanian officials meet to discuss transferring U.S. control of the Panama Canal to Panama.
- On June 28, Israel occupies Jerusalem, a city sacred to Jews, Christians and Muslims.
- On July 4, Britain's House of Commons decriminalizes private homosexual acts between consenting adults.
- On July 24, President Charles de Gaulle of France proclaims "Long live free Quebec" during a visit to Canada.
- On July 25, in Turkey, Pope Paul VI becomes the first Pope to enter an Eastern Orthodox church.
- In August, a man who had returned from a trip to Africa dies of a mysterious illness in Marburg, Germany. Physicians discover in him a new virus, which they name Marburg.
- On August 3, President Lyndon Johnson announces that the United States will send forty-five thousand to fifty thousand more troops to Vietnam.
- From August 6 to August 7, five supporters of Fidel Castro hijack a Columbian plane and force it to land in Cuba.
- On August 27, India sets up camps for nearly five hundred Tibetans who fled their country under persecution from China's Red Guards.
- On September 14, molecular biologists Vincent M. Sarich and Allan C. Wilson stun the anthropological community by announcing that the genetic clock of U.S. chemist and Nobel laureate Linus Pauling puts the divergence of the line leading to humans and the line leading to the African apes at five million years ago. Before this announcement, anthropologists had estimated the divergence at some twenty to thirty million years ago.

- On September 17, riots at a soccer game in Kayseri, Turkey, kill forty-two people and injure more than six hundred.
- On September 20, Britain launches the luxury liner the *Queen Elizabeth II.*
- On September 23, the Soviet Union agrees to continue military and economic assistance to North Vietnam.
- On September 24, the Organization of American States agrees to fight Cuban-promoted revolutionary activities in the Western Hemisphere.
- In October, molecular biologists Charles T. Caskey, Richard E. Marshall, and Marshall W. Nirenberg find that the genetic code is essentially the same in guinea pigs, toads, and bacteria, evidence that all life shares a common ancestor, a tenet of evolutionary biology.
- On October 9, Bolivian troops execute Cuban revolutionary Che Guevara.
- On October 18, the Soviet Union lands a spacecraft on Venus, revealing that the atmosphere consists largely of carbon dioxide and that temperatures range from 104 to 536° Fahrenheit.
- On October 21, Israeli archaeologists announce the discovery of a new Dead Sea scroll.
- On October 26, the shah of Iran proclaims himself king of kings and his wife Iran's first crowned queen.
- On October 31, Queen Elizabeth II announces the elimination of membership in the House of Lords by heredity.
- On December 3, Dr. Christiaan Barnard performs the world's first successful heart transplant on Louis Washkansky in Cape Town, South Africa.
- On December 11, Britain and France unveil the first supersonic airliner, the Concorde.
- On December 17, Prime Minister Harold Holt of Australia disappears while swimming and is assumed dead.
- On December 21, heart-transplant recipient Louis Washkansky dies of pneumonia.

1968

- Japan's gross national product (GNP) climbs 12 percent, making it second only to the United States.
- On January 1, C. Day Lewis becomes Great Britain's poet laureate.
- On January 5, the Czechoslovak Communist Party elects Alexander Dubcek as its first secretary, a move toward political liberalization in Czechoslovakia.
- On January 12, Simon & Schuster publishes the late German theologian Martin Buber's *A Believing Humanism.*
- On January 21, the North Vietnamese attack the U.S. Marines base at Kesanh.
- On January 23, North Korean patrol boats capture the U.S. intelligence-gathering ship *Pueblo.*
- On January 30, North Vietnamese and Viet Cong forces attack every provincial city including Saigon in South Vietnam in the Tet offensive.
- On January 31, the Viet Cong capture the U.S. embassy in Saigon. U.S. marines retake the embassy in a six-hour battle.
- In February, engineers complete the Aswan Dam in Egypt.

- On February 6, Sweden grants asylum to six U.S. soldiers opposed to the Vietnam War.
- On February 6, Soviet officials forbid a literary magazine from publishing Russian novelist Aleksandr Solzhenitsyn's *The Cancer Ward.*
- In March, molecular biologist Werner Arber discovers that some enzymes can cut sequences of nucleotide bases from a strand of DNA.
- From March 8 to March 11, thousands of students in Poland fight police in protests against Communist Party involvement in cultural matters.
- On March 16, Lt. William L. Calley Jr. orders soldiers to massacre hundreds of men, women, and children in My Lai, a South Vietnamese village.
- On April 6, voters elect Pierre Trudeau leader of Canada's Liberal Party.
- On April 21, the International Olympic Committee excludes South Africa from the 1968 games as punishment for its oppression of blacks.
- On April 23, in shifting to a decimal monetary system, Britain issues its first five-and ten-pence coins.
- On April 27, Britain legalizes most abortions.
- In May, Britain's Theatres Act ends censorship of literature and drama.
- In June, geologist Elso S. Barghoorn finds amino acids in three-billion-year-old rocks, raising the possibility that life is 3 billion years old.
- On June 26, the United States returns Iwo Jima to Japan after more than twenty-three years of U.S. administration.
- On July 29, Pope Paul VI urges Catholics to limit the size of their families only by abstinence or the rhythm method.
- From August 20 to August 22, Warsaw Pact troops invade Czechoslovakia.
- On August 22, in Columbia, Pope Paul VI becomes the first Pope to visit South America.
- On September 29, Greek voters support a new constitution that strips the king of most of his power.
- On October 9, police arrest five Soviet citizens for protesting the invasion of Czechoslovakia.
- On December 16, the Spanish government rescinds its 1492 expulsion of Jews from Spain.
- On December 27, the United States announces it will sell fifty fighter jets to Israel.

1969

- On January 12, some five thousand people march in London to protest discrimination against nonwhites.
- On February 6, Palestinians elect Yasser Arafat chair of the executive committee of the Palestine Liberation Organization.
- On March 17, Golda Meir is sworn in as premier of Israel.
- On March 19, The Museum of Modern Art in New York City purchases the art collection of the late expatriate writer Gertrude Stein for $6 million.
- On April 28, Charles de Gaulle resigns as president of France after voters reject his constitutional reforms.

- On June 5, the Soviet Writers' Union expels Russian novelist Aleksandr Solzhenitsyn.

- On July 1, Queen Elizabeth II makes her son Charles Prince of Wales and Earl of Chester.

- On July 7, Canada's House of Commons decrees French the second official language.

- On July 14, El Salvadoran troops invade Honduras.

- On July 20, U.S. astronauts make the first manned landing on the Moon.

- On July 22, Generalissimo Francisco Franco of Spain names Prince Juan Carlos as his successor.

- On July 31, Pope Paul VI is the first Pope to visit Africa.

- On September 3, North Vietnamese president Ho Chi Minh dies at age seventy-nine. For half a century, he had kept alive Vietnamese dreams of independence.

- In October, the Swedish Royal Academy awards the Nobel Prize in literature to Irish dramatist and novelist Samuel Beckett.

- On October 17, the Bolivian government nationalizes Bolivia Gulf Company, a subsidiary of the Gulf Oil Corporation.

- On October 31, a U.S. marine hijacks a jet from California to Rome in the first transatlantic hijacking.

1

THE ARTS

MILLIE JACKSON

Entries are arranged in chronological order by date of primary source. For entries with one primary source, the entry title is the same as the primary source title. Entries with more than one primary source have an overall entry title, followed by the titles of the primary sources.

Kill a Mockingbird; Flannery O'Connor, *The Violent Bear It Away;* John O'Hara, *Sermons and Soda-Water;* Sylvia Plath, *The Colossus;* Anne Sexton, *To Bedlam and Part Way Back;* John Updike, *Rabbit, Run.*

POPULAR SONGS: Paul Anka, "Puppy Love"; Ray Charles, "Georgia on My Mind"; Chubby Checker, "The Twist"; Elvis Presley, "Are You Lonesome Tonight?" and "It's Now or Never"; Johnny Preston, "Running Bear."

1961

- The Museum of Modern Art holds a retrospective exhibit of the work of Mark Rothko.

- Robert A. Heinlein's *Stranger in a Strange Land* becomes the first science-fiction novel to appear on *The New York Times* best-seller list.

- On January 20, poet Robert Frost reads his poem "Dedication" at John Kennedy's inauguration, confirming his status as America's most widely known poet.

- On January 27, soprano Leontyne Price first performs at the New York Metropolitan Opera.

- On July 29, ten paintings worth three hundred thousand dollars are stolen from the private collection of G. David Thompson of Pittsburgh; others (including a Picasso) are damaged.

- On August 28, a contract dispute concerning the musicians at the Metropolitan Opera in New York is settled when the musicians and the company agree to abide by binding arbitration by Secretary of Labor Arthur Goldberg.

- On November 13, cellist Pablo Casals performs at a White House dinner honoring Puerto Rican governor Luis Muñoz Marín.

MOVIES: *The Absent-Minded Professor,* starring Fred Mac-Murray; *Breakfast at Tiffany's,* starring Audrey Hepburn and George Peppard; *El Cid,* starring Charlton Heston; *The Hustler,* starring Paul Newman and Jackie Gleason; *Judgment at Nuremberg,* starring Montgomery Clift; *The Misfits,* directed by John Huston and starring Clark Gable and Marilyn Monroe; *101 Dalmatians,* Disney animation; *Splendor in the Grass,* directed by Elia Kazan and starring Natalie Wood and Warren Beatty; *West Side Story,* starring Richard Beymer and Natalie Wood.

FICTION: James Baldwin, *Nobody Knows My Name;* Edwin O'Connor, *The Edge of Sadness;* John Hawkes, *The Lime Twig;* Joseph Heller, *Catch-22;* Allen Ginsberg, *Kaddish and Other Poems;* John O'Hara, *Assembly;* Robert A. Heinlein, *Stranger in a Strange Land;* Bernard Malamud, *A New Life;* Walker Percy, *The Moviegoer;* Harold Robbins, *The Carpetbaggers;* J. D. Salinger, *Franny and Zooey;* Isaac Bashevis Singer, *The Spinoza of Market Street;* John Steinbeck, *The Winter of Our Discontent; Irving Stone,* The Agony and the Ecstasy; *Leon Uris,* Mila 18.

POPULAR SONGS: Ray Charles, "Hit the Road, Jack"; Jimmy Dean, "Big Bad John"; Dion, "Run-around Sue"; the Kingston Trio, "Where Have All the Flowers Gone?"; the Marvelettes, "Please, Mr. Postman"; Roy Orbison, "Cryin'"; the Shirelles, "Will You Still Love Me Tomorrow?"; the Tokens, "The Lion Sleeps Tonight."

Important Events in the Arts, 1960–1969

1960

- The second annual Photography in the Fine Arts Project is held at the IBM Gallery in New York; it is twice as big and occupies three times as much space as the original.

- Leslie Fiedler's controversial *Love and Death in the American Novel* quickly becomes one of the best-known books in the history of American literary criticism.

- *Astounding Science Fiction,* one of the most popular science-fiction magazines since the 1930s, changes its name to *Analog.*

- Motown Records is formed by Berry Gordy, who intends that this record label will become the "sound of young America."

- On January 3, the Moscow State Symphony begins a successful seven-week tour of the United States at Carnegie Hall in New York. It is the first Soviet orchestra to perform in the United States.

- In March, seven of the eight major film studios are crippled by an actors' strike.

- On March 4, baritone Leonard Warren collapses and dies during a performance of *La Forza del Destino* at the Metropolitan Opera House in New York.

- On March 16, the merger of Alfred A. Knopf, Inc., and Random House, Inc., is completed, with Random in control.

- On July 3, the city council of Newport, Rhode Island, votes to cancel remaining performances at the annual Newport Jazz Festival due to riots led by drunken high-school and college students.

- On November 2, Dimitri Mitropoulos, who had been the conductor of the Minneapolis Symphony Orchestra and the New York Philharmonic, collapses and dies while conducting at La Scala Opera House in Milan, Italy.

MOVIES: *The Apartment,* directed by Billy Wilder and starring Jack Lemmon and Shirley MacLaine; *Elmer Gantry,* starring Burt Lancaster and Jean Simmons; *Little Shop of Horrors,* directed by Roger Corman; *Psycho,* directed by Alfred Hitchcock and starring Anthony Perkins; *Spartacus,* directed by Stanley Kubrick and starring Kirk Douglas, Tony Curtis, Peter Ustinov, and Jean Simmons.

FICTION: John Barth, *The Sot-Weed Factor;* E. L. Doctorow, *Welcome to Hard Times;* John Hersey, *The Child Buyer;* Jack Kerouac, *Lonesome Traveler;* Harper Lee, *To*

1962

- William S. Burroughs's novel *Naked Lunch* (1959), initially published in Paris, is published in America for the first time.

- Claes Oldenburg creates his soft sculpture *Two Cheeseburgers with Everything.*

- After the death of Clara Langhorne Clemens Samossoud, the last surviving child of Mark Twain, his antireligious *Letters from the Earth* is published for the first time, as a book edited by Bernard De Voto.

- On May 30, Benny Goodman begins a six-week tour of Russia in Moscow arranged by the U.S. State Department. Some jazz aficionados feel a more respected all-around musician such as Duke Ellington should represent America, while others think a younger, more "modern" musician would be more appropriate.

- On September 25, Philharmonic Hall, the first completed building of the Lincoln Center for the Performing Arts in New York, is inaugurated by Leonard Bernstein and the New York Philharmonic. First Lady Jacqueline Kennedy is guest of honor.

- On October 25, John Steinbeck is announced as the 1962 recipient of the Nobel Prize in literature.

- On December 12, French minister of culture André Malraux announces that France will loan the United States Leonardo da Vinci's *Mona Lisa* for a short period for an American touring exhibit.

MOVIES: *The Birdman of Alcatraz,* starring Burt Lancaster; *Days of Wine and Roses,* starring Jack Lemmon and Lee Remick; *Dr. No,* starring Sean Connery; *Lawrence of Arabia,* directed by David Lean and starring Peter O'Toole; *Lolita,* directed by Stanley Kubrick and starring James Mason; *The Manchurian Candidate,* starring Laurence Harvey, Frank Sinatra, and Angela Lansbury; *The Music Man,* starring Robert Preston and Shirley Jones; *Mutiny on the Bounty,* starring Marlon Brando and Trevor Howard; *To Kill a Mockingbird,* starring Gregory Peck; *What Ever Happened to Baby Jane?,* starring Joan Crawford and Bette Davis.

FICTION: James Baldwin, *Another Country;* William S. Burroughs, *The Ticket That Exploded;* Ken Kesey, *One Flew Over the Cuckoo's Nest;* Jack Kerouac, *Big Sur;* Vladimir Nabokov, *Pale Fire;* Katherine Anne Porter, *Ship of Fools;* J.D. Salinger, *Franny and Zooey;* Anne Sexton, *All My Pretty Ones;* Isaac Bashevis Singer, *The Slave;* Kurt Vonnegut, Jr., *Mother Night;* Irving Wallace, *The Prize;* Herman Wouk, *Youngblood Hawk.*

POPULAR SONGS: Tony Bennett, "I Left My Heart in San Francisco"; Gene Chandler, "Duke of Earl"; Ray Charles, "I Can't Stop Loving You"; the Four Seasons, "Big Girls Don't Cry" and "Sherry"; Little Eva, "The Loco-Motion"; Bobby "Boris" Pickett, "The Monster Mash"; Elvis Presley, "Return to Sender"; Neil Sedaka, "Breaking Up Is Hard to Do."

1963

- John Cleland's erotic eighteenth-century-style novel *Memoirs of a Woman of Pleasure,* better known as *Fanny Hill,*

is banned in several cities, but the courts declare it not to be obscene. Meanwhile, a bookseller in New Orleans is arrested for selling James Baldwin's novel *Another Country.*

- A member of the New York Public Library board of trustees borrows and burns the children's book *My Mother Is the Most Beautiful Woman in the World,* Rebecca Reyher's retelling of a Russian folktale, due to the book containing passages "favorable to Russia." He is suspended from the board for six weeks or until he replaces the book.

- Andrew Wyeth becomes the first painter to receive the Presidential Medal of Freedom.

- On January 8, Leonardo da Vinci's *Mona Lisa* is shown at the National Gallery in Washington, D.C., the first time the painting has ever appeared outside the Louvre in Paris. During its three-and-a-half-week stay it attracts five hundred thousand visitors. When the painting moves to New York, 23,872 people show up on a rainy day to see it.

- On May 7, the Guthrie Theatre in Minneapolis, the first major regional theater in the Midwest, opens.

- In July, actor and folk singer Theodore Bikel and folk singers Pete Seeger and Bob Dylan go to Greenwood, Mississippi to sing "We Shall Overcome" and other politically oriented songs during the voter registration campaign.

- On July 28, at the March on Washington, folk group Peter, Paul, and Mary sing "Blowing in the Wind" and "If I Had a Hammer."

MOVIES: *The Birds,* directed by Alfred Hitchcock and starring Tippi Hedren; *Cleopatra,* starring Elizabeth Taylor and Richard Burton; *Hud,* starring Paul Newman; *It's a Mad Mad Mad Mad World,* directed by Stanley Kramer; *Lilies of the Field,* starring Sidney Poitier; *The Nutty Professor,* starring Jerry Lewis; *Tom Jones,* starring Albert Finney.

FICTION: James Baldwin, *The Fire Next Time;* Taylor Caldwell, *Grandmother and the Priests;* Allen Ginsberg, *Reality Sandwiches;* Bernard Malamud, *Idiots First;* Mary McCarthy, *The Group;* Sylvia Plath, *The Bell Jar;* Thomas Pynchon, *V.;* J. D. Salinger, *Raise High the Roofbeam, Carpenters, and Seymour: An Introduction;* John Updike, *The Centaur;* Kurt Vonnegut, Jr., *Cat's Cradle.*

POPULAR SONGS: The Angels, "My Boyfriend's Back"; the Beach Boys, "Surfin' U.S.A."; Johnny Cash, "Ring of Fire"; the Chiffons, "He's So Fine" and "One Fine Day"; the Crystals, "Then He Kissed Me"; the Four Seasons, "Walk Like a Man"; Leslie Gore, "It's My Party"; the Kingsmen, "Louie, Louie"; Steve Lawrence, "Go Away, Little Girl"; Peter, Paul and Mary, "Blowin' in the Wind" and "Puff, the Magic Dragon"; the Singing Nun, "Dominique"; Bobby Vinton, "Blue Velvet."

1964

- *A Moveable Feast,* Ernest Hemingway's memoirs of his early years in Paris, is published.

- Pop art comes into vogue as exemplified by *Vicki! I-I Thought I Heard Your Voice* a painting by artist Roy Lichtenstein.

- After three years of court battles in various states, the U.S. Supreme Court rules that Henry Miller's novel *Tropic of Cancer* is not obscene.

• *The Deputy,* by German playwright Rolf Hochhuth, is picketed at its New York performance by Catholics outraged at its suggestion that Pope Pius XII had tacitly allowed the Nazis to commit genocide during World War II.

• On February 28, jazz pianist Thelonious Monk is featured in a cover story in *Time* magazine.

• In May, after remodeling, the Museum of Modern Art reopens with a new gallery, named the Steichen Photography Center after Edward Steichen, its photography department director from 1947 to 1962.

MOVIES: *Becket,* starring Richard Burton and Peter O'Toole; *Dr. Strangelove or: How I Learned to Stop Worrying and Love the Bomb,* directed by Stanley Kubrick and starring Peter Sellers, George C. Scott, and Slim Pickens; *Goldfinger,* starring Sean Connery; *Mary Poppins,* starring Julie Andrews and Dick Van Dyke; *My Fair Lady,* starring Rex Harrison and Audrey Hepburn; *Zorba the Greek,* starring Anthony Quinn.

FICTION: Louis Auchincloss, *The Rector of Justin;* Saul Bellow, *Herzog;* Thomas Berger, *Little Big Man;* Richard Brautigan, *A Confederate General from Big Sur;* William S. Burroughs, *Nova Express;* John Cheever, *The Wapshot Scandal;* James Gould Cozzens, *Children and Others;* John Hawkes, *Second Skin;* Bel Kaufman, *Up the Down Staircase;* Ken Kesey, *Sometimes a Great Notion;* Leon Uris, *Armageddon.*

POPULAR SONGS: The Animals, "The House of the Rising Sun"; Louis Armstrong, "Hello, Dolly!"; the Beach Boys, "Fun, Fun, Fun" and "I Get Around"; the Beatles, "Can't Buy Me Love," "A Hard Day's Night," "I Feel Fine," "I Want to Hold Your Hand," "She Loves You," and "Twist and Shout"; Manfred Mann, "Do Wah Diddy Diddy"; Martha and the Vandellas, "Dancing in the Street"; Dean Martin, "Everybody Loves Somebody"; Roy Orbison, "Pretty Woman"; the Supremes, "Where Did Our Love Go?" and "Baby Love"; the Temptations, "The Way You Do the Things You Do"; Mary Wells, "My Guy."

1965

• A three-person music jury suggests that the advisory board for the Pulitzer Prizes grant jazz musician, composer, and bandleader Duke Ellington a special citation for his lifework. The board rejects the recommendation, leading one jury member to voice his dissatisfaction with the decision publicly. Ellington, 66, shrugs it off: "Fate doesn't want me to be too famous too young," he says.

• The Metropolitan Museum in New York stages a successful exhibit, "Three Centuries of American Painting," of more than four hundred works from those of colonial times to those by Jasper Johns, Robert Rauschenberg, and Mark Rothko.

• More than seventy thousand listeners attend the first of the New York Philharmonic's free concerts in Central Park.

• Malcolm Little publishes his story of racial persecution and rebirth in *The Autobiography of Malcolm X.*

• On April 26, Charles Ives's *Symphony No. 4* (1916) is performed in its entirety for the first time by the American Symphony Orchestra, conducted by Leopold Stokowski. A

grant is required to finance the extra rehearsals needed for the extremely difficult piece.

MOVIES: *Cat Ballou,* starring Lee Marvin and Jane Fonda; *Doctor Zhivago,* directed by David Lean and starring Omar Sharif and Julie Christie; *The Greatest Story Ever Told,* starring Max Von Sydow, Charlton Heston, and Telly Savalas; *A Patch of Blue,* diected by Guy Green and starring Sidney Poitier and Shelley Winters; *Ship of Fools,* directed by Stanley Kramer and starring Vivien Leigh, Lee Marvin, Simone Signoet, and Jose Ferrer; *The Sound of Music,* starring Julie Andrews and Christopher Plummer; *A Thousand Clowns,* directed by Fred Coe and starring Jason Robards and Barbara Harris; *Thunderball,* starring Sean Connery.

FICTION: Robert Coover, *The Origin of the Brunists;* Frank Herbert, *Dune;* Jerzy Kosinski, *The Painted Bird;* Norman Mailer, *An American Dream;* Cormac McCarthy, *The Orchard Keeper;* Flannery O'Connor, *Everything That Rises Must Converge.*

POPULAR SONGS: Fontella Bass, "Rescue Me"; the Beach Boys, "California Girls" and "Help Me, Rhonda"; the Beatles, "Eight Days a Week," "Ticket to Ride," and "Yesterday"; James Brown, "Papa's Got a Brand New Bag"; the Byrds, "Turn! Turn! Turn!"; Petula Clark, "Downtown"; Bob Dylan, "Like a Rolling Stone"; Four Tops, "I Can't Help Myself"; The McCoys, "Hang On, Sloopy"; Roger Miller, "King of the Road"; the Righteous Brothers, "Unchained Melody" and "You've Lost That Lovin' Feelin'"; the Rolling Stones, "Get Off of My Cloud" and "(I Can't Get No) Satisfaction"; Sonny and Cher, "I Got You Babe"; the Supremes, "Stop! In the Name of Love"; the Temptations, "My Girl"; Dionne Warwick, "What the World Needs Now."

1966

• Jazz pianist Earl Hines tours the Soviet Union, sponsored by the U.S. State Department. The tour is a tremendous success: in thirty-five concerts in eleven cities Hines plays for nearly one hundred thousand jazz fans.

• *The Sound of Music* (1965), having earned $70 million in one year, becomes the top-grossing movie in American motion-picture history.

• Berry Gordy, Jr., the founder of Motown, changes the name of the Supremes to Diana Ross and the Supremes.

• Folk singer Arlo Guthrie writes "Alice's Restaurant," a ballad about his arrest for littering and his attempts to avoid the draft.

• The Beach Boys release their *Pet Sounds* album.

• On May 11, Joseph H. Hirschhorn donates his art collection, including fifty-six hundred paintings, drawings, and sculptures, to the United States. The collection's value is appraised at $50 million.

• On December 8, Paul Mellon donates his collection of British rare books, paintings, drawings, and prints to Yale University. The collection's value is appraised at more than $35 million.

MOVIES: *Batman,* starring Adam West, Burt Ward, Burgess Meredith, Cesar Romero, Frank Gorshin, and Lee Meriwether; *The Chase,* starring Marlon Brando, Robert Redford, and Jane Fonda; *The Group,* starring Candice Bergen; *One Million Years B.C.,* starring Raquel Welch; *The Russians Are Coming, The Russians Are Coming,* directed by Norman Jewison and starring Carl Reiner, Eva Marie Saint, Alan Arkin, Brian Keith, and Jonathan Winters; *The Sand Pebbles,* directed by Robert Wise and starring Steve McQueen, Richard Crenna and Candice Bergen; *Who's Afraid of Virginia Woolf?,* starring Richard Burton, Elizabeth Taylor, George Segal, and Sandy Dennis.

FICTION: John Barth, *Giles Goat-Boy;* Truman Capote, *In Cold Blood;* William H. Gass, *Omensetter's Luck;* Bernard Malamud, *The Fixer;* Thomas Pynchon, *The Crying of Lot 49;* Kurt Vonnegut, *Mother Night.*

POPULAR SONGS: The Beach Boys, "Good Vibrations"; the Beatles, "Eleanor Rigby," "Paperback Writer," and "We Can Work It Out"; the Lovin' Spoonful, "Did You Ever Have to Make Up Your Mind?" and "Summer in the City"; Loretta Lynn, "Don't Come Home a-Drinkin' (with Lovin' on Your Mind)"; the Mamas and the Papas, "Monday, Monday"; the Monkees, "I'm a Believer" and "Last Train to Clarksville"; Napoleon XIV, "They're Coming to Take Me Away, Ha Ha"; Staff Sgt. Barry Sadler, "The Ballad of the Green Berets"; Simon and Garfunkel, "I Am a Rock" and "The Sounds of Silence"; Frank Sinatra, "Strangers in the Night"; Nancy Sinatra, "These Boots Are Made for Walkin'"; Percy Sledge, "When a Man Loves a Woman"; the Supremes, "You Can't Hurry Love"; the Troggs, "Wild Thing"; the Young Rascals, "Good Lovin'."

1967

• M-G-M Studios turns down a $10 million offer to broadcast *Gone with the Wind* on television.

• Anne Sexton wins the Pulitzer Prize for her book of poetry *Live or Die.*

• On February 18, the National Gallery of Art in Washington arranges to purchase Leonardo da Vinci's *Ginevra dei Benci* from Prince Franz Joseph of Liechtenstein for $5–6 million, the highest price at that time for a single painting.

• From April 8 to April 10, the Academy Awards ceremony, slated for April 8, is postponed two days due to the April 9 funeral of Martin Luther King, Jr., who was killed four days before, when five participants say they will not attend if the show goes on as planned. Academy president Gregory Peck also cancels the Governors' Ball.

• On April 26, Pablo Picasso's *Mother and Child* sells for $532,000, the highest price to that time for a single painting by a living artist.

• In December, unable to compete with television news, the last of the movie newsreel companies, Universal News, closes.

MOVIES: *Bonnie and Clyde,* starring Warren Beatty and Faye Dunaway; *Cool Hand Luke,* starring Paul Newman; *The Dirty Dozen,* directed by Robert Aldrich and starring Lee Marvin, Robert Ryan, Telly Savalas, John Cassavetes, Ernest Borgnine, and Jim Brown;*The Graduate,* starring Dustin Hoffman and Anne Bancroft; *Guess Who's Coming to Dinner,* starring Sidney Poitier, Spencer Tracy, and Katharine Hepburn; *In Cold Blood,* directed by Richard

Brooks and starring Robert Blake and Scott Wilson; *In the Heat of the Night,* starring Sidney Poitier and Rod Steiger; *The Jungle Book,* Disney animation.

FICTION: Donald Barthelme, *Snow White;* Richard Brautigan, *Trout Fishing in America;* Norman Mailer, *Why Are We in Vietnam?;* Chaim Potok, *The Chosen;* William Styron, *The Confessions of Nat Turner;* Leon Uris, *Topaz;* Gore Vidal, *Washington, D.C.*

POPULAR SONGS: The Doors, "Light My Fire"; Aretha Franklin, "Respect" and "(You Make Me Feel Like) A Natural Woman"; Bobbie Gentry, "Ode to Billie Joe"; Arlo Guthrie, "Alice's Restaurant"; Engelbert Humperdinck, "Release Me"; Jefferson Airplane, "Somebody to Love" and "White Rabbit"; Procol Harum, "A Whiter Shade of Pale"; Smokey Robinson and the Miracles, "I Second That Emotion"; the Rolling Stones, "Let's Spend the Night Together" and "Ruby Tuesday"; Tommy James and the Shondells, "I Think We're Alone Now"; the Turtles, "Happy Together"; Frankie Valli, "Can't Take My Eyes Off of You."

1968

• The Academy of Motion Picture Arts and Sciences announces that it will no longer offer separate Oscars for films in color and in black and white because of the rapidly shrinking number of black-and-white films. Separate awards had been given in cinematography since 1939, art direction since 1940, and costume design since 1948.

• Bosley Crowther, the influential film critic of *The New York Times,* retires after disagreeing with most critics and moviegoers over *Bonnie and Clyde* (1967), which he disliked and the public loved.

• *Switched-On Bach,* an album of music by Johann Sebastian Bach performed on the Moog synthesizer by Walter (later, after a sex change, Wendy) Carlos, is popular with classical listeners as well as young people. A second album the following year, *The Well-Tempered Synthesizer,* is equally successful.

• *Hair,* the American tribal love rock musical opens at the Biltmore Theatre and epitomizes a generation.

MOVIES: *Barbarella,* starring Jane Fonda; *Charly,* directed by Ralph Nelson and starring Cliff Robertson and Claire Bloom; *Funny Girl,* starring Barbra Streisand; *The Green Berets,* directed by and starring John Wayne; *The Lion in Winter,* starring Katharine Hepburn and Peter O'Toole; *Night of the Living Dead,* directed by George Romero; *The Odd Couple,* starring Jack Lemmon and Walter Matthau; *Planet of the Apes,* starring Charlton Heston and Roddy McDowall; *The Producers,* directed by Mel Brooks and starring Zero Mostel and Gene Wilder; *Rachel, Rachel,* directed by Paul Newman and starring Joanne Woodward; *Romeo and Juliet,* directed by Franco Zeffirelli and starring Leonard Whiting and Olivia Hussey; *Rosemary's Baby,* directed by Roman Polanski and starring Mia Farrow; *The Thomas Crown Affair,* directed by Norman Jewison and starring Steve McQueen and Faye Dunaway; *2001: A Space Odyssey,* directed by Stanley Kubrick and starring Keir Dullea.

FICTION: James Baldwin, *Tell Me How Long the Train's Been Gone;* John Barth, *Lost in the Funhouse: Fiction for*

Print, Tape, Live Voice; Richard Brautigan, *In Watermelon Sugar;* Robert Coover, *The Universal Baseball Association, Inc., J. Henry Waugh, Prop.;* James Gould Cozzens, *Morning Noon and Night;* N. Scott Momaday, *House Made of Sawn;* Ronald Sukenick, *Up;* John Updike, *Couples;* Gore Vidal, *Myra Breckinridge.*

POPULAR SONGS: The Beatles, "Hey Jude"; James Brown, "Say It Loud (I'm Black and I'm Proud)"; the Doors, "Hello, I Love You"; Marvin Gaye, "I Heard It through the Grapevine"; Bobby Goldsboro, "Honey"; Ohio Express, "Yummy Yummy Yummy"; the Rascals, "People Got to Be Free"; Otis Redding, "(Sittin' on) The Dock of the Bay"; Jeannie C. Riley, "Harper Valley P.T.A."; the Rolling Stones, "Jumpin' Jack Flash"; Simon and Garfunkel, "Mrs. Robinson"; Steppenwolf, "Born to Be Wild"; Dionne Warwick, "Do You Know the Way to San Jose?"

1969

• Ten-year retrospectives are held featuring the work of pop artists Claes Oldenburg (at the Museum of Modern Art) and Roy Lichtenstein (at the Guggenheim Museum).

• Twenty-five writers at *Newsday,* convinced that they could write a best-selling sex novel of the type popular at the time, create *Naked Came the Stranger* by "Penelope Ashe"—which indeed became a best-seller.

• In response to the new MPAA ratings system, many newspapers either refuse to advertise X-rated movies or list only the title, rating, and theater for such films.

• A music festival, featuring rock bands, folk singers, and sitar player Ravi Shankar, is held in Max Yasgur's muddy pasture and brings over 450,000 people to Woodstock, New York for three days of music.

MOVIES: *Bob and Carol and Ted and Alice,* directed by Paul Mazursky and starring Natalie Wood, Dyan Cannon, Robert Culp, and Elliott Gould; *Butch Cassidy and the Sundance Kid,* starring Paul Newman and Robert Redford; *Easy Rider,* starring Peter Fonda, Dennis Hopper, and Jack Nicholson; *Goodbye, Mr. Chips,* starring Peter O'Toole; *Hello Dolly!,* directed by Gene Kelly and starring Barbara Streisand, Walter Matthau, and Louis Armstrong; *The Love Bug,* starring Dean Jones and Buddy Hackett; *Midnight Cowboy,* starring Dustin Hoffman and Jon Voight; *The Prime of Miss Jean Brodie,* starring Maggie Smith; *Take the Money and Run,* directed by Woody Allen and starring Woody Allen; *True Grit,* starring John Wayne; *The Wild Bunch,* directed by Sam Peckinpah and starring William Holden and Ernest Borgnine.

FICTION: Robert Coover, *Pricksongs and Descants;* Ursula K. Le Guin, *The Left Hand of Darkness;* N. Scott Momaday, *The Way to Rainy Mountain;* Vladimir Nabokov, *Ada, or Ardor;* Joyce Carol Oates, *Them;* Mario Puzo, *The Godfather;* Ishmael Reed, *Yellow Back Radio Broke Down;* Philip Roth, *Portnoy's Complaint;* Ronald Sukenick, *The Death of the Novel and Other Stories;* Kurt Vonnegut, Jr., *Slaughterhouse-Five.*

POPULAR SONGS: The Archies, "Sugar, Sugar"; the Beatles, "Get Back"; Johnny Cash, "A Boy Named Sue"; Creedence Clearwater Revival, "Proud Mary"; Bob Dylan, "Lay Lady Lay"; the Fifth Dimension, "Aquarius/Let the Sunshine In"; Merle Haggard, "Okie from Muskogee"; Peter, Paul and Mary, "Leaving on a Jet Plane"; Elvis Presley, "Suspicious Minds"; Frank Sinatra, "My Way"; B.J. Thomas, "Raindrops Keep Falling on My Head"; Stevie Wonder, "My Cherie Amour"; Tommy James and the Shondells, "Crimson and Clover."

To Kill a Mockingbird
Novel

By: Harper Lee

Date: 1960

Source: Lee, Harper. *To Kill a Mockingbird.* Philadelphia: Lippincott, 1960. 40th Anniversary Edition, New York: HarperCollins, 1999, 169–177.

About the Author: Nelle Harper Lee (1926–) was born and raised in Monroeville, Alabama. As a child, she became fond of writing. However, *To Kill a Mockingbird* is her only published book, earning her the Pulitzer Prize for fiction in 1961. The daughter of a lawyer, Lee studied law at the University of Alabama and attended Oxford University in England. ■

Introduction

To Kill a Mockingbird was published in 1960, not long after the landmark 1954 Supreme Court case *Brown v. Board of Education* and during a time of increasing civil rights unrest. The Brown decision created a law to integrate schools. This was particularly controversial in the South. It was also a time of great social change in the United States, and a novel about the racial injustices of 1930s Alabama carried a powerful message to its readers.

To Kill a Mockingbird tells two tales, both set in Maycomb, Alabama. Scout Finch, the narrator, reflects on three years of her childhood in Maycomb. The daughter of a lawyer, Scout, her brother Jem, and friend Dill play games and try to catch a glimpse of Boo Radley, a misunderstood outcast in Maycomb. The parallel story tells of Tom Robinson's legal case. Atticus Finch, the children's father, takes the case to defend Tom, a black man accused of raping a white woman. Though there is little chance of winning because of the time period, Atticus still believes that he should do the right thing. The children learn about the ugly side of the town as well as their father's heroism. Tom, who is convicted despite his innocence, is killed trying to escape prison as he awaits his second trial. The fact that justice was not served carries a powerful message to the children. The themes of racism and class are portrayed in both stories. The importance of family, community, and region is also depicted.

Director Alan Pakula watches production of *To Kill a Mockingbird.* Beside him is the author of the novel, Harper Lee. AP/WIDE WORLD PHOTOS. REPRODUCED BY PERMISSION.

Atticus Finch, a lawyer, statesman, and the father of Scout and Jem, relays the message of the novel. After Scout has a fight at school, he tells her, "You never really understand a person until you consider things from his point of view—until you climb into his skin and walk around in it" (33). He also tells Jem, "Shoot all the bluejays you want, if you can hit 'em, but remember it's a sin to kill a mockingbird" (103). Both quotes reflect the importance of respecting all beings, especially the innocent. Justice and doing right are honored above all other values.

Significance

To Kill a Mockingbird is one of the most frequently taught books in U.S. high schools. A 1991 survey by the Library of Congress and the Book of the Month Club named it the second-most influential book in Americans' lives, after the Bible. And in a *Library Journal* poll, librarians across the country named it the best novel of the century. It has sold 30 million copies worldwide, been translated into more than forty languages, and been made into an Academy Award-winning movie starring Gregory Peck. Although Harper Lee denies that *Mockingbird* is autobiographical, many of the incidents it portrays are close to her own life experience and to the time period in Alabama history.

To Kill a Mockingbird received many favorable reviews upon its publication. Harding Lemay, in the *New York Herald Tribune* (July 10, 1960, 5) wrote: "Harper Lee makes a valiant attempt to combine two dominant themes of contemporary Southern fiction—the recollection of childhood among village eccentrics and the

Gregory Peck, in a scene from *To Kill a Mockingbird,* delivers his closing argument to a jury. THE KOBAL COLLECTION. REPRODUCED BY PERMISSION.

spirit-corroding shame of the civilized white Southerner in the treatment of the Negro." Richard Sullivan, of the *Chicago Sunday Tribune* labeled it "a novel of strong contemporary national significance." Phoebe Adams, of *The Atlantic Monthly,* was critical of Lee's book because she did not realize that Scout was reflecting on her childhood. She read the narrator as a six-year-old child who was unbelievable.

Both literary and legal scholars have written about *To Kill a Mockingbird.* While literary scholars tend to highlight the narrative and character development in the book, legal scholars often debate whether Atticus Finch truly is a model lawyer. Some argue that his character is a standard for the legal profession, while others view him as a tragic figure because of his decision not to prosecute Boo Radley. A historical analysis of the work draws parallels between the Scottsboro Trial (a notorious case in which a group of African American boys were tried for the rape of a white girl) and Tom Robinson's case. All-

white male juries and the threat of lynching those on trial were common factors. The book also presents important lessons about justice and the composition of juries during the 1930s.

To Kill a Mockingbird has become a classic in American literature. The story is engaging in itself; however, the parallels between law and the history of the American South has made this book an interesting read for many generations.

Primary Source

To Kill a Mockingbird [excerpt]

SYNOPSIS: This excerpt from *To Kill a Mockingbird* revolves around the events leading up to Tom Robinson's trial. Suspecting trouble, Atticus spends the night outside the jail where Robinson is being held, and his children go to watch over him. When Atticus is confronted by a gang of men who have come for Robinson, Scout runs to her father's side. Recognizing one of the men in the gang, Scout addresses him politely as she has been taught by her father. This simple act relieves the tension between Atticus and the gang.

"I'm going out for a while," he said. "You folks'll be in bed when I come back, so I'll say good night now."

With that, he put his hat on and went out the back door.

"He's takin' the car," said Jem.

Our father had a few peculiarities: one was, he never ate desserts; another was that he liked to walk. As far back as I could remember, there was always a Chevrolet in excellent condition in the carhouse, and Atticus put many miles on it in business trips, but in Maycomb he walked to and from his office four times a day, covering about two miles. He said his only exercise was walking. In Maycomb, if one went for a walk with no definite purpose in mind, it was correct to believe one's mind incapable of definite purpose.

Later on, I bade my aunt and brother good night and was well into a book when I heard Jem rattling around in his room. His go-to-bed noises were so familiar to me that I knocked on his door: "Why ain't you going to bed?"

"I'm goin' downtown for a while." He was changing his pants.

"Why? It's almost ten o'clock, Jem."

He knew it, but he was going anyway.

"Then I'm goin' with you. If you say no you're not, I'm goin' anyway, hear?"

Jem saw that he would have to fight me to keep me home, and I suppose he thought a fight would antagonize Aunty, so he gave in with little grace.

I dressed quickly. We waited until Aunty's light went out, and we walked quietly down the back steps. There was no moon tonight.

"Dill'll wanta come," I whispered.

"So he will," said Jem gloomily.

We leaped over the driveway wall, cut through Miss Rachel's side yard and went to Dill's window. Jem whistled bob-white. Dill's face appeared at the screen, disappeared, and five minutes later he unhooked the screen and crawled out. An old campaigner, he did not speak until we were on the sidewalk. "What's up?"

"Jem's got the look-arounds," an affliction Calpurnia said all boys caught at his age.

"I've just got this feeling," Jem said, "just this feeling."

We went by Mrs. Dubose's house, standing empty and shuttered, her camellias grown up in weeds and johnson grass. There were eight more houses to the post office corner.

The south side of the square was deserted. Giant monkey-puzzle bushes bristled on each corner, and between them an iron hitching rail glistened under the street lights. A light shone in the county toilet, otherwise that side of the courthouse was dark. A larger square of stores surrounded the courthouse square; dim lights burned from deep within them.

Atticus's office was in the courthouse when he began his law practice, but after several years of it he moved to quieter quarters in the Maycomb Bank building. When we rounded the corner of the square, we saw the car parked in front of the bank. "He's in there," said Jem.

But he wasn't. His office was reached by a long hallway. Looking down the hall, we should have seen *Atticus Finch, Attorney-at-Law* in small sober letters against the light from behind his door. It was dark.

Jem peered in the bank door to make sure. He turned the knob. The door was locked. "Let's go up the street. Maybe he's visitin' Mr. Underwood."

Mr. Underwood not only ran *The Maycomb Tribune* office, he lived in it. That is, above it. He covered the courthouse and jailhouse news simply by looking out his upstairs window. The office building was on the northwest corner of the square, and to reach it we had to pass the jail.

The Maycomb jail was the most venerable and hideous of the county's buildings. Atticus said it was like something Cousin Joshua St. Clair might have designed. It was certainly someone's dream. Starkly out of place in a town of square-faced stores and steep-roofed houses, the Maycomb jail was a miniature Gothic joke one cell wide and two cells high, complete with tiny battlements and flying buttresses. Its fantasy was heightened by its red brick facade and the thick steel bars at its ecclesiastical windows. It stood on no lonely hill, but was wedged between Tyndal's Hardware Store and *The Maycomb Tribune* office. The jail was Maycomb's only conversation piece: its detractors said it looked like a Victorian privy; its supporters said it gave the town a good solid respectable look, and no stranger would ever suspect that it was full of niggers.

As we walked up the sidewalk, we saw a solitary light burning in the distance. "That's funny," said Jem, "jail doesn't have an outside light."

"Looks like it's over the door," said Dill.

A long extension cord ran between the bars of a second-floor window and down the side of the building. In the light from its bare bulb, Atticus was sitting propped against the front door. He was sitting in one of his office chairs, and he was reading, oblivious of the nightbugs dancing over his head.

I made to run, but Jem caught me. "Don't go to him," he said, "he might not like it. He's all right, let's go home. I just wanted to see where he was."

We were taking a short cut across the square when four dusty cars came in from the Meridian highway, moving slowly in a line. They went around the square, passed the bank building, and stopped in front of the jail.

Nobody got out. We saw Atticus look up from his newspaper. He closed it, folded it deliberately, dropped it in his lap, and pushed his hat to the back of his head. He seemed to be expecting them.

"Come on," whispered Jem. We streaked across the square, across the street, until we were in the shelter of the Jitney Jungle door. Jem peeked up the sidewalk. "We can get closer," he said. We ran to Tyndal's Hardware door—near enough, at the same time discreet.

In ones and twos, men got out of the cars. Shadows became substance as light revealed solid shapes moving toward the jail door. Atticus remained where he was. The men hid him from view.

"He in there, Mr. Finch?" a man said.

"He is," we heard Atticus answer, "and he's asleep. Don't wake him up."

In obedience to my father, there followed what I later realized was a sickeningly comic aspect of an unfunny situation: the men talked in near-whispers.

"You know what we want," another man said. "Get aside from the door, Mr. Finch."

"You can turn around and go home again, Walter," Atticus said pleasantly. "Heck Tate's around somewhere."

"The hell he is," said another man. "Heck's bunch's so deep in the woods they won't get out till mornin'."

"Indeed? Why so?"

"Called 'em off on a snipe hunt," was the succinct answer. "Didn't you think a'that, Mr. Finch?"

"Thought about it, but didn't believe it. Well then," my father's voice was still the same, "that changes things, doesn't it?"

"It do," another deep voice said. Its owner was a shadow.

"Do you really think so?"

This was the second time I heard Atticus ask that question in two days, and it meant somebody's man would get jumped. This was too good to miss. I broke away from Jem and ran as fast as I could to Atticus.

Jem shrieked and tried to catch me, but I had a lead on him and Dill. I pushed my way through dark smelly bodies and burst into the circle of light.

"H-ey, Atticus!"

I thought he would have a fine surprise, but his face killed my joy. A flash of plain fear was going out of his eyes, but returned when Dill and Jem wriggled into the light.

There was a smell of stale whiskey and pigpen about, and when I glanced around I discovered that these men were strangers. They were not the people I saw last night. Hot embarrassment shot through me: I had leaped triumphantly into a ring of people I had never seen before.

Atticus got up from his chair, but he was moving slowly, like an old man. He put the newspaper down very carefully, adjusting its creases with lingering fingers. They were trembling a little.

"Go home, Jem," he said. "Take Scout and Dill home."

We were accustomed to prompt, if not always cheerful acquiescence to Atticus's instructions, but from the way he stood Jem was not thinking of budging.

"Go home, I said."

Jem shook his head. As Atticus's fists went to his hips, so did Jem's, and as they faced each other I could see little resemblance between them: Jem's soft brown hair and eyes, his oval face and snug-fitting ears were our mother's, contrasting oddly with Atticus's graying black hair and square-cut features, but they were somehow alike. Mutual defiance made them alike.

"Son, I said go home."

Jem shook his head.

"I'll send him home," a burly man said, and grabbed Jem roughly by the collar. He yanked Jem nearly off his feet.

"Don't you touch him!" I kicked the man swiftly. Barefooted, I was surprised to see him fall back in real pain. I intended to kick his shin, but aimed too high.

"That'll do, Scout." Atticus put his hand on my shoulder. "Don't kick folks. No—" he said, as I was pleading justification.

"Ain't nobody gonna do Jem that way," I said.

"All right, Mr. Finch, get 'em outa here," someone growled. "You got fifteen seconds to get 'em outa here."

In the midst of this strange assembly, Atticus stood trying to make Jem mind him. "I ain't going," was his steady answer to Atticus's threats, requests, and finally, "Please Jem, take them home."

I was getting a bit tired of that, but felt Jem had his own reasons for doing as he did, in view of his prospects once Atticus did get him home. I looked around the crowd. It was a summer's night, but the men were dressed, most of them, in overalls and denim shirts buttoned up to the collars. I thought they must be cold-natured, as their sleeves were unrolled and buttoned at the cuffs. Some wore hats pulled firmly down over their ears. They were sullen-looking, sleepy-eyed men who seemed unused to late hours. I sought once more for a familiar face, and at the center of the semi-circle I found one.

"Hey, Mr. Cunningham."

The man did not hear me, it seemed.

"Hey, Mr. Cunningham. How's your entailment gettin' along?"

Mr. Walter Cunningham's legal affairs were well known to me; Atticus had once described them at length. The big man blinked and hooked his thumbs in his overall straps. He seemed uncomfortable; he cleared his throat and looked away. My friendly overture had fallen flat.

Mr. Cunningham wore no hat, and the top half of his forehead was white in contrast to his sun-scorched face, which led me to believe that he wore one most days. He shifted his feet, clad in heavy work shoes.

"Don't you remember me, Mr. Cunningham? I'm Jean Louise Finch. You brought us some hickory nuts one time, remember?" I began to sense the futility one feels when unacknowledged by a chance acquaintance.

"I go to school with Walter," I began again. "He's your boy, ain't he? Ain't he, sir?"

Mr. Cunningham was moved to a faint nod. He did know me, after all.

"He's in my grade," I said, "and he does right well. He's a good boy," I added, "a real nice boy. We brought him home for dinner one time. Maybe he told you about me, I beat him up one time but he was real nice about it. Tell him hey for me, won't you?"

Atticus had said it was the polite thing to talk to people about what they were interested in, not about what you were interested in. Mr. Cunningham displayed no interest in his son, so I tackled his entailment once more in a last-ditch effort to make him feel at home.

"Entailments are bad," I was advising him, when I slowly awoke to the fact that I was addressing the entire aggregation. The men were all looking at me, some had their mouths half-open. Atticus had stopped poking at Jem: they were standing together beside Dill. Their attention amounted to fascination. Atticus's mouth, even, was half-open, an attitude he had once described as uncouth. Our eyes met and he shut it.

"Well, Atticus, I was just sayin' to Mr. Cunningham that entailments are bad an' all that, but you said not to worry, it takes a long time sometimes . . . that you all'd ride it out together . . ." I was slowly drying up, wondering what idiocy I had committed. Entailments seemed all right enough for living-room talk.

I began to feel sweat gathering at the edges of my hair, I could stand anything but a bunch of people looking at me. They were quite still.

"What's the matter?" I asked.

Atticus said nothing. I looked around and up at Mr. Cunningham, whose face was equally impassive. Then he did a peculiar thing. He squatted down and took me by both shoulders.

"I'll tell him you said hey, little lady," he said.

Then he straightened up and waved a big paw. "Let's clear out," he called. "Let's get going, boys."

As they had come, in ones and twos the men shuffled back to their ramshackle cars. Doors slammed, engines coughed, and they were gone.

I turned to Atticus, but Atticus had gone to the jail and was leaning against it with his face to the wall. I went to him and pulled his sleeve. "Can we go home now?" He nodded, produced his handkerchief, gave his face a going-over and blew his nose violently.

"Mr. Finch?"

A soft husky voice came from the darkness above: "They gone?"

Atticus stepped back and looked up. "They've gone," he said. "Get some sleep, Tom. They won't bother you any more."

From a different direction, another voice cut crisply through the night: "You're damn tootin' they won't. Had you covered all the time, Atticus."

Mr. Underwood and a double-barreled shotgun were leaning out his window above *The Maycomb Tribune* office.

It was long past my bedtime and I was growing quite tired; it seemed that Atticus and Mr. Underwood would talk for the rest of the night, Mr. Underwood out the window and Atticus up at him. Finally Atticus returned, switched off the light above the jail door, and picked up his chair.

"Can I carry it for you, Mr. Finch?" asked Dill. He had not said a word the whole time.

"Why, thank you, son."

Walking toward the office, Dill and I fell into step behind Atticus and Jem. Dill was encumbered by the chair, and his pace was slower. Atticus and Jem were well ahead of us, and I assumed that Atticus was giving him hell for not going home, but I was wrong. As they passed under a streetlight, Atticus reached out and massaged Jem's hair, his one gesture of affection.

Further Resources

BOOKS

Bloom, Harold, ed. *Harper Lee's "To Kill a Mockingbird."* Philadelphia: Chelsea House, 1999.

Johnson, Claudia Durst. *"To Kill a Mockingbird": Threatening Boundaries.* New York: Twayne, 1994.

———. *Understanding "To Kill a Mockingbird": A Student Casebook to Issues, Sources and Historic Documents.* Westport, Conn.: Greenwood, 1994.

PERIODICALS

Adams, Phoebe. "To Kill a Mockingbird." *Atlantic Monthly,* August 1960, 98–99.

Dare, Tim. "Lawyers, Ethics, and *To Kill a Mockingbird.*" *Philosophy and Literature* 25, 2001, 127–141.

Johnson, Claudia. "The Secret Courts of Men's Hearts: Code and Law in Harper Lee's *To Kill a Mockingbird.*" *Studies in American Fiction* 19, 1991, 129–140.

Lemay, Harding. "To Kill a Mockingbird." *New York Herald Tribune Book Review,* July 10, 1960, 5.

Sullivan, Richard. "To Kill a Mockingbird." *Chicago Sunday Tribune,* July 17, 1960, 1.

WEBSITES

"Harper Lee: 1926." EducETH. Available online at http://www.educeth.ch/english/readinglist/leeh; website home page: http://www.educeth.ch/english (accessed March 18, 2003).

Prody, Kathleen, and Nicolet Wheatery. *"To Kill a Mockingbird*: An Historical Perspective." American Memory digital primary source collection, Library of Congress. Available online at http://memory.loc.gov/ammem/ndlpedu/lessons/98/mock/intro.html; website home page: http://memory.loc.gov (accessed March 18, 2003).

"To Kill a Mockingbird & Harper Lee." Available online at http://mockingbird.chebucto.org (accessed March 18, 2003).

AUDIO AND VISUAL MEDIA

To Kill a Mockingbird. Directed by Robert Mulligan. Original release, Universal, 1962. Collector's Edition DVD/VHS. Universal Studios Home Video.

"Heroine at Home"
Interview

By: Gerald Fitzgerald

Date: February 4, 1961

Source: Fitzgerald, Gerald. "Heroine at Home." *Opera News,* February 4, 1961, 14–15.

About the Author: Gerald Fitzgerald was an associate editor for *Opera News* when he interviewed Leontyne Price in 1961. *Opera News* is a publication issued by the Metropolitan Opera Guild. The magazine appears weekly during the opera season and includes information about programs at the Metropolitan Opera in New York, as well as articles about opera. ∎

Introduction

Opera in the 1960s was dominated by white performers. Although a few African American singers came before her at the Metropolitan Opera, Leontyne Price, born in 1927, was the first African American female to become an operatic star there. When Price made her debut at the Metropolitan Opera in 1961, it was still located between Broadway and Seventh Avenue, and Thirty-ninth and Fortieth Streets. Her counterparts at the Met were Zinka Milanov, Maria Callas, Beverly Sills, Eileen Farrell, and Joan Sutherland, all great singers in their own right.

Throughout the twentieth century, opera houses staged mainly the traditional Italian and German operas. In the earlier part of the century, opera, a drama that is sung, merged with oratorio, a dramatic or narrative or piece that is not intended for the stage. Today, in contrast to earlier generations, opera is marked by more elaborate sets and a higher level of dramatic performance on the part of singers. In many articles and interviews, however, Price acknowledged that she was not much of an actress, for when she began her career, opera was more of a presentational than dramatic art form; the singer simply faced front and delivered the music. Price's voice, though, took over where her acting stopped, and the memories of her performances are filled with descriptions of the strong vocal presentation.

Significance

Leontyne Price has been graced with many titles, among them "La diva di tutte le dive" (opera's foremost goddess) and "La prima donna assoluta." She earned these titles through her training, her hard work and, most of all, her performances both abroad and at the Metropolitan Opera in New York City.

Price was born in Laurel, Mississippi, where she grew up singing at the Methodist church. She did not aspire to a career in opera, though she remembers listening to the Saturday-afternoon Metropolitan Opera Broadcasts as a child. Her voice was discovered in college when she filled in as a soloist. From there, she went to Julliard and her operatic career began.

As she tells Fitzgerald in the interview, Price spent much of the 1950s traveling and honing her art. By the time the article was published, Price would have made her January 27, 1961 debut at the Metropolitan Opera. The Metropolitan began employing African American singers in 1955, beginning with Marian Anderson and Robert McFerrin. None who came before her, however, had commanded the attention that Price did. She was cast in Verdi's *Il Trovatore*, and, playing the role of Leonora, she was cheered for forty-two minutes by the audience. The ovation is still a record at the Met. She sang four more roles during the 1961 season. These roles were the beginning of a career at the Met which lasted until 1985.

Leontyne Price sang in the opening performance at the new Metropolitan Opera House in 1966 when she appeared in Samuel Barber's *Antony and Cleopatra*. She performed 174 times at the two Metropolitan locations. Leontyne Price's debut in 1961 remains the performance that demonstrated she would be one of the greatest opera singers of the twentieth century.

Primary Source

"Heroine at Home"

SYNOPSIS: Gerald Fitzgerald met with Leontyne Price in her New York apartment. After several years of traveling to perform, she was back at home in New York City. She recalls previous performances and her training, and anticipates her Metropolitan Opera debut, January 27, 1961. The interview precedes her triumphant Metropolitan Opera debut in Verdi's *Il Trovatore*. The opera was broadcast on February 4, 1961, on the Texaco Metropolitan Opera Radio Network.

Opera singer Leontyne Price made her debut in a San Francisco production of *Dialogues of the Carmelites* in 1957. THE ESTATE OF CARL VAN VECHTEN. REPRODUCED BY PERMISSION.

Opera News visited Leontyne Price one brisk, sunny January day at her three-story home in lower Manhattan, situated on one of those lovely old streets that somehow have escaped the onslaught of super-highways, factories and cracker-box sky-scraping apartments. Though it was 12:30, Miss Price was still in the process of waking up. "Sam Barber took me night-clubbing last night," she hastened to explain, "and did we have fun! I never laughed so much in all my life." At that moment the electric coffee percolator signaled that breakfast was ready.

"Do you drink so early in the morning?" asked the beturbaned Miss Price with a sly smile. Receiving an affirmative, she poured a cup and then settled down in her peacefully modern living room to discuss her career. "My personal life has been absolutely nil for six years now, and I'm simply basking in the glory of having nothing to do for three whole weeks before my debut." For the past half-dozen years the soprano literally has lived out of a suitcase. Recital and opera engagements, good-will missions for ANTA to India and Australia, television, recording sessions and a European career have given her scarcely a moment to herself. Her success has been so complete that she is now in an enviable position to select only those engagements that satisfy her artistically and show her gifts to best advantage.

"Oh, no!" she replied, when asked if she had always wanted to be a singer. "I always did have an opera bug, played records and listened to the Metropolitan broadcasts, but no one knew I had a voice until I was in college. In my home town [Laurel, Mississippi], I was the local Girl Friday for my high-school glee club, community sings, Sunday school and church—just about anywhere a pianist was needed. Miss McInnis was my teacher, and of course she and my mother, bless her heart, always looked on me as a prodigy, mostly out of love. You might say I was someone of local note. Anyway, I was very impressed with myself."

Her father, James Anthony Price, a carpenter, and his wife, a county nurse, sent both Leontyne and her brother through college. Because she wanted to be a music teacher, the girl chose Central State in Wilberforce, Ohio, where she was called upon to replace a soprano in the glee club. "I suddenly found myself doing a lot of solo work, and by my senior year Anna M. Terry and Charles Wesley of the school urged me to try for a Juilliard scholarship."

Since both Price children were in college at the same time, Leontyne's New York study was aided by her lifelong friends the Alexander Chisholms of Laurel, one of Mississippi's leading families. "My folks and the Chisholms have been involved with one another since before I was born," the soprano recalled. "How do you explain such a thing? You can't; it just *is.* I always say I have two complete, warm, wonderful families. It is from them, aside from God, that I have drawn the strength for the success I've had."

Juilliard? "Oh, I had a good time at Juilliard!" she laughed. "In the opera workshop I was simply fascinated with Nella in *Gianni Schicchi*! And the Second Lady in *The Magic Flute*—I was just thrilled to be chosen to do that!" To this day Leontyne's only voice teacher remains the school's Florence Page Kimball. During her final year there, Frederic Cohen cast her as Mistress Ford in *Falstaff,* a step that led directly to her engagement, in 1952, on Broadway and in Paris for Virgil Thomson's *Four Saints in Three Acts,* and after that as Bess in the Breen revival of *Porgy and Bess.*

How many Besses did she sing? "I really never counted them—at least four a week for two and a half years, on the road and on Broadway." It was the Gershwin opera that introduced her to baritone William Warfield, her husband. How do they resolve a marriage that entails two careers and long separations? "You talk it over in advance and then accept it for what it is. It's very fast-moving and difficult. Bill and I are not a team, you know, but we take great pride in each other's work."

The soprano's large eyes beamed when the conversation returned to her climb to fame. "*Tosca* [1955 over NBC-TV] was my first real stab at grand opera," she recalled. "I've Peter Herman Adler and Samuel Chotzinoff to thank for their enthusiasm and encouragement. And Mr. Gutman [who translated the opera for television]. He is the most immaculate man I've ever known; it was fun every day just to see how much neater he'd be than the day before!"

In 1956 Leontyne sang Pamina on NBC's *Magic Flute* and added to her long list of world premieres of contemporary music, which already boasted works by Poulenc, John La Montaine, Stravinsky and Barber *(Prayers of Kierkegaard).* At her Town Hall debut in 1954, Barber had accompanied her in his cycle *Hermit Songs.* More operatic dates began to creep into her schedule. She played Handel's Cleopatra to Cesare Siepi's Caesar with the American Opera Society, and in 1957 she made her official stage debut in San Francisco as Mme. Lidoine in Poulenc's *Carmelites;* she has since been heard there as Aida, Leonora in *Trovatore* and Donna Elvira and in the title role of Orff's *Die Kluge.* At the Chicago Lyric Opera, always quick to snap up fresh talent, she has portrayed Liù, Thais, Aida and Cio-Cio-San.

"But it was the last three years in Europe that really clinched my operatic career," she said. "I owe everything there to Herbert von Karajan, who launched me at the Vienna Staatsoper. When I left the United States, I had relatively little dramatic experience behind me. In Vienna, Verona and at Covent Garden and La Scala, I had to pretend authority and pick things up as I went along. How proud I was to have Giulietta Simionato as my Amneris! And how much I learned from her economy of movement and dignity of gesture." During these difficult "growing pains," Leontyne was studying, performing and recording many of her roles simultaneously—hard work that is now paying off.

What lies ahead? Italophile to the core, the soprano hopes some day to own a *villetta* outside Rome. And in opera? "Well, this Metropolitan debut is what I call a palpitating experience; all my family and friends from the other side of the Mason-Dixon Line will be here. Except my brother George: he's a captain in the army, stationed in Germany." Her debut past, the soprano will go on to four other roles at the Metropolitan this season—Donna Anna, Liù, Cio-Cio-San and "that Ethiopian bit," Aida—and then learn something new, probably Leonora in *La Forza del Destino* or Amelia in *Ballo*. Karajan has promised to restage *Salome* for her in Vienna whenever she agrees to sing (and dance) the title role.

"But that's in the future," declared Leontyne Price, finishing her coffee. "Meanwhile, being at the Metropolitan means moving back into my home and rediscovering fabulous New York—home life, at long last!"

Further Resources

BOOKS

Jackson, Paul. *Sign-Off for the Old Met: The Metropolitan Opera Broadcasts, 1950–1966*. Portland, Ore.: Amadeus Press, 1997.

de Lerma, Dominque-Rene. "Leontyne Price." In *Black Women in America: An Historical Encyclopedia*, vol. 2. Brooklyn, N.Y.: Carlson, 1993, 941–943.

Randel, Don Michael. *Harvard Concise Dictionary of Music*. Cambridge, Mass.: Harvard University Press, 1978.

PERIODICALS

Blier, Steven. "Time after Time." *Opera News*, October 1996, 10–14, 64.

"Voice like a Banner Flying." *Time*, March 10, 1961, 58–63.

WEBSITES

"Leontyne Price." Available online at http://www2.worldbook .com/features/aamusic.html/price.htm> (accessed April 6, 2003).

"Today in History." Available online at http://memory.loc.gov /ammem/today/feb10.html (accessed April 6, 2002).

AUDIO AND VISUAL MEDIA

Verdi, Giuseppe. *Il trovatore; Il trovatore. Brani scelti*. Milano: Arkadia, CDKAR 228.2. Compact disc. 1992.

———. *Il trovatore*. Oakhurst, N.J.: Musical Heritage Society, 525286M. Compact disc. 1970, 1998.

The American Dream

Play script

By: Edward Albee

Date: 1961

Source: Albee, Edward. *The American Dream and The Zoo Story: Two Plays by Edward Albee*. New York: Signet, 1963, 57–61.

About the Author: By the time Edward Albee (1928–) established himself as a playwright in the 1960s, he had been writing for several years. *The Zoo Story*, published in 1959,

was his first successful one-act play and was one of many that addressed disillusionment and family life. Albee's awards include the 1967 Pulitzer Prize for *A Delicate Balance* and a 1996 Kennedy Center Honor. He is best known for the play *Who's Afraid of Virginia Woolf?* ∎

Introduction

The American Dream, a one-act play, premiered January 24, 1961, at York Playhouse in New York City. Five characters—Mommy, Daddy, Grandma, Mrs. Barker, and "Young Man"—convey the satiric comedy of Albee's version of the American Dream. The set is simple, with only a few pieces of furniture and frames on the walls with no pictures in them. Mommy and Daddy, a middle-aged couple, appear in the opening moments of the play, waiting for someone to visit. Mommy chatters about a hat she bought and Daddy pretends to listen. The conversation is absurd and shallow. Mommy, in particular, seeks satisfaction in her life, but she has not found it in anything, including the color of her hat.

Many Americans still held on to the ideal of the American Dream—particularly the belief in ever increasing material prosperity—in the early 1960s. Later in the decade, as the dream faded because of the numerous social problems such as war, drug use, and racism, Albee's play and attitudes came closer to how many Americans viewed life. In the preface to the play, Albee wrote, "The play is an examination of the American Scene, an attack on the substitution of artificial for real values in our society, a condemnation of complacency, cruelty, emasculation, vacuity; it is a stand against the fiction that everything in this slipping land of ours is peachy-keen."

The other three characters enter the play: Grandma, Mrs. Barker, and the Young Man. Grandma, the moral interpreter, reveals Mommy's shallowness and cynicism. Mrs. Barker, the woman's club president and former adoption agency representative, is the awaited visitor. She does not seem to know why she is there until Grandma provides a detailed account of how Mommy and Daddy dismembered their adopted son because he was not perfect. Then she recalls selling them their "bumble of joy." The Young Man, who enters last, represents the satisfaction of the American Dream. He is a perfect physical specimen who is emotionally cold and empty.

Significance

Edward Albee was the first American playwright to adapt the conventions of Theater of the Absurd, a European form, which "springs from a feeling of deep disillusionment, the draining away of the sense of meaning and purpose in life." For example, Romanian playwright Eugene Ionesco's *The Bald Soprano*, a play that defies all logic in its catalog of meaningless platitudes, was one of the inspirations for *The American Dream*. The 1960s,

Edward Albee's plays often criticized American society's preoccupation with material gain. **THE LIBRARY OF CONGRESS.**

riddled with war, assassinations and violence, disillusioned a generation of American playwrights who followed in Albee's footsteps.

Upon its debut in 1961, *The American Dream* received mixed reviews. While some critics praised the play for its insight into the contemporary mind-set, John Gassner (in "Edward Albee," *Contemporary Literary Criticism,* vol. 3. Detroit: Gale Research, 1975, 6) wrote, "The trouble with Albee's acutely original play, *The American Dream,* is that its bizarre Ionesco details don't add up to an experience."

Recent critics explore the breakdown in conventional dramatic language. Matthew Roudane writes, "In both text and performance, Albee's technical virtuosity emanates from an ability to capture the values, personal politics, and perceptions of his characters through language." ("Edward Albee [28 March 1928–]," *American Playwrights Since 1945: A Guide to Scholarship, Criticism, and Performance,* ed. Philip C. Kolin [New York: Greenwood, 1989]) Humorously uncomfortable moments, such as Mommy's invitation for Mrs. Barker to remove her dress, portray a breakdown in communication. Anne Paolucci notes that "humor, in Albee, becomes a trap; to laugh at any of these things is to laugh at our own expense" (*From Tension to Tonic: The Plays of Edward Albee.* [Washington, D.C.: Bagehot Council, 2000]).

Grandma interests most critics. Paolucci sees her as Prospero, while Erwin Beck claims she fits the archetype of R.W.B. Lewis's *The American Adam.* ("Allegory in Edward Albee's *The American Dream,*" available online at http://www.goshen.edu/facultypubs/DREAM.html). Don D. Moore sees her as "King Lear's fool." ("Albee's *The American Dream,*" *The Explicator* 30, 1972, item 44.)

Though the play was written in the early 1960s, it still resonates with audiences today as a play about our time. *The American Dream* is considered one of Edward Albee's major works because it challenged the status quo and made audiences think about life behind the masks.

Primary Source

The American Dream [excerpt]

SYNOPSIS: This excerpt is from the opening scene of *The American Dream.* Mommy and Daddy are seated in armchairs in the living room of their apartment. The conversation mimics Ionesco's opening of *The Bald Soprano.* It is not clear at this point that Mommy and Daddy are waiting for the representative from the adoption agency rather than someone to fix something in the apartment. The scene recreates the typically absurd conversation of Mommy and Daddy.

The Players:

Mommy

Daddy

Grandma

Mrs. Barker

Young Man

The Scene:

A living room. Two armchairs, one toward either side of the stage, facing each other diagonally out toward the audience. Against the rear wall, a sofa. A door, leading out from the apartment, in the rear wall, far stage-right. An archway, leading to other rooms, in the side wall, stage-left.

At the beginning, Mommy and Daddy are seated in the armchairs, Daddy in the armchair stage-left, Mommy in the other.

Curtain up. A silence. Then:

Mommy: I don't know what can be keeping them.

Daddy: They're late, naturally.

Mommy: Of course, they're late; it never fails.

Daddy: That's the way things are today, and there's nothing you can do about it.

Mommy: You're quite right.

Daddy: When we took this apartment, they were quick enough to have me sign the lease; they were quick enough to take my check for two months' rent in advance . . .

Mommy: And one month's security . . .

Daddy: . . . and one month's security. They were quick enough to check my references; they were quick enough about all that. But now! But now, try to get the icebox fixed, try to get the doorbell fixed, try to get the leak in the johnny fixed! Just try it . . . they aren't so quick about *that.*

Mommy: Of course not; it never fails. People think they can get away with anything these days . . . and, of course they can. I went to buy a new hat yesterday. *(Pause)* I said, I went to buy a new hat yesterday.

Daddy: Oh! Yes . . . yes.

Mommy: Pay attention.

Daddy: I *am* paying attention, Mommy.

Mommy: Well, be sure you do.

Daddy: Oh, I am.

Mommy: All right, Daddy; now listen.

Daddy: I'm listening, Mommy.

Mommy: You're sure!

Daddy: Yes . . . yes, I'm sure, I'm all ears.

Mommy: *(Giggles at the thought; then)* All right, now. I went to buy a new hat yesterday and I said, "I'd like a new hat, please." And so, they showed me a few hats, green ones and blue ones, and I didn't like any of them, not one bit. What did I say? What did I just say?

Daddy: You didn't like any of them, not one bit.

Mommy: That's right; you just keep paying attention. And then they showed me one that I did like. It was a lovely little hat, and I said, "Oh, this is a lovely little hat; I'll take this hat; oh my, it's lovely. What color is it?" And they said, "Why, this is beige; isn't it a lovely little beige hat?" And I said, "Oh, it's just lovely." And so, I bought it. *(Stops, looks at Daddy)*

Daddy: *(To show he is paying attention)* And so you bought it.

Mommy: And so I bought it, and I walked out of the store with the hat right on my head, and I ran spang into the chairman of our woman's club, and she said, "Oh, my dear, isn't that a lovely little hat? Where did you get that lovely little hat? It's the loveliest little hat; I've always wanted a wheat-colored hat *myself.*" And, I said, "Why, no, my dear; this hat is beige; beige." And she laughed and said, "Why no, my dear, that's a wheat-colored hat . . . wheat. I know beige from wheat." And I said, "Well, my dear, I know beige from wheat, too." What did I say? What did I just say?

Daddy: *(Tonelessly)* Well, my dear, I know beige from wheat, too.

Mommy: That's right. And she laughed, and she said, "Well, my dear, they certainly put one over on you. That's wheat if I ever saw wheat. But it's lovely, just the same." And then she walked off. She's a dreadful woman, you don't know her; she has dreadful taste, two dreadful children, a dreadful house, and an absolutely adorable husband who sits in a wheel chair all the time. You don't know him. You don't know anybody, do you? She's just a dreadful woman, but she *is* chairman of our woman's club, so naturally I'm terribly fond of her. So, I went right back into the hat shop, and I said, "Look here; what do you mean selling me a hat that you say is beige, when it's wheat all the time . . . wheat! I can tell beige from wheat any day in the week, but not in this artificial light of yours." They have artificial light, Daddy.

Daddy: Have they!

Mommy: And I said, "The minute I got outside I could tell that it wasn't a beige hat at all; it was a wheat hat." And they said to me, "How could you tell that when you had the hat on the top of your head?" Well, that made me angry, and so I made a scene right there; I screamed as hard as I could; I took my hat off and I threw it down on the counter, and oh, I made a terrible scene. I said, I made a terrible scene.

Daddy: *(Snapping to)* Yes . . . yes . . . good for you!

Mommy: And I made an absolutely terrible scene; and they became frightened, and they said, "Oh, madam; oh, madam." But I kept right on, and finally they admitted that they might have made a mistake; so they took my hat into the back, and then they came out again with a hat that looked exactly like it. I took one look at it, and I said, "This hat is wheat-colored; wheat." Well, of course, they said, "Oh, no, madam, this hat is beige; you go outside and see." So, I went outside, and lo and behold, it *was* beige. So I bought it.

Daddy: *(Clearing his throat)* I would imagine that it was the same hat they tried to sell you before.

Mommy: *(With a little laugh)* Well, of course it was!

Daddy: That's the way things are today; you just can't get satisfaction; you just try.

Mommy: Well, *I* got satisfaction.

Daddy: That's right, Mommy. *You did* get satisfaction, didn't you?

Mommy: Why are they so late? I don't know what can be keeping them.

Further Resources

BOOKS

Esslin, Martin. *Theatre of the Absurd.* Garden City, N.Y.: Doubleday, 1969.

Glassner, John. "Edward Albee." In *Contemporary Literary Criticism.* vol. 3. Detroit: Gale Research, 1975, 6.

Gussow, Mel. *Edward Albee: A Singular Journey, a Biography.* New York: Simon and Schuster, 1999.

Roudane, Matthew C. "Edward Albee (28 March 1928–)." In *American Playwrights Since 1945: A Guide to Scholarship, Criticism, and Performance.* Ed. Philip C. Kolin. New York: Greenwood, 1989, 1–27.

Paolucci, Anne. *From Tension to Tonic: The Plays of Edward Albee.* Washington, D.C.: Bagehot Council, 2000.

PERIODICALS

Miller, Jordan Y. "Myth and the American Dream: O'Neill to Albee."*Modern Drama* 7, 1964, 190–198.

Moore, Don D. "Albee's *The American Dream.*" *The Explicator* 30, 1972, item 44.

WEBSITES

Beck, Ervin. "Allegory in Edward Albee's *The American Dream.*" Available online at http://www.goshen.edu/facultypubs /DREAM.html (accessed March 25, 2003).

Catch-22

Novel

By: Joseph Heller

Date: 1961

Source: Heller, Joseph. *Catch-22.* New York: Simon & Schuster, 1996, 186–188, 190–192.

About the Author: Joseph Heller (1923–1999) was born in Brooklyn, New York. In the U.S. Army Air Force in World War II (1939–45), he served as a bombardier on B-25s and flew sixty missions in North Africa and Italy. In 1948 he earned a bachelor's degree from New York University and in 1949 a master's from Columbia University. He began publishing while he was a student. Heller is the author of novels, short stories, plays and screenplays. ∎

Introduction

Novels about World War II increased in popularity in the decade of the 1960s. *Catch-22* by Joseph Heller is frequently grouped with Norman Mailer's *The Naked and the Dead* and James Jones' *From Here to Eternity* as important World War II novels. The latter two books, however, differ in tone and purpose from Heller's story. Mailer and Jones wrote realistic novels similar to Ernest Hemingway's war novels. Heller's novel, though set in World War II, contains elements of both classical and modern writers, including absurdists who captured what they viewed as a kind of insanity of modern life. His writing reveals the restlessness of American youth, the satire and the alienation of a generation in a postmodern world. He turned to a new form and a new manner of looking at the postmodern world in ways similar to such contemporaries as Ken Kesey, Kurt Vonnegut, and Thomas Pynchon.

Heller's planning and writing are significant for this novel. Early drafts were entitled *Catch-18.* Between starting and finishing the novel, Heller had given up writing and is quoted as saying, "I wanted to write something that was very good and I had nothing good to write. So I wrote nothing." During the time he was not writing, he read Evelyn Waugh, Céline, Nathaniel West, and Vladimir Nabokov. Heller also created two schematics on desk blotters as he developed the nonlinear plot of *Catch-22.* "The overviews illustrate Heller's passion for order and detail. According to David M. Craig in *Tilting at Mortality: Narrative Strategies in Joseph Heller's Fiction* (Detroit: Wayne State University Press, 1997, 263), "Viewed through the lens of the blotter *Catch-22* has as many interrelated plot strands as a Victorian novel does, each possessing its own developmental logic and integrity."

Significance

The novel received mixed reviews upon publication. While reviewers like Julian Mitchell praised the novel for its richness and artistry, others found the satire of the novel too extreme to the point that it overwhelms the story. At a conference celebrating the twenty-fifth anniversary of its publication, John W. Aldridge said, "it is only in fairly recent years that we have begun to learn how to read this curious book" ("Catch-22 Twenty-five Years Later." *Michigan Quarterly Review* 24, no. 2, Spring 1987, 379). The book is indeed curious and innovative in its style, its presentation of characters, and its message, and it must be read carefully in order to understand Yossarian's actions at the end.

Catch-22 quickly moved from a popular novel of the 1960s to a classic of American literature. Heller introduced a new phrase into the language—catch-22, which is a situation that presents paradoxical choices, usually brought on by authority figures or someone above the person caught in the "catch-22." In the novel, the "catch" is an Air Force regulation that says that a man is insane if he willingly flies dangerous combat missions, but if he makes a formal request to be relieved of such missions, he thereby proves his sanity, making him ineligible to be relieved. Even when the person understands what is happening, the situation seems confusing. Yossarian, the main character in Heller's novel, is caught in these situations throughout the book, as are other characters. As the novel opens, he is in the hospital, editing letters to be sent to soldiers. Words are blotted out, and Yossarian makes a game of this tedious chore. Language is diminished to a code that the enemy can take as a threat, and Yossarian arbitrarily deletes words and parts of speech and substitutes "Washington Irving" for his own name. The humor is missed by the higher-ups who assign this duty.

Primary Source

Catch-22 [excerpt]

SYNOPSIS: Yossarian, the main character of the novel, finds his way to the dispensary once again. Advice from an English doctor provides Yossarian with a new excuse to escape duties in the unit—this time his problem is with his liver, a more difficult diagnosis than appendicitis. This is typical throughout the novel: Each time, Yossarian finds a new ailment that can provide a few days rest in the dispensary.

The Soldier Who Saw Everything Twice

Yossarian owed his good health to exercise, fresh air, teamwork and good sportsmanship; it was to get away from them all that he had first discovered the hospital. When the physical-education officer at Lowery Field ordered everyone to fall out for calisthenics one afternoon, Yossarian, the private, reported instead at the dispensary with what he said was a pain in his right side.

"Beat it," said the doctor on duty there, who was doing a crossword puzzle.

"We can't tell him to beat it," said a corporal. "There's a new directive out about abdominal complaints. We have to keep them under observation five days because so many of them have been dying after we make them beat it."

"All right," grumbled the doctor. "Keep him under observation five days and *then* make him beat it."

They took Yossarian's clothes away and put him in a ward, where he was very happy when no one was snoring nearby. In the morning a helpful young English intern popped in to ask him about his liver.

"I think it's my appendix that's bothering me," Yossarian told him.

"Your appendix is no good," the Englishman declared with jaunty authority. "If your appendix goes wrong, we can take it out and have you back on active duty in almost no time at all. But come to us with a liver complaint and you can fool us for weeks. The liver, you see, is a large, ugly mystery to us. If you've ever eaten liver you know what I mean. We're pretty sure today that the liver exists, and we have a fairly good idea of what it does whenever it's doing what it's supposed to be doing. Beyond that, we're really in the dark. After all, what is a liver? My father, for example, died of cancer of the liver and was never sick a day of his life right up till the moment it killed him. Never felt a twinge of pain. In a way, that was too bad, since I hated my father. Lust for my mother, you know."

"What's an English medical officer doing on duty here?" Yossarian wanted to know.

The officer laughed. "I'll tell you all about that when I see you tomorrow morning. And throw that silly ice bag away before you die of pneumonia."

Yossarian never saw him again. That was one of the nice things about all the doctors at the hospital; he never saw any of them a second time. They came and went and simply disappeared. In place of the English intern the next day, there arrived a group of doctors he had never seen before to ask him about his appendix.

"There's nothing wrong with my appendix," Yossarian informed them. "The doctor yesterday said it was my liver."

"Maybe it is his liver," replied the white-haired officer in charge. "What does his blood count show?"

"He hasn't had a blood count."

"Have one taken right away. We can't afford to take chances with a patient in his condition. We've got to keep ourselves covered in case he dies." He made a notation on his clipboard and spoke to Yossarian. "In the meantime, keep that ice bag on. It's very important."

"I don't have an ice bag on."

Joseph Heller, author of *Catch-22*. PHOTOGRAPH BY JERRY BAUER. REPRODUCED BY PERMISSION.

"Well, get one. There must be an ice bag around here somewhere. And let someone know if the pain becomes unendurable."

At the end of ten days, a new group of doctors came to Yossarian with bad news: he was in perfect health and had to get out. He was rescued in the nick of time by a patient across the aisle who began to see everything twice. Without warning, the patient sat up in bed and shouted,

"I see everything twice!"

A nurse screamed and an orderly fainted. Doctors came running up from every direction with needles, lights, tubes, rubber mallets and oscillating metal tines. They rolled up complicated instruments on wheels. There was not enough of the patient to go around, and specialists pushed forward in line with raw tempers and snapped at their colleagues in front to hurry up and give somebody else a chance. A colonel with a large forehead and horn-rimmed glasses soon arrived at a diagnosis.

"It's meningitis," he called out emphatically, waving the others back. "Although Lord knows there's not the slightest reason for thinking so."

"Then why pick meningitis?" inquired a major with a suave chuckle. "Why not, let's say, acute nephritis?"

"Because I'm a meningitis man, that's why, and not an acute-nephritis man," retorted the colonel. "And I'm not going to give him up to any of your kidney birds without a struggle. I was here first."

In the end, the doctors were all in accord. They agreed they had no idea what was wrong with the soldier who saw everything twice, and they rolled him away into a room in the corridor and quarantined everyone else in the ward for fourteen days. . . .

That was the most illogical Thanksgiving he could ever remember spending, and his thoughts returned wishfully to his halcyon fourteen-day quarantine in the hospital the year before; but even that idyll had ended on a tragic note: he was still in good health when the quarantine period was over, and they told him again that he had to get out and go to war. Yossarian sat up in bed when he heard the bad news and shouted,

"I see everything twice!"

Pandemonium broke loose in the ward again. The specialists came running up from all directions and ringed him in a circle of scrutiny so confining that he could feel the humid breath from their various noses blowing uncomfortably upon the different sectors of his body. They went snooping into his eyes and ears with tiny beams of light, assaulted his legs and feet with rubber hammers and vibrating forks, drew blood from his veins, held anything handy up for him to see on the periphery of his vision.

The leader of this team of doctors was a dignified, solicitous gentleman who held one finger up directly in front of Yossarian and demanded, "How many fingers do you see?"

"Two," said Yossarian.

"How many fingers do you see now?" asked the doctor, holding up two.

"Two," said Yossarian.

"And how many now?" asked the doctor, holding up none.

"Two," said Yossarian.

The doctor's face wreathed with a smile. "By Jove, he's right," he declared jubilantly. "He *does* see everything twice."

They rolled Yossarian away on a stretcher into the room with the other soldier who saw everything twice and quarantined everyone else in the ward for another fourteen days.

"I see everything twice!" the soldier who saw everything twice shouted when they rolled Yossarian in.

"I see everything twice!" Yossarian shouted back at him just as loudly, with a secret wink.

"The walls! The walls!" the other soldier cried. "Move back the walls!"

"The walls! The walls!" Yossarian cried. "Move back the walls!"

One of the doctors pretended to shove the wall back. "Is that far enough?"

The soldier who saw everything twice nodded weakly and sank back on his bed. Yossarian nodded weakly too, eyeing his talented roommate with great humility and admiration. He knew he was in the presence of a master. His talented roommate was obviously a person to be studied and emulated. During the night, his talented roommate died, and Yossarian decided that he had followed him far enough.

"I see everything once!" he cried quickly.

A new group of specialists came pounding up to his bedside with their instruments to find out if it was true.

"How many fingers do you see?" asked the leader, holding up one.

"One."

The doctor held up two fingers. "How many fingers do you see now?"

"One."

The doctor held up ten fingers. "And how many now?"

"One."

The doctor turned to the other doctors with amazement. "He does see everything once!" he exclaimed. "We made him all better."

"And just in time, too," announced the doctor with whom Yossarian next found himself alone, a tall, torpedo-shaped congenial man with an unshaven growth of brown beard and a pack of cigarettes in his shirt pocket that he chain-smoked insouciantly as he leaned against the wall. "There are some relatives here to see you. Oh, don't worry," he added with a laugh. "Not your relatives. It's the mother, father and brother of that chap who died. They've traveled all the way from New York to see a dying soldier, and you're the handiest one we've got."

Further Resources

BOOKS

Craig, David M. *Tilting at Mortality: Narrative Strategies in Joseph Heller's Fiction.* Detroit: Wayne State University Press, 1997.

Merrill, Robert. *Joseph Heller.* Boston: Twayne, 1987.

Potts, Stephen W. *'Catch-22': Antiheroic Antinovel.* Boston: Twayne, 1989.

PERIODICALS

Aldridge, John W. "*Catch-22* Twenty-five years Later." *Michigan Quarterly Review* 24, no. 2, Spring 1987, 379–386.

Green, Daniel. "A World Worth Laughing At: *Catch-22* and the Humor of Black Humor." *Studies in the Novel* 27, no. 2, 1995, 186–196.

WEBSITES

'Catch-22' Study Guide. Available online at: http://www.bellmore-merrick.k12.ny.us/catch22.html (accessed January 2, 2003).

"Joseph Heller Archive." Available online at: http://www.sc.edu/library/spcoll/amlit/heller.html (accessed January 27, 2003).

AUDIO AND VISUAL MEDIA

Catch-22. Directed by Mike Nichols. Paramount Home Video. DVD and Videocassette, 1970.

"All My Pretty Ones"
Poem

By: Anne Sexton

Date: 1962

Source: Sexton, Anne. *All My Pretty Ones.* Boston: Houghton Mifflin, 1962, 4–5.

About the Author: Anne Sexton (1928–1974) began writing poetry in 1957 as part of therapy for psychological disorders. She studied with numerous well-known poets in workshops, including W.D. Snodgrass and Robert Lowell. She then taught poetry at Harvard, Radcliff, Oberlin College, and Boston University. After several failed attempts, she committed suicide in 1974. ∎

Introduction

Poetry changed in style and subject in the 1950s and 1960s. The academically trained poets of the era challenged their mentors in order to find their own voices. Anne Sexton, though not university trained, became a major voice in the generation of poets who began publishing during this time. She lived in the Boston area, a city rich with poetry and opportunities for poets. She participated first in an Adult Education seminar led by John Holmes. From this seminar evolved a workshop group that would be important for Sexton's growth as a poet. The group included Maxine Kumin, George Starbuck, Sam Albert, and Holmes.

Poet Anne Sexton in her home in Weston, Massachusetts.
© BETTMANN/CORBIS. REPRODUCED BY PERMISSION.

Sexton is generally grouped with such writers as Sylvia Plath and Robert Lowell as a "confessional poet." Although she wrote of things from her life, her poetry was not necessarily about her life. This school of poetry concentrated on autobiographical subjects, emotional reactions, and psychoanalysis. Topics were treated subjectively rather than objectively. *All My Pretty Ones,* her second volume of poetry, was published in 1962. While her first volume of poetry recreated the experience of what she called "madness," the second volume tried to explore its causes. The volume contains poems about death, love, and loss. The poems carry on the thematic content of the first volume, but are technically more developed. While she loosened her style in this volume, she also included poems in such traditional forms such as the sonnet and elegy.

Significance

Anne Sexton wrote about subjects most authors would avoid because they were so deeply personal. *All My Pretty Ones,* nominated for a National Book Award in 1963, sped Sexton on her way to recognition as a talented voice of her generation.

Male and female reviewers, including established poets, responded differently to her work. Female re-

viewers such as May Swenson and Louise Bogan praised the volume for its unique exploration of psychological truths from a feminine perspective. Thom Gunn, however, found her symbolism superficial, and Ian Hamilton feared that she would become "yet another cult-figure of neurotic breakdown, valued not for what she has written but for what her suffering seems to sympotamatize" (quoted in J.D. McClatchy, *Anne Sexton: The Artist and Her Critics* [Bloomington: Indiana University Press, 1978], 127). Anne Sexton's work overcame the fears of the male reviewers, and she stands as an important voice in American poetry and letters.

Anne Sexton's second volume of poetry demonstrates her growth as a poet. The poetic structure is more developed; she takes more risks with subjects and themes. Her poetry puts readers on edge, challenging them with unpleasant moments of life as she translates her pain into verse. *All My Pretty Ones* remains an important volume in Sexton's oeuvre and in the development of poetry in the 1960s.

Primary Source

"All My Pretty Ones"

SYNOPSIS: "All My Pretty Ones," the title poem, demonstrates the process of transforming painful subjects into art. The poem explores a personal subject, her parents' death and what to do with their possessions as it reaches deeper to explore relationships. Sexton goes beyond the poet's voice to the father's voice and to the mother's euphemisms for his alcoholism. She examines the impact of their lives on her own but not in a morbid fashion.

Father, this year's jinx rides us apart
where you followed our mother to her cold slumber;
a second shock boiling its stone to your heart,
leaving me here to shuffle and disencumber
you from the residence you could not afford:
a gold key, your half of a woolen mill,
twenty suits from Dunne's, an English Ford,
the love and legal verbiage of another will,
boxes of pictures of people I do not know.
I touch their cardboard faces. They must go.

But the eyes, as thick as wood in this album,
hold me. I stop here, where a small boy
waits in a ruffled dress for someone to come . . .
for this soldier who holds his bugle like a toy
or for this velvet lady who cannot smile.
Is this your father's father, this commodore
in a mailman suit? My father, time meanwhile
has made it unimportant who you are looking for.
I'll never know what these faces are all about.
I lock them into their book and throw them out.

This is the yellow scrapbook that you began
the year I was born; as crackling now and wrinkly
as tobacco leaves: clippings where Hoover outran

the Democrats, wiggling his dry finger at me
and Prohibition; news where the *Hindenburg* went
down and recent years where you went flush
on war. This year, solvent but sick, you meant
to marry that pretty widow in a one-month rush.
But before you had that second chance, I cried
on your fat shoulder. Three days later you died.

These are the snapshots of marriage, stopped in
places.
Side by side at the rail toward Nassau now;
here, with the winner's cup at the speedboat races,
here, in tails at the Cotillion, you take a bow,
here, by our kennel of dogs with their pink eyes,
running like show-bred pigs in their chain-link pen;
here, at the horseshow where my sister wins a prize;
and here, standing like a duke among groups of
men.
Now I fold you down, my drunkard, my navigator,
my first lost keeper, to love or look at later.

I hold a five-year diary that my mother kept
for three years, telling all she does not say
of your alcoholic tendency. You overslept,
she writes. My God, father, each Christmas Day
with your blood, will I drink down your glass
of wine? The diary of your hurly-burly years
goes to my shelf to wait for my age to pass.
Only in this hoarded span will love persevere.
Whether you are pretty or not, I outlive you,
bend down my strange face to yours and forgive you.

Further Resources

BOOKS

Hall, Caroline King Barnard. *Anne Sexton.* New York: Twayne, 1989.

McClatchy, J.D., ed. *Anne Sexton: The Artist and Her Critics.* Bloomington, Ind.: Indiana University Press, 1978.

McGowan, Philip. "Anne Sexton" and "All My Pretty Ones." In *Encyclopedia of American Poetry: The Twentieth Century.* Ed. Eric L. Haralson. Chicago: FitzRoy Dearborn, 2002, 656–659.

PERIODICALS

Jones, Gregory. "The Achievement of Anne Sexton." *Hollins Critic* 21, no. 3, 1984, 1–13.

McGowan, Philip. "Uncovering the Female Voice in Anne Sexton." *Revista canaria de estudios ingleses* 37, 1998, 125–141.

Middlebrook, Diane Wood. "Housewife into Poet: The Apprenticeship of Anne Sexton." *New England Quarterly* 56, no. 4, 1983, 483–503.

WEBSITES

"Anne Sexton." Available online at http://www.poets.org/poets /poets.cfm?prmID=14 (accessed January 2, 2003).

"Anne Sexton (1928–1974)." Available online at http://www .english.uiuc.edu/maps/poets/s_z/sexton/sexton.htm (accessed January 2, 2003).

The Civil Rights Movement in Art

"An Appeal to You from . . . to March on Washington"

Flyer

By: March on Washington for Jobs and Freedom
Date: 1963
Source: "An Appeal to You from . . . to March on Washington." *March on Washington,* ARVF, Special Collections, Michigan State University, 1963.
About the Movement: The March on Washington for Jobs and Freedom was organized by several leading civil rights advocates, including Dr. Martin Luther King, Jr. Conceived by A. Phillip Randolph, the march took place August 28, 1963. ∎

"Blowin' in the Wind"

Song

By: Bob Dylan
Date: 1962
Source: Dylan, Bob. "Blowin' in the Wind." *The Peter Paul and Mary Song Book.* New York: Pepamar Music Corp., n.d., 44–45.
About the Author: Bob Dylan (1942–) was born Robert Allen Zimmerman in Duluth, Minnesota. Dylan was interested in music from an early age, and in 1960 moved to New York City to perform folk music. His first album appeared in 1962. Within a year he was internationally famous for his powerful, popular, and politically charged folk music. Dylan songs such as "Blowin' in the Wind" and "The Times They Are A-Changin'" became anthems of the social movements of the 1960s. Dylan continued to write, record, and tour into the twenty-first century, working in a many different genres. Dylan's innovations in style and lyrics had enormous influence on other musicians; he is often considered one of the most important figures in twentieth-century popular music and culture.

Introduction

Participants in the 1960s civil rights movement sought equal access and opportunities for all citizens of the United States. Activities included sit-ins, marches, and protests. Organizers and participants spent years formulating plans, appealing to political figures, and fighting for their causes. A. Philip Randolph began thinking about a march in the 1940s when he was the president of the Brotherhood of Sleeping Car Porters, a labor union. The march was conceived as a potent means of bringing attention to issues that the country needed to address, but it was averted when President Franklin Delano Roosevelt signed an order on June 25, 1941, banning discrimination in employing workers in the defense industry.

Peter, Paul and Mary perform during the 1963 March on Washington, at which over 250,000 people gathered in a protest for civil rights. NATIONAL ARCHIVES AND RECORDS ADMINISTRATION.

The civil rights movement, though, survived and developed through the 1950s and into the 1960s. The movement had many components, including the protest song. Such folksingers as Pete Seeger and Woody Guthrie sang folk music and union songs in the 1950s. The tradition was carried on by Bob Dylan, Peter, Paul and Mary, and Joan Baez in the 1960s. Some argue that folk music is not political, while others argue that there is a political message in the songs and ballads of these and other singers, especially in the early 1960s.

What is certain is that folk music, advocates for civil rights, and politicians all converged on a Wednesday afternoon in August 1963 for the same purpose. The March on Washington was in support of jobs and voting rights. Thousands of protesters from throughout the country traveled to Washington to participate. Peter, Paul and Mary, Bob Dylan, and Joan Baez all appeared on the stage that afternoon with Dr. Martin Luther King, Jr., who delivered his famous "I Have a Dream" speech to the crowd. Change did not occur as immediately as the crowd would have wished, but the Civil Rights Act eventually became law under the administration of Lyndon B. Johnson.

Significance

The significance of the song "Blowin' in the Wind" and the March on Washington for Jobs and Freedom is multi-layered. Bob Dylan composed the song, which was first recorded on his 1963 album, *The Freewheelin' Bob Dylan.* The song was recorded over sixty times, including one recording by Peter, Paul and Mary, one of the most popular singing groups in the United States at the time of the march. Their single of "Blowin' in the Wind" was on the *Billboard* magazine chart at number 5 the week of the march and had been on the charts for ten weeks. At the March on Washington, Peter, Paul and Mary, who were committed to their political beliefs and performed at many functions supporting the civil rights movement, performed both "Blowin' in the Wind" and "The Hammer Song" ("If I had a hammer . . ."). The song's lyrics carry the message on everyone's minds that day: How long will it be before all men and women are free to live in a land that proclaims freedom as a value?

The March on Washington for Jobs and Freedom was, of course, the central event of the day. Organizers had taken spent time preparing and sending out literature

1963

An Appeal to You from

JAMES FARMER
Congress of Racial Equality

MARTIN LUTHER KING
Southern Christian
Leadership Conference

JOHN LEWIS
Student Non-violent
Coordinating Committee

A. PHILLIP RANDOLPH
Negro American Labor Council

ROY WILKINS
National Association for the
Advancement of Colored People

WHITNEY YOUNG
National
Urban League

to MARCH ON WASHINGTON

WEDNESDAY AUGUST 28, 1963

America Faces a crisis...

Millions of Negroes are denied freedom...

Millions of citizens, black and white, are unemployed...

Discrimination and economic deprivation plague the nation and rob all people, Negro and white, of dignity and self-respect. As long as black workers are disenfranchised, ill-housed, denied education and economically depressed, the fight of white workers for a decent life will fail.

Thus we call on all Americans to join us in Washington:

♦ to demand the passage of effective civil rights legislation which will guarantee to all

. . . decent housing

. . . access to all public accommodations

. . . adequate and integrated education

. . . the right to vote

♦ to prevent compromise or filibuster against such legislation

♦ to demand a federal massive works and training program that puts all unemployed workers, black and white, back to work

♦ to demand an FEP Act which bars discrimination by federal, state and municipal governments, by employers, by contractors, employment agencies and trade unions

♦ to demand a national minimum wage, which includes all workers, of not less than $2.00 an hour.

In your community, groups are mobilizing for the March. You can get information on how to go to Washington from civil rights organizations, religious organizations, trade unions, fraternal organizations and youth groups.

JOIN THE MARCH ON WASHINGTON FOR JOBS AND FREEDOM
and become part of the great American revolution for human freedom and justice Now.

National Office—

MARCH ON WASHINGTON FOR JOBS AND FREEDOM

170 West 130 Street   **New York 27, New York**
FIlmore 8-1900

Cleveland Robinson
Chairman, Administrative Committee

Bayard Rustin
Deputy Director

Primary Source

"An Appeal to You from . . . to March on Washington"

SYNOPSIS: The flyer provides the sponsors and the pledge for the participants. The March on Washington for Jobs and Freedom showed support for civil rights legislation and for the end of discrimination against blacks in jobs, housing, and education. COURTESY OF MICHIGAN STATE UNIVERSITY LIBRARIES, SPECIAL COLLECTIONS.

Marcher's Pledge

Standing before the Lincoln Memorial on the 28th day of August, in the centennial year of emancipation, I affirm my complete personal commitment for the struggle for jobs and freedom for all Americans.

To fulfill that commitment, I pledge that I will not relax until victory is won.

I pledge that I will join and support all actions undertaken in good faith in accord with time-honored democratic tradition of nonviolent protest, or peaceful assembly and petition and of redress through the courts and the legislative process.

I pledge to carry the message of the March to my friends and neighbors back home and to arouse them to an equal commitment and an equal effort. I will march and I will write letters. I will demonstrate and I will vote. I will work to make sure that my voice and those of my brothers ring clear and determined from every corner of our land.

I will pledge my heart and mind and my body, unequivocally and without regard to personal sacrifice, to the achievement of social peace through social justice.

SOURCE: Saunders, Doris E., ed. *The Day They Marched.* Chicago: Johnson, 1963.

explaining the reasons for the march and the logistics of traveling to Washington, D.C. King's speech inspired the crowd and the nation, and Roy Wilkins, executive secretary of the National Association for the Advancement of Colored People, delivered remarks about employment and equal access to jobs. CBS televised the events of the entire day, including the march from the Washington Monument to the Lincoln Memorial.

Primary Source

"Blowin' in the Wind"

SYNOPSIS: Bob Dylan's song lyrics poignantly and symbolically ask how long it will be before all Americans enjoy equal access to the promise of the United States. The answer to the questions the song raises are "blowin' in the wind," suggesting, perhaps, that winds of changed are sweeping over the nation.

How many roads must a man walk down before you call him a man?
Yes, 'n' How many seas must a white dove sail before she sleeps in the sand?

Yes, 'n' How many times must the cannon balls fly before they're forever banned?

The answer, my friend, is blowin' in the wind,
The answer is blowin' in the wind.

How many times must a man look up before he can see the sky?
Yes, 'n' How many ears must one man have before he can hear people cry?
Yes, 'n' How many deaths will it take 'till he knows that too many people have died?

The answer, my friend, is blowin' in the wind,
The answer is blowin' in the wind.

How many years can a mountain exist before it's washed to the sea?
Yes, 'n' How many years can some people exist before they're allowed to be free?
Yes, 'n' How many times can a man turn his head pretending he just doesn't see?

The answer, my friend, is blowin' in the wind,
The answer is blowin' in the wind.

Further Resources

BOOKS

Goldsmith, Peter D. *Making People's Music: Moe Asch and Folkways Records.* Washington, D.C.: Smithsonian Institution Press, 1998.

Gray, Michael. *Song and Dance Man: The Art of Bob Dylan.* New York: St. Martin's Press, 1981.

Saunders, Doris E., ed. *The Day They Marched.* Chicago: Johnson, 1963.

PERIODICALS

"As 200,000 Marched in Washington." *U.S. News & World Report,* September 9, 1963, 38–44.

Crawford, K. "Some Crowd." *Newsweek,* September 9, 1963, 31.

WEBSITES

March on Washington, August 28, 1963. Available online at http://www.jointcenter.org/selpaper/themarch.htm (accessed March 2, 2003).

Ruhlmann, William. "Peter, Paul and Mary: A Song to Sing All Over this Land." Available online at http:/www.peterpaulmary.com/history/ruhlmann1.htm (accessed April 6, 2003).

AUDIO AND VISUAL MEDIA

"Final Plans for the March on Washington for Jobs and Freedom (Organizing Manual No. 2)." *March on Washington,* ARVF, Special Collections, Michigan State University.

Wilkins, Roy. *"March on Washington" For Jobs and Freedom: News Release. March on Washington,* ARVF, Special Collections, Michigan State University.

The Birds

Movie still

By: Alfred Hitchcock.

Date: 1963

Source: "The Birds." Alfred Hitchock, director. 1963. The Kobal Collection, Image no. BIRD005AB. Available online at http://www.picture-desk.com/kobal-collection (accessed April 6, 2003).

About the Artist: Alfred Hitchcock (1899–1980) was born and raised in England. By the time he moved to the United States in 1939 and became a citizen, he had already directed successful psychological thrillers. Major films include *Rear Window* (1954), *Psycho* (1960), *Rebecca* (1940), and *Frenzy* (1972). He always appeared in his own films in a nonspeaking cameo role. In addition to directing films, Hitchcock hosted two television series, *Alfred Hitchcock Presents* (1959–1962) and *The Alfred Hitchcock Hour* (1963–1965). ∎

Introduction

Alfred Hitchcock was a well-known filmmaker when he directed *The Birds* in 1963, principally because of *Psycho* (1960), which had thrilled and terrified American moviegoers. Hitchcock films were marked by the macabre and the unusual cinematic techniques, in contrast to the musicals, westerns, and romances that were still popular in the 1960s. Despite his popular success, few critics really appreciated Hitchcock's work, and he was overlooked by the Academy of Motion Pictures and by critics until the 1970s.

Hitchcock's film was adapted from a Daphne du Maurier short story. In the film, birds attack citizens in

The promotional poster for Alfred Hitchcock's *The Birds*. THE KOBAL COLLECTION/UNIVERSAL. REPRODUCED BY PERMISSION.

a California coastal town. Melanie Daniels, portrayed by Tippi Hedren, meets Mitch Brenner, portrayed by Rod Taylor, in a pet store. Melanie, a rich girl from San Francisco, is attracted to Mitch and decides to visit him at his seaside home in Bodega Bay. She takes two lovebirds as a gift, which she winds up giving to his sister, Cathy (played by Veronica Cartwright), as a birthday gift. The bird attacks begin soon after and cause the family and Melanie to be prisoners in the house. Melanie is severely attacked in the attic. Because of her injuries, they are forced to leave. The movie ends with the car driving away from the once benign seaside town.

Evil birds had appeared in several films prior to Alfred Hitchcock's production of *The Birds*. The 1956 Japanese film *Rodan* featured giant, terrifying birds, as did the 1957 U.S. film *The Giant Claw*. Hitchcock loaded *Psycho* with bird images, including having the lead character Norman Bates stuff the creatures. There were also kinder uses of birds in previous films, as in *Conflict of Wings,* a 1953 British film that used a bird sanctuary as a background, and Shirley Temple's 1940 film *Blue Bird.*

Significance

The Birds was the culmination of Alfred Hitchcock's fascination with birds. Hitchcock, in an effort to avoid seeming predictable, was trying to surprise audiences by the time he made this film, so he began the story as a light romantic comedy that seemed irrelevant to the dark, eerie story that follows. Donald Spoto (*The Art of Alfred Hitchcock: Fifty Years of His Motion Pictures* [New York: Doubleday, 1976], 385) writes that the film is like a "dark, lyric poem about the fragility of our supposedly ordered world, and the chaos which is ready to burst in and shatter our expectations." This mirrors Hitchcock's own view of the world. The birds are symbolic for the "unacknowledged invisible forces of destruction and disorder" that surrounds us (Spoto, 388).

The Highest Grossing Films of the 1960s

1. The Sound of Music (1965)
2. 101 Dalmatians (1961)
3. The Jungle Book (1967)
4. Doctor Zhivago (1965)
5. The Graduate (1967)
6. Mary Poppins (1964)
7. Butch Cassidy and the Sundance Kid (1969)
8. Thunderball (1965)
9. Cleopatra (1963)
10. Funny Girl (1968)

SOURCE: "The Decade's All-Time Box Office Leaders." Available online at http://www.filmsite.org/boxoffice2.html; website home page: http://www.filmsite.org/ (accessed May 27, 2003).

Primary Source

The Birds

SYNOPSIS: Tippi Hedren made her debut as an actress with a starring role in *The Birds*. This still photograph from the film suggests the horror people can feel when nature seems to have turned on humanity. THE KOBAL COLLECTION/UNIVERSAL. REPRODUCED BY PERMISSION.

The techniques that Hitchcock used in the film are what make it a classic, however. He took advantage of Technicolor and used red extensively in the film. Red, the color of blood, is used for clothing, a mailbox, children's hair, and a house. The use of ordinary birds—seagulls, crows, sparrows, and finches—as the attackers also make the film significant. These birds were a mixture of mechanical birds and hundreds of live, trained birds. Tippi Hedren was "placed daily in a cage-like room on the soundstage" (Spoto, 392) and had real birds thrown towards her for several of the scenes. Hedren called it the "worst week of her life" (Spoto, 392).

Critics have interpreted the film in different ways. Some see it as part of a trilogy of films that includes *Psycho* and *Marnie*. Bernard F. Dick ("Hitchcock's Terrible

Mothers," *Literature/Film Quarterly* 28, no. 4, 2000, 242) calls the film a "cold war parable." He notes the interlocking motifs of stuffed birds and real birds that connect the film with films like *Psycho*. The women in the film are viewed as caged birds, all vying for Mitch's attention. Each one is helpless is her own way.

The Birds, along with several other Hitchcock films, appears on the American Film Institute's 100 Years–100 Thrills list. It is the brilliant technical practices that make the film one to watch.

Further Resources

BOOKS

Armstrong, Richard, and Mary Willems Armstrong. "Birds." *Encyclopedia of Film Themes, Settings and Series.* Jefferson, N.C.: McFarland, 2001, 26–27.

Bellour, Raymond. *The Analysis of Film.* Bloomington, Ind.: Indiana University Press, 2000.

Spoto, Donald. *The Art of Alfred Hitchcock: Fifty Years of His Motion Pictures.* New York: Doubleday, 1976.

PERIODICALS

Dick, Bernard F. "Hitchcock's Terrible Mothers." *Literature/Film Quarterly* 28, no. 4, 2000, 238–249.

Morris, Christopher. "Reading the Birds and 'The Birds.'" *Literature/Film Quarterly* 28, no. 4, 2000, 250–258.

WEBSITES

Alfred Hitchcock: Behind the Silhouette. Available online at http://www.moma.org/exhibitions/1999/hitchcock/overview.html (accessed February 27, 2003).

The Birds. Available online at http://www.filmsite.org/bird.html (accessed February 27, 2003).

AUDIO AND VISUAL MEDIA

The American Film Institute Salute to Alfred Hitchcock. Directed by Marty Pasetta. Worldvision Home Video. Videocassette, 1989.

The Birds. Directed by Alfred Hitchcock. Universal Pictures. DVD, 1963.

Maurice Sendak with Max and the monsters from *Where the Wild Things Are.* GETTY IMAGES. REPRODUCED BY PERMISSION.

Where the Wild Things Are

Fictional work

By: Maurice Sendak

Date: 1963

Source: Sendak, Maurice. *Where the Wild Things Are.* New York: HarperCollins, 1984.

About the Artist: Maurice Sendak (1928–) is the youngest of three children born to Jewish immigrants in Brooklyn, New York. As a child, he drew scenes of his immigrant neighborhood. Formal art training took place at the Art Students League in New York. Sendak has illustrated other authors' works but prefers writing and illustrating his own material. Sendak was the first American to win the Hans Christian Anderson Award, for *In the Night Kitchen* (1970). ■

Introduction

Although nineteenth century children's books had been vivid and sometimes frightening, twentieth century parents and children were accustomed to milder topics than monsters in the bedroom. Maurice Sendak's *Where the Wild Things Are,* a 1964 Caldecott Award winner, opened the doors for more honesty in children's literature.

Max, the main character, is a mischievous child who disobeys his mother. In the opening pages, the monster's picture on the wall reveals that Max has ventured to the land of the wild things before. Because of his behavior, his mother calls Max a Wild Thing and sends him to bed without supper. Max dreams, and his room slowly turns into the land of Wild Things. When Max cries "BE STILL," he gains authority over the wild things, or the forces of his imagination—he frightens what should frighten him. In one scene, Max and the Wild Things play in the trees of the forest. Slowly Max learns that he misses those he loves and sails back home to his own room and a warm dinner. Even though he takes off his hood, Max remains in his wolf suit, a promise of more adventures.

Sendak has written that *Where the Wild Things Are* is about how children master their feelings and come to grips with realities in their livers. The earliest version of the book was about horses, but Sendak said that he was not able to draw horses very well, so after some time, he came up with "things" as a substitute. In the final version, his story drew on his own childhood realities, fears, and imagination. He describes his relatives who came for Sunday dinner and who inspired the drawings for the wild things. They "would lean way over with their bad teeth and hairy noses, and say something threatening like 'You're so cute I could eat you up'" (quoted in Selma G. Lane, *The Art of Maurice Sendak* [New York: Abrams, 1980], 88).

Significance

In his Caldecott acceptance speech, Maurice Sendak said that children have "to combat an awful fact

till Max said "BE STILL!"
and tamed them with the magic trick

Primary Source

Where the Wild Things Are (1 OF 3)

SYNOPSIS: When Max shouts "BE STILL" to the monsters, he is reversing roles, becoming an authority figure like his mother rather than a child. In the following excerpt, the monsters obey Max and all of them begin to dance and yell in what is known as the "rumpus scene," a wild and fun game that nevertheless remains in Max's room. FROM *WHERE THE WILD THINGS ARE* BY MAURICE SENDAK. HARPERCOLLINS PUBLISHERS, 1963. COPYRIGHT © 1963 BY MAURICE SENDAK. COPYRIGHT RENEWED 1991 BY MAURICE SENDAK. REPRODUCED BY PERMISSION OF THE ILLUSTRATOR.

of childhood: the fact of their vulnerability to fear, anger, hate, frustration—all the emotions that are an ordinary part of their lives and that they can perceive only as ungovernable and dangerous forces" (quoted in John Cech, *Angels and Wild Things: The Archetypal Poetics of Maurice Sendak* [University Park, Pa: Pennsylvania State University Press, 1995], 120). To do this, children turn to fantasy. Through the exploration of fantasy and the forces that influence children's lives, Sendak changed the world of picture books forever.

The book drew critical attention when it appeared in 1963. Some early reviewers felt that the book would

frighten and even disturb children. Others, however, took a more positive view by noting the depth and sheer power of the book and its images. Recent critics have analyzed the psychological aspects of the book. Jennifer Shaddock, for instance, calls it the child's version of Joseph Conrad's *Heart of Darkness* while recognizing that it is "historically and culturally indebted to nineteenth-century adventure/explorer narrative" ("Where the Wild Things Are: Sendak's Journey into the Heart of Darkness," *Children's Literature Association Quarterly* 22, no. 4, 1997, 155). Raymond Jones, writing about the five stages of Max's journey, asserts

Primary Source

Where the Wild Things Are (2 of 3)

Max hangs from a tree with a monster. FROM *WHERE THE WILD THINGS ARE* BY MAURICE SENDAK. HARPERCOLLINS PUBLISHERS, 1963. COPYRIGHT © 1963 BY MAURICE SENDAK. COPYRIGHT RENEWED 1991 BY MAURICE SENDAK. REPRODUCED BY PERMISSION OF THE ILLUSTRATOR.

that, "a circular dream journey gives *Where the Wild Things Are* significant literary form and meaning" ("Maurice Sendak's *Where the Wild Things Are:* Picture Book Poetry," in *Touchstones: Reflections on the Best in Children's Literature,* vol. 3, ed. Perry Nodelman [West Layfayette, Ind.: Children's Literature Association, 1989], 125). Jones also analyzes Sendak's poetic form as well as his graphical form. In the 1980s, Maurice Sendak and Oliver Knussen adapted the book as an opera.

Forty years after its publication, *Where the Wild Things Are* stands as a classic in children's literature. Though Max and his Wild Things may frighten the grown-ups, they still delight children.

Further Resources

BOOKS

Cech, John. *Angels and Wild Things: The Archetypal Poetics of Maurice Sendak.* University Park, Pa: Pennsylvania State University Press, 1995.

Hentoff, Nat. "Among the Wild Things." In *Only Connect: Readings on Children's Literature,* ed. Shelia Egoff, G.T. Stubbs, and L.F. Ashley. New York: Oxford University Press, 1969, 323–346.

Jones, Raymond. "Maurice Sendak's *Where the Wild Things Are:* Picture Book Poetry." In *Touchstones: Reflections on the Best in Children's Literature,* vol. 3, ed. Perry Nodelman. West Layfayette, Ind.: Children's Literature Association, 1989, 122–131.

Lane, Selma G. *The Art of Maurice Sendak* New York: Abrams, 1980.

Primary Source

Where the Wild Things Are (3 OF 3)

More monsters hang in the trees. FROM *WHERE THE WILD THINGS ARE* BY MAURICE SENDAK. HARPERCOLLINS PUBLISHERS, 1963. COPYRIGHT © 1963 BY MAURICE SENDAK. COPYRIGHT RENEWED 1991 BY MAURICE SENDAK. REPRODUCED BY PERMISSION OF THE ILLUSTRATOR.

PERIODICALS

Bodmer, George R. "Sendak into Opera: *Wild Things* and *Higglety Pigglety Pop!*" *The Lion and the Unicorn* 16, 1992, 167–175.

Shaddock, Jennifer. "*Where the Wild Things Are:* Sendak's Journey into the Heart of Darkness." *Children's Literature Association Quarterly* 22, no. 4, 1997–98, 155–159.

WEBSITES

"Maurice Sendak." Available online at http://www.northern.edu /hastingw/sendak.htm (accessed April 6, 2003).

"Maurice Sendak." Available online at http://www.barclayagency .com/sendak.html (accessed April 6, 2003).

"Maurice Sendak—video clip." Available online at http://www .scils.rutgers.edu/~kvander/mauricesendak.html (accessed April 6, 2002).

AUDIO AND VISUAL MEDIA

Where the Wild Things Are. Narrated by Peter Schickele. New York: Scholastic Inc. Cassette tape. 1989.

Where the Wild Things Are. Ballet. New York: CRI. Compact disc. 2000.

Where the Wild Things Are (puzzle). Montclair, N.J.: Briarpatch, 1999.

Where the Wild Things Are. Directed by Gene Deitch. Weston Woods Studios. Videocassette. 1988.

Where the Wild Things Are: A Fantasy Opera. Conducted by Oliver Knussen. Home Vision. Videocassette. 1985.

Wild Thing Doll: Max. San Francisco, Calif.: Determined Productions, 1985.

"A Hard Day's Night"

Song

By: John Lennon and Paul McCartney

Date: 1964

Source: Lennon, John, and Paul McCartney. "A Hard Day's Night." In *Things We Said Today: The Complete Lyrics and a Concordance to The Beatles' Songs, 1962–1970.* Edited by Colin Campbell and Allan Murphy. Ann Arbor, Mich.: Pierian Press, 1980. 19.

About the Artist: John Lennon (1940–1980) and Paul McCartney (1942–) composed much of the music for the British rock group The Beatles, which also included George Harrison and Ringo Starr. The Beatles' first American tour began February 7, 1964, at the Coliseum in Washington, D.C. During their time together, The Beatles had twenty number one singles in the United States. They were inducted into the Rock and Roll Hall of Fame in Cleveland, Ohio, in 1988. ∎

Introduction

Throughout the 1950s, American performers such as Elvis Presley, Chuck Berry, Buddy Holly, and Jerry Lee Lewis had been the stars of rock and roll and rhythm and blues. Beginning in the early 1960s, this changed with the British Invasion, which hit the shores of the United States with the tour by The Beatles and their appearance on the *Ed Sullivan Show* in February 1964. British bands and singers, including Cream, Herman's Hermits, The Dave Clark Five, Chad and Jeremy, and Petula Clark, joined The Beatles in changing the sound of rock and pop music. Yet the influences did not proceed in one direction, as American musicians influenced The Beatles. John Lennon cited Elvis Presley as having an influence on The Beatles, and the Quarry Men, the band John Lennon began before The Beatles, often performed songs by Elvis. Likewise, The Beatles shared common bonds with the Beach Boys, whose surf sound had reached the top of the charts before The Beatles made their first trip to the United States.

Lennon and McCartney wrote "A Hard Day's Night" specifically for the film by the same name. The song appeared as a single, as the first song on an album by the same name, and in the film, as well as in compilation albums. The song is a typical Beatles' lyric about love and wanting to be with the one you love.

Significance

The Beatles first appeared in the United States in February 1964, and they were an instant hit with fans. "A Hard Day's Night" debuted in London on July 10, 1964, and became the third single to reach number one on the British charts. On July 13, 1964, the single was released in the United States, where it also reached number one on the charts. The album, released in Great Britain on August 10, 1964, contained a number of new songs written by Lennon and McCartney and was the group's only album to feature songs by the two exclusively. The album had been released in the United States on June 26, 1964, with a different mixture of tracks. The million-copy-selling song was awarded the Grammy for Best Performance by a Vocal Group for 1964.

This is a unique song among The Beatles' repertoire because it was used as an album title and became the title for their first movie. The black-and-white film was shot with a relatively low budget, unlike later films or MTV videos of the 1980s and beyond. In the film, they travel from town to town by train to perform. Paul's grandfather, played by William Brambell, appears and stirs up trouble between the road manager and his assistant and finally, between Ringo and the rest of the band. What makes this song stand out is the combination of the film and song. The film, reissued in 2003, is considered to be one of the first music videos. Though performers such as Elvis Presley had cashed in on movies in the 1950s, *A Hard Day's Night* was different, for it topped both the British and American charts for fifty weeks.

Primary Source

"A Hard Day's Night"

> **SYNOPSIS:** "A Hard Day's Night" is the title song for The Beatles' 1964 film and album by the same title. The film, directed by Richard Lester, is a pseudo-documentary. The song chronicles missing a love while the singer is working. Home is the goal because that's where "everything seems to be right."

It's been a hard day's night
And I been working like a dog
It's been a hard day's night
I should be sleeping like a log
But when I get home to you
I find the things that you do
Will make me feel alright.

You know I work all day
To get you money to buy you things
And it's worth it just to hear you say
You're gonna give me everything
So why on earth should I moan
'cos when I get you alone
You know I feel OK.

When I'm home everything seems to be right
When I'm home feeling you holding me tight, tight, yeah.

It's been a hard day's night
And I been working like a dog
It's been a hard day's night,
I should be sleeping like a log

Paul McCartney, George Harrison, Ringo Starr, and John Lennon—The Beatles—run down an empty alley in the film *A Hard Day's Night.*
© BETTMANN/CORBIS. REPRODUCED BY PERMISSION.

But when I get home to you
I find the things that you do
Will make me feel alright.
(Ow)

So why on earth should I moan
'cos when I get you alone
You know I feel OK.

When I'm home everything seems to be right
When I'm home feeling you holding me tight, tight,
  yeah.

Oh, It's been a hard day's night
And I been working like a dog
It's been a hard day's night
I should be sleeping like a log
But when I get home to you
I find the things that you do
Will make me feel alright
You know I feel alright
You know I feel alright.

Further Resources

BOOKS

Buskin, Richard. *The Complete Idiot's Guide to The Beatles.* New York: Alpha Books, 1998.

Everett, Walter. *The Beatles as Musicians: Revolver Through the Anthology.* New York: Oxford University Press, 1999.

Harry, Bill. *The Ultimate Beatles Encyclopedia.* New York: Hyperion, 1992.

PERIODICALS

Anders, Allison. "A Hard Day's Fight." *Sight and Sound* 9, no. 10, 1999, 58–59.

"Report from Hiram." *The New Yorker,* August 22, 1964, 25–27.

WEBSITES

"BeatleLinks—The Beatles Internet Resource Guide." Available online at: http://www.beatlelinks.net/links/ (accessed February 26, 2003).

"The Beatles Ultimate Experience Database: The Movies. *A Hard Day's Night.*" Available online at http://www.geocities.com/~beatleboy1/dbmovies.html (accessed February 25, 2003).

AUDIO AND VISUAL MEDIA

The Beatles: The Making of "A Hard Day's Night." Repnet, Videocassette, 1995.

A Hard Day's Night. Directed by Richard Lester. Walt Disney Home Video. Videocassette. 1964.

Crying Girl
Painting

By: Roy Lichtenstein

Date: 1964

Source: Lichtenstein, Roy. *Crying Girl.* 1964. Roy Lichtenstein Foundation. Available online at http://www.lichtenstein-foundation.org/3352.htm (accessed January 7, 2003).

About the Artist: Roy Lichtenstein (1923–1997), a painter, sculptor, and printmaker, was born in New York City. His first art education took place at the Arts Student League in New York. He later earned a bachelor's degree and master of fine arts from Ohio State University. During the 1950s, the theme of much of his work was American history and the conquest of the Wild West. In the 1960s, he began creating pop art based on comics. ∎

Introduction

In the 1950s and 1960s, pop art became an international movement in painting, sculpture, and printmaking, though the term itself originated in London. Pop art was meant to appeal to a mass audience and be mass produced. Artists who were part of this movement include Lawrence Alloway, Richard Hamilton, David Hockney, Jim Dine, and Andy Warhol. The movement emerged in the United States in the 1960s, though artists had started to experiment during the decade before. When asked to define pop art, Roy Lichtenstein said, "I don't know—the use of commercial art as subject matter in painting, I suppose. It was hard to get a painting that was despicable enough so that no one would hang it—everybody was hanging everything" (G.R. Swenson, "Roy Lichtenstein," in *Pop Art Redefined,* ed. John Russell and Suzi Gablik [New York: Frederick A. Praeger, 1969], 92). Mass media, commercial products, anything industrial—objects from all of these became subjects for pop artists, who expected their work to fade away and not be of interest to future generations. Some were right, but artists like Andy Warhol and Roy Lichtenstein continue to draw interest.

In the 1960s, Lichtenstein broke away from his earlier style of art and began imitating comic art in paintings, adopting a simple style based on popular culture subjects. Because series were popular in this movement, Lichtenstein created a series that included "Crying Girl," much as Andy Warhol created a series of Campbell's Soup cans. The multiple versions of images reflected the interest the artists had in consumer culture. The movement of pure pop art was short-lived, ending around 1964, though variations of pop art became popular after that time.

Significance

"Crying Girl," reproduced here, is one of many crying girls Lichtenstein created. This one is without a "bub-

Artist Roy Lichtenstein stands with one of a series of his paintings on display at a gallery in New York City, 1964. The full text of the paintings read "As I opened fire I knew why Tex had not buzzed. If he had the enemy would have been warned that my ship was below them . . ."
© CORBIS. REPRODUCED BY PERMISSION.

ble" quotation characteristic of comic-book art, but it still portrays the sad, blond girl who is familiar in many of Lichtenstein's works. His paintings, including "Crying Girl," had a defined subject, even if it was a tongue-in-cheek look at the world. Painting women in distress may have been a response to his marriage breaking up in the early 1960s; however, he never spoke about his private life in public. Blonds crying appeared in "Drowning Girl," "Frightened Girl," and "Hopeless" as well. The repetition of the image is significant and one aspect that makes Lichtenstein's work memorable.

The pointillist technique (a pointing consisting of small dots rather than conventional brushstrokes), along with his sense of humor, became a signature style for Lichtenstein. Critics did not appreciate his work at first, dismissing it as inartistic. Yet the public judged otherwise. The image of "Crying Girl," as well as other Lichtenstein paintings, remains familiar to the public today. His work is still reproduced on T-shirts, greeting cards, posters, and other popular culture products. Original artwork by Roy Lichtenstein has been sold for millions of dollars and hangs in museums throughout the world.

Primary Source

Crying Girl

SYNOPSIS: *Crying Girl* hangs in the Milwaukee Art Museum in Milwaukee, Wisconsin. It measures forty-six by forty-six inches and was created with enamel on steel. The vivid yellow and red and the heavy black outlines are typical of Lichtenstein's work during this period. The crying girls who appeared in many of Lichtenstein's paintings were inspired by DC Comics' *Girls' Romances* and *Secret Hearts*. © ESTATE OF ROY LICHTENSTEIN. REPRODUCED BY PERMISSION.

Further Resources

BOOKS

Alloway, Lawrence. *American Pop Art.* New York: Collier, 1974.

———. *Roy Lichtenstein.* New York: Abbeville Press, 1983.

Kimmelman, Michael. *Portraits: Talking with Artists at the Met, The Modern, The Louvre and Elsewhere.* New York: Random House, 1998.

Livingstone, Marco. "Pop Art." *Dictionary of Art,* vol. 25. Edited by Jane Turner. New York: Grove, 1996, 231–233.

Swenson, G.R. "Roy Lichtenstein." In *Pop Art Redefined.* Edited by John Russell and Suzi Gablik. New York: Praeger, 1969, 92–94.

PERIODICALS

Hall, David. "Roy Lichtenstein, 1923–1997." *Art Monthly,* November 1997, 23.

WEBSITES

The Roy Lichtenstein Foundation. Available online at http://www.lichtensteinfoundation.org/ (accessed January 18, 2003).

Dutchman

Play script

By: LeRoi Jones

Date: 1964

Source: Jones, LeRoi. *Dutchman and The Slave.* New York: William Morrow, 1964, 3–7.

About the Author: LeRoi Jones (1934–), who changed his name to Amiri Baraka in 1968, writes about African Americans living in a white world. Early in his career, he wrote plays and essays. Since the 1980s, he has concentrated on writing poetry and nonfiction. As an African American nationalist in the 1960s, Baraka was an advocate for African American arts and aesthetics. His work is confrontational and demands reactions from his audiences. ∎

Introduction

Following a trip to Cuba in 1960, LeRoi Jones realized the political power of the arts. Through drama, he provided a message to the audience about his vision of life in the United States for the African American man. In 1964, he had five plays produced, including *Dutchman.* He envisioned a new African American arts movement, one that would depict a United States that few whites saw but in which many African Americans lived.

Dutchman opened in January 1964 at Village South Theatre in New York City. Like most of Jones' plays, this one ran off-Broadway. It reopened at the Cherry Lane Theatre in March 1964 and at that time was noticed by the critics, including *The New Yorker*'s Edith Oliver, who wrote that Jones "has a kind of deadly wit and passionate wild comedy that are his alone" (April 4, 1964, 78–79).

The play repeats a familiar theme in Jones' early work: a white woman tormenting an African American man. In *Dutchman,* Clay, a young African American man, is riding the Manhattan subway on his way to a party. Lula, an attractive white woman, catches his eye through the window and then boards the subway and sits by Clay. They alternately seduce and annoy one another during the slow ride. In the end, Lula knifes Clay and the fellow passengers help her throw him off the train.

Significance

Dutchman, the Obie winner for 1964, is still considered one of LeRoi Jones' most significant works. The one-act play interprets the world of Clay through Lula's eyes, right or wrong, just as the white world stereotypes African Americans in the United States. *Dutchman* portrays what Jones and Larry Neal wrote about in the anthology *Black Fire:* "Our literature, our art and our music are moving closer to the forces motivating Black America. You can hear it everywhere, especially in music, a surging new sound. . . . Black literature must become an

integral part of the community's lifestyle. And I believe that it must also be integral to the myths and experiences underlying the total history of black people" (*Black Fire: An Anthology of Afro-American Writing* [New York: William Morrow, 1968], 653). The African American arts movement was revolutionary, depicting a United States few had experienced.

Critics have interpreted the play through many lenses. The Flying Dutchman story, the biblical story of Adam and Eve, and psychological interpretations have all been applied to the brief relationship between Clay and Lula. Jerome Klinkowitz claims that the theme of the play is African American identity and its existence in the world ("LeRoi Jones (Imamu Amiri Baraka): *Dutchman* as Drama," *Negro American Literature Forum* 7, 1973, 122). Other critics noted symbolic items used in the play: the sunglasses Lula wears as a disguise of friendship, the apple she offers Clay as temptation, and the books representing the written culture meant for white society.

Although the play is nearly forty years old, it continues to be produced across the United States in small theaters. The message is just as powerful today as when it originally appeared in New York.

Primary Source

Dutchman [excerpt]

> **SYNOPSIS:** In the opening scene of *Dutchman,* Clay, a twenty-year-old African American man, is sitting alone on the subway looking into space. At one of the stops, he glances through the window and sees Lula, a thirty-year-old white woman. They smile at one another and Lula enters the train and sits by him. As they begin to banter back and forth, Lula acts like she knows more about Clay than expected.

Characters

Clay, twenty-year-old Negro

Lula, thirty-year-old white woman

Riders of coach, white and black

Young Negro

Conductor

In the flying underbelly of the city. Steaming hot, and summer on top, outside. Underground. The subway heaped in modern myth.

Opening scene is a man sitting in a subway seat, holding a magazine but looking vacantly just above its wilting pages. Occasionally he looks blankly toward the window on his right. Dim lights and darkness whistling by against the glass. (Or paste the lights, as admitted props, right on the subway windows. Have them move, even dim and

Actors Shirley Knight and Al Freeman, Jr., appeared in *Dutchman,* the film based on LeRoi Jones' (right) play, which premiered in April 1967 in New York. **AP/WIDE WORLD PHOTOS. REPRODUCED BY PERMISSION.**

flicker. But give the sense of speed. Also stations, whether the train is stopped or the glitter and activity of these stations merely flashes by the windows.) The rest of the car is outfitted as a complete subway car. But only his seat is shown. There might be, for a time, as the play begins, a loud scream of the actual train. And it can recur throughout the play, or continue on a lower key once the dialogue starts.

The train slows after a time, pulling to a brief stop at one of the stations. The man looks idly up, until he sees a woman's face staring at him through the window; when it realizes that he man has noticed the face, it begins very premeditatedly to smile. The man smiles too, for a moment, without a trace of self-consciousness. Almost an instinctive though undesirable response. Then a kind of awkwardness or embarrassment sets in, and the man makes to look away, is further embarrassed, so he brings his eyes to where the face was, but by now the train is moving again, and the face would seem to be left bethind by the way the man turns his head to look back through the other windows at the slowly fading platform. He smiles then; more comfortably confident, hoping perhaps that his memory

of this brief encounter will be pleasant. And then he is idle again.

Scene I

Train roars. Lights flash outside the windows.

Lula enters from the rear of the car in bright, skimpy summer clothes and sandals. She carries a net bag full of paper books, fruit, and other anonymous articles. She is wearing sunglasses, which she pushes up on her forehead from time to time. Lula is a tall, slender, beautiful woman with long red hair hanging straight down her back, wearing only loud lipstick in somebody's good taste. She is eating an apple, very daintily. Coming down the car toward Clay.

She stops beside Clay's seat and hangs languidly from the strap, still managing to eat the apple. It is apparent that she is going to sit in the seat next to Clay, and that she is only waiting for him to notice her before she sits.

Clay sits as before, looking just beyond his magazine, now and again pulling the magazine slowly back and forth in front of his face in a hopeless effort to fan himself. Then he sees the woman hanging there beside him and he looks up into her face, smiling quizzically.

Lula: Hello.

Clay: Uh, hi're you?

Lula: I'm going to sit down. . . . O.K.?

Clay: Sure.

Lula: *(Swings down onto the seat, pushing her legs straight out as if she is very weary)* Oooof! Too much weight.

Clay: Ha, doesn't look like much to me. *(Leaning back against the window, a little surprised and maybe stiff)*

Lula: It's so anyway. *(And she moves her toes in the sandals, then pulls her right leg up on the left knee, better to inspect the bottoms of the sandals and the back of her heel. She appears for a second not to notice that Clay is sitting next to her or that she has spoken to him just a second before. Clay looks at the magazine, then out the black window. As he does this, she turns very quickly toward him.)* Weren't you staring at me through the window?

Clay: *(Wheeling around and very much stiffened)* What?

Lula: Weren't you staring at me through the window? At the last stop?

Clay: Staring at you? What do you mean?

Lula: Don't you know what staring means?

Clay: I saw you through the window . . . if that's what it means. I don't know if I was staring. Seems to me you were staring through the window at me.

Lula: I was. But only after I'd turned around and saw you staring through that window down in the vicinity of my ass and legs.

Clay: Really?

Lula: Really. I guess you were just taking those idle potshots. Nothing else to do. Run your mind over people's flesh.

Clay: Oh boy. Wow, now I admit I was looking in your direction. But the rest of that weight is yours.

Lula: I suppose.

Clay: Staring through train windows is weird business. Much weirder than staring very sedately at abstract asses.

Lula: That's why I came looking through the window . . . so you'd have more than that to go on. I even smiled at you.

Clay: That's right.

Lula: I even got into this train, going some other way than mine. Walked down the aisle . . . searching you out.

Clay: Really? That's pretty funny.

Further Resources

BOOKS

Bonner, Thomas Jr. "Amiri Baraka (LeRoi Jones) (7 October 1934–)." *American Playwrights Since 1945.* Edited by Philip C. Kolin. New York: Greenwood, 1989.

Jones, LeRoi, and Larry Neal, eds. *Black Fire: An Anthology of Afro-American Writing* New York: William Morrow, 1968.

Olaniyan, Tejumola. *Scars of Conquest/Masks of Resistance: The Invention of Cultural Identities in African, African-American, and Caribbean Drama.* New York: Oxford University Press, 1995.

PERIODICALS

Klinkowitz, Jerome. "LeRoi Jones (Imamu Amiri Baraka): *Dutchman* as Drama." *Negro American Literature Forum* 7, 1973, 123–126.

Nelson, Hugh. "LeRoi Jones' *Dutchman:* A Brief Ride on a Doomed Ship." *Educational Theatre Journal* 20, no.1, 1968, 33–59.

Oliver, Edith. "Over the Edge." *The New Yorker,* April 4, 1964, 78–79.

Weisgram, Dianne H. "LeRoi Jones' *Dutchman:* Inter-racial Ritual of Sexual Violence." *American Image: A Psychoanalytical Journal of Culture, Science and the Arts* 29, 1972, ON.

WEBSITES

"Amiri Baraka." Available online at http://www.english.uiuc.edu /maps/poets/a_f/baraka/baraka.htm (accessed January 18, 2003.)

AUDIO AND VISUAL MEDIA

Dutchman. Directed by Anthony Harvey. Image Entertainment. Videocassette, 1967.

Creek
Painting

By: Robert Rauschenberg

Date: 1964

Source: Rauschenberg, Robert. *Creek.* 1964. Detroit Institute of Arts. Available online at http://www.dia.org/collections/twenty/69.48.html (accessed February 20, 2003).

Painter and graphic artist Robert Rauschenberg, 1966. © HULTON-DEUTSCH COLLECTION/CORBIS. REPRODUCED BY PERMISSION.

About the Artist: Robert Rauschenberg (1925–) is considered one of the most influential artists of the 1960s. He is noted for departing from abstract expressionism and for questioning relationships between art and life. He studied art at the Kansas City Art Institute, at Academie Julian in Paris, and at Black Mountain College near Asheville, North Carolina. Rauschenberg had a retrospective exhibition in 1963 at the Jewish Museum in New York City. ■

Introduction

Robert Rauschenberg's combined understanding of art and music helped him form his unique and innovative techniques. He developed his artistic style during the 1950s and was one of the leaders in the visual arts during the 1950s and 1960s. Like his counterparts in the field, he defied the style of the abstract expressionists. He is credited with influencing the pop art of Andy Warhol and Roy Lichtenstein, though he is not a pop artist himself. Many prominent artists worked in studios near one another in New York, including Rauschenberg, Jasper Johns, John Cage, Lichetenstein, and Warhol.

Rauschenberg's oft-quoted philosophy is revealing: "Painting relates to both art and life. Neither can be made. (I try to act in that gap between the two)" (quoted in Mary Lynn Kotz, *Rauschenberg: Art and Life* [New York: Abrams, 1990], 7). This philosophy and his further questioning of the artistic aesthetics and techniques of the late twentieth century turned out to be the key to his influential career. He was not afraid to go against the norm. In the 1950s, he spent periods of time painting all white and then all black canvases. These experiments helped form his questions about messages in the media, which led to silkscreen paintings in the 1960s.

Rauschenberg's silkscreen technique developed in the early 1960s when he noticed the use of found objects in collages. *Creek* is an example of one silkscreen painting from this period. Rauschenberg stated, "I was bombarded with TV sets and magazines, by the excess of the world. I thought an honest work should incorporate all of these elements, which were and are a reality" (quoted in Kotz, 99). The collages are a blend of photography, newspaper, magazines, and painting juxtaposed to create metaphors about life, which carry from painting to painting.

Significance

Rauschenberg's techniques are as significant as his work. Although silkscreen techniques were not new, the way Rauschenberg used them was new. In the late 1950s, he frequently started by using his own photography and newspaper or magazine photographs in his work. Quotations from the press were used to make statements about life and art. These were enlarged before they were arranged on the silkscreens. "Once he had the silkscreens

Primary Source

Creek

SYNOPSIS: Robert Rauschenberg's entire career and artistic innovations are significant to the artistic movements during the last half of the twentieth century. His silkscreen paintings marked a new level of experimentation, which is his trademark in the art world. *Creek* is a screen print in oil on canvas. The gift from W. Hawkins Ferry to the Detroit Institute of Arts measures six by eight feet. CREEK, 1964. ROBERT RAUSCHENBERG. GIFT OF W. HAWKINS FERRY. PHOTOGRAPH © 1987 THE DETROIT INSTITUTE OF ARTS. © ROBERT RAUSCHENBERG/LICENSED BY VAGA, NEW YORK, NY.

in hand, he would place them on a canvas laid out on his floor and force viscous inks through the images on the porous silk onto the canvas with a squeegee. He would then paint around the screened images" (Kotz, 103). This technique allowed him the freedom to alter the sizes and colors of his images. In silkscreens he found a way to "reflect life's 'extremely random order that cannot be described as accidental'" (Kotz, 103).

"Creek," like many Rauschenberg silkscreens, appears to be an abstract from a distance. When it is viewed closely, the images can be detected. The Statue of Liberty is alongside images from Rubens' "Venus before the Mirror." Images of space flight and urban landscapes are also included in this painting, as well as sea vessels and an observatory. Rauschenberg placed images beside one another randomly; however, when viewed as a whole they reveal his thoughts on the world. The images are metaphors for the power of love and human feats. He once said, "There is no reason not to consider the world as one gigantic painting" (quoted in Lawrence Alloway, *American Pop Art* [New York: Collier, 1969], 55). The past and present coincide in *Creek* to reflect a timelessness of images and ideas. Brushstrokes and the colors selected reflect Rauschenberg's training as an artist, while the selection of images reflects his nonhierarchical approach to art. He is a fearless artist who will try anything.

Further Resources

BOOKS

Alloway, Lawrence. *American Pop Art.* New York: Collier, 1969.

Kotz, Mary Lynn. *Rauschenberg: Art and Life.* New York: Abrams, 1990.

Tomkins, Calvin. *Off the Wall: Robert Rauschenberg and the Art World of Our Time.* Garden City, N.Y.: Doubleday, 1980.

PERIODICALS

Swenson, G.R. "Rauschenberg Paints a Picture." *ARTnews,* April 1963, 44–47, 65–67.

Tomkins, Calvin. "Profiles: Robert Rauschenberg." *The New Yorker,* February 29, 1964, 39–40.

WEBSITES

"Robert Rauschenberg." Available online at http://www.guggen heimcollection.org/site/artist_work_md_1332.html; website home page: http://www.guggenheimcollection.org (accessed February 20, 2003).

"Robert Rauschenberg on the Internet." Available online at http://www.artcyclopedia.com/artists/rauschenberg_robert.html; website home page: http://artcyclopedia.com/ (accessed February 20, 2003).

AUDIO AND VISUAL MEDIA

American Art in the Sixties. Directed by Michael Blackwood. New York: Blackwood Productions. Videocassette. 2000.

Robert Rauschenberg: Inventive Genius. Directed by Karen Thomas et al. New York: Fox Lorber Associates. Videocassette. 1999.

Vietnam Poetry

"Driving through Minnesota during the Hanoi Bombings"; "At a March against the Vietnam War"

Poems

By: Robert Bly

Date: 1967

Source: Bly, Robert. *The Light Around the Body.* New York: Harper & Row, 1967, 34, 37.

About the Author: Robert Bly (1926–) was born in Madison, Minnesota. From 1944 to 1946, he served in the U.S. Navy. Following World War II, he attended St. Olaf College and Harvard University, where he earned his bachelor's degree. He also earned a master's degree from the Iowa Writers Workshop. Bly, who cofounded American Writers Against Vietnam, wrote and spoke against the war. He published a literary magazine, several volumes of poetry, and the book *Iron John: A Book About Men,* which was an international best-seller. ∎

Introduction

Warfare changed during the twentieth century, and so did poetry about the experience. World War I poetry often provided a physical description from the soldier-poets in the trenches who had not yet been disillusioned. During World War II, soldiers and poets were spread across many fronts, and their poetry took on a character of resignation and endurance for war. Vietnam changed the meaning of war and the reasons for war. More civilians wrote poetry to voice opinions about the Vietnam War than had during previous wars. Poets such as Allen Ginsberg, Lawrence Ferlinghetti, and Denise Levertov openly expressed political feelings and ideas in their verse. Groups of poets held read-ins and protests, but some wondered if they were doing any good. Although Robert Bly wrote with the same fervor about the Vietnam War and other societal injustices, he stood apart from his contemporaries because he made people uneasy, lacked the connections and support of some of the major poetic movements in 1960s, and was inspired by foreign poetry.

The Light Around the Body, Bly's second book of poetry, is divided into five sections, which overlap in theme. Everyone is fair game for Bly—the president, the president's cabinet, ordinary men and women. Bly opens the volume with an epigraph by Jacob Boehme that speaks of the inward and outward man. He balances these perspectives in the volume, describing both public and private visions. Bly "has learned to use the resources of the inner life to energize his work in the outward world" (James F. Mersmann, *Out of the Vietnam Vortex: A Study of Poets and Poetry against the War* [Lawrence: University Press of Kansas, 1974], 121–122).

Significance

Critical reviews of Robert Bly's work have been mixed. While some critics find Bly superficial, others praise his poetry and compare him to such contemporary poets as James Wright, Louis Simpson, and W.S. Merwin. In 1969, he received the National Book Award for Poetry for *The Light Around the Body.* In his acceptance speech, he criticized institutions, including book publishers and the Catholic Church, for not working to end the war in Vietnam. He stated, "As Americans, we have always wanted the life of feeling without the life of suffering" and questioned our right to "congratulate ourselves on our cultural magnificence." Bly gave his thousand-dollar award to Resistance, an organization committed to the draft-resistance movement. David Ignatow, a fellow poet, described the speech. "For me the moment meant a complete and overwhelming affirmation and vindication of all that Robert stood for as a crusading, visionary figure in the literary world and in the politics of our nation. . . . It was Robert's finest hour and we who were attached to him through admiration, faith and common goals were affirmed through him and made to feel our significance before the world" (quoted in Fred

Moramarco and William Sullivan, *Containing Multitudes: Poetry in the United States since 1950* [New York: Twayne, 1998], 106–107). Robert Bly's voice remains important in American poetry today.

Primary Source

Vietnam Poetry

SYNOPSIS: These two poems are representative of Robert Bly's works about Vietnam. Minnesota's summer greenness is contrasted with the horror of bombs in the first poem. The second poem describes the contrasts of calmness and threats of war and America's Puritan past. The march held in Washington, November 27, 1965, drew 35,000 protestors. Both emphasize atonement for what the United States has done in war.

"Driving through Minnesota during the Hanoi Bombings"

We drive between lakes just turning green;
Late June. The white turkeys have been moved
To new grass.
How long the seconds are in great pain!
Terror just before death,
Shoulders torn, shot
From helicopters, the boy
Tortured with the telephone generator,
"I felt sorry for him,
And blew his head off with a shotgun."
These instants become crystals,
Particles
The grass cannot dissolve. Our own gaiety
Will end up
In Asia, and in your cup you will look down
And see
Black Starfighters.
We were the ones we intended to bomb!
Therefore we will have
To go far away
To atone
For the sufferings of the stringy-chested
And the small rice-fed ones, quivering
In the helicopter like wild animals,
Shot in the chest, taken back to be questioned.

"At a March against the Vietnam War"

Washington, November 27, 1965

Newspapers rise high in the air over Maryland

We walk about, bundled in coats
     and sweaters in the late November sun

Looking down, I see feet moving
Calmly, gaily,
Almost as if separated from their bodies

But there is something moving in the dark
  somewhere
Just beyond
The edge of our eyes: a boat

Poet Robert Bly. **PHOTO BY GREG BOOTH. COURTESY OF ROBERT BLY.**

Covered with machine guns
Moving along under trees

It is black,
The hand reaches out
And cannot touch it—
It is that darkness among pine boughs
That the Puritans brushed
As they went out to kill turkeys

At the edge of the jungle clearing
It explodes
On the ground

We long to abase ourselves

We have carried around this cup of darkness
We have longed to pour it over our heads

We make war
Like a man anointing himself

Further Resources

BOOKS

Davis, William V., ed. *Critical Essays on Robert Bly.* New York: G.K. Hall, 1992.

Mersmann, James F. *Out of the Vietnam Vortex: A Study of Poets and Poetry against the War.* Lawrence, Kan.: University Press of Kansas, 1974.

Moramarco, Fred, and William Sullivan. *Containing Multitudes: Poetry in the United States since 1950.* New York: Twayne, 1998.

PERIODICALS

Davis, William V. "Affinity and Judgment: The Private and Public Poems of Robert Bly's Early Career." *Notes on Contemporary Literature* 20, no. 1, 1990, 7–9.

Lense, Edward. "The Assyrian Lion Above the Soybean Fields: Bly's *The Light Around the Body* as Prophecy against the Vietnam War." *Journal of American Culture* 16, no. 3, 1993, 89–95.

WEBSITES

"About the Vietnam War (1960–1975)." Available online at http://www.english.uiuc.edu/maps/vietnam/vietnamwar.htm (accessed January 6, 2003).

Bly, Robert. "Acceptance of the National Book Award for Poetry" (1969). Available online at http://www.english.uiuc.edu /maps/poets/a_f/bly/award.htm (accessed January 6, 2003).

Bushell, Kevin. "Leaping into the Unknown: The Poetics of Robert Bly's Deep Image." Available online at http://ebbs .english.vt.edu/olp/gs/1.2/bushell.html (accessed January 6, 2003).

Red Cube

Sculpture

By: Isamu Noguchi

Date: 1968

Source: Noguchi, Isamu. *Red Cube,* 1968, red painted steel. Marine Midland Bank, 140 Broadway, New York City. Available online at: http://www.noguchi.org/redcube.htm (accessed February 26, 2003).

About the Artist: Isamu Noguchi (1904–1988) was born in Los Angeles but grew up in Japan and Indiana. In 1927, he was awarded a Guggenheim Fellowship. He studied in Paris, where he was a studio assistant for Constantin Brancusis. Noguchi began creating public sculpture in the 1930s. Both Eastern and Western traditions influence Noguchi's sculpture and architectural work. ■

Introduction

Isamu Noguchi created public sculpture in the form of plazas, gardens, furniture, and interiors. He ignored the usual artistic boundaries, blending the art with something that would be useful to the public. His philosophies predate Robert Rauschenberg's juxtapositions of art and life. He had developed a love for hand tools and natural materials as a child growing up in Japan. These early passions translated into his later development of simple spaces and sculptures that provided places of respite for the public.

Influences on Noguchi include Alexander Calder and David Smith. Contemporaries include Stuart Davis and Willem de Kooning. These men were more abstract and concentrate on aesthetic presentations, while Noguchi took a more commercial approach to his work. Smith, for

Isamu Noguchi designed a number of large-scale sculptures to grace public plazas. © **CORBIS. REPRODUCED BY PERMISSION.**

example, was trained as a painter and later turned to welded metal and stainless steel sculptures. He was the first American artist to create welded metal sculptures. De Kooning concentrated on painting, and was influenced by Pablo Picasso. The Constructivist movement, which began in the 1920s in Russia and spread to the rest of Europe, also influenced Noguchi's work. The artists in this movement work across mediums and relied on abstract, formal, impersonal geometrical lines and planes and worked with modern materials such as plastic and metal.

Significance

Isamu Noguchi's *Red Cube* stands outside the Marine Midland Bank Building on Broadway in New York City. This sculpture is one example of the public sculptures that Noguchi has built throughout the world. His philosophies about public sculptures and public space make his work particularly important. In the 1950s, he began working with corporate space to create meaningful experiences for viewers and workers. While many of these spaces involve gardens and landscaping, just as many involve sculpture like the one outside the Marine Midland Bank Building. He believed that everything was sculpture.

Noguchi's words on sculpture provide further clues as to why pieces like *Red Cube* are important: "New concepts of the physical world and of psychology may give

Primary Source

Red Cube

SYNOPSIS: *Red Cube* stands twenty-four feet high and balances on a point. It is made of red painted steel, and the brightly colored cube contrasts with the skyscrapers that surround it. © MICHAEL S. YAMASHITA/CORBIS. REPRODUCED BY PERMISSION.

insights into knowledge, but the visible world, in human terms, is more than scientific truths. It enters our consciousness as emotion as well as knowledge; trees grow in vigor, flowers hang evanescent, and mountains lie somnolent—with meaning. The promise of sculpture is to project these inner presences into forms that can be recognized as important and meaningful in themselves. Our heritage is now the world. Art for the first time may be said to have a world consciousness" (Noguchi website, http://www.noguchi.org). Art provides relief from

the stresses of modern life. Noguchi's success was in integrating the aesthetically pleasing sculptures into the corporate world.

Further Resources

BOOKS

Altshuler, Bruce. *Isamu Noguchi.* New York: Abbeville, 1994.

Hunter, Sam. *Isamu Noguchi.* Seattle, Wash.: Bryan Ohno Editions in association with the University of Washington Press, 2000.

Turner, Jane, ed. "Constructivism." In *The Dictionary of Art*, vol. 7. New York: Grove, 1996, 767–772.

PERIODICALS

Gruen, John. "The Artist Speaks: Isamu Noguchi." *Art in America* 56, 1968, 28–31.

Hunter, Sam. "Isamu Noguchi: 'I know nothing about anything, and that's why I'm so free.'" *ARTnews* 77, no. 5, 1978, 124–130.

WEBSITES

The Isamu Noguchi Garden Museum. Available online at http://www.noguchi.org/index.html (accessed February 26, 2003).

New York City Images. Available online at http://www.greatgridlock.net/NYC_Images/midland2.html (accessed February 26, 2003).

AUDIO AND VISUAL MEDIA

Isamu Noguchi. Directed by Michael Blackwood. Blackwood Productions. Film. 1971.

House Made of Dawn
Novel

By: N. Scott Momaday

Date: 1968

Source: Momaday, N. Scott. *House Made of Dawn*. New York: Harper & Row, 1968, 5–9.

About the Author: N. Scott Momaday (1934–) was born in Lawton, Oklahoma. He is a Kiowa Indian but grew up with the Navaho and Jemez Pueblo traditions as well. He studied at the University of New Mexico and later earned a master's degree and a Ph.D. from Stanford University. Momaday's fiction and poetry are rich in Native American oral traditions. ■

Introduction

N. Scott Momaday's 1969 Pulitzer Prize for *House Made of Dawn* was a landmark for Native American literature and writers. The Pulitzer Prize jury explained their choice as follows: "In the words of one of the members of the jury, 'eloquence and intensity of feeling, its freshness of vision and subject, its immediacy of theme,' and because an award to its author might be considered as recognition of the arrival on the American literary scene of a matured, sophisticated literary artist from the original Americans" (quoted in Matthew Schubnell, *N. Scott Momaday: The Cultural and Literary Background* [Norman: University of Oklahoma Press, 1985], 93). The publisher hardly remembered this first book of Momaday's. Critics misunderstood the title and the content. They understood the cultural background of neither Momaday nor his characters.

In form, *House Made of Dawn* is a *bildungsroman*, or novel about the growth and formation of a protagonist. Such novels have been popular since the late eighteenth century, but Momaday's novel challenges the

traditional format because of the Native American influences. Alienation is a common theme in the literature of the 1960s. Authors such as John Updike, Ken Kesey, and Kurt Vonnegut all created characters who were trying to find their way in the world; however, they did not have to fight the cultural differences Abel, the lead character in Momaday's novel, has to fight.

House Made of Dawn is Abel's story, but it is also the story of his family and friends. Abel is caught between the world of his family, which honors the land and the rhythm of the seasons, and the world he experienced when he was in the military. He meets people who are outsiders to the Native American world. Some are helpful, others take advantage of him. He suffers in the new industrial world of the West Coast until he finally returns to his grandfather's house.

Significance

Momaday addressed the problems of assimilation in the world and integration in the tribe through Abel's character in *House Made of Dawn*. His interpretation of Abel's life is told from the combined background of Navaho, Pueblo, and Kiowa traditions. These Native American references are important to an understanding of the book. Momaday uses a fragmented narrative style that represents the difficulties of his characters. Use of precise sacred language, parts of traditional songs and, most importantly, the importance of the land make this an authentic book.

In the years since the novel was published, critics have reacted in various ways to it, and the book in some critics' view became more controversial in later years than it was when it was first published. Critics still have problems with how to read the juxtaposition of the modernist structure with native traditions. Despite these issues, Momaday's novel is influential as a work about Native Americans and for inspiring a resurgence in publishing literature by and about a diverse culture that many Americans do not know well.

Primary Source

House Made of Dawn [excerpt]

> **SYNOPSIS:** Place is immediately important in the opening chapter of *House Made of Dawn*. The river, the valley, and the way the sun strikes the ground are all described to give the reader a sense of Francisco's surroundings. The old man remembers the past as he drives his roan mares to the river. The chapter concludes with his grandson Abel returning home, drunk and sick.

July 20

The river lies in a valley of hills and fields. The north end of the valley is narrow, and the river runs down from the mountains through a canyon. The sun strikes the canyon floor only a few hours each day, and in winter the snow remains for a long time in the crevices of the walls. There is a town in the valley, and there are ruins of other towns in the canyon. In three directions from the town there are cultivated fields. Most of them lie to the west, across the river, on the slope of the plain. Now and then in winter, great angles of geese fly through the valley, and then the sky and the geese are the same color and the air is hard and damp and smoke rises from the houses of the town. The seasons lie hard upon the land. In summer the valley is hot, and birds come to the tamarack on the river. The feathers of blue and yellow birds are prized by the townsmen.

The fields are small and irregular, and from the west mesa they seem an intricate patchwork of arbors and gardens, too numerous for the town. The townsmen work all summer in the fields. When the moon is full, they work at night with ancient, handmade plows and hoes, and if the weather is good and the water plentiful they take a good harvest from the fields. They grow the things that can be preserved easily: corn and chilies and alfalfa. On the town side of the river there are a few orchards and patches of melons and grapes and squash. Every six or seven years there is a great harvest of *piñones* far to the east of the town. That harvest, like the deer in the mountains, is the gift of God.

It is hot in the end of July. The old man Francisco drove a team of roan mares near the place where the river bends around a cottonwood. The sun shone on the sand and the river and the leaves of the tree, and waves of heat shimmered from the stones. The colored stones on the bank of the river were small and smooth, and they rubbed together and cracked under the wagon wheels. Once in a while one of the roan mares tossed its head, and the commotion of its dark mane sent a swarm of flies into the air. Downstream the brush grew thick on a bar in the river, and there the old man saw the reed. He turned the mares into the water and stepped down on the sand. A sparrow hung from the reed. It was upside down and its wings were partly open and the feathers at the back of its head lay spread in a tiny ruff. The eyes were neither open nor closed. Francisco was disappointed, for he had wished for a male mountain bluebird, breast feathers the pale color of April skies or of turquoise, lake water. Or a summer tanager: a prayer plume ought to be beautiful. He drew the reed from the sand and cut loose the horsehair from the sparrow's feet. The bird fell into the water and was carried away in the current. He turned

Pulitzer Prize winner N. Scott Momaday. © UPI/CORBIS-BETTMANN. REPRODUCED BY PERMISSION.

the reed in his hands; it was smooth and nearly translucent, like the spine of an eagle feather, and it was not yet burned and made brittle by the sun and wind. He had cut the hair too short, and he pulled another from the tail of the near roan and set the snare again. When the reed was curved and strung like a bow, he replaced it carefully in the sand. He laid his forefinger lightly on top of the reed and the reed sprang and the looped end of the hair snapped across his finger and made a white line above the nail. *"Sí, bien hecho,"* he said aloud, and without removing the reed from the sand he cocked it again.

The sun rose higher and the old man urged the mares away from the river. Then he was on the old road to San Ysidro. At times he sang and talked to himself above the noise of the wagon: *"Yo heyana oh . . . heyana oh . . . heyana oh . . . Abelito . . . tarda mucho en venir. . . ."* The mares pulled easily, with their heads low. He held a vague tension on the lines and settled into the ride by force of habit. A lizard ran across the road in front of the mares and crouched on a large flat rock, its tail curved over the edge. Far away a whirlwind moved toward the river, but it soon spun itself out and the air was again perfectly still.

He was alone on the wagon road. The pavement lay on a higher parallel at the base of the hills to the east. The trucks of the town—and those of the lumber camps at Paliza and Vallecitos—made an endless parade on the highway, but the wagon road was used now only by the herdsmen and planters whose fields lay to the south and west. When he came to the place called Seytokwa, Francisco remembered the race for good hunting and harvests. Once he had played a part; he had rubbed himself with soot, and he ran on the wagon road at dawn. He ran so hard that he could feel the sweat fly from his head and arms, though it was winter and the air was filled with snow. He ran until his breath burned in his throat and his feet rose and fell in a strange repetition that seemed apart from all his effort. At last he had overtaken Mariano, who was everywhere supposed to be the best of the long-race runners. For a long way Mariano kept just beyond his reach; then, as they drew near the corrals on the edge of the town, Francisco picked up the pace. He drew even and saw for an instant Mariano's face, wet and contorted in defeat . . . *"Se dió por vencido"* . . . and he struck it with the back of his hand, leaving a black smear across the mouth and jaw. And Mariano fell and was exhausted. Francisco held his stride all the way to the Middle, and even then he could have gone on running, for no reason, for only the sake of running on. And that year he killed seven bucks and seven does. Some years afterward, when he was no longer young and his leg had been stiffened by disease, he made a pencil drawing on the first page of a ledger book which he kept with his store of prayer feathers in the rafters of his room. It was the likeness of a straight black man running in the snow. Beneath it was the legend "1889."

He crossed the river below the bridge at San Ysidro. The roan mares strained as they brought the wagon up the embankment and onto the pavement. It was almost noon. The doors of the houses were closed against the heat, and even the usual naked children who sometimes shouted and made fun of him had gone inside. Here and there a dog, content to have found a little shade, raised its head to look but remained outstretched and quiet. Well before he came to the junction, he could hear the slow whine of the tires on the Cuba and Bloomfield road. It was a strange sound; it began at a high and descending pitch, passed, and rose again to become at last inaudible, lost in the near clatter of the rig and hoofs—lost even in the slow, directionless motion of the flies. But it was recurrent: another, and another; and he turned into the intersection and drove on to the trading post. He had come about seven miles.

At a few minutes past one, the bus came over a rise far down in the plain and its windows caught for a moment the light of the sun. It grew in the old man's vision until he looked away and limped around in a vague circle and smoothed the front of his new shirt with his hands. "Abelito, Abelito," he repeated under his breath, and he glanced at the wagon and the mares to be sure that everything was in order. He could feel the beat of his heart, and instinctively he drew himself up in the dignity of his age. He heard the sharp wheeze of the brakes as the big bus rolled to a stop in front of the gas pump, and only then did he give attention to it, as if it had taken him by surprise. The door swung open and Abel stepped heavily to the ground and reeled. He was drunk, and he fell against his grandfather and did not know him. His wet lips hung loose and his eyes were half closed and rolling. Francisco's crippled leg nearly gave way. His good straw hat fell off and he braced himself against the weight of his grandson. Tears came to his eyes, and he knew only that he must laugh and turn away from the faces in the windows of the bus. He held Abel upright and led him to the wagon, listening as the bus moved away at last and its tires began to sing upon the road. On the way back to the town, Abel lay ill in the bed of the wagon and Francisco sat bent to the lines. The mares went a little faster on the way home, and near the bridge a yellow dog came out to challenge them.

Further Resources

BOOKS

Nelson, Robert M. *Place and Vision: The Function of Landscape in Native American Fiction.* New York: Peter Lang, 1993.

Scarberry-Garcia, Susan. *Landmarks of Healing: A Study of House Made of Dawn.* Albuquerque, N.M.: University of New Mexico, 1990.

Schubnell, Matthew. *N. Scott Momaday: The Cultural and Literary Background* Norman, Okla.: University of Oklahoma Press, 1985.

PERIODICALS

Landrum, Larry. "The Shattered Modernism of Mamoday's *House Made of Dawn.*" *Modern Fiction Studies* 42, no. 4, Winter 1996, 763–786.

Selinger, Bernard. "*House Made of Dawn:* A Positively Ambivalent Bildungsroman," *Modern Fiction Studies* 45, no.1, Spring 1999, 38–68.

Sprauge, Marshall. "House Made of Dawn." *The New York Times Book Review,* June 9, 1968, 5.

WEBSITES

"N. Scott Momaday." Available online at http://www.english .uiuc.edu/maps/poets/m_r/momaday/momaday.htm; website home page: http://www.english.uiuc.edu (accessed January 19, 2003).

"Native American Author: N. Scott Momaday." Available online at http://www.ipl.org/div/natam/bin/browse.pl/A50; website home page: http://www.ipl.org (accessed January 19, 2003).

AUDIO AND VISUAL MEDIA

House Made of Dawn. Directed by Richardson Morse. New Line Studios. Videocassette, 1996.

Momaday, N. Scott. *House Made of Dawn.* Recorded Books, Audiocassette.

———. *N. Scott Momaday Reads from "House Made of Dawn."* AAPL, Audiocassette.

Slaughterhouse-Five
Novel

By: Kurt Vonnegut

Date: 1969

Source: Vonnegut, Kurt. *Slaughterhouse-Five or The Children's Crusade: A Duty-Dance with Death.* New York: Delacorte Press, 1969; reprinted New York: Delta, 1999, 29–35.

About the Author: Kurt Vonnegut Jr. (1922–) was born in Indianapolis, Indiana. His major works include *Mother Night* (1962), *Cat's Cradle* (1963) and *Bluebeard* (1988). Both a novelist and short story writer, Vonnegut became a cult writer during the 1960s. He is also a social critic who analyzes how science and technology affect our lives. ∎

Author Kurt Vonnegut, 1971. **AP/WIDE WORLD PHOTOS. REPRODUCED BY PERMISSION.**

Introduction

Slaughterhouse-Five or The Children's Crusade: A Duty-Dance with Death relates the story of Billy Pilgrim, a chaplain's assistant in World War II (1939–45) who is present at the bombing of Dresden, Germany. An estimated 135,000 civilians were killed in this bombing, where Vonnegut was also a soldier. Both Pilgrim and Vonnegut were devastated by this event. The book is framed with Vonnegut's personal recollections about being a prisoner of war in Dresden. The tragedy, the governmental lies, and the pain that survived within are accounted for in both his personal sections and in the story itself. Vonnegut tells Billy Pilgrim's story in episodes, past, present, and future.

Kurt Vonnegut's audience was largely composed of young people until *Slaughterhouse-Five* was published. The 1969 novel drew attention as the country became increasingly disillusioned with the Vietnam War, and Kurt Vonnegut suddenly became a well-known author with his seventh novel. It took Vonnegut twenty years to write this novel. He realized that a traditional narrative structure would not work to tell the story of destruction and

modern war. The novel is structured somewhat like Joseph Heller's *Catch-22.* Yossarian in Heller's novel and Billy Pilgrim in Vonnegut's both have painful memories of death that they must learn to cope with in order to live. Both are antiwar novels.

Significance

Until *Slaughterhouse-Five* was published, Vonnegut was mainly an underground writer. The significance of the work lay partially in its relationship to Vonnegut's own experiences in World War II. Like Billy Pilgrim, his narrator, he was there. Vonnegut worked on the novel for over twenty years, trying to tell the story of what happened during the firebombing of Dresden, Germany, in 1945.

The contrast to John Bunyan's eighteenth century *The Pilgrim's Progress,* an allegorical work about man's pilgrimage through life, is not an accident. Billy invents his own kind of heaven in the alien planet of Tralfamadore. Everything is good there, and the bad moments of life are erased. The story is nonlinear and episodic. Since Billy Pilgrim becomes "unstuck in time," he narrates in short spurts depending on if he is in the present, past, or future. Essentially this is his pilgrimage to recover from the horrors of war. Many people were having similar experiences in Vietnam when the novel was published. The timing of the publication increased the novel's popularity.

Vonnegut was speaking for a "silent generation," according to Robert Scholes, who reviewed the book for *The New York Times Book Review*. Scholes realized, as did other reviewers, that the comic episodes are important because they allow Vonnegut and the reader to contemplate horrific events. Granville Hicks was one of many reviewers who compared Vonnegut's humor to Mark Twain's humor. He wrote that "Vonnegut's satire sweeps widely, touching on education, religious, advertising and many other subjects" ("Literary Horizons," *Saturday Review,* March 29, 1969, 25). The book has endured and become an American classic. On the twenty-fifth anniversary of its publication, Alan Cheuse said, "And after 25 years, we can still respond to its deep felt cry for sanity in a world we never made and hark in all the more to its famous four word refrain that signifies the trivial and the devastating passage of all things, 'and so it goes'" (Alan Cheuse, "25th Anniversary of 'Slaughterhouse Five' Released," *All Things Considered,* March 17, 1994).

Primary Source

Slaughterhouse-Five [excerpt]

SYNOPSIS: "Billy Pilgrim has come unstuck in time." This revelation allows Billy to experience the past, present, and future again and again. In Chapter 2, the reader meets Billy. We begin to learn about his ordinary American life as an optometrist in Illium, New York, and about his extraordinary experiences traveling back and forth through time, trying to understand his own life and the world.

Listen:

Billy Pilgrim has come unstuck in time.

Billy has gone to sleep a senile widower and awakened on his wedding day. He has walked through a door in 1955 and come out another one in 1941. He has gone back through that door to find himself in 1963. He has seen his birth and death many times, he says, and pays random visits to all the events in between.

He says.

Billy is spastic in time, has no control over where he is going next, and the trips aren't necessarily fun. He is in a constant state of stage fright, he says, because he never knows what part of his life he is going to have to act in next.

•••

Billy was born in 1922 in Ilium, New York, the only child of a barber there. He was a funny-looking child who became a funny-looking youth—tall and weak, and shaped like a bottle of Coca-Cola. He graduated from Ilium High School in the upper third of his class, and attended night sessions at the Ilium School of Optometry for one semester before being drafted for military service in the Second World War. His father died in a hunting accident during the war. So it goes.

Billy saw service with the infantry in Europe, and was taken prisoner by the Germans. After his honorable discharge from the Army in 1945, Billy again enrolled in the Ilium School of Optometry. During his senior year there, he became engaged to the daughter of the founder and owner of the school, and then suffered a mild nervous collapse.

•••

He was treated in a veteran's hospital near Lake Placid, and was given shock treatments and released. He married his fiancée, finished his education, and was set up in business in Ilium by his father-in-law. Ilium is a particularly good city for optometrists because the General Forge and Foundry Company is there. Every employee is required to own a pair of safety glasses, and to wear them in areas where manufacturing is going on. GF&F has sixty-eight thousand employees in Ilium. That calls for a lot of lenses and a lot of frames.

Frames are where the money is.

•••

Billy became rich. He had two children, Barbara and Robert. In time, his daughter Barbara married another optometrist, and Billy set him up in business. Billy's son Robert had a lot of trouble in high school, but then he joined the famous Green Berets. He straightened out, became a fine young man, and he fought in Vietnam.

Early in 1968, a group of optometrists, with Billy among them, chartered an airplane to fly them from Ilium to an international convention of optometrists in Montreal. The plane crashed on top of Sugarbush Mountain, in Vermont. Everybody was killed but Billy. So it goes.

While Billy was recuperating in a hospital in Vermont, his wife died accidentally of carbon-monoxide poisoning. So it goes.

•••

When Billy finally got home to Ilium after the airplane crash, he was quiet for a while. He had a terrible scar across the top of his skull. He didn't resume practice. He had a housekeeper. His daughter came over almost every day.

And then, without any warning, Billy went to New York City, and got on an all-night radio program devoted to talk. He told about having come unstuck in time. He said, too, that he had been kidnapped by a flying saucer in 1967. The saucer was from the planet Tralfamadore, he said. He was taken to Tralfamadore, where he was displayed naked in a zoo, he said. He was mated there with a former Earthling movie star named Montana Wildhack.

■ ■ ■

Some night owls in Ilium heard Billy on the radio, and one of them called Billy's daughter Barbara. Barbara was upset. She and her husband went down to New York and brought Billy home. Billy insisted mildly that everything he had said on the radio was true. He said he had been kidnapped by the Tralfamadorians on the night of his daughter's wedding. He hadn't been missed, he said, because the Tralfamadorians had taken him through a time warp, so that he could be on Tralfamadore for years, and still be away from Earth for only a microsecond.

Another month went by without incident, and then Billy wrote a letter to the Ilium *News Leader,* which the paper published. It described the creatures from Tralfamadore.

The letter said that they were two feet high, and green, and shaped like plumber's friends. Their suction cups were on the ground, and their shafts, which were extremely flexible, usually pointed to the sky. At the top of each shaft was a little hand with a green eye in its palm. The creatures were friendly, and they could see in four dimensions. They pitied Earthlings for being able to see only three. They had many wonderful things to teach Earthlings, especially about time. Billy promised to tell what some of those wonderful things were in his next letter.

■ ■ ■

Billy was working on his second letter when the first letter was published. The second letter started out like this:

> The most important thing I learned on Tralfamadore was that when a person dies he only *appears* to die. He is still very much alive in the past, so it is very silly for people to cry at his funeral. All moments, past, present, and future, always have existed, always will exist.

The Tralfamadorians can look at all the different moments just the way we can look at a stretch of the Rocky Mountains, for instance. They can see how permanent all the moments are, and they can look at any moment that interests them. It is just an illusion we have here on Earth that one moment follows another one, like beads on a string, and that once a moment is gone it is gone forever.

When a Tralfamadorian sees a corpse, all he thinks is that the dead person is in bad condition in that particular moment, but that the same person is just fine in plenty of other moments. Now, when I myself hear that somebody is dead, I simply shrug and say what the Tralfamadorians say about dead people, which is "So it goes."

■ ■ ■

And so on.

Billy was working on this letter in the basement rumpus room of his empty house. It was his housekeeper's day off. There was an old typewriter in the rumpus room. It was a beast. It weighed as much as a storage battery. Billy couldn't carry it very far very easily, which was why he was writing in the rumpus room instead of somewhere else.

The oil burner had quit. A mouse had eaten through the insulation of a wire leading to the thermostat. The temperature in the house was down to fifty degrees, but Billy hadn't noticed. He wasn't warmly dressed, either. He was barefoot, and still in his pajamas and a bathrobe, though it was late afternoon. His bare feet were blue and ivory.

The cockles of Billy's heart, at any rate, were glowing coals. What made them so hot was Billy's belief that he was going to comfort so many people with the truth about time. His door chimes upstairs had been ringing and ringing. It was his daughter Barbara up there, wanting in. Now she let herself in with a key, crossed the floor over his head, calling, "Father? Daddy, where are you?" And so on.

Billy didn't answer her, so she was nearly hysterical, expecting to find his corpse. And then she looked into the very last place there *was* to look— which was the rumpus room.

Further Resources

BOOKS

Allen, William Rodney. *Understanding Kurt Vonnegut.* Columbia, S.C.: University of South Carolina Press, 1991.

Schatt, Stanley. *Kurt Vonnegut, Jr.* Boston: Twayne, 1976.

PERIODICALS

Hicks, Granville. "Literary Horizons." *Saturday Review,* March 29, 1969, 25.

Matheson, T.J. "This Lousy Little Book": The Genesis And Development of *Slaughterhouse-Five* as Revealed in Chapter One." *Studies in the Novel* 16, no. 2, Summer 1984, 228–240.

Scholes, Robert. "Slaughterhouse–Five." *The New York Times Book Review,* April 6, 1969, 1, 23.

WEBSITES

Cheuse, Alan. "25th Anniversary of 'Slaughterhouse Five' Released." *All Things Considered,* March 17, 1994. Available online at http://www.duke.edu/~crh4/vonnegut/sh5/sh5_npr .html (accessed January 18, 2003).

VonnegutWeb. "Slaughterhouse-Five." Available online at http://www.duke.edu/~crh4/vonnegut/sh5/index.html (accessed January 18, 2003).

AUDIO AND VISUAL MEDIA

Slaughterhouse–Five. Directed by George Roy Hill. Image Entertainment. DVD, 1972.

"Arthur Mitchell and the Dance Theater of Harlem"

Magazine article

By: Olga Maynard

Date: March 1970

Source: Maynard, Olga. "Arthur Mitchell and the Dance Theater of Harlem." *Dance Magazine,* March 1970, 52–64. ∎

Introduction

Harlem had been a place of artistic innovation and cultural experimentation in the 1920s. Artists, poets, and writers had all called Harlem home and had drawn their inspiration from its surroundings. By the time Arthur Mitchell was born in 1934, the Harlem Renaissance was over. He recalls that he was rebellious and restless and that he came under that influence of a street gang. Education and dance saved him, however. In the 1930s and 1940s, it was not common to see African Americans in dance other than jazz or tap, so Mitchell had no role models in ballet. His dance education began with a scholarship to the High School for Performing Arts in New York and continued at the School of American Ballet with Lincoln Kirstein and George Balanchine. He broke new ground when he became the first African American male to join the New York City Ballet in 1955. He would become a pioneer and the role model for future generations. He remained in the troupe for fifteen years and became a principal dancer. Janet Collins had been the first African American prima ballerina, dancing at the Metropolitan Opera House between 1951–1954.

By the time the profile of Arthur Mitchell and the Dance Theater of Harlem appeared in *Dance Magazine*

in March 1970, the school was established. Mitchell's program had drawn attention from the media. He wanted to prove that African Americans could succeed in ballet and that an African American ballet company could become a reality. He said that all he needed was money, work, and love. His passion for dance and for making his dream come true are obvious in his interview with Olga Maynard.

Significance

Mitchell became the ballet's equivalent to Jackie Robinson in baseball in breaking the color barrier when he joined the New York City Ballet. Mitchell had a vision for teaching other African Americans to dance, however. In 1968, when he was departing for Brazil and heard the news of Dr. Martin Luther King, Jr.'s death, he realized that he needed to follow his vision back home to Harlem. In 1969, he founded the Dance Theater of Harlem as a school and the first African American ballet company.

Mitchell had financial help from the Ford Foundation. Karel Shook (1920–1985) an internationally recognized ballet teacher, joined Mitchell as associate artistic director. They also relied on assistance and advice from Kirstein and Balanchine. Together they drew talented students and dancers. Thirty students came the first month, but within a few months the numbers swelled to four hundred. Mitchell believed that the professional company had to remain African American until it proved its success, saying that he saw no point in subjecting African American dancers to the rigors of classical ballet training if they had no chance to perform.

The importance of Arthur Mitchell's dream has not been overlooked. All of the programs associated with the Dance Theater of Harlem are renowned throughout the world. The company held the first public performance in 1971. It has since become integrated. The company has performed at the White House, produced television shows, and given performances throughout the world. The school's curriculum has expanded and draws seven hundred students a year. Mitchell continues to direct the Dance Theater of Harlem.

Primary Source

"Arthur Mitchell & The Dance Theater of Harlem"

> **SYNOPSIS:** Arthur Mitchell knew that it was a myth that African Americans could not become ballet dancers. He had proven that myth incorrect with his own career. In 1968, he realized that he must return to Harlem and begin a dance program. This profile of Arthur Mitchell outlines his philosophy, his dream, and how they was shaped into reality.

"Ballet is the noble way of dancing; is nobility a virtue of the white dancer alone, and not of the black? Ballet is the classical theatre dance, but have you seen African dances—what could be more classic than a Watusi dancer? In the Dance Theater of Harlem we will prove that there is no difference, except color, between a black ballet dancer and a white ballet dancer."

The Negro dancer Arthur Mitchell was talking to me in the Church of the Master, an apt place in which to expound a gospel, and Mitchell, in immaculate white turtle-neck shirt, looked like a priest in mufti. No ordained man could be more passionately committed to a cause, with more evangelistic fervor than Mitchell for his black ballet. Three months earlier, Mitchell and his Associate Artistic Director, Karel Shook, had moved their faculty and students from temporary quarters in Greenwich Village to a home in the Church of the Master on Morningside Avenue, and the Dance Theater of Harlem was born as school and company. "It *had* to be in Harlem," says Mitchell. "The arts belong to the people and we must carry the arts to the people, not wait for the people to come to the arts. We are training black dancers for a black ballet. Where else would it be, if not in Harlem?"

Mitchell has found an ideal site, facing the park, adjacent to the new annex into which the Church of the Master will move, leaving the Dance Theater to occupy the old building as studios, work rooms and theatre—and when the theatre opens, converted from the church, Mitchell will have returned it to its oldest, profoundest function. Where a congregation sat, an audience will gather, for the Dance Theater of Harlem. In December, when I visited Mitchell, his Dance Theater had already assumed a magical, and blessed, aura for a great many persons in Harlem.

Currently, the classes and weekly lecture-performances are in one large studio. "When the Church moves into the annex, we will expand our schedules," said Mitchell. "I feel that everyone should be allowed to dance. A certain category of students, whose gifts make them suited to professional dance, will be developed for the company. But other students, young and adult, want to dance for personal pleasure. Besides, we need to develop American ballet audiences, while we are developing dancers and companies . . . Eventually, we will have total theatre here and our students will train in every aspect of it. We have projected classes in stage lighting, sewing for costumes, carpentry for making sets, and the Kodak people are planning to set up a lab to teach photography."

Arthur Mitchell was a premier ballet dancer who took on a wide variety of roles on stage. THE ESTATE OF CARL VAN VECHTEN. REPRODUCED BY PERMISSION.

The Dance Theater came into being, Mitchell told me, through a Ford Foundation grant ($151,000 of which he must match) and the help of Lincoln Kirstein and George Balanchine, with whom he is closely associated in the New York City Ballet. "I went to them for help; who else? When you are hungry, you go to the hand that feeds you, right! And they are the best in our business, as is Betty Cage, the company manager, so who could better advise me on a ballet school and company? Lincoln is Chairman of our Board; Balanchine is Vice President." The Board, Mitchell mischievously remarks, is fully integrated among black and white members (some famed in the theatre) and in related arts: actress Cicely Tyson is an active Board member, singer Leontyne Price is on the Advisory Board. The school is integrated. "*This* school did not need to prove itself; only look at the faculty!" Under Mitchell, Shook, Mary Hinkson, Tanaquil Le Clercq, Thelma Hill, Pearl Reynolds, Mirielle Brianne and James Truitt, a human rainbow is being taught to dance. Students in skin shades ranging from alabaster through honeyed beiges and browns into the rare ebony stand at the barre as replica of innumerable other classes, the world over, in the *danse d'école.* Mitchell advocates ballet, the *danse noble,* as the professional dancer's primary and most important training. He has incorporated other forms (as is obvious in the faculty) because he believes that virtuoso training is the dance heritage of the 20th century American dancer.

"With our specialized training and approach to dance," he explained, "our dancers will command a repertory that includes the most sophisticated classicism, as in Balanchine ballets, and the 'primitive' forms. Our dancers will be complete ballet *artists!*"

Realistically, Mitchell prefers to discuss what he has accomplished, since September, rather than describe potentials, although they appear great.

"Arthur has already realized a great dream, for many of us," said Karel Shook. "It is the culmination of my own thirty years of work, in dozens of little studios, with black children. For the first time I am working with dancers who accept the stage as the goal of the classroom. For the first time, the black American ballet dancer can see ballet as a *performing* art."

Shook, a well-known dancer, choreographer, ballet master and teacher, left a lifetime of work in the United States in 1959, to become ballet master and choreographer of the Netherlands National Ballet. On a summer vacation in 1968, he was guest teacher at the Harlem School of the Arts, the project headed by Negro singer Dorothy Maynor . . . , where Mitchell headed the dance division. Shook and Mitchell are close friends, from years past when Mitchell studied under Shook (who then headed the ballet wing of the Katharine Dunham School). "I was immensely impressed by what Arthur was doing," said Shook, "all the more because he is one of my pupils. A teacher's only immortality is in his pupils. When one of them succeeds in accomplishing what Arthur has, then that is the teacher's reward!"

"Karel is truly important to this project," said Mitchell. "I have a very great commitment to the New York City Ballet; that is where Arthur Mitchell the *danseur* was made. For fifteen years I have worked under a genius, George Balanchine. That's where I got the authority, and the sense of the artist's personal dignity, without which I could not direct the Dance Theater of Harlem. When I have to leave it, I know that it is safe in Karel's hands—we share the same principles and aims.

"Each member of our project, in his or her way, is necessary to it! For the dancers, this is not a place to take class—it is their true home. They do everything that is needed, from answering the telephone to sweeping the floor, and they exist on pittances. Although our grant allows me to maintain a salaried company, they work more for love than money. Our scholarship students attend Professional Children's School, so that they can work at their ballet training six hours a day.

"Work never harmed anyone, providing the work was toward something you aspired to. Our dancers have every incentive to work hard, and they are lucky in having very fine teachers. I think that Karel Shook is one of the greatest ballet teachers alive. And we work in a very healthy atmosphere, psychologically. We are here only because we love ballet and because we love each other. The Man upstairs loves us, too! I have never seen a greater outpouring of love than is being given to the Dance Theater of Harlem. People come through that door and say to me: 'Arthur, what can we do to help?' Miraculously, God has sent us everyone we needed. Poor people come up to me and put a dollar in my hand and say: 'Use it for the Dance Theater.' All this makes me know that Harlem can be beautiful again. Harlem was once beautiful, a cultural magnet through the great jazz artists who influenced American dance and music so much! That is why I mean to involve the whole community in this project, to make one world for our dancers and the people out there in the streets of Harlem . . ."

Can he? Well, he has succeeded in everything to which he has turned his hand, not to mention a deft foot, since he broke upon us, a dark, dazzling star, in the New York City Ballet fifteen years ago. Mitchell is the first black dancer to become a principal artist in a world famed ballet; he is a senior premier of America's greatest classical company. A virtuoso, with mercurial temperament, he has danced, choreographed, acted and sung through every theatrical media, from classical ballet and opera into musicals, in several countries. In 1968 he smashed the American television tabu against a black dancer partnering a white one, when he and Suzanne Farrell appeared on the "Tonight Show" ("and in living color, darling!"), in the sensuous *pas de deux* from *Slaughter on Tenth Avenue,* which Balanchine mounted on them in the New York City Ballet. Still with his alma mater, Mitchell worked in Brazil as *premier danseur,* choreographer and company director, of a company brought into being for him by a Brazilian millionaire. "But here I am today," he said wryly, in New York in December, "two blocks from where I was born!"

What has made Arthur run, or dance, out of the ghetto into the white ballet and back to the ghetto, again? Arthur Adam Mitchell's childhood was classic for his race, in his time and place. The eldest of five children, of an absent father and an over-worked mother, he went to work early ("as soon as I could carry a shoe-shine box") and depended on himself for everything, even his entertainment. "I was the main support of our family before I was into my teens, but I always loved to sing and dance. Those were the only recreations of poor people, before TV!" At ten, his elders in a Police Athletic Glee Club urged him to seek training but no real encouragement was given him until his junior high school guidance teacher suggested he try for a scholarship at the School of Performing Arts. Mitchell throws back his handsome head and shouts with laughter at the memory. "All the kids had prepared nice little dances but *I had guts!* I went on in a routine an old vaudeville man, Tom Nip, taught me: *Steppin' Out With My Baby.* The SPA judges certainly didn't expect it. I stunned them!" They gave him a scholarship.

He was no sooner a student than he was a bona fide dancer, in the modern dance troupes of Natanya Neumann and Shirley Broughton, and in his senior year went to Paris in a revival of the Gertrude Stein-Virgil Thomson opera *Four Saints in Three Acts.* On his return home, he was faced with the most crucial decision of his eighteen years. He was offered a scholarship to Bennington College, then the arbiter of modern dance training, where he would have been the first male student. And Lincoln Kirstein, a director of SPA, offered him a scholarship to study ballet at the School of American Ballet, under a faculty that was a facsimile of the Russian Imperial Ballet School.

"Like every black student, I had been shoved into modern dance class. I didn't know much about ballet, had never thought of becoming a *danseur.* Lincoln put it to me with brutal frankness. He told me I would have to work twice as hard as anyone in

my class, to prove that I could meet the requirements. And that if I hoped to get into a company like New York City Ballet I would have to recognize how high the standards were. So I took the challenge!"

He continued to perform in modern idiom and was in Europe with the John Butler Company in 1955, when the New York City Ballet wired him an invitation to join the company, as soloist, replacing Jacques D'Amboise (who had gone to Hollywood) in *Western Symphony.* A casting novelty, perhaps, in the first season, Mitchell very soon demanded respect as the *danseur.* In 1957 he created a role, which Balanchine choreographed for him, in *Agon,* the most precedent-shattering classical work of the era. Since then, Mitchell has dazzled American, European and Russian audiences, partnering every major ballerina in the New York City Ballet from Diana Adams to Suzanne Farrell.

Sometimes, his very presence (as the Dark Angel in Balanchine's *Orpheus*) has infused a singular quality; often, he has given a ballet and a ballerina new dimensions, as in John Taras' *Piege de Lumiere,* with Maria Tallchief. On occasion, Mitchell's personal brilliance has ignited his company, and won for it tumultuous applause, as in Moscow with Allegra Kent, and, more recently, in Paris with Suzanne Farrell.

Mitchell candidly admits that he likes to be first, likes to create roles, as he has done in *Agon,* and, an incomparable Puck, in *A Midsummer Night's Dream.* He delighted in appearing in *Bugaku* and *Metastaseis & Pithoprakta* because, he says, "I love Balanchine's choreography; it is beautiful and difficult." Always, he has leaped to meet a challenge. It *matters,* more than he will freely admit, that he has been cast in *Allegro Brilliante, Divertimento,* and *The Four Temperaments,* and that he, unlike the majority of black American dancers, is not relegated to jazz roles. He may have longed, especially after dancing the lead, most beautifully, in *Afternoon of a Faun,* to become another *Apollo,* to take part in *Liebeslieder Walzer,* to partner the Sugar Plum Fairy . . . But he is not pining now. Having brought a black ballet school and company into existence, Willie Mae Mitchell's eldest is on top of his world. And the driving ambition that lifted Arthur Mitchell to the highest ranks of his profession is now urging the Harlem dancers.

His extraordinary vitality, his engagingly sunny disposition, have always made Mitchell an Ariel, to me. I was now meeting a new Mitchell, serious, almost patriarchal, leader of a devoted flock, and, it was very obvious, a growing band of astute admirers. The Wednesday "Open House" lecture-performances, begun to lure the Harlem community into the Dance Theater, have grown so popular (especially with neighborhood schools) that Mitchell is now obliged to carefully schedule them. Here, two worlds meet—as in December when, while infants from a Head Start program sat on the floor of the gallery, chairs accommodated, among others, the dowager Mrs. Gimbel, Mrs. Dorothy Hammerstein, actress Benay Venuta, and producer (The Damned) Luchino Visconti.

Mitchell is on easy terms with the elite of society and theatre, and he says: "I am not ashamed to brag about the Dance Theater of Harlem, and I love to show if off! We already have good reviews, from appearances we have made (reported monthly in Dance Magazine), and I have been asked to stage a season. But we are not ready for a proper season yet; when we are, I hope to have it in our own theatre."

"There is only one danger, as I see it." said Mitchell soberly, "and that is the temptation to move too fast. I have to resist it all the time, from well-meaning people to whom 'black is beautiful.' For us, it is *ballet* that is beautiful! I will never let this company capitalize on its uniqueness as a 'black' company. *It must stand as a ballet company.* My standards are very high. Look what I belong to: the New York City Ballet! I will not lower my standards, or betray the standards of the people who made Arthur Mitchell the ballet artist. I am very demanding of my dancers but *they* want high standards, because this is their company . . . it was not formed to feed one dancer's fat ego. Fortunately, we have many professional dancers, who set a good example for the younger ones.

"The professional dancers in the company came to me of their own accord, when they heard that the Dance Theater was forming, from American and European companies, where they felt themselves to be 'novelties,' without a chance of performing in real repertoire. Some of them had given up ballet altogether and gone into other forms of theatre. They were like fingers without a hand; now we have the hand . . .

"A certain success has come to us very early, and that makes us aspire to greater things. White dancers have asked to join us and I tell them we must first prove that there *are* black ballet dancers; when we are accepted, then we will integrate the company, as we have integrated the school. We have to prove beyond the shadow of a doubt that it is talent and training, not color, that makes a ballet dancer."

The irrepressible Mitchell humor wells up, in explosive laughter, but now and then there is somber regret for black dancers "wasted in American ballet, because they never had a chance to prove themselves as artists."

"I have taught for a long time," mused Mitchell, "at Dunham's, for Karel, at the Jones-Haywood School in Washington, D.C. (which has a big Negro enrollment) at the Harlem School of the Arts, before teaching in our own school. I know that little black kids, from the worst slums in this country, love ballet; it's the first order and beauty to come into their lives. And I believe that there are black dancers with the physique, temperament and stamina and everything else it takes to produce what we call the 'born' ballet dancer. The babies from the Head Start program will come to us when they are old enough, because we are *here,* right where they live in Harlem. For now, my chief concern is with the older dancers, because for them this is the last chance, while their bodies are still pliable, to be trained in ballet. We are breaking the rules in this school because we have to . . . we are making dancers in much less time than the book tells you it takes. When people tell me it can't be done, I invite them here, to show them dancers performing in my ballets who, in any other school in the country, would still be standing facing the barre. I feel that if we can put men on the moon, then we can make ballet dancers, because ballet is a man-made art. There are 22 million black Americans and I believe that in 11% of our population there is enormous potential for ballet dancers. Until now, no one has gone looking for them and when they themselves tried to become ballet artists they were told they had no opportunity in America.

"The biggest problem for the black American ballet dancer has been a lack of identity. People have to identify with something if they aspire to it! I would see black children at the ballet and hear them say: 'But there are no black people in it!' and mothers would try to comfort their kids by saying: 'O, wait! One will be coming out soon . . . ' But I was the first black dancer in New York City Ballet in 1955 and fifteen years later I am still the only one. When I was teaching in Washington I encouraged a marvelously talented boy, Sylvester Campbell, but he could not get work at home, so he went to Europe—and in the

Netherlands Ballet he was cast in premier roles, Albrecht in *Giselle* and Prince Siegfried in *Swan Lake.* If *Swan Lake* was the only classical ballet, it would prove that there *are* Black Swans! What is there in the terminology that implies that a 'ballerina' and a 'danseur noble' must be white in color? It's talent and training, not the shade of your skin, that makes a ballet dancer!"

Before we parted, Mitchell told me: "I helped organize an interracial dance company with Paul Taylor and others for a Spoleto Festival once, and I tried to take a black American company to participate in the first World Festival of Negro Arts in Senegal, in 1966, but we could not raise the money for the trip. After Martin Luther King was assassinated, and there were all the eulogies, I asked myself: Arthur Mitchell, what can *you* do? When you pay homage you do the thing you do best: if you make music, you beat your drum; if you are a singer, you sing; if you are a dancer, you dance.

"Once I made up my mind to it, all it needed was money, work,—and love, to get the Dance Theater of Harlem started. We are so very lucky, not only in our grant, and the help individuals have given us, but in the dedication we have inspired. Tanaquil Le Clercq, who had never taught before, came to work with us. Miracles keep happening! When I was teaching at the Harlem School of the Arts (which Mitchell left, when his project became too big to be contained in another organization), one day a substitute pianist came to us. As soon as I heard her play I cried: 'Who are you? Where have you come from?' (ejaculations that have been made to Tania Leon since she arrived from Cuba) and I found that she was an accomplished musician and composer. Now Tania is one of us and my ballet *Tones* is set to her original score.

"So much love and work have gone into starting the Dance Theater of Harlem that, with God's help, it will succeed. We have to prove that a black ballet school and a black ballet company are the equal of the best of their kind, anywhere in the world. I am giving the dancers the same chance Kirstein and Balanchine gave me, and on exactly the same terms:

they have to match, and maybe surpass, the standards set for white ballet dancers."

I left Arthur Mitchell standing in the doorway of the Church of the Master, which will soon be the entrance to the Dance Theater of Harlem. And I thought: if he is right, and he may well be, this is the beginning of a dark and brilliant splendor in American ballet.

Further Resources

BOOKS

Dils, Ann, and Ann Cooper Albright, eds. *Moving History/Dancing Cultures: A Dance History Reader.* Middletown, Conn.: Wesleyan University Press, 2001.

Thorpe, Edward. *Black Dance.* Woodstock, N.Y.: Overlook Press, 1990.

PERIODICALS

Fleming, Robert. "Arthur Mitchell and His Harlem Crusade." *American Visions* 7, no. 2, April 1992, 48–50.

"Man of Dedication and Talent." *Saturday Review,* October 19, 1968, 49–50.

WEBSITES

"Dance Theater of Harlem: A Neoclassical Dance Company." Available online at http://dancetheaterofharlem.com/index.asp (accessed January 19, 2003).

"Mitchell Founds the Dance Theater Of Harlem, 1968." *DISCovering World History.* Gale Research, 1997. Reproduced in History Resource Center. Farmington Hills, Mich: Gale Group. Available online at http//galenet.galegroup.com/servlet/HistRC/ (accessed April 7, 2003).

AUDIO AND VISUAL MEDIA

Mitchell, Arthur, and Ed Bradley. *The Dance Theater of Harlem.* Films for the Humanities. Videocassette. 1995.

"Success!" *Newsweek,* October 23, 1961, 62.

WEBSITES

Frank Loesser: Official Website. Available online at http://www.frankloesser.com/home.htm (accessed January 19, 2003).

AUDIO AND VISUAL MEDIA

How to Succeed in Business Without Really Trying. RCA, 1961. (Original cast recording.)

How to Succeed in Business Without Really Trying. RCA, 1995. (Revival recording.)

Loesser, Frank. *How to Succeed in Business Without Really Trying.* Directed by David Swift. MGM/UA Studios. DVD and Videocassette, 1967.

2

BUSINESS AND THE ECONOMY

JONATHAN MARTIN KOLKEY

Entries are arranged in chronological order by date of primary source. For entries with one primary source, the entry title is the same as the primary source title. Entries with more than one primary source have an overall entry title, followed by the titles of the primary sources.

Important Events in Business and the Economy, 1960–1969

1960

- The American farm population is 15.6 million or 8.7 percent of the total U.S. population.
- Defense spending and veterans' benefits account for nearly $50 billion or 56 percent of the federal budget and 10 percent of the Gross National Product (GNP).
- Lillian Vernon publishes their first mail-order catalogue.
- The median family income (in 1971 dollars) is $7,688.
- The per-capita national debt stands at $1,582.
- The U.S. automobile industry begins to shift to compact cars in response to falling sales and increased foreign imports.
- U.S. businesses spend $1 billion on computers.
- U.S. advertisers spend $1.6 billion on television commercials.
- In January, African Americans are ¼ of United Auto Workers members.
- On January 1, U.S. consumer debt totals $56 billion.
- On January 1, women make only 60 percent the income of men.
- On January 4, the longest steel strike in U.S. history ends when steel companies and the United Steel Workers agree on a wage increase.
- On May 15, taxes reach 25 percent of earnings, according to a Tax Foundation report that combines federal, state, and local taxes.
- On July 30, Congress allocates $2.9 billion for highway construction.
- On November 16, President Dwight Eisenhower orders an end to overseas spending whenever possible to stop the outflow of gold from the United States.
- On November 18, Chrysler discontinues production of the De Soto automobile, which it had manufactured since 1928.

1961

- General Dynamics loses $143 million.
- In January, demand for U.S. steel falls below 40 percent capacity.
- From February 6 to February 7, a U.S. district judge convicts twenty-nine manufacturers of electrical equipment of price-fixing.
- On February 23, the costliest airline strike in history ends.
- On May 5, President Kennedy signs the Fair Labor Standards Act increasing the minimum wage from $1.00 to $1.15 in September 1961 and to $1.25 in September 1963.

1962

- Sociologist Michael Harrington publishes *The Other America,* a condemnation of an economy that made the U.S. the world's richest nation but kept the poor in misery.
- Controversy engulfs the use of nudity in advertising when Christina Paolozzi, a twenty-two-year-old model, appears nude in a full-page color ad in *Harper's Bazaar.*
- On January 18, a contract between electrical workers and New York City employers establishes a twenty-five-hour workweek, with five overtime hours.
- On January 27, President John Kennedy issues an executive order guaranteeing federal employees the right to unionize.
- On March 1, a federal district court orders E. I. Du Pont de Nemours and Company to divest itself of sixty-three million shares of General Motors stock in the biggest antitrust case to date.
- On April 10, United States Steel announces a 3.5 percent price hike ($6 per ton) after signing a new union contract.
- On May 19, the U.S. Supreme Court affirms the Celler-Kefauver Amendment in blocking a merger between Brown Shoe Company and retail chain Kinney Shoes on the grounds that the merger would have stifled competition and innovation.
- On May 28, the New York Stock Exchange loses nearly $21 billion, the greatest proportion of total value lost since October 19, 1919.
- On July 10, American Telephone and Telegraph and Bell Telephone Laboratories launch *Telstar,* a communications satellite to relay live television pictures from Andover, Maine, to Britain and France.
- On July 27, in a price-fixing case, General Electric agrees to pay $7.5 million in damages for excess profits.
- On September 15, President John Kennedy signs into law a $900 million public-works bill for projects in poor areas.
- On October 4, Congress passes the Trade Expansion Act, to promote overseas trade through tariff reductions.

1963

- Avon returns 34.3 percent on investments, the highest among *Fortune 500* companies.
- Five percent of automobiles sold in the United States are foreign imports.
- Two U.S. companies for the first time register more than $1 billion in profits. GM has a profit of $1.6 billion and Standard Oil of New Jersey a profit of $1 billion.
- On January 26, longshoremen end a strike that had crippled shipping for nearly a month and costs more than $800 million.
- On March 31, the 114-day New York City newspaper strike ends.

- On June 3, the U.S. Supreme Court rules that the agency-shop labor contract in which an employee is not required to join a union but must still pay dues is constitutional.
- On June 10, President John Kennedy signs a bill requiring equal pay for equal work regardless of sex.
- On July 1, the United Brotherhood of Carpenters, the largest U.S. building-trade union, orders its locals to end racial discrimination on construction sites.

1964

- Encyclopaedia Britannica purchases G. and C. Merriam Company.
- On February 26, the Tax Reduction Act reduces personal and corporate income taxes.
- On April 16, Texas Gulf Sulphur Company announces a discovery of copper, silver, and zinc in Ontario, Canada.
- On June 14, United Steelworkers and eleven steel companies sign an agreement to end racial discrimination in the steel industry.
- On July 2, President Lyndon Baines Johnson signs the Civil Rights Act of 1964 banning racial discrimination in public places and employment.
- On August 5, Congress creates the National Commission on Technology, Automation and Economic Progress to study the effects of automation on unemployment.
- On August 30, President Lyndon Johnson signs the Equal Opportunity Act, creating the Job Corps and providing $950 million for youth programs, community-action antipoverty measures, and small-business loans.
- On September 25, the United Auto Workers, after success in contract negotiations with Ford and Chrysler, strike General Motors when negotiations fail.
- In November, Ford introduces the Mustang for the 1965 model year.

1965

- The GNP climbs from $628 billion to $672 billion, a 7 percent increase over the previous year.
- IBM spends $5 billion developing its third-generation computer, the 360.
- On January 1, union membership is 18.5 million.
- On May 9, eight hundred retirees of the Fifth Avenue Coach Lines in New York City receive a record arbitration award of more than $9 million.
- In July, the U.S. Labor Department reports unemployment at 4.2 percent, an eight-year low.
- On November 10, Alcoa, the largest U.S. aluminum producer, and three other companies scrap plans to raise the price of aluminum 2 percent when the government announces it will sell a portion of its aluminum stockpile.
- In December, the number of color televisions in the United States tops 5 million.
- On December 5, the Federal Reserve Board raises the discount rate from 4 percent to 4.5 percent, the highest rate in

thirty-five years, in an attempt to curb inflation by contracting the money supply.

1966

- Branch bank offices account for almost 65 percent of all bank offices and control 70 percent of U.S. banking resources.
- In January, Studebaker ceases production of cars.
- Teachers across the United States stage thirty-six walkouts.
- On February 9, the New York Stock Exchange reaches the peak of a three-and-a-half-year bull market; the Dow Jones industrial average climbs to 995, the highest to that date.
- On March 22, General Motors president James Roche apologizes to Ralph Nader before a Senate subcommittee for spying on him. Nader's book, *Unsafe at Any Speed* (1965), condemned GM's Corvair as dangerous.
- On April 6, headed by César Chavez, the National Farm Workers Union, which had struck California grape growers since September 1965, wins recognition as the bargaining agent for farmworkers of Schenley Industries.
- On April 13, Pan American Airways announces it will build twenty-five new Boeing 747 jets by 1969. The new jet can carry up to five hundred passengers.
- On June 8, the National Football League and the American Football League announce their merger, effective in 1970.
- On July 1, Medicare begins federally-subsidized medical coverage for Americans at least 65 years old.
- On July 15, the U.S. Supreme Court in *United States v. Von's Grocery Company* stops Von's, a Los Angeles, California retail grocery-store chain with only 4.7 percent of area sales and Shopping Bag from merging.
- On September 9, President Lyndon Johnson signs the Traffic Safety Act, establishing safety standards for automobiles.
- On October 7, the Dow Jones industrial average falls to 744, the worst decline since 1962.
- On October 15, Congress creates the U.S. Department of Transportation.
- On December 31, Boeing rather than Lockheed wins the supersonic transport contract (SST).

1967

- Congress appropriates $69.9 billion for defense, due largely to the Vietnam War.
- On January 1, there are 1.8 million retail stores in the United States.
- On January 15, the U.S. Commerce Department announces that the GNP rose by 5.4 percent in 1966.
- On March 10, the New York Stock Exchange has its second largest trading day to date, exceeded only by October 29, 1929.
- On May 11, the one hundred millionth telephone is installed in the United States.
- On June 30, the United States and forty-five other nations sign the General Agreement on Tariffs and Trade (GATT)

in Geneva, Switzerland. The treaty reduces tariffs among these nations to encourage trade.

- On July 5, the Federal Communications Commission (FCC) orders American Telephone and Telegraph (AT&T) to decrease its long-distance and overseas telephone rates by $120 million per year.

- On July 26, a three-month strike by the United Rubber Workers ends when the union signs a three-year contract with the largest U.S. tire manufacturers.

- On September 6, nearly 160,000 members of the United Auto Workers strike the Ford Motor Company when their contract expires.

1968

- On January 1, the average price of a new single-family home is $26,600.

- On January 15, the U.S. Supreme Court allow the New York Central and Pennsylvania railroads to merge as the Penn-Central, creating the largest U.S. railroad.

- In February, geologists discover oil in Prudhoe Bay, Alaska.

- On February 19, nearly half of Florida's public-school teachers walk off the job in the first statewide teachers' strike to date.

- On April 18, 178,000 members of the Communications Workers Union strike the Bell Telephone System for the first time in its history.

- On June 13, investors trade a record 2,350,000 shares on the New York Stock Exchange.

- On June 28, President Lyndon Johnson signs into law a 10 percent income-tax surcharge and a $6 billion cut in federal spending.

- On July 1, the United Auto Workers separates from the AFL-CIO.

- On July 30, eleven steel producers reach agreement with the United Steel Workers of America.

- On November 2, Reader's Digest buys publishing firm Funk and Wagnalls.

- In December, 3.3 percent unemployment is the lowest since the Korean War.

1969

- The American farm population declines to 10.3 million or 5.1 percent of the total U.S. population.

- Control Data Corporation has the highest average growth of any *Fortune 500* company for the decade—48.4 percent.

- The GNP rises to $932.3 billion, a 7.7 percent increase over last year.

- On February 26, GM recalls 4.9 million possibly defective cars and trucks, the largest automobile recall to date.

- On June 9, the prime lending rate peaks at a record 8.5 percent.

- On July 1, Congress passes the Truth-in-Lending Act, requiring disclosure of all pertinent information to someone requesting a bank loan.

- On July 23, consumer prices rise 6.4 percent since January 1, the largest increase since 1951.

- On October 18, the U.S. Department of Health, Education, and Welfare bans the use of cyclamates (artificial sweeteners).

- On November 20, the Department of Agriculture announces a plan to phase out use of the insecticide DDT.

- On December 17, the Dow Jones industrial average hits its low of the year at 769.93.

Franchises and Small Businesses

"Franchise Selling Catches On"

Magazine article

By: *Business Week*

Date: February 6, 1960

Source: "Franchise Selling Catches On." *Business Week,* February 6, 1960, 90–94.

About the Publication: Founded in 1929, *Business Week* provides information on global business, technology, small business, investing, and electronic commerce. The magazine also covers finance, labor and production, corporate news and investment policies, and the effects of legislative and regulatory developments on commerce. *Business Week* is published by McGraw-Hill.

"How Small Business Cuts Its Throat"

Magazine article

By: George S. Odiorne

Date: April 1960

Source: Odiorne, George S. "How Small Business Cuts Its Throat." *Harper's,* April 1960, 46–50.

About the Author: George S. Odiorne is acknowledged as the father of the M.B.O. (Management by Objective) movement. A former dean of the University of Massachusetts (Amherst) School of Business and of the University of Utah, College of Business, Odiorne has also held positions at American Can Company and General Mills. He has consulted, written, and lectured extensively on the peculiar problems faced by small business. ■

Introduction

The American people have always held a soft spot in their hearts for the small business and small businessperson. In a nation often suspicious of excessive concentrations of political or economic power—whether government or corporate—small business seemed the perfect antidote. So much of small business was purely local in character that it represented the pillars of community in thousands of towns and hamlets sprinkled across the country. Indeed, in many areas the proprietors of small businesses guided local government—often as an extension of the various service clubs and charitable organizations that they sponsored.

In addition, small business represented a major vehicle for Americans, particularly from the working or lower middle classes, to enter or move up in the middle class itself. It is safe to say that this ability to become a small business owner constituted a crucial part of the so-called "American dream" for many, along with home ownership and a college education.

During the first half of the twentieth century, governments at various levels often tried to protect small businesses from competition with big business. This period featured at least some scattered enforcement of the antitrust statutes—especially against the most blatant corporate offenders seeking to stifle open competition. And at the behest of the small business community, many states passed so-called "fair-trade" laws that prevented large chain stores from offering consumers sizable price discounts, obtained through volume buying, which could easily undercut the local merchant.

Significance

Nonetheless, by 1960 it had become painfully apparent that the best days for traditional small businesses had long since passed. A number of demographic and technological factors contributed to this decline. The shift in the nation's population, away from central cities (and away from main streets in small towns) towards the burgeoning suburbs, served to focus the country's retail and service trade towards new malls and shopping centers complete with giant outlets offering both deep discounts and nationally cultivated reputations. The subtle inflation that returned around 1960 (and escalated dramatically after 1965) forced consumers to become far more cost conscious. The revival of world trade from the decades of the Great Depression and World War II (1939–1945) resulted in a flood of cheap foreign products entering into American markets, which, among other things, served to give the public an appetite for lower prices. Finally, the tremendous proliferation of chain stores and franchises crowded out many older, community-based independent businesspeople who lacked the capital and contacts to compete effectively with larger economic units.

As traditional small business was dying, however, a new form of business enterprise—the franchise—experienced spectacular growth. Indeed, the 1960s can be considered the breakthrough era for franchising in fast food, home repair, and other areas of the economy. To some, the franchise proliferation was a welcome sight, for it continued the American entrepreneurial spirit (albeit in a slightly different form) by facilitating upward social mobility. And attaching oneself to a larger corporation gave access to technical support and mass advertising that had previously been unavailable to small scale enterprises.

Regrettably, the downside was that franchise holders who had cast their lot with the corporation lacked the true sense of independence that had characterized owner-operator proprietorship. Decisions concerning products, services, and pricing could be made hundreds or even thousands of miles away without regard to local conditions. And franchisees often proved a poor substitute for the old time, small business "boosters" who, for all their faults, often remained the backbone of numerous American communities. Then, too, the advent of huge national outlets tended to destroy a significant number of well paying owner-operator positions and replace them with an army of minimum wage jobs. By century's end, this replacement of small business with franchising was doubtless a prominent factor in the increasing disparity of income and wealth distribution in the United States.

Primary Source

"Franchise Selling Catches On"

> **SYNOPSIS:** This article describes the surge in business franchising that was underway in 1960. The nature of franchising is described, for the public was not necessarily familiar with franchising at the time. As the article notes, while chain stores had been in existence for decades they were now increasing rapidly in type and numbers.

"We are witnessing a new surge of small, independent enterprise. But, if we're going to be good, we've got to be good. That's why we're here."

Thus roughly you might paraphrase the thinking at a meeting in New York's Coliseum last week. Representatives of some 40 franchising corporations, blanketing 25,000 franchise holders, gathered to midwife and baptize the International Franchise Assn. According to A. I. Tunick, president of Chicken Delight chain of carry-out and delivery dinner outlets, and first president of the association, the group has two chief aims: to win recognition for franchising as a major method of merchandising and to set up a code of ethics.

The meeting coincided with a Start Your Own Business show . . . , also at the Coliseum. About 65 exhibitors—not all of them franchise operators—sought to entice would-be entrepreneurs with their wares: rotisserie stands, doughnut-making equipment, laundry services. Timed to coincide with the

meeting was the release of the first issue of Modern Franchising, published quarterly by Factual Publications, Inc., to keep franchising companies up to date on developments in the field, and to tell aspiring dealers of opportunities.

Pioneers

The far-flung car dealerships and strings of gasoline stations across the country remind the business world that franchising has been around a long time. Big names such as Western Auto Supply, Ben Franklin Variety Stores, Howard Johnson have thrived under a franchise setup. But since World War II, and especially in the last three years, franchising has leapt forward. Rogers Sherwood, editor of the monthly National Franchise Reports, reckons maybe 50,000 independent businessmen are doing a job under some kind of franchising umbrella. Tunick figures that 100,000 would be a conservative amount.

The first Directory of Franchising Organizations, compiled from Sherwood's reports, lists almost 200 franchise concerns—from bookkeeping services through baby safety equipment, cosmetics, drive-in and carry-out food operations, motels, pancake shops, soft-serve ice cream stands, swimming pools, all the way to water softeners. Enticing names such as Dog N' Suds, Dunkin' Donuts of America, Pelton's Spudnuts, 7 Steers Specialty Restaurants spot the directory list.

How It Works

The franchising formula varies from one operation to another. Basically, though, it's a system set up by a manufacturer or purveyor of services, which sets up under a single brand name a chain of small businessmen, who buy some of their equipment and supplies from the franchisers and run their own show—with some strings. To get a franchise, the dealer may pay a franchise fee—most of them under $10,000, some as low as $10—or he may simply make a downpayment on the equipment or plan. Usually, too, he pays a fee or royalty on his own sales. Franchising as the association defines it, Tunick says, is not a one-shot deal. A continuing relationship between franchise and franchisee marks operations of its members.

For the franchising company, this setup offers quick, assured distribution and expansion at relatively low cost—since the franchise holder himself puts up some of the investment. The franchiser keeps title to the name and basic product or service rights. Because the franchise holder runs the business himself, the franchiser gets a dealer who is both cost and sales conscious.

For the franchise holder, the setup gives him some independence with the security of a tested business. His capital investment is relatively small— and financing comes easier with a big concern backing him. In effect, he gets the buying edge of a big chain, the parent's promotion and management knowhow. In some cases, he gets the plus of direct-from-manufacturer price. Sherwood estimates that bulk buying gives the dealer savings of anywhere from 30% to 50%. While he is subject to quality and other controls, he is basically a man on his own.

Postwar Spurt

The first big spurt in franchise retailing came right after World War II. During the war, Tunick explains, GIs lived with two dreams: the little white cottage they were going to own, and the prospect of a job with no boss to hound them. With their bonuses in their pockets, they constituted a fine potential for the franchiser.

The 1957–58 recession gave franchising another boost. Men lost their jobs, or got scared. They wanted a security—and they wanted it in an easy-to-handle package.

Expanded credit is a major factor in contributing to franchising's growth, thinks J. J. Connolly, president of Roll-A-Grill Corp. of America, and a director of the association. Credit allows the little man to take part in the kind of enterprise that a Frank Woolworth built up for himself in the old days, he says.

In the last few months, several newcomers— large and small—have moved in. In November, Frank G. Shattuck Co. announced a new Franchise Div., for operation of Schrafft's restaurants, chiefly tied into new motel operations. . . . And last week, an ad in the New York Times urged people to go into the Franchised Art Galleries business.

I. Problems

While the new association insists that it is one of the few industry groups that didn't come into being primarily to deal with a problem, mushroom growth has brought problems aplenty in some lines. The soft ice cream field is a good case in point.

Right after the war, according to the Soft Serve Dairy Products Assn., there were only about 100 soft-serve stands in the country; today there are something like 18,000. This development came so fast,

A young girl samples some Dairy Queen ice cream. The number of Dairy Queen and other fast food restaurant franchises grew considerably after World War II. GETTY IMAGES. REPRODUCED BY PERMISSION.

says Harry Kimpel, executive secretary of the association, that some franchise chains didn't organize properly. "A lot of smart operators saw an opening to make some money, and with a little solid promoting, set up stands wherever they could."

They would grant franchise, regardless of the candidate's own potential or the potential of his market—and leave him to his own plight after a day or two of training.

Tricks

Fly-by-night operators sometimes deliberately chose poor locations. They would pocket the franchise holder's downpayment—maybe $3,000 to $5,000—and move on to another location. Some operators charged their franchisees different royalties, another factor making for friction. Some tricked ma and pa stands with a promise of an exclusive franchise—and neglected to mention that the same parent company might operate stands under different brand names, which might spring up across the street.

As a result, says Kimpel, turnover in the soft-serve business is about 25% a year. One industry

A deserted store in Cripple Creek, Colorado. © PIERRE PERRIN/CORBIS SYGMA. REPRODUCED BY PERMISSION.

source estimates that one-third of the big stands are in trouble.

II. Who's Who

Nevertheless, several big organizations operate successfully in the soft-serve field—with names such as Carvel, Dairy Queen, Dari-Delite, Tastee-Freez. Now that the country is saturated with stationary stands, in some markets at least, mobile units, equipped to serve a variety of dishes from trucks, are burgeoning. Mr. Softee, Inc., and Dairy Dan have gone this route—and some of the older companies are taking to the road as choice sites get crowded.

Services, Too

While the food field ranks first in the franchising field, services are coming up fast. ServiceMaster and Duraclean, carpet cleaners, have set up large franchised systems.

Home service organizations—the directory lists four—have sprouted and spread through franchised outlets. Allied Homeowners Assn., or Roslyn, N.Y., has opened up in 6 cities. National Home Owners

Club, in Chicago, has 24 franchises. Development of this group took an odd turn. Bozell & Jacobs, public relations consultants, got interested in franchising when it had such franchise operations as Midas Mufflers as clients. Now Bozell & Jacobs is half-owner of National Home Owners Club.

III. Case Study

A closer look at Chicken Delight shows how this kind of operation works.

Chicken Delight got its start in 1952 when Tunick, a scrap dealer, turned his $25,000 investment in a defunct Rock Island (Ill.) manufacturing plant into a food operation. The plant had been making conduction cookers—but couldn't sell them. "We couldn't find anyone who wanted to buy the appliance," Tunick says, "but the chicken we used one day to demonstrate it was a hit." So the first Chicken Delight outlet was born. Today, there are over 160 outlets in 40 states and Canada, and Tunick hopes to double that number this year.

Chicken Delight offers four dishes—specified by franchise agreement: chicken, fish, shrimp, and ribs.

All are prepared by a special process called conduction or searing. They are served in dinner-size or snack-size portions—about 80% of them delivered to the homes in trucks equipped to keep the food hot en route.

Cost

The total cost of setting up an outlet runs to about $12,000. Chicken Delight charges no franchise fee, but it does require the operator to put up at leats $5,000. "We want him to have a definite financial interest," Tunick explains. The parent company helps the dealer get financing.

The franchise holder buys his equipment—cookers, fryers, trays, and the like—from Chicken Delight, which manufactures the basic units. He also buys from the parent the batter that is a specialty of the house, and packaging—which means paper plates, napkins that the dinner is served in. Chicken Delight's total initial equipment sales—including a starting supply of batter, packing, and promotion aides—come to about $8,000.

Contract

Well aware of the troubles the soft-serve industry fell into, Tunick relies on a strong franchise agreement. He maintains territorial divisions—down to the last block. "We give our men a two-mile radius guarantee in cities," he says, "which usually means between 50,000 and 75,000 potential customers. In small towns, one man has exclusive rights to the area."

The contract also spells out down to the last two ounces of chicken and last grain of salt what's to be included in each meal. The company checks from time to time to make sure the franchise holder is keeping his side of the bargain. He must buy his food—other than what Chicken Delight supplies—from sources that meet the company's standards.

The company supervisor in the area—there are eight in all—helps the dealer negotiate the lease for his property, do any remodeling, install the special equipment; the supervisor stays with the novice operator for his first week. Tunick estimates that it costs an operator 69¢ to put a dinner together. Retail price is flexible, but it runs about $1.45—for a gross profit of 53%. Chicken Delight makes its profit from equipment, packaging, at 12¢ a dinner, and batter, at about 20¢ a lb.

The contract calls for a minimum of 500 sales a week; the average dealer sells about 1,000, Tunick says.

Variations

Other operations run a bit differently. Diary Dan's mobile soft-serve units, for example, operate through distributors, who screen would-be operators, get a commission on truck sales, control the sources, and get a royalty on sales—like the parent concern. Some big motel and restaurant operations, such as Howard Johnson and Holiday Inns, charge a relatively large franchise fee, and a royalty on room rentals.

Though franchised operations may lend themselves to part-time work, nobody undersells the kind of job a successful dealer must do. "The good franchise holder earns his keep," says Tunick. In fact, one secret of the system's success, he says, is that "the man who owns his business finds the 25th hour in the day to make it work."

Primary Source

"How Small Business Cuts Its Throat" [excerpt]

> **SYNOPSIS:** Odiorne's article explores the condition of independent small businessmen in 1960. In his view, the typical small businessman is doomed to failure because of inexperience and incompetence. He backs this view up with statistics showing that almost all small businesses fail, and calls for an end to government subsidies for small businesses.

Last year the Junior Chamber of Commerce in a Midwestern city awarded the citation "young man of the year" to one of its number, and in doing so quietly marked the end of a period in our history. The young chap selected was as clean-cut as any previous recipient. His grip was as firm, and he met your eye with a clear and serious look. The only thing that made him different in the past lay in the route by which he had climbed to the top.

His success story began with a loan backed by the U. S. Small Business Administration. Then with skill and aggressiveness this youngster had obtained a sizeable government contract which was open only to small businesses by Defense Department directive. His profits were helped along through an accelerated write-off of his equipment for tax purposes. His rise to the top followed immediately. Admittedly, this fellow showed perspicacity and more than average skill in negotiating the red tape required to rally such support for his firm. Still his story puts a reverse-English upon our "rags-to-riches" tradition which might cause many an old-style free enterpriser to rest uneasily in his grave.

Statistics and politics have combined to exalt the small businessman in Washington eyes in recent years. While large corporate profits have soared, the little fellow has been caught by low profits. As casualties multiplied, it because difficult if not impossible for the survivors to get credit from conventional sources. The Small Business Administration (until 1958 a temporary executive agency) did its best with business and disaster loans but found itself unable to cope with the rising tide of failures. In 1958 Congress voted $260 million tax relief for small business. Even so, the rate of failures kept mounting. Last year Congress created Small Business Investment Companies operating under the supervision of the SBA which provides funds when necessary.

Essentially bi-partisan, these measures have been enthusiastically supported by both the Democratic Congress and the Republican Administration. The small businessman, it would seem, is acquiring a privileged position in Washington comparable to the farmer's. Actually, however, there is a big difference between the two. The farmer is subsidized for hardships resulting from superior ability to produce. In most instances the small businessman is shored up with tax money because of his incompetence in management. And the present pattern of government aid does nothing constructive about converting a losing small business into a stable and profitable one. The Small Business Investment Companies in fact merely assuage symptoms without getting at the underlying malady which is partly a matter of hard economics, partly the fruit of the small businessman's peculiar philosophy and limitations. A high mortality rate is almost inevitable.

The odds are that only one in five small businesses will survive ten years. In fact, the median age of 4,500,000 firms in this country is seven. Three hundred fifty thousand will go broke this year and another 370,000 will change hands.

Despite these hazards, some 400,000 new ones are likely to get rolling in the next twelve months. Each founder will—in all probability—be confident that, with just a little capital, he can become a Henry Ford, a Buck Duke, or a John D. Rockefeller, starting in a corner grocery or tiny machine shop. Unlike a ball-player, actor, or painter, he does not feel that he needs any special talent, training or experience. Pluck and grit—nowadays called motivation—will suffice. Flanked by a Loyal Woman, he shouts "invictus" as he pours his life savings down the rat hole. If he has no capital of his own he can always borrow from a bank, friends, relatives, or the Small Business Administration.

What he can't borrow is the ability to run a business successfully. In fact, he is very likely doomed from the outset by his incompetence as a manager and his persistence in clinging to outworn ways of doing business. Typically, the small businessman stretches his limited capital too far, overextends credit in order to get customers, overloads himself with slow-moving stock, has no knowledge of the market or of his competitors, doesn't know how to raise money when he needs it, doesn't know the principles of good management and wouldn't use them if he did.

There is always a wolf at his door called "working capital." Because he needs it so badly he can't get it from the sale of stocks and bonds. His principal source is a too-meager profit, which he must plow back if his company is going to grow. High taxes keep him from accumulating funds, the inheritance tax takes a large bite between generations, and risk money is scarce. He depends chiefly upon commercial lenders and banks which, when he needs them most, also dry up on him.

Dun and Bradstreet, the master scorekeeper of business failures, has found that more than nine out of ten small business failures were caused by lack of experience or incompetence. The newspaper ads which show businesses offered for sale "for reasons of health" are often deceptive—poor health accounted for only 2.5 per cent of the failures. The bulk of them were the result of competitive weaknesses, inadequate sales, and above all, inexperience.

In the *Harvard Business Review,* L. T. White of Cities Service Corporation has listed these cardinal mistakes of small businessmen: (1) failing to create customers; (2) keeping inadequate records; (3) being emotional about credit and purchases. The typical small businessman who fails sees his job as "running a shop." Often he keeps his records and results secret not only from his wife and tax people, but from himself, and judges his credit risks by hunch. . . .

Such are the obstacles in the world of the small businessman. His rewards are mainly psychic. He has no boss breathing over him and sets his own hours—which are nearly twice as long as a paid employee's. In theory he comes and goes as he pleases and has the enviable right to tell any man to go to hell. This is seldom expedient, however, if the man happens to be a big customer, a banker, a supplier of hard-to-get material, or one of his own salesmen. Even so, the small businessman likes his work. If he is able to make a decent wage, he may even become enamored of the illusion of independence and full economic freedom.

Actually, what he hankers for is not economic freedom but the kind of monopoly once held by the general store in my home town near Haverhill, Massachusetts. With the advent of the Model T, my mother joyfully waved farewell to his exorbitant prices and drove off to buy her groceries at the A & P ten miles away. A similar kind of monopoly is enjoyed by the corner delicatessen which stays open till eleven when every other store in town is closed, and will send a boy around with a case of beer when needed. By working an ungodly number of hours the owner manages to make a living—but he is unlikely to do more.

Psychologically the small businessman tends to identify with the tycoons of another era—such as Edison, Carnegie, and Sewell Avery. Still dreaming of the day when the lonely inventor working in his cellar could found an industrial empire, he declines to face up to the long gestation period of research and the investment of time, equipment and specialized skills now required to develop a marketable new product.

An incurable optimist, he is impatient with the frictions which impede his spacious future and judges every law by how it affects his brand of free private enterprise. His voice—increasingly strident and of dwindling influence—is heard through the National Association of Manufacturers, which describes 80 per cent of its members as "small manufacturers" even though one third have over 500 employees. (In truth, no one is quite sure just what a small business is. The term includes the corner grocer, pharmacist, tavern owner, automobile dealer, and independent milkman. It also embraces any firm with less than 500 employees, by Defense Department definition.) It is, in any event, the lesser fry who dominate the NAM's committees and espouse their peculiar form of reaction and rural nostalgia. They tend to be, as John H. Bunzel puts, it, deeply suspicious "of anything that is alien to their preferred pattern of living, whether it be the intrusion of foreign ideologies into the American scene or the upsetting of tradition and stability as a result of the spread of new ideas and the mingling of different cultures and people" . . .

Of the three Goliaths threatening the small business David, the unions are probably the least interested in him. Early AFL leaders are said to have felt that "the small guy has nothing to give," and today's super-unionists seem to agree. Occasionally the large unions find themselves on the same side on an issue with a small company. But by and large the economics of big unionism require big plants and work forces. . . .

If the government stopped subsidizing this overpopulated and wrongly oriented segment of the economic community, business failures might surge upward, it is true. But continued subsidy on a long-term basis might be even worse. From the viewpoint of simple economics everyone pays when subsidies are used to bolster the incompetent. A rise, of, say, 10 per cent in business failures is unlikely to have the dire impact on the economy which is often cited as the reason for farm subsidy. On the other hand, there is ample evidence that subsidizing inefficiency maintains prices at higher levels than if the marginal businesses were wiped out. More importantly from the viewpoint of small business itself, a point-blank exposure to the workings of the free market might bring home the necessity of changed attitudes and increased professionalism in the conduct of its affairs. . . .

It is unlikely, however, that many small businesses will try this kind of therapy so long as the government continues to apply artificial respiration. Once the pulmotor is cut off, however, there might be some changes. More conversions will take place on the Road to Ruin than the road to almost everywhere else. Of all the subsidies which have come out of Washington, we have in the Small Business program the purest example of a subsidy of archaic thinking. With a decade or more of global economic warfare facing us this is an expensive luxury.

Further Resources

BOOKS

Bean, Jonathan J. *Beyond the Broker State: Federal Policies Towards Small Business, 1936–1961.* Chapel Hill: University of North Carolina Press, 1996.

Birkeland, Peter M. *Franchising Dreams: The Lure of Entrepreneurship in America.* Chicago: University of Chicago Press, 2002.

Dicke, Thomas S. *Franchising in America: The Development of a Business Method, 1840–1980.* Chapel Hill: University of North Carolina Press, 1992.

PERIODICALS

Feinstein, Robert. "Franchising: Where It Came From, Where It's Going." *Barron's,* August 25, 1980, 30–31.

Vinnell, Reuben, and R.T. Hamilton. "A Historical Perspective on Small Firm Development." *Entrepreneurship: Theory and Practice* 23, no. 4, 5–20.

WEBSITES

Chowhdury, Jaffor, and David C. Adams. "The Most Pressing Problems of Small Businesses: Some Observations Based on Two Sample Surveys." Small Business Advancement National Center. Available online at http://www.sbaer.uca .edu/Research/1989/SBIDA/89sbi091.htm; website home page: http://www.sbaer.uca.edu/ (accessed April 22, 2003).

Saldarini, Katy. "Big Federal Spenders Stiff Small Businesses." GovExec.com. Available online at http://www.govexec.com /dailyfed/0499/040999k3.htm; website home page: http:// www.govexec.com/ (accessed April 22, 2003).

"How the Old Age Market Looks"

Magazine article

By: *Business Week*

Date: February 13, 1960

Source: "How the Old Age Market Looks." *Business Week,* February 13, 1960, 72, 77–78.

About the Publication: Founded in 1929, *Business Week* provides information on global business, technology, small business, investing, and electronic commerce. The magazine also covers finance, labor and production, corporate news and investment policies, and the effects of legislative and regulatory developments on commerce. *Business Week* is published by McGraw-Hill. ∎

Introduction

By 1960 the American people began waking up to one of the most significant economic and demographic transformations in the history of the United States. Senior citizens, perhaps the poorest group in the country as late as 1940, were well on their way towards becoming one of the wealthiest. At century's end, those over sixty-five had revolutionized their own economic, social, and political status in truly remarkable fashion.

Traditionally, when the typical worker retired, his or her income fell dramatically. Often forced to liquidate savings and other assets that they had accumulated when illness struck, many elderly slipped into poverty.

All of this began to change during the late 1930s. The landmark Social Security Act of 1935 established a system of old age assistance. A subsequent decision in 1940 allowed workers who had paid in for only five years to begin receiving benefits, and for years the system paid out to this initial group of retirees far more money than they had ever paid in taxes into Social Security. Then, too, various levels of government passed tax breaks to help seniors, who began flexing their political muscle as a recognized pressure group. This financial bonanza en-

acted at the expense of the rest of the population would be augmented in 1965 with the creation of Medicare. In the late 1970s, seniors in various states, including California, voted to freeze their own property taxes. By century's end, social security and Medicare combined had even eclipsed defense as the single largest expenditure in the federal government's annual budget. All in all, "gray power" took its place alongside other recognizable special interest groups.

Meanwhile, other long-term trends tended to enhance elderly wealth. Advances in medical science lengthened human life, thereby increasing the size of the senior class, which further served to increase its political clout. The widespread prosperity enjoyed by Americans during the years 1940–1973 provided good wages along with relatively generous pension benefits courtesy of U.S. corporations awash with cash, who remained free from the type of cutthroat global competition that became a conspicuous feature of the U.S. economy at century's end. With generally high wages and a lack of competition from immigrants, and not yet facing the full brunt of job-destroying automation, workers often had surplus funds to invest in stocks and bonds. Finally, the general rise in the value of real estate benefited the older generation, which had purchased its property for much less money at some earlier date. All these economic factors provided many of the elderly with a secure nest egg, though many more still struggled.

Significance

By 1960 seniors had become a recognized niche market. Savvy businesspeople sought to relieve them of some of their disposable income with senior housing projects, packaged vacation cruises, specialized recreation, entertainment, and the like. Ingenious marketing strategies were employed to sell to seniors in much the same fashion when earlier in the century a definable women's and later a youth market had been first identified and cultivated. On some level, the elderly circa 1960 represented one of the last great untapped marketing frontiers.

Meanwhile, the discovery of the senior market reflected a major change in the way that the American people chose to view old age. In an earlier era, the elderly kept more to the background so as to make room for the younger generation. As healthcare improved and people began to live longer, more active lives, however, the elderly didn't slow down into retirement. Many began to carry out in their retirement the travel, hobbies, and other activities they had been too busy to pursue in their earlier years. Thus, the purchasing power of the elderly did not fall off with retirement, but remained steady for many years to come, leading to the emergence of the elderly as a significant factor in the U.S. economy.

Primary Source

"How the Old Age Market Looks"

SYNOPSIS: America's senior citizens, once one of the poorest groups of people, on average saw their economic, social, and political status markedly enhanced by various government policies enacted since the 1930s. These measures included social security, Medicare, and a host of assorted tax breaks, subsidies, and other measures. Additional factors, such as demographic trends and the introduction of new technology, also served to improve the financial condition of the nation's older citizens. One result of the emergence of this new senior economic clout was the discovery by U.S. business around 1960 of a distinctive "senior" market for products and services.

The nation's oldest citizens, now making their influence strongly felt as a political force . . . , represent also a sizeable and growing market that already numbers 16-million-odd potential customers in the over-65 group. And there are signs that U.S. business, which has largely thought of the multiplying ranks of the elderly as merely "more of the same" in market terms, is beginning to recognize the market possibilities in the group's special needs, and to make a pitch for it.

Yet the oldsters still have a long way to go before their dollars will count in the marketplace as their votes do on election day—as a Seattle merchant, summing up a bit bluntly today's prevailing attitude of retailers, emphasizes: "The way the older population is growing, I suppose we'll want to do something for it someday, but we're not doing anything now."

Hurdles

A basic deterrent, of course is that much of this group has only a minimum to spend. Some 80% of it has money income of under $2,000; only about 5% have over $5,000.

But marketers must take other hazards in their stride, too.

"Older people do the same things younger people do. They golf, they garden, they play bridge. You can't say, "This golf set is for older people, or these bridge cards," comments a Portland (Ore.) retailer. Except for health needs, the elderly want the same things their younger brothers want.

Maybe the toughest hazard of all is psychological. Says Lipman Wolfe & Co., Portland department store, "The quickest way I can think of to make sure a sale would flop would be to advertise, 'This dress

A senior couple gets ready for a day on a Santa Monica beach. In the 1960s marketers realized the possibilities with a generation who had time and money to spend. © **JOSEPH SCHWARTZ COLLECTION/CORBIS. REPRODUCED BY PERMISSION.**

is for ladies 65 and over'." No one wants to be pegged as an ancient. "You can't merchandise to this group," says Lane Bryant, New York specialty store.

For different reasons, manufacturers feel much the same way. Like retailers, they are anxious to sell to all age groups—and too close an identification of their wares with the older group might prove the kiss of death for younger customers.

Yet signs of change are evident.

Even the Seattle merchant who is doing nothing about the group now concedes he may have to someday. Most retailers recognize the sheer numerical heft of the market. Detroit businessmen, for example, detect some stirrings in the air.

Barriers to good merchandizing will give way as the experts learn more about the psychology of the oldsters, they believe.

Here and there, a retailer is already doing a job. "We have become keenly aware of the importance of keeping pace with the unprecedented growth in the percentage of persons now at or near 65," says Fred Meyer, head of a Northwestern drug, variety, and food chain. "We have made this a subject of extreme study and experimentation, and have changed much in our operation to meet what we consider a coming revolution in retail trade. . . . There's a wide difference between the demands of the new generation and the old, and unless the store caters to the whims of both, it's bound to lose trade."

Spurs

Two things—besides numerical growth—are abetting the changes.

First, short of cash though the bulk of the group is, it has more money than it used to have. As private pension plans expand, more personnel are retiring with a healthy nest egg. One company pays out to retirees from its thrift fund—to which employees contribute—amounts ranging from $18,000 to "10 or 20 times that"—in addition to the pension.

Second, better economic times mean earlier retirement in many cases. The "older" population is growing younger. It still has the urge to enjoy activity. Thus, it has more money. It has more energy. And it has what it always had only more so: time.

Marketers in some fields are already cashing in.

Housing ranks tops in most cities. True, a good deal of the housing activity is still sponsored by government, church, or union. But private business is getting into the act, too. Last week, FHA issued regulations for a new program that could generate up to 150,000 or 200,000 apartment starts a year. The new program, which allows private builders to make a profit on rental apartments for elder tenants, was authorized last September in the 1959 housing law. Up till then, only nonprofit organizations could go into this.

Florida to Detroit

Housing is Florida's most important industry for the aged. The Mackle brothers of General Development Corp. rate as the No. 1 builder for the oldsters in the country.

In Arizona, Youngtown, a development some 16 miles from Phoenix, has about 1,000 houses, priced at $8,200 and up. Nearby, a brand-new development, Del Webb's Sun City, catering to customers of 50 and over, sold over 200 homes the first few days after opening on Jan. 1. Prices: from $8,500 to $11,300.

Detroit's Holtzman & Silverman, residential builders, went the whole hog on a development 20 miles west of the city, with homes priced just under $11,000. The concern admits, though, that sales have been slow. Another company, C. W. Babcock & Sons, specializes in co-ops for the elderly. Last year it sold 140 such units, twice the number it sold the year before. Initial payment calls for $10,500 for a 2-room setup, with $30 a month covering maintenance except electricity.

Life-Leasing

The life-lease contract is growing in popularity. This is the deal where the customer pays a sum— it ranges from $5,000 to perhaps $30,000 or more, depending on the amount of luxury and service involved—plus monthly payments.

Coverage varies: in many places, these payments provide food and shelter for the rest of the consumers' lives. Some places—Pacific Homes, for one, nonprofit operator in the Southwest of several such developments for the Methodist Church—include medical care.

Hotels to Trailer

In Florida, Charles Lavin has specialized in reconverting old hotels—and Detroit is going that trail, too. Maimi and Seattle see a potential in plush hotels for retirees.

Trailers are growing as a solution to the housing problem. The National Assn. of Mobile Home Manufacturers estimates that 10% of those living in or owning trailers are retired—out of 3.4 million trailers in use in the country. A swish trailer park, Sunnyvale, near San Francisco draws a sizable chunk of its market from the over-60 group, by the simple expedient of allowing no children or pets.

What They Want

Builders—both public and private—have clearer ideas of what this market wants. Here, as in other lines, the Mackles say, the oldsters resent being categorized. They liked it fine when younger people began to flock to their Pompano Highlands development, designed especially for the elderly.

Transportation is a must, all agree. Arizona's Youngtown has a special weekly bus that takes residents to downtown Phoenix for a day's outing. A Denver project too far from bus service did not pan out.

If transportation is sketchy, then the community must offer all facilities at its doorstep. Ideally, it should, anyway. Webb's Sun City is one of several that feature a shopping center, swimming pool, golf, and motels.

With more people retiring before 65, demand for jobs is strong. The Mackles hope to create an industrial park at Port Charlotte to provide employment. In St. Petersburg, many take hotel jobs—Lavin employs residents of his hotel projects—or they run taxis. If they have money, they buy real estate, or an orange grove. Companies such as Hotpoint train their older employees on maintenance of Hotpoint appliances so that, come the day, they will be able to find work.

But a tiny fraction of the retired actually find work. Products and services catering to the leisure market can find rich diggings in this field.

Travel

Thomas Cook & Son, big travel agency, reports that its business with older people has more than doubled since the end of World War II, while its overall business has grown some 60%.

Cruises—long, leisurely, comfortable—have a strong appeal. The longer the cruise, the higher the average age, the Grace Line reports. Figures on passports issued and renewed during the July-September period in 1959 (the latest available) show that almost 19% went to holders aged 60 and over, against 13% the year before. While the actual numbers are small, there was a startling 93% increase in passport holders over 76 in that period.

Sports, Outdoor and In

For those to whom such living comes too high, fishing seems to rate tops in communities well supplied with oldsters. Gardening, boating, golf—and especially shuffleboard—all have strong adherents in Florida. In St. Petersburg, classes in boating flourish. B. E. Webb, of Webb's City, big St. Petersburg retailer, estimates his "Plant City" garden and shrub department sells some $1 million a year.

Another major Florida sport appears to be playing the stock market. "I live a half a mile from the bay and a half a mile from my broker," reports one contented retiree. St. Petersburg has more than 20 brokers' offices—a record, it thinks, for a city its size.

Detroit has a distinct, but undocumented, hunch that its compact cars appeal to the older driver. Handrails for tubs are a best seller in that city. An Atlanta concern is successfully marketing Fayd, a product that claims to eradicate the brown spots that come with age. Cosmeticians and beauty parlors (St. Petersburg is rich in these) also flourish; hair colorists find the elderly particularly rewarding—though youngsters are deep in this business, too.

Health products—drugs, and the like—of course find a warm reception. Webb's in St. Petersburg says vitamins are its best seller; it advertises them at a saving. Sonotone Corp. is test-marketing two vitamin formulas, one for persons over 50, one for younger people. Miami has 13 health food stores.

Insurance companies are beginning to cash in on the demand for hospitalization policies that are open-end on age and physical condition. . . .

When it comes to apparel, retailers all but give up. You simply sell on an individual basis, they say. What you can do, points out Lane Bryant, is offer more of the half-sizes that older women are apt to wear—and design them with more style, more color. Webb's notes a run on sport shirts and caps. Oldsters relax in their attire when they stop working, it believes. Most stores feel older women want whatever is the mode. "She'll wear shorts, by golly, if 'they' are wearing shorts," says a Lane Bryant spokesman.

A few big stores feature events that draw older customers—without making a big point of it. Rich's in Atlanta entertains customers over 80 on its annual birthday party. The Emporium in San Francisco continues to let the senior citizens hold their hobby show there. But for direct promotion, a gray-haired model in a fashion show or an older couple in a cruise ad about does it.

Yet the Seattle pharmacy that has studied this market closely feels it pays to stock for the older people. They want long-wearing clothes; they want old standbys in the drug lines; they don't go for faddy foods, Fred Meyer reports. Further, grandmother is a pushover for the grandchildren. She'll spend to the utmost on toys for the younger generation. And Meyer has stocked his stores accordingly.

Meyer plays up heavily courtesy from his employees to the older folks, to the point of giving them physical assistance if it's required. "Many of them live in rooms or an apartment or in the old home by themselves," he says. "A visit to the neighboring store is a lark—and it is our policy to try in every way to make it just that."

Further Resources

BOOKS

Goldstein, Sidney. *Consumption Patterns of the Aged*. Philadelphia: University of Pennsylvania, 1960.

Wise, David A. ed. *Inquiries in the Economics of Aging*. Chicago: University of Chicago Press, 1998.

PERIODICALS

Resener, Marilyn. "Targeting the Old Folks; Florida Leads the Way in Marketing to the Elderly." *Newsweek,* January 6, 1986, 54.

Sebastian, Pamela. "Selling to Seniors Means Changes at the Shelf and the Curb, Grocers Say." *The Wall Street Journal,* April 16, 1992, A1.

WEBSITES

"Marketing Your Company to Seniors: An Overview." Senior-Mag. Available online at http://www.seniormag.com/business /marketingtoseniors.htm; website home page: http://www .seniormag.com/ (accessed April 24, 2003).

"The 10 Commandments for Selling to Seniors." Suddenly Senior. Available online at http://www.suddenlysenior.com /10commandmentsadsenior.html; website home page: http:// www.suddenlysenior.com/ (accessed April 24, 2003).

"The Welfare State"

Nonfiction work

By: Barry M. Goldwater

Date: 1960

Source: Goldwater, Barry M. "The Welfare State." Chapter Eight in *The Conscience of a Conservative,* by Barry M. Goldwater. New York: MacFadden Capitol Hill, 1960, 70–77.

About the Author: Barry Morris Goldwater (1909–1998), a native of Arizona, served in the United States Senate from 1953 to 1965 and again from 1969 to 1987. He was the unsuccessful Republican presidential nominee in 1964, losing in a landslide to Democratic incumbent Lyndon B. Johnson (served 1963–1969). Goldwater is considered the father of the modern American conservative movement known as the "New Right." ■

Introduction

The year 1960 marked the beginning of a new epoch in American political history with the sudden emergence of a vigorous Conservative movement that became known as the "New Right." And the hitherto obscure Arizona Republican United States senator Barry M. Goldwater became the New Right's first great national leader. In actuality, Goldwater helped launch a crusade that had been germinating during the late 1950s. However, Goldwater served as the personal symbol of the right's resurgence in the United States. Indeed, a straight line connects Goldwater in 1960 with the triumphant Ronald Reagan (served 1981–1989) of 1980.

Although the Republicans had occupied the White House since Dwight D. Eisenhower's (served 1953–1961) landslide 1952 Presidential election victory, many staunch Conservatives in the G.O.P. ("Grand Old Party,"

the traditional Republican nickname) had never felt comfortable with the easy-going, often moderate Ike. Meanwhile, the increasingly restless Southern wing of the Democratic Party appeared ripe for defection from a national party that had become too liberal for Southern tastes—especially regarding civil rights issues. Hence by 1960 one can detect the outlines of a major political realignment involving the United States' two main parties that wound up taking a dozen years to accomplish. The outlines of this new configuration continue to dominate the United States in the early 2000s.

Significance

Perhaps the most significant intellectual event of this political realignment was the 1960 publication of Barry Goldwater's powerful manifesto, *The Conscience of a Conservative.* Rejecting the trimming conservatism of the 1950s Republican Party under Eisenhower, which essentially accepted Franklin D. Roosevelt's (served 1933–1945) New Deal reforms of the 1930s that marked the rise of the national welfare state, Goldwater took an unabashedly free market stance, demanding an end to various layers of government regulation. Goldwater wished to dismantle the huge federal government that had mushroomed since the 1930s. Moreover, he rejected the welfare state, lecturing farmers on why they needed to be weaned off government subsidies, while lecturing workers on why they should accept the demise of social security in favor of a system of private pensions or acquiesce in a restriction of their hard fought rights to join unions, bargain collectively, and strike. In short, Goldwater circa 1960 declared war on both the complacent business-as-usual Democrats and Republicans.

Nonetheless, Goldwater's ultimate fate serves to highlight an old truism that leadership is an indispensable ingredient for the success of any political movement. Goldwater, it seems, turned out to be somewhat miscast as the initial leader of the New Right. In fact, his fundamental political instincts were not, in truth, nearly as conservative as was the philosophy expounded in his book, *The Conscience of a Conservative,* which, it turned out, had been largely ghostwritten. One true New Rightist, California congressman and 1972 American Independent Party presidential nominee 1972 John Schmitz, once quipped: "I had once doubted that Goldwater had ever written his book. Now I doubt that he ever actually read it!"

In the end, the task fell to Ronald Reagan, a far better politician blessed with a more appealing personality than Goldwater, to translate some of the Arizona Senator's ideas (especially involving business and the economy) into practice. The charismatic Reagan would prove the perfect vehicle for the enactment of many parts of the conservative/New Right agenda.

Primary Source

"The Welfare State" [excerpt]

SYNOPSIS: In this chapter from his highly provocative book, *The Conscience of a Conservative*, Arizona Senator and soon-to-be unsuccessful Republican presidential nominee Barry M. Goldwater fires the opening salvo in the New Right's attack against the American welfare state that, he alleges, had suffocated the nation's business and its economy since the 1930s.

As a leader of the new conservative movement Barry Goldwater opposed further growth of the federal government. **THE LIBRARY OF CONGRESS.**

For many years it appeared that the principal domestic threat to our freedom was captioned in the doctrines of Karl Marx. The collectivists—non-Communists as well as Communists—had adopted the Marxist objective of "socializing the means of production." And so it seemed that if collectivization were imposed, it would take the form of a State owned and operated economy. I doubt whether this is the main threat any longer. . . .

The currently favored instrument of collectivization is the Welfare State. The collectivists have not abandoned their ultimate goal—to subordinate the individual to the State—but their strategy has changed. They have learned that Socialism can be achieved through Welfarism quite as well as through Nationalization. They understand that private property can be confiscated as effectively by taxation as by expropriating it. They understand that the individual can be put at the mercy of the State—not only by making the State his employer—but by divesting him of the means to provide for his personal needs and by giving the State the responsibility of caring for those needs from cradle to grave. Moreover, they have discovered—and here is the critical point—that *Welfarism is much more compatible with the political processes of a democratic society.* Nationalization ran into popular opposition, but the collectivists feel sure the Welfare State can be erected by the simple expedient of buying votes with promises of "free" hospitalization, "free" retirement pay and so on . . . The correctness of this estimate can be seen from the portion of the federal budget that is now allocated to welfare, an amount second only to the cost of national defense.

I do not welcome this shift of strategy. Socialism-through-Welfarism poses a far greater danger to freedom than Socialism-through-Nationalization precisely because it *is* more difficult to combat. The evils of Nationalization are self-evident and immediate. Those of Welfarism are veiled and tend to be postponed. People can understand the consequences of turning over ownership of the steel industry, say, to the State; and they can be counted on to oppose such a proposal. But let the government increase its contribution to the "Public Assistance" program and we will, at most, grumble about excessive government spending. The effect of Welfarism on freedom will be felt later on—after its beneficiaries have become its victims, after dependence on government has turned into bondage and it is too late to unlock the jail.

But a far more important factor is Welfarism's strong emotional appeal to many voters, and the consequent temptations it presents the average politician. It is hard, as we have seen, to make out a case for State ownership. It is very different with the rhetoric of humanitarianism. How easy it is to reach the voters with earnest importunities for helping the needy. And how difficult for Conservatives to resist these demands without appearing to be callous and contemptuous of the plight of less fortunate citizens. Here, perhaps, is the best illustration of the failure of the Conservative demonstration.

I know, for I have heard the questions often. Have you no sense of social obligation? the Liberals ask. Have you no concern for people who are out of work? for sick people who lack medical care? for children in overcrowded schools? Are you unmoved by the problems of the aged and disabled? Are you *against* human welfare?

The answer to all of these questions is, of course, no. But a simple "no" is not enough. I feel certain that Conservatism is through unless Conservatives can demonstrate and communicate the difference between being concerned with these problems and believing that the federal government is the proper agent for their solution.

The long range political consequences of Welfarism are plain enough: as we have seen, the State that is able to deal with its citizens as wards and dependents has gathered unto itself unlimited political and economic power and is thus able to rule as absolutely as any oriental despot.

Let us, however, weigh the consequences of Welfarism on the individual citizen.

Consider, first, the effect of Welfarism on the donors of government welfare—not only those who pay for it but also the voters and their elected representatives who decide that the benefits shall be conferred. Does some credit redound on them for trying to care for the needs of their fellow citizens? Are they to be commended and rewarded, at some moment in eternity, for their "charity?" I think not. Suppose I should vote for a measure providing for free medical care: I am unaware of any moral virtue that is attached to my decision to confiscate the earnings of X and give them to Y.

Suppose, however, that X approves of the program—that he has voted for welfarist politicians with the idea of helping his fellow man. Surely the wholesomeness of his act is diluted by the fact that he is voting not only to have his own money taken but also that of his fellow citizens who may have different ideas about their social obligations. Why does not such a man, instead, contribute what he regards as his just share of human welfare to a private charity?

Consider the consequences to the recipient of welfarism. For one thing, he mortgages himself to the federal government. In return for benefits—which, in the majority of cases, he pays for—he concedes to the government the ultimate in political power—the power to grant or withhold from him the necessities of life as the government sees fit. Even more important, however, is the effect on him—the elimination of any feeling of responsibility for his own welfare and that of his family and neighbors. A man may not immediately, or ever, comprehend the harm

thus done to his character. Indeed, this is one of the great evils of Welfarism—that it transforms the individual from a dignified, industrious, self-reliant *spiritual* being into a dependent animal creature without his knowing it. There is no avoiding this damage to character under the Welfare State. Welfare programs cannot help but promote the idea that the government *owes* the benefits it confers on the individual, and that the individual is entitled, by right, to receive them. Such programs are sold to the country precisely on the argument that government has an *obligation* to care for the needs of its citizens. Is it possible that the message will reach those who vote for the benefits, but not those who receive them? How different it is with private charity where both the giver and the receiver understand that charity is the product of the humanitarian impulses of the giver, not the due of the receiver.

Let us, then, not blunt the noble impulses of mankind by reducing charity to a mechanical operation of the federal government. Let us, by all means, encourage, those who are fortunate and able to care for the needs of those who are unfortunate and disabled. But let us do this in a way that is conducive to the spiritual as well as the material well-being of our citizens—and in a way that will preserve their freedom. Let welfare be a private concern. Let it be promoted by individuals and families, by churches, private hospitals, religious service organizations, community charities and other institutions that have been established for this purpose. If the objection is raised that private institutions lack sufficient funds, let us remember that every penny the federal government does *not* appropriate for welfare is potentially available for private use and without the overhead charge for processing the money through the federal bureaucracy. Indeed, high taxes, for which government Welfarism is so largely responsible, is the biggest obstacle to fund raising by private charities.

Finally, if we deem public intervention necessary, let the job be done by local and state authorities that are incapable of accumulating the vast political power that is so inimical to our liberties.

The Welfare State is *not* inevitable, as its proponents are so fond of telling us. There is nothing inherent in an industrialized economy, or in democratic processes of government that *must* produce de Tocqueville's "guardian society." Our future, like our past, will be what we make it. And we can shatter the collectivists' designs on individual freedom if we will impress upon the men who conduct our affairs this one truth: that the material and spiritual sides of man are intertwined; that it is impossible for the State to assume responsibility for one without intruding on the essential nature of the other; that if we take from a man the personal responsibility for caring for his material needs, we take from him also the will and the opportunity to be free.

Further Resources

BOOKS

Edwards, Lee. *Goldwater: The Man Who Made a Revolution.* Washington, D.C.: Regnery, 1995.

Goldberg, Robert Alan. *Barry Goldwater.* New Haven, Conn.: Yale University Press, 1995.

Perlstein, Rick. *Before the Storm: Barry Goldwater and the Unmaking of the American Consensus.* New York: Hill and Wang, 2001.

PERIODICALS

Castle, David S. "Goldwater's Presidential Candidacy and Political Realignment." *Presidential Studies Quarterly* 20, no. 1, Winter 1990, 103–110.

McCain, John. "Barry Goldwater, Patriot and Politician." *The Washington Post,* May 30, 1998, E1.

WEBSITES

"Goldwater's 1964 Acceptance Speech." The Washington Post Company. Available online at http://www.washingtonpost .com/wp-srv/politics/daily/may98/goldwaterspeech.htm; website home page: http://www.washingtonpost.com (accessed April 21, 2003).

AUDIO AND VISUAL MEDIA

Barry Goldwater: Photographs & Memories. Narrated by Hugh Downs. VHS, 1998. Bonneville Worldwide.

Dr. Martin Luther King, Jr.'s Address to the AFL-CIO Convention

Speech

By: Martin Luther King, Jr.

Date: December 11, 1961

Source: King, Martin Luther, Jr. Speech Delivered at the Fourth Constitutional Convention o\ =the AFL-CIO held in Miami Beach, Florida, December 7–13, 1961. Published in *Proceedings of the Fourth Constitutional Convention of the AFL-CIO, Vol. I: Daily Proceedings.* Washington, D.C.: American Federation of Labor and Congress of Industrial Organization, 1961, 283–288.

About the Author: The Reverend Dr. Martin Luther King, Jr. (1929–1968), scion of a prominent Atlanta, Georgia, African-American family, received his Ph.D. at Boston University. He then returned to his native South to serve as an

ordained minister. As a pastor of a Birmingham, Alabama, church, he became active in the campaign for civil rights. From 1960 until his assassination in Memphis, Tennessee, King was widely regarded as the country's most eloquent spokesperson for the movement. He was awarded the Noble Peace Prize in 1964. His birthday, commemorated in mid-January, is an American national holiday. ■

Introduction

For two centuries the American working class has been divided by race, ethnicity, and religion—and employers have repeatedly taken advantage of this situation. Indeed, this factor perhaps best explains why the labor union movement in the United States has been the weakest of any major industrial nation. Many unions have taken pains to label their organizations "brotherhoods"—not just as a catchy slogan, but to emphasize to the workers themselves that unless they remained strongly bonded, their union efforts will fall prey to the divisions inherent in such a diverse society as the United States.

Historically, perhaps nowhere else has this working class tension been so pronounced as that often exhibited between whites and African Americans. The scramble for scarce jobs often exacerbated the ever-present racial antagonism. Hungry African Americans, with little stake in the then-current socio-political arrangement, gladly accepted work as replacements for striking whites. Meanwhile, many whites, including desperate immigrants—themselves from impoverished backgrounds—clung tenaciously to their "whiteness" as their one perceived asset in the bitter struggle for existence.

Many labor leaders understood this dynamic and sought to neutralize its adverse impact. Union organizers knew that employers tended to split the ranks of labor by playing off one group against another. This was particularly true in the American South, where the strict color bar easily overshadowed any thoughts of union solidarity. Indeed, southern white workers firmly endorsed racial segregation and expected in return to be rewarded with jobs based on the privilege of being white.

Significance

It was therefore altogether fitting that the United States' best-known civil rights crusader, the Reverend Dr. Martin Luther King, Jr., should travel south to Miami Beach, Florida, in December 1961 to address the American Federation of Labor/Congress of Industrialization (AFL-CIO), the nation's premier twentieth century labor organization. Although praising organized labor for its longtime political support for the cause of racial equality, Dr. King gently chided his hosts for their failure to convince their rank-and-file members that African Americans should be seen as a firm ally in the campaign against the reactionary forces on the political right that were determined to cripple or destroy outright the union movement, and in the process economically hurt workers—white and African American alike—instead of viewing African Americans solely as competitors for jobs.

Indeed, the overall record of the American labor movement on the race issue was hardly progressive. Even the Democratic Party, which championed civil rights during the 1960s, had earlier in the pre-Civil War period featured an unholy coalition of Southern slaveholding plantation owners and Northern white workingmen, including impoverished Irish immigrants. The cynical planters reminded white workers that they, the slaveowners, were the workers' best friends, because, unlike the Northern abolitionists who advocated liberating African Americans, the plantation owners would make certain to keep African Americans in slavery and forever confined to the South. If emancipated, slaveowners warned, Southern African Americans would surely relocate North in search of work. Ironically enough, by 1961—the year of King's AFL-CIO speech and the one hundredth anniversary of the start of the Civil War, this demographic shift had actually come to pass: African Americans living outside the South were well on their way towards outnumbering those left behind.

As King had predicted, the reactionaries situated on the political right sought to alienate organized labor from fellow members of the Democratic Party—the African Americans. They were helped along by fiery Alabama governor George C. Wallace, who had theatrically stood in the schoolhouse door to prevent integration at the University of Alabama. True to form as an opportunistic demagogue, in the spring of 1964 Wallace entered several Democratic presidential primaries and managed to garner a substantial percentage of the white working class vote. For the next dozen years, the so-called "Wallace factor" played havoc with the Democrats. Jimmy Carter won the White House in 1976 by appealing to both to white workers and African Americans as a whole. But four years later the Republicans under Ronald Reagan made this white working class/African American rift a permanent feature of contemporary American politics. It appears in retrospect that Dr. King knew well of what he spoke.

Primary Source

Dr. Martin Luther King, Jr.'s Address to the AFL-CIO Convention [excerpt]

SYNOPSIS: Legendary civil rights leader Reverend Dr. Martin Luther King, Jr., addressed the December 1961 AFL-CIO Convention in an effort to persuade organized labor to take a greater interest in the African American struggle for equality. Dr. King noted that reactionary political enemies of labor, bent on

exacerbating racial tensions, have historically sought to drive a wedge between white workers and blacks, who instead should be allies in a progressive coalition.

Less than a century ago the laborer had no rights, little or no respect, and led a life which was socially submerged and barren.

He was hired and fired by economic despots whose power over him decreed his life or death. The children of workers had no childhood and no future. They, too, worked for pennies an hour and by the time they reached their teens they were worn-out old men, devoid of spirit, devoid of hope and devoid of self-respect. Jack London described a child worker in these words: "He did not walk like a man. He did not look like a man. He was a travesty of the human. It was a twisted and stunted and nameless piece of life that shambled like a sickly ape, arms loose-hanging, stoop-shouldered, narrow-chested, grotesque and terrible." American industry organized misery into sweat shops and proclaimed the right of capital to act without restraints and without conscience.

Victor Hugo, literary genius of that day, commented bitterly that there was always more misery in the lower classes than there was humanity in the upper classes. The inspiring answer to this intolerable and dehumanizing existence was economic organization through trade unions. The worker became determined not to wait for charitable impulses to grow in his employer. He constructed the means by which a fairer sharing of the fruits of his toil had to be given to him or the wheels of industry, which he alone turned, would halt and wealth for no one would be available.

This revolution within industry was fought mercilessly by those who blindly believed their right to uncontrolled profits was a law of the universe, and that without the maintenance of the old order catastrophe faced the nation. . . .

Labor's next monumental struggle emerged in the thirties when it wrote into federal law the right freely to organize and bargain collectively. It was now apparently emancipated. The days when workers were jailed for organizing, and when in the English Parliament Lord Macauley had to debate against a bill decreeing the death penalty for anyone engaging in a strike, were grim but almost forgotten memories. Yet, the Wagner Act, like any other legislation, tended merely to declare rights but did not deliver them. Labor had to bring the law to life by exercis-

To honor the memory of Dr. Martin Luther King, Jr. labor union members join civil rights activists in a march in Memphis in April 1969, a year after King's death. © **FLIP SCHULKE/CORBIS. REPRODUCED BY PERMISSION.**

ing its rights in practice over stubborn, tenacious opposition. It was warned to go slow, to be moderate, not to stir up strife. But labor knew it was always the right time to do right, and it spread its organization over the nation and achieved equality organizationally with capital. The day of economic democracy was born.

Negroes in the United States read this history of labor and find it mirrors their own experience. We are confronted by powerful forces telling us to rely on the good will and understanding of those who profit by exploiting us. They deplore our discontent, they resent our will to organize, so that we may guarantee that humanity will prevail and equality will be exacted. They are shocked that action organizations, sit-ins, civil disobedience, and protests are becoming our every day tools, just as strikes, demonstrations and union organization became yours to insure that bargaining power genuinely existed on both sides of the table. We want to rely upon the goodwill of those who oppose us. Indeed, we have brought forward the method of non-violence to give an example of unilateral goodwill in an effort to evoke it in those who have not yet felt it in their hearts. But we know that if we are not simultaneously organizing our strength

we will have no means to move forward. If we do not advance, the crushing burden of centuries of neglect and economic deprivation will destroy our will, our spirits and our hopes. In this way labor's historic tradition of moving forward to create vital people as consumers and citizens has become our own tradition, and for the same reasons.

This unity of purpose is not an historical coincidence. Negroes are almost entirely a working people. There are pitifully few Negro millionaires and few Negro employers. Our needs are identical with labor's needs, decent wages, fair working conditions, livable housing, old age security, health and welfare measures, conditions in which families can grow, have education for their children and respect in the community. That is why Negroes support labor's demands and fight laws which curb labor. That is why the labor-hater and labor-baiter is virtually always a twin headed creature spewing anti-Negro epithets from one mouth and anti-labor propaganda from the other mouth. . . .

Labor today faces a grave crisis, perhaps the most calamitous since it began its march from the shadows of want and insecurity. In the next ten to twenty years automation will grind jobs into dust as it grinds out unbelievable volumes of production. This period is made to order for those who would seek to drive labor into impotency by viciously attacking it at every point of weakness. Hard core unemployment is now an ugly and unavoidable fact of life. Like malignant cancer, it has grown year by year and continues its spread. But automation can be used to generate an abundance of wealth for people or an abundance of poverty for millions as its human-like machines turn out human scrap along with the machine scrap as a by-product of production. Our society, with its ability to perform miracles with machinery has the capacity to make some miracles for men—if it values men as highly as it values machines.

To find a great design to solve a grave problem labor will have to intervene in the political life of the nation to chart a course which distributes the abundance to all instead of concentrating it among a few. The strength to carry through such a program requires that labor know its friends and collaborate as a friend. If all that I have said is sound, labor has no firmer friend than the 20 million Negroes whose lives will be deeply affected by the new patterns of production. . . .

Labor, which made impatience for long-delayed justice for itself a vital motive force, cannot lack understanding of the Negro's impatience. It cannot speak with the reactionaries calm indifference, of progress around some obscure corner not yet possible even to see. There is a maxim in the law—justice too long delayed, is justice denied. When a Negro leader who has a reputation of purity and honesty which has benefited the whole labor movement criticizes it, his motives should not be reviled nor his earnestness rebuked. Instead, the possibility that he is revealing a weakness in the labor movement which it can ill afford, should receive a thoughtful examination. A man who had dedicated his long and faultless life to the labor movement cannot be raising questions harmful to it any more than a life-long devoted parent can become the enemy of his child. The report of a committee may smother with legal constructions a list of complaints and dispose of it for the day. But if it buries a far larger truth it has disposed of nothing and made justice more elusive. Discrimination does exist in the labor movement. It is true that organized labor has taken significant steps to remove the yoke of discrimination from its own body. But in spite of this, some unions, governed by the racist ethos, have contributed to the degraded economic status of the Ne-

gro. Negroes have been barred from membership in certain unions, and denied apprenticeship training and vocational education. In every section of the country one can find local unions existing as a serious and vicious obstacle when the Negro seeks jobs or upgrading in employment. Labor must honestly admit these shameful conditions, and design the battle plan which will defeat and eliminate them. In this way, labor would be unearthing the big truth and utilizing its strength against the bleakness of injustice in the spirit of its finest traditions.

How can labor rise to the heights of its potential statesmanship and cement its bonds with Negroes to their mutual advantage?

First: labor should accept the logic of its special position with respect to Negroes and the struggle for equality. Although organized labor has taken actions to eliminate discrimination in its ranks, the standard for the general community, your conduct should and can set an example for others, as you have done in other crusades for social justice. You should root out vigorously every manifestation of discrimination so that some internationals, central labor bodies or locals may not besmirch the positive accomplishments of labor. I am aware this is not easy nor popular—but the 8 hour day was not popular nor easy to achieve. Nor was outlawing anti-labor injunctions. But you accomplished all of these with a massive will and determination. Out of such struggle for democratic rights you won both economic gains and the respect of the country, and you will win both again if you make Negro rights a great crusade.

Second: The political strength you are going to need to prevent automation from becoming a moloch, consuming jobs and contract gains, can be multiplied if you tap the vast reservoir of Negro political power. Negroes given the vote, will vote liberal and labor because they need the same liberal legislation labor needs. . . .

If you would do these two things now in this convention—resolve to deal effectively with discrimination and provide financial aid for our struggle in the South,—this convention will have a glorious moral deed to add to an illustrious history.—

The two most dynamic and cohesive liberal forces in the country are the labor movement and the Negro freedom movement. Together we can be architects of democracy in a South now rapidly industrializing. Together we can re-tool the political structure of the South, sending to Congress steadfast liberals who, joining with those from Northern industrial states, will extend the frontiers of democracy for the whole nation. Together we can bring about the day when there will be no separate identification of Negroes and labor. There is no intrinsic difference as I have tried to demonstrate. Differences have been contrived by outsiders who seek to impose disunity by dividing brothers because the color of their skin has a different shade. I look forward confidently to the day when all who work for a living will be one with no thought to their separateness as Negroes, Jews, Italians or any other distinctions. . . .

There is a little song that we sing in the movement taking place in the South. It goes something like this. "We shall overcome. We shall overcome. Deep in my heart I do believe we shall overcome." And somehow all over America we must believe that we shall overcome and that these problems can be solved. They will be solved before the victory is won.

Further Resources

BOOKS

Nelson, Bruce. *Divided We Stand: American Workers and the Struggle for Black Equality.* Princeton, N.J.: Princeton University Press, 2001.

Branch, Taylor. *Parting the Waters: America in the King Years, 1954–63.* New York: Simon & Schuster, 1988.

WEBSITES

"Martin Luther King Jr. Tribute." *Life Magazine.* Available online at http://www.life.com/Life/mlk/mlk.html; website home page: http://www.life.com/Life/ (accessed April 18, 2003).

Sylvester, Melvin. "A Tribute to Dr. Martin Luther King, Jr." Available online at http://www.liu.edu/cwis/cwp/library/mlking.htm; website home page: http://www.liu.edu/liu_start.html (accessed April 18, 2003).

"A New World for Working Women"

Journal article

By: William F. Schnitzler

Date: August 1963

Source: Schnitzler, William F. "A New World For Working Women." *American Federationist* 70, No. 1, August 1963, 18–22.

About the Author: William F. Schnitzler, the Secretary-Treasurer of the AFL-CIO in the early 1960s, had long been interested in the concerns of women in the workforce. Schnitzler served on President John F. Kennedy's (served 1961–1963) landmark Commission on the Status of Women,

which, by exploring many concerns of working women—in particular, the question of "equal pay for equal work"—helped launch the next wave of the feminist movement. ■

Introduction

American women, curiously enough, have had to liberate themselves twice during the twentieth century. On the initial occasion, a time that coincided roughly with the Progressive era, women entered the professions, attended colleges and universities in record numbers and, at long last, obtained the right to vote in 1920. By all accounts, the American woman should have been launched on a path that would have ultimately led to eventual economic and social equality with men.

Then the Great Depression struck the country in 1929. With astronomically high unemployment—in some instances approaching thirty percent—men, as the usual head of households, were given preference for scarce jobs. It seemed unfair for some families to have a pair of breadwinners while others had none. Meanwhile, diminished career opportunities had an impact on women's college and university enrollment. Despite the temporary return of women briefly into the workforce during World War II (1939–1945)—recall Rosie the Riveter—the role of women in the workplace lessened.

The unprecedented economic prosperity enjoyed during the period of 1945–1960, coupled with the "baby boom" and the resulting preoccupation with marriage and motherhood, further served to stifle feminist progress. This state of affairs was, in fact, well chronicled by author Betty Friedan in her consciousness-raising book, *The Feminist Mystique* (1963). Thus there appears to have been much simmering discontent behind the myth of the contented 1950s suburban "happy homemaker."

Significance

Prospects for the complete liberation of American women brightened considerably after 1960 as a new generation of college and university-educated women began entering the workforce en masse. Behind this employment surge lay certain long-range societal trends. The temporarily high birthrates that had characterized the post-World War II "baby boom" diminished somewhat after 1960, in part due to the introduction of the birth control pill. Also, an expanding economy (and an enhanced role for government) created millions of new positions devoted to what became known as "people processing," such as teaching, child care, social work, and health care—fields that had always been predisposed toward female employment. In addition, the gradual rise in the cost of living that began after 1960 forced many otherwise satisfied housewives into the workforce in order to supplement their family income.

The political climate turned sharply liberal with the election of Democrat John F. Kennedy (served 1961–1963) to the White House in November 1960. In fact, Kennedy unwittingly gave feminists a huge boost when he appointed his landmark Commission on the Status of Women. Kennedy, himself seemingly indifferent to the issue, bent to mild political pressure for a token investigation. But the commission in 1963 issued a groundbreaking report that endorsed the concept of "equal pay for equal work"—in hindsight, a significant step. The equal pay issue impacted the women already in the workforce who, in the years ahead, would become the driving force behind the women's liberation movement that surfaced by the end of the decade.

Primary Source

"A New World For Working Women" [excerpt]

SYNOPSIS: Although hardly appreciated at the time, the year 1963 saw the launching of a new phase of the ongoing twentieth century feminist movement—the quest for economic and social equality. The year 1963 is justly remembered, of course, for the publication of Betty Friedan's call-to-arms, *The Feminist Mystique.* But another 1963 event, the Report by President Kennedy's Commission on the Status of Women, helped publicize the concept of "equal pay for equal work." In the following selection national union leader William Schnitzler, himself a member of that commission, discusses various issues facing the United States' working women.

Beneath the issues relating to the status of women is an undercurrent of a rather rigid and constrictionist set of notions about "the role of women"—sometimes sweepingly summed up in the phrase, "woman's place is in the home."

Unfortunately, this phrase and many of the ideas associated with it often constitute simply an excuse for not facing up to the aspirations, wishes and problems of more than half the human race. Sometimes it is an excuse for the most callous types of discrimination and injustice and for the most regrettable waste of individual talents and abilities.

It can be used as an excuse for not paying women full wages when they work; for discriminating against them in opportunities for jobs and for advancement; for discouraging high educational attainment; and for limiting occupational choices. The establishment of child care facilities for the children of working mothers can be neglected or even opposed on the ground that they merely make it easy for women to abandon home responsibilities.

Certainly the actual truth is that women have two roles—one inside the home and the other outside it. And the problem for most women is that of making a satisfactory combination of the two rather than being asked to decide, once and for all, on one or the other. Recognition of this fact is implicit in the Executive Order which established the President's Commission on the Status of Women. The Commission was charged with the responsibility for "developing recommendations for overcoming discrimination in government and private employment on the basis of sex and for developing recommendations for services which will enable women to continue their role as wives and mothers while making a maximum contribution to the world around them."

One of the most startling statistics of twentieth century America has been the extraordinary increase in the number of women who work in paid employment.

In the year 1890, for example, about 4 million women were "gainfully employed," most of them in domestic service or in "home manufactures" for which outside employers paid them directly. They made up only 17 percent of the female population aged 10 and over.

In the year 1962, an average of 24.5 million women were in the labor force and they made up 37 percent of women aged 14 and over. Industrial homework had virtually disappeared and domestic service in private homes was no longer the principal occupation of working women. The largest set of occupations for women today is in clerical work.

Women in 1890 made up only about one-sixth of the workforce. Today they account for one-third.

Perhaps even more striking than the simple increase in numbers of women at work have been two other facts: (1) the increase in the number of older women at work and (2) the number of married women at work. The change has been particularly rapid since 1940. Women over 35 now account for 58 percent of all women at work and married women for 56 percent of the female workforce. (Almost 70 percent of married women at work are past the age of 35.)

What these statistics mean is that over the past 70 years a vastly changed way of life has been evolving for women—a fact probably not yet widely and consciously appreciated or taken into account. It means that women generally can no longer take it for granted that they will work just a few years before getting married and then settle down for a singleminded, lifelong career of homemaking. And it is

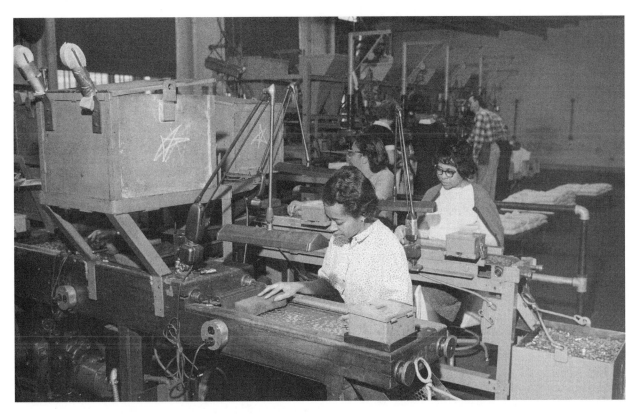

Female employees make coins at the Philadelphia mint. © BETTMANN/CORBIS. REPRODUCED BY PERMISSION.

no longer a reasonable assumption that the only event that will return them to the labor force is the death of the husband or separation from him.

The facts suggest a much different kind of picture: women will work a few years before marriage, leave employment during the period when their children are young—and then come back to work. By no means will all women follow this pattern but a great many of them will. If they do not return to the labor force, there is every likelihood they will undertake unpaid, volunteer civic activity outside the home. . . .

Furthermore the earnings of married women have become an essential part of the family budget for millions of families, making the difference between whether the family can barely make ends meet or whether it can live at a level approximating a decent standard of living. . . .

There is simply no way to turn the clock back, even if it were desirable. The work of women has become essential to the operation of the economy, to the maintenance of consumer purchasing power and to the economic stability of millions of families. This is not the most desirable solution in all circumstances. In many instances, it means that a woman must to go work whether she wants to or

not, under pressure of family economic needs and regardless of equally pressing demands in the home, involving the care of young children. Ideally, wage and employment levels should be maintained at high enough standards to afford the family a genuine choice with respect to a wife's work. . . .

At the same time, it is also true that paid employment is a source of satisfaction for many women. It would be naive to suppose that all women prefer to stay at home whenever they can and that they never go to work except under the most severe economic pressure. For many women, especially after the children are no longer extremely young or have left home altogether, useful outside employment provides a needed source of activity and interest and makes use of skills and talents not generally called for within the four walls of the home.

Yet no one will deny that the revolutionary shift of women into paid employment over the past 60 years has brought its problems and heartbreaks as well. It has called for many adjustments in the workplace to accommodate women and it has called for many adjustments by women to carry their dual responsibilities to a home and to a job or other outside activity with the least possible disruption to either. And despite the economic pressures and demands that have taken women into the workplace, they have not always found themselves welcome: often they have suffered from discriminatory practices in much the same way as other "minority" groups.

One ancient discrimination suffered a body blow on June 10, 1963, when President Kennedy signed into law the new Federal Equal Pay Act, forbidding employers in interstate commerce from discriminating in pay rates on the basis of sex. This law says that when men and women do equal work, they are to receive equal pay. . . .

Many women simply are not properly prepared for future jobs to begin with, because it is widely assumed that women will not, or should not, need to work in their adult lives. Although as many girls as boys graduate from high school—more, in fact—a far smaller proportion goes on to college. This is an obvious waste of available brainpower. The individual loses the satisfaction of using it—and also an ultimate contribution to society at large is lost. Of those who do to go college and into graduate work, a very large proportion prepare themselves for or are steered into the traditional "women's fields" of teaching and social work. . . .

Sometimes women's opportunities are very openly limited by designated lists of "women's jobs"—carrying lower pay rates than those open to men. Even when no such formal lists are in evidence, job segregation nonetheless may be enforced as a practical matter, with women simply not being accepted or considered eligible for various types of work. It just may not be "customary" to promote a woman to a supervisory position, for example.

Further Resources

BOOKS

Blackwelder, Julia Kirk. *Now Hiring: The Feminization of Work in the United States, 1900–1995.* College Station: Texas A&M University Press, 1997.

Hart, Vivien. *Bound by Our Constitution: Women, Workers, and the Minimum Wage.* Princeton, N.J.: Princeton University Press, 1994.

Kessler-Harris, Alice. *A Woman's Wage: Historical Meanings and Social Consequences.* Lexington: University Press of Kentucky, 1990.

PERIODICALS

Kerber, Linda K. "'I Was Appalled': The Invisible Antecedents of Second-Wave Feminism." *Journal of Women's History* 14, no. 2, Summer 2002, 90–102.

WEBSITES

"International Archives of the Second Wave of Feminism." Academic Indexing Service. Available online at http://home.att.net/~celesten/2ndwave.html; website home page: http://home.att.net/~celesten/ais.html (accessed April 18, 2003).

AUDIO AND VISUAL MEDIA

Step-By-Step: Building a Feminist Movement: 1941–1977. Directed by Joyce Follet. VHS, 1998.

"The Black Revolution: Letters to a White Liberal"

Journal article

By: Thomas Merton

Date: December 1963

Source: Thomas Merton, "The Black Revolution: Letters to a White Liberal," *Ramparts* 2, no. 3, Christmas 1963, 7, 8, 10, 11, 17.

About the Author: Thomas Merton (1915–1968), born in France, had no particular religious instruction and lived a rambunctious early life, but converted to Catholicism at the age of twenty-three. He spent twenty-seven years at the Abbey of Our Lady of Gethsemani in Kentucky, as a Trappist monk, and became an extraordinary essayist, theologian, poet, and social activist. Merton was a leading activist against the Vietnam War (1964–1975). His writings (more than 70 books) blended insightful contemporary political analysis with classical philosophical themes. ∎

Introduction

The civil rights movement of the early 1960s raised hopes that the United States might finally come to grips with its terrible racial history and extend equality and a measure of social justice to the nation's long suffering African American community. Indeed, the eloquent words of the Reverend Dr. Martin Luther King, Jr., speaking as he did of a color blind United States, made it appear that the whole ugly legacy could be resolved in amicable fashion. The landmark Civil Rights Bill of 1964 and the Voting Rights Act of 1965 appeared to cement what were almost, in some circles, utopian dreams.

But, regrettably, a darker side to the nation's race crisis lurked just below the surface. Stretching back to Thomas Jefferson, many prominent Americans speculated about the country's future racial dynamics. In his Notes on the State of Virginia, Jefferson warned that the African American slaves, if ever emancipated, would be animated, not by the spirit of forgiveness, but of retaliation. At best, he suggested a strict separation of the races after the abolition of slavery—should it occur. Jefferson suggested the forced removal of African Americans to some destination outside the country. In the 1780s Jefferson envisioned a semi-autonomous African American republic, populated with ex-American slaves, being founded along United States side of the Gulf of Mexico. By 1816 the focus of Jefferson's attention had shifted to sending the freed American African Americans back to Africa.

Significance

With this background in mind, a few perceptive observers felt that the harmonious prospects for African American liberation in the 1960s was oversold and instead anticipated great troubles. Of course, unreconstructed racists and segregationists, many from the deep southern states, strenuously opposed integration. But an occasional white liberal also acknowledged potential problems.

Thomas Merton was one of those white liberals who warned that integration would entail enormous difficulties. Merton recognized that not all African Americans were inspired by Dr. King's vision nor thrilled by his rhetoric. Merton had in mind the growing contingent of African American nationalists who, by 1963, were beginning to receive notice in the national press and who favored a radically different agenda.

A real sticking point, in Merton's estimation, concerned economics. For even normally well-intentioned liberals were hardly willing to give way in the face of militant African American demands if they entailed any significant inconvenience (especially financial) to themselves. The costs of integration, northern liberals intuitively understood, would be born by others, most notably poor whites in the South and white workers in the North—two groups who had known even back in pre-Civil War days that any slave emancipation, should it happen, would, of necessity, be at their expense. Indeed the economic issues at the heart of the civil rights crisis were well nigh impossible to reconcile.

The Civil Rights Act of 1964 deliberately rejected racial quotas or minority preferences. The explicit stipulation that no reverse discrimination as an instant remedy to redress centuries of oppression would be tolerated represented a key ingredient in the final passage of the measure. (Affirmative action, quotas, and minority preference came about later as the result of administrative decrees, bureaucratic mandate, or court rulings, and not the result of legislative action.) The bill would surely never had been enacted had the white community been informed of plans for reverse racism. But this was exactly what many African Americans had come to expect. And as Merton had predicted back in 1963, this tension born of disparate goals, many of them economic, guaranteed that the African American struggle for equality would be a long, hard road.

Primary Source

"The Black Revolution: Letters to a White Liberal" [excerpt]

SYNOPSIS: Thomas Merton, noted political activist and social critic, reminds readers that the Civil Rights revolution, then shifting into high gear, may not accommodate the needs and expectations of the white community, which, in actuality, has little or no comprehension of the deeper social and economic issues involved in the quest to secure African American liberation.

[T]he inner conflicts and contradictions of the South are not to be taken as a justification for the smugness with which the North is doing just as poor a job, if not a worse job, of defending the Negro's rights as a person. The race "problem" is something which the southerner cannot escape. Almost half the population of the South are Negroes. Though there are greater concentrations of Negroes in northern slums, yet northern Negroes can be treated as if they were not there at all. For years, New Yorkers have been able to drive to Westchester and Connecticut without going through Harlem, or even seeing it, except from a distant freeway. The abuses thus tolerated and ignored are sometimes as bad and worse than anything in the South.

It is clear that our actual decisions and choices, with regard to the Negro, show us that we are not in fact interested in the rights of several million persons, who are members and citizens of our society and are in every way loyal Americans. They pay taxes, fight for the country and do as well as anybody else in meeting their responsibilities. And yet we tolerate shameful injustices which deprive them, by threats and by actual violence, of their right to vote and to participate actively in the affairs of the nation.

Here I can see you will protest. You will point to the Supreme Court decisions that have upheld Negro rights, to education in integrated colleges and schools. It seems to me that our motives are judged by the real fruit of our decisions. What have we done? We have been willing to grant the Negro rights on paper, even in the South. But the laws have been framed in such a way that in every case their execution has depended on the good will of white society, and the white man has *never failed,* when left to himself, to block or obstruct or simply forget the necessary action without which the rights of the Negro cannot be enjoyed in fact. Hence, when laws have been passed and then contested, and then dragged through all the courts, and then finally upheld, the Negro is still in no position to benefit by them without, in each case, entering into further interminable lawsuits every time he wants to exercise a right that is guaranteed to him by law.

In effect, we are not really giving the Negro a right to live where he likes, eat where he likes, go

Protestors picket outside an Atlanta restaurant whose owner's firm stance against serving black patrons is stated in the window. THE LIBRARY OF CONGRESS.

to school where he likes, or work where he likes, but only *to sue the white man who refuses to let him do these things.* If every time I want a Coca Cola I have to sue the owner of the snack bar, I think I will probably keep going to the same old places in my ghetto. That is what the Negro, until recently has done. Such laws are without meaning unless they reflect a willingness on the part of white society to implement them. . . .

I think there is possibly some truth in the accusation that we are making laws simply because they look nice on the books. Having them there, we can enjoy the comfort of pointing to them, reassuring our own consciences, convincing ourselves that we are all that we claim to be, and refuting the vicious allegations of hostile critics who question the sincerity of our devotion to freedom.

But at the same time, when our own personal interests and preferences are concerned, we have no

intention of respecting the Negro's rights in the concrete. North or South, integration is always going to be not on our street but "somewhere else." That perhaps accounts for the extraordinary zeal with which the North insists upon integration in the South, while treating the northern Negro as if he were invisible, flatly refusing to let him take shape in full view, lest he demand the treatment due to a human person and a free citizen of this nation. That is why the Negro now insists on making himself just as obviously visible as he possibly can. That is why he demonstrates. He has come to realize that the white man is not interested in the rights of the Negro, but in the white man's own spiritual and material comfort.

. . . [W]e have little genuine interest in human liberty and in the human person. What we are interested in, on the contrary, is the unlimited freedom of the corporation. When we call ourselves the "free world," we mean first of all the world in which *business* is free. And the freedom of the person comes only after that, because, in our eyes, the freedom of the person is dependent on money. That is to say, without money, freedom has no meaning. And therefore the most basic freedom of all is the freedom to make money. If you have nothing to buy or sell, freedom is, in your case, irrelevant. In other words, what we are really interested in is not *persons,* but *profits.* Our society is organized first and foremost with a view to business, and wherever we run into a choice between the rights of a human person and the advantages of a profit-making organization, the rights of the person will have difficulty in getting a hearing. Profit first, people afterward.

You ask me, indignantly, to confirm these vicious allegations?

It appears that one aspect of the Negro demonstrations that is being taken most seriously in the South is that *they hurt business.* As long as there was talk only of "rights," and of "freedom" (concepts which imply *persons*), the Negro movement was taken seriously chiefly by crackpots, idealists, and members of suspicious organizations thought to be under direct control of Moscow, like the NAACP. But still, all this talk of Negro rights, especially when accompanied by hymn-singing and religious exhortations, could hardly be taken seriously.

It was only when money became involved, that the Negro demonstrations finally impressed themselves upon the American mind as being real.

We claim to judge reality by the touchstone of Christian values, such as freedom, thought, the spirit, faith, personalism, etc. In actual fact we judge them by commercial values: sales, money, price, profits. It is not the life of the spirit that is real to us, but the vitality of the *market.* Spiritual values are to us, in actual fact, meaningless unless they can be reduced to terms of buying and selling. But buying and selling are abstract operations. Money has no ontological reality: it is a pure convention. Admittedly it is a very practical one. But it is in itself completely unreal, and the ritual that surrounds money transactions, the whole liturgy of marketing and profit, is basically void of reality and of meaning. Yet we treat it as the final reality, the absolute meaning, in the light of which everything else is to be judged, weighed, evaluated, "priced."

Thus we end up by treating persons as objects for sale, and therefore as meaningless unless they have some value on the market. A man is to us nothing more or less than "what he is worth." He is

"known" to us as a reality when he is known to be solvent by bankers. Otherwise he has not yet begun to exist.

Our trouble is that we are alienated from our own personal reality, our true self. We do not believe in anything but money and the power or the enjoyment which come from the possession of money. We do not believe in ourselves, except in so far as we can estimate our own worth, and verify, by our operations in the world of the market, that our subjective price coincides with what society is willing to pay for us.

And the Negro? He has so far been worth little or nothing.

Until quite recently there was no place for him in our calculations, unless perhaps we were landlords—unless we had *real* estate—in Harlem. That of course was another matter, because the Negro was really quite profitable to us. And yet we did not think of profit as coming to us from the beings of flesh and blood who were crowded into those rooms. On the contrary, it came to us from the only thing that was *real*—our estate. The Negro was so shadowy, so unreal, that he was nothing more than the occasion for a series of very profitable transactions which gave us a good solid reality in our own eyes and in the eyes of our society.

But now, suddenly, we have discovered that there are some real Negroes. For them to be real, they must have the same kind of reality as ourselves. Reality is estimated in terms of (financial) worth. And so we discover that there are a few Negroes who have money.

Why has this rich Negro suddenly earned the grace of our benevolent attention? Because he is a person, because he has brains, because of the fantastic talents which alone could enable him to be a professional success against such inhuman odds? None of this. It is now to our interest to recognize him, because we can use him against the others. So now, when the Negro claims he wants to take his full part in American society as a *person,* we retort: you already are playing your part as a person: "Negroes over the years," we now declare, "*have had a rapid rise in income*" (a nice vague statement, but it satisfies the mind of anyone who believes in money); "*Large numbers of Negroes drive high-priced cars.*" Another beautiful act of faith! But here we come with "exact figures":

"It is estimated that there are now thirty-five Negro millionaires in the United States."

What are these statements supposed to mean? Simply that there is no need for the Negro to make such a fuss, to demonstrate, to fight for recognition as a person. He has *received that recognition already.* "Thirty-five Negroes are millionaires." (Thirty-five out of Twenty Million!) "Large numbers" drive "high-priced cars." What more do you want? These are indications that the Negro has all he needs, for he has "opportunities," he can make money and thus become real.

What opportunities?

Even though a Negro millionaire may live in a "fine residential neighborhood" he is still living in a ghetto, when he moves in, the whites move out. The neighborhood is taken over by Negroes, and even if they are millionaires, their presence means that a neighborhood is no longer "fine." For a white man it is no longer even "residential."

So that even when he is worth a million, a Negro cannot buy himself, in the land of the free, the respect that is given to a human person. . . .

Much as it might distress southerners, the fact that a Negro may now sit down next to a white woman at a snack bar and order a sandwich is still somewhat short of revolution. . . .

We must admit that the southern politicians are much more fully aware of the revolutionary nature of the situation than are those northern liberals who blithely suppose that somehow the Negroes (both north and south) will gradually and noiselessly "fit in" to white society exactly as it is, with its affluent economy, the mass media, its political machines, its professional thoughtlessness and its middle class suburban folkways. . . .

So much for the South. But what about the North? Northern Negroes are already able to put some of their own men into office: but this is only the beginning of what is suddenly becoming a very conscious and concerted drive for real political power. This drive is going to be more and more accelerated by the problem of jobs. With five million unemployed officially acknowledged in 1963, with no indications other than that this figure *must grow,* and with repeated strikes and protests in which Negroes demand to be hired along with whites, there is going to be violent conflict over the limited number of jobs. With the best will in the world, nobody is going to be able to give jobs to Negroes without taking them away from whites, and there is no indication, at the moment, that the whites intend to retire *en masse* and spend the rest of their lives watching TV so that the Negroes may carry on the work, and collect the paychecks, of the nation.

This represents, whether we like it or not, a radical threat to our present system—a revolutionary situation. And furthermore it accentuates the already clearly defined lines dividing the two sides in the conflict. This means that the Negro is going to continue to be what he has decidedly become: aggressively aware of the power and impact on white society of mere *threat* of revolutionary violence. . . .

This is the radical challenge of Negro nonviolence today. This is why it is a source of uneasiness and fear to all white men who are attached to their security. If they are forced to listen to what the Negro is trying to say, the whites may have to admit that *their prosperity is rooted to some extent in injustice and in sin.* And, in consequence, this might lead to a complete re-examination of the political motives behind all our current policies, domestic and foreign, with the possible admission that we are wrong. Such an admission might, in fact, be so disastrous that its effects would dislocate our whole economy and ruin the country. These are not things that are consciously admitted, but they are confusedly present in our thoughts and fears. They account for the passionate and mindless desperation with which we plunge this way and that, trying to evade the implications of our present crisis.

Further Resources

BOOKS

Baldwin, James. *The Fire Next Time.* New York: Dial Press, 1963.

Lubell, Samuel: *White and Black: Test of a Nation.* New York: Harper & Row, 1964.

PERIODICALS

Alexis, Marcus. "The Economics of Racism." *The Review of Black Political Economy* 26, no. 3, Winter 1999, 51–76.

Novoa, Jose. "At Times, the Problem is Economics, Not Racism." *Los Angeles Times,* September 28, 1997, M2.

WEBSITES

"Martin Luther King, Jr.'s Leadership of the American Civil Rights Movement, 1955–1968. Martin Luther King Jr. National Historic Site. Available online at http://www.nps.gov/malu/hrs/HRS2.HTM; website home page: http://www.nps.gov/malu/ (accessed April 22, 2003).

"The Manpower Revolution"

Journal article

By: George G. Kirstein

Date: February 10, 1964

Source: Kirstein, George G. "The Manpower Revolution." *The Nation* 198, no. 7, February 10, 1964, 140–142.

About the Author: George G. Kirstein (1909–1986) was a well known writer on various facets of business and the economy. He specialized in labor issues and in 1968 published his best known book, *The Rich; Are They Different?*, that restates novelist F. Scott Fitzgerald's immortal question about the relationship of people of great wealth to the rest of society. He was also publisher and editor of *The Nation,* a venerable left-leaning periodical established in 1865 that covers current affairs. ∎

Introduction

Although turn-of-the-century science fiction had speculated on the prospect of machines replacing human beings in virtually all facets of daily life, the fantasy appeared to be reality by the 1960s. Indeed, a great movie of 1968, Stanley Kubrick's *2001: A Space Odyssey,* featured thinking computers that dared to challenge man for supremacy.

Of course, the Industrial Revolution had long featured machines replacing men at various tasks. And when back-breaking labor was eliminated, the movement was seen as liberating. The wave of automation that swept the United States after 1960, however, was not so favorably viewed. Robots on the assembly line and computers in the office threatened to wipe out whole categories of well-paying jobs. Indeed, dramatic cost savings was a primary reason for the introduction of labor-saving devices into any given industry. Positions ranging from automobile assembly line welders to typesetters to lowly office file clerks found themselves eventually automated out of careers.

Significance

One would have expected greater political and social opposition to rampant automation. After all, even the early Industrial Revolution had produced the anti-technology Luddites. But the impact of automation was blunted because job-eliminating innovations did not come all at once. For example, many low level blue collar assembly jobs were lost in the 1970s as robots became more sophisticated. Then the next wave of automation transformed offices during the 1980s.

Is contemporary American society as a whole better off when, in the name of efficiency, so many jobs (many of them well paying) are eliminated in the name of technological progress? This controversy was drama-tized regarding the automobile industry in the 1970s in an exchange between Lee Iacocca, then president of Chrysler Motors, and Douglas Fraser, president of the United Auto Workers Union (UAW). The two men could be described as friendly enemies, for although personally amicable, they nonetheless often engaged in hard bargaining—especially during contract negotiations. Jointly viewing a demonstration of the latest cost saving, automobile assembly line, robotic technology that threatened to displace auto workers, Iacocca turned to Fraser and teased his rival about the large number of union positions that could be eliminated. Fraser shot back: "But, Lee, then who will have the money to buy your cars?" In essence, every discussion involving the impact of automation ultimately boils down to this fundamental question.

Primary Source

"The Manpower Revolution," [excerpt]

SYNOPSIS: Labor union authority and author George G. Kirstein explores some of the implications of the automation revolution that swept through the United States during the early 1960s and has continued right down to the early 2000s. Starting with blue collar workers, the relentless replacement of men and women by cost saving machines eventually struck the white collar sector as well as the professional class.

Few major problems in our nation's history have been more easily predictable, or more universally predicted, than the unemployment crisis which lies just ahead of us. Despite this, the unemployment rate may have to rise to 10 per cent of the work force or higher before we decide to make a national issue out of the national problem resulting from the simultaneous impacts on our society of cybernation and the population growth. It is human nature to postpone the facing of tomorrow's problems until tomorrow dawns, but it is midnight now as far as our unemployment problems are concerned. That the rate will rise to 10 per cent, or to 15 per cent or even 20 per cent is conceded by experts who extrapolate from present trends. There is agreement on the danger of the events that face us, but no consensus on what should be done to avoid a repetition of the peak joblessness of the thirties. George Meany says of automation, "There is no element of blessing in it. It is rapidly becoming a real curse to society." Other spokesmen of labor, pointing to the ever-dwindling number of workers required to produce for America's needs, forecast a gloomy future. But like other problems that man creates for himself, there are alternative courses of action which, if debated and tested, could not only avert calamity, but even hold promise of a future richer than any era we have experienced.

The facts are known, and the forecasts of the experts are available in convenient form to anyone who is willing to take the few hours necessary to read them. A Senate subcommittee, chaired by Joseph Clark of Pennsylvania, held extensive hearings throughout 1963 on every aspect of our current manpower and our future prospects. . . . [B]ecause there was little controversy or conflicting evidence regarding the dangers that lie just ahead, some major aspects of the problem can be set forth rather briefly.

First automation, or the more precise word cybernation, is defined as the combination of a computer which does man's planning and a machine which performs the work man wishes to have done. It is a combination that will make much of man's present labor unnecessary and irrelevant. One must keep in mind that any task or series of tasks that can be defined by man can be performed by the computer and the machine working in harmony. No matter how complex the various steps required to produce a finished product, if men can describe those steps exactly, computers can be programmed to give the appropriate signals to machines which will perform the tasks precisely as desired, and with far less chance of error than if they were performed by human hands. Probably it will never be worth while to cybernate such jobs as cutting grass, making beds, etc. However, any repetitive task which can be described, no matter how complex the description, lends itself to cybernation.

All of us are aware of examples of displaced manpower of the type Walter Reuther cited to the committee: the engine block of a Ford car. For the old Model T, with thousands of men on the assembly line, it took three weeks to machine an engine block. In the Ford plant that was automated in 1950, each of the much more complex engine blocks can be completed without human participation in 14.6 minutes. And the problem is highlighted when one realizes that this plant's automated equipment is today completely obsolete.

But since I was familiar with this well-publicized kind of miracle, I was more interested in what one witness described as a typical shopping incident of the future. The housewife wheels her purchases to the supermarket packing counter as she does now. The cashier totals her purchases, presses a lever, and her account at any nearby bank is debited for the total. No bills, no checks, no charge accounts, no mailing, no postal delivery, no envelopes—just a finger movement by the clerk. The point is that we are only at the beginning of the development. Present obsolete computers in auto and steel manufacturing work on a cycle of 3/10 of a millionth of a second—that is every 3/10 of a millionth of a second the electronic brain can give a new instruction to the machine. The computers now on the drawing boards have a cycle 1,000 times faster—3/10 of a billionth of a second. . . .

Translating the kindred process of the cybernetic revolution into terms of the jobs required in the future to reduce the unemployment rate to 4 per cent and then hold it there, the experts come up with the following figures. By mid-1964 (only six months from now) we shall require 5.2 million additional jobs—1.2 million to reduce unemployment from the current rate to 4 per cent; 1.2 million to employ the projected normal annual increase in the labor force; 800,000 to employ the added workers who would be drawn back into the labor force if opportunities were available, and 2 million to absorb the workers released from their present employment by technological advances. According to the usually reliable research staff of the United Auto Workers, in the ten years of the 1960s we shall need 41 million new jobs, or 80,000 new jobs every week. Of this 80,000, 25,000 jobs are required to employ new people entering the labor force and 45,000 to give employment to those displaced by technological advances. To give some idea of the scope of this challenge, in the fifteen years between 1947 and 1962, 10 million persons were added to employment rolls, but during the same period the labor force grew by 13 million. The problem before us in terms of the 1947–62 experience is to quadruple the new job opportunities in two-thirds of the time. Small wonder that one commentator can write, "Full employment has to be discarded as a national goal."

As these figures show, more than half of the coming unemployment problem will be caused by the expanding numbers of young men and women looking for their first jobs. For example, last year 1 million more people passed their sixteenth birthdays than did so in 1962. As a result of this invasion of the labor market by increasing legions of inexperienced youngsters, the unemployment rate among the sixteen-to-twenty-one-year age group is more than 13 per cent, compared to the 5.8 rate for the country as a whole. Only one out of every fourteen in our present labor force is in the sixteen-to-twenty-

An engineer stands next to a Mobot, manufactured by the Hughes Aircraft Company to use in areas of work that are too hazardous for humans. © HULTON-DEUTSCH COLLECTION/CORBIS. REPRODUCED BY PERMISSION.

one-age group, but this group accounts for almost one out of every five of the unemployed.

It is not only lack of previous job experience that makes these young folks less desirable as employees; in too many cases it is lack of education as well. Of the 26 million young people entering the labor force, 7.5 million, or fully 29 per cent, will have left school before graduating, and of these, 2.5 million will have dropped out before completing the eighth grade. Indeed, there are at present 23 million Americans eighteen years of age and older who have completed less than eight years of schooling. The relevance of these figures to job opportunities was disclosed by a 1961 study which showed a 9 per cent unemployment rate for those who did not complete high school. In contrast, the unemployment rate for high school graduates was below 4 per cent and for those with some college training it was around 2 per cent. Income figures, of course, parallel job opportunities. The median income range

for those with less than eight years' schooling is $2,275; $5,550 for high school graduates; $7,700 for college graduates.

Of all the groups in the communities whose future job opportunities are blighted by lack of education, the Negro and other non-white citizens are particularly affected. First we handicap the Negro by providing poorer schools; then by discriminatory hiring practices we deny him an opportunity to use even those skills he does manage to develop. The result in terms of unemployment statistics is evidence of how adversely the system works. In an overall unemployment rate of approximately 6 per cent, the non-white rate is between 12 and 13 per cent. In short, the Negro rate of unemployment is twice the national average and has been for years. Negroes comprise 11 per cent of the labor force but they make up 22 percent of the unemployed.

Before turning to the various solutions that have been suggested for these problems, it is worth asking what is a generally acceptable employment rate. President Johnson, like President Kennedy, seems to feel that if we could reduce unemployment to 4 per cent, we should be doing as well as could be hoped. In Scandinavia and in other European countries which are today experiencing full employment about one-half of 1 per cent of the population, from one handicap or another, is unemployable. Our own unemployment ratios have fluctuated between 1.2 per cent and 1.9 per cent in war years when maximum production plus the armed services absorbed all available manpower. These facts are included for the sake of completeness rather than for suggesting such low rates as a realistic objective. The brutal facts are that our rate is near 6 per cent, that it is rising and that it will continue to rise until it becomes unacceptably high. Then and only then, presumably, will action be taken on a sufficiently imaginative scale to reverse the trend.

Many different solutions have been offered to the problems arising out of the situation that human labor is fast becoming a surplus commodity in our, for the most part, affluent and increasingly cybernated society. Some of these are radical in the classic sense that they would require revision of most of our economic concepts. Robert Theobald, for example, testified before Senator Clark's committee along the same lines that he set forth in the special issue of *The Nation* entitled "Abundance." The burden of his carefully documented message was that pursuit of an ever-increasing number of job opportunities is a hopeless search for a dissolving mirage, and that subsistence income must be assumed by constitutional guarantee to each citizen of an affluent state whether work is available to him or not. John Kenneth Galbraith, although not a witness before the Manpower Revolution subcommittee, faced the problem some years ago in *The Affluent Society.* In all too brief outline, Galbraith's Cyclically Graduated Compensation scheme provides for fairly high unemployment compensation when jobs are unavailable, and a lowered level of jobless payments when work awaits the job seeker. Unlike Theobald, Galbraith believes that, for the most part and for as far as one can see, payment for man's labor will continue as the ordinary method of distributing the national income, and he suggests one sensible approach for those who are unable to participate in the economic structure.

Walter Reuther's major suggestion to the committee was for the establishment of economic planning of the general type that has proved successful in a number of European countries including Sweden and France. Other suggested devices varied all the way from a campaign to reduce the birth rate, presented by the spokesman for Planned Parenthood, to relocation schemes to thin out population in such disastrously affected areas as Appalachia. No witness voiced the idea that the cybernetic revolution should be slowed down by some kind of legislation, nor were any of the hopelessly outdated and irrelevant variations of the Luddite philosophy set forth.

The most depressing aspect of the testimony was the general consensus, expressed specifically by almost all government spokesmen, that the solution to our future unemployment problems can be found in the old idea that if there could only be a greater rate of growth accompanied by more consumer demand, production would spurt forward and sufficient jobs would be created to achieve acceptably full employment. All these official spokesmen agreed on the necessity for a tax cut, in the belief that increased purchasing power would promptly touch off a spending boom. But this tried and true solution is no solution at all to the new problems posed by the combined population growth and cybernation. The very experts who espoused the increased growth, increased production, theory testified that, with the new machines hitched up to the new computers, almost any product could be made in almost infinite quantities without a human hand being involved in the process. One cannot help but conclude that the experts who cling to the theory that 4 or 5 per cent growth per year in our Gross National Product will solve all our manpower problems do not even believe their own parallel testimony on cybernetics. They cannot have it both ways. Either we are becoming a society in which cybernated factories will turn out with no human assistance all the lipsticks, chrome-plated automobiles, washing machines, etc., which have become the necessities of our culture, and therefore we must think in terms of such a greatly changed and improved society that man's minds and energies will be engaged in new tasks. Or else increased consumption in itself will somehow require men's skills to produce the wanted items. They can't be right in both of their contrasting visions.

Further Resources
BOOKS

Cohen, Barbara G.F., ed. *Human Aspects in Office Automation.* New York: Elsevier, 1984.

Garson, Barbara. *The Electronic Sweatshop: How Computers are Transforming the Office of the Future Into the Factory of the Past.* New York: Simon & Schuster, 1988.

Greenbaum, Joan M. *Windows on the Workplace: Computers, Jobs, and the Organization of Office Work in the Late Twentieth Century.* New York: Cornerstone Books, 1995.

PERIODICALS

Hitomi, Katsundo. "Automation—Its Concept and a Short History." *Technovation* 14, no. 2, March 1994, 121–128.

Meyer, Steve. "'An Economic Frankenstein': UAW Workers' Responses to Automation at the Ford Brook Plant in the 1950s." *Michigan History* 28, no.1, Spring 2002, 63–89.

WEBSITES

Azar, Beth. "Danger of Automation: It Makes Us Complacent." American Psychological Association: Psychology Online. Available online at http://www.apa.org/monitor/jul98/auto .html; website home page: http://www.apa.org/ (accessed April 22, 2003).

"LBJ and Big Strikes—Is Rail Fight a Pattern?"

Magazine article

By: *U.S. News & World Report*

Date: April 27, 1964

Source: "LBJ and Big Strikes—Is Rail Fight a Pattern?" *U.S. News & World Report,* April 27, 1964, 99–101.

About the Publication: Established in 1933, the monthly *U.S. News & World Report* covers national and international political, economic, and business developments. The magazine also includes advice on investment and personal financial management. Its annual ranking report of U.S. colleges and universities is widely consulted. ∎

Introduction

In the United States during the nineteenth century, business invariably held the upper hand over labor. And when the two clashed, the American government at every level invariably sided with business. In fact, as capital's last line of defense, the U.S. Army had intervened directly to break strikes, first in 1877 involving the Baltimore & Ohio Railroad and again in 1894 during the Pullman Strike. It mattered little which political party, Republican or Democrat, had occupied the White House. In 1877 Republican president Rutherford B. Hayes (served 1877–1881) had sided with the employers. In 1894 it was Democratic president Grover Cleveland (served 1885–1889) who sent in the troops.

In fall 1902, however, President Theodore Roosevelt (served 1901–1909) broke new ground with his handling of a threatened nationwide coal miner's strike. Refusing to support either business or labor in this dispute pitting coal mine owners against union workers, Roosevelt instead claimed to represent the "public interest," and, as

such, acted with dispatch. With winter fast approaching, a coal strike would paralyze industry and deprive citizens of what was then the most widely-used heat source. Roosevelt summoned leaders from both sides to the White House. By utilizing the power and prestige of the presidency, Roosevelt personally brokered a settlement to avoid a walkout and disruption of coal deliveries. Needless to say, the American public appreciated Roosevelt's timely intervention.

Significance

President Lyndon B. Johnson (served 1963–1969) faced a similar crisis in April 1964 when an imminent walkout by railway workers threatened the nation with an equally crippling rail strike. And true to the tradition of Theodore Roosevelt, Johnson requested the presence of the railway management and the union officials, who appeared to be at loggerheads, with no settlement in sight. Nonetheless, once ensconced inside the White House, both sides wilted under the pressure of the president who personally applied his considerable persuasive powers—the "Johnson treatment," as it was known.

Journalist David Halberstam, in his acclaimed book *The Best and the Brightest* (1972), considers this episode one of the high points of the Johnson presidency. Particularly impressive, in Halberstam's judgment, was the means by which Johnson had bridged the chasm between allegedly irreconcilable economic interests. Meanwhile, the value of face-to-face negotiations once again proved effective.

Equally important, by April 1964 it had become apparent that conservative Arizona senator Barry M. Goldwater was sweeping towards the Republican Party presidential nomination. Supported by a powerful, fresh conservative movement—the "New Right"—Goldwater would be the first major party presidential nominee since Alf Landon had challenged Franklin D. Roosevelt (served 1933–1945) back in 1936 to run a campaign directed against the then-dominant moderate/liberal American political consensus. Goldwater's positions served to polarize the nation by race, social class, and economic interest. Unabashedly pro-business, Goldwater even advocated repealing some of the labor statutes of the 1930s guaranteeing workers the right to join unions, bargain collectively, and engage in strikes.

In contrast, Johnson seemed to epitomize the then-prevailing consensus in American politics. And as Halberstam remarks, Johnson's handling of the abortive 1964 railway strike was a shining, if fleeting, moment when hopes were raised that a permanent accommodation might be reached between capital and labor, and that all good things were possible in the United States. One year later, the fledgling consensus frayed as the civil rights movement faced renewed obstacles, the return of inflation drove new wedges between business and its workers and between producers and consumers, and the United States became further mired in the Vietnam War (1964–1975).

Primary Source

"LBJ and Big Strikes—Is Rail Fight a Pattern?"

SYNOPSIS: In the style of Theodore Roosevelt, President Lyndon B. Johnson in April 1964 intervened directly to avert a potentially crippling railway strike. When railway management and union officials reached an apparent impasse, and as a nationwide work stoppage loomed, Johnson acted with uncommon dispatch. The following selection describes this episode, surely one of the high water marks of the Johnson administration.

Lyndon B. Johnson's personal effort to head off a railroad strike has set a new style for Presidents in the handling of labor disputes.

As a result, this question is being raised by employers and labor leaders:

Will the President personally take charge of other major strike threats as he took charge of the negotiations in the railroad case?

There was some concern that Mr. Johnson, indeed, had set a pattern for the future.

What is different about the Johnson style? Why is it causing concern?

Labor officials of previous Democratic Administrations say they have never seen anything like it before.

Actual negotiations between railroad officials and union leaders have been held in White House offices, opening in the Cabinet Room on April 10.

No precedents?

Labor experts say they recall no previous instances in which bargaining sessions were carried on at the White House over such an extended period.

Past Presidents, notably Mr. Truman and Mr. Kennedy, on occasion called union men and employers to the White House to put pressure on them to settle. The White House in the past also has imposed settlement terms when the parties themselves could not agree.

Former President Eisenhower, in contrast, attempted to follow a hands-off policy in labor controversies.

Mr. Johnson, in the rail dispute, kept both sides guessing what his next move might be if the parties remained hopelessly deadlocked. There were hints, however, that Congress might be called upon to pass legislation calling for compulsory arbitration.

One of those who saw risks in the new Johnson style once was a high official who was deeply involved in many labor disputes that got to the White House.

"There is always a danger when a President gets involved in a labor dispute," this former official said. "If he does it for one dispute and not another, he gets criticized. If those in a dispute get the idea that the White House may intervene, they won't make any concessions in the early stages of bargaining."

Another veteran negotiator put it this way: "When the President took personal charge of the actual negotiations, and kept them right in the White House, he put himself smack in the center of the mediation, and put his personal prestige on the line.

"This could have been avoided by Mr. Johnson, if he had merely urged both sides to go back and negotiate a peace. That's what other Presidents have done. He could have left the mediation up to his Labor Secretary and others.

"Now, this means that when the next big dispute develops, the industry and union will expect Mr. Johnson to take over the job of mediating it. They will be afraid to work out their own agreement if they think he may call them in for White House peace-making."

LBJ's moves watched.

President Johnson's methods in the rail dispute did not go unnoticed by union leaders and employers in other industries.

Paul Hall, head of the AFL-CIO's maritime department, accused the President of "forcing" the rail unions into compulsory arbitration.

One of the next big labor crises could come in a field in which Mr. Hall has a personal interest—the docks on the East and Gulf coasts.

Contracts between the International Longshoremen's Association, headed by Thomas W. Gleason, and the shipping companies expire in September, and expiration of these contracts could lead to a major strike.

Such a strike, if it comes, would quickly and seriously interfere with the nation's economy. Export and import trade would immediately come to a halt.

President Lyndon Johnson (center) shakes hands with Roy Davidson, railway union spokesman (left) and J.E. Wolfe, chief negotiator for the railroads (right) in front of the White House after the settlement of railroad work rules on April 23, 1964. AP/WIDE WORLD PHOTOS. REPRODUCED BY PERMISSION.

If that happened, Mr. Johnson might once again feel that he had to step into the dispute.

More widely noted than the shipping negotiations is the dispute that is building up between the United Auto Workers Union and the auto manufacturers over the UAW's demands. The union's contracts with General Motors, Ford and Chrysler expire on August 31.

Wary of intervention.

Although the UAW and the auto companies are widely apart on contract issues, they do agree on one thing—they want to settle their own dispute.

"We're foursquare for nonintervention," said one union official. "The less government, the better."

Said an auto executive: "I don't care who the President is, he's going to intervene in case of a railstrike. But that doesn't mean anything about our negotiations. A rail strike would shut down the county in a matter of hours. An auto strike certainly wouldn't."

In Detroit, the argument was made that White House intervention in auto negotiations wouldn't be necessary. "Maybe in steel, or public utilities," as one source put it, "but not in autos."

There appeared to be less certainty in Washington than in Detroit, however, that Mr. Johnson would not intervene in autos, especially if a long industry-wide strike should develop.

Concern was expressed in other quarters over the extent of Mr. Johnson's role in the rail negotiations and what it might lead to.

You can get an idea of the Johnson style, and the response of some union leaders, from an article written by one who heard the President's appeal for postponement of the strike that had been set for April 10.

The author, Roy E. Davidson, head of the Locomotive Engineers, wrote in his union's newspaper:

"You don't defy the President of the United States when he makes a request of you.

"You don't defy the President when he is obviously sincere, deeply concerned, even humble . . . when he pleads that he is a new President and should have at least the same opportunity his predecessors had . . . when he appeals to your patriotism and says all genuine Americans will appreciate your forebearance.

"There are those who will quarrel with the explanation, who will say it is inadequate, who will accuse me and other chief executives of lacking spine.

"I would ask them to consider the consequences of defying the President in the first request he has made in the dispute, of incurring his enmity at this stage, of inviting repressive legislation without having exhausted yet another chance for collective bargaining."

On the night of April 9, it took more than two hours of the kind of appeal reflected by Mr. Davidson to win over the union leaders. The railroads had agreed to the President's proposal for a truce, to give him time to try to work out a settlement in the work-rules controversy that had been going on for five years.

Before the truce was agreed upon, the President and the union leaders were reported to have exchanged some sharp words. One who was there said the union men talked to Mr. Johnson "like he was the president of a railroad."

President on hand.

On the morning of April 10, actual negotiations began in the White House Cabinet room, and Mr. Johnson was there. In the days that followed, he moved in and out of the negotiating sessions.

The President surprised the negotiators by moving cordially among them and, with a smile, asking: "Why don't you fellows get together?"

"The President acted like he did when he was majority leader of the Senate," said one who knows him well. During his years in that role, Mr. Johnson was noted for his ability to win support for legislation by his powers of persuasion.

Two outside mediators—George W. Taylor and Theodore W. Kheel—were brought in. The President imposed secrecy on both sides, but the broad outlines of what was going on behind the White House doors leaked out.

What emerged was a picture of deep personal participation by the President in the actual negotiations. It was the extent of this personal involvement that made the Johnson method so different in its style.

Out of it all came expressions of concern that the President was setting a pattern that might bring many other major labor disputes to the White House. It was feared by some that such a pattern ultimately might lead to Government-imposed contracts.

Further Resources

BOOKS

Bernstein, Irving. *Guns or Butter: The Presidency of Lyndon Johnson.* New York: Oxford University Press, 1996.

Evans, Rowland, and Robert Novak. *Lyndon B. Johnson: The Exercise of Power: A Political Biography.* New York: New American Library, 1966.

Halberstam, David. *The Best and the Brightest.* New York: Random House, 1972.

PERIODICALS

Barrett, Wayne M. "LBJ: The White House Years." *USA Today Magazine,* January 1991, 36–45.

WEBSITES

"The Johnson Tapes." Discovery Communications. Available online at http://tlc.discovery.com/tlcpages/johnsontapes /johnsontapes.html; website home page: http://tlc.discovery .com/ (accessed April 23, 2003).

"Boom in the Desert: Why It Grows and Grows"

Magazine article

By: *U.S. News & World Report*

Date: May 25, 1964

Source: "Boom in the Desert—Why It Grows and Grows." *U.S. News & World Report,* May 25, 1964, 46–52.

About the Publication: Established in 1933, the monthly *U.S. News & World Report* covers national and international political, economic, and business developments. The magazine also includes advice on investment and personal financial management. Its annual ranking report of U.S. colleges and universities is widely consulted. ■

Introduction

The southwestern U.S. states of Arizona, Nevada, and New Mexico experienced an economic boom in the 1960s. Four critical factors led to this region's exciting economic expansion: technology advances; favorable business climates; attractive and available land; and innovative growth policies.

Technology lessened the impact of the main obstacles to living in much of the Southwest: oppressive heat and a lack of water. The availability of central air conditioning in homes during the 1960s made living in hot climates considerable more comfortable and practical for a large portion of the population, especially retirees. Car travel to the region was also much easier after the advent of air conditioning, allowing the region's tourist attractions to benefit from the American public's increased leisure time and disposable income. Technological advances in irrigation, together with the construction of man-made lakes, also aided the economic expansion by enabling farming and the construction of new communities in previously uninhabitable areas.

A second major factor in the economic boom was the favorable business climate in these states. Nevada and Arizona were "right to work" states—where employees cannot be required to join a union—generally resulting in lower wages. Combined with low taxes—Nevada has never had a state income tax for individuals or corporations and has no property taxes—inexpensive land, and low construction costs, the states were perfectly positioned to attract employers seeking reduced costs and less government regulation. Starting from scratch, businesses were able to build affordable, large factories, incorporating technological advances, and attract a dedicated workforce.

The third factor was attractive, inexpensive, and available land. Unlike in many cities across the United States, prime real estate in Southwestern urban areas was available for new construction in the 1960s. Plentiful land allowed the development of many golf courses, retirement communities, and new homes. Workers could live close to work, yet still be close enough to the "Wild West" to fully enjoy the outdoors in rugged, beautiful desert scenery or skiing and other winter sports in the mountains of the three states.

A final important factor in the economic growth of the Southwest was the innovative growth plan adopted by the three states, each focusing successfully in different areas. Nevada cast its lot with gambling and tourism as the state's main industries. Its gambling establishment began to cater more to families, especially in Las Vegas, with impressive results. Also, low airfares during the 1960s brought more tourists to Nevada. Arizona focused on building its economic base, including constructing numerous retirement communities, golf courses, and tourist attractions, capitalizing on its low humidity, beautiful terrain, and the Grand Canyon. New Mexico, home of the Las Alamos Research Center—where the atom bomb was developed—focused on public education as a tool for training the skilled workers needed for the new economy. New Mexico spent the highest percentage of any state budget on public education during the 1960s.

Significance

As a region, the Southwest generally enjoyed excellent economic expansion from the 1960s through the end of the century, boasting the nation's highest growth rates in population and economic development. In addition to the factors resulting in the 1960s economic boom, the region has benefited from attracting ever-increasing numbers of retirees relocating from colder climates, increased tourism, favorable trade treaties, including NAFTA and GATT, as well as a developing Mexican economy.

During the 1990s, Nevada's population grew more than sixty-six percent, by far the highest growth rate of any state. Despite increased competition for legalized gaming in Atlantic City and Indian casinos across the country, the Nevada gaming industry flourished. Nevada's focus on gambling paid off handsomely, attracting serious gamblers, recreational gamblers, tourists, and families looking for a fun vacation.

During the 1990s, Arizona's population grew nearly forty percent, second only to Nevada. Arizona also has attracted an increasing number of retirees. While realizing an increase in tourism, Arizona focused on building its economic base.

New Mexico experienced population and economic growth since the 1960s, but much less than have Arizona and Nevada. During the 1990s, New Mexico's population grew twenty percent, twelfth highest in the nation. With its favorable business climate and low degree of state regulation on business, New Mexico realized slow but steady growth, during the last forty years of the twentieth century.

Primary Source

"Boom in the Desert—Why It Grows and Grows" [excerpt]

> **SYNOPSIS:** In this article *U.S. News & World Report* examines the economic boom experienced by Arizona, New Mexico, and Nevada during the 1960s, and the different approach of each state to build for the future.

The Success Saga of Nevada, New Mexico, Arizona

The great American desert, once regarded as a vast wasteland, waterless and forbidding, today is the scene of an expanding boom.

Boom times spread over three States—Nevada, New Mexico and Arizona. In each State, the base for growth and opportunism has a different foundation.

In New Mexico, it's the "think and theory business"—brains—on which the future is being built.

Nevada, growing in population and glamour, has cast its lot with gambling.

Arizona is the desert State of industry, retirement and recreation.

Water everywhere in the desert is a problem. Yet water shortages generally are being overcome, or there is hope of future solution. Where temperatures above 100 degrees were a problem, air conditioning is providing the answer.

Everywhere there is sunshine—80 to 85 per cent of the daylight hours in the year. Humidity is low, usually 15 per cent or less, generally assuring comfort for people with sinus trouble or asthma.

All through this desert empire, contrasts are sharp.

Even the term "desert" is a bit misleading. Most of it is surprisingly varied in terrain and in plant and animal life. The horizon almost everywhere is etched with mountains. At sunset, their shadows sometimes lean east nearly 40 miles across the flat desert floor.

In Arizona in the spring, you can go from 80 or 90-degree temperatures in Phoenix to snow in Flagstaff, 125 miles away, at an altitude of 6,900 feet. Some of the country's great commercial forests are in Arizona.

You don't need air conditioning in much of New Mexico, most of which sits high on a plateau. In winter, eight ski centers operate at elevations up to 12,000 feet.

Nevada has four distinct seasons in the northern part of the State. Temperature variations of 50 degrees within 24 hours have been reported in Reno. Southern Nevada is a dry desert, where annual rainfall is 3 to 15 inches.

Arizona has on its borders the two largest man-made lakes in the United States—Lake Mead behind Hoover Dam, and Lake Powell behind the new Glen Canyon Dam, both on the Colorado River. It is a common sight to see autos towing boats, heading for newly created recreation centers.

Nevada tops the nation in rate of population increase. Arizona leads in rate of industrial growth. New Mexico has the best per capita record in public spending for higher education, keystone of the space-age industry.

It's here in the desert that year-round living, a new American way of life, is being developed to its fullest degree. Increasingly, it's a life in self-contained communities planned from the ground up in attractive, historic and scenic surroundings. This, too, is part of the boom.

A visitor checking into a hotel in Las Vegas gets these first impressions: Although it's 8:30 in the morning, near the registration desk people are crowded around the gambling tables, trying their luck at blackjack and craps. In his room a few minutes later, the phone rings and the voice of room service says: "The management would like to welcome you with a drink; may I take your order?"

Gambling, and the tourist business it generates, has set off in Nevada the greatest population explosion any State has ever had. In the three years since the census of 1960, Nevada's population soared from 285,000 to an unofficial estimate of 442,000 last October—a 55 per cent jump. The most optimistic forecasts are for 705,000 Nevadans by 1970 and perhaps 1,200,000 by 1975.

The surprising thing about this explosion is that it is occurring with only a slight increase in industry. Nevada today has a mere 6,700 manufacturing workers, less than one fifth the national average in proportion to population.

Entertainment and resort living, backed by gambling, is the big Nevada growth stimulator. It is a business that, around the clock, has many ways of separating visitors from their money while they are having a good time. You can take in an elaborate stage show at a hotel for the price of a single drink. The management knows it will get its money back, and more, at the gaming tables later.

Nickels to dollars.

There is one slot machine for every 22 Nevada residents. You can play one, two, or three machines with one handle—for nickels, dimes, quarters, half dollars and dollars. At the Mint, a place on Las Vegas's Fremon Street, one recent afternoon the wife of a construction worker from Arizona played a row of four $1 machines for more than two hours. She hit six jackpots and several lesser payoffs. If she had known when to stop, she would have been one of the few lucky ones who come out ahead.

Here is how a slot machine works in Nevada:

The standard machine has three rows of 20 symbols on a cylinder—cherries, bells, oranges, etc.—for 8,000 possible combinations. In 8,000 plays, on average, the machine will return 5,300 coins to the player in small payoffs, usually three to 10 coins. Another 2,000 coins are returned in jackpots—a preset payoff adjusted by the casino to suit itself. This leaves 700 coins. From these, the State is paid taxes that range from 3 to 5.5 per cent. The rest goes for local taxes, operating expenses and profit.

In 1963, Nevada collected 13.5 million dollars in gambling taxes, or 28 per cent of its general-fund revenues. Nevada ranks seventh in the country among States with income from gambling. But, "What is peanuts to a big State like California," with a multibillion-dollar budget, "is caviar to Nevada,"

Tourists and taxis cruise Fremont Street in downtown Las Vegas in 1967. © BETTMANN/CORBIS. REPRODUCED BY PERMISSION.

says a Las Vegas casino operator. Nevada's budget is 106 million dollars for the current year.

Nevada has no personal or corporate income taxes; no admissions, warehouse, inheritance or gift taxes. It calls itself "the storm cellar for the tax weary." The gambling industry opposes more production industry in the State for fear that manufacturing might someday become sufficiently important for gambling to be voted out of existence.

Attractions for nongamblers.

Gambling is being served up in increasingly attractive settings. It remains the main lure but is no longer the sole attraction. The Dunes Hotel in Las Vegas is getting a 22-story addition that will have a floor of shops, a ballroom and a "Top of the Strip" restaurant with no gambling. A 40-acre "Vegaland"—modeled after California's Disneyland—is opening this month.

More families are coming to Las Vegas for vacations, and children are often seen at dinner with their parents. Now, says a hotel official, "the showgirls put on clothes for the dinner show, take them off for the late show." . . .

Reno was known as the divorce capital of the U. S. long before gambling brought Nevada added

publicity. Six weeks' residence for divorce still is important business. But now marriage is still bigger business. Last year, Washoe County had 23,361 marriages, compared with 4,306 divorces. In Las Vegas, there's a sign: "$15 Cupid Wedding Chapel, Free Corsages to Every Bride." A justice of the peace in Las Vegas is estimated to be making $75,000 a year, mostly by performing marriage ceremonies.

The outlook for Nevada is for continued boom so long as California keeps growing. The president of Rocketdyne, a division of North American Aviation, Inc., which has large land holdings for rocket-test purposes near Reno, says, "The potential for growth here in northern Nevada is the same as in southern California."

Federal spending is sizable in Nevada, mostly in Clark County. The bulk of it is spent by the AEC: 186 million last year, supporting some 7,300 workers. Spending for the next fiscal year by this agency is due to drop a bit. Las Vegas, however, expects to continue to grow.

"We're like the playroom off the kitchen," says a casino operator, "only 50 jet minutes from Los Angeles, where 60 per cent of our business comes from. Las Vegas is in its infancy. It's destined to become a world playground."

New Mexico's boom is tied to the "think and theory business" more than anything else. A laboratory, a computer or an office dominated by a blackboard and chalk are the trademarks of this "business."

In 1945, New Mexico ushered in the atomic age when the first nuclear bomb was exploded at Los Alamos. Now, space-age activities are spread out over the State's vast emptiness. Increasingly, it is attracting people and activities that gather around research facilities and universities.

Albuquerque has become a national center for firms developing teaching machines and programs. Research at the University of New Mexico has increased more than five times in terms of dollar contracts since 1959. One third of the degrees granted by the university last year were for advanced studies. New Mexico has one doctor of philosophy for every 350 adults—highest ratio for any State in the nation. . . .

"In-laws can pop in."

Los Alamos, birthplace of the nuclear bomb, today has a population of nearly 14,000. Some 3,875 of these are employes of the University of California, which operates the Los Alamos Scientific Laboratory.

The security fence and guarded gates that once shut off the installation are gone. Emphasis now is on peaceful uses of atomic energy. Subdividers have moved in. Some residents feared that opening up Los Alamos would let in crime. None has developed. But at least one scientist there is unhappy: "Now my in-laws can pop in on us without warning."

It is at Los Alamos that 96 per cent of all nuclear-fission and fusion warheads in the U.S. arsenal were developed. Los Alamos is, after the Sandia Corporation, which handles the ordnance phases of the nuclear-weapons program, the largest of the many federal facilities that have made New Mexico a vast research-and-development laboratory for the space age. Facilities for recording, tracking, sighting and recovery of missiles dot many square miles of the State.

At White Sands Missile Range, more than 15,000 missiles have been tested since 1946. A new, 25-million-dollar project, with a peak of 900 workers, is under way for testing escape equipment for the Apollo moon vehicle.

Land prices have risen less in New Mexico, with large, private land holdings, than in Arizona and Nevada. A State-owned 59,464-acre ranch, leased at 5 cents an acre a year, was sold in January for $36 an acre. Near Deming, half-acre "ranchettes" are offered for $249. Homes for less than $10,000 can be found in the Albuquerque area.

Life in New Mexico is close to nature. It has a touch of *mañana* about it. Wide-brimmed hats and Levi's seen on the streets of Albuquerque are worn regularly by people who work on the land, not in imitation of the pioneers of the Wild West. In New Mexico, the yesterday of history and the tomorrow of the space age are combined in living today.

Factories in the desert—and a healthful climate for year-round recreation outdoors—are the chief catalysts for Arizona's amazing growth.

The rate of Arizona's population rise has consistently exceeded that of the nation. It matches the rate of California since 1900, when that State had almost the number of people in Arizona today—1.6 million. Arizonans foresee an eventual increase to match California's present total of nearly 18 million. One projection is for 2.2 million people by 1970.

In the first 15 years after World War II, Arizona gained 315 per cent in manufacturing jobs. Florida was second among the States with 135 per cent. Last year, manufacturing output was more than 10 times the 86-million-dollar value of manufactures in 1946. Phoenix has become the third-largest electronics producer, after Los Angeles and San Francisco and ahead of San Diego.

Top executives cite these attractions for new industry:

An adequate labor supply exists in all but the highest-skilled and professional fields. Newcomers to the State usually take any work offered until their skill is in demand. Recently, a plastics manufacturer wanted to move to Tucson. No mold setters were listed by the employment office. An advertisement brought replies from 17 men with the needed skill. They had been working at other jobs.

Productivity is high. Absenteeism is lower than in the more industrialized States. Workers can count on good weather for their days off. In the hot summers, workers from uncooled homes are glad to be in air-conditioned plants.

An electronics employer says, "We feel we get higher productivity here, even though we can't prove it. Our foremen don't spend their time looking for people or policing them. People in the plant think of the business as 'we,' rather than 'them' and 'us.'"

A "right to work" law has been in effect since 1947. Union activity and membership are low in Arizona, except in mining and construction. Major employers such as General Electric, AiResearch, Sperry and Motorola are not unionized. Labor-management relations are almost uniformly good.

The business climate is attractive, too. "We offer a cohesive welcome from the city and county for any prospective industry." says a Chamber of Commerce official in Tucson. "We also make every effort to keep happy those that we already have." A General Electric official says, "We're very impressed with the progressive air of the area."

. . . A revival of mining contributes to over-all expansion. This is a reversal of a long downtrend, when richer ore bodies and surface geology were exhausted. Since the war, new techniques for exploration and working of low-grade ores have revived the industry. Kennecott in Arizona is producing 60,000 tons of copper a year from mines that once were abandoned. Copper output in Arizona in 1962 was 644,000 tons—more than half the U. S. total.

A breakthrough in consumer-goods manufacturing is under way in the Phoenix area, which now has enough people to support local production. Phoenix has passed the half-million mark and its metropolitan area—Maricopa County—has 840,000 people. Tucson's population recently passed the 300,000 mark. This despite the fact that Hughes Aircraft, one of the city's major employers, is down to 2,200 workers from a peak of 5,800 in 1959. . . .

For new city—old palms.

Lake Havasu City is expected to become western Arizona's largest city after Yuma. Already, 5 million dollars has been spent on development. A hotel has been completed; wells have been drilled for the needs of 15,000 people. The first 2,300 of 11,000 mature palm trees are being planted along main streets. A plant of the McCulloch Corporation, a California-based producer of chain saws and outboard motors, is being built. It will provide 500 jobs initially—perhaps 4,000 in time. The community is being publicized as "a Palm Springs with water."

It is in this way that new life is being built on the desert. Often, the building is from scratch. "We have clean, new cities," says a State official. "They are dynamic in character, and growing."

And Arizona—as well as the rest of the desert—is growing with them.

Further Resources

BOOKS

Denton, Sally, and Roger Morris. *The Money and the Power: The Making of Las Vegas and Its Hold on America, 1947–2000.* New York: Knopf, 2001.

Luckingham, Bradford. *Phoenix: The History of a Southwestern Metropolis.* Tucson: University of Arizona Press, 1989.

Moehring, Eugene P. *Resort City in the Sunbelt: Las Vegas, 1930–2000.* Reno: University of Nevada Press, 2000.

PERIODICALS

Dalton, Joyce. "New Mexico: A Rich Mix of Culture and Striking Scenic Beauty." *Travel Weekly,* August 3, 1952, 20.

Gooley, Toby B. "The Southwest: America's NAFTA Crossroads." *Logistics Management & Distribution Report* 37, no. 10, 69–73.

WEBSITES

"Arizona History." azcentral.com. Available online at http://www.azcentral.com/news/specials/azhistory/histindex.html; website home page: http://www.azcentral.com/ (accessed April 23, 2003).

"Chambers of Commerce & Convention & Visitors Bureaus in the United States." National Chamber of Commerce and Convention & Visitors Bureau Directory. Available online at http://www.2chambers.com (accessed June 10, 2003). *This site contains links to comprehensive information on states, including economic and demographic statistics.*

"Las Vegas History." Las Vegas Chamber of Commerce. Available online at http://www.lvchamber.com/las_vegas/history.htm; website home page: http://www.lvchamber.com/ (accessed April 23, 2003).

"Towns & Cities of the Southwest." New Mexico Ranch Directories. Available online at http://newmexicoranch.com/southwestern/towns-cities/index.htm; website home page: http://wedirectyou.com/southwestern/ (accessed April 23, 2003).

Unsafe at Any Speed
Nonfiction work

By: Ralph Nader

Date: 1965

Source: Nader, Ralph. *Unsafe at Any Speed.* New York: Grossman, 1965, vii–xi.

About the Author: Ralph Nader (1934–), author, attorney, and most visible spokesperson for the consumer protection/product safety movement, first became widely known in 1965 because of his neo-muckraking classic, *Unsafe at Any Speed*—a scathing indictment of the American automobile industry's lackadaisical record on safety. During the 1970s Nader shifted his focus to various environmental concerns. He ran as the Green Party presidential nominee in 2000. ■

Introduction

In the "muckraking" investigative journalism tradition that was revived during the 1960s, attorney and consumer crusader Ralph Nader undoubtedly stands out as the nation's single most electric and controversial personality. Nader almost singlehandedly took on the largest American manufacturing industry—the automobile industry—and won.

Nader's experience with his principle nemesis General Motors, the world's largest automobile manufacturer, was typical of the problems faced by modern-day muckrakers. In his book, *Unsafe at Any Speed,* Nader presented solid research demonstrating the automobile industry's appalling lapses in safety design. But not only did his data come under fire, Nader himself became the object of personal attack. Indeed, General Motors committed a terrible public relations blunder by hiring private detectives to follow Nader and invade his privacy, in order to "dig up some dirt," instead of dealing squarely with the damaging substance of his allegations. Investigators found nothing embarrassing to report since Nader, himself virtually an ascetic in his personal life with no discernible vices, lived a monkish existence. The sordid details of this campaign to spy on Nader surfaced at a United States Senate hearing that quickly turned into a nightmare for the automobile giant.

Significance

Nader's efforts soon merged with a larger crusade, a consumer protection/product safety movement. The results were striking. Nader and his cohorts succeeded in placing corporate America on the defensive. With their veracity successfully challenged and their misdeeds chronicled, big business had no choice but to face an angry public and pledge reforms. Meanwhile, Nader and other activists learned to make ample use of the courts by instituting and winning lawsuits designed to force corporate wrongdoers to stop their unsavory practices. All told, American consumers gained new leverage to force corporations to adhere to a higher standard of conduct and accountability.

Primary Source

Unsafe at Any Speed [excerpt]

SYNOPSIS: In the preface to his controversial book, Nader recounts the financial and social consequences of unsafe products produced by the American automobile companies General Motors, Ford, and Chrysler, which, he contends, steadfastly refused to place any importance on the physical well-being of passengers or pedestrians.

For over half a century the automobile has brought death, injury, and the most inestimable sorrow and deprivation to millions of people. With Medea-like intensity, this mass trauma began rising sharply four years ago reflecting new and unexpected ravages by the motor vehicle. A 1959 Department of Commerce report projected that 51,000 persons would be killed by automobiles in 1975. That figure will probably be reached in 1965, a decade ahead of schedule.

A transportation specialist, Wilfred Owen, wrote in 1946, "There is little question that the public will not tolerate for long an annual traffic toll of forty to fifty thousand fatalities." Time has shown Owen to be wrong. Unlike aviation, marine, or rail transportation, the highway transport system can inflict tremendous casualties and property damage without in the least affecting the viability of the system. Plane crashes, for example, jeopardize the attraction of flying for potential passengers and therefore strike at the heart of the air transport economy. They motivate preventative efforts. The situation is different on the roads.

Highway accidents were estimated to have cost this country in 1964, $8.3 billion in property damage, medical expenses, lost wages, and insurance overhead expenses. Add an equivalent sum to comprise roughly the indirect costs and the total amounts to over two per cent of the gross national product. But these are not the kind of costs which fall on the builders of motor vehicles (excepting a few successful law suits for negligent construction of the vehicle) and thus do not pinch the proper foot. Instead, the costs fall to users of vehicles, who are in no position to dictate safer automobile designs.

In fact, the gigantic costs of the highway carnage in this country support a service industry. A vast array of services—medical, police, administrative, legal, insurance, automotive repair, and funeral—stand equipped to handle the direct and indirect consequences of accident injuries. Traffic accidents create economic demands for these services running into billions of dollars. It is in the post-accident response that lawyers and physicians and other specialists labor. This is where the remuneration lies and this is where the talent and energies go. Working in the area of prevention of these casualties earns few fees. Consequently our society has an intricate organization to handle direct and indirect aftermaths of collisions. But the true mark of a humane society must be what it does about *prevention* of accident injuries, not the cleaning up of them afterward.

Unfortunately, there is little in the dynamics of the automobile accident industry that works for its reduction. Doctors, lawyers, engineers and other specialists have failed in the primary professional ethic: to dedicate themselves to the prevention of accident-injuries. The roots of the unsafe vehicle problem are so entrenched that the situation can be improved only by the forging of new instruments of citizen action. When thirty practicing physicians picketed for safe auto design at the New York International Automobile Show on April 7, 1965, their unprecedented action was the measure of their desperation over the inaction of the men and institutions in government and industry who have failed to provide the public with the vehicle safety to which it is entitled. The picketing surgeons, orthopedists, pediatricians and general practitioners marched in protest because the existing medical, legal, and engineering organizations have defaulted.

A great problem of contemporary life is how to control the power of economic interests which ignore the harmful effects of their applied science and technology. The automobile tragedy is one of the most serious of these man-made assaults on the human body. The history of that tragedy reveals many obstacles which must be overcome in the taming of any mechanical or biological hazard which is a by-product of industry or commerce. Our society's obligation to protect the "body rights" of its citizens with vigorous resolve and ample resources requires the precise, authoritative articulation and front-rank support which is being devoted to civil rights.

This country has not been entirely laggard in defining values relevant to new contexts of a technology laden with risks. The postwar years have witnessed a historic broadening, at least in the courts, of the procedural and substantive rights of the injured and the duties of manufacturers to produce a safe product. Judicial decisions throughout the fifty states have given living meaning to Walt Whitman's dictum, "If anything is sacred, the human body is sacred." Mr. Justice Jackson in 1953 defined the duty of the manufacturers by saying, "Where experiment or research is necessary to determine the presence or the degree of danger, the product must not be tried out on the public, nor must the public be expected to possess the facilities or the technical knowledge to learn for itself of inherent but latent dangers. The claim that a hazard was not foreseen is not available to one who did not use foresight appropriate to his enterprise."

It is a lag of almost paralytic proportions that these values of safety concerning consumers and economic enterprises, reiterated many times by the ju-

Activist and author Ralph Nader sought to institute changes in business and environmental policy. AP/WIDE WORLD PHOTOS. REPRODUCED WITH PERMISSION.

dicial branch of government, have not found their way into legislative policy-making for safer automobiles. Decades ago legislation was passed, changing the pattern of private business investments to accommodate more fully the safety value on railroads, in factories, and more recently on ships and aircraft. In transport, apart from the motor vehicle, considerable progress has been made in recognizing the physical integrity of the individual. There was the period where railroad workers were killed by the thousands and the editor of *Harper's* could say late in the last century: "So long as brakes cost more than trainmen, we may expect the present sacrificial method of car-coupling to be continued." But injured trainmen did cause the railroads some operating dislocations; highway victims cost the automobile companies next to nothing and the companies are not obliged to make use of developments in science-technology that have demonstrably opened up opportunities for far greater safety than any existing safety features lying unused on the automobile companies' shelves.

A principal reason why the automobile has remained the only transportation vehicle to escape being called to meaningful public account is that the public has never been supplied the information nor offered the quality of competition to enable it to make effective demands through the marketplace and through government for a safe, non-polluting and efficient automobile that can be produced economically. The consumer's expectations regarding automobile innovations have been deliberately held low and mostly oriented to the very gradual annual style changes. The specialists and researchers outside the industry who could have provided the leadership to stimulate this flow of information by and large chose to remain silent, as did government officials.

The persistence of the automobile's immunity over the years has nourished the continuance of that immunity, recalling Francis Bacon's insight: "He that will not apply new remedies must expect new evils, for time is the greatest innovator."

The accumulated power of decades of effort by the automobile industry to strengthen its control over car design is reflected today in the difficulty of even beginning to bring it to justice. The time has not come to discipline the automobile for safety; that time came over four decades ago. But that is not the cause to delay any longer what should have been accomplished in the nineteen-twenties.

Further Resources

BOOKS

McCarry, Charles. *Citizen Nader.* New York: Saturday Review Press, 1972.

Nader, Ralph, Mark Green, and Joel Seligman. *Taming the Giant Corporation.* New York: Norton, 1976.

PERIODICALS

Gates, David. "Nader the Raider Marches On." *Newsweek,* February 20, 1984, 9–10.

Goldman, T.R. "The Long Ranger: Fueled by Single-Minded Determination and a Well-Developed Sense of Outrage, Ralph Nader Created the Modern Consumer Law Movement." *American Lawyer* 21, no. 11, December 1999, 100–103.

WEBSITES

The Nader Page. Available online at http://www.nader.org/ (accessed April 18, 2003).

"Salon Brilliant Careers: Citizen Nader." Salon.com. Available online at http://www.salon.com/bc/1999/01/26bc2.html; website home page: http://www.salon.com/ (accessed April 18, 2003).

"Hamburger University"

Magazine article

By: Nancy Fraser

Date: October 21, 1966

Source: Fraser, Nancy. "Hamburger University." *Life Magazine,* October 21, 1966, 100. ∎

Introduction

Few social institutions reflect the changes in the daily lives of the American people as does the fast food revolution. During the 1960s, Americans became a people "on the go"—especially with the entry of a significant number of women into the country's workforce. The McDonald's hamburger corporation became the leader of several chains that could tabulate meals served into the billions.

Social critics love to decry this transformation in the American public's dining habits. Many feel that much of the fast food cuisine ranges from dubious to dreadful, as well as being potentially harmful to one's appearance— if not to one's health. Moreover, this trend caused the demise of countless independent restaurants scattered throughout the country, that once provided a richness of diversity, to be replaced by uniform products. In some measure, this change reflects the breakdown of lingering regionalism in favor of a more homogenized national culture—although the death of the proverbial neighborhood "greasy spoon" is not mourned by many.

Some observers have raised legitimate concerns that the fast food revolution signaled the demise of the traditional family-centered, home cooked meal—and all this entails. The family dining table was a key element in socialization and in fostering parent/child bonding. But for harried parents, exhausted from the workday and lacking time to prepare meals, fast food is a convenient alternative. As long as more Americans work longer hours, and convenience remains the watchword, fast food will continue to be the choice of many.

Significance

The unquestioned pioneer of the American fast food revolution is the McDonald's hamburger corporation. The brainchild of former milkshake salesman Ray Kroc, McDonald's was, by some accounts, feeding a full ten percent of the country's population on any given day in the mid-1970s. Kroc understood the secret of success—becoming one of the first to adopt the franchise model so as to offer local entrepreneurs a stake in the corporation. And with regards to the product line itself, McDonald's patrons ordered from a standardized menu that guaranteed a familiar meal anywhere in the nation. No more need to risk the daily special at the nearest roadside diner when venturing into parts unknown.

Of course, the downside of the McDonald's model had become a paradigm for some of the worst trends in American life by the end of the twentieth century. The term "flipping burgers" stands for a host of thoroughly demeaning, mind-numbing dead-end jobs, that are not solely restricted to the fast-food trade. The label "McJobs" has entered the national debate as a codeword for such positions. The huge advertising budget and popularity of fast food has resulted in a large portion of the population regularly partaking of low nutritional food saturated with salt, sugar, fat, and chemical preservatives.

Primary Source

"Hamburger University."

> **SYNOPSIS:** The McDonald's hamburger corporation, as the trendsetter in the mid- to late twentieth century American (and worldwide) fast-food revolution, has produced interesting innovations at every step of the way. One of the first to grab public attention centered around "Hamburger University," a state-of-the-art training facility for McDonald's managers, that served to underscore founder Ray Kroc's commitment to quality management.

It's 9 a.m. in the Chicago suburb of Elk Grove Village, and Professor Ray Stibeck, refreshed and ready for another day of teaching, strides briskly to the front of his classroom. He clears his throat and announces dramatically: "Gentlemen, the average American *likes* hamburgers!"

His students nod hopefully. They are new holders of franchises from McDonald's Corporation, a chain of 800-odd drive-ins which sells more hamburgers than anyone else in the world. And they are in Elk Grove Village for an intensive three-week course at Hamburger University, the company's training academy built right into a fully operational customer-satisfying stand marked by the familiar golden arches that are McDonald's trademark. Upon graduation they hurry home with a parchment diploma, their Master's degree in Hamburgerology—and a determination to do their loyal best to prove worthy of it.

Ravenous Americans are now buying 600 million 15-cent hamburgers a year from McDonald's. With 53,000 tons of French fries, 125 million milk shakes and lake-sized quantities of soft drinks and coffee figured in, this is expected to bring the company and its franchises a gross revenue of $240 million this year—far too big a nugget to entrust to the whims of any untrained short-order cook. But it takes more than a proper education to keep McDonald's out in front; it also takes science.

Here at Hamburger U., which is a working model of McDonald's "units" everywhere, the kitchen fairly hums with space-age gadgetry. There are computer-like controls over the fry cookery; dispensers for squirting precisely the right amount of catsup, mustard, and dried onion flakes onto premeasured hamburger patties to delight the standardized American palate; instruments for testing the solidity of raw potatoes, the specific gravity of milk shakes and the fattiness of raw meat (and thereby the honesty of wholesale butchers with whom the franchisees have to deal).

Also central to the chain's success is company *espirit.* "Everybody at McDonald is *so enthusiastic,*" said one official, standing at attention in the morning sun as the gold-and-white H.U. banner was run up the pole in the alma mater's parking area.

It is to instill the proper spirit as well as teach the art and science of Hamburgerology that the company employs Ray Stibeck. He is dean and ranking professor at H.U. and his awesome responsibilities are very much on his mind when he plunges into his first lecture of the day, Patties and Buns. By then, his class, of about 25, has completed its half-hour Hamburger Quiz (*Q.* What is the most important ingredient of a McDonald burger? *A.* Tender Loving Care). After collecting the quizzes, the professor says:

"Hamburgers are the foundation of our *entire* structure. We want to make *sure* our foundation doesn't crumble!" He whirls around to the blackboard and writes out the Secret Meat Specifications: so much U.S. No. 1 Grade Chuck. So much plate beef. So much fat. He turns to face the class, and his expression is thoughtful. "Gentlemen," he says, "grill a patty. Taste it. Break it apart. By breaking it apart, we can have a better understanding of our patty."

An assistant brings up a tray of cooked patties. The ones on the right are underdone; on the left, overdone; and in the middle, just right. "The average person he likes his hamburger with a *semipink* center. He doesn't want it raw . . . curled up . . . dried out . . . rubbery." Stibeck snatches a patty from the middle row and pops it into his mouth. "Now I'll practice what I preach and *taste* it. It's good. Real good. It has *zipple* to it!" He passes the tray around the room. "Any questions? If not, it's about that there now time. So we'll take a break and come back for buns.

Speedee the Chef was McDonald's mascot until 1962. Since then characters such as Ronald McDonald, Hamburglar and the Fry Guys have sought to make the restaurant more appealing to children. **THE ADVERTISING ARCHIVE LTD. REPRODUCED BY PERMISSION.**

Fifteen minutes later, the professor is back on the podium, dwarfed by a big carton of buns. After a student has read the McDonald's Secret Bun Specifications, he begins pulling them one by one from the box, pointing out imperfections: blisters, spots, splotches of flour. Cupped buns. Squeezed buns. Lopsided buns. The professor winces. "What can you do about this, fellows? Talk to your bun purveyor! Tell him to *get on the ball!*" Smiling he pulls out a perfect bun. "Here it is—Exhibit A! Perfect contours! Perfect *resiliency!* She bounces right back for me! You can see the beautiful concave shape, the *symmetry.* The whole ball of wax!" The professor ends his lecture: "Gentlemen, visit your bun plant. It's an education. You no longer look at a bun as a bun. It takes on new *meaning* for you. . . ."

Now it's lunch time. Some of the students belly up to the order window and call for hamburgers. Others—on the day this reporter was present—make a beeline for the restaurant at the motel next door.

Exactly at 12:53 Professor Stibeck makes an announcement: "Operations Lab will begin in two minutes! Time to scrub up!" At Hamburger U., every

lecture is backed up by practical laboratory experience. ("We don't miss a trick here!")

Inside the kitchen five students are lined up ready to start. They approach the Fry Area, where the professor shows them why McDonald's French fries are "the world's finest."

"Gentlemen, a McDonald's French fry is done when it's *golden brown* in color, or emits a sound like leaves rustling in a stiff breeze. . . ." He grabs the salt shaker: "A *medium* amount of salt is all that's suggested, fellows. When you break in a new fry man, if this kid likes salt, he'll *really* put it on. So watch it." The filling of the bag is a "one-shot deal," says the professor. "Your ultimate goal is a full bag. . . ." He asks a student to try filling."Atta boy," he coos. "That's it—fresh and hot. If customers burn their lips a little bit, they're happy. The *one* time they're happy to get a little burned . . . now let's swing around and fry some burgers." His students have already read the 55 pages on Hamburger Fabrication in their 300-page Operations Manual. "A well-dressed bun is everyone's responsibility," he shouts, whirling around to the condiment tray. "In the event that the condiment spills over the side, we suggest you use a pickle to remove it, then dress the bun with the same pickle. . . . Our operation is a pennies operation. And why do we center the pickle? Because no matter *where* the customer bites, he'll taste a portion of pickle!"

A windowman yells for a "Grill," a hamburger without one or more of the standard ingredients. The students have already been advised in their manuals how to handle this crisis diplomatically: "Although our operation is not *geared* for grills, we must *not* discourage them. Your main concern is to *educate* customers. . . . Say 'Sir, the burgers that are *ready* come with everything. We would be pleased to prepare a special for you. It will take *only* four minutes.' This is very positive. It states the facts in a positive way, and cannot be interpreted as argumentative or attempting to talk the customer out of what he wants."

The lab session ends. The students look a little dazed. But Professor Stibeck is still fresh and enthusiastic. "It's the challenge," he explains. "If I can *hammer* home [he pounds his fist into his hand] to these guys the McDonald's trinity—Quality, Service, Cleanliness—it gives me great satisfaction. Why does a doctor get up in the middle of the night to make a house call? It's not the five or six bucks he gets. It's the *satisfaction* of his job. . . ." He hurries away to prepare for the next day's session in fries, cooked to emit just the right leaf-rustling sound.

Further Resources

BOOKS

Kroc, Ray, with Robert Anderson. *Grinding It Out: The Making of McDonald's.* Chicago: Henry Regnery, 1977.

Love, John F. *McDonald's Behind the Arches.* New York: Bantam, 1986.

PERIODICALS

D'Aulaire, Per Ola, and Emily D'Aulaire. "60 Billion Burgers—and Counting." *Reader's Digest,* December 1987, 39–42.

Fishwick, Marshall. "Ray and Ronald Girdle the Globe." *Journal of American Culture* 18, no. 1, Spring 1995, 13–29.

Nelson, Anne V. "Putting Muscle in McJobs." *Working Woman* 20, no.1, January 1995, 11

WEBSITES

"The McDonald's History Page." McDonald's Corporate Information. Available online at http://www.mcdonalds.com /corporate/info/history/index.html; website home page: http:// www.mcdonalds.com/countries/usa/ (accessed April 20, 2003).

Peters, Cynthia. "Treating Teens Contemptuously: The Retail Squeeze." Available online at http://csf.colorado.edu/mail /psn/2001/msg00631.html; website home page: http://csf .colorado.edu/ (accessed April 20, 2003).

"The Real Masters of Television"

Magazine article

By: Robert Eck

Date: March 1967

Source: Eck, Robert. "The Real Masters of Television." *Harper's,* March 1967, 45–52.

About the Author: Robert Eck, a writer of media advertising copy for many years, also served as a radar operator in the U.S. Army Signal Corps. ∎

Introduction

Although plenty of terrible programming flashed across the nation's airwaves during the 1950s, the decade is rightly saluted as the so-called "Golden Age" of television. The period featured much live programming, plus outstanding educational and cultural shows of the type that in the early 2000s are conspicuously absent from network channels, having been banished either to public television or to various cable stations. Indeed, during the 1950s there aired probably just enough high quality shows to foster the illusion that television—a medium with an admittedly fantastic potential—might actually promote a burst of enlightenment. By one account, a 1950s broadcast of Shakespeare's play *Hamlet* garnered more viewers than had seen the play performed live in

the preceeding three and a half centuries. Whether true or not, it was hoped that television, then still in its infancy, might actually fulfill its early promise.

By the early 1960s, critics began to doubt that television was headed in the right direction. The Kennedy administration in 1961 appointed Chicago lawyer Newton Minow to the chairmanship of the Federal Communications Commission (FCC). In Minow's immortal and oft-repeated lament, television was a "vast wasteland." Meanwhile, the three major networks held a virtual stranglehold on programming. The FCC, which had been established in 1934 to regulate radio and later television in the public interest, became a pawn of the broadcast industry even to the point of using the government's power to grant or revoke licenses in order to stifle competition. This situation was particularly egregious in many parts of the nation where little or no viewer choice existed. Politically connected Lyndon Johnson, U.S. senator, vice president, and then president (served 1963–1969), employed his enormous clout to restrict competition in Austin, Texas, for the benefit of his wife, Lady Bird Johnson, who happened to own the only station in town. Others seeking broadcasting licenses were summarily rejected.

Significance

Not only did cronyism and political favoritism play a decisive role in the granting of broadcast licenses, but the entire television industry waged a relentless, and temporarily successful, battle against newcomers. For instance, the technology had existed since the 1950s to introduce UHF broadcasting and cable, which would accommodate many additional channels, but these innovations were delayed by a federal government unwilling to face up to an established broadcast industry determined to preclude interlopers. As a consequence, an entire generation of television viewers had only CBS, NBC, and ABC from which to choose their programming, and little else.

By 1967 television critics were dismayed. The tube had sunk to new depths as inane programming, geared to the "lowest common denominator"—that is, aimed to attract the largest group of people at the cheapest cost to advertisers—flooded the nation's airwaves. Meanwhile, alternatives had not yet appeared. Public television was in its infancy; in fact, it was often spoken of disparagingly as "educational television." The rich diversity of PBS programming did not really emerge until around 1970.

In truth, if 1950s television can be considered the "Golden Age," the 1960s, although one of the most tumultuous decades on record, showed little or none of this increased consciousness in terms of prime time entertainment programming. To say that television remained out of touch with then-contemporary reality was an understatement. Television in the 1960s could not aptly be labeled "bad"—it was merely irrelevant.

Primary Source

"The Real Masters of Television" [excerpt]

> **SYNOPSIS:** Author Robert Eck discusses a question that would coninue to be asked for more than half a century: "Why is network television so bad?" In the following article, published in 1967, Eck comes to the not surprising conclusion that a lack of competition, more than anything else, explains the poor programming. Writing when he did in 1967, the federal government still restricted the sale of broadcast licenses and delayed the adoption of new technology, such as cable, while only grudgingly experimenting with UHF.

Why can't commercial television be improved? After all, its diseases seem to be no mystery. Everyone knows it is infested by evil advertising men who befoul the programs with their greedy touch. Their dupes, the sponsors, are for the most part a group of well-meaning, affluent bumblers—misguided souls who need instruction in cultural responsibility . . . The networks they deal with are stupid bureaucracies, dominated by frightened vice-presidents, natural enemies of everything that is fresh and intelligent. To make matters worse, all three idiot species are being bamboozled by a fourth: the audience researcher, a charlatan who has persuaded them he can take a continuous count of the nation's many millions of television viewers, either by telephoning the homes or bugging the sets of a thousand or two families whose identities are shrouded in mystery. By contrast to these fools and villains, there are a few exemplary sponsors who, out of the sheer goodness of their enlightened hearts, pay for the programs you and I like. And waiting in the wings is a benevolent government, needing only stronger prompting to move onstage and straighten out the mess.

If these familiar figures of cocktail-party folklore even came close to representing the actualities of commercial television, there might be some room for improvement. But they do not. They are a collection of wishes, falsehoods, and semi-truths, embodied in explanatory myths. As we shall see, it is not because of these myths but because of the more complex realities underlying them that commercial television is as amenable to reform as the adult Bengal tiger.

The Myth of the Evil Adman's Influence

While it has become fashionable among intellectual liberals to lay the sins of our materialism at the doorstep of the advertising agent, today's television programming is one sin he can rightly disclaim. He has virtually nothing to say about it. There was a time when he was a grand panjandrum of programming, but that was thirty years ago, in the heyday of radio, when advertising agencies literally produced the programs their clients sponsored. . . .

Although the business patterns of radio carried over into the early days of television, by the mid-1950s the television networks succeeded in taking away from the advertising men the controls they had historically exercised over program material. In this, the networks had no choice. Not only were television shows far more difficult to produce than radio shows, but television itself was rapidly growing into a business far more vast and risky—a business in which the profits (and the eventual existence) of a network depended not on its ability to cozen sponsors but to deliver measurable audience. Programming—the means of doing this—could not be left in the hands of outsiders, semiprofessionals, men to whom entertainment was only a sideline.

For the same reasons, production of television shows shifted from Chicago and New York to the foothills of the Santa Monica mountains. The moviemakers out there were not only the most expert producers of mass entertainment but also the most efficient. The money put into a live production is gone the moment the floodlights die, but films can be sold and resold, again and again, both here and abroad. A filmed TV series can be profitable even if it loses money on its first run.

Nowadays, the networks make a practice of inviting advertisers and their agencies to preview the prototype films of such series (the pilots), but that's about as far as it goes. Admen do not put programs on the air, don't materially change them once they're on, and don't take them off.

The Myth of the Audience-counting Charlatans

Nothing about television has been the subject of so much childish pique and wishful thinking as the rating services which undertake to measure television audiences. Inside the business, they are hated and feared, because their tabulations can make a man a potential millionaire or a failure in a matter of weeks. Outside, they are distrusted by many egocentric citizens who refuse to believe that

Actors Michael Landon (left) and Lorne Greene on the set of *Bonanza,* the most popular show during the 1966–1967 television season. **AP/WIDE WORLD PHOTOS. REPRODUCED BY PERMISSION.**

the viewing habits of a small group of strangers could possibly reflect their own and, by the same token, the nation's. These are the people who, in the words of a disgusted research director, "think you have to drink the whole quart of milk to discover it is sour."

The plain truth about audience counting is that nobody in his right mind would spend millions out of a private, corporate, political, or charitable purse to propel images into an uncharted void. Even the BBC uses random samples of its audience for guidance. And while random sampling can always be attacked because it only approaches perfection, so can a literal head-count. The more heads that must be counted, the more chances there are for human error in interviewing and arithmetic. This is why the Bureau of the Census sometimes prefers random sampling to a total count. . . .

A shocking thing has happened to most old-fashioned television sponsors. They have disap-

peared. In their place is a heartless scheme called a scatter plan. Except in moments of extreme frustration, nobody in the business ever wanted a sponsor to vanish. A few years ago, in fact, the networks would only sell the commercial use of a weekly show to a regular weekly sponsor or, at most, to two alternating sponsors. However, the supply of companies with enough advertising money to buy television time this way is limited. NBC and CBS, then the undisputed leaders of the field, were able to attract such large advertisers without undue difficulty. But it was a different matter for ABC. Lacking the programming, the audience, and the stations to get all the large sponsors it needed, ABC began selling off its unsponsored time *à la carte,* offering smaller advertisers the chance to buy a minute here and a minute there. . . .

For all his arrogant foibles, the old-time sponsor usually took a proprietary pride in his show. It was more apt to be a manifestation of his vanity than an accurate reflection of the show's intrinsic worth, but it did exist and it could be appealed to. It has been replaced by the depersonalized processes of an audience market, in which viewers by the millions are counted, sorted, graded, and sold to specification at so much a thousand head. There is not much to be gained by writing a letter of praise—or disgust—to a scatter plan. . . .

The Myth of the Stupid Bureaucratic Networks and Their Frightened Vice-Presidents

"Television is a triumph of equipment over people and the minds that control it are so small you could put them in the navel of a flea and still have room beside them for a network vice-president's heart."

When Fred Allen said that in 1952, he was suffering from an illusion still shared by millions who assume from the nature of most television programming that the networks are in the communications and entertainment business.

They are not.

It is true they deal in communications and entertainment. It is true that millions of words are annually printed to describe television programming. . . . [A] network president . . . collects no subscriptions and has no box office. He gets every cent of his money from advertisers. The network he operates is a gigantic, electronic medicine wagon with a Hollywood cast, whose entire reason for being lies in its ability to gather millions of men, women, and children to see and hear the advertiser's pitch.

The networks' business is the audience-delivery business, and if their vice-presidents are frightened men, they have good reason to be. They are involved in a unique and frightening enterprise. Their customer, the typical television advertiser, is a maker of package goods. His products (soda pop, soap, prepared foods, etc.) cost little, are bought often, and are used in every home. His audience requirements are limitless and unrelated to cultural or socioeconomic levels. He wants as much audience as he can get as cheap as he can get it. . . .

The Myth of the Benevolent Governmental Power

During his tenure as crusading chairman of the Federal Communications Commission, Newton Minow, with strong support from the press, managed to badger the networks into carrying slightly more public-service programming. He also managed to convey to the public the impression that the federal government was capable of improving the quality of commercial television.

That is mostly a false impression. Not only is the power to regulate program content specifically denied the Commission under section 326 of the Federal Communications Act; it is doubtful that any such power could exist because of the practical difficulties that lie in the way of defining it. To put up a stop sign at a traffic intersection, and require everyone to come to a full stop before crossing, is a perfectly workable arrangement. But to put up a sign saying "good judgment," and to pass a law requiring everyone to use good judgment before crossing, verges on nonsense. Yet the problem of defining good judgment at an intersection is trivial beside the problem of defining good judgment in the construction of the 7,000 hours of programming each station broadcasts in the course of a year.

What the government can do—and has done very little—is encourage alternatives to commercial network television. With Minow cheering it on, Congress did pass a law requiring that all new TV sets be capable of receiving ultra-high frequency signals. This was done in order to stimulate establishment of UHF stations, but whether these will ever provide an attractive alternative to the networks remains to be seen. The two UHF stations in my area fill their time with ancient, sub-B movies, sportscasts, travelogues, old BBC programs, and the Manion Forum.

The FCC could, but probably will not, improve educational television by approving the Ford Foundation plan to form a nonprofit corporation to manage the forthcoming domestic communications satellite. This plan would give educational television its first national hookup free, plus a badly needed $30 million a year out of the satellite's commercial revenues.

Again, by encouraging that fifteen-year-old orphan, pay-TV, the FCC might help create a desirable alternative to present commercial programming. A year ago, after studying the 1965 petition of Zenith Radio Corporation—which, with RKO General, has been running a long-term pay-TV experiment in Hartford, Connecticut—the Commission declared itself ready to authorize national pay-TV, subject to comment from those affected by it. At this writing, it had not acted, but favorable action was expected.

The common denominator of these alternatives is that all of them—UHF, satellite communications, pay-TV—are products of advances in a sophisticated and rapidly accelerating technology. This technology itself eventually may supply the most flexible and practical alternative to commercial television in the form of a simple, low-cost video recorder-player for home use. There now exists a small recorder which uses ordinary quarter-inch audio tape to record and play back both color and black-and-white television programs. Invented by Marvin Camras of the Illinois Institute of Technology's Research Institute, it is capable of recording or playing two hours of unbroken material and could be made to sell for less than $300. In essence, the video recorder (and someday there will be even easier and cheaper forms of it) is an alternative not only to commercial television, but also to pay-TV, for widespread ownership of recorders would result in a video recording industry and in the sale, rental, and library loan of recorded television programs of much the same general range as today's audio recordings. The effective differences between commercial television, pay-TV, and video recording can be put this way: no matter how much you might like to see a special television production of *Der Frieschütz,* you are not likely to see it on commercial television. In the improbable event that it does appear, it will do so just once, on a Saturday or Sunday afternoon, and it will be thoroughly fractured by commercials. Your chances of seeing it on pay-TV would probably not be a great deal better. If it should be programmed, there would be no commercials, but you would have to watch it on one of the few days it was being presented. With video recorders and recordings, your chances of seeing *Der Frieschütz* would be quite good. You could rent it without any commercials and watch it any time of the day you pleased.

Unfortunately, however, this agreeable prospect lies some distance in the future—by five, ten, or fifteen years. Right now, the large electronics firms are too busy making color sets for the multitudinous majority who dote on commercial television to worry about making recorders for the minority who do not.

And until video recording or some other alternative is realized, we will continue to be stuck with commercial television, which will continue to grind its repetitive, skillful, predictable way. Television reviewers will angrily scold, instructively praise, and loudly hope. Television producers will brag about hairbreadth advances over mediocrity. Television executives will count their cultural contributions and discuss their frequently magnificent public-information programs. Do not be deceived. Critics and defenders alike are symbiotically linked to the great audience-delivery systems. Those systems are married to cost-per-thousand, compelled to the pursuit of total audience, and—with factories in Hollywood, main

offices in New York, gala introductory promotions each fall, and franchised dealers throughout the country—are among Amerca's biggest and most successful mass-production businesses.

Further Resources

BOOKS

Barnouw, Erik. *Tube of Plenty: The Evolution of American Television.* New York: Oxford University Press, 1990.

Friendly, Fred W. *Due to Circumstances Beyond Our Control. . . .* New York: Random House, 1967.

Marc, David. *Demographic Vistas: Television in American Culture.* Philadelphia: University of Pennsylvania Press, 1996.

PERIODICALS

"The Silly Seasons: 1960s." *People,* Summer 1989 (special issue), 108–118.

WEBSITES

"Newton N. Minow: 'Television and the Public Interest.'" American Rhetoric. Available online at http://www.americanrhetoric.com/speeches/newtonminow.htm; website home page: http://www.americanrhetoric.com/ (accessed April 23, 2003).

"Television in the 1960s." Nostalgia Central. Available online at http://www.nostalgiacentral.com/60/60tv.htm; website home page: http://www.nostalgiacentral.com/ (accessed April 23, 2003).

"Team Effort"

Magazine article

By: Thomas Gordon Platt

Date: July 7, 1969

Source: Platt, Thomas Gordon. "Team Effort." *Newsweek,* July 7, 1969, 55–56. ∎

Introduction

The Russians shocked the world by launching the satellite Sputnik, the first man-made object to orbit the earth, on October 4, 1957. And on April 12, 1961, Russian cosmonaut, Yuri Gagarin, became the first man in space—weeks before American astronaut, Alan Shepherd, traveled in space. In response to these Russian achievements, President John F. Kennedy (served 1961–1963) announced an ambitious space program to a joint session of Congress and the world on May 25, 1961. Its goal was to put an American on the moon by the end of the 1960s. Beating the Russians to the moon became a top priority, a matter of special national importance—and pride—at the pinnacle of the Cold War.

To realize the space program's goal, several space centers were constructed. Often selected for political reasons, the sites of these new space centers experienced significant growth. NASA built the largest of these projects, Manned Spacecraft Center—later renamed Lyndon B. Johnson Space Center (JSC) shortly after President Johnson's (served 1963–1969) death in 1973—in a suburb of Houston, Texas, and it opened in October 1961. By the end of the 1960s, 4,500 were employed at JSC, and another 9,000 were employed locally by the 125 industries doing business with NASA that had settled in the region. The other new space stations experienced similar growth and also attracted aerospace contractors to locate nearby.

The space centers significantly impacted these regions. The aerospace industry dominated the local economies, as NASA provided contractors with jobs and a rich source of revenue. Even local housing and education were affected. The large influx of well-paid astronauts, scientists, engineers, and other highly skilled workers led to the construction of affluent neighborhoods. Area schools also reflected the aerospace presence in the community by emphasizing math and science.

President Kennedy's goal was realized when Apollo 11 landed on the moon on July 29, 1969, and American astronauts Neil Armstrong and Buzz Aldrin walked on the moon's surface. The space program's impact, however, went far beyond its achievements in space. The increased government spending on the space program, together with the efforts of the talented NASA workers, led to an unprecedented growth in research and technological innovation in many business sectors that continues into the twenty-first century.

Significance

The short-term impact of the space program and its new space centers was stunning. Attracting, empowering, and fully funding the United States' most talented workers, NASA and the aerospace industry conquered space travel in a few short years. In addition to cooperating effectively with its contractors, NASA integrated technology and innovative management practices long before most American businesses.

The space program's value extends far beyond Cold War considerations. The long-term impact of the space program has been as stunning as its accomplishment of putting a man on the moon. NASA expanded the scope of the space centers' mission after accomplishing their primary goal, transforming them into important centers of research and technological innovation for the United States' scientific and business communities.

Technology developed by the space program has lead to countless innovations and product improvements—including the discovery of smoke detectors, cordless tools, scratch-resistant eyeglasses, thermal cloth-

ing, and satellite communications. NASA operates its Technology Transfer & Commercialization Office to make its technology available to the scientific and business communities and to stimulate the economy. It also conducts important experiments that can only be done in space to advance scientific knowledge.

Primary Source

"Team Effort"

> **SYNOPSIS:** *Newsweek* writer Thomas Gordon Platt describes the individuals working at NASA's Manned Spacecraft Center and the center's impact on the region. The article also reflects the uncertainty of space center employees of their fate after their mission of landing a man on the moon is accomplished.

Houston: A Place Where 13,000 Men Can Feel Like They Are Columbus

From the moment Apollo 11 lifts off from Cape Kennedy, a communications network of unprecedented sophistication and speed will electronically shrink the enormous distance separating tracking stations on earth and the moonbound spaceship to the scale and closeness of an intimate conversation. The center of this system—and the brains of Apollo 11— is the Mission Operations Control Room of NASA's Manned Spacecraft Center near Houston. TV viewers will catch a glimpse of crew-cut, short-sleeved, laconic technicians in the windowless control room and in the first and lowest of four tiers of communications equipment—known as "the trench." In it sit the retro-fire officer, the flight dynamics officer ("fido"), the guidance control officer ("guido"), and the booster systems and extravehicular activities officer. Behind them is the flight director, who coordinates the entire worldwide operation. For the Apollo 11 mission, five flight directors have been named (they will take different shifts). The over-all operations head is Christopher Columbus Kraft Jr., an unflappable presence who has supervised sixteen manned Mercury and Gemini flights as well as the flights of Apollos 7, 8, 9, and 10. "This," as the clipped communications exchanges go, "is Apollo control."

This is also the place where the space age has touched down most pervasively on earth. Many of the 4,500 employees at the Manned Spacecraft Center as well as the 9,000 employees of 125 private firms doing business with NASA live as well as work close together in the Clear Lake area, a table-flat mosaic of a half dozen new communities. The communities in part owe their existence to NASA's 1961 decision to build a space center near Houston—a

NASA Mission Operations Control Room on the second day of the Apollo 11 lunar landing mission. A photo of Neil Armstrong aboard the Apollo 11 is transmitted to the room as the spacecraft neared the moon. © BETTMANN/CORBIS. REPRODUCED BY PERMISSION.

move partly due to the influence of the late Albert Thomas, a Houston congressman who was chairman of the powerful House subcommittee that holds NASA's purse strings. Perhaps two-thirds of the residents are non-Texans. "Many of the spaceworkers have come down here being very skeptical," says one observer. "For some of them, Houston just was not San Francisco or Boston."

The economic impact of the center on Houston has been at most marginal, but psychologically the effects are everywhere: the Astrodome, the Houston Astros, and even the Space City Directive Agency. So far, the area has come to the center more than the other way around. About 200 students from 35 nearby schools take administrative and technical courses at the MSC. A few astronauts, like Curt Michel and Don Lind, both Ph.D's, are research associates at Rice University, and some 325 full-time MSC employees take courses at the University of Houston—either at the downtown campus, or the Clear Lake Center now temporarily located in a NASA building. But on the whole the spaceworkers feel that the MSC is their university. "What you have to know to survive around here you can't learn in any other course," says Glynn S. Lunney, an Apollo 11 flight director.

The Artisans of the Space Age

It is as though the spaceworker community were itself a Little America outpost—self-sufficient and isolated. The speech is distinct, a combination of sports metaphors and engineering jargon. A Ph.D. will speak of "the team effort" and explain that the flight "is really the World Series for us." Secretaries will answer questions with a "negative" instead of a "no" on the phone. "Everyone, even the women, seems to talk about the space effort," says one young wife. "At a party, someone will ask: 'How are you?' And you'll say, 'The LM 10 is in the check-out stage'." The community has one common goal, and seemingly everyone shares in its realization. "I know I personally feel good when a flight goes well," says Chester A. Vaughan, 32, a liquid-propulsion engineer. "We're a fairly close-knit group," agrees Ralph Everett, 36, deputy chief of MSC Computer Analysis Division. "We work in a place where 13,000 men can feel like Columbus." Indeed, few technological industries today offer such chances for personal fulfillment. "There is an almost artisan satisfaction here because these men see almost immediately the effects of what they've been doing," says Dr. Richard I. Evans, a social psychologist at the University of Houston.

Salary scales are comfortable: from $10,000 to $27,000 yearly for astronauts and other MSC scientists. A division chief, who will coordinate dozens of MSC engineers and prime contractors, makes between $20,000 to $25,000 yearly. Each astronaut receives additional income from a group contract with Life magazine, which may amount to $16,000 a year during the next few years. But on the whole there are no wide disparities in standards of living. The community tends to be oriented toward its children, to vote Republican and to play the stock market in the $100 to $200 lot. NASA has hired 150 blacks at the center—less than 4 per cent of the total work force—and has tried to hire more. But, says NASA, the specialized requirements disqualify many applicants.

Since budget cuts have brought new hiring practically to a standstill, MSC and the surrounding community will probably remain ingrown. The community has, in fact, an elite structure almost completely dictated by the No. 1 business. The astronauts are the stars, though they are not on the whole star-struck by the limelight. "The astronaut families do sort of stick together," says one young woman, "but it's not a rigid thing. If an astronaut throws a party and invites only other astronauts and wives, that's about a hundred people."

The community is tenaciously goal-oriented. The children get high marks in a school system that emphasizes science and math, subjects their parents have excelled in all their life. Special labs prepare students of the Clear Creek High School, which serves all the MSC communities, for the stiff national competition for college entrance, and an average of 8.6 per cent of the junior class have qualified as semifinalists in the last three years of the National Merit Scholarship competition.

The Cutting Edge of Error

Men in the space community are under a great deal of pressure to perform. "Most of these space industries now operate under a principle of what they call 'zero defects'," says Prof. Evans. "At one time they would allow for a small margin of error, but now they operate on the notion that there is no room for error. It has a definite psychological effect—like a group of students ready to take a Ph.D. exam." And in addition to the pressure of work, there is the added insecurity of not knowing whether a particular project will be scrubbed.

"Our job is practically done for Apollo, and the agency hasn't decided where to go," says Enoch M.

Jones, 36, an engineer at the center. "Everyone's very worried about the future, particularly guys like me who have been with the program for ten years. But a lot of us aren't going to wait around for a few years for some guy to announce a new national goal in space." Adds astronaut Lind: "The space program has become the pet gripe for everyone. How can we put a man on the moon, people say, and not make a can opener that works? We have all sorts of enemies after our money. But you can't cut back on the program much more without dissolving this team, and we're at a minimum now."

One of the more reflective MSC engineers is Dave Greenshields, 36, chief of the thermal-technology branch. Since graduation from the University of Texas in 1955 Greenshields has worked on the government's space program, first as a research engineer at Langley, in Virginia, and now in Houston. At the center he helped develop the heat shield for the Apollo spacecraft, a research and development project that took years to design, test, and approve. His wife, Pat, is a Democratic Party worker. "Sometimes I feel like I'm the only Democrat in town," she says. Greenshields himself designed his family's $30,000 home, but he says he'd prefer to live in an apartment in an urban environment. "There's no real sense of tradition here," explains Dave, "no grandmothers nearby." And Mrs. Greenshields adds, "We frequently escape on weekends to New Orleans or San Antonio."

In Search of the Frontier

If Greenshields finds the area somewhat uncongenial, then why does he stay? One reason is that he doesn't discern any national project around of equivalent challenge. "Are we supposed to live like ants in a tree, with the human race confined to one little rock floating in one small corner of the universe?" he asks. "My cosmological picture is this: If we don't get off, we'll eat the earth up eventually and die."

Greenshields is an engineer whose job, he says, is to solve a problem—any problem—efficiently. In fact, he wouldn't object to turning the attention of the center to poverty and urban blight to "help straighten the nation out," as he puts it. In his opinion, the MSC is essentially a well organized problem-solving machine that could turn from landing a man on the moon to cleaning up the ghettos and be just as successful. Moreover, he says, some of the lessons that the spaceworkers have learned might well be applied by domestic problem solvers. "We've found," he says, "that some problems just can't be solved head-on. Sometimes you have to leave them unsolved for a while, work on some others, and then come back to them from a slightly different angle. And, also, it's silly to get stuck on one problem and not go on to others if you're getting nowhere."

A great many spaceworkers wholeheartedly concur with the Greenshields philosophy, not only because they think it is fundamentally correct but also because they are true believers in the power of positive technology. They feel that the only way they can fail is if they are given no mission to perform. The dread of inactivity hangs heavy over MSC. It is a trait, as the historian Frederick Jackson Turner pointed out decades ago, ingrained in the American character and reflected in the restless search for new frontiers to conquer.

Further Resources

BOOKS

Bilstein, Roger E. *The American Aerospace Industry: From Workshop to Global Enterprise.* New York: Twayne, 1996.

Bromberg, Joan Lisa. *NASA and the Space Industry.* Baltimore, Md.: Johns Hopkins University Press, 1999.

Schefter, James L. *The Race: The Uncensored Story of How America Beat Russia to the Moon.* New York: Doubleday, 1999.

Walsh, Patrick J. *Echoes Among the Stars: A Short History of the U.S. Space Program.* Armonk, N.Y.: Sharpe, 2000.

Periodicals

"Fortieth Anniversary: Technology Utilization Program." *Spin-off,* 2002. Available online at http://www.jsc.nasa.gov/er/seh /spin02.pdf; website home page: http://www.jsc.nasa.gov (accessed June 8, 2003). *This links to a 157–page special edition of a NASA journal that details the technological advances discovered as a result of the space program.*

WEBSITES

"Decision to Go to the Moon: President John F. Kennedy's May 25, 1961 Speech before a Joint Session of Congress." NASA History Office. Available online at http://history.nasa.gov /moondec.html; website home page: http://history.nasa.gov (accessed June 8, 2003). *This site contains the audio and text of President Kennedy's speech, together with links to many criticald documents and reports on the space program.*

Johnson Space Center Website. Available online at http://www .jsc.nasa.gov/info/aboutjsc/html; website home page: http:// www.jsc.nasa.gov (accessed June 8, 2003).

"NASA Centers and Responsibilities." Kennedy Space Center Science, Technology, and Engineering. Available online at http://science.ksc.nasa.gov/shuttle/technology/sts-newsref /centers.html#centers; website home page: http://science.ksc .nasa.gov/ (accessed April 19, 2003).

Space Center Houston: Official Visitor's Center of NASA's Johnson Space Center. Available online at http://www .spacecenter.org (accessed June 8, 2003).

3

EDUCATION

MILLIE JACKSON

Entries are arranged in chronological order by date of primary source. For entries with one primary source, the entry title is the same as the primary source title. Entries with more than one primary source have an overall entry title, followed by the titles of the primary sources.

Important Events in Education, 1960–1969

1960

• Myron Lieberman's *The Future Of Public Education* predicts a revolution in all aspects of education in the coming decade.

• On January 1, ninety percent of high-school principals were men and 85 percent of elementary-school teachers were women.

• On February 20, African American students in Greensboro, North Carolina, stage a sit-in by filling seats at a lunch counter to protest refusals to serve seated African Americans.

• On May 13, demonstrating San Francisco students are rebuffed with fire hoses at city hall as they protest a House Un-American Activities Committee hearing.

• On November 1, Congress passes a general aid-to-education bill, the first in the twentieth century.

• On November 12, the U.S. Justice Department warns Louisiana governor Jimmie Davis against blocking desegregation of public schools.

• On November 13, a special session of the Louisiana legislature approves steps to avoid school desegregation in New Orleans.

• On December 4, African American New Orleans minister Floyd Foreman continues to escort his five-year-old daughter to an integrated neighborhood school despite abuse from onlookers.

1961

• Classrooms and qualified teachers are in shortage throughout the U.S.

• President John F. Kennedy's school legislation fails due to the controversy over proposed federal aid to private schools.

• On January 10, two African American students enroll at the University of Georgia.

• On January 13, the University of Georgia's first two African American students are suspended following riots. University officials are directed to reinstate them.

• On March 20, the U.S. Supreme Court declares unconstitutional Louisiana's attempts to halt desegregation.

• On May 6, Attorney General Robert Kennedy, speaking at the University of Georgia, vows strict enforcement

of civil rights laws, including the integration of public schools.

• In November, students from several eastern colleges spend Thanksgiving picketing the White House to protest resumption of nuclear weapons testing.

1962

• On January 11, President John F. Kennedy, in his State of the Union Address, reaffirms his commitment to enact school legislation that failed in 1961.

• On February 6, Congress hears President John F. Kennedy's "Special Message on Education" with additional proposals: scholarships to upgrade the quality of teaching and aid for adult illiterates and handicapped children.

• In April, New York teachers strike for one day to protest years of overcrowding and low pay.

• On June 25, the U.S. Supreme Court rules that reading of an official prayer in New York public schools violates the Establishment Clause of the First Amendment.

• On July 8, the U.S. Department of Health, Education and Welfare proposes a study of television's effect on schoolchildren.

• On July 14, Anthony Celebrezze replaces Abraham Ribicoff as Secretary of Health, Education and Welfare when Ribicoff runs for Senate.

• On July 20, the U.S. Supreme Court in *Engle v. Vitale* bars public schools from sponsoring prayer and Bible reading as violations of the Establishment Clause of the First Amendment.

• On July 26, a federal judge orders Prince Edward County, Virginia, schools to open, three years after they closed to defy an order to integrate.

• On August 31, Roman Catholic officials in Buras, Louisiana, close an integrated parochial school under threat of violence.

• On September 20, Mississippi Governor Ross Barnett defies a federal court in refusing to admit James Meredith as the first African American student at the University of Mississippi.

• On September 24, the University of Mississippi agrees to admit James Meredith. Mississippi Governor Ross Barnett threaten to arrest any federal official who intervenes to force Mississippi schools, including the University of Mississippi, to integrate.

• On September 26, Misssissippi Lt. Gov. Paul Johnson prevents James Meredith from enrolling at "Ole Miss," the University of Mississippi.

• On September 28, a federal court finds Mississippi Governor Ross Barnett in contempt of the federal court order to integrate Mississippi public schools.

• On September 29, a federal court finds Mississippi Lieutenant Governor Paul Johnson in contempt for blocking the integration of Mississippi public schools.

• On September 30, James Meredith is escorted onto campus; federal troops are ordered there as rioting and shooting break out.

- On October 1, after fifteen hours of rioting which leaves two dead, James Meredith enrolls at the University of Mississippi.

1963

- In January, Alabama Governor George Wallace vows never to allow an African American student to attend the University of Alabama.

- On January 28, without incident Harvey Gantt registers as the first African American student at Clemson College in South Carolina.

- On June 5, without incident the second African American student, Cleve McDowell, enters the University of Mississippi Law School.

- On June 11, Alabama Governor George Wallace steps aside, after threatening defiance of the federal desegregation order, as two African American students register at the University of Alabama.

- On July 1, the U.S. Court of Appeals prohibits Powhatan County, Virginia, schools from closing as Prince Edward County had done in 1959 to prevent integration.

- On August 11, one of the two African American students at the University of Alabama withdraws.

- On August 14, Virginia governor Albertis Harrison details private financing to educate seventeen hundred African American children in Prince Edward County who had had no schooling since 1959.

- On August 18, James Meredith is the first African American to receive a B.A. from the University of Mississippi.

- On September 8, the United Federation of Teachers accepts a new contract, averting a strike by New York teachers.

- On September 24, the University of Mississippi expels its only African American student, Cleve McDowell, for carrying a gun on campus.

- On November 19, President John F. Kennedy thanks National Education Association members in the Rose Garden for help in passing the aid-to-higher-education bill.

- On December 16, President Lyndon B. Johnson signs the education bill into law, saying "The enactment of this measure is a monument to President Kennedy," who had been assassinated on November 22.

1964

- The number of classrooms under construction lags 124,000 behind need.

- More than ten thousand portable classrooms near U.S. schools handle overflow students.

- On January 8, in his State of the Union Address President Lyndon Baines Johnson unveils his $97.9 billion budget, with increased spending for public education as a hallmark.

- On February 22, the United States and the Soviet Union sign the fourth two-year agreement on educational, technological, and scientific exchanges.

- On March 12, ten thousand New York residents march on the board of education building to protest the loss of neighborhood schools due to desegregation.

- On May 25, the U.S. Supreme Court orders Prince Edward County, Virginia, schools to reopen.

- On November 19, in his first speech after the election President Lyndon B. Johnson calls education the "prime investment" of the future.

- In December, Students for a Democratic Society (SDS), a coalition of students at the University of California, Berkeley, calls for demonstrators against the Vietnam War to converge on Washington, D.C.

- On December 3, at the University of California, Berkeley, a three-month dispute between student activists and the administration climaxes as police arrest 796 students sitting in at the administration building.

1965

- Fifty new community colleges are built.

- On January 23, U.S. Air Force Secretary Eugene Zuckert announces that one hundred cadets at the Air Force Academy were involved in a cheating scandal.

- On January 25, the new federal budget is $2.2 billion over spending in 1964, with the largest expansion in welfare and education spending since the New Deal.

- In February, police arrest one thousand African American schoolchildren in Selma, Alabama, for participating in Martin Luther King, Jr.'s nonviolent voter-registration campaign.

- On March 5, arsonists burn to the ground the Freedom School, one of first integrated schools, in Indianola, Mississippi.

- From March 24 to March 25, some three thousand students and faculty participate in a teach-in at the University of Michigan in Ann Arbor, Michigan. They participate in workshops, listen to lectures, and debate the objectives and possible outcomes of the Vietnam War.

- On March 29, President Lyndon B. Johnson orders Central Intelligence Agency (CIA) director Richard Helms to trace the source of funding for university teach-ins and college protests against the Vietnam War. Johnson believed communist China or the Soviet Union were funding the protests, but Helms could find no communist link.

- On April 7, President Lyndon B. Johnson visits Johns Hopkins University in Baltimore, Maryland to reassure students, the males of whom are of draft age, of his desire to negotiate an end to the Vietnam War.

- On April 9, Congress enacts a $1.3 billion school-aid bill after the Senate, in a 73-18 vote, passes it without amendments.

- On April 17, twenty-five thousand demonstrators, many of them college students, answer the SDS call in December 1964, gathering in Washington, D.C. to protest the Vietnam War.

- On April 19, U.S. Federal Bureau of Investigation (FBI) director J. Edgar Hoover dispatches agents to the University of California, Berkeley to undermine SDS.

- On May 15, students at 122 U.S. colleges and universities participate in a national Vietnam Teach-in, watching television debates by university scholars and Johnson administration officials on the objectives and possible outcomes of the Vietnam War.

• On May 30, Vivian Malone becomes the first African American graduate of the University of Alabama.

• From July 20 to July 21, the White House Conference on Education, with 709 participants and 200 observers, symbolizes President Lyndon B. Johnson's commitment to education.

• On September 2, the U.S. Senate votes 79-3 to pass a $4.7 billion higher-education bill with grants for needy students.

• On November 20, the chancellor and academic dean of City University of New York (CUNY) as well as the presidents of Brooklyn and Hunter Colleges, branch colleges of CUNY, resign to protest a four-hundred-dollar fee to city residents for tuition. Previously CUNY had charged no tuition to New York City residents.

1966

• Ivy League schools intensify recruitment of African American students.

• The number of enrolled students in graduate programs has doubled to 570,000 since 1957.

• On February 19, Protestant Union Theological Seminary and Jesuit Fordham University agree to share professors, credits, and libraries.

• On March 3, veterans serving after January 31, 1955 receive new educational benefits as President Lyndon B. Johnson signs the Veteran's Readjustment Act.

• On March 9, President Lyndon B. Johnson relaxes travel restrictions to Communist China, allowing scholars to travel and study there.

• On May 12, University of Chicago students take over the administration building to protest the university's cooperation with the selective service system.

• On June 6, a sniper shoots James Meredith, the University of Mississippi's first African American graduate, as he walked from Memphis, Tennessee, to Jackson, Mississippi, to encourage voter registration.

• On October 20, Congress approves $6.2 billion in aid for elementary and secondary education.

1967

• The University of Texas chancellor asserts that the attention on disadvantaged children ignores the needs of gifted students.

• On January 14, the Hunt Report, "A Bill of Rights for Children," is released; it cites the waste of human potential due to disastrous child-rearing patterns in poor families.

• On June 30, President Lyndon B. Johnson's task force on education recommends new and expanded federal programs to include a "moon shot" effort in curriculum and instruction to assure that all children learn the three Rs.

• On December 15, House-Senate conferees agree to Texas senator Yarborough's bilingual education bill.

1968

• Congress aims to renew, extend, and amend the three giant higher-education acts of the past decade.

• On January 25, Secretary of Health, Education, and Welfare John Gardner resigns after citing misgivings about the inadequacies of the Great Society.

• In March, Alabama Governor George Wallace, running for president as the candidate of the American Independent Party, promises voters that he will restore segregation in public schools.

• On November 18, the New York United Federation of Teachers votes to end its strike after five weeks of closed schools.

• On December 4, the U.S. Justice Department orders the Union, New Jersey, school board to integrate its schools, the first attack against segregation in northern schools.

1969

• Nine million children from low-income families receive aid for education through Title I.

• Some 716,000 children are in Head Start programs.

• More than 4 million high-school and 845,000 technical students are in federally supported vocational education programs.

• On March 17, the U.S. Supreme Court affirms in *Tinker v. Des Moines Independent School District* that states, not the federal government, bear the primary responsibility of educating children.

• On April 22, City College in New York (CCNY), a branch college of CUNY, closes after 150 African American and Puerto Rican students blockade one campus.

• On May 7, a battle between African American and white students at CCNY injures seven.

• On May 15, the California National Guard, with tear gas and shotguns, breaks up a protest at the University of California, Berkeley, over the university's seizure of property that students were using as a "people's park."

• On May 15, the National Education Association and the American Federation of Teachers create a joint local, the United Teachers of Flint in Flint, Michigan.

• In December, fifty thousand children in schools with individual instruction programs receive individual packets in math and reading. Each child has a study program geared to his or her learning needs.

ployer and employee relations, and the debate over what is right versus what is wrong with education.

Significance

Myron Lieberman was one of many educational theorists of the time to challenge the effectiveness of public education in the United States. He believed that radical changes had to be made in the power structure of education in order to realize change in the way students learned. Further, Lieberman believed that "public schools [did] not develop critical thinking, good citizenship, social competence, or creative skills." The predictions that Myron Lieberman made in *The Future of Public Education,* as well as his continuing body of work, make him an important scholar in the field of education.

Lieberman's thought-provoking work challenged those who wanted to concentrate on philosophy and methodology. He criticized many of the organizational principles of education in America. *The Future of Public Education* condemns local control of schools, which became popular and necessary during the preceding decades. It also attacks teacher education and certification requirements. Christopher Jencks, writing for *The New Republic,* called Lieberman's work "the most lucid and comprehensive analysis now available." Jencks notes that Lieberman was trying to chart a "revolution among teachers" similar to the one that occurred in medicine after the Civil War (1861–1865). Lieberman maintained that teachers suffered from being seen as civil servants, rather than as trained professionals able to make intelligent decisions about education. Rather than appeal to the public for input, as so many of his colleagues were doing, Lieberman called for a strong professional teachers' organization. At the time he wrote this book, his views were unique. At the beginning of the twenty-first century, teachers' unions are stronger and input from teachers about school curricula is considered more important than it was at the beginning of the 1960s.

Lieberman did not just criticize the American educational system. He was and is an active participant in improving schools and promoting professionalism among teachers. He has served as a teachers' union president and is considered an expert on teachers' unions and bargaining.

Primary Source

The Future of Public Education [excerpt]

SYNOPSIS: In this chapter, titled "What the Problem Is Not," Myron Lieberman challenges traditional ideas about what will improve American education. He argues that philosophy, vision of a good life, and public opinion are not the central issues. Rather, Lieberman insists that Americans should agree on

---

The Future of Public Education

Nonfiction work

By: Myron Lieberman

Date: 1960

Source: Lieberman, Myron. "What the Problem Is Not." In *The Future of Public Education.* Chicago: University of Chicago Press, 1960, 15–25.

About the Author: Myron Lieberman (1919–) was born in St. Paul, Minnesota. He served in the U.S. Army during World War II (1939–1945), and after earning a Ph.D. at the University of Illinois in 1952, he began a career as an educator. Lieberman has been a high school and college instructor as well as a negotiator and consultant for many educational groups. ∎

Introduction

Both World War II and the Korean War (1950–1953) affected school funding in the United States. Because of the difficult economic conditions, government funds were diverted from schools and used to fund the military. Local and state government took over the responsibility for school funding and control, causing disparity among school districts. However, this was only part of the problem with education in America at the time.

Educational theorists of the late 1950s and early 1960s wanted to return to the emphasis on "the three Rs"—reading, writing, and arithmetic. Reports were issued and books written about the subject. Many of the theorists of the time believed in the primary importance of educational philosophy. But in his book *The Future of Education,* published in 1960, Myron Lieberman insisted on the need for changes in the *organization* of the American educational system, rather than a change in the nation's educational philosophy. This controversial approach drew attention to his ideas.

In the book, Lieberman called for major changes in the power structure of American education. He argued that the main problem in the educational system was that everyone put his or her own interests first. *The Future of Education* addressed several points, among them the issue of local control of schools, teacher education, em-

common, national goals for education, even though public schools are under state and local control. He also advocates that teachers have a stronger role in the schools.

What the Problem Is Not

The most important educational issue of our time is what should be the purposes of public education. This problem is "philosophical" in nature, in the sense that our answer to it will eventually depend on our vision of the good life and our conceptions of the nature of man, society, truth, ultimate reality, and other philosophical concepts. The determination of the purposes of education is essentially a matter for public rather than professional action.

I wish to dissent from all three of these propositions. The purpose of this chapter is to explain why they are fallacious and how belief in them has been harmful to public education in the United States.

Regardless of whether the determination of the broad purposes of education is *the* major problem of public education, there can be little doubt that most educational theorists think that it is. One of the "critics" writes:

> The point I am making is that despite a sometimes fundamental philosophical cleavage, the traditionalists and the modernists believed in content, in a body of subject matter to be taught, but parted company on matters of method. This is no longer the main debate in American education; the controversy today is between those who continue to believe that the cultivation of intelligence, moral as well as intellectual, is inextricably bound up with the cultural heritage and accumulated knowledge of mankind, and those who feel that education's primary task is to adjust the individual to the group, to see that he responds "satisfactorily" to the stresses and strains of the social order.

A recent textbook by four well-known professors of education asks and answers itself:

> Why should the teacher know anything about the social role of the school?

> First, most of the educational disputes now taking place in many communities center about the essential purpose of the school.

Paul Woodring, a widely known educational theorist who is not identified with any particular school of educational thought, comments:

> Today we are engaged in a great national debate over the aims and purpose of education, a debate that has included vigorous criticism of existing schools and of the philosophy of education which lies behind them.

And later, after proposing that "the proper aim of education is to prepare the individual to make wise decisions," he says:

> If we can agree on this as our aim, our educational planning will be greatly simplified and the great American debate over education can move on to a profitable discussion of the best means for reaching our goals.

The point of view expressed in these quotations is too common to require further documentation. Nevertheless, despite its wide acceptance in the educational world, I believe that it represents a basic fallacy in our approach to educational problems.

It is true that no *statement* of the broad purposes of education has been accepted by the American people as a whole, but this does not mean that there is widespread disagreement about these purposes. There is a difference between agreement with a particular statement of purpose and agreement upon the purposes themselves. It is possible to have either of these things without the other. To the best of my knowledge, the American people as a whole have never agreed formally to a statement of the functions of *any* profession. Nevertheless, the professions are not unduly handicapped by a lack of agreement as to their general purposes. This fact suggests that the absence of any widespread formal agreement on the broad purposes of education must be interpreted very cautiously.

Certainly, there are disagreements concerning the broad purposes of education, just as there are some disagreements concerning the objectives of the medical profession, the legal profession, the engineering profession, the civil service, and many other occupational groups. Sometimes these disagreements present extremely difficult problems for the individual in a given field. Many scientists working on the atomic bomb had grave doubts concerning the purpose of their work. Lawyers are often confronted with situations which force them to decide whether their function is to advance the interests of their client or to see that justice is done. Other examples could be cited. Furthermore, I would agree that in specific instances conflict over the broad purposes of education does constitute a serious problem. My point is that these instances are too infrequent to be regarded as our major educational problem.

Since education is a state and local responsibility in the United States, some people contend that there is no reason why the American people as a whole should agree on its general objectives. Some even go so far as to assert that it would be dangerous to have widespread agreement on the purposes of education. Nevertheless, I believe that the American people are in substantial agreement that the purposes of education are the development of critical thinking, effective communication, creative skills, and social, civic, and occupational competence.

If there is widespread agreement on the broad purposes of education, why do so many people believe that disagreement in this area is so pervasive? The most important reason is the confusion over what are purposes and what are the means of achieving them. In this connection, bear in mind that school subjects are means of achieving certain purposes; they are not the purposes themselves. When we disagree about the inclusion of a subject in the curriculum, the disagreement may or may not arise out of disagreement over educational objectives.

The point of the preceding paragraph is an extremely important one; I shall elaborate upon it on several occasions in later chapters. Here let me suggest a simple example to illustrate the point and to bring out its importance. I believe that one of the objectives of public education is to develop critical thinking. To achieve this purpose, I believe that the study of logic and scientific method should be introduced into the public school curriculum. I also happen to believe that the world history courses so often given at the tenth-grade level are largely a waste of time.

I am not concerned now with defending either of these recommendations. For the sake of argument on the main issue, concede that I am completely mistaken in thinking that the study of logic and scientific method would be more conducive to critical intelligence than tenth-grade world history. I do not see, however, how anyone can question my categorical assertion that I accept and advocate the broad purpose of developing critical thinking. The important issue is whether the study of logic and scientific method would facilitate the development of critical thinking more than the study of world history.

This example suggests that a great deal of argument popularly labeled "controversy over the broad purposes of education" really concerns the means of achieving agreed-upon objectives. This confusion results from the fact that educational theory has not provided a clear-cut demarcation between purposes and the means of achieving them. At this point the reader may ask: "What difference does it make if the disagreement is labeled one of purpose or one of means? Isn't the important fact

the one of disagreement, not what it is labeled?" My answer is that in this context, the way we label the disagreement is more important than the fact of disagreement.

Ultimately, the determination of the broad purposes of education is one for our entire society to make. The choice of means is one for the teaching profession to decide. If there is no clear-cut understanding of what are objectives and what are means, people think they are arguing about one when they are really arguing about the other. Naturally, as a result of this confusion, people tend to exaggerate the extent of disagreement over purposes. What is more important, this confusion encourages the public to make decisions concerning means which in its own best interests should be made by teachers. *To generalize: it makes a tremendous difference whether we classify a disagreement as one of purpose or as one of means, because the mode of classification has a crucial bearing on who should settle the disagreement.*

Consider again, for a moment, a few sentences from the education textbook already cited:

> In school after school, the teachers and principal are attacked by vociferous groups of citizens who think that the three R's are not given enough time, or that the conventional subjects are neglected, or that the school is not emphasizing moral and spiritual values, or that false and dangerous economic and political doctrines are being taught. . . . Each of these attacks reflects a public concern with what the school is attempting to do. *Each one presupposes that the school should serve one function rather than another—that the role of the school is to teach the fundamental skills and the conventional subjects,* or to develop moral and spiritual character, or to maintain the *status quo* or even the *status quo ante* in economics and politics, and so on.

This quotation illustrates exactly the kind of confusion I am talking about. A controversy over whether "the three R's are not given enough time" is not necessarily a conflict over the function of public education. Such controversy does *not* "presuppose that the school should serve one function rather than another." Assuming that it does so only confuses teachers and laymen alike into exaggerating the extent of disagreement over the objectives of education and encourages massive interference with academic freedom. If educators themselves tell citizens to debate and settle the amount of time given to the three R's on the grounds that this problem is one of broad purpose, they have in effect abandoned their professional claim to autonomy in this matter. And, in general, academic freedom is muddled away by educators more than it is trampled upon by laymen.

Exaggeration of the extent of disagreement over purposes is compounded by a tendency to assume that people who advocate different subjects in the curriculum necessarily advocate different objectives for education. People often agree on what is purpose and what are means, but then erroneously regard a difference in means as reflecting a difference in purpose. Sometimes it is, but often it is not. Disagreement over the inclusion of a subject may simply reflect differing estimates of its usefulness in achieving an agreed-upon purpose.

Although disagreement over educational purposes is neither the pervasive nor the all-important problem that it is often thought to be, there are some extremely important analytical and practical problems directly related to this problem. In order to effectuate any objective, teachers must develop a set of intermediate objectives which will provide direction for their efforts in the classroom. It is at this point—the point of professional translation of broad purposes into a coherent educational program—that we have some of our major unsolved problems. The failure of the teaching profession to implement certain broad purposes of education has understandably but mistakenly led to the belief that teachers have abandoned these purposes. A failure in performance has come to be regarded as one of intent instead of capability.

For example, one of the objectives of education may be to develop the ability to communicate effectively. However, the first-grade teacher can contribute to this purpose only by setting certain specific goals, such as a vocabulary of so many words or an ability to write the letters of the alphabet, for her students. The English teacher in the high school also contributes to the same broad objective but only by setting intermediate objectives which are different from those set by elementary-school teachers: he works toward such intermediate objectives as an understanding of grammar, an ability to locate sources of information, an appreciation of literary classics, and so on.

Some of the intermediate objectives of the high-school teacher will appear to be the same as those of the elementary-school teacher. For instance, both will accept increasing the pupil's vocabulary as an intermediate objective. In practice, however, the words and concepts taught by one will be different from those taught by the other. Indeed, all teachers should have as one of their broad objectives the development of effective communication. All may contribute toward this objective by increasing the vocabulary of their students. However, each teacher will have a different vocabulary to teach. The history teacher will introduce such new concepts as feudalism or the Industrial Revolution, the physics teacher will introduce such new ones as velocity and ergs, and so on.

The problem here is that the teachers have failed to establish sets of intermediate objectives which would clarify how they propose to fulfil the general objectives of education. The discussion of objectives is usually concerned with the general ones, but this is not where the problem lies. It lies in establishing consistent, defensible, and attainable intermediate objectives which can serve as the basis for evaluating the progress made by the profession.

Let me illustrate this point by examples from other occupations. One of the broad aims of the medical profession is to prolong life. In carrying out this objective, the medical profession has eliminated most communicable causes of death. Of communicable diseases, only tuberculosis and pneumonia are still major causes of death, and the advances made in checking these are impressive. Thus, in 1900 the death rate per 100,000 persons from tuberculosis was 194.4; in 1952 it was only 16.1. In 1900 the death rate per 100,000 persons from pneumonia was 175.4; in 1952 it was 30.5. Again, bear in mind that other communicable diseases have been eliminated entirely or reduced to a negligible factor.

Thus, in carrying out its general purpose of prolonging life, the medical profession has concentrated upon the major causes of death at any given time. Obviously, as some are eliminated, other causes become major. Today, degenerative diseases have largely replaced communicable diseases as the major causes of death, and the medical profession is now beginning to eliminate or substantially reduce the death rate from these. As it succeeds, still other diseases will become major causes of death, and they in turn will be subjected to intensive research with a view to their elimination or substantial reduction.

By thus going from one specific intermediate objective to another, the medical profession has achieved outstanding success in fulfilling one of its broad purposes, the prolongation of life. In the United States, life expectancy at birth was approximately 40 years in 1800, 49 years in 1900, close

Students work on an assignment in an integrated classroom, 1965. In the early 1960s, theorists including Myron Lieberman challenged the effectiveness of public education in the United States, believing that radical changes had to be made to improve the power structure of education. © JACK MOEBES/CORBIS. REPRODUCED BY PERMISSION.

to 60 years by 1925, and close to 70 years by 1950. Indeed, the success of the medical profession in eliminating one after another of the leading causes of death has led the profession to question whether there are any insuperable biological limits to human life. At any rate, there is every reason to expect greater and greater success in prolonging human life, but always through concrete intermediate goals which lead to the broad goal itself.

Perhaps one other example will be useful. Physicists have as their general purpose the achievement of an understanding of the laws of matter and motion. Their field is usually regarded as encompassing mechanics, heat, electricity, light, and sound. Now, although the general purpose of physicists has remained unchanged for centuries, in recent years they have achieved dazzling success in its fulfilment.

For example, when Einstein discovered that $e = mc^2$, he made an enormous contribution to the understanding of the laws of matter and motion. Other physicists have solved one after another of the basic theoretical problems of physics. But the point is that these gains have been achieved because physicists, collectively and individually, have continually set and achieved strategic intermediate objectives which would implement the broad purpose of their profession.

Getting back to education, we see that it too has broad purposes, such as the development of an ability to communicate effectively. Such a purpose is analogous to the general purpose of prolonging life or of increasing our understanding of matter and motion. But whereas doctors and physicists have progressive and feasible intermediate objectives, teachers do not. Therein is a problem of purpose, albeit not the problem which agitates so many of our post-Sputnik philosophers of education.

Let me illustrate what might be done. A student who is capable of earning an engineering degree is ordinarily capable of learning calculus by the time he finishes high school. In practice, such students are not even exposed to calculus until their second or third year in college. Teachers might well accept, as one of their intermediate objectives, the objective of having all students of a certain ability level and career pattern master calculus by the time they have finished high school.

Many interrelated problems would have to be solved to accomplish this intermediate objective. For instance, there are thousands of small high schools which have only one or a very few students capable of learning calculus. Some of these schools have no trained mathematics teachers, and there is little chance that a school system is going to employ a highly paid teacher for a handful of students. Thus, to achieve the proposed objective, it might be necessary to reduce drastically the number of high schools so that the remaining ones could offer appropriate courses with a reasonable teacher-pupil ratio. Obviously, changes in teacher education, in teachers' salaries, in the high-school curriculum, and in many other aspects of education would also be necessary to achieve the suggested intermediate objective. None of these changes is impossible or even impractical, given able leadership.

There are many kinds of intermediate objectives which teachers might set for themselves. Some of them would not involve any improvement in the performance of students. Instead, they would involve only an improvement in the productivity of teachers. Everyone is aware of the fact that maturational factors limit what can be taught to young children. The same student who is capable of learning calculus in the twelfth grade is not capable of learning it in the elementary grades. Of course, when we say that young children cannot learn better or faster, we never know for certain whether we are dealing with a stubborn and eradicable fact of life or with our ignorance of the learning process. In any case, when it is unreasonable to set higher goals for the students, teachers should concentrate upon ways and means of utilizing a smaller number of teachers to accomplish a given educational result. Just as in other fields, productivity may be increased either by a constant labor force which expands its output or by a constant output achieved

through a decreasing labor force. In most occupations there are exciting frontiers in both directions. Teachers, however, seem unable to make much progress in either.

It is important to recognize that intermediate objectives should be set by the professions, not by the public. The medical profession is best qualified to decide what specific hypotheses should be subjected to research in order to advance the broad purpose of prolonging life. Surely, physicists are the persons best qualified to decide which particular investigations will deepen our understanding of matter and motion. And in education teachers are, or should be, the persons best qualified to decide what proximate objectives of education should be pursued to fulfil its broad purposes. Unfortunately, while the doctors are making rapid advances in reducing pain and prolonging life, while scientists are exploring the vast reaches of the universe and the nature of the tiniest particles, while our industrialists and our labor force are achieving exciting advances in productivity, in short, while one occupational group after another is soaring to new heights, the teachers seem unable to get off the ground.

Why are the frontiers of public education so static? Why is education lost in a Sargasso Sea, so that from one generation to the next the schools are involved in the same dreary problems with the same dreary kinds of persons advocating the same dreary positions? Partly, I think, because of the misplaced, often pseudo-profound, concern with the broad purposes of education. This concern is the other side of a coin which reveals a shocking unwillingness and inability on the part of teachers at all levels and of all subjects to evaluate their own work.

Are schools today more effective (by any criterion) than they were *x* number of years ago? This question is important. We cannot evaluate public education without confronting it. Nevertheless, despite the fact that the question is often asked, there is a remarkable lack of systematic reliable data to answer it. The truth is that there is little rigorous evaluation of public education.

We have little evidence to show that the schools today are much more effective than those of an earlier day. Neither do we have much evidence to confirm the belief that there has been a sweeping deterioration in public education. But the important point is that the absence of systematic evaluative data is more remarkable than any conclusion to be drawn from whatever data we have.

Further Resources

BOOKS

Conant, James B. *The American High School Today: A First Report to Interested Citizens.* New York: McGraw-Hill, 1959.

Hutchins, Robert M. *Some Observations on American Education.* Cambridge: University Press, 1956.

Kridel, Craig. "Eight-Year Study." In *Encyclopedia of Education,* 2nd ed. New York: Macmillan Reference, 2003, 707–709.

PERIODICALS

Duncan, James Kelly. "A Right Way to Teach?" *The Journal of Teacher Education* 12, 1961, 310–313.

Jencks, Christopher. "A Teachers' Revolution." *The New Republic* 142, no. 4, January 25, 1960, 19–20.

Woodring, Paul. "Academic Nay to Reform by the Lay." *Saturday Review,* February 13, 1960, 54–55.

WEBSITES

"Dr. Myron Lieberman: Chairman, Education Policy Institute." Education Policy Institute. Available online at http://www.educationpolicy.org/resumml.htm; website home page: http://www.educationpolicy.org (accessed April 3, 2003).

Reflecting on *Sputnik:* Linking the Past, Present and Future of Education Reform. Available online at http://www.nas.edu/sputnik/index.htm (accessed February 24, 2003).

On Knowing: Essays for the Left Hand

Essay

By: Jerome Bruner

Date: 1962

Source: Bruner, Jerome. "The Act of Discovery." In *On Knowing: Essays for the Left Hand.* Cambridge: Harvard University Press, 1962, 81–85.

About the Author: Jerome S. Bruner (1915–) is a well-known psychologist and educator. In 1960, he cofounded the Center for Cognitive Studies at Harvard. Bruner was also involved in the MACOS (Man: A Course of Study) project, an attempt to produce a comprehensive curriculum based on behavioral sciences. Bruner has been a prolific author, writing several important works in the field of cognitive science. ∎

Introduction

Jerome Bruner was one of many psychologists studying the areas of thinking and learning in the 1950s and 1960s. He came to believe that "learning is an active process in which learners construct new ideas or concepts based upon their current/past knowledge." At the heart of the theory, called constructivist theory, is Socratic learning, or encouraging students to discover their own answers and principles. This is a quite different approach than rote learning and memorization, and it influenced instruction in schools.

Bruner's theories differed from those if his contemporaries, B.F. Skinner and Jean Piaget. Skinner's theory of operant behavior was based on reward and punishment. If people (or animals) are rewarded for a correct response and punished for an incorrect one, then they learn to give the correct response. Piaget's research centered on the question of how knowledge grows. He formulated theories of developmental and cognitive psychology that explain children's thinking versus adults' thinking.

On Knowing: Essays for the Left Hand is one of Jerome Bruner's many works. Published in 1962, it is a collection of essays concerned with aesthetic, or artistic, topics as well as didactic, or instructive, themes. Though originally written as separate pieces, the essays form a cohesive whole that explains how Bruner's theories developed in the early 1960s.

Significance

Bruner's theories were important to the development of both educational theory and school curricula in the 1960s and thereafter. *On Knowing: Essays for the Left Hand* explores how we know, and how we shape what we know. Three themes emerge from the essays, which Bruner wrote over the course of five years: the shape of experience, the quest for clarity, and the idea of action.

Bruner states in the book's introduction that he has long been fascinated by the theories of the right hand versus the left hand. The right hand denotes the doer, symbolizing order and lawfulness, while the left hand represents the dreamer. Bruner applies this idea to psychology and the study of learning. As a science, psychology searches for the exact answer—a right-hand approach. Bruner's pursuit of understanding knowledge forces him to think differently and to approach discovery with an open mind—in other words, from the left hand. The left cannot be divorced from the right, Bruner asserts. Scientific explanations are not always complete without artistic or creative explanations—and vice-versa. Knowledge includes both types of thinking.

In November of 1962, Eliseo Vivas, a philosopher and university professor, reviewed the book favorably in the *The New York Times Book Review.* In the review, he points out that "Bruner discusses the matters not narrowly within his discipline." This makes the book interesting and important, but perhaps overly broad. In *On Knowing,* Bruner explores education, Freud, and human control of behavior, as well as art and creativity. In linking these topics, he attempts to draw the humanities and science closer together.

Primary Source

On Knowing: Essays for the Left Hand [excerpt]

SYNOPSIS: In his chapter on "The Act of Discovery," Bruner writes, "Discovery, like surprise, favors the well-prepared mind." In other words, discovery does not just happen—it is based on and builds upon what has been learned before. The chapter explores how children discover and learn, and how they use their prior knowledge to construct new meanings.

The Act of Discovery

Maimonides, in his *Guide for the Perplexed*, speaks of four forms of perfection that men might seek. The first and lowest form is perfection in the acquisition of worldly goods. The great philosopher dismisses this on the ground that the possessions one acquires bear no meaningful relation to the possessor: "A great king may one morning find that there is no difference between him and the lowest person." A second perfection is of the body, its conformation and skills. Its failing is that it does not reflect on what is uniquely human about man: "he could (in any case) not be as strong as a mule." Moral perfection is the third, "the highest degree of excellency in man's character." Of this perfection Maimonides says: "Imagine a person being alone, and having no connection whatever with any other person; all his good moral principles are at rest, they are not required and give man no perfection whatever. These principles are only necessary and useful when man comes in contact with others." The fourth kind of perfection is "the true perfection of man; the possession of the highest intellectual faculties. . . ." In justification of his assertion, this extraordinary Spanish-Judaic philosopher urges: "Examine the first three kinds of perfection; you will find that if you possess them, they are not your property, but the property of others. . . . But the last kind of perfection is exclusively yours; no one else owns any part of it."

Without raising the question of whether moral qualities exist without reference to others, it is a conjecture much like the last of Maimonides' that leads me to examine the act of discovery in man's intellectual life. For if man's intellectual excellence is the most his own among his perfections, it is also the case that the most personal of all that he knows is that which he has discovered for himself. How important is it, then, for us to encourage the young to learn by discovery? Does it, as Maimonides would say, create a unique relation between knowledge and its possessor? And what may such a relation do for a man—or, for our purposes, a child?

The immediate occasion for my concern with discovery is the work of the various new curriculum projects that have grown up in America during the last few years. Whether one speaks to mathematicians or physicists or historians, one encounters repeatedly an expression of faith in the powerful effects that come from permitting the student to put things together for himself, to be his own discoverer.

First, I should be clear about what the act of discovery entails. It is rarely, on the frontier of knowledge or elsewhere, that new facts are "discovered" in the sense of being encountered, as Newton suggested, in the form of islands of truth in an uncharted sea of ignorance. Or if they appear to be discovered in this way, it is almost always thanks to some happy hypothesis about where to navigate. Discovery, like surprise, favors the well-prepared mind. In playing bridge, one is surprised by a hand with no honors in it and also by one that is all in one suit. Yet all particular hands in bridge are equiprobable: to be surprised one must know something about the laws of probability. So too in discovery. The history of science is studded with examples of men "finding out" something and not knowing it. I shall operate on the assumption that discovery, whether by a schoolboy going it on his own or by a scientist cultivating the growing edge of his field, is in its essence a matter of rearranging or transforming evidence in such a way that one is enabled to go beyond the evidence so reassembled to new insights. It may well be that an additional fact or shred of evidence makes this larger transformation possible. But it is often not even dependent on new information.

Very generally, and at the risk of oversimplification, it is useful to distinguish two kinds of teaching: that which takes place in the *expository mode* and that in the *hypothetical mode*. In the former, the decisions concerning the mode and pace and style of exposition are principally determined by the teacher as expositor; the student is the listener. The speaker has a quite different set of decisions to make: he has a wide choice of alternatives; he is anticipating paragraph content while the listener is still intent on the words; he is manipulating the content of the material by various transformations while the listener is quite unaware of these internal options. But in the hypothetical mode the teacher and the student are in a more cooperative position with respect to what in linguistics would be called "speaker's decisions." The student is not a bench-bound listener, but is taking a part in the formulation and at times may play the principal role in it. He will be aware of alternatives and may even have an "as if" attitude toward these, and he may evaluate information as it comes. One cannot describe the process in either mode with great precision of detail, but I think it is largely the hypothetical mode which characterizes the teaching that encourages discovery.

Consider now what benefits might be derived from the experience of learning through discoveries that one makes oneself. I shall discuss these under four headings: (1) the increase in intellectual potency, (2) the shift from extrinsic to intrinsic rewards, (3) the learning of the heuristics of discovering, and (4) the aid to conserving memory.

Intellectual potency

I should like to consider the differences among students in a highly constrained psychological experiment involving a two-choice machine. In order to win chips, they must depress a key either on the right or the left side of the apparatus. A pattern of payoff is designed so that, say, they will be paid off on the right side 70 percent of the time, on the left 30 percent, but this detail is not important. What is important is that the payoff sequence is arranged at random, that there is no pattern. There is a marked contrast in the behavior of subjects who think that there is some pattern to be found in the sequence— who think that regularities are discoverable—and the performance of subjects who think that things are happening quite by chance. The first group adopts what is called an "event-matching" strategy in which the number of responses given to each side is roughly commensurate to the proportion of times that it pays off: in the present case, 70 on the right to 30 on the left. The group that believes there is no pattern very soon settles for a much more primitive strategy allocating *all* responses to the side that has the greater payoff. A little arithmetic will show that the lazy all-and-none strategy pays off more if the environment is truly random: they win 70 percent of the time. The event-matching subjects win about 70 percent on the 70-percent payoff side (or 49 percent of the time there) and 30 percent of the time on the side that pays off 30 percent of the time (another 9 percent for a total take-home wage of 58 percent in return for their labors of decision).

But the world is not always or not even frequently random, and if one analyzes carefully what the event matchers are doing, one sees that they are trying out hypotheses one after the other, all of them containing a term that leads to a distribution of bets on the two sides with a frequency to match the actual occurrence of events. If it should turn out that there

Psychologist Dr. Jerome S. Bruner, Cambridge, Massachusetts, 1965. Bruner's theories attempt to draw science and the humanities closer together. He believes that scientific explanations are not always complete without artistic or creative explanations—that knowledge includes both types of thinking. **AP/WIDE WORLD PHOTOS. REPRODUCED BY PERMISSION.**

is a pattern to be discovered, their payoff could become 100 percent. The other group would go on at the middling rate of 70 percent.

What has this to do with the subject at hand? For the person to search out and find regularities and relationships in his environment, he must either come armed with an expectancy that there will be something to find or be aroused to such an expectancy so that he may devise ways of searching and finding. One of the chief enemies of search is the assumption that there is nothing one can find in the environment by way of regularity or relationship. In the experiment just cited, subjects often fall into one of two habitual attitudes: either that there is nothing to be found or that a pattern can be discovered by looking. There is an important sequel in behavior to the two attitudes.

Further Resources
BOOKS
Bruner, Jerome S., Jacqueline J. Goodnow, and George A. Austin. *A Study of Thinking.* New York: John Wiley & Sons, 1956.

PERIODICALS

Geisinger, Robert W. "The Discovery Variable: What is It?" *Psychology: A Journal of Human Behavior* 5, no. 1, 1968, 2–9.

Vivas, Eliseo. "Doing and Dreaming." *The New York Times Book Review,* November 16, 1962, 48.

WEBSITES

"Jerome Bruner." The Psi Cafe: A Psychology Resource Site. Available online at: http://www.psy.pdx.edu/PsiCafe /KeyTheorists/Bruner.htm#; website home page: http:// www.psy.pdx.edu (accessed April 4, 2003).

Smith, M.K. "Jerome S. Bruner and the Process of Education," 2002. The Encyclopedia of Informal Education. Available online at: http://www.infed.org/thinkers/bruner.htm; website home page: http://www.infed.org (accessed April 4, 2003).

The Community of Scholars
Nonfiction work

By: Paul Goodman

Date: 1962

Source: Goodman, Paul. "Society and School." In *The Community of Scholars.* New York: Random House, 1962, 46–52.

About the Author: Paul Goodman (1918–1972) was born in New York City and spent most of his career as a poor and itinerant teacher. He first received widespread notice with his book *Growing Up Absurd,* which was published in 1960. This paved the way for further publications, many on education. Goodman taught at several institutions and worked as a lay psychotherapist with the New York Institute for Gestalt Therapy. He was politically active during the 1960s. He also wrote fiction and poetry. His political beliefs influenced both his fiction and nonfiction works. ∎

Introduction

In the early 1960s, there were no shortages of studies about what aspects of the American educational system needed to be improved. The problem was how to make those improvements and who would pay for them. James Conant's 1961 *Slums and Suburbs: A Commentary on Schools in Metropolitan Areas* recognized the problems of violence in schools but did not address how to remedy it. *The American College,* a collection of essays, asked a number of questions about college education in America. The authors treated the problems mainly as social ills, rather than addressing the problems in the classroom.

Paul Goodman's *Community of Scholars,* published in 1962, called for education to take place in a small setting. Having visited more than thirty colleges around the country, Goodman felt that he had a unique perspective on higher education in America. Based on his experiences with students, faculty, and administrators at the university level, he concluded that faculty and students do not have the same goals, and that administrators do not aspire to please either group.

Goodman differentiated between the goals of scholarly research and the goals of society. Good, safe schools with well-educated teachers are of utmost importance to society, as are an affordable education, but these are not always what colleges and universities desire, Goodman argued. He attacked many well-known educational theorists in his book. James Coleman, James Bruner, and James Conant are particular targets, as was the Carnegie Foundation.

Significance

Paul Goodman's radical notions did not sit well with college administrators or faculty members. His ideas reflected the counterculture of the 1960s much more than the mainstream. A number of reviewers were critical of Goodman's book, calling it "unevenly written" and even "deeply flawed."

Even so, Goodman was able to communicate to the general public the alienation he felt as an intellectual and saw in university students. The problems on U.S. campuses that Goodman pointed out in *The Community of Scholars* were quite real. The divides between faculty and students deepened at some universities as the 1960s progressed, while other universities implemented experimental programs to meet the changing student population's needs. Paul Goodman's ideas were extreme for the day and still are, but they are an interesting study in the radical thinking of the 1960s.

Primary Source

The Community of Scholars [excerpt]

SYNOPSIS: In this chapter, "Society and School," Paul Goodman makes one of his favorite points: education will happen spontaneously. Children will learn, as will older students, despite what they are taught in school. What they learn, however, may coincide with the goals of the institution. Goodman also discusses ideals versus realities of education and of society's approach to education.

Society and School

Let us now lay the stress the other way, not on the schools in society, but on society and its schools. Education is an instrument of social needs, and by and large—except for the rather large factors of human recalcitrance and ignorant notions of what methods can possibly work—the powers of society get the education they want and that they deserve.

Writers on education can concentrate on social needs that are socially taken for granted: how to teach Reading or Citizenship, or even Driving. More grandly—for the Carnegie Corporation—an author can address himself to the need, in our corporate conformity, to encourage Excellence. More realistically, he can study, like James Coleman, how to manipulate Adolescent Culture so as to achieve goals useful for the adults. Professor Bruner has produced a good book on the current problem, How to educate for science. The advantage of this social-problems approach is that it is practical; the context is agreed, the powers of society need only to be convinced that one has a better technique.

A more philosophical approach is to start with the proposition that society educates inevitably, to continue itself, and that the kind of education is a function of the kind of society. This is, of course, the line that John Dewey took in *Democracy and Education.* He specified kinds of society; chose more desirable social purposes, e.g., democracy, progress; and so he arrived at the method and curriculum of the best kind of school. With such an approach, the practical problem is to get society to establish or reform its schools for its own good. On the whole, the history of progressive education has not been a cheerful one. Its ideas and methods have been stolen and bastardized precisely to strengthen the dominant system of society rather than to change it. Nevertheless, it is immortal: in its modern form it has revived for two hundred years and is reviving again with a salutary dash of A. S. Neil to counteract Dewey's propensity for order.

My own bias, however, is that education is going on spontaneously anyway; it is itself part of the kaleidoscope of society. Youngsters are imitating and identifying, aspiring to grow up, asking why, demanding show me how. Adults are demonstrative, helpful, ideal, or seeking to mold, exploit, or get a following. Spontaneous learning-and-teaching can be more or less efficient; it may be better or worse for its participants; but as with any other exciting function, the burden of proof of its defects lies on those who would interfere with it. I have been concentrating on one of its most complex and remarkable manifestations, the community of scholars of a *studium generale*. Such a college or university is a highly artificial product; yet it is profitable, I think, to regard it also as a highly natural convention, as shown by its long history. From this point of view, the practical social problem is often, not how to get society to establish good schools, but, as we have seen,

Paul Goodman's *Community of Scholars* (1962) attacked many well-known educational theorists of the day and proposed radical notions of revolution in education. **GETTY IMAGES. REPRODUCED BY PERMISSION.**

how to keep it from enslaving or destroying whatever good education happens to be occurring. When society's schools interfere too much with education, we must keep open the question whether *they* do more harm than good. *Most of our colleges being what they are, I fear that many of the best youth would get a better, though very imperfect, education if they followed their impulse and quit; and certainly many teachers ought to be more manly even if they risk getting fired.* (In my opinion, the risks are not so great as they fear. They do not push nearly as far as they could safely go.)

Education is motivated through and through by social needs. Culturally, there *are* no nonsocial needs. The professions require licenses; certain skills are marketable; rhetoric and dialectic are learned for leadership; the arts and sciences are useful. Yet it makes an enormous difference if it is directly society that uses the schools to train youth for its needs, or if it is directly the scholars that use the schools to learn or teach what they practically want to know or profess. When seminaries are founded to train ministers or our present universities are heavily subsidized to train military engineers, the social needs exist in the school as "goals of the administration" and this adds many complications: the scholars must be motivated, disciplined, evaluated. But when students who want to be lawyers or doctors find themselves a faculty, or masters with something important to profess attract disciples, the case is simpler: the goals are implicit and there is no problem of motivation. When the goals are in the administration, the teaching and learning are not likely to be for keeps, they are "lessons" (few of us remember many hours in our schooling that were not "lessons"). Teaching and learning for keeps has a very different tone; it can be troubling and even horribly upsetting, but what a pity it is that the nearest that most students ever come to emotional agitation is in cramming for examinations, and that many teachers never come near it at all. At college age, most young people do not know what they want, they must be exposed to new possibilities. But their ignorance, confusion, and seeking are not "academic" and ought to be addressed for keeps. This is what they came for. I remember a farm boy at the University of Vermont, complaining that he had come to college to be shaken in his religious faith, and the school had failed him.

■ ■ ■

Let us make a list of the implicit goals *of* the scholars and the extrinsic goals of society *for* them.

The implicit aims of the community of scholars have been: (1) To pass on and further, to grow up to and master, the arts and sciences. (2) To advance one's chosen career. Or, in less traditional societies where young people have less sense of vocation, to develop each youth's capacities and powers until he finds himself. (This includes unmaking the limitations and prejudices that he came with.) (3) To learn the philosophical bearings of one's vocation or profession in the universe of discourse, by contact with others in a *studium generale.* For example—a gruesomely important contemporary example—to learn to be not a housing engineer but a master of the social and civil functioning of housing and a lover of neighborhood beauty. (4) Finally, to have a community away from home and out of the economic mainstream, for imitating the veterans, for transferring oedipal affections and getting free of them, for friendship and sexual exploration in favorable circumstances, for self-government. Such are the implicit goals of the scholars.

On the other hand, the goals that society expects the scholars to pursue have been: (5) To fit the young for a useful life by teaching them acceptable attitudes and marketable skills. (6) To continue civilized society by manning its fundamental professions, religion, and government. (7) More narrowly, to train the young as apprentices for immediate service, as, at present, to win a war, to work for the corporations or the State. (8) And indeed, to get the scholars to affirm with their authority the social ideology, whatever it happens to be.

These two sets of aims, scholastic and social, are not always compatible. The social goals are not always, are even rarely, the ideal goals of culture and humanity. Society is often impatient with the doctrines and morals of university communities. A narrow professionalism is likely to conflict with scientific thoroughness and philosophical breadth. Placement in the workaday world has little to do with a student's capacities or vocation. In all such conflicts, of course, the members of an academic community are also members of society and internally divided against themselves. Students, pushed by their ambitious families and attracted by lucrative careers, may not be interested in the learning that their best professors want to give them. And on the other hand, goal-oriented professors are resisted by students who are not convinced that this academic torture is education for themselves. Also, professors sell out both teaching and research to engage in contractual research, and sometimes they follow the grants and leave the community flat. Mostly, however, it is the role of the administrators to see to it that the scholars fulfill their functions as, in Justice Minton's phrase, "a part of ordered society."

When society is wise, however, it tries to use its schools less wastefully, to benefit by the youngness of the young and the independence and learning of the scholars: (9) To prepare in a regular way for society's progressive change, by improving the next generation of the electorate. (10) To have in the disinterested scholars a critical standard for ordinary affairs. (11) And even, to invite the scholars to inquire and pragmatically experiment in social as well as physical problems.

These are the purposes—on which I have quoted Coleridge, Kant, and Dewey—that provide a better constitutional relation between society and school. If the schools are used for free growth, criticism, and social experiment, the socializing of the young becomes a two-way transaction: the young grow up into society, and society is regularly enlivened, made sensible, and altered by the fact that the young must grow up into it. Such social purposes preserve the community of scholars from becoming incestuous and merely academic. And with such purposes, society has its growth as organically part of itself, like the cambium of a tree.

Perhaps this is what Jefferson meant by the need of a revolution every twenty years, every new generation.

Further Resources

BOOKS

Dennis, Lawrence E., and Joseph F. Kauffman, eds. *The College and the Student: An Assessment of Relationships and Responsibilities in Undergraduate Education by Administrators, Faculty Members, and Public Officials.* Washington, D.C.: American Council on Education, 1966.

Sanford, Nevitt, ed. *The American College.* New York: John Wiley & Sons, 1962.

PERIODICALS

Goodman, Paul. "Freedom and Learning: The Need for Choice." *Saturday Review* 51, May 18, 1968, 73–75.

Jencks, Christopher. "Paul Goodman's Anarchism." *The New Republic* 147, November 17, 1962, 23–25.

Pace, C. Robert. [Review.] *Teachers College Record* 65, no. 3, December 1963, 288–289.

Selden, William K. "Administration as the Villain." *Saturday Review* 45, December 15, 1962, 61.

WEBSITES

"Nature Heals: The Psychological Essays of Paul Goodman." The Gestalt Therapy Page. Available online at http://www.gestalt.org/goodman.htm; website home page: http://www.gestalt.org (accessed April 4, 2003).

"Paul Goodman." Anarchy Archives. Available online at http://dwardmac.pitzer.edu/Anarchist_Archives/bright/goodman; website home page: http://dwardmac.pitzer.edu/Anarchist_Archives/index.html (accessed April 4, 2003).

"Paul Goodman: Writing on the Web." The Preservation Institute. Available online at http://www.preservenet.com/theory/Goodman.html; website home page: http://www.preservenet.com (accessed April 4, 2003).

Educated American Women: Self-Portraits

Nonfiction work

By: Eli Ginzberg and Alice M. Yohalem

Date: 1966

Source: Ginzberg, Eli, and Alice M. Yohalem. *Educated American Women: Self-Portraits.* New York: Columbia University Press, 1966, 1–9.

About the Author: Eli Ginzberg (1911–2002) was born in New York City. The son of a Talmudist scholar, Ginzberg

was drawn to education. He earned degrees from the University of Heidelberg, the University of Grenoble, and Columbia University. In 1935 he joined the Graduate School of Business at Columbia as a faculty member. Ginzberg published widely on economics, healthcare, and education. ■

Introduction

Women's education was not a new idea in the 1940s and 1950s; in fact, women were attending college in increasing numbers. But society still expected women to marry and raise a family, and it was assumed that mothers would not work at a full-time job outside the home.

Published in 1966, *Educated American Women: Self-Portraits,* by Eli Ginzberg and Alice M. Yohalem, was the third volume based on a study of graduate students at Columbia University between 1940–1945 and 1959–1951. Data was collected in 1961 and 1963. The first volume, titled *Talent and Performance,* concentrates on male graduate students. The study began as one of both male and female subjects, but it became apparent that the questions prepared for the first volume did not fit women's lifestyles. The second volume is based on a nine-page questionnaire geared towards women's lives. The research team also provided space for women to write about situations in their lives that did not correspond with the questions. The resulting volume, *Life Styles of Educated Women,* which details the lives of 311 women, was published in 1966. The vast amount of data that Ginzberg and his colleagues collected also provided the material for *Educated American Women: Self-Portraits,* published the same year.

Significance

Educated American Women: Self-Portraits focuses on a generation of women caught in society's mixed and changing expectations. On one hand, the post–World War II (1939–1945) economy provided greater educational opportunities for most Americans, including the middle class. On the other hand, the primary roles of women were still considered to be homemaker and mother.

Several factors make Ginzberg and Yohalem's volume noteworthy. Perhaps most important is the realization by researchers early in their work that women required different questions than men. As the introductory chapter of the book points out, life is interrupted and reinterpreted in different ways for women than for men, even when their talents are equal. Women in this era were still expected to put a husband's career first. It was rare that the woman's career would be the reason that a family's life would change or be uprooted.

The profiles in *Educated American Women* demonstrate that expectations were beginning to change but still had a long way to go. The introduction cites six factors that changed women's lives in the twentieth century: an increase in job opportunities for women; the expansion of secondary school and college education; the increase of women in the workforce during World War II; knowledge of birth control techniques; new labor-saving household appliances and technology; and a shift in men's attitudes about working women. As the introduction explains, the twenty-six profiles are divided into four categories, according to the patterns their lives had taken: planners, recasters, adapters, and unsettled.

Rosemary F. Deen, who wrote about *Educated American Women: Self-Portraits* in the June 23, 1967, issue of *Commonweal*, saw the profiles as "paradigms which permit us to see the operation of choice." Thelma McCormack, a university instructor who reviewed the book in *The Nation* in 1976, concluded that the definitions of work and leisure must be changed for all in society, not just women.

Taken together, the profiles provide a snapshot of women's lives during an era when expectations were in flux. The women of the 1950s were developing into the activists of the 1960s. Many of the women portrayed risked safe lives for more fulfilling ones. The profiles add to the history not only of women's lives, but also of American lives. The study was repeated in 1974. Questionnaires were sent to all participants who could be located. The results were published by the Radcliffe Institute for Advanced Study.

Primary Source

Educated American Women: Self-Portraits [excerpt]

SYNOPSIS: The introduction to this collection of twenty-six women's life histories, published in 1966, is appropriately titled "A World in Change." It provides an overview of the factors that affected women's lives in the twentieth century and the types of lifestyles or life patterns that resulted from these influences.

A World in Change

The lives that women and, for that matter, men, lead reflect two sets of major forces. The first is composed of the external environment with its complex of opportunities and constraints. The second reflects the values and goals of the individual who, always with some margins for discretion, must determine what he most wants and the price he is willing to pay for it.

The extent of transformation which takes place in the role of women is an important index of the rate of social change. The more rigid the society, the more fixed is the pattern of life which women must follow. In the United States, major changes have occurred in the structure and functioning of society during the present century, and these have led to fundamental transformations in the patterning of women's lives.

Changes in the lives of educated women in the post-World War II decades can be appreciated only against a background of the more important changes that took place during the preceding generations in the world of work on the one hand and in the home on the other.

By the turn of this century the United States was well on the way to becoming an industrialized urban society. The majority of the population lived in urban centers. The factory system was well established. The tertiary stage of economic development—the expansion of the service sector—was proceeding rapidly while the number engaged in agriculture was nearing its peak and manufacturing was still experiencing a rapid growth.

As our society became more urbanized and as the service sector of the economy grew, the restricted life pattern followed by most women began to give way. Six factors can be singled out that have cumulatively changed the basic structure of woman's relationship to the world of work.

The first and possibly the most important factor has been the development of a great number of jobs which are particularly well suited to women. These have sprouted in many different sectors of the economy. In manufacturing, there has been a marked shift from heavy to light work, which means that women are able to meet physical demands, sometimes even better than men. Expansion of retail trade and of the communications industry also has increased opportunities for women workers. In addition the beginning of this century saw the rapid growth of the educational and health industries, for which women are well suited.

A second factor has been the expansion of secondary school and college education. Unlike European girls, girls in the United States have long shared with boys access to education. As free educational opportunities have been expanded, girls as well as boys have had access to them, surely through high school. As a matter of fact, for many decades, more girls than boys have graduated from high school. While the proportion of female graduates is reversed in college, young women have long comprised a significant minority of the college population. The increased educational achievement of women has given a double stimulus to the employment of women. Many young women are undoubtedly stimulated to find an outlet in work for the knowledge and skills which they have acquired, and in turn their education and training make them a potentially attractive manpower resource.

The ways in which people behave are changed by new ideas which come to dominate a society. Prior to World War I it was generally believed and accepted that the place of a married woman was at home. But wars have a way of uprooting hallowed traditions; with the manpower scarcities of World War I, some of the prejudice against married women working out of the home dissolved. The post-war era witnessed the removal of additional constraints that had previously shackled women. But the real breakthrough came when the manpower needs of World War II propelled many married women out of their homes and into factories and offices.

A further factor in removing these constraints has been the diffusion of the knowledge of birth control techniques throughout much of the population, with a corresponding decline in the average size of families. This has also made it possible for women to determine when to have children. No longer must a woman devote three or more decades to child rearing. She can collapse the span of years previously devoted to maternal responsibilities. And many have done just that.

Closely related to the foregoing has been the lightening of the burdens of homemaking as a result of the steady and substantial rise in the standard of living and steady advances in the technology of housekeeping, previously so time-consuming and physically exhausting. While women, if they wish, can continue to fill their days by taking care of their homes, electrical appliances and packaged foods permit them to economize markedly on the time and energy which they previously devoted to domestic duties. And many have taken advantage of the opportunities thus presented to reallocate their time and get jobs outside the home.

The sixth change that has contributed to accelerating the entry or reentry of married women into the world of work has been the shift in the attitudes of men. In the past many husbands objected to their wives' working because, among other reasons, they thought it reflected on their ability to support their families. This is no longer true. Some men still discourage it but, since so many married women now work—about 13 million have some kind of job during the course of a year—and since society at large tolerates, even approves of, the new trend, we may

Students sit in class at Howard University, Washington, D.C., during the 1960s. The 1960s saw women increasingly enrolling in higher education and taking on roles other than the traditional ones of homemaker and mother. © BETTMANN/CORBIS. REPRODUCED BY PERMISSION.

assume that few men actually oppose their wives' working. Among educated men, the number who now encourage their wives to take jobs is probably greater than the number opposed to their working, since they are more likely to recognize the need for fulfillment outside the home.

These then are the principal forces that have been operating since the beginning of this century to change the larger environment which shapes the lives and work of all women. Such radical transformations in the environment have had a most important effect on the way in which women today set their sights and order their lives.

However, these broad changes in the environment at large merely set the limits within which plans and adaptations are carried out. A second set of forces, individual values and goals, is of equal importance in influencing a woman's style of life. The specific life patterns that a woman develops depend on three strategic variables: the shaping of her personality, the immediate circumstances of her adult life, and the way in which she responds to these circumstances.

Although a woman's genetic endowment is, of course, crucial to the character of her personality, the environment in which she grows up determines in considerable measure the type of goals and values she develops. The most significant influence is the family into which she is born and reared. Her parents play a large role in the determination of the amount and type of education she acquires and this, in turn, affects her interests and outlook. Her parents' values influence her definition of her future role. They can encourage the development of a goal which stresses a career or marriage, or a balance between a career and marriage. They can provide a home that stimulates the development of ideas, interests, and capacities or one that furnishes limited opportunities for self-realization.

Other persons, adults and peers, also play important roles in personality development. So, too, do such institutions as schools, churches, and recreational groups, whose programs may affect the shape of a young girl's aspirations. Eventually, from all the influences to which she has been exposed, each woman develops a set of values and goals which contributes to the pattern and direction of her life.

No matter what plan a young woman develops for her life and work, her ability to realize her goals will be influenced by the circumstances of her adult life. If she remains single, she usually has no choice but to support herself by engaging in full-time work. If she marries while she is in school, her husband's income may help to determine the extent of her education, since she may have to interrupt her own studies to help him to complete his. After she has her children, her husband's earnings will largely determine whether she can afford household help which in turn will affect her ability to hold a job.

Her husband's career may impose limitations on her own work. If he is transferred frequently, it may be difficult even for a well-prepared woman to pursue her career systematically because of limited opportunities in many communities. A woman often marries a man in the same or an allied field and she may find that many institutions, especially colleges and universities, will not hire more than one member of a family.

The husband himself can also exercise a determining influence on the patterning of his wife's work and life. If he holds a negative attitude about a woman's working, he may interpose so many objections that his wife will forego a career in order to save the marriage. Another husband may take a diametrically opposite stance; he may push his wife

into further education and work even though she prefers to remain at home with her children.

Another significant set of circumstances results from the presence of children. Depending on the number and, particularly, the ages of her children, a woman is under more or less pressure to adjust the pattern of her life to their needs and demands. While, as we have noted, a woman can regulate the number and spacing of her children, she cannot always predict the constraints and pressures that a growing family may exert on her plans for a career.

We see, then, that her husband's income, his job, his attitudes, and the needs of her children all go far to determine the character of a woman's activities. In addition, there are restrictions due to the fact that many employers are reluctant to hire women.

The third determining factor is the response that a woman makes to the particular circumstances she encounters. There are many different ways in which women can cope with the same objective circumstances. For instance, one woman may decide to work only if taking a job will yield the family a net increment in income. Another may decide to work as long as taking a job costs her nothing. In a family with some margins, a woman may work even if her salary does not cover the expenses incurred by her employment.

Some women are willing to leave their children to the care of a maid; others will work only if a close relative cares for the children; still others insist upon bringing up their children themselves.

Some women who want to combine home and work will put forth a great amount of physical and emotional effort in order to meet their responsibilities in each sphere. Others will not or cannot expend so much energy and time; they either cut down their obligations at work or cut corners in their homemaking or make adjustments in both. Some mothers wish to spend their free time in paid employment; others choose to utilize their skills and pursue their interests by engaging in volunteer work or in creative leisure activities; still others think of homemaking and child rearing as full-time activities.

These are some of the many different ways in which women respond to given sets of circumstances. Their responses are determined by a type of balance sheet of sacrifices and rewards. This reflects, first, the importance each woman attaches to realizing specific values and accomplishing specific goals in the various areas of her life. In addition, the entries reflect the costs which she ascribes to different actions which she must take to realize her values and goals.

Before the turn of the century alternative patterns of life were determined to a great extent by a more or less rigid environment. A woman who had completed higher education could generally pursue a career only at the cost of foregoing marriage and a family. If she married she had to withdraw from work and devote her abilities and energies to raising her children and participating in voluntary activities. Her alternatives were a career *or* marriage.

Because of the revolutionary changes which have taken place in the environment, these limited alternatives have been significantly broadened. A woman is now able to work while she is studying, before her marriage, after she marries, while her children are very young, after they enter school, or after they have grown up. Or she may decide not to work. Moreover, even if she decides to follow one pattern, she can shift to another. For example, if she finds that her decision to work while her children are very young is unsatisfactory she may resign from her job. Or the reverse may happen. She may stop working at the birth of her first child anticipating that she will remain out of the labor market until her youngest child enters grade school, only to find that she cannot tolerate a life of total domesticity.

The highly educated women in our study were graduate students at Columbia University at some time during the six years following World War II. They include fellows, scholarship winners, and other students with high academic standing, as described in the Preface. This study is a part of the results of a broader study of talented persons undertaken by the Conservation of Human Resources Project at Columbia University in the early 1960s. From our study of the women in this group, we were able to identify four major patterns of life. The patterns were revealed through our examination of the women's anticipations as they were clarified with time, of the actions they took as their lives progressed, and of the relationship between their goals and the realities they confronted. Each pattern is distinctive, but within each there is a great variety of goals and values, of life circumstances and of responses. The twenty-six portraits in this volume have been organized according to these four life styles.

The first group is called the *planners.* These are women who usually know what they want fairly early and who arrange their lives in order to realize their goals. They take advantage of opportunities which bring them closer to their objectives and they avoid becoming enmeshed in situations and circumstances that could deflect them. Many of their actions are conscious and deliberate, but much is outside their direct knowledge and control. Nevertheless, a retrospective view of the way in which the lives of this group unfold reveals an underlying consistency in their decision-making.

Next come the *recasters.* These women, like the planners, know what they want and set out to accomplish their objectives. But, at some point, they encounter opportunities which permit them to consider more attractive goals or they come face to face with obstacles that force reconsideration of their original aims. At this point, they reopen the entire question of their life plans and make changes in them.

The third type of pattern is that of the *adapters,* so named because they recognize early the inherent fluidity of a woman's life and avoid committing themselves irrevocably to any particular goal. They have preferences but their planning is deliberately open. They want to be in a position to respond flexibly to the circumstances and conditions which they encounter. They are less strongly committed to any particular pattern of work or life than either the planners or the recasters except for a commitment to adapt, which is a stance in its own right.

The fourth and last type is the *unsettled.* This is a composite group of women who start as planners or adapters but who have not satisfactorily resolved their search for a meaningful career or marriage or both. They are still groping. Some made early decisions about work or marriage but found them unworkable. Now they must search for new and more satisfactory solutions.

Twenty-six life histories cannot possibly cover all the variations within these four major groups. The examples which we will present are illustrative rather than exhaustive. They portray the ways in which some women in each category have shaped their lives. As we noted earlier, they were selected because they are informative and interesting, not necessarily because they are representative.

We shall present descriptions of the general characteristics of each type and we shall summarize some of the more important features of the self-portraits that illustrate the type. We hope that in this manner we will isolate significant elements in the succession of life stories without distracting from the intrinsic interest of the autobiographical material.

Further Resources

BOOKS

Solomon, Barbara M. *In the Company of Educated Women: A History of Women and Higher Education in America.* New Haven: Yale University Press, 1985.

PERIODICALS

Deen, Rosemary F. "Educated American Women: Self-Portraits." *Commonweal* 86, June 23, 1967, 396.

McCormack, Thelma. "Styles in Educated Females." *The Nation* 204, January 23, 1967, 117–118.

Rosen, Ruth. "The Female Generation Gap: Daughters of the Fifties and the Origin of Contemporary American Feminists." In *U.S. History as Women's History: New Feminist Essays.* Chapel Hill: The University of North Carolina, 1991, 313–334.

WEBSITES

"Lifestyles of Educated Women." Murray Research Center, Radcliffe Institute for Advanced Study. Available online at http://www.radcliffe.edu/murray/data/ds/doc0070.htm; website home page: http://www.radcliffe.edu/murray (accessed April 7, 2003).

Children of Crisis: A Study of Courage and Fear

Study

By: Robert Coles

Date: 1967

Source: Coles, Robert. *Children of Crisis: A Study of Courage and Fear.* Boston: Little, Brown and Company, 1967, 363–368.

About the Author: Robert Coles (1929–) was born in Boston. After graduating from Harvard University (1950), he earned a medical degree at Columbia University (1954) and served a number of residencies in the field of child psychiatry. He was an Air Force neuropsychiatrist from 1958 to 1960. He has since worked as a child psychiatrist, professor at Harvard Univerity, and writer of more than fifty books exploring the development of children. His work focuses especially on social justice for children. In 2003, he was the James Agee Professor of Social Ethics at Harvard. ∎

Introduction

As an Air Force neuropsychiatrist stationed in Mississippi in 1958, Robert Coles began to notice the injustices and power issues that occurred between the races. He embarked on a study of the social stress from the effects of desegregation. The goal of his research was "to describe certain lives," especially the way political and social stresses affected those lives. Coles sought to explain the motivations for people's actions. Why do young people participate in sit-ins? Why do mobs of white adults taunt small African American children who just want to go to school? He looked for the answers to his questions through personal interviews and observations of life in communities throughout the southern United States.

Many social scientists approach research with carefully made plans. Studies are controlled for variables, researchers map a method and compile a set of questions for subjects to answer. Coles approached his study of life in the South during the early 1960s in a different way. He spent eight years crisscrossing the region, observing, interviewing, and participating in the lives of the people he studied.

Coles did not discriminate in the groups he studied. He talked to the children who were the first to integrate southern schools, he listened to segregationists; he sought out students who participated in sit-ins and the "freedom rides" of the Civil Rights movement. Robert Coles approached human beings rather than a set of data. He did not seek merely to explain a problem. His subjects were individuals with their own stories and points of view.

Significance

Robert Coles' study resulted in the series *Children of Crisis.* Five volumes, published 1967–1978, explore the lives of Americans—members of minority groups as well as members of the white majority. The result is a compelling portrait of a period in American history. Coles won the Pulitzer Prize, among other awards, for the collection. He considers two later volumes to be part of the series: *The Moral Life of Children* (1986) and *The Political Life of Children* (1986).

It was the first book in the series, however, that changed the way Coles approached research. In preparing *A Study in Courage and Fear,* Coles had to gain the trust of people who never talked to white men. He had to be sensitive to the feelings of African American families who were under fire for allowing their children to attend formerly all-white schools and those of the white families who kept their children in the same schools.

Author Walker Percy and reviewer Maxine Greene both praised Coles' work. Percy wrote that Coles "does not fit the mold" of most researchers and that he "keeps his theory and his ideological spectacles in his pocket and spends his time listening to the people and trying to understand them." Greene said the book "makes us *see*" the diversity of the people and the situations they endured. Educator Alan Wieder called the work "exceptional" and applauded Coles for challenging stereotypes. Wieder wrote that Coles provided "evidence of intelligence and vitality [in Black America] to which much of White America is still blind."

In the midst of the chaos of the 1960s, Robert Coles found the true voices of Southern America. The first book, and the subsequent volumes, provide a snapshot of how life was, not just a theoretical treatise on race or desegregation. The volumes provide valuable insight into a time and its people.

Primary Source

Children of Crisis: A Study of Courage and Fear
[excerpt]

> **SYNOPSIS:** In this chapter, titled "The Place of Crisis," Robert Coles examines the experiences and behaviors of African American families and individuals in the American South during the 1960s. The people Coles interviewed sought to improve their lives. They demonstrated resiliency and did what they could to change conditions in their lives.

The Place of Crisis

I once asked a Negro youth involved in the sit-in movement whether the intense commitment he displayed could be explained satisfactorily by his sensitivity to the social and economic injustice he saw everywhere. We had been over the territory often before, and he knew where to begin: "Not completely, I guess. There's always something else going on—in your *own* life, I guess. Isn't that what you keep on coming back to, every time we talk? I was thinking, though, the other day: there's a *lot* going on in everybody's life all the time. What makes people respond to what they do—rather than respond to something else? I mean, I have a million complexes and hang-ups, and each one of them might be pushing me in a different direction. So why do I finally decide to follow one lead, and not another? It isn't necessarily how strong you feel about something that makes you go do it. If that were the case, I'm surprised I didn't go on a rampage years ago and pick a fight with every white man around. I remember hating every white man in sight, without knowing a thing about them. I must have been nine or ten when I first remember feeling like that.

"It must be that something makes sense to you at a time when you need it to make sense, and then you go do it. (For a lot of reasons it makes sense, and then you have something to do that satisfies all the reasons.) It has to be something you *can* do though; that is, unless you want to waste your life by going in for the useless or the weird—you can *always* do those—that will change nothing and no one will notice."

Certainly a lot of people were noticing what he and others like him were doing—including the lawyer from Mississippi just quoted. I do not think that my

Robert Coles stands outside his office at Harvard University, May 19, 1981. Coles' Pulitzer Prize–winning *Children of Crisis* (1967) explores the lives of American children and paints a compelling portrait of a period in American history. AP/WIDE WORLD PHOTOS. REPRODUCED BY PERMISSION.

curiosity had much to do with initiating their curiosity. In the midst of change they wanted to talk about its causes, and about the motivations of those who were opponents—fighters and resisters. Again and again I have had to remind myself—and be reminded by those I was "studying"—that my job was neither the clinician's nor the contemporary historian's nor the political scientist's, but some hard-to-define and often confusing mixture of them all. If the people I knew were mostly "like everybody else" (that is, not sick) they were also different because of their public activity, their partisanship, or their mere existence—that is, the time and place they were fated to live and, as one Southerner put it to me, "stand by and see everything change so fast you can hardly keep yourself from getting dizzy." While some may wonder whether in truth—and in the long run—there was or will be that much change, the vertigo of that Southerner has been shared by others all over the region, whatever the shade of their opinions or skin. As a matter of fact an impatient and outraged Negro youth in Mississippi told me—in 1966—that "it's *all* in the mind, what's happening here. We get excited and have our marches

Two African American girls sit barefoot on the threshhold of their door. Robert Coles interviewed Southerners such as these girls to expose the injustices they faced as well as their humanity. **THE LIBRARY OF CONGRESS.**

and stir up dust and become elated and then feel as lousy as can be, and nothing really changes in the end. A few more people are registered. A few schools have one or two black faces. That's all, and that's nothing, really—except for you to study and see what happens, to us and to the children, I guess."

It must be clear by now that the closer we look at human behavior, the more nonpsychiatric influences must be summoned to "explain" what turns out to be a rather complicated and not always obvious connection between the life of the mind and the life of the world. Those two lives, be it remembered, are but convenient abstractions to aid our thinking about an *intensely shared continuity* that actually exists. You will remember Ruby. . . . Her father once said to me: "They say it's not us, it's the poverty; then they say, it's not the poverty, it's the way we are, and our bad family life, so if we were different, we could shake it all off, the poverty. To me it's all the same package and the same rope with a big knot tied around it. You can touch the knot there and say that's the cause, but it's the whole knot, and then it's the rope, and then the

package—and the package, it was made for the rope, it was shaped so it doesn't know what to do without that rope. So that's how I see it. The rope and the package, they're together, just like this house and the backyard mean so much to Ruby, as you can see in her pictures." Perhaps his metaphors are mixed and ambiguous; they are also more subtle than the substance of some theories of human development.

Whatever Ruby and her father may think about race and poverty, a series of historical changes eventually became for them a trial and a chance for personal effort and advance, or collapse and disaster. I have not shirked reporting Ruby's symptoms, or those of her race's older leaders. Yet it must be said that under grave stress she and they have somehow done more than persist, more than endure. They have prevailed in the way that Faulkner knew they would by summoning every bit of their humanity in the face of every effort made to deny any of it to them. In so doing they have become more than they were, more than they themselves thought they were, and perhaps more than anyone watching them can quite put to word: bearers and makers of tradition; children who in a moment—call it existential, call it historical, call it psychological—took what they had from the past, in their minds, out of their homes, and made of *all* those possessions something else: a change in the world, and in themselves, too.

Of course the example of these lives can mislead us, and there are many who are all too eager for just that to be done. No matter how precise the language used to describe these people and their deeds there are those who will take any words, any lives as grist for one or another propaganda mill. Say that certain children under certain circumstances have shown courage and survived danger impressively well, and you are suddenly a bland advocate of all sorts of tribulations for children. Or you are an optimist—deliberate or naïve. Perhaps, worst of all, you may be labeled a propagandist, kept by any one of many groups to rationalize suffering, or to rob heroism of its dignity with one more revelation that what is, after all, can only appear to be.

In one of his papers on identity Erik Erikson says: "In order to find an anchor point for the discussion of the universal genetics of identity, however, it would be well to trace its development through the life histories or through significant life episodes of 'ordinary' individuals—individuals whose lives have neither become professional autobiographies . . . nor case histories. . . ." That is what I have tried to do.

We live in a time when Negroes and the rest of us have come into possession of new slogans and phrases: "the Negro family" and "black power" are two examples. Each generation has to assert its own destiny, through language among other ways. It is certainly possible to see how thoroughly familiar the meaning of either of those expressions was to earlier generations. When the impressively literate social scientists of 1930 or 1940 did their work—in Chapel Hill, in New Orleans, in John Dollard's "southern town," in the "deep South" of Davis and Gardner in the midst of the "cotton culture" once described, the "mill villages" of Herring or the Negroes Odum and Johnson heard singing "workaday songs"—they all spoke again and again of the mean, harsh living that the Southern poor had to endure, and particularly the Negroes among them. As sociologists and anthropologists or psychologists, these writers did not confine themselves to a careful description of poverty; they consistently showed what it does to fathers and mothers, to children and grandchildren. Fear, hate, hunger and utter separation from the rest of the community establish an atmosphere that inevitably affects the child and the parent every day and profoundly. That it is controversial or comes as a surprise to anybody in America that the Negro family has had its special horrors to face—and has paid a high price in doing so—is perhaps the most interesting revelation to emerge from the "new" discussion of the Negro family. The arguments about the Negro family or "black power" show again how the obvious can become the controversial: every Negro family has to come to terms with the distinct fact of the Negro's relative powerlessness in American society; and political facts become psychological ones when a jobless man tells his hard-pressed wife that their hungry rat-bitten children will simply have to keep on living that way—and perpetuating such an inheritance over the generations. At least we might admit that the real problem is not whether Negro families have to endure and suffer special strains, or whether Negroes need more—much more—power, but what our political system can (or cannot) do to solve the hurt and weakness some of its citizens not only feel, but possess as a reliable, unalleviated curse.

I want to emphasize one observation I have consistently made in the South: in the region where he is still most numerous, most humble, isolated and poorest, the Negro has shown remarkable adaptive resiliency and assertiveness, given the right social or political circumstances. I have seen enough Ne-

---

Children of Crisis:
A Five-Volume Series

Vol. 1: *A Study in Courage and Fear* (1967)

Vol. 2: *Migrants, Sharecroppers, Mountaineers* (1971)

Vol. 3: *The South Goes North* (1971)

Vol. 4: *Eskimos, Chicanos, Indians* (1978)

Vol. 5: *Privileged Ones: The Well-Off and the Rich in America* (1978)

---

gro children over a long enough time to realize that their family tragedy starts not in the first years of infancy and early childhood, but in those later years when the world's restrictions become decisive antagonists to the boy or girl—saying "no" to them about everything, teaching them finally to transform those refusals into a judgment of their worth as individuals and as citizens. As Erikson pointed out a long time ago, however impoverished and lowly their position in American society, Negro mothers are generally warm and affectionate, almost desperately so. Even among the poorest tenant farmers, even among families who couldn't be living deeper in the ghetto, infants receive the constant attention of their mothers—while young boys and girls are kept close and watched hard. I am not arguing against the practice of birth control by the poor, but I wonder how many of us understand what the presence of a new child means to many of our poorest mothers—indeed to the men in their lives and to their other children.

Further Resources
BOOKS
Erikson, Erik. *Identity and the Life Cycle.* New York: International Universities Press, 1959.

Freud, Anna. *Normality and Pathology in Childhood.* New York: International Universities Press, 1965.

PERIODICALS
Ellmann, Mary. "Psychiatry & Prejudice." *Commentary,* November 1967, 91–94.

Greene, Maxine. "The Humanity of Desegregation." *Saturday Review,* June 17, 1967, 66–67.

Percy, Walker. "The Doctor Listened." *The New York Times Book Review,* June 25, 1967, 7.

Wieder, Alan. "Robert Coles Reconsidered: A Critique of the Portrayal of Blacks as Culturally Deprived." *The Journal of Negro Education* 50, no. 4, Fall 1981, 381–388.

Learning to Read: The Great Debate
Study

By: Jeanne S. Chall

Date: 1967

Source: Chall, Jeanne S. *Learning to Read: The Great Debate.* New York: McGraw-Hill, 1967, 187–190.

About the Author: Jeanne S. Chall (1921–1999) was born in Poland and became a naturalized United States citizen. Chall earned degrees from City College in New York (B.B.A., 1941) and Ohio State University (M.A., 1947; Ph.D., 1952). A psychologist, she dedicated her life to teaching, especially to teaching reading and discovering how to improve methods of reading instruction. Chall taught at various institutions and finished her career at Harvard University, where the reading lab is named in her honor. ■

Introduction

In the late 1950s and early 1960s, debates raged about the best way to teach children to read. Rudolf Flesch's best-selling *Why Johnny Can't Read,* published in 1955, criticized the "sight-word" method popularized by reading series such as those featuring Dick and Jane.

Jeanne S. Chall. Chall's *Learning to Read: The Great Debate* (1967) was an important work contributing to the debate on how best to teach children to read—a debate that still continues. **AP/WIDE WORLD PHOTOS. REPRODUCED BY PERMISSION.**

Teachers who had been trained in the 1930s emphasized whole word and sentence recognition as well as silent reading. These methods were effective in teaching some children to read, but not all.

The United States was in a period of change. Inner cities were full of poor schools, while middle-class white families were moving to the suburbs. Science and scientific methods were at the forefront of educational debate as a result of the launch of the Soviet satellite *Sputnik I.* Methods of teaching reading, it was felt, had to catch up to the times.

Jeanne S. Chall was already a proven scholar and researcher when she was commissioned by the Carnegie Foundation to conduct a three-year study on the methods being used to teach reading across the country. Between 1962 and 1965, she visited many schools and talked to teachers and administrators. Chall and her team also analyzed reading series being used in the schools. Among the questions they explored were: How are teachers using the books? How effective are the texts? What kind of training do teachers need to use the books? Are teachers just relying on methods they had learned in college? The pros and cons of teaching phonics versus the sight-word methods were also examined in the course of the study.

The result of this study was the landmark book, *Learning to Read: The Great Debate,* published in 1967. Chall makes it clear in the book's introductory section that one study cannot answer all the questions regarding the best way to teach reading to all children. In the study she analyzes methods of reading instruction employed between 1910 and 1965. She delves into the debates of the day as well as the research regarding reading. She also investigates what happens in the classroom when children are taught to read. In general, Chall favors phonics but acknowledges the need for practice.

In "What Is a Basal-Reading Series?," a chapter in *Learning to Read,* Chall examines the pros and cons of such series. As she explains in the chapter, the publishers of these series provided school systems with "a total reading program" consisting of teachers' manuals, collections of stories and other excerpts for children to read, workbooks with exercises that helped students improve their reading skills and comprehension, and various tests, charts, and other teaching aids. These series, prepared by teams of experts, influenced the way reading was taught in American classrooms. Scott, Foresman's *New Basic Reading Program* and Ginn's *Ginn Basic Readers* were among the most popular series in the 1950s and 1960s.

Significance

Chall's study was important for reading teachers and educators in general. It answered questions and quelled some of the debate about reading instruction methods among some teachers and researchers, while laying the groundwork for future research. Reviewers in 1967 recognized the importance of Chall's work. J.C. MacCampbell wrote in *Library Journal:* "This is a book educators concerned with reading instruction have needed for years" and "[It] will provide solutions that may enable educators and laymen to come to grips with problems in reading instruction."

Chall's book—accessible, well researched, and including extensive bibliographies and appendixes on reading texts—has become a cornerstone from which further research extended. Chall recognized that not all children learn to read the same way, and that while phonics, which emphasizes the sounds of individual letters, works for many, the whole-language method, popularized in the 1980s, works for others. Noted educator Diane Ravitch, in a tribute to Chall upon her death, remarked that, "Jeanne Chall's significant contributions to this field changed the course of the debate about reading in the last third of the twentieth century."

Primary Source

Learning to Read: The Great Debate [excerpt]

> **SYNOPSIS:** This chapter, "What is a Basal-Reading Series?" describes the series, which were part of almost every child's education in the 1950s and 1960s. In her book, Jeanne S. Chall examines the good and bad aspects of these series.

What Is a Basal-Reading Series?

Let us say that you have never seen a basal-reading series, but have only read about them in the newspaper, *Life,* or *Look.* You would have no reason to think that such a series is anything more than a collection of silly sentences like "Look, look, look," or "Go, go, go!"

Actually, a basal-reading series is one of the most expensive and extensive ventures a publisher can undertake. It attempts to give teachers and pupils a "total reading program" embodying a system for teaching reading (in the teachers' manuals), a collection of stories and selections for pupils to read (the readers), and exercises for additional practice (the workbooks).

The series generally starts with a prereading program (one, two, or three "reading-readiness" books for kindergarten and/or grade 1). Then come the "graded" readers: three or more small paper-covered books (the preprimers), which are followed by the first hard-covered book (the primer) and then a first reader (the 1–2 book). Typically, these five (sometimes six) books are used by children in the first grade, although

Something Pretty

Mother said, "Look, look.
See this."

"Oh, oh," said Sally.
"It is pretty."

"Yes, yes," said Jane.
"Mother looks pretty."

21

Jeanne Chall selected and reprinted "Something Pretty" as an example of a basal reader in her discussion. This is the first page of that story, taken from *The New Fun with Dick and Jane* (1956). ILLUSTRATION FROM "SOMETHING PRETTY" IN *THE NEW FUN WITH DICK AND JANE* BY GRAY, MONROE, ARTLEY, ARBUTHNOT AND GRAY. COPYRIGHT © 1956 BY SCOTT, FORESMAN AND COMPANY. USED BY PERMISSION OF PEARSON EDUCATION, INC.

some advance through them faster, and some slower. The typical basal-reading series has a book for each half of the second grade—the 2–1 and 2–2 books. Similar breaks are made for the third through the sixth grades. Some companies have readers for the seventh and eighth grades of elementary school or the ninth grade of junior high school.

With each reader goes a workbook—a "consumable," paper-covered book containing a variety of exercises. Each reader also has a teachers' guidebook (a manual on how to teach from the readers and workbooks). Schools can also purchase accompanying charts, tests, and other aids with each series. In addition, some publishers offer supplementary readers and subject-matter textbooks coordinated with the basal-reading program.

I was reminded of how bulky a basal series and related materials can be when the generous editor

"Look, Sally," said Jane.

"Here is something pretty.

Something pretty for you and me."

"Oh, Jane," said Sally.

"I want something.

I want something red.

I want something blue."

22

Page two of "Something Pretty." ILLUSTRATION FROM
"SOMETHING PRETTY" IN *THE NEW FUN WITH DICK AND JANE*
BY GRAY, MONROE, ARTLEY, ARBUTHNOT AND GRAY.
COPYRIGHT © 1956 BY SCOTT, FORESMAN AND COMPANY.
USED BY PERMISSION OF PEARSON EDUCATION, INC.

of one of the series I analyzed wanted to know how much space I had in my office before sending his complete reading program for grades 1, 2, and 3. Fortunately, I decided that only the *core* of the program was required. Had I wanted to analyze the complete program, including all the various aids, I would have needed a storage room!

Influence of the Basal Series

The basal series are very widely used. Two studies—the Columbia Reading Study by Allen Barton and David Wilder (1964) and the Harvard Report on Reading by Mary Austin and Coleman Morrison (1963)—found that these materials are used almost universally by American classroom teachers of the first three grades. After surveying over fifteen hundred elementary school teachers, Barton and Wilder wrote:

> Reading instruction in almost all schools starts from a similar basis: basal readers from

a graded series are used by 98 percent of first grade teachers and by 92 to 94 percent of second and third grade teachers on "all or most days of the year." (pp. 378–379)

Even more impressive than their widespread use is the influence these materials have on teachers and administrators. Barton and Wilder note that 63 percent of the teachers they studied in grades 1 through 3 considered the reading series and their accompanying teachers' manuals a "very important" influence on their beliefs about the teaching of reading—even more important than their practice teaching experience, their own reading of books and articles on reading, and their undergraduate courses on teaching methods.

The Columbia Reading Study findings on attitudes toward the teachers' manuals substantiate this influence. From 66 to 70 percent of elementary school teachers either "strongly" or "mostly" agreed with the statement: "The suggestions to teachers found in reading manuals are based on definite scientific proof." Only 7 percent either "mostly" or "strongly" disagreed.

Elementary school principals followed the same pattern: 58 percent either "strongly" or "mostly" agreed with the statement. Only 9 percent either "mostly" or "strongly" disagreed. Indeed, during my own school visits I found more than one principal who believed strongly that if his teachers would only follow the basal-reader manuals, he would have no reading problems in his school.

Interestingly, reading experts were not as convinced as teachers and principals of the "scientific basis" of the teachers' manuals. Only 32 percent either "strongly" or "mostly" agreed with the statement; 46 percent either "mostly" or "strongly" disagreed.

Barton and Wilder (1964) summarize their findings as follows:

> The teachers believe that the suggestions to teachers found in reading manuals are based on "definite scientific proof": almost no teachers disagree. But the experts . . . are much less impressed by the scientific status of reading manuals; almost half disagree with the statement that they are based on "definite scientific proof," and only a third agree "mostly." The experts thus think much less highly of their own product, in a sense; perhaps the teachers have been oversold—and the principals are almost as sold as the teachers. (p. 382)

In any event, for all practical purposes American reading instruction is basal-series reading instruction.

Producing a Basal Series

A series is written by a team of specialists. The head of the team, the senior author, is usually a person of recognized authority and stature in the reading field. Most often he is a professor of education.

The basal-reader "teams" work differently. Some series are planned and supervised by the senior author, with different team members assuming responsibility for different assignments. Under such an arrangement, professional writers, teachers who have become writers, and regular classroom teachers write, adapt, and select the stories that are included in the readers. Usually, the classroom teachers write the manuals.

In one of the larger companies, a permanent staff writes the stories in the readers, the workbook exercises, and the teachers' manuals. Their "head" does not work on a royalty basis, as do the senior authors of other series, but acts as a consultant. However, he too plans and approves all parts of the program.

All basal-series teams pride themselves on cooperative effort. The larger the company, the more specialists involved—reading experts, psychologists, linguists, people with degrees in literature, and so on.

The editor of one series emphasized that producing a basal series is such an extensive enterprise that no one author could possibly do it:

> Creative ideas must come from different people. Even the books suggested as supplementary reading at the end of the various lessons in our series are gone over by five people before they are listed. The books and the manuals are composites. About ten full-time writers, editors, and artists are involved. No one person is responsible.

The financial investment in a series is, of course, enormous. No one whom I or my associates interviewed would give an actual cost figure. However, when I mentioned 1 million dollars (a figure the American Textbook Council gave in 1950 as the basic investment in a basal-reading series), the editor of one series said that this amount may cover the primer— *one* of the *six* basic books in his first-grade program! "It is hard to give a definite figure," he explained, "because we don't know what to include. We have a staff. Others pay royalties, so their investment may seem lower. The cost for an entire series is probably within the range of 10 to 20 million dollars."

One large publishing house devoted five years to its series' first-grade program alone. It took an illustrator two full years to do just the primer. He produced one illustration a week, a painting from a photographer's model. In the words of the editor: "You can't put that kind of quality into something that you sell one copy of."

Further Resources

BOOKS

Robinson, H. Alan, ed. *Recent Developments in Reading.* Chicago: The University of Chicago Press, 1965.

Smith, Nila Barton. *American Reading Instruction: Special Edition.* Newark, Del.: International Reading Association, 2002.

PERIODICALS

Clymer, Theodore. "What Do We Know About the Teaching of Reading?" *Educational Leadership* 24, no. 5, February 1967, 389–391.

Huck, Charlotte S. "The Changing Character of Basic Reading Materials." *Educational Leadership* 22, no. 6, March 1965, 377–381, 439.

"A Tribute to Jeanne Chall." *American Educator,* Spring 2001, 16–23.

WEBSITES

"Beyond the Reading Wars: How to Raise a Generation of Readers." *Harvard Education Letter.* Available online at http://www.edletter.org/past/issues/1999-so/forum.shtml; website home page: http://www.edletter.org (accessed April 8, 2003).

Jeanne Chall Reading Lab. Available online at http://www.gse.harvard.edu/~litlab/index.html; website home page: http://www.gse.harvard.edu (accessed April 8, 2003).

Death at an Early Age
Memoir

By: Jonathan Kozol

Date: 1967

Source: Kozol, Jonathan. *Death at an Early Age: The Destruction of the Hearts and Minds of Negro Children in the Boston Public Schools.* Boston: Houghton Mifflin, 1967, 1–7.

About the Author: Jonathan Kozol (1936–) spent his career advocating for the illiterate and the homeless. Harvard-educated and an Oxford University Rhodes scholar, he taught fourth grade in a Boston public school in 1964–65. Kozol has been working with students in poor urban neighborhoods ever since. Kozol's many books document the problems associated with poverty and lack of education. ∎

Introduction

De facto segregation was one of the most difficult issues faced by the city of Boston in the 1960s. Although the Boston School Committee developed a policy that would allow a student to attend any school with an open

Principal Martin Feeney (left) blocks African American students from entering an elementary school in Boston, Massachusetts, 1965. The students were bussed from a crowded school in a poor African American neighborhood. **AP/WIDE WORLD PHOTOS. REPRODUCED BY PERMISSION.**

seat, it was very difficult for minority students to find transportation.

Parents in Roxbury, the predominantly black Boston neighborhood in which Jonathan Kozol taught, became concerned about the quality of their children's education. In 1962–1963, they formed a group called "The Higginson School District Parents." Soon the Roxbury community as a whole started to question the unequal treatment of African American students in the Boston public schools.

In 1964, the Commonwealth of Massachusetts ordered a racial census of schools, and the legislature passed a bill meant to correct racial imbalances. The legislature also ordered a study to find out what was happening in the schools. The results of the study were issued in 1965. Titled *Because It Is Right Educationally,* the Kiernan Report, as it was called, found that fifty-five schools in the state, including forty-five Boston schools, had student bodies that were more than 50 percent non-white. The report concluded that this was harmful to students' development and reinforced prejudices.

Significance

Death at an Early Age documents many of the discriminatory practices that Roxbury parents had begun to question. At the school where Kozol taught, he did not even have a proper classroom. There were no books and no supplies, and students were regularly abused. Through his vivid, firsthand descriptions—such as the heartbreaking story of Stephen, recounted in the book's first chapter—Kozol brought attention to what was taking place in Boston's poorer, predominantly black public schools.

Death at an Early Age won the National Book Award in 1968. Robert Coles, a writer, educator, and child psychiatrist, noted that the "reader will find out about the cynicism, condescension, outright racism, and severely anti-intellectual attitudes that Mr. Kozol quite easily and openly encountered as a teacher among teachers." Reviewer Peter Schrag wrote in 1969 that Kozol's book and others such as Herbert Kohl's *36 Children* "are forcing, for the first time, a real confrontation with the abiding problems of urban schools."

In 1972, a decade after the Higginson School District Parents group was formed, the Boston NAACP filed a lawsuit. The result of *Morgan et al v. Hennigan et al* was a 1974 court order that finally forced the Boston school system to integrate its schools.

In *Death at an Early Age* Kozol describes the year he spent teaching fourth grade in a Roxbury school. The report is both disturbing and heartbreaking and remains an important personal record of what happened to many

African American children in the Boston Public Schools during the 1960s. The book includes documents from the Boston School Committee and the *Boston Globe,* which provide additional information about the city's school system at the time. Reissued in 1990, *Death at an Early Age* is a powerful piece of history—one teacher's and one school's experiences that were symbolic of a complex national problem.

Primary Source

Death at an Early Age [excerpt]

SYNOPSIS: The first chapter of Jonathan Kozol's book about his experiences as a teacher in a predominantly black Boston public school tells the story of Stephen. A battered and unwanted foster child, Stephen does not perform well in school, but he shows promise as an artist. The art teacher, who stifles the boy's creativity, is typical of the teachers depicted in the book. Like most of the other teachers in Kozol's school, she does not believe in the children she teaches.

Stephen is eight years old. A picture of him standing in front of the bulletin board on Arab bedouins shows a little light-brown person staring with unusual concentration at a chosen spot upon the floor. Stephen is tiny, desperate, unwell. Sometimes he talks to himself. He moves his mouth as if he were talking. At other times he laughs out loud in class for no apparent reason. He is also an indescribably mild and unmalicious child. He cannot do any of his school work very well. His math and reading are poor. In Third Grade he was in a class that had substitute teachers much of the year. Most of the year before that, he had a row of substitute teachers too. He is in the Fourth Grade now but his work is barely at the level of the Second. Nobody has complained about the things that have happened to Stephen because he does not have any mother or father. Stephen is a ward of the State of Massachusetts and, as such, he has been placed in the home of some very poor people who do not want him now that he is not a baby any more. The money that they are given for him to pay his expenses every week does not cover the other kind of expense—the more important kind which is the immense emotional burden that is continually at stake. Stephen often comes into school badly beaten. If I ask him about it, he is apt to deny it because he does not want us to know first-hand what a miserable time he has. Like many children, and many adults too, Stephen is far more concerned with hiding his abased condition from the view of the world

Jonathan Kozol waits to testify before the Senate subcommittee of Employment, Manpower and Poverty, Washington, D.C., October 25, 1967. With his *Death at an Early Age* (1967), Kozol documented discriminatory practices and brought attention to what was taking place in Boston's poorer, predominantly black public schools.
© BETTMANN/CORBIS. REPRODUCED BY PERMISSION.

than he is with escaping that condition. He lied to me first when I asked him how his eye got so battered. He said it happened from being hit by accident when somebody opened up the door. Later, because it was so bruised and because I questioned him, he admitted that it was his foster mother who had flung him out onto the porch. His eye had struck the banister and it had closed and purpled. The children in the class were frightened to see him. I thought that they also felt some real compassion, but perhaps it was just shock.

Although Stephen did poorly in his school work, there was one thing he could do well. He was a fine artist. He made delightful drawings. The thing about them that was good, however, was also the thing that got him into trouble. For they were not neat and orderly and organized but entirely random and casual, messy, somewhat unpredictable, seldom according to the instructions he had been given, and—in short—real drawings. For these drawings, Stephen received considerable embarrassment at the hands of the Art Teacher. This person was a lady no longer very young who had some rather fixed values and opinions about children and about teaching. Above all, her manner was marked by unusual confidence. She seldom would merely walk into our class but seemed always to sweep into it. Even for myself, her advent, at least in the beginning of the year, used to cause a wave of anxiety. For she came into our class generally in a mood of self-assurance and of almost punitive restlessness which never made one confident but which generally made me wonder what I had done wrong. In dealing with Stephen, I thought she could be quite overwhelming.

The Art Teacher's most common technique for art instruction was to pass out mimeographed designs and then to have the pupils fill them in according to a dictated or suggested color plan. An alternate approach was to stick up on the wall or on the blackboard some of the drawings on a particular subject that had been done in the previous years by predominantly white classes. These drawings, neat and ordered and very uniform, would be the models for our children. The art lesson, in effect, would be to copy what had been done before, and the neatest and most accurate reproductions of the original drawings would be the ones that would win the highest approval from the teacher. None of the new drawings, the Art Teacher would tell me frequently, was comparable to the work that had been done in former times, but at least the children in the class could try to copy good examples. The fact that they were being asked to copy something in which they could not believe because it was not of them and did not in any way correspond to their own interests did not occur to the Art Teacher, or if it did occur she did not say it. Like a number of other teachers at my school and in other schools of the same nature, she possessed a remarkable self-defense apparatus, and anything that seriously threatened to disturb her point of view could be effectively denied.

How did a pupil like Stephen react to a teacher of this sort? Alone almost out of the entire class, I think that he absolutely turned off his signals while she was speaking and withdrew to his own private spot. At his desk he would sit silently while the Art Teacher was talking and performing. With a pencil, frequently stubby and end-bitten, he would scribble and fiddle and cock his head and whisper to himself throughout the time that the Art Teacher was going on. At length, when the art lesson officially began, he would perhaps push aside his little drawing and try the paint and paper that he had been given, usually using the watercolors freely and the paint-

brush sloppily and a little bit defiantly and he would come up with things that certainly were delightful and personal and private, and full of his own nature.

If Stephen began to fiddle around during a lesson, the Art Teacher generally would not notice him at first. When she did, both he and I and the children around him would prepare for trouble. For she would go at his desk with something truly like a vengeance and would shriek at him in a way that carried terror. "Give me that! Your paints are all muddy! You've made it a mess. Look at what he's done! He's mixed up the colors! I don't know why we waste good paper on this child!" Then: "Garbage! Junk! He gives me garbage and junk! And garbage is one thing I will not have." Now I thought that that garbage and junk was very nearly the only real artwork in the class. I do not know very much about painting, but I know enough to know that the Art Teacher did not know much about it either and that, furthermore, she did not know or care anything at all about the way in which you can destroy a human being. Stephen, in many ways already dying, died a second and third and fourth and final death before her anger.

Sometimes when the Art Teacher was not present in our classroom, and when no other supervisory person happened to be there, Stephen would sneak up to me, maybe while I was sitting at my desk and going over records or totaling up the milk money or checking a paper, so that I would not see him until he was beside me. Then, hastily, secretly, with mystery, with fun, with something out of a spy movie, he would hand me one of his small drawings. The ones I liked the most, to be honest, were often not completely his own, but pictures which he had copied out of comic books and then elaborated, amended, fiddled with, and frequently added to by putting under them some kind of mock announcement ("I AM THE GREATEST AND THE STRONGEST") which might have been something he had wished. I think he must have seen something special and valuable about comic books, because another thing that he sometimes did was just cut out part of a comic book story that he liked and bring it in to me as a present. When he did this, as with his paintings and drawings, he usually would belittle his gift by crumpling it up or folding it up very tiny before he handed it to me. It was a way, perhaps, of saying that he didn't value it too much (although it was clear that he did value it a great deal) in case I didn't like it.

If the Art Teacher came upon us while he was slipping me a picture he had drawn, both he and I were apt to get an effective lashing out. Although she could be as affectionate and benevolent as she liked with other children, with Stephen she was almost always scathing in her comments and made no attempt at seeming mild. "He wants to show you his little scribbles because he wants to use you and your affection for him and make you pity him but we don't have time for that. Keep him away. If you don't, I'll do it. I don't want him getting near you during class."

Further Resources

BOOKS

Advisory Committee on Racial Imbalance and Education. *Because It Is Right Educationally, Parts 1 and 2*. Boston, Mass.: State Board of Education, 1965. ERIC Document 001117.

Pearson, Jim B., and Edgar Fuller, eds. *Education in the States: Historical Development and Outlook*. Washington, D.C.: National Education Association, 1969.

United States Commission on Civil Rights, Massachusetts Advisory Committee. *Report on Racial Imbalance in the Boston Public Schools*. Washington, D.C.: The Commission, 1965. ERIC Document 001521.

PERIODICALS

Coles, Robert. "Do They Know What They Do?" *The New York Times Book Review*, October 1, 1967, 1.

Kaufman, Polly Welts. "Building a Constituency for School Desegregation: African-American Women in Boston, 1962–1972." *Teachers College Record* 92, no. 4, Summer 1991, 619–631.

Schrag, Peter. "Schooldays." *Commentary: A Jewish Review* 45, January 1968, 71–74.

WEBSITES

"Jonathan Kozol Archive." Learntoquestion.com. Available online at http://www.learntoquestion.com/vclass/seevak /groups/2002/sites/kozol/Seevak02/ineedtogoHOMEPAGE /homepage.htm; website home page: http://www .learntoquestion.com (accessed April 8, 2003).

36 Children
Memoir

By: Herbert Kohl

Date: 1967

Source: Kohl, Herbert. *36 Children*. New York: The New American Library, 1967, 3–8.

About the Author: Herbert Kohl (1937–) spent his career exploring alternatives to traditional education. He was educated at Harvard, Oxford, and Teacher's College, Columbia University. Kohl taught in a New York City school for two years in the 1960s. His 1969 book *The Open Classroom: A*

Practical Guide to a New Way of Teaching discusses teaching methods that help students discover what is meaningful to them. Kohl's educational philosophy emphasizes respect and honesty with students. ■

Introduction

In the mid-1960s, slightly over 50 percent of New York state's children attended urban schools. These were often schools, as one observer described them in 1969, "hampered by financial stringency, and, in recent years, by the growing resentment of minority groups isolated in a particular school or area." These numbers and problems did not only occur in New York, they were common in cities across the United States. City schools, and especially inner-city schools, were frequently understaffed and lacking in supplies and books. The school districts gave up on the children who attended these schools, labeling them "nonverbal" and incapable of learning.

In her 1965 article "Poverty and the School," Muriel Crosby points out one of the major problems of inner-city schools and their students. She describes "poverty so crushing that the body, spirit and mind often reflect its effects early in life." She goes on to discuss the mixed blessing of mobility—those who can leave the inner city do. As a result, the schools as well as other services suffer. By the mid-1960s, some federal aid programs had been instituted to address problems in American education. These programs only addressed part of the problem, however. Some, like the National Defense Education Act, bypassed the real issues of inner-city schools. The NDEA provided money for science, math, and foreign-language programs, but inner-city schools had far more basic needs.

In his 1967 book *36 Children*, Herbert Kohl chronicles the highs and lows of his experiences teaching sixth grade for two years in Harlem. Kohl describes his frustrations with discipline, lack of books that were meaningful, and the problems that his students carried with them to school. He records how he learned to teach this group of children. Instead of rigid insistence on approaches that were not working, Kohl found ways that did work. He challenged the children to reveal their interests and took advantage of what have come to be called "teachable moments." When a child called another "psyche," Kohl taught about mythology. When science or reading interests were discovered, he found or provided appropriate materials.

Significance

The roots of the educational philosophies that Kohl expands upon in his later works are evident in *36 Children*. The students he meets on his first day as a teacher are not incapable of learning, he concludes. What they need, he says, are opportunity, respect, and a belief that they can learn.

Reviewers and educators admired Kohl's honesty about his experiences. They praised him for using language and writing to inspire his students to learn. Kohl's work proves that a "teacher can learn to be a liberator," wrote Frances and David Hawkins in the *Harvard Educational Review*. Joseph Featherstone called *36 Children* a work that "gives an honest and illuminating description of how a teacher works." A book review in *Time* says that Kohl "conveys one teacher's joy in the potential of his students and his despair at a system that beats them down."

Kohl's book was one of many in the 1960s that provided readers with a look at the day-to-day workings of inner-city schools. Kohl's *36 Children* and Jonathan Kozol's *Death at an Early Age* are often discussed together. Kohl and Kozol were classmates at Harvard, and both went on to teach in inner-city schools and write books about their experiences. Kohl's book is more personal, while Kozol's emphasizes his frustrations with the larger system. Each book, however, is an important piece of the history of education in the 1960s.

For a time Kohl's views fell out of favor—they were considered too far-out and impossible to repeat by most teachers. But *36 Children* was reprinted in 1988 with a new introduction, so a new generation of readers could learn from the successes and failures of Kohl's students.

Primary Source

36 Children [excerpt]

SYNOPSIS: In the first chapter of his book, Herbert Kohl describes the apprehension of entering his new classroom in a Harlem public school. He faces 36 sixth-grade students who had known "years of judgment" but little of encouragement. The chapter describes his first tentative steps to gain their trust.

My alarm clock rang at seven thirty, but I was up and dressed at seven. It was only a fifteen-minute bus ride from my apartment on 90th Street and Madison Avenue to the school on 119th Street and Madison.

There had been an orientation session the day before. I remembered the principal's words. "In times like these, this is the most exciting place to be, in the midst of ferment and creative activity. Never has teaching offered such opportunities . . . we are together here in a difficult situation. They are not the easiest children, yet the rewards are so great—a smile, loving concern, what an inspiration, a felicitous experience."

I remembered my barren classroom, no books, a battered piano, broken windows and desks, falling plaster, and an oppressive darkness.

I was handed a roll book with thirty-six names and thirty-six cumulative record cards, years of judgments already passed upon the children, their official personalities. I read through the names, twenty girls and sixteen boys, the 6-1 class, though I was supposed to be teaching the fifth grade and had planned for it all summer. Then I locked the record cards away in the closet. The children would tell me who they were. Each child, each new school year, is potentially many things, only one of which the cumulative record card documents. It is amazing how "emotional" problems can disappear, how the dullest child can be transformed into the keenest and the brightest into the most ordinary when the prefabricated judgments of other teachers are forgotten.

The children entered at nine and filled up the seats. They were silent and stared at me. It was a shock to see thirty-six black faces before me. No preparation helped. It is one thing to be liberal and talk, another to face something and learn that you're afraid.

The children sat quietly, expectant. *Everything must go well; we must like each other.*

Hands went up as I called the roll. Anxious faces, hostile, indifferent, weary of the ritual, confident of its outcome.

The smartest class in the sixth grade, yet no books.

"Write about yourselves, tell me who you are." (I hadn't said who I was, too nervous.)

Slowly they set to work, the first directions followed—and if they had refused?

Then arithmetic, the children working silently, a sullen, impenetrable front. *To talk to them, to open them up this first day.*

"What would you like to learn this year? My name is Mr. Kohl."

Silence, the children looked up at me with expressionless faces, thirty-six of them crowded at thirty-five broken desks. *This is the smartest class?*

Explain: they're old enough to choose, enough time to learn what they'd like as well as what they have to.

Silence, a restless movement rippled through the class. *Don't they understand? There must be something that interests them, that they care to know more about.*

A hand shot up in the corner of the room.

"I want to learn more about volcanoes. What are volcanoes?"

The class seemed interested. I sketched a volcano on the blackboard, made a few comments, and promised to return.

"Anything else? Anyone else interested in something?"

Silence, then the same hand.

"Why do volcanoes form?"

And during the answer:

"Why don't we have a volcano here?"

A contest. The class savored it, I accepted. Question, response, question. I walked toward my inquisitor, studying his mischievous eyes, possessed and possessing smile. I moved to congratulate him, my hand went happily toward his shoulder. I dared because I was afraid.

His hands shot up to protect his dark face, eyes contracted in fear, body coiled ready to bolt for the door and out, down the stairs into the streets.

"But why should I hit you?"

They're afraid too!

Hands relaxed, he looked torn and puzzled. I changed the subject quickly and moved on to social studies—How We Became Modern America.

"Who remembers what America was like in 1800?"

A few children laughed; the rest barely looked at me.

"Can anyone tell me what was going on about 1800? Remember you studied it last year. Why don't we start more specifically? What do you think you'd see if you walked down Madison Avenue in those days?"

A lovely hand, almost too thin to be seen, tentatively rose.

"Cars?"

"Do you think there were cars in 1800? Remember that was over a hundred and fifty years ago. Think of what you learned last year and try again. Do you think there were cars then?"

"Yes . . . no . . . I don't know."

She withdrew, and the class became restless as my anger rose.

At last another hand.

"Grass and trees?"

The class broke up as I tried to contain my frustration.

Herbert Kohl. Kohl's 1967 book *36 Children* chronicles the highs and lows of his experiences teaching sixth grade for two years in Harlem: students who had known "years of judgment" but little of encouragement. © BY JERRY BAUER. REPRODUCED BY PERMISSION.

"I don't know what you're laughing about—it's the right answer. In those days Harlem was farmland with fields and trees and a few houses. There weren't any roads or houses like the ones outside, or street lights or electricity. There probably wasn't even a Madison Avenue."

The class was outraged. It was inconceivable to them that there was a time their Harlem didn't exist.

"Stop this noise and let's think. Do you believe that Harlem was here a thousand years ago?"

A pause, several uncertain Noes.

"It's possible that the land was green then. Why couldn't Harlem also have been green a hundred and fifty or two hundred years ago?"

No response. The weight of Harlem and my whiteness and strangeness hung in the air as I droned on, lost in my righteous monologue. The uproar turned into sullen silence. A slow nervous drumming began at several desks; the atmosphere closed as intelligent faces lost their animation. Yet I didn't understand my mistake, the children's rejection of me and my ideas. Nothing worked, I tried to joke, command, play—the children remained joyless until the bell, then quietly left for lunch.

There was an hour to summon energy and prepare for the afternoon, yet it seemed futile. What good are plans, clever new methods and materials, when the children didn't—wouldn't—care or listen? Perhaps the best solution was to prepare for hostility and silence, become the cynical teacher, untaught by his pupils, ungiving himself, yet protected.

At one o'clock, my tentative cynicism assumed, I found myself once again unprepared for the children who returned and noisily and boisterously avoided me. Running, playing, fighting—they were alive as they tore about the room. I was relieved, yet how to establish order? I fell back on teacherly words.

"You've had enough time to run around. Everybody please go to your seats. We have work to begin."

No response. The boy who had been so scared during the morning was flying across the back of the room pursued by a demonic-looking child wearing black glasses. Girls stood gossiping in little groups, a tall boy fantasized before four admiring listeners, while a few children wandered in and out of the room. I still knew no one's name.

"Sit down, we've got to work. At three o'clock you can talk all you want to."

One timid girl listened. I prepared to use one of the teacher's most fearsome weapons and last resources. Quickly white paper was on my desk, the blackboard erased, and numbers from 1 to 10 and 11 to 20 appeared neatly in two columns.

"We're now going to have an *important* spelling test. Please, young lady"—I selected one of the gossipers—"what's your name? Neomia, pass out the paper. When you get your paper, fold it in half, put your heading on it, and number carefully from one to ten and eleven to twenty, exactly as you see it on the blackboard."

Reluctantly the girls responded, then a few boys, until after the fourth, weariest, repetition of the directions the class was seated and ready to begin— I thought.

Rip, a crumpled paper flew onto the floor. Quickly I replaced it; things had to get moving.

Rip, another paper, rip. I got the rhythm and began quickly, silently replacing crumpled papers.

"The first word is *anchor*. The ship dropped an *anchor*. Anchor."

"A what?"

"Where?"

"Number two is *final*. *Final* means last, *final*. Number three is *decision*. He couldn't make a *decision* quickly enough."

"What *decision*?"

"What was number two?"

"*Final.*"

I was trapped.

"Then what was number one?"

"*Anchor.*"

"I missed a word."

"Number four is *reason*. What is the *reason* for all this noise?"

"Because it's the first day of school."

"Yeah, this is too hard for the first day."

"We'll go on without any comments whatever. The next word is—"

"What number is it?"

"—*direction*. What *direction* are we going? *Direction.*"

"What's four?"

The test seemed endless, but it did end at two o'clock. What next? Once more I needed to regain my strength and composure, and it was still the first day.

"Mr. Kohl, can we please talk to each other about the summer? We won't play around. Please, it's only the first day."

"I'll tell you what, you can talk, but on the condition that everyone, I mean *every single person in the room*, keeps quiet for one whole minute."

Teacher still had to show he was strong. To prove what? The children succeeded in remaining silent on the third attempt; they proved they could listen. Triumphant, I tried more.

"Now let's try for thirty seconds to think of one color."

"You said we could talk!"

"My head hurts, I don't want to think anymore."

"It's not fair!"

It wasn't. A solid mass of resistance coagulated, frustrating my need to command. The children would not be moved.

"You're right, I'm sorry. Take ten minutes to talk and then we'll get back to work."

For ten minutes the children talked quietly; there was time to prepare for the last half hour. I looked over my lesson plans: Reading, 9 to 10; Social Studies, 10 to 10:45, etc., etc. How absurd academic time was in the face of the real day. *Where to look?*

"You like it here, Mr. Kohl?"

I looked up into a lovely sad face.

"What do you mean?"

"I mean do you like it here, Mr. Kohl, what are you teaching us for?"

What?

"Well, I . . . not now. Maybe you can see me at three and we can talk. The class has to get back to work. All right, everybody back to your seats, get ready to work."

She had her answer and sat down and waited with the rest of the class. They were satisfied with the bargain. Only it was I who failed then; exhausted, demoralized, I only wanted three o'clock to arrive.

"It's almost three o'clock and we don't have much time left."

I dragged the words out, listening only for the bell.

"This is only the first day, and of course we haven't got much done. I expect more from you during the year . . ."

The class sensed the maneuver and fell nervous again.

"Take out your notebooks and open to a clean page. Each day except Friday you'll get homework."

My words weighted heavy and false; it wasn't my voice but some common tyrant or moralizer, a tired old man speaking.

"There are many things I'm not strict about but homework is the one thing I insist upon. In my class *everybody always* does homework. I will check your work every morning. Now copy the assignment I'm putting on the blackboard, and then when you're finished, please line up in the back of the room."

What assignment? What lie now? I turned to the blackboard, groping for something to draw the children closer to me, for something to let them know I cared. *I did care!*

"Draw a picture of your home, the room you live in. Put in all the furniture, the TV, the windows and doors. You don't have to do it in any special way but keep in mind that the main purpose of the picture should be to show someone what your house looks like."

The children laughed, pointed, then a hand rose, a hand I couldn't attach to a body or face. They all looked alike. I felt sad, lonely.

"Do you have to show your house?"

Two boys snickered. *Are there children ashamed to describe their homes?—have I misunderstood again?* The voice in me answered again.

"Yes."

"I mean . . . what if you can't draw, can you let someone help you?"

"Yes, if you can explain the drawing yourself."

"What if your brother can't draw?"

"Then write a description of your apartment. Remember, *everybody always* does homework in my classes."

The class copied the assignment and lined up, first collecting everything they'd brought with them. The room was as empty as it was at eight o'clock. Tired, weary of discipline, authority, school itself, I rushed the class down the stairs and into the street in some unacknowledged state of disorder.

The bedlam on 119th Street, the stooped and fatigued teachers smiling at each other and pretending *they* had had no trouble with their kids relieved my isolation. I smiled too, assumed the comfortable pose of casual success, and looked down into a mischievous face, the possessed eyes of the child who had thought I would hit him, Alvin, who kindly and thoughtfully said: "Mr. Kohl, how come you let us out so early today? We just had lunch . . ."

Crushed, I walked dumbly away, managed to reach the bus stop and make my way home. As my weariness dissolved, I only remembered of that first day Alvin and the little girl who asked if I liked being "there."

Further Resources

BOOKS

Kohl, Herbert. *The Open Classroom: A Practical Guide to a New Way of Teaching.* New York: Vintage, 1969.

Pearson, Jim B., and Edgar Fuller, eds. *Education in the States: Historical Development and Outlook.* Washington, D.C.: National Education Association, 1969.

Stone, James C., and Frederick W. Schneider. *Commitment to Teaching: Teaching in the Inner City.* New York: Crowell, 1970.

PERIODICALS

Crosby, Muriel. "Poverty and the School." *Educational Leadership* 22, no. 7, May 1965, 536–539.

Featherston, Joseph. "Ghetto Classroom." *The New Republic* 157, no. 25, December 16, 1967, 23–28.

Hawkins, Frances, and David Hawkins. "36 Children." *Harvard Educational Review* 38, no. 3, 1968, 617–622.

"How to Get Through." *Time* 91, January 19, 1968, 34–36.

WEBSITES

Kohl, Herbert. "New Teachers and Social Justice." Interview with the National Education Association. NEA Today Online. Available online at http://www.nea.org/neatoday /0103/intervw.html; website home: page http://www.nea.org (accessed April 9, 2003).

Identity: Youth and Crisis
Monograph, Table

By: Erik H. Erikson
Date: 1968
Source: Erikson, Erik H. *Identity: Youth and Crisis.* New York: W.W. Norton, 1968, 91–96.
About the Author: Erik H. Erikson (1902–1994) was born in Germany and trained at the Vienna Psychoanalytic Institute. He moved to the United States in 1933 as the political climate worsened in Europe. Erikson had a private psychiatric practice, worked at the Austin Riggs Center in Massachusetts, and taught at Harvard. Erikson's work on child and human development is considered significant in the field of psychoanalysis. ∎

Introduction

In the preface of Erik H. Erikson's *Identity: Youth and Crisis,* he tells a story about one of his professors' lectures on ego boundaries, which concludes with the question "Now—have I understood myself?" He maintains that he continues to ask himself that question as he explores the concept and meaning of identity.

Identity: Youth and Crisis draws upon two decades of Erikson's work. The chapters were originally written as essays, lectures for a variety of audiences, or notes about his research. Works were combined to avoid repetition of ideas. The revisions of these essays allowed Erikson to rethink the ideas he had developed over twenty years. In this book, he reflects on the changes in society and the historical events that had occurred in the 1950s and early 1960s. Erikson's work moves beyond the training he had in Vienna under the guidance of Anna Freud. The development of his ideas, especially about youth, can be traced in these essays.

Significance

Erik Erikson's book on youth and crisis was published at a point when the public—not just academics and psychiatrists—were becoming an audience for psychological writing. This shift is important, not only for Erikson and other writers of psychology, but also for the growth of the paperback industry. It made books like Erikson's readily available as texts for college students and professors. This was a significant factor for *Identity: Youth and Crisis.* Norton, the publisher, paid a $500,000 advance, which it thought it would recover with the paperback market. The hardcover alone sold more than 10,000 copies the first year it came out. By the 1970–1971 academic year, nearly 31,000 paperbacks were purchased. The book sold more copies than any of Erikson's other books except *Childhood and Society,* his best work, which was published in 1950.

Reviewers either embraced the book or were lukewarm toward it. It is not Erikson's best writing, but it does draw a long period of research together in one volume. Chandler Brossard, writing for *The Nation,* stated that the book had "bad logic" and argued that "Being" was more important than "Identity." He thought Erikson did not realize that what he observed resulted from political changes in society. Samuel H. Miller and Robert A. Nisbet found much to like about the book, however. Miller, reviewing for *The Christian Century,* wrote that the book "enlarges our vision and presents a perspective from which we may judge both ourselves and others." After joking that nearly all undergraduates now had an "identity crisis," Nisbet acknowledged that the book was "well worth attention" and that "Erikson has been one of the key figures in the American fields of depth psychology and the study of human development."

Erikson's ideas were not always popular with his colleagues. Pure Freudians thought that he disregarded the importance of the id, or the unconscious, in development and behavior. He was also accused of being "overly optimistic." Research designs dependent upon observation and theories about the influence of society on the identity were also criticized. Despite these criticisms, Erik H. Erikson is acknowledged as influential in the fields of psychological and psychoanalytical theory and practice in the twentieth century. *Identity: Youth and Crisis* explores the themes that would dominate Erikson's work for the rest of his life. It is also a notable volume because it helps readers gain a sense of what identity means in a modern world.

Primary Source

Identity: Youth and Crisis [excerpt]: Monograph

> **SYNOPSIS:** Erik Erikson's theory on the eight stages of life is presented in this chapter, "The Life Cycle: Epigenesis of Identity." His theories began with Freud but delved into concepts from embryology, such as epigenesis, a chain of developmental stages in which an organism develops parts in sequence. Erikson maintained that people's personalities de-

velop in eight stages. In each stage, according to Erikson, a conflict must be faced and solved.

The Life Cycle: Epigenesis of Identity

Among the indispensable co-ordinates of identity is that of the life cycle, for we assume that not until adolescence does the individual develop the prerequisites in physiological growth, mental maturation, and social responsibility to experience and pass through the crisis of identity. We may, in fact, speak of the identity crisis as the psychosocial aspect of adolescing. Nor could this stage be passed without identity having found a form which will decisively determine later life.

Let us, once more, start out from Freud's far-reaching discovery that neurotic conflict is not very different in content from the "normative" conflicts which every child must live through in his childhood, and the residues of which every adult carries with him in the recesses of his personality. For man, in order to remain psychologically alive, constantly re-resolves these conflicts just as his body unceasingly combats the encroachment of physical deterioration. However, since I cannot accept the conclusion that just to be alive, or not to be sick, means to be healthy, or, as I would prefer to say in matters of personality, *vital,* I must have recourse to a few concepts which are not part of the official terminology of my field.

I shall present human growth from the point of view of the conflicts, inner and outer, which the vital personality weathers, re-emerging from each crisis with an increased sense of inner unity, with an increase of good judgment, and an increase in the capacity "to do well" according to his own standards and to the standards of those who are significant to him. The use of the words "to do well" of course points up the whole question of cultural relativity. Those who are significant to a man may think he is doing well when he "does some good" or when he "does well" in the sense of acquiring possessions; when he is doing well in the sense of learning new skills and new knowledge or when he is not much more than just getting along; when he learns to conform all around or to rebel significantly; when he is merely free from neurotic symptoms or manages to contain within his vitality all manner of profound conflict.

There are many formulations of what constitutes a "healthy" personality in an adult. But if we take up only one—in this case, Marie Jahoda's definition, according to which a healthy personality *actively*

Erik Homburger Erikson, March 1975. Building on Sigmund Freud's theories, Erikson developed a stage theory of human development and identity that has made a significant impact on the field of education. © TED STRESHINSKY/CORBIS. REPRODUCED BY PERMISSION.

masters his environment, shows a certain *unity of personality,* and is able to *perceive* the world and himself *correctly*—it is clear that all of these criteria are relative to the child's cognitive and social development. In fact, we may say that childhood is defined by their initial absence and by their gradual development in complex steps of increasing differentiation. How, then, does a vital personality grow or, as it were, accrue from the successive stages of the increasing capacity to adapt to life's necessities—with some vital enthusiasm to spare?

Whenever we try to understand growth, it is well to remember the *epigenetic principle* which is derived from the growth of organisms *in utero.* Somewhat generalized, this principle states that anything that grows has a ground plan, and that out of this ground plan the parts arise, each part having its time of special ascendancy, until all parts have arisen to form a functioning whole. This, obviously, is true for fetal development where each part of the organism has its critical time of ascendance or danger of defect. At birth the baby leaves the chemical exchange of the womb for the social exchange system of his

Stages in the Development of the Personality

Stage	Age (Years)							
	1	2	3	4	5	6	7	8
VIII								INTEGRITY vs. DESPAIR
VII							GENERATIVITY vs. STAGNATION	
VI						INTIMACY vs. ISOLATION		
V	Temporal Perspective vs. Time Confusion	Self-Certainty vs. Self-Consciousness	Role Experimentation vs. Role Fixation	Apprenticeship vs. Work Paralysis	IDENTITY vs. IDENTITY CONFUSION	Sexual Polarization vs. Bisexual Confusion	Leader- and Followership vs. Authority Confusion	Ideological Commitment vs. Confusion of Values
IV				INDUSTRY vs. INFERIORITY	Task Identification vs. Sense of Futility			
III			INITIATIVE vs. GUILT		Anticipation of Roles vs. Role Inhibition			
II		AUTONOMY vs. SHAME, DOUBT			Will to be Oneself vs. Self-Doubt			
I	TRUST vs. MISTRUST				Mutual Recognition vs. Autistic Isolation			

SOURCE: Table from Erikson, Erik H. "The Life Cycle: Epigenesis of Identity," *Identity: Youth and Crisis,* W. W. Norton: New York, 1968, 94.

Primary Source

Identity: Youth and Crisis: Table

SYNOPSIS: This table from Erik Erikson's *Identity: Youth and Crisis* (1968) shows his stages in personality development.

society, where his gradually increasing capacities meet the opportunities and limitations of his culture. How the maturing organism continues to unfold, not by developing new organs but by means of a prescribed sequence of locomotor, sensory, and social capacities, is described in the child-development literature. As pointed out, psychoanalysis has given us an understanding of the more idiosyncratic experiences, and especially the inner conflicts, which constitute the manner in which an individual becomes a distinct personality. But here, too, it is important to realize that in the sequence of his most personal experiences the healthy child, given a reasonable amount of proper guidance, can be trusted to obey inner laws of development, laws which cre-

ate a succession of potentialities for significant interaction with those persons who tend and respond to him and those institutions which are ready for him. While such interaction varies from culture to culture, it must remain within "the proper rate and the proper sequence" which governs all epigenesis. Personality, therefore, can be said to develop according to steps predetermined in the human organism's readiness to be driven toward, to be aware of, and to interact with a widening radius of significant individuals and institutions.

It is for this reason that, in the presentation of stages in the development of the personality, we employ an epigenetic diagram analogous to the one employed in *Childhood and Society* for an analysis of Freud's psychosexual stages. It is, in fact, an implicit purpose of this presentation to bridge the theory of infantile sexuality (without repeating it here in detail) and our knowledge of the child's physical and social growth.

The diagram is presented on p. 94. The double-lined squares signify both a sequence of stages and a gradual development of component parts; in other words, the diagram formalizes a progression through time of a differentiation of parts. This indicates (1) that each item of the vital personality to be discussed is systematically related to all others, and that they all depend on the proper development in the proper sequence of each item; and (2) that each item exists in some form before "its" decisive and critical time normally arrives.

If I say, for example, that a sense of basic trust is the first component of mental vitality to develop in life, a sense of autonomous will the second, and a sense of initiative the third, the diagram expresses a number of fundamental relations that exist among the three components, as well as a few fundamental facts for each.

Each comes to its ascendance, meets its crisis, and finds its lasting solution in ways to be described here, toward the end of the stages mentioned. All of them exist in the beginning in some form, although we do not make a point of this fact, and we shall not confuse things by calling these components different names at earlier or later stages. A baby may show something like "autonomy" from the beginning, for example, in the particular way in which he angrily tries to wriggle his hand free when tightly held. However, under normal conditions, it is not until the second year that he begins to experience the whole critical alternative between being an autonomous creature and being a dependent one, and it is not until then that he is ready for a specifically new encounter with his environment. The environment, in turn, now feels called upon to convey to him its particular ideas and concepts of autonomy in ways decisively contributing to his personal character, his relative efficiency, and the strength of his vitality.

It is this encounter, together with the resulting crisis, which is to be described for each stage. Each stage becomes a crisis because incipient growth and awareness in a new part function go together with a shift in instinctual energy and yet also cause a specific vulnerability in that part. One of the most difficult questions to decide, therefore, is whether or not a child at a given stage is weak or strong.

Perhaps it would be best to say that he is always vulnerable in some respects and completely oblivious and insensitive in others, but that at the same time he is unbelievably persistent in the same respects in which he is vulnerable. It must be added that the baby's weakness gives him power; out of his very dependence and weakness he makes signs to which his environment, if it is guided well by a responsiveness combining "instinctive" and traditional patterns, is peculiarly sensitive. A baby's presence exerts a consistent and persistent domination over the outer and inner lives of every member of a household. Because these members must reorient themselves to accommodate his presence, they must also grow as individuals and as a group. It is as true to say that babies control and bring up their families as it is to say the converse. A family can bring up a baby only by being brought up by him. His growth consists of a series of challenges to them to serve his newly developing potentialities for social interaction.

Each successive step, then, is a potential crisis because of a radical change in perspective. Crisis is used here in a developmental sense to connote not a threat of catastrophe, but a turning point, a crucial period of increased vulnerability and heightened potential, and therefore, the ontogenetic source of generational strength and maladjustment. The most radical change of all, from intrauterine to extrauterine life, comes at the very beginning of life. But in postnatal existence, too, such radical adjustments of perspective as lying relaxed, sitting firmly, and running fast must all be accomplished in their own good time. With them, the interpersonal perspective also changes rapidly and often radically, as is testified by the proximity in time of such opposites as "not letting mother out of sight" and "wanting to be independent." Thus, different capacities use different opportunities to become full-grown components of the ever-new configuration that is the growing personality.

Further Resources

BOOKS

Coles, Robert. *Erik H. Erikson: The Growth of His Work.* Boston: Little, Brown, 1970.

"Erikson, Erik Homburger." In *Biographical Dictionary of Psychology.* New York: Routledge Reference, 1997. 170–172.

Friedman, Lawrence J. *Identity's Architect: A Biography of Erik H. Erikson.* New York: Scribner, 1999.

PERIODICALS

Brossard, Chandler. "Making Life Tougher." *The Nation,* June 3, 1968, 734–736.

Miller, Samuel H. "Mysteries of Selfhood." *The Christian Century,* April 17, 1968, 486.

Nisbet, Robert A. "A Sense of Personal Sameness." *The New York Times Book Review,* March 31, 1968, 1, 48.

WEBSITES

Boeree, C. George. "Erik Erikson." Shippensburg University. Available online at http://www.ship.edu/~cgboeree/erikson .html; website home page: http://www.ship.edu (accessed April 9, 2003).

Don't Mourn—Organize!: SDS Guide to Community Organizing

Pamphlet

By: Students for a Democratic Society

Date: 1968

Source: Students for a Democratic Society. *Don't Mourn—Organize!: SDS Guide to Community Organizing.* San Francisco and Chicago: Movement Press, 1968, 2–3. Reproduced in Digital & Multimedia Center, Michigan State University Libraries. Available online at http://lib0131.lib.msu.edu /dmc/radicalism/public/all/dontmournorganize/AEW.pdf; website home page: http://lib0131.lib.msu.edu (accessed April 18, 2003).

About the Organization: Students for a Democratic Society (SDS) was a national left-wing organization. It was originally organized in 1946 as the Student Department of the League for Industrial Democracy. It reorganized at a meeting held in Port Huron, Michigan, in June 1962. Tom Hayden, one of the early leaders, drafted the *Port Huron Statement,* the manifesto for the group. Students involved in SDS led protests against the Vietnam War and social injustices throughout the 1960s. ■

Introduction

According to a 1970 report of the President's Commission on Campus Unrest, Students for a Democratic Society "called on students to work for a society where all men would more fully control their own lives and social institutions." In April 1965, the group organized a march in Washington; twenty thousand people gathered at the Washington Monument to protest U.S. involvement in Vietnam.

Following the April 1965 demonstration, membership in SDS rose dramatically, from about fifteen hundred members in forty chapters to more than two thousand in eighty chapters. Charismatic leaders attracted new recruits to the organization. By 1966–1967, the mass media attention brought a new cohort of members and leadership to SDS. Prior to this, SDS had relied on its own flyers, leaflets, and pamphlets to spread information and ideas and to recruit new members. These publications were passed out on campuses and distributed at meetings and demonstrations.

SDS demonstrations grew more violent as the war in Vietnam (1964–1975) escalated. In addition to U.S. presence in Vietnam, SDS held protests against the draft; on-campus recruitment by corporations such as Dow Chemical Company, which manufactured napalm; the presence of ROTC on college campuses; and economic conditions faced by poor Americans. By the late 1960s, SDS had split into several factions, including more violent groups such as the Weather Underground, also known as the Weathermen.

Significance

Students for a Democratic Society published pamphlets as a way of training and recruiting participants. These documents were published by the national organization and its local chapters. Although ephemeral in nature, copies of many of the pamphlets and flyers survive in university special collections around the country and in digital collections on the Internet. Pamphlets such as "Don't Mourn—Organize!" provide insights into the philosophies and tactics that SDS leaders promoted as part of the student radical movement of the 1960s.

"Don't Mourn—Organize!" includes copies of five articles published individually by SDS during 1967 and 1968. The articles explore issues of race and war in addition to instructing volunteers on how to effectively organize people. They call on young, white students and young professional adults to organize draft-resistance centers and economic projects in poor and ghetto areas. The writers of the articles believed that people would take a stand on issues that affected their lives—like the draft— if they were educated about the political motives behind those issues. They believed that "the resistance can draw together those people who seek real power to deflect the war."

An important aspect of "Don't Mourn—Organize!" is the fact that it encourages community-based programs. SDS moved beyond college campuses in 1967–1968 in an attempt to gain a broader influence. It was thought that organizers would gain the trust of minorities and poor whites by living in their communities. This was considered vital in order for the revolution to succeed.

SDS was an important part of the radical movement of the 1960s. In the end, the organization collapsed because there were too many factions, and the participants were divided between pursuing nonviolent vs. violent means of protest. However, the literature printed by the Students for a Democratic Society influenced a generation during a volatile decade in America.

The University of Michigan chapter of Students for a Democratic Society march through downtown Ann Arbor calling for a student strike to protest the Vietnam War, November 1968. As the 1960s drew to a close, more and more students across the country united in protest against the war.
© BETTMANN/CORBIS. REPRODUCED BY PERMISSION.

Primary Source

"Don't Mourn—Organize!: SDS Guide to Community Organizing" [excerpt]

SYNOPSIS: This essay, titled "We've Got to Reach Our Own People," was one of five articles reproduced in this 1968 pamphlet. The writer maintains that reaching minority and poor populations cannot be accomplished by mainstream government or social programs. Symbolic marches and protests can't solve the problems either, it asserts. A grassroots effort to become part of the community is necessary for protests of unjust treatment to result in action.

We've Got to Reach Our Own People

There is a movement now in this country that it makes sense to describe as a resistance. What a year ago was merely a slogan has begun to take shape at induction centers, in the corners of small offices, in the character and style of increasing amounts of anti-war work and the consciousness of growing numbers of people that they can create a real opposition to the Johnson Regime. There is still a great deal of confusion and groping. The resistance exists at the fringe—on the edge of the student movement and the university community, at the margin of the poor and decaying communities where the offices and apartments of most of the resistors are to be found.

This article outlines a program of resistance; it seeks to clarify objectives and describe a way in which part of the resistance can root itself in poor white and lower paid working class communities; it attempts to suggest the urgency, need and potential for establishing those roots now.

We Choose Resistance

Much of the anti-war movement, regardless of rhetoric, seems predicated on the assumption that existing power is legitimate and that the regular channels of political opposition are sufficient to end the war. For that reason it has concentrated on proving that there is substantial, growing public sentiment against the war (through large demonstrations, petitions, newspaper ads, referenda, etc.) and it has done this quite effectively. Its method has concentrated on antiwar propaganda and education and symbolic appeals to power. Even the most militant, civil disobedience advocates have generally directed their energy toward a Gandhian confrontation with and appeal to power.

We are convinced that power throughout this society is illegitimate and will continue to be basically unresponsive to public opinion and normal political pressure. That conviction *forces* us to a conception of resistance—an effort to impede and disrupt the functioning of the military/political machinery wherever it is local and vulnerable. We join a resistance movement out of no great optimism about its capacity to end the war; indeed we call this a resistance, not a revolution, because entrenched power is too strong to be broken. At best a resistance can delay and harass, strengthening the internal conflicts that make the war costly, aiding marginally the Vietnamese whose prosecution of the war is the most critical determinant of its outcome; at best a resistance sets seeds throughout the country of a movement aimed directly at imperialism and domestic exploitation.

What we do believe, however, is that the resistance can draw together those people who seek real power to deflect the war. We believe that a resistance can draw together people who are sufficiently detached from the integrative social mechanisms of this country so that they could never participate in a propaganda/symbolic-confrontation-oriented movement. In this sense, we think the resistance can make available to many people who are now denied it, a credible (believable, possible) form of opposition to the war.

Working Class & Poor

It is here that the war hits hardest. It is young men from these communities who do most of the dying in Vietnam and it was their fathers and brothers who did most of the dying in Korea. It is their unions that will be surpressed in the name of the war effort, their wage gains that will be erased by war inflation, their checks that will feel hardest the squeeze of a war tax. And it is also the token programs of relief, job training, school improvement, and rent supplement that will be cut off in their communities because of the war.

But it is here that the anti-war movement has had least experience and least success. Paradoxically, the people most brutalized by material and social exploitation, the people pushed unceasingly through the processing of school, military and job seem unmoved by the anti-war effort. Partly this is

explained by the massive, unthinking, unchallenged racism and patriotism (anti-communism) which these communities share with the rest of white America and which must be broken if a movement is to succeed. But more important, we feel that these are exactly the communities that will not be reached by the symbolic, propaganda tactics of the current sense of *real gain,* a sense that political activity represents more than the demonstration of disaffection. It is in these communities that a resistance makes most sense.

Because grievances are so deep, so much a part of the marginal economic and social web of people's lives, the movement of opposition, once triggered could be very powerful. We choose to work here because people do have a deep sense of exploitation that can lead them to identify not only with their own struggle, but with oppressed people everywhere. It makes sense to talk in these communities about the need and right of self-defense and self-preservation and to speak of democracy as the unadorned right of people to make the most important decisions about their lives. There is little of the legalism and formalism that can paralyze other sectors of the society, but rather a profound but segmented anger that can be kindled and united by the existence of a credible opposition to the war.

We Choose the Draft

The draft and the war are issues now, everywhere. There is no need to manufacture them or convince people of their importance; the conviction is implanted twenty times a day by television, radio, papers, conversations and the visible signs of war inflation and pressure—not the least of which is the caskets rolling back into the community from Vietnam. Unlike some of the other things community projects have tried to work on, there is no need to produce "consciousness" about this issue.

We want to focus on the draft because it is the *most important and most tangible* manifestation of the war in most people's lives. Hardly anyone exists in a lower class working community who does not have friends or close relatives who are in the army or threatened by it. Coming into the community with a program that will help people deal with this problem, that will keep themselves or their friends or their children or their loved ones out of the damned war, cuts through to the very heart of the issue. It is a way of fighting back, a method of self-defense, and it makes the opportunity for opposition credible and compelling.

Unlike many issues, the draft is important enough so that people will take a stand and accept the risks that that implies. It is only when an issue or movement is so important that the good average American will take a stand against his neighbor or his bowling team or the men he drinks with or works next to that you have a chance for a significant social movement. Revolutions always tear communities apart. It is that tearing that represents the splitting of the social fabric which has held people in belligerent allegiance to their country in spite of their disaffection. Very few of the issues we have organized around have been that powerful. This one is.

And although opposition to the war will divide a community in very important ways, it will unite it in others. There are few issues that will unify a marginal community across its fractured status and economic lines. For example, the antagonism between workers and welfare recipients frequently keeps them from working together. But the draft cuts across those lines. It can bring the welfare mother, worker, parent, young person into one cause and into a common sense of themselves and their position as opponents.

The clarity of this issue and its importance, can strengthen the opposition to other institutions when they are used to suppress it. When the school expels students for forming a high school draft resistance league, the general anger of the community about the school has a foundation and anchor that the abstractness of the "school problem" may have prevented from forming before.

Further Resources

BOOKS

Myers, R. David. *Toward a History of the New Left: Essays From Within the Movement.* Brooklyn, N.Y.: Carlson Publishing, Inc., 1989.

President's Commission on Campus Unrest. *The Report on the President's Commission on Campus Unrest.* Washington, D.C.: U.S. Government Printing Office, 1970.

Unger, Irwin. *The Movement: A History of The American New Left, 1959–1972.* New York: Harper & Row, 1974.

PERIODICALS

Hayden, Tom, and Dick Flacks. "The Port Huron Statement at 40." *The Nation* 275, no. 5, August 5, 2002, 18–21.

Herf, Jeffrey. "Striking a Balance: Remembering 1968 and After." *Partisan Review* 66, no. 2, Spring 1999, 280–289.

WEBSITES

Erickson, Christian W. "Shock Wave: Transnational University-Based New Left Revolts in the United States, France and Mexico." Available online at http://trc.ucdavis.edu/erickson/mru/intro.htm (accessed April 9, 2003).

"Port Huron Statement of the Students for a Democratic Society." Michigan State University. Available online at http://coursesa.matrix.msu.edu/~hst306/documents/huron.html; website home page: http://www.msu.edu/home (accessed April 9, 2003).

As the Seed Is Sown
Report

By: Office of Economic Opportunity

Date: 1968

Source: Office of Economic Opportunity. *As the Seed Is Sown.* Washington, D.C.: Office of Economic Opportunity, 1968, 23–25.

About the Organization: The Office of Economic Opportunity (OEO) was formed under the *Economic Opportunity Act* of 1964, part of President Lyndon B. Johnson's "Great Society" initiative. Johnson (served 1963–1969) insisted on a new office to run the programs because he did not want them to become lost in established departments. Created in August 1964, the Office of Economic Opportunity oversaw Title VI, one of six sections of the *Economic Opportunity Act.* Programs under Title VI included VISTA (Volunteers In Service To America) and Project Head Start, an educational program for disadvantaged preschool children and their families. ∎

Introduction

The Office of Economic Opportunity, headed by Sargent Shriver, dispersed its first grants in January 1965. Shriver had been the chief of the Peace Corps, a program instituted by President John F. Kennedy (served 1961–1963). Head Start was created in mid-February 1965 as a way to increase disadvantaged children's readiness for learning in school. In addition to educational programs for preschool children, Head Start provided medical services for poor children, assistance for parents, and training programs for Head Start staff. It ran both summer and year-round programs.

Guidelines for the Head Start program were developed by experts from a number of fields—pediatrics, public health, child development, education, child psychiatry, and psychology. Head Start programs were run by public schools and community action groups. Requirements for the program included meeting the conditions of Title IV of the Civil Rights Act of 1964, which mandated the desegregation of public schools, and that ninety percent of the total enrollment met the poverty guidelines.

The Head Start Program was rushed into operation by June 1965 to take advantage of the summer vacation, when unused school buildings and schoolteachers were available. During that first summer, more than 500,000 children participated. In the early years of Head Start, longitudinal studies of the program, in which a set of subjects are examined over time, were not available. The success of the program was documented through data collection and annual reports. Some of these assessments were based on speculative assumptions and anecdotal evidence.

Significance

After the first couple of years, the Head Start program started facing questions about its lasting effects. Would a short-term program really be able to improve children's chances in schools and effectively train staff and parents? These were the questions that the annual reports issued by the Office of Economic Opportunity attempted to answer.

As the Seed Is Sown, the OEO's 1968 annual report, offers data about the Head Start program at the end of its third full year. According to the report, just under half of the children in the program were African American, and almost half of the children served in the first year were from homes with no books, toys, crayons, or other educational items normally found in middle-class homes. Partnerships, especially with the medical community, had strengthened the program, the report stated. Adults who had taken advantage of training opportunities or college courses reported on how the programs had made a difference for them. According to the annual report, Head Start had reached two million preschool children, involved families in their communities, and engaged 325,000 people as volunteers.

Researchers had to wait for more scientific evidence of lasting success, however. The program served children between the ages of three and five years, so when the 1968 annual report was issued, its graduates were only in kindergarten or the first or second grade. There had not been time to prove lasting effects of educational or social intervention. But despite the lack of longitudinal evidence in 1968, Head Start was deemed a success. Sargent Shriver, it was generally felt, provided facts that "proved skeptics wrong."

Head Start is considered one of the only successful programs launched under the OEO. It was moved to the Department of Health, Education and Welfare in July 1969. The program continues to serve children and their families through the Department of Health and Human Services.

Primary Source

As the Seed Is Sown [excerpt]

SYNOPSIS: The Office of Economic Opportunity's 1968 Annual Report describes various aspects of the Head Start program, providing statistics about the number of children it serves. The report also notes the need for longitudinal studies that would provide more reliable data about the effectiveness of the program.

Head Start

Academic Opportunities for Head Start Adults

In its third full year of operation, Project Head Start initiated a new careers program—Supplementary Training—which gives full year staff members the opportunity of earning college degrees, provides them with more skills which they may apply in the classrooms, and most importantly, gives them a future.

Developed under an OEO-Head Start contract to Educational Projects, Inc., of Washington, D.C., Supplementary Training, in its first year, involved 150 colleges and universities in 47 states and Puerto Rico, and more than 350 community action agencies and Head Start delegate agencies.

Over 3500 non-professional and 1800 professional staff members, while continuing to work in Head Start, have now successfully obtained college credit hours.

A major breakthrough has thus been achieved in meeting the very real need for a cadre of experienced, qualified personnel in Early Childhood Education and related areas.

Equally important, Head Start is achieving institutional change. Participating colleges and universities have adopted more flexible admissions policies and have rearranged the presentation of curricula material so as to make it easier going at first for those persons long out of school and new to college-level course work, without sacrificing high-level standards. Such changes show promise of becoming permanent features of the higher educational establishment.

Reports show that the trainees' morale and motivation to pursue new careers within and outside of Head Start as well as job competence have substantially increased as a result of this program. From Adams State College in Alamosa, Colorado, one young woman a non-professional, writes, "I did not desire to continue my education after I graduated from high school. Today, ten years later, I suddenly get a strong thirst for education. Supplementary Training is giving me a boost; it is giving me confidence that I can do college work and that some day I may receive a degree."

Parent and Child Centers

A new Demonstration program—Parent and Child Centers, planned and developed in 1967 in

Four small children sit on the floor with their teacher at a Head Start program. In addition to educational programs for preschool children, Head Start provided medical services for poor children, assistance for parents, and training programs for staff. © **BETTMANN/CORBIS. REPRODUCED BY PERMISSION.**

partnership with HEW, the Department of Labor and HUD, became operational last year. Designed to serve the needs of the very young child—under 3 years of age—and his entire family, 29 Projects are in various stages of operational development; i.e., recruiting and hiring staff members; conducting staff pre-service training in conjunction with their university affiliates or functioning as planned with full enrollment of families and children.

Parent and Child Centers, normally operating as part of a more comprehensive neighborhood center, will focus heavily on *preventing* developmental problems and will give even greater emphasis than Head Start to reinforcing parental skills and involvement with their children.

Parent Participation

Parent Involvement—one of the cornerstones of the program—has been significantly strengthened this past year as the result of a pilot training program for staff leaders and the publication of a major curriculum manual, first of its kind in the field. *The Curriculum For Training in Parent Participation And Involvement* is a basic text for trainers engaged

in teaching both professional and non-professional personnel the art of successfully developing strong parent participation programs. It evolved from a 15-month staff training program, planned and conducted by the Child Study Association of America under a contract with Project Head Start.

New Partnership

The pediatricians of America and Project Head Start began a new partnership this past year with the American Academy of Pediatrics. This organization is accepting a major responsibility for ensuring that the health services of Head Start are effective, of high quality and meet the serious health needs of impoverished children, their families and the communities in which they live.

The response to the Academy's call for consultants in the fall of 1967 was far greater than anticipated. As the year progressed, reports from the 600 pediatricians who were named as consultants revealed an overwhelming concern for *all* aspects— not just the medical—of the Head Start program.

The Academy itself deserves credit for much of this "total" sense of commitment for it began its consulting program by holding eight regional orientation meetings, each designed to thoroughly acquaint trainees not only with the philosophy, objectives, guidelines and administration of the Head Start program, but with *all* the programs of the Office of Economic Opportunity.

Is Head Start a Success?

Because of the time-consuming process of gathering, assimilating and digesting data, summary reports of both national and small scale studies of the summer 1965–1967 programs have only recently been completed. It is now possible to make some statements about the kinds of people and organizations whom Head Start programs involve and some tentative conclusions about the impact which the Program has had on them.

The Children and Their Families

Data show that:

- Head Start is a national program. About the same number of children are enrolled in northern, southern, eastern and western states, although the southeastern states tend to have the highest proportion of children and the far western states the lowest proportion.

- About 45 percent of the full year children and about 40 percent of the summer children are Negro; about 35 percent of the full year children and about 40 percent of the summer children are Caucasian. About 12 percent are Spanish-speaking (Mexican-American or Puerto Rican families) and about 4 percent are American Indian. Other groups such as Oriental and Eskimo represent small proportions of Head Start children.

- About the same number of boys and girls are enrolled in the program.

- About 78 percent of the fathers and 95 percent of the mothers are living with the children.

- Less than 8 percent of the fathers and 5 percent of the mothers had attended college; about 22 percent of the fathers and 26 percent of the mothers had only graduated from high school.

- Most of fathers are employed, with the majority of employed fathers (85 percent) in laboring or operative trades. Despite this source of income, only about 65 percent of the mothers are able to stay home.

- About 65 percent of the summer programs and about 30 percent of the full-year are operated by the public schools. The balance are operated by community action agencies, churches and other private non-profit organizations.

The Program

Some Aspects of School Readiness

One of Head Start's main objectives is to increase a child's readiness for learning in school. One component of school readiness is general learning ability—"intelligence"—a quality difficult to measure under ideal circumstances. Newer approaches to determining intelligence "quotients" stress importance of environment in such determinations. These approaches imply that many features in the poverty environment can retard the development of traditional and testable areas of intelligence. The enrichment of Head Start, which can provide a more middle-class experience, could therefore raise scores on standard intelligence tests. It has generally been found that children who attend Head Start advance in measures of intelligence to significantly higher levels. Although not yet on a par with middle-class children, their scores show relatively high gains over a relatively brief period.

Reasons for these changes are open to several interpretations. For example, it is possible that the Head Start experience does not directly modify the general intelligence of the child but succeeds rather in cultivating particular skills through training practice. Experience with warm, interested adults may also enhance the child's performance. It is also possible that Head Start experience enables children to become more task-oriented, more responsive to both the tester and the materials. Whatever the reasons for the rise in intelligence test scores, the increase in I.Q. ratings may be considered a promising outcome.

Are These Gains Sustained?

There has been much discussion of the so-called "fade-out" phenomenon in the advances made by Head Start children. This appears to be a mislabelling of what may occur. In general, rate of growth of Head Start children *slows down* in public school, permitting children without the Head Start experience to approach the Head Start child's level. This "catch up" is not a loss in test performance but rather a maintaining of a score or a very slow increase in performance achieved. Since children at this age serve as models for each other, it is possible that Head Start children may even help the others come up to their level. In one study, it was found that with a classroom composed of more than 50 percent Head Start children, the teacher could complete the curriculum more rapidly than where there were only few or no children with Head Start experience in her class. Other factors seem to influence the extent to which gains are sustained: Head Start children who entered middle-class schools, whose parents were voluntary participants rather than "recruited," whose parents were judged more involved in the program and who had younger brothers and sisters in the program tended to have higher levels of performance than other Head Start children. At this point, data suggest that Head Start gains are not lost but that the initial advantage of Head Starters over non-Head Starters is not sustained for most of the Head Start programs and the public schools studied.

Still another interesting pattern of findings about the durability of Head Start's beneficial effects has been suggested in studies revealing a later "bloom" of Head Start children during the second year after their Head Start experience.

This may be related to the quality of the public school program, or to the changing nature of curricular demands and tasks as the child grows older. More importantly, it is possible that Head Start's most important real benefit to a child may be a set of attitudes, values, and habits which permit him to continue to make full use of his opportunities to learn, rather than merely a set of specific school-related skills.

Medical-Dental Care

Low-income children have less access to medical and dental care; the proportion of Head Start children who saw physicians during the past year increased, however, from 50 percent in summer 1965 to 65 percent in summer 1967. In the 1967 summer and full-year programs, about 25 percent had one or more conditions which needed treatment.

Diagnostic services seem to be improving. Greater efforts have been made to ensure medical and dental, visual and hearing follow-up treatment for children in the program.

■ ■ ■

The need for further research in Head Start is clear. The preliminary indications of success need to be confirmed by more rigorous studies, especially studies which are longitudinal in design and which employ national samples and control groups. We need to know exactly how Head Start has best achieved its successes, what impact the program has on a child's physical health and on his social-emotional development, on his family and home environment, and on the community of which the program is part.

During the past three years, efforts to develop new techniques for measuring these previously unmeasured variables have been initiated, and new programs of research are being undertaken to evaluate Head Start's effects on neighborhoods and communities, as well as upon social institutions, community welfare facilities, public education and the collective social conscience.

Further Resources

BOOKS

Hellmuth, Jerome, ed. *Disadvantaged Child: Head Start and Early Intervention.* New York: Brunner/Mazel Publishers, 1968.

Payne, James S., et al. *Head Start: A Tragicomedy with Epilogue.* New York: Behavioral Publications, 1973.

Unger, Irwin, and Debi Unger. *LBJ: A Life.* New York: John Wiley & Sons, 1999.

Zigler, Edward, and Jeanette Valentine, eds. *Project Head Start: A Legacy of the War on Poverty.* New York: The Free Press, 1979.

PERIODICALS

Hechinger, F.M. "Dispute over the Value of Head Start." *The New York Times,* April 20, 1969, sec. E, 11.

"Intelligence: Is There a Racial Difference?" *Time,* April 11, 1969, 54, 59.

Richmond, Julius B. "Communities in Action: A Report on Project Head Start." *Reading Teacher* 19, no. 5, February 1966, 323–331.

WEBSITES

Head Start Information & Publication Center. Available online at http://www.headstartinfo.org/infocenter/infocenter.htm (accessed April 9, 2003).

A Writer Teaches Writing: A Practical Method of Teaching Composition

Guidebook

By: Donald M. Murray

Date: 1968

Source: Murray, Donald M. *A Writer Teaches Writing: A Practical Method of Teaching Composition.* Boston: Houghton Mifflin Co., 1968, 1–3.

About the Author: Donald M. Murray (1924–) began his career as a journalist. He won a Pulitzer Prize in 1954 for editorial writing in the *Boston Herald.* He was a professor of English at the University of New Hampshire, where he inaugurated a journalism program and helped establish a graduate program in composition studies. Murray also has been a writing coach for several newspapers. He is the author of several books on writing and writing instruction as well as a novel and a collection of poems. As of 2003, he continued to write a column for the *Boston Globe.* ∎

Introduction

Composition as a field of study began to develop in the early 1960s. Many in the field mark the 1963 publication of *Research in Written Composition,* by Richard Braddock, Richard Lloyd-Jones, and L. Schoer, as the beginning point. Up until then, composition and rhetoric had been the responsibility of the English department. Freshman English as a standard college course began around the end of the nineteenth century. These courses focused on what Patricia Bizzell and Bruce Herzberg describe in their book *The Rhetorical Tradition* as "technical skill in grammar and usage, paragraph coherence, and exercises in the modes of discourse—description, narration, exposition, and argumentation."

In the twentieth century, literature was added to writing courses to give students something to write about in their papers. Colleges continued teaching writing in this manner through most of the twentieth century, and some continue to teach writing this way. Changes in writing instruction developed as researchers and writers started to realize the value of a personal voice in writing. The model for the "new" approach was the way professional writers did their work.

Donald M. Murray was one of the early advocates of teaching writing by writing. He did not try to train students to be professional writers; he tried to help them discover the process of writing by finding their own voices. In 1965, the New England School Development Council invited Murray to help develop a new approach to writing instruction for high school teachers. Murray met with a group of experienced teachers, then developed a program based on how effective writers worked. The result was the first edition of *A Writer Teaches Writing.*

Murray's book, and his body of work, is based on his own experiences as a writer. He encourages teachers to be writers and to write along with their students. Through his methods, students are encouraged just to write, instead of being concerned about the errors on their papers which are corrected or the grades they receive. The first chapter of Murray's book outlines the seven skills a writer needs. This is followed by a section on how the teacher should approach writing instruction: as a listener, as a coach, and as a writer.

Significance

Donald Murray's *A Writer Teaches Writing* presented a new alternative to the traditional way of teaching writing through the analysis of prose models. His approach changed many teachers' methods of teaching writing and the way many students learned to write. There are those who do not like Murray's methods. He has been called a "reactive" teacher. Advocates of "reactive" teaching, including Peter Elbow and William E. Coles, want students to use what they already know and the skills they have. Teachers then "react" or comment on the content first before moving on to the technical aspects of writing. Teachers who prefer assigned topics and teaching specific writing skills find Murray's method unacceptable.

Many teachers, however, are advocates of Murray's methods, which he revised in the 1985 edition of his book. As one teacher has pointed out, Murray teaches "having *human contact* with our students, one-to-one as people, not just 'knowledgeable contact.'" Perhaps the most important idea that Donald Murray promotes is continuing to learn—as a writer, as a student, and as a teacher.

Primary Source

A Writer Teaches Writing: A Practical Method of Teaching Composition. [excerpt]

> **SYNOPSIS:** In this excerpt from a chapter titled "The Writer's Seven Skills," Donald Murray discusses how writers come up with their ideas. A sense of discovery, exploration, and openness are all essential to writers in search of a topic, he says.

"The Writer's Seven Skills"

How does the writer write?

We must be able to answer this question to teach writing effectively. But we cannot discover how the writer works merely by studying what he has left on the page. We must observe the act of writing itself to expose to our students the process of writing as it is performed by the successful writer.

The successful writer is the person who conveys information, ideas and experience across the barriers of time and distance. The writer may be a novelist, a salesman, a lawyer, a historian, a member of the League of Women Voters, an engineer, a journalist, a general, a philosopher, a politician, an advertising copywriter, a union official, a businessman, a scientist. Those categories simply identify the material he has to communicate, they do not indicate whether he is a writer or not. The man who creates an effective memo is as much a writer as the man who produces an effective sonnet. We should isolate and identify the fundamental skills of the writer, who is able to take an idea from his brain and transplant it into the minds of people beyond the range of his voice.

We teach the student to write because he has to be a writer, revealing his knowledge to his teachers before he is allowed to graduate. Once the student becomes a working member of our complex society he will probably write reports, letters, proposals, memoranda, in order to work with people beyond his office and his community.

The student can learn to write if he is encouraged to discover and to practice the publishing writer's basic skills. It is the job of the writing teacher to create a climate in which his students can experience the act of writing as it is performed by the professional writer.

Writing is exploration—discovery of meaning, discovery of form—and the writer works back and forth, concentrating on one of the writer's seven basic skills at a time, so that he can discover what he has to say and how to say it more efficiently. The act of writing is complicated, but in the tidal conflict between the artist's freedom and the craftsman's discipline there is a consistent pattern of work which can be identified and passed on to the student writer.

The student writer and his teacher, however, must first understand what every writer knows: there are no absolute laws of composition. Each principle of writing may be broken to solve a particular problem in a specific piece of work. The only test a writer applies to a page is the craftsman's question, "Does it work?" But in making language work—forcing it to carry its burden of meaning to the reader—most writers discover they have to practice, consciously or subconsciously, the following seven skills.

He Discovers a Subject

The writer knows what he has to say determines how he says it. He takes part in a constant search for subject, for he has discovered the strength of his writing will depend directly on the vigor of his thinking. Content and form, form and content—which comes first? The answer has to be content. Form is not an empty jug into which the writer pours meaning; form grows out of meaning, so much so that many writers come to believe that form, in a very real sense, is meaning.

Most of a writer's time is spent trying to perceive his subject. His business is perception—to see

and to understand so that he can make the reader see. Elizabeth Bowen in "The Roving Eye" . . . , has described the process by which the imaginative writer finds his subject. We should realize that non-"creative" writers are also "see-ers." What the lawyer tries to do when he sits down to write a brief is to bring the case into perspective, into focus. The person who is writing a police report, an account of a Ladies Aid meeting, a memorandum on a new sales process, is trying to see the subject so clearly that he can make the reader see it equally well.

How does the writer develop a sense of subject so that he can identify a good subject? This process of spotting, developing, shaping and completing a subject may be described as what happens when an idea is developed into a thought. The idea is quick, fragile, a passing thing. For example, an idea might be that our town needs a school for high school graduates who cannot afford to go away to college but who have not yet developed into college material. That is an idea. A thought is a well-considered proposal for the establishment of a two-year community college. This thought would have some firm indication of the need, of the way in which a college could be founded and supported. The difference between an idea and a thought might be described as the difference between a kiss and marriage.

The writer gets ideas by spending part of his time in a state of open susceptibility. One person has said that a writer is a man with his skin off. He is particularly aware, uniquely receptive to impressions and ideas. He reads, he listens, he looks, he tastes, he touches. He is in contact with life in an uncritical way, accepting life; he hears what his students really say; he watches how the town develops as the shopping center is built on the outside of town; he sees the silent, threatening signs of a developing street fight late on an August night.

The writer is sensitive, but not in any dainty, limp-wristed sort of way. If one is going to be sensitive, aware of life, caring, then one must be tough. The writer is sensitive the way high-speed film is sensitive. It is the best film and the toughest film which can record the horror and the beauty of life. The novelist, the company speechwriter, the newspaperman, the scholar—all writers—should first of all be able to see, to listen, to record and accept what is happening around them.

The writer is not looking for ideas so much as he is trying to handle the ones he has. He feels that the ocean of ideas will overwhelm him. In the same way, some aphasic children cannot be taken to a

---

The Writer's Seven Skills

1. He Discovers a Subject
2. He Senses an Audience
3. He Searches for Specifics
4. He Creates a Design
5. He Writes
6. He Develops a Critical Eye
7. He Rewrites

SOURCE: Murray, Donald M. *A Writer Teaches Writing: A Practical Method of Teaching Composition.* Boston: Houghton Mifflin Co., 1968.

---

supermarket for the impressions made on their brains by the lights, the colors, the sounds, the cold of the air-conditioning, the clatter and the chatter, the shapes and forms, are all a jumble. The children panic because their damaged brains cannot sort out the difference between an unimportant and an important sound. The writer escapes a similar confusion and panic by seeing patterns in the jumble of impressions. He ties ideas together and sees relationships as he is on the way to developing a thought.

Mozart used the same notes as other composers, but he saw many more connections or relationships. This is how the writer builds. He sees a connection between a production statistic, a new development in transportation, the findings of a market report; and he weaves these all together into a thought: we should develop a new product. The man in the company, the community, or the government agency who is given the task of writing is usually the person who not only sees more, but sees patterns. The writer is the person who brings order to disorder. That is his most important job, to create order where disorder existed. The ghost-writer, for example, does not just rearrange the words of the person for whom he is writing; he puts together ideas for the person for whom he is writing; he creates a pattern, an order, a form.

As the writer searches for his subject he goes through a focusing process, developing a vague idea into a well-aimed thought. Lucile Vaughan Payne in her book *The Lively Art Of Writing,* talks very effectively about the informed opinion. This is what the writer has, a focused generalization. He has worked from specifics, from unrelated ideas to a synthesis, a generalization, but not toward, as the inexperi-

enced writer seems to think, a vague generalization. The writer's generalizations are nailed down, they are well-made and documented; they have been built, thought through, constructed, composed. This is why we use the term "composition," an old-fashioned but a good word for writing. The subject is composed when the writer has achieved a sense of completeness in his thinking, when he has been able to put a frame around the picture, fitting everything inside that frame which belongs there and ruthlessly discarding that which does not belong there.

The writer finds his subject by being open to ideas, by making connections between ideas, by defining that connection in a focused generalization. He builds a thought on the page which is so well-constructed that the reader will accept it as his own.

Further Resources

BOOKS

Bizzell, Patricia, and Bruce Herzberg. *The Rhetorical Tradition: Readings from Classical Times to the Present.* Boston: Bedford Books, 1990.

Ede, Lisa. "Teaching Writing." In *An Introduction to Composition Studies.* New York: Oxford University Press, 1991, 118–134.

Tate, Gary, and Edward P.J. Corbett. *The Writing Teacher's Sourcebook.* 2nd ed. New York: Oxford University Press, 1988.

PERIODICALS

Romano, Tom. "The Living Legacy of Donald Murray." *English Journal,* January 2000, 74–79.

Zirinsky, Driek. "'Mucking About in Language, I Save My Soul': An Interview with Donald Murray." *Writing on the Edge* 4, no. 2, Spring 1993, 11–23.

WEBSITES

Understanding Composition and Rhetoric. College of Liberal Arts, University of Central Oklahoma. Available online at http://www.libarts.ucok.edu/english/rhetoric/rhetoric/index.html; website home page: http://www.libarts.ucok.edu (accessed April 9, 2003).

The Strawberry Statement—Notes of a College Revolutionary

Memoir

By: James S. Kunen

Date: 1969

Source: Kunen, James S. *The Strawberry Statement: Notes of a College Revolutionary.* New York: Random House, 1969, 4–7.

About the Author: James S. Kunen (1948–) was born in Boston. He attended Andover prior to enrolling at Columbia University. Kunen is the author of four books. He works as freelance writer, contributing to magazines such as *US, Atlantic, New York,* and *Sports Illustrated.* ∎

Introduction

In the 1940s and 1950s, protests were uncommon on college campuses. This changed in the fall of 1964, when administrators at Berkeley enforced a rule prohibiting political groups from collecting money and recruiting members. When a nonstudent activist was arrested on October 1, a sit-in began that lasted for thirty-two hours. Attention from the media encouraged other students in their protests.

Reasons for student protests varied from campus to campus, but three common issues emerged: American involvement in Vietnam; racial inequality; and the "unresponsiveness" of the federal government and university administrations and their "repressive" reaction to student demands. Increasingly radical groups such as Students for a Democratic Society (SDS) became involved in the protests. They clashed not only with college administrations and police, but also with conservative groups of students on campus.

James S. Kunen documented the 1968 uprising at Columbia. It began over two issues: The university's plans for building a gymnasium in Morningside Heights and Columbia's membership in the Institute for Defense Analysis, an organization that consisted of twelve universities that conducted research for the Pentagon. The protest, organized by SDS, started with a march to the gym site, where students presented a list of demands. In the end, protesters occupied five campus buildings over an eight-day period. Seven hundred people were arrested, and one hundred were injured after the police were called to end the takeover.

Kunen, who participated in the protest, approached the task of recording his impressions as a journalist. The notes he kept in a spiral notebook were first published as articles in *New York* magazine under the pseudonym Simon Kunen. The title for the book comes from a statement made by one of the deans at Columbia, who said that students' opinions on university matters have about as much significance as their telling him they like or dislike strawberries.

Significance

In his book, James Kunen covers the weeks leading up to the uprising and the subsequent violence, providing both background information and his personal impressions about Columbia president Grayson Kirk; Mark Rudd, president of Columbia's SDS chapter; the IDA; and the controversial gym. But the book is not solely about the 1968 protest. Kunen also writes about other aspects of his life as a college student, including his girlfriend, his feelings about long hair, and what happened after the spring of 1968.

Most reviewers admired Kunen's writing. Henry S. Resnik wrote in the *Saturday Review* that "the book is laced with a dry wit and humor that would have done Huck and Holden proud." But some reviewers were disturbed by Kunen's lack of historical understanding. Anthony R. Dolan, writing in the *National Review,* stated that the book's "historical perspective is nonexistent" and that Kunen does not understand the progress institutions have made. Still, he says that the "book is, unhesitatingly, a triumph."

James S. Kunen's book is a college student's diary from the Vietnam era. As such it is a valuable piece of history. Although it should not be read as a comprehensive view of what every 1960s college radical thought, *The Strawberry Statement* does provides one person's narrative of events that led to violence and changed a university's course of action. The book remains in print more than three decades after it was first published.

Primary Source

The Strawberry Statement—Notes of a College Revolutionary [excerpt]

> **SYNOPSIS:** In the introductory chapter of *The Strawberry Statement,* James Kunen reveals "Who We Are"—the "we" being the student radicals at Columbia University—and "How the Book Was Written." The text is personal and often humorous, reflecting Kunen's thoughts and observations during the turbulent years at Columbia and in America.

Who We Are

People want to know who we are, and some think they know who we are. Some think we're a bunch of snot-nosed brats. It's difficult to say really who we are. We don't have snot on our noses. What we do have is hopes and fears, or ups and downs, as they are called.

A lot of the time we are very unhappy, and we try to cheer ourselves up by thinking. We think how lucky we are to be able to go to school, to have nice clothes and fine things and to eat well and have money and be healthy. How lucky we are really. But we remain unhappy. Then we attack ourselves for self-pity, and become more unhappy, and still more unhappy over being sad.

We're unhappy because of the war, and because of poverty and the hopelessness of politics, but also because we sometimes get put down by

A professor finds an entrance blocked as students at Columbia University stage a sit-in when they took over four buildings in a protest demonstration, April 1968. Seven hundred people were arrested, and one hundred were injured after the police were called to end the protest. © **BETTMANN/CORBIS. REPRODUCED BY PERMISSION.**

girls or boys, as the case may be, or feel lonely and alone and lost.

And who we are is people in New York City.

New York is the most exciting city in the world, and also the cruddiest place to be that I can conceive of. The city, where when you see someone on the subway you know you will never see him again. The city, where the streets are dead with the movement of people brushing by, like silt in a now-dry riverbed, stirred by the rush of a dirty wind. The city, where you walk along on the hard floor of a giant maze with walls much taller than people and full of them. The city is an island and feels that way; not enough room, very separate. You have to walk on right-angle routes, can't see where you're going to, only where you are, can only see a narrow part of sky, and never any stars. It's a giant maze you have to fight through, like a rat, but unlike the rat you have no reward awaiting you at the end. There is no end, and you don't know what you're supposed to be looking for.

And unlike the rat, you are not alone. You are instead lonely. There is loneliness as can exist only in the midst of numbers and numbers of people who don't know you, who don't care about you, who won't let you care about them.

Everywhere you walk you hear a click-clack. The click-clack of your walking never leaves you, reminding you all the time that you are at the bottom of a box. The earth is trapped beneath concrete and tar and you are locked away from it. Nothing grows.

All of this makes us sad. And all of this is at Columbia, is Columbia, for Columbia is New York. Leaving the school or its city really doesn't help. Once you live in New York you are locked in the city, and the city is locked in you.

On the beach or in the woods the click-clack follows you, and you carry pavement beneath your feet. The walls are all around, for you have lived with people and away from them. You know the story on the world; you see how far people are. And you feel quite sad.

But sadness is not despair so long as you can get angry. And we have become angry at Columbia. Not having despaired, we are able to see things that need to be fought, and we fight. We have fought, we are fighting, we will fight.

How the Book Was Written

Writing a book is a lot like having a baby; they both involve bringing something into the world that wasn't there before, and they're both a pain in the ass.

This book was written on napkins and cigarette packs and hitchhiking signs. It was spread all over, but so is my mind. I exhibit a marked tendency to forget things. I can remember only three things at a time. If I think of a fourth thing, I forget the first. Like a cigarette machine. You take one pack out— all the rest fall down a notch. Exactly analogous in every salient detail.

The best, truest way to read this book would be to rip it up and throw the scraps all over your house. Then, later, should you come across a piece, read it, or don't read it, depending upon how you feel. Or, better, save it until four o'clock in the morning when you would rather do almost anything else, and read it then. Above all, don't spend too much time reading it because I didn't spend much time writing it.

You will notice that a great deal of this book simply relates little things I've done and thought. It may seem completely irrelevant to Columbia. That's the way it goes.

Further Resources

BOOKS

Fact-Finding Commission on Columbia Disturbances. *Crisis at Columbia: Report of the Fact-Finding Commission Appointed to Investigate the Disturbances at Columbia University in April and May, 1968.* New York: Vintage Books, 1968.

President's Commission on Campus Unrest. *The Report on the President's Commission on Campus Unrest.* Washington, D.C.: U.S. Government Printing Office, 1970.

Unger, Irwin. *The Movement: A History of the American New Left, 1959–1972.* New York: Harper & Row, 1974.

PERIODICALS

Dolan, Anthony R. "Charm and Confusion." *National Review* 21, October 7, 1969, 1019–1020.

Resnik, Henry S. "The Revolution Biz." *Saturday Review* 52, May 17, 1969, 84–85.

Solotaroff, Theodore. "Holden Caulfield Meets the Movement." *The New Republic* 160, no. 18, May 3, 1969, 23–26

WEBSITES

"Columbia '68." Barnard Electronic Library and Teaching Laboratory. Available online at http://beatl.barnard.columbia.edu/Columbia68/ website home page: http://beatl.barnard.columbia.edu (accessed April 9, 2003).

da Cruz, Frank. "Columbia University 1968." Columbia University Academic Information Systems. Available online at http://www.columbia.edu/acis/history/1968.html; website home page: http://www.columbia.edu (accessed April 9, 2003).

Grinberg, Ronnie, and Zpora Perry. "Columbia '68: The Issues, The Participants." Barnard Electronic Library and Teaching Laboratory. Available online at http://beatl.barnard.columbia.edu/students/his3464y/grinberg%2Bperry/68.html; website home page: http://beatl.barnard.columbia.edu (accessed April 9, 2003).

AUDIO AND VISUAL MEDIA

The Strawberry Statement. Original release, 1970. Directed by Stuart Hagmann. MGM Home Entertainment, 1991, VHS.

4

FASHION AND DESIGN

EUGENIA F. BELL, SONIA G. BENSON

Entries are arranged in chronological order by date of primary source. For entries with one primary source, the entry title is the same as the primary source title. Entries with more than one primary source have an overall entry title, followed by the titles of the primary sources.

Important Events in Fashion, 1960–1969

1960

- Already an important designer of women's clothing, Pierre Cardin begins to create fashions for men, pioneering a trend away from the standard of the gray flannel suit.
- Anthony Traina, of well-known clothing-design label Traina-Norell, dies, leaving Norman Norell on his own.
- First Lady Jacqueline Kennedy influences women's fashion.
- General Motors, Ford, and Chrysler introduce compact models—the Corvair, Falcon, and Valiant, respectively—in order to combat the growing foreign small-car export market.

1961

- Mary Quant opens a second Bazaar in Knightsbridge, based on the same concept that had propelled the highly successful King's Road boutique in 1955—youth-oriented fun.
- After working for many years under haute couture figure Cristóbal Balenciaga, André Courrèges sets up his own house of fashion design.
- New words are: anchorman, sit-in, cosmonaut, bluegrass, laser, and compact car.
- Mini skirts are first introduced in couture houses by Marc Bohan at Dior and by Courrèges.
- Eero Saarinen's design for the TWA terminal at New York International Airport, built in the shape of an eagle about to take off into flight, nears completion. The architect dies on September 1.
- In a recession-ridden production year, only compact cars show a gain in sales. Overall, the American auto industry's sales are down 25 percent, but sales of compacts are up 9 percent.
- A revival of interest in Art Nouveau furniture, fabrics, and wallpaper takes place, influenced partly by a Museum of Modern Art exhibition.
- Jane Jacobs publishes *The Death and Life of Great American Cities,* which lambastes large-scale, utopian urban-design plans for American cities.

1962

- Yves St. Laurent opens his own couture house after having worked as head designer at the House of Dior for five years following Dior's death.

- The Council of Fashion Designers of America is founded as a nonprofit organization designed to further American fashion design as an industry, establishing basic codes of professional decorum. Norman Norell is the first president.
- Jacqueline Kennedy redecorates the White House under supervision of the National Fine Arts Commission. She shows the results of the project in a televised tour.
- Splashdown and status report are the new words showing up in conversation.
- More automobiles are produced in America during the model year than in any other year except 1955. General Motors cars average about 55 percent of the industry's total sales.

1963

- Fashions from Mary Quant and other Chelsea designers cross the Atlantic Ocean, with exports beginning to account for a large percentage of total sales.
- Vidal Sassoon creates short, geometrically inspired bob hairstyles to complement Quant's youthful concepts in fashion.
- Mary Quant receives the London *Sunday Times* International Award for the revolutionary directions in which she has taken British—as well as international—fashion.
- Waistless dresses called shifts are popular, particularly for casual wear.
- Joseph Salerno's United Church in Rowington, Connecticut, represents a burgeoning new freedom of expression in architecture, with its swooping, pointed roofline.
- The Museum of Modern Art, once an example of relative freedom in architectural design, is remodeled by Philip Johnson so as to impose symmetry.
- Many American automakers enlarge their "compact" cars in both weight and length, despite the growing trend toward smaller, particularly foreign, models.
- New words are: rat fink, Beatlemania, and fake out.

1964

- In London, Barbara Hulanicki starts Biba, a mail-order fashion business that becomes a landmark boutique for the youth market. Biba is based on the concept of cheap clothing meant to be thrown away when a particular fad changes.
- Courrèges stirs up the fashion world with innovative and youth-spirited collections that include over-the-knee skirts. His Space Age collection, in particular, causes excitement.
- .The popular new dances among young people are the Frug, Monkey, Dog, Swim, and Watusi.
- Ford introduces a new car called the Mustang at the New York World's Fair, spawning the popular trend of "pony cars"—a name that applies to the Firebird, the Camaro, and a few other small, sporty models.
- The quintessentially 1950s fin finally disappears from cars—with a final run from Cadillac, the automaker that had introduced it in 1948.

- Front seat belts become standard equipment in American cars.

- Battered child syndrome is a new phrase to describe an old problem.

1965

- Puritan Fashions, an American clothing manufacturer, imports a new fashions from London designers, including the youth-oriented fashions of Quant and of Tuffin and Foale. Clothing is presented in splashy shows rather than in the more elegant manner of traditional shows.

- The Studebaker company, started by Henry and Clement Studebaker, shows its final model, the Daytona.

- The federal government passes the Motor Vehicle Air Pollution Act, which regulates automobile design, often at considerable expense to automakers.

- Paul Young opens the first shop in the United States exclusively for mod fashions—Paraphernalia, located in New York City. His shop imports youth-spirited European clothing.

- Robert Venturi completes a residence in Chestnut Hill, Pennsylvania, that experiments with resolving architectural-design contradictions in a manner that will later be called postmodern.

- Ford's Mustang scores bigger sales than any other American auto model. Sales of all other compacts slip.

- Op-art and Mondrianesque patterns appear on dress fabrics in youthful clothing designs.

- Silicon chips are introduced.

- The Houston Astrodome, the first domed, air-conditioned stadium, is opened on April 9.

- Designed by Eero Saarinen, the Gateway Arch, six hundred and thirty feet of stainless steel, is completed in St. Louis to commemorate the spirit of American pioneers who went West. Saarinen does not live to see it; he died September 1, 1961.

1966

- Mary Quant is given the Order of the British Empire (OBE) in honor of the phenomenal success of her export market.

- Yves St. Laurent's collections include pop-art-influenced fashions.

- The federal government passes the National Traffic and Motor Safety Act due to rising public concern regarding automobile safety.

- California sets pollution standards for cars.

- Fads include Batman, Ouija boards, and astrology.

- New words that describe what's happening are: Black Power, flower children, hippies, flash cube, and glitch.

- The first phase of the Salk Institute for Biological Research in La Jolla, California—designed by Louis I. Kahn—is completed.

- The British Society for the Preservation of the Mini Skirt demonstrates outside the couture house of Christian Dior in

September in order to protest a forthcoming collection that includes long coats and dresses.

1967

- Unisex clothes begin to show up in most of the major designers' fashion collections.

- Laura Ashley opens her first shop, in London.

- Faye Dunaway wears tailored flannel trousers in the movie *Bonnie and Clyde,* prompting a turn to men's tailoring in women's clothing.

- The House of Dior creates a resort ensemble consisting of a see-through chain-mail tunic and bikini bathing suit.

- Chevrolet introduces the two-seat Camaro SS to counter the threatening popularity of the Ford Mustang.

- Only 55.23 percent of cars that are nine years old on July 1, 1967, compared to 80.70 percent of nine-year-old cars on July 1, 1965, are still on the road—a consequence of the implementation of planned product obsolescence in order to stimulate the market artificially.

- R. Buckminster Fuller's geodesic dome is a center of attention at Expo '67 in Montreal.

- The latest fads are: psychedelic stuff, Mickey Mouse watches, and saunas.

- Some college campuses now have coed dorms.

1968

- Efforts are made by certain established couturiers to replace the mini, offering maxi- and midi-length clothing as alternatives. Many women reject both, though some accept the maxi as a wearable coat length.

- Cristóbal Balenciaga, perhaps the premier Paris couturier of the 1950s and teacher of Courrèges, closes his couture house. He is said to have remarked, "The life that supported the couture is finished. Real couture is a luxury which is just impossible to do anymore."

- DuPont introduces a silklike synthetic fabric called Quiana.

- American Motors brings out the AMX in order to join the highly profitable pony-car craze. Although Craig Breedlove establishes several speed records with this car, there is not much faith in the ability of American Motors to produce a high-performance car, and the design is short-lived.

- The Volkswagen Beetle reaches record sales of 569,292 in the United States.

- Popular hairdos are the Afro and corn rows.

- Men's ties get wider.

- The one-hundred-story John Hancock Building in Chicago by Skidmore, Owings and Merrill becomes world's tallest building. It contains 825,000 square feet of office space.

- In January, the federal government begins to require expensive crash tests and emissions tests for new American auto models.

1969

- "Hot pants" (the name was not coined until 1971) make their first appearance. They are introduced as something to wear underneath a split mid-length skirt, but women wear them alone instead.

• The "nude look" is popular on beaches, with crocheted cotton bathing suits and jeweled breastplates that are worn without a T-shirt underneath.

• Danilio Silvestri comes out with a transparent ball of acrylic that opens up into a chair, to be used by the growing pop culture as home furnishing.

• Architect Richard Foster designs a rotating residence, which makes a complete turn in forty-eight minutes.

• AMC's Hornet and Ford's Maverick are Detroit's first real challenges to the subcompact-car market, which is virtually monopolized by foreign competitors.

• The air bag is developed and implemented as a crash-safety device.

• New words are: headhunter, uppers, downers, and command module.

"Space Needle at World's Fair"

Photograph

By: John Graham

Date: 1961

Source: White, Timothy. "Space Needle at World's Fair." Corbis. Image no. U1319299A. Available online at http://www.corbis.com (accessed May 29, 2003).

About the Architect: John Graham (1908–1991) was born in Seattle, Washington, the son of the well-known architect John Graham, Sr. Graham Jr. is best known for designing the Seattle Space Needle. After graduating from Yale with a degree in fine arts, Graham worked briefly in merchandising before going on to the field of architecture in New York City. In 1946, when his father retired as the head of the family architecture firm, Graham returned to Seattle, where he stepped into his father's position. Combining his business experience with his architectural skills, Graham became a tremendous force in shaping Seattle's commercial environment. ■

Introduction

When Graham took over as the head of his father's firm, the booming post-World War II economy was changing the face of cities and towns nationwide. As the relatively new phenomenon of suburbs sprouted up, Graham recognized the need for large new commercial centers outside the cities. Collaborating with Seattle-based department store president Rex Allison, Graham put together revolutionary plans for suburban shopping centers all over the United States. His first mall, Seattle's Northgate Center, was a smashing success, and Graham's firm led the way in the explosion of shopping mall development and design in the United States. Graham was also greatly respected for his leadership in renovating the downtown business district of Seattle.

Significance

As the 1960s began, plans were underway for a futuristic structure to dominate the Century 21 Exposition at the 1962 Seattle World's Fair. Seattle businessman Edward E. Carlson (1911–1990) had the original idea for what would eventually become the Space Needle. His

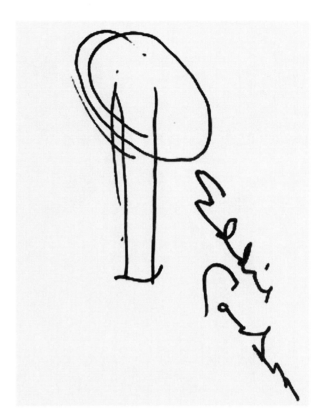

A doodle by Eddie Carlson, Seattle's 1962 World's Fair commissioner. The original doodle, written on a placemat in 1959, was the first conceptual drawing of what would become the Space Needle. This is a re-creation from 1987. **COURTESY OF HISTORYLINK.ORG. REPRODUCED BY PERMISSION.**

concept was based on the Stuttgart Tower in Germany. Carlson at first sketched out his idea on a placemat in a coffeehouse—a balloon-like structure on a stick that stood out against the city's skyline. The design was eventually turned over to Graham and his firm. Rather than the balloon shape, Graham worked out a spaceship shape atop the tower's legs. Much work was done by Graham and his team before a compromise design was in place; at that point, the fair was only eighteen months away.

Following many struggles to finance the project—at a cost of $4.5 million—and to find the property on which to build—a mere 120 by 120 square foot site—construction began, with only one year left until the fair opened. The scope was challenging: 5,850 tons of concrete and steel, resting on a 30-foot foundation. Because the concrete foundation weighed as much as the steel building, the center of gravity was at ground level. Balancing the five-level disk atop the Needle, with its revolving restaurant and observation deck, was an architectural feat. Amazingly, only a one horsepower electric motor was required to rotate the disk in which the restaurant sat because the engineering of the top of the Needle was so precise. In keeping with the futuristic theme of the fair,

Primary Source

"Space Needle at World's Fair"

SYNOPSIS: On the opening day of the 1962 World's Fair, President John F. Kennedy delivered an address to initiate the fair and its tribute to the future. The Space Needle was the enduring symbol of the fair, and subsequently became the main symbol of the city of Seattle. Other highlights of the fair—models of "future homes" and "TV telephones," for example— also celebrated "Century 21." © BETTMANN/CORBIS. REPRODUCED BY PERMISSION.

the paint colors used on the structure were "Astronaut White," "Orbital Olive," "Re-entry Red," and "Galaxy Gold." The 605-foot tall Space Needle was rapidly completed. The structure was finished in December 1961—four months before the official opening of the World's Fair on April 21, 1962.

Although the Space Needle drew some criticism at first, it quickly became the familiar symbol of Seattle. During the World's Fair, nearly 20,000 people a day rode the elevators to the top of the Needle to see the panoramic views of the city. More than 2.3 million people visited the structure during the course of the fair. The building still attracts thousands of tourists annually. Built to withstand heavy winds, earthquakes, and lightening, the Space Needle remains a dominant sight on the Seattle skyline in the twenty-first century.

In April 1999, the Seattle Landmarks Preservation Board approved the Space Needle for landmark status on the basis of all six of its designation criteria, including architectural and historical merit and physical prominence.

Further Resources

BOOKS

Clausen, Meredith L. *Shaping Seattle Architecture: A Historical Guide to the Architects.* Edited by Jeffrey Karl Ochsner. Seattle: University of Washington Press, 1994, 258–263.

Crowley, Walt. *National Trust Guide Seattle.* New York: John Wiley & Sons, 1998.

Duncan, Don *Meet Me at the Center: The Story of Seattle Center from the Beginnings to 1962 Seattle World's Fair to the 21st Century.* Seattle: Seattle Center Foundation, 1992, 43–44.

WEBSITES

Howard S. Wright Construction Co. "Space Needle Construction." Available online at http://www.hswright.com (accessed May 6, 2003).

"Space Needle." Skyscrapers.com. Available online at http://www.skyscrapers.com/re/en/wm/bu/119476/; website home page: http://www.skyscrapers.com (accessed May 6, 2003).

The Death and Life of Great American Cities

Nonfiction work

By: Jane Jacobs

Date: 1961

Source: Jacobs, Jane. *The Death and Life of Great American Cities.* New York: Random House, 1961.

About the Author: Jane Jacobs (1916–) was born in Scranton, Pennsylvania, the daughter of a doctor and a schoolteacher. After working briefly as a reporter for the *Scranton*

Tribune, Jacobs went to New York City to work as a writer. She took a job with *Architectural Forum* magazine in 1952, beginning her decades-long study of urban architecture and planning. After denouncing some of the major U.S. architects and their widely accepted views on urban planning in her 1961 book *The Death and Life of Great American Cities,* Jacobs immigrated to Toronto, Canada, in the late 1960s with her husband and three children. ∎

Introduction

When Jacobs went to work for *Architectural Forum* in 1952, her position with the magazine as well as life in New York's Greenwich Village provided a close perspective of postwar urban renewal. Jacobs, who had no training as an urban planner, developed strong personal philosophies about city life. She believed that modern planners, who were building highways and skyscrapers in American cities, were ruining the heart of those cities—their neighborhoods and street life. In 1961, she published her book *The Death and Life of Great American Cities,* eloquently arguing that modernist urbanism was a failure. Her views were in complete opposition to some of the most prestigious architects of the time. Because she lacked formal training in urban planning, Jacobs was ridiculed by the establishment for her views.

Undaunted by the criticism, Jacobs led other New Yorkers in opposing Robert Moses, New York City's infamous urban planner, when he sought to run a freeway through Washington Square in Greenwich Village. They won the fight against the freeway, and a growing movement against the modern urban forces took hold. By the mid 1960s, Jacob's interests expanded out to other social and economic concerns.

Significance

In her book, Jane Jacobs insists that successful cities are built from street life—from the hustle and bustle of people coming and going at all hours for every conceivable reason. Reasoning that busy streets were safer than quiet ones, Jacobs was ahead of her time in understanding that the city planning of the early 1960s would lead to the empty downtown plazas that had, in fact, become common by the 1980s. "Life begets life," Jacobs wrote. Warning against single-purpose zoning, she advocated mixed-use development in rebuilding a city neighborhood. She believed that lively city neighborhoods are good for the urban economy. In order to create a lively city neighborhood, she recommended mixing things up: old buildings with new buildings; and public parks and offices with commercial properties and private homes. She wrote, "Almost nobody travels willingly from sameness to sameness and repetition to repetition, even if the physical effort required is trivial."

A New Orleans residential neighborhood in 1967. © CHARLES E. ROTKIN/CORBIS. REPRODUCED BY PERMISSION.

Primary Source

The Death and Life of Great American Cities
[excerpt]

SYNOPSIS: In her book, Jacobs emphasizes the neighborhood. In this passage she describes what she means by the successful neighborhood and provides keys to achieving it.

Lately a few planners, notably Reginald Isaacs of Harvard, have daringly begun to question whether the conception of neighborhood in big cities has any meaning at all. Isaacs points out that city people are mobile. They can and do pick and choose from the entire city (and beyond) for everything from a job, a dentist, recreation, or friends, to shops, entertainment, or even in some cases their children's schools. City people, says Isaacs, are not stuck with the provincialism of a neighborhood, and why should they be? Isn't wide choice and rich opportunity the point of cities?

This is indeed the point of cities. Furthermore, this very fluidity of use and choice among city people is precisely the foundation underlying most city cultural activities and special enterprises of all kinds. Because these can draw skills, materials, customers or clienteles from a great pool, they can exist in extraordinary variety, and not only downtown but in other city districts that develop specialties and characters of their own. And in drawing upon the great pool of the city in this way, city enterprises increase, in turn, the choices available to city people for jobs, goods, entertainment, ideas, contacts, services.

Whatever city neighborhoods may be, or may not be, and whatever usefulness they may have, or may be coaxed into having, their qualities cannot work at cross-purposes to thoroughgoing city mobility and fluidity of *use,* without economically weakening the city of which they are a part. The lack of either economic or social self-containment is natural and necessary to city neighborhoods—simply because they are parts of cities. Isaacs is right when he implies that the conception of neighborhood in cities is meaningless—so long as we think of neighborhoods as being self-contained units to any significant degree, modeled upon town neighborhoods.

But for all the innate extroversion of city neighborhoods, it fails to follow that city people can therefore get along magically without neighborhoods. Even the most urbane citizen does care about the atmosphere of the street and district where he lives, no matter how much choice he has of pursuits outside it; and the common run of city people do depend greatly on their neighborhoods for the kind of everyday lives they lead. . . .

The street neighborhoods of a city have still another function in self-government, however, and a vital one: they must draw effectively on help when trouble comes along that is too big for the street to handle. This help must sometimes come from the city as a whole, at the other end of the scale. This is a loose end I shall leave hanging, but ask you to remember.

The self-government functions of streets are all humble, but they are indispensable. In spite of much experiment, planned and unplanned, there exists no substitute for lively streets.

How large is a city street neighborhood that functions capably? If we look at successful street-neighborhood networks in real life, we find this is a meaningless question, because wherever they work best, street neighborhoods have no beginnings and ends setting them apart as distinct units. The size even differs for different people from the same spot, because some people range farther, or hang around more, or extend their street acquaintance farther than others. Indeed, a great part of the success of these neighborhoods of the streets depends on their overlapping and interweaving, turning the corners. This is one means by which they become capable of economic and visual variation for their users. Residential Park Avenue in New York appears to be an extreme example of neighborhood monotony, and so it would be if it were an isolated strip of street neighborhood. . . .

Districts have to help bring the resources of a city down to where they are needed by street neighborhoods, and they have to help translate the experiences of real life, in street neighborhoods, into policies and purposes of their city as a whole. . . .

A city's collection of opportunities of all kinds, and the fluidity with which these opportunities and choices can be used, is an asset—not a detriment—for encouraging city-neighborhood stability.

Further Resources

BOOKS

Jacobs, Jane. *The Economy of Cities.* New York: Random House, 1969.

PERIODICALS

Duneier, Mitchell. "Joys in the Hood: Interview with Jane Jacobs." *The New York Times,* April 9, 2000, 33.

WEBSITES

Kunstler, Jim. "Jane Jacobs Interviewed by Jim Kunstler." Available online at http://www.kunstler.com/mags_jacobs1.htm; website home page: http://www.kunstler.com (accessed May 6, 2003).

Rochon, Lisa. "Jane Jacobs at 81." *Metropolis Magazine,* April 1998. Available online at http://www.metropolismag.com/html/content_0498/ap98jane.htm; website homepage: http://www.metropolismag.com/ (accessed June 2, 2003).

AUDIO AND VISUAL MEDIA

Cities. Bullfrog Films. Videocassette, 2000.

"Preliminary Studies for Studebaker Avanti"

Sketches

By: Raymond Loewy

Date: 1961

Source: Loewy, Raymond. "Preliminary studies for Studebaker Avanti." March 22, 1961. *American Treasures of the Library of Congress: Reason Gallery C, Transportation and Technology.* Available online at http://www.loc.gov/exhibits/treasures/trr027.html; website home page: http://www.loc.gov (accessed May 6, 2003).

About the Designer: Raymond Loewy (1893–1986) was born and raised in Paris, France. After brief schooling in engineering in France, Loewy became a soldier in World War I. After the war he moved to the United States, becoming an American citizen soon after arriving in New York in 1919. Starting his career as a window dresser for big department stores, he opened his own product design firm in 1930. Loewy designed products with an intention to make them sell. He believed that, all else being equal, the better-looking products would sell best. Among the fruits of his varied and highly prolific career were many corporate logos (or transformed logos), such as the Lucky Strike, Coca Cola, and Shell logos. His contributions to the industrial design canon include the S1 and T1 locomotives, the Greyhound Bus, the Frigidaire refrigerator, the design of Air Force One, and the interior of NASA's Skylab. Loewy's many automotive designs for Studebaker in the 1950s and 1960s are considered innovative, even by modern standards. ∎

Introduction

Loewy worked as a consultant for Studebaker Corporation for decades, beginning in 1936. His firm had designed the Starliner, considered among the United States' first sports cars, for Studebaker in 1953. In 1961, Studebaker had been in decline for some time. Its new president, Sherwood Egbert, asked Loewy to design a car that could bring Studebaker back into competition. He was looking for a sporty car that would appeal to younger drivers. Egbert asked that the car be built on the chassis model of the Studebaker Lark and that a model be

Primary Source

"Preliminary Studies for Studebaker Avanti" (1 OF 2)

SYNOPSIS: Raymond Loewy, a prolific and innovative industrial engineer best known for his enduring logo designs for Shell, Coca Cola, and Lucky Strike, and for his industrial designs for the Greyhound Bus and International Harvester, was also a legend in automobile design. His Avanti, designed for Studebaker, was considered a work of art by people in the automobile industry. THE LIBRARY OF CONGRESS.

Primary Source

"Preliminary Studies for Studebaker Avanti" (2 OF 2)

The sixth of twelve preliminary study drawings of the 1961 Studebaker Avanti by Raymond Loewy. THE LIBRARY OF CONGRESS.

produced within 40 days. Loewy returned to his home in California and assembled a design team. He quickly produced a full-scale clay model for the Avanti that was immediately accepted when he presented it to the Studebaker board in late April 1961.

Significance

Loewy had been an advocate of streamlining in design since the 1930s. Studebaker, on the other hand, was known for its large, heavy cars. With the Avanti, Loewy stuck to the principles of streamlining, paving the way for the smaller sports cars that were to follow. Many called the Avanti a true work of art. All the lines were sleek and smooth, from the grilleless nose to the fastback rear. It was a luxurious little sports car, with contoured leather bucket seats and a leather padded roll bar. Its body was made of fiberglass. The car quickly set speed records and was highly praised throughout the auto industry. When news of its release became public, orders poured in.

Even with the success of the new sports car, the Studebaker Corporation could not survive. The company folded in 1964. A Studebaker dealer named Nathan Altman so believed in the Avanti that he and an associate, Leo Newman, set out to manufacture the car themselves, buying buildings and equipment from the collapsing Studebaker. The two entrepreneurs formed the Avanti Motor Corporation in South Bend, Indiana. In 1965, they produced 45 cars that sold for $6,500 each. Altman died in 1976. At that time Avanti was producing about 150 cars per year. The company was sold two more times before it closed completely in 1991.

Further Resources

BOOKS

Loewy, Raymond. *Industrial Design.* New York: Overlook Press, 1979.

Tretiack, Philippe. *Raymond Loewy and Streamlined Design.* New York: Universe/Vendome, 1999.

PERIODICALS

Kichen, Steve. "Raymond Loewy's Four-door Avanti." *Forbes* 144, October 2, 1989, 180.

Obituary. *Road & Track* 38, December 1986, 116D.

Mary Quant

Photograph

By: Mary Quant
Date: 1962
Source: AP/Wide World Photos. Image No. APHS105. Available online at http://www.apwideworld.com (accessed June 3, 2003).

Quant on Her Impact on Fashion

"I think that I broke the couture stranglehold that Chanel, Dior and the others had on fashion, when I created styles at the working-girl level. It all added up to a democratization of fashion and entertainment. . . . It was very gratifying to see that not only did the mods of the sixties want my clothes, but so did the grandees and the millionaires. They had everything else . . . but they hadn't any fun clothes. . . . Snobbery went out of fashion, and in the shops you found duchesses jostling with typists to buy the same dresses. Fashion had become the great leveler."

SOURCE: Quant, Mary. In Hotchner, A.E. *Blown Away: The Rolling Stones and the Death of the Sixties.* New York, N.Y.: Simon & Schuster, 1990.

About the Designer: Mary Quant (1934–) was born in Kent, England. In 1955, she opened Bazaar, a boutique in the Chelsea section of London, where she sold clothing designed for the youth market. In order to keep her store supplied with clothes that suited her strong sense of style, Quant began designing her own. Quant's clothes were bold and provocative and always sported her trademark, a five-petaled daisy. As a designer, Quant was among the creators of the London-based "mod" look of the 1960s. While her most memorable product is probably the miniskirt (which she may not have invented, but certainly popularized), she was also renowned for revealing crocheted tops, hot pants, vinyl boots, striking geometric patterns, colored tights, and hip belts. Quant also developed unprecedented colors in cosmetics. Designers quickly began to follow in her footsteps, and consequently fashion in the 1960s exploded in a riot of color, sensuality, and shorter hemlines. ■

Introduction

Quant is considered one of the true pioneers of the British "mod" revolution in fashion of the 1960s. Taking her sense of style from the avant-garde movement, with its new music and poetry and its Op and Pop art, Quant invented truly daring styles. London became the world's fashion center and Quant was London's premier designer. The model Twiggy quickly rose to fame wearing Quant's fashions, popularizing the new look and taking it well beyond the realm of the urban elite. In fact, the look Quant created was directed to the working girl (or boy) of London, but appealed to people in every walk of life. Quant's influence rapidly spread across the Atlantic at a time when young Americans, spellbound by the Beatles and the Rolling Stones, were taking many of their cues from Britain. In London's *Sunday Times,* a critic wrote of Quant, "It is given to a fortunate few to be born at the right time, in the right place, with the right talents. In recent fashion, there are three: Chanel, Dior and Mary Quant."

Primary Source

Mary Quant

SYNOPSIS: Quant's miniskirts and minidresses were all the more marketable because the designer herself could wear them to advantage. She seemed to personify her own fashion values, keeping up with the latest trends in hair and makeup. Here Quant (right) and three models pose in an Arkansas clothing shop in 1968. AP/WIDE WORLD PHOTOS. REPRODUCED BY PERMISSION.

During the 1960s, the very youthful Mary Quant was the peer of her young customers. She wasn't just creating the ideas for the bold new looks, she convincingly wore the new haircuts (Vidal Sassoon cut her hair) and the bold new makeup that the trend-setting models, celebrities, and stars were wearing. David Bailey, the decade's most famous photographer, often took photos of Mary adorned in her own styles. She seemed to represent 1960s style, rather than just design it.

Significance

Inspired by her design innovations, other designers of the 1960s took her lead with elements of style: geometric patterns; vibrant colors and mixes of colors, such as shades of purple and chartreuse; and "wet look"

dresses made of shiny vinyl, cellophane, or paper. The 1960s had a distinctive look for which it will always be remembered; designs intended to shock or provoke or otherwise renounce conformity: dresses with pieces cut out, revealing skin, or dresses covered with mirrored glass; enormous bellbottoms, fur vests, go-go boots, prints from India, micro-miniskirts, midi skirts, maxi skirts, ruffled shirts, and Nehru jackets. Quant played an enormous role in transforming the fashion of the decade.

Further Resources

BOOKS

Quant, Mary. *Quant by Quant.* New York: Putnam, 1967.

PERIODICALS

Adburgham, Alison. "Interview." *Guardian,* London, October 10, 1967.

Dougherty, Steve. "As Hemlines Rise, So Do the Fortunes of Mini Mogul Mary Quant." *People Weekly* 29, April 4 1988, 107–108.

"Interior of the T.W.A. Flight Center"

Photograph

By: G.E. Kidder Smith

Date: 1962

Source: "Interior of the T.W.A. Flight Center." 1962. Corbis. Image no. GE002291. Available online at http://www.corbis.com (accessed June 14, 2003).

About the Architect: Eero Saarinen (1910–1961) was born in Helsinki, Finland, the son of artist Loja Saarinen and co-founder and first president of the Cranbrook Academy of Art, the renowned Finnish architect Eliel Saarinen. The younger Saarinen emigrated to the United States with his family in 1923. He began his studies in Paris, majoring in sculpture. Although this art education was to inform all his later work, after one year he turned to architecture, which he studied at Yale University. After graduating, Saarinen worked in his father's architectural firm and taught at Cranbrook, outside of Detroit, Michigan. Although he would later be known for his architecture, Saarinen was involved with some very successful furniture design projects early in his career, including work on popular chair designs with the well-known furniture designer Charles Eames in 1937. He worked in his father's firm until 1950, when his father died, but remained behind the scenes in architecture until near the end of his life. ∎

Primary Source

"Interior of the T.W.A. Flight Center"

SYNOPSIS: An interior photograph of the T.W.A. terminal after its completion. Saarinen's interior design was praised for its attractive and functional style. The T.W.A. terminal is considered one of his greatest works. © G.E. KIDDER SMITH/CORBIS. REPRODUCED BY PERMISSION.

Introduction

Working in his father's firm, Saarinen may have been overshadowed by his father's work. In 1947, however, he won a design competition for the Jefferson National Expansion Memorial Arch in St. Louis. In this project, his inclinations as an architect in his own right were given their first play. The St. Louis Gateway Arch was a triumph. In 1955, he designed the General Motors Technical Center in Warren, Michigan, and later the John Deere headquarters in Illinois. These designs were influenced by the functionality and lack of ornament of the Bauhaus style of architecture, but also took a new direction. Drawing on his education in sculpture, Saarinen infused his architectural designs with a unique sense of color, form, and material. His work bridged the gulf between Bauhaus's bare functionality and aesthetic expressionism.

Significance

Saarinen's union of aesthetic and functional design reached its climax in one of his last works, the T.W.A Terminal at New York's John F. Kennedy Airport. The terminal is considered by many to be one of the outstanding examples of modernist design and Saarinen's greatest architectural legacy. Like Grand Central Station in an earlier era, the building had style and elegance, designed to make an international traveler feel luxurious and pampered rather than pushed and hurried. Viewed from outside, the building looks like a bird in flight with wings extended, although Saarinen always claimed its form was an abstract symbol of flight and not a representation of anything. The building is made of concrete braced by an invisible web of reinforcing steel. Its upward curving lines, or curvilinear style, and its bands of skylights created attractive, spacious halls. The dining facilities, clubs, and lounges were elegantly and artfully outfitted, offering "jet set" style to travelers as well as great views of the runways. *Progressive Architecture* magazine extolled the interior design of the building as "the most original in decades."

When Saarinen died in 1961, the building was still a year from being completed. Since that time it has become an icon in American architecture. In 1994, the building was designated a New York landmark. In 2001, however, the Port Authority of New York planned to build a new terminal, which was to curve around the old one. The existing terminal would be made into a museum or a restaurant. The T.W.A. Terminal, beloved by many, had a very strong group of defenders who strongly protested the Port Authority's plans.

Further Resources

BOOKS

Saarinen, Eero. *Eero Saarinen on His Work: A Selection of Buildings Dating from 1947 to 1964.* New Haven: Yale University Press, 1964.

Stoller, Ezra. *The T.W.A. Terminal.* New York: Princeton Architectural Press, 2000.

PERIODICALS

Muschamp, Herbert. "Stay of Execution for a Dazzling Airline Terminal." *The New York Times,* November 6, 1994, 31.

A Report on Principles and Guidelines for Historic Preservation in the United States

Report

By: National Trust for Historic Preservation

Date: October 31, 1964

Source: *A Report on Principles and Guidelines for Historic Preservation in the United States.* Washington, D.C.: The National Trust for Historic Preservation, 1964.

About the Organization: The National Trust for Historic Preservation is a private nonprofit organization founded in 1949. Its mission is "helping people protect the irreplaceable." The Trust identifies areas and structures of national significance for special recognition and protection in accordance with various acts of Congress, including the National Historic Preservation Act. The Trust revitalizes blighted downtown areas, and works with the U.S. Congress and the courts to ensure legislation that will preserve U.S. historic treasures. ■

Introduction

Attempts to preserve historic buildings and properties go back at least 200 years in U.S. history, but lacked a central organizing group until the 1940s. At that time, a grassroots citizens group concerned with preservation nationwide began to discuss the urgent need for a national organization to support all the local efforts to rescue historical landmarks. Through ignorance or inertia, many of these monuments were either sold and torn down or allowed to fall into ruin. Historic downtown areas in cities had an especially low rate of survival when modern businesses demanded new buildings and roadways. In 1947, this group of concerned citizens formed a private nonprofit organization called the National Council for Historic Sites and Buildings. On October 26, 1949, President Harry Truman signed legislation that ratified the organization under the name of the National Trust for

The exterior corner of Frank Lloyd Wright's Robie House. The house, designed for Frederick C. Robie and his young family, was completed in 1910.
© G.E. KIDDER SMITH/CORBIS. REPRODUCED BY PERMISSION.

Historic Preservation. At that time, the Trust's mission was to locate, acquire, renovate, and manage landmark properties. Its mission would later expand to include educating the public, helping local preservation groups with direction and funding, and initiating many special programs nationwide. Over the years, the organization raised funds and gained legislative support for preservation projects ranging from homes designed by Frank Lloyd Wright to southern plantations of historical import.

What had once been a handful of interested parties soon grew into widespread public support for historic preservation in America. In 1952 the Trust began publishing a newsletter now known as *Preservation* magazine, documenting cases of preservation efforts. In 1960 the National Parks Service collaborated with the Trust in creating a limited list of landmarks that would eventually become the National Register of Historic Places, identifying historically significant properties and making them available to the public. The list was, and still is, managed by the National Parks Service. In 1964, the architecture program at New York City's Columbia University began offering graduate studies in the field of historic preservation.

Significance

By 1964, the nation was developing and expanding at a rapid rate, and the Trust deemed it time to press Congress for a comprehensive new national act to define policy and enforce preservation. The Trust therefore produced a report in which it outlined the goals of the preservation movement and formulated principles and guidelines that could be used to promote "voluntary citizen action." The report, which was delivered to Congress, set out definitive ways to classify historical sites and described how to restore and maintain them.

In 1966, Congress passed into law the National Historic Preservation Act (NHPA), as created from the National Trust for Historic Preservation's report. The NHPA provided for federal funding of the Trust. Under the act, each state was compelled to create a historical preservation office and review board. The National Register of Historic Places was officially chartered as the basis of preservation management. Buildings that were included in this database became a national treasure. Whether or not their properties produced income, owners of properties deemed national treasures could receive a 25 percent tax credit towards rehabilitating their home,

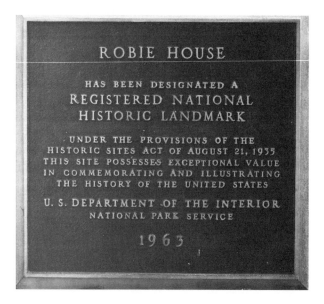

This plaque marks the Robie House as a registered national historic site.
© SANDY FELSENTHAL/CORBIS. REPRODUCED BY PERMISSION.

as long as their improvements met government standards. Today, the Trust administers 21 historic sites, and in some cases, has saved those sites from development or destruction.

Primary Source

A Report on Principles and Guidelines for Historic Preservation in the United States. [excerpt]

> **SYNOPSIS:** *A Report on Principles and Guidelines for Historic Preservation in the United States* defines: the kinds of historic sites to be preserved; the modern mission of preservation; and the standards for determining historic status. It also proposes methods of engaging ordinary citizens and historic site owners to voluntarily join in the effort.

Objectives and Scope of the Preservation Movement

Since World War II, a new generation of Americans has awakened to the importance of historic preservation and in so doing they are giving the movement strong new impetus and broader scope. Once concerned primarily with saving and restoring notable individual buildings as historic house museums, the movement now seeks to perpetuate our much wider heritage of history and architecture as an irreplaceable part of the living fabric and beauty of our communities. Once supported chiefly by historians and antiquarians, the movement now extends into all walks of life and touches the work of planners, architects, public officials, realtors, landscape architects, writers, artists, lawyers, bankers,

publishers and all citizens concerned with maintaining the character and integrity of their surroundings.

Modern preservation is, therefore, directed toward perpetuating architectural and aesthetic as well as historic and patriotic values; historic districts as well as individually notable buildings; "living monuments" as well as historic house museums; grounds and settings, including historic gardens, town squares and traditional open space as well as historic architecture; open air museums and historic villages including characteristic architecture which cannot be preserved in place; archeological sites, including prehistoric villages, earthen mounds, pueblos and other ancient ruins, as well as historic sites with foundations and artifacts of successive periods; and objects and interior furnishings from the decorative arts including books and documents, which illuminate our past and inspire the present.

To achieve these wider objectives, the modern preservation movement requires new tools and techniques, and a fresh outlook abreast of the opportunities as well as the complex pressures which are today molding community and national life in the United States.

Responsibility and Organization for Historic Preservation

Preservation of our common cultural heritage is a moral obligation which rests squarely on the shoulders of every citizen. Regardless of contemporary pressures and distractions, each generation has a profound responsibility to preserve undiminished the historical and artistic heritage it has received from the past, and from new increments, and pass the total heritage on, unimpaired, to the next generation. Wisely conserved these cumulative evidences of the past constitute a powerful physical, moral, and spiritual activating force, making an indispensable contribution to the artistic and cultural life of the nation, and to the broader world civilization of which it is a part.

In the United States, with our dedication to voluntary citizen action, and under our Federal system of government, the common effort to conserve our heritage requires joint participation of individual citizens, interested voluntary organizations, private donors and foundations, and all levels of government—local, state, and national. Within the common effort, certain broad areas of special responsibility may be identified.

Further Resources

BOOKS

Moore, Arthur. *The Powers of Preservation: New Life for Urban Historic Places.* New York: McGraw-Hill, 1998.

Tyler, Norman. *Historic Preservation: An Introduction to Its History, Principles, and Practice.* New York: W.W. Norton and Co., 1999.

PERIODICALS

Czarnecki, John E., and Tom Connors. "Preserving Wright's and Richardson's Chicago Area Icons." *Architectural Record* 188, no.10, October 2000, 46.

"Preservation: A Special Issue." *Architectural Record* 179, March 1991, 48–49, 52–59, 62–69, 87–163.

WEBSITES

"National Register of Historic Places." National Parks Service .com. Available online at http://www.cr.nps.gov/nr/; website home page: http://www.cr.nps.gov (accessed May 16, 2003).

"National Trust Historic Sites." NationalTrust.org. Available online at http://www.nationaltrust.org/national_trust_sites /list.html; website home page: http://www.nationaltrust.org (accessed May 16, 2003).

"Polaroid Automatic 101"

Magazine advertisement

By: Henry Dreyfuss

Date: 1964

Source: "Polaroid Automatic 101." Advertising Archive. Image no. 30510333.

About the Designer: Henry Dreyfuss (1904–1972) was born in Brooklyn, New York. He was exposed to design as a child in his family's theatrical design supply business. In 1924, Dreyfuss apprenticed with the well-known set designer, Norman Bel Geddes. Over the next four years he produced hundreds of stage sets as Bel Geddes' employee before striking out on his own in 1928. His company—Henry Dreyfuss Associates—although originally concerned with stage design, quickly turned its focus to industrial design. With his strong emphasis on creating machinery that functioned well with human anatomy and psychology and his uniquely practical approach to innovation, Dreyfuss achieved almost instant success in designing mass-produced items. After Dreyfuss's wife became terminally ill, in 1972 Dreyfuss brought about both of their deaths using carbon monoxide. ∎

Introduction

Not long after starting his own company, Dreyfuss won a design competition sponsored by Bell Laboratories. He began work as a consultant for the company in 1930. His Model 302 telephone became the classic phone for the period 1937–1950. He would continue to create some of the United States' most widely used telephones through the end of the 1950s, including the Princess, a small phone with the mouthpiece and dial placed together in the handset, which was successfully marketed in a variety of colors to teenage girls. During the period from the 1930s to the 1950s, Dreyfuss also designed a refrigerator for General Electric and a best-selling alarm clock for Westclox. In the same period, he worked for New York Central Railroad, first creating the long-distance travel Mercury diesel locomotive and going on to design—from engine to interior décor—the luxury liner called the Twentieth Century Limited that traveled between New York and Chicago.

In 1953, Dreyfuss designed Minneapolis-based Honeywell's groundbreaking circular wall thermostat. He had begun experimenting with the round thermostat back in 1940, but its complexities and World War II had impeded his progress. In 1960, after designing tractors for Deere and Company for years, Dreyfuss was involved in creating a groundbreaking tractor design that was appealing to farmers for its bold new look, but especially for its comfortable seat. Dreyfuss also assisted in the design of the 1947 grand failure, the ConvAIRCAR, an automobile that could fly but was doomed from the start by its costliness and major safety concerns.

Perhaps as much as any of his designs, Dreyfuss is remembered for his approach to industrial design. His design concepts provided a much-needed link between the consumer and practical business needs. He was particularly interested in making things that took into consideration the physical limitations of the human body, and was a pioneer in what is now called "ergonomics." His autobiography, which was published in 1955, was appropriately called *Designing for People.*

Significance

The camera illustrated in this 1964 advertisement—the Polaroid Automatic 101—issued a developing print immediately after the photographer took a picture. It was the first of many Polaroid products Dreyfuss designed, or assisted in designing. His Polaroid Automatic 101 was much smaller than previous models and yet it was still easy to use. Notably, Dreyfuss was the designer of the innovative single-button shutter control mechanism of the Automatic 100, which took the picture with a single movement.

Dreyfuss's work with the Polaroid Corporation exemplified the kind of relationship between an industrial engineer and a corporation that could lead to prestige and profits for the company and better value for consumers. In 1964, the Automatic 101 model shown here retailed for $164.95. But automatic cameras quickly became easier to use and less expensive. Within a year,

Show-off.

This is the finest automatic camera Polaroid has ever produced.

It's a terrible show-off.

Worse yet, it will turn you into one.

Like all Polaroid Color Pack Cameras, it will deliver a color print in 60 seconds. A pretty flashy act in itself.

But this model has a few other tricks up its sleeve. (It's all done with a sensitive electric eye and a remarkable transistorized shutter.)

For instance. Load the camera with black and white film. Turn off all the lights, except perhaps a candle or night-light near the subject. *Without flash*, it will give you a perfect time exposure. Automatically. (Great for portraits of dinner guests, sleeping kids, pretty girls by the fire.)

This one's pretty impressive too. Load with color film, add the flash and start shooting. The electric eye will read the light of the flash and set the exposure. Automatically. You never have to worry about special distance settings.

What else? It produces beautiful close-ups with the close-up and portrait attachments. It has a triplet lens, a superimposed-image, coupled range-finder, 2 exposure ranges for color, 2 for black and white. It's light. Compact. Fast-loading.

But don't say we didn't warn you. Once it's in the house, you're going to be unbearable.

Primary Source

"Polaroid Automatic 101"

SYNOPSIS: Dreyfuss frequently collaborated with Edwin Land to produce innovative cameras for Polaroid. The Polaroid Automatic 101 was one of the first Polaroid products Dreyfuss designed. The camera could issue a developing print immediately after the photo was taken. Dreyfuss's last innovation for Polaroid was the 1972 SX-70, the first folding instant camera. THE ADVERTISING ARCHIVE, LTD. REPRODUCED BY PERMISSION.

the new Polaroid Automatic 104 came out, priced at $59.95.

Dreyfuss's impact was to make products more consumer-friendly and consumers more design-aware. The pioneering designer helped to establish the Industrial Designers Society of America, becoming its first president. In 1960, he published a second book focusing on design, *The Measures of Man*. This book provides a comprehensive study of the human body, analyzing average shapes and sizes. Dreyfuss detailed how the human body works with products ranging from chairs to cameras. The book is an essential part of any industial designer's library and has frequently been updated and reissued.

Further Resources

BOOKS

Flinchum, Russell. *Henry Dreyfuss, Industrial Designer: The Man in the Brown Suit*. New York: Rizzoli, 1997.

Olshaker, Mark. *The Instant Image: Edwin Land and the Polaroid Experience*. New York: Stein and Day, 1978.

PERIODICALS

Margolies, Jane. "The Human Factor." *House Beautiful* 139, March 1997, 68

Rich, Frank. "20th Century Unlimited. Henry Dreyfuss Retrospective at the Cooper-Hewitt." *The New York Times,* March 20, 1997, A25.

WEBSITES

"Henry Dreyfuss Directing Design." Cooper-Hewitt National Design Museum, Smithsonian Institution. Available online at http://ndm.si.edu/EXHIBITIONS/hd/exhibition.html; website home page: http://ndm.si.edu (accessed May 6, 2003).

The Beatles Arrive in the United States

Photograph

By: Associated Press

Date: 1964

Source: The Beatles Arrive in the United States. 1964. AP/Wide World Photos. Image No. 340331. Available online at http://www.apwideworld.com (accessed June 3, 3003).

About the Organization: The Associated Press (AP) was formed in 1848 in New York when ten men representing six newspaper publishers decided to pool their efforts and share the expenses of gathering international news. As years passed, the newspapers in the collective developed their technology together. Because of the pooled resources of the AP, the international community gets more news, in a timely manner, about major events occurring globally. ■

Introduction

In 1960, a musical band made up of art students from Liverpool changed its name from the Quarry Men to the Beatles. The membership of the band would still undergo a couple of changes, but it was as the Beatles in the early 1960s that it changed the world of rock music—and the way many teenagers looked and thought—forever.

The Beatles were a huge cultural phenomenon in Britain and elsewhere in Europe before they were a hit in the United States. From the start, it was not only their music that profoundly affected their fans. Their style, with their narrow suits and ties, Chelsea boots, and, at that time, wildly unconventional hairstyles, also took hold. London, already considering itself a fashion center, easily adapted to the look.

On February 9, 1964, 73 million Americans sat transfixed in front of their television sets as the Beatles made their first U.S. appearance on the *Ed Sullivan Show*. In the concerts that followed, girls screamed and swooned at every gesture the Beatles made. Boys, on the other hand, were more likely to imitate the band members. The Beatles' "mop-top" haircut spread quickly in the United States, making long hair fashionable here for the first time since the eighteenth century. Until the arrival of the Beatles in the United States, most young men had kept their hair trimmed above their ears. The Beatles brought to America a new way of thinking about music and a new, controversial social message, both of which were reflected by their unique sense of style.

Significance

Stu Sutcliffe was the bass player of the Quarry Men/Beatles for a period in 1960. Around the time he was leaving the band, he had his hair cut by his girlfriend, German artist Astrid Kirchner. Kirchner combed his hair forward rather than back, and then cut it in a mop-like fashion. (Although she later claimed it was her invention, other art students in Liverpool remember the haircut as a trend at that time, called the "Julius Caesar.") The other Beatles laughed at Sutcliffe when they first saw his new haircut, but then all but drummer Pete Best decided to cut their hair in the same way, in a cut that was similar to a bowl-cut. As the Beatle's popularity soared, so too did the popularity of the Beatles haircut among young men. The style became known as the "fringe-cut" and the "mop-top."

The mop-top style does not seem long or messy by early twenty-first century standards, but in 1964 it was nothing less than shocking. The name "mop-top" is itself derogatory, evoking the shaggy strands of a floor mop. When young men wore their hair loose and long, it outraged parents and teachers across the country. The Beatles'

Primary Source

The Beatles Arrive in the United States

SYNOPSIS: The Beatles brought more than music to pop culture of the 1960s. Their haircut, known as the mop-top, fringe cut, or simply "Beatles hair," was one of the most significant and enduring styles of the decade. AP/WIDE WORLD PHOTOS. REPRODUCED BY PERMISSION.

haircuts made news and shaped policy in a way that makes little sense today. Reviewers of early Beatles appearances in the United States never failed to comment on their hair, as if the hair and not the music or the crazed fans was the main story. Schools prohibited Beatle haircuts (and so some enterprising individuals began producing Beatle wigs). Hair became a political standard: long hair signified nonconformity and even became a reflection of leftist politics. There were even Beatles hair care products.

Further Resources

BOOKS

Echols, Alice. *Shaky Ground: The '60s and Its Aftershocks.* New York: Columbia University Press, 2002.

Farber, David and Beth Bailey. *The Columbia Guide to America in the 1960s.* New York: Columbia University Press, 2001.

Kimball, Roger. *The Long March: How the Cultural Revolution of the Sixties Changed America.* San Francisco: Encounter Books, 2000.

"Colors Courageous"

Magazine article

By: *Gentleman's Quarterly*

Date: February 1965

Source: "1965: Colors Courageous." *Gentleman's Quarterly,* February 1965. Reproduced in Kidwell, Claudia B., and Margaret C. Christman. *Suiting Everyone: The Democratization of Clothing in America,* Washington, D.C.: Smithsonian Institution Press, 1974, 187.

About the Publication: Since its first issue, *Gentleman's Quarterly (GQ)* has been known as the premier style guide for men. The monthly magazine offers articles on a variety of topics besides fashion, including finance, food and entertainment, technology, celebrity profiles, sports, and travel. *GQ* is considered more upscale and better written than the majority of men's magazines. Still, it maintains its popularity year after year for its role as a bible of men's fashion. ∎

Introduction

In the 1950s, conformity was the rule in men's fashion. Professional attire of the decade was predominantly the gray flannel suit. Businessmen tended to dress conservatively, in drab and very limited styles. But even as gray flannel, blue pinstripe, and tweed suits prevailed, the 1950s saw the beginnings of change in men's fashion, with items such as bright plaid sports jackets, colored dress shirts, and Bermuda shorts finding a new market. By the end of the 1950s, a significant portion of men's clothing was made from the new synthetic materials. Synthetic blend shirts bearing the welcome "drip dry" labels were available to replace cotton shirts that required laborious pressing after each wash.

The conservatism of the 1950s gave way during the 1960s and 1970s. With the civil rights movement, the protest against the war in Vietnam, the sexual revolution, and other social upheavals, people began to see themselves in new ways that were reflected in their clothing.

Primary Source

"Colors Courageous"

SYNOPSIS: In the mid-1960s, men's fashion—even for businessmen—started to break from the gray-flannel-suit mold. Men's wear was revolutionized with brighter colors, new fabrics, and shirt and jacket options. The men's clothing industry presented consumers with mass-produced clothing in a variety of styles and prices, giving men many more fashion options than their fathers had ever known. © CONDE NAST PUBLICATIONS, INC. REPRODUCED BY PERMISSION.

Styles became more simple and youthful. Women's styles, in particular, experienced many new influences. Men's clothes in the United States were less noticeably altered in the early 1960s. Unless a man wanted to follow the British "mod look" lead, with its tapered pants and narrow ties, there were not many choices out there. The designer Pierre Cardin, recognizing this, created an American version of the European styles, with his tight-fitting clothes. Blue jeans, also very fitted, became immensely popular for recreation and informal wear among the middle classes, where once they had been considered work clothes.

Significance

By the mid-1960s the designers of men's clothing began to bring the new fashion sense to the basic business suit. Suits, still in demand in most business and professional environments, were designed for some amount of personal expression. Bright colors, double-breasted jackets, the Nehru jacket, colorfully patterned ties, and turtleneck sweaters worn under suits were among the new options for men. The time was ripe for the "Peacock Revolution"—a phrase popularized in this country by columnist George Frazier—of men's fashion. Men were given the opportunity to be vain: to dress more creatively and colorfully than their fathers had ever dreamed. The new movement, which had begun in London, encompassed an array of new looks. Men's clothing items came in purples and oranges, flower prints, and velvet fabric combinations.

The men's fashion industry of the mid-1960s boomed. In the past, many suits had been custom made, but in the 1960s, mass-produced wear became widespread. It was more affordable and offered enough variety to reflect personal tastes. The concept of men's style itself was just beginning to be acceptable for the average man, who could consult the growing supply of men's magazines for an update on the latest in suit styles or low-maintenance fabrics. Men's jewelry added another accessory option. By mid-decade, many men were sporting chains and rings. These colorful male fashion trends lasted into the 1970s.

Further Resources

BOOKS

Esquire Fashions for Men. New York: Harper and Row, 1966.

Hayward, Catherine. *Man about Town.* London: Hamlyn, 2001.

Lois, George. *Covering the '60s: The Esquire Era.* New York: Monacelli Press, 1996

PERIODICALS

Hochswender, Woody. "The Hourglass of Fashion." *Esquire,* January 1994, 86–87.

"The Future Is Now in Chicago"

Magazine article

By: *Progressive Architecture*
Date: 1965
Source: "The Future Is Now in Chicago." *Progressive Architecture* 46, no. 5, May 1965, 55. ∎

Introduction

Skidmore, Owings & Merrill (SOM), established in Chicago in 1936, was one the largest architecture firms operating in the United States in the mid-1960s. With offices in New York and Chicago, SOM became a leader in the design of skyscrapers and corporate buildings.

Bruce John Graham was born in 1925 in La Cumbre, Colombia. After graduating from the University of Pennsylvania with a degree in architecture in 1948, Graham worked in a Chicago architecture firm for several years before joining the Chicago office of Skidmore, Owings & Merrill. There, as chief of design and, after 1960, general partner, Graham set to work on the design of high-rise structures, which soon became his specialty. Graham played a leading role in establishing the design principles that would affect commercial architecture in Chicago during the 1960s. Though he never actually studied with him, he was an enthusiastic follower of Ludwig Mies van der Rohe—a leader in the Internationalist style whose steel and glass buildings had become prominent in the Chicago skyline in the 1950s and 1960s.

Significance

From 1965 to 1969, Graham joined forces with SOM's highly respected structural engineer, Fazlur Kahn, to design the John Hancock Tower. The skyscraper was to be situated within a high-rise section of Chicago's downtown area on the shore of Lake Michigan. The project called for multiple uses for the space within, and Graham decided that a tapered building, with a wide base for commercial use and a narrowing top for offices and homes, would be the most efficient use of space. The building was to be 100 floors tall, and within its frame would lie a small world, complete with stores, services, homes, parking, and recreation.

The structure Graham envisioned for the building was a steel tube. In his book *Bruce Graham of SOM*, Graham described his desire to design the building with its structure exposed to view, referring back to the principles of his mentor, Mies van der Rohe: "It was as essential to us to expose the structure of this mammoth as it is to perceive the structure of the Eiffel Tower, for Chicago, honesty of structure has become a tradition." Together Graham and Kahn developed the distinctive bracing criss-crosses on the facade of a tapered tube. The first 5 floors of the building are commercial, floors 6–12 are parking, 13–41 are office space; floors 42–92 are apartments, and the top 7 floors are service-oriented, with an observatory, television and mechanical stations, and a restaurant. The tower also has shops, offices, a hotel, a swimming pool, an ice rink, a post office, and a refuse collection agency.

Primary Source

"The Future Is Now in Chicago"

SYNOPSIS: The John Hancock Center is the tallest multifunction building in the world. From 1968 to 1973 it was Chicago's tallest building. Made possible by new technology in steel products and engineering software, the design used less than 30 pounds of steel per square foot, the amount traditionally used in a building half its height. At the time it was built, there was a sense among the American public that the world was about to change dramatically and that modern architects could do almost anything.

Chicago, Ill—It's as if someone had said "Okay, see these buildings in the Sunday supplement article about futuristic architecture: we're going to build them." First came the Marina Towers, then the U.S. Gypsum Building: next came plans for the First National Bank Building, and now we have the John Hancock Center by SOM. All these Chicago buildings, like Hollywood starlets, are distinguished by their shapes. But each, in its own way, has a more distinct personality.

The $95-million John Hancock Center, for which ground was broken last month, is shaped like a giant three-dimensional A, tapering from a 41,000-sq-ft base (which takes up 41 per cent of its site) to a 16,000-sq-ft cap. On completion in 1968, it will also be the second-tallest building in the world. Rising 1100 ft above North Michigan Avenue and East Chestnut Street in downtown Chicago, it will provide parking, offices, and apartments in 100 stories and 2.8 million sq ft of interior space. The first two stories will house office and apartment lobbies, then will come six floors of parking, entered at the third story from circular ramps, providing parking space for 1100 cars. From the ninth to the forty-fourth floors will be offices, and above them 49 floors of apartments—750 in all. The forty-fourth story is what the rental brochures will no doubt call

The John Hancock Building rises 1,100 feet above downtown Chicago.
© CHARLES E. ROTKIN/CORBIS. REPRODUCED BY PERMISSION.

a lobby-in-the-sky for apartment residents, complete with swimming pool, specialty and service shops. Toward the top of the building will be located a restaurant and public observation areas: the two top stories will house mechanical equipment. The exterior is structural steel and tinted glass, with steel braces exposed and arranged much like those in a fire tower.

Chicago, which has been talking as well as doing something about looking to the future, is seemingly engaged in an architectural race for height. Although the city can spread almost endlessly onto the surrounding Illinois plains. its radial growth is already being hampered by congested transportation. To build upward at the center is a logical and expedient move. The newly completed Civic Center is 700 ft high and currently the tallest building in town. When completed, the First National Bank Building will be 800 ft. and the John Hancock Center will be one-third higher than that. There has even been talk about reviving Frank Lloyd Wright's plans for a mile-high structure there. The way Chicago has been behaving lately, talk is close to action. And after all, why not?

Further Resources

BOOKS

Graham, Bruce. *Bruce Graham of SOM.* New York: Rizzoli, 1989.

Stoller, Ezra. *The John Hancock Building.* New York: Princeton Architectural Press, 2001.

PERIODICALS

"Chicago's 'Big John' Hancock Tower Still Stands Tall on the World's Skyline." *Architectural Record* 187, no. 5, May 1999, 154.

Williams, A.R. "Chicago's Hancock Center." *National Geographic* 175, February 1989, 174–185.

The Whitney Museum of American Art

Architectural design

By: Marcel Breuer

Date: 1966

Source: Goldberg, Jeff. The Whitney Museum of American Art. Traditional Fine Arts Online Inc. Available online at http://www.tfaoi.com/am/12am/12am23.jpg; website home page: http://www.tfaoi.com (accessed May 3, 2003).

About the Architect: Marcel Breuer (1902–1981) was born in the provincial town of Pécs, Hungary. He began his architectural studies in Vienna, but was soon drawn to the Bauhaus School in the Weimar and Dessau. There, he studied and taught during the 1920s, specializing in furniture design. His tubular steel chairs, developed during this period, are now considered furniture classics. Upon leaving Bauhaus, Breuer started his own architectural firm in Berlin. In the 1930s he left Nazi Germany and moved to London, where he worked for F.R.S. Yorke and the renowned Bauhaus architect Walter Gropius. At Gropius's invitation, Breuer moved to the United States to take an academic position at Harvard University's School of Design. Breuer later formed his own practice—Marcel Breuer and Associates—in New York, with offices in Europe to handle overseas commissions. He won the AIA Gold Medal in 1968 and died in New York in 1981. ∎

Introduction

By the time Breuer left the Bauhaus at the end of the 1920s, he was one of the best-known designers in Europe, particularly noted for his tubular steel furniture. But he was making his mark in designing residences and commercial buildings as well, and had been influenced greatly by his Bauhaus exposure to the great architects of the International Style: Le Corbusier, Mies van der Rohe, and Walter Gropius. From 1937 through World War II, Gropius and Breuer formed a partnership while on faculty at Harvard. Their work together is said to have revolutionized American housing design.

In 1946 Breuer set up his own firm, with offices in New York and Paris. At first his firm focused on residential projects. Later it would branch out to include some of the great institutional buildings. In 1952, Breuer designed the UNESCO Headquarters in Paris, and in 1954 he began work on Saint John's Abbey in Collegeville, Minnesota. His European commissions soared.

The Whitney Museum of Art, commissioned in 1963, is considered Breuer's greatest architectural legacy—though he is probably most often remembered for his furniture design. As a furniture designer, he focused on mass production, making designs that were available to everyone: inexpensive, useful, and clean in form and function. His belief in industrial design and modern technology made him a prominent leader of the International Style movement, and this was an important basis for his architecture as well, and is readily observed in the Whitney Museum design.

Significance

In 1963, Breuer was commissioned to design the Whitney Museum's third home in New York in 35 years, which was to house a collection of modern American art. The collection had been initiated with a donation by Gertrude Vanderbilt Whitney in 1914. Moving north from its first location, Vanderbilt's townhouse on West 8th Street, the museum had already moved once to West 54th. The Whitney trustees in 1963 wished to build the museum on a comparatively small southeast corner site at Madison Avenue and 75th Street. Their main interest in the design was that this building would not only exhibit innovative and experimental modern art—the museum building itself was to be a work of modern art.

Breuer was given a very short timeframe to put a design together and there were few changes to his original concept. His creation had the look a one big unit of concrete: a cantilevered cube covered in granite. Windows were in multiple shapes and spaced irregularly. The hard, modernist look is in bold contrast to the elegant brownstone residential buildings around it. Inside, the museum is set up for the changing exhibits. There are three floors with large, open gallery space, set up with movable walls and changeable lighting.

The look of the Whitney was not immediately appreciated by the public or critics when it was completed in 1966. Its overall appearance was considered harsh, somber, and brutal, and it had completely broken with traditions in museum architecture. It has since been recognized as a prime example of the innovations of modern architecture. In fact, locals and preservationists came to the defense of Breuer's design in 1985, when an expansion designed by architect Michael Graves was proposed. Protestors claimed Graves's design was incompatible with Breuer's, and the addition was canceled.

Primary Source

The Whitney Museum of American Art

SYNOPSIS: The Whitney Museum of American Art is architect Marcel Breuer's most enduring building design, although it was criticized by many when it was completed in 1966. Breuer's daring design paved the way for innovation in later museum architecture. PHOTO © JEFF GOLDBERG/ESTO. ALL RIGHTS RESERVED.

Further Resources

BOOKS

Gatje, Robert. *Marcel Breuer: A Memoir.* New York: Moncelli, 2000.

Stoller, Ezra. *The Whitney Museum of American Art.* New York: Princeton Architectural Press, 2000.

PERIODICALS

"Whitney Museum of American Art." *A+U: Architecture and Urbanism,* December 1994, 308–315.

"Whitney Opens." *Progressive Architecture* 47, October 1966, 238–241.

WEBSITES

Marcel Breuer. Available online at http:// www.marcelbreuer .org (accessed May 6, 2003).

"Marcel Breuer, a Centennial Celebration." Archives of American Art. Available online at http://artarchives.si.edu/exhibits /breuer/buildings.htm; website home page: http://artarchives .si.edu (accessed May 6, 2003).

Cutout Dresses

Clothing style

By: Rudy Gernreich

Date: 1967

Source: "The Costume Institute." Metropolitan Museum of Art. Available online at http://www.metmuseum.org/collections/department.asp?dep=8; website home page: http://www.metmuseum.org (accessed May 3, 2003).

About the Designer: Rudy Gernreich (1922–1985), was born in Austria. In 1938, as the Nazis came to power, Gernreich, a Jew, fled from Vienna at the age of 16. He made his way to Los Angeles, where he began his remarkable career in clothing design. During the 1950s, Gernreich designed costumes for movie stars such as Lana Turner and Eva Marie Saint. He was also an avid gay rights activist, a cofounder of the Los Angeles chapter of the Mattachine Society, which was established in 1951 to educate the public about homosexuality, assist gay men, effect changes in social attitudes towards gays, and secure the repeal of laws discriminating against gays. But it was his role in changing the course of modern fashion design in the 1960s for which Gernreich is most remembered. His topless swimsuit, the transparent dress, and his androgynous separates and suits created a minor revolution in the way people dressed. ∎

Introduction

Some of Gernreich's most controversial work were clothes that freed women from the bones and stays and other understructures that had long constrained their bodies. As early as the 1950s, he was designing unconstructed bathing suits—suits without boning or artificial supports—for women. He is also credited with designing the first soft, transparent bra, often called the "no bra"

bra, departing from the hard pointy bras of the 1950s. In the late 1960s his infamous topless swimsuits were banned from beaches and denounced by the Pope.

In the 1960s, London fashion designers were exercising considerable influence on American fashion. The trends coming across the Atlantic included shocking colors and experimental fabrics, which Gernreich thoroughly embraced in his own designs. He was a pioneer in combining hot pinks with oranges, purples with reds, and dots with stripes. At the same time, he was a gifted draper who appreciated beautiful, realistic clothes. He liked to play the provocateur, and this has often overshadowed what many consider his genius and artistry of design. Model Peggy Moffitt said of the designer, " . . . He invented a modern way of dressing for the latter part of the twentieth century, just as Chanel had done for the earlier part of the century."

Gernreich had designed and introduced many trends in women's fashion before he came out with his cutout dress. He is credited with many firsts: knitted tube dresses; the androgynous or unisex look; thong bathing suits; and many others. While most of his work would not raise an eyebrow in the early twenty-first century, Gernreich's fashions provoked storms of controversy and media coverage when introduced in the 1960s.

Significance

In 1967, Gernreich was elected to the Fashion Hall of Fame. A fashion critic praised him for "the best fad that didn't sell—his topless bathing suit—and for taking things off or out of clothes," referring not only to his removal of the understructures of the swimwear and bras, but also to his cutting out part of the material that covered the body in the cutout dress.

In the cutout dress, a clear vinyl band exposes a small area of the wearer's skin below the dress. The dress was featured on the cover of *Time* magazine in 1967 with a story on Gernreich. The designer's famous line was noted: "A woman today can be anything she wants to be—a Gainsborough or a Reynolds or a Reynolds Wrap."

The cutout dress appealed to those women who enjoyed the shocking and innovative elements in fashion design. But Gernreich was not only about shocking; his dresses were also beautifully made. He is well remembered for the careful craftsmanship of his clothing as well as the timeliness of his provocative design visions.

Further Resources

BOOKS

Moffitt, Peggy. *The Rudy Gernreich Book.* New York: Rizzoli, 1991.

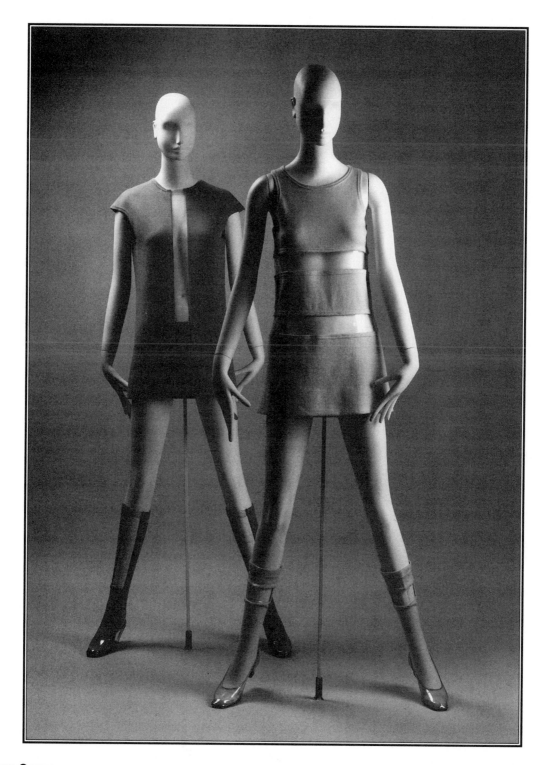

Primary Source

Cutout Dresses

SYNOPSIS: Rudy Gernreich's cutout dresses raised many an eyebrow in the 1960s, but these designs are considered classics today and have been inducted into museum collections and fashion halls of fame. *ENSEMBLE(S),* 1967, DESIGNED BY RUDI GERNREICH (AMERICAN, BORN AUSTRIA, 1922–1985) WOOL, PLASTIC, NYLON, LEATHER. THE METROPOLITAN MUSEUM OF ART, GIFT OF LÉON BING AND ORESTE F. PUCCIANI, 1988 (1988.74.1A-F; 1988.74.2A-E) PHOTOGRAPH, ALL RIGHTS RESERVED, THE METROPOLITAN MUSEUM OF ART.

PERIODICALS

Horyn, Cathy. "The Shock Heard Round the World." *Vanity Fair* 453, May 1998, 122–124.

Shields, Jody. "Rudi Gernreich Was a Designer Ahead of His Time, as a New Book Illustrates." *Vogue* 181, December 1991, 98.

Ford Foundation Building

Architectural design

By: Kevin Roche and John Dinkeloo

Date: 1967

Source: Kidder Smith, G.E. Ford Foundation Building. 1967. Corbis. Image no. GE001745. Available online at http://www.pro.corbis.com (accessed May 3, 2003).

About the Architects: John Dinkeloo (1918–1981) was born in Holland, Michigan. He studied at the University of Michigan School of Architecture, after which he worked for Skidmore, Owings, and Merrill as a structural engineer. He joined the firm of Eero Saarinen in 1950, making partner five years later. In 1966 he entered into partnership with Kevin Roche in Hamden, Connecticut.

Kevin Roche was born in Dublin, Ireland. He studied architecture at University College in Dublin, graduating in 1945. Not long after graduating, he went to work at the firm of Michael Scott, one of Ireland's premier architects. In 1948 he traveled to the United States to take a graduate class at the Illinois Institute of Technology in Chicago, taught by the renowned Bauhaus architect Mies van der Rohe. Roche worked for architect Eero Saarinen's firm from 1951 to 1961 and then entered into a partnership with John Dinkeloo in 1966. He received the Pritzker Architecture Prize in 1982. ■

Introduction

From the time of their meeting at the architectural firm of Eero Saarinen and Associates in Bloomfield, Michigan, in the early 1950s, Kevin Roche and John Dinkeloo became a creative team, producing an astonishing output of civic and corporate architecture for more than two decades. With Roche's skill at creating simple designs and Dinkeloo's expertise at technical engineering, they were able to unite highly sculptural form with intricate structure and break many of the molds in modernist architecture. During the 1950s, Dinkeloo was head of production for Saarinen's firm and Roche was the chief designer. When Saarinen died in September 1961, Dinkeloo and Roche were suddenly faced with the task of completing ten major projects that were already in progress. These included the T.W.A. Terminal at John F. Kennedy International Airport, Dulles International Airport, Deere and Company Headquarters, the St. Louis Arch, and CBS Headquarters.

Under the pressure of these major projects, the Roche-Dinkeloo partnership flourished. Roche acted as the principal designer while Dinkeloo was the expert in construction and technology. Together throughout the 1960s and 1970s they created many highly acclaimed buildings that became celebrated examples of late modernist architecture. The commission for the Ford Foundation Building was one of their first as a team.

Significance

The design and construction phase of the Ford Foundation took place between 1963 and 1968. Setting out to create a humane environment for the country's largest philanthropic organization, the architects departed from the spare and abstract forms of the International Style and the typical New York office tower. The goal of the design for this building was to create space in which the individual worker or visitor could identify "with the aims and intentions of the group," according to Dennis Sharp, author of *Twentieth Century Architecture: A Visual History*. The Roche-Dinkeloo solution was a box-like structure composed of glass, brown South Dakota granite, and rust-colored steel set around a very large twelve-story atrium, with windows in every office looking out over the exotic plant life in the center and into the windows of their co-workers' offices around them. The building was set at angles on the corner of Forty-second and Forty-third Streets in order to capture the southern light. Roche stated that the building "creates an appropriate environment for its occupants, a space that allows members of the Foundation staff to be aware of each other—to share their common aims and purposes, and that assists them in fostering a sense of working family" (Yukio, Futagawa, ed. *Kevin Roche, John Dinkeloo and Associates, 1962-1975.*)

The Ford Foundation headquarters building features a public garden that remains a refuge in the bustling city to this day. The softening of lines and spaces of the building was a departure from the spare corporate image of late-modernist office buildings, and was a welcome break. *New York Times* architecture critic Ada Louise Huxtable described the building as "probably one of the most romantic environments ever devised by corporate man." Many architects and critics hailed it as the best building of 1960s New York City, and its atrium has been copied by numerous corporate centers and hotels (notably the Hyatt Group) in the ensuing years. The design stood up well over the years, as the building was unchanged as of 2003 and has remained the headquarters of the Ford Foundation since it opened. In 1995, the building received the American Institute of Architects' 25-Year Award for enduring significance and for being one of New York City's few true modernist landmarks.

Primary Source

Ford Foundation Building

SYNOPSIS: The design for the Ford Foundation headquarters in New York City included an enormous, twelve-story atrium that all the offices faced. This humane urban environment designed by the architecture firm of Roche-Dinkeloo was a welcome departure from the functional "less is more" approach to corporate architecture of the modernist era. © G.E. KIDDER SMITH/CORBIS. REPRODUCED BY PERMISSION.

The team of Roche-Dinkeloo's list of achievements together after the Ford Foundation includes the Oakland Museum and the United Nations Plaza.

Further Resources

BOOKS

Futagawa, Yukio, ed. *Kevin Roche, John Dinkeloo and Associates, 1962-1975.* New York: Architectural Book Publishing Co., 1977.

Sharp, Dennis. *Twentieth Century Architecture: A Visual History.* New York: Facts on File, 1991.

PERIODICALS

Boyer, M. Christine. "Reflections on a Glass." *Design Book Review,* no.13, Fall 1987, 34–37.

"A Foundation's Atelier: The Ford Foundation Building." *Industrial Design* 15, no. 2, March 1968, 26–27.

"Tie Dye Booth"

Clothing style

By: Charles Harbutt

Date: 1969

Source: Harbutt, Charles. "Tie Dye Booth." Actuality, Inc. Reprinted in Brash, Sarah and Loretta Britten, eds. *Our American Century, Turbulent Years: The 60s,* Richmond, Va.: Time-Life Books, 1998, 175. ∎

Introduction

Historians do not know exactly where or when tie-dying began. The craft is a method of dying patterns into materials by tying them in such a way that parts of the fabric will not absorb any dye, creating various patterns. Tie-dying existed in the T'ang Dynasty (618–906 C.E) in China. It was known as *Shibori* in Japan during the Nara Period (552–794 C.E.). Tie-dye also existed in the histories of Indonesia and Peru. In India, tie-dye is known as

Primary Source

"Tie Dye Booth"

SYNOPSIS: During the 1960s the ancient art of tie-dyeing became one of the major fashion statements of the hippie movement. The favored dress at rock concerts, and worn by many a rock star, tie-dyed t-shirts, dresses, blouses, and bandanas lent color to the free-spirited generation. The "tie dye" booth pictured here was at the famous Woodstock music festival.

PHOTOGRAPH BY CHARLES HARBUTT. © 1989 CHARLES HARBUTT/ACTUALITY INC., NEW YORK. REPRODUCED BY PERMISSION OF THE PHOTOGRAPHER.

Bandhana. (*Bandhana* means "to tie" and is the origin of the English word "Bandana.") In the craft of Bandhana, pieces of cloth are skillfully pinched and tied with small cotton threads to produce small spots on the fabric.

In the United States, tie-dye, along with peace symbols, love-ins, and huge rock festivals, has been associated almost wholly with the hippie movement of the late 1960s. The craft itself may have been introduced to this country by Peace Corps volunteers returning from a country where it was practiced. During the youth movement of the 1960s, reviving old ethnic crafts was an alternative to joining the establishment. Tie-dye became a dramatic fashion statement and, with its wild colors and free forms, a true sign of the times.

Significance

As the 1960s progressed, the "psychedelic" generation arose, inspired not only by hallucinogenic drugs but also by an overwhelming desire to question authority and rebel against convention. Particularly important in those times were war protests, civil rights demonstrations, and other grassroots movements. For those involved, the social revolution of the 1960s changed everything from sexual mores to eating habits to music to attire. As the tie-dyed t-shirt, with its wild colors and patterns, became a popular item, it stood in stark contrast to the button-down or the polo shirt. Tie-dyed clothes were worn by many of the rock stars of the 1960s, including Jimi Hen-

drix and Janis Joplin, but none were more associated with the phenomenon than the Grateful Dead.

Because tie-dying could be done at home or by amateurs, it allowed style statement without participating in the capitalistic world of fashion. A home dyer simply needed to purchase an inexpensive and readily available clothes dye, a t-shirt, and some rubber bands. In fact, RIT dye came with instructions for tie-dying right in the package.

Tie-dye had its limits, particularly because the old dyes often bled profusely in the wash, ruining other clothes and leaving a dull blur of faded colors across the tie-dyed shirt. There have been many later variations on tie-dying, all with better dyes and more variations in pattern, but the later fads have been more commercial and nostalgic. For better or worse, the spirit of nonconformity and rebellion the tie-dyed apparel once symbolized has never again taken quite the same form.

Further Resources

BOOKS

Belfer, Nancy. *Batik and Tie-Dye Techniques.* New York: Dover, 1992.

Singer, Margo and Mary Spyrou. *Textile Arts: Multicultural Traditions.* Worcester, Mass.: Davis Publications, 2000.

PERIODICALS

"Hippies Meet Yuppies as a New Generation is Fit to be Tie-Dyed." *People Weekly* 28, August 24, 1987, 65.

5

GOVERNMENT AND POLITICS

PAUL G. CONNORS

Entries are arranged in chronological order by date of primary source. For entries with one primary source, the entry title is the same as the primary source title. Entries with more than one primary source have an overall entry title, followed by the titles of the primary sources.

Important Events in Government and Politics, 1960–1969

1960

- On January 2, Senator John F. Kennedy of Massachusetts announces that he will challenge Senator Hubert H. Humphrey of Minnesota for the Democratic Party nomination for president. Kennedy is the first major Catholic contender since Alfred E. Smith in 1928.

- On January 18, President Eisenhower submits a balanced budget for the fourth consecutive year. Federal revenue estimates project a $4.1 billion surplus.

- On February 1, African American college students begin a sit-in at a whites-only lunch counter in Greensboro, N.C., introducing a form of civil rights protest that spreads to other southern cities.

- On March 3, Michigan Governor G. Mennen "Soapy" Williams announces that he will not run for reelection. He is the only six-term governor in United States history.

- On May 7, the United States State Department confirms Soviet allegations that an American U-2 spy plane has been shot down over Russia and its pilot Francis Gary Powers has been captured.

- On May 10, Senator John F. Kennedy wins the West Virginia primary, proving that he can attract support in a predominantly Protestant state.

- On May 24, the United States Air Force launches the Midas II satellite that will alert the United States to a surprise Soviet missile attack.

- On June 26, Republican Senator Barry Goldwater of Arizona, dismissing criticism of America's handling of the U-2 controversy, states that the U-2 mission is "one of the great victories we have achieved over communism since the second World War."

- On July 13, the Democratic National Convention nominates Senator Kennedy for president on the first ballot. Lyndon B. Johnson is nominated for vice president the next day.

- On July 27, the Republican National Convention nominates Vice President Richard M. Nixon for president. The party platform includes a promise to continue school desegregation. The next day, the convention nominates United Nations Ambassador Henry Cabot Lodge for vice president.

- On August 27, the Atomic Energy Commission announces that the United States has detonated 169 nuclear devices since the summer of 1945.

- On August 29, the United States Department of Agriculture announces that the average American farmer produces enough food to feed twenty-four persons. This is a 100 percent increase in agricultural productivity since 1930.

- On September 26, Kennedy and Nixon meet in the first televised debate between presidential candidates.

- On October 14, President Eisenhower, age seventy, becomes the oldest man in American history to serve as president.

- On November 8, Kennedy defeats Nixon in the presidential election by less than 1 percent of the total vote. Kennedy is the first Roman Catholic and the youngest man to become president.

- On November 23, the House of Representatives of Louisiana passes a resolution attacking President Eisenhower for "making common cause with the communist conspiracy" by allowing court-ordered desegregation of New Orleans public schools.

1961

- On January 17, President Eisenhower gives his farewell address, warning Americans of the potential danger to democracy from the nation's large and powerful military-industrial complex.

- On January 20, President Kennedy, in his inaugural address, asks his fellow Americans to "ask not what your country can do for you—ask what you can do for your country."

- On March 1, Kennedy establishes the Peace Corps by executive order.

- On March 6, President Kennedy creates the Equal Employment Opportunity Commission to eliminate racism in the federal work place.

- On March 29, the Twenty-third Amendment to the United States Constitution is enacted. The amendment grants Washington, D.C. residents the right to vote in presidential elections.

- On April 10, the Dow-Jones Industrial Average soars to a record 692.06. The previous high of 685.47 was reached on January 5, 1960.

- On May 5, Alan Shepard, the thirty-seven-year-old Naval Commander, becomes the first American astronaut as he pilots the Project Mercury capsule to an altitude of 115 miles.

- On May 9, Congress passes a bill raising the minimum wage to $1.25 an hour and extends its coverage to an additional 3.6 million workers.

- On May 20, the United States Commerce Department announces that the average American family household income rose to sixty-nine hundred dollars in 1960, an increase of three hundred dollars over the previous year.

- On May 27, the United States Department of Transportation, Federal Highway Administration announces that motor vehicle registrations rose to a record 73,895,274 in 1960.

- On September 1, William Z. Foster, three-time United States Communist Party presidential candidate, dies in Moscow at the age of 80.

• On September 23, President Kennedy nominates Thurgood Marshall to the United States Second Circuit Court of Appeals bench.

1962

• On January 10, Congress convenes with Democrats holding a 64-36 majority in the Senate and a 258-174 majority in the House.

• On January 11, 77 percent of Americans approve of President Kennedy's performance in office.

• On April 11, United States Steel and seven other steel companies announce price increases. Kennedy reacts strongly, and three days later the price increase is rescinded.

• On August 11, seventy-nine percent of Americans approve of religious observances in public schools.

• On August 14, President Kennedy signs legislation appropriating $3.74 billion for NASA.

• On October 1, James Meredith enrolls at the University of Mississippi as federal troops battle thousands of protesters.

• On October 16, President Kennedy signs legislation giving businesses a 7 percent tax credit.

• On November 20, President Kennedy issues an executive order prohibiting racial and religious discrimination in federal and federally-assisted housing.

• On December 14, Kennedy proposes across-the-board tax cuts to stimulate the economy and reduce unemployment.

1963

• On February 28, President Kennedy gives his first special message on civil rights. He requests Congress to strengthen the voting rights provisions of the 1957 and 1960 Civil Rights Acts.

• On March 29, President Kennedy signs legislation providing for a four-year extension of the military draft law.

• On May 23, President Kennedy signs legislation appropriating $15 billion for missiles, aircraft, and ships.

• On June 10, President Kennedy signs legislation requiring equal pay for equal work regardless of gender.

• On August 28, over two hundred thousand civil rights supporters march on Washington and listen to Dr. Martin Luther King, Jr.'s now-famous "I have a dream" speech.

• On October 11, the President's Commission on the Status of Women reports that under current law women are discriminated against in terms of jury status and personal property rights.

• On November 22, President Kennedy is assassinated in Dallas. Vice President Lyndon B. Johnson becomes president.

• On November 29, President Johnson appoints Supreme Court Chief Justice Earl Warren to investigate President Kennedy's assassination.

1964

• On January 8, President Johnson declares a "War on Poverty" in his State of the Union message.

• On January 23, the Twenty-fourth Amendment to the United States Constitution, barring the poll tax in federal elections, is ratified as South Dakota becomes the thirty-eighth state to approve the measure.

• On February 18, Secretary of Defense Robert McNamara testifies before the House Armed Services Committee that he hopes to withdraw most of the fifteen thousand troops from South Vietnam by the end of 1965.

• On May 22, President Johnson, in a commencement address at the University of Michigan, announces his "Great Society" program to revitalize cities and expand educational and economic opportunities to minorities.

• On June 10, the United States Senate invokes the cloture rule, ending a southern filibuster designed to prevent a vote on the civil rights bill—the first time cloture has successfully been invoked on civil rights legislation.

• On June 25, President Johnson orders the United States Navy to join in the search for three missing civil rights workers near Philadelphia, Mississippi.

• On July 2, President Johnson signs the Civil Rights Act of 1964.

• On July 10, FBI Director J. Edgar Hoover publicly announces that 140 federal agents have been sent to Mississippi to protect civil rights workers.

• On July 15, the Republican National Convention nominates Arizona Senator Barry Goldwater for president on the first ballot. The next day, Representative William Miller of New York is nominated for vice president.

• On August 10, President Johnson signs the Gulf of Tonkin Resolution.

• On August 20, Johnson signs the War on Poverty Act, along with an act that provides free legal counsel to poor defendants in federal criminal proceedings.

• On August 26, the Democratic National Convention nominates President Johnson for president and Minnesota Senator Hubert H. Humphrey for vice president.

• On August 31, President Johnson signs into law an act expanding nationwide the food stamp program.

• On September 27, the Warren Commission releases its report on the assassination of President Kennedy. It concludes that Lee Harvey Oswald acted alone.

• On November 3, President Johnson carries 61 percent of the popular vote to defeat Barry Goldwater in a landslide.

1965

• On January 17, President Johnson announces eighty-eight War on Poverty legislative measures.

• On January 25, President Johnson sends Congress a budget containing the largest expansion of social welfare programs since President Franklin Roosevelt's New Deal.

• On March 6, the United States sends 3,500 troops to Vietnam; earlier forces had consisted primarily of military advisers and support personnel.

• On April 11, President Johnson signs into law a $1.3 billion education act.

- On July 28, President Johnson orders fifty thousand soldiers to Vietnam and doubles the military draft.
- On July 30, President Johnson signs into law the Medicare Act for the elderly.
- On August 6, President Johnson signs into law the 1965 Voting Rights Act.
- On October 15, demonstrations against the Vietnam War occur in forty U.S. cities.

1966

- On February 4, televised hearings on the war in Vietnam are begun by the Senate Foreign Relations Committee, chaired by Arkansas Senator J. William Fulbright.
- On March 25, the United States Supreme Court rules that Virginia's poll tax is unconstitutional.
- On June 7, the California Republican Party Convention nominates Ronald Reagan, the former Hollywood actor, for governor.
- On July 27, the FBI reports that the crime rate has increased 46 percent in the past five years even though the nation's population has only increased 8 percent.
- On October 4, United States Senate Republicans call President Johnson's War on Poverty programs a "boondoggle."
- On November 25, President Johnson signs into law a $1 billion appropriation to aid children of poor families.

1967

- On January 25, newly elected California Governor Ronald Reagan denounces out of control government spending.
- On January 13, the United States Public Health Service ends funding to Alabama because the state has failed to comply with the 1964 Civil Rights Act.
- On February 10, the Twenty-fifth Amendment to the United States Constitution, which provides a procedure for the performance of a president's duties in case of disablement, is ratified.
- On June 30, California Governor Reagan approves the largest budget in state history.
- On July 24, President Johnson orders federal troops to stop rioting and looting in Detroit.
- On December 15, President Johnson signs into law an act prohibiting discrimination on the basis of age against workers between the ages of forty and fifty-five.

1968

- On March 12, Minnesota Senator Eugene McCarthy, an antiwar candidate, comes in a close second to President Johnson in the New Hampshire Democratic primary.
- On March 31, President Johnson announces to a national television audience that he is halting the bombing of North Vietnam; he invites North Vietnam to begin peace negotiations and announces he will not run for reelection.
- On April 4, civil rights leader Martin Luther King, Jr., is murdered in Memphis, Tennessee. Riots occur in many U.S. cities.
- On June 5, New York Senator Robert F. Kennedy, the younger brother of former President John F. Kennedy, is assassinated in Los Angeles after winning the California Democratic Primary.
- On July 7, President Johnson signs into law an act making it a federal crime to desecrate the United States flag.
- On August 8, the Republican National Convention nominates Richard M. Nixon for president and Maryland Governor Spiro Agnew for vice president.
- On August 28, the Democratic National Convention nominates Vice President Hubert H. Humphrey for president as demonstrators battle police outside the convention hall in Chicago. The next day, the convention nominates Senator Edmund Muskie for vice president.
- On November 5, Richard Nixon is elected president of the United States.

1969

- On January 17, President Johnson says that his biggest regret was not achieving peace in Vietnam.
- On June 19, President Nixon approves of the FBI's use of occasional wiretaps.
- On June 23, Warren Burger becomes Chief Justice of the United States Supreme Court, succeeding the retiring Earl Warren.
- On July 19, Senator Edward "Ted" Kennedy drives off a highway, plunging his car into a pond and killing a woman passenger. He leaves the scene of the accident and fails to report it to police.
- On November 15, 250,000 march in Washington, D.C., to protest the Vietnam War.
- On December 27, President Nixon announces his support to raise taxes to balance the federal budget.

Berlin Crisis

Llewellyn Thompson Telegram to Dean Rusk, May 27, 1961

Telegram

By: Llewellyn Thompson

Date: May 27, 1961

Source: Thompson, Llewellyn. Telegram to Dean Rusk, May 27, 1961. The National Security Archive, George Washington University. Available online at http://www.gwu.edu /~nsarchiv/nsa/publications/berlin_crisis/bcdoc.html; website home page: http://www.gwu.edu/~nsarchiv/ (accessed April 2, 2003).

About the Author: Llewellyn Thompson (1904–1972) was born in Las Animas, Colorado. In 1929, after graduating from the University of Colorado, he entered the U.S. Foreign Service. In 1941, he was dispatched to Moscow and witnessed firsthand the Nazi siege. From 1957 to 1962 and from 1966 to 1969, he was the U.S. ambassador to the Soviet Union, serving presidents Dwight D. Eisenhower (served 1953–1961), John F. Kennedy (served 1961–1963), Lyndon B. Johnson (served 1963–1969), and Richard M. Nixon (served 1969–1974).

Maxwell Taylor Memorandum to Lyman L. Lemnitzer, September 19, 1961

Memorandum

By: Maxwell D. Taylor

Date: September 19, 1961

Source: Taylor, Maxwell D. Memorandum to Lyman L. Lemnitzer, September 19, 1961. The National Security Archive, George Washington University. Available online at http://www.gwu.edu/~nsarchiv/NSAEBB/NSAEBB56/; website home page: http://www.gwu.edu/~nsarchiv (accessed April 2, 2003).

About the Author: Maxwell D. Taylor (1901–1987) was born in Keystesville, Missouri. A graduate of West Point, Taylor commanded the 101st Airborne Division and was the first general to land in Normandy on D Day during World War II (1939–1945). After serving as the military governor of Berlin from 1949 to 1951, Taylor commanded the U.S.

General Maxwell Taylor meets with President John F. Kennedy in the Oval Office on June 28, 1961. © BETTMANN/CORBIS. REPRODUCED BY PERMISSION.

Eighth Army in the Korean War (1950–1953). Following a brief retirement, he was appointed chairman of the Joint Chiefs of Staff by President Kennedy in 1961. Under President Johnson, Taylor played an active role in escalating U.S. involvement in Southeast Asia. From 1964 to 1965, he served as the ambassador to South Vietnam. ■

Introduction

At the end of World War II, the Soviet Union, the United States, England, and France carved up Nazi Germany and its capital Berlin into four occupation zones. The Soviets occupied the eastern portion of the county, as well as a sector of Berlin. Western Germany was divided among the Americans, the British, and the French, each of whom also occupied a sector of Berlin. Because the German capital was located deep within Soviet-occupied Germany, the Russians controlled air and ground access to Berlin.

Initially, Russia granted the allies access to Berlin. Tensions between the Soviets and Americans worsened, however, when the latter played an important role in the creation of the democratic and capitalist Federal Republic of Germany (FRG).

In the late 1940s, as the FRG economy improved, people fled the economically depressed German Democratic Republic (GDR), which the Soviets created to counter the FRG, for opportunities in the West. By 1950, approximately 1.6 million GDR refugees had poured into the FRG. The exodus continued unabated throughout the 1950s. In 1960 alone, two hundred thousand people fled from the GDR for the FRG. To Soviet premier Nikita

U.S. Ambassador to Russia Llewellyn Thompson, 1966.
© BETTMANN/CORBIS. REPRODUCED BY PERMISSION.

Khrushchev, West Germany, with its dynamic economy, civil liberties, and alliance with the Western allies, was a serious threat not only to the GDR, its satellite state, but also to the Soviet sphere of influence in Eastern Europe.

On November 10, 1958, Khrushchev brought Europe to the brink of war when he ordered the allies to withdraw their forces from West Berlin within six months. At the end of this period, the Soviets would turn over its Berlin occupation rights to the GDR. If this occurred, then the allies would have to negotiate access to Berlin with the GDR. To solve this problem, Khrushchev called on the United States to recognize the GDR and for the two Germanys to sign a peace treaty. If the United States refused, then the East Germans would cut off allied air and surface traffic to Berlin.

Significance

Unable to persuade the Eisenhower administration to pull out of Berlin, Khrushchev renewed his ultimatum two weeks before President Kennedy's inauguration. The Soviet Union threatened "resolute measures" if the United States did not sever its ties to Berlin.

The Berlin crisis brought the United States and the Soviet Union as close to war as it would reach prior to the better-known Cuban missile crisis. In the summer of 1961, Khrushchev closed the border between East and West Berlin. In turn, Kennedy dispatched forty thousand additional troops to Europe.

Tensions were heightened that July when thirty thousand more refugees fled to West Berlin. The continued exodus of refugees was a devastating indictment of the moral and economic failings of communism. To stem the tide, Khrushchev ordered thirty thousand combat and engineer troops to seal off West Berlin with a twenty-eight-mile concrete wall, what would become known as the Berlin Wall. This was important because when Kennedy did not order U.S. forces to tear it down, an emboldened Khrushchev resumed nuclear testing and pursued aggressive tactics in Cuba. The U.S. military and political stance on Berlin remained firm, however. After several more months of stand-off, Khruschev backed down from his demands.

While the crisis was over, the issues that caused it would not be resolved until 1972 when the Soviets and Americans recognized East and West Germany as separate nations and Western access to Berlin was guaranteed. In 1989, the Berlin Wall, the symbol of the Cold War, was torn down and the "Evil Empire" collapsed shortly thereafter.

Primary Source

Llewellyn Thompson Telegram to Dean Rusk, May 27, 1961 [excerpt]

SYNOPSIS: In a secret telegram to Secretary of State Dean Rusk, Llewellyn Thompson, U.S. Ambassador to the Soviet Union, assesses the ongoing crisis over Berlin. Thompson states that if the United States did not concede West Berlin to the East Germans, then the "chances of war or ignominious western retreat are close to 50-50." He notes that the Soviet's have substantial military advantages in a conflict over Berlin.

While I agree in main with analysis contained Berlin Reftel I do not believe this is whole story. I not only do not believe Khrushchev has necessity of reporting progress on Berlin to Party Congress but believe he will deliberately wish to put off crisis until after he has further consolidated his position at Congress. However I consider K has so deeply committed his personal prestige and that of Soviet Union to some action on Berlin and German problems that if we take completely negative stand suggested by Berlin, this would probably lead to developments in which chances of war or ignominious Western retreat are close to 50-50. Situation is not changed by fact it is of K's own making. However, I believe there is real suspicion here that we and/or West Germans hope to develop position in which we can use force or threat of force to bring down Soviet Empire in Eastern Europe. Both sides consider other would not risk war over Berlin. Danger arises from fact that if K carries out his declared intentions and we carry out ours, situation likely get out of control and military as well as political prestige would become involved making retreat for either side even more difficult. Soviets have strong nerves and far greater cohesion with their allies. Geography and local balance of forces are in their favor. Assuming we are prepared carry our policy through to end and K found he had misjudged us, would probably be too later for retreat. . . .

Primary Source

Maxwell Taylor Memorandum to Lyman L. Lemnitzer, September 19, 1961

SYNOPSIS: This memo was written on behalf of President Kennedy by General Maxwell Taylor. It questions Chairman of the Joint Chiefs of Staff Lyman L. Lemnitzer (the head of the U.S. military) on the president's nuclear options should the Berlin Crisis escalate to war. The possibility of a first strike, a surprise nuclear attack on the Soviet Union, is raised. The memo also makes clear that Kennedy is concerned about his ability to control U.S. forces in a nuclear war should one begin.

The White House
Washington

Memorandum to General Lemnitzer

The President has asked me to pass the attached list of questions to you for transmission to General Power.

He would like General Power to respond to these questions at their meeting tomorrow, September 20th.

Maxwell D. Taylor

Strategic Air Planning

Question #1. I understand the strategic attack plan now contains 16 "options." I gather the impression, however, that such option merely indicates an increase in the size force that is launched. Is it possible to get some alternatives into the plan soon, such as having alternative options for use in different situations? For example, the present plan is based on the "optimum mix" concept. Is it now possible to exclude urban areas or governmental controls, or both, from attack? If not, how soon could you develop a plan which contains such options? Can whole areas, such as China, or the European satellites be eliminated from attack? If so, at what risk?

Question #2. Berlin developments may confront us with a situation where we may desire to take the initiative in the escalation of conflict from the local to the general war level.

a. Could we achieve surprise (i.e., 15 minutes or less warning) under such conditions by examining our present plan?

b. How would you plan an attack that would use a minimum-sized force against Soviet long range striking power only, and would attempt to achieve tactical surprise? How long would it take to develop such a plan?

c. Would it be possible to achieve surprise with such a plan during a period of high tension?

d. Would not an alternative first strike plan, even if only partially successful when implemented, leave us in a better position than we would be if we had to respond to an enemy first strike?

e. What second strike capability would probably be left to the Soviets after such an attack, assuming full, and partial, success?

f. Is this idea of a first strike against the Soviet's long-range striking power a feasible one?

Question #3. A surprise attack aimed at destroying the long-range striking power of the USSR would leave a sizeable number of MRBMs facing Europe.

a. Would the inclusion of these MRBMs in the initial attack so enlarge the target list as to preclude tactical surprise?

b. If so, is it possible to plan an immediate follow-on attack which would strike these targets before the first attack was completed? In particular, would our European land and sea-based air forces be suitable for this task?

Question #4. I am concerned over my ability to control our military effort once a war begins. I assume I can stop the strategic attack at any time, should I receive word the enemy has capitulated. Is this correct?

Question #5. Although one nuclear weapon will achieve the desired results, I understand that, to be assured of success, more than one weapon is programmed for each target. If the first weapon succeeds, can you prevent additional weapons from inflicting redundant destruction? If not, how long would it take to modify your plan to cover this possibility?

Question #6. What happens to the planned execution of our strategic attack if the Alert Force is launched and several hours later it is discovered that it has been launched on a false alarm? How vulnerable would we be, and how soon would the U.S. be in a position to attack the USSR?

Question #7. After the Alert Force has been launched, how do I know that our remaining forces are being used to best advantage. Are these follow-on forces automatically committed to predetermined targets, or do we have means of getting damage assessments to direct their attacks?

Question #8. Give the European situation, some of SACEUR's tactical fighters now scheduled for atomic attacks may be employed for conventional support of ground forces instead. Can other forces take over the responsibility of hitting SACEUR's atomic targets without jeopardizing the success of the plan materially?

Further Resources

BOOKS

Beschloss, Michael. *The Crisis Years: Kennedy and Khrushchev, 1960–1963.* New York: Edward Burlingame, 1991.

Kaplan, Fred. *The Wizards of Armageddon.* New York: Simon and Schuster, 1983.

Trachtenberg, Marc. *History and Strategy.* Princeton, N.J.: Princeton University Press, 1991.

PERIODICALS

Broderick, Jim. "Berlin and Cuba: Cold War Hotspots." *History Today* 48, December 1997, 23.

Kaplan. Fred. "JFK's First-Strike Plan." *The Atlantic Monthly,* October 2001. Available online at http://www.theatlantic .com/issues/2001/10/kaplan.htm; website home page: http:// www.theatlantic.com (accessed April 2, 2003).

WEBSITES

"Cold War International History Project Electronic Bulletin." The National Security Archive, George Washington University. Available online at http://www.gwu.edu/~nsarchiv /CWIHP/cwihp.htm; website home page: http://www.gwu .edu/~nsarchiv (accessed April 2, 2003).

"First-Strike Options and the Berlin Crisis, September 1961." The National Security Archive, George Washington University. Available online at http://www.gwu.edu/~nsarchiv /NSAEBB/NSAEBB56/; website home page: http://www .gwu.edu/~nsarchiv (accessed April 2, 2003).

The Port Huron Statement of the Students for a Democratic Society

Statement

By: Tom Hayden and Students for a Democratic Society
Date: June 1962

Source: Hayden, Tom, and Students for a Democratic Society. *The Port Huron Statement of the Students for a Democratic Society.* New York: Students for a Democratic Society, 1962. Available online at http://coursesa.matrix.msu.edu /~hst306/documents/huron.html (accessed April 2, 2003).

About the Author: Tom Hayden (1939–), born in Royal Oak, Michigan, is one of the best-known student radicals of the 1960s. He was the cofounder of Students for a Democratic Society (SDS). In the 1980s, Hayden decided to change the United States from within the political system. In 1982, he was elected to the California Assembly. Ten years later, he was elected to the state senate. He served until 1999, when he had to step down because of the California senate's term-limit regulations. ∎

Introduction

The 1960s witnessed the first active student movement since the 1930s. In part, this movement was attributable to the demographic patterns following World War II (1939–1945) and the rise of the baby boomer generation. In 1940, only 15 percent of all youth between the ages of eighteen and twenty-one attended college. In contrast, between 1950 and 1964, this number more than doubled.

One reason that a significant segment of this generation was receptive to radicalism is that it had been educated by New Deal liberals. From grade school through high school, baby boomers were taught that the role of government was to regulate the economy, redistribute the wealth from the rich to the disadvantaged, and protect the personal liberties of all citizens. This was important because when baby boomers matured in the 1960s, they blamed the government for failing to live up to its responsibilities. They wondered how a country as rich and powerful as the United States could not eradicate poverty and racism and end Cold War militarism.

At the 1960 Democratic Convention, the New Frontier rhetoric of John F. Kennedy (served 1961–1963) inspired and galvanized baby boomers. Though his political platform presented an extensive list of domestic social reforms, his administration's commitment to these ideals was thwarted by foreign affairs and the lack of support from southern Democrats. Consequently, hundreds of thousands of baby boomers became disillusioned with "traditional" politics and turned to radical alternatives.

In the winter of 1961, Tom Hayden, a twenty-year-old University of Michigan student, met with sixty fellow radicals from several other universities in Port Huron, Michigan. Together, they established the SDS. To distinguish themselves from the "Old Left," a mixture of communists, socialists, and anarchists of the 1930s and 1940s, they dubbed their movement the "New Left." They also penned the Port Huron statement. By articulating a thoughtful radical agenda, they sought to unify student radicals into a mass movement.

Significance

Influenced by the aggressive, confrontational tactics of the civil rights movement, the SDS staged marches, sit-ins, and other grassroots demonstrations on college campuses. In 1964, it helped organize the first major student protest, the Free Speech Movement, at the University of California, Berkeley, after college officials banned students from distributing leaflets and other political activities. In April 1965, the SDS launched a massive protest against the Vietnam War (1964–1975), recruiting twenty thousand people for a rally in Washington, D.C. Afterward, SDS chapters were organized on more than three hundred campuses.

That same year, Hayden went to Hanoi, Vietnam, in protest of the war. While his visit resulted in the release of three American prisoners of war, his overt support for the Vietcong was viewed as traitorous by many Americans on the home front.

The rapid growth of the SDS created chaos and division within the movement, so much so that it collapsed in 1969. In October 1969, Hayden organized the remnants of the SDS into the Weathermen, a small revolutionary terrorist group that called for a "war of liberation" against "Amerikkka." That fall, the group rampaged through Chicago for four days, overturning cars and smashing store windows.

When the clash finally ended, six members of the Weathermen had been shot and sixty-eight had been arrested. When no popular support was ensured for their Marxist ideology, the terrorist group went underground. Between 1970 to 1975, the group was implicated in approximately twenty bombings. Although the Weathermen disbanded in 1976, individual members continued their destructive actions into the early 1980s. In the mid-1970s, however, Hayden himself became involved in mainstream politics. After an unsuccessful campaign for a U.S. Senate seat in California, he was elected to the state assembly as a Democrat.

Primary Source

The Port Huron Statement of the Students for a Democratic Society [excerpt]

SYNOPSIS: The Port Huron statement, which was the founding manifesto of the SDS, provides a reflective analysis of the Cold War and the materialistic apathy of postwar American culture. Its main thesis calls on students to engage in "participatory democracy," meaning the transfer of political power from democratic institutions to individuals and communities. Though the pamphlet was not formally published, the organization made twenty thousand copies and sold them nationwide for thirty-five cents each.

Tom Hayden testifies before the President's Commission on Violence in Washington D.C., on October 23, 1968. AP/WIDE WORLD PHOTOS. REPRODUCED BY PERMISSION.

We are people of this generation, bred in at least modest comfort, housed now in universities, looking uncomfortably to the world we inherit.

When we were kids the United States was the wealthiest and strongest country in the world: the only one with the atom bomb, the least scarred by modern war, an initiator of the United Nations that we thought would distribute Western influence throughout the world. Freedom and equality for each individual, government of, by, and for the people— these American values we found good, principles by which we could live as men. Many of us began maturing in complacency.

As we grew, however, our comfort was penetrated by events too troubling to dismiss. First, the permeating and victimizing fact of human degradation, symbolized by the Southern struggle against racial bigotry, compelled most of us from silence to activism. Second, the enclosing fact of the Cold War, symbolized by the presence of the Bomb, brought awareness that we ourselves, and our friends, and millions of abstract "others" we knew more directly because of our common peril, might die at any time. We might deliberately ignore, or avoid, or fail to feel all other human problems, but not these two, for these were too immediate and crushing in their impact, too challenging in the demand that we as individuals take the responsibility for encounter and resolution.

While these and other problems either directly oppressed us or rankled our consciences and became our own subjective concerns, we began to see complicated and disturbing paradoxes in our surrounding America. The declaration "all men are created equal . . . rang hollow before the facts of Negro life in the South and the big cities of the North. The proclaimed peaceful intentions of the United States contradicted its economic and military investments in the Cold War status quo.

We witnessed, and continue to witness, other paradoxes. With nuclear energy whole cities can easily be powered, yet the dominant nation-states seem more likely to unleash destruction greater than that incurred in all wars of human history. Although our own technology is destroying old and creating new forms of social organization, men still tolerate meaningless work and idleness. While two-thirds of mankind suffers undernourishment, our own upper classes revel amidst superfluous abundance. Although world population is expected to double in forty years, the nations still tolerate anarchy as a major principle of international conduct and uncontrolled exploitation governs the sapping of the earth's physical resources. Although mankind desperately needs revolutionary leadership, America rests in national stalemate, its goals ambiguous and tradition-bound instead of informed and clear, its democratic system apathetic and manipulated rather than "of, by, and for the people."

Not only did tarnish appear on our image of American virtue, not only did disillusion occur when the hypocrisy of American ideals was discovered, but we began to sense that what we had originally seen as the American Golden Age was actually the decline of an era. The worldwide outbreak of revolution against colonialism and imperialism, the entrenchment of totalitarian states, the menace of war, overpopulation, international disorder, supertechnology—these trends were testing the tenacity of our own commitment to democracy and freedom and our abilities to visualize their application to a world in upheaval.

Our work is guided by the sense that we may be the last generation in the experiment with living. But we are a minority—the vast majority of our people regard the temporary equilibriums of our society and world as eternally-functional parts. In this is perhaps

the outstanding paradox: we ourselves are imbued with urgency, yet the message of our society is that there is no viable alternative to the present. Beneath the reassuring tones of the politicians, beneath the common opinion that America will "muddle through," beneath the stagnation of those who have closed their minds to the future, is the pervading feeling that there simply are no alternatives, that our times have witnessed the exhaustion not only of Utopias, but of any new departures as well. Feeling the press of complexity upon the emptiness of life, people are fearful of the thought that at any moment things might thrust out of control. They fear change itself, since change might smash whatever invisible framework seems to hold back chaos for them now. For most Americans, all crusades are suspect, threatening. The fact that each individual sees apathy in his fellows perpetuates the common reluctance to organize for change. The dominant institutions are complex enough to blunt the minds of their potential critics, and entrenched enough to swiftly dissipate or entirely repel the energies of protest and reform, thus limiting human expectancies. Then, too, we are a materially improved society, and by our own improvements we seem to have weakened the case for further change.

Some would have us believe that Americans feel contentment amidst prosperity—but might it not better be called a glaze above deeply felt anxieties about their role in the new world? And if these anxieties produce a developed indifference to human affairs, do they not as well produce a yearning to believe there is an alternative to the present, that something can be done to change circumstances in the school, the workplaces, the bureaucracies, the government? It is to this latter yearning, at once the spark and engine of change, that we direct our present appeal. The search for truly democratic alternatives to the present, and a commitment to social experimentation with them, is a worthy and fulfilling human enterprise, one which moves us and, we hope, others today. On such a basis do we offer this document of our convictions and analysis: as an effort in understanding and changing the conditions of humanity in the late twentieth century, an effort rooted in the ancient, still unfulfilled conception of man attaining determining influence over his circumstances of life.

Values

Making values explicit—an initial task in establishing alternatives—

is an activity that has been devalued and corrupted. The conventional moral terms of the age, the politician moralities—"free world," "people's democracies"—reflect realities poorly, if at all, and seem to function more as ruling myths than as descriptive principles. But neither has our experience in the universities brought us moral enlightenment. Our professors and administrators sacrifice controversy to public relations; their curriculums change more slowly than the living events of the world; their skills and silence are purchased by investors in the arms race; passion is called unscholastic. The questions we might want raised—what is really important? can we live in a different and better way? if we wanted to change society, how would we do it?—are not thought to be questions of a "fruitful, empirical nature," and thus are brushed aside.

Unlike youth in other countries we are used to moral leadership being exercised and moral dimensions being clarified by our elders. But today, for us, not even the liberal and socialist preachments of the past seem adequate to the forms of the present. Consider the old slogans; Capitalism Cannot Reform Itself, United Front Against Fascism, General Strike, All Out on May Day. Or, more recently, No Cooperation with Commies and Fellow Travellers, Ideologies Are Exhausted, Bipartisanship, No Utopias. These are incomplete, and there are few new prophets. It has been said that our liberal and socialist predecessors were plagued by vision without program, while our own generation is plagued by program without vision. All around us there is astute grasp of method, technique—the committee, the ad hoc group, the lobbyist, that hard and soft sell, the make, the projected image—but, if pressed critically, such expertise is incompetent to explain its implicit ideals. It is highly fashionable to identify oneself by old categories, or by naming a respected political figure, or by explaining "how we would vote" on various issues.

Theoretic chaos has replaced the idealistic thinking of old—and, unable to reconstitute theoretic order, men have condemned idealism itself. Doubt has replaced hopefulness—and men act out a defeatism that is labeled realistic. The decline of utopia and hope is in fact one of the defining features of social life today. The reasons are various: the dreams of the older left were perverted by Stalinism and never recreated; the congressional stalemate makes men narrow their view of the possible; the

specialization of human activity leaves little room for sweeping thought; the horrors of the twentieth century, symbolized in the gas-ovens and concentration camps and atom bombs, have blasted hopefulness. To be idealistic is to be considered apocalyptic, deluded. To have no serious aspirations, on the contrary, is to be "toughminded."

In suggesting social goals and values, therefore, we are aware of entering a sphere of some disrepute. Perhaps matured by the past, we have no sure formulas, no closed theories—but that does not mean values are beyond discussion and tentative determination. A first task of any social movement is to convenience people that the search for orienting theories and the creation of human values is complex but worthwhile. We are aware that to avoid platitudes we must analyze the concrete conditions of social order. But to direct such an analysis we must use the guideposts of basic principles. Our own social values involve conceptions of human beings, human relationships, and social systems.

We regard men as infinitely precious and possessed of unfulfilled capacities for reason, freedom, and love. In affirming these principles we are aware of countering perhaps the dominant conceptions of man in the twentieth century: that he is a thing to be manipulated, and that he is inherently incapable of directing his own affairs. We oppose the depersonalization that reduces human beings to the status of things—if anything, the brutalities of the twentieth century teach that means and ends are intimately related, that vague appeals to "posterity" cannot justify the mutilations of the present. We oppose, too, the doctrine of human incompetence because it rests essentially on the modern fact that men have been "competently" manipulated into incompetence—we see little reason why men cannot meet with increasing skill the complexities and responsibilities of their situation, if society is organized not for minority, but for majority, participation in decision-making.

Men have unrealized potential for self-cultivation, self-direction, self-understanding, and creativity. It is this potential that we regard as crucial and to which we appeal, not to the human potentiality for violence, unreason, and submission to authority. The goal of man and society should be human independence: a concern not with image of popularity but with finding a meaning in life that is personally authentic: a quality of mind not compulsively driven by a sense of powerlessness, nor one which unthinkingly adopts status values, nor one which represses all threats to its habits, but one which has full, spontaneous access to present and past experiences, one which easily unites the fragmented parts of personal history, one which openly faces problems which are troubling and unresolved: one with an intuitive awareness of possibilities, an active sense of curiosity, an ability and willingness to learn.

This kind of independence does not mean egoistic individualism—the object is not to have one's way so much as it is to have a way that is one's own. Nor do we deify man—we merely have faith in his potential.

Human relationships should involve fraternity and honesty. Human interdependence is contemporary fact; human brotherhood must be willed however, as a condition of future survival and as the most appropriate form of social relations. Personal links between man and man are needed, especially to go beyond the partial and fragmentary bonds of function that bind men only as worker to worker, employer to employee, teacher to student, American to Russian.

Loneliness, estrangement, isolation describe the vast distance between man and man today. These dominant tendencies cannot be overcome by better personnel management, nor by improved gadgets, but only when a love of man overcomes the idolatrous worship of things by man.

As the individualism we affirm is not egoism, the selflessness we affirm is not self-elimination. On the contrary, we believe in generosity of a kind that imprints one's unique individual qualities in the relation to other men, and to all human activity. Further, to dislike isolation is not to favor the abolition of privacy; the latter differs from isolation in that it occurs or is abolished according to individual will. Finally, we would replace power and personal uniqueness rooted in possession, privilege, or circumstance by power and uniqueness rooted in love, reflectiveness, reason, and creativity.

As a social system we seek the establishment of a democracy of individual participation, governed by two central aims: that the individual share in those social decisions determining the quality and direction of his life; that society be organized to encourage independence in men and provide the media for their common participation.

In a participatory democracy, the political life would be based in several root principles:

- that decision-making of basic social consequence be carried on by public groupings;

- that politics be seen positively, as the art of collectively creating an acceptable pattern of social relations;

- that politics has the function of bringing people out of isolation and into community, thus being a necessary, though not sufficient, means of finding meaning in personal life;

- that the political order should serve to clarify problems in a way instrumental to their solution; it should provide outlets for the expression of personal grievance and aspiration; opposing views should be organized so as to illuminate choices and facilities the attainment of goals; channels should be commonly available to related men to knowledge and to power so that private problems—from bad recreation facilities to personal alienation—are formulated as general issues.

The economic sphere would have as its basis the principles:

- that work should involve incentives worthier than money or survival. It should be educative, not stultifying; creative, not mechanical; selfdirect, not manipulated, encouraging independence; a respect for others, a sense of dignity and a willingness to accept social responsibility, since it is this experience that has crucial influence on habits, perceptions and individual ethics;

- that the economic experience is so personally decisive that the individual must share in its full determination;

- that the economy itself is of such social importance that its major resources and means of production should be open to democratic participation and subject to democratic social regulation.

Like the political and economic ones, major social institutions—cultural, education, rehabilitative, and others—should be generally organized with the well-being and dignity of man as the essential measure of success.

In social change or interchange, we find violence to be abhorrent because it requires generally the transformation of the target, be it a human being or a community of people, into a depersonalized object of hate. It is imperative that the means of violence be abolished and the institutions—local, national, international—that encourage nonviolence as a condition of conflict be developed.

These are our central values, in skeletal form. It remains vital to understand their denial or attainment in the context of the modern world.

Further Resources

BOOKS

Harrington, Michael. *The Other America: Poverty in the United States.* New York: Macmillan, 1962.

Hayden, Tom. *Reunion: A Memoir.* New York: Random House, 1988.

Horowitz, David, and Peter Collier. *Destructive Generation: Second Thoughts About the Sixties.* New York: Summit, 1989.

PERIODICALS

Hayden, Tom, and Dick Flacks. "The Port Huron Statement at 40." *The Nation,* August 5, 2002.

Zeitz, Joshua. "Back to the Barricades." *American Heritage* 52, no. 7, October 2001, 70–75.

WEBSITES

"A Trip Through the Sixties: The Anti-war Movement." Hippyland. Available online at http://www.hippy.com/php/article.php?sid=203; website home page: http://www.hippy.com/php/index.php (accessed April 2, 2003).

"WWW-VL: History: USA: 1960–1969." WWWVL The World Wide Virtual Library History: Central Catalogue, University of Kansas. Available online at http://www.ku.edu/history/VL/USA/ERAS/20TH/1960s.html; website home page: http://www.ku.edu/history/VL (accessed April 2, 2003).

"U-2 Photography of Soviet MRBM Site in Cuba, October 1962"

Photograph

By: Strategic Air Command

Date: October 1962

Source: Strategic Air Command. "U-2 Photography of Soviet MRBM site in Cuba, October 1962." October 1962. Available online at http://www.cia.gov/csi/studies/winter98-99/page14.gif. Reproduced in Orlov, Alexander. "A 'Hot' Front in the Cold War: the U-2 Program-A Russian Office Remembers." *Studies in Intelligence,* Winter 1998–1999. Available online at http://www.cia.gov/csi/studies/winter98-99/art02.html (accessed April 10, 2003).

About the Organization: In 1946, after a sweeping reorganization of the U.S. Army Air Forces, the Strategic Air Command (SAC) was created. Its mission was to conduct long-range offensive operations, including maximum-range reconnaissance, in any part of the world. During the Cold War, SAC was in charge of the nation's vast nuclear arsenal. In 1992, with the demise of the Soviet Union, SAC was disbanded. ■

Introduction

In January 1959, after a six-year war of liberation, a revolutionary movement led by Fidel Castro toppled the government of General Fulgencio Batista, a brutal Latin American dictator in Cuba. Although President Dwight D. Eisenhower (served 1953–1961) recognized the Castro government, he became increasingly concerned when Castro suppressed civil liberties and criticized the United States in several harsh-sounding speeches.

In February 1960, Cuban relations with the Soviets grew closer after they entered into a trade agreement that allowed the latter to purchase sugar at discounted rates. In retaliation, the United States prohibited the importation of Cuban sugar, effectively cutting 80 percent of Cuban exports to the United States. Later that fall, Cuba nationalized $1 billion in U.S. private interests on the island.

In December 1960, Cuba openly aligned itself with the Soviets. The following January, President John F. Kennedy (served 1961–1963) vowed to check communist expansion, particularly in Latin America. That April, fourteen hundred anti-Castro exiles, who had been trained and equipped by the CIA, invaded Cuba. The exiles believed that the Cuban people would follow their lead and help overthrow Castro. When the exiles landed at the Bay of Pigs, however, the popular uprising failed to materialize and the invaders were crushed. Castro imprisoned about twelve hundred of the invaders and arrested two hundred thousand suspected American sympathizers on the island. Afterward, Castro announced that he was a Marxist and further strengthened relations with the Soviets.

In November 1961, the Kennedy administration authorized Operation Mongoose, a major covert action aimed at overthrowing the Cuban dictator. The program involved four hundred Americans at CIA offices in Miami, two thousand Cubans, a private navy of speedboats, and an annual budget of $50 million. The operation sought to establish the internal overthrow of the Castro regime through sabotage, infiltration, and psychological warfare activities around October 1962. If necessary, the U.S. military would have intervened.

Significance

On October 14, 1962, the United States received the first hard evidence that the Soviet Union had deployed medium-range ballistic missile sites in Cuba and that the missiles could have been fully operational within two weeks. The next thirteen days encompassed the most dangerous episode in recorded history.

On October 16, President Kennedy met with fourteen members of the Executive Committee of the National Security Council to discuss different responses. The three principal options were: resolve the matter diplomatically through negotiations with Castro and

Primary Source

"U-2 Photography of Soviet MRBM Site in Cuba, October 1962"

SYNOPSIS: In October 1962, the CIA's authority of reconnaissance flights over Cuba was transferred to SAC. That same month, Major Richard Heyser of the 4080th Strategic Reconnaissance Wing piloted the top-secret U-2 flight over western Cuba that obtained solid proof of medium-range ballistic nuclear missiles in Cuba. PHOTO NO. PX66-20;7. IN THE JOHN F. KENNEDY LIBRARY.

Soviet premier Nikita Khrushchev; a naval blockade of Cuba, preventing the landing of more weapons; or a military air attack against the missiles, to be followed by an invasion. Fearing that diplomacy would not work and a military strike would provoke Soviet nuclear retaliation, Kennedy opted for the naval blockade on October 23. This strategy worked, because as the Soviet Union pulled its missiles out of Cuba, the United States withdrew its missiles from Turkey, which was strategically near to the Soviet Union, and agreed not to invade Cuba.

In 1992, U.S. officials learned just how close the situation had come to nuclear war. At a conference with former Soviet officials and Cubans, it was learned that

in addition to medium-range ballistic missiles, the Soviets had deployed nine tactical nuclear missiles to be used against any U.S. invasion force. Moreover, Soviet commanders in Cuba had the authority to fire those weapons without further direction from Moscow. This would have led to a nuclear holocaust.

Further Resources

BOOKS

Blight, James G., and David A. Welch. *On the Brink: Americans and Soviets Reexamine the Cuban Missile Crisis.* New York: Hill and Wang. 1989.

Kennedy, Robert. *Thirteen Days: A Memoir of the Cuban Missile Crisis.* New York: Norton, 1969.

McGeorge, Bundy. *Danger and Survival: Choices About the Bomb in the First Fifty Years.* New York: Random House, 1988.

PERIODICALS

Allyn, Bruce J., et al. "Essence of Revision: Moscow, Havana, and the Cuban Missile Crisis." *International Security* 14, 1989–1990.

Muckerman, Joseph E., II. "Bay of Pigs Revisited." *Military Review* 50, April 1971, 77–85.

WEBSITES

"Cuban Missile Crisis." National Security Agency. Available online at http://www.nsa.gov/docs/cuba; website home page: http://www.nsa.gov/ (accessed April 2, 2003).

"The Cuban Missile Crisis, 1962: The 40th Anniversary." The National Security Archive, George Washington University. Available online at http://www.gwu.edu/~nsarchiv/nsa/cuba_mis_cri/; website home page: http://www.gwu.edu/~nsarchiv/ (accessed April 2, 2003).

"The Desolate Year"

Essay

By: Monsanto Chemical Company

Date: October 1962

Source: Monsanto Chemical Company. "The Desolate Year." *Monsanto Magazine,* October 1962.

About the Organization: In 1901, the chemist John Francis Queeny founded the Monsanto Chemical Company. Headquartered near St. Louis, Missouri, the company soon became a leading manufacturer of industrial chemicals. Since 1940, the company has consistently ranked among the top ten chemical companies in the United States. Among its most controversial products was dichlorodiphenyl trichloroethane (DDT), a powerful and effective insecticide. ∎

Introduction

Public health experts regard DDT as the greatest life-saving chemical ever developed. One consequence of its success is that it became the most widely applied chemical in human history. DDT is effective because unlike other pesticides it destroys hundreds of different types of insects over a prolonged period of time.

It saved the lives of countless American soldiers during World War II (1939–1945) by clearing South Pacific islands of malaria-causing insects. After the war, this "atom bomb of insecticides" was made available to civilian populations throughout the world. In the United States, DDT was widely used by farmers and urban homeowners to eradicate pests. In fact, it became so popular that in 1962 alone, Americans applied over 350 million pounds of the substance.

Unbeknownst to the scientific community, however, DDT's toxic residue polluted most of the nation's major rivers, ground water, fish, migratory birds, wild animals, and dairy products. It was also absorbed in the fatty tissues of humans and was believed to cause cancer and inflict genetic damage.

In the summer of 1962, the influential *The New Yorker* magazine serialized Rachel Carson's *Silent Spring* prior to its September publication. Carson, a best-selling author, naturalist, and former marine biologist with the U.S. Fish and Wildlife Service, sparked perhaps the most bitter scientific controversy since Charles Darwin and his book *The Origin of Species* in 1859.

In the book's apocalyptic opening chapter, Carson imagined how indiscriminate spraying could destroy an entire area. She contended that since the 1940s, over two hundred pesticides were created, making the world unfit for habitation. She blamed the scientific community for failing to conduct adequate research to assess the long-term risk of pesticide exposure. Also, she criticized the Department of Agriculture for permitting aerial spraying without notifying the public, and the Food and Drug Administration for requiring only minimal tolerance limits, which contributed to higher exposure to wildlife and humans.

Significance

Silent Spring soon became a national sensation as journalists across the nation focused on the dangers of DDT. By the end of October, it was selling over six hundred thousand copies.

Despite the book's popularity with the American people, it was savaged by its opponents. Amid the tensions of the Cold War, some questioned Carson's patriotism, accusing her of being a communist dupe. *Time* magazine charged that the book was plagued with "oversimplifications and downright errors." The federal government refuted her evidence, using Carson's gender to ridicule her science by referring to her as a "hysterical female." Carson was also attacked by chemical and agricultural industries, who doubled their public relations budgets to refute the book, and by their supporters in the press. In response to the claims made in *Silent Spring,* Monsanto published "The Desolate Year," which portrayed a world in which Nature ran amok over the human population due to the disuse of pesticides like DDT.

Nevertheless, Carson had the support of the general public and President John F. Kennedy (served 1961–1963), who ordered an investigation into the alleged abuses cited in *The New Yorker* series. In May 1963, the President's Science Advisory Committee released its report "Use of Pesticides." The report corroborated most of Carson's analysis and therefore became an official endorsement of her overall position.

The day after the report was released, the Senate began hearings on environmental hazards. One witness portrayed DDT risks as potentially more serious than nuclear fallout. The committee's work led to the creation of the Environmental Protection Agency in 1972, which was given the authority to regulate pesticides and set tolerance limits. DDT was banned in the United States the same year.

Primary Source

"The Desolate Year"

SYNOPSIS: In October 1962, Monsanto published "The Desolate Year," a parody of *Silent Spring*. Without mentioning Carson's book, the article adopted her poetic style, foretelling the horrors to be faced if the United States was DDT-free for one year. "Nothing short of trillions" of pests would despoil "every square foot of land, every square yard, every acre" of the United States. Monsanto sent five thousand copies of this article free of charge to media outlets across the nation.

Life-slowing winter lay on the land that New Year's Day, the day that Nature was left to seek her own balance. Great drifts of snow cloaked the vast northland, and across the midsection of the country a thinner crust of whiteness was pierced by drab brown of brush and stone, naked tree, fence row and corn stubble.

Except for man's own small islands of sound and movement, most living creatures were silent, asleep. So it was that the grim reality of that defenseless year first sank home in the warm sub-tropics of lower Florida and California, Arizona and Texas.

It was warm that day in the citrus groves around Miami, and the glowing warmth drew a buzzing, harmless-looking fly from its place of rest. And she—for this was a female—was drawn into the golden air by some power that spanned the eons, that further drew her among the trees, and eventually to one weighted with growing grapefruit. The Mediterranean fruit fly turned her stilleto-like appendage into the first grapefruit, and when a tiny hole had been bored neatly through the rind, she sent an egg inside. Then she went to another, and another, taking no count of the 800 globes she had desecrated. Others of her kind, warmed and driven by the same purpose, followed; some further infested the holes she had bored, others sank new wells of their own.

Quietly, then, the desolate year began. Not many people seemed aware of danger. After all, in the winter, hardly a housefly was about. What could a few

bugs do, here and there? How could the good life depend upon something so seemingly trivial as a bug spray? Where *were* the bugs, anyway?

The bugs were everywhere. Unseen. Unheard. Unbelievably universal. On or under every square foot of land, every square yard, every acre, and county, and state and region in the entire sweep of the United States. In every home and barn and apartment house and chicken coop, and in their timbers and foundations and furnishings. Beneath the ground, beneath the waters, on and in limbs and twigs and stalks, under rocks, inside trees and animals and other insects—and, yes, inside man.

The most numerous and ferocious of all mankind's visible natural enemies lurked quietly that day, waiting. They weren't to be counted in the thousands, or millions, or billions. Nothing short of *trillions*, at least, could begin to account for their numbers. They were there, as eggs or larvae or pupae or voracious adults—waiting.

In a small subterranean cubicle, hardly large enough for a man to move about in: 100,000 mosquito mothers-to-be, ready to follow those only basic drives of the insect, to live and reproduce. In one cornfield: tens of thousands of caterpillars, snug in the balsa-like interior of fodder into which they'd fed. Along the sunnier south side of a single fence row in the Midwest: more thousands of tiny white-winged black chinch bugs. Scattered and broadcast across fields and meadows and ranges throughout the country: uncountable masses of grass-hopper eggs and nymphs. Waiting.

But there is no more waiting for an insect when sun's warmth stirs it from its lethargy. Nor need there by any waiting when the warmth is otherwise available.

Thus, even as the Florida citrus grower stood petrified, a pierced and wormy grapefruit in his hand and the frightening Medfly flitting through his trees, a New York housewife caused more widespread alarm. Her apartment was crawling with ticks—supposedly harmless dog ticks that her pet had transferred there from Central Park. What could she do?

What *could* she do? For, without pesticides, the pest control firms had automatically gone out of business. Of a sudden, some of the starkness of the times dawned on other people. No more protection against moths in clothing, furniture, carpets; no weapon but a fly swatter against rampant bedbugs, silverfish, fleas, slithering cockroaches and spreading ants. More people shuddered, then, and still the desolate year was young.

Desperation grew in Florida; infested trees were hacked and burned and the diseased fruit consigned to the flames. The Medfly produced and reproduced and spread, bent on making every orange and lemon and grapefruit over millions of acres so massively infested with maggots that humans would not ship or can or freeze or eat them.

Other insects brought other diseases to the ruined citrus, and the Floridians could not even find consolation in the fact that the great burden of scales and blights, blisters and scabs was likewise killing off rival groves in California and Arizona.

The garrote of Nature rampant began to tighten. The winter vegetables of the sunlands were barely marketable. But the next early crop was plagued. First to feed were the unseen cutworms, rasping off tender stalks below the ground. Then the mites and aphids, and the pretty butterflies that winged over the fields—and dropped eggs onto cabbage and cauliflower and broccoli and kale. Green worms, tan ones, striped ones, spotted ones, all hungry and eating, leaving their various residues in labyrinthine runways inside fruit and in crotch of stripped stalk. Finally, the beetles and bugs and skeletonizers ripped the leaves from potatoes and bush beans and limas, and their fellow workers in the field invaded hull and pod, and infested them with eggs and other matter.

So went the fresh, clean vegetables.

So went sweet corn, for that year hardly an ear from corner to corner of the nation brimmed with just its own sweet juice. If its stalk and ear escaped the harsh attack of the borers, along came the earworm, hatching from eggs that a brown-gray moth slipped into the receptive silks alongside the life-giving pollen. Her worm-children ate and defecated and ate more, working from the tender small kernels down into the large firm ones.

So the farmers planted and cultivated, and too often the harvest was garbage. The men at the packing plants and canning plants groaned. How could such refuse, even though whittled and carved and cored by hand, be cleaned and processed and pass for good food?

Inspectors for the Food and Drug Administration asked the same question, and were stumped for an answer. They couldn't approve food products containing what some of these did. But people had to eat. As food grew scarcer, prices spiraled.

It was a problem that grew; things got much worse that year. For now spring came to America—an extremely lively spring.

Insecticide is used to control mosquitoes alongside a church in Missouri in 1954. © CORBIS. REPRODUCED BY PERMISSION.

Genus by genus, species by species, subspecies by innumerable sub-species, the insects emerged. Creeping and flying and crawling into the open, beginning in the southern tier of states and progressing northward. They were chewers, and piercer-suckers, spongers, siphoners and chewer-lappers, and all their vast progeny were chewers—rasping, sawing, biting maggots and worms and caterpillars. Some could sting, some could poison, many could kill.

Hard-pressed men of the U.S. Department of Agriculture, besieged with pleas for help, could only issue advisories to rake and burn, to plant late or early, to seek the more resistant strains. But when insects and diseases took over anyway, there was no recourse.

In nook and cranny and open field where plants were just in bud, the insects bred and re-bred, cross-bred and in-bred. Some didn't breed at all, or need to; females simply produced more females which gave birth to more hordes of females. . . .

Some people retreated to the coolness of the mountains to pitch their tents, although life outdoors was beset by whirring gnats, flies and mosquitoes that summer. Among them was a man who had returned from a sojourn in the Far East. One day, he was stricken by an old foe that had returned violently—malaria.

While he suffered, the mosquitoes kept biting, and as each keen proboscis siphoned off his blood it also sucked in deadly gametocytes that were in the red corpuscles. Inside the mosquitoes, after a complicated reproductive cycle, microscopic organisms split and multiplied within their own expanding walls until, after two weeks, the walls broke. Out of each came thousands of minute sporozoites to circulate through the host insect, to settle in the salivary glands.

Unmolested, the mosquitoes whined over the mountainside, piercing and sucking. Each time a proboscis plunged into a camper, a droplet of saliva was forced in, too—Nature's way to make the blood flow freely. And in some of the droplets, there lived malaria.

Half a dozen campers, infected by the first onslaught of the host mosquitoes, suffered the fiendish torture of chills and fever and the hellish pain of the world's greatest scourge. Eventually, nearly three dozen people were brought down, and no one knew how many mosquitoes had bitten how many of the new patients, and so had become able to spread the outbreak further. Who could curb the mosquitoes?

South and West, in the miles and miles of cotton fields, the situation went beyond control. The worst plant-loving demon of them all chewed into the tender squares of young cotton plants. The long-snouted boll weevil, tragically belying her comical mien, inserted one egg into each of the meekly vulnerable buds after she ate, and the eggs ushered in disaster.

Three days as eggs, ten as greedy larvae hollowing out square and boll, four more as pupae, and the new boll weevil generation bored its way out, mated, and sought out every undamaged boll to deposit more eggs. Not very many bolls were left for them, however, because the bollworm—thief of several aliases—had moved in, too, chewing its way in and out of boll after boll. Nor had these co-wreckers

the fields to themselves; the dreaded pink bollworm broke from the confines where it had been fought desperately for 50 years and joined in to destroy the seeds themselves.

So went the vital cotton crop. So went the apples and pears and peaches; they had no chance from the start, because the numbers and deadliness of the insect enemies of fruit and berries were simply overwhelming—a bewildering battery of scales, aphids, mites, borers, curculios, moths, maggots, hoppers, thrips, beetles, slugs, flies, chafers, worms, rollers, grubs and weevils.

A plant plague came too, that year, adding its weight to the growing burden. Weed and insect raced each other for strawberry patch, garden plot and field of grain. They both emerged as victors in the jungle-like snarl of the strawberry runners and thick stands of wheat and rye. Tough grasses—crab, foxtail and Johnson—grew sometimes as rapidly as corn, and whole fields were abandoned to them. Thistles and wild oats could not be pulled successfully by hand in the grain and flax fields; it would have been far too costly, anyway.

Unneeded and unwanted insect reserves poured into the fray, and for man the outlook became bleak, indeed. For now came the turn of the grasshopper, most awesome plague of the plains and heartlands of America.

The hoppers never had been shy, and this year they rushed on, unchecked, in churning, boiling clouds that blotted the sun. Arizona, Colorado, Nebraska, Oklahoma, Kansas, Missouri. A hundred of them to the square yard. The remains of alfalfa, clover, soybeans and garden vegetables, already ravaged by their "own" caterpillars, seed midges, plant lice, mites, slugs and skippers, were pillage for the grasshoppers. In many places, the clicking swarms completely denuded the land of vegetation, and moved on.

On they went into the cornlands of the Midwest. But much of the corn was already doomed, doomed from the time the ant-aphid teams moved in to feed on its roots until the European borer wriggled and ate in the stalks and the earworms lay waste to the milky kernels.

The Eastern truck farmers had to give up, too. Tomatoes, sweet peppers, beans, sweet corn, cucumbers, melons—deformed, wormy, rotting on the vine. Half their tomato crop disappeared in the wilting yellow and brown leaves of blight alone, and the worm-makers sought every break in the skin of the fruit that lived.

Beetle and worm fed on top and tuber of the potato, from Idaho to Maine. Then the really notorious villain, Ireland's awful late blight, took over, and the firm brown "spuds" were gone, turned into black slime.

Enough? No; it should be remembered well, this terrible year of the insect and rodent and weed. How the termites felled innumerable buildings, destroyed a state's valuable papers, wiped out a library, brought a service station tumbling down. How the great forests wilted; how tent caterpillars stripped every leaf from 800 acres of trees in one place, and masses of beetles beneath the bark killed off 6,000 pine trees in another.

The mosquitoes were everywhere, and no one knows what harm they did—60,000 cases of "breakbone fever" in Galveston and Houston alone. Half a million cases in Texas. How many others across the country? How many epidemics, and what kind, did they cause? Yellow fever hung like a spectre over that enormous "receptive area" of the southern U.S., and public health officials dreaded the day when some infected person might arrive at a dock or airport in that region. Only the mosquito, transmitter of a dozen human diseases, could launch an epidemic of deadly yellow fever. . . .

Finally, of course, there was the chilling news that spread as a wracked nation surveyed the damage: there could be no falling back on much of the surplus food in storage. Practically no farm commodity could be stored in its natural form and not be vulnerable to contamination by other dozens of kinds of insects and their numerous aides. Rats and mice multiplied prodigiously. Freed from pesticidal opposition, they, too, burgeoned in elevator, bin and crate. And what was left was hardly food.

What, at the end of such a year, would be the fate of the United States of America?

Not Fiction . . . *Fact*

The terrible thing about the "desolate year" is this: Its events are not built of fantasy. *They are true.*

All of them, fortunately, did not take place in a single year, because so far man has been able to prevent such a thing. But all the major events of the "desolate year" have actually occurred. They have occurred in the United States. They could repeat themselves next year in greatly magnified form simply by removing this country's chemical weapons against pests.

Further Resources

BOOKS

Brooks, Paul. *The House of Life: Rachel Carson at Work.* Boston: Houghton Mifflin, 1972.

Carson, Rachel. *Silent Spring.* Boston: Houghton Mifflin, 1962.

Lear, Linda J. *Rachel Carson: Witness for Nature.* New York: Henry Holt, 1997.

PERIODICALS

Bailey, Ronald. "Silent Spring at 40: Rachel Carson's Classic Is Not Aging Well." *Reasononline,* June 12, 2002. Available online at http://reason.com/rb/rb061202.shtml (accessed April 2, 2003).

Lear, Linda J. "Rachel Carson's Silent Spring." *Environmental History Review* 17, Summer 1993, 23-48.

WEBSITES

RachelCarson.org. Available online at http://rachelcarson.org (accessed April 2, 2003).

The Rachel Carson Homestead. Available online at http://www.rachelcarsonhomestead.org (accessed April 2, 2003).

"Smoker on the Street Largely Defiant"
Newspaper article

By: Douglas Robinson

Date: January 12, 1964

Source: Robinson, Douglas. "Smoker in the Street Largely Defiant." *The New York Times,* January 12, 1964.

About the Author: Luther Terry (1911–1985) was born in Red Level, Alabama. In 1935, he graduated from Tulane University with a doctorate in medicine. Besides being an expert in cardiovascular clinical investigation, Terry was also a faculty member at Washington University, the University of Texas, and Johns Hopkins Medical School. He also served as the U.S. surgeon general and the assistant director of the National Heart Institute. ■

Introduction

Tobacco is a plant that is indigenous to North and South America. It is believed that tobacco began growing in the Americas in 6000 B.C. It is also believed that in 1 B.C. pre-Columbian Americans began to use tobacco for smoking and chewing. In October 1492, American Indians gave Christopher Columbus tobacco leaves for a present. Afterward, sailors brought the weed back to Europe where they, like the American Indians, believed that tobacco was a cure-all for everything from toothaches to cancer.

By 1612, tobacco for pipe smoking, chewing, and snuffing was in such demand in Europe that it became colonial America's first important export crop. In fact,

Surgeon General Dr. Luther L. Terry (middle) releases the report of the Surgeon General's Advisory Committee on Smoking and Health while two other members of the committee look on. The document was America's first widely publicized official recognition that cigarette smoking is a cause of cancer and other serious diseases. © BETTMANN/CORBIS. REPRODUCED BY PERMISSION.

extensive tobacco cultivation in North America fueled the demand first for indentured servants and eventually for slave labor.

It was not until the 1930s that scientists ascertained a statistical correlation between smoking and cancer, resulting in death and various diseases. However, no causal relationship had been proven. By the mid-1940s, cigarette sales reached an all time high. During World War II (1939–1945), tobacco companies sent millions of free and addictive cigarettes to American soldiers. Once the soldiers returned stateside, they had become loyal customers.

In 1952, *Reader's Digest* published "Cancer by the Carton," which for the first time widely revealed the dangers of smoking to the general public. The impact of the article was profound. Within a year, cigarette sales slumped for the first time in more than two decades.

In response, the tobacco industry established the Tobacco Industry Research Committee, which funded studies denying that smoking was related to cancer. The industry also began mass marketing filtered and low tar cigarettes that promised a "healthier" smoke. Cigarette sales promptly boomed as 68 percent of adult males and 32 percent of adult females regularly smoked in 1955.

Significance

In 1957, the U.S. Public Health Service announced that prolonged cigarette smoking was a causative factor in lung cancer. Two years later, the influential *Journal of the American Medical Association* confirmed the finding. In 1961, President John F. Kennedy (served 1961–1963) authorized U.S. surgeon general Luther Terry to establish an advisory committee to study the widespread implications of tobacco use.

Surgeon General Terry chose a committee of ten advisors, all of whom had not taken a public position on the relationship between smoking and cancer. With the assistance of 144 consultants, the committee reviewed 7,000 articles, including 3,000 research reports.

In 1964, the committee released a 387-page report that reiterated the fact that smoking was a causative factor in lung cancer. The report stated that in comparison to nonsmokers, the average male smoker had approximately a nine- to tenfold risk of developing lung cancer and heavy smokers at least a twentyfold risk. It revealed that regular smoking increased one's chances of dying in any given year by 70 percent. Moreover, it noted that since 1900 annual per capita cigarette consumption had dramatically increased from fifty cigarettes to almost four thousand in 1962. As a result, lung cancer deaths, which were less than three thousand in 1930, increased to forty-one thousand in 1962.

Unlike past smoking-related studies, the surgeon general's report made banner headlines across the nation and was featured on broadcast network news. Anti-smoking advocates seized on the publicity to target cigarettes and tobacco manufacturers as public health problem number one. Consequently, the report was a watershed event, altering the public's perception toward smoking. From 1964 to 1997, smoking rates of American adults dropped from 46 percent to 25 percent.

Primary Source

"Smoker on the Street Largely Defiant"

SYNOPSIS: After the release of Surgeon General Terry's report, *The New York Times* conducted a series of interviews to learn the initial reaction to the report. In the majority of these man-on-the-street interviews, the respondents were "largely defiant," refusing to quit smoking. This bravado was short-lived as antismoking advocates eventually persuaded thousands of smokers to kick the habit.

But Some Concede They're Frightened by the Report

Confessions of a lack of will power and sheer defiance were among the most frequent reactions yesterday to the Federal report finding the use of cigarettes a peril to health.

There were exceptions. "The report frightens me." . . . "It scares the hell out of me." . . . "I'm through." . . . "I guess I'll cut down" were some of the minority reports.

Many of those interviewed refused to give their names and said they considered the matter of smoking a private affair.

Underlying the responses of many was the unstated certainty that, after all, the odds were really against that popular American "the other guy."

A group of men in a tavern near Radio City Music Hall, fortified, perhaps, by their surroundings, agreed that they would not give up cigarette smoking.

"I can stop drinking, but not smoking," one man said.

The bartender, too, said he would not stop. Asked why, in the face of the Government report, he replied: "Because I've got strong lungs."

Tried Several Times

In the theater district, a man puffing on an unfiltered cigarette answered "Not at all" when asked if he would now stop smoking. Pressed for a reason, he said, "I love these stinkers."

Other street interviews firmly established the trend that many persons had tried to turn over a new leaf but had failed.

"I wish I could give them up, but I can't," said Donald Alagma of West Orange, N.J. "I've tried on and off several times, but it doesn't work."

He said he had smoked one pack of cigarettes a day for 20 years.

Joseph Bernard of Manhattan said that he, too, had tried to stop smoking several times.

"It's a difficult habit to break, but I might try again," he said, reaching into his pocket for one of the 40 cigarettes a day he smokes.

An unidentified working girl smiled proudly and said she had stopped smoking for six hours after having read the report.

The manager of a tobacco shop at 46th Street and Broadway, Edwin Shelansky, said that "so far, the talk of cancer hasn't cut our business at all." He said he expected a temporary drop in business.

Mr. Shelansky said he smoked both a pipe and cigarettes and would continue.

Norman Clark of Elmhurst Queens, said the report didn't frighten him.

"Everybody needs a certain amount of pleasure," he said, "and smoking is a little pleasure I think I'll continue."

Four Packs a Day

A Brooklyn resident, Charles Singer of Sheepshead Bay, said he had been smoking four packs a day for 35 years and simply hadn't the will power to stop.

"It's gotten so bad," he said, "that I smoke two cigarettes in the morning when I get up before I do anything else," he said.

Paul Moran, a sales representative of Mineola, L.I., said he was "not yet decided" on whether the report would persuade him to quit.

"You have the feeling, of course, that certain things happen to 'the other fellow' and won't happen to you," he said.

Across the nation, the responses varied according to people. A Baltimore policeman vowed to cut down cigarette smoking. A man in Charleston Va., demonstrated sheer bravado. "See this pack with three cigarettes?" he said. "When they're gone, I'm through."

Further Resources

BOOKS

Kluger, Richard. *Ashes to Ashes: America's Hundred-Year Cigarette War, the Public Health, and the Unabashed Triumph of Philip Morris.* New York: Knopf, 1996.

Koop, C. Everett. *Koop: The Memoirs of America's Family Doctor.* New York: Random House, 1991.

Sullen, Jacob. *For Your Own Good: The Anti-smoking Crusade and the Tyranny of Public Health.* New York: The Free Press, 1998.

PERIODICALS

Housman, Michael. "Smoking and Health: The 1964 U.S. Surgeon General's Report As a Turning Point in the Anti-smoking Movement." *Harvard Health Policy Review* 2, no. 1, Spring 2001. Available online at http://hcs.harvard.edu/~epihc/currentissue/spring2001/housman.html; website home page: http://hcs.harvard.edu/~epihc/ (accessed April 2, 2003).

Schuman, Leonard M. "The Origins of the Report of the Advisory Committee on Smoking and Health to the Surgeon General." *Journal of Public Health Policy* 2, March 1981, 19–27.

WEBSITES

"History of Tobacco." Institute on Race, Health Care and the Law, University of Dayton School of Law. Available online at http://academic.udayton.edu/health/syllabi/tobacco/history.htm; website home page: http://academic.udayton.edu/health (accessed April 2, 2003).

"Reports of the Surgeon General." U.S. National Library of Medicine. Available online at http://sgreports.nlm.nih.gov/NN/B/B/M/Q/segments.html; website home page: http://www.nlm.nih.gov/ (accessed April 2, 2003).

"The Great Society"

Speech

By: Lyndon B. Johnson

Date: May 22, 1964

Source: Johnson, Lyndon B. "The Great Society." May 22, 1964. *Public Papers of the Presidents of the United States:* *Lyndon B. Johnson, 1963–64.* Vol. 1. Washington, D.C.: U.S. Government Printing Office, 1964, 704–707. Reproduced in CNN Cold War Historical Documents. Available online at http://www.cnn.com/SPECIALS/cold.war/episodes/13/documents/lbj/; website home page: http://www.cnn.com/SPECIALS/cold.war/ (accessed April 2, 2003).

About the Author: Lyndon B. Johnson (1908-1973) was born near Stonewall, Texas. After a brief stint at teaching, Johnson was elected to the U.S. House of Representatives in 1935 and two years later to the U.S. Senate. In 1954, he was named majority leader, the most powerful member of the Senate. Following the assassination of John F. Kennedy (served 1961–1963), Johnson was sworn in as the thirty-sixth president (served 1963–1969). He won reelection in 1964, but chose not to run in 1968. ∎

Introduction

In 1937, Franklin D. Roosevelt (served 1933–1945) estimated that 33 percent of the nation was "ill-housed, ill-clad, ill-nourished." To help alleviate suffering, Congress enacted a welfare program that made payments to widows with children. By 1956, the number of Americans living below the poverty line, a government standard of minimum subsistence based on income and family size, dropped to 23 percent.

Despite this decline, from 1950 to 1960 the number of children on welfare had increased from 1.6 million to 2.4 million. Moreover, statisticians made a direct correlation between low income and poor health. Government statistics revealed that 4 percent of middle class families were chronically ill. In contrast, 16 percent of poor families were unhealthy. In addition, the poor were disproportionately afflicted with mental illness, drug addiction, and crime.

In 1962, Michael Harrington wrote the influential book *The Other America.* Harrington argued that as middle class Americans moved out of urban America to the suburbs, poverty became "less visible." Furthermore, the poor had become alienated from mainstream society, no longer believing in the American dream and were on the verge of giving up. If the United States hoped to rescue the underclass, Harrington contended, the middle class had to become actively involved.

In order the assist the poor, President John F. Kennedy (served 1961–1963), as part of his New Frontier platform, proposed an array of new social programs, including federal money for education, medical care for the aged, urban mass transit, and a federal Department of Urban Affairs. For the most part, Kennedy's domestic agenda was stymied by congressional southern Democrats. After Kennedy's assassination, President Lyndon B. Johnson continued his predecessor's reform agenda.

The Great Society consisted of numerous programs passed between 1964 and 1967 that were designed to expand the social welfare system and eliminate poverty. A committed New Dealer, Johnson sought to create a record of domestic achievement comparable to Roosevelt's. Unlike the New Deal, however, the Great Society was launched amid a period of economic prosperity.

Significance

The most ambitious of Johnson's legislative agenda was the Economic Opportunity Act of 1964, which declared a "war on poverty." This act combined the progressive welfare state with the conservative notion of self reliance by giving the poor the opportunity to improve themselves. The act created the Job Corps, which provided the poor with vocational training.

In 1965, the government created Medicare, which provided federal funding for older Americans' medical costs. In 1966, the government established Medicaid, which extended medical funding to welfare recipients.

Johnson also sponsored the Elementary and Secondary Education Act, which sought to improve education by providing federal funding to cash-strapped public school districts. The rationale behind the program was that children in city slums and impoverished rural areas were educationally deprived and therefore needed supplemental funding. In the related Head Start program, additional funding was directed toward preschool children. The program contributed to improving children's health by ensuring medical examinations and good meals.

In 1964, Congress appropriated $1 billion to the Great Society and another $2 billion the following two years. Afterward, funding was limited because fiscal resources were directed toward the Vietnam War (1964–1975).

The overall success of the Great Society was mixed. Whereas Head Start was a success, the Elementary and Secondary Education Act failed, as many districts funneled federal revenue to cover ordinary expenses and student performances did not significantly improve. The Job Corps was a dismal failure as training costs were high and relatively few trainees completed the courses. Medicare and Medicaid provided medical treatment for millions, but because the government picked up the tab, health care costs skyrocketed. Nevertheless, from 1963 to 1968 the proportion of Americans living below the poverty line dropped from 20 percent to 13 percent.

Primary Source

"The Great Society"

SYNOPSIS: On May 22, 1964, President Johnson gave his "Great Society" speech before eighty thousand people, the largest commencement ever attended at the University of Michigan. Johnson challenged students to build a Great Society "a place where the city of man serves not only the needs of the body and the demands of commerce, but the desire for beauty and the hunger for community."

President Hatcher, Governor Romney, Senators McNamara and Hart, Congressmen Meader and Staebler, and other members of the fine Michigan delegation, members of the graduating class, my fellow Americans:

It is a great pleasure to be here today. This university has been coeducational since 1870, but I do not believe it was on the basis of your accomplishments that a Detroit high school girl said, "In choosing a college, you first have to decide whether you want a coeducational school or an educational school."

Well, we can find both here at Michigan, although perhaps at different hours.

I came out here today very anxious to meet the Michigan student whose father told a friend of mine that his son's education had been a real value. It stopped his mother from bragging about him.

I have come today from the turmoil of your capital to the tranquillity of your campus to speak about the future of your country.

The purpose of protecting the life of our nation and preserving the liberty of our citizens is to pursue the happiness of our people. Our success in that pursuit is the test of our success as a nation.

For a century we labored to settle and to subdue a continent. For half a century we called upon unbounded invention and untiring industry to create an order of plenty for all of our people.

The challenge of the next half century is whether we have the wisdom to use that wealth to enrich and elevate our national life, and to advance the quality of our American civilization.

Your imagination, your initiative and your indignation will determine whether we build a society where progress is the servant of our needs, or a society where old values and new visions are buried under unbridled growth. For in your time we have the opportunity to move not only toward the rich society and the powerful society, but upward to the Great Society.

The Great Society rests on abundance and liberty for all. It demands an end to poverty and racial injustice, to which we are totally committed in our time. But that is just the beginning.

The Great Society is a place where every child can find knowledge to enrich his mind and to enlarge his talents. It is a place where leisure is a welcome chance to build and reflect, not a feared cause of boredom and restlessness. It is a place where the city of man serves not only the needs of the

President Lyndon Johnson and Lady Bird Johnson meet members of the Fletcher family of Inez, Kentucky, in April 1964. Johnson declared a "War on Poverty" as central to building the Great Society. © BETTMANN/CORBIS. REPRODUCED BY PERMISSION.

body and the demands of commerce but the desire for beauty and the hunger for community.

It is a place where man can renew contact with nature. It is a place which honors creation for its own sake and for what it adds to the understanding of the race. It is a place where men are more concerned with the quality of their goals than the quantity of their goods.

But most of all, the Great Society is not a safe harbor, a resting place, a final objective, a finished work. It is a challenge constantly renewed, beckoning us toward a destiny where the meaning of our lives matches the marvelous products of our labor.

So I want to talk to you today about three places where we begin to build the Great Society—in our cities, in our countryside, and in our classrooms.

Many of you will live to see the day, perhaps 50 years from now, when there will be 400 million Americans—four-fifths of them in urban areas. In the remainder of this century urban population will double, city land will double, and we will have to build homes, highways and facilities equal to all those built since this country was first settled. So in the next 40 years we must rebuild the entire urban United States.

Aristotle said: "Men come together in cities in order to live, but they remain together in order to live the good life." It is harder and harder to live the good life in American cities today.

The catalog of ills is long: There is the decay of the centers and the despoiling of the suburbs. There is not enough housing for our people or transportation for our traffic. Open land is vanishing and old landmarks are violated.

Worst of all expansion is eroding the precious and time-honored values of community with neighbors and communion with nature. The loss of these values breeds loneliness and boredom and indifference.

Our society will never be great until our cities are great. Today the frontier of imagination and innovation is inside those cities and not beyond their borders.

New experiments are already going on. It will be the task of your generation to make the American city a place where future generations will come, not only to live but to live the good life.

I understand that if I stayed here tonight I would see that Michigan students are really doing their best to live the good life.

This is the place where the Peace Corps was started. It is inspiring to see how all of you, while you are in this country, are trying so hard to live at the level of the people.

A second place where we begin to build the Great Society is in our countryside. We have always prided ourselves on being not only America the strong and America the free, but America the beautiful. Today that beauty is in danger. The water we drink, the food we eat, the very air that we breathe, are threatened with pollution. Our parks are overcrowded, our seashores overburdened. Green fields and dense forests are disappearing.

A few years ago we were greatly concerned about the "Ugly American." Today we must act to prevent an ugly America.

For once the battle is lost, once our natural splendor is destroyed, it can never be recaptured. And once man can no longer walk with beauty or wonder at nature, his spirit will wither and his sustenance be wasted.

A third place to build the Great Society is in the classrooms of America. There your children's lives will be shaped. Our society will not be great until every young mind is set free to scan the farthest reaches of thought and imagination. We are still far from that goal.

Today, 8 million adult Americans, more than the entire population of Michigan, have not finished five years of school. Nearly 20 million have not finished eight years of school. Nearly 54 million—more than one quarter of all America—have not even finished high school.

Each year more than 100,000 high school graduates, with proved ability, do not enter college because they cannot afford it. And if we cannot educate today's youth, what will we do in 1970 when elementary school enrollment will be 5 million greater than 1960? And high school enrollment will rise by 5 million. College enrollment will increase by more than 3 million.

In many places, classrooms are overcrowded and curricula are outdated. Most of our qualified teachers are underpaid, and many of our paid teachers are unqualified. So we must give every child a place to sit and a teacher to learn from. Poverty must not be a bar to learning, and learning must offer an escape from poverty.

But more classrooms and more teachers are not enough. We must seek an educational system which grows in excellence as it grows in size. This means better training for our teachers. It means preparing youth to enjoy their hours of leisure as well as their hours of labor. It means exploring new techniques of teaching, to find new ways to stimulate the love of learning and the capacity for creation.

These are three of the central issues of the Great Society. While our government has many programs directed at those issues, I do not pretend that we have the full answer to those problems.

But I do promise this: We are going to assemble the best thought and the broadest knowledge from all over the world to find those answers for America. I intend to establish working groups to prepare a series of White House conferences and meetings—on the cities, on natural beauty, on the quality of education, and on other emerging challenges. And from these meetings and from this inspiration and from these studies we will begin to set our course toward the Great Society.

The solution to these problems does not rest on a massive program in Washington, nor can it rely solely on the strained resources of local authority. They require us to create new concepts of cooperation, a creative federalism, between the national capital and the leaders of local communities.

Woodrow Wilson once wrote: "Every man sent out from his university should be a man of his nation as well as a man of his time."

Within your lifetime, powerful forces, already loosed, will take us toward a way of life beyond the realm of our experience, almost beyond the bounds of our imagination.

For better or for worse, your generation has been appointed by history to deal with those problems and to lead America toward a new age. You have the chance never before afforded to any people in any age. You can help build a society where the demands of morality, and the needs of the spirit, can be realized in the life of the nation.

So, will you join in the battle to give every citizen the full equality which God enjoins and the law requires, whatever his belief, or race, or the color of his skin?

Will you join in the battle to give every citizen an escape from the crushing weight of poverty?

Will you join in the battle to make it possible for all nations to live in enduring peace—as neighbors and not as mortal enemies?

Will you join in the battle to build the Great Society, to prove that our material progress is only the foundation on which we will build a richer life of mind and spirit?

There are those timid souls who say this battle cannot be won; that we are condemned to a soulless wealth. I do not agree. We have the power to shape the civilization that we want. But we need your will, your labor, your hearts, if we are to build that kind of society.

Those who came to this land sought to build more than just a new country. They sought a new world. So I have come here today to your campus to say that you can make their vision our reality. So let us from this moment begin our work so that in the future men will look back and say: It was then, after a long and weary way, that man turned the exploits of his genius to the full enrichment of his life.

Thank you. Goodbye.

Further Resources

BOOKS

Harrington, Michael. *The Other America: Poverty in the United States.* New York: Macmillan, 1962.

Kearns, Doris. *Lyndon Johnson and the American Dream.* New York: Harper and Row, 1976.

Murray, Charles. *Losing Ground: American Social Policy, 1950-1980.* New York: Basic, 1984.

PERIODICALS

Califano, Joseph A., Jr. "What Was Really Great About the Great Society: The Truth Behind the Conservative Myths." *Washington Monthly,* October 1999. Available online at http://www.washingtonmonthly.com/features/1999/9910 .califano.html; website home page: http://www.washington monthly.com (accessed April 2, 2003).

Fumento, Michael. "Is the Great Society to Blame? If Not, Why Have Problems Worsened Since '60s?" *Investor's Business Daily,* June 19, 1992. Available online at http://www .fumento.com/greatsociety.html (accessed April 2, 2003).

WEBSITES

"LBJ and the Power of the Presidency." CNN.com. Available online at http://www.cnn.com/US/9610/17/lbj.day3/index .html; website home page: http://www.cnn.com (accessed April 2, 2003).

"Lyndon B. Johnson: The War on Poverty President." The American President. Available online at http://www .americanpresident.org/kotrain/courses/lbj/lbj_in_brief.htm; website home page: http://www.americanpresident.org /home6.htm (accessed April 2, 2003).

"Report of the President's Commission on the Assassination of President Kennedy"

Report

By: Earl Warren

Date: September 1964

Source: Warren, Earl. "Report of the President's Commission on the Assassination of President Kennedy." President's Commission on the Assassination of President Kennedy, September 1964. Available online at http://www.jfk-assassination .de/WCR/wcr1.html#p2; website homepage: http://www.jfk -assassination.de/ (accessed April 2, 2003).

About the Author: Earl Warren (1891–1974) was born and raised in California. He was the governor of California from 1943 to 1953. That same year, President Dwight D. Eisenhower (served 1953–1961) appointed him chief justice of the U.S. Supreme Court. The Warren Court was most famous for issuing the 1954 decision *Brown v. Board of Education of Topeka,* which unanimously ruled that school segregation was unconstitutional. He retired from the bench in 1969. ■

Introduction

Unlike the vast majority of twentieth century Irish Catholics, John F. Kennedy had a privileged upbringing. His father, Joseph, was a millionaire businessman who served as President Franklin D. Roosevelt's (served 1933–1945) head of the Securities and Exchange Commission and as the U.S. ambassador to Great Britain. After the death of John's older brother Joe, Joseph groomed John for the presidency.

Blessed with a sharp, inquisitive mind, intelligence, good looks, and charisma, Kennedy drew on his Irish Catholic heritage, an important advantage in predominately Catholic Massachusetts. Kennedy was also an attractive political candidate because he was a bona fide World War II hero.

In 1946, Kennedy won election to the U.S. House of Representatives. After serving three terms, he was elected to the U.S. Senate. At the age of forty-three, Kennedy was looking to become the youngest man ever elected to the U.S. presidency and the nation's first Irish Catholic president.

In 1960, his Republican opponent was Richard M. Nixon, who served as President Eisenhower's vice president for eight years. In November, Kennedy won the electoral vote 303 to 219, but the popular vote was extremely close, 34,227,000 to 34,109,000. If a few thousand votes in Texas or Illinois, where confirmed voter fraud had occurred, had gone the other way, Nixon would have won the election.

For a thousand days, President Kennedy (served 1961–1963) projected an aura of dynamism, idealism, and glamor. Americans enjoyed pictures of their active president playing touch football on the White House lawn, sailing with his wife, Jacqueline, and romping with his children in the executive office. Kennedy was so popular that in June 1963, 59 percent of those surveyed claimed to have cast ballots for him in 1960. This figure approached 70 percent nearly six months later.

Significance

On November 22, 1963, despite a flagging economy, many believed that Kennedy would win reelection. With an eye toward the 1964 election, Kennedy visited Dallas, Texas. He and Jacqueline rode in an open convertible, basking in the applause of thousands of wellwishers. As the motorcade passed the Texas School Book Depository, an assassin fatally shot the president.

Within thirty minutes of the shooting, 68 percent of American adults learned that Kennedy had been killed. Millions watched *Air Force One* return to Washington, D.C., transporting the president's coffin and his widow in her bloodstained clothes.

Lee Harvey Oswald, who had returned to the United States after defecting to the Soviet Union three years earlier, was arrested after killing a Dallas policeman. Though no one witnessed Oswald firing the rifle from the upper floor of the book depository, substantial evidence tied him to the crime. Before Oswald was arraigned, Jack Rudy, a local nightclub owner, murdered him.

Between Oswald's Soviet connections and the fact that he was murdered in broad daylight while supposedly in police custody, many were not convinced that Oswald acted alone, nor that he masterminded the assassination. One week after the assassination, President Lyndon B. Johnson (served 18963–1969) issued Executive Order No. 11130, which appointed the President's Commission on the Assassination of President Kennedy. Johnson appointed Supreme Court chief justice Earl Warren to head the commission, and it is also referred to as the Warren Commission. On December 13, 1963, Congress passed Senate Joint Resolution No. 137, allowing the commission to subpoena witnesses and obtain evidence concerning any matter relating to the investigation. In the end, the commission took testimony from 552 witnesses and compiled twenty-six volumes of hearing proceedings.

In September 1964, the Warren Commission issued its official report on the Kennedy assassination. It concluded that Oswald acted alone in killing Kennedy, and that Jack Ruby also acted alone when he killed Oswald. Neither man, according to the Warren Report, was part of a larger conspiracy to assassinate the president.

Nevertheless, doubts persisted. Almost as soon as the report was published, some were questioning its conclusions and presenting their own explanations for the two killings. Most notably, in 1979, a congressional investigation raised serious concerns about the Warren report, concluding that there was a "probable conspiracy," with two gunmen firing four shots.

Primary Source

"Report of the President's Commission on the Assassination of President Kennedy" [excerpt]

SYNOPSIS: In these excerpts, the commission presents its opinion that Lee Harvey Oswald, acting alone, shot Kennedy. The evidence supporting this is summarized, and Oswald's potential motives are explored. The death of Oswald and the flaws in President Kennedy's protection are also examined.

1. The shots which killed President Kennedy and wounded Governor Connally were fired from the sixth floor window at the southeast corner of the Texas School Book Depository. This determination is based upon the following:

Witnesses at the scene of the assassination saw a rifle being fired from the sixth-floor window of the Depository Building, and some witnesses saw a rifle in the window immediately after the shots were fired.

The nearly whole bullet found on Governor Connally's stretcher at Parkland Memorial Hospital and the two bullet fragments found in the front seat of the Presidential limousine were fired from the 6.5-millimeter Mannlicher-Carcano rifle found on the sixth floor of the Depository Building to the exclusion of all other weapons.

The three used cartridge cases found near the window on the sixth floor at the southeast corner of the building were fired from the same rifle which fired the above-described bullet and fragments, to the exclusion of all other weapons.

The windshield in the Presidential limousine was struck by a bullet fragment on the inside surface of the glass, but was not penetrated.

The nature of the bullet wounds suffered by President Kennedy and Governor Connally and the location of the car at the time of the shots establish that the bullets were fired from above and behind the Presidential limousine, striking the President and the Governor as follows:

President Kennedy was first struck by a bullet which entered at the back of his neck and exited through the lower front portion of his neck, causing a wound which would not necessarily have been lethal. The President was struck a second time by a bullet which entered the right-rear portion of his head, causing a massive and fatal wound.

Governor Connally was struck by a bullet which entered on the right side of his back and traveled downward through the right side of his chest, exiting below his right nipple. This bullet then passed through his right wrist and entered his left thigh where it caused a superficial wound.

There is no credible evidence that the shots were fired from the Triple Underpass, ahead of the motorcade, or from any other location.

2. The weight of the evidence indicates that there were three shots fired.

3. Although it is not necessary to any essential findings of the Commission to determine just which shot hit Governor Connally, there is very persuasive evidence from the experts to indicate that the same bullet which pierced the President's throat also caused Governor Connally's wounds. However, Governor Connally's testimony and certain other factors have given rise to some difference of opinion as to this probability but there is no question in the mind of any member of the Commission that all the shots which caused the President's and Governor Connally's wounds were fired from the sixth floor window of the Texas School Book Depository.

4. The shots which killed President Kennedy and wounded Governor Connally were fired by Lee Harvey Oswald. This conclusion is based upon the following:

The Mannlicher-Carcano 6.5-millimeter Italian rifle from which the shots were fired was owned by and in the possession of Oswald.

Oswald carried this rifle into the Depository Building on the morning of November 22, 1963.

Oswald, at the time of the assassination, was present at the window from which the shots were fired.

Shortly after the assassination, the Mannlicher-Carcano rifle belonging to Oswald was found partially hidden between some

(PLEASE TYPE OR PRINT)

PASSPORT APPLICATION

DEPARTMENT OF STATE
FORM APPROVED
BUDGET BUREAU NO. 47-R051.1

(Before Completing this Application, Read Information for Passport Applicants on Page 4)

(Passport Office Use Only)

A

PART I - TO BE COMPLETED BY ALL APPLICANTS

(First name) LEE (Middle name) HARVEY (Last name) OSWALD

I, _____, a citizen of the United States, do hereby apply to the Department of State for a passport.

MAIL PASSPORT TO

STREET P.O. BOX 30061

CITY NEW ORLEANS STATE LA.

IN CARE OF (IF NECESSARY) _____

DATE OF BIRTH (Month, day, year) Oct. 18, 1939 PLACE OF BIRTH NEW ORLEANS, LA

HEIGHT 5 FT. 11 IN. | HAIR BR. | EYES GREY | APPROXIMATE DATE OF DEPARTURE OCT-JAN

VISIBLE DISTINGUISHING MARKS NONE | OCCUPATION Photographer

MY PERMANENT RESIDENCE (Street address, City, State) (If same as in mailing block, write "Same") 757 FRENCH ST. NEW ORLEANS, LA | COUNTY OF RESIDENCE USA

P 0 9 2 5 2 6

PASSPORT ISSUED

JUN 25 '63

DEPARTMENT OF STATE
NEW ORLEANS, LA.

R | D | O | DF

B

PERSONS TO BE INCLUDED IN PASSPORT

This section to be completed only if wife or husband is to be included in applicant's passport (Include photographic likenesses in group photo)

(WIFE'S) (HUSBAND'S) FULL LEGAL NAME

(WIFE'S) (HUSBAND'S) LAST U. S. PASSPORT WAS OBTAINED FROM

LOCATION OF ISSUING OFFICE | DATE OF ISSUANCE | NUMBER
☐ SUBMITTED HEREWITH
☐ OTHER DISPOSITION (STATE)

This section to be completed only if children are to be included in applicant's passport (Include photographic likenesses in group photo)

NAME IN FULL | PLACE OF BIRTH (City, State) | DATE OF BIRTH | RESIDED IN THE U. S. FROM TO

TO BE PRINTED IN FULL

C

STAPLE ONE PHOTO BELOW
DO NOT MAR FACE

HAVE YOU PREVIOUSLY APPLIED FOR A U. S. PASSPORT? (If answer is "Yes", complete box below)
☐ YES ☐ NO

MY LAST U. S. PASSPORT WAS OBTAINED FROM (Note: If included in another's passport, state name of bearer):

LOCATION OF ISSUING OFFICE LOS ANGELOS, CALIF | DATE OF ISSUANCE SEPT 10, 1959

NUMBER: 1733242 · C † A - 3

☑ SUBMITTED FOR CANCELLATION
☐ OTHER

Commission Exhibit No. 781

JUN-24-63 600004 LT ACHFPT 9.00

(Passport Office Use Only)

JUN-24-63 600004 LT ACHEXN 1.00

Lee H. Oswald

FEE EXEC. TWX POST.

FORM DSP-11
5-62

(OVER - YOU MUST COMPLETE PAGE 2)

D-3

Front page of a passport application for Lee Harvey Oswald, dated June 1963. This document was submitted as evidence to the Warren Commission for the assassination of President John Kennedy. © CORBIS. REPRODUCED BY PERMISSION.

cartons on the sixth floor and the improvised paper bag in which Oswald brought the rifle to the Depository was found close by the window from which the shots were fired.

Based on testimony of the experts and their analysis of films of the assassination, the Commission has concluded that a rifleman of Lee Harvey Oswald's capabilities could have fired the shots from the rifle used in the assassination within the elapsed time of the shooting. The Commission has concluded further that Oswald possessed the capability with a rifle which enabled him to commit the assassination.

Oswald lied to the police after his arrest concerning important substantive matters.

Oswald had attempted to kill Maj. Gen. Edwin A. Walker (Resigned, U.S. Army) on April 10, 1963, thereby demonstrating his disposition to take human life.

5. Oswald killed Dallas Police Patrolman J.D. Tippit approximately 45 minutes after the assassination. This conclusion upholds the finding that Oswald fired the shots which killed President Kennedy and wounded Governor Connally and is supported by the following:

Two eyewitnesses saw the Tippit shooting and seven eyewitnesses heard the shots and saw the gunman leave the scene with revolver in hand. These nine eyewitnesses positively identified Lee Harvey Oswald as the man they saw.

The cartridge cases found at the scene of the shooting were fired from the revolver in the possession of Oswald at the time of his arrest to the exclusion of all other weapons.

The revolver in Oswald's possession at the time of his arrest was purchased by and belonged to Oswald.

Oswald's jacket was found along the path of flight taken by the gunman as he fled from the scene of the killing.

6. Within 80 minutes of the assassination and 35 minutes of the Tippit killing Oswald resisted arrest at the theater by attempting to shoot another Dallas police officer.

7. The Commission has reached the following conclusions concerning Oswald's interrogation and detention by the Dallas police:

Except for the force required to effect his arrest, Oswald was not subjected to any physical coercion by any law enforcement officials. He was advised that he could not be compelled to give any information and that any statements made by him might be used against him in court. He was advised of his right to counsel. He was given the opportunity to obtain counsel of his own choice and was offered legal assistance by the Dallas Bar Association, which he rejected at that time.

Newspaper, radio, and television reporters were allowed uninhibited access to the area through which Oswald had to pass when he was moved from his cell to the interrogation room and other sections of the building, thereby subjecting Oswald to harassment and creating chaotic conditions which were not conducive to orderly interrogation or the protection of the rights of the prisoner.

The numerous statements, sometimes erroneous, made to the press by various local law enforcement officials, during this period of confusion and disorder in the police station, would have presented serious obstacles to the obtaining of a fair trial for Oswald. To the extent that the information was erroneous or misleading, it helped to create doubts, speculations, and fears in the mind of the public which might otherwise not have arisen.

8. The Commission has reached the following conclusions concerning the killing of Oswald by Jack Ruby on November 24, 1963:

Ruby entered the basement of the Dallas Police Department shortly after 11:17 a.m. and killed Lee Harvey Oswald at 11:21 a.m.

Although the evidence on Ruby's means of entry is not conclusive, the weight of the evidence indicates that he walked down the ramp leading from Main Street to the basement of the police department.

There is no evidence to support the rumor that Ruby may have been assisted by any members of the Dallas Police Department in the killing of Oswald.

The Dallas Police Department's decision to transfer Oswald to the county jail in full public view was unsound.

The arrangements made by the police department on Sunday morning, only a few hours before the attempted transfer, were inadequate. Of critical importance was the fact that news media representatives and others were not excluded from the basement even after the police were notified of threats to Oswald's life. These deficiencies contributed to the death of Lee Harvey Oswald.

9. The Commission has found no evidence that either Lee Harvey Oswald or Jack Ruby was part of any conspiracy, domestic or foreign, to assassinate President Kennedy. The reasons for this conclusion are:

The Commission has found no evidence that anyone assisted Oswald in planning or carrying out the assassination. In this connection it has thoroughly investigated, among other factors, the circumstances surrounding the planning of the motorcade route through Dallas, the hiring of Oswald by the Texas School Book Depository Co. on October 15, 1963, the method by which the rifle was brought into the building, the placing of cartons of books at the window, Oswald's escape from the building, and the testimony of eyewitnesses to the shooting.

The Commission has found no evidence that Oswald was involved with any person or group in a conspiracy to assassinate the President, although it has thoroughly investigated, in addition to other possible leads, all facets of Oswald's associations, finances, and personal habits, particularly during the period following his return from the Soviet Union in June 1962.

The Commission has found no evidence to show that Oswald was employed, persuaded, or encouraged by any foreign government to assassinate President Kennedy or that he was an agent of any foreign government, although the Commission has reviewed the circumstances surrounding Oswald's defection to the Soviet Union, his life there from October of 1959 to June of 1962 so far as it can be reconstructed, his known contacts with the Fair Play for Cuba Committee and his visits to the Cuban and Soviet Embassies in Mexico City during his trip to Mexico from September 26 to October 3, 1963, and his known contacts with the Soviet Embassy in the United States.

The Commission has explored all attempts of Oswald to identify himself with various political groups, including the Communist Party, U.S.A., the Fair Play for Cuba Committee, and the Socialist Workers Party, and has been unable to find any evidence that the contacts which he initiated were related to Oswald's subsequent assassination of the President.

All of the evidence before the Commission established that there was nothing to support the speculation that Oswald was an agent, employee, or informant of the FBI, the CIA, or any other governmental agency. It has thoroughly investigated Oswald's relationships prior to the assassination with all agencies of the U.S. Government. All contacts with Oswald by any of these agencies were made in the regular exercise of their different responsibilities.

No direct or indirect relationship between Lee Harvey Oswald and Jack Ruby has been discovered by the Commission, nor has it been able to find any credible evidence that either knew the other, although a thorough investigation was made of the many rumors and speculations of such a relationship.

The Commission has found no evidence that Jack Ruby acted with any other person in the killing of Lee Harvey Oswald.

After careful investigation the Commission has found no credible evidence either that Ruby and Officer Tippit, who was killed by Oswald, knew each other or that Oswald and Tippit knew each other. Because of the difficulty of proving negatives to a certainty the possibility of others being involved with either Oswald or Ruby cannot be established categorically, but if there is any such evidence it has been beyond the reach of all the investigative agencies and resources of the United States and has not come to the attention of this Commission.

10. In its entire investigation the Commission has found no evidence of conspiracy, subversion, or disloyalty to the U.S. Government by any Federal, State, or local official.

11. On the basis of the evidence before the Commission it concludes that Oswald acted alone. Therefore, to determine the motives for the assassination of President Kennedy, one must look to the assassin himself. Clues to Oswald's motives can be found in his family history, his education or lack of it,

The 6.5 mm Mannlicher-Carcano owned by Lee Harvey Oswald. The weapon was presented with the Warren Commission's report on Kennedy's assassination. © CORBIS. REPRODUCED BY PERMISSION.

his acts, his writings, and the recollections of those who had close contacts with him throughout his life. The Commission has presented with this report all of the background information bearing on motivation which it could discover. Thus, others may study Lee Oswald's life and arrive at their own conclusions as to his possible motives. The Commission could not make any definitive determination of Oswald's motives. It has endeavored to isolate factors which contributed to his character and which might have influenced his decision to assassinate President Kennedy. These factors were:

His deep-rooted resentment of all authority which was expressed in a hostility toward every society in which he lived;

His inability to enter into meaningful relationships with people, and a continuous pattern of rejecting his environment in favor of new surroundings;

His urge to try to find a place in history and despair at times over failures in his various undertakings;

His capacity for violence as evidenced by his attempt to kill General Walker;

His avowed commitment to Marxism and communism, as he understood the terms and developed his own interpretation of them; this was expressed by his antagonism toward the United States, by his defection to the Soviet Union, by his failure to be reconciled with life in the United States even after his disenchantment with the Soviet Union, and by his efforts, though frustrated, to go to Cuba. Each of these contributed to his capacity to risk all in cruel and irresponsible actions.

12. The Commission recognizes that the varied responsibilities of the President require that he make frequent trips to all parts of the United States and abroad. Consistent with their high responsibilities Presidents can never be protected from every potential threat. The Secret Service's difficulty in meeting its protective responsibility varies with the activities and the nature of the occupant of the Office of President and his willingness to conform to plans for his safety. In appraising the performance of the Secret Service it should be understood that it has to do its work within such limitations. Nevertheless, the Commission believes that recommendations for improvements in Presidential protection are compelled by the facts disclosed in this investigation.

The complexities of the Presidency have increased so rapidly in recent years that the Secret Service has not been able to develop or to secure adequate resources of personnel and facilities to fulfill its important assignment. This situation should be promptly remedied.

The Commission has concluded that the criteria and procedures of the Secret Service designed to identify and protect against persons considered threats to the president were not adequate prior to the assassination.

1. The Protective Research Section of the Secret Service, which is responsible for its preventive work, lacked sufficient trained personnel and the mechanical and technical assistance needed to fulfill its responsibility.

2. Prior to the assassination the Secret Service's criteria dealt with direct threats against the President. Although the Secret Service treated the direct threats against the President adequately, it failed to recognize the necessity of identifying other potential sources of danger to his security. The Secret Service did not develop adequate and specific criteria defining those persons or groups who might present a danger to the President. In effect, the Secret Service largely relied upon other Federal or State agencies to supply the information necessary for it to fulfill its preventive responsibilities, although it did ask for information about direct threats to the President.

The Commission has concluded that there was insufficient liaison and coordination of information between the Secret Service and other Federal agencies necessarily concerned with Presidential protection. Although the FBI, in the normal exercise of its responsibility, had secured considerable information about Lee Harvey Oswald, it had no official responsibility, under the Secret Service criteria existing at the time of the President's trip to Dallas, to refer to the Secret Service the information it had about Oswald. The Commission has concluded, however, that the FBI took an unduly restrictive view of its role in preventive intelligence work prior to the assassination. A more carefully coordinated treatment of the Oswald case by the FBI might well have resulted in bringing Oswald's activities to the attention of the Secret Service.

The Commission has concluded that some of the advance preparations in Dallas made by the Secret Service, such as the detailed security measures taken at Love Field and the Trade Mart, were thorough and well executed. In other respects, however, the Commission has concluded that the advance preparations for the President's trip were deficient.

1. Although the Secret Service is compelled to rely to a great extent on local law enforcement officials, its procedures at the time of the Dallas trip did not call for well-defined instructions as to the respective responsibilities of the police officials and others assisting in the protection of the President.

2. The procedures relied upon by the Secret Service for detecting the presence of an assassin located in a building along a motorcade route were inadequate. At the time of the trip to Dallas, the Secret Service as a matter of practice did not investigate, or cause to be checked, any building located along the motorcade route to be taken by the President. The responsibility for observing windows in these buildings during the motorcade was divided between local police personnel stationed on the streets to regulate crowds and Secret Service agents riding in the motorcade. Based on its investigation the Commission has concluded that these arrangements during the trip to Dallas were clearly not sufficient.

The configuration of the Presidential car and the seating arrangements of the Secret Service agents in the car did not afford the Secret Service agents the opportunity they should have had to be of immediate assistance to the President at the first sign of danger.

Within these limitations, however, the Commission finds that the agents most immediately responsible for the President's safety reacted promptly at the time the shots were fired from the Texas School Book Depository Building.

Further Resources

BOOKS

Reeves, Thomas C. *A Question of Character: A Life of John F. Kennedy.* New York: The Free Press, 1991.

Schlesinger, Arthur M., Jr. *A Thousand Days: John F. Kennedy in the White House.* Boston: Houghton Mifflin, 1965.

Schwartz, Bernard. *The Warren Court: A Retrospective.* New York: Oxford University Press, 1996.

PERIODICALS

"Pulling Back the Curtain." *The Atlantic Monthly,* November 14, 2002. Available online at http://www.theatlantic.com /unbound/interviews/int2002-11-18.htm; website home page: http://www.theatlantic.com (accessed April 2, 2003).

Stark, Steven. "The Cultural Meaning of the Kennedys: Why JFK Has More in Common with Elvis than FDR." *The Atlantic Monthly,* January 1994. Available online at http:// www.theatlantic.com/unbound/flashbks/pres/stark.htm; website home page: http://www.theatlantic.com (accessed April 2, 2003).

WEBSITES

"John F. Kennedy: The Charismatic President." The American President. Available online at http://www.americanpresi-dent.org/kotrain/courses/jfk/jfk_in_brief.htm; website home page: http://www.americanpresident.org (accessed April 2, 2003).

John F. Kennedy Library and Museum. Available online at http://www.jfklibrary.org/ (accessed April 2, 2003).

"Aggression from the North"

Paper

By: Dean Rusk

Date: February 27, 1965

Source: Rusk, Dean. "Aggression from the North." State Department White Paper on Vietnam, February 27, 1965. Reproduced in CNN Cold War Historical Documents. Available online at http://www.cnn.com/SPECIALS/cold.war/episodes /11/documents/white.paper/; website home page: http://www .cnn.com/SPECIALS/cold.war/ (accessed April 2, 2003).

About the Author: Dean Rusk (1909–1994) was born in Cherokee County, Georgia. In 1940, the Rhodes Scholar entered the army as an infantry captain and rose to the rank of colonel. In 1946, he joined the State Department and was appointed assistant secretary of state for Far Eastern affairs in 1950. In 1961, President Lyndon B. Johnson (served 1963–1969) appointed him secretary of state. From 1970 to 1984, he served as a professor of international law at the University of Georgia. ∎

Introduction

For centuries, the Indochinese peninsula, which rounds the southeastern corner of Asia, had been subjected to foreign occupation. At the end of the nineteenth century, the part of peninsula now known as Vietnam was a French colony. In 1940, when Japan invaded Vietnam, it left the French administration intact. When Japan surrendered in 1945, France reasserted its claim over Vietnam.

The following year, the communist Ho Chi Minh and nationalist rebels proclaimed independence from Asian and European colonialism. When the French rejected their political aspirations, Vietnam, with assistance from China, launched an eight-year struggle of liberation.

To counter communist Chinese assistance, President Harry S. Truman (served 1945–1953) provided economic and military assistance to the French. However, the French were defeated by the rebels and, in 1954, they reached a peace agreement with Ho Chi Minh. Vietnam would be partitioned along the seventeenth parallel, with the northern half under control of the rebels. France would withdraw from the southern half of Vietnam, leaving it under the control of a native democracy.

Fearing that the communists would gain control in South Vietnam as well as the North, from 1955 to 1961, President Dwight D. Eisenhower (served 1953–1961) provided $200 million annually in assistance to South Vietnam Military advisors were sent to the capital, Saigon, to train the South Vietnamese army. As time passed, the American commitment to establish a stable bulwark against communist aggression grew.

When President Lyndon B. Johnson took office in 1963, he escalated the Vietnam conflict. In January 1964, he ordered the U.S. Army to increase covert actions against the North. That March, he began planning air strikes. In August, American naval forces conducted surveillance missions off the North Vietnamese coast and bombarded coastal islands to provide cover for South Vietnamese attacks.

When the North repelled the attacks, President Johnson went on television to announce that the North attacked the USS *Maddox,* a destroyer located in the international waters of the Gulf of Tonkin. Johnson claimed that the attack was "unprovoked." To prevent future attacks, Johnson, without consulting Congress, publicized that American warplanes were engaged in battle.

The next day, he pressured Congress to immediately pass a retroactive joint resolution that authorized him to take all measures necessary to protect the armed forces. Congress adopted the so-called "Gulf of Tonkin" resolution almost unanimously.

Significance

On February 13, 1965, Johnson authorized Operation Rolling Thunder, named after a Protestant hymn. The operation called for a protracted bombing campaign designed to cripple the North Vietnamese economy and force them to negotiate. Between 1965 and 1968, the United States dropped 800 tons of bombs a day on the North. This aerial onslaught was three times the amount that had fallen on Europe, Asia, and Africa in World War II (1939–1945). The bombing had little effect on the Vietcong's (the pro-communist forces in the South) ability to wage war. If anything, it intensified the Vietcong's willingness to fight.

Two captured Vietcong suspects are surrounded by South Vietnamese army soldiers while an American soldier looks on, 1965. The White Paper on Vietnam defended the presence of U.S. troops in Vietnam. © TIM PAGE/CORBIS. REPRODUCED BY PERMISSION.

Operation Rolling Thunder was the first phase of the United States' involvement in the Vietnam War (1964–1975), the longest war in the nation's history. By the end of 1965, there were 184,000 Americans in the field, 385,000 a year later, and 485,000 the following year. In 1968, the number exceeded 538,000.

Consequently, the United States was engaged in a war that Congress never officially declared, and that proved increasingly unpopular. The war resulted in the death of fifty-seven thousand Americans and three hundred thousand wounded, and it cost taxpayers $150 billion. Despite its great cost, the U.S. intervention in Vietnam was a failure, with the entire country falling to the communists in 1975.

Vietnam was the first war that the United States ever lost, and had far-reaching and long-lasting effects on the country. In 1973, Congress took action to try and prevent future "undeclared wars" by passing the War Powers Act, which requires the president to report any use of military force within forty-eight hours and directs hostilities to cease within sixty days unless Congress declares war. Another legal change arising from the war was the abolishment of the military draft. In a wider sense, the expe-

rience of the Vietnam War made Americans less trusting of the government and the military, and less willing to intervene in future conflicts.

Primary Source

"Aggression from the North"

SYNOPSIS: Two weeks after the authorization of Operation Rolling Thunder, Secretary of State Dean Rusk released this paper. The paper views the war through the lens of the Cold War, as part of the Soviet and Chinese conspiracy to install Third World communist regimes. It fails to recognize that the war was also fueled by nationalist aspirations to reunify the partitioned nation and overthrow foreign occupiers.

South Vietnam is fighting for its life against a brutal campaign of terror and armed attack inspired, directed, supplied, and controlled by the Communist regime in Hanoi. This flagrant aggression has been going on for years, but recently the pace has quickened and the threat has now become acute.

The war in Vietnam is a new kind of war, a fact as yet poorly understood in most parts of the world. Much of the confusion that prevails in the thinking of many people, and even governments, stems from this basic misunderstanding. For in Vietnam a totally new brand of aggression has been loosed against an independent people who want to make their way in peace and freedom.

Vietnam is not another Greece, where indigenous guerrilla forces used friendly neighboring territory as a sanctuary.

Vietnam is not another Malaya, where Communist guerrillas were, for the most part, physically distinguishable from the peaceful majority they sought to control.

Vietnam is not another Philippines, where Communist guerrillas were physically separated from the source of their moral and physical support.

Above all, the war in Vietnam is not a spontaneous and local rebellion against the established government.

There are elements in the Communist program of conquest directed against South Vietnam common to each of the previous areas of aggression and subversion. But there is one fundamental difference. In Vietnam a Communist government has set out deliberately to conquer a sovereign people in a neighboring state. And to achieve its end, it has used every resource of its own government to carry out its carefully planned program of concealed aggression. North Vietnam's commitment to seize control of the South is no less total than was the commitment of the regime in North Korea in 1950. But knowing the consequences of the latter's undisguised attack, the planners in Hanoi have tried desperately to conceal their hand. They have failed and their aggression is as real as that of an invading army.

This report is a summary of the massive evidence of North Vietnamese aggression obtained by the Government of South Vietnam. This evidence has been jointly analyzed by South Vietnamese and American experts.

The evidence shows that the hard core of the Communist forces attacking South Vietnam were trained in the North and ordered into the South by Hanoi. It shows that the key leadership of the Vietcong (VC), the officers and much of the cadre, many of the technicians, political organizers, and propagandists have come from the North and operate under Hanoi's direction. It shows that the training of essential military personnel and their infiltration into the South is directed by the Military High Command in Hanoi. In recent months new types of weapons have been introduced in the VC army, for which all ammunition must come from outside sources. Communist China and other Communist states have been the prime suppliers of these weapons and ammunition, and they have been channeled primarily through North Vietnam.

The directing force behind the effort to conquer South Vietnam is the Communist Party in the North, the Lao Dong (Workers) Party. As in every Communist state, the party is an integral part of the regime itself. North Vietnamese officials have expressed their firm determination to absorb South Vietnam into the Communist world.

Through its Central Committee, which controls the Government of the North, the Lao Dong Party directs the total political and military effort of the Vietcong. The Military High Command in the North trains the military men and sends them into South Vietnam. The Central Research Agency, North Vietnam's central intelligence organization, directs the elaborate espionage and subversion effort. . . .

Under Hanoi's overall direction the Communists have established an extensive machine for carrying on the war within South Vietnam. The focal point is the Central Office for South Vietnam with its political and military subsections and other specialized agencies. A subordinate part of this Central Office is the liberation Front for South Vietnam. The front was formed at Hanoi's order in 1960. Its principle function is to influence opinion abroad and to create the false impression that the aggression in South Vietnam is an indigenous rebellion against the established Government.

For more than 10 years the people and the Government of South Vietnam, exercising the inherent right of self-defense, have fought back against these efforts to extend Communist power south across the 17th parallel. The United States has responded to the appeals of the Government of the Republic of Vietnam for help in this defense of the freedom and independence of its land and its people.

In 1961 the Department of State issued a report called A Threat to the Peace. It described North Vietnam's program to seize South Vietnam. The evidence in that report had been presented by the Government of the Republic of Vietnam to the International Control Commission (ICC). A special report by the ICC in June 1962 upheld the validity of that evidence. The Commission held that there was "sufficient evidence to show beyond reasonable doubt" that North Vietnam had sent arms and men into South Vietnam to carry out subversion with the aim of overthrowing the legal Government there. The ICC found the authorities in Hanoi in specific violation of four provisions of the Geneva Accords of 1954.

Since then, new and even more impressive evidence of Hanoi's aggression has accumulated. The Government of the United States believes that evidence should be presented to its own citizens and to the world. It is important for free men to know what has been happening in Vietnam, and how, and why. That is the purpose of this report. . . .

The record is conclusive. It establishes beyond question that North Vietnam is carrying out a carefully conceived plan of aggression against the South. It shows that North Vietnam has intensified its efforts in the years since it was condemned by the International Control Commission. It proves that Hanoi continues to press its systematic program of armed aggression into South Vietnam. This aggression violates the United Nations Charter. It is directly contrary to the Geneva Accords of 1954 and of 1962 to which North Vietnam is a party. It is a fundamental threat to the freedom and security of South Vietnam.

The people of South Vietnam have chosen to resist this threat. At their request, the United States has taken its place beside them in their defensive struggle.

The United States seeks no territory, no military bases, no favored position. But we have learned the meaning of aggression elsewhere in the post-war world, and we have met it.

If peace can be restored in South Vietnam, the United States will be ready at once to reduce its military involvement. But it will not abandon friends who want to remain free. It will do what must be done to help them. The choice now between peace and continued and increasingly destructive conflict is one for the authorities in Hanoi to make.

Further Resources

BOOKS

Halberstam, David. *The Making of the Quagmire.* New York: Random House, 1965.

Karnow, Stanley. *Vietnam: A History.* New York: Penguin, 1991.

McNamara, Robert. *In Retrospect: The Tragedy and Lessons of Vietnam.* New York: Times Books, 1995.

PERIODICALS

Hellman, John. "Vietnam and the Hollywood Genre Film: Inversions of American Mythology in the Deer Hunter and Apocalypse Now." *American Quarterly* 34, 1982, 398–418.

Wilson, William. "I Prayed to God That This Thing Was Fiction." *American Heritage,* February 1990, 44–53.

WEBSITES

"Vietnam Online." The American Experience, Public Broadcasting Service. Available online at http://www.pbs .org/wgbh/amex/vietnam/refer/index.html; website home page: http://www.pbs.org/wgbh/amex (accessed April 2, 2003).

"Vietnam War Bibliography." Edwin E. Moïse, History Department, Clemson University. Available online at http:// hubcap.clemson.edu/~eemoise/bibliography.html; website home page: http://hubcap.clemson.edu/~eemoise/ (accessed April 2, 2003).

Martin Luther King, Jr.

"I Have a Dream"
Speech

By: Martin Luther King, Jr.

Date: August 28, 1963

Source: King, Martin Luther, Jr. "I Have a Dream." Address delivered at the Lincoln Memorial, Washington, D.C., August 28, 1963. Transcript available online at http://www.stanford .edu/group/King/publications/speeches/address_at_march_on _washington.pdf; website home page: http://www.stanford .edu/group/King (accessed July 30, 2003).

"The American Dream"
Sermon

By: Martin Luther King, Jr.

Date: July 4, 1965

Source: King, Martin Luther, Jr. "The American Dream." July 4, 1965. In *A Knock at Midnight: Inspiration From the Great Sermons of Reverend Martin Luther King, Jr.* Clayborne Carson and Peter Holloran, eds. New York: IPM/ Warner Books, 1998. Available online at http://www.stanford .edu/group/King/sermons/650704_the_american_dream.html; website homepage: http://www.stanford.edu/group/King (accessed April 2, 2003).

About the Author: Martin Luther King, Jr. (1929-1968), was born in Atlanta, Georgia. His grandfather, William, was a Baptist minister and founding member of the Atlanta chapter of the National Association for the Advancement of Colored People (NAACP). His father, Martin Luther King, Sr., succeeded William as pastor of Ebenezer Baptist Church and was a civil rights leader. In 1955, Martin Luther King, Jr., earned a doctorate in theology from Boston University. Afterward, he returned to the South, becoming the pastor of Dexter Avenue Baptist Church in Montgomery, Alabama. ∎

Introduction

On December 1, 1955, Rosa Parks, a seamstress and secretary of the Montgomery chapter of the NAACP, refused to obey local rules mandating the segregation of buses. Four days later, African American residents organized a bus boycott and nominated Martin Luther King, Jr., as the leader of the newly established Montgomery Improvement Association.

In February 1956, city officials mistakenly believed that they could suppress the demonstration by obtaining indictments of 115 boycott leaders. Instead, the move boomeranged, attracting widespread national publicity to the otherwise local controversy. King emerged as an instant celebrity, drawing financial and moral support from across the nation. The following November, the U.S. Supreme Court ruled in *Browder vs. Gayle* that busing segregation laws were unconstitutional.

King's philosophy and theology were heavily influenced by the preaching of the Indian Mohandas Gandhi. Through nonviolent resistance and redemptive suffering, Gandhi championed the rights of the "untouchables," who occupied the lower rung of India's rigid and unjust caste system. Like Gandhi, King rejected violence as immoral and used nonviolent resistance as a moral weapon to transform race relations in the United States. Seeking to build on the success of the Montgomery bus boycott, King and other southern African American pastors founded the Southern Christian Leadership Conference (SCLC).

In April 1963, King and the SCLC led a massive demonstration in Birmingham, Alabama. Eugene Conner, the city's commissioner of public safety, responded with using vicious dogs, electric cattle prods, and high-pressure fire hoses that wrenched bricks from buildings. The horrifying scene was broadcast to living rooms across the country. President John F. Kennedy (served 1961–1963) noted that Conner had done as much for the civil rights movement as Abraham Lincoln.

In August 1963, King and other prominent black leaders organized the March on Washington, D.C., to pressure Congress to pass a civil rights bill. On the steps of the Lincoln Memorial, before a crowd of more than 250,000 blacks and whites, King spellbound the throng with his memorable "I Have a Dream Speech."

Significance

The March on Washington affirmed King's position, especially among white liberals, as the leading speaker for the African American cause. King's reputation continued to grow. In 1963, he was *Time* magazine's Man of the Year and the next year he won the Nobel Peace Prize.

Afterward, King became more radical. He alienated President Lyndon B. Johnson (served 1963–1969), the most pro-civil rights leader in the nation's history, by denouncing the Vietnam War (1964–1975). He also became a strident critic of capitalism, calling for major economic reforms that would guarantee annual incomes for all.

On April 3, 1968, King was in Memphis, Tennessee, lending moral support to striking black sanitation workers. The next evening, he was assassinated by the white supremacist James Earl Ray. King's death set off a spasm of racial violence in more than 125 cities in 28 states. In the nation's capital, President Johnson ordered twenty thousand regular troops and twenty-four thousand National Guardsmen to the cities to keep order. In less than three weeks, forty-six people were dead, twenty-six hundred were injured, and more than twenty-one thousand were arrested.

For a brief time, it appeared that King's death had destroyed the very ideals he had hoped would heal the nation's racial wounds. King's legacy is as controversial as his death. To most whites, King is a celebrated hero who had successfully integrated the races. Indeed, in 1986 his birthday became a national holiday. Many African Americans, including King's family, however, believe that Ray was innocent and that the government conspired to kill King because of his growing radicalism. There is no convincing proof, however, that Ray was innocent or that the government conspired to assassinate King.

Primary Source

"I Have a Dream"

> **SYNOPSIS:** On August 28, 1963, Martin Luther King, Jr., delivered his "I Have a Dream" speech on the steps of the Lincoln Memorial in Washington, D.C.

[Editor's note: the remarks in parentheses are spoken by the audience.]

I am happy to join with you today in what will go down in history as the greatest demonstration for freedom in the history of our nation. [*applause*]

Five score years ago, a great American, in whose symbolic shadow we stand today, signed the Emancipation Proclamation. This momentous decree came as a great beacon light of hope to millions of Negro slaves who had been seared in the flames of withering injustice. It came as a joyous daybreak to end the long night of their captivity.

But one hundred years later, the Negro still is not free. [*Audience response:*] *(My Lord)* One hundred years later, the life of the Negro is still sadly crippled by the manacles of segregation and the chains of discrimination. One hundred years later, the Negro lives on a lonely island of poverty in the midst of a vast ocean of material prosperity. One hundred years later *(My Lord)* [*applause*], the Negro is still languished in the corners of American society and finds himself an exile in his own land. And so we've come here today to dramatize a shameful condition.

In a sense we've come to our nation's capital to cash a check. When the architects of our republic wrote the magnificent words of the Constitution and the Declaration of Independence *(Yeah)*, they were signing a promissory note to which every American was to fall heir. This note was a promise that all men, yes, black men as well as white men, would be guaranteed the "unalienable Rights of Life, Liberty, and the pursuit of Happiness." It is obvious today that America has defaulted on this promissory note insofar as her citizens of color are concerned. Instead of honoring this sacred obligation, America has given the Negro people a bad check, a check which has come back marked "insufficient funds." [*sustained applause*]

But we refuse to believe that the bank of justice is bankrupt. *(My Lord)* [*laughter*] *(Sure enough)* We refuse to believe that there are insufficient funds in the great vaults of opportunity of this nation. And so we've come to cash this check *(Yes)*, a check that will give us upon demand the riches of freedom *(Yes)* and the security of justice. [*applause*]

We have also come to this hallowed spot to remind America of the fierce urgency of Now. This is no time *(My Lord)* to engage in the luxury of cooling off or to take the tranquilizing drug of gradualism. [*applause*] Now is the time to make real the promises of democracy. *(My Lord)* Now is the time to rise from the dark and desolate valley of segregation to the sunlit path of racial justice. Now is the time [*applause*] to lift our nation from the quicksands of racial injustice to the solid rock of brotherhood. Now is the time [*applause*] to make justice a reality for all of God's children.

It would be fatal for the nation to overlook the urgency of the moment. This sweltering summer of the Negro's legitimate discontent will not pass until there is an invigorating autumn of freedom and equality. Nineteen sixty-three is not an end but a beginning. And those who hope that the Negro needed to blow off steam and will now be content will have a rude awakening if the nation returns to business as usual. [*applause*] There will be neither rest nor tranquility in America until the Negro is granted his citizenship rights. The whirlwinds of revolt will continue to shake the foundations of our nation until the bright day of justice emerges.

But there is something that I must say to my people, who stand on the warm threshold which leads into the palace of justice: In the process of gaining our rightful place, we must not be guilty of wrongful deeds. Let us not seek to satisfy our thirst for freedom by drinking from the cup of bitterness and hatred. *(My Lord)* [*applause*] We must forever conduct our struggle on the high plane of dignity and discipline. We must not allow our creative protest to degenerate into physical violence. Again and again, we must rise to the majestic heights of meeting physical force with soul force. The marvelous new militancy which has engulfed the Negro community must not lead us to a distrust of all white people, for many of our white brothers, as evidenced by their presence here today, have come to realize that their destiny is tied up with our destiny. [*applause*] And they have come to realize that their freedom is inextricably bound to our freedom. We cannot walk alone.

And as we walk, we must make the pledge that we shall always march ahead. We cannot turn back. There are those who are asking the devotees of civil rights, "When will you be satisfied?" *(Never)*

We can never be satisfied as long as the Negro is the victim of the unspeakable horrors of police brutality. We can never be satisfied [*applause*] as long as our bodies, heavy with the fatigue of travel, cannot gain lodging in the motels of the highways and the hotels of the cities. [*applause*] We cannot be satisfied as long as the Negro's basic mobility is from a smaller ghetto to a larger one. We can never be satisfied as long as our children are stripped of their selfhood and robbed of their dignity by signs stating "for whites only." [*applause*] We cannot be satisfied as long as a Negro in Mississippi cannot vote and a Negro in New York believes he has nothing for which to vote. *(Yes)* [*applause*] No, no, we are not satisfied and we will not be satisfied until "justice rolls down like waters and righteousness like a mighty stream." [*applause*]

I am not unmindful that some of you have come here out of great trials and tribulations. *(My Lord)* Some of you have come fresh from narrow jail cells. Some of you have come from areas where your quest for freedom left you battered by the storms of persecution *(Yes)* and staggered by the winds of police brutality. You have been the veterans of creative suffering. Continue to work with the faith that unearned suffering is redemptive. Go back to Mississippi *(Yes)*, go back to Alabama, go back to South Carolina, go back to Georgia, go back to Louisiana, go back to the slums and ghettos of our northern

The Reverend Dr. Martin Luther King, Jr., speaks at a press conference in Miami, Florida, August 16, 1965. King delivered a speech insprired by Thomas Jefferson's Declaration of Independence one month earlier. AP/WIDE WORLD PHOTOS. REPRODUCED BY PERMISSION.

cities, knowing that somehow this situation can and will be changed. *(Yes)* Let us not wallow in the valley of despair.

I say to you today, my friends [*applause*], so even though we face the difficulties of today and tomorrow, I still have a dream. *(Yes)* It is a dream deeply rooted in the American dream.

I have a dream that one day *(Yes)* this nation will rise up and live out the true meaning of its creed: "We hold these truths to be self-evident, that all men are created equal." *(Yes)* [*applause*]

I have a dream that one day on the red hills of Georgia, the sons of former slaves and the sons of former slave owners will be able to sit down together at the table of brotherhood.

I have a dream that one day even the state of Mississippi, a state sweltering with the heat of injustice *(Well)*, sweltering with the heat of oppression, will be transformed into an oasis of freedom and justice.

I have a dream *(Well)* [*applause*] that my four little children will one day live in a nation where they will not be judged by the color of their skin but by the content of their character. *(My Lord)* I have a dream today. [*applause*]

I have a dream that one day, down in Alabama, with its vicious racists, with its governor having his lips dripping with the words of "interposition" and "nullification" *(Yes)*, one day right there in Alabama little black boys and black girls will be able to join hands with little white boys and white girls as sisters and brothers. I have a dream today. [*applause*]

I have a dream that one day "every valley shall be exalted *(Yes)*, and every hill and mountain shall be made low; the rough places will be made plain, and the crooked places will be made straight *(Yes)*; and the glory of the Lord shall be revealed, and all flesh shall see it together." *(Yes)*

This is our hope. This is the faith that I will go back to the South with. *(Yes)* With this faith we will be able to hew out of the mountain of despair a stone of hope. *(Yes)* With this faith we will be able to transform the jangling discords of our nation into a beautiful symphony of brotherhood. *(Talk about it)* With this faith *(My Lord)* we will be able to work together, to pray together, to struggle together, to go to jail together, to stand up for freedom together, knowing that we will be free one day. [*applause*] This will be the day [*applause continues*], this will be the day when all of God's children *(Yes)* will be able to sing with new meaning:

My country 'tis of thee *(Yes)*, sweet land of liberty, of thee I sing.

Land where my fathers died, land of the pilgrim's pride *(Yes)*

From every mountainside, let freedom ring!

And if America is to be a great nation, this must become true.

And so let freedom ring *(Yes)* from the prodigious hilltops of New Hampshire.

Let freedom ring from the mighty mountains of New York.

Let freedom ring from the heightening Alleghenies of Pennsylvania. *(Yes, That's right)*

Let freedom ring from the snow-capped Rockies of Colorado. *(Well)*

Let freedom ring from the curvaceous slopes of California. *(Yes)*

But not only that: Let freedom ring from Stone Mountain of Georgia. *(Yes)*

Let freedom ring from Lookout Mountain of Tennessee. *(Yes)*

Let freedom ring from every hill and molehill of Mississippi. *(Yes)*

From every mountainside, let freedom ring. [*applause*]

And when this happens [*applause continues*], when we allow freedom to ring, when we let it ring from every village and every hamlet, from every state and every city *(Yes)*, we will be able to speed up that day when all of God's children, black men and white men, Jews and Gentiles, Protestants and Catholics, will be able to join hands and sing in the words of the old Negro spiritual:

Free at last! *(Yes)* Free at last!

Thank God Almighty, we are free at last! [*applause*]

Primary Source

"The American Dream"

SYNOPSIS: On July 4, 1965, King delivered his "The American Dream" speech before his Atlanta congregation. The speech focuses on the Declaration of Independence's guarantee that "all men are created equal." King's growing economic radicalism is evident in his discussion of "classism" and his demand for higher wages for the poor. He also reminds his congregation that full political and economic equality can only be attained through nonviolent means. The parenthetical remarks are the responses of his congregation to his speech.

I planned to use for the textual basis for our thinking together that passage from the prologue of the book of Job where Satan is pictured as asking God, "Does Job serve thee for nought?" And I'd like to ask you to allow me to hold that sermon [*"Why Serve God?"*] in abeyance and preach it the next time I am in the pulpit in order to share with you some other ideas. This morning I was riding to the airport in Washington, D.C., and on the way to the airport the limousine passed by the Jefferson monument, and Reverend Andrew Young, my executive assistant, said to me, "It's quite coincidental that we would be passing by the Jefferson Monument on Independence Day." You can get so busy in life that you forget holidays and other days, and it had slipped my mind altogether that today was the Fourth of July. And I said to him, "It is coincidental and quite significant, and I think when I get to Atlanta and go to my pulpit, I will try to preach a sermon in the spirit of the founding fathers of our nation and in the spirit of the Declaration of Independence." And so this morning I would like to use as a subject from which to preach: "The American Dream." *(Yes, sir)*

It wouldn't take us long to discover the substance of that dream. It is found in those majestic words of the Declaration of Independence, words lifted to cosmic proportions: "We hold these truths to be self-evident, that all men are created equal, that they are endowed by God, Creator, with certain inalienable Rights, that among these are Life, Liberty, and the pursuit of Happiness." This is a dream. It's a great dream.

The first saying we notice in this dream is an amazing universalism. It doesn't say "some men," it says "all men." It doesn't say "all white men," it says "all men," which includes black men. It does not say "all Gentiles," it says "all men," which includes Jews. It doesn't say "all Protestants," it says "all men," which includes Catholics. *(Yes, sir)* It doesn't even say "all theists and believers," it says "all men," which includes humanists and agnostics.

Then that dream goes on to say another thing that ultimately distinguishes our nation and our form of government from any totalitarian system in the world. It says that each of us has certain basic rights that are neither derived from or conferred by the state. In order to discover where they came from, it is necessary to move back behind the dim mist of eternity. They are God-given, gifts from His hands. Never before in the history of the world has a sociopolitical document expressed in such profound, eloquent, and unequivocal language the dignity and the worth of human personality. The American dream reminds us, and we should think about it anew on this Independence Day, that every man is an heir of the legacy of dignity and worth.

Now ever since the founding fathers of our nation dreamed this dream in all of its magnificence—to use a big word that the psychiatrists use—America has been something of a schizophrenic personality, tragically divided against herself. On the one hand we have proudly professed the great principles of democracy, but on the other hand we have sadly practiced the very opposite of those principles.

But now more than ever before, America is challenged to realize its dream, for the shape of the world today does not permit our nation the luxury of an anemic democracy. And the price that America must pay for the continued oppression of the Negro and other minority groups is the price of its own destruction. *(Yes it is)* For the hour is late. And the clock of destiny is ticking out. We must act now before it is too late.

And so it is marvelous and great that we do have a dream, that we have a nation with a dream; and to forever challenge us; to forever give us a sense of urgency; to forever stand in the midst of the "is-ness" of our terrible injustices; to remind us of the "oughtness" of our noble capacity for justice and love and brotherhood.

This morning I would like to deal with some of the challenges that we face today in our nation as a result of the American dream. First, I want to re-iterate the fact that we are challenged more than ever before to respect the dignity and the worth of all human personality. We are challenged to really believe that all men are created equal. And don't misunderstand that. It does not mean that all men are created equal in terms of native endowment, in terms of intellectual capacity—it doesn't mean that. There are certain bright stars in the human firma-ment in every field. *(Yes, sir)* It doesn't mean that every musician is equal to a Beethoven or Handel, a Verdi or a Mozart. It doesn't mean that every physi-cist is equal to an Einstein. It does not mean that every literary figure in history is equal to Aeschylus and Euripides, Shakespeare and Chaucer. *(Make it plain)* It does not mean that every philosopher is equal to Plato, Aristotle, Immanuel Kant, and Friedrich Hegel. It doesn't mean that. There are in-dividuals who do excel and rise to the heights of ge-nius in their areas and in their fields. What it does mean is that all men are equal in intrinsic worth. *(Yes)*

You see, the founding fathers were really influ-enced by the Bible. The whole concept of the imago dei, as it is expressed in Latin, the "image of God," is the idea that all men have something within them that God injected. Not that they have substantial unity with God, but that every man has a capacity to have fellowship with God. And this gives him a uniqueness, it gives him worth, it gives him dignity. And we must never forget this as a nation: there are no gradations in the image of God. Every man from a treble white to a bass black is significant on God's keyboard, precisely because every man is made in the image of God. One day we will learn that. *(Yes)* We will know one day that God made us to live to-gether as brothers and to respect the dignity and worth of every man.

This is why we must fight segregation with all of our nonviolent might. *(Yes, sir; Make it plain)* Seg-regation is not only inconvenient—that isn't what makes it wrong. Segregation is not only sociologi-cally untenable—that isn't what makes it wrong. Seg-regation is not only politically and economically unsound—that is not what makes it wrong. Ulti-mately, segregation is morally wrong and sinful. To use the words of a great Jewish philosopher that died a few days ago, Martin Buber, "It's wrong be-cause it substitutes an 'I-It' relationship for the 'I-Thou' relationship and relegates persons to the status of things." That's it. *(Yes, sir)*. . . .

And I tell you this morning, my friends, the rea-son we got to solve this problem here in America: Be-cause God somehow called America to do a special job for mankind and the world. *(Yes, sir; Make it plain)* Never before in the history of the world have so many racial groups and so many national backgrounds as-sembled together in one nation. And somehow if we can't solve the problem in America the world can't solve the problem, because America is the world in miniature and the world is America writ large. And God set us out with all of the opportunities. *(Make it plain)* He set us between two great oceans; *(Yes, sir)* made it possible for us to live with some of the great natural resources of the world. And there he gave us through the minds of our forefathers a great creed: "We hold these truths to be self-evident, that all men *(Yes, sir)* are created equal." . . .

I submit to you when I took off on that plane this morning, I saw men go out there in their over-alls. *(Yes, sir, Every time)* I saw them working on things here and there, and saw some more going out there to put the breakfast on there so that we could eat on our way to Atlanta. *(Make it plain)* And I said to myself that these people who constitute the ground crew are just as significant as the pilot, because this plane couldn't move if you didn't have the ground crew. *(Amen)* I submit to you that in Hugh Spaulding or Grady Hospital, *(Preach it)* the woman or the man who goes in there to sweep the floor is just as significant as the doctor, *(Yes)* because if he doesn't get that dust off the floor germs will begin to circulate. And those same germs can do injury and harm to the human being. I submit to you this morning *(Yes)* that there is dignity in all work *(Have mercy)* when we learn to pay people decent wages. Whoever cooks in your house, whoever sweeps the floor in your house is just as significant as anybody who lives in that house. *(Amen)* And everybody that we call a maid is serving God in a significant way. *(Preach it)* And I love the maids, I love the people who have been ignored, and I want to see them get the kind of wages that they need. And their job is no longer a menial job, *(No, sir)* for you come to see its worth and its dignity.

Are we really taking this thing seriously? "All men are created equal." *(Amen)* And that means that every man who lives in a slum today *(Preach it)* is just as significant as John D., Nelson, or any other Rockefeller. Every man who lives in the slum is just as significant as Henry Ford. All men are created equal, and they are endowed by their Creator with certain inalienable rights, rights that can't be separated from you. [clap] Go down and tell them, *(No)* "You may take my life, but you can't take my right to life. You may take liberty from me, but you can't take my right to liberty. You may take from me the desire, you may take from me the propensity to pursue happiness, but you can't take from me my right to pursue happiness." *(Yes)* "We hold these truths to be self-evident that all men are created equal and endowed by their Creator with certain inalienable Rights and among these are Life, Liberty, and the pursuit of Happiness." *(Yes, sir)* . . .

And I would like to say to you this morning what I've tried to say all over this nation, what I believe firmly: that in seeking to make the dream a reality we must use and adopt a proper method. I'm more convinced than ever before that nonviolence is the way. I'm more convinced than ever before that violence is impractical as well as immoral . . . We can stand up before our most violent opponent and say: We will match your capacity to inflict suffering by our capacity to endure suffering. We will meet your physical force with soul force. *(Make it plain)* Do to us what you will and we will still love you. We cannot in all good conscience obey your unjust laws, because noncooperation with evil is as much a moral obligation as is cooperation with good, and so throw us in jail. *(Make it plain)* We will go in those jails and transform them from dungeons of shame to havens of freedom and human dignity. Send your hooded perpetrators of violence into our communities after midnight hours and drag us out on some wayside road and beat us and leave us half-dead, and as difficult as it is, we will still love you. *(Amen)* Somehow go around the country and use your propaganda agents to make it appear that we are not fit culturally, morally, or otherwise for integration, and we will still love you. *(Yes)* Threaten our children and bomb our homes, and as difficult as it is, we will still love you. *(Yeah)* . . .

We have a great dream. *(Great dream)* It started way back in 1776, and God grant that America will be true to her dream.

About two years ago now, I stood with many of you who stood there in person and all of you who were there in spirit before the Lincoln Monument in Washington. *(Yes)* As I came to the end of my speech there, I tried to tell the nation about a dream I had. I must confess to you this morning that since that sweltering August afternoon in 1963, my dream has often turned into a nightmare; (Lord) I've seen it shattered. . . . I've seen my dream shattered as I've walked the streets of Chicago *(Make it plain)* and seen Negroes, young men and women, with a sense of utter hopelessness because they can't find any jobs. And they see life as a long and desolate corridor with no exit signs. And not only Negroes at this point. I've seen my dream shattered because I've been through Appalachia, and I've seen my white brothers along with Negroes living in poverty. *(Yeah)* And I'm concerned about white poverty as much as I'm concerned about Negro poverty. *(Make it plain)*

So yes, the dream has been shattered, *(Amen)* and I have had my nightmarish experiences, but I tell you this morning once more that I haven't lost the faith. *(No, sir)* I still have a dream *(A dream, Yes, sir)* that one day all of God's children will have food and clothing and material well-being for their bodies, culture and education for their minds, and freedom for their spirits. *(Yes)*

I still have a dream this morning: *(Yes)* one day all of God's black children will be respected like his white children.

I still have a dream this morning *(Yes)* that one day the lion and the lamb will lie down together, and every man will sit under his own vine and fig tree and none shall be afraid.

I still have a dream this morning that one day all men everywhere will recognize that out of one blood God made all men to dwell upon the face of the earth.

I still have a dream this morning *(Yes, sir)* that one day every valley shall be exalted, and every mountain and hill will be made low; the rough places will be made plain, and the crooked places straight; and the glory of the Lord shall be revealed, and all flesh shall see it together.

I still have a dream this morning *(Amen)* that truth will reign supreme and all of God's children will respect the dignity and worth of human personality. And when this day comes the morning stars will sing together *(Yes)* and the sons of God will shout for joy.

"We hold these truths to be self-evident that all men *(All right)* are created equal, that they are endowed by their Creator with certain inalienable Rights, *(Yes, sir)* that among these are Life, Liberty, and the pursuit of Happiness."

We open the doors of the church now. If someone needs to accept Christ, *(Yes, sir)* this is a marvelous opportunity, a great moment to make a decision. And as we sing together, we bid you come at this time by Christian experience, baptism, watch care. But come at this moment, become a part of this great Christian fellowship and accept Christ *(Yes, sir)* as your personal savior.

Further Resources

BOOKS

Garrow, David J. *Bearing the Cross: Martin Luther King Jr., and the Southern Christian Leadership Conference.* New York: Morrow, 1986.

Lewis, David L. *King: A Critical Biography.* New York: Praeger, 1970.

Posner, Gerald L. *Killing the Dream: James Earl Ray and the Assassination of Martin Luther King, Jr.* New York: Random House, 1998.

PERIODICALS

Carson, Clayborne. "Martin Luther King, Jr. As Scholar: A Re-examination of His Theological Writings." *Journal of American History* 78, June 1991.

Colaiaco, James A. "The American Dream Unfulfilled: Martin Luther King, Jr., and the 'Letter from the Birmingham Jail.'" *Phylon* 45, no. 1, 1984, 1-18.

WEBSITES

American Rhetoric. Available online at http://www.americanrhetoric.com. *This site contains audio recordings and transcriptions of King's speeches and sermons.*

Martin Luther King Jr. and the Civil Rights Movement. Available online at http://seattletimes.nwsource.com/mlk/king/ (accessed April 2, 2003).

Federal Role in Traffic Safety: Hearings Before the Senate Subcommittee on Executive Reorganization of the Committee on Government Operations

Testimony

By: Ralph Nader

Date: February 1966

Source: Nader, Ralph. Testimony to the U.S. Senate Subcommittee on Executive Reorganization of the Committee on Government Operations. *Federal Role in Traffic Safety: Hearings Before the Senate Subcommittee on Executive Reorganization of the Committee on Government Operations.* 89th Congress, 2nd session, February 1966, 1265–1270.

About the Author: Ralph Nader (1934–) was born in Winsted, Connecticut. In 1955, after graduating from Princeton University, he attended Harvard Law School. While still in school, he became interested in cases involving automobile injuries, so much so that he wrote the article "The Safe Car You Can't Buy." In 1963, he quit his private practice and with one suitcase hitchhiked to Washington, D.C. ■

Introduction

In October 1959, General Motors (GM), responding to the growing popularity of the economical German-made Volkswagen Beetle in the United States, began designing the Chevrolet Corvair. The car was a first for Chevrolet because it was powered by an air-cooled, six-cylinder engine. The engine was referred to as a "flat six" because the cylinders were horizontally configured instead of the typical *V* design. Not only was the engine design unique, but GM engineers, emulating the European Porsche and Volkswagen, placed the Corvair's engine in the rear. In 1962, the first Corvair convertible was sold.

In March 1965, U.S. Senator Abraham Ribicoff, chair of the Senate Subcommittee on Executive Reorganization, launched an investigation of automobile safety. The federal government had imposed safety regulations on passenger ships, Pullman train cars, and airplanes, yet the automobile industry had been left largely unregulated.

That November, Ralph Nader authored the book *Unsafe at Any Speed.* The first sentence of the book reads, "For over a half a century the automobile has brought death, injury, and the most inestimable sorrow and deprivation to millions of people."

Nader slammed GM for investing only $1 million of its $20.7 billion, or two-hundredths of 1 percent, in profits on collision research. As an example of GM's neglect, Nader cited the Corvair. In making a case for government regulation, Nader claimed that the Corvair's design was so flawed that it fishtailed easily and was prone to rollover when cornering sharply.

Outraged, GM hired private detectives to scour Nader's personal life for indiscretions, eventually accusing him of being gay and anti-Semitic. When GM's smear campaign was revealed, Nader successfully sued the corporation for $425,000. Due to this publicity, Nader's claims gained credibility. Ironically, GM, which prior to the publication of the book planned to end Corvair production in 1966, felt compelled to continue producing the poor-selling model. It was not until the 1969 model year that production was halted.

Significance

In June 1966, the Senate subcommittee released its long awaited report. It indicated that automobile safety defects were more pervasive than the public realized.

These defects, combined with the increase in both the number of bigger and faster automobiles and the number of miles people traveled each year in them, caused the rate of motor vehicle deaths and injuries to skyrocket. By 1965, the annual death toll in motor vehicle accidents was at fifty thousand, making automobiles the leading cause of accidental death for all age groups and the overall leading cause of death for the population below the age of forty-four.

After the release of the report, President Lyndon B. Johnson (served 1963–1969) called highway deaths "the gravest problem before this nation-next to the war in Vietnam." That September, Johnson signed the National Traffic and Motor Vehicle Safety Act and the Highway Safety Act, both of which mandated safety features on every car sold. Two years later, the government created the National Highway Traffic Safety Administration (NHTSA).

As a result of these laws, nineteen federal safety regulations went into effect on January 1, 1968. The regulations significantly reduced traffic fatalities. Between 1968 and 1979, the annual motor vehicle death rate decreased 35.2 percent, from 5.4 to 3.5 deaths per 100 million vehicle miles. Of all the safety regulations, however, the most important and effective safety standard was the seatbelt. Seatbelts that attached across both the lap and the shoulder reduced the probability of serious injury in an accident by 64 percent and of fatalities by 32 percent for front-seat occupants.

In 1972, the NHTSA conducted its own investigation of the Corvair. It found, after extensive tests, that the vehicle handled sharp turns just as well as other light domestic cars sold in the same period. Furthermore, it reported that the car was no more prone to rollover than its competitors.

Ralph Nader testifies before the Senate Commerce subcommittee, March 22, 1966. © BETTMANN/CORBIS. REPRODUCED BY PERMISSION.

Primary Source

Federal Role in Traffic Safety: Hearings Before the Senate Subcommittee on Executive Reorganization of the Committee on Government Operations [excerpt]

> **SYNOPSIS:** Nader testified before a Senate committee that through manipulative advertising automobile manufacturers compounded their product's serious safety problems. For example, he states that "aggressive and ferocious" model names such as "Panther" or ads referring to potential Buick Skylark owners as "human cannonballs" caused impressionable teenagers to drive negligently, which directly contributed to increased death rates.

Annual Model Change

[Mr. Nader:] The car buyer pays over $700, according to a study by MIT, Harvard, and University of Chicago economists, when he buys a new car for the cost of the annual model change, which is mostly stylistic in content. Consider how much safer today's automobile would be if over the past few decades the car buyer received annually a substantial safety advance, both in the operational and crash worthy aspects of the automobile, for that $700 payment.

Instead cars are being built which standing can kill adult and child pedestrians who fall or are inadvertently pushed into their sharp points and edges. Children playing have struck cars, like we all have when we were children, and there is quite a difference between striking a flat rear end of a car and the dagger fin of a Cadillac. A little girl in Kensington, Md., was killed by just such a dagger fin a few years ago.

And passengers die in collisions at speeds as low as 5 miles per hour.

Is it any wonder that at present rate at least one out of every two living Americans will either be killed or injured in an automobile collision? For those with a lifespan of 70 years ahead of them, the probabilities are considerably higher. Yet the orgy of expenditure for style, which is charged to the consumer every year, as entirely standard equipment, continues unabated. A style change for the rear end of a Mustang, for example, will cost the manufacturer close to $50 million.

There are those rare instances when the impressive containment of public self-criticism by auto executives exhaust itself temporarily. Such an instance occurred in January 1964 when Donald Frey a perceptive vice president of Ford Motor Co., told a gathering of auto engineers:

> I believe that the amount of product innovation successfully introduced into the automobile is smaller today than in previous times and is still falling. The automatic transmission was the last major innovation of the industry.

The automatic transmission, you may recall, was first adopted on a mass-production basis in 1938–39. Henry Ford II seemed troubled by this same lack of innovation when he told the same audience:

> When you think of the enormous progress of science over the last two generations, it is astonishing to realize that there is very little about the basic principles of today's automobiles that would seem strange and unfamiliar to the pioneers of our industry. . . . What we need even more than the refinement of old ideas is the ability to develop new ideas and put them to work.

The smog-ridden people of Los Angeles for many years have been troubled by the same thought as they struggled against an intransigent, unified industry that produced millions of little pollution factories on wheels and refused to apply the necessary remedial engineering to clean them up. Apparently, diagnosis is far from treatment. The 1966 Ford advertisements boast of "engineering magic." The expectant reader, rushing to read on, learns that this "magic" is composed of an optional stereosonic tape system and a station wagon tailgate that swings open for people and pulls down for cargo. With such "magic" our space endeavors would have gotten us no further to the moon than Mount Everest.

The annual model change ritual is not meaningful innovation for the public safety and welfare; its purpose is to "stir the animal" in the car buyer. It is aimed not at the reason of men but at their ids and hypogastria. Can there be anything less than a fundamental contempt for the consumer in the following advertisements:

Senator Curtis: I don't like to interrupt—

Mr. Nader: Yes, sir.

Senator Curtis: But I don't understand your language. "It is aimed not at the reason of men but at their ids and hypogastria." If I ever bought a car for those reasons nobody explained it to me. What does that mean?

Mr. Nader: The ids refer to, in traditional psychology, Senator, to that part of the subconscious which generates the aggressive instincts of man. The hypogastria refers to the lower region of the human abdomen. I shall give examples which will indicate just what I mean.

Senator Curtis: The ids refer to the subconscious aggressive pattern.

Mr. Nader: Yes, sir.

Senator Curtis: I want a car that I can really hit somebody and smash him dead, is that what you mean?

Auto Advertising

Mr. Nader: Well, you see, I am referring to the stimulants by the advertisements in the industry, Senator Curtis, the types of ads you see that say, "Let go of this trigger," and some other examples which I have here such as asking the reader of a Buick Skylark ad headed, "Son of Gun," asking this reader— and I quote from the ad:

> Ever prodded a throttle with 445 pound-feet of torque coiled tightly at the end of it? Do that with one of these; you can start billing yourself as the human cannonball.

Another example taken from the radio: Teenagers can turn on the radio and hear an ad that begins with a deep growl. Is it a cue for Tarzan of the Apes? An announcement of a circus coming to town? By no means. It is the Pontiac widetrack tiger and the announcer urges the listener to come on down and ride the tiger at "Tiger Country," formerly known as your Pontiac dealer.

A 1966 Buick Riviera ad tries this sensual effect:

> If there are two things that romantic Italians love, one of them is automobiles. Dashing, dramatic automobiles. Now, some people think Italy has a monopoly on the red-blooded cars that make hearts beat faster and the adrenalin flow. But those people have another think coming. The tuned car is here, Con Brio.

Other ads urge the potential driver to "drive it like you hate it."

Senator Curtis: Like you what?

Mr. Nader: "Like you hate it" or after spelling out the 400-plus horsepower, advising that "it's cheaper than psychiatry."

While the recent spate of Ford "safety ads," in response to a growing public outrage over unsafe design, urge the reader to "cultivate a safety state of mind . . . thinking safety," (and GM is doing the same) Ford continues to name its cars with such aggressive and ferocious titles as Comet, Meteor, Thunderbird, Cobra, Mustang (Mustang means "a wild, unbreakable horse"), and Marauder (which means literally "one who pillages and lays waste the countryside"). There is also the Plymouth Fury and Barracuda, the Oldsmobile Cutlass, and the Buick Wildcat—to name a few. And coming soon to join the menagerie on the highways are the Mercury Cougar and the Chevrolet Panther.

Senator Curtis: Now, let me ask you what does the name of an automobile have to do with the solid construction there or lack thereof?

Mr. Nader: It has to do with the problem that is before us, Senator, in two ways: One, it is a part of the communication of the concept of the automobile to the public. That communication comes heavily from the automobile manufacturers, I would say almost overwhelmingly. When impressionable people, particularly teenagers, are consistently exposed to this type of aggressive power and sensual insinuation it might have some transferral effect.

Senator Simpson: May I interrupt right here?

Mr. Nader: Yes, sir.

Senator Simpson: This doesn't happen in any other industry, or does it?

Mr. Nader: In transportation, sir?

Senator Simpson: In any kind.

Mr. Nader: In the cosmetics industry there may be rather imaginative titles, but I know of no other industry, besides the auto industry, that involves such a serious safety problem that engages in aggressive and provoking advertisements dealing with the operation and use of its products.

Incidentally, I might add that a tremendous amount of interest in research goes into the automobile company's choice of these names, that is when you want to choose whether to call a car a Panther or not you don't just pick it out of the dictionary. You search the literature to see the context in which the word

"Panther" was and is used, and the image that the Panther gives in fiction, nonfiction, hunting materials, and so forth.

Senator Simpson: What would you be suggesting, just doing away with its advertising?

Mr. Nader: I would suggest—and in this rare instance, Senator Simpson, many automobile executives are in agreement with me—I would suggest that this advertising be toned down and that it be more informative and less provocative.

Senator Simpson: This committee has advocated that since its inception.

Mr. Nader: Pardon, sir?

Senator Simpson: This committee has advocated that since its inception.

Mr. Nader: I understand that, sir. I hope it will be listened to in the immediate future.

The second answer to your question is that it reflects a good deal about the automobile manufacturers' view of the automobile. When they consistently live in this dreamboat fairyland the operating atmosphere leans in this direction. The more they get into a type of fashion industry syndrome in producing a form of transportation that kills so many people, the more they are going to go away from the quality and functional aspects in their own thinking within the industry, and the more they are going to go to the fashion, the ephemeral, the trivial, and the superficial aspects—so that these words are not only a method of communication, they are also symptoms of the type of orientation within the industry.

Senator Curtis: You kind of lost me. I listen to radio and they tell me to put a tiger in my tank.

Does that make me a dangerous driver? Does it change the structure of the automobile I drive, if I would say not to that ad, and still not drive with utmost care, would it give me immunity?

Mr. Nader: Senator, the reception of the audience to the advertisements is not a uniform one. I would be the first to agree that you would not be within the most impressional class of receivers of this information.

Senator Curtis: You mean I am rather stupid?

Mr. Nader: No: on the contrary. This affects mostly, Senator—

Senator Curtis: But do you contend that the ad, and I don't even know what gasoline company promotes this, telling me to put a tiger in their tank, somehow contributes to automobile accidents and fixes the responsibility on manufacturers of gasoline and manufacturers of automobiles. What is your opinion on that?

Mr. Nader: Yes, Senator. Let me answer it this way: Unless the manufacturers have done studies which show no connection between the content of their advertising and the attitudes and behaviors of those who listen to and read their advertisement, then they are acting as imprudent businessmen. That is when you tell somebody that if he gets behind the wheel he can start labeling himself as a human cannonball, unless you have done studies that show no connection, the presumption is that there is some connection, that it is without any utility or any redeeming value whatsoever.

Senator Curtis: Would you go so far as to say that when an automobile company shows their car being driven or observed by a beautiful girl, that that is contributing to the divorce rate in the country?

Mr. Nader: I am restricting myself to the casualty rate, sir.

Senator Curtis: No; let me ask you. You have come up here with ideas and gastro-something or others, and unfolded something that is going on here. I want to ask you, in your approach to the psychology of advertising, are you contending that automobile manufacturers who show a nice shiny car driven by an attractive young lady, and if she gets out of the car or she looks at it or she exclaims concerning it, that that is contributing to the divorce rate in the country?

Mr. Nader: I wouldn't know, Senator. But I would say this: that anybody who—

Senator Curtis: You think it might, then?

Mr. Nader: Pardon?

Senator Curtis: You think it might?

Mr. Nader: It may and it may not. Unless there are studies that show there are not, I wouldn't engage in such advertising. I wouldn't on the one hand urge drivers to think safety, and then expose them to this type of advertising.

Senator Curtis: You advocate a lot of sophisticated type of thought control.

Mr. Nader: Pardon, sir?

Senator Curtis: You seem to advocate a rather sophisticated type of thought control.

Mr. Nader: No. I simply advocate a rather unsophisticated type of sanity in advertising copy. I hope you have the opportunity, Senator, to discuss this question with automobile executives who uniformly deplore this type of advertising, but say that if they don't do it their competitor will do it. They don't try to defend it themselves.

People Must be Heard

As Prof. Jeffrey O'Connell of the University of Illinois Law School asked recently in a letter to the New York Times, detailing some of these calculated appeals to power, speed and other aggressive instincts: "Shall the wolves be shepherds?"

The answer to this question must be "No." It must be "No" for two independently sufficient reasons.

First, a genuine democracy has to provide for the participation of the public in decisions relating to technology whose use is so fraught with tragedy to millions of people. There is an old Roman adage which says: "Whatever touches all should be decided by all." The automobile touches us all in the most ultimate ways. The safety the motorist gets when he buys his car should not be determined solely by manufacturers—especially a tightly knit few—whose interests are necessarily one of profit-parochialism. A democratic policy should not permit an industry to unilaterally decide how many years it wishes to hold back the installation of superior braking systems, safer tires, fuel tanks that do not rupture and incinerate passengers in otherwise survivable accidents—collapsible steering columns, safer instrument panels, steering assemblies, seat structures and frame strengths, or to engage in a stylistic orgy of vehicle-induced glare, chrome eyebrow bumpers and pedestrian impalers—to take only a few examples of many. Instead the amount of safety should be determined, and I stress this, by fuller dialog and resolution clash of values of the entire democratic community. This is hardly a new idea. Our country has applied such a philosophy long ago to other areas of safety—safety codes for buildings and factories, food and drug regulations, safety standards for aircraft, ships and trains, "safety" examinations for professional skills. However inadequate such rules and their administration are, they do represent progress when contrasted with the alternatives. They also represent society's decision that democratic participation is to extend to hazardous economic activities or products.

In the area of automobile design, this public participation to raise continuously the operational and crash worthy safety of motor vehicles does not exist. The automobile has been the "sacred cow." Because of the attenuated competition of a concentrated industry, product choices are being made, in effect, for the consumer by the manufacturers to the extent that they have muted the market signals which consumers would have ideally in exercising their choice or expressing their wishes. More significant, the public has not been able to make its collective judgments felt through the governmental process. This is the case because both the automobile and its maker are in the uniquely privileged position of being outside the law. . . .

Further Resources

BOOKS

Bollier, David. *Citizen Action and Other Big Ideas: A History of Ralph Nader and the Modern Consumer Movement.* Washington, D.C.: Center for Study of Responsive Law, 1991.

Nader, Ralph. *Unsafe at Any Speed: The Designed-in Dangers of the American Automobile.* New York: Grossman, 1965.

Whiteside, Thomas. *The Investigation of Ralph Nader: General Motors vs. One Determined Man.* New York: Arbor House, 1972.

PERIODICALS

Rowe, Jonathan. "Ralph Nader Reconsidered." *The Washington Monthly* 17, no. 2, March 1985.

Van Tune, C. "1965 Corvair Corsa Turbo." *Motor Trend* 42, August 1990, 122-124.

WEBSITES

"Corvair Museum." Corvair Society of America. Available online at http://www.corvair.org/cmuseum.html; website home page: http://www.corvair.org (accessed April 2, 2003).

The Nader Page. Available online at http://www.nader.org/ (accessed April 2, 2003).

Three Years in Mississippi
Nonfiction work

By: James Meredith

Date: 1966

Source: Meredith, James. *Three Years in Mississippi.* Bloomington: Indiana University Press, 1966, 209–214.

About the Author: James Meredith (1933–), the grandson of a slave, grew up on an eighty-four-acre farm near Kosciusko,

Mississippi. From 1951 to 1960, he served in the U.S. Air Force and rose to the rank of staff sergeant. In 1961, he graduated from the all-black Jackson State University. In 1962, Meredith, feeling a personal responsibility to overturn White Supremacy, became the first African American to enroll at the 114-year old, all-white University of Mississippi. ∎

Introduction

In the wake of the Civil War (1861–1865), Radical Republicans abolished slavery in the Thirteenth Amendment and advanced the ideal of racial equality in the Fourteenth and Fifteenth Amendments. For much of the next century, this moral crusade lapsed into apathy. It was not until the Montgomery bus boycott and the emergence of Martin Luther King, Jr., in 1955 that the civil rights movement breathed life into the moribund constitutional promises.

In November 1956, the U.S. Supreme Court upheld a lower court ruling in *Browder vs. Gayle,* in which it declared that segregation on buses unconstitutional. The boycott was significant because it not only had given national visibility to the injustices heaped on southern blacks, but it also demonstrated the effectiveness of mass mobilization. Despite this important victory, the leaders of the civil rights movement altered their tactics in the 1960s. Instead of passively protesting segregation and racial discrimination through boycotts, they became confrontational, directly challenging racist institutions.

James Meredith was an integral member of the civil rights movement. In January 1961, he filled out his application to enroll in the University of Mississippi. Previously, African Americans who tried to gain admittance were denied. In fact, some applicants had been jailed, committed to mental institutions, or hounded from the state. That May, the school denied Meredith's application. Unlike other applicants, Meredith challenged the school to defend its practices in court.

In February 1962, a lower federal court dismissed Meredith's complaint and ruled that he was not denied admission because of his race. Meredith appealed the decision to the U.S. Fifth Circuit Court of Appeals. On June 25, 1962, his twenty-ninth birthday, the court ruled that that from the moment the school discovered Meredith was African American it engaged in a "carefully calculated campaign of delay, harassment, and masterly inactivity." It overturned the decision and ordered the school to enroll Meredith in the autumn session. The decision was appealed to the U.S Supreme Court, which upheld the appeals court decision.

Significance

For more than a year, the high-profile Meredith saga had fixated the state. The legislature was called into a special midnight session to enact a law specifically

President John F. Kennedy delivers a speech on September 30, 1962, via television and radio, asking that University of Mississippi students and state residents accept the enrollment of James Meredith.

© BETTMANN/CORBIS. REPRODUCED BY PERMISSION.

aimed at preventing Meredith from enrolling. Furthermore, Governor Ross Barnett issued a proclamation that the state was sovereign and directed the university to defy the court order. Barnett even had himself appointed university registrar and personally refused Meredith's admission.

On September 30, 1962, President John F. Kennedy ordered the university to admit Meredith and deployed 123 deputy federal marshals, 316 border policemen, and 97 federal prison guards on or near the campus to protect Meredith. When Meredith arrived on campus to register, federal forces were attacked by two thousand rioters who were armed with guns, bricks, bottles, and Molotov cocktails. The violence continued until President Kennedy sent thirty thousand federal troops to secure the campus. In the end, two people died, thirty marshals were shot, and forty-eight American soldiers were injured.

The incident has been called the "biggest domestic military crisis of the twentieth century." Yet, Meredith had integrated perhaps the most racist institution in the nation and graduated with a political science degree the following year.

In response to the Meredith ordeal, which he recounted in *Three Years in Mississippi,* southern white

voters, who had been the backbone of the Democratic Party since the Civil War, started to bolt in large numbers to the Republican Party. This political backlash became apparent in the 1962 congressional election campaign. That year, the Republican vote in the South had risen from 660,000 in 1958, the previous off-year election, to more than 2 million. In Alabama, Senator Lister Hill, a Democrat, faced his first Republican challenger in thirty-seven years and won by less than 1 percent of the vote.

Primary Source

Three Years in Mississippi [excerpt]

SYNOPSIS: In late September 1962, Meredith flew from Memphis to Oxford, Mississippi, the home of the University of Mississippi. He then proceeded to Baxter Hall for the night. Meredith's account of his raucous first couple of days is surprising because of its lack of emotionalism. His matter-of-fact style projects an aura of calm in what must have been a terrifying time.

The Final Preparations

The call now went out all over the United States for U.S. marshals, border patrolmen, and federal prison guards. As political appointees in their local areas, the marshals were not fighting men, nor were all of them trained in the art of riot or mob control. The usual background for a marshal is some form of police work. Moreover, due to the unusual nature of this assignment, it was necessary for the chiefs to have training sessions at Millington Naval Air Station for the marshals.

The marshals brought back some exciting tales about their training-school experiences. One of the problems was the fact that no one could distinguish a marshal from anyone else. The newsmen took immediate advantage of this and joined their ranks. One newsman, less (or more) astute than the others, secured a horse. He somehow convinced the navy guard that he was an inspector and proceeded to the practice area where he reviewed and recorded the action of the trainees and took numerous photographs. Somebody got suspicious and apprehended the horseman. Two of the other newsmen in the ranks then began to feel uncomfortable, especially when the marshals started to look suspiciously at the cameras that they carried instead of guns. They broke out of the ranks and ran for the fence. The military might have its shortcomings but they keep good fences around their installations, and the newsmen were caught. The government was in a worse predicament after they were caught than it had been before. The two newsmen were well-known correspondents for the nation's biggest news media. What would the government do with them? It finally brought them back to the barracks and asked me if I would let them interview me. I had been carefully shielded from the press up to then. I don't know if the newsmen demanded me as an alternative or if the government offered me as a bribe.

In the meantime, the Army was moving in, in great force. The entire Naval Station had been turned into a drill field. One of the most notable things to me was that Negro officers and men were with the army units. Many of the drill sergeants were Negro non-commissioned officers.

No More Advisers

After the last futile attempt to enroll, it was evident that I would become more and more isolated. Finally, on September 29 the moment came when I was left on my own. There were no more advisers at this point. Of course, I could understand the position of the NAACP Legal Defense and Educational Fund, since the case was completely out of the legal field now and they were so far removed from the scene and the pertinent facts, that it would have been unwise for them to advise me to go or not to go.

The Deal

Adding everything up and weighing it, I am absolutely sure that my greatest uncertainty was over the talk about a deal between the federal government and the state of Mississippi. Any one thinking about this matter afterwards might fail to understand or appreciate my apprehension regarding a possible deal during this crucial period. It must always be remembered that I was a Negro in Mississippi and I was acutely aware of my history as a Negro. The Negro had existed for a long time; the whites had existed for a long time; the federal union had existed for a long time; the state of Mississippi had existed for a long time; and the question that we now faced—the extension of citizenship rights to the Negro—was not new. Certainly, there must have been deals made in the past between the federal government and Mississippi. How could I, a Negro, who had never once received my due, and who knew of not one single occasion where any of my foreparents on the Negro side had received his due, not be concerned about this prospect, especially when no official of the federal government would commit himself or his government as to the exact extent of its involvement?

The Flight from Memphis to Oxford

It was Sunday. Barnett had had his greatest day of triumph the day before at the "Ole Miss" football game in Jackson, and General Walker had issued his famous call for volunteers to come to Mississippi. Activity was at a peak at Millington. We would go today. Late in the afternoon we boarded the "Ole Miss" special. Ironically, it was the first time we had changed planes. The Florida pilot had had to return home; we had a new plane and a new pilot, but the three traveling companions—McShane, Doar, and Meredith—were the same. We took off and arrived in Oxford before the final clearance was given; we had to circle the airport for some time before the word came from Washington to land.

The First Night

When we landed, the Oxford airport was unrecognizable. There were rows of Air Force and other planes, mostly transport planes, and hundreds of marshals. The two most noticeable things were the floodlights and the tense atmosphere. We unboarded and hurried through a host of men wearing U.S. deputy marshal armbands, all of whom seemed to close in on us. We then slowly proceeded in a caravan to Baxter Hall and arrived there between dusk and darkness. The campus was completely vacated. There were no obvious signs that school was in session. The entire student body had either caught the "Barnett Special" train to Jackson or found their own means of getting to the football game. Without ceremony, we moved into Baxter Hall to spend the first night; there was not even a dorm chief present to give me the rules of the hall.

My Rooms in Baxter Hall

I suppose you could call it an apartment. Since they knew some government men would be staying with me, I had been assigned two bedrooms, a living room, and a bathroom. The first thing that I did was make my bed. When the trouble started, I could not see or hear very much of it. Most of the events occurred at the other end of the campus, and I did not look out the window. I think I read a newspaper and went to bed around ten o'clock. I was awakened several times in the night by the noise and shooting outside, but it was not near the hall, and I had no way of knowing what was going on. Some of the students in my dormitory banged their doors for a while and threw some bottles in the halls, but I slept pretty well all night.

I woke up about 6:30 in the morning and looked out and saw the troops. There was a slight smell of tear gas in my room, but I still did not know what had gone on during the night. I did not find out, until some marshals came and told me how many people were hurt and killed.

Some newspapermen later asked me if I thought attending the university was worth all this death and destruction. The question really annoyed me. Of course, I was sorry! I hadn't wanted this to happen. I believe it could have been prevented by responsible political leadership in Mississippi. As for the federal government, the President and the Attorney General had all the intelligence facilities at their disposal, and I believe that they handled it to the best of their knowledge and ability. I think it would have been much worse if they had waited any longer. Social change is a painful thing, but the method by which it is achieved depends upon the people at the top. Here they were totally opposed—the state against the federal government. There was bound to be trouble, and there was.

The Registration

There was no lingering or turning back now. At eight o'clock the three of us—McShane, Doar, and Meredith—with a retinue of marshals and soldiers left Baxter Hall for the Lyceum Building to get on with the long-delayed business of my registering as a student at the University of Mississippi. The signs of strife and warfare from the night before were everywhere. But at this moment the power of the United States was supreme. Even the Mississippi National Guard had proven without a doubt that its first loyalty was to the Commander-in-Chief of the Armed Forces of the United States—the President.

The border patrol car in which we rode to the administration building was a shattered example of the violence of social change. We had used this car to make our first attempt to enroll on September 20, 1962, and then it had been a spotless, unmarred specimen. Now it was battered and smashed: bullet holes had riddled the sides; the windows were all shot out. McShane sent one of the deputies back into Baxter Hall to get a couple of Army blankets to put over the back seat so that we could sit down. The marshals had suffered also. It would have been hard to find one who did not bear some mark of the process of violent change: Bandages, bruises, and limps were the rule.

We entered through the back door of the Lyceum Building. Fortunately, I did not know that it was the back door at the time; otherwise, I would have had to confront the question of whether this was a concession to the Mississippi "way of life." It was a dis-

mal day. Even the newsmen were spiritless. Inside the room behind a desk sat Ellis, the Registrar. He was a lone stand-out, the only man on the scene with spirit—a spirit of defiance, even of contempt, if not hatred. Doar stated our purpose and the Registrar pointed to a group of forms to be filled out by me. I looked at them and filled out all but one—my class-schedule form. As I studied it, obviously Ellis knew what was on my mind. One course on my schedule not only was a duplicate of one with the same title which I had already completed with the grade of A, but when I got to the class, I found that the instructor was using the very same textbook. Ellis said to me, "Meredith (he is the only official at the university who did not address me with the usual title of courtesy), you may as well sign." I tried to discuss the matter with him, but it was no use. I signed and decided to take the matter up through other channels. The schedule was later changed to suit my needs.

We left the room. The press had been patient and I consented to stop and talk briefly with them. There was not too much to ask and less to say. The first question asked me was, "Now that you are finally registered, are you happy?" I could only express my true feeling that, "This is no happy occasion." Truly, this was no time for joy.

On my way out of the Lyceum Building, I encountered my first Negro. What would his reaction be? What would our relationship be? What would be our communication? He had his cleaning tools, as all Negroes on the campus must keep them visible, and under one arm was tucked a broom. As I walked past, he acted as if he had not even noticed anything unusual on the campus, but just as I passed he touched me with the handle of his broom and caught my eye. I got the message. Every Negro on the campus was on my team. Every black eye would be watching over me at the University of Mississippi. Later on, I got to know this fellow very well. He told me that he just had to let me know that they were with me all the way, and to bump me with the broom handle was the best way he could think of to communicate with me. . . .

The First Class

At nine I attended my first class; it was a course in Colonial American History. I was a few minutes late and was given a seat at the back of the room. The professor was lecturing on the English background, conditions in England at the time of the colonization of America, and he pretended to pay no

James Meredith is escorted by U.S. Marshals after enrolling at the University of Mississippi on October 1, 1962. AP/WIDE WORLD PHOTOS. REPRODUCED BY PERMISSION.

special attention when I entered. When the U.S. marshals decided to come inside the room, however, he asked them to remain outside. This was a precedent that was followed during my entire stay at the university. I think there were about a dozen students in class. One said hello to me and the others were silent. I remember a girl—the only girl there, I think—and she was crying. But it might have been from the tear gas in the room. I was crying from it myself.

I had three classes scheduled that day. I went to two; the third did not meet because there was too much tear gas in the room.

Return to Baxter Hall

This day, October 1, 1962, was a turning point in my three years in Mississippi. The first phase—to breach the system of "White Supremacy"—had been accomplished; even if I only had a toehold in the door, the solid wall had been cracked.

The return up the hill to Baxter Hall, after attending the classes, also marked a turning point in my own personal struggle to contribute what I could

to the fight for human freedom and dignity. I felt a sudden release of pressure that I perhaps cannot put into words. I recall that I remarked to John Doar about this feeling of relief, and he did not seem to understand at all. Perhaps this was not the time for philosophizing, since I was the only one who had gotten any rest the night before. But I had the feeling that my personal battle was over. The pressure from that inner doubt, always present in one's mind, that one's best might not be good enough, was now released. The often debated question of whether or not I would break before the system bulged no longer troubled my mind.

To me, it seemed that the ultimate outcome was relatively insignificant; whether or not I went on to graduate appeared to be a minor issue. The important thing was that I had the privilege of choice. At the same time I was aware that Negroes recognized only "Success" and "Titles," and I had bypassed the title several times, knowing full well that if I should fail in this effort, I would be soon forgotten. However, as we slowly ascended the hill toward Baxter Hall, it appeared to me that the particular steps that

I had chosen to take in an effort to carry out the mandate of my Divine Responsibility had been proper and timely.

Further Resources

BOOKS

Doyle, William. *An American Insurrection: The Battle of Oxford, Mississippi, 1962.* New York: Doubleday, 2001.

Martin, John Barlow. *The Deep South Says Never.* New York: Ballantine, 1957.

PERIODICALS

"Battle of Words on Who Is to Blame: Accounts by Top Federal and State Officials." *U.S. News and World Report,* October 15, 1962.

"Though the Heavens Fall: Race Riot at University of Mississippi." *Time,* October 12, 1962.

WEBSITES

"African American Odyssey: The Civil Rights Era." American Memory Historical Collections for the National Digital Library, Library of Congress. Available online at http://memory.loc.gov/ammem/aaohtml/exhibit/aopart9.html; website home page: http://memory.loc.gov/ammem/ (accessed April 2, 2003).

"Ole Miss, 40 Years Later: Weighing the Impact of a Watershed in Desegregation." National Public Radio, October 1, 2002. Available online at http://discover.npr.org/features/feature.jhtml?wfId=1150902; website home page: http://www.npr.org (accessed June 2, 2003).

"Mutual Deterrence"

Speech

By: Robert S. McNamara

Date: September 18, 1967

Source: McNamara, Robert S. "Mutual Deterrence." September 18, 1967. Reproduced in CNN Cold War Historical Documents. Available online at http://www.cnn.com/SPECIALS/cold.war/episodes/12/documents/mcnamara.deterrence/; website home page: http://www.cnn.com/SPECIALS/cold.war/ (accessed April 2, 2003).

About the Author: Robert S. McNamara (1916–), born in San Francisco, California, earned a master's in business administration from Harvard University. McNamara served in the military during World War II (1939–1945) as a supply and management expert. In 1946 he joined Ford Motor Company as an efficiency expert. By 1960 he was president of Ford. In 1961, McNamara was appointed Secretary of Defense. Serving until 1968, Secretary McNamara oversaw much of the United States' early involvement in the Vietnam War (1964–75). From 1968 until 1981, McNamara was president of the World Bank internationl development agency. Subsequent to this he served on corporate boards and wrote extensively on foreign policy. ■

Introduction

During the Cold War years, President Dwight D. Eisenhower (served 1953–1961) and the North Atlantic Treaty Organization (NATO) anticipated Soviet conventional forces rushing through the Fulda Gap, across the German plains, and overwhelming the Western democracies.

To counter this threat, Eisenhower, who considered NATO ground troops too expensive to deploy, sought to deter Soviet aggression with nuclear weapons. The president's assumption was that if Moscow invaded West Germany, the United States would turn Moscow into a smoking crater two hours later. This strategy was called the doctrine of massive retaliation.

There were, however, two major problems with this doctrine. First, it provided no alternative responses to Soviet confrontations that were limited in scope. For example, in 1953, when the Soviets suppressed an anticommunist rebellion in East Berlin, the Soviets knew that the United States would not counter with a nuclear strike. The second flaw in the doctrine was evident in 1957 when the Soviets launched their first intercontinental ballistic missile, which had the capability of reaching the United States. Now that the United States was vulnerable to a Soviet nuclear strike, the massive retaliation doctrine lost credibility with the United States' European allies. No matter what American policy makers said to the contrary, the Europeans knew that the United States was not prepared to risk the fate of New York for that of Berlin.

In October 1961, Soviet premier Nikita Khrushchev demonstrated to the world that the Russians had reached nuclear parity with the United States by exploding the largest bomb that the world had ever seen to date. The explosion, which was the equivalent of more than fifty million tons of dynamite and more than all explosives used in World War II, knocked people off their feet fifty miles away.

Significance

With the Soviets possessing long-range missiles and stockpiling nuclear warheads, President John F. Kennedy's (served 1961–1963) secretary of defense Robert S. McNamara devised a new military doctrine. Believing that nuclear arms served no military purpose other than as exorbitantly expensive deterrents, McNamara at first refused military requests to allocate defense dollars for nuclear weapons systems. Instead, he favored the doctrine of flexible response. Under this doctrine, The United States' conventional forces in Europe were bolstered, giving the military multiple nonnuclear options to deal with a crisis.

In 1962, in the aftermath of the Soviet's withdrawal of nuclear missiles from Cuba, Khrushchev embarked on a massive nuclear arms buildup. By 1967, McNamara had come to the realization that nuclear disarmament was not realistic and that the only way that nuclear war could be averted was by the threat of mutual assured destruction (MAD).

The basic concept of MAD is simple: No one would dare start a nuclear war if they knew that it would lead in turn to their own destruction. Thus if the Soviet Union and the United States both had huge numbers of nuclear weapons, ready to be fired on short notice, then neither could afford to start a nuclear war with the other.

By 1969, the Soviet Union and the United States were spending a combined $50 million a day on nuclear armaments. For over a decade, the two superpowers continued to aggressively build weapons, eventually resulting in each nation possessing thousands of nuclear warheads, with the capability of destroying all life on Earth.

Since a war between the United States and the Soviet Union did not occur during this period, MAD can be considered a success of sorts. However it is impossible to say if it was really MAD that prevented a war, or other factors. One thing is certain, the massive arms build-up that was part of the MAD strategy was very expensive. And while it might be preventing war, the thought that both the United States and the Soviet Union were prepared to destroy mankind on a moment's notice was disturbing to many people.

When President Ronald Reagan (served 1981–1989) was elected in 1980, he decided that the American people should no longer have to live under the constant fear of a massive Soviet attack. In March 1983, he signed National Security Decision Directive 85, which ended the country's complete dependence on MAD and moved toward the development of the Strategic Defense Initiative (SDI), also known as "Star Wars." This system would position large numbers of space satellites to detect the launch of Soviet missiles and shoot them down. It was controversial, in part because of its enormous expense and partly because by giving the United States a defense against nuclear attack it would end MAD and create the possibility of U.S. nuclear attacks against which no response could be made. SDI was never implemented on a significant scale, as the Soviet Union first took steps to improve relations with the United States during the 1980s and then, in the 1990s, the nation collapsed entirely.

Primary Source

"Mutual Deterrence"

> **SYNOPSIS:** In his speech, McNamara explains the mutually assured destruction (MAD) doctrine as a defense against nuclear war. He stresses that the United States will never allow the Soviet Union to

Defense Secretary Robert McNamara speaks at a press conference at the Pentagon, September 7, 1967. He argued that if the Soviets knew that an attack on the United States would guarantee the equivalent destruction of the USSR, then the Soviets would be less likely to attack.
© BETTMANN/CORBIS. REPRODUCED BY PERMISSION.

develop "first strike" capability, meaning that the United States is committed to developing a nuclear arsenal so large and powerful that even if many of its weapons are destroyed in a surprise attack, it will retain the ability to destroy its enemies. Since anyone who launches a nuclear attack on the United States will face "assured destruction," no one will do so.

In a complex and uncertain world, the gravest problem that an American Secretary of Defense must face is that of planning, preparation and policy against the possibility of thermonuclear war. It is a prospect that most of mankind understandably would prefer not to contemplate. For technology has now circumscribed us all with a horizon of horror that could dwarf any catastrophe that has befallen man in his more than a million years on earth.

Man has lived now for more than twenty years in what we have come to call the Atomic Age. What we sometimes overlook is that every future age of man will be an atomic age, and if man is to have a future at all, it will have to be one overshadowed with the permanent possibility of thermonuclear holocaust. About that fact there is no longer any doubt. Our freedom in this question consists only in facing the matter rationally and realistically and discussing actions to minimize the danger.

No sane citizen, political leader or nation wants thermonuclear war. But merely not wanting it is not enough. We must understand the differences among actions which increase its risks, those which reduce them and those which, while costly, have little influence one way or another. But there is a great difficulty in the way of constructive and profitable debate over the issues, and that is the exceptional complexity of nuclear strategy. Unless these complexities are well understood rational discussion and decision-making are impossible.

One must begin with precise definitions. The cornerstone of our strategic policy continues to be to deter nuclear attack upon the United States or its allies. We do this by maintaining a highly reliable ability to inflict unacceptable damage upon any single aggressor or combination of aggressors at any time during the course of a strategic nuclear exchange, even after absorbing a surprise first strike. This can be defined as our assured-destruction capability.

It is important to understand that assured destruction is the very essence of the whole deterrence concept. We must possess an actual assured-destruction capability, and that capability also must be credible. The point is that a potential aggressor must believe that our assured-destruction capability is in fact actual, and that our will to use it in retaliation to an attack is in fact unwavering. The conclusion, then, is clear: if the United States is to deter a nuclear attack in itself or its allies, it must possess an actual and a credible assured-destruction capability.

When calculating the force required, we must be conservative in all our estimates of both a potential aggressor's capabilities and his intentions. Security depends upon assuming a worst plausible case, and having the ability to cope with it. In that eventuality we must be able to absorb the total weight of nuclear attack on our country—on our retaliatory forces, on our command and control apparatus, on our industrial capacity, on our cities, and on our population—and still be capable of damaging the aggressor to the point that his society would be simply no longer viable in twentieth-century terms. That is what deterrence of nuclear aggression means. It means the certainty of suicide to the aggressor, not merely to his military forces, but to his society as a whole.

Let us consider another term: first-strike capability. This is a somewhat ambiguous term, since it could mean simply the ability of one nation to attack another nation with nuclear forces first. But as it is normally used, it connotes much more: the elimination of the attacked nation's retaliatory second-strike forces. This is the sense in which it should be understood.

Clearly, first-strike capability is an important strategic concept. The United States must not and will not permit itself ever to get into a position in which another nation, or combination of nations, would possess a first-strike capability against it. Such a position not only would constitute an intolerable threat to our security, but it obviously would remove our ability to deter nuclear aggression.

We are not in that position today, and there is no foreseeable danger of our ever getting into that position. Our strategic offensive forces are immense: 1,000 Minuteman missile launchers, carefully protected below ground; 41 Polaris submarines carrying 656 missile launchers, with the majority hidden beneath the seas at all times; and about 600 long-range bombers, approximately 40 percent of which are kept always in a high state of alert.

Our alert forces alone carry more than 2,200 weapons, each averaging more than the explosive equivalent of one megaton of TNT. Four hundred of these delivered on the Soviet Union would be sufficient to destroy over one-third of her population and one-half of her industry. All these flexible and highly reliable forces are equipped with devices that ensure their penetration of Soviet defenses.

Now what about the Soviet Union? Does it today possess a powerful nuclear arsenal? The answer is that it does. Does it possess a first-strike capability against the United States? The answer is that it does not. Can the Soviet Union in the foreseeable future acquire such a first-strike capability against the United States? The answer is that it cannot. It cannot because we are determined to remain fully alert and we will never permit our own assured-destruction capability to drop to a point at which a Soviet first-strike capability is even remotely feasible.

Is the Soviet Union seriously attempting to acquire a first-strike capability against the United States? Although this is a question we cannot answer with absolute certainty, we believe the answer is no. In any event, the question itself is—in a sense—irrelevant: for the United States will maintain and, where necessary strengthen its retaliatory forces so that, whatever the Soviet Union's intentions or actions, we will continue to have an assured-destruction capability vis a vis their society.

Further Resources

BOOKS

Gaddis, John Lewis. *Strategies of Containment: A Critical Appraisal of Postwar American National Security.* Cambridge: Oxford University Press, 1982.

Halberstam, David. *The Best and the Brightest.* New York: Random House, 1972.

Roherty, James H. *Decisions of Robert S. McNamara: A Study of the Role of the Secretary of Defense.* Miami: University of Miami Press, 1970.

PERIODICALS

Cannon, Lou. "Reagan's Big Idea." *National Review,* February 22, 1999, 40.

Krepon, Michael. "Are Missile Defenses MAD? Will New U.S. Missile Defenses Zap the Nuclear Stalemate Born of Mutual Assured Destruction? They Are Neither That Good a Shot Nor That Bad a Strategy." *Foreign Affairs* 74, January 1995, 19.

WEBSITES

"MAD 1960–1972." CNN Cold War Historical Documents. Available online at http://www.cnn.com/SPECIALS/cold.war/episodes/12; website home page: http://www.cnn.com/SPECIALS/cold.war/ (accessed April 2, 2003).

"Nuclearfiles.org: A Project of the Nuclear Age Peace Foundation." Nuclear Age Peace Foundation. Available online at http://www.nuclearfiles.org/index.html (accessed April 2, 2003).

Codes of Conduct and the My Lai Massacre

"Nine Rules"; "The Enemy in Your Hands"; "Guidance for Commanders in Vietnam"

Codes of conduct

By: Military Assistance Command, Vietnam

Date: September 1967

Source: Military Assistance Command, Vietnam. "Nine Rules," "The Enemy in Your Hands," and "Guidance for Commanders in Vietnam." September 1967. Available online at http://www.law.umkc.edu/faculty/projects/ftrials/mylai/myl_wmac.htm; website home page: http://www.law.umkc.edu/faculty/projects/ftrials/ftrials.htm (accessed April 2, 2003).

About the Organization: The Military Assistance Command, Vietnam (MACV) was established in February 1962. Originally, its presence in Vietnam was to be short-lived,

departing once the Vietcong (VC) rebellion was defeated. As the American presence in South Vietnam increased, however, so too did MACV's responsibilities. MACV controlled all U.S. military operations, coordinated U.S. intelligence operations, and assisted South Vietnam to maintain internal security. ■

Introduction

In 1967, the United States was in the midst of an undeclared war in Southeast Asia. At issue was Vietnam (or Indochina). Formerly a French colony, the region had been split into two countries in 1954 after Communist rebels succeeded in driving out the French. The Communists, led by Ho Chi Minh, were in command of North Vietnam. South Vietnam was put under control of anti-Communist Ngo Dinh Diem. The region was to be reunified and democratic elections held in 1956. The United States feared that the popular Minh would win these elections, however, and supported Diem's efforts to keep South Vietnam independent. Fighting soon broke out between South Vietnam and the pro-Communist Viet Cong (VC) guerillas inside of South Vietnam. Over the next decade the United States committed an ever increasing amount of men and material to supporting the South, eventually becoming heavily involved in the ground fighting in South Vietnam while also launching air raids against the North.

The U.S. military found the VC to be a difficult enemy to fight because of their guerilla tactics. The VC avoided the large, decisive battles that American troops were trained for, instead striking unexpectedly where U.S. forces were weak and then hiding in the jungle, an environment U.S. troops were unfamiliar with. Instead of trying to capture and hold ground they moved about frequently, making them very difficult to find and attack. The VC also made extensive use of snipers, mines, and other traps. Supported by many in the South Vietnamese population, they could often get supplies in villages or blend in among the civilian population there.

All of these factors made fighting the VC a difficult and demoralizing task for U.S. troops. Men were injured or killed by enemies that they seldom saw or were able to fight back against with full force. In all wars there is a tendency for soldiers to dehumanize their enemies, to see them as less than human and undeserving of any respect or humane treatment. The conditions U.S. soliders were experiencing in Vietnam encouraged this sort of sentiment. Yet the United States was committed by treaties and its own morals to protect innocent people and to treat captured enemy troops humanely.

Starting in September 1967, Military Assistance Command, Vietnam (MACV) provided two hours of instructions on the rights of VC prisoners to all U.S. armed forces personnel. In addition, it issued the wallet-size

P-14   SP4 Dustin (Haeberle B&W)

A soldier of Charlie Company sets fire to a thatch-covered hut during the massacre at My Lai on March 16, 1968. As many as 500 unarmed civilians were killed and the village was detroyed. **DOUBLE DELTA INDUSTRIES, INC.**

pocket card "Nine Rules," which encouraged soldiers to "treat women with politeness and respect" and make "personal friends" among the "common people." It also issued the pocket cards "The Enemy In Your Hands," which ordered soldiers to comply with the Geneva Prisoner of War Convention, and "Guidance for Commanders in Vietnam," which listed objectives for field commanders. All of these were attempts to maintain the discipline and professionalism of U.S. troops in Vietnam.

Significance

The failure of MACV's efforts can be seen in the tragedy of My Lai. In November 1967, U.S. forces engaged the VC in a vicious battle in the hills of Dak To. The nearby village of My Lai also witnessed fighting while the VC heavily mined and booby trapped the surrounding paddy fields and jungle. In December, Charley Company of the First Battalion arrived in Vietnam. Throughout February and March of the next year, VC mines and traps inflicted significant casualties on the company. To the Americans' mounting frustration, however, they had yet to directly encounter the enemy.

On March 14, a small squad from Charley Company ran into another booby trap, killing a popular sergeant. Following the next day's memorial service, Captain Ernest L. Medina, a career military officer, discussed the following day's mission. Medina informed his men that the VC's formidable Forty-eighth Battalion was in the vicinity of My Lai. He stated that the company would finally engage the enemy, razing and torching its homes, killing its livestock, and poisoning its wells. It is not clear, however, whether or not Medina ordered that My Lai's citizens be attacked.

On the morning of March 16, nine helicopters carrying Charlie Company landed about a quarter of a mile from My Lai. When Charley Company entered the village, it did not encounter any VC or any males of military age. Without receiving a single round of enemy fire, several members of the company randomly opened fire on anything that moved. A middle-aged man was thrown down a well to be followed by a grenade. Twenty women, who were kneeling in prayer, were executed. Between seventy and eighty old men, women, and children were pushed into a drainage ditch and shot point blank. At one point, a two-year-old child escaped and was pitched back into the ditch and killed. In four brief hours, My Lai was destroyed and most of its inhabitants were murdered. In total, approximately five hundred people were killed there, apparently none of them members of the VC.

Not all of the Americans present at My Lai participated in the massacre. While the atrocity unfolded below him, helicopter pilot Hugh Thompson landed between fleeing villagers and hard-charging Americans. Thomp-son shepherded the villagers onto other gunships, ordering his crew to turn their guns on his countrymen if they intervened.

Initially, the military covered up the massacre. The army reported that the operation was a great success with 128 enemy soldiers dead and one American casualty. In December 1968, Ronald Ridenhour, a former soldier, reported the incident to a congressman, who pressed for an investigation. The following September, Lieutenant William Calley, who commanded the operation, was charged with 109 murders. Two months later, the massacre was reported in *The New York Times*. The truth about My Lai was soon known to the American public. In March 1971, Calley was found guilty of executing twenty-two Vietnamese in the longest court martial in American history. In 1974, his sentence was reduced from life imprisonment to parole.

The My Lai massacre not only raised important questions of whether or not the bloodbath was an isolated incident, but it also stoked the fires of the antiwar movement on the home front.

Primary Source

"Nine Rules"; "The Enemy in Your Hands";
"Guidance for Commanders in Vietnam"

SYNOPSIS: These three codes of conduct were issued to U.S. servicemen and officers in Vietnam. They reminded the troops of their duty as professional soldiers to respect the Geneva Prisoner of War Convention of 1949 and treat prisoners humanely. In addition, they stressed that troops should act with restraint and respect when dealing with Vietnam's civilian population. Had these rules been followed, the My Lai massacre of March 16, 1968, would not have occurred.

Nine Rules

Rules

The Vietnamese have paid a heavy price in suffering for their long fight against the communists. We military men are in Vietnam now because their government has asked us to help its soldiers and people in winning their struggle. The Viet Cong will attempt to turn the Vietnamese people against you. You can defeat them at every turn by the strength, understanding, and generosity you display with the people. Here are nine simple rules:

1. Remember we are guests here: We make no demands and seek no special treatment.

2. Join with the people! Understand their life, use phrases from their language and honor their customs and laws.

3. Treat women with politeness and respect.

4. Make personal friends among the soldiers and common people.

5. Always give the Vietnamese the right of way.

6. Be alert to security and ready to react with your military skill.

7. Don't attract attention by loud, rude or unusual behavior.

8. Avoid separating yourself from the people by a display of wealth or privilege.

9. Above all else you are members of the U.S. Military Forces on a difficult mission, responsible for all your official and personal actions. Reflect honor upon yourself and the United States of America.

The Enemy in Your Hands

As a member of the U.S. Military Forces, you will comply with the Geneva Prisoner of War Convention of 1949 to which your country adheres. Under these Conventions:

You can and will:

- Disarm your prisoner.

- Immediately search him thoroughly.

- Require him to be silent.

- Segregate him from other prisoners.

- Guard him carefully.

- Take him to the place designated by your commander.

You cannot and must not:

- Mistreat your prisoner.

- Humiliate or degrade him.

- Take any of his personal effects that do not have significant military value.

- Refuse him medical treatment if required and available.

ALWAYS TREAT YOUR PRISONER HUMANELY

KEY PHRASES

English–Vietnamese

Halt . . . . Dung Lai

Lay down your gun . . . . Buong sung xuong

Put up your hands. . . . . Dua tay len

Keep your hands on your head. . . Dau tay len dau

I will search you. . . . . Toi Kham ong

Do not talk . . . . Lai dang kia

Turn Right . . . . Xay ben phai

Turn Left. Xay ben trai

1. *Handle him firmly, promptly, but humanely.*

The captive must be disarmed, searched, secured and watched. But he must also be treated at all times as a human being. He must not be tortured, killed, mutilated, or degraded, even if he refuses to talk. If the captive is a woman, treat her with all respect due her sex.

2. *Take the captive quickly to security.*

As soon as possible evacuate the captive to a place of safety and interrogation designated by your commander. Military documents taken from the captive are also sent to the interrogators, but the captive will keep his personal equipment except weapons.

3. *Mistreatment of any captive is a criminal offense. Every soldier is personally responsible for the enemy in his hands.*

It is both dishonorable and foolish to mistreat a captive. It is also a punishable offense. Not even a beaten enemy will surrender if he knows his captors will torture or kill him. He will resist and make his capture more costly. Fair treatment of captives encourages the enemy to surrender.

4. *Treat the sick and wounded captive as best you can.*

The captive saved may be an intelligence source. In any case he is a human being and must be treated like one. The soldier who ignores the sick and wounded degrades his uniform.

5. *All persons in your hands, whether suspects, civilians, or combat captives, must be protected against violence, insults, curiosity, and reprisals of any kind.*

Leave punishment to the courts and judges. The soldier shows his strength by his fairness and humanity to the persons in his hands.

Guidance for Commanders in Vietnam

1. Make the welfare of your men your primary concern with special attention to mess, mail, and medical care.

2. Give priority emphasis to matters of intelligence, counter-intelligence, and timely and ac-

curate reporting.

3. Gear your command for sustained operations: keep constant pressure on the enemy.

4. React rapidly with all force available to opportunities to destroy the enemy; disrupt enemy bases, capturing or destroying his supply caches.

5. Open up methodically and use roads, waterways, and the railroad; be alert and prepared to ambush the ambusher.

6. Harass enemy lines of communication by raids and ambushes.

7. Use your firepower with care and discrimination, particularly in populated areas.

8. Capitalize on psywar opportunities.

9. Assist in "revolutionary development" with emphasis on priority areas and on civic action wherever feasible.

10. Encourage and help Vietnamese military and paramilitary units; involve them in your operations at every opportunity.

11. Be smarter and more skillful than the enemy; stimulate professionalism, alertness and tactical ingenuity; seize every opportunity to enhance training of men and units.

12. Keep your officers and men well informed, aware of the nine rules for personnel of MACV, and mindful of the techniques of communist insurgency and the role of free world forces in Vietnam.

13. Maintain an alert "open door" policy on complaints and sensitivity to detection and correction of malpractice.

14. Recognize bravery and outstanding work.

15. Inspect frequently units two echelons below your level in insure compliance with the foregoing.

Further Resources

BOOKS

Caputo, Philip. *A Rumor of War.* New York: Holt, Rinehart and Winston, 1977.

Herring, George G. *America's Longest War.* New York: McGraw-Hill, 1996.

Moore, Harold G. *We Were Soldiers Once . . . And Young: Ia Drang, the Battle That Changed the War in Vietnam.* New York: Random House, 1992.

PERIODICALS

Range, Peter. "Rusty Calley: Unlikely Villain." *Time,* April 12, 1971.

Smith, Jack P. "Death in the Ia Drang Valley." *Saturday Evening Post,* January 28, 1967.

WEBSITES

"Into the Dark: The My Lai Massacre." Crime Library. Available online at http://www.crimelibrary.com/notorious _murders/mass/lai/index_1.html; website home page: http:// www.crimelibrary.com/index.html (accessed April 2, 2003).

"The My Lai Courts-Martial 1970." Famous Trials, University of Missouri, Kansas City, School of Law. Available online at http://www.law.umkc.edu/faculty/projects/ftrials/mylai /mylai.htm; website home page: http://www.law.umkc.edu (accessed April 2, 2003).

"President Lyndon B. Johnson's Address to the Nation Announcing Steps to Limit the War in Vietnam and Reporting His Decision Not to Seek Reelection"

Speech

By: Lyndon B. Johnson

Date: March 31, 1968

Source: Johnson. Lyndon B. "President Lyndon B. Johnson's Address to the Nation Announcing Steps to Limit the War in Vietnam and Reporting His Decision Not to Seek Reelection." March 31, 1968. In *Public Papers of the Presidents of the United States: Lyndon B. Johnson, 1968–69.* Vol. 1. Washington, D.C.: U.S. Government Printing Office, 1970.

About the Author: Lyndon B. Johnson (1908–1973) was born near Stonewall, Texas. In 1930, he earned a degree from South West Texas State Teachers College. After teaching English in Houston, he worked as a congressional staffer in Washington, D.C. In 1937, he was elected to the U.S. House of Representatives. In 1955, his Senate colleagues elected him majority leader, the most powerful member of the Senate. In 1960, he was elected vice president of the United States, and later served as president. ■

Introduction

In the 1964 election, Lyndon B. Johnson ran against Senator Barry Goldwater from Arizona. A hawkish anti-communist, Goldwater once joked about tossing a nuclear bomb into the Kremlin's bathroom. During the campaign, Johnson, running as the peace candidate, said, "We are not going to send American boys nine or ten thousand miles away from home to do what Asian boys ought to be doing for themselves."

Johnson won the election by the largest margin of popular votes in American history, forty-three million to twenty-seven million. The landslide victory afforded Johnson (served 1963–1969) the opportunity to pass much of his liberal domestic agenda. However, after 1966 financial funding for his Great Society programs was consumed by the Vietnam War (1964–1975). Although Johnson regretted prematurely ending what would be his domestic policy legacy, he feared losing South Vietnam to the communists and forever being tarred a coward or an appeaser.

In mid-1965, Johnson was an extremely popular figure. Within two years, however, his public approval ratings plummeted from 70 percent to 40 percent. Johnson's slide in popularity mirrored the United States' increasing involvement in Vietnam. From November 1965 to March 1968, the number of American troops in Vietnam increased from 175,000 to over 500,000.

Opposition to the war affected the 1968 presidential campaign when Senator Eugene McCarthy, a Democrat from Wisconsin, made an extraordinary decision to challenge the incumbent wartime president. Running as the antiwar alternative, McCarthy drew considerable support in February 1968 following the Vietcong's (VC) Tet offensive against South Vietnam. VC forces attacked thirty-six of the forty-four provincial capitals and five of the six major cities, including Saigon. The offensive, though a military blunder, contradicted U.S. government statements that it was winning the war and bolstered the antiwar movement.

Significance

After the Tet offensive, support for the manner in which Johnson was managing the war fell from 56 percent to 28 percent. In March 1968, Johnson won the first Democratic primary election in New Hampshire. McCarthy, however, received an unprecedented 42 percent of the vote. Recognizing that the president was vulnerable, Senator Robert Kennedy of New York, who had earlier decided not to run, announced his own candidacy.

The beginning and end of Johnson's presidency were shrouded in grave adversity. He was suddenly elevated to the presidency by the assassination of his predecessor and later chose not to run for reelection because of the United States' escalating involvement in the Vietnam War.

After taking office, Johnson advanced John F. Kennedy's (served 1961–1963) idealism through his Great Society programs and civil rights legislation. However, his management of the war helped usher in an era of increased public suspicion toward the federal government. In the fall of 1968, the Democrat Hubert Humphrey lost to Richard M. Nixon, who claimed to have a "secret plan" to end the bloodshed. The war, however, dragged on for several more years. On January 22, 1973, John-son died, one day before the Paris Peace Accords ending the Vietnam War were concluded.

Primary Source

"President Lyndon B. Johnson's Address to the Nation Announcing Steps to Limit the War in Vietnam and Reporting His Decision Not to Seek Reelection" [excerpt]

SYNOPSIS: On March 31, 1968, Johnson became a casualty of the Vietnam War. Before a surprised nationwide audience, he announced that he would not seek reelection. He vowed to devote the remainder of his term to a quest for peace. On May 10, 1968, preliminary peace talks between the United States and North Vietnam began in Paris.

Finally, my fellow Americans, let me say this:

Of those to whom much is given, much is asked. I cannot say and no man could say that no more will be asked of us.

Yet, I believe that now, no less than when the decade began, this generation of Americans is willing to "pay any price, bear any burden, meet any hardship, support any friend, oppose any foe to assure the survival and the success of liberty."

Since those words were spoken by John F. Kennedy, the people of America have kept that compact with mankind's noblest cause.

And we shall continue to keep it.

Yet, I believe that we must always be mindful of this one thing, whatever the trials and the tests ahead. The ultimate strength of our country and our cause will lie not in powerful weapons or infinite resources or boundless wealth, but will lie in the unity of our people.

This I believe very deeply.

Throughout my entire public career I have followed the personal philosophy that I am a free man, an American, a public servant, and a member of my party, in that order always and only.

For 37 years in the service of our Nation, first as a Congressman, as a Senator, and as Vice President, and now as your President, I have put the unity of the people first. I have put it ahead of any divisive partisanship.

And in these times as in times before, it is true that a house divided against itself by the spirit of faction, of party, of region, of religion, of race, is a house that cannot stand.

This sketch depicts Lyndon Johnson during his address to the nation in which he announces he will not seek reelection, 1968. © FRANKLIN MCMAHON/CORBIS. REPRODUCED BY PERMISSION.

There is division in the American house now. There is divisiveness among us all tonight. And holding the trust that is mine, as President of all the people, I cannot disregard the peril to the progress of the American people and the hope and the prospect of peace for all peoples.

So, I would ask all Americans, whatever their personal interests or concern, to guard against divisiveness and all its ugly consequences.

Fifty-two months and 10 days ago, in a moment of tragedy and trauma, the duties of this office fell upon me. I asked then for your help and God's, that we might continue America on its course, binding up our wounds, healing our history, moving forward in new unity, to clear the American agenda and to keep the American commitment for all of our people.

United we have kept that commitment. United we have enlarged that commitment.

Through all time to come, I think America will be a stronger nation, a more just society, and a land of greater opportunity and fulfillment because of what we have all done together in these years of unparalleled achievement.

Our reward will come in the life of freedom, peace, and hope that our children will enjoy through ages ahead.

What we won when all of our people united just must not now be lost in suspicion, distrust, selfishness, and politics among any of our people.

Believing this as I do, I have concluded that I should not permit the Presidency to become involved in the partisan divisions that are developing in this political year.

With America's sons in the fields far away, with America's future under challenge right here at home, with our hopes and the world's hopes for peace in the balance every day, I do not believe that I should devote an hour or a day of my time to any personal partisan causes or to any duties other than the awesome duties of this office—the Presidency of your country.

Accordingly, I shall not seek, and I will not accept, the nomination of my party for another term as your President.

But let men everywhere know, however, that a strong, a confident, and a vigilant America stands ready tonight to seek an honorable peace—and stands ready tonight to defend an honored cause—whatever the price, whatever the burden, whatever the sacrifice that duty may require.

Thank you for listening.

Good night and God bless all of you.

Further Resources

BOOKS

Dallek, Robert. *Flawed Giant: Lyndon Johnson and His Times, 1961–1973.* New York: Oxford University Press, 1998.

Halberstam, David. *The Best and the Brightest.* New York: Random House, 1969.

Kearns, Doris. *Lyndon Johnson and the American Dream.* New York: Harper and Row, 1976.

PERIODICALS

Dallek, Robert. "Lyndon Johnson and Vietnam: The Making of a Tragedy." *Diplomatic History* 20, 1996, 147–163.

Nelson, Justin A. "Drafting Lyndon Johnson: The President's Secret Role in the 1968 Democratic Convention." *Presidential Studies Quarterly* 30, 2000, 688–713.

WEBSITES

"Lyndon Baines Johnson." Presidents of the United States (POTUS), Internet Public Library. Available online at http://www.ipl.org/ref/potus/lbjohnson.html; website home page: http://www.ipl.org/ref/potus/ (accessed April 2, 2003).

"Lydon B. Johnson: The War on Poverty President." The American President. Available online at http://www.americanpresident.org/kotrain/courses/lbj/lbj_in_brief.htm; website home page: http://www.americanpresident.org (accessed April 2, 2003).

6

LAW AND JUSTICE

SCOTT A. MERRIMAN

Entries are arranged in chronological order by date of primary source. For entries with one primary source, the entry title is the same as the primary source title. Entries with more than one primary source have an overall entry title, followed by the titles of the primary sources.

Important Events in Law and Justice, 1960–1969

1960

- On June 26, the Supreme Court decides *Hannah v. Slawson,* which allows the Civil Rights Commission to keep secret the identities of persons submitting complaints, to protect them from retaliation.

- In December, President John F. Kennedy announces his choice for attorney general, his brother Robert F. Kennedy.

1961

- On May 20, after a white mob attacks a racially-mixed group of bus riders known as "Freedom Riders," Attorney General Kennedy sends four hundred marshals and other law enforcement officials to Montgomery, Alabama, to restore order.

- On May 29, the Supreme Court holds in *Braunfeld v. Brown* that Pennsylvania's Sunday Closing Law did not violate the Free Exercise Clause of the First Amendment. The high court reaches the same conclusion in *McGowan v. Maryland.*

- On June 5, the Supreme Court issues the *Scales v. United States* opinion holding that membership in a Communist organization advocating the violent overthrow of the government is not protected by the First Amendment.

- On June 19, in *Mapp v. Ohio,* the Supreme Court applies the exclusionary rule to illegal searches and seizures by state police, meaning that illegally obtained evidence must be excluded in state criminal proceedings.

- On November 20, in *Hoyt v. Florida,* the Supreme Court rules that a Florida statute excluding women from juries unless they volunteer for service is constitutional.

- In November, the Civil Rights Commission releases its second report. Its five volumes recount disturbing episodes of police brutality against African Americans in both the North and South. It calls for federal grants to upgrade police forces and for new laws allowing victims of such violence to sue local governments for damages.

1962

- On March 26, in *Baker v. Carr,* the Supreme Court enunciates the principal of one man, one vote, and opens the courts to citizens seeking to challenge electoral district apportionment schemes.

- On March 31, associate justice Charles E. Whittaker steps down from the Supreme Court.

- On April 16, Byron White is sworn in as associate justice of the Supreme Court.

- On June 25, in *Engel v. Vitale,* the Supreme Court rules that a nondenominational prayer read at the start of a school day in a public school violates the Establishment Clause of the First Amendment.

- On August 14, the Great Mail Robbery occurs on Cape Cod Highway in Massachusetts. The thieves get away with over $1.5 million in cash, making it the biggest cash heist in U.S. history.

- On August 28, Justice Felix Frankfurter resigns from the Supreme Court.

- On October 1, Arthur Goldberg joins the Supreme Court.

1963

- On February 18, in *Kennedy v. Mendoza-Martinez,* the Supreme Court holds that the Selective Training and Service Act of 1940, which divested U.S. citizens of their citizenship for remaining outside the United States during a time of war or national emergency in order to avoid the draft, violated the Fifth and Sixth Amendments.

- On February 25, in *Edwards v. South Carolina,* the Supreme Court holds that police violated the First and Fourteenth Amendment rights of African Americans peacefully demonstrating on the South Carolina State House grounds.

- On March 18, the *Gideon v. Wainwright,* decision by the Supreme Court requires that states provide legal counsel for criminal defendants who cannot afford to hire their own attorney.

- On June 12, Mississippi civil rights leader Medgar Evers is gunned down by segregationist Byron De La Beckwith.

- On June 17, in *Abbington v. Schempp,* the Supreme Court reaffirms that prayer in state supported schools violates the separation of church and state.

- On June 17, in *Sherbert v. Verner,* the Supreme Court rules that a woman could collect unemployment benefits after she was fired for refusing to work on Saturdays, due to her religious beliefs.

- On September 2, Alabama Governor George Wallace uses state troopers to prevent the integration of Tuskegee High School.

- On September 10, twenty African American students enter public schools in three Alabama cities, following a standoff between federal officials and Alabama Governor George Wallace.

- On September 15, a bomb explodes in the largest African American church in Birmingham, Alabama, killing four girls, and igniting protests and more violence.

- On November 22, President Kennedy is shot and killed in Dallas. Lee Harvey Oswald is arrested shortly thereafter. He is charged later in the day.

- On November 24, Oswald is shot to death by nightclub owner Jack Ruby. The event is captured live by television cameras filming Oswald's transfer to the county jail.

1964

- On February 17, in *Wesberry v. Sanders,* the Supreme Court requires that congressional districts must all have approximately the same population.

- On March 9, in *New York Times v. Sullivan,* the Supreme Court establishes constitutional standards for libel law, making it difficult for public officials to win libel suits. The court rules the First Amendment protects the publication of all statements, even false ones, except when statements are made with actual malice.

- On March 13, Kitty Genovese is stabbed and killed in Queens, New York, while dozens hear but do nothing.

- On March 14, a Dallas, Texas, jury finds Jack Ruby guilty of murdering Lee Harvey Oswald.

- In June, the Boston Strangler begins a killing spree which soon holds the city in the grip of terror.

- On June 15, the *Malloy v. Hogan* decision by the Supreme Court makes the Fifth Amendment applicable to the states.

- On June 15, in *Reynolds v. Sims,* the Supreme Court requires that both houses of state legislatures must be apportioned on the basis of population.

- On June 21, three civil rights workers are murdered in Mississippi. Their bodies are found six weeks later. Eight Klu Klux Klan members serve time on federal conspiracy charges.

- On June 22, *Escobedo v. Illinois* is decided by the Supreme Court, which requires that a suspect have access to an attorney during interrogation.

- On October 28, Harold Burton, retired associate justice, dies.

- On October 29, thieves steal the Star of India and other treasures from the American Museum of Natural History in New York.

- On November 23, in *Garrison v. Louisiana,* the Supreme Court applies its new libel standard to criminal libel suits as well.

- On December 3, eight hundred students are arrested at the University of California at Berkley, for staging a sit-in.

- On December 14, *Heart of Atlanta Motel, Inc. v. United States* is decided by the Supreme Court, upholding the Civil Rights Act of 1964 and holding that motels and hotels have no right to choose their customers and may not turn someone away based upon race. The court reaches the same conclusion in *Katzenbach v. McClung,* regarding restaurants that serve interstate customers.

1965

- On January 18, in *Cox v. Louisiana,* the Supreme Court rules that a statutory disturbance of the peace conviction, for a peaceable demonstration that contains speech that may potentially incite violence, infringes on a demonstrator's First Amendment rights.

- On February 21, Malcom X, former Black Muslim leader, is shot to death in New York by Black Muslim assassins.

- On February 22, retired Supreme Court justice Felix Frankfurter, appointed by President Franklin Roosevelt, dies.

- On March 7, state police and a sheriff's posse break up a civil rights march in Selma, Alabama.

- On March 11, James J. Reeb, a white minister from Boston, dies from a beating by whites in Selma, Alabama.

- On April 5, in *Pointer v. Texas,* the Supreme Court applies the Sixth Amendment's confrontation clause to the states.

- On April 9, Sherman Minton, former associate justice of the Supreme Court from 1949 to 1956, dies.

- On April 28, the *Griffin v. California* decision by the Supreme Court holds that, when a criminal defendant exercises his constitutional right not to testify, the prosecution cannot comment on this fact to the jury.

- On June 7, in *Griswold v. Connecticut,* the Supreme Court recognizes a constitutional right of privacy in striking down a law that prohibited giving contraceptives to married couples.

- On July 25, Justice Goldberg resigns from the Supreme Court in order to become ambassador to the United Nations.

- On August 11, rioting and looting break out in the Watts section of Los Angeles. Thirty-four will be killed and more than one thousand injured over the next week.

- On October 4, Abe Fortas is sworn in as an associate justice of the Supreme Court.

1966

- On January 17, in *Evans v. Newton,* the Supreme Court holds that a public park cannot be segregated.

- On February 23, in *Brown v. Louisiana,* the Supreme Court rules that police violated First and Fourteenth Amendment rights of African Americans arrested for participating in a peaceful sit-in at a public library.

- On March 7, in *South Carolina v. Katzenbach,* the Supreme Court upholds the constitutionality of the Voting Rights Act of 1965.

- On March 24, in *Harper v. Virginia State Board of Elections,* the Supreme Court finds state poll taxes unconstitutional.

- On June 6, in *Sheppard v. Maxwell,* the Supreme Court rules that Dr. Sam Sheppard did not receive a fair trial due to massive publicity surrounding his prosecution for the murder of his pregnant wife.

- On June 6, James Meredith is shot and wounded while walking on a Mississippi highway to encourage African American voter registration.

- On June 13, in *Miranda v. Arizona,* the Supreme Court requires that individuals in police custody be informed of their right to counsel and right against self-incrimination.

- On June 20, in *Schmerber v. California,* the Supreme Court holds that a blood test does not violate the Fifth Amendment right against self-incrimination.

- On July 14, Richard Speck kills eight student nurses in their Chicago dormitory.

- On August 1, Charles Whitman goes on a shooting spree from a clock tower on the University of Texas campus, killing fifteen and wounding thirty-one.

• On November 16, Dr. Sam Sheppard is acquitted at his second trial of murdering his pregnant wife.

1967

• On January 9, the Supreme Court rules in *Time, Inc. v. Hill* that the First Amendment protects a publication from liability for damages against a party absent a finding of malicious intent on the part of a publisher, even if the statements are otherwise false or inaccurate.

• On January 18, Albert DeSalvo, the self-confessed "Boston Strangler, " is convicted of sexual assault and armed robbery.

• On May 15, in *In Re Gault*, the Supreme Court establishes procedural protections for juveniles in court.

• On May 29, in *Afroyim v. Rusk*, the Supreme Court rules that a federal law that revokes a naturalized citizen's citizenship without consent violates both the Fifth and Fourteenth Amendments.

• In June, boxer Muhammad Ali, who has changed his name from Cassius Clay, is tried and convicted for refusing induction into the U.S. Army.

• On June 12, in *Loving v. Virginia*, the Supreme Court declares that antimiscegenation laws, (laws prohibiting the marriage of people of different races) are unconstitutional.

• On June 12, in *Walker v. Birmingham*, the Supreme Court upheld the arrests of Martin Luther King, Jr., Ralph Abernathy, and others, for marching in a demonstration, after a state court had ordered them not to.

• On June 12, Justice Clark retires from the Supreme Court.

• On July 13, race riots erupt in Newark; twenty-seven people die during the four days of riots.

• On July 23, race riots erupt in Detroit. Forty-three people are killed.

• On October 2, Thurgood Marshall joins the Supreme Court, becoming the first African American justice.

• On December 18, in *Katz v. United States*, the Supreme Court rules that police must obtain a search warrant before wiretapping a public phone booth.

1968

• On February 8, three college students die in a confrontation with highway patrolmen in Orangeburg, S.C. The students were protesting at a whites-only bowling alley.

• On April 1, in *Avery v. Midland*, the Supreme Court extends its one man, one vote requirement to local governmental elections.

• On April 4, civil rights leader Martin Luther King, Jr., is assassinated in Memphis.

• In May, President Johnson nominates Justice Abe Fortas to replace retiring chief justice Earl Warren.

• On May 20, in *Duncan v. Louisiana*, the Supreme Court rules that an accused is entitled to a jury trial under the Sixth Amendment where the possible penalty which may be imposed upon conviction is a two-year imprisonment, even though in this case defendant was only sentenced to sixty days in prison.

• On May 27, in *United States v. O'Brien*, the Supreme Court recognizes symbolic speech as protected by the First Amendment. However, the decision also recognizes that certain limitations can be placed on this right.

• On June 3, pop artist Andy Warhol is shot and wounded by Valerie Solanas in New York.

• On June 5, Senator Robert F. Kennedy is shot in Los Angeles; he dies the next day. Sirhan Sirhan is arrested in the shooting.

• On June 8, James Earl Ray is arrested in London as he disembarks from a flight.

• On June 10, in *Terry v. Ohio*, the Supreme Court upholds a "stop and frisk" search of three men who appeared to be casing a store for a robbery.

• On June 17, in *Jones v. Alfred H. Mayer Co.*, the Supreme Court prohibits racial discrimination in purchase, lease, sale, and conveyance of property.

• In August, Vietnam War and civil rights protestors clash with police as they disrupt the Democratic party National Convention in Chicago, Illinois.

1969

• On February 24, in *Tinker v. Des Moines*, the Supreme Court upholds the right of high school students to protest the Vietnam War by wearing black armbands.

• On March 10, in Memphis, James Earl Ray pleads guilty to the assassination of Martin Luther King, Jr.

• On March 10, in *Alderman v. United States*, the Supreme Court holds that the exclusionary rule only applies to the person whose rights were violated by an illegal search.

• On April 7, in *Stanley v. Georgia*, the Supreme Court rules that private possession of obscene materials is not a crime under the First and Fourteenth Amendments.

• On April 17, Sirhan Sirhan is convicted of assassinating Senator Robert F. Kennedy. On April 23, the jury returns a death sentence, which is later reduced to life imprisonment.

• On April 21, in *Shapiro v. Thompson*, the Supreme Court prohibits residency requirements for welfare benefits by states on the grounds that they violate the fundamental right to travel.

• On May 14, Justice Fortas resigns from Supreme Court amid allegations of wrongdoing involving his acceptance and subsequent return of a fee from a charitable foundation controlled by the family of an indicted stock manipulator. Fortas denied any wrongdoing.

• On June 16, in *Powell v. McCormick*, Congressman Adam Clayton Powell wins the right to be seated in Congress, after his colleagues in the House of Representatives voted to exclude him.

• On June 23, Chief Justice Warren retires.

• On June 23, Warren Burger is confirmed as the new chief justice.

• On June 23, the Supreme Court rules in *Chimel v. California* that police may only search in the vicinity of a person when executing an arrest warrant at a suspect's home, and that a full search of the premises is prohibited by the Fourth Amendment.

• On June 23, in *Benton v. Maryland,* the Supreme Court applies Double Jeopardy protection to state criminal proceedings.

• On August 9, the Manson "Family" commits five grisly murders at the home of filmmaker Roman Polanski. The next day, they murder Leno and Rosemary LaBianca at their Los Angeles home.

• In November, President Nixon's nomination of Clement Haynsworth to the Supreme Court is rejected by the Senate.

The Enemy Within

Nonfiction work

By: Robert F. Kennedy

Date: 1960

Source: Kennedy, Robert F. *The Enemy Within.* New York: Harper & Row, 1960, 320–325.

About the Author: Robert F. Kennedy (1925–1968), the younger brother of President John F. Kennedy (served 1961–1963), was educated at Harvard and the University of Virginia Law School. He served as an assistant to Joseph McCarthy and as counsel to the McClelland Committee. After helping manage his brother's successful election campaigns, he served as U.S. attorney general. As a senator from New York, he was running for president in 1968 when he was assassinated. ∎

Introduction

Crime has long been a sordid part of American life, but what constitutes a crime has varied over time. In the early years of the colonies, for example, witchcraft was a crime. Additionally, the government's attitude toward crime has varied. Following the Civil War (1861–1865), for instance, thousands of lynchings were carried out, particularly in the South, and most of the victims were African Americans. The state governments, however, were not overly interested in pursuing the killers, and few were ever arrested, much less tried, for lynching. As the twentieth century progressed, society and the authorities adopted a tougher stance against crime.

A type of crime that garners a great deal of public attention is "organized crime," referring to the enterprises of criminal organizations that exist for the sole purpose of making money through crime. The amount of organized crime has often depended on historical circumstances. For instance, organized crime ran rampant in the 1920s, as it made large amounts of money providing liquor, which had been made illegal by Prohibition. During the 1930s and 1940s, the focus turned away from organized crime, but in the 1950s, interest returned, and many people believed that organized crime had infiltrated America's labor unions. A select committee was appointed by the Senate to investigate, and Robert Kennedy was the counsel for this committee.

Significance

Later in the 1950s, Robert Kennedy managed his brother's successful campaign for the presidency. After John F. Kennedy's inauguration, he appointed Robert U.S. attorney general and conducted a campaign against organized crime. However, he was stifled because of difficulties he had with J. Edgar Hoover, the longtime director of the FBI. After JFK's assassination in 1963, Robert Kennedy remained attorney general in the Johnson administration before he was elected to the U.S. Senate from New York in 1964. While running for president in 1968, he was assassinated by Sirhan Sirhan in June 1968.

One of Kennedy's targets as attorney general was Jimmy Hoffa, the president of the Teamsters Union. Hoffa fought off a number of investigations and survived one major trial. However, in 1967 he was convicted of tax evasion and began serving time in prison. In 1971, he was pardoned by President Richard Nixon (served 1969–1974); part of the pardon agreement was that Hoffa have nothing to do with the union until 1980. Hoffa disappeared in 1975 and was widely presumed to have been murdered.

Organized crime continued to be a concern in the last thirty years of the century. The mafia in New York City was targeted in a number of high-profile prosecutions, most of which eventually were successful. However, many crime figures had to be tried several times because the first trials almost inevitably ended in mistrials, hung juries, or acquittals. Even forty years after Hoffa and Kennedy, organized crime remained a concern for the government.

Primary Source

The Enemy Within [excerpt]

> **SYNOPSIS:** Kennedy first argues that America at the time was winning the war on crime. He discusses the prosecution of organized crime figures, the positive steps labor unions have taken to clean up criminal activity, and the laws that have been passed against crime. He closes by noting that more changes need to be made, but that America can win if it returns to the idealism that has marked its history.

In the long run, the legislation and the awakening of the public are what are important. It is not sufficient to get rid of a Dave Beck or a Jimmy Cross or a Hoffa without passing a law to deal with the problem that has been uncovered. The honest elements of organized labor, the Meanys and Dubinskys, recognize this.

And Hoffa's days are numbered. Because of recent court decisions the Teamster monitors have the power to press for his removal. I believe they will. Even if this does not prove true, a man with Hoffa's power and position, and so corrupt, cannot survive in a democratic society if democracy itself is going to survive. I believe the country, not Hoffa, will triumph.

The investigators themselves can also take a great amount of satisfaction from the knowledge that their work often shook the foundations of a community and even of a state.

Duffy's and McShane's investigation in Tennessee brought about five convictions of important Teamster officials, the impeachment of a judge, and the removal of several public officials from office. It was a No. 1 news story in the state and it caused a tremendous impact.

Bellino's investigation of Dave Beck in Seattle knocked from a position of power a major political figure who, more than any one man, had dominated the state's affairs.

Lee Nulty's investigation of Local 107 of the Teamsters had a tremendous effect on Philadelphia.

Walter Sheridan's investigations in Indianapolis and St. Louis; Langenbacher's investigation in Pontiac, Michigan; Pierre Salinger's investigation in San Francisco; Adlerman's and Calabrese's in Portland; Willse's, Kelly's, May's, Tierney's, Constandy's investigations in New York; Ralph Mills's in Miami; Sinclair's in Gary, Indiana; Kopecky's in Chicago; and the work of others elsewhere had tremendous impact; and I regret that I have not had space to deal with all of them.

More than twenty individuals, labor leaders, management people, gangsters and others directly involved in the investigations have been convicted and sentenced to prison terms as a result of the work of these men.

And as this is written there are other encouraging developments. As a result of the work of the Committee, indictments are pending against some of Mr. Hoffa's closest associates, including international vice president John O'Rourke of New York, international trustee Raymond Cohen of Philadelphia, William Presser of Cleveland, Anthony Provenzano of New Jersey, Mike Singer of Los Angeles, Barney Baker now located in Chicago, Theodore Cozza of Pittsburgh, Vincent Squillante of New York, and Harry Gross of Miami and New York. Cornelius Noonan, an official of the ILA, is under indictment along with Gross in New York.

Jimmy Hoffa takes an oath at a Senate labor racket hearing in 1965. He later served a five-year prison term, during which he remained president of the Brotherhood of Teamsters. © HULTON-DEUTSCH COLLECTION/CORBIS. REPRODUCED BY PERMISSION.

Maurice Hutcheson, international president of the Carpenters Union, faces a contempt of Congress indictment in Washington.

Whether any of these cases results in conviction, the fact that the Justice Department and state authorities brought some of these matters to the attention of grand juries indicates that positive action has replaced lethargy in the attitude of government toward this important area of corruption.

The labor movement itself has had a drastic overhaul. The Teamsters have been expelled from the AFL-CIO and other unions have been placed under suspension or their officers have been removed.

There is tremendous satisfaction obviously in the fact that Congress has passed legislation that will deal with the abuses we have uncovered. Under the new law labor unions no longer will be able to file false or incomplete reports of their financial and administrative affairs. These matters must now be reported in detail to the Secretary of Labor and no longer may be concealed from union members or the general public.

Union officials no longer will be able to engage in secret conflict-of-interest deals. Management officials no longer can hide anti-union expenditures or make secret payments to labor "consultants," such as Nathan Shefferman, to do their dirty work. All such arrangements must be reported.

When our investigation began one hundred Teamster locals were under trusteeship and some had been for fifteen years—which means it had been that long since rank and file members were allowed to have any voice in running their own local affairs. Provisions of the bill deal with dictatorial trusteeships such as those practiced by the Teamsters and by the Operating Engineers, which kept two local unions shackled for twenty-nine years. The law sets up minimum standards for imposing trusteeships and provides for freeing locals from improper trusteeships.

Fair election procedures and a secret ballot are provided union members under this law. Now Federal and administrative action can be taken to overturn unfair elections, and there must be elections of International officers at least every five years and local officers every three.

The bill also seeks to rid the labor movement of ex-convicts such as many of the unsavory characters Jimmy Hoffa employs in his "palace guard." It blocks ex-convicts from serving as union officers for five years following their release from prison.

It sets up machinery for recovering misappropriated union funds and provides criminal penalties for embezzlement of union money. Under the statute every officer now must be bonded and a labor union may not lend more than $2,000 of its money to a union official.

It prohibits offering or accepting bribes in labor-management relations and provides for criminal prosecution in cases of violence or the threat of violence that might deprive a union member of his rights. The law as passed corrected some obvious weaknesses in the Landrum-Griffin Bill which passed the House of Representatives in 1959. For example, under that bill a broadly drawn section outlawed all union contract provisions designed to protect working men and women from sweatshop competition. Had it been passed into law, racketeers operating run-away sweatshops could have infringed on the rights of honest union workers—and would have been protected by the law.

The House and Senate conferees who developed the new bill made major improvements in the House

measure; I am convinced that we have a far better and a fairer bill because of that conference.

Obviously, the law still is not perfect. Just as large corporations, such as General Motors and U.S. Steel have different problems from small retail establishments, so do small and large unions have different problems. Laws regulating business recognize these differences. The newly passed labor law falls with equal weight on all unions, regardless of their strength or economic bargaining position. The restrictions on picketing in the new measure are desirable where a strong union wields its power in a socially irresponsible manner and for all practical purposes forces membership on employees who may or may not wish to join the union. On the other hand, these same restrictions will work to the detriment of small, weak unions whose sole weapon in the face of determined employer resistance to union activity is a peaceful picket line. This provision will have a seriously adverse effect on the development of responsible trade unionism, particularly in the unorganized sectors of the economy. This is most unfortunate. However, I am extremely pleased that a law was passed. For the most part it is a good law and one that is absolutely essential.

The sordid dishonesty uncovered by the McClellan Committee is a reflection on all Americans, for it cuts across all segments of our economic life—labor, management, the law, the press. The new labor bill is a big step forward, but it cannot be considered an end-all; we cannot afford to sit back and with smug satisfaction assume that the job has been done. The revelations of the McClellan Committee were, in my estimation, merely a symptom of a more serious moral illness.

In the fall of 1959, I spoke at one of the country's most respected law schools. The professor in charge of teaching ethics told me the big question up for discussion among his students was whether as a lawyer you could lie to a judge. Evidently, things are not going to improve. I told the professor and said later in my speech that I thought we had all been taught the answer to that question when we were six years old.

And yet two children, eight and twelve year old, were corrupted during the course of the TV quiz programs, and many older people who were approached also accepted the crooked arrangement.

For our nation to survive in the period of heightened international competition, we must reaffirm some of the basic values of our forebears, values that are deeply rooted in the history of our country and in its rise to a position of strength and respect in the community of nations.

The tyrant, the bully, the corrupter and corrupted are figures of shame. The labor leaders who became thieves, who cheated those whose trust they had accepted, brought dishonor on a vital and largely honest labor movement. The businessmen who succumbed to the temptation to make a deal in order to gain an advantage over their competitors perverted the moral concepts of a free American economic system.

Neither the labor movement nor our economic system can stand this paralyzing corruption. Premier Khrushchev has said that we are a dying house, a decadent society. That he says it does not make it true. But that corruption, dishonesty and softness, physical and moral, have become widespread in this country there can be no doubt.

The great events of our nation's past were forged by men of toughness, men who risked their security and their futures for freedom and for an ideal. The foot soldiers at Valley Forge, the men who marched up Cemetery Hill and those who stood by their guns at the summit, the men who conquered the West, the Marines who fought at Belleau Woods and at Tarawa did not measure their sacrifices in terms of self-reward. And because of what they and countless others like them achieved, we are now a powerful and prosperous country.

But have the comforts we have bought, the successes we have won, the speeches that we make on national holidays extolling American bravery and generosity so undermined our strength of character that we are now unprepared to deal with the problems that face us? The records of the McClellan Committee are studded with disturbing signs that we are not prepared. Dangerous changes are taking place in the moral fiber of American society.

These are uncertain times for the United States. People say, But what can we do? We must all begin to take a greater interest in our national affairs and let our legislators know where we stand on the important issues that arise. We must take new interest in the running of our communities, the operations of our schools, and in such important matters as the physical, mental and spiritual fitness of our children. A recent survey shows that, even in democratic unions, less than 12 per cent of the membership attend the meetings with any regularity. The men to whom the unions belong must take a role in the running of them. And certainly an ethical prac-tices code such as the AFL-CIO has adopted should be introduced by management groups such as the Chamber of Commerce and the National Association of Manufacturers.

It seems to me imperative that we reinstill in ourselves the toughness and idealism that guided the nation in the past. The paramount interest in self, in material wealth, in security must be replaced by an actual, not just a vocal, interest in our country, by a spirit of adventure, a will to fight what is evil, and a desire to serve. It is up to us as citizens to take the initiative as it has been taken before in our history, to reach out boldly but with honesty to do the things that need to be done.

To meet the challenge of our times, so that we can later look back upon this era not as one of which we need be ashamed but as a turning point on the way to a better America, we must first defeat the enemy within.

Further Resources

BOOKS

Edelman, Peter B. *Searching for America's Heart: RFK and the Renewal of Hope.* Boston: Houghton Mifflin, 2001.

Goldfarb, Ronald L. *Perfect Villains, Imperfect Heroes: Robert F. Kennedy's War Against Organized Crime.* New York: Random House, 1995.

Sloane, Arthur A. *Hoffa.* Cambridge, Mass.: MIT Press, 1992.

Thomas, Evan *Robert Kennedy: His Life.* New York: Simon and Schuster, 2000.

WEBSITES

Robert F. Kennedy, Senate Counsel; Jimmy Hoffa, Teamsters President. Available online at http://www.historychannel.com /speeches/archive/speech.b/cgi-bin/frameit.cgi?p=http%3A _163.html; website home page: http://www.historychannel .com (accessed January 23, 2003).

AUDIO AND VISUAL MEDIA

Fox, Stephen R., Bill Kurtis, David Royle, and David Osterland. *Mafia: The Definitive History of the Mob in America,* vol. 2, *The Kennedys and the Mob.* New York: Arts & Entertainment Home Video, 1993.

Mapp v. Ohio
Supreme Court decision

By: Thomas C. Clark; William O. Douglas; John Marshall Harlan

Date: June 19, 1961

Source: Clark, Thomas C., William O. Douglas, and John Marshall Harlan *Mapp v. Ohio,* 367 U.S. 643. Available

online at http://caselaw.lp.findlaw.com/scripts/getcase
.pl?navby=case&court=us&vol=367&page=643; website home
page: http://caselaw.lp.findlaw.com (accessed June 11, 2003).

About the Authors: Thomas C. Clark (1899–1977) was
named U.S. attorney general in 1945 and served on the U.S.
Supreme Court from 1949 to 1967.

John Marshall Harlan (1899–1971) spent most of his precourt
legal career working on Wall Street. In 1955, President
Dwight Eisenhower (served 1953–1961) appointed Harlan to
the Supreme Court, where he served until 1971.

William O. Douglas (1898–1980), at age forty, was one of
the youngest men ever to be appointed to the Supreme Court,
and his thirty-six-year tenure on the Court was the longest in
history. ■

Introduction

During the early days of America, a sizable number
of colonists made their living by smuggling goods into
the United States. The British wanted to end this practice and issued general warrants allowing any area to be
searched and any illegal items to be seized. This practice
angered the colonists and was one of the grievances that
led to the American Revolution. As the Constitution was
being drafted, some wanted protection against the government's carrying out similar searches. As a result, the
Bill of Rights included the Fourth Amendment, which requires that "the right of the people to be secure . . . against
unreasonable searches and seizures, shall not be violated,
and no Warrants shall issue, but upon probable cause . . .
and particularly describing the place to be searched, and
the persons or things to be seized."

The amendment, though, provides no penalty when
it is violated, and throughout the nineteenth century
courts generally allowed the use of evidence seized illegally. In 1886, the Supreme Court overturned a conviction and excluded from a trial papers that had been seized
without a warrant, but it was not until 1914 that the
Supreme Court created the "exclusionary rule," which
states that evidence seized without a warrant cannot be
used in trial in a federal court. It was unclear, though,
whether that rule was integral to the Fourth Amendment.
In 1949 and again in 1954, the Supreme Court refused to
apply the Fourth Amendment against the states and force
the states not to use evidence seized without a warrant.
The issue arose again in the *Mapp* case.

Significance

In this case, the Supreme Court applied the exclusionary rule against the states, creating a uniform procedure in all prosecutions: Evidence seized without a
warrant cannot be used. It should be noted that the evidence used to obtain Dollree Mapp's conviction for obscenity was not what the police were looking for when
they entered her boarding house—they were searching
for gambling evidence. Further, the police lied to Mapp

about having a warrant. Since *Mapp*, exceptions to the
exclusionary rule have been created. The exclusionary
rule applies only to evidence used against a person whose
Fourth Amendment rights have been violated. The same
evidence can be used to prosecute other defendants. Evidence seized illegally may be used if the police can prove
that the evidence would have been "inevitably discovered" through normal police procedures. Finally, evidence is allowed in some cases if the police seized it
acting in "good faith" under an improperly issued warrant if the police did not know that the warrant had been
issued improperly.

In 1984, the Supreme Court upheld a conviction
based on evidence that had been seized with a warrant
even though the warrant was not supported by probable
cause. The Court held that searches should be voided only
if the officers did not have a reasonable belief that probable cause existed for the warrant. The court "weighed"
the benefits gained by society from the arrest versus the
costs to the person whose rights were violated, and decided to err on the side of society. Since 1984, the Warren Burger and William Rehnquist courts have continued
to narrow the exclusionary rule and have now recognized
at least five major exceptions to it, in addition to those
noted above.

Primary Source

Mapp v. Ohio [excerpt]

> **SYNOPSIS:** Justice Clark, writing for the majority,
> notes the growing use of the exclusionary rule and
> holds that all evidence seized without a warrant
> should be excluded, whether in state or federal
> court. Clark then states that government should
> follow its own rules, even if criminals occasionally
> go free. In concurring, Justice Douglas castigates
> the lawlessness of the search. Justice Harlan dis-
> sents, arguing that this case deals only with
> whether this search was reasonable and whether
> there was a constitutional basis for extending the
> exclusionary rule.

Mr. Justice Clark delivered the opinion of the
Court.

. . . the Supreme Court of Ohio found that her
conviction was valid though "based primarily upon
the introduction . . . of . . . books and pictures un-
lawfully seized during an unlawful search of defendant's home. . . ."

At the trial no search warrant was produced by
the prosecution, nor was the failure to produce one
explained or accounted for. . . .

The State says that even if the search were
made without authority, or otherwise unreasonably,

it is not prevented from using the unconstitutionally seized evidence at trial, citing *Wolf v. Colorado . . .* in which this Court did indeed hold "that in a prosecution in a State court for a State crime the Fourteenth Amendment does not forbid the admission of evidence obtained by an unreasonable search and seizure." . . .

The Court in *Wolf* first stated that "[t]he contrariety of views of the States" on the adoption of the exclusionary rule of Weeks was "particularly impressive" . . . ; and, in this connection, that it could not "brush aside the experience of States which deem the incidence of such conduct by the police too slight to call for a deterrent remedy . . . by overriding the [States'] relevant rules of evidence." . . . While in 1949, prior to the *Wolf* case, almost two-thirds of the States were opposed to the use of the exclusionary rule, now, despite the *Wolf* case, more than half of those since passing upon it, by their own legislative or judicial decision, have wholly or partly adopted or adhered to the Weeks rule. . . . Significantly, among those now following the rule is California, which, according to its highest court, was "compelled to reach that conclusion because other remedies have completely failed to secure compliance with the constitutional provisions. . . ."

We hold that all evidence obtained by searches and seizures in violation of the Constitution is, by that same authority, inadmissible in a state court.

Since the Fourth Amendment's right of privacy has been declared enforceable against the States through the Due Process Clause of the Fourteenth, it is enforceable against them by the same sanction of exclusion as is used against the Federal Government. Were it otherwise, . . . the freedom from state invasions of privacy would be so ephemeral and so neatly severed from its conceptual nexus with the freedom from all brutish means of coercing evidence as not to merit this Court's high regard as a freedom "implicit in the concept of ordered liberty." At the time that the Court held in *Wolf* that the Amendment was applicable to the States through the Due Process Clause, the cases of this Court, as we have seen, had steadfastly held that as to federal officers the Fourth Amendment included the exclusion of the evidence seized in violation of its provisions. Even *Wolf* "stoutly adhered" to that proposition. . . . Therefore, in extending the substantive protections of due process to all constitutionally unreasonable searches—state or federal—it was logically and constitutionally necessary that the exclusion doctrine— an essential part of the right to privacy—be also

Dollree Mapp, owner of a boarding house, was convicted for possessing pornographic materials that she claimed were left behind by a boarder. Her conviction was appealed to the Supreme Court because the warrant police used to search her house was for an entirely unrelated investigation. **AP/WIDE WORLD PHOTOS. REPRODUCED BY PERMISSION.**

insisted upon as an essential ingredient of the right newly recognized by the *Wolf* case. In short, the admission of the new constitutional right by *Wolf* could not consistently tolerate denial of its most important constitutional privilege, namely, the exclusion of the evidence which an accused had been forced to give by reason of the unlawful seizure. To hold otherwise is to grant the right but in reality to withhold its privilege and enjoyment. . . .

There are those who say, as did Justice . . . Cardozo, that under our constitutional exclusionary doctrine "[t]he criminal is to go free because the constable has blundered." . . . In some cases this will undoubtedly be the result. But, as was said in *Elkins,* "there is another consideration—the imperative of judicial integrity." . . . The criminal goes free, if he must, but it is the law that sets him free. Nothing can destroy a government more quickly than its failure to observe its own laws, or worse, its disregard of the charter of its own existence. As Mr. Justice Brandeis, dissenting, said in *Olmstead:* "Our Government is the potent, the omnipresent teacher. For good or for ill, it teaches the whole people by its example. . . . If the Government becomes a lawbreaker, it breeds contempt for law; it invites every man to become a law unto himself; it invites anarchy." Nor can it lightly be assumed that, as a practical matter, adoption of the exclusionary rule fetters law enforcement. . . .

The ignoble shortcut to conviction left open to the State tends to destroy the entire system of constitutional restraints on which the liberties of the people rest. Having once recognized that the right to privacy embodied in the Fourth Amendment is enforceable against the States, and that the right to be secure against rude invasions of privacy by state officers is, therefore, constitutional in origin, we can no longer permit that right to remain an empty promise. Because it is enforceable in the same manner and to like effect as other basic rights secured by the Due Process Clause, we can no longer permit it to be revocable at the whim of any police officer who, in the name of law enforcement itself, chooses to suspend its enjoyment. Our decision, founded on reason and truth, gives to the individual no more than that which the Constitution guarantees him, to the police officer no less than that to which honest law enforcement is entitled, and, to the courts, that judicial integrity so necessary in the true administration of justice.

The judgment of the Supreme Court of Ohio is reversed and the cause remanded for further proceedings not inconsistent with this opinion.

Reversed and remanded. . . .

Mr. Justice Douglas, concurring.

Though I have joined the opinion of the Court, I add a few words. This criminal proceeding started with a lawless search and seizure. The police entered a home forcefully, and seized documents that were later used to convict the occupant of a crime. . . .

When we allowed States to give constitutional sanction to the "shabby business" of unlawful entry into a home . . . we did indeed rob the Fourth Amendment of much meaningful force. . . .

The only remaining remedy, if exclusion of the evidence is not required, is an action of trespass by the homeowner against the offending officer. Mr. Justice Murphy showed how onerous and difficult it would be for the citizen to maintain that action and how meagre the relief even if the citizen prevails. . . . The truth is that trespass actions against officers who make unlawful searches and seizures are mainly illusory remedies.

Without judicial action making the exclusionary rule applicable to the States, *Wolf v. Colorado* in practical effect reduced the guarantee against unreasonable searches and seizures to "a dead letter," as Mr. Justice Rutledge said in his dissent. . . .

Wolf v. Colorado . . . was decided in 1949. The immediate result was a storm of constitutional controversy which only today finds its end. I believe that this is an appropriate case in which to put an end to the asymmetry which *Wolf* imported into the law. . . . It is an appropriate case because the facts it presents show—as would few other cases—the casual arrogance of those who have the untrammelled power to invade one's home and to seize one's person. . . .

Mr. Justice Harlan, whom Mr. Justice Frankfurter and Mr. Justice Whittaker join, dissenting.

In overruling the *Wolf* case the Court, in my opinion, has forgotten the sense of judicial restraint which, with due regard for stare decisis, is one element that should enter into deciding whether a past decision of this Court should be overruled. Apart from that I also believe that the *Wolf* rule represents sounder Constitutional doctrine than the new rule which now replaces it. . . .

In this posture of things, I think it fair to say that five members of this Court have simply "reached out" to overrule *Wolf.* With all respect for the views of the majority, and recognizing that stare decisis carries different weight in Constitutional adjudication than it does in nonconstitutional decision, I can perceive no justification for regarding this case as an appropriate occasion for re-examining *Wolf.* . . .

Thus, even in a case which presented simply the question of whether a particular search and seizure was constitutionally "unreasonable"—say in a tort action against state officers—we would not be true to the Fourteenth Amendment were we merely to stretch the general principle of individual privacy on a Procrustean bed of federal precedents under the Fourth Amendment. But in this instance more than that is involved, for here we are reviewing not a determination that what the state police did was Constitutionally permissible (since the state court quite evidently assumed that it was not), but a determination that appellant was properly found guilty of conduct which, for present purposes, it is to be assumed the State could Constitutionally punish. Since there is not the slightest suggestion that Ohio's policy is "affirmatively to sanction . . . police incursion into privacy" . . . what the Court is now doing is to impose upon the States not only federal substantive standards of "search and seizure" but also the basic federal remedy for violation of those standards. For I think it entirely clear that the Weeks exclusionary rule is but a remedy which, by penalizing past official misconduct, is aimed at deterring such conduct in the future.

I would not impose upon the States this federal exclusionary remedy. The reasons given by the majority for now suddenly turning its back on *Wolf* seem to me notably unconvincing. . . .

The preservation of a proper balance between state and federal responsibility in the administration of criminal justice demands patience on the part of those who might like to see things move faster among the States in this respect. Problems of criminal law enforcement vary widely from State to State. . . . For us the question remains, as it has always been, one of state power, not one of passing judgment on the wisdom of one state course or another. In my view this Court should continue to forbear from fettering the States with an adamant rule which may embarrass them in coping with their own peculiar problems in criminal law enforcement. . . .

The point, then, must be that in requiring exclusion of an involuntary statement of an accused, we are concerned not with an appropriate remedy for what the police have done, but with something which is regarded as going to the heart of our concepts of fairness in judicial procedure. The operative assumption of our procedural system is that "Ours is the accusatorial as opposed to the inquisitorial system. Such has been the characteristic of Anglo-American criminal justice since it freed itself from practices borrowed by the Star Chamber from the Continent whereby the accused was interrogated in secret for hours on end." . . . The pressures brought to bear against an accused leading to a confession, unlike an unconstitutional violation of privacy, do not,

apart from the use of the confession at trial, necessarily involve independent Constitutional violations. What is crucial is that the trial defense to which an accused is entitled should not be rendered an empty formality by reason of statements wrung from him, for then "a prisoner . . . [has been] made the deluded instrument of his own conviction." . . . That this is a procedural right, and that its violation occurs at the time his improperly obtained statement is admitted at trial, is manifest. For without this right all the careful safeguards erected around the giving of testimony, whether by an accused or any other witness, would become empty formalities in a procedure where the most compelling possible evidence of guilt, a confession, would have already been obtained at the unsupervised pleasure of the police. . . .

I regret that I find so unwise in principle and so inexpedient in policy a decision motivated by the high purpose of increasing respect for Constitutional rights. But in the last analysis I think this Court can increase respect for the Constitution only if it rigidly respects the limitations which the Constitution places upon it, and respects as well the principles inherent in its own processes. In the present case I think we exceed both, and that our voice becomes only a voice of power, not of reason.

Further Resources

BOOKS

Alderman, Ellen, and Caroline Kennedy. *In Our Defense: The Bill of Rights in Action.* New York: Morrow, 1991.

Greenhalgh, William W. *The Fourth Amendment Handbook: A Chronological Survey of Supreme Court Decisions,* 2nd ed. Chicago: Criminal Justice Section, American Bar Association, 2002.

Hall, John Wesley. *Search and Seizure,* 3rd ed. Charlottesville, Va.: Lexis, 2000.

LaFave, Wayne R. *Search and Seizure: A Treatise on the Fourth Amendment,* 3rd ed. St. Paul, Minn.: West, 1996.

Levy, Leonard Williams. *Origins of the Bill of Rights.* New Haven, Conn.: Yale University Press, 1999.

Raskin, Jamin B. *We the Students: Supreme Court Decisions For and About Students.* Washington: CQ Press, 2000.

Stephen, John A. *Officer's Search and Seizure Handbook.* New York: Lexis, 2000.

WEBSITES

Background Summary and Questions—Landmark Supreme Court Cases, Mapp v. Ohio. Available online at http://www.landmarkcases.org/mapp/background3.html; website home page: http://www.landmarkcases.org (accessed January 23, 2003).

Engel v. Vitale

| Supreme Court decision

By: Hugo L. Black; William O. Douglas; Potter Stewart

Date: June 25, 1962

Source: Black, Hugo L., William O. Douglas, and Potter Stewart *Engel v. Vitale,* 370 U.S. 421. Available online at http://caselaw.lp.findlaw.com/scripts/getcase.pl?navby=case &court=us&vol=370&page=421; website home page: http://caselaw.lp.findlaw.com (accessed March 15, 2003).

About the Authors: Hugo Lafayette Black (1886–1971) was appointed to the Supreme Court in 1937 after serving two terms in the U.S. Senate. His term was generally distinguished by his support of civil rights.

William O. Douglas (1898–1980) was an activist, liberal justice who served longer on the Supreme Court than any justice in history.

Potter Stewart (1885–1985) was a pragmatist and a moderate on the Court who, in reference to pornography, coined the famous statement that although he could not define it, "I know it when I see it." ∎

Introduction

The First Amendment states, in part, that "Congress shall make no law respecting the establishment of religion, or prohibiting the free exercise thereof." However, what exactly the founders meant by that clause has occasioned debate throughout much of the twentieth century. Many of the original states had a state-supported church, with taxes being paid to support it, but the nation's founders strongly believed in keeping the state out of the church's business and vice-versa. The issue of separation of church and state did not arise to any great extent during the nineteenth century because Congress did not enact many laws that directly affected religion and because the Bill of Rights, of which the First Amendment is a part, was held to apply only to the federal government. Thus, it did not affect the states, which generally had greater involvement in issues of religion.

In the twentieth century, this began to change. In 1925, the First Amendment was found applicable to the states, so the actions of the state as they affected religion became a constitutional issue. Education increased in importance, as by the middle of the twentieth century the expectation became that everyone would graduate from high school. Religion, too, grew in importance during the Cold War with the atheistic communists of the Soviet Union. The phrase "under God" was added to the Pledge of Allegiance, said in most schools, as part of this struggle, and few people publicly questioned the promotion of religion by schools with the Pledge and a prayer to start most days. One of those few filed suit, and the case came before the Supreme Court as *Engel v. Vitale.*

Significance

In *Engel v. Vitale,* the Supreme Court ruled that mandated prayer in the public schools was unconstitutional. Although the form of prayer in question was nonsectarian and did not promote any particular religion, it promoted a monotheistic, Western view of religion, even among atheists and agnostics. The state of New York argued further that the prayer was voluntary. The Court, though, rejected this argument, noting that the pressures of conformity forced recitation and that if freedom of religion means freedom to not have a religion, then any prayer interferes. The Court's ruling provoked a firestorm of controversy throughout America. Many conservative commentators, from the 1960s to today, link the beginning of the downfall of America with this ruling. This decision, along with ones allowing flag-burning, have provoked more attempts at constitutional amendments reversing them than any other Court decisions.

The next year, the Supreme Court struck down a school program of Bible readings and recitation of the Lord's Prayer. The Court upheld the loaning of textbooks to religious schools, however, as this did not "excessively entangle" the church and the state. Similarly, a tax exemption for churches was allowed for similar reasons. The state has generally been allowed to issue rules affecting religious issues if no "excessive entanglement" results, if the law has a secular purpose, and the rule neither hinders nor helps religion. Laws allowing or mandating a moment of silence, school prayers, and the posting of the Ten Commandments in schools, even though popular in some areas, have nearly always been struck down as violating the First Amendment.

Primary Source

Engel v. Vitale [excerpt]

SYNOPSIS: Black, who wrote the majority opinion, surveys the history of the state's involvement in religion and holds that the state's promulgation of an officially allowable prayer to start the schoolday violates the First Amendment. Douglas concurs, arguing that any state financing or support of religion is illegal. Stewart dissents, noting that the phrase "wall of separation" is nowhere found in the Constitution.

Mr. Justice Black delivered the opinion of the Court.

The respondent Board of Education . . . acting in its official capacity under state law, directed the School District's principal to cause the following prayer to be said aloud by each class in the presence of a teacher at the beginning of each school day:

Students at a San Antonio high school pray, two days after the *Engel v. Vitale* ruling that held that the recitation of an official prayer in public schools violated the First Amendment. © BETTMANN/CORBIS. REPRODUCED BY PERMISSION.

Almighty God, we acknowledge our dependence upon Thee, and we beg Thy blessings upon us, our parents, our teachers and our Country.

This daily procedure was adopted on the recommendation of the State Board of Regents, a governmental agency created by the State Constitution to which the New York Legislature has granted broad supervisory, executive, and legislative powers over the State's public school system. . . .

There can, of course, be no doubt that New York's program of daily classroom invocation of God's blessings as prescribed in the Regents' prayer is a religious activity. It is a solemn avowal of divine faith and supplication for the blessings of the Almighty. . . . We . . . think that the constitutional prohibition against laws respecting an establishment of religion must at least mean that in this country it is no part of the business of government to compose official prayers for any group of the American people to recite as a part of a religious program carried on by government.

It is a matter of history that this very practice of establishing governmentally composed prayers for

religious services was one of the reasons which caused many of our early colonists to leave England and seek religious freedom in America. . . .

It is an unfortunate fact of history that when some of the very groups which had most strenuously opposed the established Church of England found themselves sufficiently in control of colonial governments in this country to write their own prayers into law, they passed laws making their own religion the official religion of their respective colonies. . . . In 1785–1786, those opposed to the established Church, led by James Madison and Thomas Jefferson, who, though themselves not members of any of these dissenting religious groups, opposed all religious establishments by law on grounds of principle, obtained the enactment of the famous "Virginia Bill for Religious Liberty" by which all religious groups were placed on an equal footing so far as the State was concerned. Similar though less far-reaching legislation was being considered and passed in other States.

By the time of the adoption of the Constitution, our history shows that there was a widespread awareness among many Americans of the dangers of a union of Church and State. These people knew, some of them from bitter personal experience, that one of the greatest dangers to the freedom of the individual to worship in his own way lay in the Government's placing its official stamp of approval upon one particular kind of prayer or one particular form of religious services. . . . The Constitution was intended to avert a part of this danger by leaving the government of this country in the hands of the people rather than in the hands of any monarch. But this safeguard was not enough. Our Founders were no more willing to let the content of their prayers and their privilege of praying whenever they pleased be influenced by the ballot box than they were to let these vital matters of personal conscience depend upon the succession of monarchs. The First Amendment was added to the Constitution to stand as a guarantee that neither the power nor the prestige of the Federal Government would be used to control, support or influence the kinds of prayer the American people can say—that the people's religious must not be subjected to the pressures of government for change each time a new political administration is elected to office. Under that Amendment's prohibition against governmental establishment of religion, as reinforced by the provisions of the Fourteenth Amendment, government in this country, be it state or federal, is without power to prescribe by law any particular form of prayer which is to be used as an official prayer in carrying on any program of governmentally sponsored religious activity.

There can be no doubt that New York's state prayer program officially establishes the religious beliefs embodied in the Regents' prayer. The respondents' argument to the contrary, which is largely based upon the contention that the Regents' prayer is "non-denominational" and the fact that the program, as modified and approved by state courts, does not require all pupils to recite the prayer but permits those who wish to do so to remain silent or be excused from the room, ignores the essential nature of the program's constitutional defects. Neither the fact that the prayer may be denominationally neutral nor the fact that its observance on the part of the students is voluntary can serve to free it from the limitations of the Establishment Clause, as it might from the Free Exercise Clause, of the First Amendment, both of which are operative against the States by virtue of the Fourteenth Amendment. Although these two clauses may in certain instances overlap, they forbid two quite different kinds of governmental encroachment upon religious freedom. The Establishment Clause, unlike the Free Exercise

Clause, does not depend upon any showing of direct governmental compulsion and is violated by the enactment of laws which establish an official religion whether those laws operate directly to coerce nonobserving individuals or not. This is not to say, of course, that laws officially prescribing a particular form of religious worship do not involve coercion of such individuals. When the power, prestige and financial support of government is placed behind a particular religious belief, the indirect coercive pressure upon religious minorities to conform to the prevailing officially approved religion is plain. But the purposes underlying the Establishment Clause go much further than that. Its first and most immediate purpose rested on the belief that a union of government and religion tends to destroy government and to degrade religion. . . . The Establishment Clause thus stands as an expression of principle on the part of the Founders of our Constitution that religion is too personal, too sacred, too holy, to permit its "unhallowed perversion" by a civil magistrate. Another purpose of the Establishment Clause rested upon an awareness of the historical fact that governmentally established religions and religious persecutions go hand in hand. . . . It was in large part to get completely away from this sort of systematic religious persecution that the Founders brought into being our Nation, our Constitution, and our Bill of Rights with its prohibition against any governmental establishment of religion. The New York laws officially prescribing the Regents' prayer are inconsistent both with the purposes of the Establishment Clause and with the Establishment Clause itself.

It has been argued that to apply the Constitution in such a way as to prohibit state laws respecting an establishment of religious services in public schools is to indicate a hostility toward religion or toward prayer. . . . It is neither sacrilegious nor antireligious to say that each separate government in this country should stay out of the business of writing or sanctioning official prayers and leave that purely religious function to the people themselves and to those the people choose to look to for religious guidance.

It is true that New York's establishment of its Regents' prayer as an officially approved religious doctrine of that State does not amount to a total establishment of one particular religious sect to the exclusion of all others. . . . To those who may subscribe to the view that because the Regents' official prayer is so brief and general there can be no danger to religious freedom in its governmental establishment, however, it may be appropriate to say in the words of James Madison, the author of the First Amendment:

> [I]t is proper to take alarm at the first experiment on our liberties. . . . Who does not see that the same authority which can establish Christianity, in exclusion of all other Religions, may establish with the same ease any particular sect of Christians, in exclusion of all other Sects? . . .

Mr. Justice Douglas, concurring.

It is customary in deciding a constitutional question to treat it in its narrowest form. Yet at times the setting of the question gives it a form and content which no abstract treatment could give. The point for decision is whether the Government can constitutionally finance a religious exercise. Our system at the federal and state levels is presently honeycombed with such financing. Nevertheless, I think it is an unconstitutional undertaking whatever form it takes. . . .

Mr. Justice Stewart, dissenting.

A local school board in New York has provided that those pupils who wish to do so may join in a brief prayer at the beginning of each school day, acknowledging their dependence upon God and asking His blessing upon them and upon their parents, their teachers, and their country. The Court today decides that in permitting this brief nondenominational prayer the school board has violated the Constitution of the United States. I think this decision is wrong.

The Court does not hold, nor could it, that New York has interfered with the free exercise of anybody's religion. . . .

With all respect, I think the Court has misapplied a great constitutional principle. I cannot see how an "official religion" is established by letting those who want to say a prayer say it. On the contrary, I think that to deny the wish of these school children to join in reciting this prayer is to deny them the opportunity of sharing in the spiritual heritage of our Nation.

. . . For we deal here not with the establishment of a state church, which would, of course, be constitutionally impermissible, but with whether school children who want to begin their day by joining in prayer must be prohibited from doing so. Moreover, I think that the Court's task, in this as in all areas of constitutional adjudication, is not responsibly aided by the uncritical invocation of metaphors like the "wall of separation," a phrase nowhere to be found in the Constitution. What is relevant to the is-

sue here is not the history of an established church in sixteenth century England or in eighteenth century America, but the history of the religious traditions of our people, reflected in countless practices of the institutions and officials of our government.

At the opening of each day's Session of this Court we stand, while one of our officials invokes the protection of God. . . . The Court today says that the state and federal governments are without constitutional power to prescribe any particular form of words to be recited by any group of the American people on any subject touching religion. . . . In 1954 Congress added a phrase to the Pledge of Allegiance to the Flag so that it now contains the words "one Nation under God, indivisible, with liberty and justice for all."

. . . Since 1865 the words "IN GOD WE TRUST" have been impressed on our coins.

Countless similar examples could be listed, but there is no need to belabor the obvious. It was all summed up by this Court just ten years ago in a single sentence: "We are a religious people whose institutions presuppose a Supreme Being." . . .

I do not believe that this Court, or the Congress, or the President has by the actions and practices I have mentioned established an "official religion" in violation of the Constitution. And I do not believe the State of New York has done so in this case. What each has done has been to recognize and to follow the deeply entrenched and highly cherished spiritual traditions of our Nation—traditions which come down to us from those who almost two hundred years ago avowed their "firm Reliance on the Protection of divine Providence" when they proclaimed the freedom and independence of this brave new world.

I dissent.

Further Resources

BOOKS

Ball, Howard. *Hugo L. Black: Cold Steel Warrior.* New York: Oxford University Press, 1996.

Ball, Howard, and Phillip J. Cooper. *Of Power and Right: Hugo Black, William O. Douglas, and America's Constitutional Revolution.* New York: Oxford University Press, 1992.

Eastland, Terry. *Religious Liberty in the Supreme Court: The Cases That Define the Debate over Church and State.* Washington, D.C.: Ethics and Public Policy Center, 1993.

Frank, John Paul. *Inside Justice Hugo L. Black: The Letters.* Austin, Tex.: Jamail Center for Legal Research, the University of Texas at Austin, 2000.

PERIODICALS

Blackmun, Harry A. "Certain Southerners on the Supreme Court." *The Georgia Journal of Southern Legal History* 1, no. 2, Fall/Winter 1991, 379–394.

Gerhardt, Michael J. "A Tale of Two Textualists: A Critical Comparison of Justices Black and Scalia." *Boston University Law Review* 74, no.1, January 1994, 25–66.

WEBSITES

"Introduction to the Engel v. Vitale Court Case." Available online at http://usinfo.state.gov/usa/infousa/facts/democrac/47 .htm; website home page: http://www.usinfo.state.gov (accessed January 21, 2003).

Gideon v. Wainwright

Supreme Court decision

By: Hugo L. Black

Date: March 18, 1963

Source: Black, Hugo L. *Gideon v. Wainwright,* 372 U.S. 335. Available online at http://caselaw.lp.findlaw.com/scripts /getcase.pl?navby=case&court=us&vol=372&page=335; website home page: http://caselaw.lp.findlaw.com (accessed June 11, 2003).

About the Author: Hugo L. Black (1886–1971) graduated from the University of Alabama Law School in 1906. His first major political race was a successful one for the U.S. Senate in 1926. After serving two terms in the Senate, Black was appointed to the U.S. Supreme Court in 1937. There was some opposition to his appointment because he had admitted to being a member of the Ku Klux Klan in the 1920s, but his term was distinguished by his support of civil rights. ∎

Introduction

The right of an accused criminal to hire defense counsel is enshrined in the American Constitution. The Sixth Amendment states that "in all criminal prosecutions, the accused shall enjoy the right . . . to have the Assistance of Counsel for his defense." However, many people cannot afford counsel. Since 1790, a defendant in a federal capital case who cannot afford to pay a lawyer can request counsel and the court will appoint up to two; this safeguard, however, does not apply to noncapital cases. Another problem for those being tried in state court was that the Sixth Amendment applied only to the federal government and not to the states.

In the twentieth century, though, interpretations of the right to counsel evolved. In capital cases in state courts, the Supreme Court held in 1932 that the right to counsel was part of a fair trial, and thus began to apply the Sixth Amendment to the states. The Court held that the right to counsel was part of due process and thus protected by the Fourteenth Amendment. On the federal level, the Supreme Court held in *Johnson v. Zerbst* (1938) that counsel had to be appointed, if the defendant could not afford it, unless the right to counsel was waived. However, most criminal cases were and are in state court,

not federal court. The right to counsel in state court in noncapital cases was first stated in 1942, when the Supreme Court held that the right to counsel was not a fundamental part of a fair trial in all criminal cases. The Supreme Court expanded the mandatory right to counsel in certain circumstances, but not all. The general right to counsel in all felony criminal cases came before the Court again in *Gideon v. Wainwright.*

Significance

Clarence Gideon had prepared his own appeal to the Supreme Court, claiming a right to counsel. Although he wrote his legal brief while in prison, it caught the eye of the Court. After appointing him counsel to represent him, the Court voted favorably on his appeal. When he was retried in a lower court, Gideon was freed. The assistance of counsel proved to be essential to his case, as the counsel was able to counter the evidence against him.

The right to counsel for all defendants was only one of the due process rights the Warren Court (as the Supreme Court under Chief Justice Earl Warren was known, 1953–1969) created or expanded in the 1960s. In the famous *Miranda* case in 1966, the Court required authorities to read an accused his/her rights at the time of arrest. These increased rights for the accused outraged many conservatives and helped lead to the conservative ascendancy of the 1970s and 1980s. Conservative justices, though, did not reverse the *Gideon* decision. In fact, the Burger Court (under Chief Justice Warren Burger, 1969–1986), which followed the Warren Court, first expanded the right to counsel to all cases that could lead to imprisonment, not just all felony cases. However, the right was not expanded to people in lineups who had not been indicted. The Rehnquist Court (under Chief Justice William Rehnquist, 1986–), which followed the Burger Court, has somewhat restricted the rights of the accused, including allowing some coerced confessions and some limitations on the *Miranda* warnings, but it has not reversed the ruling in *Gideon.*

Primary Source

Gideon v. Wainwright [excerpt]

SYNOPSIS: In this excerpt, Black, who wrote the majority opinion, points out that Gideon asked for a lawyer at trial. The Sixth Amendment right to counsel is a fundamental right that the states are obligated to uphold. Black closes by noting that states have great financial resources to prove people guilty, and the only way one can have a fair trial is to have counsel.

Mr. Justice Black delivered the opinion of the Court.

Petitioner was charged in a Florida state court with having broken and entered a poolroom with intent to commit a misdemeanor. This offense is a felony under Florida law. Appearing in court without funds and without a lawyer, petitioner asked the court to appoint counsel for him, whereupon the following colloquy took place:

> The Court: Mr. Gideon, I am sorry, but I cannot appoint Counsel to represent you in this case. Under the laws of the State of Florida, the only time the Court can appoint Counsel to represent a Defendant is when that person is charged with a capital offense. I am sorry, but I will have to deny your request to appoint Counsel to defend you in this case.
>
> The Defendant: The United States Supreme Court says I am entitled to be represented by Counsel.

Put to trial before a jury, Gideon conducted his defense about as well as could be expected from a layman. . . . The jury returned a verdict of guilty, and petitioner was sentenced to serve five years in the state prison. . . . Since 1942, when *Betts v. Brady* . . . was decided by a divided Court, the problem of a defendant's federal constitutional right to counsel in a state court has been a continuing source of controversy and litigation in both state and federal courts. To give this problem another review here, we granted certiorari. . . .

The facts upon which Betts claimed that he had been unconstitutionally denied the right to have counsel appointed to assist him are strikingly like the facts upon which Gideon here bases his federal constitutional claim. . . . Betts was denied any relief, and on review this Court affirmed. It was held that a refusal to appoint counsel for an indigent defendant charged with a felony did not necessarily violate the Due Process Clause of the Fourteenth Amendment, which for reasons given the Court deemed to be the only applicable federal constitutional provision.. . . .

Treating due process as "a concept less rigid and more fluid than those envisaged in other specific and particular provisions of the Bill of Rights," the Court held that refusal to appoint counsel under the particular facts and circumstances in the *Betts* case was not so "offensive to the common and fundamental ideas of fairness" as to amount to a denial of due process. Since the facts and circumstances of the two cases are so nearly indistinguishable, we think the *Betts v. Brady* holding if left standing would require us to reject Gideon's claim that the Constitution guarantees him the assistance

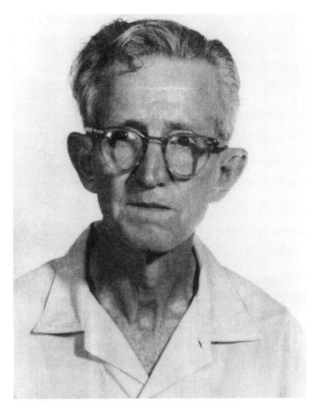

Clarence Earl Gideon, said to be a homeless drifter, was accused of breaking and entering into a pool hall. He wrote his own appeal of his case to the Supreme Court from prison, where he had been sentenced to a five-year term. **AP/WIDE WORLD PHOTOS. REPRODUCED BY PERMISSION.**

of counsel. Upon full reconsideration we conclude that *Betts v. Brady* should be overruled.

. . . The Sixth Amendment provides, "In all criminal prosecutions, the accused shall enjoy the right . . . to have the Assistance of Counsel for his defence." We have construed this to mean that in federal courts counsel must be provided for defendants unable to employ counsel unless the right is competently and intelligently waived. Betts argued that this right is extended to indigent defendants in state courts by the Fourteenth Amendment. In response the Court stated that, while the Sixth Amendment laid down "no rule for the conduct of the States, the question recurs whether the constraint laid by the Amendment upon the national courts expresses a rule so fundamental and essential to a fair trial, and so, to due process of law, that it is made obligatory upon the States by the Fourteenth Amendment." . . .

We think the Court in *Betts* had ample precedent for acknowledging that those guarantees of the Bill of Rights which are fundamental safeguards of liberty immune from federal abridgment are equally protected against state invasion by the Due Process Clause of the Fourteenth Amendment. This same principle was recognized, explained, and applied in *Powell v. Alabama,* . . . (1932), a case upholding the right of counsel, where the Court held that despite sweeping language to the contrary in *Hurtado v. California,* . . . (1884), the Fourteenth Amendment "embraced" those "'fundamental principles of liberty and justice which lie at the base of all our civil and political institutions,'" even though they had been "specifically dealt with in another part of the federal Constitution." . . . In many cases other than *Powell* and *Betts,* this Court has looked to the fundamental nature of original Bill of Rights guarantees to decide whether the Fourteenth Amendment makes them obligatory on the States. Explicitly recognized to be of this "fundamental nature" and therefore made immune from state invasion by the Fourteenth, or some part of it, are the First Amendment's freedoms of speech, press, religion, assembly, association, and petition for redress of grievances. For the same reason, though not always in precisely the same terminology, the Court has made obligatory on the States the Fifth Amendment's command that private property shall not be taken for public use without just compensation, the Fourth Amendment's prohibition of unreasonable searches and seizures, and the Eighth's ban on cruel and unusual punishment. On the other hand, this Court in *Palko v. Connecticut,* . . . (1937), refused to hold that the Fourteenth Amendment made the double jeopardy provision of the Fifth Amendment obligatory on the States. In so refusing, however, the Court, speaking through Mr. Justice Cardozo, was careful to emphasize that "immunities that are valid as against the federal government by force of the specific pledges of particular amendments have been found to be implicit in the concept of ordered liberty, and thus, through the Fourteenth Amendment, become valid as against the states" and that guarantees "in their origin . . . effective against the federal government alone" had by prior cases "been taken over from the earlier articles of the federal bill of rights and brought within the Fourteenth Amendment by a process of absorption." . . .

We accept *Betts v. Brady*'s assumption, based as it was on our prior cases, that a provision of the Bill of Rights which is "fundamental and essential to a fair trial" is made obligatory upon the States by the Fourteenth Amendment. We think the Court in *Betts* was wrong, however, in concluding that the Sixth Amendment's guarantee of counsel is not one of these fundamental rights. Ten years before *Betts*

v. Brady, this Court, after full consideration of all the historical data examined in *Betts,* had unequivocally declared that "the right to the aid of counsel is of this fundamental character." *Powell v. Alabama,* . . . (1932). While the Court at the close of its *Powell* opinion did by its language, as this Court frequently does, limit its holding to the particular facts and circumstances of that case, its conclusions about the fundamental nature of the right to counsel are unmistakable. Several years later, in 1936, the Court reemphasized what it had said about the fundamental nature of the right to counsel in this language:

> We concluded that certain fundamental rights, safeguarded by the first eight amendments against federal action, were also safeguarded against state action by the due process of law clause of the Fourteenth Amendment, and among them the fundamental right of the accused to the aid of counsel in a criminal prosecution. . . .

And again in 1938 this Court said:

> [The assistance of counsel] is one of the safeguards of the Sixth Amendment deemed necessary to insure fundamental human rights of life and liberty. . . . The Sixth Amendment stands as a constant admonition that if the constitutional safeguards it provides be lost, justice will not `still be done.' . . .

In light of these and many other prior decisions of this Court, it is not surprising that the *Betts* Court, when faced with the contention that "one charged with crime, who is unable to obtain counsel, must be furnished counsel by the State," conceded that "[e]xpressions in the opinions of this court lend color to the argument. . . ." The fact is that in deciding as it did—that "appointment of counsel is not a fundamental right, essential to a fair trial"—the Court in *Betts v. Brady* made an abrupt break with its own well-considered precedents. In returning to these old precedents, sounder we believe than the new, we but restore constitutional principles established to achieve a fair system of justice. Not only these precedents but also reason and reflection require us to recognize that in our adversary system of criminal justice, any person haled into court, who is too poor to hire a lawyer, cannot be assured a fair trial unless counsel is provided for him. This seems to us to be an obvious truth. Governments, both state and federal, quite properly spend vast sums of money to establish machinery to try defendants accused of crime. Lawyers to prosecute are everywhere deemed essential to protect the public's interest in an orderly society. Similarly, there are few defendants charged with crime, few indeed, who fail to hire the best lawyers they can get to prepare and present their defenses. That government hires lawyers to prosecute and defendants who have the money hire lawyers to defend are the strongest indications of the widespread belief that lawyers in criminal courts are necessities, not luxuries. The right of one charged with crime to counsel may not be deemed fundamental and essential to fair trials in some countries, but it is in ours. From the very beginning, our state and national constitutions and laws have laid great emphasis on procedural and substantive safeguards designed to assure fair trials before impartial tribunals in which every defendant stands equal before the law. This noble ideal cannot be realized if the poor man charged with crime has to face his accusers without a lawyer to assist him. A defendant's need for a lawyer is nowhere better stated than in the moving words of Mr. Justice Sutherland in *Powell v. Alabama:*

> The right to be heard would be, in many cases, of little avail if it did not comprehend the right to be heard by counsel. Even the intelligent and educated layman has small and sometimes no skill in the science of law. If charged with crime, he is incapable, generally, of determining for himself whether the indictment is good or bad. He is unfamiliar with the rules of evidence. Left without the aid of counsel he may be put on trial without a proper charge, and convicted upon incompetent evidence, or evidence irrelevant to the issue or otherwise inadmissible. He lacks both the skill and knowledge adequately to prepare his defense, even though he have a perfect one. He requires the guiding hand of counsel at every step in the proceedings against him. Without it, though he be not guilty, he faces the danger of conviction because he does not know how to establish his innocence. . . .

The Court in *Betts v. Brady* departed from the sound wisdom upon which the Court's holding in *Powell v. Alabama* rested. Florida, supported by two other States, has asked that *Betts v. Brady* be left intact. Twenty-two States, as friends of the Court, argue that *Betts* was "an anachronism when handed down" and that it should now be overruled. We agree.

The judgment is reversed and the cause is remanded to the Supreme Court of Florida for further action not inconsistent with this opinion.

Reversed.

Further Resources

BOOKS

Ball, Howard, and Phillip J Cooper. *Of Power and Right: Hugo Black, William O. Douglas, and America's Constitutional Revolution.* New York: Oxford University Press, 1992.

Lewis, Anthony. *Gideon's Trumpet.* New York: Random House, 1964.

Meador, Daniel John. *Preludes to Gideon; Notes on Appellate Advocacy, Habeas Corpus, and Constitutional Litigation.* Charlottesville, Va.: Michie, 1967.

PERIODICALS

Surkiewicz, Joe. "Is There a Civil Gideon in Our Future?: Yes, Say Legal Experts Who Are Laying the Groundwork for a Test Case." *Daily Record,* June 23, 2001, 13A–14A.

WEBSITES

Gideon v. Wainwright. Available online at http://exchanges .state.gov/education/engteaching/pubs/AmLnC/br67.htm; website home page: http://www.exchanges.state.gov (accessed January 16, 2003).

AUDIO AND VISUAL MEDIA

Agronsky, David, and Anthony Lewis. *Gideon's Trumpet: The Poor Man and the Law.* New York: CBS Television Network, 2000.

New York Times Co. v. Sullivan

Supreme Court decision

By: William J. Brennan; Hugo Black; Arthur Goldberg

Date: March 9, 1964

Source: Brennan, William J., Hugo Black, Arthur Goldberg. *New York Times v. Sullivan*, 376 U.S. 254. Available online at http://caselaw.lp.findlaw.com/scripts/getcase.pl?navby=case &court=us&vol=376&page=254; website home page: http:// caselaw.lp.findlaw.com (accessed June 11, 2003).

About the Authors: William Brennan (1906–1997) received his law degree from Harvard. He was appointed to New Jersey's highest court in 1952 and to the Supreme Court in 1957.

Hugo Lafayette Black (1886–1971) was appointed to the Supreme Court in 1937 after serving in the U.S. Senate. His term was distinguished by his support of civil rights.

Arthur Joseph Goldberg (1908–1990) passed the bar at age twenty, was appointed secretary of labor in 1960, and served on the Supreme Court from 1962 to 1965, resigning to accept a post as ambassador to the United Nations. ∎

Introduction

The First Amendment states, in part, that "Congress shall make no law . . . abridging the freedom of speech, or of the press." The question of freedom of the press was not extensively litigated in U.S. federal courts before 1900. During the Civil War (1861–1865), laws were passed limiting freedom of the press, but the U.S. Supreme Court never ruled on the validity of the legislation. Further, the First Amendment was held to limit only the federal government, not state governments.

Police Commissioner L.B. Sullivan (second left) and his attorneys celebrate his libel suit victory against *The New York Times* in Montgomery, Alabama. The 1960 ruling was overturned by the U.S. Supreme Court in 1964. © BETTMANN/CORBIS. REPRODUCED BY PERMISSION.

Around 1900, however, the issue of freedom of the press began to be litigated more often. In World War I (1914–1918), the Espionage and Sedition Acts restricted the freedom of the press, and these laws were upheld by the Supreme Court. In the 1920s, the Supreme Court expanded the protection of the freedom of the press by applying the First Amendment against the states. In *Near v. Minnesota* (1931), for example, the Court struck down a Minnesota statute that allowed any defamatory, malicious, or scandalous newspaper to be suppressed. The ability of individuals to win libel lawsuits was kept relatively intact, though. In the early 1960s, *New York Times* published an advertisement that stated that the city fathers of Montgomery, Alabama, had mistreated civil rights protesters. Some of the statements in the ad were misleading, causing a Montgomery city commissioner to sue the *Times* for libel, and he won a $500,000 judgment.

Significance

In *New York Times Co. v. Sullivan,* the Supreme Court crafted a new standard for libel cases. To win a libel case, a public official had to show "actual malice" on the part of the paper. This meant that the paper had to publish a false, defamatory statement "with knowledge that it was false or with reckless disregard of whether it was false or not." This rule applied only to public officials, though, and the Warren Court (as the Supreme Court was known under Chief Justice Earl Warren, 1953–1969) soon limited the rule to public officials who had the power and responsibility to create policy. Later, in two 1967 cases, public figures were required to show "highly unreasonable conduct" on the part of the publisher. There was no clear agreement on this issue, though, as the Supreme Court justices issued a large number of conflicting opinions in these cases.

In the 1970s, 1980s, and 1990s, the courts refused to extend the "actual malice" test to private individuals. Newsworthy statements that were not defamatory were allowed to be published. This expansion of freedom of the press helped to bring about the press investigation that partially uncovered the Watergate scandal during the administration of President Richard Nixon (served 1969–1974). It also helped to keep light shining on civil rights issues. The Rehnquist Court (1986–) shifted the inquiry from whether or not one was a public figure or public official to whether or not the allegedly defamatory statement involved a matter of public concern. If the statement did not, then the person suing for damages did not have to prove that the publishing agent printed the statement knowing it was false. The general rule of *New York Times Co. v. Sullivan* has been upheld and has strengthened the press, although with qualifications.

Primary Source

New York Times Co. v. Sullivan [excerpt]

> **SYNOPSIS:** Writing for the majority, Justice Brennan examines the issue of libel, stating that it deserves some First Amendment protection. He establishes the actual malice test: statements must be made falsely with knowledge of that falsity or with reckless disregard for it. Black concurs: the First Amendment creates an absolute ban on libel suits by public officials. Goldberg also concurs: the First Amendment gives an absolute right to criticize.

Mr. Justice Brennan delivered the opinion of the Court. . . .

It is uncontroverted that some of the statements contained in the paragraphs were not accurate descriptions of events which occurred in Montgomery. Although Negro students staged a demonstration on the State Capitol steps, they sang the National Anthem and not "My Country, 'Tis of Thee." . . .

Respondent made no effort to prove that he suffered actual pecuniary loss as a result of the alleged libel. . . .

Under Alabama law as applied in this case, a publication is "libelous per se" if the words "tend to injure a person . . . in his reputation" or to "bring [him] into public contempt" . . . . Once "libel per se" has been established, the defendant has no defense as to stated facts unless he can persuade the jury that they were true in all their particulars. . . . His privilege of "fair comment" for expressions of opinion depends on the truth of the facts upon which the comment is based. . . . Unless he can discharge the burden of proving truth, general damages are presumed, and may be awarded without proof of pecuniary injury. . . . Good motives and belief in truth do not negate an inference of malice, but are relevant only in mitigation of punitive damages if the jury chooses to accord them weight. . . .

The question before us is whether this rule of liability, as applied to an action brought by a public official against critics of his official conduct, abridges the freedom of speech and of the press that is guaranteed by the first and Fourteenth Amendments. . . . Like insurrection, contempt, advocacy of unlawful acts, breach of the peace, obscenity, solicitation of legal business, and the various other formulae for the repression of expression that have been challenged in this court, libel can claim no talismanic immunity from constitutional limitations. It must be measured by standards that satisfy the First Amendment.

The general proposition that freedom of expression upon public questions is secured by the First Amendment has long been settled by our decisions. . . . The First Amendment, said Judge Learned Hand, "presupposes that right conclusions are more likely to be gathered out of a multitude of tongues, than through any kind of authoritative selection. To many this is, and always will be, folly; but we have staked upon it our all." . . .

Thus we consider this case against the background of a profound national commitment to the principle that debate on public issues should be uninhibited, robust, and wide-open, and that it may well include vehement, caustic, and sometimes unpleasantly sharp attacks on government and public officials. . . . The present advertisement, as an expression of grievance and protest on one of the major public issues of our time, would seem clearly to qualify for the constitutional protection. The question is whether it forfeits that protection by the falsity of some of its factual statements and by its alleged defamation of respondent.

Authoritative interpretations of the First Amendment guarantees have consistently refused to recognize an exception for any test of truth—whether administered by judges, juries, or administrative officials—and especially one that puts the burden of proving truth on the speaker. . . . The constitutional protection does not turn upon "the truth, popularity, or social utility of the ideas and beliefs which are offered." . . . As Madison said, "Some degree of abuse is inseparable from the proper use of every thing; and in no instance is this more true than in that of the press." . . .

Injury to official reputation affords no more warrant for repressing speech that would otherwise be free than does factual error. Where judicial officers are involved, this Court has held that concern for the dignity and reputation of the courts does not justify the punishment as criminal contempt of criticism of the judge or his decision. . . .

If neither factual error nor defamatory content suffices to remove the constitutional shield from criticism of official conduct, the combination of the two elements is no less inadequate. This is the lesson to be drawn from the great controversy over the Sedition Act of 1798 . . . which first crystallized a national awareness of the central meaning of the First Amendment. . . .

Although the Sedition Act was never tested in this Court, the attack upon its validity has carried the day in the court of history. . . .

What a State may not constitutionally bring about by means of a criminal statute is likewise beyond the reach of its civil law of libel. . . .

The constitutional guarantees require, we think, a federal rule that prohibits a public official from recovering damages for a defamatory falsehood relating to his official conduct unless he proves that the statement was made with "actual malice"—that is, with knowledge that it was false or with reckless disregard of whether it was false or not. . . .

Analogous considerations support the privilege for the citizen-critic of government. It is as much his duty to criticize as it is the official's duty to administer. . . .

We conclude that such a privilege is required by the First and Fourteenth Amendments.

Mr. Justice Black, with whom Mr. Justice Douglas joins, concurring.

I concur in reversing this half-million-dollar judgment against the New York Times Company and the four individual defendants. . . . I base my vote to reverse on the belief that the First and Fourteenth Amendments not merely "delimit" a State's power to award damages to "public officials against critics of their official conduct" but completely prohibit a State from exercising such a power. . . . Unlike the Court, therefore, I vote to reverse exclusively on the ground that the Times and the individual defendants had an absolute, unconditional constitutional right to publish in the Times advertisement their criticisms of the Montgomery agencies and officials. . . .

The half-million-dollar verdict does give dramatic proof, however, that state libel laws threaten the very existence of an American press virile enough to pub-

Justice William O. Douglas argued that the "clear and present danger" text could be manipulated to limit free speech. © BETTMANN/CORBIS. REPRODUCED BY PERMISSION.

lish unpopular views on public affairs and bold enough to criticize the conduct of public officials. . . .

One of the acute and highly emotional issues in this country arises out of efforts of many people, even including some public officials, to continue state-commanded segregation of races in the public schools and other public places, despite our several holdings that such a state practice is forbidden by the Fourteenth Amendment. Montgomery is one of the localities in which widespread hostility to desegregation has been manifested. This hostility has sometimes extended itself to persons who favor desegregation, particularly to so-called "outside agitators," a term which can be made to fit papers like the Times, which is published in New York. The scarcity of testimony to show that Commissioner Sullivan suffered any actual damages at all suggests that these feelings of hostility had at least as much to do with rendition of this half-million-dollar verdict as did an appraisal of damages. Viewed realistically, this record lends support to an inference that instead of being damaged Commissioner Sullivan's political, social, and financial prestige has likely been enhanced by the Times' publication. . . .

In my opinion the Federal Constitution has dealt with this deadly danger to the press in the only way possible without leaving the free press open to destruction—by granting the press an absolute immunity for criticism of the way public officials do their public duty. . . .

I agree with the Court that the Fourteenth Amendment made the First applicable to the States. This means to me that since the adoption of the Fourteenth Amendment a State has no more power than the Federal Government to use a civil libel law or any other law to impose damages for merely discussing public affairs and criticizing public officials. The power of the United States to do that is, in my judgment, precisely nil. Such was the general view held when the First Amendment was adopted and ever since. Congress never has sought to challenge this viewpoint by passing any civil libel law. It did pass the Sedition Act in 1798, which made it a crime—"seditious libel"—to criticize federal officials or the Federal Government. As the Court's opinion correctly points out, however . . . that Act came to an ignominious end and by common consent has generally been treated as having been a wholly unjustifiable and much to be regretted violation of the First Amendment. Since the First Amendment is now made applicable to the States by the Fourteenth, it no more permits the States to impose damages for libel than it does the Federal Government.

We would, I think, more faithfully interpret the First Amendment by holding that at the very least it leaves the people and the press free to criticize officials and discuss public affairs with impunity. This Nation of ours elects many of its important officials; so do the States, the municipalities, the counties, and even many precincts. These officials are responsible to the people for the way they perform their duties. . . . To punish the exercise of this right to discuss public affairs or to penalize it through libel judgments is to abridge or shut off discussion of the very kind most needed. This Nation, I suspect, can live in peace without libel suits based on public discussions of public affairs and public officials. But I doubt that a country can live in freedom where its people can be made to suffer physically or financially for criticizing their government, its actions, or its officials. . . . An unconditional right to say what one pleases about public affairs is what I consider to be the minimum guarantee of the First Amendment.

I regret that the Court has stopped short of this holding indispensable to preserve our free press from destruction. . . .

Mr. Justice Goldberg, with whom Mr. Justice Douglas joins, concurring in the result. . . .

In my view, the First and Fourteenth Amendments to the Constitution afford to the citizen and to the press an absolute, unconditional privilege to criticize official conduct despite the harm which may flow from excesses and abuses. The prized American right "to speak one's mind," . . . about public officials and affairs needs "breathing space to survive." . . . The right should not depend upon a probing by the jury of the motivation of the citizen or press. The theory of our Constitution is that every citizen may speak his mind and every newspaper express its view on matters of public concern and may not be barred from speaking or publishing because those in control of government think that what is said or written is unwise, unfair, false, or malicious. In a democratic society, one who assumes to act for the citizens in an executive, legislative, or judicial capacity must expect that his official acts will be commented upon and criticized. Such criticism cannot, in my opinion, be muzzled or deterred by the courts at the instance of public officials under the label of libel. . . .

I strongly believe that the Constitution accords citizens and press an unconditional freedom to criticize official conduct. It necessarily follows that in a case such as this, where all agree that the allegedly defamatory statements related to official conduct, the judgments for libel cannot constitutionally be sustained.

Further Resources

BOOKS

Eastland, Terry. *Freedom of Expression in the Supreme Court: The Defining Cases.* Washington: Rowman and Littlefield, 2000.

Hopkins, W. Wat. *Actual Malice: Twenty-five Years after Times v. Sullivan.* New York: Praeger, 1989.

———. *Mr. Justice Brennan and Freedom of Expression.* New York: Praeger, 1991.

Irons, Peter H. *Brennan vs. Rehnquist: The Battle for the Constitution.* New York: Knopf, 1994.

Lewis, Anthony. *Make No Law: the Sullivan Case and the First Amendment.* New York: Random House, 1991.

Rosenkranz, E. Joshua, and Bernard Schwartz. *Reason and Passion: Justice Brennan's Enduring Influence.* New York: Norton, 1997.

VanBurkleo, Sandra F., Kermit Hall, and Robert J Kaczorowski. *Constitutionalism and American Culture: Writing the New Constitutional History.* Lawrence: University Press of Kansas, 2002.

WEBSITES

The New York Times v. Sullivan. Available online at http://faculty-web.at.nwu.edu/commstud/freespeech/cont/cases/nytsullivan.html; website home page: http://www.faculty-web.at.nwu.edu (accessed January 21, 2003).

Atlanta Motel v. U.S.
Supreme Court decision

By: Thomas C. Clark; William O. Douglas

Date: December 14, 1964

Source: Clark, Thomas C., and William O. Douglas. *Atlanta Motel v. United States,* 379 U.S. 241. Available online at http://caselaw.lp.findlaw.com/scripts/getcase.pl?navby=case&court=us&vol=379&page=241; website home page: http://caselaw.lp.findlaw.com (accessed June 11, 2003).

About the Authors: Thomas C. Clark (1898–1980), a native of Texas, was appointed U.S. attorney general in 1945. He served on the U.S. Supreme Court from 1949 to 1967. William O. Douglas (1899–1977) was one of the youngest men ever to be appointed to the Supreme Court and served the longest of any justice: thirty-six years. He was an independent who was more concerned about being right than being in the majority. ∎

Introduction

After the Civil War (1861–1865), some steps were taken to improve the status of African Americans. The Thirteenth Amendment ended slavery; the Fourteenth Amendment guaranteed due process, equal protection under the law, and equal privileges and immunities to all persons; and the Fifteenth Amendment guaranteed that the right to vote would not be denied on the basis of race. The precise meaning of those amendments was not immediately clear, however. In 1873, the U.S. Supreme Court held that the "privileges and immunities" referred to in the Fourteenth Amendment were limited, applying only to the actions of the federal government. In 1883, the Supreme Court held that equal protection under the law applied to state action, not the actions of private citizens. Finally, in 1896, the Supreme Court upheld the "separate but equal" doctrine in the landmark case *Plessy v. Ferguson.*

The Supreme Court upheld this doctrine until 1954. That year, in *Brown v. Board of Education,* the Court overturned *Plessy* by ruling that separate but equal facilities in education were unconstitutional. The Court continued to prohibit racial discrimination, but on a case-by-case basis until Congress began to take action in outlawing discrimination. The 1957 Civil Rights Act was

An NAACP member and civil rights activist holds a sign urging an end to the whites-only policy at Atlanta hotels and restaurants. Nearby a Klansman passes out flyers to supporters of segregation, as part of the KKK's counter-initiative against NAACP efforts. July 4, 1962. **AP/WIDE WORLD PHOTOS. REPRODUCED BY PERMISSION.**

the first civil rights act passed in seventy-five years. However, the scope of this act was limited, since the Civil Rights Commission it created could only recommend legislation and provide for jury trials for those accused of some violations of civil rights. In the pro-segregation South, this meant that few convictions would be forthcoming. President John F. Kennedy (served 1961–1963) called for new civil rights legislation, but only after his assassination did President Lyndon Johnson (served 1963–1969) push through the Civil Rights Act of 1964, which used the commerce clause of the Constitution (which gave Congress power over interstate commerce) to ban racial segregation and discrimination in activities that affected interstate commerce. One of the earliest tests of this act was *Atlanta Motel v. U.S.*

Significance

In its decision, the Supreme Court unanimously upheld the constitutionality of the Civil Rights Act of 1964. The Court applied a two-prong test that was the same test applied to other regulations of commerce: whether the activity regulated is "commerce" and whether the regulation serves a legitimate government interest. In his de-

cision, Justice Clark ruled that the answer to both questions was yes. Justice Douglas, concurring, suggested that the legislation should have been based on the Fourteenth Amendment's allowance of legislation to enforce the rights extended by the amendment.

Since 1964, Congress has continued to use the commerce clause to enact legislation only tangentially related to commerce. For instance, Congress invoked its commerce power to criminalize the possession of weapons near school zones. Although the Supreme Court has generally upheld such regulations, it struck down gun criminalization in this instance as overstepping the bounds of congressional power. The Rehnquist Court (the Supreme Court under Chief Justice William Rehnquist, 1986–), though, has been more restrictive about Congress's power under the commerce clause. Still, Congress continued to pass civil rights legislation. Among the most important laws are theVoting Rights Act of 1965, which removed impediments to voting for almost three million African American voters, and the Civil Rights Act of 1968, which prevented housing discrimination. The Court has upheld both of these laws.

Primary Source

Atlanta Motel v. U.S. [excerpt]

SYNOPSIS: Justice Clark first states that Congress has the power to regulate commerce and any discrimination that develops there. Douglas concurs, agreeing that Congress has the power to act in this way, but expresses a belief that the banning of discrimination would have been better accomplished under the Fourteenth Amendment rather than through the commerce clause.

Mr. Justice Clark delivered the opinion of the Court. . . .

The sole question posed is, therefore, the constitutionality of the Civil Rights Act of 1964 as applied to these facts. The legislative history of the Act indicates that Congress based the Act on [Section] 5 and the Equal Protection Clause of the Fourteenth Amendment as well as its power to regulate interstate commerce under Art. I, 8, cl. 3, of the Constitution.

The Senate Commerce Committee made it quite clear that the fundamental object of Title II was to vindicate "the deprivation of personal dignity that surely accompanies denials of equal access to public establishments." At the same time, however, it noted that such an objective has been and could be readily achieved "by congressional action based on the commerce power of the Constitution." S. Rep. No. 872, supra, at 16–17. Our study of the legislative record, made in the light of prior cases, has brought us to the conclusion that Congress possessed ample power in this regard, and we have therefore not considered the other grounds relied upon. This is not to say that the remaining authority upon which it acted was not adequate, a question upon which we do not pass, but merely that since the commerce power is sufficient for our decision here we have considered it alone. . . .

The Basis of Congressional Action

While the Act as adopted carried no congressional findings the record of its passage through each house is replete with evidence of the burdens that discrimination by race or color places upon interstate commerce. . . . This testimony included the fact that our people have become increasingly mobile with millions of people of all races traveling from State to State; that Negroes in particular have been the subject of discrimination in transient accommodations, having to travel great distances to secure the same; . . . and that these conditions had become so acute as to require the listing of available lodging for Negroes in a special guidebook which was itself "dramatic testimony to the difficulties" Negroes encounter in travel. . . . These exclusionary practices were found to be nationwide, the Under Secretary of Commerce testifying that there is "no question that this discrimination in the North still exists to a large degree" and in the West and Midwest as well. . . . This testimony indicated a qualitative as well as quantitative effect on interstate travel by Negroes. . . . This was the conclusion not only of the Under Secretary of Commerce but also of the Administrator of the Federal Aviation Agency who wrote the Chairman of the Senate Commerce Committee that it was his "belief that air commerce is adversely affected by the denial to a substantial segment of the traveling public of adequate and desegregated public accommodations." . . . We shall not burden this opinion with further details since the voluminous testimony presents overwhelming evidence that discrimination by hotels and motels impedes interstate travel.

The Power of Congress Over Interstate Travel

The power of Congress to deal with these obstructions depends on the meaning of the Commerce Clause. Its meaning was first enunciated 140 years ago by the great Chief Justice John Marshall in *Gibbons v. Ogden*. . . .

In short, the determinative test of the exercise of power by the Congress under the Commerce Clause is simply whether the activity sought to be regulated is "commerce which concerns more States than one" and has a real and substantial relation to the national interest. Let us now turn to this facet of the problem. . . .

The same interest in protecting interstate commerce which led Congress to deal with segregation in interstate carriers and the white-slave traffic has prompted it to extend the exercise of its power to gambling, . . . to criminal enterprises, . . . to deceptive practices in the sale of products, . . . to fraudulent security transactions, . . . to misbranding of drugs, . . . and to racial discrimination by owners and managers of terminal restaurants. . . .

That Congress was legislating against moral wrongs in many of these areas rendered its enactments no less valid. In framing Title II of this Act Congress was also dealing with what it considered a moral problem. But that fact does not detract from the overwhelming evidence of the disruptive effect that racial discrimination has had on commercial intercourse. It was this burden which empowered Congress to enact appropriate legislation, and, given this basis for the exercise of its power, Congress was not restricted by the fact that the particular obstruction to interstate commerce with which it was dealing was also deemed a moral and social wrong.

It is said that the operation of the motel here is of a purely local character. But, assuming this to be true, "[i]f it is interstate commerce that feels the pinch, it does not matter how local the operation which applies the squeeze." . . .

Thus the power of Congress to promote interstate commerce also includes the power to regulate the local incidents thereof, including local activities in both the States of origin and destination, which might have a substantial and harmful effect upon that commerce. One need only examine the evidence which we have discussed above to see that Congress may—as it has—prohibit racial discrimination by motels serving travelers, however "local" their operations may appear.

Nor does the Act deprive appellant of liberty or property under the Fifth Amendment. The commerce power invoked here by the Congress is a specific and plenary one authorized by the Constitution itself. The only questions are: (1) whether Congress had a rational basis for finding that racial discrimination by motels affected commerce, and (2) if it had such a basis, whether the means it selected to eliminate that evil are reasonable and appropriate. . . .

We find no merit in the remainder of appellant's contentions, including that of "involuntary servitude." . . . We could not say that the requirements of the Act in this regard are in any way "akin to African slavery." . . .

We, therefore, conclude that the action of the Congress in the adoption of the Act as applied here to a motel which concededly serves interstate travelers is within the power granted it by the Commerce Clause of the Constitution, as interpreted by this Court for 140 years. It may be argued that Congress could have pursued other methods to eliminate the obstructions it found in interstate commerce caused by racial discrimination. But this is a matter of policy that rests entirely with the Congress not with the courts. How obstructions in commerce may be removed—what means are to be employed—is within the sound and exclusive discretion of the Congress. It is subject only to one caveat—that the means chosen by it must be reasonably adapted to the end permitted by the Constitution. We cannot say that its choice here was not so adapted. The Constitution requires no more.

Affirmed. . . .

Mr. Justice Douglas, concurring. . . .

Though I join the Court's opinions, I am somewhat reluctant here . . . to rest solely on the Commerce Clause. My reluctance is not due to any conviction that Congress lacks power to regulate commerce in the interests of human rights. It is rather my belief that the right of people to be free of state action that discriminates against them because of race . . ." occupies a more protected position in our constitutional system than does the movement of cattle, fruit, steel and coal across state lines." . . .

Hence I would prefer to rest on the assertion of legislative power contained in [Section] 5 of the Fourteenth Amendment which states: "The Congress shall have power to enforce, by appropriate legislation, the provisions of this article"—a power which the Court concedes was exercised at least in part in this Act.

A decision based on the Fourteenth Amendment would have a more settling effect, making unnecessary litigation over whether a particular restaurant or inn is within the commerce definitions of the Act or whether a particular customer is an interstate traveler. Under my construction, the Act would apply to all customers in all the enumerated places of public accommodation. And that construction would put

an end to all obstructionist strategies and finally close one door on a bitter chapter in American history. . . .

I think the Court is correct in concluding that the Act is not founded on the Commerce Clause to the exclusion of the Enforcement Clause of the Fourteenth Amendment. . . .

Thus while I agree with the Court that Congress in fashioning the present Act used the Commerce Clause to regulate racial segregation, it also used (and properly so) some of its power under §5 of the Fourteenth Amendment.

I repeat what I said earlier, that our decision should be based on the Fourteenth Amendment, thereby putting an end to all obstructionist strategies and allowing every person—whatever his race, creed, or color—to patronize all places of public accommodation without discrimination whether he travels interstate or intrastate.

Further Resources

BOOKS

Cortner, Richard C. *Civil Rights and Public Accommodations: The Heart of Atlanta Motel and McClung Cases.* Lawrence: University Press of Kansas, 2001.

Horwitz, Morton J. *The Warren Court and the Pursuit of Justice: A Critical Issue.* New York: Hill and Wang, 1998.

Loevy, Robert D. *The Civil Rights Act of 1964: The Passage of the Law That Ended Racial Segregation.* Albany, N.Y.: State University of New York Press, 1997.

Powe, L.A. Scot. *The Warren Court and American Politics.* Cambridge, Mass.: Belknap Press of Harvard University Press, 2000.

Schwartz, Bernard. *The Warren Court: A Retrospective.* New York: Oxford University Press, 1996.

PERIODICALS

Webster, McKenzie. "The Warren Court's Struggle with the Sit-in cases and the Constitutionality of Segregation in Places of Public Accommodations." *Journal of Law and Politics* 17, no. 2, Spring 2001, 373–407.

WEBSITES

Debating Key Issues: Can Discrimination In Private Facilities Be Prohibited? Available online at http://www.phschool.com /curriculum_support/black_history/lessons/strategy1.html; website home page: http://www.phschool.com (accessed January 21, 2003).

Griswold v. Connecticut

Supreme Court decision

By: William O. Douglas; Arthur J. Goldberg; Hugo L. Black

Date: June 7, 1965

Source: Douglas, William O., Arthur J. Goldberg and Hugo L. Black. *Griswold v. Connecticut,* 381 U.S. 479. Available online at http://caselaw.lp.findlaw.com/scripts/getcase.pl?navby =case&court=us&vol=381&page=479; website home page: http://caselaw.lp.findlaw.com (accessed June 11, 2003).

About the Authors: William O. Douglas (1898–1980) was an activist, liberal justice who served longer on the Supreme Court than any justice in history.

Arthur Joseph Goldberg (1908–1990) passed the bar at age twenty, was appointed secretary of labor in 1960, and served on the Supreme Court from 1962 to 1965, resigning to accept a position as ambassador to the United Nations.

Hugo Lafayette Black (1886–1971) was appointed to the Supreme Court in 1937 after serving in the U.S. Senate. His term was distinguished by his support of civil rights. ∎

Introduction

For most of its first century, the United States considered the issue of birth control and the number of children to bear to be a matter between a husband and wife. The federal government became involved in decisions involving birth control with the 1873 Comstock Act, which forbid "obscene" materials from being sent through the interstate mails. This act was promoted by and named after Anthony Comstock, an anti-vice crusader, and was enforced against the distributors of birth control information, among other targets. Similar laws were passed in other states, including Connecticut, whose law banned not only the use of birth control devices but even materials discussing them. Some of these laws were rooted in concerns that "less desirable" immigrant Catholic families from eastern and southern Europe were having more children than Protestant families. Despite these laws, by the end of the nineteenth century the average number of children per family had dropped to four, as fewer children were needed on the farm and to work in industry.

In the early 1900s, Margaret Sanger and other reformers advocated informing the public about birth control, but Sanger was arrested multiple times for her efforts. In 1916, the federal government indicted Sanger under the Comstock Act for sending birth control information through the mail, and although the charges were dropped, in *People v. Sanger* (1918) the New York Court of Appeals upheld the constitutionality of a state law prohibiting the selling of contraceptive devices or the discussion of them. Despite her arrests, Sanger remained active and founded Planned Parenthood to advance her views. Doctors, though, were generally hostile to artificial birth control until 1937, when the American Medical Association reversed its stand against contraception. In the 1960s, social attitudes favored individual freedom, and new birth control devices, such as the Pill, were developed. The director of Connecticut's Planned Parenthood division baited the police into arresting him because he wanted to test Connecticut's anti-birth control law in the court system.

Significance

In *Griswold v. Connecticut,* the Supreme Court struck down the state's law, ruling that the right to privacy denied the state the right to ban the use of artificial contraception. The Court stated that all married couples had the right to privacy, with different justices finding that right in different constitutional amendments. William Douglas, for example, reasoned that certain amendments had "penumbras," or shadows, that created a "zone of privacy," while Arthur Goldberg found the right to privacy in the Ninth Amendment. Hugo Black, though, dissented from the majority, holding that the court cannot create rights that are not enumerated in the Constitution. Many Court observers agreed, arguing that Douglas and the majority were creating "rights" that had no constitutional basis.

The "zone of privacy" was invoked eight years later in *Roe v. Wade,* the landmark Supreme Court case that affirmed a woman's right to have an abortion. Although the Court has slightly narrowed its decision in *Roe,* various attempts to severely restrict abortion rights, even to overturn the Court's decision, have failed. Further, the Court has upheld a right to privacy as it pertains to other issues. While the Court upheld a state law against sodomy in 1986, even that issue was up for Court reexamination in 2003. This right to privacy, essentially created in *Griswold,* still exists today.

Primary Source

Griswold v. Connecticut [excerpt]

SYNOPSIS: Justice Douglas first points out that privacy is not specifically mentioned in the Constitution. He then surveys past cases that have inferred a right to privacy from various constitutional amendments. Justice Goldberg concurs but locates that right to privacy in the Ninth Amendment rather than in "penumbras" coming from a variety of amendments. In his dissent, Justice Black states that there is no fundamental right to privacy in the Constitution and that the court cannot simply create such a right.

Mr. Justice Douglas delivered the opinion of the Court. . . .

Coming to the merits, we are met with a wide range of questions that implicate the Due Process

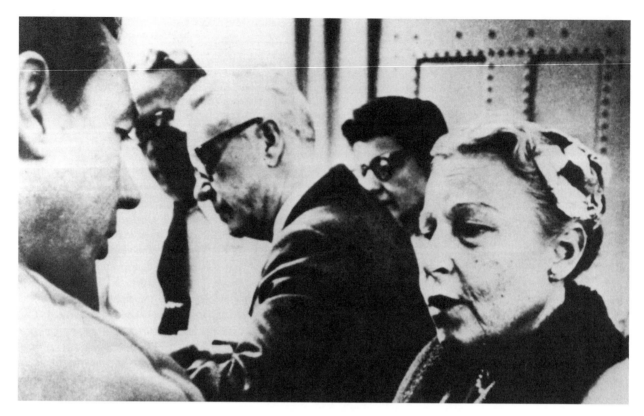

Executive director of Planned Parenthood of Connecticut, Estelle Griswold speaks with Dr. Charles Lee Buxton, Yale professor of obstetrics and gynecology. Griswold and Buxton opened an illegal birth control clinic to prompt their arrest and to subsequently bring Connecticut's ban on birth control into trial. **PLANNED PARENTHOOD OF CONNECTICUT. REPRODUCED BY PERMISSION.**

Clause of the Fourteenth Amendment. . . . We do not sit as a super-legislature to determine the wisdom, need, and propriety of laws that touch economic problems, business affairs, or social conditions. This law, however, operates directly on an intimate relation of husband and wife and their physician's role in one aspect of that relation.

The association of people is not mentioned in the Constitution nor in the Bill of Rights. The right to educate a child in a school of the parents' choice—whether public or private or parochial—is also not mentioned. Nor is the right to study any particular subject or any foreign language. Yet the First Amendment has been construed to include certain of those rights.

. . . The right of freedom of speech and press includes not only the right to utter or to print, but the right to distribute, the right to receive, the right to read . . . and freedom of inquiry, freedom of thought, and freedom to teach—indeed the freedom of the entire university community. . . . Without those peripheral rights the specific rights would be less secure. . . .

In *NAACP v. Alabama* . . . , we protected the "freedom to associate and privacy in one's associ-

ations," noting that freedom of association was a peripheral First Amendment right. Disclosure of membership lists of a constitutionally valid association, we held, was invalid "as entailing the likelihood of a substantial restraint upon the exercise by petitioner's members of their right to freedom of association." . . . In other words, the First Amendment has a penumbra where privacy is protected from governmental intrusion. In like context, we have protected forms of "association" that are not political in the customary sense but pertain to the social, legal, and economic benefit of the members. . . .

Those cases involved more than the "right of assembly"—a right that extends to all irrespective of their race or ideology. . . . The right of "association," like the right of belief . . . is more than the right to attend a meeting; it includes the right to express one's attitudes or philosophies by membership in a group or by affiliation with it or by other lawful means. Association in that context is a form of expression of opinion; and while it is not expressly included in the First Amendment its existence is necessary in making the express guarantees fully meaningful.

The foregoing cases suggest that specific guarantees in the Bill of Rights have penumbras, formed by emanations from those guarantees that help give them life and substance. . . . Various guarantees create zones of privacy. The right of association contained in the penumbra of the First Amendment is one, as we have seen. The Third Amendment in its prohibition against the quartering of soldiers "in any house" in time of peace without the consent of the owner is another facet of that privacy. The Fourth Amendment explicitly affirms the "right of the people to be secure in their persons, houses, papers, and effects, against unreasonable searches and seizures." The Fifth Amendment in its Self-Incrimination Clause enables the citizen to create a zone of privacy which government may not force him to surrender to his detriment. The Ninth Amendment provides: "The enumeration in the Constitution, of certain rights, shall not be construed to deny or disparage others retained by the people." . . .

We have had many controversies over these penumbral rights of "privacy and repose." . . .

The present case, then, concerns a relationship lying within the zone of privacy created by several fundamental constitutional guarantees. And it concerns a law which, in forbidding the use of contraceptives rather than regulating their manufacture or sale, seeks to achieve its goals by means having a maximum destructive impact upon that relationship. Such a law cannot stand in light of the familiar principle, so often applied by this Court, that a "governmental purpose to control or prevent activities constitutionally subject to state regulation may not be achieved by means which sweep unnecessarily broadly and thereby invade the area of protected freedoms." *NAACP v. Alabama.* . . . Would we allow the police to search the sacred precincts of marital bedrooms for telltale signs of the use of contraceptives? The very idea is repulsive to the notions of privacy surrounding the marriage relationship.

We deal with a right of privacy older than the Bill of Rights—older than our political parties, older than our school system. Marriage is a coming together for better or for worse, hopefully enduring, and intimate to the degree of being sacred. It is an association that promotes a way of life, not causes; a harmony in living, not political faiths; a bilateral loyalty, not commercial or social projects. Yet it is an association for as noble a purpose as any involved in our prior decisions.

Reversed. . . .

Mr. Justice Goldberg, whom the Chief Justice and Mr. Justice Brennan join, concurring. . . .

The Court stated many years ago that the Due Process Clause protects those liberties that are "so rooted in the traditions and conscience of our people as to be ranked as fundamental." . . .

This Court, in a series of decisions, has held that the Fourteenth Amendment absorbs and applies to the States those specifics of the first eight amendments which express fundamental personal rights. The language and history of the Ninth Amendment reveal that the Framers of the Constitution believed that there are additional fundamental rights, protected from governmental infringement, which exist alongside those fundamental rights specifically mentioned in the first eight constitutional amendments.

The Ninth . . . Amendment . . . was proffered to quiet expressed fears that a bill of specifically enumerated rights could not be sufficiently broad to cover all essential rights and that the specific mention of certain rights would be interpreted as a denial that others were protected. . . .

Madison and Story make clear that the Framers did not intend that the first eight amendments be construed to exhaust the basic and fundamental rights which the Constitution guaranteed to the people.

While this Court has had little occasion to interpret the Ninth Amendment, "[i]t cannot be presumed that any clause in the constitution is intended to be without effect." In interpreting the Constitution, "real effect should be given to all the words it uses." To hold that a right so basic and fundamental and so deep-rooted in our society as the right of privacy in marriage may be infringed because that right is not guaranteed in so many words by the first eight amendments to the Constitution is to ignore the Ninth Amendment and to give it no effect whatsoever. Moreover, a judicial construction that this fundamental right is not protected by the Constitution because it is not mentioned in explicit terms by one of the first eight amendments or elsewhere in the Constitution would violate the Ninth Amendment. . . .

I do not mean to imply that the Ninth Amendment is applied against the States by the Fourteenth. Nor do I mean to state that the Ninth Amendment constitutes an independent source of rights protected from infringement by either the States or the Federal Government. Rather, the Ninth Amendment shows a belief of the Constitution's authors that fundamental rights exist that are not expressly enumerated in the

Social Implications of the *Griswold v. Connecticut* Decision

In November 1961 two Connecticut detectives, responding to a complaint by James Morris, a Roman Catholic resident of New Haven, conducted an investigation of the Planned Parenthood of Connecticut clinic in that city. The clinic's director, Estelle Griswold, readily admitted that the clinic was violating the Connecticut law, passed in 1879, which banned the sale, distribution, or use of contraceptive materials. Although it was usually ignored by authorities, the statute was occasionally used to arrest and prosecute individuals who sold contraceptives or operated family-planning clinics.

Following the investigation Griswold and her clinic's doctor, Charles Lee Buxton, were arrested on charges of distributing contraceptives and abetting others—the patients who came into the clinic for medical treatment and advice—in their use. The Planned Parenthood center was temporarily closed, and Griswold and Buxton each had to pay a $100 fine. The arrests and closure inaugurated a four-year legal battle that wound its way through the Connecticut courts and eventually to the U.S. Supreme Court in March 1965. The court issued its decision in *Griswold v. Connecticut,* authored by William O. Douglas, on June 7. 1965. In overturning the Connecticut statute, the court declared that the First Amendment to the U.S. Constitution protected individual privacy from governmental intrusion, a right that extended to the choice of married couples to use contraceptives. Although the First Amendment did not explicitly detail this right, Douglas explained that it, like all of the amendments in the Bill of Rights, created a "penumbra," or umbrella of associated rights, which included a right to privacy.

Although conservative critics disagreed with Douglas's description of a "penumbra" of rights not explicitly detailed in the Constitution, his decision became one of the most important in Supreme Court history. Similar reasoning would be used to give unmarried people the right to use contraceptive devices in *Eisendtadt v. Baird* in 1972. The following year the Supreme Court would also include a woman's right to an abortion as a matter of privacy in the 1973 case *Roe v. Wade.* In *Bowers v. Hardwick* in 1986, the Court rejected a challenge to a Georgia sodomy law, thereby deciding not to extend the right of privacy, which originated in the *Griswold* decision, to gays. In upholding the constitutionality of the Georgia law, which outlawed sodomy regardless of the gender of the participants, the Court found that states could criminalize sexual behavior even if it took place between consenting adults in their own homes.

Griswold v. Connecticut was a key decision in the Supreme Court's trend toward protecting individual civil liberties from government interference. In practical terms the decision made various means of contraception more readily available in the United States, a factor that may have also helped to overturn traditional mores that prohibited sexual relations outside of marriage. The decision also signaled the declining influence of religious organizations on American society over topics such as family planning and premarital sex. In giving women more control over their reproductive choices, *Griswold* was also a boon to the women's movement, which viewed access to contraception and abortion as important individual rights.

first eight amendments and an intent that the list of rights included there not be deemed exhaustive. . . . The Ninth Amendment simply shows the intent of the Constitution's authors that other fundamental personal rights should not be denied such protection or disparaged in any other way simply because they are not specifically listed in the first eight constitutional amendments. I do not see how this broadens the authority of the Court; rather it serves to support what this Court has been doing in protecting fundamental rights. . . .

The entire fabric of the Constitution and the purposes that clearly underlie its specific guarantees demonstrate that the rights to marital privacy and to marry and raise a family are of similar order and magnitude as the fundamental rights specifically protected.

Although the Constitution does not speak in so many words of the right of privacy in marriage, I cannot believe that it offers these fundamental rights no protection. The fact that no particular provision of the Constitution explicitly forbids the State from disrupting the traditional relation of the family—a relation as old and as fundamental as our entire civilization—surely does not show that the Government was meant to have the power to do so. Rather, as the Ninth Amendment expressly recognizes, there are fundamental personal rights such as this one, which are protected from abridgment by the Government though not specifically mentioned in the Constitution.

. . . The vice of the dissenters' views is that it would permit such experimentation by the States in the area of the fundamental personal rights of its citizens. I cannot agree that the Constitution grants such power either to the States or to the Federal Government. . . .

In sum, I believe that the right of privacy in the marital relation is fundamental and basic—a personal right "retained by the people" within the meaning of the Ninth Amendment. Connecticut cannot constitutionally abridge this fundamental right, which is protected by the Fourteenth Amendment from infringement by the States. I agree with the Court that petitioners' convictions must therefore be reversed. . . .

Mr. Justice Black, with whom Mr. Justice Stewart joins, dissenting.

. . . There is no single one of the graphic and eloquent strictures and criticisms fired at the policy of this Connecticut law either by the Court's opinion or by those of my concurring Brethren to which I cannot subscribe—except their conclusion that the evil qualities they see in the law make it unconstitutional. . . .

The Court talks about a constitutional "right of privacy" as though there is some constitutional provision or provisions forbidding any law ever to be passed which might abridge the "privacy" of individuals. But there is not. . . .

I like my privacy as well as the next one, but I am nevertheless compelled to admit that government has a right to invade it unless prohibited by some specific constitutional provision. For these reasons I cannot agree with the Court's judgment and the reasons it gives for holding this Connecticut law unconstitutional.

. . . While I completely subscribe to the holding of *Marbury v. Madison,* 1 Cranch 137, and subsequent cases, that our Court has constitutional power to strike down statutes, state or federal, that violate commands of the Federal Constitution, I do not believe that we are granted power by the Due Process Clause or any other constitutional provision or provisions to measure constitutionality by our belief that legislation is arbitrary, capricious or unreasonable, or accomplishes no justifiable purpose, or is offensive to our own notions of "civilized standards of conduct." Such an appraisal of the wisdom of legislation is an attribute of the power to make laws, not of the power to interpret them. The use by federal courts of such a formula or doctrine or whatnot to veto federal or state laws simply takes away from Congress and States the power to make laws based on their own judgment of fairness and wisdom and transfers that power to this Court for ultimate determination—a power which was specifically denied to federal courts by the convention that framed the Constitution. . . .

If any broad, unlimited power to hold laws unconstitutional because they offend what this Court conceives to be the "[collective] conscience of our people" is vested in this Court by the Ninth Amendment, the Fourteenth Amendment, or any other provision of the Constitution, it was not given by the Framers, but rather has been bestowed on the Court by the Court.

Further Resources

BOOKS

Ball, Howard, and Phillip J. Cooper. *Of Power and Right: Hugo Black, William O. Douglas, and America's Constitutional Revolution.* New York: Oxford University Press, 1992.

Dixon, Robert Galloway. *The Right of Privacy; a Symposium on the Implications of Griswold v. Connecticut, 381 U.S. 497 (1965).* New York: Da Capo Press, 1971.

Douglas, William O. *The Court Years, 1939–1975: The Autobiography of William O. Douglas.* New York: Random House, 1980.

Garrow, David J. *Liberty and Sexuality: The Right to Privacy and the Making of Roe v. Wade.* New York: Macmillan, 1994.

Nelson, Deborah. *Pursuing Privacy in Cold War America.* New York: Columbia University Press, 2002.

WEBSITES

The Impact of Legal Birth Control and the Challenges that Remain. Available online at http://www.plannedparenthood .org/library/facts/griswolddone.html; website home page: http://www.plannedparenthood.org (accessed March 16, 2003).

Miranda v. Arizona

Supreme Court decision

By: Earl Warren

Date: June 13, 1966

Source: Warren, Earl. *Miranda v. Arizona,* 384 U.S. 436. Available online at http://caselaw.lp.findlaw.com/scripts/getcase .pl?navby=case&court=us&vol=384&page=486; website home page: http://caselaw.lp.findlaw.com (accessed June 11, 2003).

About the Author: Earl Warren (1891–1974) received his bachelor's degree from the University of California in 1912 and his law degree there two years later. After three years in private practice, he joined the army in 1917, then began a career in government as deputy city attorney for Oakland. From 1945 to 1953, he was governor of California. He became chief justice of the U.S. Supreme Court in 1953, a position he held until 1969. The Warren Court is synonymous with expansion of civil rights and civil liberties. ∎

Introduction

The Bill of Rights, added to the U.S. Constitution in 1791, outlines the rights of all Americans, but the meaning

Ernesto Miranda (right) leaves a Phoenix court with his attorney. Miranda confessed to raping a girl after police misled him to believe they had sufficient evidence against him. Though the Supreme Court held that his confession was inadmissible, Miranda was later retried and found guilty of the crime on evidence uncovered later. © BETTMANN/CORBIS. REPRODUCED BY PERMISSION.

and extent of those rights was not always apparent, especially in criminal cases. The average person involved in the criminal justice system could not always be expected to know and understand those rights, particularly because, until the 1960s, different criminal procedures and constitutional protections applied at the state and federal levels, creating in effect fifty-one different sets of constitutional protections. Further, the police often had incentives for encouraging people not to assert their rights, especially the right to remain silent or to contact an attorney, because police officers with higher rates of cleared cases were promoted and commended. It also remained unclear whether the Constitution required that accused persons be informed of their rights.

In the 1960s, the Warren Court began increasing the constitutional protections for criminal defendants and applying the same level of constitutional protections to defendants whether they were in state or federal court. In 1963, the Warren Court, following the recommendation of twenty-three states that were unsure about when indigent defendants should be appointed counsel, held that the right to counsel was fundamental to a fair trial. In 1964, the Court applied the right against self-incrimination, which had existed for decades in federal court, to state court matters. That same year, it held that a con-

fession obtained when a defendant was not able to consult a lawyer and was not informed of the right to remain silent was inadmissible in state courts. Finally, in 1966, in *Miranda,* the Supreme Court considered whether in all cases the police were required to inform defendants of their rights.

Significance

The Supreme Court concluded that defendants must be informed of their rights: their right to remain silent and the fact that statements they made might be used against them, their right to consult an attorney, and their right to have an attorney appointed if they could not afford one. This warning is generally known as the "*Miranda* warning." The Supreme Court has generally upheld the *Miranda* warning in the thirty-seven years since it has been announced. Some conservative politicians and "law and order" advocates have denounced the Miranda requirement as a way for criminals to "get off" and have linked it with a rise in the crime rate. However, social science research has found no such link, and it is clear that the number of coerced confessions by innocent defendants has decreased.

For example, the Supreme Court in 1977 threw out a confession that was made without the assistance of counsel and without a *Miranda* warning, even though the confession was unsolicited. In later years, though, the Supreme Court slightly narrowed the *Miranda* requirement by allowing the confession of a mentally ill defendant and a confession obtained through police misrepresentation. In the 1990s, the Rehnquist Court generally continued these trends. It held that while a coerced confession could not be used against a defendant, the use of such a confession in a trial did not automatically create grounds for reversal, as the "totality of the circumstances" needed to be considered. The Court suggested that the admission of such a confession might simply be a "harmless error."

Primary Source

Miranda v. Arizona [excerpt]

SYNOPSIS: Justice Warren, writing for the majority, first argues that the purpose of interrogation is to force a confession. He suggests that the privilege against self-incrimination is important and available throughout the judicial process. To safeguard one's rights, Warren holds, the defendant must be informed of his rights before interrogation begins, including the right to remain silent and the right to counsel. Warren suggests that individual rights exist and should not be "weighed" against those of society.

Mr. Chief Justice Warren delivered the opinion of the Court. . . .

An understanding of the nature and setting of . . . in-custody interrogation is essential to our decisions today. The difficulty in depicting what transpires at such interrogations stems from the fact that in this country they have largely taken place incommunicado. From extensive factual studies undertaken in the early 1930's, including the famous Wickersham Report to Congress by a Presidential Commission, it is clear that police violence and the "third degree" flourished at that time. . . .

. . . [W]e stress that the modern practice of in-custody interrogation is psychologically rather than physically oriented. . . . Interrogation still takes place in privacy. Privacy results in secrecy and this in turn results in a gap in our knowledge as to what in fact goes on in the interrogation rooms. . . .

. . . [T]he setting . . . observed in practice becomes clear. In essence, it is this: To be alone with the subject is essential to prevent distraction and to deprive him of any outside support. The aura of confidence in his guilt undermines his will to resist. He merely confirms the preconceived story the police seek to have him describe. Patience and persistence, at times relentless questioning, are employed. To obtain a confession, the interrogator must "patiently maneuver himself or his quarry into a position from which the desired objective may be attained." When normal procedures fail to produce the needed result, the police may resort to deceptive stratagems such as giving false legal advice. It is important to keep the subject off balance, for example, by trading on his insecurity about himself or his surroundings. The police then persuade, trick, or cajole him out of exercising his constitutional rights.

Even without employing brutality, the "third degree" or the specific stratagems described above, the very fact of custodial interrogation exacts a heavy toll on individual liberty and trades on the weakness of individuals. . . .

It is obvious that such an interrogation environment is created for no purpose other than to subjugate the individual to the will of his examiner. This atmosphere carries its own badge of intimidation. To be sure, this is not physical intimidation, but it is equally destructive of human dignity. The current practice of incommunicado interrogation is at odds with one of our Nation's most cherished principles—that the individual may not be compelled to incriminate himself. Unless adequate protective devices are employed to dispel the compulsion inherent in custodial surroundings, no statement obtained from the defendant can truly be the product of his free choice. . . .

We sometimes forget how long it has taken to establish the privilege against self-incrimination, the sources from which it came and the fervor with which it was defended. . . .

Thus we may view the historical development of the privilege as one which groped for the proper scope of governmental power over the citizen. . . . All these policies point to one overriding thought: the constitutional foundation underlying the privilege is the respect a government—state or federal—must accord to the dignity and integrity of its citizens. . . .

Today, then, there can be no doubt that the Fifth Amendment privilege is available outside of criminal court proceedings and serves to protect persons in all settings in which their freedom of action is curtailed in any significant way from being compelled to incriminate themselves. We have concluded that without proper safeguards the process of in-custody interrogation of persons suspected or accused of crime contains inherently compelling pressures which work to undermine the individual's will to resist and to compel him to speak where he would not otherwise do so freely. In order to combat these pressures and to permit a full opportunity to exercise the privilege against self-incrimination, the accused must be adequately and effectively apprised of his rights and the exercise of those rights must be fully honored. . . .

At the outset, if a person in custody is to be subjected to interrogation, he must first be informed in clear and unequivocal terms that he has the right to remain silent. For those unaware of the privilege, the warning is needed simply to make them aware of it—the threshold requirement for an intelligent decision as to its exercise. More important, such a warning is an absolute prerequisite in overcoming the inherent pressures of the interrogation atmosphere. It is not just the subnormal or woefully ignorant who succumb to an interrogator's imprecations, whether implied or expressly stated, that the interrogation will continue until a confession is obtained or that silence in the face of accusation is itself damning and will bode ill when presented to a jury. Further, the warning will show the individual that his interrogators are prepared to recognize his privilege should he choose to exercise it. . . .

The warning of the right to remain silent must be accompanied by the explanation that anything said can and will be used against the individual in court. This warning is needed in order to make him aware not only of the privilege, but also of the consequences of forgoing it. It is only through an awareness of these consequences that there can be any assurance of real understanding and intelligent exercise of the privilege. Moreover, this warning may serve to make the individual more acutely aware that he is faced with a phase of the adversary system— that he is not in the presence of persons acting solely in his interest.

The . . . right to have counsel present at the interrogation is indispensable to the protection of the Fifth Amendment privilege under the system we delineate today. . . . Thus, the need for counsel to protect the Fifth Amendment privilege comprehends not merely a right to consult with counsel prior to questioning, but also to have counsel present during any questioning if the defendant so desires. . . .

An individual need not make a pre-interrogation request for a lawyer. While such request affirmatively secures his right to have one, his failure to ask for a lawyer does not constitute a waiver. No effective waiver of the right to counsel during interrogation can be recognized unless specifically made after the

warnings we here delineate have been given. The accused who does not know his rights and therefore does not make a request may be the person who most needs counsel. . . .

Accordingly we hold that an individual held for interrogation must be clearly informed that he has the right to consult with a lawyer and to have the lawyer with him during interrogation under the system for protecting the privilege we delineate today. . . . If an individual indicates that he wishes the assistance of counsel before any interrogation occurs, the authorities cannot rationally ignore or deny his request on the basis that the individual does not have or cannot afford a retained attorney. The financial ability of the individual has no relationship to the scope of the rights involved here. The privilege against self-incrimination secured by the Constitution applies to all individuals. The need for counsel in order to protect the privilege exists for the indigent as well as the affluent. . . .

In order fully to apprise a person interrogated of the extent of his rights under this system then, it is necessary to warn him not only that he has the right to consult with an attorney, but also that if he is indigent a lawyer will be appointed to represent him. Without this additional warning, the admonition of the right to consult with counsel would often be understood as meaning only that he can consult with a lawyer if he has one or has the funds to obtain one. The warning of a right to counsel would be hollow if not couched in terms that would convey to the indigent—the person most often subjected to interrogation—the knowledge that he too has a right to have counsel present. . . .

Once warnings have been given, the subsequent procedure is clear. If the individual indicates in any manner, at any time prior to or during questioning, that he wishes to remain silent, the interrogation must cease. At this point he has shown that he intends to exercise his Fifth Amendment privilege; any statement taken after the person invokes his privilege cannot be other than the product of compulsion, subtle or otherwise. Without the right to cut off questioning, the setting of in-custody interrogation operates on the individual to overcome free choice in producing a statement after the privilege has been once invoked. If the individual states that he wants an attorney, the interrogation must cease until an attorney is present. At that time, the individual must have an opportunity to confer with the attorney and to have him present during any subsequent questioning. If the individual cannot obtain an attorney and he indicates that he wants one before speaking to police, they must respect his decision to remain silent. . . .

The warnings required and the waiver necessary in accordance with our opinion today are, in the absence of a fully effective equivalent, prerequisites to the admissibility of any statement made by a defendant. . . . The principles announced today deal with the protection which must be given to the privilege against self-incrimination when the individual is first subjected to police interrogation while in custody at the station or otherwise deprived of his freedom of action in any significant way. It is at this point that our adversary system of criminal proceedings commences, distinguishing itself at the outset from the inquisitorial system recognized in some countries. Under the system of warnings we delineate today or under any other system which may be devised and found effective, the safeguards to be erected about the privilege must come into play at this point.

Our decision is not intended to hamper the traditional function of police officers in investigating crime. . . .

To summarize, we hold that when an individual is taken into custody or otherwise deprived of his freedom by the authorities in any significant way and is subjected to questioning, the privilege against self-incrimination is jeopardized. Procedural safeguards must be employed to protect the privilege, and unless other fully effective means are adopted to notify the person of his right of silence and to assure that the exercise of the right will be scrupulously honored, the following measures are required. He must be warned prior to any questioning that he has the right to remain silent, that anything he says can be used against him in a court of law, that he has the right to the presence of an attorney, and that if he cannot afford an attorney one will be appointed for him prior to any questioning if he so desires. Opportunity to exercise these rights must be afforded to him throughout the interrogation. After such warnings have been given, and such opportunity afforded him, the individual may knowingly and intelligently waive these rights and agree to answer questions or make a statement. But unless and until such warnings and waiver are demonstrated by the prosecution at trial, no evidence obtained as a result of interrogation can be used against him.

A recurrent argument made in these cases is that society's need for interrogation outweighs the privilege. This argument is not unfamiliar to this Court. . . .

In announcing these principles, we are not unmindful of the burdens which law enforcement officials must bear, often under trying circumstances. We also fully recognize the obligation of all citizens to aid in enforcing the criminal laws. This Court, while protecting individual rights, has always given ample latitude to law enforcement agencies in the legitimate exercise of their duties. The limits we have placed on the interrogation process should not constitute an undue interference with a proper system of law enforcement. As we have noted, our decision does not in any way preclude police from carrying out their traditional investigatory functions.

Further Resources

BOOKS

Cray, Ed. *Chief Justice: A Biography of Earl Warren.* New York: Simon and Schuster, 1997.

Horwitz, Morton J. *The Warren Court and the Pursuit of Justice: A Critical Issue.* New York: Hill and Wang, 1998.

Leo, Richard A., and George C. Thomas. *The Miranda Debate: Law, Justice, and Policing.* Boston: Northeastern University Press, 1998.

Powe, L.A. Scot. *The Warren Court and American Politics.* Cambridge, Mass.: Belknap Press of Harvard University Press, 2000.

Schwartz, Bernard. *The Warren Court: A Retrospective.* New York: Oxford University Press, 1996.

Warren, Earl. *The Memoirs of Earl Warren.* Garden City, N.Y.: Doubleday, 1977.

White, Welsh S. *Miranda's Waning Protections: Police Interrogation Practices after Dickerson.* Ann Arbor, Mich.: University of Michigan Press, 2001.

Wice, Paul B. *Miranda v. Arizona: "You Have the Right to Remain Silent."* New York: Franklin Watts, 1996.

WEBSITES

Miranda vs Arizona: The Crime That Changed American Justice. Available online at http://www.crimelibrary.com/classics4/miranda/8.htm; website home page: http://www.crimelibrary.com/ (accessed January 21, 2003).

Loving v. Virginia
Supreme Court decision

By: Earl Warren

Date: June 12, 1967

Source: Warren, Earl. *Loving v. Virginia,* 388 U.S. 1. Available online at http://caselaw.lp.findlaw.com/scripts/getcase.pl?navby=case&court=us&vol=388&page=1; website home page: http://caselaw.lp.findlaw.com (accessed June 12, 2003).

About the Author: Earl Warren (1891–1974) received his bachelor's degree from the University of California in 1912 and his law degree there two years later. After three years in private practice, he joined the army in 1917, then began a career in government as deputy city attorney for Oakland. From 1945 to 1953, he was governor of California. He became chief justice of the U.S. Supreme Court in 1953, a position he held until 1969. The Warren Court is synonymous with expansion of civil rights and civil liberties. ∎

Introduction

Ever since the first Africans were brought to the United States in chains, there has been a strong concern among some whites about "race purity." With the end of slavery after the Civil War (1861–1865), concerns over interracial relations increased, leading to laws against interracial marriages. In the public's mind, widespread lynchings of African Americans were justified because, it was thought, African American men desired white women and had to be strongly dissuaded from acting on those desires. In truth, few of the crimes even alleged against blacks in lynchings were rapes. Lynching was much more about power than sex.

At the beginning of the twentieth century, laws against "miscegenation," or interracial marriage, were strengthened. In Virginia, for example, the definition of a "colored" person was changed. Previously, a person who was one-fourth black was legally considered "colored." The new law changed that proportion to one-sixteenth. In 1958, two Virginians, Richard Loving, a white, and Mildred Jeter, an African American, married in Washington, D.C. Their marriage was considered illegal in Virginia, so they were arrested when they returned home. They were given a one-year sentence, with the sentence suspended on condition that they leave Virginia and never return. They appealed their conviction, and their case, *Loving v. Virginia*, made its way to the U.S. Supreme Court.

Significance

The Supreme Court unanimously struck down the Virginia law. The Court concluded that the right to marriage and to procreation were fundamental rights, and therefore the state could not interfere with them. The Court's decision had an immediate widespread effect—antimiscegenation laws in fifteen states besides Virginia were struck down.

The *Loving* decision was consistent with the Warren Court's defense of fundamental rights and of privacy, even though "privacy" is not a right specifically enumerated in the Constitution. In *Griswold v. Connecticut*, for example, the Warren Court cited the right to privacy in striking down a state law banning the use of contraceptives. Later, in *Roe v. Wade*, the Court ruled that a woman has a fundamental right to an abortion because state interference with that right would violate her right

to privacy. In 2003, the Court agreed to reexamine the issue of state laws criminalizing sodomy. In the meantime, states have not attempted to recriminalize interracial marriage, in part because of changing social attitudes and in part because larger numbers of African Americans were able to exercise their right to vote.

Primary Source

Loving v. Virginia [excerpt]

SYNOPSIS: Chief Justice Warren, writing for the unanimous Court, first surveys the facts of the case and notes that Virginia defends the law as applying equally to all races. Warren then holds that to establish a classification system based on race, the state must show that the law is necessary to accomplish a permissible state objective, which Virginia was unable to do. Warren concludes that the law is invalid because its only purpose is to make racial classifications and deny due process of law.

Mr. Chief Justice Warren delivered the opinion of the Court.

This case presents a constitutional question never addressed by this Court: whether a statutory scheme adopted by the State of Virginia to prevent marriages between persons solely on the basis of racial classifications violates the Equal Protection and Due Process Clauses of the Fourteenth Amendment. For reasons which seem to us to reflect the central meaning of those constitutional commands, we conclude that these statutes cannot stand consistently with the Fourteenth Amendment.

On January 6, 1959, the Lovings pleaded guilty to the charge and were sentenced to one year in jail; however, the trial judge suspended the sentence for a period of 25 years on the condition that the Lovings leave the State and not return to Virginia together for 25 years. He stated in an opinion that:

> Almighty God created the races white, black, yellow, malay and red, and he placed them on separate continents. And but for the interference with his arrangement there would be no cause for such marriages. The fact that he separated the races shows that he did not intend for the races to mix. . . .

The central features of this Act, and current Virginia law, are the absolute prohibition of a "white person" marrying other than another "white person" . . . .

In upholding the constitutionality of these provisions in the decision below, the Supreme Court of Appeals of Virginia referred to its 1955 decision in

After getting married in Washington, D.C., Mildred and Richard Loving were arrested in their home in Virginia, where interracial marriage was banned. AP/WIDE WORLD PHOTOS. REPRODUCED BY PERMISSION.

Naim v. Naim. . . . In *Naim,* the state court concluded that the State's legitimate purposes were "to preserve the racial integrity of its citizens," and to prevent "the corruption of blood," "a mongrel breed of citizens," and "the obliteration of racial pride," obviously an endorsement of the doctrine of White Supremacy. . . . The court also reasoned that marriage has traditionally been subject to state regulation without federal intervention, and, consequently, the regulation of marriage should be left to exclusive state control by the Tenth Amendment.

While the state court is no doubt correct in asserting that marriage is a social relation subject to the State's police power, . . . the State does not contend in its argument before this Court that its powers to regulate marriage are unlimited notwithstanding the commands of the Fourteenth Amendment. . . . Instead, the State argues that the meaning of the Equal Protection Clause, as illuminated by the statements of the Framers, is only that state penal laws containing an interracial element as part of the definition of the offense must apply equally to whites and Negroes in the sense that members of each race are punished to the same degree. Thus, the State contends that, because its miscegenation statutes punish equally both the white and the Negro participants in an interracial marriage, these statutes, despite their reliance on racial classifications, do not constitute an invidious discrimination based upon race. The second argument advanced by the State assumes the validity of its equal application theory. The argument is that, if the Equal Protection Clause does not outlaw miscegenation statutes because of their reliance on racial classifications, the question of constitutionality would thus become whether there was any rational basis for a State to treat interracial marriages differently from other marriages. On this question, the State argues, the scientific evidence is substantially in doubt and, consequently, this Court should defer to the wisdom of the state legislature in adopting its policy of discouraging interracial marriages.

Because we reject the notion that the mere "equal application" of a statute containing racial classifications is enough to remove the classifications from the Fourteenth Amendment's proscription of all invidious racial discriminations, we do not accept the State's contention that these statutes should be upheld if there is any possible basis for concluding that they serve a rational purpose. . . .

In the case at bar, . . . we deal with statutes containing racial classifications, and the fact of equal application does not immunize the statute from the very heavy burden of justification which the Fourteenth Amendment has traditionally required of state statutes drawn according to race.

The State argues that statements in the Thirty-ninth Congress about the time of the passage of the Fourteenth Amendment indicate that the Framers did not intend the Amendment to make unconstitutional state miscegenation laws. . . . While these statements have some relevance to the intention of Congress in submitting the Fourteenth Amendment, it must be understood that they pertained to the passage of specific statutes and not to the broader, organic purpose of a constitutional amendment. As for the various statements directly concerning the Fourteenth Amendment, we have said in connection with a related problem, that although these historical sources "cast some light" they are not sufficient to resolve the problem; "[a]t best, they are inconclusive. . . ." We have rejected the proposition that the debates in the Thirty-ninth Congress or in the state legislatures which ratified the Fourteenth Amendment supported the theory advanced by the State, that the requirement of equal protection of the laws is satisfied by penal laws defining offenses based on racial classifications so long as white and Negro participants in the offense were similarly punished. . . .

The clear and central purpose of the Fourteenth Amendment was to eliminate all official state sources of invidious racial discrimination in the States. . . .

There can be no question but that Virginia's miscegenation statutes rest solely upon distinctions drawn according to race. The statutes proscribe generally accepted conduct if engaged in by members of different races. Over the years, this Court has consistently repudiated "[d]istinctions between citizens solely because of their ancestry" as being "odious to a free people whose institutions are founded upon the doctrine of equality." . . . At the very least, the Equal Protection Clause demands that racial classifications, especially suspect in criminal statutes, be subjected to the "most rigid scrutiny," *Korematsu v. United States*, . . . (1944), and, if they are ever to be upheld, they must be shown to be necessary to the accomplishment of some permissible state objective, independent of the racial discrimination which it was the object of the Fourteenth Amendment to eliminate. Indeed, two members of

this Court have already stated that they "cannot conceive of a valid legislative purpose . . . which makes the color of a person's skin the test of whether his conduct is a criminal offense."

There is patently no legitimate overriding purpose independent of invidious racial discrimination which justifies this classification. The fact that Virginia prohibits only interracial marriages involving white persons demonstrates that the racial classifications must stand on their own justification, as measures designed to maintain White Supremacy. We have consistently denied the constitutionality of measures which restrict the rights of citizens on account of race. There can be no doubt that restricting the freedom to marry solely because of racial classifications violates the central meaning of the Equal Protection Clause.

These statutes also deprive the Lovings of liberty without due process of law in violation of the Due Process Clause of the Fourteenth Amendment. The freedom to marry has long been recognized as one of the vital personal rights essential to the orderly pursuit of happiness by free men.

Marriage is one of the "basic civil rights of man," fundamental to our very existence and survival. . . . To deny this fundamental freedom on so unsupportable a basis as the racial classifications embodied in these statutes, classifications so directly subversive of the principle of equality at the heart of the Fourteenth Amendment, is surely to deprive all the State's citizens of liberty without due process of law. The Fourteenth Amendment requires that the freedom of choice to marry not be restricted by invidious racial discriminations. Under our Constitution, the freedom to marry, or not marry, a person of another race resides with the individual and cannot be infringed by the State.

These convictions must be reversed.

It is so ordered.

Further Resources

BOOKS

Cray, Ed. *Chief Justice: A Biography of Earl Warren.* New York: Simon and Schuster, 1997.

Gordon-Reed, Annette. *Race on Trial: Law and Justice in American History.* New York: Oxford University Press, 2002.

Horwitz, Morton J. *The Warren Court and the Pursuit of Justice: A Critical Issue.* New York: Hill and Wang, 1998.

Irons, Peter H., and Stephanie Guitton. *May It Please the Court: The Most Significant Oral Arguments Made Before the Supreme Court since 1955.* New York: New Press, 1993.

Moran, Rachel F. *Interracial Intimacy: The Regulation of Race and Romance.* Chicago: University of Chicago Press, 2001.

Powe, L.A. Scot. *The Warren Court and American Politics.* Cambridge, Mass.: Belknap Press of Harvard University Press, 2000.

Schwartz, Bernard. *The Warren Court: A Retrospective.* New York: Oxford University Press, 1996.

WEBSITES

Civil Rights Movement #19: Loving v. Virginia and the Roots of Social Segregation. Available online at http://www.africana .com/blackboard/bb_his_000158.htm; website home page: http://www.africana.com (accessed January 21, 2003).

For Us, the Living
Memoir

By: Myrlie Evers

Date: 1967

Source: Evers, Mrs. Medgar, with William Peters. *For Us, the Living.* Garden City, N.Y.: Doubleday, 1967, 297–304.

About the Author: Myrlie Evers (1933?–), now Myrlie Evers-Williams, was the first woman to head the NAACP. After her husband, Medgar Evers, was murdered, she moved to California, working for the Claremont Colleges and running for public office. She also worked for Atlantic Richfield and was a commissioner on the Board of Public Works in the city of Los Angeles. She was instrumental in bringing her husband's killer, Byron de la Beckwith, to justice in 1994. ■

Introduction

After the Civil War (1861–1865), the Fourteenth and Fifteenth Amendments to the Constitution, often called the civil rights amendments, were enacted. The Fourteenth Amendment guaranteed equal treatment under the law, and the Fifteenth guaranteed the right to vote regardless of race. These amendments, however, were not fully enforced. In 1896, for example, the Supreme Court allowed "separate but equal" facilities for blacks and whites, but in many parts of the country, particularly the segregated South, the systems were far from equal.

African Americans did not accept this discrimination. In 1909, African Americans and whites formed the National Association for the Advancement of Colored People (NAACP), which aimed to challenge legal discrimination in the courts. Notable among this organization's successes was *Brown v. Board,* the landmark case in which the U.S. Supreme Court declared that segregation in education was unconstitutional. Many southern whites mobilized against this decision, slowing its implementation despite the resistance of NAACP chapters throughout the South. During this period, Medgar Evers was the field secretary of the Mississippi chapter of the

NAACP field secretary Medgar Evers was shot and killed outside his home after an integration rally on June 12, 1963. **AP/WIDE WORLD PHOTOS. REPRODUCED BY PERMISSION.**

NAACP and was active in fighting for civil rights. On June 12, 1963, President John F. Kennedy (served 1961–1963) gave a nationally televised speech on civil rights, which Evers watched at NAACP headquarters. When he returned home, he was assassinated in an ambush. His wife remembers that day in *For Us, the Living.*

Significance

Evers' assassination on the same day as Kennedy's speech kept the focus on civil rights and Mississippi. Kennedy, though, was unable to get his civil rights bill through Congress, where it was languishing when he was assassinated in November 1963. His successor, Lyndon B. Johnson (served 1963–1969), pledged to continue Kennedy's effort. Johnson was more skilled in congressional maneuvering than Kennedy, and many people felt more favorable toward Kennedy after his death. Both of these factors helped Kennedy's bill pass Congress as the 1964 Civil Rights Act. Johnson followed up this legislation with the 1965 Voting Rights Act and the 1968 Civil Rights Act guaranteeing equal treatment in housing.

These pieces of legislation forever changed the face of America. The Voting Rights Act allowed millions of African Americans to register to vote, changing southern politics. The Democratic Party in the South, long the party of segregation, now became the party of African Americans. Elected officials began to listen to them. The 1964 Civil Rights Act officially desegregated the South and led to a more integrated society. The 1968 act led to improved chances for housing, although discrimination still occurs.

Myrlie Evers eventually received some measure of justice. Byron de la Beckwith, Medgar Evers' assassin, was tried twice in the 1960s, but both trials resulted in hung juries. Beckwith was finally retried in 1994 and convicted. He died in prison in 2001 while serving a life term.

Primary Source

For Us, the Living [excerpt]

> **SYNOPSIS:** Myrlie Evers details the day's events including her husband's departure, President Kennedy's speech that night, her husband's return home, the shooting, and the discovery of her husband's body on the driveway.

Next morning I was up at five o'clock, creeping silently from the bedroom to iron shirts for Medgar. With the telephone ringing every few minutes all day, I had fallen far behind in my housework and had been ironing a shirt each morning for Medgar to wear that day. Today I was resolved to get ahead, and by the time he woke I had ten freshly ironed shirts neatly hung on hangers, the way he liked them. I took them to the bedroom and found him staring at the ceiling again. He smiled as I came in.

I held out the shirts. "See what I did this morning?"

"You're awfully smart."

"Aren't you going to thank me?"

He smiled and beckoned, and I went over and sat on the bed, and he squeezed me.

"I'm still waiting," I said.

And then he said, "I thank you for ironing all the shirts, but I'm not going to need them."

"Oh, come on," I said, getting up. "It's time to get out of bed."

I didn't know it until later, but Medgar had kept some things from me. Just the day before, Dr. Felix Dunn, president of the Gulfport NAACP, had called to tell him to be careful, to have someone see him home each night, to arrange for guards around the house. A white lawyer, sympathetic to the NAACP, had told Dr. Dunn an attempt was going to be made on Medgar's life, and while Dr. Dunn couldn't prove it, he wanted Medgar to know and to prepare for it.

After breakfast, Medgar kissed us all and went to the car. As usual I followed him to the door. At the open car door, he stood a moment and looked out across the street at the vacant lot with the high grass and overgrown bushes. Because I didn't want him to know I had seen this, I went back to the children at the table.

He came through the door a moment later, came back to the table, and kissed us all again. I felt a twinge of panic. At the door once more, he turned and looked pleadingly at me, his shoulders slumped, his face a mirror of conflicting emotions. "Myrlie, I don't know what to do. I'm so tired I can't go on, but I can't stop either."

I ran to him and held him, and we stood like that for a moment. Then he kissed me and walked out the door, got into the car and drove off. I prayed that he would somehow get through this one more day.

It was quite a day. As far behind as I was in my housework, I couldn't seem to get started. There were postponed projects wherever I looked, but I couldn't concentrate, and I'd find myself sitting somewhere, thinking, worrying, trying to see some way out. Medgar called three times that afternoon, once right after the televised "schoolhouse door" confrontation on the campus of the University of Alabama between Governor George Wallace of Alabama and Deputy U.S. Attorney General Nicholas Katzenbach. He was happy about Governor Wallace's surrender and the subsequent admission to the university of its first two Negro students since Autherine Lucy: Vivian Malone and James Hood.

The first two times he called he talked to the children. The third time I jokingly accused him of loafing. He asked what I meant. "Well, you've called three times today. I didn't think you'd have the time."

"I'll take the time," he said, "to check on my family."

I told him I was tired and was thinking of missing the mass meeting that night. I asked him if he needed me.

"No," he said, "you stay home and rest. You need the sleep."

I told him I'd rest and then fix him something to eat when he got home. I could hear someone enter his office then, and Medgar laughed at something that was said. "I've got to go, honey. See you tonight. I love you."

"All right," I said. "Take care." Those were our last words to each other.

■ ■ ■

Medgar had told me that President Kennedy was speaking on civil rights that night, and I made a mental note of the time. We ate alone, the children and I. It had become a habit now to set only four places for supper. Medgar's chair stared at us, and the children, who had heard about the President's address to the nation, planned to watch it with me. There was something on later that they all wanted to see, and they begged to be allowed to wait up for Medgar to return home. School was out, and I knew that Van would fall asleep anyway, so I agreed.

We moved the television set into my bedroom, and I stretched out on the bed, the children clustered on the floor out of range of the window. When President Kennedy appeared, all three children fell silent, knowing despite their youth that he was going to be talking about them.

He spoke of the events at the University of Alabama that afternoon, congratulated the students who had kept the peace by acting responsibly. He spoke of the ideals of the founding fathers; that all men were created equal and said that the rights of all men were diminished when the rights of one were threatened.

"Today," he said, "we are committed to a worldwide struggle to promote and protect the rights of all who wish to be free. And when Americans are sent to Vietnam or West Berlin, we do not ask for whites only. It ought to be possible, therefore, for American students of any color to attend any public institution they select without having to be backed up by troops.

"It ought to be possible for American consumers of any color to receive equal service in places of public accommodation, such as hotels and restaurants and theaters and retail stores, without being forced to resort to demonstrations in the street, and it ought to be possible for American citizens of any color to register and to vote in a free election without interference or fear of reprisal."

I felt that he was talking directly about our Capitol Street boycott, our voter registration drives, and suddenly I felt very close to the President of the United States. The children listened intently.

"We are confronted primarily with a moral issue," he said. "It is as old as the Scriptures and as clear as the American Constitution.

"The heart of the question is whether all Americans are to be afforded equal rights and equal opportunities, whether we are going to treat our fellow Americans as we want to be treated. If an American, because his skin is dark, cannot eat lunch in a restaurant open to the public, if he cannot send his children to the best public school available, if he cannot vote for the public officials who represent him, if, in short, he cannot enjoy the full and free life which all of us want, then who among us would be content to have the color of his skin changed and stand in his place? Who among us would then be content with the counsels of patience and delay?"

I thought of Medgar, watching the address somewhere, and my heart filled with the joy I knew he would be feeling at these words. Medgar had said something very like this in his television speech three weeks earlier.

"We face, then, a moral crisis as a country and as a people," President Kennedy said. "It cannot be met by repressive police action. It cannot be left to increased demonstrations in the streets. It cannot be quieted by token moves or talk. It is a time to act in the Congress, in your state and local legislative body, and, above all, in all of our daily lives."

He outlined the program of legislation that was to become the Civil Rights bill of 1964, asking Congress for a law to open places of public accommodation to all, a law to accelerate the pace of school desegregation, a law to protect the right to vote.

"This is one country," he said. "It has become one country because all of us and all the people who came here had an equal chance to develop their talents.

"We cannot say to ten per cent of the population that you can't have that right; that your children can't have the chance to develop whatever talents they have; that the only way that they are going to get their rights is to go into the streets and demonstrate. I think we owe them and we owe ourselves a better country than that. . . ."

It was a moving speech, the most direct and urgent appeal for racial justice any President of the United States had ever made. It moved me and gave me hope and made what Medgar was doing seem more important than ever before. I remember wondering what the white people of Mississippi were thinking as I lay back on the bed and the children switched the set to another channel. I must have drifted off into a light sleep, because I woke, later, to settle an argument over which program was to be watched next. Then, still buoyed up by the President's words, I relaxed, to watch with the children. Darrell heard the car first.

"Here comes Daddy."

We listened to the familiar sound of the car. I roused myself as the tires reached the gravel driveway, stretched, and then heard the car door close. I wondered what Medgar would have to say about the speech, and I sat up on the bed.

A shot rang out, loud and menacing. The children, true to their training, sprawled on the floor. I knew in my heart what it must mean.

I flew to the door, praying to be wrong. I switched on the light. Medgar lay face down at the doorway drenched with blood.

I screamed, went to him, calling his name.

There was another shot, much closer, and I dropped to my knees. Medgar didn't move.

The children were around me now, pleading with him. "Please, Daddy, please get up!"

Behind Medgar on the floor of the carport were the papers he had dropped and some sweatshirts. Crazily, across the front of one, I read the words, "Jim Crow Must Go." In his hand, stretched out toward the door, was the door key. There was blood everywhere.

I left the children and ran to the telephone. I dialed "O" and tried to breathe and screamed at the operator for the police and gave her the address and ran back outside.

The Youngs were there and the Wellses and more people were coming and someone had turned Medgar over and he was breathing heavily, in short spurts, and his eyes were open, but they were set and unmoving.

I called and called to him, but if he heard me he showed no sign.

I heard the children being led away, screaming and crying for their father, and I remember some men carrying the mattress from Rena's bed from the house, putting Medgar on it and carrying him to Houston Wells' station wagon. I followed and tried to get in beside him, still calling to him, but they held me back, and as the car pulled off, I fell trying to reach him, and someone picked me up and I ran back into the house. There had been a police car in front of the Wells' car as it tore away through the night, but I had not yet seen a policeman.

I ran to the living room and fell to my knees and prayed. I prayed for Medgar and I fought for breath and I prayed that God's will be done and I sobbed and I prayed that whatever happened I would be able to accept it.

Someone found me there, and I got up and ran to the telephone and called Attorney Young's house where Gloster Current was staying. "They've killed my husband!" I screamed. "They've killed my husband!"

A woman took the telephone from me, and I wandered off to the bedroom, dazed with grief. One of the women followed and found me packing Medgar's toothbrush and some pajamas for the hospital and asking out loud how many pairs he would need.

Jean Wells took my arm and said that Dr. Britton had called from Ole Miss Hospital. Medgar had regained consciousness. I searched the room for my clothes and began to dress.

Then Hattie Tate came in the door and looked at me and I knew.

"Is he gone?"

She couldn't speak. She tried but she couldn't speak. She turned and ran from the room, and I slumped like a marionette whose strings had been cut.

■ ■ ■

I called Aunt Myrlie in Vicksburg. "Medgar has been shot. He's dead." She screamed and dropped the telephone.

I called Charles in Chicago and spoke to his wife, Nan. She said, "Oh no!"

And then everything became a blur.

Further Resources

BOOKS

Jackson, James E. *At the Funeral of Medgar Evers in Jackson, Mississippi: A Tribute in Tears and a Thrust for Freedom.* New York: Publisher's New Press, 1963.

Massengill, Reed. *Portrait of a Racist: The Man Who Killed Medgar Evers?* New York: St. Martin's Press, 1994.

Morris, Willie. *The Ghosts of Medgar Evers: A Tale of Race, Murder, Mississippi, and Hollywood.* New York: Random House, 1998.

Nossiter, Adam. *Of Long Memory: Mississippi and the Murder of Medgar Evers.* Reading, Mass.: Addison-Wesley, 1994.

Vollers, Maryanne *Ghosts of Mississippi: The Murder of Medgar Evers, the Trials of Byron de la Beckwith, and the Haunting of the New South.* Boston: Little, Brown, 1995.

WEBSITES

Medgar Wiley Evers. Available online at http://www.mec .cuny.edu/presidents_office/mwe/medgar_evers.htm; website home page: http://www.mec.cuny.edu (accessed January 23, 2003).

AUDIO AND VISUAL MEDIA

Reiner, Rob, Alec Baldwin, Whoopi Goldberg, and James Woods. *Ghosts of Mississippi.* Columbia Pictures, 1996.

Brandenburg v. Ohio

Supreme Court decision

By: William O. Douglas

Date: June 9, 1969

Source: Douglas, William O. *Brandenburg v. Ohio,* 395 U.S. 444. Available online at http://caselaw.lp.findlaw.com/scripts /getcase.pl?navby=case&court=us&vol=395&page=444; website home page: http://caselaw.lp.findlaw.com (accessed June 12, 2003).

About the Author: William O. Douglas (1898–1980), at age forty, was one of the youngest men ever to be appointed to the Supreme Court, and after thirty-six years (1939–1975), his tenure was the longest in Supreme Court history. As a child, he recovered from polio by walking outside, which fostered his love of the environment. Prior to his appointment to the Supreme Court, he was chairman of the Securities and Exchange Commission. He was an independent justice often described as more concerned with being right than having other justices vote with him. ∎

Introduction

During the eighteenth and nineteenth centuries, the federal government issued few laws that affected issues of free speech. Two that did, the Alien and Sedition Acts, were never tested in the Supreme Court. Similarly, the Supreme Court never ruled on the validity of laws and executive orders affecting free speech during the Civil War (1861–1865). Further, prior to the twentieth century, the Court held that the First Amendment, which guarantees freedom of speech, was limited to actions by the federal government, not the states.

Around the beginning of the twentieth century, however, the issue of free speech began to attract more attention. During World War I (1914–1918), the Espionage and Sedition Acts and other legislation restricted free speech rights, and the Supreme Court, in six cases that came before it, held that this legislation was constitutional if the banned speech presented "a clear and present danger." In three of these cases, though, Justices Oliver Wendell Holmes and Louis Brandeis dissented, arguing that the legislation infringed freedom of speech. In the 1920s, the Supreme Court expanded the protection of freedom of speech by applying the First Amendment against the states. The Court continued this expansion in the 1930s by overturning legislation that prohibited the use of a red flag, which at the time was regarded as a symbol of communism and anarchy. In the 1950s, the Supreme Court for a time was influenced by the fear of communist expansion, generally allowing governmental repression of free speech. In 1957, though, the court limited the government's power to restrict free speech by holding that advocating ideas could not be banned, only advocating illegal acts. It was in this context that the Court heard *Brandburg v. Ohio* in 1969.

Significance

In *Brandenburg,* the Court reviewed the conviction of a Ku Klux Klan member under the Ohio Criminal Syndicalism Act. The Court voided this conviction, holding that advocating the use of force could be banned only when doing so "is directed to inciting or producing imminent lawless action." Justice Douglas, in his concurrence with the majority opinion, went further, arguing that the "clear and present danger" standard, which had been used to judge when speech could be banned since World War I, should be overruled and that political speeches should be "immune from prosecution." While his view was never adopted by the Court, the *Brandenburg* standard is much more protective of free speech than the "clear and present danger" test. During World War I and the Red Scare of the 1920s, the Court upheld bans on the advocacy of illegal ideas if those ideas were seen to produce a danger. *Brandenburg,* though, requires not only the advocacy of force but also that resulting danger be immediate.

Since 1969, the Supreme Court's decisions have largely been consistent with *Brandenburg.* At least two attempts to ban flag-burning were struck down by the Court as violations of the First Amendment, and in 1992 the Court held that a law forbidding the burning of a cross for racist purposes violated the First Amendment.

Primary Source

Brandenburg v. Ohio [excerpt]

> **SYNOPSIS:** The Court's decision first surveys past cases and states that laws criminalizing speech can only criminalize advocacy of "imminent lawless" action. Because the Ohio law does not do this, it violates the Constitution. In his concurrence, Douglas agrees with the ruling but argue that the "clear and present danger" standard should be done away with, as it is unclear and allows unpopular speech to be suppressed. Speech, in Douglas's view, should be banned only when it becomes an "overt act."

The appellant, a leader of a Ku Klux Klan group, was convicted under the Ohio Criminal Syndicalism statute for "advocat[ing] . . . the duty, necessity, or propriety of crime, sabotage, violence, or unlawful methods of terrorism as a means of accomplishing industrial or political reform" and for "voluntarily assembl[ing] with any society, group, or assemblage of persons formed to teach or advocate the doctrines of criminal syndicalism. . . . He was fined $1,000 and sentenced to one to 10 years' imprisonment. . . .

The Ohio Criminal Syndicalism Statute was enacted in 1919. . . . In 1927, this Court sustained the constitutionality of California's Criminal Syndicalism Act, . . . the text of which is quite similar to that of the laws of Ohio. *Whitney v. California,* . . . The Court upheld the statute on the ground that, without more, "advocating" violent means to effect political and economic change involves such danger to the security of the State that the State may outlaw it. . . . But *Whitney* has been thoroughly discredited by later decisions. See *Dennis v. United States* . . . These later decisions have fashioned the principle that the constitutional guarantees of free speech and free press do not permit a State to forbid or proscribe advocacy of the use of force or of law violation except where such advocacy is directed to inciting or producing imminent lawless action and is likely to incite or produce such action. As we said in *Noto v. United States* . . . "the mere abstract teaching . . . of the moral propriety or even moral necessity for a resort to force and violence, is not the same as preparing a group for violent action and steeling it to such action." . . . A statute which fails to draw this distinction impermissibly intrudes upon the freedoms guaranteed by the First and Fourteenth Amendments. It sweeps within its condemnation speech which our Constitution has immunized from governmental control. . . .

Measured by this test, Ohio's Criminal Syndicalism Act cannot be sustained. The Act punishes persons who "advocate or teach the duty, necessity, or propriety" of violence "as a means of accomplishing industrial or political reform"; or who publish or circulate or display any book or paper containing such advocacy; or who "justify" the commission of violent acts "with intent to exemplify, spread or advocate the propriety of the doctrines of criminal syndicalism"; or who "voluntarily assemble" with a group formed "to teach or advocate the doctrines of criminal syndicalism." Neither the indictment nor the trial judge's instructions to the jury in any way refined the statute's bald definition of the crime in terms of mere advocacy not distinguished from incitement to imminent lawless action.

Accordingly, we are here confronted with a statute which, by its own words and as applied, purports to punish mere advocacy and to forbid, on pain of criminal punishment, assembly with others merely to advocate the described type of action. Such a statute falls within the condemnation of the First and Fourteenth Amendments. The contrary teaching of *Whitney v. California,* supra, cannot be supported, and that decision is therefore overruled.

Reversed. . . .

Mr. Justice Douglas, concurring.

While I join the opinion of the Court, I desire to enter a caveat.

The "clear and present danger" test was adumbrated by Mr. Justice Holmes in a case arising during World War I—a war "declared" by the Congress, not by the Chief Executive. The case was *Schenck v. United States* . . . where the defendant was charged with attempts to cause insubordination in the military and obstruction of enlistment. The pamphlets that were distributed urged resistance to the draft, denounced conscription, and impugned the motives of those backing the war effort. The First Amendment was tendered as a defense. Mr. Justice Holmes in rejecting that defense said:

> The question in every case is whether the words used are used in such circumstances and are of such a nature as to create a clear and present danger that they will bring about the substantive evils that Congress has a right to prevent. It is a question of proximity and degree.

. . .

In the 1919 Term, the Court applied the *Schenck* doctrine to affirm the convictions of other dissidents in World War I. *Abrams v. United States,* . . . was one instance. Mr. Justice Holmes, with whom Mr. Justice Brandeis concurred, dissented. While adhering to *Schenck,* he did not think that on the facts a case for overriding the First Amendment had been made out:

> It is only the present danger of immediate evil or an intent to bring it about that warrants Congress in setting a limit to the expression of opinion where private rights are not concerned. Congress certainly cannot forbid all effort to change the mind of the country. . . .

The dissents in *Abrams* . . . show how easily "clear and present danger" is manipulated to crush what Brandeis called "[t]he fundamental right of free men to strive for better conditions through new legislation and new institutions" by argument and discourse . . . even in time of war. Though I doubt if the "clear and present danger" test is congenial to the First Amendment in time of a declared war, I am certain it is not reconcilable with the First Amendment in days of peace.

The Court quite properly overrules *Whitney v. California* . . . which involved advocacy of ideas which the majority of the Court deemed unsound and dangerous. Mr. Justice Holmes, though never formally abandoning the "clear and present danger" test, moved closer to the First Amendment ideal when he said in dissent in *Gitlow v. New York.* . . .

> Every idea is an incitement. It offers itself for belief and if believed it is acted on unless some other belief outweighs it or some failure of energy stifles the movement at its birth. The only difference between the expression of an opinion and an incitement in the narrower sense is the speaker's enthusiasm for the result. Eloquence may set fire to reason. But whatever may be thought of the redundant discourse before us it had no chance of starting a present conflagration. If in the long run the beliefs expressed in proletarian dictatorship are destined to be accepted by the dominant forces of the community, the only meaning of free speech is that they should be given their chance and have their way.

We have never been faithful to the philosophy of that dissent. . . .

Out of the "clear and present danger" test came other offspring. Advocacy and teaching of forcible overthrow of government as an abstract principle is immune from prosecution. *Yates v. United States.* . . . But an "active" member, who has a guilty knowledge and intent of the aim to overthrow the Government by violence, . . . may be prosecuted. . . . And the power to investigate, backed by the powerful sanction of contempt, includes the power to determine which of the two categories fits the particular witness. . . . And so the investigator roams at will through all of the beliefs of the witness, ransacking his conscience and his innermost thoughts. . . .

I see no place in the regime of the First Amendment for any "clear and present danger" test, whether strict and tight as some would make it, or free-wheeling as the Court in *Dennis* rephrased it.

When one reads the opinions closely and sees when and how the "clear and present danger" test has been applied, great misgivings are aroused. First, the threats were often loud but always puny and made serious only by judges so wedded to the status quo that critical analysis made them nervous. Second, the test was so twisted and perverted in *Dennis* as to make the trial of those teachers of Marxism an all-out political trial which was part and parcel of the cold war that has eroded substantial parts of the First Amendment.

Action is often a method of expression and within the protection of the First Amendment.

Suppose one tears up his own copy of the Constitution in eloquent protest to a decision of this Court. May he be indicted? . . .

Last Term the Court held in *United States v. O'Brien* . . . that a registrant under Selective Service who burned his draft card in protest of the war in Vietnam could be prosecuted. The First Amendment was tendered as a defense and rejected, the Court saying:

> The issuance of certificates indicating the registration and eligibility classification of individuals is a legitimate and substantial administrative aid in the functioning of this system. And legislation to insure the continuing availability of issued certificates serves a legitimate and substantial purpose in the system's administration. . . .

But O'Brien was not prosecuted for not having his draft card available when asked for by a federal agent. He was indicted, tried, and convicted for burning the card. And this Court's affirmance of that conviction was not, with all respect, consistent with the First Amendment. . . .

One's beliefs have long been thought to be sanctuaries which government could not invade. *Barenblatt* [*v. United States*] is one example of the ease with which that sanctuary can be violated. The lines drawn by the Court between the criminal act of being an "active" Communist and the innocent act of being a nominal or inactive Communist mark the difference only between deep and abiding belief and casual or uncertain belief. But I think, that all matters of belief are beyond the reach of subpoenas or the probings of investigators. That is why the invasions of privacy made by investigating committees were notoriously unconstitutional. That is the deep-seated fault in the infamous loyalty-security hearings which, since 1947 when President Truman launched them, have processed 20,000,000 men and women. Those hearings were primarily concerned with one's thoughts, ideas, beliefs, and convictions. They were the most blatant violations of the First Amendment we have ever known.

The line between what is permissible and not subject to control and what may be made impermissible and subject to regulation is the line between ideas and overt acts.

The example usually given by those who would punish speech is the case of one who falsely shouts fire in a crowded theatre.

This is, however, a classic case where speech is brigaded with action. See *Speiser v. Randall* . . . They are indeed inseparable and a prosecution can be launched for the overt acts actually caused. Apart from rare instances of that kind, speech is, I think, immune from prosecution. Certainly there is no constitutional line between advocacy of abstract ideas as in *Yates* and advocacy of political action as in *Scales* [*v. United States*]. The quality of advocacy turns on the depth of the conviction; and government has no power to invade that sanctuary of belief and conscience.

Further Resources

BOOKS

Ball, Howard, and Phillip J Cooper. *Of Power and Right: Hugo Black, William O. Douglas, and America's Constitutional Revolution.* New York: Oxford University Press, 1992.

Douglas, William O. *The Court Years, 1939–1975: The Autobiography of William O. Douglas.* New York: Random House, 1980.

Eastland, Terry. *Freedom of Expression in the Supreme Court: The Defining Cases.* Washington, D.C.: Rowman and Littlefield, 2000.

Horwitz, Morton J. *The Warren Court and the Pursuit of Justice: A Critical Issue.* New York: Hill and Wang, 1998.

Parker, Richard A. *Free Speech on Trial: Communication Perspectives on Landmark Supreme Court Decisions.* Tuscaloosa, Ala.: University of Alabama Press, 2003.

Powe, L.A. Scot. *The Warren Court and American Politics.* Cambridge, Mass.: Belknap Press of Harvard University Press, 2000.

Schwartz, Bernard. *The Warren Court: A Retrospective.* New York: Oxford University Press, 1996.

WEBSITES

Legislation: Prior Restraint. Available online at http://www.stanford.edu/~dalmassi/CS201/prior_restraint.html; website home page: http://www.stanford.edu (accessed January 21, 2003).

Chicago Trial Testimony

Testimony

By: Allen Ginsberg

Date: 1969

Source: Ginsberg, Allen. *Chicago Trial Testimony.* San Francisco: City Lights, 1975, 3–10.

About the Author: Allen Ginsberg (1926–1997) was one of the best known writers of the Beat Movement and one of the few who continued to influence culture up until his death in the 1990s. His poem "Howl," along with his friend Jack Kerouac's *On the Road,* became leading literary influences on the Beats. He was politically active in the 1960s, leading the antiwar movement. He remained culturally active and continued to write until his death. ∎

Introduction

The United States has fought many wars in its past, provoked varying levels of opposition. The War of 1812 was heavily opposed by the Federalist Party, which collapsed after the United States won the war. The Civil War (1861–1865), too, met with opposition in both the North and the South. The Democrats, whom Lincoln called Copperheads, opposed Lincoln's efforts, and many Southerners opposed seccession from the Union. Opposition to American involvement in World War I (1914–1918) was widespread, and draconian laws were passed to restrict that opposition. Even World War II (1939–1945), often referred to as "the last good war," met with some opposition, particularly as war loomed in the 1930s. In the 1950s, McCarthyism silenced many who objected to the aims and tactics of the Cold War.

To contain the spread of communism in Asia, the United States committed large numbers of troops to Vietnam in a long and bloody struggle that would cost fifty-eight thousand American lives. As the number of Americans questioning the nation's involvement in Vietnam grew, a vocal antiwar movement emerged. Thousands of antiwar protesters gathered in Chicago during the 1968 Democratic National Convention, which nominated Humbert Humphrey. Richard Daley, mayor of Chicago, violently cracked down on the protesters, often in full view of cameras that broadcast riots into American living rooms. Eight men, later reduced to seven, known as the "Chicago 7"—Abbie Hoffman, Jerry Rubin, David Dellinger, Rennie Davis, Tom Hayden, John Froines, Lee Weiner, and Bobby Seale—were charged with violating the 1968 Anti-Riot Act by traveling "in interstate commerce . . . with the intent to incite . . . a riot." Poet Allen Ginsberg, in his own distinct style, testified in their defense, explaining what the protests aimed to accomplish.

Significance

Five of the seven defendants were convicted on the charges of inciting a riot. Two of their lawyers, including William Kunstler, and some of the defendants were also held in contempt of court. Both the contempt charges and the charges of violating the Anti-Riot Act were later overturned by the Seventh Circuit Court of Appeals. The antiwar movement, especially the more radical fringe that Ginsberg and many of the Chicago 7 represented, brought a great deal of attention to the movement, but it had little direct effect on the political process. Humbert Humphrey was still nominated, and his plan for the war was to negotiate a withdrawal. Richard Nixon, the Republican candidate, wanted "Peace with Honor" and claimed to have a secret plan for winning the war in Vietnam. George Wallace, a third-party candidate, took a strong stand against protesters and urged the use of any weapon needed, including nuclear weapons, in Vietnam. Nixon won the election and attempted to turn control of the war over to the Vietnamese, which failed. The United

States finally had to withdraw from Vietnam. The official reason given for this withdrawal was military failure rather than the effects of antiwar protesters.

Ginsberg continued to be a radical poet until his death in 1997. William Kunstler, the Chicago 7 lawyer, defended radical causes until his death in 1995. Several of the Chicago 7, though, turned more mainstream; Jerry Rubin, for example, took a job on Wall Street, and Tom Hayden became a California state senator.

Primary Source

Chicago Trial Testimony [excerpt]

SYNOPSIS: Ginsberg opens his testimony with a description of his participation in the San Francisco "Be-In," after which he notes what Abbie Hoffman intended to have occur at the protest in Chicago. Ginsberg then refers to discussions he had with Jerry Rubin about these same protests. The testimony closes with Ginsberg talking about some of the activities planned for the Chicago demonstrations. Throughout there are clashes by the lawyers and the court. [The format of this primary document has been changed to improve readability.]

Mr. Weinglass: Mr. Ginsberg, do you know the defendant Jerry Rubin?

Mr. Ginsberg: Yes, I do.

Mr. Weinglass: Could you identify him seated here in this courtroom?

Mr. Ginsberg: Yes, the gentlemen with the Indian headband.

Mr. Weinglass: How long have you known Jerry Rubin?

Mr. Ginsberg: Four and a half years.

Mr. Weinglass: Do you recall where it was that you first met him?

Mr. Ginsberg: In Berkeley and San Francisco in 1965 during the time of the anti-Vietnam war marches in Berkeley.

Mr. Weinglass: Were you associated with Mr. Rubin in that anti-war march?

Mr. Ginsberg: Yes, we worked together.

Mr. Weinglass: Did you have any further occasion in the year of 1967 to be associated with Mr. Rubin?

Mr. Ginsberg: Yes. I saw him again at the Human Be-in in San Francisco. We shared the stage with many other people.

Mr. Weinglass: Would you describe for the court and jury what the Be-in in San Francisco was?

Allen Ginsberg was one of the pioneers of the Beat literary movement of the 1950s and 1960s. AP/WIDE WORLD PHOTOS. REPRODUCED BY PERMISSION.

Mr. Ginsberg: A large assembly of younger people who came together to—

Mr. Foran: Objection, your Honor.

The Court: Just a minute. I am not sure how you spell the Be-in

Mr. Weinglass: B–E—I–N, I believe. Be-in.

Mr. Ginsberg: *Human* Be-in.

The Court: I really can't pass on the validity of the objection because I don't understand the question.

Mr. Weinglass: I asked him to explain what a Be-in was. I thought the question was directed to that possible confusion. He was interrupted in the course of the examination.

Mr. Foran: I would love to know also but I don't think it has anything to do with this lawsuit.

Mr. Weinglass: Well, let's wait and find out.

Mr. Foran: This is San Francisco in 1967.

The Court: I will let him, over the objection of the government, tell what a Be-in is.

Mr. Ginsberg: A gathering together of younger people aware of the planetary fate that we are all

Chicago Seven members address a press conference in 1970; left to right (front) Rennie Davis, Jerry Rubin, and Abbie Hoffman, (back) Lee Weiner, Bob Lamb (who was not part of Chicago Seven) and Thomas Hayden. **AP/WIDE WORLD PHOTOS. REPRODUCED BY PERMISSION.**

sitting in the middle of, imbued with a new consciousness and desiring of a new kind of society involving prayer, music and spiritual life together rather than competition, acquisition and war.

Mr. Weinglass: Did you have occasion—and was that the activity that was engaged in in San Francisco at this Be-in?

Mr. Ginsberg: There was what was called a gathering of the tribes of all of the different affinity groups, political groups, spiritual groups, Yoga groups, music groups and poetry groups that all felt the same crisis of identity and crisis of the planet and political crisis in America, who all came together in the largest assemblage of such younger people that had taken place since the war in the presence of the Zen Master Suzuki that I mentioned before, in the presence of a number of Tibetan Buddhists and Japanese Zen Buddhists and in the presence of the rock bands and the presence of Timothy Leary and Mr. Rubin.

The Court: Now having had it explained to me, I will hear from you.

Mr. Foran: I object, your Honor.

The Court: I sustain the objection.

Mr. Foran: Your Honor, I will refrain from moving to have the jury directed to disregard it.

Mr. Weinglass: If your Honor please—

Mr. Kunstler: It isn't so funny that it has to be laughed at by the U.S. Attorney.

Mr. Foran: Your Honor—

Mr. Kunstler: I think the objection can be stated—

Mr. Ginsberg: Sir—

The Court: You will get another question.

Mr. Kunstler: I will let Mr. Weinglass—

Mr. Weinglass: In answering that objection, I think within the last hour the court has heard the prosecutor examine extensively a prior witness on another demonstration which occurred in October of 1967. I think we are talking about public meetings at which these defendants were present during the year 1967.

The Court: I will let my ruling stand. Ask another question.

Mr. Weinglass: Now during the—later on in the year of 1967 did you have occasion to meet again with the defendant Jerry Rubin?

Mr. Ginsberg: Yes.

Mr. Weinglass: And what was that meeting concerning?

Mr. Ginsberg: We met in a cafe in Berkeley and discussed his mayoral race for the City of Berkeley. He had run for mayor.

Mr. Weinglass: Did you have any participation in that campaign?

Mr. Ginsberg: I encouraged it, blessed it.

Mr. Weinglass: Now do you know the defendant Abbie Hoffman?

Mr. Ginsberg: Yes.

Mr. Weinglass: Do you see him seated here at that table?

Mr. Ginsberg: Yes.

Mr. Weinglass: Would you identify him for the jury?

Mr. Ginsberg: At the corner of the table on your right with the wine-colored jacket.

Mr. Weinglass: For how long have you known Abbie Hoffman?

Mr. Ginsberg: Since late in 1967, I believe.

Mr. Weinglass: Now calling your attention to the month of February, 1968, did you have occasion in that month to meet with Abbie Hoffman?

Mr. Ginsberg: Yeah.

Mr. Weinglass: Do you recall the precise day of that meeting?

Mr. Ginsberg: No. Sometime mid-February, I think.

Mr. Weinglass: Do you recall where that meeting took place?

Mr. Ginsberg: In my apartment in New York.

Mr. Weinglass: Now were there any other persons present?

Mr. Ginsberg: No.

Mr. Weinglass: Did you have a conversation with Abbie Hoffman?

Mr. Ginsberg: Yes.

Mr. Weinglass: Could you relate to the jury what was discussed between you and Mr. Hoffman at that meeting?

Mr. Ginsberg: We talked about the possibility of extending the feeling of humanity and compassion of the Human Be-in in San Francisco to the City of Chicago during the time of the political convention, the possibility of inviting the same kind of younger people and the same kind of teachers who had been at the San Francisco Human Be-in to Chicago at the time of the convention in order to show some different new planetary life style than was going to be shown to the younger people by the politicians who were assembling.

Mr. Weinglass: Now when you say, "We discussed," did Mr. Hoffman indicate to you what his intention was with respect to that discussion?

Mr. Foran: Objection, leading and suggestive.

The Court: I sustain the objection.

Mr. Weinglass: Do you recall what Mr. Hoffman said in the course of that conversation?

Mr. Ginsberg: Yippie—among other things. He said that politics had become theatre and magic; that it was the manipulation of imagery through mass media that was confusing and hypnotizing the people in the United States and making them accept a war which they did not really believe in; that people were involved in a life style which was intolerable to the younger folk, which involved brutality and police violence as well as a larger violence in Viet Nam, and that ourselves might be able to get together in Chicago and invite teachers to present different ideas of what is wrong with the planet, what we can do to solve the pollution crisis, what we can do to solve the Viet Nam war, to present different ideas for making the society more sacred and less commercial, less materialistic, what we could do to uplevel or improve the whole tone of the trap that we all felt ourselves in as the population grew and as politics became more and more violent and chaotic.

Mr. Weinglass: Did he mention to you specifically any teachers that he had in mind for coming to Chicago?

Mr. Foran: Objection.

The Court: I sustain the objection.

Mr. Weinglass: Did you hear him mention the names of Mr. Burroughs, Mr. Olson and other teachers?

Mr. Ginsberg: Burroughs, Olson and Mr. Fuller.

The Court: Mr. Witness—

Mr. Foran: Objection to the leading and suggestive question.

The Court: I sustain the objection and I strike the answer and direct the jury to disregard it.

Mr. Weinglass: Mr. Ginsberg, does you prior answer exhaust your recollection as to what Mr. Hoffman said at that meeting?

Mr. Ginsberg: Yes.

Mr. Weinglass: Do you recall him mentioning anything about rock and roll bands?

Mr. Ginsberg: Yes.

Mr. Weinglass: What did he say about rock and roll bands?

Mr. Ginsberg: Well, he said that he was in contact with John Sinclair who was the leader of the MC 5 rock and roll band and John Sinclair and Ed Sanders of the Fugs would collaborate together and invite a lot of rock and roll people, popular music such as Arlo Guthrie—Phil Ochs was also mentioned by Mr. Hoffman. Mr. Hoffman asked me if I could contact the Beatles or Bob Dylan and tell them what was afoot and ask them if they could join us so that we could actually put on a really beautiful thing that would turn everybody on in the sense of like uplift everybody's spirit and show actually what we were actually feeling as far as delight instead of the horror that was surrounding us.

Mr. Weinglass: Now did he ascribe any particular name to that project?

Mr. Ginsberg: Festival of Life.

Mr. Weinglass: Did he ask you to take any active role in the Festival of Life?

Mr. Foran: Objection, you Honor. Can't Mr. Weinglass—

The Court: I sustain the objection.

Mr. Foran: I mean, those are all the leading and suggestive questions, your Honor, and I object to them. They are improper.

The Court: I have already sustained the objection.

Mr. Weinglass: After he spoke to you, what, if anything was your response to his suggestion?

Mr. Ginsberg: I was worried as to whether or not the whole scene would get violent. I was worried whether we would be allowed to put on such a situation. I was worried whether, you know, the Government would let us do something that was funnier or prettier or more charming than what was going to be going on in the convention hall.

Mr. Foran: I object and ask that it be stricken. It was not responsive.

The Court: Yes. I sustain the objection.

Mr. Ginsberg: Sir, this is—that was our conversation.

The Court: I direct the jury to disregard the last answer of the witness.

Mr. Weinglass: Your Honor, I would like to—

Mr. Ginsberg: How can I phrase that then because that was our—

Mr. Weinglass: Your Honor, I would like to be informed by the Court how that answer was not responsive to that question. It seemed to me to be directly responsive.

Mr. Foran: Your Honor, he asked him what he said and he answered by saying what he was wondering.

The Court: Worry.

Mr. Ginsberg: Oh, I am sorry, then. I said to Jerry that I was worried about violence—

The Court: I have ruled on the objection. Ask another question if you like.

Mr. Weinglass: Now during that same month, February of 1968, did you have occasion to meet with Jerry Rubin?

Mr. Ginsberg: I spoke to Jerry Rubin on the phone, I believe.

Mr. Weinglass: Did you call him or did he call you?

Mr. Ginsberg: I called him.

Mr. Weinglass: Do you recall where you called him at?

Mr. Ginsberg: His house, his apartment on the Lower East Side in New York.

Mr. Weinglass: Did you have his home phone number?

Mr. Ginsberg: Yes.

Mr. Weinglass: Was it that number that you dialed?

Mr. Ginsberg: Yes.

Mr. Weinglass: And who answered?

Mr. Ginsberg: Jerry did. I asked if could speak with Jerry Rubin and he said "That's me," and I recognized his voice.

Mr. Weinglass: Had you talked to Jerry Rubin prior to this occasion by telephone?

Mr. Ginsberg: Yes, often.

Mr. Weinglass: How many times approximately had you talked to him before telephone since knowing him?

Mr. Ginsberg: Oh, ten, twelve.

Mr. Weinglass: Could you recognize his voice?

Mr. Ginsberg: Yes.

Mr. Weinglass: Did you recognize his voice in the course of this telephone conversation?

Mr. Ginsberg: Yes.

Mr. Weinglass: Now do you recall what was discussed during that telephone conversation?

Mr. Ginsberg: Yes.

Mr. Weinglass: Will you relate to the Court and jury what Jerry Rubin said to you.

Mr. Ginsberg: Jerry told me that he and others were going to Chicago to apply for permission from the city government for a permit to hold a Festival of Life and that he was talking with John Sinclair about getting rock and roll bands together and other musicians and that he would report back to me and try to find a good place near where we could either meet delegates and influence delegates or where we could have like some kind of central location in the city where people could sleep overnight so we could actually invite younger people to come or come ourselves with knapsacks and sleeping bags, somewhat as turned out at the Woodstock Festival this year.

Mr. Foran: I object to this, your Honor. He would have had a hard time saying that.

The Court: The reference to the Woodstock Festival may go out and the jury is directed to disregard it.

Mr. Ginsberg: Sir, the imagination that we had of it—

The Court: Will you excuse me, sir? I am not permitted to engage in a colloquy with the witness.

Mr. Ginsberg: I am just trying to clarify the data that I know.

The Court: A lawyer is asking you questions. You just answer them as best you can.

Mr. Weinglass: Did Mr. Rubin in the course of that conversation indicate what activities were planned for Chicago during the Democratic Convention?

Mr. Ginsberg: Yes. He said that he thought it would be interesting if we could set up tents and areas within the park where kids could come and sleep, and set up little schools like ecology schools, music schools, political schools, schools about the Viet Nam war, to go back into history, schools with yogis.

He suggested that I contact whatever professional breathing exercise Yogi Swami teachers I could find and invite them to Chicago and asked if I could contact Burroughs and ask Burroughs to come also to teach non-verbal, non-conceptual feeling states.

Mr. Weinglass: Now you indicated a school of ecology. Could you explain to the Court and jury what that is?

Mr. Ginsberg: Ecology is the interrelation of all the living forms on the surface of the planet involving the food chain, that is to say, whales eat plankton; littler organisms in the ocean eat tiny microscopic organisms called plankton; larger fishes eat smaller fish, octopus or squid eat shellfish which eat plankton; human beings eat the shellfish or squid or smaller fish which eat the smaller tiny micro-organisms.

Mr. Foran: That is enough, your Honor.

The Court: You say that is enough?

Mr. Foran: I think that the question is now responsive. I think that—

The Court: Yes. We all have a clear idea now of what ecology is.

Mr. Ginsberg: Well, the destruction of ecology is what would have been taught. That is, how it is being destroyed by human intervention and messing it up with pollution.

Mr. Weinglass: Now you also indicated that Mr. Rubin mentioned non-verbal education. Will you explain what that is to the Court and jury.

Mr. Ginsberg: Most of our consciousness, since we are continually looking at images on television and listening to words, reading newspapers, talking in courts as this, most of our consciousness is filled with language, with a kind of matter babble behind the ear, a continuous yackety-yack that actually prevents us from breathing deeply in our bodies and sensing more subtly and sweetly the feelings that we actually do have as persons to each other rather than as to talking machines.

Further Resources

BOOKS

Dellinger, David T., and Bobby Seale. *Chicago Conspiracy Contempt Briefs*. New York: Distributed by the Center for Constitutional Rights, 1970.

Dellinger, David T. *In the Matter of David T. Dellinger, Abbott H. Hoffman, Jerry C. Rubin and William M. Kunstler, Defendants-Appellants*. Chicago: United States Law Printing, 1974.

Draper, Timothy Dean, David Paul Nord, and Timothy J. Gilfoyle. *Revisiting 1968*. Chicago: Chicago Historical Society, 2002.

Epstein, Jason. *The Great Conspiracy Trial: An Essay on Law, Liberty, and the Constitution*. New York: Random House, 1970.

Feiffer, Jules. *Pictures at a Prosecution: Drawings and Text from the Chicago Conspiracy Trial*. New York: Grove Press, 1971.

Jezer, Marty. *Abbie Hoffman, American Rebel*. New Brunswick, N.J.: Rutgers University Press, 1992.

Schultz, John. *The Chicago Conspiracy Trial*. New York: Da Capo Press, 1993.

WEBSITES

The Trial of the Chicago 7. Available online at http://www.law.umkc.edu/faculty/projects/ftrials/Chicago7/chicago7.html; website home page: http://www.law.umkc.edu (accessed January 23, 2003).

Helter Skelter: The True Story of the Manson Murders

Memoir

By: Vincent Bugliosi

Date: 1974

Source: Bugliosi, Vincent, with Curt Gentry. *Helter Skelter: The True Story of the Manson Murders*. New York: Norton, 1974, 173–177.

About the Author: Vincent Bugliosi (1933–) received his law degree from UCLA. He was a successful prosecutor, losing just one out of 106 felony cases that he tried. After his fame from the Manson murder trial and his successful book about it, *Helter Skelter*, he continued to prosecute cases and occasionally write books about them. In the 1990s, he published popular books on the O.J. Simpson case, the Paula Jones–Bill Clinton lawsuit, and the 2000 presidential election. ∎

Introduction

Outlaw gangs have been active throughout American history. Quantrill's Raiders during the Civil War (1861–1865) were primarily bandits, and the Jesse James gang is part of American folklore. In the twentieth cen-

tury, the Black Hand was rumored to have entered the country to create havoc, and anarchist groups struck at America through violence. During the Roaring Twenties, organized crime was active in the illegal liquor trade. Generally, any murders that these and other gangs committed were motivated either by money or the desire to make a political statement. On some level, they made sense or could at least be explained.

The 1960s was a period marked by a number of notorious and highly publicized crimes that seemed to make no sense. The decade began with the cases of Richard Hickock and Perry Smith, who broke into a home in Kansas and murdered four people in a failed burglary attempt. Their case was made famous by Truman Capote's best-selling book *In Cold Blood*. Near the end of the decade, another senseless violent crime riveted the nation. On the night of August 9, 1969, the followers of Charles Manson broke into a Los Angeles mansion and brutally murdered actress Sharon Tate, who was eight months pregnant, coffee heiress Abigail Folger, and three others. Graffiti was scrawled on the walls with the victims' blood. The following night, the same group broke into a Hollywood home and stabbed to death a wealthy couple, Rosemary and Leno LaBianca. Together, the two sets of murders are usually referred to as the Tate-LaBianca murders. What attracted Americans' attention was the bizarre and cultish nature of the group that carried out the killings.

Significance

Susan Atkins, one of the members of the Manson "family" convicted of the crimes, showed indifference throughout the trial. Her explanation of why Manson had his followers kill did not really satisfy or comfort many. Manson believed that songs by the Beatles carried messages of a coming race war and that if he could touch off the war through murder, then he and his followers could hide in the desert while it occurred. The most frightening aspects of this murder spree for many Americans was the bizarre psychological purpose for which the crimes were carried out and Manson's total psychological control over those who committed the crimes, including Atkins, Leslie Van Houten, Patricia Krenwinkel, and Charles "Tex" Watson. Many Americans who were disturbed by the counterculture movement of the 1960s pointed to the Manson family murders as examples of its decline.

Manson and the three women involved in the killings were all convicted of murder in 1971 in a widely followed trial prosecuted by Vincent Bugliosi. Tex Watson was convicted in a separate trial. All were sentenced to death, but their death sentences were commuted in 1972 when the U.S. Supreme Court declared all existing state death penalty statutes unconstitutional in *Furman v.*

Georgia (new death penalty statutes have been established in 38 states since then). All five have been denied parole several times. The four family members have all expressed remorse and tried to help people outside prison. Manson, though, continues to blame the establishment for his "persecution." His next parole hearing will be in 2007 when he is age seventy-two.

Primary Source

Helter Skelter: The True Story of the Manson Murders [excerpt]

SYNOPSIS: Bugliosi details the grand jury proceedings in the Manson murder trial. First, Susan Atkins testifies how she met Manson and how he took control of her. Next she discusses how Manson programmed her and what he had her do. The testimony closes with the discussion of the murders at the Tate residence.

December 5, 1969

"Sorry. No comment." Although grand jury proceedings are by law secret—neither the DA's Office, the witnesses, nor the jurors being allowed to discuss the evidence—this didn't keep the reporters from trying. There must have been a hundred newsmen in the narrow hallway outside the grand jury chambers; some were atop tables, so it looked as if they were stacked to the ceiling.

In Los Angeles the grand jury consists of twenty-three persons, picked by lot from a list of names submitted by each Superior Court judge. Of that number twenty-one were present, two-thirds of whom would have to concur to return an indictment. The proceedings themselves are usually brief. The prosecution presents just enough of its case to get an indictment and no more. Though in this instance the testimony would extend over two days, the "star witness for the prosecution" would tell her story in less than one.

Attorney Richard Caballero was the first witness, testifying that he had informed his client of her rights. Caballero then left the chambers. Not only are witnesses not allowed to have their attorneys present, each witness testifies outside the hearing of the other witnesses.

The Sergeant at Arms[:] "Susan Atkins."

The jurors, seven men and fourteen women, looked at her with obvious curiosity.

Aaron informed Susan of her rights, among which was her right not to incriminate herself. She waived them. I then took over the questioning, establishing that she knew Charles Manson and tak-

Prosecutors Vincent Bugliosi (left) and Paul Fitzgerald confer during the LaBianca-Tate murder trial. **AP/WIDE WORLD PHOTOS. REPRODUCED BY PERMISSION.**

ing her back to the day they first met. It was over two years ago. She was living in a house on Lyon Street in the Haight-Ashbury district of San Francisco, with a number of other young people, most of whom were into drugs.

A. " . . . and I was sitting in the living room and a man walked in and he had a guitar with him and all of a sudden he was surrounded by a group of girls." The man sat down and began to play, "and the song that caught my attention most was 'The Shadow of Your Smile,' and he sounded like an angel."

Q: "You are referring to Charles Manson?"

A: "Yes. And when he was through singing, I wanted to get some attention from him, and I asked him if I could play his guitar . . . and he handed me the guitar and I thought, 'I can't play this,' and then he looked at me and said, 'You can play that if you want to.'

"Now he had never heard me say 'I can't play this,' I only thought it. So when he told me I could play it, it blew my mind, because he was inside my head, and I knew at that time that he was something

Charles Manson was convicted of planning the seven murders carried out by his "family" and was originally given the death penalty. **ARCHIVE PHOTOS. REPRODUCED BY PERMISSION.**

that I had been looking for . . . and I went down and kissed his feet."

A day or two later Manson returned to the house and asked her to go for a walk. "And we walked a couple blocks to another house and he told me he wanted to make love with me.

"Well, I acknowledged the fact that I wanted to make love with him, and he told me to take off my clothes, so I uninhibitedly took off my clothes, and there happened to be a full-length mirror in the room, and he told me to go over and look at myself in the mirror.

"I didn't want to do it, so he took me by my hand and stood me in front of the mirror, and I turned away and he said, 'Go ahead and look at yourself. There is nothing wrong with you. You are perfect. You always have been perfect.'"

Q: "What happened next?"

A: "He asked me if I had ever made love with my father. I looked at him and kind of giggled and I said, 'No.' And he said, 'Have you ever thought about making love with your father?' I said, 'Yes.' And he told me, 'All right, when you are making love . . .

picture in your mind that I am your father.' And I did, I did so, and it was a very beautiful experience."

Susan said that before she met Manson she felt she was "lacking something." But then "I gave myself to him, and in return for that he gave me back to myself. He gave me the faith in myself to be able to know that I am a woman."

A week or so later, she, Manson, Mary Brunner, Ella Jo Bailey, Lynette Fromme, and Patricia Krenwinkel, together with three or four boys whose names she couldn't remember, left San Francisco in an old school bus from which they had removed most of the seats, furnishing it with brightly colored rugs and pillows. For the next year and a half they roamed—north to Mendocino, Oregon, Washington; south to Big Sur, Los Angeles, Mexico, Nevada, Arizona, New Mexico; and, eventually, back to L.A., living first in various residences in Topanga Canyon, Malibu, Venice, and then, finally, Spahn Ranch. En route others joined them, a few staying permanently, most only temporarily. According to Susan, they went through changes, and learned to love. The girls made love with each of the boys, and with each other. But Charlie was complete love. Although he did not have sex with her often— only six times in the more than two years they were together—"he would give himself completely."

Q: "Were you very much in love with him, Susan?"

A: "I was in love with the reflection and the reflection I speak of is Charlie Manson's."

Q: "Was there any limit to what you would do for him?" . . .

A: "No."

I was laying the foundation for the very heart of my case against Manson, that Susan and the others would do anything for him, up to and including murder at his command.

Q: "What was it about Charlie that caused you girls to be in love with him and to do what he wanted you to do?"

A: "Charlie is the only man I have ever met . . . on the face of this earth . . . that is a complete man. He will not take back-talk from a woman. He will not let a woman talk him into doing anything. He is a man."

Charlie had given her the name Sadie Mae Glutz because "in order for me to be completely free in my mind I had to be able to completely forget the past. The easiest way to do this, to change identity, is by doing so with a name."

According to Susan, Charlie himself went under a variety of names, calling himself the Devil, Satan, Soul.

Q: "Did Mr. Manson ever call himself Jesus?"

A: "He personally never called himself Jesus."

Q: "Did you ever call him Jesus?" From my questioning the night before, I anticipated that Susan would be evasive about this, and she was.

A: "He represented a Jesus Christ-like person to me."

Q: "Do you think Charlie is an evil person?"

A: "In your standards of evil, looking at him through your eyes, I would say yes. Looking at him through my eyes, he is as good as he is evil, he is as evil as he is good. You could not judge the man."

Although Susan didn't state that she believed Manson was Christ, the implication was there. Though I was at this time far from understanding it myself, it was important that I give the jury some explanation, however partial, for Manson's control over his followers. Incredible as all this was to the predominantly upper-middle-class, upper-middle-aged grand jurors, it was nothing compared to what they would hear when she described those two nights of murder.

I worked up to them gradually, having her describe Spahn Ranch and the life there, and asking her how they survived. People gave them things, Susan said. Also, they panhandled. And "the supermarkets all over Los Angeles throw away perfectly good food every day, fresh vegetables and sometimes cartons of eggs, packages of cheese that are stamped to a certain date, but the food is still good, and us girls used to go out and do 'garbage runs.'"

DeCarlo had told me of one such garbage run, when, to the astonishment of supermarket employees, the girls had driven up in Dennis Wilson's Rolls-Royce.

They also stole—credit cards, other things.

Q: "Did Charlie ask you to steal?"

A: "No, I took it upon myself. I was—we'd get programmed to do things."

Q: "Programmed by Charlie?"

A: "By Charlie, but it's hard for me to explain it so that you can see the way—the way I see. The words that would come from Charlie's mouth would not come from inside him, [they] would come from what I call the Infinite."

And sometimes, at night, they "creepy-crawled."

Q: "Explain to these members of the jury what you mean by that."

A: "Moving in silence so that nobody sees us or hears us . . . Wearing very dark clothing . . ."

Q: "Entering residences at night?"

A: "Yes."

They would pick a house at random, anywhere in Los Angeles, slip in while the occupants were asleep, creep and crawl around the rooms silently, maybe move things so when the people awakened they wouldn't be in the same places they had been when they went to bed. Everyone carried a knife. Susan said she did it "because everybody else in the Family was doing it" and she wanted that experience.

These creepy-crawling expeditions were, I felt sure the jury would surmise, dress rehearsals for murder.

Q: "Did you call your group by any name, Susan?"

A: "Among ourselves we called ourselves the Family." It was, Susan said, "a family like no other family."

I thought I heard a juror mutter, "Thank God!"

Q: "Susan, were you living at Spahn Ranch on the date of August the eighth, 1969?"

A: "Yes."

Q: "Susan, on that date did Charlie Manson instruct you and some other members of the Family to do anything?"

A: "I never recall getting any actual instructions from Charlie other than getting a change of clothing and a knife and was told to do exactly what Tex told me to do."

Q: "Did Charlie indicate to you the type of clothing you should take?"

A: "He told me . . . wear dark clothes."

Susan ID'd photos of Watson, Krenwinkel, and Kasabian, as well as a photo of the old Ford in which the four of them left the ranch. Charlie waved to them as they drove off. Susan didn't notice the time, but it was night. There was a pair of wire cutters in the back seat, also a rope. She, Katie, and Linda each had a knife; Tex had a gun and, she believed, a knife too. Not until they were en route did Tex tell them, to quote Susan, that they "were going to a house up on the hill that used to belong to Terry Melcher, and the only reason why we were going to that house was because Tex knew the outline of the house."

Q: "Did Tex tell you why you four were going to Terry Melcher's former residence?"

Matter-of-factly, with no emotion whatsoever, Susan replied, "To get all of their money and to kill whoever was there."

Q: "It didn't make any difference who was there, you were told to kill them; is that correct?"

A: "Yes."

They got lost on the way. However, Tex finally recognized the turnoff and they drove to the top of the hill. Tex got out, climbed the telephone pole, and, using the wire cutters, severed the wires. (LAPD still hadn't got back to me regarding the test cuts made by the pair found at Barker.) When Tex returned to the car, they drove back down the hill, parked at the bottom, then, bringing along their extra clothing, walked back up. They didn't enter the grounds through the gate "because we thought there might be an alarm system or electricity." To the right of the gate was a steep, brushy incline. The fence wasn't as high here. Susan threw over her clothing bundle, then went over herself, her knife in her teeth. The others followed.

They were stowing their clothing in the bushes when Susan saw the headlights of a car. It was coming up the driveway in the direction of the gate. "Tex told us girls to lie down and be still and not make a sound. He went out of sight . . . I heard him say 'Halt.'" Susan also heard another voice, male, say "Please don't hurt me, I won't say anything." "And I heard a gunshot and I heard another gunshot and another one and another one." Four shots, then Tex returned and told them to come on. When they got to the car, Tex reached inside and turned off the

lights; then they pushed the car away from the gate, back up the driveway.

I showed Susan a photo of the Rambler. "It looked similar to it, yes." I then showed her the police photograph of Steven Parent inside the vehicle.

A: "That is the thing I saw in the car."

There were audible gasps from the jurors.

Q: "When you say 'thing,' you are referring to a human being?"

A: "Yes, human being."

The jurors had looked at the heart of Susan Atkins and seen ice.

Further Resources

BOOKS

Cooper, David Edward. *The Manson Murders: A Philosophical Inquiry.* Cambridge, Mass.: Schenkman, 1974.

Endleman, Robert. *Jonestown and the Manson Family: Race, Sexuality, and Collective Madness.* New York: Psyche Press, 1993.

Faith, Karlene. *The Long Prison Journey of Leslie Van Houten: Life Beyond the Cult.* Boston: Northeastern University Press, 2001.

George, Edward, and Dary Matera. *Taming the Beast: Charles Manson's Life Behind Bars.* New York: St. Martin's Press, 1998.

Manson, Charles, and Nuel Emmons. *Manson in his Own Words.* New York: Grove Press, 1986.

Terry, Maury. *The Ultimate Evil: An Investigation Into a Dangerous Satanic Cult.* New York: Bantam Books, 1989.

WEBSITES

The Trial of Charles Manson. Available online at http://www.law.umkc.edu/faculty/projects/ftrials/manson/manson.html; website home page: http://www.law.umkc.edu (accessed January 23, 2003).

7

LIFESTYLES AND SOCIAL TRENDS

TIMOTHY G. BORDEN

Entries are arranged in chronological order by date of primary source. For entries with one primary source, the entry title is the same as the primary source title. Entries with more than one primary source have an overall entry title, followed by the titles of the primary sources.

Important Events in Lifestyles and Social Trends, 1960–1969

1960

- Enovid 10, the first oral contraceptive pill, is first sold at fifty-five cents a pill.

- The nation's population is nearing 180 million. The U.S. Census Bureau finds that Nevada, Florida, Alaska, Arizona, and California have the largest population growth of the United States.

- More than a third of women work outside the home, up from 25 percent in the 1940s.

- Some two thousand computers are at work in American businesses, performing tasks that were once human functions.

- Felt-tip pens, artificial tanning cream, and Astroturf are among the year's new products.

- On February 1, students from a nearby university stage a sit-in at a whites-only lunch counter in Greensboro, North Carolina. The passive, nonviolent tactic to integrate public facilities quickly spreads to cities across the South.

- On April 9, *Southern School News* reports that six years after the Supreme Court's desegregation ruling, only 6 percent of the South's schools are integrated.

- On April 17, young civil rights activists meet at Shaw University in Raleigh, North Carolina, to establish the Student Nonviolent Coordinating Committee (SNCC).

- On September 26, the first of four presidential debates between candidates Richard Nixon and John F. Kennedy is watched by a television audience of seventy-five million Americans. Just over one month later, Kennedy defeats Nixon by a slender margin, less than 120,000 votes.

1961

- Americans are marrying at a younger age than at any time this century. Fifty years ago men averaged 25.1 years old, and women 21.2 years, on their wedding day. Today the average male marries at 22.8 years of age. The average bride is 20.3 years old. A Gallup Poll of 16-to-21-year-old girls finds that almost all those interviewed expect to be married by age 22 and that most want four children.

- The "twist" is introduced on TV's *American Bandstand* by Chubby Checker, who sings the song for which the dance is named. Unlike many earlier dance sensations, it becomes popular among adults as well as teens.

- Yo-yos become a national craze after yo-yo experts demonstrate their skills on television.

- Timothy Leary and Richard Alpert, two psychology professors, are fired from Harvard University because of their experiments with hallucinogens.

- Ray Kroc buys out the McDonald brothers and opens two hundred McDonald's restaurants in southern California.

- On February 23, the use of birth control to limit the size of a couple's family is endorsed by the National Council of Churches.

- In May, Freedom Rides to desegregate interstate bus travel begin. They continue throughout the summer.

- On May 5, the federal minimum wage is raised $.25 to $1.25 an hour.

- From May 21 to May 22, a bus carrying Freedom Riders is attacked by an angry mob in Montgomery, Alabama. On May 24, the Freedom Riders arrive safely in Jackson, Mississippi, and are promptly jailed.

- On July 19, President Kennedy calls on public schools to improve the physical fitness of the nation's youth. He urges each school to develop a program of basic exercise and physical achievement.

1962

- Rachel Carson's *Silent Spring* is published, alerting the public to the dangers that pesticides being used in the environment are getting into the human food chain.

- On February 20, Astronaut John Glenn orbits the earth three times.

- On February 26, the U.S. Supreme Court rules that the practice of segregation in transportation facilities is unconstitutional.

- On June 25, a New York law permitting recitation of an official prayer in the state's public school is ruled unconstitutional by the Supreme Court.

- In July, the activist group Students for a Democratic Society (SDS) is organized in a meeting at Port Huron, Michigan. The group issues the *Port Huron Manifesto,* pledging itself to radical political action to achieve social change.

- On September 29, the longest-running musical in Broadway's history, *My Fair Lady,* closes after 2,717 performances.

- On October 1, President Kennedy sends three thousand federal troops to the University of Mississippi to enforce the admission of James Meredith, Ole Miss's first African American student.

1963

- Betty Friedan's *The Feminine Mystique* is published. In her book she argues that women are bored and unfulfilled as housewives, and that they must work outside the home to fully develop their identities.

- The general population trends of recent decades are illustrated when California passes New York to become the nation's most populous state.

- "Piano wrecking" becomes a popular campus pastime.

- Fourteen thousand people are arrested in seventy-five southern cities in civil rights demonstrations during the year.

- "Hootenannies"—concerts by folk singers which include audience participation—become popular.

- On January 4, Pope John XXIII is named *Time* magazine's "Man of the Year."

- On June 11, Governor George Wallace stands aside and permits the enrollment of two African American students, Vivian Malone and James Hood, at the University of Alabama. The governor's action ends a long struggle with Attorney General Robert Kennedy over this issue. But Wallace vows that he will continue to defy other federal orders to end segregation.

- On June 12, civil rights leader Medgar Evars is shot and killed by white racists in Jackson, Mississippi.

- On July 1, the U.S. Post Office launches the use of a five-digit code to help route the mail. It is called the Zone Improvement Plan Code, or ZIP Code.

- On August 28, more than two hundred thousand demonstrators gather on the Mall in front of the Lincoln Memorial in Washington, D.C., to pressure Congress for passage of a civil rights law. The rally is electrified by a speech delivered by the Reverend Dr. Martin Luther King, Jr., who tells the crowd "I have a dream."

- On September 10, President Kennedy federalizes the Alabama National Guard and again forces Governor Wallace to end his obstruction of integration. This time the issue is the desegregation of Huntsville's public schools.

- On September 15, a racially motivated church bombing in Birmingham, Alabama, leaves four young African American girls dead.

- On October 22, about 225,000 students stay home in a one-day boycott to protest segregation in Chicago's public schools. Chicago schools are not segregated by law, as are schools in the South, but instead because of settlement patterns in the city. Racially segregated neighborhoods produce neighborhood schools in which the pupils are largely of one race.

- On November 22, President Kennedy is assassinated in Dallas.

1964

- On January 11, the U.S. Surgeon General issues a warning that cigarette smoking is a leading cause of lung cancer, bronchitis, heart and other diseases. He says that "remedial action" is needed to combat this health hazard. In June the Federal Trade Commission announces that warning labels will be required on all cigarette packs starting in 1965.

- In February, the British singing group The Beatles arrive in the United States, launching Beatlemania and the "British Invasion" in popular music.

- On July 2, in a televised ceremony, President Lyndon Johnson signs the most sweeping civil rights act in American history into law.

- In July, race riots in New York over the police shooting of a 15-year-old African American boy, result in six deaths, hundreds of injuries, and more than a thousand arrests.

- On August 4, the United States begins bombing North Vietnam, citing as justification the attack on a U.S. destroyer in the Gulf of Tonkin.

- From September 30 to October 4, students at the University of California, Berkeley, stage a sit-in at the campus administration building and trap a police car trying to leave with an arrested demonstrator for more than thirty hours, thus beginning the free speech movement.

- On October 14, Dr. Martin Luther King, Jr., is awarded the Nobel Peace Prize and donates the prize money to the civil rights movement.

1965

- The nation's annual birth rate falls to nineteen births per one thousand people, the lowest since 1940.

- Latino labor leader and civil rights activist César Chavez goes on a twenty-five day fast to call attention to the plight of the nation's farmworkers. Many shoppers boycott grapes at the supermarket to support the strike he leads against grape growers.

- I Ching from Asia, Krishna Consciousness from India, and the Beatles and James Bond from Great Britain are all imported fads in America. Domestic fads include "go-go girls" in boots and miniskirts and dating services in which couples are matched by a computer.

- Wham-O introduces the Superball.

- On February 21, Malcolm X is assassinated while speaking in Harlem.

- On March 6, police attack thirty-two hundred civil rights demonstrators near Selma, Alabama, as they are marching on the state capital. Pictures of the brutal attack are broadcast on television news and rally national support for the civil rights movement. When the march is finally resumed and completed on March 25, the number of marchers has grown to more than twenty-five thousand.

- On August 6, President Johnson signs the Voting Rights Act. The law bans poll taxes, literacy tests, and other devices that some states have used for nearly a century to deny African Americans their constitutional right to vote.

- From August 11 to August 14, race riots in south central Los Angeles leave thirty-four dead, more than a thousand injured, and millions of dollars in property damage.

- On October 3, the United States ends the system on which immigration has been based since the 1920s. Although immigration from any nation is limited to 20,000 per year, a specific quota for each nation will no longer be enforced. In addition the total number of immigrants admitted is increased to 120,000 a year from the Western Hemisphere and 170,000 from the rest of the world.

- From October 15 to October 16, protests against the Vietnam War are held in forty cities around the nation.

- On December 8, Delta Airlines puts the first DC-9 passenger jet into service.

1966

- Possession, manufacture, and distribution of LSD is made illegal.

- The Black Panther Party for Self-Defense is organized in San Francisco by Huey P. Newton and Bobby Seale.

- The National Organization for Women (NOW) is established. It calls for "full equality between the sexes" and "true equality for all women in America."

- The first annual Conference on Black Power, organized by Adam Clayton Powell, is held.

- The television series *Batman* debuts, quickly becoming a national sensation.

- New to the nation this year are stereo cassette decks, tape cartridges, and credit cards that can be used to charge purchases from many different merchants. The U.S. Department of the Interior issues the first Rare and Endangered Species List.

- Americans' consumption of potato chips has jumped from 6.3 pounds per person per year in 1958 to 14.2 pounds to date.

- Nearly half the eleven million TVs sold this year are color sets.

- From March 25 to March 27, International Days of Protest Against the War in Vietnam are held; seven American cities participate.

- On May 15, a rally in Washington, D.C. against the Vietnam War draws sixty-three thousand protestors. Ten thousand picket the White House.

- In July, Martin Luther King, Jr. leads the civil rights campaign north to Chicago. Whites riot in opposition to King's presence and in reaction to his call for ending racial discrimination in the North. He returns in September to much the same reception.

- In September, days of rioting and racial violence rock Atlanta. The events dramatize the split that has developed in the civil rights movement between radical young militants and more moderate, nonviolent older leaders.

- On November 3, national standards for the labeling of the contents of packaged products are ordered to be established.

1967

- British supermodel Twiggy arrives in New York, and thinness is confirmed as the new fashion standard.

- Muhammad Ali is stripped of his heavyweight championship title for refusing to report for the military draft. He is arrested, given a five-year prison sentence, and fined one hundred thousand dollars. His conviction is later overturned.

- The Gathering of Tribes for the Human Be-In is held at Golden Gate Park in San Francisco, inaugurating the Summer of Love.

- Long-playing, or LP record albums begin outselling single 45 rpm records.

- On April 2, a report reveals that 16 percent of African American students in eleven southern states are attending integrated schools.

- On April 15, protests against the Vietnam War draw 50,000 demonstrators in San Francisco and as many as 400,000 in New York. On May 13, a counter demonstration in New York in support of the war attracts 70,000 demonstrators.

- On June 19, a federal judge orders the end of segregation in the public schools of Washington, D.C.

- In July, five-day race riots in Newark, New Jersey, and Detroit leave nearly seventy-five people dead, more than a thousand injured, and hundreds of millions of dollars in property damage. Rioting also occurs in Boston, Philadelphia, Cincinnati, New York and more than sixty other cities during the month. Experts blame the poor housing and unemployment that plague the nation's inner cities.

- On October 21, antiwar demonstrators march on the Pentagon in Washington; protestors include child-care expert Dr. Benjamin Spock, linguist Noam Chomsky, and poet Robert Lowell.

1968

- Feminists stage a rowdy protest against the Miss America pageant in Atlantic City, New Jersey.

- Four permanent three-day weekends are created by shifting the Washington's Birthday, Memorial Day, Columbus Day, and Veterans Day holidays to Mondays.

- The government sharply cuts back on its practice of deferring young men from service in the armed forces because of their occupation or college enrollment.

- In February, polls indicate that only 35 percent of Americans support President Johnson's policies.

- On April 4, Martin Luther King Jr., is assassinated, sparking a week of rioting in more than one hundred cities around the country.

- In April, five thousand students led by SDS president Mark Rudd take over Columbia University and demand a greater voice in its governance. The students seize five campus buildings and hold them for a week before the occupation is ended by about one thousand police.

- On June 5, Attorney General Robert Kennedy is assassinated.

- On November 6, students at San Francisco State University go on strike and call for reforms. Four months of student unrest follow.

- On November 14, Yale University admits women.

1969

- The first automatic teller machine (ATM) is installed by the Chemical Bank in New York.

- A huge oil slick contaminates the coast of Santa Barbara, California.

- On January 21, a government study reports that hunger, malnutrition, and unhealthy living conditions are widespread in the United States.

- On April 9, four hundred students at Harvard University seize buildings on campus as part of a campus-wide strike; police break up the demonstration after seventeen hours.

Nearly 450 other colleges and universities also experience strikes or are forced to close during the year. Students' demands range from easing admissions policies to major changes in academic programs.

• On July 20, *Apollo 11* astronaut Neil Armstrong becomes the first man to walk on the moon. Armstrong and Buzz Aldrin are on the moon for twenty-one hours.

• From August 15 to August 17, the Woodstock Music and Art Fair—"An Aquarian Exposition, Three Days of Peace and Music"—is held in Bethel, New York, with some four hundred thousand in attendance.

• On November 15, the largest anti-war demonstration in the capital's history takes place when 250,000 protestors march from the Capitol Building to the Washington Monument. Nearly 200,000 rally in San Francisco on the same day.

• On December 6, Hell's Angels acting as security guards stab a concertgoer to death while the Rolling Stones are playing onstage at the Altamont Music Festival in San Francisco.

The Politics of Race, Civil Rights, and Segregation

"The 1963 Inaugural Address of Governor George C. Wallace"

Speech

By: George C. Wallace

Date: January 14, 1963

Source: Wallace, George. "The 1963 Inaugural Address of Governor George C. Wallace." Alabama Department of Archives and History. Available online at http://www.archives .state.al.us/govs_list/inauguralspeech.html; website home page: http://www.archives.state.al.us (accessed June 2, 2003).

About the Author: George Corley Wallace (1919–1998) was born in Clio, Alabama. He became a staunch segregationist and won the election for Alabama governer in 1962. During his first term a series of divisive racial confrontations took place. Reelected as governor for a fourth and final time in 1982, Wallace eventually disavowed his segregationist views and attracted a majority of African American votes in his final run for office. The politician also staged two unsuccessful, yet highly symbolic, runs for the presidency in 1968 and 1972, when he was shot and paralyzed.

Soul on Ice

Nonfiction work

By: Eldridge Cleaver

Date: 1968

Source: Cleaver, Eldridge. *Soul on Ice.* New York: Dell, 1968, 80–81, 83–84.

About the Author: Eldridge Cleaver (1935–1998) was arrested numerous times for theft while growing up in California. Convicted of a series of rapes, Cleaver served time in Folson Prison from 1957 to 1966. Upon his release he published *Soul on Ice,* written while he completed his sentence. As the minister for information for the Black Panthers, based in Oakland, California, Eldridge emerged as one of the Black Power movement's leading spokespersons. ∎

Introduction

In 1958 George Wallace entered the Alabama Governor's race as a respected circuit court judge and past state legislative representative who had a relatively liberal record on race relations. Avoiding the strident segregationalist tactics of his opponent, who welcomed an endorsement by the Ku Klux Klan in a successful bid to get white votes, Wallace was soundly defeated in the Democratic primary. As he told aides in private, "I was out-niggered [in the election], and I won't be out-niggered again," a vow he put into practice in his next gubernatorial run.

Elected in November 1962 on a platform of racial segregation in defiance of federal pressure to integrate public facilities, Governor George Wallace became the South's leading advocate of states' rights to preserve racial segregation in the 1960s. At his inauguration to the Alabama governor's office in 1963, he urged the (white) people of Alabama "to rise to the call of freedom-loving blood that is in us and send our answer to the tyranny that clanks its chains upon the South," a clear reference to his defiance of federal court orders to end racial segregation.

In the chapter "The White Race and Its Heroes," Eldridge Cleaver traces the historical roots of racism that gave rise to political leaders such as George Wallace. Unyielding in his condemnation of such segregationalist tactics, Cleaver issues a passionate appeal for all people, regardless of race, to overcome the entrenched racism that he views as pervasive in American society. Cleaver also puts his analysis of racism in an international context, comparing the history of America with the Holocaust in Nazi Germany and the dropping of the atomic bombs on Japan during World War II. Although Wallace and Cleaver both rely on historical references in describing their vision of the American nation, then, their interpretations of the nation's past yield profoundly different calls to action.

Significance

In June 1963, just months after he took office, Governor Wallace became the leading symbol of segregation when he stood on the steps of a University of Alabama building to prevent two African American students from registering for classes. In response, President John F. Kennedy placed the Alabama National Guard under federal supervision so that the students could enter the university. Although Wallace's attempt to enforce segregation had failed, his action transformed him into a national leader of opposition to the Civil Rights movement. Wallace took his power as a symbol of conservative values to the national arena in 1968, when he made an unsuccessful run for the presidency that helped to put Richard M. Nixon into the White House by splitting the Democratic vote.

As Wallace rose to national political prominence in the 1960s, Eldridge Cleaver also came to the forefront of America's racial politics. After his release from prison in 1966, Cleaver joined the Black Panther Party for

Alabama governor George C. Wallace in 1965. Wallace was an opponent of the civil rights movement of the 1960s and fought to maintain segregation in his state. AP/WIDE WORLD PHOTOS. REPRODUCED BY PERMISSION.

Self-Defense in Oakland, California as the group's minister of information. Under the leadership of Cleaver, Huey P. Newton, and Bobby Seale, the Black Panthers demanded health care, housing, employment, and education reforms. Although it was perceived by some as a racial separatist group, the Black Panthers insisted that the group's work could only be achieved through a cross-racial coalition. A target of numerous federal and local police investigations designed to discredit its leadership and weaken its influence, the group also called for investigations into police brutality. Cleaver, who went into exile after a run-in with the police in 1968, was expelled from the Black Panthers in February 1971 over ideological differences, and the group's popularity declined through the 1970s. Once the leading Black Power organization—even though its membership never reached more than 5,000 people—the Black Panthers disbanded in 1982.

Primary Source

"The 1963 Inaugural Address of Governor George C. Wallace" [excerpt]

> SYNOPSIS: In his gubernatorial inauguration speech, George Wallace invokes the region's history in a call

to his fellow white Southerners to resist federal efforts to integrate public institutions. His pledge to enforce "segregation forever" as a matter of states' rights became one of the infamous rallying cries of those opposed to the Civil Rights movement in the 1960s.

This is the day of my Inauguration as Governor of the State of Alabama. And on this day I feel a deep obligation to renew my pledges, my covenants with you . . . the people of this great state.

General Robert E. Lee said that "duty" is the sublimest word on the English language and I have come, increasingly, to realize what he meant. I SHALL do my duty to you, God helping . . . to every man, to every woman . . . yes, to every child in this state. I shall fulfill my duty toward honesty and economy in our State government so that no man shall have a part of his livelihood cheated and no child shall have a bit of his future stolen away.

I have said to you that I would eliminate the liquor agents in this state and that the money saved would be returned to our citizens . . . I am happy to report to you that I am now filling orders for several hundred one-way tickets and stamped on them are these words . . ."for liquor agents . . . destination: . . . out of Alabama." I am happy to report to you that the big-wheeling cocktail-party boys have gotten the word that their free whiskey and boat rides are over . . . that the farmer in the field, the worker in the factory, the businessman in his office, the housewife in her home, have decided that the money can be better spent to help our children's education and our older citizens . . . and they have put a man in office to see that it is done. It shall be done. Let me say one more time. . . . no more liquor drinking in your governor's mansion.

I shall fulfill my duty in working hard to bring industry into our state, not only by maintaining an honest, sober and free-enterprise climate of government in which industry can have confidence . . . but in going out and getting it . . . so that our people can have industrial jobs in Alabama and provide a better life for their children.

I shall not forget my duty to our senior citizens . . . so that their lives can be lived in dignity and enrichment of the golden years, nor to our sick, both mental and physical . . . and they will know we have not forsaken them. I want the farmer to feel confident that in this State government he has a partner who will work with him in raising his income and increasing his markets. And I want the laboring man to know he has a friend who is sincerely striving to better his field of endeavor.

I want to assure every child that this State government is not afraid to invest in their future through education, so that they will not be handicapped on every threshold of their lives.

Today I have stood, where once Jefferson Davis stood, and took an oath to my people. It is very appropriate then that from this Cradle of the Confederacy, this very Heart of the Great Anglo-Saxon Southland, that today we sound the drum for freedom as have our generations of forebears before us done, time and time again through history. Let us rise to the call of freedom-loving blood that is in us and send our answer to the tyranny that clanks its chains upon the South. In the name of the greatest people that have ever trod this earth, I draw the line in the dust and toss the gauntlet before the feet of tyranny . . . and I say . . . segregation today . . . segregation tomorrow . . . segregation forever.

The Washington, D.C. school riot report is disgusting and revealing. We will not sacrifice our children to any such type school system—and you can write that down. The federal troops in Mississippi could be better used guarding the safety of the citizens of Washington, D.C., where it is even unsafe to walk or go to a ballgame—and that is the nation's capitol. I was safer in a B-29 bomber over Japan during the war in an air raid, than the people of Washington are walking to the White House neighborhood. A closer example is Atlanta. The city officials fawn for political reasons over school integration and THEN build barricades to stop residential integration—what hypocrisy!

Let us send this message back to Washington by our representatives who are with us today . . . that from this day we are standing up, and the heel of tyranny does not fit the neck of an upright man . . . that we intend to take the offensive and carry our fight for freedom across the nation, wielding the balance of power we know we possess in the Southland. . . . that WE, not the insipid bloc of voters of some sections . . . will determine in the next election who shall sit in the White House of these United States . . . That from this day, from this hour . . . from this minute . . . we give the word of a race of honor that we will tolerate their boot in our face no longer. . . . and let those certain judges put *that* in their opium pipes of power and smoke it for what it is worth.

Hear me, Southerners! You sons and daughters who have moved north and west throughout this na-

tion. . . . we call on you from your native soil to join with us in national support and vote . . . and we know . . . wherever you are . . . away from the hearths of the Southland . . . that you will respond, for though you may live in the fartherest reaches of this vast country . . . your heart has never left Dixieland.

And you native sons and daughters of old New England's rock-ribbed patriotism . . . and you sturdy natives of the great Mid-West . . . and you descendants of the far West flaming spirit of pioneer freedom . . . we invite you to come and be with us . . . for you are of the Southern spirit . . . and the Southern philosophy . . . you are Southerners too and brothers with us in our fight.

Primary Source

Soul on Ice [excerpt]

SYNOPSIS: Analyzing America's history of race relations in an international context, Cleaver examines the economic and social forces that maintained racism as a force in modern American life. Unlike Wallace, who sees a proud history of individual freedom in the history of the country, Cleaver argues that America's political and economic leaders have long used racism to prevent the ideals of equality and opportunity from being realized by many Americans.

The separate-but-equal doctrine was promulgated by the Supreme Court in 1896. It had the same purpose domestically as the Open Door Policy toward China in the international arena: to stabilize a situation and subordinate a non-white population so that racist exploiter could manipulate those people according to their own selfish interests. These doctrines were foisted off as *the epitome of enlightened justice, the highest expression of morality.* Sanctified by religion, justified by philosophy and legalized by the Supreme Court, separate-but-equal was enforced by day by agencies of the law, and by the KKK & Co. under cover of night. Booker T. Washington, the Martin Luther King of his day, accepted separate-but-equal in the name of all Negroes. W. E. B. DuBois denounced it.

Separate-but-equal marked the last stage of the white man's flight into cultural neurosis, and the beginning of the black man's frantic striving to assert his humanity and equalize his position with the white. Blacks ventured into all fields of endeavor to which they could gain entrance. Their goal was to present in all fields a performance that would equal or surpass that of the whites. It was long axiomatic

Stokely Carmichael, head of the Student Nonviolent Coordinating Committee, speaks to a crowd of hundreds at Florida A&M University in 1967. Carmichael turned the phrase "black power" into a rallying cry for the civil rights movement. **AP/WIDE WORLD PHOTOS. REPRODUCED BY PERMISSION.**

among blacks that a black had to be twice as competent as a white in any field in order to win grudging recognition from the whites. This produced a pathological motivation in the blacks to equal or surpass the whites, and a pathological motivation in the whites to maintain a distance from the blacks. This is the rack on which black and white Americans receive their delicious torture! At first there was the color bar, flatly denying the blacks entrance to certain spheres of activity. When this no longer worked, and blacks invaded sector after sector of American life and economy, the whites evolved other methods of keeping their distance. The illusion of the Negro's inferior nature had to be maintained. . . .

A young white today cannot help but recoil from the base deeds of his people. On every side, on every continent, he sees racial arrogance, savage brutality toward the conquered and subjugated people, genocide; he sees the human cargo of the slave trade; he sees the systematic extermination of American Indians; he sees the civilized nations of Europe fighting in imperial depravity over the lands of other people—and over possession of the very people themselves. There seems to be no end to the ghastly

deeds of which his people are guilty. *GUILTY.* The slaughter of the Jews by the Germans, the dropping of atomic bombs on the Japanese people—these deeds weigh heavily upon the prostrate souls and tumultuous consciences of the white youth. The white heroes, their hands dripping with blood, are dead.

The young whites know that the colored people of the world, Afro-Americans included, do not seek revenge for their suffering. They seek the same things the white rebel wants: an end to war and exploitation. Black and white, the young rebels are free people, free in a way that Americans have never been before in the history of their country. And they are outraged.

There is in America today a generation of white youth that is truly worthy of a black man's respect, and this is a rare event in the foul annals of American history. From the beginning of the contact between blacks and whites, there has been very little reason for a black man to respect a white, with such exceptions as John Brown and others lesser known. But respect commands itself and it can neither be given nor withheld when it is due. If a man like Malcolm X could change and repudiate racism, if I myself and other former Muslims can change, if young whites can change, then there is hope for America. It was certainly strange to find myself, while steeped in the doctrine that all whites were devils by nature, commanded by the heart to applaud and acknowledge respect for these young whites—despite the fact that they are descendants of the masters and I the descendant of slave. The sins of the fathers are visited upon the heads of the children—but only if the children continue in the evil deeds of the fathers.

Further Resources

BOOKS

Brown, Elaine. *A Taste of Power: A Black Woman's Story.* New York: Pantheon Books, 1992.

Carter, Dan T. *The Politics of Rage: George Wallace, the Origins of the New Conservatism, and the Transformation of American Politics.* Baton Rouge: Louisiana State University Press, 2000.

Farber, David. *The Age of Great Dreams: America in the 1960s.* New York: Hill and Wang, 1994.

Foner, Philip S., ed. *The Black Panthers Speak.* Philadelphia: J.B. Lippincott, 1970.

Lesher, Stephan. *George Wallace: American Populist.* New York: Addison-Wesley, 1994.

Lockwood, Lee. *Conversations with Eldridge Cleaver: Algiers.* New York: McGraw-Hill, 1970.

Rout, Kathleen. *Eldridge Cleaver.* Boston: Twayne, 1991.

Seale, Bobby. *Seize the Time: The Story of the Black Panther Party and Huey P. Newton.* New York: Random House, 1970.

Van Deburg, William L. *Black Camelot: African–American Culture Heroes in Their Times, 1960-1980.* Chicago: University of Chicago Press, 1997.

———. *New Day in Babylon: The Black Power Movement and American Culture, 1965-1975.* Chicago: University of Chicago Press, 1992.

X, Malcolm. *The Autobiography of Malcolm X.* New York: Grove, 1966.

PERIODICALS

"A Fiery Soul Set Free." *Newsweek,* May 11, 1998, 72.

Johnson, Charles Richard. "A Soul's Jagged Arc." *The New York Times,* January 3, 1999, 16.

Riley, Michael. "Confessions of a Former Segregationalist." *Time,* March 2, 1972, 10.

WEBSITES

"George Wallace: Settin' the Woods on Fire." Available online at http://www.pbs.org/wgbh/amex/wallace/; website home page: http://www.pbs.org (accessed October 1, 2002).

"The 1963 Inaugural Address of Governor George C. Wallace." Available online at http://www.archives.state.al.us/govs_list /inauguralspeech.html; website home page: http://www .archives.state.al.us (accessed June 2, 2003).

"For President Kennedy: An Epilogue"

Magazine article

By: Theodore H. White

Date: December 6, 1963

Source: White, Theodore H. "For President Kennedy: An Epilogue." *Life,* December 6, 1963, 158–159.

About the Author: Theodore H. White (1915–1986) graduated from Harvard University in 1938 and worked for *Time* magazine as a foreign correspondent during World War II. He later wrote for *The New Republic* and *Collier's* before publishing a series of books on the American politcal scene, including *The Making of the President: 1960,* which won the Pulitzer Prize for general nonfiction in 1962. White remained one of America's leading political commentators until his death. ∎

Introduction

Theodore White became acquainted with the Kennedys while following the campaign that he covered in *The Making of the President: 1960.* White was working on a profile of John F. Kennedy when, on November 22, 1963, President Kennedy was assassinated in Dallas, Texas. Kennedy's widow, Jacqueline, asked White to meet with her just one week later for a private interview. Reflecting on her husband's work, she referred to the Broadway show *Camelot,* the Alan Jay Lerner-Frederick Loewe musical that depicted Sir Arthur's Knights of the Round Table in glowingly romantic terms. As White later recounted in his personal papers (quoted in Sarah Bradford's *America's Queen: The Life of Jacqueline Kennedy Onassis*), "I realized it was a misreading of history, but I was taken with Jackie's ability to frame the tragedy in such human and romantic terms. . . . All she wanted was for me to hang this *Life* epilogue on the Camelot conceit. It didn't seem like a hell of a lot to ask. So I said to myself, 'Why not? If that's all she wants, let her have it. So the epitaph of the Kennedy administration became Camelot—a magic moment in American history where gallant men danced with beautiful women, when great deeds were done and when the White House became the center of the universe."

Significance

Jacqueline Kennedy's compelling, if nostalgic, vision defined the public's memories of the Kennedy presidency for a generation. Books on the Kennedy family ranked at the top of the best-seller lists throughout the decade, and public opinion polls continued to list the late president as one the most admired leaders in American history. The assassination of the president's younger brother, Senator Robert F. Kennedy, in 1968 during his

President John F. Kennedy attends a ceremony at Arlington National Cemetery, with his son, John F. Kennedy Jr., November 18, 1963.
© BETTMANN/CORBIS. REPRODUCED BY PERMISSION.

own presidential election campaign renewed the public's sympathy and admiration for the family. It was not until decades later that reports of President Kennedy's numerous sexual indiscretions and poor health were widely circulated. Kennedy's decision to increase American involvement in Vietnam and his lack of commitment to guaranteeing the civil rights of African Americans in the South also came under renewed scrutiny by scholars, who now describe his presidency in far less glowing terms than in the past.

Although Jacqueline Kennedy's 1968 marriage to Greek multimillionaire Aristotle Onassis and subsequent years as a fixture of the international jet set somewhat diminished the public's admiration for her, she remained one of the most fascinating figures of her generation. Her death in 1994 was met by an outpouring of public grief; as the media once again made references to Camelot, Jacqueline Kennedy Onassis was laid to rest in Arlington National Cemetery next to President Kennedy.

Primary Source

"For President Kennedy: An Epilogue"

SYNOPSIS: On November 29, 1963—just one week after her husband was assassinated in Dallas—Jacqueline Kennedy conducted the last personal interview that she would give as a public figure. "The chief memory I have of her is of her composure," White later wrote in his personal notes, "of her

beauty (dressed in trim slacks, beige pullover sweater), her eyes wider than pools; and of her calm voice and total recall." The resulting article appeared in the December 6, 1963 edition of *Life* magazine.

Hyannis Port

She remembers how hot the sun was in Dallas, and the crowds—greater and wilder than the crowds in Mexico or in Vienna. The sun was blinding, streaming down; yet she could not put on sunglasses for she had to wave to the crowd.

And up ahead she remembers seeing a tunnel around a turn and thinking that there would be a moment of coolness under the tunnel. There was the sound of the motorcycles, as always in a parade, and the occasional backfire of a motorcycle. The sound of the shot came, at that moment, like the sound of a backfire and she remembers Connally saying, "No, no, no, no, no. . . ."

She remembers the roses. Three times that day in Texas they had been greeted with the bouquets of yellow roses of Texas. Only, in Dallas they had given her *red* roses. She remembers thinking, how funny—red roses for me; and then the car was full of blood and red roses.

Much later, accompanying the body from the Dallas hospital to the airport, she was alone with Clint Hill—the first Secret Service man to come to their rescue—and with Dr. Burkley, the White House physician. Burkley gave her two roses that had slipped under the President's shirt when he fell, his head in her lap.

All through the night they tried to separate him from her, to sedate her, and take care of her—and she would not let them. She wanted to be with him. She remembered that Jack had said of his father, when his father suffered the stroke, that he could not live like that. Don't let that happen to me, he had said, when I have to go.

Now, in her hand she was holding a gold St. Christopher's medal.

She had given him a St. Christopher's medal when they were married; but when Patrick died this summer, they had wanted to put something in the coffin with Patrick that was from them both; and so he had put in the St. Christopher's medal.

Then he had asked her to give him a new one to mark their 10th wedding anniversary, a month after Patrick's death.

Mourners line the streets of Washington, D.C., in 1963 as the body of assassinated president John F. Kennedy passes. © **WALLY MCNAMEE/CORBIS. REPRODUCED BY PERMISSION.**

He was carrying it when he died and she had found it. But it belonged to him—so she could not put *that* in the coffin with him. She wanted to give him something that was hers, something that she loved. So she had slipped off her wedding ring and put it on his finger. When she came out of the room in the hospital in Dallas, she asked: "Do you think it was right? Now I have nothing left." And Kenny O'Donnell said, "You leave it where it is."

That was at 1:30 p.m. in Texas.

But then, at Bethesda Hospital in Maryland, at 3 a.m. the next morning, Kenny slipped into the chamber where the body lay and brought her back the ring, which, as she talked now, she twisted.

On her little finger was the other ring: a slim, gold circlet with green emerald chips—the one he had given her in memory of Patrick.

There was a thought, too, that was always with her. "When Jack quoted something, it was usually classical," she said, "but I'm so ashamed of myself—all I keep thinking of is this line from a musical comedy.

"At night, before we'd go to sleep, Jack liked to play some records; and the song he loved most came at the very end of this record. The lines he loved to hear were: *Don't let it be forgot, that once there was a spot, for one brief shining moment that was known as Camelot."*

She wanted to make sure that the point came clear and went on: "There'll be great Presidents again—and the Johnsons are wonderful, they've been wonderful to me—but there'll never be another Camelot again.

"Once, the more I read of history the more bitter I got. For a while I thought history was something that bitter old men wrote. But then I realized history made Jack what he was. You must think of him as this little boy, sick so much of the time, reading in bed, reading history, reading the Knights of the Round Table, reading Marlborough. For Jack, history was full of heroes. And if it made him this way—if it made him see the heroes—maybe other little boys will see. Men are such a combination of good and bad. Jack had this hero idea of history, the idealistic view."

But she came back to the idea that transfixed her: *"Don't let it be forgot, that once there was a spot, for one brief shining moment that was known as Camelot—and it will never be that way again."*

■ ■ ■

As for herself? She was horrified by the stories that she might live abroad. "I'm *never* going to live in Europe. I'm not going to 'travel extensively abroad.' That's a desecration. I'm going to live in the places I lived with Jack. In Georgetown, and with the Kennedys at the Cape. They're my family. I'm going to bring up my children. I want John to grow up to be a good boy."

As for the President's memorial, at first she remembered that, in every speech in their last days in Texas, he had spoken of how in December this nation would loft the largest rocket booster yet into the sky, making us first in space. So she had wanted something of his there when it went up—perhaps only his initials painted on a tiny corner of the great Saturn, where no one need even notice it. But now Americans will seek the moon from Cape Kennedy. The new name, born of her frail hope, came as a surprise.

The only thing she knew she must have for him was the eternal flame over his grave at Arlington.

"Whenever you drive across the bridge from Washington into Virginia," she said, "you see the Lee Mansion on the side of the hill in the distance. When Caroline was very little, the mansion was one of the first things she learned to recognize. Now, at night you can see his flame beneath the mansion for miles away."

She said it is time people paid attention to the new President and the new First Lady. But she does not want them to forget John F. Kennedy or read of him only in dusty or bitter histories:

For one brief shining moment there was Camelot.

Further Resources

BOOKS

Anthony, Carl Sferrazza. *As We Remember Her: Jacqueline Kennedy Onassis in the Words of Her Family and Friends.* New York: HarperCollins, 1997.

Baldrige, Letitia. *A Lady, First: My Life in the Kennedy White House and the American Embassies of Paris and Rome.* New York: Viking, 2001.

Bradford, Sarah. *America's Queen: The Life of Jacqueline Kennedy Onassis.* New York: Viking, 2000.

Davis, John H. *Jacqueline Bouvier: An Intimate Memoir.* New York: John Wiley and Sons, 1996.

Klein, Edward. *All Too Human: The Love Story of Jack and Jackie Kennedy.* New York: Pocket Books, 1996.

Leaming, Barbara. *Mrs. Kennedy: The Missing History of the Kennedy Years.* New York: Free Press, 2001.

Schlesinger, Arthur M., Jr. *A Thousand Days: John F. Kennedy in the White House.* New York: Houghton Mifflin, 1965.

Strober, Gerald S., and Deborah H. Strober, eds. *Let Us Begin Anew: An Oral History of the Kennedy Presidency.* New York: Viking, 1993.

White, Theodore H. *The Making of the President: 1960.* Reprint. New York: Signet, 1967.

WEBSITES

"Jacqueline Lee Bouvier Kennedy." Available online at http://www.whitehouse.gov/history/firstladies/jk35.html; website home page: http://www.whitehouse.gov (accessed June 2, 2003).

The Feminine Mystique
Nonfiction work

By: Betty Friedan

Date: 1963

Source: Friedan, Betty. *The Feminine Mystique.* New York: W.W. Norton, 1963, 15–19.

About the Author: Betty Friedan (1921–), born in Peoria, Illinois, was a founding member of the National Organization of Women in 1966, the National Abortion Rights League in 1968, and the National Women's Political Caucus in 1971. The author of *"It Changed My Life": Writings on the Women's Movement* (1976), *The Second Stage* (1981), *The Fountain of Age* (1993), *Beyond Gender: The New Politics of Work and Family* (1997), and *Life So Far* (2000), Friedan remains an advocate of women's and family issues. ■

Introduction

Although job opportunities for women had expanded during World War II, many women were displaced at war's end in favor of the returning veterans. Other women willingly left the job market to become full-time home-makers and mothers, an option made possible for many families by the prosperous economy of the 1950s. Yet many wives and mothers found themselves frustrated by social attitudes that increasingly emphasized the domesticity of women during the decade at the exclusion of any other role. Images of women as capable, career-oriented professionals declined in the popular media, only to be replaced by the familiar characters of June Cleaver and Donna Reed in television situation comedies. Some social scientists even argued that advanced educational and professional training made women more frustrated once they inevitably ended up as housewives and mothers.

Like the women whose lives she researched for *The Feminine Mystique*, Friedan also felt "a strange stirring, a sense of dissatisfaction" with her suburban life as a full-time wife and mother in the 1950s. Although she enjoyed those roles, her experience of being fired from a job after requesting maternity leave left her feeling angry and isolated. After her articles on the conflicts that women felt in balancing their careers and family lives were rejected by the editors of various women's magazines, Friedan conducted an in-depth survey of her Smith College classmates to explore the topic in an extended forum. She was also eager to rebut arguments predicting that well-educated women were more prone to psychological and emotional problems because their education had given them unrealistic and unfulfilled expectations of having a life outside the home.

Significance

"I had no idea that my book would start a revolution," Friedan wrote in her 2000 memoir *Life So Far.* "Until that revolution actually came—the women's movement—new possibilities for women's lives weren't visible. But I did understand that what I had figured out—that the feminine mystique was no longer a valid guide to women's lives, that it was *obsolete*—implied monumental social change, and that my text would be very threatening to those who couldn't deal with that change, men and women." Indeed, Friedan's work, published in 1963 as *The Feminine Mystique,* not only broke down the silence of "the problem that has no name," but helped to ease the burden of domesticity that many women experienced in the 1950s and 1960s. It also served as one of the keynote documents empowering the modern women's movement, one of the vital social currents of the 1960s and beyond.

Although Friedan became the target of some conservative commentators, who argued that her views were anti-family and therefore anti-American, *The Feminine Mystique* was an instant success upon its publication in 1963. Its popularity made Friedan into a media celebrity even as she critiqued the media for perpetuating the suburban homemaker ideal. Not content to remain a social critic, Friedan plunged into the political arena as a founding member of the National Organization for Women (NOW) in 1966. As an articulate and warm personality, Friedan was a vital force in popularizing the main tenets of the modern women's movement, which included fighting against gender discrimination, legalizing abortion, and overturning traditional social attitudes that limited women's participation in public life. Spurred on by the critique offered in *The Feminine Mystique,* each of these topics was reevaluated in the 1960s.

Primary Source

The Feminine Mystique [excerpt]

SYNOPSIS: The opening chapter of *The Feminine Mystique,* "The Problem That Has No Name" describes the quiet desperation that gripped many

well-educated women who married and moved to the suburbs to raise their families in the post-World War II era. In contrast to the portrayal of blissful domesticity that appeared on television shows such as *Leave It to Beaver* and *The Donna Reed Show* and in magazine articles, advertisements, and movies, Friedan showed that marriage and motherhood did not necessarily lead to personal fulfillment.

The problem lay buried, unspoken, for many years in the minds of American women. It was a strange stirring, a sense of dissatisfaction, a yearning that women suffered in the middle of the twentieth century in the United States. Each suburban wife struggled with it alone. As she made the beds, shopped for groceries, matched slipcover material, ate peanut butter sandwiches with her children, chauffeured Cub Scouts and Brownies, lay beside her husband at night—she was afraid to ask even of herself the silent question—"Is this all?"

For over fifteen years there was no word of this yearning in the millions of words written about women, for women, in all the columns, books and articles by experts telling women their role was to seek fulfillment as wives and mothers. Over and over women heard in voices of tradition and of Freudian sophistication that they could desire no greater destiny than to glory in their own femininity. Experts told them how to catch a man and keep him, how to breastfeed children and handle their toilet training, how to cope with sibling rivalry and adolescent rebellion; how to buy a dishwasher, bake bread, cook gourmet snails, and build a swimming pool with their own hands; how to dress, look, and act more feminine and make marriage more exciting; how to keep their husbands from dying young and their sons from growing into delinquents. They were taught to pity the neurotic, unfeminine, unhappy women who wanted to be poets or physicists or presidents. They learned that truly feminine women do not want careers, higher education, political rights—the independence and the opportunities that the old-fashioned feminists fought for. Some women, in their forties and fifties, still remembered painfully giving up those dreams, but most of the younger women no longer even thought about them. A thousand expert voices applauded their femininity, their adjustment, their new maturity. All they had to do was devote their lives from earliest girlhood to finding a husband and bearing children.

By the end of the nineteen-fifties, the average marriage age of women in America dropped to 20, and was still dropping, into the teens. Fourteen million girls were engaged by 17. The proportion of

Betty Friedan, author of *The Feminine Mystique,* talks to a group in New York about discrimination based on sex in 1966. One of the leaders of the modern women's movement, Friedan challenged traditional ideas about the place of women in American society. **AP/WIDE WORLD PHOTOS. REPRODUCED BY PERMISSION.**

women attending college in comparison with men dropped from 47 per cent in 1920 to 35 per cent in 1958. A century earlier, women had fought for higher education; now girls went to college to get a husband. By the mid-fifties, 60 per cent dropped out of college to marry, or because they were afraid too much education would be a marriage bar. Colleges built dormitories for "married students," but the students were almost always the husbands. A new degree was instituted for the wives—"Ph.T." (Putting Husband Through).

Then American girls began getting married in high school. And the women's magazines, deploring the unhappy statistics about these young marriages, urged that courses on marriage, and marriage counselors, be installed in the high schools. Girls started going steady at twelve and thirteen, in junior high. Manufacturers put out brassieres with false bosoms of foam rubber for little girls of ten. And an advertisement for a child's dress, sizes 3–6x, in *The New York Times* in the fall of 1960, said: "She Too Can Join the Man-Trap Set."

By the end of the fifties, the United States birthrate was overtaking India's. The birth-control movement, renamed Planned Parenthood, was asked to find a method whereby women who had been advised that a third or fourth baby would be born dead or defective might have it anyhow. Statisticians were especially astounded at the fantastic increase in the number of babies among college women. Where once they had two children now they had four, five, six. Women who had once wanted careers were now making careers out of having babies. So rejoiced *Life* magazine in a 1956 paean to the movement of American women back to the home.

In a New York hospital, a woman had a nervous breakdown when she found she could not breast-feed her baby. In other hospitals, women dying of cancer refused a drug which research had proved might save their lives: its side effects were said to be unfeminine. "If I have only one life, let me live it as a blonde," a larger-than-life-sized picture of a pretty, vacuous woman proclaimed from newspaper, magazine, and drugstore ads. And across America, three out of every ten women dyed their hair blonde. They ate a chalk called Metrecal, instead of food, to shrink to the size of the thin young models. Department-store buyers reported that American women, since 1939, had become three and four sizes smaller. "Women are out to fit the clothes, instead of vice-versa," one buyer said.

Interior decorators were designing kitchens with mosaic murals and original paintings, for kitchens were once again the center of women's lives. Home sewing became a million-dollar industry. Many women no longer left their homes, except to shop, chauffeur their children, or attend a social engagement with their husbands. Girls were growing up in America without ever having jobs outside the home. In the late fifties, a sociological phenomenon was suddenly remarked: a third of American women now worked, but most were no longer young and very few were pursuing careers. They were married women who held part-time jobs, selling or secretarial, to put their husbands through school, their sons through college, or to help pay the mortgage. Or they were widows supporting families. Fewer and fewer women were entering professional work. The shortages in the nursing, social work, and teaching professions caused crises in almost every American city. Concerned over the Soviet Union's lead in the space race, scientists noted that America's greatest source of unused brain-power was women. But girls would not study physics: it was "unfeminine." A girl refused a science fellowship at Johns Hopkins to take a job in a real-estate office. All she wanted, she said, was what every other American girl wanted—to get married, have four children and live in a nice house in a nice suburb. . . .

If a woman had a problem in the 1950's and 1960's, she knew that something must be wrong with her marriage, or with herself. Other women were satisfied with their lives, she thought. What kind of a woman was she if she did not feel this mysterious fulfillment waxing the kitchen floor? She was so ashamed to admit her dissatisfaction that she never knew how many other women shared it. If she tried to tell her husband, he didn't understand what she was talking about. She did not really understand it herself. For over fifteen years women in America found it harder to talk about this problem than about sex. Even the psychoanalysts had no name for it. When a woman went to a psychiatrist for help, as many women did, she would say, "I'm so ashamed," or "I must be hopelessly neurotic." "I don't know what's wrong with women today," a suburban psychiatrist said uneasily. "I only know something is wrong because most of my patients happen to be women. And their problem isn't sexual." Most women with this problem did not go to see a psychoanalyst, however. "There's nothing wrong really," they kept telling themselves. "There isn't any problem."

Further Resources

BOOKS

Farber, David. *The Age of Great Dreams: America in the 1960s.* New York: Hill and Wang, 1994.

Friedan, Betty. *"It Changed My Life": Writings on the Women's Movement.* Cambridge, Mass.: Harvard University Press, 1998.

———. *Life So Far.* New York: Simon & Schuster, 2000.

Hennessee, Judith. *Betty Friedan: Her Life.* New York: Random House, 1999.

Horowitz, Daniel. *Betty Friedan and the Making of The Feminine Mystique: The American Left, The Cold War, and Modern Feminism.* Amherst, Mass.: University of Massachusetts Press, 1998.

McGowan, Barbara. "Betty Friedan and the National Organization for Women." *American Reform and Reformers.* Randall M. Miller and Paul A. Cimbala, eds. Westport, Conn.: Greenwood Press, 1996.

Meyerowitz, Joanne, ed. *Not June Cleaver: Women and Gender in Postwar America, 1945–1960.* Philadelphia: Temple University Press, 1994.

PERIODICALS

Gardels, Nathan. "The New Frontier of Feminism: Busting the Masculine Mystique." *New Perspectives Quarterly* 15, no. 1, Winter 1998, 50–52.

Wolfe, Alan. "The Mystique of Betty Friedan." *Atlantic Monthly* 284, no. 3, September 1999, 98–105.

WEBSITES

"The National Organization for Women." Available online at http://www.now.org (accessed March 30, 2003).

Automobiles of the 1960s

"If You Think Big Cars Are Back in Style, You're Right"; "The Second Best Shape in Italy"; "Superiority Complex"

Advertisements

By: Chrysler Dodge Division; Fiat Motors; General Motors Chevrolet Division

Date: 1963, 1965, 1968

Source: The Advertising Archive Ltd. Image nos. 30522839, 30523028, 30522195. ■

Introduction

At the beginning of the twentieth century only 8,000 automobiles were registered in the United States. At first considered a plaything of the rich, more efficient production techniques and installment buying transformed

Primary Source

"If You Think Big Cars Are Back in Style, You're Right"

SYNOPSIS: The Chrysler Corporation was the smallest of the Big Three, and its Dodge line was intended to appeal to budget-conscious buyers. This ad for the 1964 Dodge 880 sells the car as a good value for its price range, but with features that make it competitive with more luxurious automobiles. Simple photos and text highlight the practical appeal of this entry in the Dodge lineup. THE ADVERTISING ARCHIVE LTD. REPRODUCED BY PERMISSION.

The Second Best Shape in Italy

at the coolest little figure in its class — $2585.* That's all the money you part with for all this car, the Fiat 1500 Spider. Styled by Pininfarina, the romantic web it spins is captivating America. It's dynamic outside and a dynamo inside—a perfect expression of Italy's fabled creative energy and inspired art. Lean into a curve with Fiat's curves and know what it's like to drive this <u>five</u> forward-speed sportsman's dream. And to help you keep it humming, there are 425 parts-and-service centers in the U.S.A. This new <u>five</u>-speed Spider is waiting for you at your Fiat dealer. So what are you waiting for? *Always have at least one* **FIAT**

*Suggested price p.o.e. New York reflects reduced U.S. Excise Taxes. See the Yellow Pages for your nearest Fiat dealer. Fiat Motor Co., Inc., 500 Fifth Avenue, N. Y., N. Y. 10036

Primary Source

"The Second Best Shape in Italy"

SYNOPSIS: The largest auto maker in Italy, Fiat never became a major player in the United States—but not from a lack of trying, as this 1965 ad demonstrates. Both the 1500 Spider and the bikini-clad model are given equal prominence in the ad, and the text calls attention to "the coolest little figure in its class." Although ads for American automobiles also used sexual images in the 1960s, their approach typically did not go nearly as far in identifying the product as a sex object. THE ADVERTISING ARCHIVE LTD. REPRODUCED BY PERMISSION.

You pull up to a traffic light. Heads turn. You look in the rearview mirror. Eyes follow. Corvette's that kind of car. The kind of car that makes you feel the whole world is watching. The kind of car that brings out the driver in you. And why not? Everything's in your favor. Sleek aerodynamic fuselage. Four-wheel disc brakes. Independent suspension all around. Even V8s available up to 427 cubic inches. That's the real beauty of Corvette. It does all the work, you get all the credit.

Corvette CHEVROLET

Superiority complex.

Corvette Sting Ray Convertible, Sports Class winner of *Motor Trend's* 1968 Achievement Award

Primary Source

"Superiority Complex"

SYNOPSIS: In their attempt to capture more of the youth market, American auto makers turned out numerous "muscle cars" with high-performance engines and aggressive styling. One of the best examples arrived in the late 1960s with the re-vamped Corvette, a line that had initially been offered in the early 1950s as a small sports car. By 1968 the Corvette took its place alongside the Mustang, GTO, and Camaro as a car that was both a powerful muscle car and a status symbol. THE ADVERTISING ARCHIVE LTD. REPRODUCED BY PERMISSION.

the auto into a hallmark of American life by the 1920s. The automobile industry itself signaled the rise of America as an economic superpower, where even the working class increasingly shared in the staples of middle-class life. After all, nothing symbolized the progress and prosperity of the new industry more than Henry Ford's announcement of a Five Dollar Day for workers at his Highland Park, Michigan factory in 1914. The act, which significantly boosted workers' wages and Ford's profits through massive productivity gains, promised to bring working-class families into the consumer age.

Often called the "golden age" of the American automobile industry, the 1950s and 1960s witnessed continued growth and profits for domestic car manufacturers. Although sales of the German Volkswagen Beetle were on the rise, there was little foreign competition, particularly among the ranks of the more profitable, full-sized luxury cars that dominated the marketplace. Despite the publicity over Ralph Nader's *Unsafe at Any Speed* in 1965, auto makers in the 1960s concentrated more on annual style updates to the larger, more profitable models, rather than working on technological innovation or the introduction of smaller, more fuel-efficient cars.

There was not much demand for small cars in an era of cheap and plentiful gasoline. When Studebaker tried to compete with the Big Three—as General Motors, Ford, and Chrysler were known—by trying to find a market niche with smaller cars such as the Lark, it quickly went out of business. Nash Motors, maker of the economy-sized Rambler, only survived by merging with other smaller auto companies into the American Motors Corporation in 1959. The Big Three's most notable attempt to sell economy cars also met with disaster when the Chevrolet Corvair's manufacturing defects were exposed in *Unsafe at Any Speed.*

Significance

Although some consumers turned away from the Big Three's products, foreign auto makers held just 5 percent of the American market in 1963. By 1971, however, their share had increased to 16 percent, an ominous trend once gasoline prices skyrocketed after the OPEC oil embargoes of the early 1970s. Although many of the imported autos were luxury makes, such as the Mercedes-Benz, or sports cars from Fiat or MG, increasingly they were fuel-efficient Japanese models from Honda and Toyota.

Although domestic automobile manufacturers blamed unfair trade regulations and a supposedly high wage rate for their slumping competitiveness after the 1960s, their own decisions had laid the groundwork for the decline. In the days of little competition and a ready consumer market, the Big Three had passed numerous

opportunities to diversify their product lineup to include more compact-sized models. Convinced that the American driver would never purchase an economy car, even the smaller, less expensive domestic makes (such as the Dodge 880) were sold as aspiring full-sized luxury cars.

The Chevrolet Corvair was the most notable attempt by the Big Three to market an economy car in the 1960s, though it was also a precursor to the auto makers' missteps in the 1970s with the Ford Pinto and Chevy Vega. These were two ill-designed small cars that experienced recalls, lethal accidents, and a slew of lawsuits. Ralph Nader exposed the Corvair's crucial design flaws—with its rear-wheel drive and concentration of weight in the rear part of the vehicle, the Corvair had an increased chance of rolling over if a driver lost control while turning. After Nader reported this, General Motors eased the car out of production, even though it had corrected the problem in its later-model Corvairs. GM's heavy-handed tactics against Nader, including the use of private detectives to dig up dirt on the irreproachable crusader, backfired when the company was forced to pay a settlement to Nader for its questionable actions.

Further Resources

BOOKS

Critchlow, Donald T. *Studebaker: The Life and Death of an American Corporation.* Bloomington: Indiana University Press, 1996.

Dalrymple, Marya, ed. *Is the Bug Dead?: The Great Beetle Ad Campaign.* New York: Workman Publishing Company, 1983.

Dregni, Eric, and Karl Hagstrom Miller. *Ads That Put America on Wheels.* Osceola, Wisc.: Motorbooks International, 1996.

Flink, James J. *The Automobile Age.* Cambridge, Mass.: MIT Press, 1988.

Frank, Thomas. *The Conquest of Cool: Business Culture, Counterculture, and the Rise of Hip Consumerism.* Chicago: University of Chicago Press, 1997.

Ikuta, Yasutoshi. *Cruise O Matic: Automobile Advertising of the 1950s.* San Francisco: Chronicle Books, 1988.

Ingrassia, Paul and Joseph B. White. *Comeback: The Fall and Rise of the American Automobile Industry.* New York: Simon and Schuster, 1994.

Keller, Maryann. *Rude Awakening: The Rise, Fall, and Struggle for Recovery of General Motors.* New York: William Morrow and Company, 1989.

Nader, Ralph. *Unsafe at Any Speed: The Designed-In Dangers of the American Automobile.* New York: Grossman, 1965.

Twitchell, James B. *Twenty Ads That Shook the World: The Century's Most Groundbreaking Advertising and How It Changed Us All.* New York: Crown Publishers, 2000.

Wolfe, Tom. *The Kandy-Kolored Tangerine-Flake Streamline Baby.* New York: Farrar, Straus, and Giroux, 1965.

Latino Consciousness

"We Shall Overcome"

Newspaper article

By: César Chávez

Date: September 16, 1965

Source: Chávez, César. "We Shall Overcome." *El Malcriado.* September 16, 1965. Available online at http://www.sfsu .edu/~cecipp/cesar_chavez /venceremos.htm; website home page: http://www.sfsu.edu (accessed June 2, 2003).

"Prayer of the Farm Workers' Struggle"

Prayer

By: César Chávez

Source: Chávez, César. "Prayer of the Farm Workers' Struggle." Available online at http://www.sfsu.edu/~cecipp/cesar _chavez/prayer.htm; website home page: http://www.sfsu.edu (accessed June 2, 2003).

"The Mexican-American and the Church"

Essay

By: César Chávez

Date: Summer 1968

Source: Chávez, César. "The Mexican-American and the Church." *El Grito.* Summer 1968. Available online at http:// www.sfsu.edu/~cecipp/cesar_chavez/cesar&church.htm; website home page: http://www.sfsu.edu (accessed June 2, 2003).

About the Author: Césario (César) Estrada Chávez (1927–1993) formed the Farm Workers Association (FWA) as a self-help organization for migrant workers in Delano, California. Under Chávez's leadership, the FWA became the National Farm Workers Union (NFWU) in 1966 and conducted successful organizing drives, strikes, boycotts, and other nonviolent protests to unionize the agricultural fields and improve conditions and wages for workers. ∎

Introduction

César Chávez's family, who worked as migrant farm laborers, had been active in the National Farm Labor Union (NFLU) in the late 1940s. Although the NFLU's attempts to unionize agricultural workers in California were crushed by the power of large landowners and a hostile political climate, the experience gave Chávez the lessons in organization and mass participation that he would later use to form the United Farm Workers (UFW) union in the 1960s. Chávez also drew on his years of work in the mid-1950s as a staff member of San José's Community Service Organization (CSO). The CSO urged Mexican Americans to become active in the political process by registering them to vote and also used its authority to expose cases of police brutality against Latinos in San Jose. The third major influence in Chávez's outlook dated to his upbringing as a Roman Catholic. Inspired by his grandmother's religious stories of suffering and redemption and the dignity and symbolism of the Mass, the Church made a lasting impact on Chávez's view of labor relations as having a strong moral component. It also strengthened his resolve to use nonviolent means in *la causa* (the cause).

Although he had been offered a number of other well paying jobs, Chávez took his family to Delano, California in 1962 to work as a labor organizer at poverty-level wages. Over the next several years he often had to ask for food donations to keep his eight children sufficiently fed. Inaugurating the Farm Workers Association (FWA) as a self-help organization with a cooperative store selling tires and other items essential to migrant workers, Chávez gradually built support for a new union of agricultural workers through mass participation and grassroots involvement. He was greatly assisted by Dolores Huerta, a CSO leader from Stockton who had formed the Agricultural Workers Association in 1960 to lobby the California State Legislature to gain public assistance and pension rights for migrant workers. Huerta, a dynamic speaker whose dedication to the new union matched that of Chávez, also helped the FWA broaden its appeal to women migrant workers by making sure that their interests were reflected in the union's agenda.

Significance

The FWA—known as the United Farm Workers (UFW) union after 1966—faced the first major test of its strength in a strike against Delano-area grape growers that began in September 1965. After Filipino workers in the Agricultural Workers Organizing Committee (AWOC) struck over low wages and dangerous work conditions, the landowners attempted to bring in Latino migrant workers to take their places for the harvest. Although the UFW was not prepared to finance a strike, its members voted overwhelmingly to join the action, which spread to thirty farms around Delano. In addition to demands for better wages and improved working conditions, the cross-racial coalition of the UFW and AWOC quickly became a protest against civil rights violations that their members had suffered under the growers, who had frequently violated the law to break strikes and keep workers in line.

On March 17, 1966, Chávez led a delegation of seventy strikers on a march from Delano to the State Legislature in Sacramento. The 340-mile journey took twenty-five days, with rallies at each stop culminating in a crowd of 10,000 meeting at the Capitol building on Easter Sunday. The outpouring of support helped the unions win a contract with Schenley Vineyards, the first-ever contract signed by an agricultural grower to recognize an agricultural union as a legitimate bargaining agent. In addition to its mass rallies, the UFW also instituted a series of boycotts against grape growers who refused to bargain with the union. The call to boycott the growers helped to bring national attention and support to the UFW's cause, and the union's membership reached approximately 80,000 workers by 1971.

In addition to winning the first union contract by an agricultural union, the UFW helped to improve working conditions by stipulating safety measures against pesticides and access to clean water and sanitary facilities for workers covered by its contracts. The union also won health benefits for its members and inaugurated a pension plan for its retired members, the first such plan ever created by an agricultural union. In his role as the UFW's leader until his death in 1993, Chávez also helped to raise the consciousness of Latino workers by using the moral authority and nonviolent tactics that had earlier empowered the Civil Rights movement.

Primary Source

"We Shall Overcome"

> **SYNOPSIS:** The connection to the Civil Rights movement is obvious in the title of this piece, which appeared in the UFW's newspaper, *El Malcriado,* in 1965. In describing the start of the Delano grape-growers strike, Chávez highlights the protest as a nonviolent action in pursuit of moral, not just economic, ends. The article also demonstrates the mass participation of union and community members that helped the strikers face up to their armed opponents.

In a 400 square mile area halfway between Selma and Weedpatch, California, a general strike of farm workers has been going on for six weeks. The Filipinos, under AWOC AFL-CIO began the strike for a $1.40 per hour guarantee and a union contract. They were joined by the independent Farm Workers Association which has a membership of several thousand Mexican-Americans.

Filipino, Mexican-American and Puerto Rican workers have been manning picket lines daily for 41 days in a totally non-violent manner. Ranchers in the area, which include DiGiorgio Fruit, Schenley, and many independent growers, did not take the strike seriously at first. By the second or third week, however, they began taking another look—and striking

back. Mechanized agriculture began picketing the pickets—spraying them with sulfur, running tractors by them to create dust storms, building barricades of farm machinery so that scabs could not see the pickets. These actions not only increased the determination of the strikers, but convinced some of the scabs that the ranchers were, in fact, less than human. Scabs quit work and the strike grew.

The growers hired security guards for $43 a day. They began driving their Thunderbirds, equipped with police dogs and rifles, up and down the roads. The people made more picket signs, drew in their belts, and kept marching.

Production was down 30% and the growers began looking for more and more scabs. They went to Fresno and Bakersfield and Los Angeles to find them. They didn't tell the workers that they would be scab crews. The pickets followed them into every town and formed ad hoc strike committees to prevent scabbing. They succeeded in these towns. Within two weeks, only one bus, with half a dozen winos, escorted by a pearl gray Cadillac, drove into the strike zone. A new plan was formed. The ranchers would advertise in South Texas and old Mexico. They bring these workers in buses and the workers are held in debt to the rancher before they even arrive in town. We have a new and more difficult task ahead of us with these scabs.

As our strike has grown, workers have matured and now know why and how to fight for their rights. As the strike has grown into a movement for justice by the lowest paid workers in America, friends of farm workers have begun to rally in support of LA CAUSA. Civil rights, church, student and union groups help with food and money.

We believe that this is the beginning of a significant drive to achieve equal rights for agricultural workers. In order to enlist your full support and to explain our work to you, I would like to bring some of our pickets and meet with you.

VIVA LA CAUSA Y

VIVA LA HUELGA

Cesar Estrada Chavez
General Director,
National Farm Workers Association

Primary Source

"Prayer of the Farm Workers' Struggle"

> **SYNOPSIS:** In this undated piece, the connection between Chávez's religious beliefs and his work with

Latino migrant workers toil in a California field in 1964. AP/WIDE WORLD PHOTOS. REPRODUCED BY PERMISSION.

the UFW is obvious. Known for his absolute integrity, unstinting compassion, and self-denying lifestyle, Chávez's own life was reflected in his words.

Show me the suffering of the most miserable;
So I will know my people's plight.
Free me to pray for others;
For you are present in every person.
Help me take responsibility for my own life;
So that I can be free at last.
Grant me courage to serve others;
For in service there is true life.
Give me honesty and patience;
So that the Spirit will be alive among us.

Let the Spirit flourish and grow;
So that we will never tire of the struggle.
Let us remember those who have died for justice;
For they have given us life.
Help us love even those who hate us;
So we can change the world.
Amen.

Primary Source

"The Mexican American and the Church" [excerpt]

> **SYNOPSIS:** Chávez wrote this essay during a twenty-five-day fast in 1968 to rededicate the farm workers' movement to nonviolent methods. Chávez

ended the fast at a Mass attended by Senator Robert F. Kennedy, another civil rights activist who was assassinated in California later that year. The essay shows that Chávez was not blindly obedient to his church's hierarchy and in fact urged it to take a more responsive and activist role in helping its followers achieve social justice.

The place to begin is with our own experience with the Church in the strike which has gone on for thirty-one months in Delano. For in Delano the church has been involved with the poor in a unique way which should stand as a symbol to other communities. Of course, when we refer to the Church we should define the word a little. We mean the whole Church, the Church as an ecumenical body spread around the world, and not just its particular form in a parish in a local community. The Church we are talking about is a tremendously powerful institution in our society, and in the world. That Church is one form of the Presence of God on Earth, and so naturally it is powerful. It is powerful by definition. It is a powerful moral and spiritual force which cannot be ignored by any movement. Furthermore, it is an organization with tremendous wealth. Since the Church is to be servant to the poor, it is our fault if that wealth is not channeled to help the poor in our world. In a small way we have been able, in the Delano strike, to work together with the Church in such a way as to bring some of its moral and economic power to bear on those who want to maintain the status quo, keeping farm workers in virtual enslavement. . . .

BUT THERE ARE HUNDREDS OF THOUSANDS OF OUR PEOPLE WHO DESPERATELY NEED SOME HELP FROM THAT POWERFUL INSTITUTION, THE CHURCH, AND WE ARE FOOLISH NOT TO HELP THEM GET IT. For example, the Catholic Charities agencies of the Catholic Church has millions of dollars earmarked for the poor. But often the money is spent for food baskets for the needy instead of for effective action to eradicate the causes of poverty. The men and women who administer this money sincerely want to help their brothers. It should be our duty to help direct the attention to the basic needs of the Mexican-Americans in our society . . . needs which cannot be satisfied with baskets of food, but rather with effective organizing at the grass roots level. Therefore, I am calling for Mexican-American groups to stop ignoring this source of power. It is not just our right to appeal to the Church to use its power effectively for the poor, it is our duty to do so. It should be as natural as appealing to government . . . and we do

that often enough. Furthermore, we should be prepared to come to the defense of that priest, rabbi, minister, or layman of the Church, who out of commitment to truth and justice gets into a tight place with his pastor or bishop. It behooves us to stand with that man and help him see his trial through. It is our duty to see to it that his rights of conscience are respected and that no bishop, pastor or other higher body takes that God-given, human right away. Finally, in a nutshell, what do we want the Church to do? We don't ask for more cathedrals. We don't ask for bigger churches of fine gifts. We ask for its presence with us, beside us, as Christ among us. We ask the Church to sacrifice with the people for social change, for justice, and for love of brother. We don't ask for words. We ask for deeds. We don't ask for paternalism. We ask for servanthood.

Further Resources

BOOKS

Daniel, Cletus E. "César Chávez and the Unionization of California Farm Workers." In *Labor Leaders in America.* Melvyn Dubofsky and Warren Van Tine, eds. Urbana: University of Illinois Press, 1987.

Del Castillo, Richard Griswold, and Richard A. Garcia. *César Chávez: A Triumph of Spirit.* Norman, Okla.: University of Oklahoma Press, 1995.

Jenkins, Craig J. *The Politics of Insurgency: The Farm Workers Movement in the 1960s.* New York: Columbia University Press, 1985.

Levy, Jacques E. *César Chávez: Autobiography of La Causa.* New York: W.W. Norton & Co., 1975.

Ross, Fred. *Conquering Goliath: César Chávez at the Beginning.* Keene, Calif.: Taller Grafico, 1989.

WEBSITES

"The Rise of the UFW." Available online at http://www.ufw .org/ufw.htm; website home page: http://www.ufw.org (accessed June 2, 2003).

AUDIO AND VISUAL MEDIA

Chicano!: The History of the Mexican–American Civil Rights Movement. Volume 2: The Struggle in the Fields. 1996, NLCC Educational Mediax.

Fight in the Fields: César Chávez and the Farmworkers' Struggle. Directed by Ray Telles and Rick Tejada-Flores. 1996, Paradigm Productions.

Valley of the Dolls
Novel

By: Jacqueline Susann
Date: 1966

Source: Susann, Jacqueline. *Valley of the Dolls.* New York: Grove Press, 1966, 377–382.

About the Author: Jacqueline Susann (1918–1974), after the 1963 publication of a humorous book of sketches about her poodle, *Every Night, Josephine!,* found lasting celebrity as a writer. *Valley of the Dolls* was a publishing sensation when it appeared in 1966 and ranked as the best-selling novel of all-time by the end of the decade. Susann followed *Valley of the Dolls* with two more best-sellers, *The Love Machine* (1970) and *Once Is Not Enough* (1973). ∎

Introduction

Although she had written some plays in the 1940s and scored a major success with the book *Every Night, Josephine!* in 1963, Jacqueline Susann was an unlikely candidate as a novelist. After undergoing surgery for breast cancer in 1962, however, she became determined to publish a book that would reach a mass audience and finally deliver the fame that she had sought in a quarter-century of toiling away as a minor-league celebrity. Combing through her memories as a stage actress and television personality, Susann fictionalized many of the stories and rumors that she had picked up over the years: aging musical star Helen Lawson was a double for Susann's former confidant Ethel Merman; talented Neely O'Hara, overtaken by drug addition and mental break-downs, was based on Judy Garland; and Jennifer North, the sensual, bisexual showgirl, had her roots in actress Carole Landis, a one-time lover of Susann's who committed suicide in 1947. Although almost every major critic savaged *Valley of the Dolls* after its release in 1966, the book spent twenty-eight weeks at the top of the best-seller list and eventually ranked as the most successful first novel of any author up to that time. With more than ten million paperback copies in print by 1969, the novel was also far -and away the most popular book of the decade.

Significance

With a reference to drug dependency in its title—"dolls" being a term for the sleeping pills and amphetamines that the characters used very frequently—*Valley of the Dolls* was deliberately provocative. It was also a huge and immediate success when it appeared in bookstores, accompanied by an aggressive marketing campaign headlined by Susann herself. Susann became a fixture on television talk shows as she promoted her novel and remained a celebrity author for the rest of her life. A successful movie adaptation of *Valley of the Dolls* appeared in 1967; although it tacked on a happy ending that contrasted with Anne Wells's ambiguous acceptance of her husband's infidelities in the novel, the movie retained most of the book's more shocking moments.

Although tame by later standards, the raw language and frank descriptions of sexual encounters, drug use, and psychological traumas shocked many readers who paged through *Valley of the Dolls.* The publicity over its alleged obscenities increased its sales, opening the door to even more graphic language and topics in other novels as the decade progressed. With its graphic descriptions of the sex and drug habits of celebrities (albeit in thinly veiled form), *Valley of the Dolls* also ushered in the tabloid culture that would make such revelations commonplace in later years. Although it never earned respect from literary critics, Susann's work ranked alongside Kathleen Winsor's *Forever Amber* (1944) and Grace Metalious's *Peyton Place* (1956) as the defining novel during the decade in which it was published.

Primary Source

Valley of the Dolls [excerpt]

> **SYNOPSIS:** *Valley of the Dolls* traces the rise of Anne Wells, who comes to New York City from small-town New England in the 1940s. Along the way she befriends Neely O'Hara and Jennifer North. In addition to the compelling personal sagas of the main characters, *Valley of the Dolls* features numerous passages detailing the drug and alcohol abuse and frequent sexual encounters of the women. The following passage details one of Anne Wells's liaisons with Lyon Burke, the great love of her life.

She couldn't come to terms with herself the following day. She reached for the phone a dozen times to call Lyon and cancel the date. But she never finished dialing. Maybe it *would* fall flat. Maybe she *could* just walk away. That would solve everything. She had promised Kevin she wouldn't leave him, but she hadn't promised not to see Lyon. She *had* to see him.

They met at the Little Club at seven. He was sitting at the bar when she came in, and he sprang to his feet and led her to a table. "You're just not the type to sit at a bar," he said. He looked at her intently after they had ordered a drink. "Anne, you look marvelous. You haven't changed a bit. No, that's not true. You are much more lovely."

"You've held up fairly well too," she said wryly.

"I often wondered about you," he said. "Sometimes when I longed for you I'd console myself with crazy fantasies. I'd tell myself you were fat, with six or seven sniffly little brats clinging to your skirts. At least it got me back to the typewriter."

She laughed. "Oh, Lyon—and I used to pretend you were bald."

It was easy after that. She told him about Jennifer, carefully skirting the real truth. Somehow she

In a scene from the movie version of Jacqueline Susann's *Valley of the Dolls*, a distraught Neely O'Hara (played by Patty Duke) reaches for a bottle of pills. Susann's story of sex and drugs in Hollywood was scandalous and highly successful in the 1960s. **THE KOBAL COLLECTION/20TH CENTURY FOX. REPRODUCED BY PERMISSION.**

felt that Jennifer's legend must be kept intact—that the body beautiful should not be blemished by cancer. They discussed Neely. Henry had told him about that, but he couldn't believe it could happen to the bright-eyed Neely he had known.

"She's such an enormous talent," he said. "She's frightfully popular in England. Her pictures were quite wonderful for Hollywood products. In spite of all the tinsel and sugar candy they surrounded her with, she still emerged as a true artist. She will come out of it, won't she?"

Anne's eyes clouded. "They say she's bent for self-destruction, that her kind of illness is never really cured. It may be arrested, and with help she might be able to function again. But she'll always have that self-destructive urge. At least, that's what the doctors say."

He sighed. "Perhaps that's why I never made it big. Sometimes I think all great artists are a little balmy. I'm much too normal. I fall asleep the minute I hit the pillow, don't drink to excess and never even take an aspirin."

She laughed. "I guess I'm second-rate too. Perhaps I smoke too much, but I'm still a one-drink girl, and although I'd never admit it, I sometimes fall asleep right in the middle of the late movie."

He laughed back. "No, Anne, you're first-rate—there's no one like you. There really isn't, you know. Every girl I met, it always washed out. They just couldn't stand up to your image."

They talked through dinner about New York and the changes he noticed. He introduced her to Irish coffee and she became an instant devotee. She was still praising it when he suddenly turned to her. "It's all the same, Anne. I want to take you in my arms this moment. I feel as if we've never parted."

"I want to *be* in your arms, Lyon."

He grinned. "It's a deal. But I think it's best if I paid the check and we got the hell out of here!"

It was unbelievable. To be lying beside him, watching the smoke curl into the light of the bed lamp. . . . There had been no hesitation, no bridges to cross; they had come together in a fusion of love and desire. This was complete fulfillment. When she held him in her arms she suddenly knew it *was* important to love—more important than *being* loved. And she knew this was a decision she had to make. Lyon loved her, in his own way. Was it enough? Would she miss Kevin's tender, unselfish devotion, the one-sided way he lived for her? With Lyon she would have to be on her toes every second. Was she up to the give and take of this kind of love?

He reached out and stroked her bare back. "It was wonderful, Anne. It always was."

"For me too, Lyon—but only with you."

"Anne, there *is* Kevin Gillmore," he said quietly. He felt her stiffen and stroked her head. "It's common knowledge, darling. And everyone knows he wants to marry you." He paused. "You know I didn't just happen on the set yesterday, don't you? I made it a point to look up Jerry Richardson. I wanted to meet this Kevin Gillmore—and I wanted to see you."

She pulled away and sat up. "What was I supposed to do? Sit around all these years and pray for your return? Lyon . . . not a letter, not a word . . . nothing."

"Hush." He put his fingers across her lips. "Of course I understand. I *wanted* to write—oh, God, the letters I wrote and never mailed—but that bloody pride of mine . . . Each book would do it, I'd tell myself. Then I'd return the conquering hero and take my girl away from whatever guy she was with. But

I'm *not* the hero—and Kevin Gillmore is *not* just a guy. He's a good man, Anne, and from what I hear he's head over heels about you."

She was silent.

"If I had any character, I wouldn't see you after tonight," he said.

"Lyon!" There was fear in her voice.

He laughed aloud. "I said *if* I had any character. I'm afraid I never had very much. And seeing you made whatever shred I had go up in smoke." Then he said very seriously, "I'll be here, Anne, for the taking, any time you want me. But that's all it can be."

"What does that mean?"

"I return to London after this assignment. I have a new book in the works. The first draft is written."

"Couldn't you write here?"

"Possibly. But I couldn't live, at least not as well. I have a nice flat, and I pick up extra money doing articles. It's a different life, Anne, but I like it." Then he added, "And I earn just enough to make it possible to spend those bleak hours at the typewriter, writing what *I* want to write. It's a lonely existence, but there's always the hope that perhaps *this* is the book that will do it. I believe in my writing and what I'm trying to do, and I have you to thank for this. I've lost you because of it—but then, it probably couldn't have worked any other way. . . ."

"Why not?" she said stubbornly. "If I hadn't opened my big mouth that day in the Barberry Room—if I hadn't insisted that you write—you might have been the biggest manager in town and we'd have children and—"

"And hate one another. No, Anne, a marriage hasn't a chance when you're scrambling for success. And it probably wouldn't have worked if you had meekly submitted to that wild idea about living in Lawrenceville, either. I'm just cut out to be a loner, I guess. But I am so very glad to have this chance to be with you again. I'll cherish every second you give me, and stretch out all the memories for those rainy British nights when I'm home again." He took her in his arms, and her hurt evaporated in the incredible wonder of loving him.

It was dawn when she reached her apartment. As she slipped the key into the door, she noticed the sliver of light.

"How did you manage to tear yourself away so soon? It's not morning yet." Kevin was sitting in the living room, smoking.

She walked over and snatched the cigarette from his mouth. "You haven't smoked since your heart attack. What are you trying to prove?"

He sneered. "Why the big concern for my health? Seems to me that after tonight I have very little future."

"Kevin, why did you come here?"

"Because I knew you were with him. Tell me about it. Did he release all those inhibitions? Did you both swing from chandeliers?"

"Stop it! It's not good for you to carry on like this. Come on—if you want to stay the night, go to bed."

"Would you go to bed with me tonight?" He saw her stiffen. "If you did, you'd be a wet deck. That's the name for a girl like that. Well, would you?"

"Kevin . . . we haven't had sex since your heart attack. It's not that I've minded—I understand about your health and . . ."

"And my age—go on, say it."

"Whatever happened tonight is between Lyon and me. It has nothing to do with my feeling for you."

"Am I supposed to take that? Let Lyon play the stud, and I play the doddering faithful retainer?"

"You are my friend, part of my life . . . someone I love deeply. Lyon is something . . . different."

"Well, I won't stand for it. You'll have to choose."

"All right, Kevin," she said wearily. "If you force me . . ."

He grabbed her. "No—no! Anne, don't leave me!" He began to sob. She wanted to pull away; instead she stroked his head. It was so terrible to see a man fall apart. Was she responsible, or was it his failing health and his age?

"Kevin, I won't leave you."

"But you'll go on seeing him. Do you think I can go on like that? Knowing you come to me from his arms?"

"Kevin—" She groped for the right words. "We both know I was with Lyon. But he's going back. And he knows about you. He even said you're quite a guy."

"That's the English in him. Don't you know that? All the English are decadent. He'd probably get a kick out of sharing you."

She sighed patiently. This wasn't Kevin speaking. It was his hysterical fear. "Kevin, I'm staying with you."

"Why? Doesn't he want you?"

She turned and went into the bedroom and began to undress. It was unbelievable. History repeating itself. Kevin had suddenly looked like Allen Cooper—the same cowlike expression and the same childish rage. And once again it was Lyon who was sitting back, demanding nothing and promising nothing, while she was being torn in two. How much did she really owe Kevin? Her relationship with him had been far from thrilling. Yet throughout the entire time she had never given him cause for jealousy or concern. There had been many chances—many men younger and more attractive than Kevin—but she had ignored every advance. She had given him fourteen years of happiness—shouldn't that balance any obligation she owned him? Yet Kevin needed her. He had sat there all night, smoking. She knew how it was to sit and wait for someone. Suddenly she felt a great surge of tenderness and pity for Kevin. Oh, God, he had looked so old, so vulnerable. She couldn't hurt him.

She returned to the living room. He was sitting there, staring into space—crumpled, defeated.

She held out her arms. "Kevin, I love you. Get undressed, it's late. Get some sleep. I'm here—I'll always be here, as long as you want me."

He stumbled toward her. "You won't see him again? You won't?"

"No, Kevin. I won't see him ever again."

Further Resources

BOOKS

Ehrenreich, Barbara, et al. *Re-Making Love: The Feminization of Sex.* Garden City, New York: Anchor Press/Doubleday, 1986.

Mansfield, Irving. *Life with Jackie: The Personal Story of Jacqueline Susann.* New York: Bantam Books, 1983.

Seaman, Barbara. *Lovely Me: The Life of Jacqueline Susann.* New York: William Morrow and Company, 1987.

PERIODICALS

Davidson, Sara. "Jacqueline Susann: The Writing Machine." *Harper's,* October 1969.

Howard, Jane. "Happiness Is Being Number One." *Life,* August 19, 1966.

Purdy, Ken W. "Valley of the Dollars." *Saturday Evening Post,* February 24, 1968.

AUDIO AND VISUAL MEDIA

The Love Machine. Directed by Jack Haley, Jr. Columbia/Tristar Studios. Videocassette, 1971.

Once Is Not Enough. Directed by Guy Green. Paramount. Videocassette, 1975.

Valley of the Dolls. Directed by Mark Robson. Twentieth Century Fox. Videocassette, 1967.

Phyllis Diller

Phyllis Diller's Housekeeping Hints

Manual

By: Phyllis Diller

Date: 1966

Source: Diller, Phyllis. *Phyllis Diller's Housekeeping Hints.* Garden City, New York: Doubleday and Company, 1966, 16–17; 68–70.

Phyllis Diller's Marriage Manual

Manual

By: Phyllis Diller

Date: 1967

Source: Diller, Phyllis. *Phyllis Diller's Marriage Manual.* Garden City, New York: Doubleday and Company, 1967, 79–82.

About the Author: Phyllis Ada (Driver) Diller (1917–), insecure about her physical appearance, developed an outgoing personality and indulged her love of music by studying the piano at the Sherwood Music Conservatory in Chicago. In 1955 Diller made her stand-up debut at the Purple Onion nightclub in San Francisco. Within five years, she appeared regularly on national television as one of the few female comedians of the day. ∎

Introduction

Although her stand-up comedy routine at first relied on her musical talent with a series of impressions, Phyllis Diller quickly realized that the monologues about her domestic life were proving even more popular with audiences. As Diller refined her act, she came upon the formula that she would use for nearly the next half-century. That formula included jokes about her inability to manage her household and keep her children in line, gags about her husband's deficiencies as a breadwinner and lover, and pointed remarks about her neighbor, Mrs. Clean, who actually lived up to the ideals of suburban life with an immaculate home and well-behaved kids. To go along with her skewed take on domestic life, Diller created a persona to match. She typically wore outlandish evening clothes and dress gloves with a long cigarette holder to demonstrate an exaggerated sense of feminity. Diller also sported a disheveled hairstyle and combat boots to make the contrast between the ideal suburban housewife and her everyday reality even more obvious.

In an era still dominated by the images of domestic bliss seen on *Leave It to Beaver, The Adventures of Ozzie and Harriet,* and *The Donna Reed Show*—all of which ran well into the 1960s—Diller's take on marriage, child-rearing, and housekeeping was all the more jarring. Al-

though her marriage to Sherwood Diller ended in 1965, shortly before *Phyllis Diller's Housekeeping Hints* and *Phyllis Diller's Marriage Manual* appeared, both volumes became best-sellers. She married Ward Donovan in 1965 and divorced him a decade later. Diller also made headlines by poking fun of her face lift, which made her one of the first celebrities to acknowledge undergoing cosmetic surgery.

Significance

From her roots on the San Francisco comedy scene in the 1950s, Diller made a name for herself as one of the first nationally known female comics in the 1960s. As demonstrated in her best-selling volumes, *Phyllis Diller's Housekeeping Hints* and *Phyllis Diller's Marriage Manual,* she did so by making light of the traditional images of women as wives and mothers that dominated contemporary popular culture. In presenting a take on domestic life that upended the common assumptions of a woman's supposed natural abilities as a wife and mother, Diller presented a sharp counterpoint that verged on the subversive, even as she enjoyed mainstream success.

With her best-selling books, guest appearances on television variety shows, and starring roles in the 1966 movie, *Boy, Did I Get a Wrong Number!* with Bob Hope and the television series *The Phyllis Diller Show,* Diller confirmed her position as one of America's most popular comedians of the decade. She continued to tour with her stand-up act through 2002, when she announced her retirement from the road after almost a half-century of appearances. By that time Diller had influenced two generations of prominent female comics, including Roseanne Barr, the woman whose own take on domestic life was just as subversive.

Primary Source

Phyllis Diller's Housekeeping Hints [excerpt]

> **SYNOPSIS:** Diller's books presented parts of her stand-up routines in the form of self-help advice manuals. Typical of her comments was this advice to prospective home buyers: "Buy the house far enough away from school so your kids can't come home for lunch."

I am an immaculate housekeeper. I'm clean, but the house is a mess. I suspected I wouldn't be the perfect housewife the way I botched up the wedding cake.

They won't even sell me *Good Housekeeping* magazine. They're afraid it might be seen in my home. And I can't blame them. I'm such a lousy housekeeper even the white pages in my phone book are yellow.

I know people who are so clean you can eat off their floors. You can't eat off my table. Fang, my husband, says the only thing domestic about me is that I was born in this country.

Some women have qualities that take away the need for being a domestic expert, but unfortunately, I do not. When I stand next to Jayne Mansfield I feel like a cake with the baking powder left out.

And household ability wouldn't matter if I were a financial genius, but if I invested in a mouth wash stock, bad breath would suddenly become popular.

Besides this, I live next door to Mrs. Clean, who bleaches her *snow*. She's got dust cloths for her dust cloths. Everything at her house folds up and puts away. She has a folding ping pong table that has folding ping pong balls. She polishes her furniture so much you can see your face in it. (Now why in heaven's name would I want to do that?!) . . .

■ ■ ■

Ah! The magic of childhood! But it doesn't work. I can't make them disappear. I do wear dark glasses in the house hoping they won't recognize me.

To show how wild they are, my eight-year-old bought a bicycle with money he had saved by not smoking. I got one of them a pair of elevator shoes and sent him to school a year early. I had him going to kindergarten and two nursery schools at the same time.

One of my girls was so hard to get along with she was in a Girl Scout troop all by herself. She never smiles. She was 15 before I saw her second teeth, and then I just happened to be with her when they told her she was on Candid Camera.

None of my kids were drop outs, but they caused several drop-outs among the teachers. They are so hard to live with our next-door neighbors were ready to sell. Well, in fact, they were ready to give.

I signed up for the Foster Parents Plan, but that didn't work. I thought they'd send me some foster parents to help.

And did we have kids! We were sort of an atom bomb in the population explosion. We were having kids so long I went straight from buying Carter's baby clothes to Carter's Little Liver Pills. I was tired out all year signing their names on the Christmas cards. I finally quit having them by lying to the doctor about my age.

Comedienne and author of humor-filled advice books on marriage and domestic life, Phyllis Diller takes time out to vacation in London, England, in 1968. © **BETTMANN/CORBIS. REPRODUCED BY PERMISSION.**

Then Mrs. Clean has the nerve to say things like, "Children grow up too fast." I keep asking mine, "Why can't you be like other kids and grow up too fast?" One day she said, "If they make you so nervous, why did you have so many?" I told her I had them before I knew poodles were going to become so popular. Once she looked at my five and said sweetly, "You're so lucky. How I'd love just one of those." I said, "Frankly, that's what I would have settled for, too."

Primary Source

Phyllis Diller's Marriage Manual [excerpt]

SYNOPSIS: As with her other books, *Phyllis Diller's Marriage Manual* is based largely on her stand-up routine. Although Diller's descriptions of her mother-in-law play upon one of the standard themes of stand-up comedy, her take on the subject as a daughter-in-law brought a different perspective to the topic in the 1960s, when almost all popular comedians were male.

The Inspector General

My mother-in-law must be the probation officer I got for the crime I committed of marrying my husband. I'm surprised she isn't nicer to me. With the kind of husband her son made, you'd think she'd be afraid I'd sue her.

Every mother thinks her son is Cary Grant, and she will never believe for a minute that by being married to her son you're going through life Tourist Class. A mother-in-law always thinks of her child first and foremost. Here is an example of what I mean. A friend of mine had her baby on the way to the hospital, and the comment of her mother-in-law was, "Everything happens to George."

All mothers-in-law have a disgusting habit . . . they come to visit you.

Discount the idea of an anonymous phone call warning yours to stay away from her son's house. Try to remember, a mother-in-law doesn't need a search warrant. Every mother-in-law has phenomenal eyesight. From across the room she'll spot the olive pits in your garbage and know you've been drinking. Take the following precautions:

1. If you draw a caricature of your mother-in-law on the family blackboard, don't forget to erase it before she comes over.

2. Have an old pair of white gloves she slips on when she comes over to run along the furniture looking for dust so she won't have to ruin her good ones.

3. If you have a house like mine, send her upstairs to get something. There's a good chance she'll get lost.

4. No matter how tempted you are to do so, never salute her.

5. Be sure your mother-in-law has left the house for good before spraying with the air freshener.

Further Resources

BOOKS

Barreca, Regina. *Last Laughs: Perspectives on Women and Comedy.* New York: Gordon and Breach Publishers, 1988.

Diller, Phyllis. *Phyllis Diller Tells All About Fang.* San Francisco: Macventures, 1963.

Finney, Gail, ed. *Look Who's Laughing: Gender and Comedy.* Langhorne, Pa.: Gordon and Breach Publishers, 1994.

Horowitz, Susan. *Queens of Comedy: Lucille Ball, Phyllis Diller, Carol Burnett, Joan Rivers, and the New Generation of Funny Women.* Amsterdam: Gordon and Breach Publishers, 1997.

Walker, Nancy A. *A Very Serious Thing: Women's Humor and American Culture.* Minneapolis: University of Minnesota Press, 1988.

Wilde, Larry. *Great Comedians Talk About Comedy.* Mechanicsburg, Penn.: Executive Books, 2000.

PERIODICALS

Vellela, Tony. "Pioneer Showed Women How to Stand Up and Be Funny." *Christian Science Monitor,* March 2, 2001, 20.

WEBSITES

"Phyllis Diller Filmography and Television Appearances." Available online at http://us.indb.com (accessed January 1, 2003).

The Conservative Backlash

"Nixon's Address to the Nation on the War in Vietnam"

Speech

By: Richard M. Nixon

Date: November 3, 1969

Source: "Nixon's Address to the Nation on the War in Vietnam." Available online at http://www.watergate.info/nixon/silent-majority-speech-1969.shtml; website home page: http://www.watergate.info (accessed June 2, 2003).

About the Author: Richard M. Nixon (1913–1994) was defeated in his presidential run in 1960 and a California gubernatorial run in 1962, but he staged a political comeback in 1968 and was elected to the White House. He was reelected in 1972, but resigned on August 8, 1974, after his role was revealed in covering up a break in of the Democratic Party Committee's headquarters in the Watergate building.

The Power of the Positive Woman

Nonfiction work

By: Phyllis Schlafly

Date: 1977

Source: Schlafly, Phyllis. *The Power of the Positive Woman.* New York: Jove Publications, 1977, 213–215; 218–219.

About the Author: Phyllis McAlpin (Stewart) Schlafly (1924–) rose to prominence as a vocal and highly conservative political commentator in the 1950s. She has written and spoken extensively on topics such as the threat of the Soviet

President Richard Nixon, in a 1969 address to the nation about the war in Vietnam, suggested that a "silent majority" of the public was in support of the war effort. AP/WIDE WORLD PHOTOS. REPRODUCED BY PERMISSION.

Union, the effects of feminism on the family, and the need for less government regulation. Schlafly is most famous for her opposition to the Equal Rights Amendment (ERA) to the U.S. Constitution, a proposal to outlaw gender discrimination. Her efforts were critical in preventing the ERA from being adopted by its 1982 ratification deadline. ■

Introduction

The 1960s witnessed mass protests over civil rights, the Vietnam War, and women's liberation. Although thousands of people took part in the demonstrations on college campuses and city streets, many Americans criticized the protests as radical, dangerous, and unpatriotic. Appealing to those who were troubled by the calls for reform and change, presidential candidate Richard M. Nixon offered a "law-and-order" platform in his 1968 campaign to "the silent majority" of Americans who watched the demonstrations with apprehension. Nixon's strategy proved successful, and he narrowly won the popular vote over Democratic challenger Hubert H. Humphrey. Refining his message during his first term, Nixon won a landslide four years later over George M. McGovern with more than 60 percent of the popular vote.

Phyllis Schlafly, who maintained an image as an ordinary wife of an Illinois lawyer, was active in politics since the late 1940s when she wrote anti-New Deal arti-

cles for a banking group and did research for the anti-Communist Senator Joseph McCarthy, who was later censured by the Senate for his ethical misdeeds. In addition to her call for less government regulation and increased American military spending, Schlafly advocated a return to conservative morality in American society. A critic of the women's movement, Schlafly claimed that women had already achieved equality and did not need to demand further reforms. Schlafly also viewed feminism as a destructive force against family life and in the 1970s became the leading opponent of the Equal Rights Amendment (ERA), an attempt to add a gender anti-discrimination amendment to the U.S. Constitution. Schlafly's argument carried the day; despite a three-year extension of the ratification period, the proposed ERA expired in 1982 without being enacted.

Significance

As the appeal of conservative figures like Richard M. Nixon and Phyllis Schlafly demonstrated, not all Americans were sympathetic to the protests that swept the nation in the 1960s. Although they were often criticized for their habit of labeling their opponents unpatriotic and radical, both Nixon and Schlafly gained large followings and used that support to implement a conservative political agenda. Caught up in the habitual corruption that took him out of office in 1974, Nixon was unable to transform his landslide 1972 election victory into a lasting return of conservatism in national politics, but Schlafly capitalized on her position as the country's leading antifeminist to campaign successfully against the ERA.

The careers of Nixon and Schlafly also demonstrated the chasm between reform-minded liberals and the so-called "silent majority" of average Americans, many of whom resented the elite backgrounds and condescending tone of some of the various movements' leaders. The conflicts between "Joe Six-Pack" and the "limousine liberals" were the basis for the popular situation comedy *All in the Family,* which debuted in January 1971. Much of the show's humor derived from the verbal battles between Archie Bunker, a working-class Republican, and his liberal, college-educated son-in-law. The comedy ran through 1979, and although Bunker eventually adopted a more liberal set of views, he remained a quintessential member of the silent majority throughout the run.

In the political arena, the conservative backlash against the civil and women's rights movements and the expanded role of the government in mediating such disputes was best characterized by the failed presidential bids of Barry Goldwater in 1964 and George C. Wallace in 1968. Then-California governor Ronald Reagan would learn from their mistakes and present a milder form of conservatism in 1980 to win his first of two terms as President.

Primary Source

Nixon's Address to the Nation on the War in Vietnam [excerpt]

> **SYNOPSIS:** In these words, Nixon invokes the support of "the great silent majority" of Americans for his plans to end the country's involvement in the Vietnam War. Nixon often referred to "the silent majority" as his basis of support to draw attention away from the mass protests that often took place in the late 1960s. In this excerpt, Nixon reaffirms his vision of America as a nation with a moral destiny to fight Communism and bring democracy and prosperity to the rest of the world.

I know it may not be fashionable to speak of patriotism or national destiny these days. But I feel it is appropriate to do so on this occasion.

Two hundred years ago this Nation was weak and poor. But even then, America was the hope of millions in the world. Today we have become the strongest and richest nation in the world. And the wheel of destiny has turned so that any hope the world has for the survival of peace and freedom will be determined by whether the American people have

the moral stamina and the courage to meet the challenge of free world leadership.

Let historians not record that when America was the most powerful nation in the world we passed on the other side of the road and allowed the last hopes for peace and freedom of millions of people to be suffocated by the forces of totalitarianism.

And so tonight—to you, the great silent majority of my fellow Americans—I ask for your support.

I pledged in my campaign for the Presidency to end the war in a way that we could win the peace. I have initiated a plan of action which will enable me to keep that pledge.

The more support I can have from the American people, the sooner that pledge can be redeemed; for the more divided we are at home, the less likely, the enemy is to negotiate at Paris.

Let us be united for peace. Let us also be united against defeat. Because let us understand: North Vietnam cannot defeat or humiliate the United States. Only Americans can do that.

Fifty years ago, in this room and at this very desk, President Woodrow Wilson spoke words which caught the imagination of a war-weary world. He said: "This is the war to end war." His dream for peace after World War I was shattered on the hard realities of great power politics and Woodrow Wilson died a broken man.

Tonight I do not tell you that the war in Vietnam is the war to end wars. But I do say this: I have initiated a plan which will end this war in a way that will bring us closer to that great goal to which Woodrow Wilson and every American President in our history has been dedicated—the goal of a just and lasting peace.

As President I hold the responsibility for choosing the best path to that goal and then leading the Nation along it.

I pledge to you tonight that I shall meet this responsibility with all of the strength and wisdom I can command in accordance with your hopes, mindful of your concerns, sustained by your prayers.

Thank you and goodnight.

Primary Source

The Power of the Positive Woman [excerpt]

> **SYNOPSIS:** Like Nixon, Schlafly sees America as "the greatest country in the world," but one that is challenged to live up to its ideals while defending itself from aggression. Like Nixon, Schlafly is par-

At a December 7, 1969, "tell it to Hanoi" rally in Boston, roughly 2,000 self-proclaimed members of the "silent majority" demonstrate their support for action against the Viet Cong in Vietnam. President Nixon called on the "silent majority" of Americans to support his Vietnam policies and counter the antiwar protestors he believed to be a "vocal minority." © BETTMANN/CORBIS. REPRODUCED BY PERMISSION.

ticularly critical of the changes that took place in American society in the 1960s, which in her view have weakened the average American's patriotic commitment to "the values of God, family, and country."

The Bible tells us, "Where there is no vision, the people perish." The Positive Woman must have a vision for America that gives perspective to her goals, her hopes for the future, and her commitment to her country. The Positive Woman starts with the knowledge that America is the greatest country in the world and that it is her task to do her part to keep it that way.

By common consent over nearly two centuries, the day Americans celebrate as our most important national patriotic anniversary is the Fourth of July. The bicentennial of our nation, July 4, 1976, was not the anniversary of the signing of the United States Constitution, or the ratification of the Bill of Rights, or the start or finish of the Revolutionary War—important as all these events were. The Fourth

of July is the anniversary of the adoption of the Declaration of Independence on July 4, 1776.

This basic document of our national existence is the most perfect orientation of man to God and government outside of Holy Scripture. It is the most important document in American history and the most inspired writing in world history that ever flowed from the hand of man alone. Here is why:

(1) The Declaration of Independence is the official and unequivocal recognition by the American people of their belief and faith in God. It is a religious document from its first sentence to its last. It affirms God's existence as a "self-evident" truth that requires no further discussion or debate. The nation it creates is God's country. The rights it defends are God given. The actions of its signers are God inspired. There are four references to God—God as Creator of all men, God as the Supreme Judge, God as the source of all rights, God as our patron and protector.

(2) The Declaration of Independence declares that each of us is created equal. This means equal

before God. It does not mean that all men are born with equal abilities, and so on, as some try to claim. Nor does it mean that all men can be made equal, as Communist dogma alleges. Obviously and realistically, and as your own individuating fingerprints prove, each of God's creatures is unequal and different from every other person who have ever lived or ever will live on this earth.

(3) The Declaration of Independence proclaims that life and liberty are unalienable gifts of God—natural rights—which no person or government can rightfully take away.

(4) The Declaration of Independence proclaims that the purpose of government is to secure these unalienable individual rights and that government derives its powers from the consent of the governed. For the first time in history, government was reduced from master to servant.

The Declaration of Independence comes to us after 200 years in all its pristine purity. Whereas the United States Constitution has had to suffer the slings and arrows of some outrageous federal court interpretations and judicial distortions, neither the meddling judges nor the bungling bureaucrats have confused or distorted the Declaration of Independence. As the Declaration was in the beginning, it is now and ever shall be because it proclaims truth and facts that are not subject to change or amendment.

The Supreme Court that banned God from the public schools has not been able to censor Him out of the Declaration of Independence. The Supreme Court has forbidden public school children to declare their dependence upon God, but the Declaration of Independence pledges the firm reliance of the American people forever on the continued protection of God's Divine Providence. . . .

The paramount question confronting America is: What is our national response to this challenge? Are we building the nuclear weapons we need to enable us to live in freedom and independence in the face of the Soviet threat? Make no mistake about it, our freedom of religion, speech, and press, our independence as a nation, and our entire Judeo-Christian civilization are possible only in a world defended by America's armed forces with their nuclear weapons. Without the superiority of American defenses over every potential aggressor, there can be no freedom, independence, or civilization as we know it.

If we want to hang on to the precious vitality that built our great nation, we must teach our young peo-

ple that the pass-word of freedom is Patrick Henry's eloquent "Give me liberty or give me death"—not the plea of the handout hunter, "Gimme, gimme, gimme." If we want our independence to endure, we must teach our young people to reject the lure of the Soviet appeasers who cry, "Better Red than dead"—and instead to kindle the patriotic fervor of Nathan Hale, the young teacher who said, "I regret that I have but one life to give for my country."

Further Resources

BOOKS

Blum, John Morton. *Years of Discord: American Politics and Society, 1961-1974.* New York: W.W. Norton & Company, 1991.

Carroll, Peter N. "Phyllis Stewart Schlafly." In *Famous in America: The Passion to Succeed.* New York: Weidenfeld & Nicolson, 1989.

Carter, Dan T. *George Wallace, Richard Nixon, and the Transformation of American Politics.* Waco, Tex.: Baylor University Press, 1992.

Coontz, Stephanie. *The Way We Never Were: American Families and the Nostalgia Trap.* New York: BasicBooks, 1992.

Faludi, Susan. *Backlash: The Undeclared War Against American Women.* New York: Anchor Books, 1991.

Felsenthal, Carol. *The Sweetheart of the Silent Majority.* Garden City, NY: Doubleday and Company, 1981.

Matusow, Allen J. *The Unraveling of America: A History of Liberalism in the 1960s.* New York: Harper & Row, 1984.

Schudson, Michael. *Watergate in American Memory: How We Remember, Forget, and Reconstruct the Past.* New York: BasicBooks, 1992.

WEBSITES

"The Eagle Forum." Available online at http://www.eagle forum.org (accessed April 6, 2003).

"Richard M. Nixon." Available online at http://www.white house.gov/history/presidents/rn37.html; website home page: http://www.whitehouse.gov (accessed April 6, 2003).

Sex and the New Single Girl
Handbook

By: Helen Gurley Brown

Date: 1970

Source: Brown, Helen Gurley. "The Rich, Full Life." In *Sex and the New Single Girl.* New York: Bernard Geis Associates, 1970, 253–254, 257–258, 262–263, 273,

About the Author: Helen Gurley Brown (1922–) wrote *Sex and the Single Girl,* an advice-style book targeted to young, single, working women; it was one of the ten best-selling books of 1962. *Sex and the Office* followed in 1964, and in 1965 Gurley Brown became editor of *Cosmopolitan,* a dying general-interest magazine. After Gurley Brown revamped its format to emphasize issues of interest to single women in their twenties, the magazine's fortunes immediately rebounded. ■

Introduction

Bored with her work as an advertising copywriter, Helen Gurley Brown seized upon her husband's suggestion that she write a self-help book aimed at young, single women. The result, 1962's *Sex and the Single Girl,* sold more than two million copies in its first month of release and led to *Sex and the Office* (1964), *Outrageous Opinions* (1966), and *Sex and the New Single Girl* (1970). Often writing about her own experiences as a single, working woman until the age of thirty-seven, the volumes transformed Brown into a lifestyle guru for women who increasingly viewed marriage as only one of many possible lifestyle choices. Although each book maintained the value of landing a suitable husband through self-improvement and sacrifice, they also overturned traditional gender roles and morality by encouraging women to find independence through their working and sexual lives—including sexual experiences outside of marriage.

As editor of *Cosmopolitan* after 1965, Brown ditched the magazine's failing format of short stories, medical news, and social critiques. Going after the eighteen-to-thirty-four-year-old female reader, Brown instead mixed articles about single working women with features on birth control, divorce, and beauty tips. The two topics that *Cosmopolitan* refused to cover during Brown's tenure as editor were articles on child rearing and education.

Significance

Some viewed Brown's frank promotion of guilt-free sexuality for women—coupled with the overtly sexual images typified by her magazine cover's "Cosmo Girl"—as a powerful blow to the sexual double-standard that refused to acknowledge women's sexuality on terms equal with men's. Others argued that Brown's approach was little more than crass marketing aimed at selling books and magazines to a working-class audience that cared little for such political statements. Whatever the case, Brown emerged from the decade as one of the most influential—and entertaining—spokespersons of the sexual revolution. By the time *Sex and the New Single Girl* appeared in 1970, *Cosmopolitian* reached more than two million readers each month in the United States, with several foreign editions bringing additional doses of self-improvement and sexuality to women around the world. Building on the advertising truism that "sex sells," Brown proved that explicit sex sold even better. The "Cosmo Girl," symbolized by the sexually provocative

Helen Gurley Brown, author of *Sex and the Single Girl,* works at her typewriter, January 23, 1965. Gurley Brown encouraged single women to feel good about themselves, countering the then traditional view that unmarried women are somehow flawed. © BETTMANN/CORBIS. REPRODUCED BY PERMISSION.

model appearing on each month's cover, was single, childless, and sexually liberated, making her an archetype of the sexual revolution begun by the introduction of the birth-control pill and encouraged by the changing social mores of the 1960s. By the time America's social climate turned more conservative in the 1980s, the overt and sometimes explicit images and commentary in magazines like *Cosmopolitan* had become so commonplace that they escaped serious criticism. Brown's campaign to free women from guilt about their sexual experiences also resonated through American society as more people rejected the idea that sex should be confined to the bounds of marriage.

Primary Source

Sex and the New Single Girl [excerpt]

SYNOPSIS: Mixing advice, anecdote, and social critique, Helen Gurley Brown published several bestselling books in addition to gaining fame as the editor of *Cosmopolitan.* In "The Rich, Full Life," taken from the 1970 book *Sex and the New Single Girl,* an update of her 1962 bestseller, Gurley Brown dishes out her views on the joys of single life with a breezy confidence in the power of self-fulfillment. "You may marry or you may not," she concludes. "In today's world that is no longer the big question for women."

I never met a completely happy single woman . . . or a completely happy married one!

A single woman admittedly has a special set of problems, but I think her worst one is not the lack of someone to belong to officially but the pippy-poo, day-to-day annoyances that plague her. For example, she has purchased a secondhand TV set from a private owner, and the 400-pound bargain is waiting in the trunk of her car to be brought upstairs and hooked up. She hasn't a date until next weekend—and anyway she outweighs him by ten pounds!

Or she has called a taxi to take her to the airport for a 6 A.M. departure. The taxi is now thirty minutes late and she must be on that plane to keep an important business appointment in another city. A married woman could simply wake up a husband. That's what I did once in such a predicament. I woke up a husband next door (*and* his wife, unfortunately, or I might have had more luck) and asked if he would mind driving me to a central part of town where I could find a cab. He was anything but thrilled with the idea, considering his wife's admonitions which I could hear from the bedroom, and I can't say I really blamed her. Mercifully, my taxi arrived while he was probably wondering how to say no.

These are the frustrating little experiences that vex and humiliate a single woman from time to time; however, they are not so frequent as to make life unendurable I've jotted down a few suggestions for coping with them.

And for a finale I can't resist adding a few last thoughts on how I think a single woman can have a happier life. . . .

Don't fold up over what you read—or don't read

Many publications deal with the problems of single women in the same vein as their articles on air pollution. I read a newspaper editorial recently which stated among other philosophies: "The bachelor is only half-man or half-woman. They are to be pitied." Now really!

Still other publications—*most* others for that matter—ignore the existence of single women entirely! For example, an otherwise excellent book entitled *Emotional Problems of Living,* by Oliver S.

English and G. H. J. Pearson (Norton), lists in the index under S:

Sheep, neurosis in

Shock therapy

Siblings

    adolescent rivalry

    traumatic effects of birth of

Sioux culture

Social worker

Where would a single woman look to find something about *her,* I wonder. (Don't worry—I looked. There's nothing under U for Unmarried or under B for Bachelor girl, either.)

You see enough picture stories in national publications about couples and families to make you feel like the sole occupant of a life raft. To further depress you, the couples and families are always blueberry-pie normal, as industrious as gophers, and as much at home in the world as an egg in custard.

We know the married state *is* the normal one in our culture, and anybody who deviates from "normal" has a price to pay in nonacceptance and nonglorification. There is no one universal "normal" time, however, for participating in the normal state of marriage. Furthermore, part of what you are, at the moment, missing in marriage may be well *worth* missing! . . .

Put your guilt away

Would it surprise you to know that your most wicked and base thoughts—secret fantasies—even leanings to homosexuality, are not unusual, and should not alarm you? You may share your desire to make love to an African lion with the vicar's wife— or even the vicar! Far from making you a depraved monster, your thinking is probably not even original. This is the consensus of psychiatrists. *Doing something* about these thoughts and not merely thinking them is what makes you cuckoo!

Perhaps you will reconsider the idea that sex without marriage is dirty. This is not a plea to get you into bed—your moral code is *your* business— but if you are already involved, you might remember that sex was here a long time before marriage. You inherited your proclivity for it. It isn't some random piece of mischief you dreamed up because you're a bad, wicked girl.

The psychiatrist I mentioned before frequently shows sexually guilt-ridden patients pictures from an entomology book. All the patients can figure out at first look is that they are seeing some kind of bug. "And do you know what the bugs are doing?" the doctor asks. No, they don't know. Well, the bugs, according to the text, are Mediterranean fruit flies engaged in the act of mating. "Okay, so what?" asks the patient. And the doctor explains that, by the patient's own concept of sex, he is looking at some *very dirty pictures, indeed!*

The point is, you may be much harder on yourself than you are on other creatures of nature who are less deserving of your tolerance. When you accept yourself, with all your foibles, you will be able to accept other people, too. And you and they will be happier to be near you. (Big order, but you can fill it.) . . .

Finally

You may marry or you may not. In today's world that is no longer the big question for women. Those who capture a man, so that they can collapse with relief, spend the rest of their days shining up their status symbol and figure they never have to reach, stretch, learn, grow, face dragons or make a living again are the ones to be pitied. They, in my opinion, are the unfulfilled ones.

You, my friend, if you work at it, can be envied the rich, full life possible for the single woman today. It's a good show . . . enjoy it from wherever you are, whether it's two in the balcony or one on the aisle—don't miss *any* of it.

Further Resources

BOOKS

Ballaster, Rosalind, et al. *Women's Worlds: Ideology, Feminity, and the Woman's Magazine.* Hampshire: Macmillian Education, 1991.

Brown, Helen Gurley. *I'm Wild Again: Snippets from My Life and a Few Brazen Thoughts.* New York: St. Martin's Press, 2000.

———. *The Late Show: A Semi-wild but Practical Survival Plan for Women Over Fifty.* New York: Morrow, 1993.

———. *Outrageous Opinions.* New York: B. Geis Associates, 1966.

———. *Sex and the Office.* New York: Bernard Geis Associates, 1964.

———. *Sex and the Single Girl.* New York: Bernard Geis Associates, 1962.

Douglas, Susan J. *Where the Girls Are: Growing Up Female with the Mass Media.* New York: Times Books, 1994.

Ehrenreich, Barbara, et al. *Re-Making Love: The Feminization of Sex.* New York: Doubleday, 1986.

McCracken, Ellen. *Decoding Women's Magazines: From "Mademoiselle" to "Ms."* New York: St. Martin's Press, 1993.

PERIODICALS

Ouellette, Laurie. "Inventing the Cosmo Girl: Class Identity and Girl-style American Dreams." *Media, Culture and Society,* 21, no. 3, May 1999, 359–383.

AUDIO AND VISUAL MEDIA

Sex and the Single Girl. Directed by Richard Quine. Warner Brothers Home Video. Videocassette, 1992.

"Christopher Street Liberation Day, June 28, 1970"

Poem

By: Fran Winant

Date: 1970

Source: Winant, Fran. "Christopher Street Liberation Day, June 28, 1970." In Jay, Karla and Allen Young, eds. *Out of the Closets: Voices of Gay Liberation.* New York: Douglas Book Corporation, 1972.

About the Author: Fran Winant (1943–) has been a noted writer, artist, and activist since the early 1970s. Winant's poetry has been widely anthologized and her poetry books, *Looking at Women* (1971), *Dyke Jacket* (1976), and *Goddess of Lesbian Dreams* (1980), were published by Violet Press. Her paintings were included in *Extended Sensibilities,* the first museum show by openly gay artists in 1982 at the New Museum and received a National Endowment for the Arts Award in 1990. Active in the holistic health and spirituality community, Winant also worked as an instructor and practitioner of massage therapy in New York City. ∎

Introduction

Legislation outlawing discrimination based on religious identity, race and ethnicity, and gender was enacted in the 1960s on all levels of government, in large part due to the efforts of the Civil Rights and women's movements. In contrast, most gay advocacy groups maintained a low profile in the United States. With social prejudice and statutes outlawing gay behavior holding sway in almost every community, few activists felt safe in openly conducting an equal-rights campaign for gays as other groups had done. The atmosphere of repression reigned even in New York City, a mecca of gay life in the United States. Police routinely raided bars and clubs with a gay clientele and arrested patrons if they lacked identification or were dressed in drag (under a then-state law requiring everyone to wear at least three pieces of clothing appropriate to one's gender).

The Stonewall Inn, located at 53 Christopher Street in Greenwich Village, was one of many gay bars in New York City, but it was the only one that allowed its patrons to dance. Its owners, who were part of the Mafia,

Participants in the "Gay Pride Week" parade demonstrate during their march from Greenwich Village to a rally in Central Park on June 30, 1974. The Stonewall Riot marked the beginning of the gay political movement. © BETTMANN/CORBIS. REPRODUCED BY PERMISSION.

paid about $2,000 each week in police protection; despite this safeguard, the Stonewall was temporarily shut down every few weeks as the police rounded up anyone without identification or anyone who was engaging in sexual conduct on the premises. In addition to the resentment of being threatened with arrest for being in a gay bar, the Stonewall's patrons also had to endure the anti-gay slurs of the police during the raids.

At some point during the police raid that took place in the early morning hours of Saturday, June 28, 1969, however, some of the Stonewall's customers—led by the drag queens who were singled out for arrest—began to shout at the police. Onlookers, who saw an officer strike one of the detainees, began to throw coins at the police. The violence began to escalate as the crowd, still numbering only a few dozen people, began to pick up other objects on the street and throw them at the police, who quickly retreated back inside the Stonewall. After the bar's doorman battered the front door with an uprooted parking meter, another person squirted lighter fluid through the broken front window and tossed in a match. As the bar went up in flames at about 3:00 A.M., a tactical assault team rescued the trapped officers. Street fighting continued for another half hour before the police were able to disperse the crowd. When thousands of

protesters and curious onlookers reassembled on Saturday night, the scene was repeated as street battles took place throughout Sheridan Square.

Significance

The Stonewall Riots—as the street battles came to be known—galvanized gay men and women in New York City, who publicized the event as an example of police brutality and civil rights violations. Determined to build on the sense of a common cause generated by the incident, the city's gay leaders held the first gay-pride rally, known as the Christopher Street Liberation Day, on June 18, 1970. The event, which drew between 2,000 and 10,000 people, later came to be known as "Gay Pride Day" (or in some places, "Gay Pride Week") and spread to dozens of other cities throughout the decade. The first National Gay and Lesbian Civil Rights March in Washington, D.C. drew a crowd of 100,000 people in 1979 and lent further visibility to gay Americans in public life.

As the beginning of the modern gay rights movement, the Stonewall Riots and their aftermath also led to important legislative and social changes. In 1973 the American Psychiatric Association removed homosexuality from its list of mental illnesses; that same year, the American Bar Association endorsed a resolution to act against laws that criminalized gay behavior. Gay-rights lobbying groups were also successful in getting dozens of cities to pass legislation barring discrimination based on sexual orientation in matters of employment and housing. The gay liberation movement showed that the spirit of protest fostered by the 1960s could take many different forms. As Charles Kaiser noted in a 2000 article in *The Advocate,* "Once it became clear that the establishment could be so disastrously wrong about the [Vietnam] war, its convictions about everything else—including homosexuality—suddenly became vulnerable to determined assaults. In 2003, the United States Supreme Court struck down the sodomy laws, legalizing gay sexual expression, and affirming each individual's right to define "the pursuit of happiness" for himself or her herself.

Primary Source

"Christopher Street Liberation Day, June 28, 1970"

SYNOPSIS: Written to commemorate the first large-scale gay pride rally in the United States, which took place in New York City one year after the Stonewall Riots, Fran Winant's poem emphasizes the common humanity shared by the protesters and their onlookers. It also strikes a tone of quiet defiance in the face of social prejudice and a determination to seek social justice through collective action. Rallies were held in Los Angeles, Chicago, and Boston in 1970; a quarter century after the Stonewall Riots, gay pride rallies took place in dozens of cities with participation at some events including half a million people.

with our banners and our smiles
we're being photographed
by tourists police and leering men
we fill their cameras
with 10,000 faces
bearing witness
to our own existence
in sunlight
from Washington Maryland
Massachusetts Pennsylvania
Connecticut Ohio
Iowa Minnesota
from Harlem and the suburbs
the universities
and the world
we are women who love women
we are men who love men
we are lesbians and homosexuals
we cannot apologize
for knowing
what others refuse to know
for affirming
what they deny
we might have been

the women and men
who watched us and waved
and made fists
and gave us victory signs
and stood there after we had passed
thinking of all they had to lose
and of how society punishes
its victims
who are all of us
in the end
but we are sisters and sisters
brothers and brothers
workers and lovers
we are together

we are marching
past the crumbling old world
that leans toward us
in anguish from the pavement
our banners are sails
pulling us through the streets
where we have always been
as ghosts
now we are shouting our own words
we are a community
we are society
we are everyone
we are inside you
remember
all you were taught to forget
we are part of the new world

photographers
grim behind precise machines
wait to record
our blood and sorrow
and revolutionaries beside them
remark
love is not political
when we stand against our pain
they say
we are not standing against anything
when we demand our total lives
they wonder
what we are demanding
cant you lie
cant you lie
they whisper they hiss
like fire in grass
cant you lie
and get on with the real work

our line winds
into Central Park
and doubles itself
in a snakedance
to the top of a hill
we cover the Sheep Meadow
shouting
lifting our arms
we are marching into ourselves
like a body
gathering its cells
creating itself
in sunlight
we turn to look back

on the thousands behind us
it seems we will converge
until we explode
sisters and sisters
brothers and brothers
together

Further Resources

BOOKS

Andryszewski, Tricia. *Gay Rights.* Brookfield, Conn.: Twenty-First Century Books, 2000.

Berman, Paul. *A Tale of Two Utopias: The Political Journey of the Generation of 1968.* New York: W.W. Norton & Company, 1996.

Button, James, and Barbara A. Rienzo and Kenneth D. Wald. *Private Lives, Public Conflicts: Battles Over Gay Rights in American Communities.* Washington: CQ Press, 1997.

Creekmur, Corey K. and Alexander Doty, eds. *Out in Culture: Gay, Lesbian, and Queer Essays on Popular Culture.* Durham: Duke University Press, 1995

Jay, Karla, and Allen Young. *Out of the Closets: Voices of Gay Liberation.* New York: Douglas Book Corporation, 1972.

Jennings, Kevin, ed. *Becoming Visible: A Reader in Gay and Lesbian History for High School and College Students.* Los Angeles: Alyson Publications, 1994.

Marcus, Eric. *Making History: The Struggle for Gay and Lesbian Equal Rights: An Oral History.* New York: Harper-Collins, 1992.

Vaid, Urvashi. *Virtual Equality: The Mainstreaming of Gay and Lesbian Liberation.* New York: Anchor Books, 1995.

PERIODICALS

Kaiser, Charles. "The Man Behind Stonewall." *Advocate,* August 15, 2000, 41.

Kopkind, Andrew. "After Stonewall." *Nation,* July 4, 1994, 4.

WEBSITES

"Lambda Legal Defense and Education Fund." Available online at http://www.lambdalegal.org (accessed April 5, 2003).

AUDIO AND VISUAL MEDIA

Before Stonewall: The Making of a Gay and Lesbian Community. Directed by Greta Schiller and Robert Rosenberg. 1984, First Run Features.

Out of the Past: The Struggle for Gay and Lesbian Rights in America. Directed by Jeff Dupre. 1998, Unapix.

Stonewall 25: Global Voices of Pride and Protest. Directed by John Scagliotti. 1994, Wolfe Video.

Woodstock: The Oral History

Eyewitness accounts

By: Diana Warshawsky and Richie Havens

Date: 1989

Source: Makower, Joel, ed. *Woodstock: The Oral History.* New York: Doubleday, 1989, 7, 8–9, 10, 12–13, 14, 185–190.

About the Authors: Diana Warshawsky, like many of those who went to the Woodstock Music and Art Fair in August 1969, had little idea of the magnitude of the event that would take place. She had heard that a concert was planned in upstate New York—with a rumored appearance by Bob Dylan—and when she ran into some acquaintances who were planning on going, she joined the group. Overwhelmed by the crowded conditions of the concert, Warshawsky left the event on the second day of the festival.

Richie Havens (1941–) born in New York City, was a popular folk guitarist and singer on the city's club scene by the early 1960s. After releasing several albums in the mid-1960s, Havens found mainstream success with *Something Else Again* in 1968. In addition to his work as a recording artist and concert performer, Havens was active in environmental causes as the founder of the Natural Guard, a children's educational foundation. Still a popular concert performer, in 2002 Havens released the album *Wishing Well.* ∎

Introduction

Those who came of age in the 1960s are often described as "The Woodstock Generation" in reference to one of the decade's most notable happenings. The Woodstock Music and Art Fair was organized by two wealthy entrepreneurs, John Roberts and Joel Rosenman, and Michael Lang and Artie Kornfeld, who initially brought a proposal to the investors to build a recording studio in Woodstock, New York. All of the organizers were then in their mid-twenties. The Woodstock project quickly evolved into plans for a three-day series of art exhibitions and concerts; although it was designed as a money-making venture by its organizers, the event also would attempt to capture some of the hipness of the West Coast "be-ins," free concerts that attracted thousands of young people. When the town of Woodstock, New York, refused to grant permission for the festival, the event was moved to Bethel, about 100 miles north of New York City. The organizers anticipated that about 60,000 people would attend the three days of music and exhibitions from August 15 to 17, 1969. Advance tickets sold for $6.50 for one day or $18.00 for the entire festival.

With media reports predicting that Bob Dylan would make an appearance at Woodstock, the highways leading from New York City to Bethel quickly jammed with carloads of people on their way to the event. As an estimated 400,000 people camped on Max Yasgur's farm, where the concert was set up, a seventeen-mile traffic jam closed down the roads leading into town. Despite the crowded conditions—made worse by the rain showers that turned most of the ground into a muddy mess—the event mostly lived up to its slogan, "Three Days of Peace and Music." Despite widespread marijuana and LSD use, there were few drug-related casualties or reports of violence among the concertgoers. Although Dylan did not make his expected appearance, Janis Joplin, Jimi Hendrix, the Who; Crosby, Stills, and Nash; and Joan Baez all made memorable appearances that were later released on a live album and documentary film. Although the promoters initially lost money when most of the audience members crashed the gates instead of buying tickets at Woodstock, they recouped their investment through album sales and film grosses.

Significance

The Woodstock Festival was arguably the defining moment of the 1960s. A celebration of youth culture, the event showcased the optimism of the 1960s through its music, as well as the cooperative spirit and rebellion of the era through the prevalence of drugs and rejection of traditional propriety. Although it started out as a profit-seeking venture, the organizers' inexperience, word-of-mouth anticipation, and proximity to New York City turned Woodstock into a mass spectacle, one that was amply covered by the media. Although some observers were horrified by the overcrowding and unsanitary conditions of the festival, others had a more positive outlook. As performer Richie Havens recalled in a *Life* magazine interview in 1994 to mark the twenty-fifth anniversary of the concert, "We were touted as an angry, violent, radical generation. I knew we needed to have a festival of us, the people. Woodstock belonged to all of the people who came. History was made on a lot of levels, from the New York State Thruway being closed down for the first time, to babies being born in the field, to no violence."

Woodstock took place just days after the Manson Family murders of Sharon Tate and her friends in Los Angeles exposed the dark side of the 1960s hippie culture. Woodstock also marked the end of the 1960s as a cultural period. The Altamont Festival, held later that year in California, resulted in the death of one concertgoer who was stabbed to death by the Hell's Angels motorcycle gang during a performance by the Rolling Stones, as well as the deaths of three other people. A little more than a year after Woodstock, two of its most notable performers, Jimi Hendrix and Janis Joplin, were both dead from drug overdoses. Attempts to revive the Woodstock spirit with concerts in 1994 and 1999 met with only partial success and were criticized for being prepackaged versions of an event most memorable for its spontaneity.

Primary Source

Woodstock: The Oral History [excerpt]

SYNOPSIS: Diana Warshawsky was one of the estimated four hundred thousand people who attended Woodstock. She heard of the concert through word

of mouth and traveled cross-country with friends in part because of a (false) rumor that Bob Dylan would perform. What she found was an enormous—but mostly peaceful and happy—crowd overwhelming the roads and other infrastructure around the concert. Warshawsky's strongest memory of the music at Woodstock is of Richie Havens's opening performance. Havens's appearance and his performance of the song "Freedom" (which he made up on the spot) made him into a star. Havens himself recounts how he and his band had to be flown in and out of Woodstock by helicopter because the roads were blocked. He also recalls being greatly impressed by the size and spirit of Woodstock, an event which he—like most others—had expected to be just a typical music festival.

Diana Warshawsky

I was living in San Francisco in the Haight-Ashbury area, sort of across the panhandle from the Haight proper, and I heard that there was going to be some kind of gathering of music and it was supposed to be in New York in a place called Woodstock and had something to do with a ranch owned by Bob Dylan. That's what I heard, that's what the rumor had it. And some of the people from the area were thinking of going. I really had no idea what it was going to be; I didn't read newspapers or watch TV at the time. If it was publicized, I didn't have any inkling. It was just something that sounded pretty interesting. And so I made arrangements to go. It just worked out that people from the area were going and I arranged to go with them. . . .

There was a guy in the area that had a Volkswagen that was just like a cargo van, and it had two seats in the front and just a cargo area in the back. So although it wasn't very hospitable, you know, he took a few people, not too many—maybe four or five people, something like that, all together. But much to my good fortune the van broke down in Elko, Nevada, in the middle of the heat. It was summer and it was hot and the van broke down and there was a Volkswagen dealer in Elko, Nevada. So we went to this Elko dealer and it sounded like the repairs were going to take a couple days to do. I wasn't friendly with or didn't really know any of the people I was riding with, including the guy whose van it was. And it turned out that parked at the same Volkswagen dealer were two young men from New York who were on their way back to New York, also to go to Woodstock. They had been traveling all over the country and their Volkswagen was nice and new and had just been fully repaired, and they were ready to start off and were amenable to having me come with them and help defray expenses—you know, split

Part of the crowd at the Woodstock Festival on August 17, 1969. People are climbing one of the sound towers in the background. An estimated four hundred thousand people attended what proved to be one of the most famous events of the 1960s. **AMALIE ROTHSCHILD/CORBIS-BETTMANN. REPRODUCED BY PERMISSION.**

gas and all of that. So I ended up for the rest of the journey going in a really nice brand-new van with curtains and ice boxes, and it was really nice. It was really a comfortable trip and they were very nice people, good company. They were from Scarsdale, so they were quite affluent and I guess that's how they had this nice new van. All the people I knew had just real scroungy stuff. . . .

. . . We arrived in Scarsdale at about four in the morning and took a shower, and I was met there and found myself in a convertible with my friend and his friends heading to upstate New York. It was very strange. I remember the weather was that smoggy, real kind of hazy weather they have on the East Coast. I'd never experienced it before. It was humid, the sky looked like it was going to rain, but it was hot. It was very confusing and it seemed real strange. I remember going across probably the Verrazano Bridge and, you know, being tired and sort of weirded out. But the strangest part was when we got close to Woodstock itself. The traffic became very thick and it was bumper-to-bumper traffic all going to Woodstock, and I had no idea this was going to be such a big thing. I thought it was really going

to be basically a small gathering and I had just happened to meet up with other people that were going and it was all coincidental. It was sort of scary and frustrating. The roads narrowed to a two-lane road, the road that actually led into where we were supposed to go, and there was bumper-to-bumper traffic in that one lane going in the proper direction, but people pretty quickly became impatient and they began to use the shoulder of the road as a second lane. Then, before long, they were using the shoulder of the opposite part of the road as another lane going there, so on a two-lane road there were three lanes of traffic all headed towards Woodstock. And eventually, I seem to recall, they may or may not have taken over the whole other side of the road. In other words, the road was packed with traffic, three to four lanes streaming into this area, and I don't think that many people knew exactly where they were going. They were just following the rest of the cars figuring they'd find it. . . .

. . . We had to park pretty far away and we had sleeping bags and duffel bags and walked for a long time to get there, you know, following streams of other people all walking with their sleeping bags and duffel bags, and hot, humid. We finally arrived at the area and it was a very strange scene. It was muddy and there was some grass. It was all in browns and grays, you know, from the sky and the overcast and the humidity, and there was a huge—like a big mud puddle is all I can call it—that was as big as a small swimming pool. And all these people had their clothes off and thought they were swimming or something, I don't know. They were all bathing in this muddy water and I remember—I'll never forget this— all these muddy brown bodies, you know, bathing and sort of frolicking in this water hole. It didn't look appealing at all to me. I thought, "Boy, who knows, some people will jump at the chance to do anything." The field was huge and it was surrounded, they had it all surrounded by barbed wire, this area that the concert was taking place in. And we eventually found, with our stuff with us, you know, found a spot in this field. I guess it was sort of like a dry, grassy field. We just walked in, I guess. I don't know what the story was. Were they selling tickets? Were there supposed to be tickets? . . .

. . . It wasn't ever an out of control situation. I know they had emergency stands, you know, in case somebody was flipping out or sick or hurt or anything, and it was a very peaceful group of people. People were just happy, you know, getting stoned and just being happy to be there. But I found it very unnerving to be with this many people inside a barbed wire. And there was a helicopter flying over. I got very paranoid and I didn't like it at all. The whole situation of just being—I felt like I was trapped because I knew I couldn't get out on the road, all the traffic was swarming in one direction. I was sort of encircled by barbed wire, a helicopter flying overhead, and I didn't like the feeling. I was having a good time because of, you know, being with my friends, the person I was with, and I remember, in terms of music, I have almost no recollection of the music except that the only performer that I remember is Richie Havens. I remember him and I remember really liking that and that's it. I don't know who else performed that night. Actually, I'd be curious to know.

I do remember that when the music was over for that evening, we sort of trudged down a road and found a relatively hospitable place to unroll sleeping bags off the side of the road, and slept that night. And there was no question about the fact that I wanted to leave the next morning. And so we ended up hitchhiking out of the area back into New York City. I guess I felt the potential of danger either from within or from without. They had us all caged in the barbed wire, especially with the helicopter flying over-

head, and it seemed more like a war zone that happened to be peaceful at the moment. It was real strange and I didn't care for it. . . .

Richie Havens

I was coming back from Europe the second time and getting ready to make my third album. I had heard about Woodstock before that because Michael Lang I had known before I went away, and he had talked about doing something. I had heard that they were going to try to do something like Monterey on the East Coast. That was the image of what it was going to be like.

Now, the consciousness—we have to put it in context, because a lot of people do not have the context out of which it came philosophically. And that is that in California, they had free concerts all the time—they were called "be-ins"—so this was a kind of a be-in for the first time on the East Coast. But Woodstock was going to be a real happening on the East Coast that was more organized and less a happening for the first time. So it came out of context for the philosophy, and it had a philosophy base and not just music.

I call it a cosmic accident myself. I call it a media event, created by the media and not by the promoters, as much as they would like it to have been more in their control. What happened was created by the media. When I did come back, I heard on the radio all around the country about this festival that was going to happen on the East Coast, and the news was, "Well, they found a place to do it." And the next two days the news was, "Well, they don't have a place to do it." So, mind you, all around the country, everybody's hearing this big music news item. When there was a finality of the location, people started to leave their places then. There were people from Alaska, from California—they drove from everywhere.

I went up Friday morning and I had no problem getting there because actually we left at five in the morning and there wasn't a car on the road going up. I didn't go to the field; we went to a hotel off the highway. It was seven miles away from where the concert was going to be held. There was a Holiday Inn and a Howard Johnson's on the other side of the road. All of the groups were staying in these two hotels.

I remember being in the hotel and the so-called stage management letting everybody know what was going on, which was the road was blocked. And as of this point, nobody is going to the field, and since it was already going on the weekend, it was hard to get certain things to happen. So they called out the helicopter help and they came back and knocked: "Helicopter's going to come." And they came back and knocked again: "Helicopter's not going to come." This went on about three times and finally, I'm sitting in my room, watching TV, and I hear a helicopter landing in the driveway of the Holiday Inn, and it's one of these little bubble guys, you know, with four seats in it. And because we only had two acoustic guitars and two conga players, we went over first. That was how I got over there. And there were very few people over there. Tim Hardin was there and maybe a couple of people who weren't going to play because their bands were nowhere in sight. That was how I had to go on first, because they came and asked me to go on first. . . .

. . . I actually was afraid to go on first, basically because I knew the concert was late and I knew that people paid for this and maybe it would be a little nuts. Flying over that crowd coming in in that bubble, I knew what being nuts could mean. And I didn't want to be trampled by a billion people. So I said, "Don't put me in front of your problem like this. Don't do this to me, Michael. I'm only one guy. My bass player isn't even here." He was walking on the road for twenty-five miles because the cars were backed up. He made it as I walked off the stage, he came walking up to the stage. They'd left the car on the New York Thruway twenty-five miles back and then walked, along with a lot of other people, and they partied all the way down the line and he got there just as I got off. . . .

. . . I just saw color to the top of the hill and beyond. When my eyes went from the foot of the stage up to the top of the hill and beyond, I went right up to the sky, I went right out to where the whole thing was. The best sound that I have ever played on outdoors to date happened at Woodstock. As a matter of fact, they said they heard it ten miles away in every direction, because they put those towers up there, and it bounced through those mountains. We not only did it for the crowd there, we did it for the whole countryside at that point. So it was a modular saturation level of vibrations into the planet. This was not just in that spot, it went ten miles all around, and that's a big circle of sound wave. . . .

. . . I did about four or five encores, till I had nothing else to sing, and then "Freedom" was created right there on the stage. That's how "Freedom" was created, on the stage. It was the last thing that I could think of to sing. I made it up. It was what I

thought of, what I felt—the vibration which was freedom—which I thought at that point we had already accomplished. And I thought, "God, this is a miracle. Thank God I got to see it." My whole consciousness of the whole thing was that this was a normal festival, and I had already been too overimpressed by the Newport Folk Festival with twelve thousand people and nothing was ever going to match that. So this wasn't too unusual in its musical aspects, but it was more unusual in the people who came. The people who were up in the mountains who thought they were on vacation in the Catskills who were over fifty to their eighties brought their grandchildren, thinking it was going to be a nice musical festival, and ended up staying for three days and helping everybody out. It was families, it was the policemen in the movie saying, "Leave the kids alone," it was a time when consciousness came about. My viewpoint of it was I finally crossed over the line where I don't have to worry anymore. About the whole planet, the entire planet.

I remember walking across that bridge they built back there, and I just made it because my conga drummer's foot went through and I remember turning around and looking at him and his drums bounced—one fell off and somebody caught the other one—and his foot went through that little ramp that they had that went over that back road, and I just couldn't believe it. He was up to his thigh on one leg down in this hole. That was my picture that I saw, and I just couldn't believe it. Then they got him out of there; he was O.K. and he was worried about his drum that fell off the thing more than he was worried about himself. And we got off and then we came down the stairs and that was when my bass player walked up.

While I was onstage, a few helicopter trips came in with stuff, and at that point it could start. They started rolling the stuff up the minute I was doing my first encore actually, and starting to put it in place for the next band that was going to come on. I spent the night backstage and walking around in the side woods and at some of the crafts area, but spent the night mostly backstage. We all were jamming back there, just hanging out really, and eating a lot.

They flew us back and I got the chance to fly over the whole field in an open Army helicopter, which gave me another point of view. Which was kind of interesting because here I was, sitting against the wall with another band and my group like soldiers in an Army helicopter with our equipment, guitars sitting there. And I look down the row and I flash so heavy, "This is what it's like in Vietnam, only it's guns, right?" And I look out the door and all I see is treetops. I actually fantasized tracers coming up out of the treetops. I actually did, all the way back to the hotel because there was nothing but treetops. There was never an open field from that point back to the hotel highway section and you couldn't see the ground and that put me anywhere in the world, and I was in Vietnam in that sense. And all I could think of was, "This has got to be what it's like, man, for all those soldiers, man, flying and ducking stuff coming up out of the damn trees, you know." And that's where I was at going back.

We ended up getting back to the hotel and packing up our stuff and driving out because I was playing in Michigan the next night, that same night that I got back. So we got into the car, the station wagon that brought us, and we went out to the New York Thruway. And there was not one car on the entire Thruway because it was closed all the way back to New York. We had the entire New York Thruway to ourselves completely. In my lifetime, that's one of the biggest highlights I've ever had, is to have the entire New York Thruway closed and us driving from there back to Newark Airport straight away.

Further Resources

BOOKS

Curry, Jack. *Woodstock: The Summer of Our Lives.* New York: Weidenfeld & Nicolson, 1989.

Rosenman, Joel, with John Roberts and Robert Pilpel. *Young Men with Unlimited Capital: The Story of Woodstock.* Reprint, Houston: Scrivenery Press, 1999.

Spitz, Bob. *Barefoot in Babylon: The Creation of the Woodstock Music Festival, 1969.* Reprint, New York: W.W. Norton & Co., 1989.

Young, Jean, and Michael Lang. *Woodstock Festival Remembered.* New York: Ballantine, 1979.

PERIODICALS

Fields-Meyer, Thomas, and Patrick Rogers."Long Time Gone: It's Thirty Years Later: Do You Know Where Your Flower Children Are?" *People* 52, no. 7, August 23, 1999, 58.

Simon, Josh, and Gregory Heisler. "Back to the Garden." *Life* 17, no. 8, August 1994, 32.

WEBSITES

"1969 Woodstock Festival and Concert." Available online at http://www.woodstock69.com (accessed April 5, 2003).

"Richie Havens." Available online at http://www.allmusic.com (accessed April 5, 2003).

AUDIO AND VISUAL MEDIA

Woodstock: Three Days of Peace and Music. Directed by Michael Wadleigh. 1970, Warner Studios.

Woodstock: Three Days of Peace and Music: Twenty-Fifth Anniversary Edition. Atlantic Records, 1994.

Days of Decision: An Oral History of Conscientious Objectors in the Military During the Vietnam War

Oral history

By: Mike Ferner

Date: 1989

Source: Gioglio, Gerald R., ed. *Days of Decision: An Oral History of Conscientious Objectors in the Military During the Vietnam War.* Trenton: The Broken Rifle Press, 1989, 27–30, 63, 65, 180, 183, 188.

About the Author: Mike Ferner (1951–), born in Toledo, Ohio, struggled to reconcile the media's anti-Communist rhetoric with the moral teachings on pacifism. As a hospital corpsman in the U.S. Navy, Ferner treated soldiers from the Vietnam War who had serious injuries, and the experience deepened his opposition to the war. Ferner returned to Toledo to work as a union organizer for the Farm Labor Organizing Committee and as an activist for the Toledo Coalition for Safe Energy and the Veterans for Peace. ∎

Introduction

The United States's involvement in Vietnam was one of many foreign interventions intended to stem the influence of communism during the Cold War. A French colony that had been occupied by the Japanese during World War II, Vietnam asserted its independence under the communist rebel leader Ho Chi Minh in 1946. The French attempted to maintain control of the colony and fought Ho Chi Minh in a civil war that lasted until 1954, when they withdrew from Vietnam after a series of military defeats. During this period the United States gave the French $1 billion in aid and military equipment, but even that was not enough to keep Vietnam under France's control.

After France's defeat the region was divided into North Vietnam, led by Ho Chi Minh and other communists, and South Vietnam. The United States backed South Vietnam, installing Ngo Dinh Diem as president there, to try and stem the communists from taking over the entire country. Ngo Dinh Diem proved to be corrupt and unpopular, however, and guerilla attacks supported by North Vietnam threatened to overthrow Diem and unite the country under the communists. As the threat of a communist take-over grew, the United States increased its commitments in South Vietnam. The military buildup that began under President Eisenhower picked up pace during the Kennedy administration in the early 1960s. With the 1964 Gulf of Tonkin Resolution, President Lyndon B. Johnson received broad authority from Congress to increase America's involvement in the region and act as he saw fit to stop the spread of communism there. By early 1968 about half a million American soldiers were in Vietnam.

Although most Americans continued to support the government's declared anti-communist efforts in the military buildup in Vietnam through 1967, the television images of the war's violence gradually turned public opinion against the war. So too did reports of atrocities committed by America's South Vietnamese allies and by American troops themselves. The March 1968 My Lai Massacre, in which American soldiers killed an estimated 300–500 Vietnamese civilians, created a storm of protest among antiwar advocates. The communist's large Tet Offensive of early 1968, during which they struck deep into South Vietnam, also diminished support for the war among many Americans. They increasingly saw the war effort as a failed exercise. As a presidential candidate in 1968, Richard M. Nixon capitalized on the growing skepticism about Vietnam by pledging to reduce the number of American troops fighting there. In 1972, 150,000 American soldiers remained in the country; a January 1973 international peace settlement finally sent the rest of the troops home. In April 1975, South Vietnam fell to Communist forces, and a formal reunification of the country followed in July 1976.

Significance

It took several years for the antiwar sentiment to prevail among Americans. In 1965, after the Gulf of Tonkin Resolution was passed, 61 percent of Americans supported the intervention in Vietnam, but by 1971, the same percentage of respondents to a public-opinion survey viewed America's involvement in Vietnam as wrong. Although antiwar protests on college campuses dominated the media coverage of the war's domestic side through the 1960s, the strongest and earliest opposition to the war came from the ranks of the working class. College students were eligible for draft deferments until 1969, and young men with political connections could often arrange for service in the National Guard; others were able to have a sympathetic doctor diagnose a medical condition to get a draft exemption. Each of these factors meant that the brunt of the fighting by American troops in the Vietnam War was borne by working-class and poor men who could not escape the draft.

Some young men who lacked the resources to avoid the draft left the country as "draft dodgers." Between 50,000 and 100,000 men left the United States to evade conscription; some of them traveled to Europe, but most simply slipped over the border to Canada. Less common were the conscientious objectors, men who were exempted from service because their moral or religious beliefs forbid them from participating in war. Unless one was a member of a religion with a well-known commit-

ment to pacifism it could be very difficult to obtain conscientious objector status.

As a central conflict of the Cold War, America's experience in Vietnam showed the limits of American power on the international scene. It also demonstrated the importance of public opinion on the implementation of American foreign policy, particularly where troops were deployed in large numbers. Although the government's actions in conducting the war came under harsh scrutiny for their secrecy and lack of accountability, the war also showed mass protests by Americans could be effective in forcing a change in the government's policies—even in the face of the communist menace.

Primary Source

Days of Decision: An Oral History of Conscientious Objectors in the Military During the Vietnam War [excerpt]

SYNOPSIS: Mike Ferner is one of several conscientious objectors to the Vietnam War (1964–75) who tell their stories in *Days of Decision*. Ferner enlisted in the U.S. Navy in 1969 and served until 1972. He did so primarily because he knew that as a young man who was not attending college, he would surely be drafted into the Army if he did not enlist first. Like many Americans growing up in the 1960s, Ferner initially had mixed feelings about the war. Although he had some moral objections to warfare before he enlisted in the U.S. Navy, it was not until he witnessed firsthand the human suffering of war that he became a conscientious objector. In these passages he describes the development of his objection to the war in the context of the social changes that took place in the late 1960s and early 1970s.

I came from a family of eight kids, and for some reason, I'm kind of an oddball in terms of how we turned out. I grew up in a very small farming village just west of Toledo; we had, I think, fourteen kids in our eighth grade graduating class. So, it was very small. Being a traditional Catholic, in the early and mix-Sixties, I got a strong dose of rabid anticommunism. We were taught by over-the-hill Franciscan nuns who'd tell us jibberish horror stories about communists and how they had dominated Red China, and one thing and another. We got several Catholic publications at our house. And, in the mid-to-late Sixties when the Vietnam war was building up, there was a steady dose of things like the communists were the "bad guys" and the U.S. government was there trying to keep the peace.

In grade school I remember visiting migrant labor camps with my mom. There were a lot of migrant farm-

A soldier helps an injured Vietnamese woman at an aid station outside of Saigon in 1968. © BETTMANN/CORBIS. REPRODUCED BY PERMISSION.

workers in the area when I was growing up. My mom wanted to learn Spanish so she went to the camps. I went with her and saw the conditions that people lived in. I can remember writing our local Congressman telling him that something had to be done about those camps. They were terrible. I think that was the first activist sort of thing I did. Just little things like that. I'm a union organizer now, so organizing and activism have been a recurrent theme for me.

I didn't really fit in at school; I felt more like I stood out like a sore thumb—only because I was from a little farm town. There I was, at a Jesuit high school in Toledo, with city kids from families with higher-than-average incomes; I just never quite fit in. But, I was in the band for a few years and on the track team. I felt a need to excel for some reason. . . . To my classmates, I was known to be outspoken and quick with an opinion, even if those opinions changed every week.

Through grade school and high school I was taught two really different views of the world: the conservative, anticommunist, flag-waving view, and that which appealed to higher moral values, like "Thou shalt not kill," and concern for one's fellow man. At that point I thought the U.S. Marines were great; so, in speech class I gave a speech on how wonderful the Marines were, but then the next week I'd talk about the horrors of war.

This kind of stuff kept bouncing back and forth inside my head. I didn't know how I was going to come out of this. I was approaching high school graduation knowing I did not want to go to college, and knowing if you didn't go to college, you got drafted. I did not know, from one week to the next, whether or not I was going to enlist in the Marines, or go to Canada. I bounced back and forth between those two things all the time. I thought about this every day, all day long, some days.

At the time, I was kind of a hawk; I had full-color pictures of battleships stuck all over my wall. The only thing I knew about current events was what was reported in the mass media. My family didn't take popular magazines, although I did see *Life* magazine occasionally. But obviously, there were things from a variety of sources that made an impression on me. Also, my English teacher, a priest, talked about what was going on at the 1968 Democratic Convention and about the riots in the cities. It all seemed completely foreign to me. It really opened my eyes to think that somebody in Toledo would be concerned about what was happening in other parts of the country.

I knew there were a lot of people getting killed in Indochina. They were being blown up by ships like those I had plastered on the wall of my room. To a seventeen year old kid it looked kind of neat to see a cruiser belching orange flames out at the enemy. I would think about what it was like; but the difference was I carried it a bit further at times. I imagined what it was like when the shells exploded in a village. I don't know how or why I thought about those things, but I did. . . .

I enlisted, I wasn't drafted. I figured, as soon as I graduated I was probably going to get drafted. So, I never even went down to the draft board. That was one experience I didn't have to go through; I never had the draft physical, or anything.

I did file for CO status from Selective Service, but the draft board turned me down. I remember quoting part of *The Universal Soldier,* a song by Buffy Sainte-Marie, as part of my reason for being opposed to war. The draft board didn't even give me a hearing, just a letter stating my CO claim was rejected. They said I wasn't one of the standard religions—Quakers or other groups—that they gave CO status to. At the time, I just didn't know my own mind or what I wanted to do. Later, when I applied for discharge from the Navy, I knew what I wanted to do. It took me awhile, it took almost three-and-a-half years, but things finally became clear to me. If the Navy told me "tough luck kid, you're not a Quaker, you can't get a CO," I wouldn't have bought it. But the draft board knew what it was doing, and I wasn't sure.

Anyhow, when I graduated from high school, I was eighteen-and-a-half, and from what I knew about the Army, getting drafted wasn't something I particularly wanted to do. So, I chose something closer to what I wanted, which was the Navy. I enlisted in October 1969. . . .

My brain was really churning that first day in the military, just like it was in high school. I still felt faced with, and almost overwhelmed by, those same moral dilemmas; but now I'd taken the plunge, I was

in. Adding to this confusion was that every day lots of things happened that made no sense at all. In fact, some of the people in authority—the "lifers" we quickly learned to call them—did things that not only didn't make sense, they were downright cruel. For example, one Sunday, the only day of the week you could kind of relax, a lifer who wasn't even in authority over our company brought his girlfriend through the barracks. Just to impress her, I guess, he had us all down doing push-ups as he barked commands. . . .

Early on in boot camp we had to drill with our "pieces," rifles that didn't work; but we still had to drill with them, learn the "Manual of Arms" and so forth. I was thinking, you know, "Why am I doing this bullshit. What is the purpose of this nonfunctional rifle?" It just angered me. I knew I was going to be a hospital corpsman and I didn't have to know what those things were about, but yet, I had to drill. And I started thinking, "What would happen if I refused to drill with the pieces?" It wasn't until later that I realized how closely connected the hospital corps was in spirit, and in function, to the combat troops.

Hospital corpsman training was at Great Lakes, too. We got our training manuals on the first day, and there, in the introduction to the book, it said something that smacked me right in the face: "The purpose of the Naval Hospital Corps is to keep as many men at as many guns for as many days as possible." That was the first day! In the introduction to the book! I said, "Boy, I'm going to have problems with this. I'm not going to be able to salve my conscience doing this." Things progressed from there. . . .

I worked at the Great Lakes Hospital for a year-and-a-half. During that time I began to question the militaristic part of me that had been real strong when I was younger. Bits and pieces of that remained. It took a long time to work through this, and to finally decide that war was wrong—that it was not the thing to do. In the meantime, I continued to have other, contradictory thoughts, like, the war represented a historical period and I should experience it to the max.

Now, I worked on a psychiatric ward and a neurosurgery ward, and I saw a lot of brain and nerve damage caused by battle wounds. In the surgery ward we pieced guys back together who were only a couple of years older than I was. Those guys had pieces of their heads missing, and stuff like that—I worked on those kinds of cases for a year-and-a-half—and, as I talked to more and more Vietnam vets, it really began to sink in. I slowly began to challenge a lot of the views I had about duty, God, and country; that is, what duty was and how we should carry it out.

■ ■ ■

In my CO application, I basically talked about the experiences I had patching guys up, thinking that something was wrong there, and how I wasn't going to be part of it. When you file for CO status, they send you to a line officer, a chaplain and a psychiatrist. While I was waiting for the boat to come back I did my psychiatrist interview. My first reaction was to question the whole process. I thought, "These guys think I'm nuts, because I don't want to participate in this crazy, fuckin' war; but obviously, they're the crazy ones."

When the boat came back I saw the chaplain and the line officer. The interviews went really well. The psychiatrist and the chaplain recommended that I get out. But the officer listened to my story, read my application and wrote a report that said, "Mike is sincere, but he should not be discharged, he should get noncombatant status and finish his tour." I had ten months left in my four-year tour when my claim was rejected. . . .

This is what happened. My lawyer contacted the Bay area Congressmen; they, in turn, wrote telegrams to the Secretary of the Navy, the Commander of the Pacific Fleet and to the captain of my boat. Boy, you talk about the shit hitting the fan. It hit the fan royally! The next morning I was called down to Personnel and processed out of the Navy. The Personnel clerk told me, "The captain said to get the fuck off the ship." I was escorted, with a military guard, out the gates of the Naval Base. I was so elated, you couldn't have brought me down to the ground if you had skyhooks to pull me down. . . .

While I was in the Navy I worked with the American Friends Service Committee, the Quaker peace organization. I went to their San Francisco office and learned how to write press releases, how to leaflet, and how to talk to reporters.

I also stuck with the ACLU case brought against the Navy for not allowing me to petition on the *USS Hancock.* The case was called "Allan versus Monger." Monger was the captain of the ship. The case had to be brought by another serviceman since I was no longer in the military. So, my friend who helped me petition had the nerve to allow his name to be put on it. We beat them at the first level of federal court. They appealed, and we won again.

There were a couple of other First Amendment cases that became part of this case. There was another petition case from the *USS Ranger,* and one from an Air Force captain raising the issue of hair length as a matter of personal expression. So, the ACLU combined these cases. We went through all the appeal processes, and eventually it went to the Supreme Court. But, the case was not heard on my issue, nor the *USS Ranger* petition case—it was heard on the haircut issue. The petition cases would win or lose on that issue. By this time, there had been enough reactionary appointments to the Supreme Court that we lost. We went that far, but we didn't make it.

I got discharged at the end of March 1973 and my boat sailed back to Vietnam in May. I joined the protest that was held as the boat sailed out of San Francisco Bay. It was kind of an emotional moment for me, because of the guys I knew who were going back to Vietnam.

I continued working with the American Friends Service Committee until I left California in September 1973. The peace treaty had been signed and things were beginning to wind down. So, even though I really wanted to stay in California, I packed up my wife and daughter and went back to Ohio.

I wasn't in Ohio a week when I felt all this fervor and interest that made me want to do something. But, there was nothing going on, there was no peace movement that I knew of. Well, I saw an environmentalist on the nightly news who was trying to do something about water pollution. So, I hooked-up with him, asked him if he wanted some help, and worked on that particular issue for a little while.

Then I started reading about nuclear power and nuclear waste, and I realized something was drastically wrong. Normally, I would not have questioned it, but I knew the public was being lied to about Vietnam; so, I had a very jaundiced view about other things that came from official channels.

The more I looked into nuclear power, the screwier it seemed. In 1975, I helped form an organization called the Toledo Coalition for Safe Energy. The process of working on safe energy issues and reading about other social issues brought me in contact with a guy who worked with the American Federation of State, County and Municipal Employees. I asked him about the union and what they were working on. He told me they were trying to organize a hospital in Toledo. So, I offered to give him a hand. Before I knew it, I was in there talking to

A large anti-war movement developed in the United States in response to military actions in Vietnam. This anti-Vietnam War poster plays on the traditional Army recruiting poster with its picture of Uncle Sam saying "I Want You!" **THE ADVERTISING ARCHIVE LTD. REPRODUCED BY PERMISSION.**

the employees trying to get them to join the union. That campaign didn't work, but I began to look into unions more.

I slowly began to see connections between safe energy, environmentalism, jobs, and labor issues. After I'd been in the safe energy movement for several years it became clear to me that job issues, and the kinds of energy policies we pursued, were very much related. What turned out to be good for the environment, also turned out to be the best way to create jobs.

More and more, I had trouble fitting into the normal scheme of things. I didn't think my CO experience caused me difficulties adjusting, in fact I kind of wrote the experience off as an interesting chapter that was behind me. But when I got out of the Navy, I fit the "angry young man" picture pretty well. The things that were supposed to be important—like a job and family responsibilities—seemed to pale next to what I felt were burning social issues that demanded attention.

Before long my marriage hit the rocks. My wife told me she'd try and stick by me, even though it was becoming clearer that I wasn't going to be able to balance staying married and being a traditional breadwinner. It might sound odd to some people that there could be something more important than your family, but after my experience in the Navy, there were things I felt I needed to do, things that, more and more, were not related to my family.

A society that was ruining the environment seemed pretty screwed up to me, especially when such a thing was accepted without people fighting back. So, I fought for the things I believed were important; and I felt more at peace when I spoke out on things that were too important to ignore.

I've faced many frustrations in the safe energy and the labor movements, but it's good work, because it's doing something for other people. A lot of times it seems like I'm banging my head against a wall, but there are lots of good reasons not to despair. Things still get crazy and hectic, but these days I feel much better.

I see myself as part of a long line of activists that fight for social justice. I'll probably never see the things come about that we are working for, but to simply work towards them is a worthwhile goal. I might live to be fifty or sixty or eighty and I'll keep doing this. Along the way, I'll try to have as much fun as I can with the people I'm doing it with, and that'll be my reward.

On another level, I have signed the Pledge of Resistance as a way of protesting U.S. involvement in Central America. I saw Ron Kovic [author of *Born On The Fourth Of July*] speak at a peace rally a couple of years ago, and I was in tears. He compared what's going on in Central America with Vietnam. I could never say what he said as well as he did, but in my heart I feel the same.

I joined Veterans For Peace (VFP) because the group made sense to me. Unlike the Veterans of Foreign Wars and the American Legion, which tend to support the administration and the Pentagon, VFP is interested in trying to change U.S. policies to be less militaristic. VFP members are doing this as vets, claiming a right to speak out, because we have served in the military, and we know there is a better way.

VFP members speak at local high schools about the military, Vietnam and U.S. foreign policy. This is something that is very important and very rewarding. It gives me a chance to talk about the real causes of social unrest in places like Central America, what happens when we take our government's say at face value, and what alternatives exist.

I also went to Guatemala, Honduras and Nicaragua with VFP. We saw the conditions there, and we listened to the U.S. embassy officials. They gave us the same rationale for U.S. involvement in Central America that I heard before and during the Vietnam war. I saw VFP members, combat veterans from Vietnam, stand up to these embassy officials. We told them they were lying to the American public, and that we would do our damnedest to see that they didn't get away with it. These veterans for peace were the truest patriots I've ever seen.

So, this government isn't going to do it again, not without discovering that people won't stand for it. You see, I've never forgotten that people in power are vulnerable, it was a sweet day when I learned this. Whether it's standing up to the Navy, trying to organize employees, going up against the officials of some utility company, or whatever, those kinds of people can't scare me.

Further Resources

BOOKS

Appy, Christian G. *Working Class War: American Combat Soldiers and Vietnam.* Chapel Hill: University of North Carolina Press, 1993.

Blum, John Morton. *Years of Discord: American Politics and Society, 1961–1974.* New York: W.W. Norton & Company, 1991.

Farber, David. *The Age of Great Dreams: America in the 1960s.* New York: Hill and Wang, 1994.

Kovic, Ron. *Born on the Fourth of July.* New York: McGraw-Hill, 1976.

Matusow, Allen J. *The Unraveling of America: A History of Liberalism in the 1960s.* New York: Harper & Row, 1984.

Tollefson, James. *The Strength Not to Fight: An Oral History of Conscientious Objectors of the Vietnam War.* Boston: Little, Brown & Co., 1993.

Zinn, Howard. "The Impossible Victory: Vietnam." In *A People's History of the United States.* Reprint New York: Harper & Row, 1990.

AUDIO AND VISUAL MEDIA

Born on the Fourth of July. Directed by Oliver Stone. 1989, Universal.

What You Can Do for Your Country: An Oral History of the Peace Corps

Oral histories

By: Roger Landrum, Lynda Edwards, Robert Marshall, and George McDaniel

Date: 1991

Source: Schwarz, Karen, ed. *What You Can Do for Your Country: An Oral History of the Peace Corps.* New York: William Morrow & Co., 1991, 37, 42, 76–77, 117–118, 120–121, 123.

About the Authors: Roger Landrum, Lynda Edwards, Robert Marshall, and George McDaniel entered the Peace Corps with similar expectations and left with different perspectives on their experience. All were profoundly moved by the cross-cultural impact of their tours, yet they looked back with varying degrees of their initial enthusiasm and idealism intact. For some, the differences between the Peace Corps's stated goals and the reality of their assignments left them somewhat cynical about the experience. Others emerged with a renewed commitment to community and international development. ∎

Introduction

During a campaign stop at the University of Michigan in October 1960, Democratic candidate John F. Kennedy spontaneously asked the crowd of students if they would be willing to devote years of their lives to helping people in less developed countries. His off-the-cuff remarks drew a thunderous response; after Kennedy was elected president, forming an international public service program became a priority of the new administration. Although private groups, typically missionary organizations, had undertaken such efforts in the past, the new program would be the first large-scale sustained effort by the federal government to promote international understanding through community development. As Kennedy declared in his inaugural address on January 20, 1961, "To those people in the huts and villages of half the globe struggling to break the bonds of mass misery, we pledge our best efforts to help them help themselves, for whatever period is required—not because the communists may be doing it, not because we seek their votes, but because it is right. If a free society cannot help the many who are poor, it cannot save the few who are rich." Shortly after taking office, Kennedy signed an executive order creating the Peace Corps, and the first volunteers to Ghana and Tanzania left in August 1961 to begin their assignments.

In an era when international travel was not yet a common experience, the Peace Corps was a symbol of Kennedy's "New Frontier," a reference to his administration's social and legislative agenda that included an ambitious space program. The program also embodied Kennedy's pragmatic idealism; although its chief goal was to help train workers in local communities in less developed nations, the Peace Corps was also designed to foster goodwill toward America wherever its volunteers went. By the time Kennedy was assassinated in late 1963, 7,300 Peace Corps volunteers were stationed in forty-four countries, with half working in the field of education.

Significance

Typical of most new endeavors, the Peace Corps endured some well-publicized criticism of its first efforts. As most of its volunteers came from the ranks of the white, college-educated, middle class, some viewed it as an elitist organization that could not hope to reach out to poor people in other countries. Others pointed to the difficulty in sustaining Peace Corps projects in the long run, as the typical tour of duty lasted less than two years. Still others questioned whether the government should have funded such a project in the first place, particularly in countries run by repressive dictatorships. Some volunteers added to the criticism by noting that many of their projects were unrealistic to undertake or not feasible to complete with the resources available at the local level. Despite the criticism, the Peace Corps remained one of the most popular government programs of the decade and was kept in place by later administrations. As the embodiment of the optimism of the 1960s, the Peace Corps may have been President Kennedy's most enduring legacy.

Although it was founded with the intent to counter the international influence of communism during the Cold War, the Peace Corps expanded into eastern Europe after the fall of the Soviet Union in the early 1990s. Forty years after its founding, the Peace Corps remained active with 7,000 volunteers in seventy countries. As of 2003, more than 165,000 Peace Corps volunteers had served in 135 countries. The Peace Corps was also the model for a domestic version of the program, AmeriCorps, which was established by the National and Community Service Act of 1993. Like the Peace Corps, AmeriCorps matched volunteers in the areas of education, public health and safety, and the environment with existing local community programs.

Primary Source

What You Can Do for Your Country: An Oral History of the Peace Corps [excerpt]

> **SYNOPSIS:** These excerpts from *What You Can Do for Your Country* tell the stories of four Peace Corps volunteers. Roger Landrum was one of the first Peace Corps volunteers to go abroad, teaching in

Nigeria from 1961 to 1963. Lynda Edwards served in the Dominican Republic from 1964 to 1966. She faced problems and misunderstandings because of local customs, but used this experience to start an informal women's health program for local women. Robert Marshall, who served in two African countries from 1968 to 1970, joined the Peace Corps to avoid the military draft. George McDaniel also joined the Peace Corps in part to avoid the military draft. He was drafted anyway, and his tour of duty to the African nation of Togo in 1968 was cut short.

Roger Landrum

I didn't go to a lot of speeches in college but I went to hear Kennedy because someone told me he was probably going to run for President. This was in 1959. I remember him quoting the line from the Robert Frost poem that went, "miles to go before I sleep," and then dashing off the stage. It was like a meteor going through the room. I followed his campaign and when he announced the Peace Corps idea, I wrote him a letter saying, "If you will do it, I will volunteer."

I grew up in rural Michigan and I'd never been overseas before. I was at my mother's house when the telegram came inviting me to train for Nigeria. I remember my hands were shaking as I opened it. I had never heard of Nigeria but I definitely felt I was participating in history. This was a new era of American participation in the world. Peace Corps volunteers were the front-line people making fresh contact with a whole bunch of newly independent nations. There was a sense of exhilaration about maybe carrying forth democracy and establishing new relations with Asia, Africa, and South America. . . .

The president of Nigeria, Nnamdi Azikiwe, told Sargent Shriver that he wanted to establish a four-year American-style university. There was only one other university in Nigeria at the time. He told Shriver he was having trouble recruiting faculty and asked him for a big contingent of teachers. The Peace Corps made up a third of the teaching staff at this new university.

They put us in these one-room cells in the student dorms. There were no screens on the windows, so whenever I turned on the light swarms of bugs came in. These three-inch rhinoceros beetles would fly in and when they hit the wall it sounded like a bomb exploding. The mattress was made of packed straw, so after a time your body position was sunk into the straw and you couldn't move.

We were a little intimated living among all these Africans and it was hard to cope. The students were

The Peace Corps' first volunteers gather outside the plane that would carry them to Ghana, in Africa, for teaching assignments, August 29, 1961.
AP/WIDE WORLD PHOTOS. REPRODUCED BY PERMISSION.

from the villages and they'd wake up when the sun rose. There would be this tremendous hubbub of noise as they headed down to the showers. They'd be chattering away at the top of their lungs and singing and turning on their radios. We never got enough sleep. One of the volunteers in our group was this very crusty veterinarian and one morning he came out of his room and yelled, "You black bastards, shut off those radios."

Africans have no sense of private property. They would go into your room when you weren't there and shuffle through your things. That was culturally appropriate behavior. Some of the volunteers threatened to quit. But the rest of us were wedded to the Peace Corps ideals and we were going to stick it out no matter how miserable it got. . . .

Lynda Edwards

The people in my barrio thought I must be a prostitute since prostitutes are the only women who live by themselves. One day a delegation of three women came to visit me and said, "Although you're a prostitute, you never get pregnant." A light bulb went on in my head and I decided that I would play along. "I have a special method," I told them, "a saline-soaked sponge." I also told them about the well-baby clinic which gave out these things and I explained the rhythm method.

After that day, the neighborhood women would come to my house one or two at a time. Some would come right out with it and ask, "Where's the clinic?" But most were a little embarrassed. "We heard that you could tell us some things about health," they would say. So we'd make small talk for a while before they broached the topic. We would talk about the weather and then get to how hard it was to feed so many children and get them all through school. "Sometimes you can limit a family," I would say. "Isn't that good?" Some women didn't know how you got pregnant. They thought you'd get pregnant if you ate spaghetti with lemon. When I explained it to them, they thought it was a tremendous joke.

Volunteers were prohibited from talking about birth control but I was discreet. If the Peace Corps told me to stop, I don't think I would have and I might have been sent home. . . .

Robert Marshall

Everyone at Harvard was very eager to find something that would get them out of the draft. Joining the reserve units was very common. Some of my friends were gorging themselves on chocolate to make their acne worse so they could get exempted on skin problems. Another guy was working on his flat feet. The Peace Corps was one of the easier options and also a noble one. It was very popular at Harvard because of the Kennedy legacy. That spirit was still around.

When I applied to the Peace Corps, I requested Thailand, the Philippines, or Malaysia because I had lived in Japan as an exchange student during my senior year in high school and had taken courses in Asian history. But I was assigned to Libya, which nobody had ever heard of at that time. Other than people in the oil business, no one had ever gone there.

I was posted to the most isolated site in the country. It took me two weeks to get there. I hitched a ride on a Land-Rover which the Ministry of Education was sending out to deliver some school books. We kept getting stuck in the sand, and since there were no roads in the desert—you follow truck tracks and the lights marking the oil fields—we got lost a couple of times.

The town of three thousand had three public buildings: the town hall, the hospital, and the schoolhouse. The Libyan government had decided that every fifth-grade student in the country was going to have two hours a day of English instruction and they invited the Peace Corps to fill those spots. That was my assignment. I lived in a room in the school and wore a suit every day, even though I had to walk three miles between the two schools where I taught.

The first month everyone in the town invited me to their homes because they felt this obligation to have me over and give me dinner. They all served spaghetti with tomato sauce and a piece of mutton. The hot spices made me sick every time. They thought I must be lonely so they'd come by and just sit in my room for hours. I resented the intrusion upon my time. I wanted to be a Peace Corps volunteer and relate to the society from nine to five. But after five, I wanted to do my own thing: prepare lessons, correct papers, listen to the BBC, read novels, and take care of my room. But time just doesn't exist for people in the desert. They'd just sit and not say anything. Sometimes they'd nibble on some sunflower seeds or I'd offer them a little can of apricot nectar and that would be my big social obligation.

I discovered the stars there. The desert is the best place to look at stars. There's no electricity so there are no lights competing with them. You see stars down to the horizon. That was exhilarating. The

mail would come every two or three weeks. Those were wonderful moments, when the mail would arrive. That kept me busy for a couple of days, reading mail and writing letters. I had one visit from a Peace Corps staff member. We played whiffle ball in the desert. The Libyans thought we were crazy.

All the men in the town worked in the oil fields. When one of the American foremen there learned I was living in this town, he asked one of the workers to bring me out on my day off. They couldn't believe an American was actually living with the Libyans. After that, I'd go out to the oil field once a month and they'd bring me into the commissary and let me take anything I wanted. Every day they'd give the workers some canned goods and a fresh loaf of bread to bring me. After a while they were sending me steaks. . . .

I wasn't all that sorry I didn't have a second year in Libya. My life in Tunisia was luxurious compared to what I'd been through in Libya. I lived in the teachers dorm, which had running water and electricity, and I ate in the student dining hall. The Tunisia volunteers were different from the Libya volunteers. They smoked dope and read Marxist literature. A friend of mine who lived in Tunis had a nice house and a housekeeper who came in every day to clean and cook his dinner. He taught English at an adult school to very wealthy people and he spent his free time reading and sitting in a café. His life there was such that he could have been in Paris.

I like to think I would have gone into the Peace Corps even if there hadn't been a Vietnam War. I had that international interest and was in no hurry to start a career. The idea of national service has always appealed to me. I think everybody should spend two years after college doing something for society.

I was proud I did the Peace Corps. I still am. I feel different. Everyone's a lawyer or an investment banker. Not everyone can go around saying, "I taught English in the Sahara Desert." . . .

George McDaniel

I was in medical school but had problems fitting in. I had taught high school previously, and was told by my draft board that if I returned to teaching, went to grad school, or joined VISTA, they'd draft me. They would not draft me if I went into the Peace Corps. I had no problem serving my country, but I was against the war.

As it turned out, the other guys in my training group for Togo, West Africa, felt the same way; they

A Peace Corps volunteer (seated, center) talks to villagers in India about a Peace Corps school-building project, 1968. © **BETTMANN/CORBIS.**
REPRODUCED BY PERMISSION.

were willing to serve their country but in the Peace Corps, not the military.

Two weeks before I left for Africa, in the spring of 1968, I got a notice from my draft board classifying me 1-A [available for military service]. I wrote to them, and they answered that there'd been a bureaucratic snafu and not to worry. . . .

I was in Niamtougou just a month when I got a letter from my draft board officially declaring me 1-A. The Peace Corps said they would take my case to the Selective Service Board of Appeals of Georgia. I'll never forget when the telegram arrived from Secretary of State Dean Rusk, notifying me that my appeal was denied. The Peace Corps then took my case to the President's Board of Appeals.

In the meantime, the rainy season was ending, and I wanted to start our projects, but I couldn't. The Peace Corps had emphasized that it was critical for volunteers to establish a foundation of trust, and if I left with projects uncompleted, the next volunteer would have a hard time getting the villagers' support. I was very bitter that my government was putting me in this position. I was playing by the rules, and my government was betraying me.

As I was waiting around, I wondered what would be the right thing to do. I didn't want to go to jail for refusing to be inducted because I hated confinement and knew I'd lose my mind. I didn't want to go to Canada because I didn't want to be prevented from ever going home. If I went to Vietnam, though, I could at least have it behind me. I could also get killed, but I had been reading Hemingway, Faulkner, the existentialist writers, and *All Quiet on the Western Front,* and I wasn't afraid of death. I thought war could be a way to confront and understand oneself, even if I ended up dying.

In October 1968, I got a telegram saying that I'd lost the presidential appeal. I wrote a nasty letter to my draft board, telling them to come and get me, and resigned from the Peace Corps. I flew to East Africa and hitchhiked around Kenya and Tanzania. I saw the lions and wildebeests on the Serengeti Plain, visited settlements of the Masai, and climbed Mount Kilamanjaro. I came home in time for Christmas and a month later was inducted. . . .

I got an Army Commendation for Valor. I thought it was undeserved because it was really just a bureaucratic thing—we all got medals. When I came back to the States, I realized that I should try to help break stereotypes—commies, gooks, niggers, Jews, pigs, rednecks. Once we stereotype a person, they become nonhuman and we can mistreat or kill them. That's the process we went through in training for Vietnam. We were killing gooks, not people.

I also came to respect the VC. They hung in there day in and day out, and believed in what they were fighting for—to run their own country.

In looking back on the two services, the Peace Corps and the Army, the Peace Corps was far more efficient. The Peace Corps trained us to learn about people, to try to think as they do in order to understand problems and solve them. But the military distanced themselves from people and did not demand the truth. *We* were right. *They* were gooks. But of course, they won.

Further Resources

BOOKS

Fischer, Fritz. *Making Them Like Us: Peace Corps Volunteers in the 1960s.* Washington: Smithsonian Institution Press, 1998.

Cobbs Hoffman, Elizabeth. *All You Need Is Love: The Peace Corps and the Spirit of the 1960s.* Cambridge, Mass.: Harvard University Press, 1998.

Redmon, Coates. *Come as You Are: The Peace Corps Story.* San Diego: Harcourt, Brace, Jovanovich, 1986.

Reeves, T. Zane. *The Politics of the Peace Corps and Vista.* Tuscaloosa: University of Alabama Press, 1988.

Rice, Gerald T. *The Bold Experiment: JFK's Peace Corps.* Notre Dame, Ind.: University of Notre Dame Press, 1985.

Searles, P. David. *The Peace Corps Experience: Challenge and Change, 1969-1976.* Lexington: University Press of Kentucky, 1997.

Schwarz, Karen. *What You Can Do for Your Country: Inside the Peace Corps: A Thirty-Year History.* New York: Anchor Books, 1993.

Weitsman, Madeline. *The Peace Corps.* New York: Chelsea House, 1989.

WEBSITES

"Inaugural Address, President John F. Kennedy." Available online at http://www.cs.umb.edu/jfklibrary/j012061.htm; website home page: http://www.cs.umb.edu (accessed April 1, 2003).

"The Peace Corps." Available online at http://www.peacecorps.gov (accessed April 1, 2003).

8

THE MEDIA

JOSEPH R. PHELAN

Entries are arranged in chronological order by date of primary source. For entries with one primary source, the entry title is the same as the primary source title. Entries with more than one primary source have an overall entry title, followed by the titles of the primary sources.

Important Events in the Media, 1960–1969

1960

- Daytime radio serials and most other network radio programming end, leaving news and special events coverage.

- On February 10, television host Jack Paar's late night talk show is cut off by NBC censors after he tells a joke they consider to be in poor taste. The next night, Paar walks off the show to protest the censorship. He does not return to the air until March 7.

- On May 19, radio disc jockey Alan Freed, who coined the term "rock 'n roll," is arrested for taking money to play certain records on his program. Famous TV disc jockey Dick Clark denies accepting such bribes. But the "payola scandal" reaches national proportions.

- On June 1, the National Council of Churches issues a report assailing television's preoccupation with sex and violence.

- On September 26, the largest television audience yet measured watches the first of four debates between presidential candidates Vice-president Richard Nixon and Senator John F. Kennedy. The power of television is demonstrated by polls showing that most who heard the debate on radio called it a draw. But television viewers, watching the vigorous, self-confident Kennedy and the haggard vice president, gave the edge to the senator.

- On November 25, CBS airs a one-hour news program called *Harvest of Shame,* documenting the working and living conditions of migrant farm workers. Reported by Edward R. Murrow, the program is a powerful piece of investigative journalism.

1961

- In January, the first presidential press conference to be broadcast live on both radio and television is held.

- In January, Edward R. Murrow leaves CBS for a position with the United States Information Agency.

- On February 1, *The New York Times* is voted the nation's best newspaper by a poll of 276 papers.

- On March 9, the Washington Post Company acquires *Newsweek* magazine.

- On May 9, FCC chairman Newton Minow's speech to the National Association of Broadcasters labels television programming "a vast wasteland."

- On July 17, John Chancellor takes over from original host Dave Garroway on NBC's *The Today Show.*

- On September 24, *Walt Disney's Wonderful World of Color* premieres on NBC.

1962

- On January 5, the *Los Angeles Mirror* and the *Los Angeles Examiner* cease publication.

- On February 14, a tour of the White House, led by First Lady Jacqueline Kennedy and televised by both CBS and NBC, is seen by more than 46 million viewers.

- On February 20, John Glenn becomes the first American to orbit the earth; Walter Cronkite leads the news coverage.

- On April 16, Walter Cronkite makes his first appearance as the anchorman of the *CBS Evening News.*

- On May 7, W. A. Swanberg is rejected as a Pulitzer Prize winner for biography by Columbia University trustees. His book *Citizen Hearst* profiles newspaper magnate William Randolph Hearst.

- On July 10, *Telstar 1,* a communications satellite, is launched; later that same day the first broadcast between the United States and Europe is made.

- In September, Legislation requiring all new televisions to be manufactured with UHF band tuners is passed.

- On September 23, ABC broadcasts its first television show in color, the animated program *The Jetsons.*

1963

- On March 31, the costliest newspaper strike in the nation's history to date comes to an end. The 114-day shutdown of all new York City newspapers has cost them more than $100 million in lost sales and advertising revenues.

- On September 2, CBS expands its evening newscast to thirty minutes from fifteen minutes.

- On November 22, President John F. Kennedy is assassinated; television news begins an unprecedented five days of complete coverage.

- On November 24, Lee Harvey Oswald, the alleged assassin of President Kennedy, is shot and killed on national television by Dallas nightclub owner Jack Ruby as police are moving Oswald from the jail. Millions of TV viewers witness the murder. Ruby is immediately arrested.

1964

- On February 9, the British singing group The Beatles appears on the Ed Sullivan Show. A record 73 million viewers watch their performance on television.

- On March 2, Fred Friendly becomes president of CBS News.

- On March 9, the U.S. Supreme Court reverses a five hundred thousand dollar libel judgment against *The New York Times.* The case arose out of an ad that appeared in the paper which made false statements about Alabama state officials. The Court rules that the Constitution protects *The Times* because the paper did not have good reason to suspect the statements were false.

• On March 25, *Relay II* satellite is launched, making transpacific broadcasting possible.

• In September, NBC becomes the first network to broadcast more than 50 percent of its programs in color.

• On October 7, NBC broadcasts the first made-for-television movie, *See How They Run,* starring John Forsythe and Jane Wyatt.

1965

• The nation's first all-news radio station begins broadcasting in New York.

• On March 6, video news cameras record police, some on horses, attacking civil rights marchers near Selma, Alabama. The marchers, lead by Dr. Martin Luther King, are headed for the capitol at Montgomery to demand voting rights for African Americans when they are blocked by the authorities at the Edmund Pettis Bridge. The sight on national television of marchers being trampled by horses and beaten by officers stuns the nation and rallies many Americans behind the civil rights movement.

• In March, the U.S. Supreme Court declares state and local censorship laws to be unconstitutional and a violation of the First Amendment's protection of free expression.

• On April 6, NASA launches Early Bird. It is the first commercial communications satellite designed to relay telephone and television signals.

• On June 7, Sony introduces the first home videotape recorder.

• On October 24, NBC becomes the first network with thirty minutes of network news every evening.

• On December 9, the first "Peanuts" television special, *A Charlie Brown Christmas,* is broadcast on CBS.

1966

• The National Association of Broadcasters advises all disc jockeys to screen all the records they play for obscene hidden drug or obscene meanings or messages

• On April 24, the final issue of the *New York Herald Tribune* is published.

1967

• In January, National Educational Television offers the first coast-to-coast educational broadcasts.

• On January 9, ABC becomes the last network to expand its news programs to thirty minutes.

• On January 15, Super Bowl I is broadcast on both CBS and NBC; CBS wins the ratings war.

• On May 4, the New York *World Journal Tribune* ceases publication.

• On June 25, the first global TV broadcast occurs live from nineteen nations on five continents. It is seen via satellite in thirty-nine nations.

• On August 27, *I Love Lucy* is finally removed from the CBS network schedule and released to local syndication.

• In November, strikes shut down Detroit's two major daily papers, the *News* and the *Free Press.* They remain closed until August 1968.

• On November 7, President Johnson signs a law authorizing public funds to support non-commercial radio and television. The stations will broadcast news, public affairs, and cultural and educational programs.

1968

• On March 5, CBS news anchorman Walter Cronkite breaks the newscasters' code of neutrality and comes out openly against the Vietnam War on national TV. In a special report on his recent trip to Vietnam, Cronkite states that he believes the war to be immoral and futile.

• In August, television provides graphic coverage of the violence that surrounds the Democratic National Convention in Chicago. The cameras capture hundreds of people, including innocent bystanders and members of the press, being beaten by police.

• On September 6, the last broadcast of fifteen-minute episodes of soap operas occurs; after a three-day break, the shows return in half-hour format.

• On September 17, *Julia* premieres on NBC; the show, starring Diahann Carroll, is the first to have an African American actor in the lead role.

• On October 13, the first live broadcast from space takes place, courtesy of *Apollo 7.*

1969

• Ron Zeigler, White House press secretary for President Richard Nixon, coins the term "photo opportunity."

• On February 8, the *Saturday Evening Post* closes after nearly 150 years of publication. The magazine returns to publish nine issues a year in the 1970s.

• On April 4, CBS cancels *The Smothers Brothers Comedy Hour* following a long conflict with the show's creators over dialogue and skits about the Vietnam War, the national government, and other "controversial" topics.

• On June 9, the Supreme Court ruling in *Red Lion Broadcasting Co. v. FCC* establishes the fairness doctrine for broadcasters.

• On November 13, Vice-president Spiro Agnew delivers a speech critical of television news. He charges that the news media is filled with liberals and that it is responsible for the spirit of negativism that he claims pervades American society.

• On December 17, singer Tiny Tim is married to Miss Vicki in a ceremony performed on Johnny Carson's *Tonight* show.

"Television and the Public Interest"

Speech

By: Newton Minow

Date: May 9, 1961

Source: Minow, Newton. "Television and the Public Interest." Speech to the National Association of Broadcasters. May 9, 1961. Reprinted online at http://www.janda.org/b20 /News/%20articles/vastwastland.htm; website home page: http://www.janda.org (accessed April 7, 2003).

About the Author: Newton Minow (1926–) was the chairman of the Federal Communications Commission (FCC) from 1961 to 1963. He served on the boards of CBS and the Corporation for Public Broadcasting. In 1987, he became the director of the Annenberg Center for Communications in Washington. ∎

Introduction

Newton Minow had worked in the Illinois state administration during Adlai Stevenson's governorship and was a leading figure in the governor's campaigns for president in 1952 and 1956. During these years, he became known to the Kennedy circle, and in 1960 he worked on the Kennedy campaign. It was no surprise, then, when Kennedy nominated Minow to the post of Federal Communications Commission (FCC) chairman.

What was a surprise, however, was how Minow became one of the principal figures in overseeing the new administration's domestic initiatives. He decided to challenge the heads of the major television networks (ABC, NBC, and CBS) to think about the broader public interest in the nature of television programming. In his first major speech to the National Association of Broadcasters on May 9, 1961, he quoted with approval the head of the association's own description of the broadcaster's mission. For broadcasting to serve the public interest, it "must have a soul and a conscience, a burning desire to excel, as well as to sell; the urge to build the character, citizenship and intellectual stature of people." Minow made the improvement of the content of television, especially children's programming, the primary concern of the FCC. While he had no statutory authority over con-

tent, Minow was determined to change the focus of programming from shallow entertainment to culture and education. To this end, he was more than willing to use the fact-finding power of the commission to hold hearings at which the doings of the television industry could be portrayed "warts and all."

Significance

As chairman, Minow went further than any federal official had ever done before in addressing the question of "quality" in broadcasting. His major accomplishment was to initiate a dialogue on the future of broadcasting, which involved both broadcasters and outsiders. Against the power of the media, Minow pitted the counterweight of the government's obligation to look out for the well-being of the American public. Minow was more than ready to use his "bully pulpit" to highlight television's shortcomings. He worked hard to gain support from legislators and network bosses for long-term solutions to the problems posed by the rapidly expanding role of the mass media in American life. As a result of Minow's energy and commitment to his task, he generated more news coverage than any other federal official except the president.

During his three-year tenure as FCC chairman, the offerings of the television networks improved only slightly in caliber and content, but Minow did succeed in bringing more high-quality programming to the small screen. He strongly supported such things as annual regular performances of great theatrical works. He also wanted to see the American public exposed to great music, including ballet and opera. But the problem remained that the networks were only providing the type of programming that viewers wanted. The television program on NBC focusing on Minow's FCC hearings received an 8.2 rating, compared with a 12.7 for the competing *Maverick* on ABC and a 23.4 for *Mister Ed* on CBS. Still, Minow's defense of quality in television programming helped lay the foundation for both the Corporation for Public Broadcasting and the Public Broadcasting System in the late 1960s. The result was such programs as *Masterpiece Theatre,* which was still running more than thirty years later, and brought productions of classic literature to the television screen on a regular basis. Further, PBS's *Sesame Street* led to an overnight change in viewers' expectations concerning the material available to young children through the medium of television.

Primary Source

"Television and the Public Interest" [excerpt]

> **SYNOPSIS:** This is possibly the most famous speech ever given by a non-cabinet-level officer in any administration. In an age when most members of the media elite had studied T.S. Eliot's bleak poem about

modern life, *The Wasteland,* in college, Minow's use of the phrase "vast wasteland" to characterize everyday fare on television had dramatic resonance.

Thank you for this opportunity to meet with you today. This is my first public address since I took over my new job. . . . It may also come as a surprise to some of you, but I want you to know that you have my admiration and respect.

I admire your courage—but that doesn't mean I would make life any easier for you. Your license lets you use the public's airwaves as trustees for 180 million Americans. The public is your beneficiary. If you want to stay on as trustees, you must deliver a decent return to the public—not only to your stockholders. So, as a representative of the public, your health and your product are among my chief concerns.

I have confidence in your health. But not in your product. **I am here to uphold and protect the public interest.** What do we mean by "the public interest?" Some say the public interest is merely what interests the public. I disagree.

When television is good, nothing—not the theater, not the magazines or newspapers—nothing is better.

But when television is bad, nothing is worse. I invite you to sit down in front of your television set when your station goes on the air and stay there without a book, magazine, newspaper, profit and-loss sheet or rating book to distract you—and keep your eyes glued to that set until the station signs off. I can assure you that you will observe a **vast wasteland.**

You will see a procession of game shows, violence, audience-participation shows, formula comedies about totally unbelievable families, blood and thunder, mayhem, violence, sadism, murder, western badmen, western good men, private eyes, gangsters, more violence and cartoons. And, endlessly, commercials—many screaming, cajoling and offending. And most of all, boredom. True, you will see a few things you will enjoy. But they will be very, very few. And if you think I exaggerate, try it.

Sentenced to prime time

Is there one person in this room who claims that broadcasting can't do better? Well, a glance at next season's proposed programming can give us little heart. Of 73 1/2 hours of prime evening time, the networks have tentatively scheduled 59 hours to categories of "action-adventure," situation comedy, variety, quiz shows and movies.

Is there one network president in this room who claims he can't do better? Well, is there at least one network president who believes that the other networks can't do better? Gentlemen, your trust accounting with your beneficiaries is overdue. Never have so few owed so much to so many.

Why is so much of television so bad? I have heard many answers: demands of your advertisers; competition for ever-higher ratings; the need always to attract a mass audience; the high cost of television programs; the insatiable appetite for programming material—these are some of them. Unquestionably these are tough problems not susceptible to easy answers.

But I am not convinced that you have tried hard enough to solve them . . . and I am not convinced that the people's taste is as low as some of you assume.

What about the children?

Certainly, I hope you will agree that ratings should have little influence where children are concerned. It used to be said that there were three great influences on a child: home, school and church. Today there is a fourth great influence, and you ladies and gentlemen control it.

If parents, teachers and ministers conducted their responsibilities by following the ratings, children would have a steady diet of ice cream, school holidays and no Sunday school. What about your responsibilities? There are some fine children's shows, but they are drowned out in the massive doses of cartoons, violence and more violence. Must these be your trademarks?

Let me make clear that what I am talking about is balance. You will get no argument from me if you say that, given a choice between a western and a symphony, more people will watch the western. I like westerns and private eyes too—but a steady diet for the whole country is obviously not in the public interest. We all know that people would more often prefer to be entertained than stimulated or informed. But your obligations are not satisfied if you look only to popularity as a test of what to broadcast. You are not only in show business; you are free to communicate ideas as well as relaxation. You must provide a wider range of choices, more diversity, more alternatives. It is not enough to cater to the nation's whims—you must also serve the nation's needs.

As Chairman of the Federal Communications Commission under President Kennedy, Newton H. Minow pushed hard for higher quality in television programing. AP/WIDE WORLD PHOTOS. REPRODUCED BY PERMISSION.

And I would add this—that if some of you persist in a relentless search for the highest rating and the lowest common denominator, you may very well lose your audience.

The 6 principles

I want to make clear some of the fundamental principles which guide me.

First: The people own the air. They own it as much in prime evening time as they do at 6 o'clock Sunday morning. For every hour that the people give you, you owe them something. I intend to see that your debt is paid with service.

Second: I think it would be foolish and wasteful for us to continue any worn-out wrangle over the problems of payola, rigged quiz shows and other mistakes of the past. There are laws on the books, which we will enforce. But there is no chip on my shoulder.

Third: I believe in the free enterprise system. I want to see broadcasting improved and I want you to do the job. I am proud to champion your cause.

It is not rare for American businessmen to serve a public trust. Yours is a special trust because it is imposed by law.

Fourth: I will do all I can to help educational television. There are still not enough educational stations, and major centers of the country still lack usable educational channels.

Fifth: I am unalterably opposed to governmental censorship. There will be no suppression of programming which does not meet with bureaucratic tastes. . . .

Sixth: I did not come to Washington to idly observe the squandering of the public's airwaves. . . . I believe in the gravity of my own particular sector of the New Frontier. There will be times perhaps when you will consider that I take myself or my job too seriously. Frankly, I don't care if you do.

Now, how will these principles be applied? Clearly, at the heart of the FCC's authority lies its power to license, to renew or fail to renew, or to revoke a license. As you know, When your license comes up for renewal, your performance is compared with your promises. I understand that many people feel that in the past licenses were often renewed pro forma. I say to you now: Renewal will not be pro forma in the future. There is nothing permanent or sacred about a broadcast license.

But simply matching promises and performance is not enough. I intend to do more. I intend to find out whether the people care. I intend to find out whether the community which each broadcaster serves believes he has been serving the public interest. You must re-examine some fundamentals of your industry. You must open your minds and open your hearts to the limitless horizons of tomorrow.

Words of wisdom

I can suggest some words that should serve to guide you:

Television and all who participate in it are jointly accountable to the American public for respect for the special needs of children, for community responsibility, for the advancement of education and culture, for the acceptability of the program materials chosen, for decency and decorum in production, and for propriety in advertising. This responsibility cannot be discharged by any given group of programs, but can be discharged only through the highest standards of respect for the American home, applied to every moment of every program presented by television. Program materials should enlarge the horizons of the viewer, provide him with wholesome entertainment, afford helpful stimulation, and remind him of the responsibilities which the citizen has toward his society.

These words are not mine. They are yours. They are taken literally from your own Television Code. They reflect the leadership and aspirations of your own great industry. I urge you to respect them as I do.

We need imagination in programming, not sterility; creativity, not imitation; experimentation, not conformity; excellence, not mediocrity. Television is filled with creative, imaginative people. You must strive to set them free.

The power of instantaneous sight and sound is without precedent in mankind's history. This is an awesome power. It has limitless capabilities for good—and for evil. And it carries with it awesome responsibilities—responsibilities which you and I cannot escape.

I urge you to put the people's airwaves to the service of the people and the cause of freedom.

Further Resources

BOOKS

Minow, Newton. *Equal Time: Private Broadcaster and the Public Interest.* New York: Atheneum, 1964.

———. *How Vast the Wasteland Now?* New York: Columbia University Press, 1991.

———. *Television's Values and the Values of Children.* Chicago: Northwestern University Press, 1995.

PERIODICALS

Sunstein, Cass. "Abandoned in the Wasteland: Children, Television and the First Amendment." *New Republic,* August 21, 1995.

WEBSITES

Federal Communications Commission. Available online at http://www.fcc.gov/ (accessed March 24, 2003).

"And Here's Johnny . . ."

Magazine article

By: *Newsweek*

Date: February 12, 1962

Source: "And Here's Johnny . . ." *Newsweek,* February 12, 1962, 80.

About the Publication: *Newsweek,* a popular weekly newsmagazine, along with hard news and analysis included short unsigned articles reporting on developments in the entertainment industry. ∎

Introduction

The Tonight Show began in 1951 in Los Angeles as a radio show starring Steve Allen. Allen and the show made the jump both to television and to New York City in 1954. After two-and-a-half years, Allen was replaced as host by Jack Paar. The show aired from 11:15 P.M. to 1:00 A.M. with several million viewers watching every night. When Jack Paar announced his retirement, he recommended Johnny Carson as his replacement. Carson was at first reluctant to give up his own successful show in order to replace a legend. When he finally did consent to take over the show, ABC would not release him from his contract, so NBC would have to use guest hosts for the six months at the risk of frittering away the high ratings earned by Paar. NBC took the chance, and this delaying tactic turned into an effective marketing ploy for the show. America grew fascinated with the comic for whom NBC was willing to wait. Moreover, the public came to enjoy the parade of guest hosts. In fact the Nielsen ratings for the show remained "at Paar" during the period leading up to Carson's takeover.

Significance

Johnny Carson took over *The Tonight Show* on October 1, 1962. A number of factors contributed to his enormous success: His opening monologue with its closing golf swing, his attention to comic detail, plus his gentlemanly treatment of guests all contributed to making him a natural for the late-night time slot. His sidekick and straight man, Ed McMahon, became an integral part of the show. Johnny's banter with band leader Doc Severenson—and when he was away, Tommy Newsome—was also a much loved aspect of the show, as was Johnny's frequent appearance as the sage and soothsayer "Karnak the Magnificent." As to his guests, it was Carson's view that if they sparkled, then so too would the show. Over the years, many of the country's greatest entertainers, plus some ordinary folks, came out from behind the stage curtain and sat between Johnny and Ed. Producer Rudy Tellez described the program's formula as "the bland leading the bland." But, combined with Carson's mildly risqué sense of humor, it worked consistently. Appearance on the Carson show could make or break a struggling performer's career, and comedians like David Letterman, Jay Leno, George Carlin, Joan Rivers, and Roseanne Barr were all fortunate enough to get their big break as a result of appearing with Johnny.

The Tonight Show's nightly format became the model for late-night television. It was initially the only show of its kind, but the other networks trotted out imitations hosted by such figures as Joey Bishop, Merv Griffin, Mike Douglas, David Frost, Virginia Graham, Phil Donahue, Dick Cavett, Joan Rivers, Alan Thicke, and

Comedian Johnny Carson in 1962, the year he became the host of CBS's *The Tonight Show.* Carson hosted the show for the next 30 years, becoming a television legend. **AP/WIDE WORLD PHOTOS. REPRODUCED BY PERMISSION.**

Chevy Chase. But despite the competition, Carson reigned supreme.

When Carson finally decided to retire a full twenty years after his move from New York to the West Coast in 1972, two established late-night comedians stood as heirs apparent. David Letterman had built a successful talk show on NBC, but comedian Jay Leno, who had been a popular guest host during Johnny's last year with the show, stepped in as Carson's natural successor in 1992. Letterman left NBC and signed with CBS to do *Late Night With David Letterman.* It is a testament to Johnny Carson's legacy that both Leno on the West Coast and Letterman on the East go head-to-head every night. There can be little doubt that a full decade after Johnny Carson's withdrawal from the scene, the late-night talk show has become an American institution.

Primary Source

"And Here's Johnny . . ."

> **SYNOPSIS:** This short article provides an early indication of why Johnny Carson was to become an institution on late-night television. Six months before taking over *The Tonight Show*, Carson insists he will

not be trying to replace Jack Paar so much as being himself.

"I got into a cab this morning; I wasn't awake yet. The driver said: 'You know what you oughta do with that show?'"

Johnny Carson, a boyish 36, raised his eyebrows and shrugged. The show he was talking about wasn't even his own—yet. But Jack Paar told his viewers last week that Carson will replace him Oct. 1 in NBC's darkest hours (11:15 p.m.-1 a.m. EST), and for the next eight months a lot more people will be telling Carson what he should do with the show.

Over a Bloody Mary next door to the New York studio where he now toils for ABC, the nominee admitted that the NBC decision had come as something of an anticlimax. "When I finally heard," he said, "I thought, 'that's interesting'." For weeks before Paar's announcement, Carson had looked like a shoo-in for the job. There was a hitch, however: Paar will leave his show at the end of March, and Carson's contract as host of ABC's daytime half-hour "Who Do You Trust?" runs through September. NBC finally decided it could wait for its chosen man.

No Break

Carson has stepped into big shoes before. A onetime writer for Red Skelton, he went on for his boss one night in 1952 when Skelton was felled in rehearsal by a breakaway prop that didn't break. The result: Carson's first network contract, with CBS. Before that, he recalled last week, "I did everything. I was on radio in the Midwest, and I had a show on the Coast." His first CBS show, with a variety-comedy format, "went over well with the critics but had trouble with ratings." After one season, it went off the air. In 1957, Carson took on "Who Do You Trust?"

"We have a game at the end to get off the air," Carson pointed out last week. "But the basis of this show, like Paar's, is interesting people. We have no end of material—even when I ask the same questions, I get different answers. Like 'How did you meet your wife?' One fellow said perfectly seriously: 'I won her in a card game'."

With a nocturnal audience, Carson foresees more stimulation. "People come on with something to say, and they can say it," he observed. "You're not under pressure to be funny all the time. There will always be a show like this, whether I do it, or Paar, or anyone else. But it would have to be done by someone who has worked with other people— someone who could be a catalyst."

Carson himself has already been a catalyst on the Paar show, substituting as host for a total of three weeks. Gentlemanly Hugh Downs, Paar's regular announcer, last week spoke warmly of the new man. "He has a great personality," said Downs, "and it's not just the one he projects on the air. If anybody had trouble with him, the trouble would be with themselves . . . A guy like Carson will probably build as fierce a following eventually as Paar has."

Whether he does or not, Carson doesn't think his fill-in experience will count for much next October. "That was a different situation—taking over Jack's show and his people," he said. "Well, I can't do the Jack Paar show. I'll do the Johnny Carson show, and I'll do the best show I can."

Further Resources

BOOKS

Cox, Stephen. *Here's Johnny! Thirty Years of America's Favorite Late- Night Entertainment.* New York: Harmony, 1992.

Haley, Alex. *The Playboy Interviews.* New York: Ballantine, 1993.

Lerner, Laurence. *King of the Night: The Life of Johnny Carson.* New York: Morrow, 1989.

PERIODICALS

Zehme, Bill. "The Man Who Retired." *Esquire,* April 29, 2002.

Zoglin, Richard. "And What a Reign It Was: In His Thirty Years, Carson Was the Best." *Time,* March 16, 1992.

WEBSITES

"The Official Johnny Carson Website." Available online at http://www.johnnycarson.com/carson/indexflash.jsp (accessed March 24, 2003).

"From Clown to Hero"

Magazine article

By: John Horn

Date: December 15, 1963

Source: Horn, John. "From Clown to Hero." *New York Herald Tribune,* December 15, 1963. Reprinted in "What Was Seen and Read. Television: a Transformation." *Columbia Journalism Review,* Winter 1964, 18–19. ∎

Introduction

On November 22, 1963, at 12:30 P.M. central standard time, President John F. Kennedy was assassinated while riding in an open motorcade in Dallas, Texas. Kennedy was killed instantly; he was pronounced dead by officials at 1:00 P.M. Yet the American people did not learn about this historic tragedy by turning on their televisions. Most people heard about the assassination from friends or on the radio. Television news reporting from the site of live events hardly existed. There were no immediate pictures of the actual assassination, and the technology didn't exist to get good images of the scene on the air quickly. By the time television had some usable footage of the event, most of America had gone to sleep. But within hours, television began to intrude on the events in a surprising way. Lee Harvey Oswald, a twenty-four-year-old Dallas resident, was arrested as a suspect in the murder of a Dallas policeman and was subsequently charged with Kennedy's murder. On Sunday, while he was being transferred from one cell to another, Jack Ruby stepped forward and fatally shot Oswald. Television crews captured the event live on national television. From that time on, the mission of television news would be to capture, and sometimes inadvertently create, news events that would be beamed into millions of homes.

In the days immediately following Kennedy's assassination, the whole world watched as the presidential coffin was taken to the White House, and then to the Capitol, where hundreds of thousands of silent mourners filed by, many in tears. More than 90 million Americans watched the television broadcast of the funeral procession from Capitol Hill to the graveside in Arlington National Cemetery. From Sunday's procession and memorial ceremonies in the Capitol through Monday's funeral with its riderless horse, Americans experienced a time of collectively shared grief as a result of television.

Significance

The Kennedy assassination changed forever the place of television in American national life. Before this time, television was seen as at best a kind of "entertainment machine" or at worst a "vast wasteland," to use the words of President Kennedy's chairman of the Federal Communications Commission, Newton Minow. Evidence for this negative view was the extent to which quiz shows, soap operas, and situation comedies dominated the programming.

During those four days of crisis in 1963, one can say that television made it possible for all Americans to experience a national event as one electronic civic community. Over the decades, television would create other "national experiences" such as the Nixon resignation and the Reagan assassination attempt. But the 1963 tragedy was the first occasion it had done so, in the process attracting the largest domestic audience in the history of the medium until then.

Although for most of those four days, reporters had kept quiet and let the events speak for themselves, from that time on the teller of the television tale would become tied up with the tale itself. Through its coverage, television had made itself part of the story, seemingly without anyone's realizing it. In the new age of reporting ushered in by the Kennedy assassination, television, by its very presence, would alter the news itself in ways never imagined in connection with print or even radio. The new medium would make its way to the center of any situation in such a way as to sometimes be as pivotal to the actual course of events as the actors in the unfolding story.

When people remembered that tragic weekend in 1963 in later years, what they recalled were the television images and the television journalists such as Walter Cronkite who broke down in tears while reporting the news of the president's death. Even those who had once distrusted this new medium somehow allowed that it "came into its own" as a result of its coverage of the Kennedy assassination. As a consequence of this event, television's hold on the public's imagination has never really been doubted since. Print and radio would never again challenge television as the public's primary source of information and authority. Television was now more than the medium of choice; it was the only medium anyone could envision conveying significant information about an important event. Thus, 1963 constitutes a dividing line in American cultural and social history. In one weekend, America had gone from a print and radio nation to a television nation, a place where it is sometimes said that if it is not on television, it did not happen.

Primary Source

"From Clown to Hero"

SYNOPSIS: This review notes how television covered the tragic events of late November 1963 and in so doing transformed itself from a "frivolous and often inane court jester" into a "national hero." It serves as a reminder that as far as the medium has come since its early days, it is always faced with finding a healthy balance between entertainment and education.

The three shots on Main and Elm Streets, Dallas, that altered the course of American history also revolutionized the shape and content of American television for four tragic and tumultuous days.

From a frivolous and often inane jester and an urgent, wheedling hawker, TV was transformed instantly to a swift recorder of stunning deeds and sorrowful rites, to electronic transportation that took all of America to scenes of infamy and miscarriage of justice in Dallas and of melancholy pomp and circumstance in Washington.

The sad journey of the slain President to his resting place, the grace and gallantry of his bereaved widow, the ceremonies of final farewell, the on-camera slaying of the suspected assassin—these staggering events were etched into minds and hearts of an America that was a television eyewitness.

The critical assaults on television's banality, frivolity, and hucksterism are often well deserved, but how can one dismiss as inconsequential or worthless a medium that is capable of spanning utter triviality to solemn magnificence?

The fact is that almost everyone underestimates television. Even television itself—specifically the three networks that dominate the medium with their owned stations, alliances with hundreds of affiliates, and national news-gathering organizations—tends to minimize its importance and public-service achievements.

Embarrassment is part of it. Television's finest hours come when normal standards and operations—the overwhelming predominance of entertainment programs and full sponsorship—are scuttled. Of necessity there must be mixed feelings when one's great moments are made possible only by repudiation of one's everyday values.

There is also the matter of responsibility. Recognition and acknowledgment of one's duties make clear one's responsibilities. Networks, which are not licensed as are stations to serve "the public interest, convenience and necessity," have kept the area of responsibilities understandably nebulous. For at a time like the solemn days following President's Kennedy's assassination, the networks remain alone, without advertisers or stations, to bear the enormous costs of news coverage. Not spelling out duties gives the networks latitude in deciding the method and length of such coverage.

The ambiguity often leads to confusion, with private prudence reining public-service eagerness. Such must have been the case on the first night of assassination coverage. With the biggest story of their lives on their hands, the New York stations of CBS and NBC reacted strangely. WCBS-TV, normally on the air all night with movies, signed off before midnight. WNBC-TV was off the air by 1 a.m., about two hours before its normal signoff. WABC-TV, like other ABC-owned stations, elected to stay on the air all night.

After that one lapse, WCBS-TV returned to continuous telecasting the next day and through the long weekend with special news programs. And WABC-TV went to earlier than normal signoff.

Three-year-old John F. Kennedy Jr. salutes his father's casket as it passes by in procession, three days after President Kennedy was assassinated on November 22, 1963. Kennedy's wife Jacqueline stands in the background, surrounded by daughter Caroline and Kennedy's brothers Edward (left) and Robert (right). **AP/WIDE WORLD PHOTOS. REPRODUCED BY PERMISSION.**

Hesitation and uncertainty are bound to be the consequences of unclear policy in the face of enormous expenditures. Public-interest news coverage is expensive. It is estimated that the four-day coverage of Presidential tragedy ran the three networks more than $3 million in direct spending and ten times that in advertising-revenue loss.

For the public, there was no question about what was appropriate action. Television offers it the unique opportunity of being on the scene of action.

The night before the funeral NBC-TV, remaining on the air through the night, recorded for America a memorable self-portrait in mourning—equal to Mr. Lincoln's train home to Springfield—by keeping cameras on the silent hundreds of thousands, both humble and great, as they shuffled silently past the bier in the Capitol rotunda. Through television, a hundred million more Americans were able to pay their respects there too . . .

Television has played a great national role. In one man's opinion, television has been a cohesive factor, perhaps the most important one, in unifying the postwar United States. By dissolving distance, it helped eliminate mid-country pockets of isolationism that once seemed so far from both oceans and from Europe and Asia. It broke down the social isolationism of the South, where Negroes and whites now appear and perform together in all living rooms as a matter of TV routine. Southern whites once protested such "Northern" behavior.

Television bound the country with common laughter at the programs of Milton Berle, Lucille Ball and other comedians. It also bound Americans through more serious concerns—the Presidential conventions and elections, the Presidential debates of 1960, the orbital flights of U. S. astronauts, and this November's funeral.

Those who have laughed and wept together in common cause are a nation. . . .

The nation has become a family through the public eye of television.

Television did not set out to accomplish this. At the beginning, all that the three big broadcasting organizations—ABC, CBS and NBC—wanted to do was to mold television more or less in the image of radio. They succeeded. Investing heavily, they rapidly established transcontinental network television. . . .

The problem remains: How can television reconcile its schizophrenic extremes?

It's not enough that the medium finally comes through in a pinch. The great expense is always a deterrent. Can't advertisers and stations, which use the air no less, somehow share extraordinary network news-coverage costs?

The schedule is so stabilized by film, tape, and sold time that it becomes increasingly difficult to pre-empt existing programs for live news coverage. Can the schedule somehow be loosened so as to encourage live public-service coverage?

In prime time, the networks' domain, news and information programs get a one-twenty-fifth share. The rest is entertainment. Can't networks do something about filling this reality gap?

Since the quiz scandals, television has been much concerned with image. It now has two: a generally amusing idler and a sometime national hero. Which will it cultivate?

Further Resources

BOOKS

Berry, Joseph P. *John F. Kennedy and the Media: The First Television President.* Lanham, Md.: University Press of America, 1987.

Greenberg, Bradley S. *The Kennedy Assassination and the American Public: Social Communication in Crisis.* Stanford, Calif.: Stanford University Press, 1965.

Mayo, John B. *Bulletin from Dallas: The President Is Dead: The Story of John F. Kennedy's Assassination as Covered by Radio and TV.* New York: Exposition Press, 1967.

WEBSITES

NARA JFK Assassination Records. Available online at http://www.archives.gov/research_room/jfk/background_jfk.html; website home page: http:// www.archives.gov (accessed March 24, 2003).

"Television and the Feminine Mystique"

Magazine article

By: Betty Friedan

Date: February 1–8, 1964

Source: Friedan, Betty. "Television and the Feminine Mystique." *TV Guide,* February 1–8, 1964, 273–275.

About the Author: Betty Friedan (1921–) was born Betty Goldstein. She graduated from Smith College in 1942 and married Carl Friedan in 1947. After publishing the revolutionary book *The Feminine Mystique* (1963) about American society's treatment of women, she became a leader of the women's liberation movement. She cofounded the National Organization for Women (NOW) and spearheaded the movement for the ratification of the Equal Rights Amendment. ∎

Introduction

When Betty Friedan's book *The Feminine Mystique* appeared in 1963, it exposed a cluster of myths about the American woman that had built up during the postwar years by social scientists, psychologists, educators, and marriage counselors. The "mystique" involved a definition of woman solely in terms of her roles as "wife, mother, love object, dishwasher, and general server of [her man's] physical needs." Friedan's book helped debunk the notion that women found fulfillment through "sexual passivity, loving service of husband and children, and dependence on men for all decisions in the world outside the home." Friedan was the first writer to show how the prevailing stereotype misrepresented the reality of women's lives in an America where by the 1960s 24 million women were working outside the home.

The success of the book led *TV Guide* to ask Friedan to examine the image of womanhood presented on television entertainment shows. Friedan's research involved scores of interviews with producers, writers, network decision makers, and advertising executives as well as viewing the shows that millions of American women watched each week. She found that on the one hand, television commercials, situation comedies, soap operas, and game shows were presenting an image of the American woman as a "stupid, unattractive, insecure little household drudge who spends her martyred, mindless, boring days dreaming of love and plotting nasty revenge against her husband. " On the other hand, dramas, documentaries, and news programs had no image of women upon which to comment because women were nonexistent in what they had to offer the viewing public.

Friedan also offered a thorough analysis of why situation comedies presented domestic married life as fundamentally a battle between the sexes. She suggested that American women resented their roles in life being automatically restricted to those of wife and mother and that it was as a result of this discontent that they spent all their time plotting revenge on their husbands. If television offerings reflected women's real-life achievements and accomplishments, then there would be a closer match between life on the small screen and the real life of America. This in turn would make it more likely that women would see themselves as fit for more than just domestic chores and service to their husbands.

Significance

While Friedan found that television left much to be desired in the way it portrayed the American woman, it was nevertheless true that by the mid-1960s some successful, intelligent, and disciplined female characters were to be seen on the small screen. In 1960, just five women had their own television shows: Shirley Temple

Barbara Feldon starred with Don Adams in the television series *Get Smart* from 1965 to 1970. Feldon played the role of the savvy Agent 99, in contrast to Adams's bumbling Agent 86. © BETTMANN/CORBIS. REPRODUCED BY PERMISSION.

Black, Dinah Shore, Loretta Young, Barbara Stanwyck, and Donna Reed. But after Friedan's book hit the best-seller lists, television showed signs of gradual change. In fairly short order, Barbara Eden was to be seen giving Larry Hagman fits in *I Dream of Genie,* while Elizabeth Montgomery was doing the same to Dick York in *Bewitched.* Barbara Feldon appeared in *Get Smart* as the unforgettable Agent 99 who was an incomparably more efficient spy than the bumbling Agent 86 named "Max," played by Don Adams. Meanwhile Ann Francis played a female detective in *Honey West,* while the free-spirited *Gidget* appeared the next year, together with Tammy Grimes playing an offbeat kind of "gal pal." In 1967, Marlo Thomas debuted in *That Girl* and Sally Field became *The Flying Nun,* both of whose leading characters were role models for independent young women at the time. The year 1968 brought viewers Diahann Carroll as the single working mom of *Julia,* while Carol Burnett began her tremendously successful variety show during that same year. But the show that most classically portrayed a single professional woman who "makes it after all" was *The Mary Tyler Moore Show,* which debuted in 1970 and went on to be the signature situation comedy of that

A publicity shot for the TV show *Mr. Novak*, a 1960s drama set in a school. Betty Friedan questioned why programs like *Mr. Novak* did not feature stronger, female characters. © BETTMANN/CORBIS. REPRODUCED BY PERMISSION.

decade. At the same time, both Moore and Burnett became the heads of successful production companies. Clearly the image of the American woman presented on television changed significantly during the 1960s. Perhaps this evolution was due in no small measure to the impact of Betty Friedan's book and the research that came out of it.

Primary Source

"Television and the Feminine Mystique" [excerpt]

> **SYNOPSIS:** In this *TV Guide* article, feminist Betty Friedan examines the images of women on network television programming and issues a call for "some heroines," female characters who function in roles other than that of housewife.

Why is there no image at all on television of the millions and millions of self-respecting American women who are not only capable of cleaning the sink, without help, but of acting to solve more complex problems of their own lives and their society? That moronic housewife image denies the 24,000,000 women who work today outside the home, in every industry and skilled profession, most of them wives who take care of homes and children too. That image also insults the millions of real American housewives, with more and more education, who shape U.S. culture, politics, art and education, by their actions in PTA, League of Women Voters and local political parties, and who help to build libraries, art galleries and theaters, from Detroit to Seattle, and even strike for peace.

Why for instance, isn't one of the leads in a program like *Mr. Novak* a woman teacher? I asked MGM executive producer Norman Felton. He explained: "If you have a woman lead in a television series, she has to be either married or unmarried. If she's unmarried, what's wrong with her? After all, it's housewives we're appealing to, and marriage is their whole life. If she's married, what's her husband doing in the background? He must not be very effective. He should be making the decisions. For drama, there has to be action, conflict. If the action is led by a woman, she has to be in conflict—with men or women or something. She has to make decisions; she has to triumph over opposition. For a woman to make decisions, to triumph over anything, would be unpleasant, dominant, masculine. After all, most women are housewives, at home with children; most women are dominated by men, and they would react against a woman who succeeded at anything."

But that housewife in the family situation comedies in only too unpleasant, dominant and masculine. She is always triumphing, not over forces in the outside world, but in that endless warfare against her own husband or children. "In comedy it's all right," Felton said. "You're not supposed to take her seriously; you laugh at her." Could there be a serious drama about a woman in the home, a housewife? "We couldn't make it dramatic—and honest," he said. "Most of a housewife's life is too humdrum. If you showed it honestly, it would be too dull to watch. Maybe you can get away with it in a hospital. After all, how many dramatic cases does a doctor or lawyer have in a year? But if you tried to do it with a housewife, no one would believe it. Everyone knows how dull the life of a housewife really is."

Thus, if television's only image of women is such a "dull" housewife, there is, in the end, no action or dramatic conflict she can engage in except that warfare with her own husband or children. Unless she gets sick and goes to the hospital, where she can die nobly of a brain tumor. "It makes sense that women are only figures of comedy," said Madelyn Martin, writer of *Lucy*. "When you think of traditional figures of comedy—the short guy, the ugly one, the man with the big nose, the Negro or Jew or member of any minority group—comedy is a way of turning their misfortune into a joke. It's a way of being accepted—'Look at me, I'm funny' and 'Don't anybody laugh at me, I'll laugh first.'"

If women are the one majority in America that resembles an oppressed minority, it's not because of actual deprivation of right, or opportunity, or human dignity, but simply because of that self-ridiculing image—the mystique of the mindless female, the passive housewife, which keeps girls and women from using their rights and opportunities and taking their own lives seriously, in time. In an examination scene in a *Mr. Novak* episode, a high school girl takes the blame for her boy friend's crib sheet to protect his future as a would-be physicist. "It's all right," she says, "let them blame it on me. I'm not going to college or anything. it won't matter to me." Why doesn't it matter to her, her own life and future? Why, in high school, does she already play the martyred, passive wife? No need to work or study in school herself, or plan her own future, the image says. All she has to do is get that boy to marry her—the sooner, the better—and he'll take care of her life.

Do anything you can to hook that man, all those images of women on television say, because you aren't or can't be a person yourself. But without studying, or working, or doing anything yourself, you can be a "housewife" at 18. And get all those expensive things for wedding presents, just like *Queen for a Day*—a lounge chair, a dishwasher, a whole set of china, baby furniture, even a free trip to the beauty parlor every week.

Is it a coincidence that millions of real girls who have grown up watching television—and seeing only that emptily "glamorous" housewife image of women—do not, in high school, have any goal of their own future except being such a passive housewife? Is it partly from lack of any self-respecting image of a woman as a person herself that so many stop their own growth in junior high to start that frantic race to "trap" a man, get pregnant in high school, or quit college to take a "housework" job in industry, to put their husbands through medical or engineering school. By seducing real girls into evading the choices, efforts, goals, which would enable them to grow to maturity and full human identity in our society, television's image of women is *creating* millions of unnecessarily mindless, martyred housewives, for whom there may never be a thrill or challenge greater than the dirty kitchen sink.

These new teen-age housewives—the growth-stunted young mothers who quit school to marry and become mothers before they grow out of bobby socks themselves—are the female Frankenstein monsters television helped create. And they may writhe forever in that tedious limbo between the kitchen sink and the television game show, living out their century-long life ahead, in a complex world which requires human purposes, commitment and efforts they never ever glimpsed. How long can even television channel their pent-up energies into vicarious love affairs with Dr. Kildare, vicarious revenge against that husband who is surely not their real enemy?

How long will boys and men love women, if this nasty, vengeful martyr is their only public image of woman, and becomes an increasingly vengeful private image? The female Frankenstein monsters, after all, are created by the minds of men. Does the new plethora of widowers, bachelor fathers, and unmarried mature men on television, who pay a maid or house-boy, or soon perhaps, a robot to get the household drudgery done, signify unconscious rebellion against that "housewife" altogether? Do they really want her for a wife? One suddenly realizes that there are no real love stories on the television screen—in the sense of the love stories that one can still see in the old movies with Ingrid Bergman, Joan Crawford, Norma Shearer, Claudette Colbert and all the rest. No love stories, no heroines—only those housewife drudges, the comic ogres who man the war between the sexes.

Television badly needs some heroines. It needs more images of real women to help girls and women take themselves seriously and grow and love and be loved by men again. And television decision-makers need to take real women more seriously—not for women's sake but for their own. Must women only be used as diaper-and-pot-holders for the male news commentators? Must they be shown only as paid or underpaid dishwashers for fear of making real housewives uncomfortable?

Further Resources

BOOKS

Friedan, Betty. *The Feminine Mystique.* New York: Dell, 1983.

———. *It Changed My Life: Writings on the Women's Movement.* New York: Random House, 1976.

Haralovitch, Mary Beth, and Lauren Rabinowitz, eds. *Television, History and American Culture: Feminist Essays.* Durham, N.C.: Duke University Press, 1999.

WEBSITES

Garber, Amy. *A Bibliography of Women on Television.* Available online at http://hoover.mcdaniel.edu/studentlist/garber .htm; website home page: http://hoover.mcdaniel.edu (accessed March 24, 2003).

"Winds of Change for Newspapers"

Magazine article

By: *U.S. News & World Report*
Date: April 25, 1966
Source: "Winds of Change for Newspapers." *U.S. News & World Report,* April 25, 1966, 67–69.
About the Publication: *U.S. News & World Report* was and still is one of the three major weekly news magazines. It regularly reports on developments in other news media such as television and newspapers. ∎

Introduction

Big-city newspapers were in decline in the 1960s. There were many causes for this, including economic expansion, population movement, the spread of higher education, and a revival in the American cinema. Suburbanization and the resultant dependence on personal cars to travel to work meant that fewer commuters were reading a newspaper on the bus or subway. Further, by the 1960s virtually every American home contained a television set, which provided news easily, instantaneously, and with compelling visuals.

It was in the large metropolitan areas with their high-circulation dailies and Sunday editions that the impact of these changes was most evident. While the population of the United States was going up, the number of large daily newspapers in the big cities was going down. But the comparative decline of the great metropolitan daily was not to be mistaken for the decline of the newspaper industry as a whole, for the number and circulation of smaller market newspapers increased. The daily newspaper endured, but the old world of the newspaper, once classically portrayed in the movie *Citizen Kane,* has had its day, and as a result newspapers have had to adapt their style and content to a different media environment. When *USA Today* was launched in the 1980s, it was meant to imitate television newsmagazine programs with its flashy style, emphasis on the visual, and its summaries of news designed for the hurried reader.

Significance

Today, the competition to be the first with the news involves less the getting of newspapers to every street corner before dawn than it does establishing a direct television link to a broadcast journalist. Yet the newspaper as a means of communication endures. Perhaps the most radical change came in the 1990s with the arrival of the Internet. But the newspapers have proven themselves ready for the challenge. In response to this revolution in communications, newspapers have gone online. Thus, the paper will be directly available to anyone who has access to

a computer if they cannot put their hands on a print copy. Rather than put the traditional newspaper out of business, the digital revolution has enabled it to reinvent itself.

American daily life has always been greatly influenced by the stage of scientific and technological development at which the country has found itself. Thus, Americans who once used to receive their messages via pony express today receive them by e-mail. In like manner, the once mighty newspaper industry has had to adapt to a media world that includes radio, television, cable, satellite, and the Internet. But it has shown itself ready to face any changes in the media environment created by rapidly advancing technology.

Primary Source

"Winds of Change for Newspapers"

> **SYNOPSIS:** This article presents an overview of the place of newspapers in the changing media world of the 1960s. With the rise of radio and television, the issue of the future of the big-city dailies had become a question mark. Would they endure in the face of the new forms of information and new habits within the American culture? While newspapers were facing competition from new media, the article notes that the smaller, more community-oriented newspapers, focusing more on the "neighborhood" needs of local readers, were most likely to be the wave of the future as far as print media was concerned.

Across the nation, dramatic changes are taking place in the basic means of public information.

Some big-city newspapers are failing. Community dailies are springing up in smaller cities and suburban areas. Total newspaper circulation, as a long-term average, is gaining.

Booming new methods of communication—including television, radio, national news and picture magazines—are strongly challenging the newspapers as vendors of news, advertising and entertainment.

Most important of all: The various mass media of public information, as a whole, are engaged in vigorous competition for the time and attention of the average citizen.

It is a significant part of a social and economic revolution going on in America, spurred by increasing prosperity, a highly mobile population, and the widest variety of educational, entertainment and recreational facilities ever available to the public.

Era of Mergers

The trend shows up again in the combination of three New York City newspapers.

With completion of that merger, there will be 5 daily newspapers and 3 Sunday papers of general circulation in Manhattan, where there were 14 dailies and 8 Sunday papers as recently as the early 1920s.

Since the end of World War II in 1945, in the 10 largest metropolitan areas of the nation, ranging from 2.2 million to 11.3 million in population, the number of big-city dailies has declined from 49 to 31.

Eighteen metropolitan newspapers have vanished in the postwar era. These included such well-known names as "The New York Sun," "The Boston Post," "The Philadelphia Record," "The Washington Times Herald," "The Detroit Times," "The Pittsburgh Sun-Telegraph," "The Chicago Times," "The San Francisco Call-Bulletin" and "The Los Angeles Examiner."

Nationwide, during the last 50 years the number of daily newspapers has fallen from a peak of 2,580 in 1914, to 1,751 at the start of 1966, while the total population of the United States has doubled.

Newspaper circulation, however, has gone up from 28,777,000 to 60,357,563 daily. Sunday circulation advanced from 16,480,000 to 48,600,090.

Still a Giant Industry

From the decline in number of papers, observers have concluded that the newspaper is "fading" in the United States.

"Nothing could be farther from the truth," asserted Robert U. Brown, publisher of "Editor & Publisher," a trade journal.

"Thirty-odd years ago, many people thought the advent of network radio spelled the doom of newspapers. It did not materialize. The newspapers that died in the 1930s did so because of the depression—not radio.

"About 15 years ago, the same thing was said about network television. But doomsday for the newspapers has not come, and will not in any foreseeable future."

Mr. Brown calls the newspaper business "a giant that few people know or understand." In addition to daily and Sunday newspapers, it includes approximately 9,000 weekly or semiweekly papers with 24 million circulation.

"It is an industry," says Mr. Brown, "with annual receipts from circulation and advertising exceeding 5 billion dollars. Its annual expenditure of over 1 bil-

---

All the Biggest U.S. Cities Have Fewer Papers Now

	Dailies 20 Years Ago	Dailies Now
New York	10	5*
Chicago	5	4
Los Angeles	4	2
Philadelphia	4	3
Detroit	3	2
Boston	7	5
San Francisco-Oakland	6	3
Pittsburgh	3	2
Washington	4	3
St. Louis	3	2
TOTAL, 10 cities	**49**	**31**

*After merger of "The Herald Tribune," "The Journal-American," and "The World-Telegram and Sun."

SOURCE: Table from "Winds of Change for Newspapers," *U.S. News and World Report.* 25 April 1966, 69.

---

lion dollars for newsprint is exceeded only by its expenditure for payrolls."

In the "Old Days"

The long-range decline in the number of daily newspapers—taken alone—does not provide a complete understanding of what has happened to mass communications in America.

In the "good old days" when every city of any consequence had three or four competing newspapers, there was no radio or television. Motion pictures were in their infancy. National news and picture magazines hadn't started.

"Of course, there was great competition between newspapers 50 or 70 years ago," Mr. Brown observed. "What most people do not realize is that many of these were not self-supporting.

"They were supported, sustained, and subsidized by utilities magnates, traction kings, beer barons, political bosses—anyone who had an ax to grind before the public.

"They fought each other tooth and nail. It was fun. But it didn't add up to good journalism. It added up to partisanship. Journalism today may not be as colorful, but it is better journalism."

Toll of the Weak

Between the great wars, depression took a heavy toll among the weaker newspapers.

Since World War II, inflation—rising costs of labor, equipment, and materials—has added to the casualty list, primarily among big-city newspapers.

Where People Get the News—Fewer Newspapers, More TV, Radio, Magazines

Number of	1920	1940	Now
Daily newspapers	2,042	1,878	1,751
Sunday newspapers	522	525	562
National magazines	146	224	268
AM radio stations	0	765	4,056
FM radio stations	0	15	1,467
Television stations	0	0	604
TOTAL	**2,710**	**3,407**	**8,708**

SOURCE: Table from "Winds of Change for Newspapers," *U.S. News and World Report*. 25 April 1966, 68.

"The New York Mirror"—a morning tabloid with the second-largest daily circulation in the country—collapsed in 1963. The collapse followed a 114-day printers' strike that shut down all New York City newspapers and caused an estimated loss of 108 million dollars in advertising revenue.

The price of newsprint—the big rolls of paper used in producing newspapers on high-speed rotary presses—went up from $78 to $135 a ton between 1945 and 1957. A single price hike of $10 a ton was blamed when "The St. Louis Star-Times" suspended publication in 1951.

Doubled Costs

Stanford Smith, general manager of the American Newspaper Publishers Association, said press costs have doubled since World War II. More equipment is necessary, including color-printing machinery.

Some newspapers agreed to share production facilities, while keeping their news and editorial operations separate. Such joint-plant arrangements are in effect in 24 cities, including Pittsburgh, St. Louis and San Francisco.

Newspapers derive around 75 per cent of their income from advertising, less than 25 per cent from circulation or sales.

Total spending on all kinds of advertising in the United States has just about tripled in the last 15 years—from 5.7 billion dollars in 1950 to 15.1 billion in 1965.

The newspaper share went up from 2.1 billion dollars to 4.4 billion. Magazines increased their share from 515 million dollars to 1.2 billion. Radio went from 605 million to 889 million.

But television—a postwar bonanza—was the only one of the major media to rise as a percentage of the total advertising take. TV receipts rose from 171 millions, or 3 per cent, in 1950, to 2.5 billions, or 16.5 per cent of the total advertising market in 1965.

Great Boom in News

Surveying the trends, Jesse Markham, Princeton University economist, found in an analysis prepared for the ANPA:

"One of the most important developments of the twentieth century is the rapid growth and spectacular change in the information-disseminating business. Only four decades ago, the public was completely dependent on the printed media for news. As recently as 1920, the home radio set was a rarity, and home television was unknown.

"By 1950, 97 out of every 100 U.S. families had at least one radio receiving set, and by 1960, 90 out of every 100 had at least one television set.

"Out of each 100 families, 86 subscribe to at least one daily newspaper, and an additional number purchase them regularly from the newsstands.

"The public has available far more news sources than constraining force of time permits it to use."

Experts agree that all major media are in competition today—not only with each other for news and advertising—but for the available time of well-to-do Americans against a host of competing attractions.

These include the time that workers spend driving to and from their jobs in millions of private automobiles, as well as leisure-time activities such as golfing, swimming, bowling, movies, gardening, bridge, backyard barbecues, home workshops, and myriad other hobbies of the affluent society.

Newspaper attrition, in recent years, has occurred mostly in the big cities. The plight of the metropolitan newspaper—in a sense—is the problem of the big cities themselves:

Flight of higher-income families to the suburbs . . . lack of mass-transit trains or buses where commuters may read . . . traffic congestion that impedes delivery by trucks.

"Closer to People"

The population trend has favored a growth of community newspapers in smaller cities and suburban areas where the newcomers become homeowners, take an interest in local affairs, and do their buying in new shopping centers with parking accommodations.

"The American press is not 'fading' as some claim and many believe," said Kenneth R. Byerly, a journalism professor of the University of North Carolina.

"It is just getting closer to the people, in that the nation's smaller city and suburban dailies are chalking up the big circulation gains."

Where Circulation Rises

In a study of newspaper circulation between 1950 and 1965, Mr. Byerly found:

Newspapers published in cities of less than 250,000 gained 28.6 per cent; an even greater growth occurred in communities of less than 50,000.

Combined circulation of newspapers in cities of more than a million population dropped off 14.4 per cent, or around 2 million copies a day.

Similar figures were reported by Jon G. Udell, director of the bureau of business research and service, University of Wisconsin, in a recent study on newsprint consumption.

"The most significant measure of newspaper growth is newsprint consumption," Mr. Udell said. Use of newsprint reflects "both changes in advertising and editorial content, and changes in circulation.

"The greatest growth of newspapers, measured by newsprint consumption, occurred in small cities and towns. The 10-year increase [1954–64] of all newspapers was 24.4 per cent. The growth of small-city newspapers was 70 per cent greater than the average for all U. S. newspapers."

In the State of Florida—where population jumped from 1.9 million in 1940 to more than 5 million now—at least 75 communities have local newspapers where none existed 10 years ago.

On Big-City Fringes

According to Mr. Byerly, there has been a "surging growth of community dailies and weeklies" around the largest metropolitan areas of the nation.

At least 40 suburban dailies ring New York City, including "Newsday" on Long Island—started in 1940—which has over 400,000 circulation now.

Downtown newspapers in Los Angeles compete with 28 suburban dailies, 150 weeklies, and over 100 shopping guides.

Similar situations prevail in varying degree in the Boston, Philadelphia, Pittsburgh, Detroit, Chicago, St. Louis and San Francisco-Oakland markets.

Most of these cities already have gone through a wringer where the number of competing metropolitan dailies is concerned. Authorities believe that, outside of one or two remaining special situations, the shaking-down process is just about over.

World at Doorstep

The postwar boom in news and advertising has brought about an expansion of worldwide news-gathering facilities, a greater variety of information services available to the public, and many technological advances in communications.

The two big, privately owned American wire services—the Associated Press and United Press International—have extended their news and photo coverage to more than 100 foreign countries.

News magazines and radio-TV networks have set up their own news bureaus in principal cities of the world.

Coverage of Capital

Before the start of the "New Deal" in 1933, the Senate and House press galleries in Washington had 364 accredited newspaper reporters. There were no separate galleries for the periodical press, photographers, or radio-TV correspondents.

Today, more than 2,000 reporters of all kinds are covering the nation's capital, including 150 women reporters, and more than 100 foreign correspondents.

William L. Rivers, University of Texas journalism professor, wrote in the spring, 1962, "Columbia Journalism Review":

"Newspapermen and wire-service reporters dominated the Washington press corps in the 1930s. . . . Today, radio, television, and magazine correspondents are quite important.

"It is notable that the newspaper correspondents, like all of the rest of the Washington press corps, are predominantly 'liberal.'

"More than 55 per cent of the correspondents consider themselves 'liberal'; 26.9 per cent call themselves 'conservatives.' Only 15.9 per cent described themselves as 'middle-roaders' or refused to label themselves."

New Techniques

News magazines have brought a new dimension in analysis and depth to news reporting, while the colorful newspaper "extra" has vanished from city

A man reads at a newsstand, 1967. By the 1960s the number of newspapers in circulation had declined dramatically from early in the century. © TED STRESHINSKY/CORBIS. REPRODUCED BY PERMISSION.

streets under the impact of spot-news broadcasts on radio and television.

One observer pointed out: "There's not even a newspaperman in the White House press office any more. The President is more concerned about making an impression on television."

Postwar advances include color printing in newspapers, higher-speed offset presses with greater capacity, composing of news copy and setting of classified ads by computer, wire movement of stock-market reports and important news texts at speeds of more than 1,000 words per minute, experiments in satellite transmission of photos, and tape-operated Teletypesetter machines.

"There has been more development in news technology than in news presentation," observed ANPA general manager Stanford Smith.

What of the future?

A News Revolution

Experts agree that the prospects are bright for every form of communications. Some authorities hint

of big changes in the print media. Again, the emphasis is on production methods—not news and editorial format or content.

Otis Chandler, publisher of "The Los Angeles Times," made this statement at a meeting of the Washington professional chapter of Sigma Delta Chi, national journalism society:

"We are just now witnessing the bare beginning of a major revolution in the world of information.

"Print—whether it be newspapers, magazines, or books—will be here in greater abundance 25 years hence, but its availability and penetration will be quite different."

Complaints, Warnings

These optimistic forecasts are being coupled with complaints about inadequate basic information in the daily press concerning national and foreign news events, and warnings about restrictive practices of labor unions.

"If you get out of New York and Washington and travel around the country, you don't find much in the daily newspapers," one veteran newsman observed.

"The newspapers have fallen down on the job of supplying basic information."

Mr. Smith claimed that some of the advantages of new labor-saving, cost-saving equipment introduced in recent years, which could help newspapers be more competitive with other media, have been "minimized by adamant attitudes of some labor unions toward preservation of needless jobs."

Turner Catledge, executive editor of "The New York Times," in a lecture to students at the University of Kansas, concluded:

"Unless we can intelligently and swiftly resolve the conflicts which are holding off the introduction into general newspaper use of modern automation, the newspaper as we know it will surely decline in significance if not, indeed, eventually disappear from the scene."

Further Resources

BOOKS

Abel, Elie, ed. *What's News: The Media in American Society.* San Francisco: Institute for Contemporary Studies, 1981.

Lindstrom, Carl. *The Fading American Newspaper.* Glouster, Mass.: Peter Smith, 1964.

Martin, Shannon. *Newspapers of Record in a Digital Age: From Hot Type to Hot Link.* Westport, Conn.: Praeger, 1998.

WEBSITES

"Print Journalism." Available online at http://www.journalism.org (accessed March 25, 2003).

"A Dialogue— Marshall McLuhan and Gerald Emanuel Stearn"

Interview

By: Marshall McLuhan and Gerald E. Stearn

Date: June 1967

Source: *Encounter,* June 1967. Reprinted in Stearn, Gerald Emanuel, ed. "A Dialogue—Marshall McLuhan and Gerald Emanuel Stearn." *McLuhan: Hot and Cool.* New York: Dial, 1967, 280–286, 287–291.

About the Author: Marshall McLuhan (1911–1980) was born in Edmonton, Alberta, Canada, studied at Cambridge University, and taught for many years at St. Michael's College at the University of Toronto. His insight that "the medium is the message" made him famous during the 1960s and 1970s. ∎

Introduction

In the 1960s, the most celebrated prophet of the electronic age and the death of book literacy was Marshall McLuhan, an eminent scholar who received his doctorate in English literature from Cambridge University. According to a *Newsweek* interview (March 6, 1967), it was during his early days of teaching that he first engaged with popular culture and the mass media. "I was confronted with young Americans I was incapable of understanding." He vowed to "get through" to them by studying their movies, radio programs and the advertisements aimed at them. The resulting book, *The Mechanical Bride: Folklore of Industrial Man,* was an attack on the "pressures" that automobile advertising, Great Books programs, and mass-market magazines exerted on the young American psyche. A decade later, in *The Gutenberg Galaxy: The Making of Typographic Man,* McLuhan argued that the invention of moveable type in the fifteenth century made western European people literate but linear. The linearity of print accounts for linear thinking in music, mathematics, and the sciences. When print superseded speech, the eye replaced the ear as the principal sensory organ encouraging individualism, which led to a fragmentation of society.

But with the dawn of the electronic age, humanity was restored to certain of its tribal ways and the world became a global village. Electronic media have brought redistribution and heightening of sensory awareness, along with an immediacy in communication that reduces the separation between thought and action and diminishes human isolation. McLuhan's purpose in writing his next book, *Understanding Media: The Extension of Man* (1962), was to call attention to how and why electronic forms of communication are reshaping civilization. Specifically, any medium is an extension of a person, and because of electricity our central nervous system has become extended outside the body. According to McLuhan, television, which is low in definition and requires audience involvement, is a "cool" medium, whereas the informative book is a "hot" medium. The participatory conditioning of a "cool" medium has implications for education. Children of the television generation are inclined more toward discovery than toward instruction.

Significance

Marshall McLuhan, the first and greatest guru of the media age, was an innovative cross-disciplinary thinker who proposed that many of the radical social changes of the twentieth century could be attributed to the effect of electronic communications. "The medium is the message," he famously asserted, by which he meant that it is the character of television, computers, and other media, far more than their content, that is reshaping civilization. McLuhan was criticized for refusing to judge whether the influences of electronic media on patterns were good or bad. In response, he argued that human beings should become informed about what is happening and equipped by awareness to fight back if so desired. "My entire concern" he told an interviewer in 1967, "is to overcome the determinism that results from the determination of people to ignore what is going on." McLuhan did not regard technological change as inevitable but insisted that if we understand the components, "we can turn it off any time we choose." He was also attacked for the assertion that the book is obsolete.

Agreeing that his books were difficult, McLuhan attempted a user-friendlier version in *The Medium is the Massage* (1967), a collection of over a hundred illustrations of how media are transforming every aspect of our lives. Moreover, he appeared frequently on television to explain his theories. In one appearance, he noted that the title was intended to draw attention to the fact that a medium is not something "neutral—it does something to people. It takes hold of them. It rubs them off, its massages them, it bumps them around." He was most vehement that we are unaware of the new media because its content is the old media. Since it is emotionally more secure to live in the old media, people look at the present through a "rear-view mirror."

Primary Source

"A Dialogue—Marshall McLuhan and Gerald Emanuel Stearn" [excerpt]

SYNOPSIS: In this interview, McLuhan clarifies some of his theories, particularly his view that the medium in which a message is conveyed significantly shapes the nature of the message. He denies that he is an "enemy of the book," maintaining that he is simply describing cultural changes brought about by the development of electronic media.

When you say that technologies are extensions of man, are they as well extensions of man's will?

In the ordinary sense of subliminal wish and drive—yes. Man, however, never intends the cultural consequences of any extension of himself.

What are we to do with all this information? How does it affect our consciousness?

When man is overwhelmed by information, he resorts to myth. Myth is inclusive, time-saving, and fast. Children are driven today into mythic thinking. When environmental effects shift beyond a certain point, everybody agrees on a new strategy.

To be conscious or unconscious is to make a certain order of experience. I possess no theory of consciousness. But that says nothing. Throughout

my work, however, I am saying that awareness is being pushed more and more out into the environment. Technology pushes human awareness out into the environment. Art becomes environment. Our environments are made of the highest levels of human consciousness.

Many readers have been shocked and confused by what they consider idiosyncratic methods in your work. For example: A number of critics suggest that your books are repetitious and, in Dwight Macdonald's words, "ultimately boring."

Macdonald's is the kind of confusion that comes to the literary mind when confronted with a drilling operation. Repetition is really drilling. When I'm using a probe, I drill. You repeat naturally when you're drilling. But the levels are changing all the time. Macdonald thinks *that's* repetition. There is a complete unawareness of what is going on in the book. . . . The idea of using facts as probes—as means of getting into new territories—is utterly alien to them. They use facts as classified data, as categories, as packages.

Literally, *Understanding Media* is a kit of tools for analysis and perception. It is to *begin* an operation of discovery. It is not the completed work of discovery. It is intended for practical use. . . .

Depth operations are natural to modern studies in all fields including psychiatry and metallurgy and structural analysis. In order to inspect any situation structurally you have to inspect it from all sides simultaneously, which is a sort of cubist gimmick. A structural approach to a medium means studying its total operation, the *milieu* that it creates—the environment that the telephone or radio or movies or the motorcar created. . . .

If you look at print not as a conveyer belt of data but as a structure somewhat different from the spoken word, somewhat different from manuscript culture, then you are at once in a world where you have to repeat yourself furiously in order to capture all facets simultaneously. The literary form is truly not adopted to simultaneity and structural awareness and this of course is inherent in the very first acts of writing in early times when a vast amount of human awareness was tossed out. Very little of the qualities of speech can be captured by written form, very little of nuance, very little of the drama and action of speech can be captured by written form whatever. But today, with the oscillograph, tape recorder, and various electronic devices, speech is being felt in depth and discovered in structural multi-facet-ness for the first time in human history. So naturally anybody who has become vividly aware of the many, many structural facets of speech, when confronted with the literary form, is aghast at its impoverished character. It's very abstract—it has eliminated most language and speech from its medium. The moment you begin to look at speech as a structure you quickly understand why writing as a structure really cannot deal with much speech. The great poets, starting with Baudelaire and Rimbaud, were quite aware of this and began to substitute all sorts of new literary techniques as a way of capturing the multi-facet-ness of speech. Symbolism discovered that in order to capture the live drama of speech you have to break up the sentence and break up language. . . .

Macdonald (and other literary critics) have never thought for one minute about the book as a medium or a structure and how it related itself to other media as a structure, politically, verbally, and so on. It's not peculiar to Macdonald. It's true of the entire academic world, of the whole journalistic world. They have never studied any medium.

Are you an "enemy of the book?" John K. Jessup (in the Yale Review) *claims that you have "sold the pass of reason and joined the assault on it." Your observations have become infatuations. . . .*

It is customary in conventional literary circles to feel uneasy about the status of the book and of literacy in our society. Macdonald and others, heaven knows, are nineteenth not twentieth-century minds. Therefore anybody who looks at it in a kind of clinical spirit is regarded as hostile, and an enemy of the book.

My own motivation in studying all media began with my commitment to literature as a profession and I quickly became aware that literature had a great many enemies. (They are all of our own making. We have created them.) I discovered that the enemies of literature needed very careful scrutiny and study if the literary man was to manage to extricate himself from this new jungle. So the literary people, I became aware, were so uneasy about the surround of enemies that any attention given to literature as such was considered unfortunate and, as Dwight Macdonald says, "gloomy." And it's a past subjunctive. Any attention to the book is regarded as unfriendly because it is felt that the book will not bear scrutiny any more. Now, in the same way, any attention to new media which are in the ascendant, whose gradient is climbing rapidly, is considered as an act of optimism. Anybody who would direct intellectual attention to a new medium must be an optimist because the rear-view look of the nine-

teenth-century mind in contemplating literature is essentially a pessimistic one. . . . The idea of stating without approval or disapproval is alien to the literary man who finds classification indispensable for order.

When Eric Goldman asked you on "The Open Mind" if media change—the electronic revolution of our time, for example—was a "good" or "bad" thing, you replied:

> Now, you see, you have slipped into the literary language of the classifier. The visual man is always trying to check things out by classification and matching.

. . .

Classification, for the literary man, is the be-all and end-all of observations. That's why Macdonald attempts to classify me. In the medical world, classification is a form of dismissal. If the doctor says it's measles, that's it, it's over with. The rest is just routine. But classification is not the beginning of the study of a problem—it's the end. . . .

There is an alternative to classification and that is exploration. This doesn't easily register with nineteenth-century minds. Most nineteenth-century minds are helpless in discussing contemporary forms. They have never acquired the verbal means of grappling with a pictorial world. Macdonald has no verbal strategies for even coping with the movies, let alone more subtle or more recent forms, like radio or television.

I'm perfectly prepared to scrap any statement I ever made about any subject once I find that it isn't getting me into the problem. I have no devotion to any of my probes as if they were sacred opinions. I have no proprietary interest in my ideas and no pride of authorship as such. You have to push any idea to an extreme, you have to probe. Exaggeration, in the sense of hyperbole, is a major artistic device in all modes of art. . . .

This question of repetition bothers them most because they are looking for values or a "point of view." Now values, insofar as they register a preference for a particular kind of effect or quality, are a highly contentious and debatable area in every field of discourse. Nobody in the twentieth century has ever come up with any meaningful definition or discussion of "value." It doesn't work any longer in economics, let alone humanist affairs. It is rather fatuous to insist upon values if you are not prepared to understand how they got there and by what they are now being undermined. The mere moralistic expression of approval or disapproval, preference or detestation, is currently being used in our world as

Canadian philosopher and communications theorist Marshall McLuhan in 1966. McLuhan held that the media of television and radio were transforming society through the manner in which they conveyed information. © BETTMANN/CORBIS. REPRODUCED BY PERMISSION.

a substitute for observation and a substitute for study. . . .

Anybody who spends his time screaming about values in our modern world is not a serious character. You might as well start screaming about a house that's burning down, shouting, "This is not the act of a serious man!" When your old world is collapsing and everything is changing at a furious pitch, to start announcing your preferences for old values is not the act of a serious person. . . . That's all these critics are saying. Their house is burning and they're saying, "Don't you have any sense of values, simply telling people about fire when you should be thinking about the serious content, the noble works of the mind?" Value is irrelevant. . . .

Many people would rather be villains than nitwits. It occurs to me just now that moral vehemence may provide ersatz dignity for our normal moronic behavior. It would be possible to extend my media analysis to include the idea that the normal human condition, when faced with innovation, is that of the brainwashed idiot who tries to introduce the painfully learned responses from one situation into new situations where they apply not at all. The reason that I refrain in the book from pointing out this obvious moral is owing to the discovery, represented by the book itself, that this helpless and witless condition of persistent irrelevance of response is unnecessary at the first moment that we recognize this pattern of response and its causes. It is this discovery that fills me with optimism. . . .

Do I "approve of 'Peyton Place' or of Jack Paar?" No! But they're trying to classify Paar with a good or bad "thing," not attempting to find out *what* he's doing or what effect he's having or what's really going on. They are trying to fit him into some sort of encyclopedia of culture. They find *concept* a much more convenient form of human activity than *precept*. They ask me to judge what I observe. Cocteau said: "I don't want to be famous. I just want to be believed." Any artist would say that he doesn't want people to agree or disagree with him. He just wants them to notice. I expect my audience to participate with me in a common act of exploration. I want observations, not agreement. And my own observation of our almost overwhelming cultural gradient toward the primitive—or involvement of all the senses—is attended by complete personal distaste and dissatisfaction. I have no liking for it.

Since, however, this new cultural gradient is the world, the *milieu,* in which I must live and which prepares the students I must teach, I have every motive to understand its constituents, its components, and its operations. I move around through these elements as I hope any scientist would through a world of disease and stress and misery. If a doctor, surgeon or scientist were to become personally agitated about any phenomenon whatever, he would be finished as an explorer or observer. The need to retain an attitude of complete clinical detachment is necessary for survival in this kind of work. It is not an expression of approval or a point of view or outlook. It's only a strategy of survival. Anybody who enters this kind of work with strong feelings of approval or disapproval, nineteenth-century-style point of view, fixed positions . . . completely polished himself off the scene as an observer. He's had it. So our literary fraternities—nineteenth-century liberals if you like—are completely helpless to even approach the material of their own culture. They are so terrified, so revolted, they don't even know how to get near it and they've never bothered to acquire the means of studying or of observing it.

This so-called primitivism—and it is so fatuous in our time, so uncritical—one of the more ridiculous aspects of Picasso, if you like—it's a form of surfboarding, just riding any old wave that happens to be around. On the other hand, primitivism, D. H. Lawrence style, has become in itself almost a form of *camp.* That is why we have suddenly abandoned it in favor of *camp,* which is a new artistic attitude toward our own junkyard. The sudden resolve to tackle our own junkyard as art work is a hopeful indication that we are prepared after all to look at the environment as that which is capable of formulation, patterning, shaping. It still lacks the awareness of what effects environments have upon us. They still seem to imagine that you can take it or leave it. . . . The idea of immunity from environments and environments created by media—so long as one concentrates upon noble content—is a cherished illusion in literary circles. . . .

Similarly, there are those who feel they can expose themselves to a hideous urban environment so long as they feel they are in a state of literary grace, as it were; that the forms of life are not in themselves communicative; that only classified data register in our apparatus. People would never dream of valuing their daily experiences in terms of what they happen to see or hear *that* day. Media like print or radio or television—which are much more environmental and pervasive forms assailing their eyes and ears all day long—these are invisible. It was only in the nineteenth century that artists, painters, and poets began to notice that it was the environmental form itself, as humanly constituted, that really provided people with the models of perception that governed their thoughts. The literary people still cherish the idea that we can fight off the sensory models imposed on our sensorium by environment, by content, by the classifiable part of the environment. . . .

As a person committed to literature and the literary tradition, I have studied these new environments which threaten to dissolve the whole of literary modality, the whole traditions of literary achievement, and I don't think that these are merely threats to classifiable literary values that can be fended off by staunch moralism or lively indignation. We have to discover new patterns of action, new strategies of survival.

This is where William Burroughs comes in with his *Naked Lunch.* When we invent a new technology, we become cannibals. We eat ourselves alive since these technologies are merely extensions of ourselves. The new environment shaped by electric technology is a cannibalistic one that eats people. To survive one must study the habits of cannibals.

Why are some critics so outraged by your work?

Any new demand on human perception, any new pressure to restructure the habits of perception, is the occasion for outraged response. Literary people prefer to deal with their world without disturbance to their perceptual life. . . . In our time the plunge through the looking glass of Lewis Carroll into the discontinuous, space-time world of electric technology has created the same sense of the plunge into the abyss, the plunge into the irrational on the part of our contemporaries that we associate with existentialism. Our contemporaries are mistaken, in many ways, as to the causes of their present discontent. On the other hand, they are not mistaken about the demands on their sensibilities and on their perceptions. To shift out of a nineteenth-century, rational space into a twentieth-century space-time, noncontinuum is an experience of great discomfort because it puts one's whole sensorium under terrible pressure.

Further Resources

BOOKS

Molinaro, Matie, Corinne McLuhan, and William Tove, eds. *Letters of Marshall McLuhan.* New York: Oxford University Press, 1988.

McLuhan, Marshall, with Eric McLuhan. *Laws of Media: The New Science.* Toronto: University of Toronto Press, 1989.

McLuhan, Eric, and Frank Zingrone, eds. *The Essential McLuhan.* New York: Basic Books, 1996.

PERIODICALS

Kenner, Hugh. "Understanding McLuhan." *National Review,* November 28, 1966, 1224–1225.

Schickel, Richard. "Marshall McLuhan: Canada's Intellectual Comet." *Harper's,* November 1965, 62–68.

WEBSITES

"Marshall McLuhan." Available online at http://www.mcluhan .utoronto.ca/marshal.htm (accessed March 24, 2003).

"Marshall McLuhan." Available online at http://www.law.pitt .edu/hibbitts/mcl.htm (accessed March 25, 2003).

"We Are Mired in Stalemate"

Television broadcast

By: Walter Cronkite Jr.

Date: February 27, 1968

Source: Cronkite, Walter. "We Are Mired in Stalemate" news broadcast. CBS television, February 27, 1968. Reprinted online at http://www.richmond.edu/~ebolt /history398/Cronkit_1968.html; website home page: http:/www.richmond.edu (accessed April 8, 2003).

Walter Cronkite, anchorman of CBS news, reports from Vietnam in 1968.
GETTY IMAGES. REPRODUCED BY PERMISSION.

About the Author: Walter Leland Cronkite Jr. (1916–), American journalist and radio and television news broadcaster, was among the preeminent group of correspondents and commentators developed by CBS News after World War II. He anchored *CBS Evening News* from 1962 to 1981 and hosted the *Universe* TV series. He was inducted into the Television Academy Hall of Fame in 1985. ∎

Introduction

On January 30, 1968, communist troops launched a surprise offensive throughout South Vietnam. The South Vietnamese capital of Saigon and the U.S. embassy were attacked for the first time. A few weeks later, the U.S. military claimed that because of the heavy losses the Viet Cong had suffered during the Tet offensive, this event was in fact a defeat for the communists. This may have been true from a military and strategic point of view, but it turned out to be beside the point politically. Prior to Tet, most Americans believed that victory in Vietnam was inevitable because of U.S. superiority in firepower and technology. But Tet turned out to be a political and propaganda victory for the communists because of the intensity and scope of the offensive. The sheer scale of what the Viet Cong and their North Vietnamese suppliers were able to do shocked Americans out of their belief that victory would come, and come soon.

A bigger shock was on the way. The prominent CBS newsman Walter Cronkite flew to Vietnam to do a special report on the Tet offensive and its implications for the war. The idea was to allow the American people to see the conflict as it appeared from the frontlines. Over the years, Cronkite had acquired a reputation for sobriety, objectivity, and perspective in his reporting. Thus, when he expressed personal emotion in front of the camera, it tended to have a disproportionate effect on the audience. When he closed his broadcast each night with his famous sign-off—"And that's the way it is . . ."—viewers felt that he was sincere and was attempting to convey to them plain, unvarnished truth.

Cronkite may have gone to Vietnam with some doubts about the military involvement, but after talking with key participants on the scene, he concluded that the war was unwinnable, and at the end of his special report to the nation on the Tet offensive, he said so: "To say that we are closer to victory today is to believe, in the face of the evidence, the optimists who have been wrong in the past. To suggest that we are on the edge of defeat is to yield to unreasonable pessimism. To say that we are mired in stalemate seems the only realistic, yet unsatisfactory conclusion." President Lyndon Johnson watched the special report with some of his staff, including his assistant, Bill Moyers. According to Moyers, when the program was over, "The President flipped off the set and said 'If I've lost Cronkite, I've lost Middle America.'" Five weeks later, on March 31, Johnson announced that he would not seek reelection. The war was to continue for seven more years, but in hindsight it became evident that Cronkite's famous statement marked the beginning of American withdrawal from Southeast Asia.

Significance

The war in Vietnam was a major turning point for Walter Cronkite and for network news generally. Cronkite was the first news anchorman to publicly oppose the war. While he may not have changed the course of the Vietnam War, President Johnson was prescient when he noted Cronkite's link with Middle America, for by the end of 1968 most of Middle America had come to share Cronkite's view.

In the 1960s, before the proliferation of cable and satellite channels, CBS, NBC, and ABC were the windows on the world for most Americans. Each night, more than 50 million Americans would watch the evening news, compared to 20 million in the early twenty-first century. While the 1960s were a golden era for network television, the decade was also a time of deep disagreements, rapid social change and often confrontational politics. In this context, television news broadcasts were voices of moderation amid chaos. They reflected middle-class values and centrist politics, mainly because the men who produced and presented them were middle class and moderate. Network television news during this era rejected extremes, cleaved to the political middle, and had as its symbolic representatives men of unquestioned journalistic excellence, experience, and integrity. In tending to a centrist perspective, the anchors and their colleagues contributed in some measure to peace and stability in both the foreign and domestic arenas. The daily arguments in their newsrooms were not about what story would be the most interesting, amusing, or titillating, but what was the most intrinsically important. As longtime CBS commentator Eric Sevareid put it: "My job is not to tell you what to think. It is to suggest what you should think about."

Primary Source

"We Are Mired in Stalemate"

SYNOPSIS: In this famous broadcast, Walter Cronkite offered his opinion that the United States was not winning (or losing) the war in Vietnam but rather was locked in a stalemate with an enemy it could not defeat militarily.

Tonight, back in more familiar surroundings in New York, we'd like to sum up our findings in Vietnam, an analysis that must be speculative, personal, subjective. Who won and who lost in the great Tet offensive against the cities? I'm not sure. The Vietcong did not win by a knockout, but neither did we. The referees of history may make it a draw. Another standoff may be coming in the big battles expected south of the Demilitarized Zone. Khesanh could well fall, with a terrible loss in American lives, prestige and morale, and this is a tragedy of our stubbornness there; but the bastion no longer is a key to the rest of the northern regions, and it is doubtful that the American forces can be defeated across the breadth of the DMZ with any substantial loss of ground. Another standoff. On the political front, past performance gives no confidence that the Vietnamese government can cope with its problems, now compounded by the attack on the cities. It may not fall, it may hold on, but it probably won't show the dynamic qualities demanded of this young nation. Another standoff.

We have been too often disappointed by the optimism of the American leaders, both in Vietnam and Washington, to have faith any longer in the silver linings they find in the darkest clouds. They may be right, that Hanoi's winter-spring offensive has been forced by the Communist realization that they could not win the longer war of attrition, and that the Communists hope that any success in the offensive will improve their position for eventual negotiations. It would improve their position, and it would also require our realization, that we should have had all along, that any negotiations must be that—negotiations, not the dictation of peace terms. For it seems now more certain than ever that the bloody experience of Vietnam is to end in a stalemate. This summer's almost certain standoff will either end in real give-and-take negotiations or terrible escalation; and for every means we have to escalate, the enemy can match us, and that applies to invasion of the North, the use of nuclear weapons, or the mere commitment of one hundred, or two hundred, or three hundred thousand more American troops to the battle. And with each escalation, the world comes closer to the brink of cosmic disaster.

To say that we are closer to victory today is to believe, in the face of the evidence, the optimists who have been wrong in the past. To suggest we are on the edge of defeat is to yield to unreasonable pessimism. To say that we are mired in stalemate seems the only realistic, yet unsatisfactory, conclusion. On the off chance that military and political analysts are right, in the next few months we must test the enemy's intentions, in case this is indeed his last big gasp before negotiations. But it is increasingly clear to this reporter that the only rational way out then will be to negotiate, not as victors, but as an honorable people who lived up to their pledge to defend democracy, and did the best they could.

This is Walter Cronkite. Good night.

Further Resources

BOOKS
Aaseng, Nathan. *Walter Cronkite*. Minneapolis, Minn.: Lerner, 1981.

Cronkite, Walter. *The Challenges of Change*. Washington, D.C.: Public Affairs Press, 1971.

Jakes, John. *Great War Correspondents*. New York: Putnam, 1967.

PERIODICALS
"Cronkite's Alarm." *Nation*, February 27, 1967, 260–261.

"Cronkite Takes a Stand." *Newsweek*, March 11, 1968, 18.

WEBSITES
"The Connection: Walter Cronkite." Available online at http://www.theconnection.org/shows/2002/10/20021018_a_main.asp; website home page: http://www.theconnection.org (accessed March 25, 2003).

"Chicago: A Post-Mortem"

Magazine article

By: Frank Reuven

Date: December 14, 1968

Source: Reuven, Frank. "Chicago: A Post-Mortem." *TV Guide,* December 14, 1968, 106–115.

About the Author: Frank Reuven (1920–) was born in Montreal, Quebec. After earning a Masters in Journalism from Columbia University in 1947, he worked for three years as a newspaper writer before joining the NBC television network. He had a long career with NBC News, first as a writer and editor and then as a producer of news programs, including the *Huntley-Brinkley Report.* He was president of the NBC News Division from 1968–1973 and again in 1982–1984. ■

Introduction

Every four years the nation's political parties hold conventions to nominate presidential and vice presidential candidates. These conventions typically serve to introduce and showcase the parties' candidates on national television. But 1968 was not a typical year. Antiwar and civil rights demonstrations had become a fact of life as Americans disagreed about the Vietnam War and measures to take to end racial discrimination. These unresolved questions ensured that there would be disturbances at both the Republican convention in Miami and the Democratic convention in Chicago. If the former was marked by unrest, the latter was disfigured by it when the news media turned their focus to the streets and parks of Chicago where protesters and police were violently confronting each other.

These tumultuous events happened when an irresistible force met an immovable object. The immovable object was Mayor Richard Daley of Chicago, an old-style Democrat boss who earlier that spring had given police orders to crack down on violent demonstrators during peace marches and the disturbances that followed the assassination of Martin Luther King Jr. The irresistible force was the young antiwar protestors who came to Chicago. The four major groups of protestors were the National Mobilization to End the War in Vietnam, led by David Dellinger and Rennie Davis; the Yippies, led by Jerry Rubin and Abbie Hoffman; Students for a Democratic Society (SDS), a campus antiwar group led by Tom Hayden; and the Coalition for an Open Convention, led by Martin Slate. All four groups had applied unsuccessfully for permits for marches, rallies, and access to the public parks for sleeping. The public assemblies were therefore illegal from the start, increasing the potential for confrontation.

These groups and their sympathizers viewed the convention as a confrontation between traditional machine politics, represented by Daley, and the new and often idealized politics of the youth activists, represented by protest leaders and, within the convention, the supporters of Eugene McCarthy. While every news organization sent reporters and journalists to cover this event, there was a parallel confrontation between establishment journalists who believed in balancing perspectives and aiming at middle-class values and a younger group of writers who were called the "new journalists." The rise of the "new journalism" in publications such as the *New Yorker, Atlantic, The Village Voice,* and *Esquire* is one of the most significant developments in this period. New Journalism was personal journalism, written without deference to the official view. *Esquire* magazine, one of the vanguards of the new journalism, sent one of its "hippest" writers, Terry Southern, accompanied by French playwright and novelist Jean Genet and author William Burroughs, to cover this clash of generational political views. Southern was disposed to hang out on the streets of Chicago with the kids rather than with the politicians in the Convention Hall.

He wrote of his experience: "We got there [Lincoln Park] around eleven and immediately sensed that there was a different atmosphere from the night before, an air of determination, and about twice as many people . . . At midnight the police begin to appear; they arrived on the opposite side of the expressway which forms the north boundary of the park, it was a solid line, shoulder to shoulder, five blocks long. Their gas masks were quite conspicuous. About twelve-thirty, one officer crossed the expressway and started issuing "final warnings" on the bullhorn. . . . In any case, when the brick hit the windshield . . . we began a leisurely withdrawal. . . . That's when the police charged. They came very fast, clubbing everyone they could catch, and firing tear-gas shells ahead of the fleeing crowd, so that it was a question of going through the gas or waiting to get clubbed."

Significance

The confrontations between the protesters and the police began on Sunday before the convention began and continued each day through Thursday night, when Hubert Humphrey was nominated. Mayor Daley posted twelve thousand police officers on the streets and called in the Illinois National Guard. Television cameras recorded a bloody riot as police arrested over five hundred people in clashes that injured more than a hundred police and a hundred demonstrators just outside the hotel where Humphrey, George McGovern, and Eugene McCarthy were staying. The antiwar protesters retreated back to Grant Park for an all-night rally just as Humphrey received the Democratic nomination for president.

The impact of the events in Chicago was felt within an already divided Democratic Party. Humphrey's standing in the polls suffered; even though he regained most of his support, there was a surge of support for the "law and order" stances of Republican candidate Richard Nixon and third-party candidate George Wallace. Humphrey lost the November election to Nixon by only 0.7 percent of the vote. Longer-term effects involved the way in which the public regarded the media and its role in covering political upheavals. Vice President Spiro T. Agnew was to lead a very popular attack on the media for encouraging the protestors and making them into heroes. More generally, arguments about the impact of mass media on protest activity were to continue for years. Davis, Hayden, Dellinger, Bobby Seale, Abbie Hoffman, Jerry Rubin, and Mobilization officials Lee Weiner and John Froines, collectively known as the Chicago Seven (after Seale's case was severed and he was tried separately), were charged with conspiracy to riot. The farthest-reaching effects of the Chicago demonstrations, however, were changes in the procedures for choosing presidential candidates, including an expanded primary system and the inclusion of more women, young people, and racial minorities among the delegates. The clashes, however, remained a major symbol of the conflict between the old and new politics.

Journalist Terry Southern covered the 1968 Democratic Convention for *Esquire* magazine. His focus was on the protestors gathered outside in the streets. © **BETTMANN/CORBIS. REPRODUCED BY PERMISSION.**

Primary Source

"Chicago: A Post-Mortem" [excerpt]

> **SYNOPSIS:** In this excerpt, the president of NBC News, Frank Reuven, responds to criticism of NBC's coverage of the 1968 Democratic Convention and the protests outside the convention.

The details of what happened in Chicago are already fading into memory, but the impressions, the memory of the emotions, will remain. What happened in Chicago seems to be this: several thousand people, mostly but not all young, came there to make their antiwar protest heard. The City of Chicago tried in every possible way to assure that they got no attention. They therefore got more attention, in the country and around the world, than they deserved or dared expect.

The reason was television: not what anybody in television did but the fact of television, the existence of television. It demonstrated the shortsightedness of planning any public event these days without taking television truly into account, because it is just plain there, and its absence would be even more obvious than its presence.

Another thing happened in Chicago that almost disappeared from public discussion the day the convention ended. The convention was a disunited one, and its disunity was patent. Controls imposed on delegates and others entitled to be there may or may not have been unusual but they seemed harsh to the delegates themselves and to the people watching at home. At the center of this storm, also, was Mayor Richard J. Daley of Chicago, delaying and then ordering adjournments, cuing and cutting off band music. The fuss over the peace demonstrators and the police has driven the troubles of the convention itself from memory. The letters make almost no mention of what happened inside the convention hall; and the polls, which show 70 or 60 or 50 percent of Americans siding with the Chicago police against the demonstrators, have not even bothered to poll the country about what they thought of the convention.

Immediately following the convention, the criticism seemed to be concentrated on charges that we had spent undue time in showing the demonstrations and the police actions in suppressing them, and that our reporters and commentators had made

Thousands of protestors gather on Michigan Avenue in Chicago, outside the hotel (not shown) where the 1968 Democratic Convention is taking place. Police and National Guardsmen (bottom) block their path. © BETTMANN/CORBIS. REPRODUCED BY PERMISSION.

statements about the police action which directly or indirectly criticized the police. This was easy to answer because it was simply not true.

The time NBC devoted to direct network coverage of the convention totaled more than 35 hours. The time devoted to the pictures of the demonstrations was 65 minutes, less than three percent of the total time. Of these 65 minutes, 30 were in prime time. (The consideration of prime time is important because Mayor Daley raised it when he demanded network time for his "reply.") Also of these 65 minutes, 12 were a resume of scenes already shown, a late-night summary of events, and clearly labeled as such. The other networks had similar experience.

I have reviewed the NBC transcript of the 65 minutes in question. To me, it is notable among other reasons for its brevity. The transcript is unusually short for 65 minutes of pictures. It showed no statement critical of the police; it showed almost no value judgments at all. It was simple descriptive material accompanying pictures. Most of the time our reporters said nothing at all, merely letting the pictures be shown. The regularly scheduled pro-

grams which NBC News produces reused some of these pictures; and the reporters gave their analyses as they often do with news events whether they have been covered live or not. Hugh Downs and others carried on a long discussion during the *Today* program.

From implying that we had shown too much, the criticism shifted in the week after Labor Day to the implication that we had not shown enough. The new and larger wave of letters, stimulated, at least in part, by Mayor Daley's public statements, were to the point that we did not show the provocation of the police which led to the action we did show; and then, to a lesser degree, that we did not describe adequately the organization and history of the demonstrations as they were developed over the months preceding the conventions. It was criticism of too little rather than too much coverage.

We have only the word of Mayor Daley and official Chicago police spokesmen as to the degree of provocation. No one denies that there was some. The transcript of our own 65 minutes mentions it prominently. To accept uncritically the evaluations of various Chicago officials about the high degree of provocation is no more justified than accepting uncritically the statements of various people in relatively high public position that there was no provocation at all. Blair Clark and Richard Goodwin, in behalf of Senator McCarthy's campaign organization, sent telegrams to the networks asking to answer Mr. Daley if he were given time on television. They detail what they consider and state was the entirely unprovoked attack by Chicago policemen on young McCarthy workers after Thursday midnight of convention week. The point of all this is that the statements by Mayor Daley and his associates about the extent to which the demonstrators provoked the police cannot be accepted without much more information and documentation.

Up until the violence, it was our conscious policy to avoid covering too much of the activities of demonstrators lest we fall into the trap of doing their advertising for them. Months of "underground newspaper" ads organizing two streams of the demonstrators were known to everyone in the news field, and little was done about it for this reason. During the actual convention coverage, little attention was paid to the demonstrations Monday and Tuesday night for the same reason. When open clashes occurred within range of our cameras, which were relatively stationary, there was no longer any responsible reason for withholding coverage.

But all this begs much more important questions. The tone of the criticism is a lack or loss of faith in television reporting itself. There is implication after implication, in the letters, in certain newspaper accounts and comments, that all this came about because of intent, because the networks wanted it this way as a sort of revenge. Revenge that the two national conventions were in different cities, revenge that floor credentials were allotted below what we considered minimum needs, revenge against a catalogue of greedy motives and mythic presences. And if the answer is No, why haven't we stopped beating our wives?

What did this? The nature of the coverage was not substantially different from the nature of the coverage in 1964, 1960 and 1956. Nor for that matter from the nature of the coverage of the Republican Convention this year. There was some criticism of what we did that week, but of manageable and expectable volume. It was more than counterbalanced by open expressions of approval and appreciation.

But in Chicago, the event itself was different, and the coverage is blamed for that. There is no logical answer available other than this one.

Since 1956 it has been our pattern to rely on four floor reporters for reporting events inside convention hall. By interviews and by statements they explain proceedings, expected developments and also currents of thought and action which otherwise would not reach the public. It is our position that the official proceedings of a convention are only a part of the journalistic record of that convention, and this has been the best method we could devise of fulfilling journalistic responsibility to find and report the rest of the story. These four floor men are augmented by reporters and mobile electronic equipment at many locations away from the convention hall, at the convention headquarters hotel, at candidates' headquarters, and at other locations.

Our equipment has improved over the years and our men have grown more experienced. But the basic structure has not changed since 1956. A third element in that basic structure, the least-known element, is a body of reporters covering each principal candidate and as many as 40 of the principal delegations.

The degree to which this entire reporting system was called on to present news material other than the official proceedings was not substantially different from 1964, although many of the letters express criticism of it in a tone which implies 1968 was

something brand-new. This is just one more instance where the criticism cannot be taken to mean what its words say. There is no doubt the critics are disaffected or hostile. But they give reasons which were just as valid in previous situations which they did not see fit to criticize.

Lately, when I have had to reply to criticism of our covering more than the official proceedings, I have often gone beyond the simple statement that there is more news at a convention than takes place at the podium and that it is our responsibility as journalists to find it and report it. We spend a great deal of time and effort every fourth year reporting that world-shaking event, the choice of the American President by the American electorate. We cover primary campaigns; the important primary elections; the election campaigns; Election Night; all in detail and depth, deploying all our men and expending network time which sheer business considerations would not necessarily justify. The national nominating conventions are not only themselves important events in this process, but they are the locales of many other events hearing upon this process, some important, some minor.

The managers of the convention have not yet learned well enough to realize what it means that television is there. They know it as a fact, but they do not appreciate it. Television is there and will always be there. Individuals working in television organizations do not make the decisive difference; the fact that television is there makes the difference. Television has been invented and developed and it exists. The politician tends to see this as giving him access to the public. Now the public has access to him. It may be, as has been said, that there were conventions in the past which were even more rigidly managed. But not when people could watch it as it happened, feel that it was they being managed.

There have also been many references, in letters and in print, to the fact that the first pictures of the Michigan Avenue demonstrations interrupted Mayor Carl Stokes of Cleveland, who was seconding the Presidential nomination of Vice President Humphrey. Usually there is an implication of some sinister purpose. Again, the explanation is far longer and more complicated than the original charge.

First of all, it is our practice to try to present the entire nominating speech of every serious nominee, unless truly major news events intervene, but to consider seconding speeches subject to much less stringent criteria for interruption. Mayor Stokes, as I say, was seconding Mr. Humphrey's nomination.

Secondly, when it became apparent that events outside the convention hall would not be available for live television broadcast because of the circumstances of the telephone-equipment-installers' strike, I set down the rule that if we could not cover live, we would cover with television tape as soon as it became available; if tape was ruled out, we should do it with film; and if film was out of the question, we might try the sound signal from walkie-talkies, and show still pictures on the television screen. But we would do what we could, as we could, to discharge our responsibility to the television audience to cover the entire story in the manner it had come to expect. That first piece of television tape was rushed by motorcycle courier from Michigan Avenue to the Merchandise Mart; screened there on a spot-check basis for technical reliability; an editor evaluated it and chose less than four minutes, which was all we could handle; and as soon as it became available, we were ready to use it. Since the speech placing Vice President Humphrey's name in nomination was still being made, we deferred the tape until the nominating speech ended, and used it instead of Mayor Stokes' seconding speech. (Later that night a videotape excerpt from the speech was used.)

Further Resources

BOOKS

Farber, David. *Chicago '68.* Chicago: University of Chicago Press, 1988.

Southern, Nile, and Josh Alan Friedman, eds. *Now Dig This: The Unspeakable Writings of Terry Southern 1950–1995.* New York: Grove, 2001.

United States Congress. House Committee on Un-American Activities. *Subversive Involvement in Disruption of 1968 Democratic National Party Convention.* Washington D.C.: Government Printing Office, 1968.

WEBSITES

Arlen, Michael, "Notes on the New Journalism" *Atlantic Monthly,* May 1972. Available online at http://www.theatlantic.com/issues/72may/newjournalism-p1.htm; website home page: http://www.theatlantic.com/ (accessed March 26, 2003).

"Chicago 1968: An Introduction." Available online at http://www.geocities.com/Athens/Delphi/1553/ (accessed March 25, 2003).

Southern, Terry. "Grooving in Chi." *Esquire,* November 1968. Available online at http://www.pbs.org/newshour/convention96/retro/southern.html; website home page: http://www.pbs.org (accessed March 25, 2003).

"Terry Southern." Available online at http://www.terrysouthern.com/home.htm (accessed March 25, 2003).

The Smothers Brothers Comedy Hour

"C.B.S. to Drop Smothers Hour; Cites Failure to Get Previews"

Newspaper article

By: Jack Gould

Date: April 3, 1969

Source: Gould, Jack. "C.B.S. to Drop Smothers Hour; Cites Failure to Get Previews." *The New York Times,* April 3, 1969.

"The Smothers Brothers Redux: A Bittersweet Reunion"

Newspaper article

By: Andy Meisler

Date: January 31, 1988

Source: Meisler, Andy. "The Smothers Brothers Redux: A Bittersweet Reunion." *The New York Times,* January 31, 1988. ■

Introduction

The Smothers Brothers Comedy Hour debuted on CBS on Sunday night in February 1967 opposite the long-standing hit NBC show *Bonanza.* Although CBS never expected the show to succeed in that time slot, the intention was to appeal to a "hipper" and more youthful audience. Against all odds, the show turned out to be a hit in its first season, knocking off the top-rated *Bonanza* in the ratings. *Time* magazine dubbed the youthful Smothers brothers "hippies with haircuts." The show tried to appeal to the divergent tastes of the increasingly polarized older and younger generations. It introduced major rock groups such as Jefferson Airplane and The Mamas and the Papas but at the same time scheduled a mainstream artist such as Jim Nabors to sing "The Impossible Dream." And when old-timers like Kate Smith visited the show, they would appear with The Beatles on the one hand and Irving Berlin on the other. The show also introduced mildly satirical sketches designed to provide commentary on contemporary political and cultural issues. It was for this reason that the Smothers would get into trouble with the network's censors.

In the second season, Pete Seeger, a previously blacklisted singer, was booked without objections from CBS. But the network balked at his proposed song, "Waist Deep in the Big Muddy," because of its references to the sitting president as a fool. CBS executives argued that such political material had no place in an entertainment show. There was such an avalanche of criticism that CBS relented, allowing Seeger to return to the show a few weeks later to sing the song without cuts. This began a cycle of provocation, reaction, and counterreaction, which was to be repeated time and again and fed Tommy Smothers' sense of mission about the show. But the more Tommy saw the show as a "mission" rather than entertainment, the more the executives at CBS feared losing control. Tom Smothers, the major creative force behind the show, enjoyed pushing the envelope in areas of political satire, off-color sexual innuendo, religious subjects, and topics considered "off beat" by the networks. He always insisted, though, that "We belonged to no political parties, we were vaudevillians."

But they were vaudevillians who had found an appreciative audience for their political and cultural comedy. In the third season, several runs-in with the network involved guest performers who chose material that was highly critical of the establishment. Harry Belafonte wanted to do a song criticizing the way the police dealt with the demonstrators at the Chicago Democratic Convention. The network axed the entire number. At another point, an entire program featuring antiwar activist Joan Baez was canceled. But it was a series of religious satires called "sermonettes" by comedian David Steinberg that ultimately caused CBS to pull the plug on the program. On April 3, 1969, with a few weeks yet to go in the television season, Robert D. Wood, president of CBS television, informed Tom Smothers by wire that they were fired. The ostensible reason was that the Smothers had not delivered an acceptable broadcast tape in time for preview by network censors and affiliated stations. The forced removal of a television series from a network schedule led to a public uproar. Tom Smothers attempted to launch a free speech campaign in Washington, D.C., to pressure the network to relent, but to no avail.

Significance

As a comedy/singing team, the Smothers Brothers reached the apex of their career with *The Smothers Brothers Comedy Hour.* Their offbeat creativity and experimentation with countercultural work in a medium aimed at the broadest possible cross-section of the population brought them great notoriety and success for a time. But the inevitable dismissal came when the television authorities concluded that the limits for satisfying the widest range of possible viewers had been reached.

In attempting to reflect some of the political and social turmoil of the era in a prime-time entertainment offering, the Smothers brothers discovered that there are limits beyond which American commercial television is not willing to go. In the 1960s, even mildly controversial material in entertainment programming could ruffle feathers to a surprising extent, given how much change

was taking place at the time. The Smothers' variety show, with its ongoing battles against network censorship, became a flash point in the debate about the relation of popular entertainment to social change.

The Smothers Brothers Comedy Hour was one of the most important pop culture phenomena of the 1960s. The show was enormously influential on the future practices of both American comedians and television programs that sought to make political satire part of their fare. Comedian Steve Martin has commented that it was on this program that he acquired 90 percent of his writing skills. *Saturday Night Live* was perhaps the most noteworthy legacy of the Smothers' groundbreaking work. Bill Maher, host of *Politically Incorrect,* and Dennis Miller, host of a late-night show on HBO named for him, owes much to the Smothers' example. But for all that, it is important to note that unlike *The Smothers Brothers Comedy Hour,* all of these shows are either aired outside prime time or on cable and specialty channels, leaving the prime-time hours on the networks to less controversial programming.

Primary Source

"C.B.S. to Drop Smothers Hour; Cites Failure to Get Previews"

SYNOPSIS: This article details the events surrounding the cancellation of *The Smothers Brothers Comedy Hour* by the CBS network, noting that the cancellation had been widely expected.

"The Smothers Brothers Comedy Hour" has been canceled for next season by the Columbia Broadcasting System, bringing to a climax months of argument over the program's content.

Robert D. Wood, president of the C.B.S. television network, notified Tom and Dick Smothers that they had committed a breach of contract by having failed to submit tomorrow night's program in time for a screening by the network and its affiliated stations last Wednesday. Mr. Wood, who made the announcement last night, said a program seen Nov. 10 would be substituted.

The Smothers Brothers, according to the announcement, "had consistently failed" to deliver tapes in time for review.

In Hollywood, Tom Smothers denied C.B.S.'s charges and said that the program originally planned for tomorrow had been seen by network reviewers there on Wednesday.

Two programs of the current season are still scheduled to be televised through April 20. Following that, the program schedule calls for reruns through June 15. A summer series that was to have been made by the Smothers Brothers production unit, Comedic Productions, Inc., and that would not have presented the brothers on camera, is now "up in the air," a network source reported.

The network had picked up the option on the Smothers Brothers for next season two weeks ago.

Mr. Wood said that the network had reason to believe the Smothers Brothers had planned to include in the program a monologue that would have been regarded as "irreverent and offensive." It would have been inappropriate, he indicated, even if this past week had not been marked by the funeral of General of the Army Dwight D. Eisenhower and Sunday were not Easter. The monologue, C.B.S. said, was to have been delivered by David Steinberg, the comedian, and was described as "a sermonette" on Solomon and Jonah. The text was not available.

In disputing C.B.S.'s contention, Tom Smothers said that Mr. Steinberg's monologue had been voluntarily deleted in advance and that he and his brother had no knowledge that their show would be scheduled after General Eisenhower's funeral on Easter Sunday.

The program, he said, complied completely with all legal obligations and the C.B.S. protests were just a pretext "to get us off the air."

Mr. Smothers added that he had never voiced objections to C.B.S. affiliates making deletions in accordance with regional taste and that a check at the Federal Communications Commission had failed to uncover any protests against the show. Mr. Smothers declined to say what his next step might be.

Publicity About Show

Cancellation of the Smothers Brothers program had been widely anticipated in the broadcasting industry after the network and the comedy team had made clear separately that they could not agree on standards and practices. Despite the substantial publicity about the disagreement, the ratings of "The Smothers Brothers Comedy Hour," seen at 9 P.M. on Sundays, had dropped this season.

The Smothers brothers realized an annual gross in excess of $4.42-million for their show, based on 26 original installments costing $170,000 a week. Of this, they paid production costs and deducted their own salaries.

Including the cost of an hour of prime time on Sunday evenings, which accrues to the network and its affiliated stations, the total investment in a single weekly Smothers brothers hour has amounted to about $375,000.

The contract provides for eight or nine reruns over the summer months, which would lift annual figures higher. The yearly total at stake, divided between the artists and the broadcasters, is in the range of $10-million.

Ratings of 'Laugh-In'

Tom and Dick Smothers, who began their show in January, 1967, were known to be upset by the higher ratings of the Dan Rowan and Dick Martin program called "Laugh-In," seen on Monday nights over the network of the National Broadcasting Company. They attributed the success of the rival show in part to what they regarded as the less stringent program standards of N.B.C.

The 32-year-old Tom Smothers, in particular, took a strong position against the war in Vietnam and also took a liberal view on religious matters. Last month, there were arguments between the team and the network over Joan Baez's expression of opposition to the war and a proposed monologue by Jackie Mason, the comedian.

Primary Source

"The Smothers Brothers Redux: A Bittersweet Reunion at CBS"

> **SYNOPSIS:** Twenty years after the cancellation of the *The Smothers Brothers Comedy Hour*, CBS and the Smothers brothers put their differences aside and aired a Smother Brother reunion show. In this article the participants in the reunion look back on the original show's cancellation.

Hollywood—On the surface, at least, the scene is innocuous. There's even a touch of naïveté in the air: on Stage 33, in the heart of CBS's huge Television City complex, several dozen middle-aged—albeit well-preserved—individuals are rehearsing an old-fashioned TV variety show.

It's "The Smothers Brothers Comedy Hour 20th Reunion Show," a one-hour special to be broadcast Wednesday at 10 P.M. Most of the writers, performers and even crew members are alumni of the original "Smothers Brothers Comedy Hour," which ran on CBS from 1967 through '69. But this show is more than just an exercise in nostalgia.

At the end of the 1968–69 season, CBS, in a move both unprecedented and unduplicated, removed "The Smothers Brothers Comedy Hour" from its schedule. Ratings weren't a problem. The action followed months of bitter contention—over such issues as censorship, the role of political satire in entertainment and overall creative control—between Tom Smothers, the "dumb" half (but offstage the intense, dominant, driving force) of the team, and the highest levels of CBS. They fought over antiwar jokes and songs, "off color" and "inappropriate" material, satirical send-ups of religion, the pre-screening of the show for affiliate stations. Their arguments were conducted even as students and blacks were demonstrating and rioting, while national leaders were being assassinated, while the country was in the midst of a divisive military conflict. That CBS, in 1988, is working hand in glove with the performers it exiled only heightens the atmosphere of ironic bemusement on the set.

The firing severely crippled the Smothers brothers' career, and the whole controversy somehow summed up the passion and contradictions of an era. For many people over 30, including Tom and Dick Smothers themselves, much effort has been spent trying to understand the lessons of that turbulent time.

In that effort, the comedians have been only partly successful. "The way I look at it now, if what happened hadn't happened to us, it would have happened to somebody else," says Tom Smothers, talking, with his brother, in his temporary Sunset Strip production office several days after the taping of the new show. "We were," he says, resignedly, "at the scene of an accident."

It's a theory held by most of those involved. Ken Kragen, the show's executive producer and the Smothers brothers' personal manager both then and now, believes that the pair were as much victims as provocateurs. The strength of their comedy, he says, lay more in their wit, well-developed comic personalities and superb timing than in their political views. "At its height, the Smothers show had maybe five minutes of controversy each week," says Mr. Kragen. "They just got caught up in the spirit of the times."

"We weren't radical chic," says Tom Smothers. "Jane Fonda embarrassed me. We belonged to no political parties. Basically, we were vaudevillians."

Tom, 51, and Dick, 49, grew up in California, and have been performing together since the late 1950's. Their act was a combination of fractured folk songs and comic sibling rivalry. Dick was the straight man. Tom, his face an ever-changing mask of paranoia, low-I.Q. cunning, shame and indigna-

tion, sabotaged all attempts at real folk singing and delivered most of the punch lines. "Mom loved you best!"—delivered as a sure-fire comeback at the slightest provocation—was his most famous.

Their popularity grew through the early 1960's, and CBS saw the clean-cut duo as a fairly safe way of connecting with the burgeoning youth market. On Feb. 5, 1967, at 10 P.M., after "The Ed Sullivan Show" and against NBC's powerhouse "Bonanza," "The Smothers Brothers Comedy Hour" made its debut. The first guest stars were Jack Benny and George Burns.

"The programming people loved us," says Tom Smothers. His brother adds: "I remember one of them coming up to us and saying, 'We want you to be controversial, but at the same time we want everyone to agree with you.'"

Cut to 1988. The studio audience, noticeably older than average, is plainly enjoying the reunion show's taped dress rehearsal. The musical performances (from the likes of Glen Campbell, John Hartford and Jennifer Warnes) are mainstream, the comedy well within the bounds of late 80's good taste. In their opening "two spot," Tom and Dick—clutching guitar and bass, as usual—get off a few clever swipes at CBS, a few more at their own expense, even a slightly risqué remark or two. Perennial Presidential candidate Pat Paulsen ("Where is the man America is looking for?") denounces his current crop of opponents. Steve Martin, who auditioned for the show in 1968 (as a performer, though he got a job as a writer), appears with Tom and Dick Smothers as a mock-smarmy star returning to his roots in a segment he wrote himself.

There's even a gray-suited CBS executive monitoring the proceedings from the control booth. He isn't really a censor: the network's program practices department was abolished several years ago. The fact that the Smotherses' old nemeses have gone the way of the dinosaurs—and, indeed, that there is precious little in the reunion special that any network would worry about in 1988—is an issue the participants politely do not address. The job of censor has shrunk from a full-time occupation to one of many duties of the program executive. "Nowadays, we leave matters of taste and content to the individual departments," says the CBS official, who declined to be quoted by name.

The seeds of destruction of the Smothers Brothers show, most agree, were planted that very first half-season. The program was an instant hit, nearly matching the ratings of "Bonanza." It was popular

Tom (left) and Dick Smothers answer questions from the press after the canceling of *The Smothers Brothers Comedy Hour.* AP/WIDE WORLD PHOTOS. REPRODUCED BY PERMISSION.

among young adults and on college campuses, clearly tapping the market it was aimed at.

"It was the only show that dealt with political issues," says Steve Martin. "It was the only show that allowed rock musicians on. It was the only show that was letting the new culture seep through to the screen. We felt prestigious. We felt like we were outside the system a little bit. Remember, I was 22."

The Smotherses' conflicts with network authority began almost immediately. In April 1967, CBS forbade them to do a sketch, written by Elaine May, making fun of movie censorship. The censors cut such "objectionable" words and lines as "hell," "damn" and "Did you get that girl in trouble?" Jokes about lung cancer—television was still accepting cigarette ads—were also taboo. Tom Smothers battled each cut fiercely, winning some, losing others.

Some controversial material, embodied in satiric concepts, not words, got through. The character of Officer Judy was a not-so-subtle satirical comment on censorship and police repression; Leigh French's character, Goldie, was obviously on drugs.

Tom Smothers insulated his young writers from the network's wrath. They never dealt with the cen-

sors personally, they were, they recall, having a wonderful time. "That's where I learned, I'd say, 90 percent of my writing skills," says Mr. Martin. "We thought back then that it was all sort of a game," says Bob Einstein, then 24, who now stars in and co-produces "The Super Dave Osborne Show" for Showtime. "We enjoyed pushing the boundaries. They couldn't take us off! We were beating the pants off 'Bonanza,' weren't we?"

The situation heated up rapidly during the summer of 1968. It was the summer of Robert Kennedy's assassination and the Democratic Convention. The Smothers brothers made a joke about President Johnson restricting foreign travel: when Dick brought up the topic, Tom leaned into the camera and said, "Okay, you guys in Vietnam—come on home!"

"These things get very heady," says Ken Kragen. "Tom got a lot of support. Most of the media really loved him. Even with all the ominous things happening, there was a feeling of invincibility. When you're young, you don't see the edge of the waterfall."

In March, CBS censored an entire program when the singer Joan Baez dedicated a song to her husband, David Harris, an antiwar activist. The end came the next week, when the brothers refused to pre-screen an episode containing an irreverent "sermonette" by the comedian David Steinberg, Robert D. Wood, the president of CBS, pulled the show off the air.

Tom Smothers didn't believe it. "I thought it was all part of the negotiating, the give and take. I thought a contract was a contract. I didn't know they were playing hardball."

In a bit of Smotherian humor, the brothers have invited William Tankersly, a distinguished-looking gray-haired man from Washington, D.C., to the taping of the reunion show. In 1969, Mr. Tankersly was CBS vice president for program practices—in other words, the head censor.

"I was the one who called the meeting that resulted in the death of the show," says Mr. Tankersly. "We did it reluctantly. Nobody wanted to lose the hour—it added sparkle to Sunday nights. But it got to that point. We had a polarized society at that time, and nobody had a very good sense of humor. They touched nerves with those jokes. And we had affiliated stations that were getting terribly upset."

Like others connected with the show, Tom Smothers believes other forces were also at work. "The political climate was changing," he says. "Nixon, the conservatives were coming in. That was when we became very dispensable to CBS."

The Smothers brothers sued CBS for $31 million, and several years later, after an eight-week trial, won about three-quarters of a million dollars. In the meantime, though, they did very little performing. "I don't remember very much about the first year after the firing," says Tom Smothers. "I do know, though, that I lost my sense of humor."

His anger, he says, gradually abated in the early 70's; his sense of humor recovered, too. "I found out that I couldn't have a nervous breakdown," he says. "I tried a couple of times, but it just didn't work out. My mind, my body wouldn't let me. I had my brother, my family to worry about instead."

Says his brother: "Sure, it was tough being out of the center of things. But we always worked." The coffee-house circuit was gone, but they played at nightclubs and colleges, using mostly nonpolitical material.

In 1975, they starred in an NBC variety show produced by Joe Hamilton, Carol Burnett's husband; as a condition of employment, they had little creative input. "It was like we were being hired to play the part of the Smothers Brothers," says Tom Smothers disgustedly. That same year, the brothers stopped performing together. "We were tired of each other," says Tom. "We were tired of our act. We were beginning to repeat ourselves. Says Dick: "I just became a private citizen. Took the family and did things with them." The two brothers became involved in producing and bottling wine.

Both performed in stage productions, separately and together for the next five years. In the early '80s, the CBS controversy farther behind them, they reformed their comedy team. They worked concerts, county fairs, conventions. Several years ago, they noticed something interesting. "The CEO's of companies, the guys who run advertising agencies, were now our age," says Tom Smothers. The pair became spokesmen for Magnavox; the unexpected popularity of their commercials, according to one CBS official, was a big factor in their being hired to do the reunion show.

They re-signed with Ken Kragen. "He picked up the phone, made a few calls, and CBS finally admitted it had made a mistake," jokes Tom Smothers.

Do the Smothers Brothers feel any residual anger at CBS? "Oh, no," says Tom Smothers. "I'm certainly bright enough to recognize exactly how it was. I can't be mad at any one individual. And I can't be mad at CBS. It's just an organization. And everybody who works in it plays musical chairs."

Whether he'd do things differently is a harder question.

"How can I answer that?" says Tom Smothers. "It's like asking somebody in the water if he's swimming. If he stops to think about it, then he isn't swimming any more.

"Given what I know now, sure, I'd change things. But how could I have back then? There was little room for tolerance. For compromise. I was in a righteous place in my mind. I felt that I was doing the right thing. You only get that feeling two or three times in your life. It's a very pure, sweet place to be."

Further Resources

BOOKS

Hendra, Tony. "Death by Committee." In *Going Too Far*. New York: Doubleday, 1987, 202–226.

Mertz, Robert. "The Smothered Brothers." In *CBS: Reflections in a Bloodshot Eye* Chicago: Playboy Press, 1975, 293–305.

O'Connor, John E., ed. *American History/American Television*. New York: Fredrick Ungar, 1983.

PERIODICALS

Bodroghkozy, Aniko. "The Smothers Brothers Comedy Hours and Youth Rebellion." *The Revolution Wasn't Televised: Sixties Television and Social Conflict*. Lynn Spigel and Michael Curtin, eds. New York: Routledge, 1998, 201–219.

Carr, Steve Allen. "On the Edge of Tastelessness: CBS, the Smothers Brothers, and the Struggle for Control." *Cinema Journal* 31, no. 4, Summer 1992, 3–24.

WEBSITES

"Smothers Brothers Home Page." Available online at http://www.smothersbrothers.com/ (accessed March 26, 2003).

"Smothers Brothers." Available online at http://www.museum.tv/archives/etv/S/htmlS/smothersbrot/smothersbrot.htm; website home page: http://www.museum.tv (accessed March 26, 2003).

"TV: An Awesome Event"

Newspaper article

By: Jack Gould

Date: July 21, 1969

Source: Gould, Jack. "TV: An Awesome Event." *The New York Times*, July 21, 1969. ∎

Introduction

On July 20, 1969, half a billion people all over the world watched on their television sets as Neil A. Armstrong, an American astronaut, climbed slowly down the ladder of his lunar landing vehicle and stepped carefully

Neil Armstrong stands next to the Lunar Module *Eagle* on the moon on July 20, 1969. About a third of the population of the world watched the moon landing on television as it happened. **NASA. REPRODUCED BY PERMISSION.**

onto the surface of the moon. He carried a plaque inscribed with the words: "Here Men from the Planet Earth First Set Foot on the Moon. We Came in Peace for All Mankind."

The *Apollo 11* moon landing was the climax of an intense thirteen-year competition in space exploration between the Soviet Union and the United States, which had begun with the orbiting of the Soviet *Sputnik,* the first artificial earth satellite, in October 1957. In 1961, President John F. Kennedy, in the wake of the Soviet successes, issued a challenge to land men on the moon before 1970 and thus give the United States preeminence in space exploration. After twenty manned missions—two to the vicinity of the moon itself—the United States was ready to achieve that goal.

The *Apollo 11* mission was launched on July 16, 1969. Aboard were Neil A. Armstrong, Colonel Edwin E. Aldrin, and Lieutenant Colonel Michael A. Collins. The command module was named *Columbia,* and the lunar module was called *Eagle.* The two separated during lunar orbit, with Collins aboard the *Columbia* and Armstrong and Aldrin aboard the *Eagle.* On July 20, at 9:18 P.M., Americans reached the moon. Landing on a rocky lunar plain called the Sea of Tranquility, Armstrong announced the arrival: "The *Eagle* has landed." Four hours later the astronauts had on space suits. Armstrong was

first to come out of the lunar module. On touching the moon's surface, he said, "That's one small step for a man, one giant leap for mankind." About a third of the population of the world watched the event on television as it happened. While Armstrong collected moon rocks and dust, Aldrin joined him. The astronauts collected samples and set up various experiments including a laser reflector. After two and a half hours, they returned to the lunar module for some needed sleep. The two astronauts in the lunar module remained on the moon's surface about twenty hours before they fired the ascent rockets and were back in lunar orbit. After rejoining Michael Collins in the command module, the three returned to Earth. At an hour past noon on July 24, the astronauts splashed down near the carrier *Hornet* in the Pacific Ocean.

Significance

After centuries of dreams and prophecies, man had set foot on another world. Standing on the lifeless, rock-studded surface he could see the earth, a blue and white hemisphere suspended in the black sky. Armstrong's first steps onto the moon's surface were cautious, almost tentative, but as time passed he and Aldrin gained confidence, jumping and loping across the barren landscape while the TV camera they had set up transmitted their movements with remarkable clarity to audiences on earth, a quarter of a million miles away. Although the astronauts planted an American flag on the moon, their feat was far more than a national triumph. It was a stunning scientific and intellectual accomplishment for all humankind.

The moon landing was of enormous significance in and of itself, but it is also notable because millions of people watched it happening. Carried live on television worldwide, the picture of Neil Armstrong in his white space suite descending the last rung of the ladder and then extending his foot onto the moon's surface is an indelible image in the minds of the millions of television viewers and a symbol of man's determination to step toward the unknown and to visually record that step. Television cameras were deployed throughout the *Apollo 11* mission so that the astronauts could tell the people of the earth what going to the moon meant to them. Thus people around the world were able to watch history unfold in a manner never before available.

Primary Source

"TV: An Awesome Event"

SYNOPSIS: In this *The New York Times* article, Gould details the events of the *Apollo 11* moon landing, focusing on the role of television in bringing the event live to viewers throughout the world.

Live Pictures of Astronauts on the Moon Leave Little Room for Words

A day of unparalleled uncertainty, marked by minutes of breathless suspense, culminated in the majestic event of live television pictures of Neil A. Armstrong becoming the first human being to place a foot on a planet other than the earth. Long hours of monitoring civilization in evolution were rewarded by a scene that will be remembered for generations.

The poet, journalist and novelist, let alone scientists, academicians, manufacturers and the man in the street, were at loss for adequate words to describe the magnitude and implications of the Apollo 11's success. Mr. Armstrong and Col. Edwin E. Aldrin Jr. of the Air Force in the Eagle lunar module may have had the right literary approach. Unostentatious declaratory descriptions can have their own nobility in contrast to strained incursions into a thesaurus.

The pictures of Mr. Armstrong and Colonel Aldrin hardly required embellishment. The inadequacy of the human language could hardly rival what the eye could see, and the individual beholder instinctively wrote his own script. It was no wonder that during the Apollo 11 highlights the talkative commentators often were mum, some reduced to tears.

An Astronaut's View

Neil Armstrong

To stand on the surface of the moon and look at the earth high over head is certainly a unique experience. Although very beautiful, it is very remote and apparently very small. You might suspect that in such a situation the observer would dismiss the earth as relatively unimportant. Paradoxically, the opposite conclusion has been reached by each of the individuals who has had the opportunity to share that view. We have all been struck by the simile to an oasis or an island. More importantly, it is the only island that we know is a suitable home for man. The importance of protecting and saving that home has never been felt more strongly. Protection seems most required, however, not from foreign aggressors or natural calamity, but from its own population.

SOURCE: *The New York Times,* January 1, 1971, 23.

Mr. Armstrong was clearly seen descending the ladder from the LM module and touching the moon's surface. He described the soft surface of the moon but said there was hard material beneath. He walked out of the fixed lunar module camera range so it was not possible to witness all his preliminary activities. The viewer could see the bag of moon particles being hoisted into the module. At one point Mr. Armstrong was seen almost running in a display of liveliness, describing walking on the Sea of Tranquility as very comfortable. In about 20 minutes he was joined by Colonel Aldrin in their further explorations.

For the viewer the highlight almost was hard to believe. The substitution of a close-up lens enabled the layman to see the helmeted figures in astonishing detail under the circumstances. When the camera cable was extended there were beautiful shots of the moon's surface as well as distinct pictures of clear angular rocks and the shadow of the lunar module. The shots of men exploring the moon gave new substance to television's old claim of enabling the people to see history in the making.

The split-screen showing the two astronauts on the moon and President Nixon from the White House was a discordant note. The occasion was a world triumph, not a time for injection of nationalistic considerations.

The long drama of reaching the moon was different from other predictable delays that television has known. Despite the oceans of unavoidable verbiage, covering the esoteric technological, social and philosophical implications of the flight, there was the compellingly hypnotic appeal of waiting to see if the lunar module would reach its goal.

The clarity of voice communication between Houston and the moon module was almost unbelievable. To the layman there was particular interest in Colonel Aldrin's immediate comments on what he could observe of the Sea of Tranquility, particularly his analysis of rock structures and the grayish environment around the moon.

From the late morning until about 4 P.M. the television medium faced one of the most difficult ordeals in its more than 20 years of operation. Contrary to announced plans, there was no live televising of the separation of the command and lunar modules; the crew had more pressing duties.

Hour after hour the commentators held forth with protracted commentaries, interviews with astronauts, scientists and equipment manufacturers here and abroad. The value of TV until the landing at 4:17 P.M. and Mr. Armstrong's arrival on the moon's surface was really in illustrating technical detail.

One instructional service were the simulations of crucial points in the Apollo adventure and full-scale mockups of the modules to explain how they operated, something much more difficult to accomplish by radio alone.

The networks—the Columbia Broadcasting System, the National Broadcasting Company and the American Broadcasting Company—all planned to be on the air continuously with Apollo news until late this evening—30 hours or more. Last night the networks did not hesitate to scrap their scheduled programs. The audience throughout the night undoubtedly will establish a rating record.

In the early stages of the long day's coverage, C.B.S. News showed a clear initiative in spot pickups, both around the United States and by satellite relay from abroad, before and after the landing. The sustained coherence of Walter Cronkite, C.B.S. anchor man, attested once again to his remarkable human endurance.

Further Resources

BOOKS

Armstrong, Neil. *First on the Moon: A Voyage with Neil Armstrong, Michael Collins and Edwin Aldrin, Jr.* Boston: Little, Brown, 1970.

Collins, Michael. *Carrying the Fire: An Astronaut's Journey.* New York: Farrar, Straus, and Giroux, 1974.

Hehner, Barabar. *First on the Moon: What It Was Like When Men Landed on the Moon.* New York: Hyperion Books, 1999.

PERIODICALS

Franzen, Gene. "One Small Drive." *American Heritage,* July–August 1994, 36.

WEBSITES

"Human Space Flight." Available online at http://spaceflight.nasa.gov/history/apollo/apollo11/; website home page: http://spaceflight.nasa.gov (accessed March 27, 2003).

The Official Apollo 11 Website. Available online at http://www.hq.nasa.gov/office/pao/History/ap11ann/introduction.htm; website home page: http://www.hq.nasa.gov (accessed March 27, 2003).

Spiro Agnew and the Liberal Media

"Television News Coverage"

Speech

By: Spiro T. Agnew

Date: November 13, 1969

Source: Angew, Spiro T. "Television News Coverage." Speech delivered in Des Moines, Iowa, November 13, 1969. Reprinted in *American Rhetoric from Roosevelt to Reagan* Halford Ross Ryan, ed. 2nd ed. Prospect Heights, Ill.: Waveland Press, 1987, 212-219. Available online at "American Rhetoric," http://www.americanrhetoric.com/speeches/spiroagnew.htm; website home page: http://www.americanrhetoric.com (accessed May 27, 2003).

"Agnew Tells Why He Says What He Says"

Interview

By: Spiro T. Agnew

Date: November 17, 1969

Source: "Agnew Tells Why He Says What He Says." *U.S. News & World Report,* November 17, 1969, 20.

About the Author: Spiro Theodore Agnew (1918–1996) entered politics as chief executive of Baltimore County in Maryland. In 1967, he was elected governor of Maryland. In 1968 he was nominated for the vice presidency on the Republican ticket with Richard M. Nixon. Reelected with Nixon in 1972, Agnew was forced to resign—the first vice president in American history to do so—on October 10, 1973, after a Justice Department investigation uncovered evidence of corruption during his years in Maryland politics. After he pleaded no contest to a charge of federal income tax evasion, he was sentenced to three years' probation and fined. ∎

Introduction

Spiro T. Agnew first came to public attention when Richard M. Nixon picked him out of the relative obscurity of state politics to be his vice-presidential running mate. "Spiro who?" asked the media, Agnew was in fact the first suburban politician to be nominated as vice president by one of the major parties. During the campaign, his gaffs and malapropisms led the media to view him as a buffoon. But to their surprise he soon proved himself to be a formidable campaigner and political figure. He quickly became known for his blunt criticisms of college students protesting the Vietnam War and of civil rights agitators and rioters. He tapped into a widespread dissatisfaction of the large group of Americans, the so-called silent majority, who felt their conservative views on law and order and patriotism were being ignored or belittled by the media and "the kids." Agnew also gained much notoriety for lashing out at his opponents with caustic phrases peppered with alliteration and words that required the press to carry dictionaries.

During his first two years in office, Agnew's popularity soared. By the middle of his first year in office, he delivered a series of speeches widely viewed by the media as a new direction in American politics. He turned his attention from the pot-smoking students on campus to the leaders of the antiwar movement whom he labeled "an effete corps of impudent snobs," "ideological eunuchs" and "vultures who sit in trees."

On November 3, President Nixon had delivered a nationally televised speech concerning U.S. policy in Vietnam, which was immediately dissected and criticized by network commentators. Nixon and his aides were enraged. Two days later, the newly appointed head of the FCC was instructed to contact the three networks and obtain transcripts of the remarks of their reporters and commentators—an unprecedented move from the White House. They then prepared a response, which Agnew delivered in a speech before Republican officials in Des Moines, Iowa on November 13, 1969. The speech attacked the nation's media as being biased in their coverage and unfair to President Nixon and his views. This was caused, in Agnew's view, by the liberal views of the relatively small number of people who decided what news to air and how to present it.

Agnew made the media elite's decisions about how to cover protests against the Vietnam War a key issue, arguing that this coverage lacked "balance." He found the media to be uncritical of the antiwar protests, ignoring their "irresponsible" positions and presenting them as "simply doing their own thing to express a desire for peace." He also presented himself as the spokesman for the "silent majority" of Americans that the liberal media ignored. The speech was followed by others, including

one in San Diego, where he famously characterized the press as "nattering nabobs of negativism."

Significance

Agnew's November 13 speech—which was broadcast live by the three networks, a highly unusual act of deference to a vice president—triggered soul-searching in the press. Walter Cronkite, for example, agreed that the news media were too heavily concentrated in New York. The networks received 150,000 communications, which ran two to one in favor of Agnew, although some of those responses were believed to have been coordinated by the Nixon administration.

In retrospect, Agnew's speeches were significant for many reasons: They set the tone for the administration's adversarial relationship with the press, a relationship that led to harassment, eavesdropping, and IRS audits that would soon be launched against Nixon's perceived enemies. These activities would eventually culminate in the Watergate break-in and cover-up and its attendant scandal. Moreover, Agnew's speech was the beginning of a new trend in American politics in which the "liberal press" would become a target for the Republican Party, a tactic employed to stunning effect by conservative politicians in the 1980s, 1990s and beyond.

Agnew's speech also led to the realization on the part of conservatives that they must establish their own network of think tanks and media outlets to counter what they considered to be the monolithic liberal bias of the academy, newspapers, magazines, radio, and television. The next decade was to see the enormous growth of conservative and libertarian think tanks such as the American Enterprise Institute, the Heritage Foundation, and the Cato Institute, as well as the rise of such conservative pundits as William Safire and Pat Buchanan.

Primary Source

"Television News Coverage" [excerpt]

SYNOPSIS: In this speech Vice President Spiro Agnew responds to critical news coverage of President Richard Nixon. He points out that a small body of people control television news coverage, and that they are using that power, in his opinion, to support their own liberal views and attack those of the Nixon administration.

Tonight I want to discuss the importance of the television news medium to the American people. No nation depends more on the intelligent judgment of its citizens. No medium has a more profound influence over public opinion. Nowhere in our system are there fewer checks on vast power. So, nowhere should there be more conscientious responsibility exercised than by the news media. The question is, Are we demanding enough of our television news presentations? And are the men of this medium demanding enough of themselves?

Monday night a week ago, President Nixon delivered the most important address of his Administration . . . When the President completed his address—an address, incidentally, that he spent weeks in the preparation of—his words and policies were subjected to instant analysis and querulous criticism. The audience of 70 million Americans gathered to hear the President of the United States was inherited by a small band of network commentators and self-appointed analysts, the majority of whom expressed in one way or another their hostility to what he had to say.

It was obvious that their minds were made up in advance. . . .

Now every American has a right to disagree with the President of the United States and to express publicly that disagreement. But the President of the United States has a right to communicate directly with the people who elected him, and the people of his country have the right to make up their own minds and form their own opinions about a Presidential address without having a President's words and thoughts characterized through the prejudices of hostile critics before they can even be digested. . . .

The purpose of my remarks tonight is to focus your attention on this little group of men who not only enjoy a right of instant rebuttal to every Presidential address, but, more importantly, wield a free hand in selecting, presenting and interpreting the great issues in our nation. First, let's define that power.

At least 40 million Americans every night, it's estimated, watch the network news. . . . According to Harris polls and other studies, for millions of Americans the networks are the sole source of national and world news. . . .

Now how is this network news determined? A small group of men, numbering perhaps no more than a dozen anchormen, commentators and executive producers, settle upon the 20 minutes or so of film and commentary that's to reach the public. . . .

Now what do Americans know of the men who wield this power? Of the men who produce and direct the network news, the nation knows practically nothing. Of the commentators, most Americans know little other than that they reflect an urbane and assured presence seemingly well-informed on every

important matter. We do know that to a man these commentators and producers live and work in the geographical and intellectual confines of Washington, D.C., or New York City. . . .

Both communities bask in their own provincialism, their own parochialism.

We can deduce that these men read the same newspapers. They draw their political and social views from the same sources. Worse, they talk constantly to one another, thereby providing artificial reinforcement to their shared viewpoints. Do they allow their biases to influence the selection and presentation of the news? . . .

The American people would rightly not tolerate this concentration of power in Government. Is it not fair and relevant to question its concentration in the hands of a tiny, enclosed fraternity of privileged men elected by no one and enjoying a monopoly sanctioned and licensed by Government? . . .

Perhaps the place to start looking for a credibility gap is not the offices of the Government in Washington but in the studios of the networks in New York. Television may have destroyed the old stereotypes, but has it not created new ones in their places? What has this passionate pursuit of controversy done to the politics of progress through local compromise essential to the functioning of a democratic society? . . .

In this search for excitement and controversy, has more than equal time gone to the minority of Americans who specialize in attacking the United States—its institutions and its citizens? . . .

Now, my friends, we'd never trust such power, as I've described, over public opinion in the hands of an elected Government. It's time we questioned it in the hands of a small unelected elite. The great networks have dominated America's airwaves for decades. The people are entitled a full accounting of their stewardship.

Primary Source

"Agnew Tells Why He Says What He Says"

SYNOPSIS: In this interview with *U.S. News & World Report*, Spiro Agnew adopts the same combative tone that characterized his speeches to urge a more fair and balanced approach by the media to the administration's policies.

Mr. Vice President, what are you trying to convey in your speeches about war protests?

The speeches came about because I kept looking for a balanced expression of opinion in the news media, and I didn't find it. I saw all the publicity about the Moratorium, and the reasons why it should be supported, and the accolades to the leaders of it. Then I began to notice that, irrespective of the fact that the leaders of the Moratorium were articulating very irresponsible positions, many people were ignoring those positions and joining the function as simply doing their own thing to express a desire for peace.

And the incongruity of this struck me, because here is a demonstration aimed principally at the foreign policy of the President, being participated in by those who didn't really disagree with his foreign policy, had none to offer of their own, but just felt like doing something to release emotions over the frustrations about the difficulty of ending the war.

And, of course, this is playing right into the hands of Hanoi, because the intransigence of the enemy is stimulated by their feeling that antiwar sentiment in this country will force the leadership into more offers of conciliation, concessions—one after another. So I felt I had to point out what this march and its effect really is all about.

Then, I was affected to some extent by a feeling of revulsion over the kind treatment that's continually given those among us who downgrade and degrade the United States. You pick a typical Eastern newspaper and you'll see that someone who has broken into a building and thrown files out the window is referred to as though he's on a spiritual crusade. That he has broken the law is not discussed.

I feel that somebody has to speak out on these subjects. I spoke out—and I'll continue to speak out. All of the alleged hand-wringing of my confreres, enthusiastically reported in the press, is not going to dissuade me one inch. I'm not going to be abrasive for the sake of abrasion, but I'm not going to go away just because some people are sucking in their breath with alarm over what I'm saying.

Were you put up to doing this as a matter of Administration policy?

No, this was all on my own initiative. The President and I never had any discussion about this. I don't think he's at all alarmed about what I've said.

Do you think you have been intemperate in your language?

You know, it's amazing to me how much I shock people.

Vice President Spiro T. Agnew created controversy with his strong attacks on critics of the Nixon administration, including what he claimed was a biased national news media. **THE LIBRARY OF CONGRESS.**

There seems to be a double standard for people who become controversial in high public office.

The people who are the most shocked about the "earthiness" of my expressions, as they call it, are those who applaud the obscenities hurled by their chosen few—those who take a staunch stand for freedom of expression in the written word bordering on pornography, and who don't seem to be at all affected by the ready availability of a form of expression that makes mine pale to insignificance.

I'm going to continue to say what I think is proper to say, and in the way I want to say it. And if I'm not reflecting the views of the people who elect me, I'm sure they'll let me know in the mail. And the mail doesn't indicate that.

What reactions have you gotten?

Here's our latest count: favorable communications, 7,122; unfavorable, 1,587. That's about 4½—almost 5—to 1. And you'd be surprised at how many people on the other side of the political fence in high public office privately are laudatory about what I've been doing. Some you'd not really expect.

How do you think you're doing with editorial writers and commentators?

Not too well, particularly in the big-city papers and the national media—but reasonably well in the hustings.

Do you think this indicates a schism in this country between the intellectual elite and the mass of people?

I don't consider the people who write for the news media intellectual elite. Sometimes I think they're about the most superficial thinkers I've ever seen.

Many of the writers—people who've been covering the Government for years—don't go below the surface for one reason: They're afraid that it will affect their ability to be opinionated if they know too much about the subject they are discussing.

They're not all this way, obviously. But some of the ones whom I've come in contact with are. The more intellectual they consider themselves, the less they know—because this is a screen, I would say, for not having to know anything.

If everybody says you're smart, you don't have to be.

Does this upset you?

One of the things that distresses me more than anything else about the handling I've had and what I call this "big-city, liberal media" is that they're intellectually dishonest in their reporting. If you say something and carefully qualify it, the qualification, after three or four repetitions, disappears. And the repetition becomes an unqualified, highly provocative statement.

Example: If I said that some of the supporters of the Moratorium were an effete corps of impudent snobs, it is reported that I said the leaders were. The next time it's reported that I said the demonstrators were. And then finally it gets down to the point where I say that all young people are impudent snobs.

Now, I've seen this over a period of my political career where—through a process of oversimplification I can't help but believe is intentional—an illusion is created in the minds of the electorate that a public figure has, in fact, said things that he never said.

How do you feel about all this?

I feel like I'm involved in a crusade, almost. And I'm going to see it through. My personal longevity politically means nothing to me when it's compared with the over-all importance of what we're confronting here. I don't want to sound overdramatic, but I feel that strongly about it. I really do.

Further Resources

BOOKS

Coyne, John R., Jr. *The Impudent Snobs: Agnew vs. the Intellectual Establishment.* New Rochelle, N.Y.: Arlington House, 1972.

Lippman, Theo. *Spiro Agnew's America.* New York: Norton, 1972.

PERIODICALS

"Attacking the Press." *Columbia Journalism Review* 40, no. 4, November–December 2001, 66.

Bruning, Fred. "The Real Problem with Today's Journalism." *McLean's,* February 20, 1995, 11.

WEBSITES

"Papers of Spiro T. Agnew." Available online at http://www .lib.umd.edu/ARCV/histmss/OnePagers/agnew.html; website home page: http://www.lib.umd.edu (accessed March 27, 2003).

"Remembering Spiro T. Agnew." Available at http://www.pbs .org/newshour/bb/remember/agnew_9-18.html; website home page: http://www.pbs.org (accessed March 27, 2003).

"Future of Non-commercial TV"

Interview

By: John Macy

Date: December 8, 1969

Source: "Future of Non-commercial TV: Exclusive Interview with John Macy, Corporation for Public Broadcasting." *U.S. News & World Report,* December 8, 1969, 94–97.

About the Author: John Macy (1917–1986) graduated from Wesleyan University in 1938, and then began a lifelong career in public service. He worked for the War Department during and after World War II, then served in the Civil Service Commission and other government agencies. He was appointed the first president of the Corporation for Public Broadcasting in 1969 and served until 1972. ■

Introduction

Public broadcasting on television and radio in the United States in the mid-1960s consisted of about a hundred local stations with little public money and no national programming. In 1967, two major foundations moved to fill this leadership vacuum. The Ford Foundation sponsored a nationally televised educational program on Sunday nights, and the Carnegie Commission published a report on the future of educational television. This report persuaded President Lyndon Johnson to make not-for-profit television and radio a part of his Great Society programs. The Carnegie Report became the basis for legislative proposals to create a national system of public broadcasting. The Public Broadcasting Act of 1967 created the Corporation for Public Broadcasting (CPB), which initially received $5 million from the federal government to go to educational television stations and to underwrite programming. Though it had little direct effect on the overall quality of television initially, the CPB at least helped guarantee an outlet for programming not regarded as commercially viable.

The corporation created the Public Broadcasting System (PBS) in 1969 to help connect the local educational-television stations. This created a program distribution network, enabling local stations to create their own programs that could then be shared with other stations and broadcast nationally. John W. Macy was named chief executive of the CPB in 1969. His first project was to develop educational shows for children. This led to the creation of The Children's Television Workshop, which produced *Sesame Street,* premiering on November 10, 1969. *Mr. Rogers' Neighborhood* soon followed and became another favorite of children and their parents. By giving PBS a niche market in children's programming, both shows were key elements in PBS's gradual success.

During these early years, PBS also looked overseas to find material for successful adult programming, buying many programs from British television outlets such as the BBC. Working with these British outlets, WGBH-Boston began to co-produce high-quality dramatic programming such as Kenneth Clark's *Civilization* and *Masterpiece Theatre.* The latter offered the "series within a series" concept in the form of *Upstairs Downstairs,* which attracted a loyal audience of adults.

National Public Radio was established in 1970 with the same rationale as public television: to bring local noncommercial stations together within a common programming framework. The late-afternoon show *All Things Considered* debuted in May 1971 and was soon praised for its in-depth coverage of news and cultural affairs. Its companion program, *Morning Edition,* made its debut in 1979.

Significance

John Macy points out in this interview that the term "educational" was dropped in favor of "public" because the nonprofit stations were viewed as providing a service much broader than classroom teaching. Coverage of local government activities such as school board meetings, local city councils, important hearings, and the like was envisioned as being one of the most important areas for local public broadcasting. Macy also notes that the very fact of being televised may have a salutary effect on the actual proceedings being broadcast. This possibility was illustrated when the San Francisco PBS affiliate devoted five of its evening hours to covering the Berkeley City Council meeting during a local urban crisis. It was suggested by some observers that this move may have served to defuse a potentially explosive situation.

In this interview, Macy looks forward to public broadcasts of Congress and of presidential campaigns. Yet this seemed unlikely to happen in the early seventies. Despite early successes and a dramatic increase in the number of public television and radio stations, the existence of public television was to be challenged in 1972 by President Nixon's veto of an important appropriations measure. This forced the system to reconsider its means of support and to lay off many employees. Public television, according to the Nixon administration, should concentrate on local programming and should be more decentralized. This approach was seen, from PBS's perspective at least, as a step backwards. Ironically PBS's extensive coverage of Congress's investigation into the Watergate cover-up and its accompanying commentary renewed interest in public television as a source of indepth news and public affairs programming such as *Washington Week in Review* and *The News Hour.*

Primary Source

"Future of Non-Commercial TV"

> **SYNOPSIS:** In this interview, John Macy, the first president of the Corporation for Public Broadcasting, describes the ambitious and idealistic plans and hopes for public broadcasting system at the time of its founding. Macy makes prophetic statements about the role that satellites will play in expanding program choices for the television audience.

Mr. Macy, what is public broadcasting?

It is broadcasting by nonprofit institutions—universities. State or local-government agencies, or local citizen groups.

Without commercial advertising?

Yes, except that, when an industrial concern puts up the money for a show that is broadcast by a public station, this assistance is recognized by a simple printed statement at the beginning and end of the show. You could consider that a form of institutional advertising.

Is public broadcasting what we used to call "educational" broadcasting?

Yes. The term "educational" has been dropped in favor of "public" because the nonprofit stations perform a service much broader than classroom teaching.

Just what sorts of programs do you plan to stress?

There is a great deal that needs to be done that we can't expect the commercial broadcaster to do.

For example, covering city-council meetings, important hearings, school-board meetings. This is one area of primary program emphasis for the local stations.

Are they doing much in this field?

More and more.

I was amused not long ago when I was in a city in the South where they had started covering the school-board meetings. In the local vernacular, the show was known as "the Tuesday night fights."

The Philadelphia station has also covered school-board meetings. I asked Richardson Dilworth, the former mayor who is now chairman of the school board, how this was going over. He said, "Well, all our members argued against it, but I notice that they showed up with blue shirts for the meeting."

I also recall that early last summer the San Francisco station devoted a full evening to the meeting of the Berkeley city council when it was considering the controversy over the so-called "people's park."

The show went on for five hours. Witnesses ranged from the extreme-right wing to the Maoists on the left. When the final vote was taken, one member had switched, and the decision, by a 5-to-4 vote, was credited with bringing peace the following day.

Did the city council act differently because it was on television?

I think they gave a gravity to their judgment, knowing they were being observed. Some officials like this coverage and some don't like it. The mayor of one city who was running for re-election, when I asked him what public broadcasting ought to do, said, "The first thing you can do is to take that city council off the air."

How about broadcasting sessions of Congress?

I'm all for it. In this age, with the importance of accountability to the public, there is no valid argument against broadcasting the major debates.

Wouldn't that be a dull show most of the time?

Essentially, we would be concerned with key debates on major national issues—issues that directly affect all citizens, such as foreign policy, taxes, education and the control of our environment, and so on. Also, it might be that, if the two houses were on camera, they might change some of their procedures.

What reactions to this idea do you get from Congress?

Not a great deal of enthusiasm.

I've also suggested that political candidates—particularly the presidential candidates—might make use of public broadcasting. As it is, the candidates spend an excessive amount of money for coverage on commercial television stations.

How did the parties respond to that suggestion?

It is a very live issue with them. Both the Republicans and Democrats have study groups on the subject. I hope and expect that public broadcasting will provide an important public service in allowing the voters to judge the candidates in 1972.

Why don't the parties jump at the idea, if it will save them a lot of money?

They're skeptical as to just how much of an audience we can deliver. The 185 nonprofit television stations are within receiving distance of about 46 million families, but I can't claim that all 46 million are watching public television.

What about State and local campaigning?

Here is where public broadcasting can make a significant contribution to public understanding of the occasionally confusing local issues, and the large number of candidates. Two grants that we made last spring went for this purpose. One was to the Los Angeles station, which put on a program on the Saturday night before the primary. That show lasted three hours and presented all 13 of the candidates for mayor. They all had their say. Then there was time for them to question each other, and for questions from the audience.

In Madison, Wis., our grant was used to provide time for all candidates for city council and school board prior to the election. The same thing has been done by the public stations in New York, Cleveland and Detroit.

In several States, the public-broadcasting stations are covering the State legislatures. For instance, the Connecticut station broadcast the closing session of the State legislature, when most of the business was done, and stayed on the air until adjournment at 2 o'clock in the morning.

In Nebraska, the State-owned station in Lincoln taped the sessions of the legislature and broadcast an edited portion each night. The service was so well received the legislature gave favorable consideration to new facilities for the station.

Many people say public broadcasting needs to do something to liven up its programs. Are you doing anything about that?

We are trying to meet that problem. We are eager to develop some personalities to make the best possible use of creative talent and television techniques and, yes, to sponsor experimentation.

Even in the field of educational programs, it is my feeling that learning does not have to be dull.

Because of a lack of adequate funds across the board, we've built up the picture of educational broadcasting as a teacher standing in front of a drape or a blackboard and going through the same scenario that he or she would go through in front of a class. Or else we've had a group of talking faces around a table. That doesn't really use the unique qualities of television.

We are paying part of the cost of a new program called "Sesame Street," which is being produced by the Children's Television Workshop. This is an approach to learning in the home for the preschool child, with emphasis on children in disadvantaged homes.

What is the idea behind that show?

Educators knew that preschool youngsters watch television 40 or 50 hours a week. The question was: Is it possible to use that means to give youngsters their first taste of schooling?

The Children's Television Workshop was formed by a group of educators, psychologists and television directors. They spent a whole year in research before they developed their first pilot program.

What did they find out?

For one thing, that the children's concentration was much greater on the commercials than on the substance of the programs they regularly watch on television. So in "Sesame Street" the teaching of letters and numbers often takes the form of jingles, such as are used in commercials.

Do you look on this program as a breakthrough for educational TV?

It's too soon to say. The show just went on the air on November 10. It will be broadcast five days a week for 26 weeks over at least 150 stations. Some will show it in the morning and afternoon, and a station in Chicago will repeat the full week's series every Saturday morning.

The Educational Testing Service, at Princeton, N. J., is going to test groups of youngsters at various times in the course of this series to see what impact it has. We need this evaluation before we decide whether to invest money in the program for a second year.

What do you know about the results of other educational programs on television?

Actual measurements of impact are disappointingly limited. Many claims were made that television would provide accelerated learning, greater reten-

tion, and lower cost of education in the school systems. I don't think there is conclusive evidence to back up any of those claims. There needs to be more research, and the corporation hopes to fill this gap.

Is the amount of classroom television increasing?

It is increasing, but not at the rate that was originally anticipated. On the average, 45 per cent of the broadcast time of all public-television stations is being devoted to beaming educational programs directly into the classroom. In addition, many stations and State networks are beaming the so-called "continuing education" programs on a variety of subjects for at-home or on-the-job study. Chicago's University of the Air has had particularly good results in bringing higher education to those who could not otherwise benefit from it.

Do you know how many people watch the public programs, and which ones are the most effective in holding an audience?

We are spending money on surveys, and we need to spend more.

We know that some people tend to look on public broadcasting as "the poverty program for the overeducated"—as having an audience that is limited to the intellectual few.

We already have strong evidence to refute that criticism. Some of our programs are drawing very substantial numbers of viewers from all parts of society. We have a program called "Mister Rogers' Neighborhood," a children's program that comes on at 5 in the afternoon. In many markets, this program has gained a strong audience following and is right up there with the commercial broadcasts. We also have instances where Julia Child with her cooking show rolls up a substantial viewership.

We need to recognize that, although the audience for some of our shows appears small in contrast to "The Sunday Night Movie," when you compare the number watching to the number you could put into Constitution Hall or Carnegie Hall or Soldier Field it's enormous. Our aim is not to compete with the commercial networks in mass audiences, with sustained viewing, but rather to provide a diversity of viewing choice and, hopefully, to offer something that is going to be meaningful, stimulating and entertaining to the people who view it.

Have you ever had a program that drew anything like the numbers that watch one of the 10 top commercial shows?

I don't believe so. But we had one program in our series called "Sounds of Summer" that included

A still from the Public Broadcasting System and Children's Television Network show *Sesame Street*, 1970. *Sesame Street* debuted in 1969 and quickly became the first hit show for the fledgling Public Broadcasting System (PBS). © UPI/CORBIS-BETTMANN. REPRODUCED BY PERMISSION.

both Arlo Guthrie and Joni Mitchell, and although it wasn't promoted any more than any other show in the series, it's very clear from the mail and from reports from the stations that it was far and away the most popular with the viewers, and had a much larger slice of the younger audience. The teen-agers and people in the low 20s tend to spurn television. They feel that it's part of "the establishment" put-on. But they knew about this program, and there were large numbers watching it.

Are you planning to sponsor other programs with broad popular appeal?

I hope we have some. I'm going to be very much interested in seeing what our research shows on the NET series production of John Galsworthy's "The Forsyte Saga."

This show had a magnificent audience in Britain; they had to change the hour of vespers in most Anglican churches because people had to see this pro-gram before they went to church. It has been acquired by Western European countries and by Iron Curtain countries. And we're already beginning to get some feedback from the showing here in this country. I was told recently that there wasn't a single printed copy of "The Forsyte Saga" in any bookstore in Washington. They were all sold out. Scribner's is bringing out a special edition to go with the show.

What impact will satellites have, when they begin to be used for television broadcasting here in the U. S.?

They will be very significant for public broadcasting The commercial networks already have their programs distributed nationwide over cables leased from the American Telephone & Telegraph Company. So they are taken care of though it is claimed that satellites will be cheaper for them than the telephone hookup. The satellites are coming on the horizon just when public broadcasting needs a reliable system of interconnection, so that we can offer shows on a network basis across the nation.

What arrangement do you have for network shows at the present time?

AT&T is providing us with interconnections for three hours of prime time five nights a week at a cost which is about 20 per cent of their normal rates. We are now negotiating with the company on a new contract for broader service. We have just received from the Federal Communications Commission a letter and order which reinforce the corporation's contention that the quality of service provided by AT&T on the interconnection should be comparable to that delivered to other customers. On the matter of the rate to be charged, the FCC has supported the corporation's representation that the congressional standard of "free or reduced rates" should be negotiated.

This FCC advice should assist the corporation in reducing the volume of pre-emption in the interconnected service. Under present arrangements, service to any of the public stations can be cut off if demands from commercial customers are too heavy. We did an extensive program on the Vietnam Moratorium on October 15, and—in action unrelated to the program—quite a number of stations were preempted, so that they could not receive the show. They got irate letters, particularly from students, on the ground that failure to show the program as advertised was a form of censorship. We also put a good deal of time and effort and money into promoting "The Forsyte Saga" and "The Advocates," and on October 19 we lost both these programs on about 19 stations because of pre-emption. We need a system that will be hardened and not preemptible.

If the answer is satellites, who should own them?

I'm completely parochial on that score. What concerns me is that we get the service—and get it free.

Frank Stanton, president of the Columbia Broadcasting System, has suggested that the three commercial networks and the Corporation for Public Broadcasting join in developing a domestic satellite system, with the commercial stations putting up the capital and public broadcasting getting free service. We're discussing how that might be achieved—whether through a new company or through the Communications Satellite Corporation, better known as Comsat.

Then the commercial broadcasters don't look on you as a dangerous rival—

No. They feel the public broadcasters are in a position to meet public needs that the commercial stations cannot meet. Both CBS and the National Broadcasting Company have contributed funds to the Corporation for Public Broadcasting.

In almost every public station I've visited, I have found some equipment donated by the commercial broadcasters.

Do they, perhaps, hope that you will become a training ground for talent that they can then hire away from you?

The whole broadcasting industry, commercial and public, requires an expansion of talent. We have a number of people who have come to us from commercial broadcasting, because they are interested in the types of programs we are doing.

In addition, the corporation is attempting to strengthen the capacity of local stations throughout the country to use their own people to produce for the national audience. This will help provide the diversity of programs that should be available in this country, as well as develop talent.

Will commercial television eventually be limited to light entertainment and sports, leaving the rest to you?

I don't expect that kind of specialization. The commercial broadcaster will continue to offer news programs and special events that only the commercial networks can do, because of the tremendous cost—the coverage of an inauguration or a space shot, for example.

But do you see your corporation becoming a kind of American BBC—owning stations and producing programs, just like the British Broadcasting Corporation?

No, the British background is wholly different.

Our system is based on the licensing of individual stations. The Corporation for Public Broadcasting owns no stations and doesn't plan to. We hope, when a national program is produced, that the local stations will run it, but in the final analysis they can elect not to. They can use the time for a program of their own that they feel is more responsive to the interests of their viewers or use other available material, without loss of revenue. I think this is an asset worth preserving.

What, then, is the role of the Corporation for Public Broadcasting, as you see it?

To do several things: to provide a national system for connecting the public stations into a network; to provide leadership and financial support for the production of a wider variety of programs, both at the national and the local level; to provide some financial support directly to local stations, so that they can continue to operate and become more effective: and lastly, to support some needed research and promotion.

How much money do you have to do all that?

The corporation had 5 million dollars from the Government in the last fiscal year, and about 2.5 million from private sources, including CBS and the Carnegie Foundation. This year, Congress has authorized 20 million, the full amount of which we'll seek in appropriations, and to which we hope to add 4 million of private funds. In addition, the local stations have their own sources of public and private funds. We estimate that public broadcasting gets about 60 million a year from all sources.

How does that compare with the resources of the commercial broadcasters?

Their gross receipts are about 3 billions a year.

Do you expect to expand your program in the future?

We believe the Corporation for Public Broadcasting will require, to meet its objectives, between 100 million and 120 million dollars a year, at the end of five years. We are making a special study of future needs, so that this estimate may have to be changed.

Where could you look for that much money?

The Carnegie Commission in a special report on public broadcasting suggested a 2 per cent excise tax on all new television sets. That would bring in about 70 million a year and would increase as the economy grows. I haven't seen any better suggestion than that, although there have been many other suggestions, and new ones are appearing every day.

If we had this assured revenue from the Government, I think we could go out and try to raise the additional income needed from foundations, corporations and other donors, particularly if there were a provision for federal matching of private contributions.

Further Resources

BOOKS

Jarvik, Lawrence Ariel. *PBS: Behind the Screen.* Rocklin, Calif.: Forum Press, 1997.

Kovitz, Roselle. *The History of Public Broadcasting.* Washington, D.C., 1987.

Macy, John. *To Irrigate a Wasteland: The Struggle to Shape a Public Television System in the United States.* Berkeley, Calif.: University of California Press, 1974.

PERIODICALS

"Meatier Than Bonanza." *Business Week,* November 4, 1967, 38.

"Whiter Public TV?" *Newsweek,* April 21, 1969.

WEBSITES

PBS home page. Available online at http://www.pbs.org/ (accessed March 27, 2003).

"The First Debate over Presidential Debates"

Magazine article

By: Frank Stanton

Date: September 15, 2000

Source: Stanton, Frank, "The First Debate over Presidential Debates." *Newsweek,* September 15, 2000, 11.

About the Author: After Frank Stanton (1908–) graduated from Ohio Wesleyan University, he was hired by CBS Radio to head its audience research department. He became president of CBS in 1946, a position he held for twenty-seven years. ∎

Introduction

During the 1960 presidential campaign, a series of four debates between the two candidates, Massachusetts Democratic senator John F. Kennedy and Republican vice president Richard M. Nixon, were televised nationally. Although television had been around since the 1940s, these were the first presidential debates to be televised and the only ones until 1976. Since that time, presidential debates have become a fixture in the campaigns.

Although television was in place by the time of the 1952 and 1956 Eisenhower-Stevenson campaigns, there were no televised debates for at least three reasons. First, in 1952 the number of viewers was too small. Second, in the 1956 rerun election four years later, there was indeed television advertising (including Eisenhower's famous slogan, "I like Ike"), but Eisenhower had no incentive to heighten the profile of his less well-known opponent. Third, as Stanton notes, the equal-time provision of the Federal Communications Act of 1934 meant that all candidates running for the White House had a right to participate in the debates. A change in the law to permit only the frontrunners to face each other would have been necessary for a debate to take place, but there was no strong sentiment in Congress for such a legal reform at that time.

In 1960, both Kennedy and Nixon were eager to seize the opportunity television provided to put their candidacies forward to the electorate. By this time, television was coming into its own as America's favorite source of news and information, and this fact was not lost on these two seasoned politicians. Both campaigns jumped at the offer by the networks of almost four hours of free nationwide airtime.

The debate most etched into the public memory from the 1960 series is the first one, where the telegenic Kennedy won the image battle. Though recovering from the flu and appearing pale, Nixon refused to use makeup in order to enhance his appearance on the screen. It was famously said that Mr. Nixon suffered from a "five o'clock shadow" because of his heavy beard, and it was thought that the darkness of his face compared unfavorably with the radiance of the young senator's. Although Nixon performed well rhetorically, Kennedy managed to convey an appealing image of youthfulness, energy, and physical poise, which convinced many that he had had the best of the televised exchange. Thus, Kennedy won the debate not on the merits but on the intangible factor of image, or what the great early twentieth-century sociologist Max Weber termed "charisma."

As might have been expected under the circumstances, these debates were not focused on serious questions of public policy. This would have required complex and detailed arguments on the part of the participants. Commentators were quick to point out this lack of serious discussion, noting, for example, that most of the second and third debates were taken up with a discussion of the strategic importance of two tiny islands just off the Chinese mainland called Quemoy and Matsu—words that were to enter the American political lexicon as a result of the debates rather than their strategic significance.

Significance

In 1960, television reached an estimated 46 million American homes, and its possibly key role in any successful electoral campaign had just begun to be appreciated. Whatever its effect on decided voters, television was seen as potentially influencing the "swing vote," or the independents who constituted between 10 and 35 percent of the electorate. And public polling-research showed that approximately 10 percent of these "swing" voters would not make up their minds until a week before the election. The key element in making use of television for political gain came to be seen as shaping of the candidate's public "image" to make a favorable impression on voters. The recognition in 1960 of the potential of "image management" to bring a candidate to power had the long-term effect of turning politics more into a matter of style than of substance. Candidates would come to spend more time with image consultants than they would studying policy details.

Although these famous encounters were called "debates," they were not really debates in a strict sense. With no formal rules of debate or a panel of judges, it was the electorate that was placed in the position of deciding for themselves who "won"—with the help of opinion leaders and media experts. Because these political pundits ap-

Frank Stanton was president of the CBS television network from 1946 to 1973. He helped organize the first-ever televised debates between presidential candidates in 1960. © BETTMANN/CORBIS. REPRODUCED BY PERMISSION.

peared to know much more about the political process than the ordinary person, they gained authority with the viewing public. Overnight, a whole industry grew up invested with the responsibility of deciding who won presidential debates, usually on the basis of image. Thus it is possible to see in the 1960 debate the origins of such things as "sound bites," spin doctors, candidate handlers, focus groups, poll takers, image makers, and media packagers, all staples in today's politics.

Primary Source

"The First Debate over Presidential Debates"

> **SYNOPSIS:** In this brief article, Frank Stanton, the former head of CBS, reveals how he was instrumental in the creation of presidential debates.

If this year's debate over presidential debates seems rough, try arranging the first televised presidential debates in American history. It took eight years!

In the early 1950s, as president of CBS, I suggested to my colleagues at the network that it would

Vice President Richard Nixon (left) and Senator John F. Kennedy (right) in the first-ever televised debate between presidential candidates, 1960. © BETTMANN/CORBIS. REPRODUCED BY PERMISSION.

be wonderful if we could have presidential debates. The problem was Section 315 of the Communications Act of 1934, which required you to give equal time to all the candidates. There were numerous bona fide candidates in the '52 campaign, so it was impossible to contemplate debates within the framework of the rules.

If Eisenhower and Stevenson had agreed to debate in '52, I would have pushed Congress to change the rules. But Eisenhower wasn't interested. In 1955 I wrote a guest column in the New York Herald-Tribune, saying that if Congress amended Section 315, CBS would provide free air time for the major candidates to debate.

By 1960 I was ready to try again. First I wanted to find out whether the potential candidates would actually debate. It was early in the year, and I went to see Nixon in the Capitol; he was vice president. His aide said, "You don't have to see him. He was a champion debater at Whittier College. He'll be terrific." So I trotted on down the hall to see my friend Lyndon Johnson, the Democratic Senate leader. Johnson saw me and said, "What the goddam hell do you want?" I said, "Have you got a minute?" At that point Jack Kennedy, who happened to have been

sitting with his back to me, turned around and said hello. I said, "If I get these rules changed, will you debate?" Johnson answered, "Why don't you ask Jack?" Jack smiled and said, "I'll do it."

Subsequently, at a Senate subcommittee hearing chaired by John Pastore, I suggested that Congress adopt a resolution to suspend Section 315 for one election. After the hearing, Pastore, along with Warren Magnuson, who chaired the full Senate Commerce Committee, agreed to support the resolution if I got the votes.

I went to work and got the Senate's support. I found no support on the House side. It was May or June, and I wanted to have this legislation passed before the conventions that summer. I knew that Gene Autry, the cowboy-actor who owned a CBS affiliate station, was close to the speaker of the House, Sam Rayburn. I talked to Gene about the resolution and asked if he could help with the speaker. He said, "I'll call you right back." He didn't, but Rayburn's office did. I got the chairman of the House Commerce Committee, Oren Harris, and the two of us went to see Rayburn. The problem was, Rayburn would have to scrap the rules of procedure to bring this thing up at the last minute. Rayburn turned to Harris and said, "Oren, have you got the votes?" Oren turned to me: "Frank, have we got the votes?" And I said yes. I didn't have any idea where the votes were. But I knew that, having gotten them on the Senate side, we could probably get them in the House. And we did. It was time to invite the candidates.

The first debate was held in the CBS studio in Chicago, an old riding academy that still had entrances which had been used for carriages. So when the candidates arrived, they drove right into the building. Nixon got there first. When he got out of the car, he banged his right knee on the door so bad that he almost went down on his knees in pain. After that, he seemed disoriented.

I escorted Nixon into the studio. The control room wanted to take some voice levels on the microphone that hung above the candidate. When Kennedy arrived, Nixon jumped up to shake his hand, and that microphone hit him right in the head.

Kennedy was bronzed beautifully, wearing a navy suit and a blue shirt. Nixon looked like death because he had been in the hospital. And you could run your hand inside his collar without touching anything—it was that loose. His color was terrible; his beard was not good and he didn't want any makeup. I felt sorry for him.

When the debate was over, I went to thank the candidates. Nixon's Secret Service man told me he was gone. I said, "Well, his coat and briefcase are right here." "Yes," he said, "he left without picking them up."

Then I went over to the room where Kennedy was. It was very dark, except for where Kennedy sat under a hanging lamp. He was on the phone speaking to someone in his immediate family. At one point he said, "Well, we sure took this one." His sleeves were wet with perspiration down to his wrists. When he hung up we shook hands and he said, "You know Dick Daley?" referring to Chicago's mayor. I hadn't even realized Daley was there. We said hello and Daley asked me if I wanted a ride downtown. As we walked down the hall he said, "You know, I'm going to change my mind and tell my men to go all out for Kennedy." He meant that he hadn't been supporting Kennedy with any enthusiasm until that debate. And his support made an enormous difference, because Illinois determined the election.

Further Resources

BOOKS

Hellweg, Susan A., Michael Pfau, and Steven R. Brydon. *Televised Presidential Debates: Advocacy in Contemporary America.* New York: Praeger, 1992.

Jamieson, Kathleen Hall, and David S. Birdsell. *Presidential Debates: The Challenge of Creating An Informed Electorate.* New York: Oxford University Press, 1988.

Kraus, Sidney. *Televised Presidential Debates and Public Policy.* Hillsdale, N.J.: Erlbaum, 1988.

WEBSITES

"Commission on Presidential Debates." Available online at http://www.debates.org/ (accessed April 7, 2003).

"Kennedy-Nixon Presidential Debates." Available online at http://www.cs.umb.edu/jfklibrary/debates-1960.html; website home page: http://www.cs.umb.edu (accessed April 7, 2003).

Tell Me a Story
Memoirs

By: Don Hewitt

Date: 2001

Source: Hewitt, Don. *Tell Me a Story: Fifty Years and 60 Minutes in Television.* New York: Public Affairs Press, 2001, 104–113.

About the Author: Don Hewitt (1922–) was a correspondent in Europe and the Pacific during World War II. Later, he became night editor of the Associated Press's Memphis bureau. He began his career with CBS News in 1948 as an associate director of *Douglas Edwards with the News,* then served as producer-director of the show for fourteen years. He later became executive producer of the *CBS Evening News with Walter Cronkite.* He created *Sixty Minutes* in 1968 and was the executive producer until his retirement. ■

Introduction

In the fall of 1968, the Columbia Broadcasting System (CBS) was at the peak of its reputation for news. A long tradition of journalists such as Edward R. Murrow, Eric Severeid, William Shirer, and Walter Cronkite made the news division of CBS the champion in ratings and in awards, first on radio and then on television. But CBS's image, while serious, was also perceived as dull. This was to change when veteran producer Don Hewitt got an idea for a new kind of television journalism that would put actual human faces on the information the news provided.

Hewitt saw that in the future, news programs were not going to survive by competing for the dwindling number of viewers who turned to television for serious fare. His idea was to go after a sizable segment of the huge entertainment audience. His old boss, Edward R. Murrow, pioneered a very popular show in which he visited famous people in their homes each week. Hewitt believed that an updated version of this format would make for a network news magazine that would be intellectually respectable and yet at the same time appeal to a broad cross-section of the audience. The show he pitched to the network was *60 Minutes*.

Hewitt picked as host for the new program the easygoing and affable Harry Reasoner. When CBS suggested a second correspondent to balance Reasoner, Hewitt thought of Mike Wallace, widely referred to as "Mike Malice" because of his hard-hitting, "take no prisoners" interviewing style. In fact, Wallace's style of interviewing was essential to the investigative aspect of the program. In the early days, he filled up two-thirds of the airtime.

Significance

60 Minutes was not an instant hit. The ratings were dismal during the first season, and nobody except Hewitt expected it to survive. It was cancelled in 1971 but reappeared the next season in different time slots without much of an impact. In fact, it was not until 1975, when CBS moved it to early Sunday night, that the show found its audience. Investigative journalists were enjoying a newly won popularity thanks to the Watergate scandal. Dan Rather joined the show that season. By 1977, *60 Minutes* had reached the top ten in ratings.

During its long history, *60 Minutes* has aired many memorable news stories and interview sessions. In its early days, it featured interviews with Eldridge Cleaver, the head of the Black Panther Party, and Captain Ernest Medina, the officer who was court-martialed for his part in the My Lai massacre during the Vietnam War. The show also capitalized on the intense public interest in the Watergate scandal by interviewing some of the principal figures caught up in the scandal and the related investigation.

In the show's most hard-hitting pieces, the questioning is sometimes relentless, giving the program an inquisitorial tone. But at the same time, the show can be credited with having uncovered numerous scandals and disreputable business practices, and even with gaining freedom for citizens wrongly convicted of crime.

Over the years, the format of *60 Minutes* became distinctive, with its verbal "table of contents," a kind of "back page column" by Andy Rooney, and its "Point Counterpoint." The success of *60 Minutes* has led to many imitators, some of them very successful in their own right, such as *20/20, Prime Time Live,* and *Dateline NBC*.

60 Minutes has had its critics, as might be expected given the controversial nature of the show. On the one hand, Mike Wallace has been criticized for turning himself into "Mike Malice" for some of his more confrontational interviews. On the other hand, Harry Reasoner was sometimes criticized for being too easygoing in his treatment of interviewees. Yet these contrasting styles in part constitute the secret of the show's success.

Primary Source

Tell Me a Story [excerpt]

SYNOPSIS: In this excerpt from his memoirs, Don Hewitt recounts the line of thought that led to the development of the first and most successful broadcast newsmagazine and the events leading up to the first broadcast.

By 1966 and 1967, I was already starting to think about a new type of personal journalism. The documentaries—*CBS Reports, NBC White Paper,* and *ABC Close Up*—all seemed to be the voice of the corporation, and I didn't believe people were interested in hearing from a corporation. They were like newspaper editorials, I thought. Do people really care about the "voice of the newspaper"? They want to read the reporting and the columnists, not the editorials.

. . .

I had entered the television age in the era of news as a public service and spent my TV adolescence serving that cause. But I had begun to realize in the '60s that TV news was going to have to pay its own way. . . .

At the same time, Ed Murrow was beginning to realize the same thing—that his and Fred Friendly's *See It Now* program was not getting the respect from the corporate brass they thought it deserved and that in some markets it was being preempted by *Amos 'n Andy*.

What to do about it? The only way Murrow could give them a show that could hold its own against the best the other networks could throw at it would be to get into the ratings game—a game he had roundly condemned as beneath serious journalists. But if we were going to please the corporation—and that was something he knew quite a bit about because he was a member of the CBS hierarchy for a while—it meant playing the game.

. . . The broadcast Murrow agreed to do was called *Person to Person,* and it concerned itself each week with visiting the homes of famous people.

We who worked on Ed's prestigious Sunday afternoon broadcast, *See It Now,* soon saw the public gravitating to *Person to Person* in the kind of numbers that frequently put it in the top ten while we languished in the cellar.

It was John Horne, the TV critic of the *New York Herald Tribune,* who coined the phrases "high Murrow" and "low Murrow" to distinguish between the two broadcasts.

Oh my God, I thought. That's the answer. Why not put them together in one broadcast and reap the benefits of being *both* prestigious and popular? . . . We could make the news entertaining without compromising our integrity.

That, in essence, was the genesis of *60 Minutes.*

It could be like the old *Life* magazine, I thought—a family friend in the home of millions of Americans each week, serious and light-hearted in the same issue. The ads didn't interrupt the stories in *Life:* You'd have a story for a few pages, then some ads, then another story. . . .

I began to tell people at the network about my notion of an hour-long program combining "high Murrow" and "low Murrow." Fred Friendly thought it was a terrible idea, but I was undeterred and kept working on refining and improving the concept. . . . Following Friendly's resignation as president of CBS News, Richard S. Salant, who came from the legal department, took over. So I wrote a note to him, asking him why in the hundreds of prime-time minutes of make-believe that CBS beamed into American living rooms each week, the network couldn't find "60 minutes" of prime time to air some reality, produced with the same flair that the entertainment division had become famous for.

Salant, hardly overwhelmed by or even vaguely interested in what I had proposed, told CBS News Vice President Bill Leonard that it was a lousy idea. "That's funny," Leonard said. "That's exactly what Friendly said." Believe it or not, that is how *60 Minutes* got born. Because anything Friendly was against, Salant was for—even if it meant turning over a prime time hour each week to me, about whom he felt, at best, lukewarm.

In early 1968, Salant reluctantly put his seal of approval on my proposed broadcast, which took its title from the phrase in my memo, "60 minutes of prime time."

"What kind of stories do you want to do?" he asked me.

"Good stories, interesting and arresting stories," I told him. I couldn't come up with anything more specific than that, except to say that we would do three a week, with style and wit, each edited down to a manageable twelve to fifteen minutes to deal with the viewers' attention span.

Mike Wallace circa 1965. The "tough-as-nails newsman," has been co-editor of *60 Minutes* since its debut on September 24, 1968. GETTY IMAGES. REPRODUCED BY PERMISSION.

We still had to make a pilot, but Salant initially balked at the cost—$25,000, which was a paltry sum in television even then. But a savvy woman named Ellen McCloy intervened. She was the daughter of John J. McCloy, one of the "wise men" who helped to shape the post–World War II order, and she had recently started work at CBS as an assistant to Salant. Ellen called, told me she loved the idea, and said she would talk Salant into going along with the money. And she did.

In the early days of television, there was an hour-long weekly series called *Four Star Playhouse,* in which Dick Powell, Ida Lupino, David Niven, and Charles Boyer formed a repertory company and each week played different parts. Any one of them could play anything. It gave me the idea that maybe I could do the same thing with reporters and cover the world that way. In effect, they would be a repertory company of freelance journalists, each dedicated to his or her story, but there would be no star out front, no master of ceremonies, no Ed Sullivan introducing the acts.

But my rep company started with a cast of only one—Harry Reasoner. He was a superb writer, personable, one of CBS's most accomplished correspondents who, I thought, could sort of publish his notes on air and take people along on his story. He had for a long while been on the *CBS Morning News* and was now on general assignment, not doing anything very exciting, just covering stories the way he had done for the *CBS Evening News* back when I was producing it. I approached him and he agreed to give the pilot a shot. . . .

With so little money for the pilot, all I could do was to cannibalize existing film from documentaries that were in the CBS library. For instance, a ten-minute piece on Bobby Kennedy taking his kids skiing was taken from an hour we had done on him. Another story we called "Two Faces of Black America" (Ed Brooke, then a Republican senator from Massachusetts, and Stokely Carmichael, one of the founders of the Student Non-Violent Coordinating Committee, or SNCC) were taken from an hour broadcast we had done on the two of them.

When the lights came up in the screening room after Salant, Leonard, and Bob Chandler, Leonard's assistant, had viewed the pilot, Salant and Leonard seemed pleased. Chandler had a feeling it wasn't quite right.

"Wouldn't it be a better broadcast," he asked, "if you paired Reasoner with another correspondent, à la Huntley and Brinkley?"

"Like who," I said belligerently, guarding my turf.

"Like Mike Wallace," Chandler said.

Holy shit, I thought, *what an idea.* They could be the real start of my rep company. Reasoner and Wallace were made for each other.

Were they ever! Good guy, bad guy. The guy you love, the guy who makes you quake. Wallace had developed a tough-guy reputation over the years, going back to a show called *Night Beat,* in which he would take on anyone and ask the questions no one else had the guts to ask. He was someone I *knew* people would be interested in hearing from.

Mike is, quite frankly, the best thing that ever happened to a television set—certainly the best thing that ever happened to *my* television set. He's a tiger, the kind of journalist who comes along once in a lifetime, and he hasn't lost a step along the way. He also brings out the best of everyone who works with him, which is a rare quality, especially in the television business.

. . .

Back in the late '60s, though, I didn't know for sure whether Mike really took the offer to be on *60*

Minutes seriously. He was so sure he was going to be CBS's next White House correspondent that he figured he could tell me anything because he could always get out of it later when his glamour job came through. So he told me yes. Mike got into the act as an afterthought—probably the most fortuitous afterthought that ever came my way or his.

. . .

Reasoner set the tone on our first broadcast, September 24, 1968, letting our audience know that this was a new form for television. "The symphony of the real world is not a monotone and while this does not mean you have to mix it all up in one broadcast, it seems to us that the idea of a flexible attitude has its attractions," Harry began. "All art is the rearrangement of previous perceptions, and we don't claim this is anything more than that, or even that journalism is an art, for that matter. But we do think this is sort of a new approach."

The new approach intentionally abjured music. If there was a forerunner to the TV newsmagazine format, it was the old newsreel, *The March of Time,* which ran in movie theaters during the 1930s and '40s. But the clips were done with music, which can be used to make editorial points as effectively as words, or they can convey a mood. . . .

We didn't want to editorialize, but we did want some sound, arresting enough to bring people in from the kitchen. And how to do it came at the end of our first broadcast in the form of a ticking stopwatch. I said, "Wait a minute, why are we wasting the ticking clock at the end?" After that, we put it at the beginning and it became our trademark.

We began in the 10–11 P.M. time slot, every other Tuesday, alternating with documentaries and opposite the top-rated ABC series *Marcus Welby, M.D.* Normally, if you didn't make it with the audience, it was thirteen weeks and out, never to return. But because Tuesday night at ten had been put aside for news and documentaries, and you could survive in that spot if you got good press, even though you got lousy numbers—which we did—could this kind of program keep its head above water in a sea of Jackie Gleasons, Lucille Balls, and Arthur Godfreys? No one really thought it could, but us. And there were times when even we had our doubts. What I wanted as much as to be good was to be different, to take viewers to places they hadn't been before and never would have had a chance to go to if it weren't for us—like Richard Nixon's hotel suite the night he watched himself being nominated the Republican candidate for president. What I remember most about that story was that when the voting was over and Nixon had the nomination and he and his cronies were congratulating one another, Pat Nixon sat in the corner completely ignored. Nobody said a word to her. Nixon never went up to her, kissed her, or put his arm around her.

I happened to mention the Pat Nixon incident to Hubert Humphrey a couple of weeks later, before we filmed him on his nomination night. The night Humphrey got the Democratic nomination, his wife, Muriel, was at the convention hall and not in the room with him. The moment Hubert became the nominee, he got up from his seat, walked to the television set and kissed Muriel's picture on the screen. Do I think that what I told him about the Nixon was why he did it? I don't have a doubt about it.

Within a few weeks of our premiere, I could start to breathe easier, because right off the bat we were a critical success. Even though our share of the audience was pitifully low, *60 Minutes* was something the right people liked, and that was something the network brass liked. As long as we stayed in the Tuesday 10–11 spot and in effect stayed out of their hair, we were good for at least a year.

I faced my first crisis less than two months later, soon after the presidential election. Nixon had defeated Humphrey, . . . and the new president-elect offered Mike Wallace the job of White House press secretary. Mike was intrigued and flattered, as anyone would be, but I told him, "That doesn't make any sense. You don't want to go from being Mike Wallace to being a press secretary, even a White House press secretary. It's the kind of job a nobody takes so he can become a somebody." I don't know if that's what convinced Mike to stick with *60 Minutes,* but shortly after that conversation he told the Nixon people thanks but no thanks.

I was so glad he did, and *60 Minutes* was on its way.

How *60 Minutes* went from just another horse in the stable to being Secretariat is something I have never been able to explain. I have said on occasion that we were successful because we generated a lot of psychic energy rubbing off on each other. And for reasons I can't explain, we are able to transmit that psychic energy through the tube every week. . . .

Every enterprise needs a Palmer Williams—someone who knows where all the bodies are buried, who knows how to convince you that what you're about to do is something you're going to regret later, and actually points you in the right direction when you lose your way. I can't recount all of the many times Palmer saved us from ourselves, but it's safe to say that without him there, we wouldn't still be here, thirty-three years later.

Further Resources

BOOKS

Campbell, Richard. *60 Minutes and the News: A Mythology for Middle America.* Urbana, Ill.: University of Illinois Press, 1991.

Gitlin, Todd. *Inside Prime Time.* New York: Pantheon Books, 1983.

Madsen, Alex. *The Power and the Politics.* New York: Dodd and Mead, 1984.

Metz, Robert. *CBS: Reflections in a Bloodshot Eye.* Chicago: Playboy Press, 1975.

PERIODICALS

"The Mellowing of Mike Malice." *Time,* January 10, 1969, 39.

"Merry Magazines." *Time,* April 11, 1969, 86.

WEBSITES

"60 Minutes." Available online at http://www.cbsnews.com /sections/60minutes/main3415.shtml; website home page: http://www.cbsnews.com (accessed March 26, 2003).

9

MEDICINE AND HEALTH

CHRISTOPHER CUMO

Entries are arranged in chronological order by date of primary source. For entries with one primary source, the entry title is the same as the primary source title. Entries with more than one primary source have an overall entry title, followed by the titles of the primary sources.

Important Events in Medicine and Health, 1960–1969

1960

- The percentage of babies delivered by cesarean section doubles in twenty years to between 5 and 6 percent.
- U.S. Department of Agriculture poultry scientist B.R. Burmeister demonstrates that a virus causes a type of cancer in chickens. His work implies that viruses may likewise cause cancer in humans.
- Laborer Billy Smith has a severed leg reimplanted, but with only temporary success.
- Debate continues over the effectiveness of inactive- versus active-virus polio vaccines.
- On January 1, physicians visit only 10 percent of patients in their homes. The other 90 percent come to the physician's office for treatment.
- On January 1, abortion is illegal in all 50 states, though 45 permit abortion when pregnancy endangers the mother's life.
- In February, Dr. Frank L. Horsfall Jr. becomes director of the prestigious Memorial Sloan-Kettering Cancer Center in New York.
- In April, a breast implant is made from silicone gel in a plastic bag.
- In May, the Food and Drug Administration approves Enovid, an oral contraceptive pill, for use in the United States.
- In July, Harvard University physician and Nobel laureate John F. Enders' measles vaccine shows promise in early tests.
- In October, surgeons use a skin graft to replace a portion of the aorta.
- In November, the Educational Council for Foreign Medical Graduates gives foreign physicians its first examination to determine their fitness to practice medicine in the U.S.

1961

- Intrauterine contraceptive devices are developed as a new form of birth control.
- In February, the Centers for Disease Control and Prevention reports outbreaks of syphilis and gonorrhea among U.S. teens.
- In March, the U.S. Supreme Court agrees to hear a case that would overturn a repressive Connecticut law preventing distribution of contraceptive advice or devices.

- In April, California recognizes equivalency between osteopaths and M.D.s.
- In May, Drs. Jack Kevorkian and Glenn Bylsma use blood from a cadaver for a transfusion.
- In August, the Food and Drug Administration approves University of Cincinnati physician Albert Sabin's oral polio vaccine.
- In November, an Ohio drug retailer, William S. Merrel Company, withdraws its application for Food and Drug Administration approval of thalidomide, a sedative, after the *British Medical Journal* reports that the drug causes birth defects.
- In December, the Centers for Disease Control and Prevention urges vaccination for mothers with Rh-negative blood to prevent their antibodies from affecting future pregnancies.

1962

- Surgeons use the Harrington-rod operation to cure scoliosis, excessive curvature of the spine.
- Oncologists use multiple-agent therapy (radiation, chemotherapy, and steroids) to treat leukemia.
- Burroughs-Wellcome Company markets the drug Allopurinol to prevent attacks of gout.
- In February, Dr. Irving S. Cooper pioneers cryosurgery (freezing) in the brain to kill a brain tumor.
- In March, Congress debates proposals that would grant the elderly health insurance.
- In June, Everett Knowles Jr. has a severed arm reimplanted.
- In September, the rubella virus is isolated.
- In December, surgeons transplant the first human kidney between nonrelatives.

1963

- Roche introduces the drug Valium.
- Body-function recorders monitor postoperative care of patients.
- The Food and Drug Administration approves several intrauterine contraceptive devices.
- In May, the first human liver transplant is performed.
- In June, the first human lung transplant is performed.
- On June 8, the American Heart Association launches a campaign warning the public of cigarette smoking's dangers.
- In September, Dr. John F. Enders announces the success of his measles vaccine.

1964

- Home kidney dialysis is introduced.
- Drs. Blakemore and Sengstaken begin using a two-part balloon to stop stomach bleeding in patients with liver disease.
- In Saint Louis, women may give birth without general anesthesia.

- A new fertility drug, Pergonal, is introduced. Twins, triplets, and other multiple births are common from its use.

- A million abortions per year are done in the United States, most of them illegally.

- A rubella outbreak sweeps the United States.

- In January, cardiologist and surgeon James D. Hardy transplants for the first time a chimpanzee heart into a human patient, who dies within one hour from heart failure.

- On January 1, some one hundred people in the U.S. receive twice-weekly kidney dialysis in a hospital at ten thousand dollars per patient.

- In March, Joseph Goodman from Connecticut becomes the first American to die of Portuguese man-of-war jellyfish stings, on Miami Beach.

- In April, Sterling Drug Company of New Jersey produces the hundred billionth Bayer aspirin tablet.

- In June, the U.S. Surgeon General declares cigarette smoking a health hazard.

- In June, the U.S. Department of Agriculture reports that some 16 million children receive federally subsidized school lunches. Many receive free lunches and none pay more than ten cents per lunch.

- On June 24, the Federal Trade Commission requires cigarette manufactures to add warning labels to cigarette packs.

- In July, Massachusetts Senator Ted Kennedy fractures his spine in an airplane crash.

1965

- The female hormone estrogen is found to prevent bone degeneration (osteoporosis).

- The rubella epidemic of 1963–1964 causes twenty thousand children to be born with birth defects.

- Soft contact lenses are invented.

- Physicians and engineers work to develop an artificial heart at three sites in the United States.

- In January, one and a half million Americans have been sterilized for birth control.

- In March, a computerized blood bank, the New York Blood Center, is set up in New York City.

- In May, "surfer's knees" is described as a medical consequence of kneeling on surfboards.

- In June, University of Chicago anthropologist F. Clark Howell identifies arthritis in the skeleton of a Neanderthal, an early man that lived between 200,000 and 30,000 years ago, demonstrating the antiquity of diseases that afflict Homo sapiens. Howell also identifies evidence of surgery in a 60,000-year-old Neanderthal skull, demonstrating the antiquity of surgery.

- On July 30, President Lyndon Baines Johnson signs into law Medicare, granting federally subsidized medical coverage to Americans at least 65 years old.

1966

- Surgeons treat a coronary-artery blockage by bypassing the blocked vessel with a vein from the patient's leg. This becomes known as coronary-artery bypass surgery.

- Brooklyn surgeons use a gas jet to remove blockages from arteries.

- Surgeons use a surgical stapler to close incisions during surgery.

- In January, dermatoglyphics (palm prints) are used in the diagnosis of congenital defects.

- On January 1, Congress requires cigarette manufactures to add to cigarette packs the warning "Caution: Cigarette Smoking May Be Hazardous to Your Health."

- On February 4, cardiologist and surgeon Adrian Kantrowitz implants the first heart pump. The patient dies the next day.

- In March, a live-virus rubella vaccine is developed.

- In March, an epidemic of children with thyroid disease is reported in Saint George, Utah, downwind from Nevada nuclear test site.

- On July 1, Medicare goes into effect.

1967

- The fertility drug Clomiphene is marketed.

- A live-virus measles vaccine is developed.

- Cook County Hospital, Chicago, hooks up a cystoscope (to look in the bladder) to a color television and videotape machine.

- The drug LSD causes chromosomes to break during meiosis and mitosis, the two types of cell division.

- Leprosy is grown in a laboratory using an armadillo.

- No American died of rabies in 1967, for the first year on record.

- In April, authorities in Evanston, Illinois, report that fluoridated water reduced cavities 58 percent over twenty years.

- In May, Colorado becomes the first state to permit abortion, but in limited cases.

1968

- A meningitis vaccine is developed and tested on military recruits.

- Tests of a new German-measles vaccine show it is safe and effective.

- Nude group psychotherapy is used in Los Angeles.

- Surgeons implant a cancerous kidney, inadvertently causing cancer in the recipient.

- The injectable drug Depo-Provera can prevent pregnancy for three months per dose.

- In January, the U.S. Public Health Service declares malnutrition among the poor to be as severe in the U.S. as in developing countries.

- On January 17, President Lyndon Baines Johnson asks Congress in his State of the Union address to grant federally subsidized medical coverage to all pregnant women and infants to age one.

- In February, alcohol is found to be the best inhibitor of premature labor.

- In March, paramedics begin to use a kidney-storage unit that can save donor kidneys awaiting transplant for up to three days.

- In May, a study links "supermales," men with an extra male (Y) chromosome, to violent crimes.

- In June, RhoGAM, for Rh-negative mothers, is marketed.

- In October, the FDA bans cyclamate (a sugar substitute), after it is found to cause cancer in lab animals.

1969

- Louisville pediatrician Billy Andrews develops a new incubator for premature babies.

- Hysterectomies, especially in women under forty, are reported to be often unnecessary.

- In June, the Food and Drug Administration approves a rubella vaccine.

- On April 4, Dr. Denton A. Cooley implants the first artificial heart in a human, Haskell Karp, at Baylor University Hospital in Texas. Karp dies the next day.

- In September, Alabama Medical College dean Clifton K. Meador begins MIST (Medical Information Telephone System) for consultations between doctors.

- On October 18, the Department of Health, Education, and Welfare bans artificial sweeteners after scientists establish their potential to cause cancer in laboratory animals.

Newsweek Letters on Abortion

Letters

By: *Newsweek*

Date: September 12, 1960; September 26, 1960

Source: Letters published in *Newsweek,* September 12, 1960, 15–17; September 26, 1960, 14–16.

About the Publication: *Newsweek* originated as *The Illustrated News Magazine,* founded in 1933 by Thomas J. Martyn, a former editor of *Time* magazine. It was published by Weekly Publication, Inc., based in Dayton, Ohio, with editorial and executive departments in New York City. Eventually the name became *News-Week,* then *Newsweek* by the end of the 1930s. In 1961, *Washington Post* publisher Philip L. Graham bought the magazine. In addition to current news events, the magazine's coverage includes art, health, science, religion, economics, and sports. ■

Introduction

In 1960, all fifty states prohibited abortion, though forty-five exempted women whose pregnancy threatened their life. Women who wanted an abortion either paid surgeons large fees, went to amateurs, or sought the procedure abroad.

State legislatures softened their opposition to abortion during the decade. Colorado led the way in permitting abortion in the case of rape or incest. Other states questioned the wisdom of forcing women to give birth to deformed babies.

The birth defects of European babies whose mothers had taken thalidomide for morning sickness made news in the United States, focusing attention on the tragedy of birth defects and the benefit of abortion as a way to avoid the lifelong suffering of parents and children. Moreover, rubella, also known as "German measles," swept the country between 1963 and 1965, causing birth defects in babies whose mothers had been infected while pregnant. The development of ultrasound enabled physicians to detect birth defects that otherwise would have escaped notice, raising the question of whether women had the right to use such knowledge to abort deformed babies.

The question polarized Americans. Liberals who took the position that government had no right to abridge the freedom of women to decide their own fate supported their right to choose whether to carry a pregnancy to term. Religious conservatives defined the beginning of life as the moment of conception. To them, abortion was murder as well as defiance of God.

Significance

On September 12 and 26, 1960, *Newsweek* magazine published thirteen letters prompted by a story on abortion in the August 15 issue. The letters ranged the gamut of opinion about the morality and legality of abortion. The correspondents included an osteopathic physician, a minister, and several others with a religious agenda. No one had a tentative opinion; each writer expressed a moral certitude that made compromise difficult, much as the harsh rhetoric over slavery made compromise impossible during the nineteenth century.

Three writers accused abortion opponents of playing God. A fourth called the laws against abortion "archaic." Yet the majority opposed abortion. Two writers equated abortion with murder. The minister stuck to the premise that life begins at conception. The osteopathic physician pointed out that parents should take responsibility for conceiving a child.

A particularly eye-opening letter came from abortion supporter Florence R. Cloud in Los Angeles, California, who blamed promiscuous women for churning out babies they neither loved nor nurtured. Abortion, she believed, could rid the country of such progeny, freeing Americans from paying taxes to agencies that cared for illegitimate children. Cloud's letter typified the rancor of the abortion debate. She did not advocate abortion by appealing to evidence or logic; rather, she demonized women with children they could not care for for burdening America with their offspring. Abortion would not become legal until the Supreme Court decision in *Roe v. Wade,* in 1973.

Primary Source

Newsweek Letters on Abortion

SYNOPSIS: In the issues of September 12 and September 26, 1960, *Newsweek* published a total of thirteen letters on abortion, with the majority in opposition. Each writer expressed a moral certitude that made compromise difficult.

A Matter of Life

The opinions expressed in your story on the abortion racket (Special MEDICINE Report, Aug. 15) demonstrate the attitude of "expedience makes

Eunice Shriver, of the Joseph P. Kennedy Jr. Foundation, during a 1967 news conference where plans for an International Conference on Abortion were announced. © BETTMANN/CORBIS. REPRODUCED BY PERMISSION.

benevolence." We fought wars over the suppression of human rights and the murder of misfits.

Andrew J. Varga
Philadelphia, Pa.

I heartily agree with Dr. Alan Guttmacher that our abortion laws are archaic and need liberalizing.

Eunice Hafford
Fillmore, Calif.

Dr. Guttmacher's suggestion that abortion laws be liberalized is a step backward, not forward.

Maryann Norton
Valley Stream, N.Y.

Where do these people get the right to play God?

Eugene R. August
Jersey City, N.J.

Being a mother, I contend that it's about time abortions became legal. States would profit tremendously from this kind of revenue. Also, monies contributed to social agencies for illegitimate-child

support amount to well over $1 million. This tax money goes to women who even promiscuously become pregnant. And the taxpayer should pay for this?

Florence R. Cloud
Los Angeles, Calif.

Why not wait until the unwanted babies are born and then do away with them? Unthinkable, isn't it?

Mrs. G. L. Morrison
Boise, Idaho

It is not within the province of a physician to determine who shall and who shall not live. A life once conceived is the responsibility of those who brought about the conception.

E. W. Ferens, D.O.
Dearborn, Mich.

Since when can the natural law be modified to allow human beings to murder for their own convenience?

Jerry Van Lancker
Camp Lejeune, N.C.

If human beings have rights, then whether they are living in the world we know or the world of their mothers' wombs, they have a right to life. Residence doesn't alter anything.

Rev. P. Robert Roche
Westbrooke, Maine

The Unwanted, Unloved

Relative to the LETTERS (Sept. 12) concerning the alteration of the abortion laws, it seems to me that several of your readers have lost the point when they complain of murder, loss of personal liberty. Is bringing into the world an unwanted and unloved child any more right than keeping a crippled calf or lamb? The individual should be allowed the choice. The severe critics of Dr. Guttmacher are attempting to play God as much as those they accuse.

Peter C. Lear
Center Sandwich, N.H.

Your readers' letters against legal abortion appall me. This is a matter, in a free country, for individuals to decide. Just who thinks he has the right to play God?

Mrs. Philip Meeske
Spring Lake, Mich.

Isn't it more humane for illegitimate babies to be aborted than to have them brought into a cold world without love?

Judith Anderson
Edgewater, N.J.

The solution lies not in weakening our laws but in strengthening the moral fiber of our nation.

Mrs. W. C. Welsh
Downey, Calif.

Further Resources

BOOKS

Abortion in Law, History & Religion. Toronto: Childbirth by Choice Trust, 1995.

Cook, Elizabeth Adell. *Between Two Absolutes: Public Opinion and the Politics of Abortion.* Boulder, Colo.: Westview, 1992.

Frohock, Fred M. *Abortion: A Case Study in Law and Morals.* Westport, Conn.: Greenwood, 1983.

Williams, Mary K. *Abortion: A Collision of Rights.* Washington, D.C.: U.S. Catholic Conference, 1972.

PERIODICALS

"The Abortion Epidemic." *Newsweek,* November 14, 1966, 92.

WEBSITES

"Abortion History." Available online at http://www.abortion essay.com/files/history.html; website home page: http://www .abortionessay.com/ (accessed March28, 2003).

"Abortion History: A History of the Abortion Controversy in the United States." About.com. Available online at http:// womenshistory.about.com/library/weekly/aa012200.htm; website home page: http://womenshistory.about.com/ (accessed March 28, 2003).

"Conservative Politics: U.S. Abortion History." About.com. Available online at http://usconservatives.about.com/cs /abortionhistory; website home page: http://usconservatives .about.com/ (accessed March 28, 2003).

"History of Abortion." Columbia Electronic Encyclopedia. Available online at http://www.factmonster.com/cc6/sci /A0856467.html; website home page: http://www.fact monster.com/ (accessed March 28, 2003).

"The History of Abortion." Heritage House '76. Available online at http://www.abortionfacts.com/history/history.asp; website home page: http://www.abortionfacts.com/ (accessed March 28, 2003).

Congressman's Report

Report

By: Morris K. Udall

Date: August 17, 1962

Source: Udall, Morris K. *Congressman's Report.* Available online at http://www.library.arizona.edu/branches/spc/udall /congrept/87th/620817.html; website home page: http://www .library.arizona.edu/ (accessed March 31, 2003).

About the Author: Morris King Udall (1922–1998) was born in St. John's, Arizona. He served 30 years in the U.S. House of Representatives. Perhaps his greatest accomplishment was the *Alaska Lands Act,* which substantially increased the size of the national park system. In 1976, Udall sought the Democratic nomination for president, losing to Jimmy Carter (served 1977–1981). He was diagnosed with Parkinson's disease in 1979, and retired from politics in 1991. ■

Introduction

The drug firm Ciba-Geigy developed Thalidomide to prevent seizures in humans. When it failed to do so in tests, Ciba-Geigy sold it to Chemie Gruenenthal, a West German pharmaceutical company.

Chemie Gruenenthal discovered that Thalidomide was an effective sedative. Unlike other sedatives, Thalidomide could be administered in large doses, without fear of killing a patient from overdose. This property made it useful as a sedative for suicidal patients. After a round of tests, the West German Ministry of Health approved Thalidomide for sale in 1958.

Once the drug was in use in West Germany and elsewhere in Europe, physicians discovered that Thalidomide also reduced morning sickness and insomnia in pregnant women. Tragically, thousands of women who took the drug delivered babies without arms or legs and with heart abnormalities, kidney problems, and deafness. Chemie Gruenenthal would continue to deny for years that Thalidomide caused these effects. In 1970, the company agreed to an out-of-court settlement with the victims.

Significance

Confident in Thalidomide's potential for profit, the William S. Merrell Company, a drug retailer in Ohio, bought the right to sell Thalidomide in the United States. In 1960, Merrell asked the Food and Drug Administration (FDA) for permission to market Thalidomide in this country, and while awaiting approval, Merrell gave the drug to 1,248 physicians for clinical trials, in accordance with U.S. law. These physicians in turn prescribed Thalidomide to more than 15,000 women.

Physician and pharmacologist Frances Kelsey had been hired by the FDA to evaluate applications for licenses for new drugs. Upon receiving Merrell's request for Thalidomide's approval, Kelsey asked the company for evidence of the drug's safety. Merrell, which had been expecting routine approval, attempted to appeal to her superiors, but Kelsey continued to resist. While awaiting evidence she would never receive, Kelsey read a February 1961 report in the *British Medical Journal* that linked

Thalidomide to nerve damage in the arms and legs. Kelsey reasoned that a drug that could paralyze peripheral nerves could also cause damage to an embryo. The report hardened Kelsey's skepticism into opposition against Thalidomide.

In November, a German pediatrician reported that Thalidomide caused birth defects. The West German Ministry of Health banned the drug on November 29, 1961. The next day Merrell withdrew its application. Udall credited Kelsey with saving "many hundreds of babies from possible deformity." President John F. Kennedy gave her the President's Award for Distinguished Federal Service, the highest distinction a federal employee can earn, as Udall noted.

As a result of the Thalidomide near-disaster, Americans wanted tougher FDA scrutiny of new drugs. Congress responded in 1962 by authorizing the FDA to reject drugs that manufacturers could not prove both safe and effective. Moreover, drug manufacturers could no longer dispense drugs to physicians prior to FDA approval.

Primary Source

Congressman's Report

SYNOPSIS: In this report, Morris K. Udall praises Frances Kelsey for withholding approval of Thalidomide, saving hundreds of babies from deformity. In addition, Udall announces his support for tougher FDA scrutiny of new drugs.

Thalidomide: A Crippling Drug Promises Greater Protection for Consumers

Thalidomide—a tranquilizer and sleep drug—has caused several hundred malformed babies in Europe and produced the Sherri Finkbine case in Arizona. But a by-product of these tragedies may be an improved set of laws affecting every American who uses prescription drugs.

Present drug laws and regulations are not as extensive as most Americans might suspect. And they are administered by a Food and Drug Administration which is understaffed.

The American manufacturer of thalidomide distributed his product to 1,248 American doctors who in turn gave it to more than 15,000 women. There was nothing illegal about this procedure. Under present FDA regulations a manufacturer need not even notify FDA when the firm sends trial samples to physicians in the "clinical investigation" phase of new drug development. Now the agency proposes to tighten its regulations to give the federal government a greater role in planning and watching the testing process.

However, FDA did keep thalidomide off the general prescription market. If it had not, thalidomide might have been prescribed by your doctor or mine and we would have had many thousands of additional women wondering about their coming babies.

Credit for this action goes to Dr. Frances Kelsey, a "bureaucrat" if you please, of the FDA. Despite considerable criticism and pressure, she kept thalidomide out of the corner drug store. Her stubborn skepticism saved many hundreds of babies from possible deformity and earned her the President's Award for Distinguished Federal Civil Service, highest honor for federal workers.

New Regulations and Laws

The thalidomide tragedy seems certain to result in better enforcement of existing laws, and passage by Congress of new laws aimed at further insuring public safety. No one wants any unnecessary regulation of any part of our lives; but failure to enact measures to protect us from preventable disasters is equally bad.

The Kefauver Investigation

Sen. Estes Kefauver of Tennessee has long been concerned with the high cost of some new miracle drugs and the laws regulating manufacture and prescription. In 1960 he held extensive hearings which disclosed a need for changes in the law. While American doctors have been scrupulously careful with new and untested products, Senator Kefauver has questioned what he believes are some manufacturers' high-pressure advertising tactics directed at doctors as well as patients.

Regarding prices, it was pointed out, for example, that prednisolone costs 1.6 cents per tablet to make, sells to wholesalers at 14.3 cents and by the time it reaches consumers the price hits 29.8 cents or 1,763 per cent above manufacturing cost. The Committee figured an arthritic patient using prednisolone steadily would pay out $30 a month for a drug which cost $1.50 to manufacture.

As a result of his studies, Senator Kefauver introduced a highly controversial bill; President Kennedy supports some of its provisions; still other proposals have been made by different members of Congress. The drug manufacturers themselves have supported some of the proposed changes while opposing others.

Some Proposals

Here are some of the important changes being considered:

- Drugs would have to be shown to be EFFECTIVE as well as meeting present requirements for safety. Since 1913, hog, sheep and cattle owners have been not only protected against dangerous serums for their livestock but against worthless ones as well. The same protection would be provided for people who buy drugs for their own use.

- New drugs would not be placed on the prescription market until FDA approved them. At present, a new-drug application is automatically effective unless FDA acts against it.

- The FDA would be authorized a 25 per cent increase in staff.

- Advertising and information sent with drugs would be required by law to clearly state possible adverse effects.

- Manufacturers with drugs on the market would be required to report any information bearing on the safety or effectiveness of these products and the government could withdraw unsafe ones immediately.

- Patents on newly developed drugs would be exclusive only for three years (as against 17 years now), after which the patent holder would have to let other firms, for a fee, make and sell the drug.

- The generic name would be prominently displayed along with the brand name. This would enable persons to know what they are buying and would mean that if more than one manufacturer makes a drug, buyers could choose the brand with the lowest price. The Kefauver committee found that one drug could be purchased for $1.75 per 100 tablets if the prescription specified its generic name of prednisone whereas it cost $17.90 for 100 tablets if prescribed by a highly advertised brand name.

- The FDA would be given greater authority to institute inspection of manufacturers.

- A better system of preventing illicit use of barbiturates (sedatives) and amphetamines (stimulants) would be instituted.

Until thalidomide Sen. Kefauver was going nowhere with his proposals. Now the picture is altered. While not all of these changes will be ap-

Thomas Yendell, 16 months old. Thomas, and thousands of other babies, suffered birth defects due to exposure to the drug Thalidomide while still in the womb. AP/WIDE WORLD PHOTOS. REPRODUCED BY PERMISSION.

proved, it is likely that before adjournment the Congress will make some needed revisions in the law. And for this, at least, we can thank thalidomide.

Further Resources

BOOKS

Roskies, Ethel. *Abnormality and Normality: The Mothering of Thalidomide Children.* Ithaca, N.Y.: Cornell University Press, 1972.

Stephens, Trent D., and Rock Brynner. *Dark Remedy: The Impact of Thalidomide and Its Revival as a Vital Medicine.* Cambridge, Mass.: Perseus Publishers, 2001.

Teff, Harvey, and Colin R. Munro. *Thalidomide: The Legal Aftermath.* Westmead, England: Saxon House, 1976.

PERIODICALS

"The Doctor and the Drug." *Newsweek,* July 30, 1962, 70.

Lear, John. "The Unfinished Story of Thalidomide." *Saturday Review,* September 1, 1962, 35–40.

Mintz, Morton. "Dr. Kelsey Said No." *Reader's Digest,* October 1962, 86–89.

WEBSITES

Spiegel, Rachel. "Thalidomide." U.S. National Institutes of Health: Research in the News. Available online at http://science-education.nih.gov/nihHTML/ose/snapshots/multimedia/ritn

/Thalidomide; website home page: http://science-education
.nih.gov/ (accessed March 31, 2003).

"Thalidomide: Important Patient Information." U.S. Food and
Drug Administration Center for Drug Evaluation and Research. Available online at http://www.fda.gov/cder/news
/thalidomide.htm (accessed February 5, 2003).

"Thalomid History." Celgene Corporation. Available online at
http://www.celgene.com/thalomid; website home page: http://
www.celgene.com/ (accessed March 31, 2003).

"Heart Transplantation in Man"

Journal article

By: James D. Hardy

Date: June 29, 1964

Source: Hardy, James D. "Heart Transplantation in Man."
Journal of the American Medical Association 188, June 29,
1964, 1132–1134, 1135, 1138–1140.

About the Author: James D. Hardy (1918–2003) grew up in
Newala, Alabama, and received a master's degree from the
University of Pennsylvania in 1942. In 1951, the university
awarded him the Master of Medical Science in physiological
chemistry. His transplant of a chimpanzee heart into a human
in 1964 made international headlines. Hardy served as chairman of the surgery department of Loma Linda Medical Center in California from 1955 until his retirement in 1987. ■

Introduction

The transplant of a heart or any other organ into a
human is complicated by the fact that the immune system recognizes a new heart or other organ in the same
way it recognizes bacteria or viruses—as a foreign invader. This recognition leads the immune system to manufacture white blood cells and antibodies to attack the
invader. While in the case of bacteria and viruses this reaction protects the body, in the case of a heart transplant
the white blood cells and antibodies may damage the
heart enough to kill the patient.

Because the immune system reacts against a new
heart, physicians must suppress it to give the new heart
a chance to work. This too has a danger. An immune system that will not attack a new heart will also not attack
pathogens, with the result that any infection may kill a
patient even if the transplant is a success.

For this reason, the first successful transplant was of
a kidney from one identical twin to another. Identical
twins are biological equivalents, leaving the immune system no way to distinguish between the original and the
new kidney. In fact, no difference exists, and the immune
system accepts the new kidney as its own.

However, few people have identical twins, and even
in such cases a heart transplant would kill one twin to
save the other. Suppression of the immune system is thus
a prerequisite of a heart transplant.

Significance

During the 1960s, physicians discovered that some
anticancer drugs suppress the immune system, making
possible a heart transplant. Meanwhile, James D. Hardy
had since 1956 experimented with heart transplants in
dogs, admitting high mortality in these tests. By the
spring of 1963, Hardy made enough progress to consider
a human heart transplant.

By December 1963, he had identified several patients
with advanced heart disease who would not live long
without a transplant. In 1964, a 68-year-old man agreed
to a transplant and Hardy found a donor with terminal
brain damage. The heart of the recipient, however, deteriorated dangerously before the brain-damaged donor
could be declared dead.

Certain that the intended recipient would die without immediate intervention, Hardy transplanted a chimpanzee's heart into him, hoping he would live long
enough to receive a human heart. The choice of a chimpanzee made sense because its heart most closely resembles that of a human. A chimpanzee's heart, however,
is smaller than a human heart. The chimpanzee heart
Hardy transplanted into the patient lacked the strength to
pump enough blood to meet the body's needs. The patient died an hour after surgery.

Hardy knew he faced long odds in transplanting a
chimpanzee's heart into a human, but believed he had no
other way of saving the patient. He admitted that such
operations have ethical consequences: to take a heart
from a live chimpanzee kills it. Hardy's transplant of a
chimpanzee's heart into a human failed, but many significant factors were learned during the operation, not the
least of which included the handling of the media. Hardy
concluded that the experience supported the feasibility of
future heart transplants in humans.

Primary Source

"Heart Transplantation in Man" [excerpt]

SYNOPSIS: In this excerpt, James D. Hardy describes
his transplant of a chimpanzee's heart into a 68-
year-old man dying of heart failure. The transplant
failed and the man died an hour after surgery.

Heart transplantation has interested many investigators. Studies of related problems were begun
in our laboratory in 1956. Webb and his associates
studied such factors as practical methods for ho-

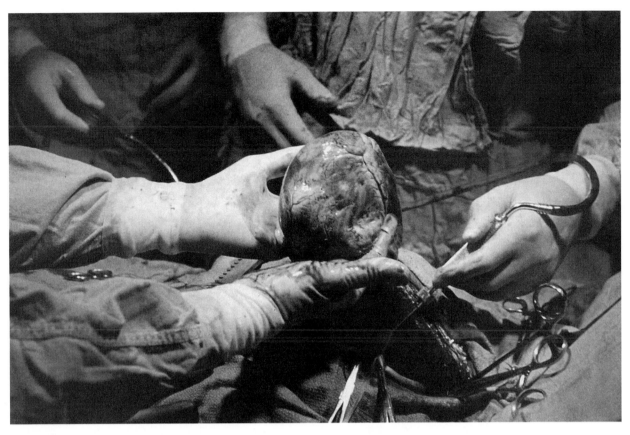

A surgery team sutures a human donor's heart into a 48-year-old-man in 1968. Although unsuccessful, Dr. James D. Hardy's heart transplant attempt in 1964 broke new ground in medicine and helped make heart transplants a reality by the end of the decade. © BETTMANN/CORBIS. REPRODUCED BY PERMISSION.

mologous cardiac transplantation, cardiopulmonary transplantation, restoration of function of the refrigerated heart, and cardiac metabolism as influenced by ischemia and refrigeration. The operative mortality was high, but extended survival of some dogs with orthotopic homotransplants was achieved. Collateral studies were conducted by other members of the department. Thus, in the spring of 1963, Webb and the senior author (J.D.H.) considered that the laboratory and clinical heart work justified a planned approach directed toward eventual heart transplantation in man. This objective, a natural outgrowth of transplantation research, was cleared with the administrative officials of the University Medical Center.

It remained for us to evaluate further the methods available for preservation of the heart during its transplantation. While resuscitation of the transplanted heart preserved with cold arrest could be achieved in most animals, it was essential that restoration of a good beat be assured for the first heart transplanted in man. Coronary artery perfusion had previously proved superior to ice slush during

aortic valve surgery in animals and in human beings and it was now re-examined. However, the coronary arteries of the dog were often too small and too variable to be perfused consistently with the equipment available, and ventricular ischemia and infarction occurred with some frequency.

Meanwhile, two operating teams had been established, one of which would obtain the heart from the donor and the other would prepare the recipient. One team continued heart transplantation in dogs (W.R.W.), but the other (J.D.H.) turned to a study of beef hearts and eventually to the use of the hearts of infant calves. It was found that the coronary arteries of even newborn calves were almost equal in size to those of the human adult, and that perfusion of both the right and left coronary arteries with cold oxygenated blood under gravity flow could routinely be achieved within three minutes from the time of excision of the organ. These small calves tolerated the supine position poorly, and ventricular fibrillation frequently occurred even before intrapericardial dissection had been initiated. Even so, the animals proved satisfactory for our purposes, in that coronary artery perfusion was regularly achieved without undue delay, following which the continuously perfused organ was transferred to an adjacent operating table and inserted into the new host who was supported with the pump oxygenator. The two operating teams were combined to complete this final insertion of the transplant. The extracorporeal circuit was primed with "sterile" but unmatched blood obtained from a slaughterhouse two hours previously, and the suture technique described by Lower and associates was employed. In contrast to experience with heart transplantation in dogs, anastomotic bleeding rarely constituted a problem in calves, whose tissues were tough and held sutures without tearing. Digitalization was found helpful when used cautiously, but on some occasions the digitalis produced heart block which often responded dramatically to the intravenous infusion of isoproterenol (Isuprel) hydrochloride.

Approximately 50 calves were used in the successful completion of 20 homotransplants. Coronary artery perfusion was found to be satisfactory in the majority of instances, but here again inadequate perfusion of either the right or the left coronary artery still occurred with sufficient frequency to be disturbing. For example, one of the catheters would become displaced at a point in the course of the operation when its reinsertion was difficult or perhaps inaccurate. Various types of sutures and chokers were employed to prevent displacement of the catheters in the unanchored heart, but none was wholly satisfactory. At this point, retrograde coronary sinus perfusion was re-examined (F.D.K.) and it became the method of choice for the remainder of the calf studies. These results were reported elsewhere, but good heart preservation and prompt resuscitation were regularly possible with this technique. While long-term survival of these very young animals was not achieved, a normal blood pressure level and sensorium were commonly restored following cardiopulmonary bypass and maintained many hours into the postoperative period. Two additional advantages of the retrograde coronary sinus gravity perfusion with chilled oxygenated blood were (1) the coronary sinus was readily accessible for immediate insertion of the single large perfusion catheter and (2) the aortic cuff of the donor heart could be left long to facilitate completion of the aortic anastomosis. The coronary sinus catheter was held in place with a choker, and through it oxygenated blood traversed the myocardial vascular bed to emerge cyanotic from the right and left coronary artery ostia.

Clinical Exploration

As the laboratory work continued and animal heart transplants came to exceed 200 in number, considerable reflection was devoted to a definition of the clinical circumstances under which heart transplantation might be ethically carried out. It was fully appreciated that, while the clinical transplantation of a nonpaired organ such as the liver had been widely accepted, transplantation of the heart would involve basic emotional factors that could be exceeded only by those of the brain. The question of heart transplantation was therefore discussed with many thoughtful persons, both physicians and laymen. In general, the reaction was favorable and one of cautious approval. All agreed that a rigid set of circumstances must exist. The donor heart presumably would be derived from a relatively young patient dying of brain damage, and the recipient must be a patient dying of terminal myocardial failure, since valvular disease might be amenable to valve replacement. But how soon after "death" of the donor could the heart be removed? If it were not done promptly, irreversible damage might have occurred. To minimize such damage it was planned to insert catheters into the femoral vessels and begin total body perfusion the instant death was announced by a physician not associated with the transplant team. It was believed that if the relatives were willing to permit use of the heart for transplantation, they probably would not object to heparinization and insertion of the peripheral catheters using local anesthesia at some point just prior to cardiorespiratory arrest. In this way, oxygenation of the body tissues could be effected while thoracotomy was performed to excise the donor heart and begin coronary sinus perfusion.

At the outset, it was expected that months, or perhaps even years, might elapse before an acceptable donor and recipient died simultaneously in the relatively small University Hospital. Furthermore, it was assumed that suitable donors would be far more rare than suitable recipients. Yet the opposite proved to be the case. In fairly rapid succession, three young men were admitted to either the University Hospital or the adjacent Veterans Hospital in late December, 1963, with fatal head lesions—trauma from a fall, a brain tumor, and a gunshot wound received in a suicide attempt. And while no potential recipient was currently hospitalized, oblique inquiry disclosed that the responsible relatives of two of these three neurosurgical patients were willing for either the heart or the kidneys to be used for transplantation. Each of these patients died after variable periods of mechanical pulmonary ventilation, a fact which raised a disturbing moral problem: When, if ever, would a physician be justified in switching off the ventilator in a patient whose voluntary respiratory effort had long since ceased, to permit the hypoxia that would be followed by cardiac arrest? We were not able to conclude that we would be willing to do this, despite the fact that at some point fruitless resuscitation efforts must cease if a viable kidney, heart, or other organ were to be obtained for transplantation to a recipient.

Meanwhile, the composition of the "donor team" and the "recipient team" had to be rearranged, made necessary by the departure on Jan 1, 1964, of one senior member to accept an academic post elsewhere.

Team Preparation

During these last weeks of December, 1963, a number of patients considered by their physicians to be in absolutely terminal heart failure were admitted and served to sharpen the orientation of the surgical group. The transplant teams, of course, had been working together in the laboratory for many months and all were well versed in their specific assignments relative to the techniques of heart transplantation. However, the anesthesiologists and the hospital operating-room scrub nurses were now brought into the program and began to participate in the laboratory procedures. Heart transplantation was performed between monkeys. The heart was also removed and replanted in the human cadaver.

Meanwhile, the complexities involved in the diagnosis of absolutely terminal shock due to myocardial failure were even more apparent. One patient was admitted to the emergency room "moribund" from acute myocardial infarction, but he recovered. Another patient admitted in deep shock from myocardial infarction improved considerably, only to die abruptly. No time would have been afforded in which to make the most meager preparations for cardiopulmonary bypass using a disposable bag oxygenator, even had a suitable donor been available. Still other similar instances made it clear that the recipient must be dying of long-standing heart disease, in which the downward course had been progressive and inexorable to a clearly discernible terminal collapse. In such a situation, the transplant would offer some possibility of life prolongation, as opposed to certain death otherwise.

As with clinical lung transplantation previously performed, specific written protocols had been drawn up for the donor team and for the recipient

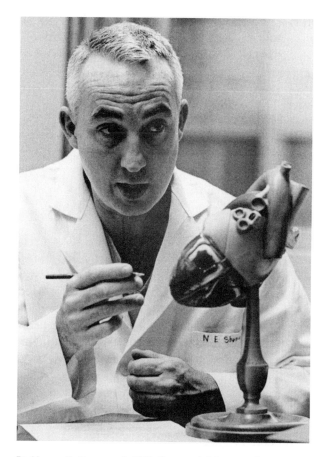

Dr. Norman E. Shumway. In 1968, Shumway led the team of surgeons who performed the first adult human heart transplant in the United States.
© UPI/CORBIS-BETTMANN. REPRODUCED BY PERMISSION.

team, and these had been distributed as confidential information to all personnel who might be immediately involved in a transplant. . . .

Further Reflection on Heart Transplantation

The realization that heart transplantation could conceivably have become a realistic possibility in this case prompted even further reflection and evaluation of our general philosophical and ethical position. It was clear that clinical heart transplantation raised psychological and emotional questions and problems which had not been major factors in the clinical transplantation of another nonpaired organ, the liver. But, on the other hand, we were not considering heart transplantation in other than the dying patient. The philosophical implications of performing any operation on a dying patient were also analyzed, and the light in which heart transplantation might be considered was assessed. First, it was noted that heroic operations are not infrequently performed on the terminally ill patient in the desperate hope, but remote chance, that life can be prolonged.

Second, an additional precedent had been set by the use of a novel extracorporeal apparatus in an attempt to support the heart of a patient dying of left ventricular inadequacy. Although it was unlikely that this mechanical support could prove adequate to the circumstances, we were in complete agreement with these investigators that the effort should have been made. . . .

Comment

Certain ramifications of the transplantation were far-reaching and merit individual comment.

What Was Accomplished

First, it was found that the heart could be effectively preserved for one hour while being transplanted into man. While cold arrest might have been employed, we had greater confidence in coronary perfusion to make possible resuscitation of the heart in the single, first clinical transplant to be attempted. The retrograde coronary sinus perfusion with cold oxygenated blood using gravity flow had been regularly effective in the infant calves, and it proved satisfactory in the clinical transplant. Second, the suture techniques widely employed for heart transplantation in experimental laboratories were adequate and otherwise acceptable. Third, a regular and forceful beat was promptly restored following defibrillation with a single weak shock of the pulse defibrillator. Actually, this was anticipated from the excellent condition of the fibrillating organ. Fourth, the transplanted heart reacted immediately to intravenously administered digoxin, as reflected in relative heart block with pulsus bigeminus. The cardiac pacemaker readily broke through this arrhythmia when the current was increased.

It was also apparent that the heart of the lower primate, at least at the chimpanzee level, is not quite large enough to support the circulatory load of the adult human being.

Collateral Issues

The secondary events extended far beyond the operative procedure and greatly exceeded anything that was anticipated by the members of the transplant team. Among these secondary issues was the management of public interest.

Public Announcement

Following the events of the previous week when a hospital employee had mistakenly informed the press that a transplant had been performed, it had become obvious that the essential facts, to be announced at one of the several imminent medical meetings, could not be suppressed. In addition, by the time the operation was over, almost 25 persons, many of them physicians, had gained entrance to the operating suite on one pretext or another, despite the fact that a doorkeeper had been placed at the only unlocked entrance. Clearly, the news would shortly be disseminated and, to announce the bare facts accurately, the director of public information decided to release a short statement. In accord with usual Medical Center policy, no member of the transplant team was to grant any interview, release any illustrative material, or be photographed, except under the formal auspices of national medical meetings. This was strictly adhered to.

Unfortunately, the first release resulted inadvertently in the need to permit another. The initial announcement did not specify that a chimpanzee heart had been used; this was to be divulged at the Sixth International Transplantation Conference a few days later. However, when it was announced in a distant city that the donor heart had been taken from a living human being, the situation had to be clarified. At this point, the university officials decided to halt piecemeal news leaks by one final announcement which included the membership of the transplant team.

Moral Issue of Clinical Heart Transplantation

The present status of clinical organ transplantation has been critically re-examined during recent months and the heart transplant has served as the model for this reassessment. Large issues are involved. The clinical homotransplantation of a cadaver kidney to attempt to save the life of a patient in terminal renal failure is accepted by most physicians, unless it be those who favor long-term dialysis for such patients. Of course, the die is not irretrievably cast in the case of renal transplantation, since the rejected kidney can be removed and life still be maintained by renal dialysis. In sharp contrast, following transplantation of the liver or the heart there can be no recovery if the organ fails to function satisfactorily, and, admittedly, the odds against chronic survival of such transplants are enormous. However, it can be expected that immunosuppressive therapy will be come increasingly effective in permitting survival of homotransplants, and the concomitant development and improvement of surgical techniques would appear to be desirable and justified in rare circumstances. We believe that such circumstances were those under which we transplanted the primate heart. For, although survival was not achieved, the situation was one in which the patient had no chance, except for the slim possibility that the transplant could be made to support the circulatory requirements and rejection could be prevented.

Much was learned in this effort to prolong life. Had the health of the lower primate heart (as contrasted with the hypoxic human cadaver heart) not been a positive favorable factor, resuscitation of the organ following its insertion might have failed. Thus, it is clear that the heart can be transplanted in man, and that with further refinements in physiology and drug therapy this operation may some day add years of life to many patients.

The general discussion which the heart transplant stimulated has had, with other factors, a penetrating influence on and within the transplantation movement. Many are reassessing their positions, reappraising their guidelines. We ourselves underestimated the extent and the vigor of the debate which was to ecenter around the use of clinical transplants—especially the use of lower primate organs. We believed then and we believe at this writing that the insertion of the chimpanzee heart, under the conditions which existed at that moment, was well within the bounds of medical ethics and morality. While the transplant did not function for as long a period as we had hoped, a great deal was learned, and this will render continuing laboratory studies more meaningful.

Summary and Conclusions

A heart transplantation operation in man was preceded by extensive heart transplantation studies in animals. It had been planned to use a human donor heart, but such an organ was not available at the moment the patient went into terminal collapse due to severe coronary atherosclerosis and hypertensive cardiovascular disease. Thus, the heart of a lower primate was used and inserted orthotopically in approximately 45 minutes.

The donor heart was well preserved during transplantation by retrograde coronary sinus perfusion with cold oxygenated blood. Once the transplant had been rewarmed by blood entering the aorta from the pump oxygenator, it was defibrillated with a single shock. The regular and forceful beat of the transplant was interrupted by pulses bigeminus which followed the intravenous injection of digoxin. However, this arrhythmia was abolished by increasing the current amplitude of the ventricular pacemaker which had been set at a rate of 100 beats per minute. The donor heart was smaller than the excised recipient heart and gradually became progressively less able to accommodate the large venous return without dilating.

This clinical heart transplantation in a most unusual set of circumstances lies within the established precedents of human transplantation of the nonpaired liver, the clinical transplantation of lower primate kidneys, and the exploration of mechanical ventricular support in a patient with terminal heart failure. Heart transplantation is confronted by the same immunologic barriers which threaten all grafts between genetically dissimilar partners. It is concluded that this experience supports the scientific feasibility of heart transplantation in man.

Further Resources

BOOKS

Thompson, Thomas. *Hearts: Of Surgeons and Transplants, Miracles and Disasters Along the Cardiac Frontier.* New York: McCall, 1971.

U.S. National Heart Institute. *Cardiac Replacement: Medical, Ethical, Psychological and Economic Implications.* Washington, D.C.: Government Printing Office, 1969.

U.S. National Institutes of Health. *Facts About Heart and Heart-Lung Transplants.* Bethesda, Md.: National Heart, Lung, and Blood Institute, 1997.

Wallwark, John. ed. *Heart and Heart-Lung Transplantation.* Philadelphia: Saunders, 1989.

PERIODICALS

Morgan, Elaine, and Elfriede Pahl. "Early Heart Transplant in a Child With Advanced Lymphoma." *Pediatric Transplantation* 6, no. 6, December 2002, 509–513.

WEBSITES

Groleau, Rick. "Operation: Heart Transplant or How to Transplant a Heart in 19 Easy Steps." Available online at http://www.pbs.org/wgbh/nova/eheart/transplant.html; website home page: http://www.pbs.org (accessed March 29, 2003).

"The History of Medicine: 1966–Present." MEDhelpNET.com. Available online at http://www.medhelpnet.com/medhist10.html; website home page: http://www.medhelpnet.com/contents.html (accessed March 29, 2003).

"LifeSharing—A History Timeline for Transplantation." Lifesharing Community Organ & Tissue Donation. Available online at http://www.lifesharing.org/timeline.html; website home page: http://www.lifesharing.org/home.html (accessed March 29, 2003).

"The Transplant Center at Fairview-University Medical Center." Fairview Health Services. Available online at http://www.fairviewtransplant.org (accessed March 29, 2003).

"Transplantation Milestones." UK Transplant. Available online at http://www.uktransplant.org.uk/about_transplants/transplantation_milestones/transplantation_milestones.htm; website home page: http://www.uktransplant.org.uk/ (accessed March 29, 2003).

Smoking and Health: Report of the Advisory Committee to the Surgeon General of the Public Health Service

Report

By: U.S. Department of Health, Education, and Welfare

Date: 1964

Source: U.S. Department of Health, Education, and Welfare. *Smoking and Health: Report of the Advisory Committee to the Surgeon General of the Public Health Service.* Washington, D.C.: Government Printing Office, 1964, 7, 8, 25, 26–27, 28–30, 31.

About the Organization: Congress created the U.S. Department of Health, Education, and Welfare in 1953 upon the recommendation of President Dwight D. Eisenhower (served 1953–1961). The department consolidated several medical and health agencies under one umbrella. Among its agencies was the Public Health Service, which examined the link between smoking and illness. ∎

Introduction

The smoking of tobacco and its relation to health has a curious history. Virginia planters exported tobacco to England and continental Europe beginning in 1617, only ten years after the founding of the Jamestown colony. King James I of England declared smoking a filthy habit. He was Scottish by birth, leading many Englishmen to disdain him as a foreigner. In an era when no government tolerated criticism, Englishmen could, without fear of arrest, express their dislike of King James by smoking tobacco.

Eager to adopt the habits of fashionable Englishmen, Americans took up smoking in the seventeenth century. Few people at that time suspected tobacco of impairing health.

During the twentieth century, vaccines and antibiotics reduced the number of deaths from infectious diseases, leaving heart disease and cancer as the two leading causes of death in the United States. Deaths from heart disease declined for unknown reasons between 1900 and 1955, when they began a climb that continued into the early twenty-first century. Cancer deaths have risen steadily since 1900. Physicians and scientists studied these trends, coming to suspect by 1960 that smoking increased the risk of both diseases.

Such suspicion worried cigarette manufacturers and tobacco farmers, who pressured Congress not to fund the Public Health Service of the U.S. Department of Health, Education, and Welfare in a study of the link between smoking and heart disease and cancer. However, in 1962, President John F. Kennedy (served 1961–1963) commissioned Surgeon General Luther L. Terry to establish

a committee to investigate the link between smoking and these diseases.

Significance

The department issued its report in 1964. The report chronicled the rise in the number of lung cancer deaths from less than 3,000 in 1930 to 41,000 in 1962. The report linked these deaths to smoking, demonstrating that tobacco smoke and tar caused cancer in laboratory animals, that autopsies of smokers revealed damage to organs including the lungs, and that smokers died more often than nonsmokers of lung cancer, bronchitis, emphysema, cancer of the larynx, oral cancer, cancer of the esophagus, ulcers, and heart disease.

The report also demonstrated that death rates increased with the number of cigarettes one smoked. The young were particularly vulnerable to the dangers of smoking, noted the report. Those who started smoking before age 20 died at younger ages than those who began after age 25.

Perhaps most important, the report identified smoking as a factor in making heart disease and cancer the leading causes of death among Americans. The report focused attention on smoking as a cause of lung cancer. Heavy smokers incur 20 times the risk of death from lung cancer than nonsmokers.

The report did little to deter smokers. Cigarette sales in 1964 fell only three percent below 1963 sales, and after an initial decline tobacco companies' stock rose.

Nor was government aggressive. Although Congress required cigarette packs to include a warning that "cigarette smoking may be hazardous to your health," President Lyndon Baines Johnson (served 1963–1969), who was so active in promoting the federal government's role in advancing health, did nothing to curb smoking.

Primary Source

Smoking and Health: Report of the Advisory Committee to the Surgeon General of the Public Health Service [excerpt]

SYNOPSIS: The U.S. Department of Health, Education, and Welfare reported in 1964 that cigarette smoking caused heart disease and cancer, the leading causes of death in the U.S. The report amassed evidence from animal experiments, autopsies of smokers, and comparisons of death rates for smokers and nonsmokers.

Impressed by the report of the Study Committee and by other new evidence, Surgeon General Leroy E. Burney issued a statement on July 12, 1957, reviewing the matter and declaring that: "The

Public Health Service feels the weight of the evidence is increasingly pointing in one direction; that excessive smoking is one of the causative factors in lung cancer." Again, in a special article entitled "Smoking and Lung Cancer—A Statement of the Public Health Service," published in the Journal of the American Medical Association on November 28, 1959, Surgeon General Burney referred to his statement issued in 1957 and reiterated the belief of the Public Health Service that: "The weight of evidence at present implicates smoking as the principal factor in the increased incidence of lung cancer," and that: "Cigarette smoking particularly is associated with an increased chance of developing lung cancer." These quotations state the position of the Public Health Service taken in 1957 and 1959 on the question of smoking and health. That position has not changed in the succeeding years, during which several units of the Service conducted extensive investigations on smoking and air pollution, and the Service maintained a constant scrutiny of reports and publications in this field.

Establishment of the Committee

The immediate antecedents of the establishment of the Surgeon General's Advisory Committee on Smoking and Health began in mid-1961. On June 1 of that year, a letter was sent to the President of the United States, signed by the presidents of the American Cancer Society, the American Public Health Association, the American Heart Association, and the National Tuberculosis Association. It urged the formation of a Presidential commission to study the "widespread implications of the tobacco problem."

On January 4, 1962, representatives of the various organizations met with Surgeon General Luther L. Terry, who shortly thereafter proposed to the Secretary of Health, Education, and Welfare the formation of an advisory committee composed of "outstanding experts who would assess available knowledge in this area [smoking vs. health] and make appropriate recommendations . . ." . . .

On July 24, 1962, the Surgeon General met with representatives of the American Cancer Society, the American College of Chest Physicians, the American Heart Association, the American Medical Association, the Tobacco Institute, Inc., the Food and Drug Administration, the National Tuberculosis Association, the Federal Trade Commission, and the President's Office of Science and Technology. At this meeting, it was agreed that the proposed work should be undertaken in two consecutive phases, as follows:

Entertainers (left to right) Jan Murray, Dean Martin, Sammy Davis Jr., and Frank Sinatra smoke after a 1961 performance at Carnegie Hall, New York City. Smoking was a fixture in American life in the 1960s, when the Surgeon General first reported on its links to cancer and heart disease. © BETTMANN/CORBIS. REPRODUCED BY PERMISSION.

Phase I—An objective assessment of the nature and magnitude of the health hazard, to be made by an expert scientific advisory committee which would review critically all available data but would not conduct new research. This committee would produce and submit to the Surgeon General a technical report containing evaluations and conclusions. . . .

Another cause for concern is that deaths from some of these diseases have been increasing with great rapidity over the past few decades.

Lung cancer deaths, less than 3,000 in 1930, increased to 18,000 in 1950. In the short period since 1955, deaths from lung cancer rose from less than 27,000 to the 1962 total of 41,000. This extraordinary rise has not been recorded for cancer of any other site. While part of the rising trend for lung cancer is attributable to improvements in diagnosis and the changing age-composition and size of the population, the evidence leaves little doubt that a true increase in lung cancer has taken place. . . .

Kinds of Evidence

1. Animal experiments

In numerous studies, animals have been exposed to tobacco smoke and tars, and to the various

A New York City billboard for Camel cigarettes shows a football player exhaling cigarette smoke, 1961. © **ROGER WOOD/CORBIS. REPRODUCED BY PERMISSION.**

chemical compounds they contain. Seven of these compounds (polycyclic aromatic compounds) have been established as cancer-producing (carginogenic). Other substances in tobacco and smoke, though not carcinogenic themselves, promote cancer production or lower the threshold to a known carcinogen. Several toxic or irritant gases contained in tobacco smoke produce experimentally the kinds of non-cancerous damage seen in the tissues and cells of heavy smokers. This includes suppression of ciliary action that normally cleanses the trachea and bronchi, damage to the lung air sacs, and to mucous glands and goblet cells which produce mucus.

2. Clinical and autopsy studies

Observations of thousands of patients and autopsy studies of smokers and non-smokers show that many kinds of damage to body functions and to organs, cells, and tissues occur more frequently and severely in smokers. Three kinds of cellular changes—loss of ciliated cells, thickening (more than two layers of basal cells), and presence of atypical cells—are much more common in the lining layer (epithelium) of the trachea and bronchi of cigarette smokers than of non-smokers. Some of the advanced lesions seen in the bronchi of cigarette smokers are probably premalignant. Cellular changes regularly found at autopsy in patients with chronic bronchitis are more often present in the bronchi of

smokers than non-smokers. Pathological changes in the air sacs and other functional tissue of the lung (parenchyma) have a remarkably close association with past history of cigarette smoking.

Population studies

Another kind of evidence regarding an association between smoking and disease comes from epidemiological studies. . . .

In the combined results from the seven studies, the mortality ratio of cigarette smokers over non-smokers was particularly high for a number of diseases: cancer of the lung (10.8), bronchitis and emphysema (6.1), cancer of the larynx (5.4), oral cancer (4.1), cancer of the esophagus (3.4), peptic ulcer (2.8), and the group of other circulatory diseases (2.6). For coronary artery disease the mortality ratio was 1.7.

Expressed in percentage-form, this is equivalent to a statement that for coronary artery disease, the leading cause of death in this country, the death rate is 70 percent higher for cigarette smokers. For chronic bronchitis and emphysema, which are among the leading causes of severe disability, the death rate for cigarette smokers is 500 percent higher than for non-smokers. For lung cancer, the most frequent site of cancer in men, the death rate is nearly 1,000 percent higher.

Other Findings of the Prospective Studies

In general, the greater the number of cigarettes smoked daily, the higher the death rate. For men who smoke fewer than 10 cigarettes a day, according to the seven prospective studies, the death rate from all causes is about 40 percent higher than for non-smokers. For those who smoke from 10 to 19 cigarettes a day, it is about 70 percent higher than for non-smokers; for those who smoke 20 to 39 a day, 90 percent higher; and for those who smoke 40 or more, it is 120 percent higher.

Cigarette smokers who stopped smoking before enrolling in the seven studies have a death rate about 40 percent higher than non-smokers, as against 70 percent higher for current cigarette smokers. Men who began smoking before age 20 have a substantially higher death rate than those who began after age 25. Compared with non-smokers, the mortality risk of cigarette smokers, after adjustments for differences in age, increases with duration of smoking (number of years), and is higher in those who stopped after age 55 than for those who stopped at an earlier age.

In two studies which recorded the degree of inhalation, the mortality ratio for a given amount of smoking was greater for inhalers than for non-inhalers.

The ratio of the death rates of smokers to that of non-smokers is highest at the earlier ages (40–50) . . . and declines with increasing age.

Possible relationships of death rates and other forms of tobacco use were also investigated in the seven studies. The death rates for men smoking less than 5 cigars a day are about the same as for non-smokers. For men smoking more than 5 cigars daily, death rates are slightly higher. There is some indication that these higher death rates occur primarily in men who have been smoking more than 30 years and who inhale the smoke to some degree. The death rates for pipe smokers are little if at all higher than for non-smokers, even for men who smoke 10 or more pipefuls a day and for men who have smoked pipes more than 30 years.

Excess Mortality

Several of the reports previously published on the prospective studies included a table showing the distribution of the excess number of deaths of cigarette smokers among the principal causes of death. The hazard must be measured not only by the mortality ratio of deaths in smokers and non-smokers, but also by the importance of a particular disease as a cause of death.

In all seven studies, coronary artery disease is the chief contributor to the excess number of deaths of cigarette smokers over non-smokers, with lung cancer uniformly in second place. For all seven studies combined, coronary artery disease (with a mortality ratio of 1.7) accounts for 45 percent of the excess deaths among cigarette smokers, whereas lung cancer (with a ratio of 10.8) accounts for 16 percent.

Some of the other categories of diseases that contribute to the higher death rates for cigarette smokers over non-smokers are diseases of the heart and blood vessels, other than coronary artery disease, 14 percent; cancer sites other than lung, 8 percent; and chronic bronchitis and emphysema, 4 percent.

Since these diseases as a group are responsible for more than 85 percent of the higher death rate among cigarette smokers, they are of particular interest to public health authorities and the medical profession. . . .

Lung Cancer

Cigarette smoking is causally related to lung cancer in men; the magnitude of the effect of cigarette smoking far outweighs all other factors. The data for women, though less extensive, point in the same direction.

The risk of developing lung cancer increases with duration of smoking and the number of cigarettes smoked per day, and is diminished by discontinuing smoking. In comparison with non-smokers, average male smokers of cigarettes have approximately a 9- to 10-fold risk of developing lung cancer and heavy smokers at least a 20-fold risk.

The risk of developing cancer of the lung for the combined group of pipe smokers, cigar smokers, and pipe and cigar smokers is greater than for non-smokers, but much less than for cigarette smokers.

Cigarette smoking is much more important than occupational exposures in the causation of lung cancer in the general population.

Further Resources

BOOKS

Cumulative Index to Health Consequences of Smoking: A Report of the Surgeon General, 1964–1982. Arlington, Va.: Information Resources Press, 1983.

U.S. Department of Health and Human Services. *The Health Consequences of Smoking: Report of the Surgeon General.* Washington, D.C.: Government Printing Office, 1982.

PERIODICALS

"The Government Report." *Time,* January 17, 1964, 42.

"One Year Later." *Time,* January 22, 1965, 58.

"The Smoking Report." *Scientific American,* February 1964, 66–67.

WEBSITES

American Lung Association. Available online at http://www.lungusa.com (accessed March 30, 2003).

"Health Issues: Surgeon General Reports." Philip Morris USA. Available online at http://www.philipmorrisusa.com/health_issues/surgeon_general_reports.asp; website home page: http://www.philipmorrisusa.com/home.asp (accessed March 30, 2003).

"Reports of Surgeon General: The 1964 Report on Smoking." U.S. National Library of Medicine. Available online at http://sgreports.nlm.nih.gov/NN/Views/Exhibit/narrative/smoking.html; website home page: http://www.nlm.nih.gov/ (accessed March 30, 2003).

"Surgeon General's Reports on Smoking and Health, 1964–2001." University of Minnesota Government Publications Library. Available online at http://govpubs.lib.umn.edu/guides/surgeongeneral.phtml; website home page: http://govpubs.lib.umn.edu/ (accessed March 30, 2003).

"Tobacco Information and Prevention Source (TIPS)." Centers for Disease Control and Prevention. Available online at http://

www.cdc.gov/tobacco/; website home page: http://www.cdc
.gov/ (accessed March 30, 2003).

President Johnson's Health Care Programs

President Lyndon B. Johnson's Remarks with President Truman at the Signing in Independence of the Medicare Bill, July 30, 1965

Speech

By: Lyndon Baines Johnson and Harry S. Truman

Date: July 30, 1965

Source: Johnson, Lyndon B., and Harry S. Truman. President Lyndon B. Johnson's Remarks with President Truman at the Signing in Independence of the Medicare Bill, July 30, 1965. *Public Papers of the Presidents of the United States: Lyndon B. Johnson, 1965,* vol. 2. Washington, D.C.: Government Printing Office, 1966, 811–815. Reprinted online at http://www.lbjlib.utexas.edu/johnson/archives.hom/speeches.hom/650730.asp; website home page: http://www.lbjlib.utexas.edu/ (accessed March 29, 2003).

About the Authors: Lyndon Baines Johnson (1908–1973) was born in Gillespie County, Texas. In 1937, he won election to the U.S. House of Representatives and in 1948 to the U.S. Senate, where he rose to majority leader. In 1960, he accepted John F. Kennedy's (served 1961–1963) offer to run as his vice president on the Democratic ticket. Kennedy's assassination in 1963 made Johnson president. Reelected in 1964, he retired from politics in 1969.

Harry S. Truman (1884–1972) was born in Lamar, Missouri. In 1934, he won election to the U.S. Senate, and in 1944 he became Franklin D. Roosevelt's (served 1933–1945) vice president. Like Johnson, Truman assumed the presidency upon the death of the incumbent, when Roosevelt died in 1945; and, as was also the case with Johnson, Truman was subsequently reelected, holding office until 1953.

President Lyndon B. Johnson's Annual Message to the Congress on the State of the Union, January 17, 1968.

Speech

By: Lyndon Baines Johnson

Date: January 17, 1968

Source: Johnson, Lyndon B. President Lyndon B. Johnson's Annual Message to the Congress on the State of the Union, January 17, 1968. *Public Papers of the Presidents of the*

United States: Lyndon B. Johnson, 1968–69, vol. 1. Washington, D.C.: Government Printing Office, 1970, 25–33. Reprinted online at http://www.lbjlib.utexas.edu/johnson/archives.hom/speeches.hom/680117.asp; website home page: http://www.lbjlib.utexas.edu/ (accessed April 1, 2003). ∎

Introduction

During the twentieth century, American businesses increasingly offered employees medical coverage as part of their compensation. However, this coverage usually ended with a worker's retirement. Yet it was during the retirement years, as people aged, that their medical expenses often surpassed their pensions.

Americans turned to the federal government for help. The liberal wing of the Democratic Party seized the issue of health care. This support allowed both President Harry S. Truman and Progressive Party candidate Henry A. Wallace to propose government-sponsored medical coverage for all Americans in the 1948 presidential election. Pundits predicted Truman would be defeated in the 1948 presidential election by Republican challenger Thomas Dewey, who opposed national health care. Truman's surprise victory led him to believe he had a mandate to guide a government-sponsored health plan through Congress.

He miscalculated. Congressional Republicans and conservative southern Democrats opposed the idea, and Truman left the White House in 1953 without any healthcare legislation. His successor, Republican Dwight D. Eisenhower (served 1953–1961), branded government-sponsored health care as socialized medicine, and the issue appeared dead. Eisenhower's successor in 1961, Democrat John F. Kennedy, supported government health care programs, but was unable to overcome opposition in Congress.

The absence of government-sponsored medical coverage for all Americans left the onus on businesses to insure their workers. The private-sector solution left retirees, children, and workers in low-paying service industries without insurance. If government were to make a difference, it would need to cover these groups, the most vulnerable in America's health care system.

Significance

Kennedy's assassination in 1963 brought Lyndon Baines Johnson, a dedicated advocate of government support for health care, to the presidency. Johnson had served in Congress since 1937 and had been Senate majority leader before becoming Kennedy's vice president. During his 23 years in Congress, Johnson had cemented friendships he could mobilize as president. As a southerner, he could more easily silence conservative opposition to a health care plan than Kennedy. Johnson could also call upon Congress to act on this issue to honor the memory and legacy of President Kennedy. Perhaps most important, Johnson understood that he could not push national health care legislation through Congress in a single thrust. His strategy would be to proceed in increments.

Johnson started by proposing aid for retired Americans, whom the private-sector solution had left without coverage. He also pushed for aid to poor families, the blind, and the disabled. He unveiled his plans for helping these groups, Medicare and Medicaid, during his 1964 presidential election campaign. His landslide victory gave him the power to push the programs through Congress, in the form of the *Social Security Act of 1965*. Political instinct led Johnson to sign the act in Independence, Missouri, the hometown of Harry S. Truman, with Truman at his side.

That day, Truman expressed pleasure at having lived long enough to see Medicare become a reality. He emphasized the justice of extending government-sponsored coverage to the aged. Johnson, for his part, praised Truman for having made medical coverage for Americans a priority.

Johnson then outlined Medicare's provisions. Taxes on both employers and employees would fund it. At age 65, Americans would begin to draw on its coverage, which would pay ninety days of hospital care per year, one hundred home visits by a nurse or physician, and beginning in 1967, one hundred days of nursing home care.

President Johnson continued to push for more federal health care aid even after Medicare and Medicaid were established. A 1967 bill raised benefits, and the government began to study the issue of expanding coverage to include the cost of perscription drugs. In his 1968 State of the Union Address, Johnson called for a third major step (Medicare and Medicaid being the first two) toward national health care. In his address, he asked Congress to expand government-sponsored medical coverage to all pregnant women and infants under the age of one.

Congress rebuffed Johnson. By 1968, Johnson's popularity had crumbled as a result of the bloody conflict in Vietnam. As American soldiers returned home in body bags, Americans turned against Johnson. With his support greatly weakened and conservative opponents strengthened, and with much of his attention centered on the Vietnam War, Johnson was unable to get his new health care program through Congress. Furthermore, with his presidency in shambles, Johnson withdrew from the 1968 presidential campaign. He would be replaced in 1969, by Republican Richard Nixon, without having achieved his goal of medical coverage for all Americans.

Although President Johnson was unable to create the broad national health care system that he had hoped for, Medicare and Medicaid marked an important shift in government policy. Although criticized for their cost and bu-

reaucracy, they have been expanded several times since their creation. For instance, in 1981, Congress extended Medicaid benefits to poor pregnant women and infants, much as Johnson had called for in 1968. In the early twenty-first century, the question of expanding Medicare to cover the cost of perscription drugs remained a major political issue. Through it all, Medicare and Medicaid helped millions of Americans receive medical care they could not have paid for otherwise.

Primary Source

President Lyndon B. Johnson's Remarks with President Truman at the Signing in Independence of the Medicare Bill, July 30, 1965 [excerpt]

SYNOPSIS: In this excerpt, Harry S. Truman and Lyndon Baines Johnson celebrate the signing of Medicare into law. Both employer and employee would fund Medicare. At age 65, Americans would begin to draw on its coverage, which would pay ninety days of hospital care per year, one hundred home visits by a nurse or physician, and beginning in 1967, one hundred days of nursing home care.

President Truman: Thank you very much. I am glad you like the President. I like him too. He is one of the finest men I ever ran across.

Mr. President, Mrs. Johnson, distinguished guests:

You have done me a great honor in coming here today, and you have made me a very, very happy man.

This is an important hour for the Nation, for those of our citizens who have completed their tour of duty and have moved to the sidelines. These are the days that we are trying to celebrate for them. These people are our prideful responsibility and they are entitled, among other benefits, to the best medical protection available.

Not one of these, our citizens, should ever be abandoned to the indignity of charity. Charity is indignity when you have to have it. But we don't want these people to have anything to do with charity and we don't want them to have any idea of hopeless despair.

Mr. President, I am glad to have lived this long and to witness today the signing of the Medicare bill which puts this Nation right where it needs to be, to be right. Your inspired leadership and a responsive forward-looking Congress have made it historically possible for this day to come about.

Thank all of you most highly for coming here. It is an honor I haven't had for, well, quite awhile, I'll say that to you, but here it is:

President Lyndon Johnson (left) signs the bill to establish Medicare, the federal government's system of health care for the elderly, on July 30, 1965. Vice President Hubert Humphrey (center) and former president Harry Truman (right) note the time. © **BETTMANN/CORBIS. REPRODUCED BY PERMISSION.**

Ladies and gentlemen, the President of the United States.

President Johnson: The people of the United States love and voted for Harry Truman, not because he gave them hell—but because he gave them hope.

I believe today that all America shares my joy that he is present now when the hope that he offered becomes a reality for millions of our fellow citizens.

I am so proud that this has come to pass in the Johnson administration. But it was really Harry Truman of Missouri who planted the seeds of compassion and duty which have today flowered into care for the sick, and serenity for the fearful.

It was a generation ago that Harry Truman said, and I quote him: "Millions of our citizens do not now have a full measure of opportunity to achieve and to enjoy good health. Millions do not now have protection or security against the economic effects of sickness. And the time has now arrived for action to help them attain that opportunity and to help them get that protection."

Well, today, Mr. President, and my fellow Americans, we are taking such action—20 years later.

And we are doing that under the great leadership of men like John McCormack, our Speaker; Carl Albert, our majority leader; our very able and beloved majority leader of the Senate, Mike Mansfield; and distinguished Members of the Ways and Means and Finance Committees of the House and Senate—of both parties, Democratic and Republican.

There are more than 18 million Americans over the age of 65. Most of them have low incomes. Most of them are threatened by illness and medical expenses that they cannot afford.

And through this new law, Mr. President, every citizen will be able, in his productive years when he is earning, to insure himself against the ravages of illness in his old age.

This insurance will help pay for care in hospitals, in skilled nursing homes, or in the home. And under a separate plan it will help meet the fees of the doctors.

Now here is how the plan will affect you.

During your working years, the people of America—you—will contribute through the social security program a small amount each payday for hospital insurance protection. For example, the average worker in 1966 will contribute about $1.50 per month. The employer will contribute a similar amount. And this will provide the funds to pay up to 90 days of hospital care for each illness, plus diagnostic care, and up to 100 home health visits after you are 65. And beginning in 1967, you will also be covered for up to 100 days of care in a skilled nursing home after a period of hospital care.

And under a separate plan, when you are 65— that the Congress originated itself, in its own good judgment—you may be covered for medical and surgical fees whether you are in or out of the hospital. You will pay $3 per month after you are 65 and your Government will contribute an equal amount.

No longer will older Americans be denied the healing miracle of modern medicine. No longer will illness crush and destroy the savings that they have so carefully put away over a lifetime so that they might enjoy dignity in their later years. No longer will young families see their own incomes, and their own hopes, eaten away simply because they are carrying out their deep moral obligations to their parents, and to their uncles, and their aunts.

And no longer will this Nation refuse the hand of justice to those who have given a lifetime of service and wisdom and labor to the progress of this progressive country.

And this bill, Mr. President, is even broader than that. It will increase social security benefits for all of our older Americans. It will improve a wide range of health and medical services for Americans of all ages. . . .

President Harry Truman, as any President must, made many decisions of great moment; although he always made them frankly and with a courage and a clarity that few men have ever shared. The immense and the intricate questions of freedom and survival were caught up many times in the web of Harry Truman's judgment. And this is in the tradition of leadership.

But there is another tradition that we share today. It calls upon us never to be indifferent toward despair. It commands us never to turn away from helplessness. It directs us never to ignore or to spurn those who suffer untended in a land that is bursting with abundance. . . .

And this is not just our tradition—or the tradition of the Democratic Party—or even the tradition of the Nation. It is as old as the day it was first commanded: "Thou shalt open thine hand wide unto thy brother, to thy poor, to thy needy, in thy land."

And just think, Mr. President, because of this document—and the long years of struggle which so many have put into creating it—in this town, and a thousand other towns like it, there are men and women in pain who will now find ease. There are those, alone in suffering who will now hear the sound of some approaching footsteps coming to help. There are those fearing the terrible darkness of despairing poverty—despite their long years of labor and expectation—who will now look up to see the light of hope and realization. . . .

There just can be no satisfaction, nor any act of leadership, that gives greater satisfaction than this.

And perhaps you alone, President Truman, perhaps you alone can fully know just how grateful I am for this day.

Primary Source

President Lyndon B. Johnson's Annual Message to the Congress on the State of the Union, January 17, 1968 [excerpt]

SYNOPSIS: In these excerpts, Lyndon Baines Johnson asks Congress to extend medical coverage to all pregnant women and to infants to age one. He informs Congress and the national audience that the United States, the world's richest nation, is ranked fifteenth among nations in infant mortality.

[Delivered in person before a joint session at 9:05 p.m.]

Mr. Speaker, Mr. President, Members of the Congress, and my fellow Americans:

I have come once again to this Chamber—the home of our democracy—to give you, as the Constitution requires, "Information of the State of the Union."

. . . Let me speak now about some matters here at home.

Tonight our Nation is accomplishing more for its people than has ever been accomplished before. Americans are prosperous as men have never been in recorded history. Yet there is in the land a certain restlessness—a questioning. . . .

Hospital and medical costs are high, and they are rising. . . .

Better health for our children—all of our children— is essential if we are to have a better America.

Last year, Medicare, Medicaid, and other new programs that you passed in the Congress brought better health to more than 25 million Americans.

American medicine—with the very strong support and cooperation of public resources—has produced a phenomenal decline in the death rate from many of the dread diseases.

But it is a shocking fact that, in saving the lives of babies, America ranks fifteenth among the nations of the world. And among children, crippling defects are often discovered too late for any corrective action. This is a tragedy that Americans can, and Americans should, prevent.

I shall, therefore, propose to the Congress a child health program to provide, over the next five years, for families unable to afford it—access to health services from prenatal care of the mother through the child's first year.

When we do that you will find it is the best investment we ever made because we will get these diseases in their infancy and we will find a cure in a great many instances that we can never find by overcrowding our hospitals when they are grown.

Further Resources

BOOKS

Adler, Gerry, et al. *Medicare 2000: 35 Years of Improving Americans' Health and Security.* Baltimore, Md.: Health Care Financing Administration, 2000.

David, Sheri I. *With Dignity: The Search for Medicare and Medicaid.* Westport, Conn.: Greenwood, 1985.

PERIODICALS

"Biggest Change Since the New Deal." *Newsweek,* April 12, 1965, 88–89.

"Medicare—How It Will Work." *Business Week,* July 31, 1965, 51–54.

"Medicare Is Launched Into a Shambles." *Life,* September 3, 1965, 52–58.

WEBSITES

Centers for Medicare & Medicaid Services. Available online at http://cms.hhs.gov (accessed March 30, 2003).

"Medicare." Social Security Administration. Available online at http://www.ssa.gov/pubs/10043.html; website home page: http://www.ssa.gov/ (accessed March 30, 2003).

"Medicare.gov—The Official U.S. Government Site for People With Medicare." Centers for Medicare & Medical Services. Available online at http://www.medicare.gov (accessed March 30, 2003).

Medicare.org: The Information Source for Medicare Information. Available online at http://www.medicare.org (accessed March 30, 2003).

"MEDLINEplus: Medicare." U.S. National Library of Medicine and the National Institutes of Health. Available online at http://www.nlm.nih.gov/medlineplus/medicare.html; website home page: http://www.nlm.nih.gov/ (accessed March 30, 2003).

"The Artificial Heart"

Journal article

By: American Medical Association

Date: September 6, 1965

Source: "The Artificial Heart." *Journal of the American Medical Association* 193, no. 10, September 6, 1965, 25–27, 28, 29, 30.

About the Organization: A group of 250 physicians and surgeons formed the American Medical Association (AMA) in 1847 in Philadelphia, Pennsylvania. Currently headquartered in Chicago, the AMA has grown to 250,000 members, including half of all U.S. physicians. The Association develops and promotes standards in medical practice, research, and education; provides advocacy for physicians and patients; and disseminates information through its *Journal of the American Medical Association (JAMA)* and other publications. ∎

Introduction

The development of vaccines and antibiotics reduced the number of deaths from infectious diseases in the first half of the twentieth century, leaving heart disease as the leading killer of Americans by 1955, according to a U.S. Department of Agriculture report. At the time, heart disease felled twice as many Americans as cancer, the second-leading killer.

The risk of heart disease increases with age, partly because the heart shrinks and loses strength as a person ages. By age seventy, the heart has lost one-third of its strength. As a person, ages the heart's valves lose their flexibility and may not close completely, allowing blood to leak back into the heart. It must therefore pump harder to circulate blood through the body.

Decline in the heart's size and strength may prevent it from pumping enough blood to meet the body's needs. This condition is heart failure and is fatal without treatment. A second danger is the accumulation of cholesterol and fat in the arteries and veins. These accumulations may block the flow of blood to a portion of the heart, damaging that portion. This condition, known as heart attack, may likewise be fatal.

Advanced states of heart disease lead to death unless the person receives a healthy heart from a donor. In the 1960s, however, few people wished to be donors upon their death. Consequently, the demand for hearts for transplant exceeded supply.

During the 1960s, physicians developed an artificial heart. Initially, they did not intend the artificial heart to be a permanent replacement for a biological heart; the hope was that it would keep a patient alive long enough to receive a heart from a donor.

Significance

In a September 1965 article, the American Medical Association (AMA) chronicled the development of an artificial heart. Domingo Liotta, a physician at Baylor University in Houston, Texas, developed the first artificial heart, which Baylor surgeons used in 1963. The patient lived only four days with the artificial heart, though the AMA asserted that the artificial heart had not contributed to the patient's death.

The AMA predicted the development of a better artificial heart before the end of 1965 and announced that the aim of physicians was to develop an artificial heart that surgeons could implant in a patient as a permanent device. William Hall, a Baylor University physician, predicted the development of such a heart by decade's end.

The development of a source to power an artificial heart was an obstacle to its success, noted the AMA. Electric motors, for example, worked as an external source of power but were too large for implantation. Frank W. Hastings, a physician at the National Institutes of Health, feared that physicians might develop an artificial heart for implantation by decade's end but fail to develop a source to power it.

Surgeon Denton A. Cooley implanted the first artificial heart in a patient in 1969, but the patient died of pneumonia and kidney failure 30 hours after implantation. By the end of the 1960s, physicians had developed an artificial heart, but it did not yet keep patients alive long enough to receive a heart from a donor.

Primary Source

"The Artificial Heart" [excerpt]

SYNOPSIS: In these excerpts from an article in its journal, the AMA reports on the development of an artificial heart for implantation in a human. The discussion examines several possible approaches, ranging from various methods of heart assistance to installation of a complete artificial heart. The problem of a portable yet durable power source is also recounted.

The first reported attempt to maintain blood circulation in the human body by means of an artificial heart was made in July 1963 by surgeons at Baylor University College of Medicine, Houston.

Using an implantable left ventricular bypass pump designed by Domingo Liotta, MD, assistant professor of surgery at Baylor, circulation was maintained in an adult male patient for almost four days.

The patient had developed left ventricular failure, transient cardiac arrest, and pulmonary edema following cardiac surgery.

The pump was placed in the patient to correct the left ventricular failure and was still working at the time the patient died of causes unconnected with its use. Cardiac status, electrocardiogram, and pulmonary edema had improved during the four days the bypass was used.

A left ventricular bypass pump of an improved design is going to be manufactured for clinical use, perhaps before the end of the year, C. William Hall, MD, assistant professor of surgery at Baylor, told *The Journal.*

"It will be used for temporary assistance of persons in acute left ventricular failure and for no other purpose," Dr. Hall said.

A nonportable, external power source will be used to drive the gas-operated pump. Gas transport in and out of the thoracic cavity will be by means of a tube brought out through the chest wall.

Patients will be hospitalized and nonambulatory.

Such temporary cardiac assistance will precede the final aim of an intensive research effort at many medical institutions today—development of a permanent, indwelling artificial heart to either replace or supplement the action of the natural human heart.

Dr. Hall has predicted that an artificial heart suitable for implantation in a human patient will be developed in from three to five years. . . .

A dual approach—development of a cardiac assistance device as well as an artificial ventricular pump—is being taken in a broad-based, coordinated research and development program at Baylor and Rice Universities, Houston. . . .

Partial cardiac support by means of an implanted left ventricular bypass was first reported in 1959 by Bert K. Kusserow, MD, University of Vermont College of Medicine, Burlington. Dr. Kusserow experimented with a small solenoid-driven diaphragm pump placed in the abdomen of dogs. Dr. Kusserow later modified this technique to externalize the pump. In 1961 he reported continued partial left ventricular bypass in an ambulatory dog for a period in excess of two days using a motor-driven extracorporeal pump.

The pump was suspended along the left chest wall by means of a harness sling. Blood was withdrawn from the left atrium by the pump and returned to the aorta via the cannulated proximal stump of

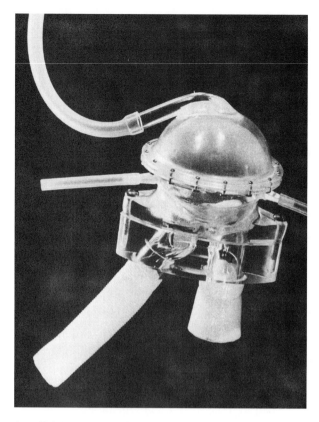

An artificial heart made of plastic. This early design, from 1966, relied on a power source from outside the body to function and was not a viable permanent replacement for a living heart. © BETTMANN/CORBIS. REPRODUCED BY PERMISSION.

the left subclavian artery. Directional flow was obtained by two appropriately placed rubber flap valves.

Moving the pump as well as the power source outside the body, while necessitating fluid-bearing connections across the chest wall, had a number of advantages, Dr. Kusserow reported. These included the possibility of direct observation, repair and replacement of pump components, reduction of tissue irritation, and greater facility for dissipation of heat.

Pump flow varied from approximately 600 to 800 ml/min and represented from 1/5 to 1/3 total cardiac output.

Moderate but significant damage to the formed elements of the blood was encountered, although hemolysis was considerably reduced by use of large bore cannulae.

Dr. Liotta's bypass pump, now brought to a high degree of sophistication, was first reported in 1962. It consists, essentially, of a double-walled tubular shunt between the left atrium and the descending aorta. A nondistensible tube of Dacron-reinforced silicone rubber (Silastic) houses a thin flexible tubular ventricle of the same material.

A pulsatile pumping action is maintained by intermittent transmission of compressed carbon dioxide under pressure into the space between the inner and outer walls of the tube, collapsing the flexible ventricle.

Recently reported modifications in this device include a pneumatically actuated inlet valve which is operated from the same pressure source used to energize the collapsible chamber.

Such a valve decreases resistance to flow, permits the pump to be stopped without danger of clot formation, and eliminates hemolysis and clotting experienced with the ball valves used previously.

An air-actuated outlet valve proved impractical since it required a separate power source. A modified Gott-Daggert type valve is used instead.

An improved method of atrial connection also reduces the possibility of clot formation, permits an unobstructed opening into the pump and does not compromise left atrial volume.

Paired electrical stimuli are used to synchronize action of the biological heart and the bypass. Pump control signals derived from the ECG were tried previously, but these proved unreliable.

As originally developed, the left ventricular bypass was intended as a temporary cardiac support measure following cardiac or aortic surgery.

Recent studies in dogs, however, indicate that the bypass can be used for prolonged maintenance not only of the systemic circulation, but of the pulmonary circulation as well.

Dr. Liotta and Dr. Hall have reported that when both ventricles of the dog were electrically fibrillated, pressure within the pulmonary circulation was maintained at a constant value to 12 to 14 mm Hg during use of a single bypass pump. Respiratory assistance to the pulmonary circulation was not necessary.

An Intraventricular Pump

In addition to left ventricular bypass, investigators at Rice and Baylor are developing an intraventricular pump. It consists of separate, air-driven, sac-type pumps for each ventricle made of Silastic. The outer walls are molded to fit the inside contours of the right and left ventricle and are reinforced with fine mesh, stainless steel screen.

Each artificial ventricle sits within the appropriate natural ventricle. The biological atrioventricular valves and their respective papillary muscles are removed and a prosthetic ball valve in each artificial ventricle sutured to the mitral and tricuspid annulus.

The Baylor-Rice group is also experimenting with a two-chamber, air-driven sac-type pump which replaces, rather than fits within, the natural ventricles.

"There are several approaches to heart replacement and it is a question of semantics as to which should be called total and which partial heart replacement," Dr. Hall said.

"You can bypass the heart using both left and right ventricular bypasses and leave the biological heart in place. You can amputate the ventricles and replace them with devices sutured to atrial remnants. You can take the whole heart out and sew the artificial device to the existing vascular structure.

"Or, you can do what we have done here. That is to develop an intraventricular pump which fits inside the natural ventricle.

"We have taken this approach because we are of the opinion that as much of the biological heart should be left intact as possible."

He gave these reasons:

1. Leaving the heart intact requires less surgery, and the operation itself is less dangerous.

2. The biological pacemaker is left intact. This is seldom diseased, and can be used to pace the artificial heart, resulting in a measure of biological control—as least with respect to rate—over cardiac output.

3. The outflow valves, the pulmonary and aortic valves, are left in place so there are two less mechanical devices to add trauma to the formed elements of the blood.

A Single Chamber Pump

Recent experiments at Baylor and at the University of Pennsylvania School of Medicine, Philadelphia, suggest that a right ventricular pump may not be necessary to sustain pulmonary circulation, at least for relatively short periods.

As mentioned previously, a left ventricular bypass pump was able to sustain both systemic and pulmonary circulation in the dog. In another experiment at Baylor, an intraventricular left ventricle pump alone was able to maintain circulation through both systems in dogs whose hearts were in fibrillation. Normal blood pressure was maintained for seven hours in one experiment, although the right heart received no support.

William S. Pierce, MD, and co-workers at the University of Pennsylvania School of Medicine, Philadelphia, have developed a single ventricular pump to maintain both systemic and pulmonary circulation. In this system, the right ventricle is bypassed by superior vena cava-pulmonary artery anastomosis. The inferior vena cava is ligated below the renal veins. The anastomosis of the thoracic inferior vena cava to the left atrium completes the circulatory modifications.

The pump is a motor-driven piston type in which a pliant diaphragm seals the piston to the cylinder wall, reducing blood trauma. Unidirectional blood flow is maintained by two one-way valves of opposite orientation. Cardiac output is responsive to left atrial pressure.

In dogs, adequate arterial oxygenation and blood flow has been maintained by this single pump for periods up to seven hours.

A single pump system has several advantages over the conventional two-pump system, Pierce and his coworkers report. These include smaller pump size, decreased power requirement, greater reliability, fewer valves, and less blood damage. . . .

Counterpulsation

The cardiac assistance measures discussed thus far have, to a greater or lesser degree, used artificial pumps to replace ventricular pumping action. There is another method of cardiac assistance which utilizes a fundamentally different hemodynamic principle called counterpulsation.

Counterpulsation is a method of augmenting arterial blood flow, while at the same time reducing the cardiac work load, by altering the pressure profile of the aortic and arterial pulses.

The arterial system is cannulated and blood withdrawn during cardiac systole, thus reducing both the pressure against which the heart works and myocardial oxygen consumption. The blood is returned during cardiac diastole, elevating the arterial pressure and the coronary blood flow. . . .

Dr. Kantrowitz found that placing the bulb end-to-side in the ascending and descending aorta, bypassing the aortic arch, produced the most marked decrease in left ventricular pressure, and the left ventricle's work load.

Modifications in this device have been reported this year. An asymmetrical U-shape replaced the ellipsoidal design. This allows the unit to be placed closer to the aortic root and takes up less space in the left chest. In addition, a slight negative pressure is applied to the tube during systolic filling to facilitate emptying of the ventricle; formerly, filling was passive.

With this improved unit, chronic and intermittent pumping (up to 104 days with 303 pumping hours) yielded a consistent reduction in left ventricular work and an increase in coronary flow with cardiac output unchanged or slightly increased. . . .

The principle of subcutaneous exteriorization eliminates the requirement for intracorporeal mechanisms and sources of energy as well as transthoracic cannulae. "It appears to be the only proposed technique which allows direct application of external pumping energy to the prosthesis," Dr. Soroff said.

Assistance vs Replacement

The counterpulsation devices and the ventricle bypass procedure are examples of the cardiac assistance approach to artificially maintaining adequate circulation of the blood. The alternative is total heart replacement. . . .

The Problem of Power

When the time comes for clinical trials of artificial hearts, they probably will be operated, at first, by some form of external power source. An adequate, long-lasting, implantable power source is still some years away.

The problem of power is, probably, the most vexing of all the difficulties encountered in development of an artificial heart.

Almost all pumping systems currently under study use conventional power units such as solenoids, electric motors, compressed air, or hydraulic fluid.

In most situations, the power must be transmitted across the chest wall either by means of wires, as is the case with electrical pumps, or through indwelling tubes in the case of gas-driven or hydraulic pumps. . . .

Nuclear power remains an intriguing but largely unexplored possibility.

In the absence of an adequate, long-lasting implantable power source the best alternative is an external power source coupled with an optimum energy transport and conversion system. Ideally, such a system would not involve electrical or tubular connections through the chest wall. . . .

An increase in life expectancy of some system components and reduction in the weight of internal components is required before it is suitable for use in humans. . . .

If pump efficiency is arbitrarily rated at 67%, and if currently available silver-zinc batteries with an energy storage to weight ratio of 110 watt-hours/kg are used, then to achieve a potential maximum blood pump output of 8 watts (the average power output of the normal biological heart during moderate heavy exercise), a patient would be required to wear 0.52 kg of batteries for each hour he wished to go between battery charges.

For a 12-hour period slightly more than 6 kg of batteries would be required, Dr. Schuder said. It would appear, therefore, that one of the first requirements is to develop an energy source with a more attractive energy storage to weight ratio.

A Unified Approach

Regardless of what approach is taken to the question of mechanically maintaining adequate blood circulation, the problems that are present must be dealt with on a concurrent, coordinated basis, says Frank W. Hastings, MD, special assistant for program planning, National Heart Institute, National Institutes of Health, Bethesda, Md.

"The development of an artificial heart must be regarded as the concurrent development of a number of subsystems," Dr. Hastings told *The Journal.* "It is false economy to develop a new blood pump without at the same time thinking about the energy systems that will be required to drive the pump. We might wind up five years from now with an excellent blood pump, but one that is incompatible with an appropriate energy system."

There also are many unanswered collateral questions, not directly concerned with development, which must be answered before large scale use of an artificial heart in human patients can become practical, he added. . . .

There are also unanswered physiological questions.

"What effect will an artificial heart have on concomitant diseases? What are the long-term effects, not only on the blood and circulation, but on all the body systems of an artificially maintained circulation?

"The all-important question is: Just how many lives will we save by using an artificial heart?"

Further Resources
BOOKS
Berger, Melvin. *The Artificial Heart.* New York: F. Watts, 1987.

DeVries, William C., and Lyle D. Joyce. *Artificial Heart*. Summit, N.J.: CIBA Pharmaceutical, 1983.

Gizzi, Peter. *Artificial Heart*. Providence, R.I.: Burning Deck, 1998.

PERIODICALS

"An Act of Desperation." *Time,* April 18, 1969, 58.

"An Artificial Heart." *Time,* April 11, 1969, 46.

Gilmore, Charles P. "Booster Pump Gives New Life to Failing Hearts." *Popular Science,* December 1965, 48–51, 194.

"Half-Heart Replacement." *Time,* November 8, 1963, 50.

"The Most Important Operation in History." *Science Digest,* July 1966, 46–49.

WEBSITES

"Artificial Heart." Available online at http://inventors.about.com /library/inventors/blartificialheart.htm?terms=artificial+ heart; website home page: http://inventors.about.com/ (accessed March 31, 2003).

"Building a Better Heart." The Franklin Institute Online. Available online at http://sln.fi.edu/biosci/healthy/fake.html; website home page: http://sln.fi.edu/ (accessed March 31, 2003).

"Artificial Heart Development." McGowan Center for Artificial Organ Development, University of Pittsburgh Medical Center. Available online at http://www.upmc.edu/mcgowan /artheart/Project01.htm; website home page: http://www .upmc.com (accessed March 31, 2003).

AUDIO AND VISUAL MEDIA

ABCNEWS Nightline: Artificial Heart. Original release, 1982. VHS, 1990. MPI Home Video.

A young boy eats a healthy piece of corn on the cob. © WILLIAM GOTTLIEB/CORBIS. REPRODUCED BY PERMISSION.

"A Daily Food Guide"

Reference work

By: Mary M. Hill

Date: 1965

Source: Hill, Mary M. "A Daily Food Guide." In *Consumers All: The Yearbook of Agriculture, 1965.* Washington, D.C: Government Printing Office, 1965, 742–743.

About the Author: Mary M. Hill joined the Department of Obstetrics and Gynecology at the U.S. Department of Agriculture's Agricultural Research Service in 1960. She specialized in child nutrition and eventually became director of the Children's Nutrition Research Center at the U.S. Department of Agriculture. ∎

Introduction

The federal government has a long history of trying to educate Americans about proper nutrition. Its first reports and pamphlets on the subject appeared around the beginning of the twentieth century, at a time when nutrition as a science was in its infancy. These reports became more detailed and accurate as scientists devel-oped a better understanding of the body's nutritional requirements.

When Lyndon Johnson became president in 1963, he placed great importance on improving the nutrition of Americans. Johnson had grown up in poverty and knew firsthand that poor nutrition weakened health. Johnson committed the federal government to a "war on poverty," an initiative that, among other goals, aimed to banish malnutrition and its diseases from the United States. America in the 1960s was more prosperous than ever before, and Johnson believed that in a land of such abundance no American should suffer the consequences of malnutrition. All Americans should enjoy robust health, the result of sound nutrition and timely medical care. Johnson felt that history would judge the United States not by the strength of its Army or the wealth of its corporations but by the degree to which it ensured the health and welfare of all its citizens.

Significance

The U.S. Department of Agriculture (USDA) was an important weapon in this campaign against malnourishment. It issued innumerable reports during the 1960s on the importance of nutrition in restoring and maintaining health. Never before had Americans had so much information about the value of nutrition in promoting health. Also, never before had the federal government been so active in promoting health through nutrition. Typical of this media blitz is "A Daily Food Guide," issued by the USDA in 1965.

The vegetable and fruit group supplied vitamins and minerals necessary to health. Mary M. Hill recommended that Americans derive all their Vitamin C from foods in this group. She listed citrus fruits and juices, strawberries, broccoli, brussels sprouts, and peppers as Vitamin C sources, downgrading the tomato, cabbage, watermelon, collard, and potatoes to "fair sources." She recommended that Americans derive half their Vitamin A from vegetables and fruit, citing broccoli, apricots, carrots, cantaloup, spinach, mango, and pumpkin as Vitamin A sources.

The meat group supplied protein, iron, thiamine, riboflavin, and niacin. Their protein content led Hill to add beans, peas, lentils, and nuts to the meat group. She emphasized the value of protein in building muscle, organs, blood, skin, and hair. Hill recommended two or three servings daily from this group.

The milk group included milk, cheese, cream, and ice cream. Like foods in the meat group those in the milk group supplied protein. In addition they supplied calcium, riboflavin, and Vitamin A.

The bread group included grains: wheat, oats, rice, and corn, and foods made from them. They supplied protein, iron, and several B vitamins. Hill recommended that Americans derive more calories from the bread group than from any other group.

The last group, "other foods," was a "wastebasket" category into which Hill tossed butter, margarine, and sugar—foods that she had not added to the other categories. Butter, for example, is a derivative of cream. One might argue that it belongs in the milk group. Margarine and sugar lacked nutrients and supplied only calories.

Primary Source

"A Daily Food Guide"

SYNOPSIS: During the Johnson Administration (1963–1969), the federal government worked hard to educate Americans about good nutrition and help them achieve it. In this article, the U.S. Department of Agriculture divided food into five groups: vegetables and fruits, meat, milk, bread, and "other." Mary M. Hill explains the contribution of each group to nutrition.

Suggestions for achieving a balanced diet are made by nutrition scientists. They translate the technical information about nutrient needs of people and the nutrient content of different kinds of food into a guide that is easy for everyone to use.

In the guide, the different foods are sorted into a few large groups on the basis of their similarity in nutrient content. Then suggestions are made for the number of servings from each food group that, with servings from the other groups, contribute the kinds and amounts of the many nutrients needed for good nutrition—a balanced diet.

An easy guide to follow is "A Daily Food Guide," . . .

It gives us as wide a choice as possible among different foods while still assuring us of a balanced diet. It gives a good deal of free choice in selecting additional foods. If we are convinced of the importance of the food we eat to the way we feel, we will welcome a guide such as this one.

Many persons want to know why particular food groups are emphasized in the guide and the names of some of the important nutrients. Such information can make choosing food for ourselves and our families more rewarding.

Foods from the milk group are relied on to provide most of the mineral calcium needs for the day. They are also dependable sources of protein and contribute riboflavin and other vitamins and minerals.

Meat, poultry, fish, and eggs from the meat group are valued for the protein, iron, and the B vitamins—thiamine, riboflavin, and niacin—they provide. This is true also of their alternates, dry beans, dry peas, and nuts.

The vegetable-fruit group is depended on to supply most of the vitamin C and vitamin A value of the diet. Yet only a relatively small number of foods are really good sources of either. To protect the nutritional value of your diet, your choices are directed toward the dark-green and deep-yellow ones for vitamin A value and to citrus fruit and a few others that are among the better sources of vitamin C.

The bread-cereal group, with its whole-grain and enriched bread and other cereal products, provides protein, iron, and the B vitamins.

Fats, oils, sugars, and sweets are not emphasized in the guide because all of them are common in every diet. Some of the fats and oils provide vitamin A, and some furnish essential fatty acids, but their chief nutritional contribution is energy value.

Some persons want to know more about foods than these general groupings tell them.

They want to know the number of calories and the amounts of specific nutrients in individual foods. For them, a booklet, "Nutritive Value of Foods," is a mine of information. They will find in it figures for the amounts of the key nutrients in common measures or servings of more than 500 items. Single copies can be had without charge from the Office of Information, U.S. Department of Agriculture.

From the figures in its tables we can also locate the better food sources of the key nutrients provided by a food group. For example, it would take about 1.5 ounces of Cheddar cheese, 1.5 cups of cottage cheese, or nearly 2 cups of ice cream to provide the amount of calcium in a cup of milk.

A fund of accurate information makes the subject of food and nutrition more meaningful to some persons—perhaps to you. That is fine.

But knowledge beyond the basic facts about your food needs is neither a prerequisite nor a guarantee to making wise food choices. A food guide can be that. Follow it. Here's to your health! . . .

Vegetable-Fruit Group

Foods Included

All vegetables and fruit. This guide emphasizes those that are valuable as sources of vitamin C and vitamin A.

Sources of Vitamin C

Good sources.—Grapefruit or grapefruit juice; orange or orange juice; cantaloup; guava; mango; papaya; raw strawberries; broccoli; brussels sprouts; green pepper; sweet red pepper.

Fair sources.—Honeydew melon; lemon; tangerine or tangerine juice; watermelon; asparagus tips; raw cabbage; collards; garden cress; kale; kohlrabi; mustard greens; potatoes and sweet potatoes cooked in the jacket; spinach; tomatoes or tomato juice; turnip greens.

Sources of Vitamin A

Dark-green and deep-yellow vegetables and a few fruits, namely: Apricots, broccoli, cantaloup, carrots, chard, collards, cress, kale, mango, persimmon, pumpkin, spinach, sweet potatoes, turnip greens and other dark-green leaves, winter squash.

Contribution to Diet

Fruits and vegetables are valuable chiefly because of the vitamins and minerals they contain. In this plan, this group is counted on to supply nearly all the vitamin C needed and over half of the vitamin A.

Vitamin C is needed for healthy gums and body tissues. Vitamin A is needed for growth, normal vision, and healthy condition of skin and other body surfaces.

Amounts Recommended

Choose 4 or more servings every day, including:

1 serving of a good source of vitamin C or 2 servings of a fair source.

1 serving, at least every other day, of a good source of vitamin A. If the food chosen for vitamin C is also a good source of vitamin A, the additional serving of a vitamin A food may be omitted.

The remaining 1 to 3 or more servings may be of any vegetable or fruit, including those that are valuable for vitamin C and vitamin A.

Count as 1 serving: ½ cup of vegetable or fruit; or a portion as ordinarily served, such as 1 medium apple, banana, orange, or potato, half a medium grapefruit or cantaloup, or the juice of 1 lemon.

Meat Group

Foods Included

Beef; veal; lamb; pork; variety meats, such as liver, heart, kidney.

Poultry and eggs.

Fish and shellfish.

As alternates—dry beans, dry peas, lentils, nuts, peanuts, peanut butter.

Contribution to Diet

Foods in this group are valued for their protein, which is needed for growth and repair of body tissues—muscle, organs, blood, skin, and hair. These foods also provide iron, thiamine, riboflavin, and niacin.

Amounts Recommended

Choose 2 or more servings every day.

Count as a serving: 2 to 3 ounces of lean cooked meat, poultry, or fish—all without bone; 2 eggs; 1 cup cooked dry beans, dry peas, or lentils; 4 tablespoons peanut butter.

Milk Group

Foods Included

Milk—fluid whole, evaporated, skim, dry, buttermilk.

Cheese—cottage; cream; cheddar-type—natural or processed.

Ice cream.

Contribution to Diet

Milk is our leading source of calcium, which is needed for bones and teeth. It also provides high-quality protein, riboflavin, vitamin A, and many other nutrients.

Amounts Recommended

Some milk every day for everyone.

Recommended amounts are given below in terms of whole fluid milk:

8-ounce cups

Children under 9 . . . . 2 to 3

Children 9 to 12 . . . . 3 or more

Teenagers . . . . = 4 or more

Adults . . . . 2 or more

Pregnant women . . . . 3 or more

Nursing mothers . . . . 4 or more

Part or all of the milk may be fluid skim milk, buttermilk, evaporated milk, or dry milk.

Cheese and ice cream may replace part of the milk. The amount of either it will take to replace a given amount of milk is figured on the basis of calcium content. Common portions of various kinds of cheese and of ice cream and their milk equivalents in calcium are:

1-inch cube cheddar-type cheese . . . = ½ cup milk

½ cup cottage cheese . . . . = ⅓ cup milk

2 tablespoons cream cheese . = 1 tablespoon milk

½ cup ice cream . . . . = ¼ cup milk

Bread-Cereal Group

Foods Included

All breads and cereals that are whole grain, enriched, or restored; *check labels to be sure.*

Specifically, this group includes: Breads; cooked cereals; ready-to-eat cereals; cornmeal; crackers; flour; grits; macaroni and spaghetti; noodles; rice; rolled oats; and quick breads and other baked goods

if made with whole-grain or enriched flour. Parboiled rice and wheat also may be included in this group.

Contribution to Diet

Foods in this group furnish worthwhile amounts of protein, iron, several of the B-vitamins, and food energy.

Amounts Recommended

Choose 4 servings or more daily. Or, if no cereals are chosen, have an extra serving of breads or baked goods, which will make at least 5 servings from this group daily.

Count as 1 serving: 1 slice of bread; 1 ounce ready-to-eat cereal; ½ to ¾ cup cooked cereal, cornmeal, grits, macaroni, noodles, rice, or spaghetti.

Other Foods

To round out meals and to satisfy the appetite everyone will use some foods not specified—butter, margarine, other fats, oils, sugars, or unenriched refined grain products. These are often ingredients in baked goods and mixed dishes. Fats, oils, and sugars are also added to foods during preparation or at the table.

These "other" foods supply calories and can add to total nutrients in meals.

Further Resources

BOOKS

Shotland, Jeffrey, and Ellen Hass. *Rising Poverty, Declining Health: The Nutritional Status of the Rural Poor.* Washington, D.C.: Public Voice, 1986.

U.S. Department of Agriculture. *Food.* Washington, D.C.: Government Printing Office, 1959.

PERIODICALS

"Oh No, It's Robert: The Five Food Groups." *Spider,* March 2003, 2–9.

Seipel, Michael. "Social Consequences of Malnutrition." *Social Work* 44, no. 5, September 1999, 416–426.

WEBSITES

"The Five Food Groups." Bodywellbeing. Available online at http://www.bodywellbeing.plus.com/pages/the%20five%20food%20groups.htm; website home page: http://www.bodywellbeing.plus.com/ (accessed March 31, 2003).

"The Five Food Groups." PageWise, Inc. Available online at http://allsands.com/Food/fivefoodgroups_bgi_gn.htm; website home page: http://www.essortment.com/ (accessed March 31, 2003).

"The Food Guide Pyramid: A Guide to Daily Food Choices." National Agricultural Library, U.S. Department of Agriculture. Available online at http://www.nal.usda.gov:8001/py/pmap.htm; website home page: http://www.nal.usda.gov/ (accessed March 31, 2003).

"School Lunches"

Essay

By: Anne G. Eifler

Date: 1965

Source: Eifler, Anne G. "School Lunches." In *Consumers All: The Yearbook of Agriculture, 1965.* Washington, D.C: Government Printing Office, 1965, 475–476.

About the Author: Anne G. Eifler earned a Ph.D. in nutrition from Iowa State University in 1958 and joined the U.S. Department of Agriculture's Agricultural Research Service as a nutritionist in 1961. She retired from the department in 1995 and died in 2002 in Ames, Iowa. ∎

Introduction

The federal government had promoted the health of Americans since Congress founded the Public Health Service in 1789. The federal commitment to health grew during the 1960s.

Lyndon Baines Johnson (served 1963–1969), who became president upon John F. Kennedy's (served 1961–1963) assassination, made the quality of Americans' health a priority. He crafted an ambitious agenda, the "Great Society," that included extending government-sponsored medical coverage to the aged and poor. In 1965 he guided Medicare through Congress, guaranteeing medical coverage to Americans at least 65 years old. The next year he persuaded Congress to enact Medicaid, which extended coverage to Americans who fell below an income threshold. In 1968 he estimated that Medicare and Medicaid covered more than 25 million Americans.

These gains did not satisfy Johnson. In 1968 he asked Congress to extend medical coverage to all pregnant women and to infants up to age one. One of the tragedies in U.S. history is that Johnson, who had done more than any other president to promote the health of Americans, sunk his health initiatives, his Great Society, into the quagmire of the Vietnam War (1964–1975). The deaths of tens of thousands of Americans in Vietnam turned the country against Johnson in 1968, leaving him unable to do anything more to benefit Americans' health. In this climate of opposition Congress refused to extend medical coverage to pregnant women and infants.

Significance

A component of Lyndon B. Johnson's health initiatives, and one that received less attention from Americans than Medicare and Medicaid, was to extend a school lunch program, which Congress had created in 1946, to all needy American children in the nation's public and private schools. Under Johnson's leadership Congress extended federally subsidized school lunches to nearly 70,000 schools in 1964, as Anne G. Eifler notes. As it always had, the U.S. Department of Agriculture administered the program.

The program invested in the health of America's children, which in turn was an investment in "community health," wrote Eifler. Well-nourished children, physicians knew, were less susceptible to infection than underfed children.

For this reason Johnson targeted the program to poor children, those prone to malnourishment. The poorest received a full subsidy: free lunches. Other children paid 5 or 10 cents depending on household income. Schools in poor neighborhoods received a federal reimbursement of 15 cents per lunch, Eifler reported.

Eifler touted the nutrition of these lunches, which included a half pint of milk, supplying protein, calcium, and Vitamin D; two ounces of meat or a protein substitute; a 3/4 cup of fruit or vegetables; a piece of vitamin-fortified, whole-grain bread; and two teaspoons of butter or enriched margarine. These lunches supplied one-third the calories, protein, minerals, and vitamins for a ten-year-old. Eifler recommended larger portions for teens and smaller portions for children under age ten so long as these portions satisfied U.S. Department of Agriculture nutritional guidelines.

Eifler emphasized the role of these lunches in fostering nutritious eating habits among children, habits that would sustain them into adulthood. Moreover these lunches would, she believed, encourage children to learn the value of nutrition in maintaining their health.

Primary Source

"School Lunches"

SYNOPSIS: In this essay Anne G. Eifler touts the role the U.S. Department of Agriculture played in the school lunch program by promoting the health of American children, particularly the poor who too often suffered malnourishment. She points out that the beneficiaries of the program extend beyond the children to include farmers, food industries, and local markets, as well as local workers who operate the programs. The program served nearly sixteen million children in 1964.

Communities and parents and producers of food, almost as much as the children themselves, gain in the national school lunch program.

Figures, impressive as they are, reveal only part of the balance sheet of the project, which was authorized by the National School Lunch Act of 1946:

Children line up for school lunches on October 16, 1962. Federal support for school lunch programs was greatly expanded by President Lyndon Johnson in the 1960s. THE LIBRARY OF CONGRESS.

Sixteen million children (one out of every three schoolchildren in the United States) in 68,500 public and nonprofit private schools in 1964 had balanced, nutritious lunches, at an average national cost to the child of 27 cents a day. Needy children, about one in ten, paid 5 or 10 cents or nothing.

The full balance sheet would bring out that two-thirds of American children do not receive lunches from the program. About half of those children are in schools that have the benefits of the program, but for one reason or another many of those in attendance do not participate. The other half of those children are in schools which have not become part of the program. Many of them are in sections where the need is greatest.

Federal, State, and local authorities stand ready to help communities and schools provide lunch service for children. For additional information, school officials should write to the State educational agency in their capital city. Since some States are able to administer the program only in public schools, private schools may be referred to an appropriate field office of the Department of Agriculture.

The community gains in the health of its children and, therefore, in time, in community health, which are matters that can be measured and proved.

For those who want another kind of assessment, I point out that 883 million dollars' worth of food was used in preparing lunches in 1964; nearly four-fifths of that amount was spent by the schools in obtaining the food in local markets. Thus the program provides good markets for local businesses, food industries, and farmers.

Employment is provided also for some 300 thousand local workers who operate the individual programs.

Local lunchrooms participating in the program receive Federal donations of abundant agricultural products and cash assistance, which amounts to more than 23 percent of the total cost of the program. Children's payments take care of more than 50 percent of the cost. State and local sources pay the rest.

Federal funds for the school lunch programs are apportioned among the States to be used in reimbursing schools for part of the cost of the foods they purchase. The amount of money each State receives is determined by two factors: School lunch participation in the State, and per capita income for the State.

Federal funds used in a State for reimbursing school lunches must be matched with funds within the State at the rate of 3 dollars for each Federal dollar. State and locally appropriated funds, children's payments, and donated goods and services may be used as matching sources.

Under this program, any nonprofit public or private school is eligible to participate. Local schools may enter into agreements with State departments of education to operate lunch programs in accordance with certain standards and regulations. They are reimbursed at the rate of 1 to 9 cents per lunch for a portion of their food expenditures.

An especially needy school, having a high proportion of children unable to pay for their lunches, may be reimbursed up to 15 cents per lunch.

The most important operating standards established for the program are: The lunches shall meet the minimum requirements of a nutritional standard based on research, and established by the Department of Agriculture; the lunch program shall be operated on a nonprofit basis; and children who are unable to pay the full price of the lunch shall be served free or at a reduced cost.

The United States Department of Agriculture is authorized by the act to purchase foods that are in plentiful supply for distribution to schools participating in the national school lunch program. These foods usually include meat and poultry items, either frozen or canned, and a variety of canned fruits and vegetables which will help to assure nutritional adequacy.

Schools also receive foods acquired in the operation of surplus-removal and price support programs.

Distribution of these foods helps the farmer by removing surpluses from the market and providing increased consumption outside of normal market channels. These foods vary in kind from time to time according to crop and market conditions.

The foods received through the various distribution programs in the Department of Agriculture provide about 7 cents' worth of food per lunch. The other foods used are purchased by the schools in local markets throughout the country.

Each month the United States Department of Agriculture supplies a list of foods which are in plentiful supply. Local schools are encouraged to use these foods in their menus.

The first of the standards—the so-called Type A pattern—guides the planning of well-balanced lunches and helps to assure the nutritional quality of the lunches. It is based on the amount of food needed to provide at least one-third of the daily nutritive requirements of 10-year-old children.

The lunches have five basic components: One-half pint of whole fluid milk; 2 ounces of meat or other protein-rich food; three-fourths cup of fruit or vegetable in at least two items; a serving of whole-grain or enriched bread; and 2 teaspoons of butter or fortified margarine.

Those five basic components form the foundation of the lunch. When those foods are used in the amounts specified and in combination with other foods needed to satisfy the appetite, the lunches generally will meet one-third of the daily nutritional needs of a child about 10 years old. Larger portions or seconds are recommended to meet the nutritional needs of teenagers. The regulations permit serving lesser amounts of certain foods in the lunch to younger children, provided the adjustment of portion is based on the lesser food needs of these children.

All schools that participate in the national school lunch program must meet the minimum requirements of the Type A pattern daily.

Besides, those who plan the lunches consider other factors, like the esthetic value of foods, the food habits of the community, the foods available in local markets, and the equipment available to produce the meal.

Communities, schools, and parents derive benefit from the education in nutrition that accompanies the food service. Nutritionists tell us that a large part of the population have diets that furnish less than the recommended amounts of various nutrients. Sometimes inadequate diets reflect a lack of knowledge of what constitutes good nutrition or of good food habits.

The lunch program helps children form good food habits and increase their knowledge of the importance of food to good health. Teachers and lunch supervisors work together to encourage children to learn to eat and enjoy a variety of foods.

Further Resources

BOOKS

Bode, Barbara. *School Lunch Program.* Washington, D.C.: Children's Foundation, 1971.

U.S. General Accounting Office. *School Lunch Program.* Washington, D.C.: Government Printing Office, 1989.

PERIODICALS

"National School Lunch Week Focuses on Nutritional Awareness." *Nation's Restaurant News,* October 28, 2002, 18.

Shell, Ellen Ruppel. "An International School Lunch Tour." *The New York Times,* February 1, 2003, A19.

WEBSITES

"Child Nutrition Home Page." U.S. Department of Agriculture, Food, Nutrition, and Consumer Services, Child Nutrition Programs. Available online at http://www.fns.usda.gov/cnd; website home page: http://www.fns.usda.gov/fncs/ (accessed March 31, 2003).

"Federal Food Programs: National School Lunch Program." Federal Research and Action Center. Available online at http://www.frac.org/html/federal_food_programs/programs/nslp.html; website home page: http://www.frac.org/ (accessed March 31, 2003).

"National School Lunch Program." Catalog of Federal Domestic Assistance. Available online at http://www.cfda.gov/public/viewprog.asp?progid=88; website home page: http://www.cfda.gov/ (accessed March 31, 2003).

"National School Lunch Program." U.S. Department of Agriculture, Food, Nutrition, and Consumer Services. Available online at http://www.fns.usda.gov/cnd/Lunch/default.htm; website home page: http://www.fns.usda.gov/fncs/ (accessed March 31, 2003).

"School Lunch Program." Andover Regional School District. Available online at http://www.andoverregional.org/id225.htm; website home page: http://www.andoverregional.org/ (accessed March 31, 2003).

"School Lunch Program." California Department of Education. Available online at http://www.cde.ca.gov/nsd/snp/lunch .htm; website home page: http://www.cde.ca.gov/ (accessed March 31, 2003).

Overweight and What It Takes to Stay Trim
Report

By: Marjorie B. Washbon and Gail G. Harrison

Date: 1969

Source: Washbon, Marjorie B., and Gail G. Harrison. *Overweight and What It Takes to Stay Trim.* In *Food For Us All: The Yearbook of Agriculture 1969.* Washington, D.C.: Government Printing Office, 1969, 304–307, 308–309.

About the Authors: Marjorie B. Washbon earned a Ph.D. in nutrition from the University of South Carolina in 1955 and was a U.S. Department of Agriculture (USDA) nutritionist between 1959 and 1992. In 1982, together with Gail G. Harrison and Helen Gifft, she co-authored the book *Nutrition, Behavior, and Change.* Gail G. Harrison was a nutritionist at the USDA during the 1960s. Currently professor and chair of the Department of Community Health Science at the University of California at Los Angeles, she has conducted research in the area of cancer prevention through dietary change. ■

Introduction

Obesity, a weight at least 20 percent above one's ideal weight, began to attract attention from physicians and scientists in the 1950s. During that decade Ercel Sherman Eppright, a scientist at Iowa State University, examined 1,200 Iowa children, identifying eleven percent of the boys and seventeen percent of the girls as obese. Charlotte M. Young of Cornell University identified twenty-three percent of first-year undergraduate males and thirty-six percent of females at Cornell as obese. A 1959 USDA report linked obesity with diabetes, liver damage, appendicitis, nephritis, cerebral hemorrhage, gallbladder infections, and heart disease.

Obesity is also related to a lack of physical fitness, a fact that attracted national attention in 1957 when a report found half of American children unable to pass a fitness test, compared to European children's success rate on the same test. Americans blamed their children's lack of fitness on the availability of cars and other labor-saving technology, and television.

A second cause was an excess of calories in the American diet. A 1965 USDA survey revealed that between 1955 and 1965 Americans' consumption of potato chips increased 83 percent. During this decade consumption of donuts, candy, and white bread, all high-

calorie foods with few if any nutrients, also increased. In 1966, the National Soft Drink Association reported that the average American drank 18 gallons of soft drinks and artificially-flavored uncarbonated beverages per year.

Significance

The problem of obesity focused attention on methods of reducing weight. Marjorie B. Washbon and Gail G. Harrison distinguished between overweight and overfat. A person may be overweight with muscles accounting for the excess. By contrast people may be overweight because their bodies carry too much fat. The goal of weight reduction is to lose fat rather than muscles, stressed Washbon and Harrison.

Not everyone can shed fat with the same ease, they noted, because not everyone has the same body type. Washbon and Harrison proposed three "extreme" types, with most people possessing some combination of two of them. One of these is the ectomorph, which has a light skeleton and small muscles. An ectomorph is thin and probably can eat much without gaining weight. Second is the endomorph, who is thick and covered with a layer of fat. Endomorphs are predisposed to gaining fat and have the most trouble losing it. Third, the mesomorph, has a large skeleton and muscles, analogous to Neanderthals. A mesomorph may tend toward being overweight because of muscle and skeletal bulk while having little fat. Like ectomorphs, mesomorphs are less likely than endomorphs to gain fat and can lose it more easily.

This division of humans into three types implies that most overfat people are endomorphs. Because one cannot change one's body type the tendency toward gaining fat may be hereditary. This does not mean that obese people can do nothing to reduce fat, only that they will struggle to do so. Washbon and Harrison stress that diet and exercise can reduce fat and build muscle even in endomorphs.

Primary Source

Overweight and What It Takes to Stay Trim
[excerpt]

> **SYNOPSIS:** In these excerpts Marjorie B. Washbon and Gail G. Harrison divide humans into three types: ectomorph, endomorph, and mesomorph. They also discuss some basic facts about weight gain and reduction, and offer several possible reasons for the difficulties encountered by many individuals attempting to lose weight.

How to lose weight, preferably without effort, receives constant attention in the press and conversation. Not all of this information is wrong; but much is a mixture of fact, half-truths, and pure imagination. How can you know what to believe, especially when the information is often presented as a "new, scientific discovery"? After all, science has progressed to voyages around the moon. Yet easy ways to lose weight are still elusive. Unravelling the mysteries of the human body is proving more difficult than conquering outer space.

An easy way to lose weight is not yet in sight nor is it realistic to expect one. There has been, however, gradual accumulation of knowledge from continual experimentation, some of which has been treated in popular writings. The purpose of this chapter is to present an overview of what we know and don't know about the causes and correction of obesity.

There are sound health reasons for a concern about weight reduction although, admittedly, much of the current interest is motivated by desire for a fashionable figure. Most people know that overweight is considered a health hazard, particularly in relation to diseases of the heart and circulatory system. Most life insurance companies charge higher rates to the grossly overweight just as they do for other high risk categories—such as smokers and the accident-prone.

The connection between extreme overweight and several diseases is well documented. It is also known that the greater the degree of obesity, the greater the risk. But it is not clear just how much excess weight—or excess fat—constitutes a danger. Neither are we sure whether the primary health risk is overweight or overfatness.

Most of us agree there is little to say in favor of overweight and most of us, too, are acquainted with some of the more basic facts about weight reduction. The implications of these facts are less well understood.

Just about everyone knows, for example, that you accumulate extra fat by taking in more food than you can use up in energy output. And, conversely, that you lose body fat when you eat less food than you require for your energy expenditure. Most people know, also, that the term used to measure energy is calories. Possibly no word in the English language is more maligned. We count calories; we regret them; we blame them.

But scientifically speaking, calories are simply units to measure energy, just as inches or miles are units to measure distance.

We need food energy. Without it, the body could not function. But keeping it functioning at a con-

stant weight requires a balance between intake and outgo. Many factors affect both sides of this energy equation.

We all use energy in two distinct ways: (1) to maintain those basic processes necessary to life, including growth and (2) to accomplish physical activity. The precise amount needed in each category varies greatly from one person to another.

By far the greatest proportion of our calorie need is accounted for by the basic, on-going processes of life—the work needed to keep the heart beating, the lungs breathing, the kidneys eliminating waste products, the cells of the body repairing themselves, new tissues being built during growth, and production of heat to keep body temperature normal. All of these processes require energy. The energy needed to maintain them is called the basal metabolic rate, or the BMR.

Many conditions affect the BMR, and thus the total caloric needs of a given individual. Among these are size, the body composition, age, and hormonal factors. The larger person, with a greater amount of muscle and bone, requires more energy for basic metabolic demands than the smaller person. Age is another influencing factor. Basal metabolic rate increases during periods of growth and decreases gradually throughout adult life.

About the only controllable factor affecting basal metabolic rate is the rare situation of hormonal imbalance. Occasionally the occurrence of thyroid insufficiency will slow BMR down. In these relatively rare and easily detected cases, therapy with thyroid hormone alleviates the condition. More often the imbalance in the energy equation must be attacked from the standpoint of food intake, exercise, or both.

Besides the BMR, the other major factor affecting energy needs is exercise. And this you can control. An important reason for the increased incidence of overweight today is the limited physical activity that everyday living demands of most of us. A conscious effort to increase our physical activity deserves more attention than it has had in the past. Even a few years ago, it was common to teach that exercise was of little or no value in weight control. Unfortunately, the erroneous ideas on which this teaching was based still persist.

One such fallacy is the notion that exercise automatically increases appetite and thus any beneficial effects are canceled out. This doesn't have to be true, especially with moderate activity. Actually, more data are available to support the opposite

THREE EXTREMES OF BODY BUILD

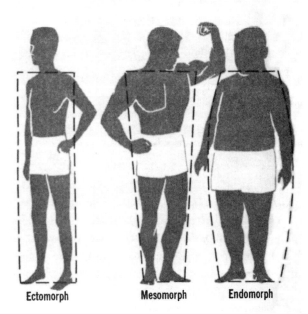

Ectomorph   Mesomorph   Endomorph

An illustration from *The Yearbook of Agriculture 1969*, illustrates natural variations in body build that can make some people naturally thin or heavy. **ILLUSTRATION FROM *FOOD FOR US ALL: THE YEARBOOK OF AGRICULTURE 1969*. WASHINGTON, D.C.: GOVERNMENT PRINTING OFFICE, 1969, 306.**

situation. That is, reducing activity to a low level may not be accompanied by less eating.

A second misconception is the belief that it takes a lot of exercise—more than most people will do—to use significant amounts of energy.

This is true enough if you are talking about the short term of a few weeks. But, over a period of months or years, even small increases in exercise can make a difference in how much you weigh, providing the activity becomes a daily habit.

Some increase in exercise is especially significant for many older folks and others whose caloric needs are low, when keeping extra weight off may seem almost an impossible problem. If such persons are to maintain their weight, the choice may rest between making the effort to get some regular exercise—or continually being a little hungry.

For the person who has always been overweight, exercise may be an even more complicated problem. The overweight teenager, for instance, may not be proficient in sports and feel self-conscious, and so he may habitually underparticipate. Thus, lack of exercise is not only contributing to his obesity; it is also a result of his obesity. A vicious circle devel-

ops that is difficult to break. Studies have also shown that the obese individual often gets less physical exercise than the person of normal weight even when engaged for the same length of time in the same sport. This is simply because he moves less.

The other side of the energy equation—the energy taken in as calories from food—is equally important. The amount of food we eat is not regulated solely by our need for calories. Would that it were! We humans are social beings, and often we eat to please our hostess, to share in the sociability, to relieve frustration, boredom, or loneliness, or just because the food is there—even if we are not particularly hungry!

We also adjust our food intake according to the expectations of society—and those expectations aren't always clear-cut and simple. Definitions of what's-good-to-do may contradict one another, creating a vague feeling of guilt. For instance, the ideal of the Clean Plate Club is still with us. The Puritan ethic of "waste not, want not" is part of our culture. Coupled with an abundance of food available, this conflicts with the ideal of a slim figure.

Because more than physical need is involved in controlling the amount we eat, many of us fail to adequately adjust our intake to our caloric need.

Much remains to be learned before all the pieces are in place in the complicated puzzle of our energy balance. Emotional, genetic, and metabolic factors may be important influences. Many of these are at present only notions in the minds of researchers— as yet a long way from being of practical value to the person who wants to lose some weight.

Most people realize there is some connection between heredity and body weight. You may have observed that overweight tends to run in families, but again the issue is not simple.

We know definitely that the body build—the general size and shape of the body, including bony structure and musculature as well as the fat distribution—is inherited. Bony structure cannot be changed, and muscle development can be changed only within rather narrow limits. It is a fact that some of us are tall, large-boned, and heavy. Others are long and lean. Still others are short, round, and stocky. Normal variations in body build are the subject of a whole science, called somatotyping. There are three basic somatotypes or extremes of body build: ectomorphy, mesomorphy, and endomorphy.

The ectomorphic individual has a long, lean body build. The skeletal structure is light and muscle development is usually small. Ectomorphs are seldom overweight, but may have the opposite problem of being too thin. They often seem to be able to eat relatively large amounts of food without gaining weight.

The mesomorphic person has a large, heavy frame and heavy muscle development. The "ideal" football player type of a person with broad shoulders and lots of muscle could be classified as mesomorphic. The scales may read high for the mesomorph because of heavy bone and muscle structure, even if he is not too fat.

The endomorphic person typically has soft, round body contours and is well covered with body fat. Endomorphs often have trouble maintaining reasonable weight.

Most of us are a combination of two of these types. An extreme ectomorph, endomorph, or mesomorph is really quite rare. But most people do exhibit one of these particular body builds predominantly.

What does all of this mean for the person who wants to lose weight? It means that overweight and overfatness may not be the same thing. A person with a large bony frame and heavy musculature is not as fat as a person of the same height and weight who has a small skeleton and less muscle development.

Understanding the difference between overweight and overfatness is important because it is the basis for setting realistic goals for weight reduction. The amount of fat on the body can be changed, but the basic body build cannot. Nor can you expect to eliminate localized fat deposits, such as heavy thighs on an otherwise non-obese person. Fat distribution of this type cannot be selectively controlled by diet or exercise.

Less well established is whether heredity affects total fatness as well as bone, muscle structure, and fat distribution. Research relating the number and size of fat cells in the body to obesity may some day help clarify the mystery of heredity and obesity. But what we do know about heredity and body build is sufficient to help us realize that what is a realistic goal for one person may not be realistic for the next. And as knowledge about the relation of heredity to body fatness increases, it may be more and more possible to identify those individuals who are predisposed to easy weight gain and to help them prevent obesity in the first place, rather than limiting our attacks on the problem to helping the person who is already too fat.

It is easy to see that some people will, because of their basic body build, have more trouble maintaining reasonable weight than others. Obesity is a physical problem, and it may be a psychological one as well; but it should not be made a moral issue. It is highly unfair to classify every individual who has a weight problem as a weak-willed glutton as our society too often does. . . .

Anyone who has tried to lose weight is acquainted with another aspect of weight reduction. Weight loss is difficult to achieve and to maintain for many people. The low rate of success, measured by continued maintenance of weight loss, is disheartening to the reducer and to the clinicians who work with the problem. There is some comfort in realizing that the picture is probably brighter than published figures show. Many who achieve success may do so upon their own without ever seeking help and thus are never counted in the statistics.

Nevertheless, there is no question that losing weight and keeping it off is an obstinate problem for many, many people. Understanding some of the reasons won't in itself correct the problem, but it may help the would-be reducer to know the challenges that he is up against.

One reason for a poor success in weight reduction programs is incomplete knowledge of the relevant facts. Let's consider a few illustrations.

Many people fail to realize that obesity has multiple causes. Take, for example, the common experience of weight gain during the first year of marriage. But what caused the excess of food? A rewardingly appreciative husband, perhaps. Should the new wife be helped to realize that she cherishes her husband more effectively by not tempting him to overeat? When obesity is long-standing, the causative factors are much more complex. Treatment requires insight beyond "eat less, exercise more."

In addition, there is a great deal of popular ignorance about the caloric value of food, despite all that has been written about it. Most people have a general idea which foods are high in calories, defined as furnishing many calories in a small amount. But there are many misconceptions.

Bread, for example, has a high calorie image. To many people, this means white bread; but whole wheat, rye, or diet bread are often thought of as substantially lower in calories. Instead, they are roughly equivalent.

Meat enjoys a low-calorie image. Meat is not low calorie in the amounts usually eaten. Calorie values in tables are usually given in 2- or 3-ounce servings. This means one small hamburger, one frankfurter, or one small pork chop. Servings are commonly twice this size. Further, many meats contain a good deal of fat which cannot be trimmed off.

One general rule about caloric content of foods may prove useful. Fat contains, weight for weight, over twice as many calories as carbohydrate or protein. Cutting down on the amount of fat in the diet (substituting skim milk for whole milk, for instance) may be the most efficient way to trim calorie intake.

Few people realize, too, that the overweight person doesn't always eat more than his slender peer. Many studies support this in the adolescent; some show it for the adult. If a person is already eating very little, further restriction may seem unrewarding unless the individual is either prepared for very slow progress or learns to adjust his activity pattern upward.

Further Resources

BOOKS

Gumbiner, Barry. *Obesity.* Philadelphia: American College of Physicians, 2001.

Professional Guide to Diseases. 6th ed. Springhouse, Penn.: Springhouse Corporation, 1998.

PERIODICALS

Crichton, Doug. "Shaping What Nature Gave You (and Us)." *Health* 17, no. 1, January-February 2003, 10.

Heaner, Martica K. "The Real-Life Body-Type Plan." *Health* 17, no. 1, January-February 2003, 114.

WEBSITES

Clark, Ron J. "How to Determine Your Genetic Limitations." Available online at http://www.promatrixtech.com/Body %20Type.htm; website home page; http://www.promatrix tech.com/ (accessed April 2, 2003).

Levinson, Robin K. "How about an Ectomorph, Mesomorph, Endomorph or Something in Between?" Available online at http://www.weightlosscontrol.com/bodytypes.htm; website home page: http://www.weightlosscontrol.com/ (accessed April 2, 2003).

"morph." Available online at http://canadacraig.homestead .com/morph.html; website home page: http://canadacraig .homestead.com (accessed April 2, 2003).

"Weight Control and Obesity Resource List for Consumers." Beltsville, Md.: U.S. Department of Agriculture, Food and Nutrition Information Center. Available online at http:/ /www.nal.usda.gov/fnic/pubs/bibs/topics/weight/consumer .html; website home page: http://www.nal.usda.gov/fnic/ (accessed June 2, 2003).

"Weight Loss for Life." Bethesda, Md.: National Institutes of Health, National Institute of Diabetes & Digestive & Kidney Diseases. Available online at http://www.niddk.nih .gov/health/nutrit/pubs/wtloss/wtloss.htm; website home page: http://www.niddk.nih.gov/index.htm (accessed June 2, 2003).

10

RELIGION

PETER J. CAPRIOGLIO

Entries are arranged in chronological order by date of primary source. For entries with one primary source, the entry title is the same as the primary source title. Entries with more than one primary source have an overall entry title, followed by the titles of the primary sources.

Important Events in Religion, 1960–1969

1960

- The Standing Conference of Orthodox Bishops in America is created to coordinate actions among the various Eastern Orthodox groups in the United States.

- On January 9, the Protestant Episcopal Church approves the use of artificial birth control.

- On April 28, the General Assembly of the Presbyterian Church, U.S. (Southern), declares that marital sexual relations without the intent of procreation are not sinful.

1961

- On January 20, President John F. Kennedy is inaugurated; he becomes the first Roman Catholic to hold the office.

- From January 22 to January 23, the National Council of Churches meets and decides to approve the use of birth control and family planning.

- On May 29, in *Two Guys from Harrison—Allentown, Inc. v. McGinley* the Supreme Court rules that a Pennsylvania law, as presently written, that requires businesses to close on Sunday does not violate the equal protection clause of the Fourteenth Amendment since the law is secular in intent and is aimed to provide workers with rest and to prevent unfair competition.

- On June 19, the Supreme Court unanimously rules in *Toresco v. Watkins* that the state of Maryland cannot require candidates for office to swear they believe in a Supreme Being. This is a religious test for office and violates the First Amendment.

1962

- On March 23, Archbishop Joseph Francis Rummel of New Orleans orders the desegregation of all diocesan schools.

- On April 16, Archbishop Rummel excommunicates three people, including the powerful politician Leander Perez, for their opposition to desegregation of Roman Catholic schools.

- On June 25, the Supreme Court, in *Engel v. Vitale,* rules that a prayer required for the public schools of New York violates the establishment of religion clause of the First Amendment.

1963

- Hebrew Union College (Reform) establishes a branch in Jerusalem.

- On May 21, the United Presbyterian Church General Assembly passes a resolution opposing compulsory school prayer and devotions. It also opposes religious displays on public sites and tax privileges for the clergy.

- On May 23, Elizabeth Ann Bayley Seton, founder of the American Sisters of Charity of Saint Joseph, is beatified by Pope John XXIII, making her eligible to become the first American-born saint.

- On June 17, the Supreme Court, in *School Board of Abington Township v. Schempp,* rules that states cannot require Bible reading in public schools.

- On December 4, the Second Vatican Ecumenical Council authorizes the use of vernacular languages, English and Spanish in the United States, in the Mass.

1964

- While participating in the Muslim pilgrimage to Mecca, Malcolm X converts from the Nation of Islam to orthodox Islam.

- *National Catholic Reporter* begins publication. This independent, lay-controlled journal becomes a major voice in Roman Catholic circles.

- On May 12, Rachel Henderlite is the first woman to be ordained by the Presbyterian Church, U.S. (Southern).

- In May, Baptists—including members of the American Baptist Convention; the National Baptist Convention of America, the National Baptist Convention, U.S.A.; and the Southern Baptist Convention in Atlantic City, New Jersey—celebrate the 150th anniversary of the first Baptist mission organization in the United States.

- On October 14, the Nobel Peace Prize is awarded to Martin Luther King, Jr., for his work in civil rights. He donates the $54,600 award to the Civil Rights movement.

1965

- The Lutheran Council in the U.S.A. is created by the three largest Lutheran bodies—the Lutheran Church in America, the Lutheran Church-Missouri Synod, and the American Lutheran Church—to coordinate their joint activities.

- On February 21, Malcolm X is assassinated as he addresses a rally in Harlem. Members of the Nation of Islam are later arrested and convicted for the crime.

- On March 11, Rev. James Reeb, a Unitarian minister from Boston, dies following a beating he had received in Selma, Alabama, on March 9. He was in Selma as part of the voting rights campaign. The men tried for the crime are later found not guilty.

- On March 30, the New York State Supreme Court rules that Black Muslims in Attica prison have the same rights to practice their religion and worship together as do Protestants, Catholics, and Jews.

- In May, the Most Reverend Harold Robert Perry is appointed auxiliary bishop of New Orleans. He is the first

African-American bishop in the Roman Catholic Church in the twentieth century and the second in the Church's history.

- On October 2, Pope Paul VI arrives in New York on a trip to the United Nations. He is the first pope to come to the United States while holding the title.

1966

- On November 18, Roman Catholic bishops announce that effective 2 December Catholics in the United States will no longer have to abstain from eating meat on Fridays, except during Lent.

1967

- On May 18, the governor of Tennessee signs into law a bill which repeals the "Monkey Law" of 1925. That law forbade public schools teaching "any theory that denied the story of divine creation of man as taught in the Bible" or "that man has descended from a lower order of animals." The "Monkey Law" led to the famous Scopes trial in Dayton, Tennessee, in 1925.

- On May 22, the General Assembly of the Presbyterian Church, U.S.A. (Northern), adopts the Confession of Faith of 1967, the first major new confession by Presbyterians since the Westminster Confession of 1647.

1968

- Troy Perry organizes the Metropolitan Community Church, a ministry for gay men and women.

- In April, the Black Catholic Clergy Caucus is organized and creates a National Office for Black Catholics.

- On April 4, Martin Luther King, Jr., is assassinated in Memphis. Riots break out in nearly 130 cities. Order is restored in some only by martial law.

- On June 16, Rabbi Yehuda Leib Levin, chief rabbi of Moscow, arrives in the United States for a two-week visit. This is the first official representation of Russian Jewry in over fifty years. His statements that Soviet Jews have full religious freedom and that there is no anti-Semitism there fail to convince many of his audiences.

- In August, the National Black Sisters Conference of black Catholic religious orders is organized.

- On November 12, the Supreme Court strikes down an Arkansas law permitting public schools to teach the Bible version of Creation but forbidding teaching any theory that "mankind ascended or descended from lower order of animals." The Court rules this is a violation of religious freedom guaranteed under the First and Fourteenth Amendments.

- On December 24, the *Apollo 8* mission begins its orbit around the moon. The three astronauts take turns reading from the first verses of Genesis in the King James Version of the Bible.

1969

- On April 26, the National Black Economic Development Conference, led by James Foreman, issues its Black Manifesto, demanding churches and synagogues pay $500 million in reparations for their complicity in racism.

- Thomas Kilgore, Jr., pastor of Second Baptist Church of Los Angeles, is elected president of the American Baptist Convention; he is the first African-American to hold that office.

- On May 26, the General Assembly of the Presbyterian Church, U.S. (Southern), passes a resolution that the theory of evolution and the traditional biblical interpretation of Creation are "not contradictory."

- On May 29, the General Assembly of the Presbyterian Church, U.S. (Southern), passes a resolution saying that citizens have a right of conscientious objection to a particular war, in the context of the times this refers to the American involvement in the Vietnam conflict.

- In May, Christ Memorial Church, St. Louis, Missouri, a predominantly white Southern Baptist Convention congregation, affiliates with the National Baptist Convention, U.S.A., apparently the first Southern Baptist Convention congregation to affiliate jointly with a predominantly African-American denomination.

- On June 10, Norman Vincent Peale, pastor of the Marble Collegiate Church, is elected president of the Reformed Church in America.

Braunfeld v. Brown

Supreme Court decision

By: Earl Warren

Date: May 29, 1961

Source: *Braunfeld v. Brown*, 366 U.S. 599 (1961). Available online at http://caselaw.lp.findlaw.com/scripts/getcase.pl ?navby=search&court;=US&case;=/us/366/599.html (accessed February 5, 2003).

About the Author: Earl Warren (1891–1974) was born in Los Angeles and graduated from the University of California law school in 1912. From 1939 to 1943, he was California's attorney general, and from 1943 to 1953, he served as its governor. Warren was appointed chief justice of the U.S. Supreme Court in 1953, a position that he held until 1969. His tenure was noted for decisions in support of civil rights and individual liberties. ■

Introduction

Jacob Braunfeld, an Orthodox Jew, closed his retail clothing store in Philadelphia on Saturdays to observe the Jewish Sabbath. Pennsylvania law declared that his store, and similar businesses, could not be open to the public on Sunday, in observance of the Christian Sabbath. Braunfeld, though, wanted to be able to open on Sundays because he was closed on Saturday. He argued that to pay his expenses and make a profit, he needed to be open six days a week. He believed that the Pennsylvania blue law mandating Sunday closings violated his freedom of religion. He also argued that mandatory Sunday closings interfered with Judaism's attempts to gain new followers. In addition, these laws gave an unfair economic advantage to those who kept their businesses open on Saturday.

The blue laws—so called because they were originally printed on blue paper—can be traced to colonial New England, when the legislatures tried to enforce moral and religious standards. Many of these laws were eventually discarded, but in some states they remained on the books. The surviving blue laws were generally aimed at regulating activities on Sunday, such as forbidding the opening of retail stores or prohibiting certain types of recreation or entertainment. Braunfeld's attorneys argued that Pennsylvania's blue laws violated the

U.S. Constitution, specifically the First Amendment. The establishment clause of the amendment says that "Congress shall make no law respecting an establishment of religion"; the free exercise clause forbids Congress from "prohibiting the free exercise thereof." The establishment clause prohibits the federal government from creating a national religion. The free exercise clause prevents the government from interfering with an individual's religious beliefs.

Braunfeld's case made it to the Supreme Court, where, by a 6–3 vote, the Court ruled that Pennsylvania's blue laws were constitutional. Writing for the majority, Warren cited several reasons for the Court's decision. First, the law did not specifically target Orthodox Judaism, nor did it prevent anyone from practicing that religion. Also, the blue laws did not force people to adopt any religious belief, nor did they make the holding of any religious belief a crime. In addition, not all Orthodox Jews were burdened by the Sunday closing laws; only those who wanted to work on that day were affected.

Significance

Although public opinion in general supported the Court's decision, those who believed in the strict separation of church and state did not, and the decision of the Court was not unanimous. Justice William O. Douglas, for example, dissented from the majority, emphasizing that even though the majority of people in America are Christians who worship God on Sunday, they do not have the right to force that practice on others. Also dissenting was Potter Stewart, who wrote that Pennsylvania's blue laws forced an Orthodox Jew to choose between economic needs and his faith. He believed that those laws trespassed on the constitutionally guaranteed right to the free exercise of religion.

Primary Source

Braunfeld v. Brown [excerpt]

SYNOPSIS: In these excerpts, the Court majority, including Chief Justice Earl Warren, ruled that Pennsylvania's blue laws, involving the forced closing of businesses on Sunday, were constitutional. These laws did not target any specific religion and placed only an indirect burden on the members of a particular religion.

Appellants are members of the Orthodox Jewish Faith, which requires the closing of their places of business and total abstention from all manner of work from nightfall each Friday until nightfall each Saturday. As merchants engaged in the retail sale of clothing and home furnishings in Philadelphia, they sued to enjoin enforcement of a 1959 Pennsylvania criminal statute which forbade the retail sale on Sundays of those commodities and other specified commodities. They claimed that the statute violated the Equal Protection Clause of the Fourteenth Amendment and constituted a law respecting an establishment of religion and that it interfered with the free exercise of their religion by imposing serious economic disadvantages upon them, if they adhere to the observance of their Sabbath, and that it would operate so as to hinder the Orthodox Jewish Faith in gaining new members. Held: The statute does not violate the Equal Protection Clause of the Fourteenth Amendment nor constitute a law respecting an establishment of religion. . . .

Mr. Chief Justice Warren announced the judgment of the court and an opinion in which Mr. Justice Black, Mr. Justice Clark, and Mr. Justice Whittaker concur.

This case concerns the constitutional validity of the application to appellants of the Pennsylvania criminal statute, enacted in 1959, which proscribes the Sunday retail sale of certain enumerated commodities. Among the questions presented are whether the statute is a law [366 U.S. 509, 601] respecting an establishment of religion and whether the statute violates equal protection. Since both of these questions, in reference to this very statute, have already been answered in the negative . . . the only question for consideration is whether the statute interferes with the free exercise of appellants' religion.

Appellants are merchants in Philadelphia who engage in the retail sale of clothing and home furnishings within the proscription of the statute in issue. Each of the appellants is a member of the Orthodox Jewish faith, which requires the closing of their places of business and a total abstention from all manner of work from nightfall each Friday until nightfall each Saturday. They instituted a suit in the court below seeking a permanent injunction against the enforcement of the 1959 statute.

Their complaint, as amended, alleged that appellants had previously kept their places of business open on Sunday; that each of appellants had done a substantial amount of business on Sunday, compensating somewhat for their closing on Saturday; that Sunday closing will result in impairing the ability of all appellants to earn a livelihood and will render appellant Braunfeld unable to continue in his business, thereby losing his capital investment; that the statute is unconstitutional for the reasons stated above.

U.S. Chief Justice Earl Warren poses in his office, Washington, D.C., March 19, 1961. Warren delivered the judgment of the Supreme Court in *Braunfeld v. Brown,* which upheld the constitutionality of a Pennsylvania law that required businesses to be closed on Sunday. **AP/WIDE WORLD PHOTOS. REPRODUCED BY PERMISSION.**

A three-judge court was properly convened and it dismissed the complaint on the authority of the Two Guys from Harrison case. . . .

Appellants contend that the enforcement against them of the Pennsylvania statute will prohibit the free exercise [366 U.S. 599, 602] of their religion because, due to the statute's compulsion to close on Sunday, appellants will suffer substantial economic loss, to the benefit of their non-Sabbatarian competitors, if appellants also continue their Sabbath observance by closing their businesses on Saturday; that this result will either compel appellants to give up their Sabbath observance, a basic tenet of the Orthodox Jewish faith, or will put appellants at a serious economic disadvantage if they continue to adhere to their Sabbath.

Appellants also assert that the statute will operate so as to hinder the Orthodox Jewish faith in gaining new adherents. And the corollary to these arguments is that if the free exercise of appellants' religion is impeded, that religion is being subjected to discriminatory treatment by the State. . . .

. . . [T]he statute at bar does not make unlawful any religious practices of appellants; the Sunday law simply regulates a secular activity and, as applied to appellants, operates so as to make the practice of their religious beliefs more expensive. Furthermore, the law's effect does not inconvenience all members of the Orthodox Jewish faith but only those who believe it necessary to work on Sunday.

And even these are not faced with as serious a choice as forsaking their religious practices or subjecting themselves to criminal prosecution. Fully recognizing that the alternatives [366 U.S. 599, 606] open to appellants and others similarly situated—retaining their present occupations and incurring economic disadvantage or engaging in some other commercial activity which does not call for either Saturday or Sunday labor—may well result in some financial sacrifice in order to observe their religious beliefs, still the option is wholly different than when the legislation attempts to make a religious practice itself unlawful.

To strike down, without the most critical scrutiny, legislation which imposes only an indirect burden on the exercise of religion, i. e., legislation which does not make unlawful the religious practice itself, would radically restrict the operating latitude of the legislature. Statutes which tax income and limit the amount which may be deducted for religious contributions impose an indirect economic burden on the observance of the religion of the citizen whose religion requires him to donate a greater amount to his church; statutes which require the courts to be closed on Saturday and Sunday impose a similar indirect burden on the observance of the religion of the trial lawyer whose religion requires him to rest on a weekday. The list of legislation of this nature is nearly limitless.

Needless to say, when entering the area of religious freedom, we must be fully cognizant of the particular protection that the Constitution has accorded it. Abhorrence of religious persecution and intolerance is a basic part of our heritage. But we are a cosmopolitan nation made up of people of almost every conceivable religious preference. These denominations number almost three hundred. *(Year Book of American Churches)* for 1958. . . .

Consequently, it cannot be expected, much less required, that legislators enact no law regulating conduct that may in some way result in an economic disadvantage to some religious sects and not to others because of the special practices of the various religions. We do not believe that such an effect is an absolute test [366 U.S. 599, 607] for determining whether the legislation violates the freedom of religion protected by the First Amendment.

Of course, to hold unassailable all legislation regulating conduct which imposes solely an indirect burden on the observance of religion would be a gross oversimplification. If the purpose or effect of a law is to impede the observance of one or all religions or is to discriminate invidiously between religions, that law is constitutionally invalid even though the burden may be characterized as being only indirect. But if the State regulates conduct by enacting a general law within its power, the purpose and effect of which is to advance the State's secular goals, the statute is valid despite its indirect burden on religious observance unless the State may accomplish its purpose by means which do not impose such a burden. See *Cantwell v. Connecticut,* supra, at pp. 304–305.

As we pointed out in *McGowan v. Maryland,* supra, at pp. 444–445, we cannot find a State without power to provide a weekly respite from all labor and, at the same time, to set one day of the week apart from the others as a day of rest, repose, recreation and tranquility—a day when the hectic tempo of everyday existence ceases and a more pleasant atmosphere is created, a day which all members of the family and community have the opportunity to spend and enjoy together, a day on which people may visit friends and relatives who are not available during working days, a day when the weekly laborer may best regenerate himself. This is particularly true in this day and age of increasing state concern with public welfare legislation.

Also, in McGowan, we examined several suggested alternative means by which it was argued that the State might accomplish its secular goals without even remotely or incidentally affecting religious freedom. Ante, at pp. 450–452. We found there that a State might well find that those alternatives would not accomplish bringing about a general day of rest. We need not examine them again here.

However, appellants advance yet another means at the State's disposal which they would find unobjectionable. They contend that the State should cut an exception from the Sunday labor proscription for those people who, because of religious conviction, observe a day of rest other than Sunday. By such regulation, appellants contend, the economic disadvantages imposed by the present system would be removed and the State's interest in having all people rest one day would be satisfied.

A number of States provide such an exemption, and this may well be the wiser solution to the problem. But our concern is not with the wisdom of legislation but with its constitutional limitation. Thus, reason and experience teach that to permit the exemption might well undermine the State's goal of providing a day that, as best possible, eliminates the atmosphere of commercial noise and activity. Although not dispositive of the issue, enforcement problems would be more difficult since there would be two or more days to police rather than one and it would be more difficult to observe whether violations were occurring.

Additional problems might also be presented by a regulation of this sort. To allow only people who rest on a day other than Sunday to keep their businesses open on that day might well provide these people with an economic advantage over their competitors who must [366 U.S. 599, 609] remain closed on that day; this might cause the Sunday-observers to complain that their religions are being discriminated against. With this competitive advantage existing, there could well be the temptation for some, in order to keep their businesses open on Sunday, to assert that they have religious convictions which compel them to close their businesses on what had formerly been their least profitable day.

This might make necessary a state-conducted inquiry into the sincerity of the individual's religious beliefs, a practice which a State might believe would itself run afoul of the spirit of constitutionally protected religious guarantees. Finally, in order to keep the disruption of the day at a minimum, exempted employers would probably have to hire employees who themselves qualified for the exemption because of their own religious beliefs, a practice which a State might feel to be opposed to its general policy prohibiting religious discrimination in hiring. For all of these reasons, we cannot say that the Pennsylvania statute before us is invalid, either on its face or as applied.

Mr. Justice Harlan concurs in the judgment. Mr. Justice Brennan and Mr. Justice Stewart concur in our disposition of appellants' claims under the Establishment Clause and the Equal Protection Clause. Mr. Justice Frankfurter and Mr. Justice Harlan have rejected appellants' claim under the Free Exercise Clause in a separate opinion.

Accordingly, the decision is Affirmed.

Further Resources

BOOKS

Schlossberg, Eli W. *The World of Orthodox Judaism.* Northvale, N.J.: Jason Aronson, 1996.

Sherman, Moshe D. *Orthodox Judaism in America: A Biographical Dictionary and Sourcebook.* Westport, Conn.: Greenwood, 1996.

Sokol, Moshe Z., ed. *Engaging Modernity: Rabbinic Leaders and the Challenge of the Twentieth Century.* Northvale, N.J.: J. Aronson, 1997.

WEBSITES

Belief Net.com. "What Orthodox Jews Believe." Available online at http://www.beliefnet.com/story/80/story_8053_1 .html; website home page: http://www.beliefnet.com/index .html (accessed February 1, 2003).

Eliezer Segal's Home Page, University of Calgary. "Varieties of Orthodox Judaism." Available online at http://www .ucalgary.ca/~elsegal/363_Transp/08_Orthodoxy.html; website home page: http://www.ucalgary.ca/~elsegal/index .html (accessed February 1, 2003).

Jewish Virtual Library. "Orthodox Judaism." Available online at http://www.us-israel.org/jsource/Judaism/ortho.html; website home page: http://www.us-israel.org/index.html (accessed February 1, 2003).

"Atheism"

Speech

By: Madalyn Murray O'Hair

Date: August 25, 1962

Source: O'Hair, Madalyn Murray. Address given at the Eighth Annual Convention of the American Rationalist Federation, August 25, 1962. Published as "Atheism" in *The American Rationalist* 17, no. 3 (September/October 1962). Available online at http://www.americanatheist.org/win99-00 /T2/atheism.html (accessed February 5, 2003).

About the Author: Madalyn Murray O'Hair (1919–1995) was born in Pittsburgh, Pennsylvania. After she served as an officer in World War II, her belief in God diminished and she became an atheist. In a case heard by the U.S. Supreme Court, she contended that prayers in public school were unconstitutional. In 1963, the Court ruled in her favor. A controversial person because of her atheism, she founded two organizations: American Atheists and United Secularists of America. ■

Introduction

Madalyn Murray O'Hair achieved national attention through a U.S. Supreme Court case in which she asserted that prayer and Bible verse readings in public schools violated the First Amendment of the Constitution. The case, *Murray v. Curlett* (1963), was consolidated with another case, *Abington School District v. Schempp* (1963). On

Madalyn E. Murray and sons William and Garth (center) leave the Supreme Court in Washington, D.C., February 27, 1963. An atheist, Murray's (later Murray O'Hair) case resulted in the Supreme Court's ruling that prayer and Bible reading in public schools was in violation of the Constitution. © BETTMANN/CORBIS. REPRODUCED BY PERMISSION.

June 17, 1963, the Court ruled that reciting Bible verses and the Lord's Prayer in public schools was unconstitutional. One year earlier, the Court in *Engel v. Vitale* (1962) had already prohibited New York State from allowing prayers in public schools.

O'Hair founded American Atheists, an organization of those who profess a nonbelief in a supernatural being or God, in 1963. Her goal was to create a group that would support freedom from religion (rather than freedom of religion), protect the constitutional rights of atheists, and defend the civil rights of atheists who spoke out about their beliefs. She and her followers also desired a society in which there would be complete and absolute separation of church and state. American Atheists summarized its chief tenet by stating that it "works for freedom from theism, the freedom from dependency on god theories." Further, "Belief in the existence of that agency is based on faith. An Atheist has no specific belief system. We accept only that which is scientifically verifiable. Since god concepts are unverifiable, we do not accept them." O'Hair was noted for her defense of materialism, a philosophical belief that viewed everything as being material and denied that the nonmaterial or the

soul existed. She frequently stated in her speeches and pamphlets: "We have to live now. No one gets a second chance. There is no heaven and no hell . . . You either make the best or the worst of what you have now, or there is nothing. Laugh at it. Hug it to you. Drain it. Build it. Have it."

O'Hair's efforts on behalf of the American Atheists made it into a national organization with its own conventions and over thirty state chapters. O'Hair also broadcasted a series of programs carried on hundreds of radio stations. American Atheists has filed lawsuits in the courts, participated in picket line protests against what it considers violations of the separation of church and state, and brought the organization's position statements to the mass media.

Significance

The public reaction to O'Hair's campaign was decidedly negative. At one point she called herself "the most hated woman in America" because of her advocacy of atheism and opposition to prayer and Bible readings in public schools.

The American Atheists, which claims about 2,000 members, presently has its headquarters in Parsippany, New Jersey. Ellen Johnson became its president in 1995 after O'Hair and two family members were reported missing. In 2001, their remains were discovered in rural Texas, and they were believed to have been murdered. Allegedly, a former office worker at American Atheists was involved in the murder plot.

Primary Source

"Atheism"

SYNOPSIS: In this speech, O'Hair discusses the history of opposition to philosophical materialism, the "ignorance and superstition" of religious belief, and the foundations of modern materialism.

The indestructible foundation of the whole edifice of Atheism is its philosophy, materialism, or naturalism, as it is also known. That philosophy regards the world as it actually is, views it in the light of the data provided by progressive science and social experience. Atheistic materialism is the logical outcome of scientific knowledge gained over the centuries.

We make a fundamental error, I think, as we tilt at the windmills of imagined gods. We need to review from where we have come, under what conditions, and to see the threshold upon which we stand now.

Our history has been marked by a ceaseless struggle against ignorance and superstition. In ancient Greece the works of the materialist philosopher Democritus, who first taught the atomic theory of matter, were destroyed. Anaxagoras was banished from Athens for being an Atheist. The materialist philosopher Epicurus, revered by the ancients for having liberated man from fear of gods and for asserting the validity of science, was for 2000 years anathematized and falsely depicted as an enemy of morality and a disseminator of vice.

The Alexandria library, housing 700,000 scientific and literary works, was burned by Christian monks in 391 A.D. Pope Gregory I (590–604) destroyed many valuable works by ancient authors. In every society there have been forces that have stood to lose by the dissemination of progressive scientific views. In the past these forces either directly persecuted progressive scientists and philosophers or sought to distort scientific discoveries so as to deprive them of their progressive, materialistic implications.

The Inquisition, a papal invention for suppressing all opposition to the Catholic Church, savagely persecuted all progressive thinkers; Giordano Bruno, Ludilio Vanini, and Galileo come readily to mind.

Voltaire was imprisoned in the Bastille, and Diderot was sent to prison. In our own country we are familiar with the story of Thomas Paine, of the Salem witch trials, of Ingersoll, of Einstein. The struggle is unceasing, as important today as during any other period of history.

We need, therefore, to see what we fight and why. We need not direct our main assault against the Bible or the Koran. We need not argue endlessly about the historicity of Jesus. We should look past trinities and angels and other theological blind alleys. We must look to materialistic philosophy which alone enables men to understand reality and to know how to deal with it.

It is true that today our kind are no longer burned at the stake, but there are many other ways of exerting pressure. Our scientists and progressive philosophers are dismissed from universities and other employment. Outspoken scientific and philosophical works are much less likely to be published than rather senseless junk. Character assassination is common. Reactionary religious propaganda is unceasingly drummed into unthinking minds through the captive media of mass communication. As always, our opponents today are formidable. But our strength lies in the positive approach of uncovering and publicizing the laws of nature and human behavior, and in applying these laws in the interest of human welfare. We need not waste our time with

endless arguments about tortuous paths of the endless labyrinths of theology.

We need to know upon what we base ourselves. Atheism is based upon a materialist philosophy, which holds that nothing exists but natural phenomena. There are no supernatural forces or entities, nor can there be any. Nature simply exists. But there are those who deny this, who assert that only mind or idea or spirit is primary. This question of the relation of the human mind to material being is one of the fundamental questions dealt with by all philosophers, however satisfactorily.

The Atheist must slice through all obfuscation to bedrock, to the basic idea that those who regard nature as primary and thought as a property (or function) of matter belong to the camp of materialism, and that those who maintain that spirit or idea or mind existed before nature or created nature or uphold nature belong to the camp of idealism. All conventional religions are based on idealism. Many varieties of idealism exist, but the apologist for idealism and opponents of materialism go under many names; we have, for instance, dualists, objective idealists, subjective idealists, solipsists, positivists, Machians, irrationalists, existentialists, neo-positivists, logical positivists, fideists, revived medieval scholastics, Thomists. And opposed to these stand alone the Atheistic materialists (or perhaps naturalists, Rationalists, freethinkers, etc.) who have no need for intellectual machinations, deceptions, or masquerades.

Whether or not the Bible is pornographic literature is only a side issue. Let us see what the Idealist camp features. The church teaches a contempt for earthly life and that to reach some imagined "heaven" is the main goal of life.

And, significantly, the church teaches that this goal can be achieved only as the reward for obedience and meekness. The church threatens the wrath of God and the torment of hell for those who dare to oppose its teaching. But Materialism liberates us, teaches us not to hope for happiness beyond the grave but to prize life on earth and strive always to improve it. Materialism restores to man his dignity and his intellectual integrity. Man is not a worm condemned to crawl in the dust, but a human being capable of mastering the forces of nature and making them serve him.

Materialism compels faith in the human intellect, in the power of knowledge in man's ability to fathom all the secrets of nature and to create a social system based upon reason and justice. Materialism's faith is in man and his ability to transform the world by his own efforts. It is a philosophy in every essence optimistic, life-asserting, and radiant. It considers the struggle for progress as a moral obligation, and impossible without noble ideals that inspire men to struggle, to perform bold, creative work.

Modern materialism—or naturalism—is linked with the everyday experience of people. It believes in experiment as the basis of knowledge, and neglects no sphere of reality. It advances itself as an ideological weapon for use in progress. It is in social life that man develops his mind and emotions, will, and conscience, and puts meaning and purpose into life. He does not closet himself in solitary prayer and dream of death as a door opening unto eternal bliss. A materialist lives a full social life and is inspired by progressive ideals; he is concerned with the problems and joys of life, not death. He is deeply involved with shaping his life as a useful member of society and contributing what he can to its progress.

The Idealist sees science and man as subordinate to religion, to "idea," and sees knowledge as subordinate to faith. The ultimate object of the idealist is to furnish evidence of the existence of "God." He lays great stress on moral questions, but the morality he preaches is one of meek submission, of passive acceptance, and thus, of justification of existing social evils. This morality substitutes prayer and appeals for divine assistance for struggle and protest against social injustice. The entire Idealist philosophy is contrived, with deliberateness, to bolster the status quo.

Ours is a time when successful struggle against this reactionary philosophy requires more than a petulant argument over the authorship of the Gospels, more than a negative attack on the totalitarian and monolithic authoritarianism of conventional religion, but rather an aggressive action program to spread the positive philosophy of materialism.

Further Resources

BOOKS

Joshi, S.T. *Atheism: A Reader.* Amherst, N.Y.: Prometheus Books, 2000.

Lewis, Joseph. *Atheism.* New York: Freethought Press Association, 1938.

Martin, Michael. *Atheism: A Philosophical Justification.* Philadelphia, Pa.: Temple University Press, 1990.

PERIODICALS

Gesalman, Anne Belli. "An Atheist's Last Rites: Investigators Lay Madalyn O'Hair Case to Rest." *Newsweek,* February 12, 2001, 27.

Moore, Art. "Madalyn Murray O'Hair's Stepchildren Seek Atheists' Revival." *Christianity Today,* March 1, 1999, 24.

"People." *The Christian Century,* April 11, 2001, 13.

WEBSITES

American Atheists. Website home page. Available online at http://www.atheists.org/ (accessed February 1, 2003).

Atheism Awareness. Website home page. Available online at http://atheismawareness.home.att.net/ (accessed February 1, 2003).

Positive Atheism Magazine. Website home page. Available online at http://www.positiveatheism.org/index.shtml (accessed February 1, 2003).

Pacem in Terris

Papal encyclical

By: Pope John XXIII

Date: April 11, 1963

Source: Pope John XXIII. *Pacem in Terris,* Rome, April 11, 1963. Available online at http://www.vatican.va/holy_father /john_xxiii/encyclicals/documents/hf_j-xxiii_enc_11041963 _pacem_en.html (accessed February 2, 2003).

About the Author: Pope John XXIII (1881–1963) was born in Sotto il Monte, Italy, as Angelo Giuseppe Roncalli. He was ordained a priest in 1904 and served as a chaplain during World War I. In 1925, he became an archbishop and served as an apostolic delegate to Bulgaria, Turkey, and Greece. In 1953, he was appointed patriarch of Venice. During his tenure as pope (1958–1963), he summoned the Second Vatican Council. ■

Introduction

Pope John XXIII issued "On Establishing Universal Peace in Truth, Justice, Charity, and Liberty" *(Pacem in Terris)* during the height of cold war tension between the West and the Soviet Union. As the world faced the threat of nuclear war, the pope wanted to play a role in helping to calm people's fears.

The aim of his encyclical was to bring about global stability. In addressing human rights abuses throughout the world, the pope condemned authoritarianism from both the political left and the political right—in both communist nations and the capitalist, Western nations. By addressing the human rights weaknesses of both sides, and through his own personal diplomacy, he was trying to convince all nations that they were equally responsible for changing their own societies and reducing the threat of war.

His concern for the promotion of human rights was apparent through his choice of subtopics for the encyclical. Under the banner of human rights and freedom, for example, he focused upon rights pertaining to moral and cultural values, the right to worship God according to one's conscience, the right to choose freely one's state in life, economic rights (having a decent job), the right of meeting and association, the right to emigrate and immigrate, political rights, reciprocity of rights and duties between persons, the right of mutual collaboration (working together), and the right of the equality of all humans. In the pope's view, some of these issues were more applicable to communist nations such as the Soviet Union, and some were more applicable to the Western nations, including the United States.

The overall message of Pope John XXIII's encyclical centered on the common bonds that united all humans. These ties were more important than the political, cultural, and racial differences that divided them. In emphasizing these common bonds, he called for an end to the arms race, gradual disarmament, and respect for basic human rights.

Significance

In their encyclicals, earlier popes had urged universal peace, truth, justice, and charity. In the eyes of many theologians and religious observers, though, the pope's emphasis on the word *liberty* made *Pacem in Terris* unique. In an April 27, 1963, article in *America* magazine, for example, Father John Courtney Murray commented that "Freedom is a basic principle of political order; it is also the political method. The whole burden of the encyclical is that the order for which the postmodern world is looking cannot be an order that is imposed by force, or sustained by coercion, or based on fear."

The pope's words were generally welcomed by many Americans. His charisma and emphasis on human rights were well received in the Catholic community and the rest of the nation. Some observers, though, were sharply critical, charging that he was too soft on communism and even suggesting that he was a "socialist pope." A column in *Life* magazine on April 26, 1963—just two weeks after the encyclical was issued—noted that the pope's critics were disturbed by the "'leftish' pronouncements in the new encyclical, including its favorable references to government welfare services, full employment, complete racial equality, the U.N., disarmament, and even the need for world government."

Primary Source

Pacem in Terris [excerpt]

> **SYNOPSIS:** In these excerpts, Pope John XXIII affirms the God-given sanctity of human rights. These rights applied to relations among individuals, between the individual and the community, and among nations. Only by respecting and obeying the law of God can

full human rights ever be achieved and peace, founded on mutual trust, be obtained. The encyclical contained 173 statements; numbers 8–27 and 37–43 are included here.

To Our Venerable Brethren the Patriarchs, Primates, Archbishops, Bishops, and all other Local Ordinaries who are at Peace and in Communion with the Apostolic See, and to the Clergy and Faithful of the entire Catholic World, and to all Men of Good Will. Venerable Brethren and Dearest Sons Health and Apostolic Benediction.

Peace on Earth—which man throughout the ages has so longed for and sought after—can never be established, never guaranteed, except by the diligent observance of the divinely established order. . . .

I. Order Between Men

8. We must devote our attention first of all to that order which should prevail among men.

9. Any well-regulated and productive association of men in society demands the acceptance of one fundamental principle: that each individual man is truly a person. His is a nature, that is, endowed with intelligence and free will. As such he has rights and duties, which together flow as a direct consequence from his nature. These rights and duties are universal and inviolable, and therefore altogether inalienable.

10. When, furthermore, we consider man's personal dignity from the standpoint of divine revelation, inevitably our estimate of it is incomparably increased. Men have been ransomed by the blood of Jesus Christ. Grace has made them sons and friends of God, and heirs to eternal glory.

Rights

11. But first We must speak of man's rights. Man has the right to live. He has the right to bodily integrity and to the means necessary for the proper development of life, particularly food, clothing, shelter, medical care, rest, and, finally, the necessary social services. In consequence, he has the right to be looked after in the event of ill health; disability stemming from his work; widowhood; old age; enforced unemployment; or whenever through no fault of his own he is deprived of the means of livelihood.

Rights Pertaining to Moral and Cultural Values

12. Moreover, man has a natural right to be respected. He has a right to his good name. He has a right to freedom in investigating the truth, and—

Pope John XXIII is welcomed by the crowds on his way to the shrines of Loreto and Assisi, Italy, October 1962. Pope John XXIII affirmed the inviolability of human rights in his encyclical *Pacem in Terris*. GETTY IMAGES. REPRODUCED BY PERMISSION.

within the limits of the moral order and the common good—to freedom of speech and publication, and to freedom to pursue whatever profession he may choose. He has the right, also, to be accurately informed about public events.

13. He has the natural right to share in the benefits of culture, and hence to receive a good general education, and a technical or professional training consistent with the degree of educational development in his own country. Furthermore, a system must be devised for affording gifted members of society the opportunity of engaging in more advanced studies, with a view to their occupying, as far as possible, positions of responsibility in society in keeping with their natural talent and acquired skill.

The Right to Worship God According to One's Conscience

14. Also among man's rights is that of being able to worship God in accordance with the right dictates of his own conscience, and to profess his religion both in private and in public. According to the clear teaching of Lactantius, "this is the very condition of our birth, that we render to the God who made us that just homage which is His due; that we ac-

knowledge Him alone as God, and follow Him. It is from this ligature of piety, which binds us and joins us to God, that religion derives its name."

Hence, too, Pope Leo XIII declared that "true freedom, freedom worthy of the sons of God, is that freedom which most truly safeguards the dignity of the human person. It is stronger than any violence or injustice. Such is the freedom which has always been desired by the Church, and which she holds most dear. It is the sort of freedom which the Apostles resolutely claimed for themselves. The apologists defended it in their writings; thousands of martyrs consecrated it with their blood."

The Right to Choose Freely One's State in Life

15. Human beings have also the right to choose for themselves the kind of life which appeals to them: whether it is to found a family—in the founding of which both the man and the woman enjoy equal rights and duties—or to embrace the priesthood or the religious life.

16. The family, founded upon marriage freely contracted, one and indissoluble, must be regarded as the natural, primary cell of human society. The

interests of the family, therefore, must be taken very specially into consideration in social and economic affairs, as well as in the spheres of faith and morals. For all of these have to do with strengthening the family and assisting it in the fulfilment of its mission.

17. Of course, the support and education of children is a right which belongs primarily to the parents.

Economic Rights

18. In the economic sphere, it is evident that a man has the inherent right not only to be given the opportunity to work, but also to be allowed the exercise of personal initiative in the work he does.

19. The conditions in which a man works form a necessary corollary to these rights. They must not be such as to weaken his physical or moral fibre, or militate against the proper development of adolescents to manhood. Women must be accorded such conditions of work as are consistent with their needs and responsibilities as wives and mothers.

20. A further consequence of man's personal dignity is his right to engage in economic activities suited to his degree of responsibility. The worker is likewise entitled to a wage that is determined in accordance with the precepts of justice. This needs stressing. The amount a worker receives must be sufficient, in proportion to available funds, to allow him and his family a standard of living consistent with human dignity. Pope Pius XII expressed it in these terms:

> Nature imposes work upon man as a duty, and man has the corresponding natural right to demand that the work he does shall provide him with the means of livelihood for himself and his children. Such is nature's categorical imperative for the preservation of man.

21. As a further consequence of man's nature, he has the right to the private ownership of property, including that of productive goods. This, as We have said elsewhere, is "a right which constitutes so efficacious a means of asserting one's personality and exercising responsibility in every field, and an element of solidity and security for family life, and of greater peace and prosperity in the State."

22. Finally, it is opportune to point out that the right to own private property entails a social obligation as well.

The Right of Meeting and Association

23. Men are by nature social, and consequently they have the right to meet together and to form as-sociations with their fellows. They have the right to confer on such associations the type of organization which they consider best calculated to achieve their objectives. They have also the right to exercise their own initiative and act on their own responsibility within these associations for the attainment of the desired results.

24. As We insisted in Our encyclical Mater et Magistra, the founding of a great many such intermediate groups or societies for the pursuit of aims which it is not within the competence of the individual to achieve efficiently, is a matter of great urgency. Such groups and societies must be considered absolutely essential for the safeguarding of man's personal freedom and dignity, while leaving intact a sense of responsibility.

The Right to Emigrate and Immigrate

25. Again, every human being has the right to freedom of movement and of residence within the confines of his own State. When there are just reasons in favor of it, he must be permitted to emigrate to other countries and take up residence there. The fact that he is a citizen of a particular State does not deprive him of membership in the human family, nor of citizenship in that universal society, the common, world-wide fellowship of men.

Political Rights

26. Finally, man's personal dignity involves his right to take an active part in public life, and to make his own contribution to the common welfare of his fellow citizens. As Pope Pius XII said, "man as such, far from being an object or, as it were, an inert element in society, is rather its subject, its basis and its purpose; and so must he be esteemed."

27. As a human person he is entitled to the legal protection of his rights, and such protection must be effective, unbiased, and strictly just. To quote again Pope Pius XII:

> In consequence of that juridical order willed by God, man has his own inalienable right to juridical security. To him is assigned a certain, well-defined sphere of law, immune from arbitrary attack. . . .

God and the Moral Order

37. Now the order which prevails in human society is wholly incorporeal in nature. Its foundation is truth, and it must be brought into effect by justice. It needs to be animated and perfected by men's love for one another, and, while preserving freedom

intact, it must make for an equilibrium in society which is increasingly more human in character.

38. But such an order—universal, absolute and immutable in its principles—finds its source in the true, personal and transcendent God. He is the first truth, the sovereign good, and as such the deepest source from which human society, if it is to be properly constituted, creative, and worthy of man's dignity, draws its genuine vitality. This is what St. Thomas means when he says:

> Human reason is the standard which measures the degree of goodness of the human will, and as such it derives from the eternal law, which is divine reason . . . Hence it is clear that the goodness of the human will depends much more on the eternal law than on human reason.

Characteristics of the Present Day

39. There are three things which characterize our modern age.

40. In the first place we notice a progressive improvement in the economic and social condition of working men. They began by claiming their rights principally in the economic and social spheres, and then proceeded to lay claim to their political rights as well. Finally, they have turned their attention to acquiring the more cultural benefits of society.

Today, therefore, working men all over the world are loud in their demands that they shall in no circumstances be subjected to arbitrary treatment, as though devoid of intelligence and freedom. They insist on being treated as human beings, with a share in every sector of human society: in the socio-economic sphere, in government, and in the realm of learning and culture.

41. Secondly, the part that women are now playing in political life is everywhere evident. This is a development that is perhaps of swifter growth among Christian nations, but it is also happening extensively, if more slowly, among nations that are heirs to different traditions and imbued with a different culture. Women are gaining an increasing awareness of their natural dignity. Far from being content with a purely passive role or allowing themselves to be regarded as a kind of instrument, they are demanding both in domestic and in public life the rights and duties which belong to them as human persons.

42. Finally, we are confronted in this modern age with a form of society which is evolving on entirely new social and political lines. Since all peoples have either attained political independence or are on the way to attaining it, soon no nation will rule over another and none will be subject to an alien power.

43. Thus all over the world men are either the citizens of an independent State, or are shortly to become so; nor is any nation nowadays content to submit to foreign domination. The longstanding inferiority complex of certain classes because of their economic and social status, sex, or position in the State, and the corresponding superiority complex of other classes, is rapidly becoming a thing of the past. . . .

Further Resources

BOOKS

Cahill, Thomas. *Pope John XXIII.* New York: Viking, 2002.

Feldman, Christian. *Pope John XXIII: A Spiritual Biography.* New York: Crossroad, 2000.

Johnson, Paul. *Pope John XXIII.* Boston: Little, Brown, 1974.

PERIODICALS

"Jewish Group Wants Pope John XXIII Declared Righteous." *America,* September 23, 2000, 5.

McBrien, Richard P. "Peasant Profundis." *America,* April 8, 2002, 23.

Twomey, Gerald S. "Anniversary Thoughts: Ten Lessons from Good Pope John." *America,* October 7, 2002, 12.

WEBSITES

O'Grady, Desmond. "Almost a Saint: Pope John XXIII." *St. Anthony Messenger.* Available online at http://www.american catholic.org/Messenger/Nov1996/feature1.asp; website home page: http://www.americancatholic.org/default.asp (acessed February 2, 2003).

Randall, Beth. "Illuminating Lives: Pope John XXIII." Available online at http://www.mcs.drexel.edu/~gbrandal/Illum_html/JohnXXIII.html (accessed February 2, 2003).

The Civil Rights Movement in Birmingham, Alabama

"Public Statement by Eight Alabama Clergymen"

Statement

By: C.C.J. Carpenter, Joseph A. Durick, Milton L. Grafman, Paul Hardin, Nolan B. Harmon, George M. Murray, Edward V. Ramage, and Earl Stallings

Date: April 12, 1963

Source: Carpenter, C.C.J., et al. "Public Statement by Eight Alabama Clergymen." *Birmingham News,* April 12, 1963.

About the Authors: The eight Alabama clergymen represented a wide spectrum of religions, including priests, bishops, ministers, and a rabbi from the Episcopalian, Catholic, Methodist, Presbyterian, Baptist, and Jewish faiths.

"Letter from a Birmingham Jail"

Letter

By: Martin Luther King Jr.

Date: April 16, 1963

Source: King, Martin Luther, Jr. "Letter from a Birmingham Jail." April 16, 1963. Available online at http://www.mlkonline.com/jail.html (accessed February 2, 2003).

About the Author: Martin Luther King Jr. (1929–1968), born in Atlanta, was ordained a Baptist minister in 1954 and received his doctorate from Boston University in 1955. Instrumental in the founding of the Southern Christian Leadership Conference in 1957, he advocated nonviolence in the Civil Rights movement. He served as a major organizer of the Montgomery bus boycott in 1956 and the March on Washington in 1963. He was awarded the Nobel Peace Prize in 1964, but four years later he was assassinated in Memphis, Tennessee. ∎

Introduction

In the spring of 1963, during a peaceful civil rights march in downtown Birmingham, Alabama, Martin Luther King Jr. found himself in a confrontation with "Bull" Connor and other city authorities. T. Eugene "Bull" Connor (1897–1973) was the commissioner of public safety in Birmingham and a leader of the city's segregationist forces. King, the leader of the Southern Christian Leadership Conference, was in Birmingham to oppose racial segregation. As a result of this confrontation, King was arrested and jailed.

At the time of the protest, Birmingham was one of the most industrialized cities in the South. With a population of about 40 percent African Americans, it was also one of the nation's most segregated cities. Two years earlier, in 1961, civil rights freedom riders—African Americans and whites who entered southern cities by bus to test the local reaction to integrated seating on that bus—had been violently attacked in Alabama. Also, Birmingham and other southern cities had been the scenes of bombings directed at African Americans and civil rights protesters.

On April 12, 1963, a group of eight Alabama clergymen issued a "Public Statement by Eight Alabama Clergymen," appealing to the African American community "to withdraw support from these demonstrations, and to unite locally in working peacefully for a better Birmingham." The clergymen supported the goals of the Civil Rights movement but opposed the tactics being employed in Birmingham. They feared that further demonstrations by King and his followers would worsen race

relations and result in deadly violence. Four days later, while in jail, King responded to this statement in a letter to his fellow clergymen explaining why he helped organize and participate in the protests. That letter, dated April 16, 1963, was the now famous "Letter from a Birmingham Jail."

Significance

"Letter from a Birmingham Jail" received international as well as national attention and has been reprinted throughout the world in newspapers, magazines, and books. The demonstrations had clearly affected many people beyond Alabama and the United States. For weeks, events in Birmingham had been a leading news item, and pictures of dogs attacking protesters and demonstrators being drenched by fire hoses were seen worldwide.

King was released after serving eight days in jail, but he continued leading massive civil rights demonstrations. Rallies were held in several African American churches for sixty-five consecutive nights, and during the day direct-action protests were conducted. By the end of the first week in May 1963, two thousand protesters had been arrested.

On May 10, 1963, a desegregation agreement affecting lunch counters, drinking fountains, and other facilities was reached and the demonstrations stopped. A permanent biracial committee was organized, demonstrators were released from jail, and more hiring of African Americans in clerical jobs was promised. It would take time for social change to take place in Birmingham and racial healing to occur. Almost forty years after these confrontations, though, the city takes pride in its Birmingham Civil Rights Institute. The institute describes itself as "a place of remembrance, revolution and reconciliation built at the site of the most tumultuous events of the Civil Rights era. More than a museum, it also serves as a forum for understanding the universal problem of racism—while chronicling the role Birmingham played in setting a people free."

Primary Source

"Public Statement by Eight Alabama Clergymen"

> **SYNOPSIS:** In response to civil rights protests in Birmingham, eight Alabama clergymen composed a statement urging restraint in the Civil Rights movement and the discontinuance of demonstrations in Birmingham. The authors explained that progress could best be achieved through negotiation and through the court system and suggested that direct action would only make the situation worse.

We the undersigned clergymen are among those who, in January, issued "An Appeal for Law and

Order and Common Sense," in dealing with racial problems in Alabama. We expressed understanding that honest convictions in racial matters could properly be pursued in the courts, but urged that decisions of those courts should in the meantime be peacefully obeyed.

Since that time there had been some evidence of increased forbearance and a willingness to face facts. Responsible citizens have undertaken to work on various problems which cause racial friction and unrest. In Birmingham, recent public events have given indication that we all have opportunity for a new constructive and realistic approach to racial problems.

However, we are now confronted by a series of demonstrations by some of our Negro citizens, directed and led in part by outsiders. We recognize the natural impatience of people who feel that their hopes are slow in being realized. But we are convinced that these demonstrations are unwise and untimely.

We agree rather with certain local Negro leadership which has called for honest and open negotiation of racial issues in our area. And we believe this kind of facing of issues can best be accomplished by citizens of our own metropolitan area, white and Negro, meeting with their knowledge and experience of the local situation. All of us need to face that responsibility and find proper channels for its accomplishment.

Just as we formerly pointed out that "hatred and violence have no sanction in our religious and political traditions," we also point out that such actions as incite to hatred and violence, however technically peaceful those actions may be, have not contributed to the resolution of our local problems. We do not believe that these days of new hope are days when extreme measures are justified in Birmingham.

We commend the community as a whole, and the local news media and law enforcement in particular, on the calm manner in which these demonstrations have been handled. We urge the public to continue to show restraint should the demonstrations continue, and the law enforcement official to remain calm and continue to protect our city from violence.

We further strongly urge our own Negro community to withdraw support from these demonstrations, and to unite locally in working peacefully for a better Birmingham. When rights are consistently denied, a cause should be pressed in the courts and in negotiations among local leaders, and not in the streets. We appeal to both our white and Negro citizenry to observe the principles of law and order and common sense.

Bishop C.C.J. Carpenter, D.D., LL.D., Episcopalian Bishop of Alabama
Bishop Joseph A. Durick, D.D., Auxiliary Bishop, Roman Catholic Diocese of Mobile, Birmingham
Rabbi Milton L. Grafman, Temple Emanu-El, Birmingham, Alabama
Bishop Paul Hardin, Methodist Bishop of the Alabama-West Florida Conference
Bishop Nolan B. Harmon, Bishop of the North Alabama Conference of the Methodist Church
Rev. George M. Murray, D.D., LL.D, Bishop Coadjutor, Episcopal Diocese of Alabama
Rev. Edward V. Ramage, Moderator, Synod of the Alabama Presbyterian Church in the United States
Rev. Earl Stallings, Pastor, First Baptist Church, Birmingham, Alabama

Primary Source

"Letter from a Birmingham Jail" [excerpt]

SYNOPSIS: In response to this statement, Martin Luther King Jr. composed his famous "Letter from a Birmingham Jail" to explain why he was active in civil rights demonstrations—primarily the failure of the courts and negotiation to address effectively the issue of civil rights.

My Dear Fellow Clergymen:

While confined here in the Birmingham city jail, I came across your recent statement calling present activities "unwise and untimely." Seldom do I pause to answer criticism of my work and ideas. If I sought to answer all the criticisms that cross my desk, my secretaries would have little time for anything other than such correspondence in the course of the day, and I would have no time for constructive work. But since I feel that you are men of genuine good will and that your criticisms are sincerely set forth, I want to try to answer your statement in what I hope will be patient and reasonable terms.

I think I should indicate why I am here in Birmingham, since you have been influenced by the view which argues against "outsiders coming in." I have the honor of serving as President of the Southern Christian Leadership Conference, an organization operating in every southern state, with headquarters in Atlanta, Georgia. We have some eighty-five affiliated organizations across the South, and one of them is the Alabama Christian Movement for Human Rights. Frequently we share staff, educational and financial resources with our affiliates. Several months ago the affiliate here in Birmingham asked us to be on call

Civil rights protesters kneel on a sidewalk after being arrested for parading without a permit, Birmingham, Alabama, May 2, 1963. Rev. Dr. Martin Luther King Jr. supported nonviolent civil disobedience and demonstrations to effect change in American society. © **BETTMANN/CORBIS.** **REPRODUCED BY PERMISSION.**

to engage in a nonviolent direct-action program if such were deemed necessary. We readily consented, and when the hour came we lived up to our promise. So I, along with several members of my staff, am here because I was invited here. I am here because I have organizational ties here.

But more basically, I am in Birmingham because injustice is here. Just as the prophets of the eighth century B.C. left their villages and carried their "thus saith the Lord" far beyond the boundaries of their home towns, and just as the Apostle Paul left his village of Tarsus and carried the gospel of Jesus Christ to the far corners of the Greco-Roman world, so am I compelled to carry the gospel of freedom beyond my own home town. Like Paul, I must constantly respond to the Macedonian call for aid.

Moreover, I am cognizant of the interrelatedness of all communities and states. I cannot sit idly in Atlanta and not be concerned about what happens in Birmingham. Injustice anywhere is a threat to justice everywhere. We are caught in an inescapable network of mutuality, tied in a single garment of destiny. Whatever affects one directly, affects all indirectly. Never again can we afford to live with the narrow, provincial "outside agitator" idea. Anyone who lives inside the United States can never be considered an outsider anywhere within its bounds.

You deplore the demonstrations taking place in Birmingham. But your statement, I am sorry to say, fails to express a similar concern for the conditions that brought about the demonstrations. I am sure that none of you would want to rest content with the superficial kind of social analysis that deals merely with effects and does not grapple with underlying causes. It is unfortunate that demonstrations are taking place in Birmingham, but it is even more unfortunate that the city's white power structure left the Negro community with no alternative.

Rev. Dr. Martin Luther King Jr. stares out the window of his cell in the Jefferson County Courthouse, Birmingham, Alabama. Four days after local religious leaders urged restraint in the Civil Rights movement, King responded to this criticism in his famous "Letter from a Birmingham Jail." © BETTMANN/CORBIS. REPRODUCED BY PERMISSION.

In any nonviolent campaign there are four basic steps: collection of the facts to determine whether injustices exist; negotiation; self-purification; and direct action. We have gone through all these steps in Birmingham. There can be no gain saying the fact that racial injustice engulfs this community. Birmingham is probably the most thoroughly segregated city in the United States. Its ugly record of brutality is widely known. Negroes have experienced grossly unjust treatment in the courts. There have been more unsolved bombings of Negro homes and churches in Birmingham that [sic] in any other city in the nation. These are the hard, brutal facts of the case. On the basis of these conditions, Negro leaders sought to negotiate with the city fathers. But the latter consistently refused to engage in good-faith negotiation.

Then, last September, came the opportunity to talk with leaders of Birmingham's economic community. In the course of the negotiations, certain promises were made by the merchants—for example, to remove the stores' humiliating racial signs.

On the basis of these promises, the Reverend Fred Shuttlesworth and the leaders of the Alabama Christian Movement for Human Rights agreed to a moratorium on all demonstrations. As the weeks and months went by, we realized that we were the victims of a broken promise. A few signs, briefly removed, returned; the others remained.

As in so many past experiences, our hopes had been blasted, and the shadow of deep disappointment settled upon us. We had no alternative except to prepare for direct action, whereby we would present our very bodies as a means of laying our case before the conscience of the local and the national community. Mindful of the difficulties involved, we decided to undertake a process of self-purification. We began a series of workshops on nonviolence, and we repeatedly asked ourselves: "Are you able to accept blows without retaliation?" "are you able to endure the ordeal of jail?" We decided to schedule our direct-action program for the Easter season, realizing that except for Christmas, this is the main shopping period of the year. Knowing that a strong economic withdrawal program would be the by-product of direct action, we felt that this would be the best time to bring pressure to bear on the merchants for the needed change.

Then it occurred to us that Birmingham's mayoralty election was coming up in March, and we speedily decided to postpone action until after election day. When we discovered that the Commissioner of Public Safety, Eugene "Bill" Connor, had piled up enough votes to be in the run-off, we decided again to postpone action until the day after the run-off so that the demonstrations could not be used to cloud the issues. Like many others, we waited to see Mr. Connor defeated, and to this end we endured postponement after postponement. Having aided in this community need, we felt that our direct-action program could be delayed no longer.

You may well ask: "Why direct action? Why sit-ins, marches, and so forth? Isn't negotiation a better path?" You are quite right in calling for negotiation. Indeed, this is the very purpose of direct action. Nonviolent direct action seeks to create such a crisis and foster such a tension that a community which has constantly refused to negotiate is forced to confront the issue. It seeks so to dramatize the issue that it can no longer be ignored. My citing the creation of tension as part of the work of the nonviolent-resister may sound rather shocking. But I must confess that I am not afraid of the word "tension." I have earnestly opposed violent tension, but there is a type of constructive, nonviolent tension which is necessary for growth. Just as Socrates felt that it was necessary to create a tension in the mind so that individuals could rise from the bondage of myths and half-truths to the unfettered realm of creative analysis and objective appraisal, so must we see the need for nonviolent gadflies to create the kind of tension in society that will help men rise from the dark depths of prejudice and racism to the majestic heights of understanding and brotherhood.

The purpose of our direct-action program is to create a situation so crisis-packed that it will inevitably open the door to negotiation. I therefore concur with you in your call for negotiation. Too long has our beloved Southland been bogged down in a tragic effort to live in monologue rather than dialogue.

One of the basic points in your statement is that the action that I and my associates have taken in Birmingham is untimely. Some have asked: "Why didn't you give the new city administration time to act?" The only answer that I can give to this query is that the new Birmingham administration must be prodded about as much as the outgoing one, before it will act. We are sadly mistaken if we feel that the election of Albert Boutwell as mayor will bring the millennium to Birmingham. While Mr. Boutwell is a much more gentle person that Mr. Connor, they are both segregationists, dedicated to maintenance of the status quo. I have hoped that Mr. Boutwell will be reasonable enough to see the futility of massive resistance to desegregation. But he will not see this without pressure from devotees of civil rights. My friends, I must say to you that we have not made a single gain in civil rights without determined legal and nonviolent pressure. Lamentably, it is an historical fact that privileged groups seldom give up their privileges voluntarily. Individuals may see the moral light and voluntarily give up their unjust posture; but as Reinhold Niebuhr has reminded us, groups tend to be more immoral than individuals.

We know through painful experience that freedom is never voluntarily given by the oppressor, it must be demanded by the oppressed. Frankly, I have yet to engage in a direct-action campaign that was "well timed" in view of those who have not suffered unduly from the disease of segregation. For years now I have heard the word "wait!" It rings in the ear of every Negro with piercing familiarity. This "Wait" has almost always meant "Never." We must come to see, with one of our distinguished jurists, that "justice too long delayed is justice denied." . . .

Further Resources

BOOKS

Blaustein, Albert P., and Robert L. Zangrando, eds. *Civil Rights and the American Negro: A Documentary History.* New York: Washington Square Press, 1968.

Dunn, John M. *The Civil Rights Movement.* New York: Lucent Books, 1998.

Higham, John, ed. *Civil Rights and Social Wrongs: Black-White Relations Since World War II.* University Park, Pa.: Pennsylvania State University Press, 1997.

PERIODICALS

Harris, William. "The Papers of Martin Luther King, Jr. Volume IV: Symbol of the Movement, January 1957–December 1958." *Journal of Southern History,* August 2002, 750.

McDonald, Dora. "Sharing the Dream: Martin Luther King Jr., the Movement, and Me." *Library Journal,* November 1, 2002, 110.

Walton, Anthony. "A Dream Deferred: Why Martin Luther King Has Yet to Be Heard." *Harper's,* August 2002, 67.

WEBSITES

National Civil Rights Museum home page. Available online at http://www.civilrightsmuseum.org/ (accessed February 2, 2003).

U.S. Department of Justice, Civil Rights Division home page. Available online at http://www.usdoj.gov/crt/crt-home.html (accessed February 2, 2003).

Western Michigan University Department of Political Science. "Timeline of the American Civil Rights Movement." Available online at http://www.wmich.edu/politics/mlk/ (accessed February 2, 2003). *This site contains links to articles on key events in the Civil Rights movement.*

"Eulogy for the Martyred Children"
Eulogy

By: Martin Luther King Jr.

Date: September 18, 1963

Source: King, Martin Luther, Jr. "Eulogy for the Martyred Children." Delivered at Sixth Avenue Baptist Church, Birmingham, Alabama, September 18, 1963. Available online at http://www.mlkonline.com/eulogy.html (accessed February 2, 2003).

About the Author: Martin Luther King Jr. (1929–1968), born in Atlanta, Georgia, was ordained a Baptist minister in 1954 and received his doctorate from Boston University in 1955. Instrumental in the founding of the Southern Christian Leadership Conference in 1957, he advocated nonviolence in the Civil Rights movement. He served as a major organizer of the Montgomery bus boycott in 1956 and the March on Washington in 1963. He was awarded the Nobel Peace Prize in 1964, but four years later he was assassinated in Memphis, Tennessee. ∎

Rev. Dr. Martin Luther King Jr. stands at the pulpit. The famous civil rights leader delivered the eulogy at the funeral service for the young victims of the Sixteenth Street Baptist Church bombing where he named them martyrs. © FLIP SCHULKE/CORBIS. REPRODUCED BY PERMISSION.

Introduction

On Sunday morning, September 15, 1963, in Birmingham, Alabama, a potent bomb exploded at the Sixteenth Street Baptist Church, killing four African American girls and injuring scores of others. The bomb was thrown into the basement of the church while Sunday school was in session. One of the victims, Carol Denise McNair, was only eleven years old. The other three were fourteen years old: Cynthia Wesley, Addie Mae Collins, and Carole Robertson.

On September 18, Dr. Martin Luther King Jr. delivered "Eulogy for the Martyred Children" at the funeral service for three of the girls. The fourth victim, Carole Robertson, was remembered at a separate funeral service. Dr. King's spiritual message to the congregation was that "they did not die in vain. God still has a way of wringing good out of evil. And history has proven over and over again that unmerited suffering is redemptive. The innocent blood of these little girls may well serve as a redemptive force that will bring new light to this dark city." Consistent with his nonviolent philosophy of civil rights action, King urged the congregation not to retaliate with violence but to continue to love their white broth-

ers. He believed that through education and God's grace, even the most misguided people would learn to respect the dignity and worth of all human beings and treat others fairly.

Over a period of several weeks earlier in the year, King had led large peaceful demonstrations and marches by civil rights workers and local African Americans. In Birmingham, approximately two thousand people were arrested, including King, who spent eight days in a Birmingham jail.

Significance

"Eulogy for the Martyred Children" was significant in helping the families of the victims deal with their loss and profound sorrow. But the tragic incident, along with King's eulogy, also had a galvanizing effect on the Civil Rights movement. Many people in the early 1960s had ignored the problems of segregation and discrimination, particularly in the South. These murders, though, exposed the depth of racial hatred to a shocked nation and convinced many people that the aims of the Civil Rights movement were justified. Ironically, the murders, calculated to intimate the African American community, gave the Civil Rights movement new supporters and financial help from church sources and other groups nationwide.

Although the deaths were tragic, the Reverend Jesse Jackson, an associate of King in the Civil Rights movement, stated later that good came out of them: "We were able to transform a crucifixion into a resurrection." Looking back on the incident, CBS news anchor Walter Cronkite, commented, "I don't think the white community realized the depth of hate until then."

It took many years to bring the murderers to justice. In 1977, Robert Edward Chambliss was convicted of one count of murder in Carol McNair's death. On May 1, 2001, Thomas Blanton, a former Ku Klux Klansman, was found guilty of the murders. Later, Bobby Frank Cherry, also a former Klansman, was found guilty of murder. The fourth main suspect, Herman Cash, died in 1994 without ever being charged.

Primary Source

"Eulogy for the Martyred Children"

SYNOPSIS: In his eulogy for the victims of the Sixteenth Street Baptist Church bombing, King emphasized that the four victims had died nobly because they were martyred for a righteous cause, the Civil Rights movement. They did not die in vain, because good will overcome evil, and the hearts of segregationists will eventually change. The document also records, in parentheses, the responses of members of the congregation.

This afternoon we gather in the quiet of this sanctuary to pay our last tribute of respect to these beautiful children of God. They entered the stage of history just a few years ago, and in the brief years that they were privileged to act on this mortal stage, they played their parts exceedingly well. Now the curtain falls; they move through the exit; the drama of their earthly life comes to a close. They are now committed back to that eternity from which they came.

These children—unoffending, innocent, and beautiful—were the victims of one of the most vicious and tragic crimes ever perpetrated against humanity. Yet they died nobly. They are the martyred heroines of a holy crusade for freedom and human dignity.

And so this afternoon in a real sense they have something to say to each of us in their death. They have something to say to every minister of the gospel who has remained silent behind the safe security of stained-glass windows. They have something to say to every politician [Audience:] (Yeah) who has fed his constituents with the stale bread of hatred and the spoiled meat of racism. They have something to say to a federal government that has compromised with the undemocratic practices of southern Dixiecrats (Yeah) and the blatant hypocrisy of right-wing northern Republicans. (Speak) They have something to say to every Negro (Yeah) who has passively accepted the evil system of segregation and who has stood on the sidelines in a mighty struggle for justice. They say to each of us, black and white alike, that we must substitute courage for caution. (Mmm) They say to us that we must be concerned not merely about who murdered them, but about the system, the way of life, the philosophy which produced the murderers. Their death says to us that we must work passionately and unrelentingly for the realization of the American dream.

And so my friends, they did not die in vain. (Yeah) God still has a way of wringing good out of evil. (Oh yes) And history has proven over and over again that unmerited suffering is redemptive. The innocent blood of these little girls may well serve as a redemptive force (Yeah) that will bring new light to this dark city. (Yeah. Mmm) The holy Scripture says, "A little child shall lead them." (Well) The death of these little children may lead our whole Southland (Well) from the low road of man's inhumanity to man to the high road of peace and brotherhood. (Yeah) These tragic deaths may lead our nation to substitute an aristocracy of character for an aristocracy of color. The spilled blood of these

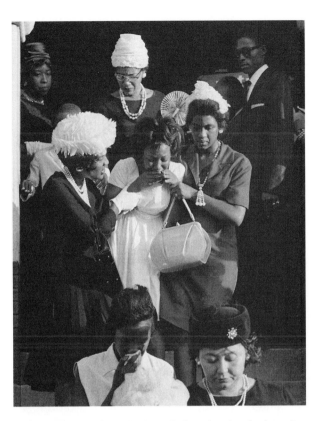

Family members comfort each other at the funeral services for three of the girls killed in the September 18, 1963, bombing of the Sixteenth Street Baptist Church, in Birmingham, Alabama. © BETTMANN/ CORBIS. REPRODUCED BY PERMISSION.

innocent girls may cause the whole citizenry of Birmingham (Yeah) to transform the negative extremes of a dark past into the positive extremes of a bright future. (Mmm) Indeed, this tragic event may cause the white South to come to terms with its conscience. (Yeah)

And so I stand here to say this afternoon to all assembled here that in spite of the darkness of this hour, (Well) we must not despair. (Well) We must not become bitter, (Yeah. That's right) nor must we harbor the desire to retaliate with violence. (Mmm) No, we must not lose faith in our white brothers. (Yeah) Somehow we must believe that the most misguided among them can learn to respect the dignity and the worth of all human personality.

May I now say a word to you, the members of the bereaved families? It is almost impossible to say anything that can console you at this difficult hour and remove the deep clouds of disappointment which are floating in your mental skies. But I hope you can find a little consolation from the universality of this experience. Death comes to every individual. There is an amazing democracy about death.

It is not aristocracy for some of the people, but a democracy for all of the people. Kings die and beggars die; rich men and poor men die; old people die and young people die. Death comes to the innocent and it comes to the guilty. Death is the irreducible common denominator of all men.

I hope you can find some consolation from Christianity's affirmation that death is not the end. Death is not a period that ends the great sentence of life, but a comma that punctuates it to more lofty significance. Death is not a blind alley that leads the human race into a state of nothingness, but an open door which leads man into life eternal. Let this daring faith, this great invincible surmise, be your sustaining power during these trying days.

Now I say to you in conclusion, life is hard, at times as hard as crucible steel. (Mmm) It has its bleak and difficult moments. Like the ever-flowing waters of the river, life has its moments of drought and its moments of flood. (Yeah) Like the ever-changing cycle of the seasons, life has the soothing warmth of its summers and the piercing chill of its winters. (Yeah) But if one will hold on, he will discover that God walks with him, (Yeah. Well) and that God is able (Yeah) to lift you from the fatigue of despair to the buoyancy of hope and transform dark and desolate valleys into sunlit paths of inner peace. (Mmm)

And so today, you do not walk alone. You gave to this world wonderful children. (Mmm) They didn't live long lives, but they lived meaningful lives. (Well) Their lives were distressingly small in quantity, but glowingly large in quality. (Yeah) And no greater tribute can be paid to you as parents, and no greater epitaph can come to them as children, than where they died and what they were doing when they died. (Yeah) They did not die in the dives and dens of Birmingham, (Well) nor did they die discussing and listening to filthy jokes. (Yeah) They died between the sacred walls of the church of God (Yeah) and they were discussing the eternal meaning (Yes) of love. This stands out as a beautiful, beautiful thing for all generations. (Yes) Shakespeare had Horatio to say some beautiful words as he stood over the dead body of Hamlet. And today, as I stand over the remains of these beautiful, darling girls, I paraphrase the words of Shakespeare (Well): Good night, sweet princesses. (Mmm) Good night, those who symbolize a new day. (Yeah) And may the flight of angels (That's right) take thee to thy eternal rest. God bless you.

Further Resources

BOOKS

Garrow, David J. *Bearing the Cross: Martin Luther King, Jr., and the Southern Christian Leadership Conference.* New York: Vintage, 1986.

King, Coretta Scott. *My Life with Martin Luther King, Jr.* New York: Holt, Rinehart, and Winston, 1969.

Washington, James M., ed. *A Testament of Hope: The Essential Writings of Martin Luther King, Jr.* San Francisco: Harper & Row, 1986.

PERIODICALS

Hopkins, Dwight N. "I May Not Get There with You: The True Martin Luther King, Jr." *African American Review,* Spring 2002, 169.

"King Speaks to the 21st Century." *Ebony,* January 2001, 53.

"The Martin Luther King, Jr. Center for Nonviolent Social Change." *Footsteps,* May 2000, 42.

WEBSITES

Holidays on the Net, "Welcome to Martin Luther King, Jr. Day on the Net." Available online at http://www.holidays.net /mlk (accessed February 2, 2003).

King Center. Website home page. Available online at http:// www.thekingcenter.com/ (accessed February 2, 2003).

Stanford University. "Martin Luther King, Jr. Papers Project." Available online at http://www.stanford.edu/group/King accessed February 2, 2003).

Gaudium et Spes (Pastoral Constitution on the Church in the Modern World)

Constitution

By: Second Vatican Council

Date: December 7, 1965

Source: Second Vatican Council. *Gaudium et Spes.* Rome, December 7, 1965. Available online at http://www.vatican.va (accessed February 4, 2003).

About the Organization: The Second Vatican Council, called by Pope John XXIII, was the twenty-first ecumenical, or general, council of the Roman Catholic Church. Beginning in 1962, one session was conducted each year for four years. Pope Paul VI called the council to closure in the fourth year. A total of 2,908 bishops and others were eligible to attend, and the average attendance at the meetings was approximately 2,200. ∎

Introduction

At the gathering of the Roman Catholic Church hierarchy at the Second Vatican Council, a multitude of social and moral problems were discussed, analyzed, and debated. The bishops, in conjunction first with Pope John

XXIII, then, after his death, with Pope Paul VI, believed that the church had a responsibility to play a more active role in helping meet the needs of people and working toward solutions to pressing social problems. To express this position, Pope Paul VI promulgated "Pastoral Constitution on the Church in the Modern World" *(Gaudium et Spes)*.

To address modern problems, the council included ten major parts in the document: (1) The Church and the Human Vocation: responding to the promptings of the Holy Spirit to what people should do with their lives. (2) The Dignity of the Human Person: recognizing the equality of women and men who were both made in the image of God. (3) The Human Community: focusing on the mutual interdependence among all people. (4) Human's Activity in the Universe: questioning the meaning and value of all the modern-day "feverish activity." (5) The Role of the Church in the Modern World: establishing a dialogue between the church and the rest of the world. (6) The Dignity of Marriage and the Family: forming the foundation of the healthy community. (7) The Proper Development of Culture: keeping it in line with God's laws. (8) Economic and Social Life: respecting the dignity and vocation of the human being. (9) The Political Community: dealing with the profound transformations in the structure and institutions of nations. (10) The Fostering of Peace: advocating the establishment of a true community of nations.

To bolster the message that not only dialogue but also action was required, the bishops stated that "one of the gravest errors of our time" was "the dichotomy between the faith which many profess and their day-to-day conduct." The roles of individual Christians and of local churches should be directed toward meeting the "pressing appeals of our times with a generous and common effort of love." The love must be put into practice in helping to change the world for the betterment of all.

Significance

In "Pastoral Constitution," the Second Vatican Council created a new attitude toward the modern world. The council called for dialogue between the church and others regardless of their religion or beliefs. This approach appealed to American Roman Catholics, as well as other Christians and non-Christians, who had endorsed the ecumenical movement, which began as an effort to promote unity among churches within Christianity, then extended to the encouragement of unity among religions.

Not everyone was satisfied with this document. Oscar Cullmann, in his book *Vatican Council II: The New Direction* (1968), wrote that the church's position in the document "is not sufficiently grounded in the specifically Christian revelation, in spite of all good intent." Albert

C. Outler, in an article in *Catholic World* (September, 1966), reacted in this way: "The greatest weaknesses of the document, I think, lie in the fact that on a great many questions, the solution of which depend so much upon experts of many different sorts, the chief reliance of the drafting commission was upon ecclesiastical scholars, clerical or lay." Outler believed that experts in sociology, economics, and political science should have helped formulate the document.

Despite some criticisms, most reactions to "Pastoral Constitution" were more favorable. Charles Moeller, in *Lumen Vitae* (September, 1966), presented a typical response when he noted that the church, in addressing people's actions in the world at large, had never before been so explicit.

Primary Source

Gaudium et Spes (Pastoral Constitution on the Church in the Modern World) [excerpt]

SYNOPSIS: The following excerpts focus upon some of the problems and changes facing the world at that time and the commitment of the church to taking an active role in working to solve these problems and direct these changes in a Christian manner. The call by the bishops of the Second Vatican Council was for Catholics to develop a new sense of service toward others. The constitution made a total of ninety-three statements, of which the first eight are excerpted.

Preface

1. The joys and the hopes, the griefs and the anxieties of the men of this age, especially those who are poor or in any way afflicted, these are the joys and hopes, the griefs and anxieties of the followers of Christ. Indeed, nothing genuinely human fails to raise an echo in their hearts. For theirs is a community composed of men. United in Christ, they are led by the Holy Spirit in their journey to the Kingdom of their Father and they have welcomed the news of salvation which is meant for every man. That is why this community realizes that it is truly linked with mankind and its history by the deepest of bonds.

2. Hence this Second Vatican Council, having probed more profoundly into the mystery of the Church, now addresses itself without hesitation, not only to the sons of the Church and to all who invoke the name of Christ, but to the whole of humanity. For the council yearns to explain to everyone how it conceives of the presence and activity of the Church in the world of today.

Therefore, the council focuses its attention on the world of men, the whole human family along with the sum of those realities in the midst of which it lives; that world which is the theater of man's history, and the heir of his energies, his tragedies and his triumphs; that world which the Christian sees as created and sustained by its Maker's love, fallen indeed into the bondage of sin, yet emancipated now by Christ, Who was crucified and rose again to break the strangle hold of personified evil, so that the world might be fashioned anew according to God's design and reach its fulfillment.

3. Though mankind is stricken with wonder at its own discoveries and its power, it often raises anxious questions about the current trend of the world, about the place and role of man in the universe, about the meaning of its individual and collective strivings, and about the ultimate destiny of reality and of humanity. Hence, giving witness and voice to the faith of the whole people of God gathered together by Christ, this council can provide no more eloquent proof of its solidarity with, a, [sic] well as its respect and love for the entire human family with which it is bound up, than by engaging with it in conversation about these various problems. The council brings to mankind light kindled from the Gospel, and puts at its disposal those saving resources which the Church herself, under the guidance of the Holy Spirit, receives from her Founder. For the human person deserves to be preserved; human society deserves to be renewed. Hence the focal point of our total presentation will be man himself, whole and entire, body and soul, heart and conscience, mind and will.

Therefore, this sacred synod, proclaiming the noble destiny of man and championing the Godlike seed which has been sown in him, offers to mankind the honest assistance of the Church in fostering that brotherhood of all men which corresponds to this destiny of theirs. Inspired by no earthly ambition, the Church seeks but a solitary goal: to carry forward the work of Christ under the lead of the befriending Spirit. And Christ entered this world to give witness to the truth, to rescue and not to sit in judgment, to serve and not to be served.(2)

Introductory Statement: The Situation of Men in the Modern World

4. To carry out such a task, the Church has always had the duty of scrutinizing the signs of the times and of interpreting them in the light of the Gospel. Thus, in language intelligible to each generation, she can respond to the perennial questions which men ask about this present life and the life to come, and about the relationship of the one to the other. We must therefore recognize and understand the world in which we live, its explanations, its longings, and its often dramatic characteristics. Some of the main features of the modern world can be sketched as follows.

Today, the human race is involved in a new stage of history. Profound and rapid changes are spreading by degrees around the whole world. Triggered by the intelligence and creative energies of man, these changes recoil upon him, upon his decisions and desires, both individual and collective, and upon his manner of thinking and acting with respect to things and to people. Hence we can already speak of a true cultural and social transformation, one which has repercussions on man's religious life as well.

As happens in any crisis of growth, this transformation has brought serious difficulties in its wake. Thus while man extends his power in every direction, he does not always succeed in subjecting it to his own welfare. Striving to probe more profoundly into the deeper recesses of his own mind, he frequently appears more unsure of himself. Gradually and more precisely he lays bare the laws of society, only to be paralyzed by uncertainty about the direction to give it.

Never has the human race enjoyed such an abundance of wealth, resources and economic power, and yet a huge proportion of the worlds citizens are still tormented by hunger and poverty, while countless numbers suffer from total illiteracy. Never before has man had so keen an understanding of freedom, yet at the same time new forms of social and psychological slavery make their appearance. Although the world of today has a very vivid awareness of its unity and of how one man depends on another in needful solidarity, it is most grievously turn into opposing camps by conflicting forces. For political, social, economic, racial and ideological disputes still continue bitterly, and with them the peril of a war which would reduce everything to ashes. True, there is a growing exchange of ideas, but the very words by which key concepts are expressed take on quite different meanings in diverse ideological systems. Finally, man painstakingly searches for a better world, without a corresponding spiritual advancement.

Influenced by such a variety of complexities, many of our contemporaries are kept from accurately identifying permanent values and adjusting them properly to fresh discoveries. As a result, buffeted between hope and anxiety and pressing one another with questions about the present course of events,

The Second Vatican Council meets in St. Peter's Basilica, Vatican City, September 1962. Vatican II addressed the concerns and problems faced by Christians in the modern age. © **DAVID LEES/CORBIS. REPRODUCED BY PERMISSION.**

they are burdened down with uneasiness. This same course of events leads men to look for answers; indeed, it forces them to do so.

5. Today's spiritual agitation and the changing conditions of life are part of a broader and deeper revolution. As a result of the latter, intellectual formation is ever increasingly based on the mathematical and natural sciences and on those dealing with man himself, while in the practical order the technology which stems from these sciences takes on mounting importance.

This scientific spirit has a new kind of impact on the cultural sphere and on modes of thought. Technology is now transforming the face of the earth, and is already trying to master outer space. To a certain extent, the human intellect is also broadening its dominion over time: over the past by means of historical knowledge; over the future, by the art of projecting and by planning.

Advances in biology, psychology, and the social sciences not only bring men hope of improved self-knowledge; in conjunction with technical methods, they are helping men exert direct influence on the life of social groups.

At the same time, the human race is giving steadily-increasing thought to forecasting and regulating its own population growth. History itself speeds along on so rapid a course that an individual person can scarcely keep abreast of it. The destiny of the human community has become all of a piece, where once the various groups of men had a kind of private history of their own.

Thus, the human race has passed from a rather static concept of reality to a more dynamic, evolutionary one. In consequence there has arisen a new series of problems, a series as numerous as can be, calling for efforts of analysis and synthesis.

6. By this very circumstance, the traditional local communities such as families, clans, tribes, villages, various groups and associations stemming from social contacts, experience more thorough changes every day.

The industrial type of society is gradually being spread, leading some nations to economic affluence, and radically transforming ideas and social conditions established for centuries.

Likewise, the cult and pursuit of city living has grown, either because of a multiplication of cities and their inhabitants, or by a transplantation of city life to rural settings.

New and more efficient media of social communication are contributing to the knowledge of events; by setting off chain reactions they are giving the swiftest and widest possible circulation to styles of thought and feeling.

It is also noteworthy how many men are being induced to migrate on various counts, and are thereby changing their manner of life. Thus a man's ties with his fellows are constantly being multiplied, and at the same time "socialization" brings further ties, without however always promoting appropriate personal development and truly personal relationships.

This kind of evolution can be seen more clearly in those nations which already enjoy the conveniences of economic and technological progress, though it is also astir among peoples still striving for such progress and eager to secure for themselves the advantages of an industrialized and urbanized society. These peoples, especially those among them who are attached to older traditions, are simultaneously undergoing a movement toward more mature and personal exercise of liberty.

7. A change in attitudes and in human structures frequently calls accepted values into question, especially among young people, who have grown impatient on more than one occasion, and indeed become rebels in their distress. Aware of their own influence in the life of society, they want a part in it sooner. This frequently causes parents and educators to experience greater difficulties day by day in discharging their tasks. The institutions, laws and modes of thinking and feeling as handed down from previous generations do not always seem to be well adapted to the contemporary state of affairs; hence arises an upheaval in the manner and even the norms of behavior.

Finally, these new conditions have their impact on religion. On the one hand a more critical ability to distinguish religion from a magical view of the world and from the superstitions which still circulate purifies it and exacts day by day a more personal and explicit adherence to faith. As a result many persons are achieving a more vivid sense of God. On the other hand, growing numbers of people are abandoning religion in practice. Unlike former days, the denial of God or of religion, or the abandonment œc [sic] them, are no longer unusual and individual occurrences. For today it is not rare for such things to be presented as requirements of scientific progress or of a certain new humanism. In numerous places these views are voiced not only in the teachings of philosophers, but on every side they influence literature, the arts, the interpretation of the humanities and of history and civil laws themselves. As a consequence, many people are shaken.

8. This development coming so rapidly and often in a disorderly fashion, combined with keener awareness itself of the inequalities in the world beget or intensify contradictions and imbalances.

Within the individual person there develops rather frequently an imbalance between an intellect which is modern in practical matters and a theoretical system of thought which can neither master the sum total of its ideas, nor arrange them adequately into a synthesis. Likewise an imbalance arises between a concern for practicality and efficiency, and the demands of moral conscience; also very often between the conditions of collective existence and the requisites of personal thought, and even of contemplation. At length there develops an imbalance between specialized human activity and a comprehensive view of reality.

As for the family, discord results from population, economic and social pressures, or from difficulties which arise between succeeding generations, or from new social relationships between men and women.

Differences crop up too between races and between various kinds of social orders; between wealthy nations and those which are less influential or are needy; finally, between international institutions born of the popular desire for peace, and the ambition to propagate one's own ideology, as well as collective greeds existing in nations or other groups.

What results is mutual distrust, enmities, conflicts and hardships. Of such is man at once the cause and the victim.

Further Resources

BOOKS

Ruokanen, Miikka. *The Catholic Doctrine of Non-Christian Religions According to the Second Vatican Council.* Leiden, The Netherlands and New York, N.Y.: E.J. Brill, 1992.

Rynne, Xavier. *Vatican Council II.* Maryknoll, N.Y.: Orbis, 1999.

Vatican Council. *The Sixteen Documents of Vatican II.* Boston: Pauline Books & Media, 1999.

PERIODICALS

Greeley, Andrew M. "The Revolutionary Event of Vatican II." *Commonweal,* September 11, 1998, 14.

Komonchak, Joseph A. "Convening Vatican II: John XXIII Calls for a Council." *Commonweal,* February 12, 1999, 10.

Ruddy, Christopher. "The American Church's Sexual Abuse Crisis: Some Thoughts from Vatican II." *America,* June 3, 2002, 7.

WEBSITES

Overkott, Cristoph, and Josef Spindelbock. "II Vatican Council: A Fulltext Search Engine." Available online at http://www.stjosef.at/council/search/; website home page: http://www.stjosef.at (accessed February 4, 2003).

RC Net. "Documents of Vatican II." Available online at http://www.rc.net/rcchurch/vatican2/ (accessed February 4, 2003).

Are You Running with Me, Jesus?

Essay, Prayers

By: Malcolm Boyd

Date: 1965

Source: Boyd, Malcolm. *Are You Running with Me, Jesus?* New York: Holt, Rinehart and Winston, 1965, 3–8, 11–15.

About the Author: Malcolm Boyd (1923–) was born in New York City. He earned his bachelor's degree at the University of Arizona in 1944 and a bachelor's of divinity degree at the Church Divinity School of the Pacific in 1954. After ordination as an Episcopal priest in 1955, he served in ministerial capacities at several churches and in chaplain positions across the country. A social activist, he has written or edited over thirty books on religion and social issues. ■

Introduction

In the 1960s, Reverend Malcolm Boyd found that some church members, as well as others who were in contact with him in his ministerial role, were telling him that praying in the traditional Christian manner was not a personally satisfying way to communicate their feelings to God. They were becoming so discouraged by customary, formulaic prayers that had been employed for centuries that they either prayed less and less or stopped praying entirely. Others continued to pray because they felt prayer was important, but they did so with little emotion, understanding, or conviction.

Boyd decided that what was needed was a more up-to-date approach to praying, using modern-day language

to fit modern-day needs. His answer to the dissatisfied Christian's prayer problem evolved into his milestone book, a collection of prayers called *Are You Running with Me, Jesus?* He had already developed prayers that he found helpful in communicating with God, and he wanted to share them with others who might find them meaningful. The book of prayers fit the culture of the 1960s, a time when religious, economic, educational, political, and family institutions were being openly challenged. The Civil Rights movement, opposition to the war in Vietnam, and the ecumenical movement were especially important in bringing about a desire for finding new ways of communicating with God through prayer.

The prayers in Boyd's book were written out of his personal experiences and grouped together into useful categories that addressed the demands of the times. Some of these categories included attainment of the free self, racial freedom, and sexual freedom. The book included prayers for living in the city or on a college campus and meditations about films, as well as for traditional themes such as meditations on the meaning of the cross. Boyd believed that nearly anyone could find some type of prayers that were suitable for his or her life situations.

Boyd summarized the meaning of prayer in this statement: "I believe that God prays in us and through us, whether we are praying or not (and whether we believe in God or not). So, any prayer on my part is a conscious response to what God is already doing in my life."

Significance

Christians found comfort and meaning in Boyd's prayers. Through them, they could comprehend that Christ would be with them wherever they may be or whatever may be happening to them, including the moment of death. Readers discovered that these prayers were not prayers for use inside a church, although they could serve well there, but for use in their personal lives as they faced the challenges of daily living. Even those who did not usually pray found Boyd's spiritual words meaningful. This new approach to praying was helpful in motivating them to at least consider the role that prayer could play in their lives. Even some non-Christians found something thought provoking in his prayers.

The public's overwhelming acceptance of *Are You Running with Me, Jesus?* was completely unexpected, especially by the author. When Boyd was approaching eighty years old, he looked back at his life and noted that writing the book was a significant turning point in his life. He remarked that his small book of prayers had "astonishingly became a national bestseller and led the way to my writing a number of other books, all of whom I love as my children."

Primary Source

Are You Running With Me, Jesus? [excerpt]

SYNOPSIS: The excerpt from the Introduction to the book presents Boyd's rationale for devising a new approach to prayer, one more consonant with the demands of modern life. The prayers excerpted are from the section "Prayers for the Free Self" and include the prayer about the fast pace of modern life that gives the book its title.

I cannot recall exactly when the idea, and way, of prayer began to change radically in my own life.

Prayer, for me, used to stand as something separate from other parts of life. But I have come to learn that real prayer is not so much talking to God as just sharing his presence. More and more, prayer and my style of life as a Christian now seem inseparable.

This assertion may seem to smack of self-righteousness, as if I have it "made." I don't mean it that way. It is simply an awareness that Christ *has* it "made," and my life is a life *in his,* not at all by any goodness or merits on my part but because of his love. Thus I am able to live in a kind of Christian nonchalance rooted in a trust of God which severs the old double-standard morality game I used to play with him. I can no longer conceive of lying to him in proper Old English or any other style of speech. I feel free to be completely myself with him. In a given situation where I know he is with me (perhaps in another person, or persons), I speak out of that deep trust and love which can spring only from a healthy, tried, and authentic freedom.

During a Freedom Ride in the Deep South in 1961, one of my fellow Episcopalian priests said: "It seems to me this is really a kind of prayer—a kind of corporate confession of sin." Some people said the Freedom Ride was essentially a sermon. But my fellow priest well expressed my feelings about being on that bus. It was a prayer.

In 1964, I attended a Roman Catholic Mass in Lebanon. During the liturgy, someone gave me the "kiss of peace," which I was to pass along to the next person. As the man on my right embraced me, he said the traditional words: "The Lord be with you." I replied with traditional correctness: "And with thy spirit." Then, turning to the man on my left, I said: "The Lord be with you." He replied—and I shall never forget the devastating honesty and directness of it: "And with you too, Malcolm." He was a layman, just then undertaking voluntary poverty, a member of a Roman Catholic group of priests and laymen with whom I was visiting Israel, the Near East, and Rome. The trip was an ecumenical encounter and discovery of singular grace. Something else had occurred to disturb and shake my prayer life.

In recent years I have had to spend much time traveling on planes from city to city, with the inevitable waiting in crowded but impersonal and lonely airports, and nights spent in innumerable faceless hotels. I came to realize that, for me, "community" was no longer an ideal but a reality, *here, now.* Each evening when I talked with groups of students, this was it—the sharing, the common life experienced together. I no longer had to seek for it; it was *given* and I had only to accept it. This molded my developing idea of prayer, too. Prayer could no longer be offered to God *up there* but to God *here;* prayer had to be natural and real, not phony or contrived; it was not about *other things* (as a rationalized fantasy or escape) but *these* things, however unattractive, jarring, or even socially outcast they might be.

God, I discovered, was not an upper-middle-class snob in a private, clublike "holy of holies" nor was he an impersonal I.B.M. machine computing petty sins in some celestial office building above the clouds. It came home to me that God was loving, in a terribly unsentimental and profound way. Every day, then, was like Good Friday's cross in demonstrating the depth and complexity and holy simplicity of his love.

I came to realize that many prayers are uttered without the prescribed forms of piety and even in a language which Puritans might, in their rigidity and lovelessness, label as profane. For example, Jerry's monologue in Edward Albee's play, *The Zoo Story,* is a prayer. If you will listen, you can hear prayers in the novels, songs, plays, and films of Samuel Beckett, Ralph Ellison, Ingmar Bergman, Saul Bellow, Bob Dylan, Tennessee Williams, James Baldwin, William Golding, Michelangelo Antonioni, Jean Genet, or John Updike. Prayer bridges the heretical gulf between the sacred and secular, the holy and profane. Of course, to hear some prayers, verbal or nonverbal, you must *listen* for what was not said.

Naïve and superstitious misconceptions about prayer have never ceased to shock me. On one occasion a forty-year-old man, an intellectual and cultural leader, confessed that he had stood in agony at his young son's grave, unable to pray because he did not know the words of a single prayer.

I am angered, as are many students and other youths, by worshipers who deny in their actions out-

Reverend Malcolm Boyd fields questions from Boston University students in 1966. Boyd's book, *Are You Running With Me, Jesus?* presented modernistic and practical prayers to help people. **AP/WIDE WORLD PHOTOS. REPRODUCED BY PERMISSION.**

side church what they "pray" about for one hour a week inside expensive Gothic or Colonial buildings. There is a hypocritical gulf between mouthing verbal prayers about Negroes and then resolutely manipulating a white power structure to keep Negroes in housing ghettos and interminable second-class citizenship.

During my stay at the Taizé Community in France, in 1957, I learned how the integrity of grace before meals was linked to an action of fasting. Prayer was offered on the fast day for persons in Asia who were literally starving to death. This grace, coupled with

fasting from lunch, expressed solidarity with them in prayer.

Some devout Christians believe that prayer is practicing the presence of God, and they find it difficult to enter into circumscribed or particular forms of prayer which seem to say, "Prayer is commencing now." Haven't they been involved in prayer all the time? On the other hand, one Christian clergyman saw things quite differently. "My prayers are addressed either to a Lord whom I do not perceive at all," he told me, "and I speak them into the void with a blind and sometimes desperate faith, or else, in my more mystical moments, with a sense of awe and wonder to Jesus Christ."

Prayer, I have learned, is more my response to God than a matter of my own initiative. I believe Jesus Christ prays *in* me as well as *for* me. But my response is sporadic, moody, now despairing, now joyful, corrupted by my self-love and desire to manipulate Christ's love. The community of Christ incarnates prayer in its essential life, and my own prayer is a part of this. But many times when I am caught up in egoism and self-pity, I forget. I find in the Psalms much the same range of mood and expression as I perceive within my own life of prayer.

God's grace is wonderful in prayer as in all other parts of human life. I remember a Sunday morning in 1964, during a trip to Mississippi to assist in Negro voter registration. At the "Freedom House" where I lived, I became deeply involved in a conversation with one of the student volunteers. She had not talked with an older person for quite some time about the things that mattered most to her, the pressing personal questions about life. She had so much to say that by the time we finished it was too late for me to attend morning worship.

It had remained in my mind that it was Sunday morning, and I had planned to attend a worship service, although I knew it must be a Negro service *or* a white one. As always, I hated this particular sinful prospect. But then, suddenly, God's grace seemed simply and beautifully manifest to me. The student and I had broken toast and eaten it, had shared the coffee. Surely God had, in his providence and merciful love, permitted us to share in communion with him.

■ ■ ■

It has been asked by some persons why this book is not entitled *Am I Running With You, Jesus?* The query overlooks the fact that my prayer life, as the state of my spirituality, is neither very respectable nor quite correct. Needless to say, I am a self-centered man, sinfully immersed in my own welfare and concerns, attempting to manipulate God, and often lost in my own self-love and self-pity. *Are You Running With Me, Jesus?* more accurately reflects the grounding, motivation, and style of my prayer life and spirituality as I grapple with imperfections and ambiguities in myself and my society.

■ ■ ■

The prayers which follow are some of my experiences in prayer. They are not meant for anyone else to recite by rote or copy as from a blueprint;

these can only be signposts, pointing toward those elements I find in church renewal and in church tradition, which can somehow be brought into a unity of worship.

Each of us is a person, with individual masks, scars, celebrations, moments of rejecting God, and experiences of conversion. Our prayers must spring from the indigenous soil of our own personal confrontation with the Spirit of God in our lives. Even for myself the words printed here are not wholly and completely those prayers. They are approximations or recollections of these, adaptations of some, and paraphrases of others. They stand for something deeper which can never be captured in writing or even fully in the spontaneously spoken word.

I have not attempted to root out the person of Malcolm Boyd from these prayers, for it was Malcolm Boyd who prayed them. Prayer must be personal, imbedded in the ground of one's own being as a person meeting God. These prayers are not intended as impersonal exhibits in a vacuum. They are the prayers of one man. It is hoped they may be useful, as signposts, to other men and women.

Prayers for the Free Self

It's morning, Jesus. It's morning, and here's that light and sound all over again

I've got to move fast . . . get into the bathroom, wash up, grab a bite to eat, and run some more.

I just don't feel like it, Lord. What I really want to do is get back into bed, pull up the covers, and sleep. All I seem to want today is the big sleep, and here I've got to run all over again.

Where am I running? You know these things I can't understand. It's not that I need to have you tell me. What counts most is just that somebody knows, and it's you. That helps a lot.

So I'll follow along, okay? But lead, Lord. Now I've got to run. Are you running with me, Jesus?

I'm crying and shouting inside tonight, Lord, and I'm feeling completely alone

All the roots I thought I had are gone. Everything in my life is in an upheaval. I am amazed that I can maintain any composure when I'm feeling like this.

The moment is all that matters; the present moment is of supreme importance. I know this. Yet in the present I feel dead. I want to anchor myself in the past and shed tears of self-pity. When I look ahead tonight I can see only futility, pain, and death.

I am only a rotting body, a vessel of disease, potentially a handful of ashes after I am burned.

But you call me tonight to love and responsibility. You have a job for me to do. You make me look at other persons whose needs make my self-pity a mockery and a disgrace.

Lord, I hear you. I know you. I feel your presence strongly in this awful moment, and I thank you. Help me onto my feet. Help me to get up.

You said there is perfect freedom in your service, Lord

Well, I don't feel perfectly free. I don't feel free at all. I'm a captive to myself.

I do what I want. I have it all my own way. There is no freedom at all for me in this, Jesus. Today I feel like a slave bound in chains and branded by a hot iron because I'm a captive to my own will and don't give an honest damn about you or your will.

You're over there where I'm keeping you, outside my real life. How can I go on being such a lousy hypocrite? Come over here, where I don't want you to come. Let me quit playing this blasphemous game of religion with you. Jesus, help me to let you be yourself in my life—so that I can be myself.

I know it sounds corny, Jesus, but I'm lonely

I wasn't going to get lonely any more, and so I kept very busy, telling myself I was serving you. But it's getting dark again, and I'm alone; honestly, Lord, I'm lonely as hell.

Why do I feel so sorry for myself? There's no reason why I should be. You're with me, and I know it. I'll be with other people in a little while. I know some of them love me very much in their own way, and I love some of them very much in mine.

But I still feel so damned lonely right now, in this minute that I'm living. I feel confused about how to get through the immediate next few steps to the other ones afterward. It's silly, but I feel this way because I'm threatened by me, and I wish I could get through me to you, clearly and with a kind of purity and integrity.

And yet, while I say this to you, I've been unkind to certain people whom you also love, and I've added to misunderstanding and confusion, and I haven't been able to make it at all nicely or properly.

Take hold of me, and connect me with these other lives, Jesus. Give me patience and love so that I can listen when I plug into these other lives. Help

me to listen and listen and listen . . . and love by being quiet and serving, and being there.

I'm scared, Jesus. You've asked me to do something I don't think I can do

I'm sure I wouldn't want to do it except that you asked me.

But I don't feel strong enough, and you know that I lack the courage I'd need. Why did you ask me to do this? It seems to me that John could do this much, much more easily, Lord. Remember, I told you I'm afraid to stand up and be criticized, Jesus. I feel naked in front of everybody, and I can't hide any part of myself.

Why can't I be quiet and have peace and be left alone? I don't see what good it will do for me to be dragged out in front of everybody and do this for you. Don't misunderstand me. I'm not saying I won't do it. I'm just saying I don't *want* to do it. I mean, how in hell *can* I do it?

You know me better than anybody does, but then you go and ask me to do something crazy like this. I can't figure you out. I wish you'd just leave me alone today, but if this is what you think is best, I'll try. I'll try. But I don't want to. Pray for me, Jesus.

Further Resources

BOOKS

Boyd, Malcolm. *Gay Priest: An Inner Journey.* New York: St. Martin's Press, 1986.

———. *Take Off the Masks: The Classic Spiritual Autobiography.* San Francisco: HarperSanFrancisco, 1993.

———. *Running with Jesus: The Prayers of Malcolm Boyd.* Minneapolis, Minn: Augsburg, 2000.

WEBSITES

Friedland, Michael B. "Giving a Shout for Freedom, Part I: The Reverend Malcolm Boyd, the Right Reverend Paul Moore, Jr., and the Civil Rights and Antiwar Movements of the 1960s and 1970s." *Nobody Gets Off the Bus: The Vietnam Generation Big Book* 5, nos. 1–4 (1994). Available online at http://lists.village.virginia.edu/sixties/HTML_docs/Texts /Scholarly/Friedland_Boyd_01.html (accessed February 4, 2003).

Hames, Jerry. "Still in the Saddle: Author Malcolm Boyd Celebrates Life as 'Elder.'" *Episcopal Life.* Available online at http://www.episcopalchurch.org/episcopal-life/StSaddle .html; website home page: http://www.episcopalchurch .orgepiscopal-life/Index.html (accessed February 4, 2003).

Shergood Forest. "Malcolm Boyd: Biography." Available online at http://shergoodforest.com/biocentral/boydm.html; website home page: http://shergoodforest.com/biocentral /biocentral.html (accessed February 4, 2003).

What's the Difference? A Comparison of the Faiths Men Live By

Theological work

By: Louis Cassels

Date: 1965

Source: Cassels, Louis. *What's the Difference? A Comparison of the Faiths Men Live By.* Garden City, N.Y.: Doubleday, 1965. Available online at http://www.religion-online.org /cgi-bin/relsearchd.dll/showbook?item_id=1623 (accessed February 4, 2003).

About the Author: Louis Cassels (1922–1974) was born in Ellenton, South Carolina. He received a bachelor's degree from Duke University in 1942 and served as a communications officer in the military from 1943 to 1946. In 1947, he became a correspondent for United Press International. He was a feature writer and author of the popular column "Religion in America" from 1955 to 1974. He was also a recipient of the prestigious Faith and Freedom Award from the Religious Heritage of America. ∎

Introduction

From his lengthy career as a newspaper religion editor and writer, Louis Cassels developed an interest in the variety of ways people from diverse cultural backgrounds expressed their beliefs about the supernatural and God. He believed that others had a similar interest, so he decided that a book that presented an overview and summary of world religions would contribute to people's understanding. From his research came *What's the Difference? A Comparison of the Faiths Men Live By,* which summarizes the vast varieties of faiths that have developed over many centuries. It discusses Judaism's survival for forty centuries and the Jewish-Christian heritage that binds these two monotheistic religions together. In analyzing the growth of Christianity, Cassels explores the impact of Catholic and Protestant differences, the denominations within Protestantism, the development of Christianity in Europe, and the Eastern Orthodox Church. Turning to faiths that originated in America, the book describes eight religious groups: the Disciples of Christ, Unitarians and Universalists, Mormans, Seventh-day Adventists, Christian Scientists, Pentecostals, the Church of the Nazarene, and Jehovah's Witnesses.

Like Judaism and Christianity, Islam is a monotheistic religion. Cassels devoted a chapter to Islam, emphasizing its growth and how it had been attracting converts in many emerging nations in Asia and Africa. In another chapter on Eastern religions, he described the importance of Hinduism to the life and faith of India and the appeal of Buddhism to Westerners as well as people from the East.

In the book's foreword, Cassels acknowledged that he was a "committed Christian, who has been nourished in the Protestant tradition." He went on: "However, I have also been trained, during more than twenty years as a wire-service reporter, to be as fair and accurate as humanly possible in presenting the other fellow's point of view," adding that his "conscience would not permit me to malign or knowingly misrepresent any person's religious faith."

Significance

What's the Difference reached a receptive American audience. Cassels was already well known to the readers of over four hundred newspapers. His fairness of presentation, objective reporting, and knowledge of the world's religions were well established. Demand for his book was bolstered by the culture of the 1960s. As the decade progressed, social movements such as the civil rights movement, antipoverty efforts, the ecumenical movement, and protests against the war in Vietnam were leading to social change. Many people, especially students and the young, became more aware of those who were different from them. Interest sprang up in different religions and the cultures they came from. A multicultural and a multireligious perspective became more important in education and the mass media. To be informed about other people's religions and cultures became a sign of progressiveness in one's thinking.

Cassels's work was so highly regarded by the public and by religion journalists that the Religion Newswriters Association named an award in his honor in 1971. The association wanted Cassels to be remembered for his kindness and encouragement to new reporters and for his high standards of journalism, especially in the field of religion.

Primary Source

What's the Difference? A Comparison of the Faiths Men Live By [excerpt]

SYNOPSIS: These excerpts from Chapter 1, "The Varieties of Faith," attempt to define the nature of religious belief and contain a summary of the three types of beliefs about God: atheism, which includes hedonism, humanism, and communism; pantheism, including animism and polytheism; and theism, represented by Judaism, Christianity, and Islam.

Everyone has a religion of some kind.

There are people who call themselves unbelievers or insist that they are "not religious." But this doesn't mean that they have found a way to live without faith. It merely reveals that they have a very narrow definition of religion, such as "going to church" or "believing in God."

A much more realistic definition is offered by the Columbia Encyclopedia. "Religion," it says, "has to do with what is most vital in the feeling, belief and performance of every human being." In other words, your religion is the set of assumptions—conscious or unconscious—on which you base your day-to-day decisions and actions.

A person may try to sidestep the religious issue by saying, "I'm an agnostic . . . I just don't know what to believe." But this dodge won't work. As the great Protestant preacher Dr. Harry Emerson Fosdick has pointed out, "you can avoid making up your mind, but you cannot avoid making up your life." Each day we are confronted with decisions, alternative courses of conduct, big choices and little choices. We may wish to suspend judgment on the ultimate meaning of human existence, but in actual fact we find ourselves compelled to act as if certain things were true and certain values more important than others. In every showdown, great or petty, we bet our lives on some hypothesis about God.

I say hypothesis to underscore the role that faith plays in all religious decisions, even those that are cynical or despairing. Religion need never be irrational, but religious convictions are always transrational, in the sense that they necessarily involve intuitions, instincts, emotions, and perceptions, as well as rational thought. We have fallen into the custom of reserving the word "faith" for religious beliefs that affirm the existence of a deity. But this is an inaccurate way of speaking. In reality, it is just as much an act of faith to assert that the universe just happens to be here as it is to say "In the beginning God created the heaven and the earth."

Basically, there are three hypotheses about God. They are called atheism, pantheism, and theism.

The Beliefs of the Atheists

The atheist stakes all on the proposition that God is just a figment of the human imagination, a name invented by prescientific man to explain what he could not understand.

The chief articles of the atheist's creed have been summarized by the British philosopher Bertrand Russell. An atheist, he says, believes "that man is the product of causes which had no prevision of the end they were achieving; that his origin, his growth, his hopes and fears, his loves and be-

liefs, are but the outcome of accidental collocations of atoms; that no fire, no heroism, no intensity of thought or feeling, can preserve an individual life beyond the grave; that all the labors of the ages, all the devotion, all the inspiration, all the noonday brightness of human genius, are destined to extinction in the vast death of the solar system. . . .

Hedonism: Faith in Pleasure

Many atheists find their positive affirmations in the attitude toward life called hedonism. The name comes from the Greek word for pleasure, and its intellectual ancestry traces back to the Greek philosophers, particularly Epicurus. The hedonist believes that enjoyment is the chief end of human existence. His creed is perfectly expressed in the ancient aphorism, "Eat, drink and be merry, for tomorrow you may die." The modern version is, "Live it up while you can; you're a long time dead." . . .

Humanism: Faith in Man

Hedonism is sometimes called the most self-centered of all religions. At the opposite pole is another atheistic religion, which attracts unselfish, generous-spirited men and women. It is called humanism.

One of its leading exponents, Sir Julian Huxley, defines a humanist as "someone who believes that Man is just as much a natural phenomenon as an animal or a plant; that his body, mind and soul were not supernaturally created, but are all products of evolution, and that he is not under the control or guidance of any supernatural being or beings, but has to rely on himself and his own powers."

Although he finds nothing else in the universe to worship, the humanist has great reverence for Man (spelled, characteristically, with a capital M). He believes that Man can invest his transitory existence with meaning and dignity by creating his own values and struggling gallantly toward them in a world that is at best indifferent and at worst hostile toward his hopes. . . .

Communism: Faith in Materialism

The largest and best organized of the atheistic religions is Communism. Some readers may be astonished to find it listed as a religion. But many close observers of the Communist movement, including FBI Director J. Edgar Hoover, have concluded that it can be understood only as a faith that demands the total allegiance of its adherents. In his authoritative study *The Nature of Communism,* Professor Robert V. Daniels says:

> The Communist Party is a sect, with beliefs, mission, priesthood and hierarchy. It is a church, in the very obvious sense that it is the institutionalization of belief. . . . Fervor, dogmatism, fanaticism, dedication, atonement and martyrdom can all be observed in the Communist movement.
>
> So far does the character of the Communist's allegiance to the movement correspond to religious commitment that we can even observe the intensely emotional phenomenon of conversion when individuals are persuaded to embrace the Communist faith. . . .

The Varieties of Pantheism

Let's pause for a brief summary: We said there are three basic hypotheses about God—atheism, pantheism, theism. We first took a look at atheism—the "no God" hypothesis—and found three principal varieties currently competing in the idea market. Now let's examine the second basic hypothesis about God—pantheism.

Pantheism's distinctive belief is summed up in its name, which is a compound of the Greek words pan (all) and theos (God). To the pantheist, "God is all and all is God." In other words, he identifies God with the universe and the universe with God.

To some pantheists, God is the all-important part of the God-universe equation. They speak of the visible, temporal world as being merely "an idea in the mind of God." Others approach from the opposite direction. They speak of God as if the word were merely a synonym for nature.

In either case, the pantheist is convinced of the "oneness" of all things, and his concept of God is "the Whole that gathers up in itself all that exists." He may use the traditional word for convenience, but for him "God" is not a proper name. It is an abstract noun, meaning "underlying principle of unity," and it has no connotations of personhood. Pantheists do not believe in a God who exists apart from the natural universe as a separate, transcendent Being. . . .

Primitive Animism

The primitive version of pantheism is called animism. Animists believe that various objects, such as stones, trees, mountains, or the sun—objects we would call inanimate—are actually suffused with supernatural spirits who must be propitiated and cajoled. The ancestor worship of Japanese Shintoism and the spiritism of South American Indians are very closely related to animism since they entail the same idea; that is, of a natural world overrun by invisible spirits.

Although Westerners tend to think of animism as a form of belief that went out with Stone-Age man, it remains today one of the world's major religions, in terms of numbers, with more than 100 million followers in Africa, Asia, Polynesia, and South America.

Classic and Modern Polytheism

Polytheism is another variety of pantheistic religion that is still strong. Polytheists believe in many different gods. The mythologies of ancient Greece and Rome are classic examples of polytheism. Both acknowledged one chief deity—the Greeks called him Zeus; the Romans, Jupiter. But his control over the universe was regarded as quite limited; other gods and goddesses were free to do pretty much as they pleased in the particular realms of nature or human activity over which they held jurisdiction. Thus, in the Roman pantheon, Mars had charge of war, Apollo took care of the sun, Neptune ruled the ocean, Ceres had the last word in agriculture, Diana in hunting, and Venus in love. Altogether, the Greeks and Romans recognized about thirty thousand gods.

In the modern world, we encounter polytheism mainly in the Oriental religions. Later we shall devote a whole chapter to these ancient faiths, which have more than 700 million adherents in Asia. But it is pertinent here to note that Hinduism is based on a pantheistic view of the universe and that in popular practice it is extremely polytheistic. By one reckoning, Hinduism has about 3 million gods—a hundred times as many as the ancient Greeks and Romans! Buddhism, an offshoot of Hinduism, is not so easily categorized. Some versions of Buddhism—those that have remained closest to the spirit of its founder, Gautama Buddha—are really more atheistic than pantheistic. But there are other types of Buddhism—the ones with the largest followings in Asia today—that have degenerated into polytheistic idol worship. . . .

The Faith in One God

Theism (or, as some prefer to say, monotheism) is professed by about 1.5 billion people—half of the world's population. This concept of God is shared by Christians, Jews, and Moslems.

Theists are united in several affirmations about the nature of God. One is expressed succinctly in the Shema Yisrael, which Jews recite at every religious service and, if possible, at the hour of death: "Hear, O Israel, the Lord our God, the Lord is One." It is echoed in the creed that every devout Moslem repeats five times a day: "There is no God but Allah." To a person who has grown up in a Christian culture, the assertion that there is only one God may sound trite and obvious. But both Judaism and Islam—the correct name for the Moslems' religion—grew up in the midst of polytheistic cultures. When the Jews and Moslems declared that there was one God, and one only, they were making a radical contradiction of what most of the people around them had always believed.

A second basic belief that is common to all theists is that God is both immanent and transcendent. To describe God as immanent is to say, with the pantheists, that He dwells within nature and particularly within the hearts and minds of men. To call Him transcendent is to say, in direct opposition to pantheism, that He is also beyond and above, utterly independent of the material universe which He has called into being, and "wholly other" than any created thing.

Theists also agree in ascribing to God the attributes of personhood. This does not mean taking an anthropomorphic view of God as a grandfatherly Being who exists somewhere "out there" in space. On the contrary, theistic scholars are the first to insist that God cannot properly be conceived a particular thing, not even as "the highest person" or "the Supreme Being." Theism's God is infinitely more than a person or a being. He is the Source of all personhood, existence, and reality, totally beyond the powers of man to comprehend or describe.

Since God transcends any of the categories of human intelligence into which we may try to fit Him, the only question is whether we do less injustice to His majesty by referring to Him in personal pronouns, or by using impersonal abstract nouns, such as "Ground of Being" and "First Cause." . . .

The Personal God

Theists speak of God in categories appropriate to personhood for two reasons. First, they believe that personality—thinking, willing, purposeful personality—is by far the highest form of existence that we have encountered in this complex universe. Therefore, it is the least inadequate frame of reference in which to speak of, or to, God. The second reason is more basic and more empirical. In their experience of God, Christians, Jews, and Moslems

have been certain that they were dealing, not with an It, but with a Thou.

And that brings us to the fourth fundamental conviction of the theistic religions. God desires to enter into a personal, I-Thou relationship with His human creatures. He loves them ("as tenderly as a mother bird loves her young," say the Moslem scriptures, the Koran) and He takes the initiative in revealing Himself to them.

The concept of a self-revealing God is one of the great practical, as well as theoretical, points of difference between pantheists and theists. The pantheist feels that it is up to him to gain such knowledge of God, or—to use a term more congenial to him—Ultimate Reality, as he can. He tends to be eclectic in his quest for wisdom, borrowing one idea from the Bible and another from the Bhagavad-Gita. But Christianity, Judaism, and Islam are "religions of revelation." They place their faith not in any human speculation about what God ought to be like, but in what they believe He has revealed about Himself. So they naturally accord great importance to the particular sacred writings, or scriptures, in which they believe God's self-revelation is authentically recorded. Islamic scholars refer to Moslems, Jews, and Christians as "people of the Book," and the phrase aptly depicts one of the most profound bonds among the theistic religions.

Further Resources
BOOKS

Cassels, Louis. *Christian Primer*. Garden City, N.Y.: Doubleday, 1964.

———. *The Real Jesus, How He Lived and What He Taught*. Garden City, N.Y.: Doubleday, 1968.

———. *The Reality of God*. Garden City, N.Y.: Doubleday, 1971.

The Secular City
Theological work

By: Harvey Cox

Date: 1965

Source: Cox, Harvey Gallagher. *The Secular City*. New York: Macmillan, 1965, 241–243, 257–258, 264–268.

About the Author: Harvey Gallagher Cox Jr. (1929–) was born in Phoenixville, Pennsylvania. He earned a bachelor's degree from the University of Pennsylvania in 1951 and a bachelor's of divinity degree from Yale in 1955. In 1963, he received a doctorate from Harvard Divinity School and was appointed professor of theology at Andover Newton Theological Seminary. He joined the Harvard University Divinity School faculty in 1965. An author of several books, he is regarded as one of the most influential Protestant theologians. ∎

Introduction

In *The Secular City,* theologian Harvey Cox expressed his view that two critical social changes were taking place in the 1960s: the escalation of urbanization and the crumbling of traditional religion. Urbanization, according to Cox, constituted a massive change in the way people lived together and "became possible in its contemporary form only with the scientific and technological advances which sprang from the wreckage of religious worldviews." Secularization marked a basic change in the way people understood their life together, and "it occurred only when the cosmopolitan confrontations of city living exposed the relativity of the myths and traditions men once thought were unquestionable." Secularization was a movement away from concerns with the hereafter to involvement with the problems of the here and now. Since the age of the secular city was an "age of no religion at all," new meanings for living had to be found.

Cox's thesis was that God still fits into the concept of the secular city: "God is first the Lord of history and only then the Head of the Church. This means that God can be just as present in the secular as in the religious realms of life." Secularization "is not the Messiah. But neither is it anti-Christ. It is rather a dangerous liberation." It posed risks "of a larger order than those it displaces. But the promise exceeds the peril, or at least makes it worth taking the risk."

Cox refers several times to the writings of German theologian Dietrich Bonhoeffer (1906–1945), who strongly influenced Cox's thinking in *The Secular City.* Bonhoeffer's book *Prisoner for God,* published posthumously in 1959, contained entries from diaries and letters he wrote while in a Nazi prison during World War II. Bonhoeffer expressed his anger and sorrow that the churches were not condemning Nazism, and he said that the churches had become no longer vital because of this inaction. He stated that a "religionless Christianity" without belief in a supernatural being could help preserve traditional Christian values regarding the dignity and sanctity of all human life. Because of his vocal opposition to the Nazis, Dietrich Bonhoeffer was executed in 1945.

Significance

The impact of *The Secular City* was almost immediate. It soon became a best-seller, and more than a million copies have been sold since 1965.

The responses from theologians were mixed. While some accepted his conclusions, others challenged his belief regarding the decline of religion in urban society. Controversy was to be the fate of the book, and for the next several decades, "secular city" debates were held in schools of theology and other public forums.

Twenty-five years after the book's publication, Cox commented that everywhere there was an "unanticipated resurgence of traditional religion." Fundamentalist movements in Islam (Middle East), Shinto (Japan), Judaism (Israel), Hinduism (India), and Christianity (America) "have raised important questions about the allegedly ineluctable process of secularization." Asking, though, if all this fundamentalism was good, Cox argued that secularization was relevant and needed to prevent "powerful religions from acting on their theocratic pretensions. It allows people to choose among a wider range of worldviews."

Primary Source

The Secular City [excerpt]

SYNOPSIS: In the following excerpts from Chapter 11, "To Speak in a Secular Fashion of God," Cox discusses the conceptualization of God within the framework of two major social transformations in the 1960s: the rise of urban civilization and the collapse of traditional religion. In addition to Bonhoeffer, he refers to three other writers who affected his thinking: Cornelis von Peursen (*Man and Reality, the History of Human Thought,* 1963), Carl Michalson (*Theology as Ontology and as History,* 1963), and Bernhard Anderson (*Understanding the Old Testament,* 1956).

On April 30, 1944, Dietrich Bonhoeffer wrote to one of his friends from his prison cell words that have both tempted and tormented theologians ever since. "We are proceeding toward a time," he wrote, "of no religion at all. . . . How do we speak of God without religion. . . . How do we speak in a secular fashion of God?"

No wonder Bonhoeffer's question bothers us. It reminds us of two incontrovertible facts. The first is that the biblical faith, unlike Buddhism, for example, must *speak* of God. It cannot withdraw into silence or cryptic aphorisms. A God to whom human words cannot point is not the God of the Bible. Bonhoeffer's question also reminds us, however, that the word *God* means almost nothing to modern secular man. His mental world and his way of using language is such that he can neither understand nor use the word *God* meaningfully. This reveals the impasse: if man cannot speak of God in the secular city, then all we have said about secularization as the work of God for man is nonsense and the whole thesis of this book is erroneous. It is clear that we must deal with this painful question of Bonhoeffer satisfactorily or all that we have said so far becomes implausible.

Significantly, Bonhoeffer himself supplies a much-needed clue for where to start in seeking to answer his question. Many years before his imprisonment he wrote this paragraph in his commentary on the Second Commandment:

> "God" is not for us a common concept by which we designate that which is the highest, holiest and mightiest thinkable, but "God" is a name. It is something entirely different when the heathen say "God" as when we, to whom God himself has spoken, say "God" . . ."God" is a name. . . . The word means absolutely nothing, the name "God" is everything.

Here Bonhoeffer drops an invaluable hint about how we should proceed. He reminds us that in the biblical tradition, we do not speak "about God" at all, either "in a secular fashion" or in any other. When we use the word *God* in the biblical sense, we are not speaking about but "naming," and that is an entirely different matter. To name is to point, to confess, to locate something in terms of our history. We can name something only by using the fund of memories and meanings we carry with us as individuals and as a species. This makes the act of naming, whether naming God or anything else, more than merely a theological or linguistic problem. Theologies and languages grow out of a sociocultural milieu. They spring from one or another epochal *manière d'être.* This makes the problem of "speaking in a secular fashion about God" in part at least a sociological problem.

But speaking about God in a secular fashion is not just a sociological problem. Since we live in a period when our view of the world is being politicized, in which, as we shall see in a moment, the political is replacing the metaphysical as the characteristic mode of grasping reality, "naming" today becomes in part also a political issue. It becomes a question of where, in the push and pull of human conflict, those currents can be detected which continue the liberating activity we witness in the Exodus and in Easter. Speaking of God in a secular fashion is also a political issue.

But the sociological and political considerations in no sense exhaust the depth of Bonhoeffer's riddle. Despite the efforts of some modern theologians to sidestep it, whether God exists or not *is* a des-

In *The Secular City,* Harvey Cox confronted the facts of secularization and urbanization in modern society and hailed them as a means toward a renewed "Christianity." **AP/WIDE WORLD PHOTOS. REPRODUCED BY PERMISSION.**

perately serious issue. All the palaver about the terms *existence* and *being* and all the sophisticated in-group bickering about nonobjectifying language cannot obscure the fact that there remains an indissoluble question after all the conceptualizations have been clarified. It is the question the Spanish philosopher Miguel Unamuno rightly felt overshadows all other questions man asks: Is man alone in the universe or not?

So Bonhoeffer's query has three parts. It is first of all a *sociological problem.* We say problem because it can be answered at that level with relatively little difficulty. It is also a *political issue.* An issue is a somewhat more demanding challenge. It requires us to take some risks and make some choices, to take sides. It necessitates our indicating where that same reality whom the Hebrews called Yahweh, whom the disciples saw in Jesus, is breaking in today. But finally, Bonhoeffer presents us with what is a *theological question.* He makes us answer for ourselves whether the God of the Bible is real or is just a rich and imaginative way man has fashioned to talk about himself. No amount of verbal clarification can set this disagreement aside. In the last analysis it is not a matter of clear thinking at all but a matter of personal decision. Luther was right: deciding on this question is a matter which, like dying, every man must do for himself.

Speaking of God as a Sociological Problem

The reason speaking about God in the secular city is in part a sociological problem is that all words, including the word *God,* emerge from a particular sociocultural setting. No language was ever handed down from heaven. When words change their meanings and become problematical, there is always some social dislocation or cultural breakdown which lies beneath the confusion. There are basically two types of such equivocality. One is caused by historical change, the other by social differentiation.

Equivocation through historical change means that the same word carries different connotations in different historical periods of a given language. The English word *let,* for example, has reversed its meaning since Shakespeare's day. When Hamlet, lunging for his father's ghost, says "I'll slay the man that *lets* me!," he means he will slay whoever tries to stop him. Equivocation through social differentiation means that in a complex society, the same word means different things in different settings. It may even mean different things for the same person, depending on where it is used. Take the word "God" by changing the society in which it has been trivialized, by moving away from the context where "God-talk" usually occurs, and by shedding the stereotyped roles in which God's name is usually intoned.

Speaking of God as a Theological Question

When all the preliminary work has been done and the ground has been cleared, the question Bonhoeffer poses is still a *theological* one. In the present theological climate it is especially important to remember this, since where theologians are not busily trying to dress God in tribal costume or enlist him in their existentialist histrionics, they may be just as avidly whittling down the fact that God does make a difference in the way men live. Their opportunity to do this arises from a new situation in theology. There have always been important similarities between biblical faith and atheism, as contrasted, for example, to belief in demons and spirits. But in our time this similarity has produced a rather novel heresy. It is a kind of atheism expressed in Christian theological terminology. This curious phenomenon is made possible by the fact that the biblical doctrine of the hiddenness of God comports so very

well, at one level at least, with contemporary atheism or, better, "nontheism." The two can easily be confused unless real care is used. Thus the hidden God or *deus absconditus* of biblical theology may be mistaken for the no-god-at-all of nontheism. Though He is very different from Godot in Samuel Beckett's play, like Godot He has the similar habit of not appearing at the times and places men appoint. Because the two have often been jumbled, it is important that we distinguish them here.

Carl Michalson describes the biblical doctrine of the hiddenness of God in these terms:

> . . . it is God's way of life to be hidden. He is *ex officio* hidden. Hiddenness is intrinsic to his nature as God. . . . The doctrine of the hiddenness of God . . . is not a counsel of despair or a concession to human finitude, but a positive description of God himself which performs a merciful service. *It prevents man both from looking for God in the wrong place* and from esteeming God's role in reality with *less than ultimate seriousness.*

This biblical God's hiddenness stands at the very center of the doctrine of God. It is so commanding that Pascal was echoing its intention when he said, "Every religion which does not affirm that God is hidden is not true." It means that God discloses himself at those places and in those ways he chooses and not as man would want. . . .

The idea of an I–You partnership between God and man is strongly hinted by the language of Galatians 4. . . . In this passage man is viewed as a son and heir. The emphasis is on *son* as opposed to child, and on *heir* as having assumed responsibility. This implies that the strictly vertical relationship which informs a father's relationship to his minor boy is discarded for the adult partnership which obtains between a grown man and his father.

Perhaps in the secular city God calls man to meet Him first of all as a "you." This has far-reaching implications. It suggests that man is not to become fascinated with God himself. Like his relationship to his work partner, man's relationship to God derives from the work they do together. Rather than shutting out the world to delve into each other's depths the way adolescent lovers do, God and man find joy together in doing a common task. Of course this type of relationship will not satisfy the man who is driven by a compulsive interest in "finding" or "experiencing" God. Such people are always dissatisfied by the admittedly sparse revelation of Himself which God has made. It is not the kind of revelation which encourages delving. God wants man to be interested not in Him but in his fellow man. . . .

But how do we name the God who is not interested in our fasting and cultic adoration but asks for acts of mercy? It is too early to say for sure, but it may well be that our English word *God* will have to die, corroborating in some measure Nietzsche's apocalyptic judgment that "God is dead." By what name shall we call the One we met both in the life of Jesus and in our present history as the liberator and the hidden one?

Perhaps we should not be anxious about finding a name. Our present fit of tonguetied verbosity, of empty and ambiguous words, will work itself out in experience, the way it always has. "The story of the word 'God,'" says Cornelis van Peursen, "is that it has no given meaning, but acquires a meaning in history. . . ." Naming was the process by which Israel drew more and more reality into history by relating it to the One who had brought them up out of Egypt. First the origin of history, then its consummation were included in this process of "radiation" by which God was named as he was encountered in the world. God manifests himself to us in and through secular events. The meaning of the word *God* will be altered or a new name will emerge as we encounter that presence in events which draws them into the history of which we are a part, the history of God's liberation of man. Secular talk of God is pointing and naming. As van Peursen says,

> . . . it is in a functional way that man comes into contact with the reality of God, that God acquires a meaning in history. . . . As the Church we have to respond to the world through our acts . . . transmitting the old message of a Name . . . which is taking on a new meaning in history, and especially in the functional history of our time.

We cannot simply conjure up a new name. Nor can we arbitrarily discard the old one. God does reveal His name in history, through the clash of historical forces and the faithful efforts of a people to discern His presence and respond to His call. A new name will come when God is ready. A new way of conceptualizing the Other will emerge in the tension between the history which has gone before us and the events which lie ahead. It will emerge as the issues of the urban civilization are drawn into that rehearsal of the past, reflection on the present, and responsibility for the future which *is* history.

This may mean that we shall have to stop talking about "God" for a while, take a moratorium on speech until the new name emerges. Maybe the name that does emerge will not be the three-letter word *God*, but this should not dismay us. Since naming is a human activity embedded in a particular sociocultural milieu, there is no holy language as such, and the word *God* is not sacred. All languages are historical. They are born and die. Presumably God will continue to live eons after English and all other present languages have been totally forgotten. It is only word magic to believe that there is some integral connection between God and any particular linguistic vocable.

If the naming we must do in the secular city requires our dispensing with the word *God* in order not to confuse the One who reveals Himself in Jesus with the gods of mythology or the deity of philosophy, it will not be the first time this has happened in the history of biblical faith. It is common knowledge that the people of Israel went through several stages in naming Him, and they may not be through yet. At various times they used the terms El Elyon, Elohim, El Shaddai, and—of course—Yahweh. They freely borrowed these designations from neighboring peoples and discarded them with what now seems to us an amazing freedom, especially in view of the enormous power inherent in names in Hebrew culture. A remarkable evidence of this daring willingness to move to new names when the historical situation warranted it is found in Exodus 6:2–3, a part of the so-called P document:

> And God [Elohim] said to Moses, "I am the Lord [Yahweh]. I appeared to Abraham, Isaac and Jacob as God Almighty [El Shaddai], but by my name the Lord [Yahweh] I did not make myself known to them."

One could write an entire history of Israel, charting its cultural and political relationships to its neighbors, by following the conflict and development in naming, both the naming of God and the naming of children. God reveals his name to man through the abrasive experiences of social change.

After the period of the Exile, the Jews again switched their nomenclature. Disturbed by the debasement of the name *Yahweh,* which was considered too holy for everyday use, they began using the word *Adonai* which is still used in synagogues.

Perhaps for a while we shall have to do without a name for God. This may seem threatening, but there are biblical precedents for it. Moses apparently felt equally uncomfortable when he was told to go down to Egypt and lead the children of Israel to freedom. He anxiously asked for the name of the One who spoke to him from the burning bush. But the answer given to him was not very comforting. His request was simply refused. He was not given a name at all, but was told rather cryptically that if the captives were curious about who had sent him, he should simply tell them that "I will do what I will do" had sent him (Exodus 3:13–14). At one time this verse was interpreted ontologically. God was revealing Himself as "being itself." But today most Hebrew scholars agree that no metaphysical description is implied. The voice from the bush gives an answer which is intended to be terse and evasive. As Bernhard Anderson says,

> Moses had asked for information about the mystery of the divine nature [the name], but this information had been withheld. Instead God made known his demand . . . and assured him that he would know who God is by what he brings to pass. In other words, the question "Who is God?" would be answered by events that would take place in the future.

The Exodus marked for the Jews a turning point of such elemental power that a new divine name was needed to replace the titles that had grown out of their previous experience. Our transition today from the age of Christendom to the new era of urban secularity will be no less shaking. Rather than clinging stubbornly to antiquated appellations or anxiously synthesizing new ones, perhaps, like Moses, we must simply take up the work of liberating the captives, confident that we will be granted a new name by events of the future.

Further Resources

BOOKS

Cox, Harvey Gallagher. *Just as I Am.* Nashville, Tenn.: Abingdon Press, 1983.

———. *Many Mansions: A Christian's Encounter with Other Faiths.* Boston: Beacon Press, 1992.

———. *The Seduction of the Spirit: The Use and Misuse of People's Religion.* New York: Simon and Schuster, 1973.

PERIODICALS

Bruder, Judith. "Interfaith Encounter." *America,* October 15, 2001, 27.

Genco, Barbara A. "Common Prayers: Faith, Family, and a Christian's Journey through the Jewish Year." *School Library Journal,* December 2001, 56.

"Hunger Pangs." *The Christian Century,* September 12, 2001, 30.

WEBSITES

"745 Boylston St." *Atlantic Online,* November 1995. Available online at http://www.theatlantic.com/issues/95nov/745.htm; website home page: http://www.theatlantic.com (accessed February 4, 2003).

Cox, Harvey. "The Secular City—Ten Years Later." Available online at http://www.religion-online.org/cgi-bin/relsearchd .dll/showarticle?item_id=1861; website home page: http://www.religion-online.org (accessed February 4, 2003).

"The Secular City 25 Years Later." Available online at http://www.religion-online.org/cgi-bin/relsearchd.dll/showarticle ?item_id=206; website home page: http://www.religion-online.org (access February 4, 2003).

World Aflame

Theological work

By: Billy Graham

Date: 1965

Source: Graham, Billy. *World Aflame.* Garden City, N.Y.: Doubleday, 1965, xiii–xvii, 254–257.

About the Author: Billy Graham (1918–), born in Charlotte, North Carolina, was ordained a Southern Baptist minister in 1939. After serving at the First Baptist Church in Western Springs, Illinois, he became a traveling "tent evangelist" noted for his charisma. He was first vice president of Youth for Christ International from 1945 to 1948 and has advised two generations of American presidents. ∎

Introduction

Graham's purpose in writing *World Aflame* was to describe the ways in which the world was "on fire" because of the many social problems consuming the social and moral fiber of America and other nations. A second purpose was to discuss the Christian's role in dealing with these problems in light of biblical teachings. Graham reminded the reader that fire can be used either to destroy humanity or symbolically purify it. He wanted to stir people out of their complacency and into moral action. He pointed out that "Man is precisely what the Bible says he is. Human nature is behaving exactly as the Bible said it would. The course of human events is flowing just as Christ predicted it would."

The biblical philosophy of man and of history, in Graham's view, is that God created the universe but that humans have rebelled against his word and directives. Even though humans rebel, God still loves them and sent his son, Jesus Christ, to redeem the human race. The Bible predicts that at some future time, the Kingdom of God, a time of world peace and goodness, will be established. But, Graham warned, until that time comes, the world would plunge from one crisis to another.

Significance

Graham used the basic content of *World Aflame* during his many evangelistic crusades in the 1960s and in the following decades. His crusades drew thousands of people both in the United States and worldwide, and millions more viewed them on television. His appeal was so universal that religious historians believed that he preached to more people about Jesus Christ than any other person in history.

The popularity of Graham's books and crusades were the result, in large part, of his focus on social problems and moral issues that concerned many people. During one of his crusades, he said, "Now the world today is in a mess. I do not need to tell you that, for you know it. Anyone who can read a newspaper or watch a television set knows that there is something wrong with the world in which we live. One of the great British philosophers, Bertrand Russell, said a few weeks ago, 'I wouldn't give you a fifty-fifty chance that one person will be on this planet forty years from today.' That is the thinking of many of our people today."

Since starting his crusades in the late 1940s, Graham has been consistently viewed as one of the most respected and trusted persons in America. Even those who disagree with his theology respect him as a person and preacher.

Primary Source

World Aflame [excerpt]

SYNOPSIS: *World Aflame* is a Christian analysis of a world filled with riots, demonstrations, threats, wars, and rebellion. The book was an attempt to bring understanding to all these problems. Graham explained why he believed the world was on a collision course and what the generation of the 1960s could do about it. The following excerpts are from the introduction and from Chapter 23, "The World of Tomorrow."

Introduction

At 5:30 A.M. on July 16, 1945, a light brighter than a thousand suns illuminated the desert sands of New Mexico. One scientist who was watching wept. "My God," he exclaimed, "we have created hell." From that day on our world has not been the same. We entered a new era of history—perhaps the last era.

This book attempts to describe our modern world on fire. Fire can either purify or destroy.

The world has been in flames before, but only in a limited sense. Today our world is a common neighborhood, all of it reachable in mere hours by physical flight and in seconds over the airwaves. This accessibility increases the spread of tension and dissension. Thus when the fires of war and lawlessness break out, they leap the national boundaries and cultural differences to become major conflagrations. The whole world is filled with riots, demon-

Famous evangelist William "Billy" Graham, 1963. Graham's *World Aflame* summarized his views about what was wrong with America and the world in the 1960s, and what good Christians should do about it. **AP/WIDE WORLD PHOTOS. REPRODUCED BY PERMISSION.**

strations, threats, wars, and with a rebellion against authority that threatens civilization itself.

It is not the purpose of these pages to identify all the different fires that change and shift with kaleidoscopic speed, but rather to examine the cause of the tensions and conditions feeding them. Newspapers, television screens, and radios portray the unfolding crises of our times. Over and over we ask ourselves, Why? What is the cause? What has happened to our world? Can we do anything about it?

It is the assumption of some *economists* that the cause of a world aflame is to be found in monetary inequities. Redistribute the wealth, they say, and we shall solve our problems. But as Justice Whittaker has pointed out: "Even the distribution of wealth would not solve or long alleviate the human problems that plague us."

It is the assumption of some *diplomats* that the cause of world tension is political and that, if we could attain good will and friendship with all nations, we should solve our problems. In the United Nations we have tried desperately to do just that. Yet the United Nations is proving to be almost as ineffectual as the old League of Nations. The diplomat ignores the evidence that international diplomacy is a record of broken dreams, broken promises, and broken treaties.

It is the assumption of some *educators* that the cause of world tension lies in the lack of knowledge and that if we can only educate every man, peace will come to the world. They say that if man knows better, he will do better. In *The Suicide of the West,* which purports to explain the meaning and destiny of liberalism, James Burnham says that this plea of the educator overlooks entirely certain facts—that Germany, long one of the great cultured nations of the world, produced a Hitler and a Himmler and that Joseph Goebbels had a Doctor of Philosophy degree. Burnham contends that highly educated people have inward drives, greeds, compulsions, passions, and a lust for power that are not eliminated by any known process of education.

It is the assumption of the *sociologist* that bad environment, in the form of poor living conditions such as urban slums and rural poverty areas, is the breeding ground of evil and trouble. Here again Burnham is right when he says that these bad environmental conditions will continue to exist because their substitutes will inevitably turn bad. A slum is not composed simply of run-down buildings. Skid rows can be torn down, but the same people remain to create new ones. Indeed, some of the greater social problems we now face are found in the more affluent areas of suburbia. We are beginning to realize that the problem is deeper than bad environment.

In this book my thesis is based on the Biblical philosophy of man and of history. The more I have traveled around the world the more convinced I have become that the Biblical revelation of man, his origin, his present predicament, and his destiny is true. This book is intentionally controversial. I hope that something of what I have written will shock readers out of apathy into the reality of our desperate condition individually and socially.

Christians must never fall into the trap of thinking that a Bible-based philosophy of world events and world destiny will parallel the world's philosophies. For example, there are few philosophers, politicians, economists, or sociologists who accept Jesus' prophetic account of history as recorded in the twenty-fourth chapter of Matthew. To one who accepts the Biblical account, it is exciting to pick up a newspaper in one hand and the Bible in the other hand and to watch the almost daily fulfillment of prophetic events. Man is precisely what the Bible says he is. Human nature is behaving exactly as the Bible said it would. The course of human events is flowing just as Christ predicted it would.

As a Christian, I am under no obligation to attempt to reconcile the Bible's teachings with modern philosophy. Biblical truth does not parallel human opinion of any generation; it usually opposes it! We are to be witnesses, not imitators. The prophets who spoke to their generations for God did not please and conform; they irritated and opposed.

The Bible's philosophy of man in history begins with God as the Creator of the universe. The Bible presents man as being in rebellion against God. This began when, in an overt act of self-will, our first parents rebelled against divine law. In this experience man ruined his divine image, became alienated from God, and started on a course of action that produced civilizations and cultures saturated with crime, lust, hate, greed, and war. The earth is a planet in rebellion.

The Bible reveals that in spite of man's rebellion God loves him. Thus God undertook the most dramatic rescue operation in cosmic history. He determined to save the human race from self-destruction, and He sent His Son Jesus Christ to salvage and redeem them. The work of man's redemption was accomplished at the cross.

Ultimately, the Bible looks into the future to foresee a new world in which peace and righteousness prevail. There is to be world peace. There is to be a new social order. There is to be a new age. There is to be a completely new man in whom will be no false pride, hate, lust, greed, or prejudice.

This will be the climax of human history. This age will be unlike anything the world has ever known. The Kingdom of God will triumph. The Scripture says: "Nevertheless we, according to his promise, look for new heavens and a new earth, wherein dwelleth righteousness" (II Pet. 3:13).

Until the coming of the new social order in God's direct intervention, the world will continue to plunge from crisis to crisis. In the midst of these trials and tribulations, we must determine which way God is moving in history—and then get in step with God!

In *World Aflame* I can touch only the high spots. I could have written an entire book on the subject of each chapter, especially in those chapters where I discuss the end of the world. I have left much unsaid. Someday I hope to write a book on the subject of "The End."

In theory, the people of the West have various forms of democracy based on a belief in God as well as on a general acceptance of moral law. However, in practice we are beginning to resemble the Marxists, who have little respect for moral law or religion. Our interests are centered in ourselves. We are preoccupied with material things. Our supreme god is technology; our goddess is sex. Most of us are more interested in getting to the moon than in getting to heaven, more concerned about conquering space than about conquering ourselves. We are more dedicated to material security than to inner purity. We give much more thought to what we wear, what we eat, what we drink, and what we can do to relax than we give to what we are. This preoccupation with peripheral things applies to every area of our lives.

World Aflame is an attempt to speak to man in his present situation, to show him how he can find victory over his environment and conquer the downward pull into the infernos of our time.

Today the whole world is on fire! These pages present what I believe to be the Biblical answer to world conflagration. . . .

The World of Tomorrow

The General Electric exhibit at the New York World's Fair of 1964 and 1965 had as its theme song, "There Will Be a Bright Tomorrow." No doubt the producers used this song with tongue in cheek considering the precarious condition of the world. But when the Christian says, "There will be a bright tomorrow," he has no reservations, for God has promised it and "there hath not failed one word of all his good promise" (I Kings 8:56).

The Christian hope is based on two worlds—this world and the next. When these two worlds are in view, we are adequately prepared for a full life here. The Christian has the hope of a life of joy, peace, and outgoing love in the midst of a world of trouble. The Christian has the hope of better living conditions as a result of Christian influence in any society or community. However, the Christian's great and ultimate hope is in the world to come. It is true that a person is not prepared to live until he is prepared to die. Emil Brunner says: "What oxygen is for the lungs such is hope for the meaning of human life." Dr. R. McNair Wilson, a cardiologist, wrote in his autobiography: "Hope is the medicine I use more than any other."

Everywhere in the Bible it is assumed that there will be a next world. The Bible does not argue for its existence or elaborately explain it. Gordon Allport says: "The future is what concerns people most of all." In describing the future of the Christian, the Apostle Paul once said: "Eye hath not seen, nor ear heard, neither have entered into the heart of man, the things which God hath prepared for them that love him" (I Cor. 2:9).

Once the Apostle Paul had a vision of heaven when he saw things "unlawful to utter." This indicates that he could not explain it adequately in language that would be understood. We cannot comprehend the wonders of the next world or correlate its knowledge to that of this world. To do so would be beyond our present capacity to understand. At the close of the Bible it is written: "And I saw a new heaven and a new earth: for the first heaven and the first earth were passed away" (Rev. 21:1).

A New Creation

Everything in respect to heaven will be new. It is described as a new creation in which we shall move in new bodies, possessed of new names, singing new songs, living in a new city, governed by a new form of government, and challenged by new prospects of eternity. The paradise that man lost will be regained, but it will be much more. It will be a new paradise, not the old one repaired and made over. When God says, "Behold, I make all things new," the emphasis is on "all things." We shall live in a brand-new world.

The traditional concept of the "heaven-dweller" is a caricature. We often think of heaven as a place where people sit at a harp, with wings sprouting from their shoulder blades. We have seen pictures of a jewel-studded halo on a man's head, an angelic look on his face, golden streets under his feet, the dazzling beauty of gates of pearl to fill his eyes. This, of course, is not the true nature of the heaven-dweller. He does not live in a static form of life.

Someone has said that on the door of heaven is inscribed: "No admission except on business." Heaven is not all rest. It is labor, adventure, excitement, employment, and engagement. The Scripture says concerning the people in heaven, that "his servants shall serve him" (Rev. 22:3). It will be much like the present life with labor and leisure, but missing all the imperfections that have destroyed the full and true meaning of life.

According to Jesus, life in the future world is related to "many mansions," a term variously understood to mean many places of sojourn, many homes, or many planets to visit. We can read much into this statement of Jesus, but to me it means active, creative, adventuresome living.

Ian McClaren wrote: "Heaven is not a Trappist monastery. Neither is it retirement on pension. No, it is a land of continual progress." Heaven will have many opportunities for endless adventure and abundant creative living.

Time magazine once described the house of the future, calling it "the New Age House." This house was "like none ever built before. Its roof was a honeycomb of tiny solar cells that use the sun's rays to heat the house, furnish all the electric power. Doors and windows opened in response to hand signals; they closed automatically when it rained. The TV set hung like a picture, flat against the wall—so did the heating and air-conditioning panels. The radio was only as big as a golf ball. The telephone was a movielike screen which projected both the caller's image and voice. In the kitchen the range broiled thick steaks in barely two minutes. Dishes and clothes were cleaned without soap or water. The house had no electrical outlets; invisible radio beams ran all appliances. At night, the walls and ceilings glowed softly with glass-encased 'light sandwiches,' which changed color at the twirl of a dial. And throughout the house, tiny, unblinking bulbs of a strange reddish hue sterilized the air and removed all bacteria."

This was written years ago, and some of this dream has already come to pass in many homes. However, the houses of heaven will be far more spectacular. They will be beyond the fondest dream of any housewife.

Sometime ago I visited Rocket City in Texas. It is one of the most fantastic developments in America. It is the place where the astronauts live and train. They showed me some of the capsule food which has been developed for spacemen to use when they go to the moon. One of the scientists laughingly said: "Maybe this is going to be the food of heaven!" The Bible does teach that there will be some kind of food peculiarly adapted to the bodies of those who will live in heaven, for the book of Revelation speaks of "a tree of life which bore twelve manner of fruits." . . .

However, the most thrilling thing to me about heaven is that Jesus Christ will be there. I will see Him face to face. I will have the opportunity to talk directly to Him and to ask Him a hundred questions that I have never had answered.

Further Resources

BOOKS
Graham, Billy. *The Faith of Billy Graham.* Anderson, S.C.: Droke House, 1968.

High, Stanley. *Billy Graham: The Personal Story of the Man, His Message, and His Mission.* New York: McGraw-Hill, 1956.

Pollock, John C. *Billy Graham: The Authorized Biography.* New York: McGraw-Hill, 1966.

PERIODICALS
Banks, Adelle M. "Graham, Calls Bigotry a Sin: Evangelist Calls for Racial Healing." *Christianity Today,* August 5, 2002, 19.

"Billy Graham: A Tribute from Friends." *Publishers Weekly,* April 1, 2002, 76.

Elliott, William J. "A Place at the Table: A Journey to Rediscover the Real Jesus with the Guidance of Various Teachers from Billy Graham to Deepak Chopra." *Publishers Weekly,* July 15, 2002, 67.

WEBSITES
Billy Graham Center archives home page. Available online at http://www.wheaton.edu/bgc/archives/archhp1.html (accessed February 4, 2003).

Billy Graham Evangelistic Association. "Decision Today." Available online at www.decisiontoday.org (accessed February 4, 2003).

Billy Graham Training Center. "The Cove." Available online at http://www.thecove.org/ (accessed February 4, 2003).

Humanae Vitae: Encyclical of Pope Paul VI on the Regulation of Birth

Papal encyclical

By: Pope Paul VI

Date: July 25, 1968

Source: Pope Paul VI. *Humanae Vitae:* Encyclical of Pope Paul VI on the Regulation of Birth. Rome, July 25, 1968. Available online at http://www.vatican.va (accessed February 5, 2003).

About the Author: Pope Paul VI (1897–1978) was born in Concesio, Italy, as Giovanni Battista Montini. He was ordained as a priest in 1920 and assigned to the Vatican diplomatic service until 1944. He became an archbishop in 1954 and a cardinal in 1958. Elected pope in 1963 after the death of Pope John XXIII, he served until he died in 1978. Pope Paul VI was known for his support of Christian unity and social reform. ∎

Introduction

Roman Catholic Church encyclicals had always expressed the belief that abortion and artificial means of birth control (for example, sterilization, birth control pills, and other contraceptive devices) were serious sins, violations of the natural law and the will of God. Before

Pope Paul VI issued *Humanae Vitae* in 1968, some Catholics and others expected that the encyclical might include some liberalization of the church's teachings. This expectation was based on the work of a commission of theologians and laymen formed by Pope John XXIII to study the issue. This commission, continued by Pope Paul VI, was to report back to the pope. A year before the encyclical was released, the press reported that most members of the commission were in favor of liberalizing the church's stance on birth control.

The encyclical, however, rejected the commission's recommendations. Pope Paul VI reasoned that because God intended the sexual act to be the means for procreation, it must always be open to the transmission of life. Birth control and abortion interfere with this natural process, although the encyclical does permit married people to take advantage of the "natural cycles immanent in the reproductive system and engage in marital intercourse only during those times that are infertile." Controlling birth in that manner, the pope said, does not in any way offend the moral principles established by God because there was no interference with the possibility, even though remote, that a life would be conceived.

Significance

Humanae Vitae turned out to be possibly the most controversial papal encyclical of the twentieth century. To many Catholics, the encyclical was very personal because it directly addressed the behaviors of Catholics rather than abstract theological issues.

As many Catholics and observers outside the church had predicted, Catholics reacted to the encyclical in one of three ways. Some wholeheartedly endorsed the pronouncement by the pope and would follow all the church's teachings on abortion and birth control without any objections. Others decided to abide by the abortion prohibition but left their decision about birth control methods up to their own conscience or their own interpretation of Christian morality. Many of these people remained true to the church's teachings in all other respects and continued to practice Catholicism by attending weekly mass. Critics of this second group called them "cafeteria Catholics," choosing which teachings they would accept and which they would reject. A third group rejected the encyclical's pronouncements about both abortion and birth control. They believed that abortion and birth control were private decisions and not open to scrutiny by the church. Some of these people continued to identify themselves as Catholics, but others gradually drifted away from the church.

Opinion polls and observations by the Roman Catholic clergy in local churches in the 1980s and 1990s found that many Catholics in America continued to dis-

agree with the church's prohibition on artificial birth control and continued to use these methods.

Primary Source

Humanae Vitae: Encyclical of Pope Paul VI on the Regulation of Birth [excerpt]

SYNOPSIS: This famous and controversial encyclical reinforced the Roman Catholic Church's opposition to abortion and "artificial means of birth control," which the church defined as immoral and opposed to natural law and the will of God. Pope Paul VI explained the distinction between "unlawful birth control methods" and "lawful therapeutic means." The encyclical consisted of thirty-one statements; statements 7 to 16 are included here.

Doctrinal Principles

7. The question of human procreation, like every other question which touches human life, involves more than the limited aspects specific to such disciplines as biology, psychology, demography or sociology. It is the whole man and the whole mission to which he is called that must be considered: both its natural, earthly aspects and its supernatural, eternal aspects. And since in the attempt to justify artificial methods of birth control many appeal to the demands of married love or of responsible parenthood, these two important realities of married life must be accurately defined and analyzed. This is what We mean to do, with special reference to what the Second Vatican Council taught with the highest authority in its Pastoral Constitution on the Church in the World of Today.

God's Loving Design

8. Married love particularly reveals its true nature and nobility when we realize that it takes its origin from God, who "is love," the Father "from whom every family in heaven and on earth is named."

Marriage, then, is far from being the effect of chance or the result of the blind evolution of natural forces. It is in reality the wise and provident institution of God the Creator, whose purpose was to effect in man His loving design. As a consequence, husband and wife, through that mutual gift of themselves, which is specific and exclusive to them alone, develop that union of two persons in which they perfect one another, cooperating with God in the generation and rearing of new lives.

The marriage of those who have been baptized is, in addition, invested with the dignity of a sacramental sign of grace, for it represents the union of Christ and His Church.

Married Love

9. In the light of these facts the characteristic features and exigencies of married love are clearly indicated, and it is of the highest importance to evaluate them exactly.

This love is above all fully human, a compound of sense and spirit. It is not, then, merely a question of natural instinct or emotional drive. It is also, and above all, an act of the free will, whose trust is such that it is meant not only to survive the joys and sorrows of daily life, but also to grow, so that husband and wife become in a way one heart and one soul, and together attain their human fulfillment.

It is a love which is total—that very special form of personal friendship in which husband and wife generously share everything, allowing no unreasonable exceptions and not thinking solely of their own convenience. Whoever really loves his partner loves not only for what he receives, but loves that partner for the partner's own sake, content to be able to enrich the other with the gift of himself.

Married love is also faithful and exclusive of all other, and this until death. This is how husband and wife understood it on the day on which, fully aware of what they were doing, they freely vowed themselves to one another in marriage. Though this fidelity of husband and wife sometimes presents difficulties, no one has the right to assert that it is impossible; it is, on the contrary, always honorable and meritorious. The example of countless married couples proves not only that fidelity is in accord with the nature of marriage, but also that it is the source of profound and enduring happiness.

Finally, this love is fecund. It is not confined wholly to the loving interchange of husband and wife; it also contrives to go beyond this to bring new life into being. "Marriage and conjugal love are by their nature ordained toward the procreation and education of children. Children are really the supreme gift of marriage and contribute in the highest degree to their parents' welfare."

Responsible Parenthood

10. Married love, therefore, requires of husband and wife the full awareness of their obligations in the matter of responsible parenthood, which today, rightly enough, is much insisted upon, but which at the same time should be rightly understood. Thus, we do well to consider responsible parenthood in the light of its varied legitimate and interrelated aspects.

With regard to the biological processes, responsible parenthood means an awareness of, and respect for, their proper functions. In the procreative faculty the human mind discerns biological laws that apply to the human person.

With regard to man's innate drives and emotions, responsible parenthood means that man's reason and will must exert control over them.

With regard to physical, economic, psychological and social conditions, responsible parenthood is exercised by those who prudently and generously decide to have more children, and by those who, for serious reasons and with due respect to moral precepts, decide not to have additional children for either a certain or an indefinite period of time.

Responsible parenthood, as we use the term here, has one further essential aspect of paramount importance. It concerns the objective moral order which was established by God, and of which a right conscience is the true interpreter. In a word, the exercise of responsible parenthood requires that husband and wife, keeping a right order of priorities, recognize their own duties toward God, themselves, their families and human society.

From this it follows that they are not free to act as they choose in the service of transmitting life, as if it were wholly up to them to decide what is the right course to follow. On the contrary, they are bound to ensure that what they do corresponds to the will of God the Creator. The very nature of marriage and its use makes His will clear, while the constant teaching of the Church spells it out.

Observing the Natural Law

11. The sexual activity, in which husband and wife are intimately and chastely united with one another, through which human life is transmitted, is, as the recent Council recalled, "noble and worthy." It does not, moreover, cease to be legitimate even when, for reasons independent of their will, it is foreseen to be infertile. For its natural adaptation to the expression and strengthening of the union of husband and wife is not thereby suppressed. The fact is, as experience shows, that new life is not the result of each and every act of sexual intercourse. God has wisely ordered laws of nature and the incidence of fertility in such a way that successive births are already naturally spaced through the inherent operation of these laws. The Church, nevertheless, in urging men to the observance of the precepts of the natural law, which it interprets by its constant doctrine, teaches that each and every marital act must

of necessity retain its intrinsic relationship to the procreation of human life.

Union and Procreation

12. This particular doctrine, often expounded by the magisterium of the Church, is based on the inseparable connection, established by God, which man on his own initiative may not break, between the unitive significance and the procreative significance which are both inherent to the marriage act.

The reason is that the fundamental nature of the marriage act, while uniting husband and wife in the closest intimacy, also renders them capable of generating new life—and this as a result of laws written into the actual nature of man and of woman. And if each of these essential qualities, the unitive and the procreative, is preserved, the use of marriage fully retains its sense of true mutual love and its ordination to the supreme responsibility of parenthood to which man is called. We believe that our contemporaries are particularly capable of seeing that this teaching is in harmony with human reason.

Faithfulness to God's Design

13. Men rightly observe that a conjugal act imposed on one's partner without regard to his or her condition or personal and reasonable wishes in the matter, is no true act of love, and therefore offends the moral order in its particular application to the intimate relationship of husband and wife. If they further reflect, they must also recognize that an act of mutual love which impairs the capacity to transmit life which God the Creator, through specific laws, has built into it, frustrates His design which constitutes the norm of marriage, and contradicts the will of the Author of life. Hence to use this divine gift while depriving it, even if only partially, of its meaning and purpose, is equally repugnant to the nature of man and of woman, and is consequently in opposition to the plan of God and His holy will. But to experience the gift of married love while respecting the laws of conception is to acknowledge that one is not the master of the sources of life but rather the minister of the design established by the Creator. Just as man does not have unlimited dominion over his body in general, so also, and with more particular reason, he has no such dominion over his specifically sexual faculties, for these are concerned by their very nature with the generation of life, of which God is the source. "Human life is sacred—all men must recognize that fact," Our predecessor Pope John XXIII recalled. "From its very inception it reveals the creating hand of God."

Pope Paul VI greets delegates, Vatican City, Rome, October, 1969. Pope Paul VI's famous and controversial encyclical *Humanae Vitae* (1968) reinforced the Catholic Church's opposition to artificial birth control. © TED SPIEGEL/CORBIS. REPRODUCED BY PERMISSION.

Unlawful Birth Control Methods

14. Therefore We base Our words on the first principles of a human and Christian doctrine of marriage when We are obliged once more to declare that the direct interruption of the generative process already begun and, above all, all direct abortion, even for therapeutic reasons, are to be absolutely excluded as lawful means of regulating the number of children. Equally to be condemned, as the magisterium of the Church has affirmed on many occasions, is direct sterilization, whether of the man or of the woman, whether permanent or temporary.

Similarly excluded is any action which either before, at the moment of, or after sexual intercourse, is specifically intended to prevent procreation—whether as an end or as a means.

Neither is it valid to argue, as a justification for sexual intercourse which is deliberately contraceptive, that a lesser evil is to be preferred to a greater one, or that such intercourse would merge with procreative acts of past and future to form a single entity, and so be qualified by exactly the same moral goodness as these. Though it is true that sometimes it is lawful to tolerate a lesser moral evil in order to avoid a greater evil or in order to promote a greater good, "it is never lawful, even for the gravest reasons, to do evil that good may come of it"—in other words, to intend directly something which of its very nature contradicts the moral order, and which must therefore be judged unworthy of man, even though the intention is to protect or promote the welfare of an individual, of a family or of society in general. Consequently, it is a serious error to think that a whole married life of otherwise normal relations can justify sexual intercourse which is deliberately contraceptive and so intrinsically wrong.

Lawful Therapeutic Means

15. On the other hand, the Church does not consider at all illicit the use of those therapeutic means necessary to cure bodily diseases, even if a foreseeable impediment to procreation should result therefrom—provided such impediment is not directly intended for any motive whatsoever.

Recourse to Infertile Periods

16. Now as We noted earlier (no. 3), some people today raise the objection against this particular doctrine of the Church concerning the moral laws governing marriage, that human intelligence has both the right and responsibility to control those forces of irrational nature which come within its ambit and to direct them toward ends beneficial to man. Others ask on the same point whether it is not reasonable in so many cases to use artificial birth control if by so doing the harmony and peace of a family are better served and more suitable conditions are provided for the education of children already born. To this question We must give a clear reply. The Church is the first to praise and commend the application of human intelligence to an activity in which a rational creature such as man is so closely associated with his Creator. But she affirms that this must be done within the limits of the order of reality established by God.

If therefore there are well-grounded reasons for spacing births, arising from the physical or psychological condition of husband or wife, or from external circumstances, the Church teaches that married people may then take advantage of the natural cycles immanent in the reproductive system and engage in marital intercourse only during those times that are infertile, thus controlling birth in a way which does not in the least offend the moral principles which We have just explained.

Neither the Church nor her doctrine is inconsistent when she considers it lawful for married people to take advantage of the infertile period but condemns as always unlawful the use of means which directly prevent conception, even when the reasons given for the later practice may appear to be upright and serious. In reality, these two cases are completely different. In the former the married couple rightly use a faculty provided them by nature. In the latter they obstruct the natural development of the generative process. It cannot be denied that in each case the married couple, for acceptable reasons, are both perfectly clear in their intention to avoid children and wish to make sure that none will result. But it is equally true that it is exclusively in the former case that husband and wife are ready to abstain from intercourse during the fertile period as often as for reasonable motives the birth of another child is not desirable. And when the infertile period recurs, they use their married intimacy to express their mutual love and safeguard their fidelity toward one another. In doing this they certainly give proof of a true and authentic love.

Further Resources

BOOKS
Hatch, Alden. *Pope Paul VI.* New York: Random House, 1966.

Hebblethwaite, Peter. *Paul VI: The First Modern Pope.* New York: Paulist Press, 1993.

Tyler, Edward T., ed. *Birth Control: A Continuing Controversy.* Springfield, Ill.: Thomas, 1967.

PERIODICALS
Sullivan, Robert E. "Paul VI: The First Modern Pope." *America,* May 1, 1993, 18.

WEBSITES
Jensen, Tom. "Birth Control." Available online at http://www.catholic-defense.com/birthcontrol.htm (accessed February 5, 2003). This site contains links to numerous articles about church history and doctrine.

McManus, Mike. "Pope Paul VI Was Right on Contraception." Available online at http://www.lifecorner.org/contraception3.html; website home page: http://www.lifecorner.org/index.html (accessed February 5, 2003).

O'Malley, Martin, Owen Wood, and Amy Foulkes. "The Pill and Us." *Backgrounder: CBC News Indepth.* Available online at http://cbc.ca/news/indepth/background/birthcontrol_pill.html; website home page: http://www.cbc.ca/ (accessed February 5, 2003).

Epperson v. Arkansas

Supreme Court decision

By: Abe Fortas

Date: November 12, 1968

Source: *Epperson v. Arkansas,* 393 U.S. 97 (1968). Available online at http://caselaw.lp.findlaw.com/scripts/getcase.pl ?court=US&navby;=case&vol;=393&invol;=97 (accessed February 4, 2003).

About the Author: Abe Fortas (1910–1982) was born in Memphis, Tennessee. After earning his law degree from Yale in 1933, he taught there until 1937. He held several government posts, including undersecretary of the interior from 1942 to 1946. He then entered private law practice. In 1965, he was appointed to the U.S. Supreme Court, where he served until 1969. ∎

Introduction

In 1928, Arkansas passed a statute that prohibited teaching in public schools and universities the theory that humans evolved from other species. Violation of the statute was a misdemeanor and left the teacher open to dismissal. In the mid-1960s, Susan Epperson, a teacher in the Little Rock school system, was assigned a textbook that contained a chapter about the principles of evolution. Since it would have been a criminal offense for her to use that chapter, she brought her case to state court, which declared that the statute violated the U.S. Constitution. Upon appeal, however, the Arkansas Supreme Court reversed the decision of the lower court. Epperson and her supporters appealed to the U.S. Supreme Court.

Justice Abe Fortas delivered the majority opinion for the Court, which found the Arkansas law unconstitutional because it violated two key provisions of the First Amendment to the Constitution: the establishment clause, which prohibits the state from imposing any particular religious creed; and the free exercise clause, which prohibits the state from interfering with a person's religious beliefs. The Court held that because the Arkansas law forced the beliefs of creationists on public school students, it violated the establishment clause. And since the law disallowed other religious explanations of the creation of humanity, it violated the free exercise clause. In sum, the Arkansas law was not neutral about religion and therefore violated the principle of separation of church and state.

A similar case arose in 1925 when teacher John Scopes was put on trial for violating Tennessee's Butler Act, which made it a crime to teach any theory that denied creationism. After teaching about evolution, Scopes was tried (in the famous "Scopes Monkey Trial"), found guilty, and fined $100, but because of a legal error, the conviction was later reversed. The Tennessee state legislature abolished the law in 1967.

Significance

In the 1960s, *Epperson v. Arkansas* definitively settled the legal issue about whether the teaching of evolution could be banned in public schools. The battle between creationists and evolutionists did not abate, however. Creationists, generally conservative Christians, base their beliefs about the creation of humans on the Bible. Some interpret the Bible literally, others less so, but all believe that God created man and woman as distinct creations, not as evolutionary descendants of apes and other primates. They hold that each species or life-form has stayed largely unchanged since God created it. They deny that any species has evolved from any other and reject theories of evolution, whether those proposed by Charles Darwin (1809–1882) in *The Origin of the Species* (1859) or by modern scientists.

Evolutionists believe that life on earth arose through the processes of evolution—that all living things, including humans, evolved from simpler organisms, including humans. Humans today are physically different from earlier humans because modern humans are the end products of millions of years of gradual change. Evolutionists consist of people from a wide variety of scientific disciplines; some believe in God, others do not. They are likely to adhere to less fundamentalist branches of Christianity, which do not see any contradiction between a belief in God and the theory of evolution.

Primary Source

Epperson v. Arkansas [excerpt]

> **SYNOPSIS:** In the following excerpts, Justice Abe Fortas presented the Court's reasons for striking down Arkansas's law prohibiting the teaching of evolution as a violation of the U.S. Constitution. The message of the court was that the state could not establish which theories concerning creation could or could not be taught in public school because to do so would violate the First Amendment of the Constitution.

Appellant Epperson, an Arkansas public school teacher, brought this action for declaratory and injunctive relief challenging the constitutionality of Arkansas' "anti-evolution" statute. That statute makes it unlawful for a teacher in any state-supported school or university to teach or to use a textbook that teaches "that mankind ascended or descended from a lower order of animals."

The State Chancery Court held the statute an abridgment of free speech violating the First and Fourteenth Amendments. The State Supreme Court, expressing no opinion as to whether the statute prohibits "explanation" of the theory or only teaching that the theory is true, reversed the Chancery Court. In a two-sentence opinion it sustained the statute as within the State's power to specify the public school curriculum. Held: The statute violates the Fourteenth Amendment, which embraces the First Amendment's prohibition of state laws respecting an establishment of religion. pp. 102–109.

a. The Court does not decide whether the statute is unconstitutionally vague, since, whether it is construed to prohibit explaining the Darwinian theory or teaching that it is true, the law conflicts with the Establishment Clause. pp. 102–103.

b. The sole reason for the Arkansas law is that a particular religious group considers the evolution theory to conflict with the account of the origin of man set forth in the Book of Genesis. pp. 103, 107–109.

c. The First Amendment mandates governmental neutrality between religion and religion, and between religion and nonreligion. pp. 103–107.

d. A State's right to prescribe the public school curriculum does not include the right to prohibit teaching a scientific theory or doctrine for reasons that run counter to the principles of the First Amendment. p. 107.

e. The Arkansas law is not a manifestation of religious neutrality. p. 109. . . .

Mr. Justice Fortas delivered the opinion of the Court.

This appeal challenges the constitutionality of the "anti-evolution" statute which the State of Arkansas adopted in 1928 to prohibit the teaching in its public schools and universities of the theory that man evolved from other species of life. The statute was a product of the upsurge of "fundamentalist" religious fervor of the twenties.

The Arkansas statute was an adaptation of the famous Tennessee "monkey law" which that State adopted in 1925. The constitutionality of the Tennessee law was upheld by the Tennessee Supreme Court in the celebrated Scopes case in 1927. The Arkansas law makes it unlawful for a teacher in any state-supported school or university "to teach the [393 U.S. 97, 99] theory or doctrine that mankind ascended or descended from a lower order of animals," or "to adopt or use in any such institution a textbook that teaches" this theory. Violation is a misdemeanor and subjects the violator to dismissal from his position.

The present case concerns the teaching of biology in a high school in Little Rock. According to the testimony, until the events here in litigation, the official textbook furnished for the high school biology course did not have a section on the Darwinian Theory. Then, for the academic year 1965–1966, the school administration, on recommendation of the teachers of biology in the school system, adopted and prescribed a textbook which contained a chapter setting forth "the theory about the origin . . . of man from a lower form of animal." [393 U.S. 97, 100]

Susan Epperson, a young woman who graduated from Arkansas' school system and then obtained her master's degree in zoology at the University of Illinois, was employed by the Little Rock school system in the fall of 1964 to teach 10th grade biology at Central High School. At the start of the next academic year, 1965, she was confronted by the new textbook (which one surmises from the record was not unwelcome to her). She faced at least a literal dilemma because she was supposed to use the new textbook for classroom instruction and presumably to teach the statutorily condemned chapter; but to do so would be a criminal offense and subject her to dismissal.

She instituted the present action in the Chancery Court of the State, seeking a declaration that the Arkansas statute is void and enjoining the State and the defendant officials of the Little Rock school system from dismissing her for violation of the statute's provisions. H. H. Blanchard, a parent of children attending the public schools, intervened in support of the action.

The Chancery Court, in an opinion by Chancellor Murray O. Reed, held that the statute violated the Fourteenth Amendment to the United States Constitution. The court noted that this Amendment encompasses the prohibitions upon state interference with freedom of speech and thought which are contained in the First Amendment. Accordingly, it held that the challenged statute is unconstitutional because, in violation of the First Amendment, it "tends to hinder the quest for knowledge, restrict the freedom to learn, and restrain the freedom to teach." In this perspective, the Act, [393 U.S. 97, 101] it held, was an unconstitutional and void restraint upon the freedom of speech guaranteed by the Constitution.

On appeal, the Supreme Court of Arkansas reversed. Its two-sentence opinion is set forth in the margin. It sustained the statute as an exercise of

Susan Epperson in her Little Rock Central High School classroom in August 1966. Epperson sued the state of Arkansas, challenging a law that prohibited the teaching of evolution. The Supreme Court struck down the Arkansas law as unconstitutional in 1968. **AP/WIDE WORLD PHOTOS. REPRODUCED BY PERMISSION.**

the State's power to specify the curriculum in public schools. It did not address itself to the competing constitutional considerations.

Appeal was duly prosecuted to this Court under 28 U.S.C. 1257. Only Arkansas and Mississippi have such "anti-evolution" or "monkey" laws on their books. There is no record of any prosecutions in Arkansas [393 U.S. 97, 102] under its statute. It is possible that the statute is presently more of a curiosity than a vital fact of life in these States. Nevertheless, the present case was brought, the appeal

as of right is properly here, and it is our duty to decide the issues presented.

At the outset, it is urged upon us that the challenged statute is vague and uncertain and therefore within the condemnation of the Due Process Clause of the Fourteenth Amendment. The contention that the Act is vague and uncertain is supported by language in the brief opinion of Arkansas' Supreme Court. That court, perhaps reflecting the discomfort which the statute's quixotic prohibition necessarily engenders in the modern mind, stated that it "expresses no opinion" as to whether the Act prohibits "explanation" of the theory of evolution or merely forbids "teaching that the theory is true." Regardless of this uncertainty, the court held that the statute is constitutional.

On the other hand, counsel for the State, in oral argument in this Court, candidly stated that, despite the State Supreme Court's equivocation, Arkansas would interpret the statute "to mean that to make a student aware of the theory . . . just to teach that there was [393 U.S. 97, 103] such a theory" would be grounds for dismissal and for prosecution under the statute; and he said "that the Supreme Court of Arkansas' opinion should be interpreted in that manner." He said: "If Mrs. Epperson would tell her students that 'Here is Darwin's theory, that man ascended or descended from a lower form of being,' then I think she would be under this statute liable for prosecution."

In any event, we do not rest our decision upon the asserted vagueness of the statute. On either interpretation of its language, Arkansas' statute cannot stand. It is of no moment whether the law is deemed to prohibit mention of Darwin's theory, or to forbid any or all of the infinite varieties of communication embraced within the term "teaching."

Under either interpretation, the law must be stricken because of its conflict with the constitutional prohibition of state laws respecting an establishment of religion or prohibiting the free exercise thereof. The overriding fact is that Arkansas' law selects from the body of knowledge a particular segment which it proscribes for the sole reason that it is deemed to conflict with a particular religious doctrine; that is, with a particular interpretation of the Book of Genesis by a particular religious group.

The antecedents of today's decision are many and unmistakable. They are rooted in the foundation soil of our Nation. They are fundamental to freedom.

Government in our democracy, state and national, must be neutral in matters of religious theory, doctrine, [303 U.S. 97, 104] and practice. It may not be hostile to any religion or to the advocacy of no-religion; and it may not aid, foster, or promote one religion or religious theory against another or even against the militant opposite. The First Amendment mandates governmental neutrality between religion and religion, and between religion and nonreligion. . . .

There is and can be no doubt that the First Amendment does not permit the State to require that teaching and learning must be tailored to the principles or prohibitions of any religious sect or dogma. In *Everson v. Board of Education,* this Court, in upholding a state law to provide free bus service to school children, including those attending parochial schools, said: "Neither [a State nor the Federal Government] can pass laws which aid one religion, aid all religions, or prefer one religion over another." 330 U.S. 1, 15 (1947).

At the following Term of Court, in *McCollum v. Board of Education,* 333 U.S. 203 (1948), the Court held that Illinois could not release pupils from class to attend classes of instruction in the religion of their choice. This, it said, would involve the State in using tax-supported property for religious purposes, thereby breaching the "wall of separation" which, according to Jefferson, the First Amendment was intended to erect between church and state. See also *Engel v. Vitale,* 370 U.S. 421 (1962); *Abington School District v. Schempp,* 374 U.S. 203 (1963).

While study of religions and of the Bible from a literary and historic viewpoint, presented objectively as part of a secular program of education, need not collide with the First Amendment's prohibition, the State may not adopt programs or practices in its public schools or colleges which "aid or oppose" any religion. Id. at 205. This prohibition is absolute. It forbids alike the preference of a religious doctrine or the prohibition [393 U.S. 97, 107] of theory which is deemed antagonistic to a particular dogma.

As Mr. Justice Clark stated in *Joseph Burstyn, Inc. v. Wilson,* "the state has no legitimate interest in protecting any or all religions from views distasteful to them. . . ." 343 U.S. 495, 505 (1950). The test was stated as follows in *Abington School District v. Schempp,* supra, at 222: "What are the purpose and the primary effect of the enactment? If either is the advancement or inhibition of religion then the enactment exceeds the scope of legislative power as circumscribed by the Constitution."

These precedents inevitably determine the result in the present case. The State's undoubted right to prescribe the curriculum for its public schools does not carry with it the right to prohibit, on pain of criminal penalty, the teaching of a scientific theory or doctrine where that prohibition is based upon reasons that violate the First Amendment. It is much too late to argue that the State may impose upon the teachers in its schools any conditions that it chooses, however restrictive they may be of constitutional guarantees. *Keyishian v. Board of Regents*, 385 U.S. 589, 605–606 (1967).

In the present case, there can be no doubt that Arkansas has sought to prevent its teachers from discussing the theory of evolution because it is contrary to the belief of some that the Book of Genesis must be the exclusive source of doctrine as to the origin of man. No suggestion has been made that Arkansas' law may be justified by considerations of state policy other than the religious views of some of its citizens. It is clear [393 U.S. 97, 108] that fundamentalist sectarian conviction was and is the law's reason for existence.

Its antecedent, Tennessee's "monkey law," candidly stated its purpose: to make it unlawful "to teach any theory that denies the story of the Divine Creation of man as taught in the Bible, and to teach instead that man has descended from a [393 U.S. 97, 109] lower order of animals." Perhaps the sensational publicity attendant upon the Scopes trial induced Arkansas to adopt less explicit language. It eliminated Tennessee's reference to "the story of the Divine Creation of man" as taught in the Bible, but there is no doubt that the motivation for the law was the same: to suppress the teaching of a theory which, it was thought, "denied" the divine creation of man.

Arkansas' law cannot be defended as an act of religious neutrality. Arkansas did not seek to excise from the curricula of its schools and universities all discussion of the origin of man. The law's effort was confined to an attempt to blot out a particular theory because of its supposed conflict with the Biblical account, literally read. Plainly, the law is contrary to the mandate of the First, and in violation of the Fourteenth Amendment to the Constitution.

The judgment of the Supreme Court of Arkansas is Reversed.

Further Resources

BOOKS

Corey, Michael Anthony. *The Natural History of Creation: Biblical Evolutionism and the Return of Natural Theology.* Lanham, Md.: University Press of America, 1995.

Durant, John R. *Darwinism and Divinity: Essays on Evolution and Religious Belief.* Oxford, New York: Blackwell, 1985.

Leone, Bruno J., ed. *Creationism vs. Evolution.* San Diego, Calif.: Greenhaven Press, 2002.

WEBSITES

Questia, the Online Library. "Creationism." Available online at http://www.questia.com/Index.jsp?CRID=creationism&OF FID;=se1 (accessed February 4, 2003). *This site contains links to books and articles on creationism.*

Syracuse University. "Evolution v. Creationism" home page. Available online at http://physics.syr.edu/courses/modules /ORIGINS/origins.html (accessed February 4, 2003). *This site contains links to numerous resources about creationism and evolution.*

Washington Post. "Education: Creationism v. Evolution." Available online at http://www.washingtonpost.com/wp-dyn /education/specials/policy/creationism/; website home page: http://www.washingtonpost.com (accessed February 4, 2003). *This site contains links to recent news articles about the debate.*

11

SCIENCE AND TECHNOLOGY

CHRISTOPHER CUMO

Entries are arranged in chronological order by date of primary source. For entries with one primary source, the entry title is the same as the primary source title. Entries with more than one primary source have an overall entry title, followed by the titles of the primary sources.

continents move on plates—hence the name continental drift.

• In October, a power station in Dresden, Illinois, becomes the first commercial nuclear power plant to use a boiling-water reactor to produce steam which spins a turbine to generate electricity.

1961

• Bell Laboratories produces the first computer designed by another computer.

• IBM markets its "golf ball" Selectric typewriter.

• Quartz iodide and quartz bromide lamps are used in film projectors. They are brighter than filament lamps and withstand higher temperatures.

• On January 31, NASA launches a chimpanzee into space. The rocket travels 5,000 mph and reaches a height of 155 miles.

• In February, the U.S. Patent Office grants Texas Instruments a patent on the first silicon chip for electronic circuits.

• In February, psychologist James V. McConnell sends a worm through a maze, then feeds it to other worms. McConnell claims, after sending these worms through the same maze, that they had absorbed the memory of the maze from the worm they ate.

• In March, the U.S. Navy launches the USS *Enterprise* aircraft carrier, powered by eight nuclear reactors. It can travel for three years and two hundred thousand miles between stops.

• In April, physicist Albert Ghiorso leads a team of researchers in producing the element lawrencium, named after American physicist and 1939 Nobel laureate Ernest O. Lawrence, at Lawrence Berkeley Radiation Laboratory in California.

• On April 12, The Soviet Union lauches Yuri Gagarin, the first man into Space with the object of being the first nation to send a man to the moon.

• In May, geneticist Marshall W. Nirenberg asserts that every three nucleotide bases in a strand of DNA code for the production of an amino acid.

• On May 5, NASA launches Alan Shepard, Jr., into space.

• On May 25, President John F. Kennedy, in his second State of the Union address, urges Congress to land a man on the moon by decade's end.

• In June, C. Roger Lynds at the National Radio Astronomy Observatory at Greenbank, West Virginia, detects radio waves from nebulae, regions in space that contain large amounts of gas and possibly stars.

• On June 29, NASA launches three satellites from one rocket for the first time in history.

• In August, the barge *Cuss I* drills 2.2 miles into the ocean bottom for samples of rock beneath the ocean floor.

• On December 11, American physicist Robert Hofstadter wins the Nobel Prize in physics for describing the structure of protons and neutrons in the nucleus of an atom.

Important Events in Science and Technology, 1960–1969

1960

• The first American use of geothermal power begins near San Francisco, employing steam under high pressure to produce electricity.

• The meter is redefined according to a wavelength in the spectrum of the gas krypton.

• On January 2, after studying a meteorite that had fallen in North Dakota in 1919, Dr. John H. Reynolds of the University of California estimates the age of the solar system to be 4.95 billion years.

• On January 12, General Electric introduces a thermoplastic tape capable of recording video and audio signals simultaneously.

• On January 23, the bathyscaphe *Trieste* plunges to the deepest part of Pacific Ocean, almost seven miles deep.

• In February, the U.S. Navy launches the USS *George Washington*, which carries sixteen Polaris missiles. The first nuclear submarine to carry nuclear warheads, it is able to attack anywhere at any time from an undetected location.

• In April, physicist Luis Alvarez identifies short-lived particles smaller than the subatomic protons, neutrons, and electrons as "resonances." The resonance might be a particle or several particles associated with each other.

• On April 1, the National Aeronautics and Space Administration (NASA) launches *Tiros 1*, the first weather satellite.

• On May 10, the USS *Triton*, a nuclear submarine, completes an eighty-four-day journey around the world without surfacing. A computer, knowing the starting point, speeds, and directions, maps its location at all times.

• In July, physicist Theodore H. Maimen develops the laser. The laser is a concentrated beam of light with sufficient energy to bore through solids.

• On August 12, NASA launches the *ECHO 1*, a communications satellite that reflects signals to receptors on earth.

• In August, astronomer Allan Sundage finds an object in a region of the sky known as 3C48 that emits radio waves.

• In August, Harvard University physicists confirm Albert Einstein's Special Theory of Relativity, which states that time ticks at different rates for objects moving at different speeds.

• In October, oceanographer Harry H. Hess proposes his theory of seafloor spreading, which corroborates the idea that

1962

- NASA abandons building the Sugar Grove radio telescope, begun in 1959, after spending $96 million. NASA had intended it to spy on the Soviets, but other satellites make Sugar Grove obsolete before NASA can complete it.

- In response to the Soviets shooting down the U-2 spy plane with Francis Gary Powers aboard in 1960, the U.S. Air Force develops the Model 147 airplane. Piloted by remote control, the plane does reconnaissance without endangering U.S. pilots.

- Kelvinator produces a dishwasher that uses neither soap nor water.

- Peter van de Kamp studies two thousand photos of Barnard's Star, looking at the "wobble" in its position over time. He concludes there is a planet orbiting the star.

- Rachel L. Carson publishes her book *Silent Spring,* which warns that insecticides and herbicides are damaging the environment.

- A molded car seat is made for children.

- Digital Equipment Corporation develops the third generation of computers.

- A braille typewriter is developed for blind people.

- In February, Harry H. Hess shows that convection currents in the Earth's mantle cause seafloor spreading. This evidence strengthens the theory of continental drift.

- On February 20, U.S. Marine Colonel John Glenn becomes the first American to orbit the Earth.

- On May 1, William Luyten of the University of Minnesota announces the discovery of the smallest known star, a white dwarf, designated LP 327-186.

- On May 2, NASA's space probe *Mariner 2* reaches Venus 109 days after its launch from Earth.

- In May, chemist Neil Bartlett produces the first noble gas compound, xenon platinum hexafluoride. Chemists had thought the noble gases were inert—incapable of combining with other atoms to form molecules

- In June, American chemist and Nobel laureate Linus Pauling and his colleague Emile Zuckerkandl show that the rate at which species accumulate mutations acts as a clock to determine how long ago two species diverged from a common ancestor.

- In July, Dr. G. Danby at Brookhaven Laboratories shows that there are two types of neutrino, a subatomic particle with no mass or electrical charge.

- On July 10, American Telegraph & Telephone and Bell Laboratories launch *Telstar,* the first privately owned communications satellite.

- In July, RCA develops the integrated circuit by putting numerous electronic circuits on a single silicon chip.

- In September, Harvard University physicists develop an atomic clock using hydrogen atoms. They predict it will remain accurate for one hundred thousand years.

- In October, Unimation markets one of the first commercially useful industrial robots.

1963

- American scientists studying residual magnetism in iron-bearing rocks from the floor of the Indian Ocean discover periodic changes in polarity, evidence that the poles have changed many times in earth's 4.5 billion-year history.

- Kodak produces the Instamatic camera, which uses a film cartridge.

- A Kodak subsidiary, Recordak Corporation, produces a system to store up to a million pages on microfilm. Any page can be enlarged within seconds.

- The Visible Man and Visible Woman models are sold.

- On March 30, NASA selects Edward J. Dwight, Jr., the first black pilot for astronaut training.

- On July 26, the communications satellite *Syncom 2* becomes the first to enter a geosynchronous orbit (matching the speed of the Earth's rotation).

- In August, the anti-xi-zero, a fundamental particle of antimatter, is discovered.

- In October, physicists Herbert Friedman and Riccardo Giacconi develop a satellite able to detect X-rays from space.

- In November, The USS *Atlantis II* photographs the ocean floor.

- In December, astronomer Maarten Schmidt finds that quasar 3C273 is moving away from earth at 29,400 miles per second.

1964

- IBM produces a new product, the word processor, a hybrid of the typewriter and the computer.

- The U.S. Navy Research Lab produces a new "Mayday" distress radio. The radio has a nickel-magnesium battery and automatically sends a distress signal on contact with sea water.

- INTELSAT is formed. It is an international venture in which countries share the cost of developing and launching communications satellites.

- Dr. Stookey at Corning Glass Works in New York develops photochromic glass.

- *Sealab I* is the first in a series of oceanographic vessels used for research.

- In March, astronomer Harold Weaver describes the first natural "cosmic maser." The extreme conditions of heat and energy in some galactic regions produce maser emissions from certain chemical ions such as the OH radical.

- In March, physicist Murray Gell-Mann identifies quarks as the building blocks of matter.

- In May, the Verrazano Narrows Bridge opens in New York City. It was then the world's largest suspension bridge.

- In June, British anthropologist Louis S. B. Leakey announces his discovery of *Homo habilis.*

- In June, the Tokyo Olympics are broadcast live to the United States via the geosynchronous *Syncom 3* satellite.

- In June, physicists Arno A. Penzias and Robert W. Wilson of Bell Labs determine that background radiation from space is left over from the "Big Bang" which started the universe.

- On July 31, the *Ranger 7* space probe relays 4,316 close-up photographs of the Moon back to Earth.

- In October, physicists James W. Cronin and Val Fitch assert that time can move toward the future or past.

1965

- The Arecibo Observatory in Puerto Rico shows that Venus rotates in the opposite direction from the other planets.

- The first fully electronic telephone exchange becomes operational in Succasunna, New Jersey. The new development by AT&T will replace human operators with machines.

- The Stanford Linear Accelerator Center becomes operational.

- A magnetic highway is demonstrated in the United States. Vehicles ride above the roadway.

- Traffic control in Chicago, New York and Detroit becomes computerized.

- A computer at the New York Stock Exchange answers questions over the telephone using an artificial voice.

- Super-8mm cassettes are developed with super-8mm movie cameras, following the lead of still picture cameras and their user-friendly technology.

- The videodisc recorder is developed.

- Ray Dolby, an American engineer, develops a way to reduce the background noise in recordings without decreasing the music's quality.

- The first American astronaut walks in space.

- Gas chromatography is used to separate rare-earth complexes.

- In January, geologist Melvin Calvin determines that chlorophyll residue in shale rock from the Sudan Formation are 2.5–2.9 billion years old. This residue is evidence for the antiquity of algae.

- On January 9, the U.S. Atomic Energy Commission invites private companies to submit proposals for the construction of nuclear power plants.

- In January, John Kemeny and Thomas Kurtz develop a new computer programming language. They call it Beginner's All-purpose Symbolic Instructional Code (BASIC).

- In February, NASA launches *Intelsat I*.

- On February 17, NASA launches the *Ranger 8* probe. It sends more than seven thousand photos of the moon back to earth.

- In June, University of Chicago anthropologist F. Clark Howell labels Neanderthal Man (an early man that lived between 200,000 and 30,000 years ago) our immediate ancestor. This claim remains controversial.

- In July, Allan Sandage discovers quasars that do not emit radio waves.

- On July 15, *Mariner 4* sends the first close-up photographs of Mars.

- On December 3, *Gemini 7* sends messages to Earth by laser.

1966

- Richard G. Doell, G. Brent Dalrymple, and Allan Cox show the Earth's magnetic field has periodic reversals.

- Radar is used to measure the polar ice thickness.

- Kodak introduces a "square" flash bulb.

- In January, *Lunar Orbiter II* photographs two million square miles of the Moon from close up.

- In March, anthropologist and author Robert Ardrey shows humans are territorial creatures like other animals. He tries to show that the desire to hold territory is more basic than any other instinct.

- On March 16, U.S. astronauts Neil Armstrong and David Scott of *Gemini 8* stage the first docking of an orbiting spacecraft.

- On June 2, *Surveyer I* makes the first moon landing. It is unmanned.

- In November, archeologists Clifford Evans and Betty J. Maggers assert that pottery from South America from 3000 B.C.E. was influenced by the Japanese, suggesting contact between South America and Japan at that time.

1967

- Computer keyboards are developed for immediate access between the operator and the computer. Punched tapes, punched cards, and magnetic tapes are no longer required.

- IBM develops a light-sensitive pen, a television screen for computers, and uses computers to assist in electronic-circuit design.

- S. Manabe and R.T. Wetherald propose that industrial pollutants increase atmospheric carbon dioxide and can cause a greenhouse effect. Manabe and Wetherald use a computer model to show that the greenhouse effect is a feature of the earth's atmosphere.

- RCA develops a compact television camera weighing 2.2 pounds.

- A cordless, battery-powered telephone is developed. It is the precursor of the cellular phone but is more complex and expensive to use.

- On January 27, a fire kills Gus Grissom, Ed White, and Roger Chaffee in their spacecraft at Cape Kennedy. The three are the first deaths in the U.S. space program.

- In February, Project Gassbuggy detonates a 2.4-kiloton nuclear charge to release natural gas in New Mexico. This is part of Project Plowshares, the use of nuclear weapons for peaceful purposes.

- On March 1, the first overseas direct dialing begins.

- In May, engineers Harold Hay and Jonathon Yellott at the University of Arizona complete a solar-powered house using roof ponds to collect and store solar energy.

- On May 11, the one hundred millionth telephone is installed in the U.S. The U.S. has half the world's phones.

- In June, physicists Steven Weinberg and Sheldon Glashow independently propose electroweak unification, stating that it should be possible to unify the four basic forces of physics into one grand theory. Physicists call this theory the Unified Field Theory or the Theory of Everything.

- On September 14, molecular biologists Vincent M. Sarich and Allan C. Wilson stun the anthropological community by announcing that the genetic clock of Linus Pauling puts the divergence of the line leading to humans and the line leading to the African apes at 5 million years ago. Before this announcement anthropologists had estimated the divergence at some twenty to thirty million years ago.

- In October, molecular biologists Charles T. Caskey, Richard E. Marshall, and Marshall W. Nirenberg find that the genetic code is essentially the same in guinea pigs, toads, and bacteria, evidence that all life shares a common ancestor, a core tenet of evolutionary biology.

- On November 9, the unmanned *Surveyor VI* makes a soft landing on the moon.

- In December, Yale University anthropologist Elwyn L. Simons determines that a skull he found in Egypt is nearly thirty million years old. Simons christens his find *Aegyptopithecus.*

- In December, physician and Nobel laureate Arthur Kornberg synthesizes DNA in a test tube.

1968

- A newly described pulsar in the Crab nebula is thought to have been the site of a supernova seen on Earth on July 4, 1054.

- Standard Telephones and Cables Co. lays a deep-sea cable capable of transmitting 720 simultaneous conversations between Florida and the Caribbean region.

- Bell Labs measures the picosecond as the duration of a single laser pulse. It is the shortest interval of time scientists have measured.

- Du Pont Corporation produces a new wallpaper from polythene. It requires special inks to produce and is the first washable wallpaper.

- Beryllium, a heat-resistant element that is lighter than steel, is used in Lockheed's C5 transport for brake disks and will later be used for heat shields in missiles and satellites.

- The Green Revolution in agriculture promises to feed a rapidly growing population by using new crop varieties and farming techniques, though some methods require the use of chemicals that harm the environment.

- J. Weber identifies gravitational waves which Albert Einstein had predicted.

- In February, the *Glomar Challenger* obtains seabed core samples from the deepest parts of the ocean. It uses a sonar beam to remain stationary above the drill site.

- In March, molecular biologist Werner Arber discovers that some enzymes can cut sequences of nucleotide bases from a strand of DNA. These strands vary in length and sequence according to the enzyme.

- On May 5, George Clark, Gordon Garmire, and William Kraushaar use the third orbiting solar observatory sent into space by NASA to detect gamma rays from the center of the Milky Way.

- In June, geologist Elso S. Barghoorn finds amino acids in three-billion-year-old rocks, raising the possibility that life is three billion years old.

- In July, work begins on the Trans-Alaska Pipeline that will transport oil in the North Slope near Prudhoe Bay on the Beaufort Sea to the ice-free port of Valdez.

- In August, a House of Representatives report declares Lake Erie dead from pollution.

- In August, molecular biologist David Zipser deciphers the last codon, a sequence of three nucleotide bases.

- On August 16, at Cape Kennedy, Florida, NASA and the U.S. Navy test the *Poseidon 3,* a new missile that can be launched from submarines.

- On October 11, *Apollo 7* begins an 11-day mission.

- In November, scientists at Cornell University map the surface of Venus using radar.

- In November, the University of Miami uses radar to pinpoint where lightning strikes occur.

- On December 21, *Apollo 8* is launched and on 24 December becomes the first manned spacecraft to orbit the moon.

1969

- The scanning electron microscope is introduced.

- Computer bubble memory is developed. This new memory stores information even when the electricity is off.

- Fermilab (the National Accelerator Lab), in Batavia, Illinois, will be one of the largest in the world and will give scientists more information about subatomic particles.

- Bell Labs makes holograms, three dimensional laser pictures.

- On January 9, a two-year U.S. Air Force study concludes that unidentified flying objects (UFOs) do not exist.

- On January 22, the Atomic Energy Commission announces the completion of the world's largest superconducting magnet.

- On July 20, American astronauts Neil Armstrong and Edwin "Buzz" Aldrin land on the Moon, walk on its surface, and return safely to Earth four days later.

- On July 31, the unmanned craft *Mariner 6* transmits close-up photographs of the surface of Mars.

- In October, astronomers John Cocke, Donald Taylor, and Michael Disney find a visible star near a (radio) pulsar in the region of space astronomers have labeled the Crab nebula.

- On November 18, Americans land on the Moon for the second time in *Apollo 12.*

- On November 20, the U.S. Department of Agriculture announces a grace period during which farmers will phase out their use of the insecticide DDT.

"Man's Deepest Dive"

Magazine article

By: Jacques Piccard

Date: August 1960

Source: Piccard, Jacques. "Man's Deepest Dive." *National Geographic* 118, August 1960, 224–239.

About the Author: Jacques Piccard (1922–) was born in Brussels, Belgium, and graduated from the Ecole Nouvelle de Suisse Romande in Lausanne, Switzerland, in 1943. He helped his father, Auguste Piccard, design the bathyscaphe *Trieste* and made his first dive in 1953. Other dives followed, and in 1960 he and U.S. Navy Lieutenant Donald Walsh descended nearly 37,000 feet, deeper than any human had gone to that date. ∎

Introduction

Like space, the depths of the ocean emerged as a new frontier during the 1960s. As astronauts grappled their way toward the moon, specially designed submarines plumbed the ocean to unprecedented depths. During the decade, the U.S. Navy tested how well Americans lived and worked underwater for the first time. The first of these projects, *Sealab I,* submerged off Bermuda in 1964 with four Americans to a depth of nearly two hundred feet and remained for nine days. The warm water off Bermuda made the location ideal, though the U.S. Navy wondered how humans would fare in cold water.

To answer this question, the U.S. Navy submerged *Sealab II* 205 feet into the Pacific Ocean off La Jolla, California, in 1965. Three ten-men crews spent fifteen days each in *Sealab II,* a twelve- by fifty-seven-foot steel cylinder. The crew leader, U.S. Navy Commander and former astronaut M. Scott Carpenter, spent thirty days in *Sealab II.* Crew members worked inside and outside in wet suits to determine how well they functioned in cold water at a depth of more than two hundred feet. In 1967, the U.S. Navy launched the last venture of the decade, *Sealab III,* which reached depths of up to six hundred feet.

Significance

Yet these depths did not compare to the dive of the *Trieste,* a specially designed ship with a spherical cabin

on its underside. Jacques Piccard's father designed the ship in Italy, and the U.S. Navy bought it in 1958. On January 23, 1960, it descended to nearly 37,000 feet, a depth no human had reached to that date, in the Pacific Ocean's Mariana Trench. In the cabin were Piccard and U.S. Navy Lieutenant Donald Walsh.

Piccard described the suspense of the long, silent descent. At one point, he and Walsh lost telephone contact with the main vessel. When they had only three hundred feet to go to reach the bottom, Piccard and Walsh knew success was only moments away. Ten minutes later they reached the ocean floor. On the bottom they became the first humans to see a fish at a depth of nearly 37,000 feet as it swam slowly toward them, passing them and disappearing into the black waters that no sunlight penetrated. At that depth, the temperature registered only 38 degrees F, and they could detect neither ocean currents nor radioactivity. The pressure of water at the ocean floor, Walsh realized, had cracked a Plexiglas window. Although Piccard and Walsh had planned to stay thirty minutes on the bottom, the crack persuaded them to return to the surface after twenty minutes, a circumstance they relayed to the crew on the surface after having reestablished telephone contact with it. Piccard recalled this conversation as the first at such depth.

The *Trieste*'s dive marked the first in a series of firsts for American science and technology in the 1960s: the first moon landing, the first laser, the isolation of the first gene, and the Federal Drug Administration's approval of the first oral contraceptive. During the 1960s, the American public and media came to view science as an agent of progress that provided abundant food, antibiotics, vaccines, and computers. The most optimistic forecasters saw no limit to what science and technology could achieve.

Primary Source

"Man's Deepest Dive" [excerpt]

SYNOPSIS: In this excerpt, Piccard described the novelty and suspense of diving to nearly 37,000 feet, the deepest any human had gone. He described the fish and shrimp he saw on the bottom of the ocean as they drew near him, then disappeared into the blackness of an ocean that was too deep for sunlight to penetrate. The discovery of cracks in a Plexiglas window forced Piccard and Walsh to surface earlier than they had planned.

We continue to descend, exceedingly slowly now. Our gasoline is still cooling, and, as more water enters the float because of the contraction of the gasoline, it makes us heavier and heavier. I feel as if these hundreds of gallons of water are passing into my veins.

President Eisenhower decorates Jacques Piccard (center) and Lt. Don Walsh at the White House on February 4, 1960. Walsh and Piccard are being honored for their record descent to 37,800 feet below the surface of the Pacific Ocean, in the Marianas Trench near Guam. The dive was made in the *Trieste*, a bathyscaphe that Piccard helped design. © **BETTMANN/CORBIS. REPRODUCED BY PERMISSION.**

The telephone has gone silent. We are perhaps too deep? The descent is silent, slow, and our eyes pass from porthole to depth finder, from depth finder to porthole. We are very near the bottom; we should reach it at any moment . . . but we continue to descend.

At 1256 hours I say to Walsh, "Don, look. Here is the bottom on the depth finder."

"Finally," Don replies.

Yes, finally—the bottom, quite distinct on the depth finder, 300 feet below us. Those 300 feet were traversed in 10 minutes; and at 1306 hours the *Trieste,* in my sixty-fifth dive, made a perfect landing on a carpet of uniform ivory color, that the sea had laid down during the course of thousands of years.

Fish Meets Sphere on Bottom

Like a free balloon on a windless day, indifferent to the almost 200,000 tons of water pressing on the cabin from all sides, balanced to within an ounce or so on its wire guide rope, slowly, surely, in the name of science and humanity, the *Trieste* took possession of the abyss, the last extreme on our earth that remained to be conquered.

And to demonstrate well all the significance of this dive, nature would have it that the *Trieste* come down on the bottom a few feet from a fish, a true fish, joined in its unknown world by this monster of steel and gasoline and a powerful beam of light. Our fish was the instantaneous reply (after years of work!) to a question that thousands of oceanographers had been asking themselves for decades.

Slowly, very slowly, this fish—apparently of the sole family, about a foot long and half as wide—moved away from us, swimming half in the bottom ooze, and disappeared into the black night, the eternal night which was its domain. . . .

Slowly also (Is everything slow, then, at the bottom of the sea?), Walsh held out his hand to me.

We remained on the bottom for 20 minutes. We took temperature measurements (about 38° F.), made measurements of a possible undersea current (none, apparently), and of radioactivity (no positive indication), and spent several minutes at the porthole. Once a shrimp swam peacefully in front of us.

As a matter of duty and to leave nothing undone, Don skeptically called the surface on the telephone:

"This is *Trieste* on the bottom, Challenger Deep. Six three zero zero fathoms. Over."

Suddenly I saw him give a start, and I was able to follow the telephone conversation.

"I hear you weakly but clearly. Please repeat the depth."

Don did so slowly. "Everything O.K." (What could go wrong?)

"Six three zero zero fathoms?"

"That is Charley." (In the seaman's jargon, Charley stands for "C" and means "correct.") "We will surface at 1700 hours," Don replied.

"Roger." (That is, "understood.")

Of course we had every reason to be pleased with this telephone conversation. On the surface our friends were reassured as to our fate, but, in particular, we had been able to perform a highly interesting experiment. The credit belonged to scientists who, after long and patient laboratory research, had succeeded in giving us a telephone unparalleled in the world. With their instrument, without wires or radio waves, we had established the first voice communication between the surface and the great depths of the ocean. . . .

Port Cracked by the Cold

"Can you switch on the rear searchlight?" Walsh asks.

"Certainly. There it is."

Don looks through the porthole. Three seconds later he leaves the viewing port.

"I know what happened, that noise, that jolt," he says quietly. "It was the big viewing port of the entry tube that cracked."

This big Plexiglas viewing port is subjected to no differences in pressure, it must have contracted more than its exterior steel frame allowed. Thanks to our rear searchlight, several cracks are clearly visible.

This little accident does not involve us in danger. But if these cracks do not close of themselves during the ascent, the tube may be difficult to empty. In that case, we may have some trouble getting out of the cabin. Perhaps we shall need to have divers install the spare window cover always carried aboard the towing vessel, but so far never needed.

For that prospect, especially in the heavy seas on the surface, we need daylight. Hence there is not a minute to lose. We do not regard with favor the chance of having to spend extra hours confined in this steel ball.

Besides, of the 30 minutes we intended to spend on the bottom, 20 have already elapsed. Regretfully we forego these last 10 minutes. We cast a final look upon this horizonless land, shining under the glow of our seachlights.

Further Resources

BOOKS
Piccard, Auguste. *In Balloon and Bathyscaphe*. London, England: Cassell, 1956.

———. *Earth, Sky and Sea*. New York: Oxford University Press, 1956.

———. *Seven Miles Down: The Story of the Bathyscaphe Trieste*. New York: Putnam, 1961.

PERIODICALS
"Achieving the Ultimate Adventure on Earth." *Life*, February 15, 1960, 110–121.

"Bathyscaphe Descends to Deepest Parts of Ocean." *Science News Letter*, February 6, 1960, 91.

Fantel, Hans. "A Longer, Deeper, Daring Quest for the Secrets of Living in the Sea." *Popular Mechanics*, September 1968, 95–99, 180–182.

"Journey to Inner Space." *Time*, September 17, 1965, 90, 95.

WEBSITES
Department of the Navy. Office of Naval Research. Science & Technology Focus. "Current Research: Submersibles—Trieste. Press Release, January 8, 1958." Available online at http://www.onr.navy.mil/focus/ocean/vessels/submersibles5.htm; website home page: http://www.onr.navy.mil/focus/ (accessed June 2, 2003).

Naval Historical Center. "Bathyscaphe *Trieste* (1958–1963) in 1959–1960." Available online at http://www.history.navy.mil/photos/sh-usn/usnsh-t/trste-b.htm; website home page: http://www.history.navy.mil/index.html (accessed February 5, 2003).

Wikipedia. "Bathyscaphe Trieste." Available online at http://www.wikipedia.org/wiki/Bathyscaphe_Trieste; website home page: http://www.wikipedia.org/wiki/Main_Page (accessed February 5, 2003).

"The Present Evolution of Man"

Journal article

By: Theodosius Dobzhansky

Date: September 1960

Source: Dobzhansky, Theodosius. "The Present Evolution of Man."*Scientific American* 203, no. 3, September 1960, 206–217.

About the Author: Theodosius Dobzhansky (1900–1975) was born in Nemirov, Ukraine, and in 1927 immigrated to the United States, where he joined Columbia University as a Rockefeller Fellow. He became a U.S. citizen in 1937 and professor of zoology at Columbia University in 1942. In 1962, he moved to Rockefeller University and in 1971 to the University of California, Davis. ∎

Introduction

According to Harvard University evolutionary biologist and historian of biology Ernest Mayr, nothing deflates pride more than the thought that humans evolved from a hairy quadruped that foraged in trees. Yet even before British naturalist Charles Darwin published *On the Origin of Species* (1859), amateur fossil hunters had begun turning up the remains of early man. In 1829 in Belgium and in 1848 in Gibraltar, they found fragments of *Homo neanderthalis* (Neanderthal man) without recognizing the significance of their finds. In 1856, quarry workers in the Neander Valley, Germany (hence the name Neanderthal), unearthed part of a cranium and arm and leg bones. A local teacher, Carl Fuhlrott, recognized the bones as the remains of an early man more robustly built than modern humans.

The search for man's ancestors had begun in earnest. More Neanderthal finds followed. Then in 1897, Dutch physician Eugene Dubois discovered a partial cranium and femur of an even more ancient man, *Homo erectus,* in Indonesia. Especially important was the 1924 find by British anatomist Raymond Dart of a toddler's skull in South Africa. He recognized it as the remains of an ancient biped with the brain the size of a chimpanzee's. Here was the earliest human ancestor, *Australopithecus africanus* (southern ape from Africa), yet discovered, and it was found in Africa, the continent Darwin had predicted as the birthplace of humanity. By 1960, the year Dobzhansky wrote his article, the fossil record of man's ancestors stretched back nearly 3 million years, and only those with a religious world view rejected belief in human evolution.

Significance

Dobzhansky wrote that all life, including human life, evolves through natural selection. Natural selection presupposes that every generation has organisms with a diversity of traits: skin and eye color, hair color and texture, height and weight. Nature selects for survival those organisms best adapted to their environment. Nature selects, for example, bats with acute hearing for survival because this trait adapts them to navigating dark caves. Those organisms best adapted to their environment survive to pass on those favorable traits to offspring. Over numerous generations, natural selection fits organisms ever more closely to their environment.

Dobzhansky wrote that humans alone are shaped not only by biological evolution but by cultural evolution. Culture is everything nongenetic, technology and language being its most conspicuous components. Humans, though, are the only animal to pass on more than genes from generation to generation, for humans also pass on culture. Dobzhansky wrote that cultural evolution was more rapid than biological evolution. Nevertheless, humans were still subject to biological evolution through natural selection. As an example, Dobzhansky noted that less intelligent humans were having more offspring than more intelligent humans. The danger as he saw it was that humans might evolve into a less intelligent species. This danger led him to urge humans to control their evolution. Humans are the only species to be aware of their evolution and are thus the only species capable of channeling it in the direction best for them.

Primary Source

"The Present Evolution of Man" [excerpt]

SYNOPSIS: In this excerpt, Dobzhansky wrote that all life, including human life, is evolving through natural selection. In addition to biological evolution, humans alone are shaped by cultural evolution. Culture is evolving faster than biology. Because humans are the only species conscious of their evolution, they are the only species capable of channeling evolution in the direction best for them.

Man still evolves by natural selection for his environment, but it is now an environment largely of his own making. Moreover, he may be changing the environment faster than he can change biologically

In tracing the evolution of man, this issue of *Scientific American* deals with a natural process that has transcended itself. Only once before, when life originated out of inorganic matter, has there occurred a comparable event.

After that first momentous step, living forms evolved by adapting to their environments. Adaptation—the maintenance or advancement of confority between an organism and its surroundings—takes

Ukrainian-born geneticist Theodosius Dobzhansky argued that because of their intelligence, human beings evolve both biologically and culturally, and that human culture can influence biological evolution. **THE LIBRARY OF CONGRESS.**

Other organisms adapt to their environments by changing their genes in accordance with the demands of the surroundings. Man and man alone can also adapt by changing his environments to fit his genes. His genes enable him to invent new tools, to alter his opinions, his aims and his conduct, to acquire new knowledge and new wisdom. . . .

For better or worse, biological evolution did not stop when culture appeared. In this final article we address ourselves to the question of where evolution is now taking man. The literature of this subject has not lacked for prophets who wish to divine man's eventual fate. In our age of anxiety, prediction of final extinction has become the fashionable view, replacing the hopes for emergence of a race of demigods that more optimistic authorities used to foresee. Our purpose is less ambitious. What biological evolutionary processes are now at work is a problem both serious and complex enough to occupy us here. . . .

There is no doubt that human survival will continue to depend more and more on human intellect and technology. It is idle to argue whether this is good or bad. The point of no return was passed long ago, before anyone knew it was happening.

But to grant that the situation is inevitable is not to ignore the problems it raises. Selection in modern societies does not always encourage characteristics that we regard as desirable. Let us consider one example. Much has been written about the differential fertility that in advanced human societies favors less intelligent over more intelligent people. Studies in several countries have shown that school children from large families tend to score lower on so-called intelligence tests than their classmates with few or no brothers and sisters. Moreover, parents who score lower on these tests have more children on the average than those who get higher marks.

We cannot put our finger on the forces responsible for this presumed selection against intelligence. As a matter of fact, there is some evidence that matters are changing, in the U. S. at least. People included in *Who's Who in America* (assuming that people listed in this directory are on the average more intelligent than people not listed there) had fewer children than the general population during the period from 1875 to 1904. In the next two decades, however, the difference seemed to be disappearing. L. S. Penrose of University College London, one of the outstanding human geneticists, has pointed out that a negative correlation between intelligence and

place through natural selection. The raw materials with which natural selection works are supplied by mutation and sexual recombination of hereditary units: the genes.

Mutation, sexual recombination and natural selection led to the emergence of *Homo sapiens.* The creatures that preceded him had already developed the rudiments of tool-using, toolmaking and cultural transmission. But the next evolutionary step was so great as to constitute a difference in kind from those before it. There now appeared an organism whose mastery of technology and of symbolic communication enabled it to create a supraorganic culture.

family size may in part be corrected by the relative infertility of low-grade mental defectives. He suggests that selection may thus be working toward maintaining a constant level of genetic conditioning for intelligence in human populations. The evidence presently available is insufficient either to prove or to contradict this hypothesis. . . .

If this article has asked many more questions than it has answered, the purpose is to suggest that answers be sought with all possible speed. Natural selection is a very remarkable phenomenon. But it does not even guarantee the survival of a species. Most living forms have become extinct without the "softening" influence of civilization, simply by becoming too narrowly specialized. Natural selection is opportunistic; in shaping an organism to fit its surroundings it may leave the organism unable to cope with a change in environment. In this light, man's explosive ability to change his environment may offer as much threat as promise. Technological evolution may have outstripped biological evolution.

Yet man is the only product of biological evolution who knows that he has evolved and is evolving further. He should be able to replace the blind force of natural selection by conscious direction, based on his knowledge of nature and on his values. It is as certain that such direction will be needed as it is questionable whether man is ready to provide it. He is unready because his knowledge of his own nature and its evolution is insufficient; because a vast majority of people are unaware of the necessity of facing the problem; and because there is so wide a gap between the way people actually live and the values and ideals to which they pay lip service.

Further Resources

BOOKS

Bowler, Peter J. *Theories of Human Evolution*. Baltimore, Md.: Johns Hopkins University Press, 1986.

Dobzhansky, Theodosius. *Mankind Evolving*. New Haven, Conn.: Yale University Press, 1962.

Gould, Stephen Jay. *Ever Since Darwin: Reflections in Natural History*. New York: Norton, 1977.

Leakey, Richard E., and Roger Lewin. *Origins: What New Discoveries Reveal about the Emergence of Our Species and Its Possible Future*. New York: Dutton, 1977.

Lewin, Roger. *In the Age of Mankind: A Smithsonian Book of Human Evolution*. Washington, D.C.: Smithsonian Books, 1988.

————. *Principles of Human Evolution: A Core Textbook*. Malden, Mass.: Blackwell Science, 1998.

Tanner, Nancy M. *On Becoming Human*. New York: Cambridge University Press, 1981.

PERIODICALS

Weaver, Kenneth F., Richard E. Leakey, and Alan Walker. "The Search for Early Man." *National Geographic,* November 1985, 560–629.

WEBSITES

American Philosophical Society. "Theodosius Dobzhansky Papers." Available online at http://www.amphilsoc.org/library/browser/d/doby.htm; website home page: http://www.amphilsoc.org/ (accessed February 5, 2003).

Lei Pi Sze, Emily. "Theodosius Dobzhansky: 1900–1975." Available online at http://emuseum.mnsu.edu/information/biography/abcde/dobzhansky_theodosius.html; website home page: http://www.emuseum.mnsu.edu/index.shtml (accessed February 5, 2003).

Walker, Phillip L., and Edward H. Hagan. "Human Evolution: The Fossil Evidence in 3D." Available online at http://www.anth.ucsb.edu/projects/human (accessed February 5, 2003).

"Special Message to the Congress on Urgent National Needs"

Message

By: John F. Kennedy

Date: May 25, 1961

Source: Kennedy, John F. "Special Message to Congress on Urgent National Needs." May 25, 1961. Available online at http://www.cs.umb.edu/jfklibrary/j052561.htm (accessed February 6, 2003).

About the Author: John Fitzgerald Kennedy (1917–1963) was born in Brookline, Massachusetts. After graduating from Harvard University in 1940, he joined the U.S. Navy in 1941 and was wounded when a Japanese destroyer sunk his patrol boat in the Pacific. At age twenty-nine, he won election to the U.S. House of Representatives and in 1952 to the U.S. Senate. He was elected president in 1960, but his term was cut short by an assassin's bullets in 1963. ∎

Introduction

In a speech to Congress on May 25, 1961, John F. Kennedy framed his desire to land a man on the moon as a "battle . . . between freedom and tyranny." This was the language of the Cold War, the hostile rivalry between the United States and the Soviet Union that shaped science and technology in both nations. During World War II, the two had been allies in fighting a common enemy, Nazi Germany. After the war, each grew suspicious of the other's intentions. The United States became alarmed when the Soviets occupied Eastern Europe and installed

President John F. Kennedy addresses Congress on May 25, 1961. Kennedy challenged Congress and the American people to recapture leadership in the space race by putting a man on the moon before the decade's end. © BETTMANN/CORBIS. REPRODUCED BY PERMISSION.

puppet governments; the Soviets feared that the United States was giving economic aid to Europe to make it dependent on American capitalism.

Each nation looked to science to give it a military and technological advantage. Both used science in an attempt to control space, for mastery of space would give either nation command of missile technology and spy satellites. In the 1950s, Americans had assumed that U.S. science and technology were superior, an assumption that collapsed in 1957 when the Soviets launched the world's first intercontinental ballistic missile and the first satellite, Sputnik. American astronomer Otto Struve voiced the fears of many Americans when he declared 1957 to be a year as momentous as 1492, when Spain surpassed Portugal as a maritime power.

Congress responded in 1958 by passing the National Defense Education Act, which funded the teaching of science, mathematics, and foreign languages in public schools. That year, too, Congress created the National Aeronautics and Space Administration (NASA), the scientific agency that was to recapture America's leadership in the space race, a race that accelerated in April 1961, when the Soviets launched the first man, Yuri Gagarin, into orbit around the earth. On May 5, 1961, the United States responded by launching Navy Commander Alan

Shepard Jr. 116 miles into space during a flight that lasted just over fifteen minutes.

Significance

These events were the prelude to Kennedy's 1961 address to Congress in which he committed the United States to recapturing leadership in the space race. He warned that the Soviets had a "head start" and that national security demanded a redoubling of U.S. efforts. As part of these efforts, Kennedy committed Congress and the American people to landing a man on the moon and safely returning him to earth before decade's end.

Although Kennedy couched his speech in the language of the cold war, he was motivated by idealism. Kennedy saw space as a new frontier, one that beckoned the energy and talents of "free men." Americans always responded to new challenges, he believed, for this was part of our national character. Great quests brought out a heroic element in man. He saw the struggle to reach the moon as a quest for "knowledge and peace." This idealism motivated him in Vienna, Austria, in 1961 and at the United Nations in 1963 to invite the Soviets to join the United States in a joint landing on the moon.

One cannot know what Kennedy might have accomplished, for his assassination in 1963 ended hopes for cooperation. Both nations tried to surpass the other in launching spacecraft into orbit for longer periods. In honor of the martyred president, President Lyndon Johnson renewed the nation's commitment to putting a man on the moon. NASA was equal to the challenge: On July 16, 1969, *Apollo 11* was launched from Cape Kennedy, Florida. Four days later, Captain Neil A. Armstrong took the first steps on the moon.

Primary Source

"Special Message to the Congress on Urgent National Needs" [excerpt]

SYNOPSIS: In this excerpt, Kennedy challenged Congress and the American people to put a man on the moon and safely return him to earth before decade's end. He appealed to the idealism of Americans by speaking of space as a new frontier. At the same time, he said, a moon landing would be a scientific triumph over the Soviet Union.

Finally, if we are to win the battle that is now going on around the world between freedom and tyranny, the dramatic achievements in space which occurred in recent weeks should have made clear to us all, as did the Sputnik in 1957, the impact of this adventure on the minds of men everywhere, who are attempting to make a determination of which road they should take. Since early in my term, our efforts in space have been under review. With the advice of the Vice President, who is Chairman of the National Space Council, we have examined where we are strong and where we are not, where we may succeed and where we may not. Now it is time to take longer strides—time for a great new American enterprise—time for this nation to take a clearly leading role in space achievement, which in many ways may hold the key to our future on earth.

I believe we possess all the resources and talents necessary. But the facts of the matter are that we have never made the national decisions or marshalled the national resources required for such leadership. We have never specified long-range goals on an urgent time schedule, or managed our resources and our time so as to insure their fulfillment. Recognizing the head start obtained by the Soviets with their large rocket engines, which gives them many months of leadtime, and recognizing the likelihood that they will exploit this lead for some time to come in still more impressive successes, we nevertheless are required to make new efforts on our own. For while we cannot guarantee that we shall one day be first, we can guarantee that any failure

Soviet pilot Yuri Gagarin sits in the cockpit of his Vostok 1 rocket before lift-off. He became the first man to orbit the Earth on April 15, 1961.
© BETTMANN/CORBIS. REPRODUCED BY PERMISSION.

to make this effort will make us last. We take an additional risk by making it in full view of the world, but as shown by the feat of astronaut Shepard, this very risk enhances our stature when we are successful. But this is not merely a race. Space is open to us now; and our eagerness to share its meaning is not governed by the efforts of others. We go into space because whatever mankind must undertake, free men must fully share.

I therefore ask the Congress, above and beyond the increases I have earlier requested for space activities, to provide the funds which are needed to meet the following national goals: First, I believe that this nation should commit itself to achieving the goal, before this decade is out, of landing a man on the moon and returning him safely to the earth. No single space project in this period will be more impressive to mankind, or more important for the long-range exploration of space; and none will be so difficult or expensive to accomplish. We propose to accelerate the development of the appropriate lunar space craft. We propose to develop alternate liquid and solid fuel boosters, much larger than any now being developed, until certain which is superior. We propose additional funds for other engine development and for unmanned explorations—explorations which are particularly important for one purpose which this nation will never overlook: the survival of the man who first makes this daring flight. But in a very real sense, it will not be one man going to the moon—if we make this judgment affirmatively, it will be an entire nation. For all of us must work to put him there.

Further Resources

BOOKS

Collins, Michael. *Liftoff: The Story of America's Adventure in Space.* New York: Grove, 1988.

Compton, William David. *Where No Man Has Gone Before: A History of the Apollo Lunar Exploration Missions.* Washington, D.C.: GPO, 1989.

Cox, Donald W. *The Space Race.* Philadelphia: Chilton, 1962.

Lewis, Richard S. *The Voyages of Apollo: The Exploration of the Moon.* New York: The New York Times Book Company, 1974.

Wilfred, John N. *We Reach the Moon.* New York: Bantam, 1969.

PERIODICALS

Johnson, Nicholas L. "Apollo and Zond—Race around the Moon?" *Spaceflight,* December 1978, 403–412.

Oberg, James E. "Russia Meant to Win the 'Moon Race.'" *Spaceflight,* November 1975, 163–171.

WEBSITES

National Aeronautics and Space Administration. "30th Anniversary of Apollo 11." Available online at http://history .nasa.gov/ap11ann/introduction.htm; website home page: http://www.history.nasa.gov (accessed June 2, 2003).

The Genesis Flood: The Biblical Record and Its Scientific Implications

Nonfiction work

By: John C. Whitcomb and Henry M. Morris

Date: 1961

Source: Whitcomb, John C., and Henry M. Morris. *The Genesis Flood: The Biblical Record and Its Scientific Implications.* Philadelphia: Presbyterian and Reformed Publishing, 1961.

About the Authors: John C. Whitcomb (1926–) was born in Philadelphia, Pennsylvania. He received a Th.D. from Grace Theological Seminary in Winona Lake, Indiana, in 1957, where he taught in the departments of Old Testament and Christian theology from 1951 to 1990. For twenty years, he was the seminary's director of doctoral studies and for ten years edited *Grace Theological Journal.* He studied and taught in China, Puerto Rico, France, Canada, and the Central African Republic.

Henry M. Morris (1918–) was born in Houston, Texas and received a Ph.D. in hydraulic engineering from the University of Minnesota in 1950. From 1957 to 1970, he chaired the department of civil engineering at Virginia Polytechnic Institute. He founded and served as director of the Institute for Creation Research, an organization that denies evolution in favor of a literal reading of Genesis. ■

Introduction

As early as 1838, British naturalist Charles Darwin began formulating his theory of evolution by natural selection. He was wary about publishing it, though, because he feared that religious leaders would attack him. French naturalist Georges Buffon had escaped censorship in the eighteenth century by floating evolution as a hypothesis he doubted. But when French naturalist Jean-Baptiste Lamarck proposed evolution as a serious theory in 1809 and British amateur scientist Robert Chambers followed suit in 1844, religious leaders savaged them.

Darwin received in 1858 a manuscript from British naturalist Alfred Russell Wallace outlining evolution by natural selection. He realized he had to publish to preserve his claim of priority. The next year, when he published *On the Origin of Species,* a storm of religious indignation swirled around him, as he had feared. At the 1860 meeting of the British Association for the Advancement of Science, Anglican bishop Samuel Wilberforce derided Darwin, yet by century's end clerics in England and on the continent had made their peace with evolution or ignored it. Only in the United States did religious opposition remain vigorous into the twentieth century.

In the United States, fundamentalists insisted on a literal reading of the account of creation recorded in the biblical book of Genesis. The initial creationist wave crested during the 1920s. Texas governor Miriam Ferguson declared that she would not "let that kind of rot go into Texas schoolbooks." In 1925, the Tennessee legislature banned the teaching of evolution in public schools, but the law backfired. When biology teacher John Scopes defied the law, attorney Clarence Darrow and Baltimore journalist Henry L. Mencken used the trial to depict creationists as intolerant and ignorant of science.

Significance

The failure of the attempt to ban the teaching of evolution in public schools led creationists to switch tactics in the 1960s. They now insisted that science supported a literal reading of Genesis. That is, creationism was a science and as such deserved a place in public schools.

In *The Genesis Flood,* John Whitcomb and Henry Morris asserted that geological evidence supported the

A replica of Noah's Ark sits at the Bronx Zoo in the spring of 1960. Whitcomb and Morris argue in *The Genesis Flood* (1961) that there was scientific evidence for the worldwide flood described in the Bible that only Noah, his family, and the animals on his Ark survived. © BETTMANN/ CORBIS. REPRODUCED BY PERMISSION.

Genesis account of a universal flood that killed all life except Noah, his family and the animals (and presumably plants, bacteria, fungi and viruses) that accompanied them on the ark. Genesis is thus as much science as religion. Yet they summarized their position with references to Genesis, I Peter, and II Peter and without a word about the putative geological evidence that corroborates the Genesis account.

The Genesis Flood reveals the weakness of creationism, at least from a scientific perspective. In the end, its proponents demonstrate that creationism rests upon faith, not science. This fact has led most scientists to dismiss creationism as religion and to affirm that religious doctrine has nothing to do with the scientific method. Creationism rests on dogma, not on a hypothesis that scientists can test.

Primary Source

Genesis Flood

SYNOPSIS: In these excerpts, Whitcomb and Morris maintain that geology corroborates the Genesis account of a universal flood. Yet as evidence they cited Scriptural passages rather than scientific evidence.

The serious-minded Christian, desiring of course to accept both the truths revealed in Scripture and the findings of science as well, thus finds himself on the horns of a dilemma. The decision as to which position is to be accepted has too often been made simply on the basis of expediency. The uniformitarian concept has, by the mere fact of its being more modern and spectacular, and because of the strong pressure toward conformity even in scientific attitudes, been uncritically accepted today by the great majority of modern geologists.

But to reach a truly logical and correct conclusion, especially on such important and fundamental problems as these, an individual should certainly be willing to make a careful and open-minded study of both types of explanations. The fact is, however, that very few modern scientists in recent years have made any kind of serious attempt to evaluate the facts of geology and other sciences in terms of their possible harmonization with the Biblical revelation of the Creation and the Flood.

This book is an exception to such conformist thinking. *The Genesis Flood* places before the reader in clear and comprehensive fashion the theological and scientific basis for a literal acceptance of the Biblical account. The authors have carefully considered and developed their arguments, supporting each of them with an abundance of recent and authoritative documentation. . . .

Summary and Conclusion

In this chapter we have attempted to establish the geographical universality of the Flood on the basis of seven major Biblical arguments: (1) the Bible says that the waters of the Flood covered the highest mountains to a depth sufficient for the Ark to float over them; (2) the Bible also informs us that this situation prevailed for a period of five months and that an additional seven months were required for the waters to subside sufficiently for Noah to disembark in the mountains of Ararat; (3) the expression "fountains of the great deep were broken up" points unmistakably to vast geological disturbances that are incompatible with the local-Flood concept, especially when these disturbances are said to have continued for five months; (4) the construction of the Ark with a capacity of at least 1,400,000 cubic feet, merely for the purpose of carrying eight people and a few animals through a local inundation is utterly inconceivable; (5) if the Flood had been limited in extent, there would have been no need for an ark at all, for there would have been plenty of time for Noah's family to escape from the danger-area, to say nothing of the birds and beasts; (6) Peter's use of the Flood as a basis for refuting uniformitarian skeptics in the last days would have been pointless if the Flood had been merely a local one, especially when we consider the cosmic setting into which he placed that cataclysm (II Pet. 3:3–7), and (7) a widely distributed human race could not have been destroyed by a local Flood.

In support of our seventh argument, we presented four Biblical reasons for the necessity of a total destruction of humanity in the days of Noah: (1) since the stated purpose of the Flood was the punishment of a sinful race, such a purpose could not have been accomplished if only a part of humanity had been affected; (2) the fact that the Flood destroyed the rest of mankind is greatly strengthened by repeated statements in Genesis, I Peter, and II Peter, to the effect that *only* Noah and his family were spared; (3) the Lord Jesus Christ clearly stated that all men were destroyed by the Flood (Luke 17:26–30), and (4) the covenant which God made with Noah after the Flood becomes meaningless if only a part of the human race had been involved.

In addition to these arguments for a total destruction of the human race except for Noah's family, we gave two reasons for believing that the human race could not have been confined to the Mesopotamian Valley at the time of the Flood: (1) the longevity and fecundity of the antediluvians would allow for a very rapid increase in population even if only 1,656 years elapsed between Adam and the Flood; and the prevalence of strife and violence would have encouraged wide distribution rather than confinement to a single locality; (2) evidence of human fossils in widely-scattered parts of the world makes it very difficult to assume that men did not migrate beyond the Near East before the time of the Flood.

The writers are firmly convinced that these basic arguments, if carefully weighed by Christian thinkers, would prove to be sufficiently powerful and compelling to settle once and for all the long-debated question of the geographical extent of the Flood. This is not to say, of course, that a universal Flood presents no serious scientific problems; for the remaining chapters of this volume are devoted largely to an examination of such problems. But we do believe that no problem, be it scientific or philosophical, can be of sufficient magnitude to offset the combined force of these seven Biblical arguments for a geographically universal Flood in the days of Noah.

Further Resources

BOOKS

Hanson, Robert W., ed. *Science and Creation: Geological, Theological, and Educational Perspectives.* New York: Macmillan, 1986.

Kitcher, Philip. *Abusing Science: The Case against Creationism.* Cambridge, Mass.: MIT Press, 1982.

Larson, Edward J. *Trial and Error: The American Controversy over Creation and Evolution.* New York: Oxford University Press, 1985.

Morris, Henry M., ed. *Scientific Creationism.* San Diego, Calif.: Creation-Life Publishers, 1974.

Zetterberg, J. Peter, ed. *Evolution versus Creationism: The Public Education Controversy.* Phoenix, Ariz.: Oryx Press, 1977.

PERIODICALS

Callaghan, Catherine A. "Evolution and Creationist Arguments." *American Biology Teacher,* June 1980, 422–427.

Cavanaugh, Michael A. "Scientific Creationism and Rationality." *Nature,* May 14, 1985, 185–189.

Gatewood, Willard B. "From Scopes to Creation Science: The Decline and Revival of the Evolution Controversy." *South Atlantic Quarterly,* Winter 1984, 363–383.

Nelkin, Dorothy. "The Science-Textbook Controversies." *Scientific American,* April 1976, 33–39.

Numbers, Ronald L. "Creationism in 20th-Century America." *Science,* February 4, 1986, 538–544.

Scott, Eugenie C., and Henry P. Cole. "The Elusive Scientific Basis of Creation Science." *Quarterly Review of Biology,* Spring 1985, 21–30.

WEBSITES

Institute for Creation Research home page. Available online at http://www.icr.org (accessed February 6, 2003).

Silent Spring

Nonfiction work

By: Rachel Carson

Date: 1962

Source: Carson, Rachel. *Silent Spring.* Boston: Houghton Mifflin, 1962, 5–9

About the Author: Rachel Louise Carson (1907–1964) was born in Springdale, Pennsylvania, and earned an M.A. from Johns Hopkins University in 1932. The previous year she had begun teaching at the University of Maryland. From 1929 to 1936 she also taught summer school at Johns Hopkins. In 1936, she joined the U.S. Bureau of Fisheries as an aquatic biologist. ∎

Introduction

Since the advent of agriculture ten thousand years ago, farmers have battled insects. This struggle became acute in the twentieth century, when rising production slashed food prices. Because farmers lived on such narrow profit margins, protecting their crops from insects meant the difference between survival and bankruptcy.

In this battle, farmers depended upon chemists to develop insecticides. The first insecticides, developed in the nineteenth century, were arsenic compounds that killed insects that ate the toxin. Then in 1939, a Swiss chemical company, J.R. Geigy, developed dichlorodiphenyltrichloroethane (DDT), the first of a new generation of insecticides that killed any insect that came in contact with it, whether or not the insect ate it. In 1942, Geigy gave samples to the U.S. Department of Agriculture (USDA). Together with the agricultural and mechanical colleges and the agricultural experiment stations, the USDA touted the value of DDT, inviting amazed farmers to tour insect-free barns sprayed with the chemical. Farmers quickly came to see DDT as their most potent weapon against insects. That decade, chemists developed other insecticides that killed on contact, the most popular being chlordane.

American farmers sank money into these new insecticides. Whereas they had spent $9.2 million on insecticides in 1939, they spent $174.6 million in 1954. American farmers were at last winning the war against insects.

Significance

Rachel Carson believed this victory came at too high a cost. She charged DDT and other chemicals with "contamination of air, earth, rivers, and sea." She warned that humans were staking their future, along with the future of other animals, plants, and the earth, on a short-term victory. Even this victory was illusory, for insects were evolving resistance to insecticides, requiring chemists to develop ever more toxic ones. "Can anyone believe it is possible to lay down a barrage of poisons on the surface of the earth without making it unfit for all life?" she asked.

In answering no, Carson laid the foundation for an environmental movement that originated in the 1960s and remains a political and social force today. During the 1960s, environmentalists joined Carson in highlighting the dangers of DDT and other chemicals, demonstrating that DDT made some birds sterile and thinned the eggshells of others. In 1972, Congress responded to these problems by banning the sale of DDT.

A man, dressed as Death, protests in San Francisco against the use of the pesticide DDT, October 1969. Congress banned the sale of DDT in 1972. © TED STRESHINSKY/CORBIS. REPRODUCED BY PERMISSION.

Meanwhile, environmentalists held the first Earth Day on April 22, 1970, to raise public awareness of the dangers of toxic chemicals. They charged that Agent Orange, a defoliant used in the Vietnam War to deprive the enemy of jungle sanctuaries, caused cancer in Vietnam veterans. They charged Hooker Company in Niagara Falls, New York, with dumping toxic chemicals into Love Canal, an unfinished nineteenth-century canal, that caused miscarriages, birth defects, and cancer. This activism owes much to Carson's concern for the earth and the diversity of life it sustains.

Primary Source

Silent Spring [excerpt]

"The Obligation to Endure"

> **SYNOPSIS:** In this excerpt, Carson warned that humans were poisoning themselves and their environment by using insecticides and other toxins that could at best win a short-term victory against insects and rodents. This victory was illusory, Carson believed, because insects evolved resistance to insecticides, forcing chemists to develop ever more potent ones.

The history of life on earth has been a history of interaction between living things and their surroundings. To a large extent, the physical form and the habits of the earth's vegetation and its animal life have been molded by the environment. Considering the whole span of earthly time, the opposite effect, in which life actually modifies its surroundings, has been relatively slight. Only within the moment of time represented by the present century has one species—man—acquired significant power to alter the nature of his world.

During the past quarter century this power has not only increased to one of disturbing magnitude but it has changed in character. The most alarming of all man's assaults upon the environment is the contamination of air, earth, rivers, and sea with dangerous and even lethal materials. This pollution is for the most part irrecoverable; the chain of evil it initiates not only in the world that must support life but in living tissues is for the most part irreversible. In this now universal contamination of the environment, chemicals are the sinister and little-recognized partners of radiation in changing the very nature of the world—the very nature of its life. Strontium 90, released through nuclear explosions into the air, comes to earth in rain or drifts down as fallout, lodges in soil, enters into the grass or corn or wheat grown there, and in time takes up its abode in the bones of a human being, there to remain until his death. Similarly, chemicals sprayed on croplands or forests or gardens lie long in soil, entering into living organisms, passing from one to another in a chain of poisoning and death. Or they pass mysteriously by underground streams until they emerge and, through the alchemy of air and sunlight, combine into new forms that kill vegetation, sicken cattle, and work unknown harm on those who drink from once pure wells. As Albert Schweitzer has said, "Man can hardly even recognize the devils of his own creation." . . .

The rapidity of change and the speed with which new situations are created follow the impetuous and heedless pace of man rather than the deliberate pace of nature. Radiation is no longer merely the background radiation of rocks, the bombardment of cosmic rays, the ultraviolet of the sun that have existed before there was any life on earth; radiation is now the unnatural creation of man's tampering with the atom. The chemicals to which life is asked to make its adjustment are no longer merely the calcium and silica and copper and all the rest of the minerals washed out of the rocks and carried in rivers to the sea; they are the synthetic creations of man's inventive mind, brewed in his laboratories, and having no counterparts in nature.

To adjust to these chemicals would require time on the scale that is nature's; it would require not merely the years of a man's life but the life of generations. And even this, were it by some miracle possible, would be futile, for the new chemicals come from our laboratories in an endless stream; almost five hundred annually find their way into actual use in the United States alone. The figure is staggering and its implications are not easily grasped—500 new chemicals to which the bodies of men and animals are required somehow to adapt each year, chemicals totally outside the limits of biologic experience.

Among them are many that are used in man's war against nature. Since the mid-1940's over 200 basic chemicals have been created for use in killing insects, weeds, rodents, and other organisms described in the modern vernacular as "pests"; and they are sold under several thousand different brand names.

These sprays, dusts, and aerosols are now applied almost universally to farms, gardens, forests, and homes—nonselective chemicals that have the power to kill every insect, the "good" and the "bad," to still the song of birds and the leaping of fish in the streams, to coat the leaves with a deadly film, and to linger on in soil—all this though the intended target may be only a few weeds or insects. Can anyone believe it is possible to lay down such a barrage of poisons on the surface of the earth without making it unfit for all life? They should not be called "insecticides," but "biocides."

The whole process of spraying seems caught up in an endless spiral. Since DDT was released for civilian use, a process of escalation has been going on in which ever more toxic materials must be found. This has happened because insects, in a triumphant vindication of Darwin's principle of the survival of the fittest, have evolved super races immune to the particular insecticide used, hence a deadlier one has always to be developed—and then a deadlier one than that. It has happened also because, for reasons to be described later, destructive insects often undergo a "flareback," or resurgence, after spraying, in numbers greater than before. Thus the chemical war is never won, and all life is caught in its violent crossfire.

Along with the possibility of the extinction of mankind by nuclear war, the central problem of our

Environmental activist Rachel Carson speaks in favor of curbing the use of chemical pesticides and the aerial spraying of crops, before a Senate subcommitee on June 4, 1963. AP/WIDE WORLD PHOTOS. REPRODUCED BY PERMISSION.

age has therefore become the contamination of man's total environment with such substances of incredible potential for harm—substances that accumulate in the tissues of plants and animals and even penetrate the germ cells to shatter or alter the very material of heredity upon which the shape of the future depends.

Some would-be architects of our future look toward a time when it will be possible to alter the human germ plasm by design. But we may easily be doing so now by inadvertence, for many chemicals, like radiation, bring about gene mutations. It is ironic to think that man might determine his own future by something so seemingly trivial as the choice of an insect spray.

All this has been risked—for what? Future historians may well be amazed by our distorted sense of proportion. How could intelligent beings seek to control a few unwanted species by a method that contaminated the entire environment and brought the threat of disease and death even to their own kind? Yet this is precisely what we have done. We have done it, moreover, for reasons that collapse the moment we examine them. We are told that the enormous and expanding use of pesticides is necessary to maintain farm production. Yet is our real problem not one of *overproduction?* Our farms, despite measures to remove acreages from production and to pay farmers *not* to produce, have yielded such a staggering excess of crops that the American taxpayer in 1962 is paying out more than one billion dollars a year as the total carrying cost of the surplus-food storage program. And is the situation helped when one branch of the Agriculture Department tries to reduce production while another states, as it did in 1958, "It is believed generally that reduction of crop acreages under provisions of the Soil Bank will stimulate interest in use of chemicals to obtain maximum production on the land retained in crops."

All this is not to say there is no insect problem and no need of control. I am saying, rather, that control must be geared to realities, not to mythical situations, and that the methods employed must be such that they do not destroy us along with the insects.

Further Resources

BOOKS

Brown, Michael H. *Laying Waste: The Poisoning of America by Toxic Chemicals.* New York: Pantheon, 1979.

Janick, Jules, et al. *Plant Agriculture.* San Francisco: W. H. Freeman, 1970.

Perkins, John. *Insects, Experts and the Insecticide Crisis: The Quest for New Pest Management Strategies.* New York: Plenum, 1982.

Shemilt, Lawrence W., ed. *Chemistry and World Food Supplies: The New Frontier.* New York: Pergamon, 1983.

PERIODICALS

Beckman, Tom J. "Farm Pesticides in Midwest Streams." *Ohio Farmer,* February 18, 1992, 78–79.

Finch, Robert H. "Agriculture's Role and Responsibility in Environmental Quality." *National Association of State Universities and Land Grant Colleges* 84, 1970, 90–94.

Peakall, David B. "Pesticides and the Reproduction of Birds." *Scientific American,* April 1970, 72–78.

Wallace, Mike. "Leaning toward the Public Sector." *Agrochemical Age,* November 1990, 12, 21–22.

WEBSITES

Harrison, Karl. "DDT, a Banned Insecticide." University of Oxford. Department of Chemistry. Available online at http://www.chem.ox.ac.uk/mom/ddt/ddt.html; website home page: http://www.chem.ox.ac.uk (accessed June 2, 2003).

Raloff, J. "The Case for DDT." *Science News* 158, no. 1, July 1, 2000, 12. Available online at http://www.sciencenews.org/20000701/bob2.asp; website home page: http://www.sciencenews.org/index.asp (accessed February 6, 2003).

The Origin of Races
Monograph

By: Carleton Coon

Date: 1962

Source: Coon, Carleton. *The Origin of Races.* New York: Knopf, 1962. Reprint, 1968, 658, 659–662.

About the Author: Carleton Stevens Coon (1904–1981) was born in Wakefield, Massachusetts, and in 1928 received a Ph.D. in anthropology from Harvard University, where he taught from 1927 to 1948. During World War II, he joined the U.S. Office of Strategic Services in Africa. In 1948, he became professor of anthropology at the University of Pennsylvania and curator of ethnology at the University Museum in Philadelphia. ∎

Introduction

A species consists of all the members of a group of plants or animals that can interbreed to produce fertile offspring. A human male and female are an example of members of a species, *Homo sapiens,* because they can have children who themselves can have offspring when they reach sexual maturity. A horse and donkey are not members of the same species because, although they can breed with each other, the mule they produce is sterile.

Below the level of species, scientists may designate subspecies, commonly called races. Members of a race should have features that unify them as a subgroup and as different from the members of another race. An example is dogs, which belong to the same species but whose breeds, or "races," have distinctive features.

American scientists in the past were keen to designate human races as a prelude to ranking them, for science needed to justify white European enslavement of black Africans and appropriation of land from Native Americans. Thomas Jefferson and Benjamin Franklin, America's leading scientists and statesmen of the eighteenth century, stressed the differences between whites and blacks that defined them as separate races. In the 1830s, Philadelphia physician Samuel Morton tried to distinguish whites from blacks and Native Americans by demonstrating that whites had larger brains than Native Americans, who in turn had larger brains than blacks. He was wrong, but whites were eager to believe him. In the mid–nineteenth century, Harvard zoologist Louis Agassiz thought whites and blacks were so different as to be nearly separate species, a view that American paleontologist Edward D. Cope supported in the 1890s.

The consensus that humans are divisible into races persisted into the twentieth century. In the 1940s, Harvard evolutionary biologist and historian of biology Ernest Mayr added the requirement that races occupy distinct geographic regions, a criterion difficult to apply to humans who had migrated by choice or the force of the slave trade beyond the areas they first occupied.

Significance

Carleton Coon maintained Mayr's emphasis on geographic distinctness, dividing humans into five races: the Caucasoids of Europe, the Mongoloids of Asia, the Australoids of Australia, the Negroids of central Africa, and the Capoids of southern Africa. Coon rooted these races deep in prehistory, asserting that they arose more than half a million years ago with *Homo erectus* and separately evolved into the five races of *Homo sapiens*. Some races became *Homo sapiens* before others. The implication was that Caucasoids did so before the other races, accounting for their superiority. Coon never doubted this superiority. He cautioned against racial intermixing, which he felt could upset the genetic equilibrium of a race. Coon thus defended the consensus that human races exist and are unequal. Although he disavowed any social or political agenda, instead claiming scientific objectivity, his certainty of Caucasoid superiority makes his claim suspect.

In fact, scientists from Jefferson to Coon were wrong. For a race to exist, its members must share most genes in common, whereas members of different races must share fewer genes with them. The Human Genome Project has revealed that human races are a fiction. Humans differ from one another in roughly 8 nucleotide bases (the molecules that build DNA) per 330, a difference that holds constant for two whites or for a white and a black or a black and an Asian. There are no genetic differences that allow scientists to divide humans into races.

Primary Source

The Origin of Races [excerpt]

SYNOPSIS: In this excerpt, Coon asserts that five human races developed at least half a million years in the past. Human races arose among *Homo erectus* and separately evolved into *Homo sapiens*, with some races reaching *Homo sapiens* before others. Members of different races, Coon asserted, should not interbreed for fear of disturbing each race's genetic equilibrium.

The Dead and The Living

My thesis is, in essence, that at the beginning of our record, over half a million years ago, man was a single species, *Homo erectus*, perhaps already divided into five geographic races or subspecies. *Homo erectus* then gradually evolved into *Homo sapiens* at different times, as each subspecies, living in its own territory, passed a critical threshold from a more brutal to a more *sapient* state, by one genetic process or another. . . .

I studied genetic theory, zoogeography, and human physiology (with special reference to adaptations to climate and culture); the history of the primates, with its marvelous record of parallelism, by which such similar creatures as the Old and the New World monkeys could evolve from different prosimians; and the record of our hominid predecessors, the Australopithecines. I also made a survey of world archaeology covering the Pleistocene. In addition, I had to explain the differences among fossil men between evolutionary characteristics and those that are racial. These efforts filled eight chapters, numerically two thirds of the book, but without them, Chapters 9 through 12 would not have been solidly grounded.

Now that the task is over, I feel that the three Eurasiatic lines—the Australoid, Mongoloid, and Caucasoid—have been traced fully enough so that future discoveries will entail no major surprises. The African material, however, is less well documented and new conclusions may be reached as new evidence becomes available.

As far as we know now, the Congoid line started on the same evolutionary level as the Eurasiatic ones in the Early Middle Pleistocene and then stood still for a half million years, after which Negroes and Pygmies appeared as if out of nowhere. The Ternefine-Tangier line has left us enough jaws and teeth to work with, only one very early but still unmeasured parietal from Ternefine, and two new pre-Mouillian skulls from Jebel Ighoud, Morocco. These skulls seem to support my hypothesis that the ancestors of the Bushmen and Hottentots originated north of the Sahara and only reached South Africa postglacially. After these skulls have been properly studied, they may also help explain why in the Middle Pleistocene North Africans resembled the earliest Mongoloids, whereas the East Africans were closest to the Caucasoids, and what role they may have played in the still enigmatic genesis of the Congoids.

We also urgently need new evidence concerning the details of the transition from the australopithecine to the human grade. The search for more early hominid fossils should be accelerated in the few suitable areas of the Old World which contain Lower Pleistocene deposits. Only when the key fossils have been found will we know where and when the major lines of human descent embarked on the separate paths that they have followed to this day.

Toward the end of the Pleistocene, after all five geographical races of man had become *sapiens* but before the two northern-most, the Mongoloid and

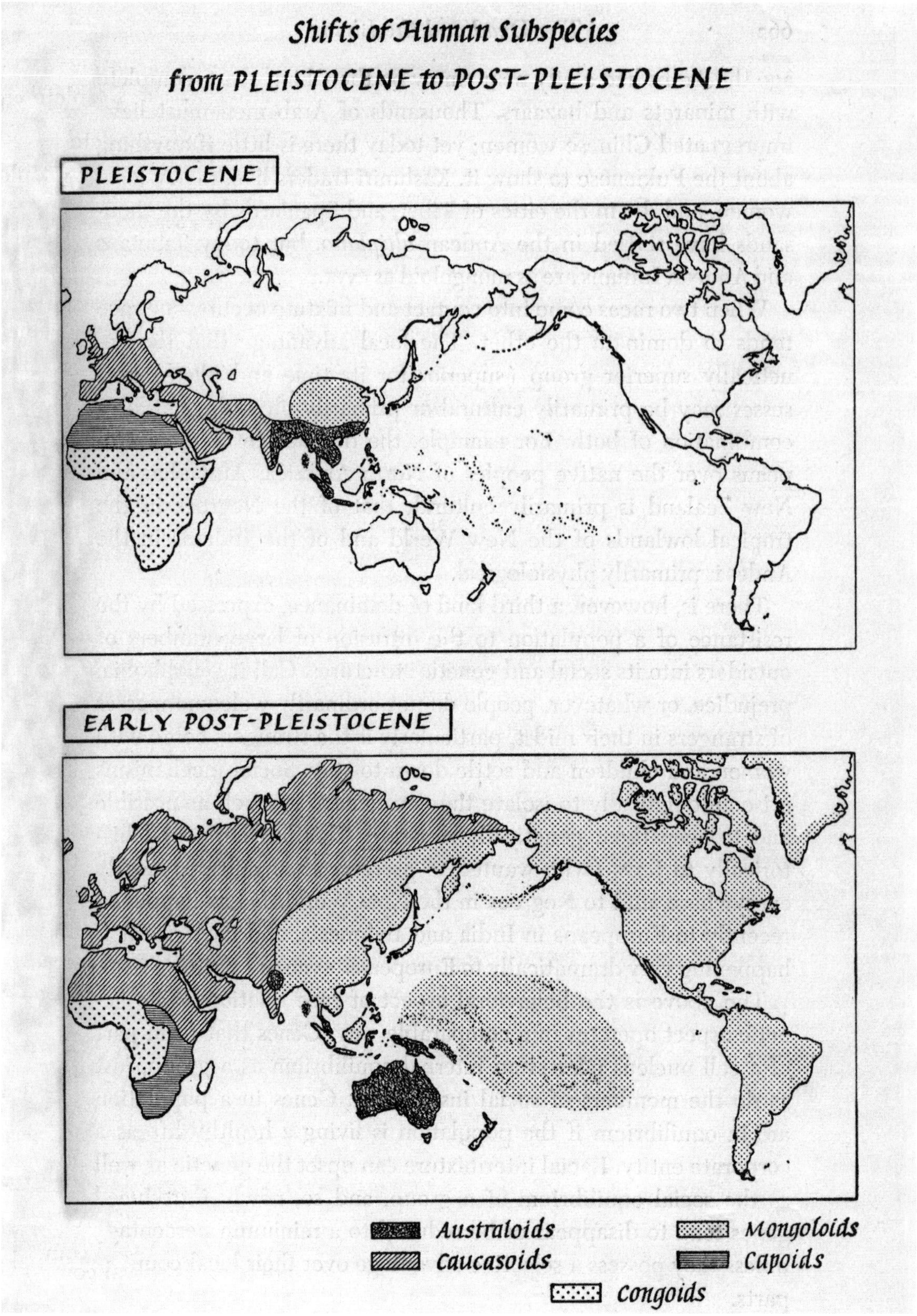

Shifts of Human Subspecies
from PLEISTOCENE to POST-PLEISTOCENE

PLEISTOCENE

EARLY POST-PLEISTOCENE

Australoids   Mongoloids
Caucasoids   Capoids
Congoids

This schematic map from Carleton S. Coon's *The Origin of Races,* shows the distribution of what he believed to be the five subspecies of humanity during most of the Pleistocene, from 500,000 to 10,000 years ago. The second map shows what happend at the end of the Pleistocene, when the Mongoloids and Caucasoids expand and burst out of their ancient territories. REPRINTED FROM COON, CARLETON S. *THE ORIGIN OF RACES.* NEW YORK: KNOPF, 1962, 661.

Caucasoid, had completed their southward invasions and expansions, each race may have contained nearly equal numbers of individuals. However, by the time agriculture and animal husbandry had been invented, by Caucasoids and Mongoloids, these two had begun to outnumber the others. With the wide spread of food production, the numerical disproportion between the races increased; and today Mongoloids and Caucasoids together constitute the vast majority of the earth's inhabitants.

The Australoids are on the decline, except among the aboriginal tribes of India; and the Bushmen and Hottentots number only tens of thousands. The Pygmies are few, but hold their own. The African Negroes, on the other hand, have shown extraordinary vitality. They have been particularly versatile in adopting new cultures wherever they have been taken, as laborers, by Caucasoids and Mongoloids, and they have become the dominant racial element in many of the tropical lowland regions of the New World, as well as of Madagascar and parts of the Arabian coast.

Once a race has become established as the principal population of a region, it has a tendency to stay there and to resist the genetic influences swept in by later invasions. Less than a thousand years ago the Arabs had a city near Amoy on the China coast, complete with minarets and bazaars. Thousands of Arab men must have impregnated Chinese women; yet today there is little if anything about the Fukienese to show it. Kashmiri traders live, marry local women, and die in the cities of Tibet, and Spaniards by the thousands have settled in the Andean *altiplano,* but today Tibetans and Andean Indians are as mongoloid as ever.

When two races come into contact and mixture occurs, one race tends to dominate the other. The local advantage that the genetically superior group (superior for its time and place) possesses may be primarily cultural or primarily physiological, or a combination of both. For example, the dominance of the Europeans over the native peoples of North America, Australia, and New Zealand is primarily cultural; that of the Negroes in the tropical lowlands of the New World and of the Indians in the Andes is primarily physiological.

There is, however, a third kind of dominance, expressed by the resistance of a population to the intrusion of large numbers of outsiders into its social and genetic structures. Call it xenophobia, prejudice, or whatever, people do not ordinarily welcome masses of strangers in their midst, particularly if the strangers come with women and children and settle down to stay. Social mechanisms arise automatically to isolate the newcomers as much as possible and to keep them genetically separate. This has happened historically to Jews (who wanted to preserve their culture) nearly everywhere, and to Negroes in the New World. It has happened recently to Europeans in India and Indonesia, and in Africa it is happening very dramatically to Europeans, even as I write.

The above is the behavioral aspect of race relations. The genetic aspect operates in a comparable way. Genes that form part of a cell nucleus possess an internal equilibrium as a group, just as do the members of social institutions. Genes in a population are in equilibrium if the population is living a healthy life as a corporate entity. Racial intermixture can upset the genetic as well as the social equilibrium of a group, and so, newly introduced genes tend to disappear or be reduced to a minimum percentage unless they possess a selective advantage over their local counterparts.

Further Resources

BOOKS

Brush, Stephen G. *The History of Modern Science: A Guide to the Second Scientific Revolution, 1800–1950.* Ames, Iowa: Iowa State University Press, 1988.

Gould, Stephen Jay. *The Mismeasure of Man.* New York: Norton, 1981.

Montagu, Ashley, ed. *The Concept of Race.* London, England: Collier, 1964.

Young, John Z. *An Introduction to the Study of Man.* Oxford: Oxford University Press, 1971.

PERIODICALS

Hoover, Dwight W. "A Paradigm Shift: The Concept of Race." *Conspectus of History,* March 1981, 82–100.

WEBSITES

Bright, Stephanie. "Carleton Coon: 1904–1981." Available online at http://emuseum.mnsu.edu/bio/abcde/coon%5Fcarleton.html; website home page: http://www.emuseum.mnsu.edu (accessed February 6, 2003).

Horus Publications. "Scientific Racism and Eugenics." Available online at http://www.horuspublications.com/guide/cu110.html; website home page: http://www.horuspublications.com/ (accessed February 6, 2003). *This site contains a list of books and articles on science and race.*

"Revolutions as Changes of World View"

Essay

By: Thomas Kuhn

Date: 1962

Source: Kuhn, Thomas S. "Revolutions as Changes of World View." In *The Structure of Scientific Revolutions.* Vol. 2 of *International Encyclopedia of Unified Science,* no. 2. Chicago: University of Chicago Press, 1962. Second edition, 1970, 111–12, 120–21, 122–23.

About the Author: Thomas Samuel Kuhn (1922–1996) was born in Cincinnati, Ohio, and received a Ph.D. in the history of science from Harvard University in 1949. He taught at Harvard, the University of California at Berkeley, Princeton University, and the Massachusetts Institute of Technology, and was a Guggenheim Fellow in 1954. ∎

Introduction

The traditional view of science is one of cumulative progress. By the steady accumulation of facts, scientists draw ever nearer to a description of reality. Science is thus progress from ignorance to ever fuller knowledge.

With few exceptions, the ancients and medieval Europeans thought, for example, that the earth was the motionless center of the universe and that the sun, moon, and planets circled around it. Only in the sixteenth and seventeenth centuries did the Polish astronomer and mathematician Nicholas Copernicus, the Italian Galileo, the German Johannes Kepler, and the British polymath Isaac Newton accumulate the facts that proved that the earth, too, was a planet and that it with the other planets revolved around the sun. Here was the exemplar of progress. Copernicus corrected the ancients by putting the sun at the center of the universe and setting the earth in circular orbit around it. Kepler corrected Copernicus by showing that the earth and the other planets traveled elliptical paths, not circles around the sun. Newton codified Kepler's discovery by calculating that the force of gravity kept the earth and the other planets in elliptical orbit around the sun. And in 1916, Albert Einstein demonstrated that what Newton had called gravity was simply the curvature of space. Any massive object, like the sun, warps space as a bowling ball curves a mattress upon which it rests, forcing the earth and the other planets to trace an ellipse around it. From Copernicus to Einstein, one comes ever closer to a full understanding of the solar system.

Significance

Thomas Kuhn disputed this traditional view of science. Much of science is what he called "normal science," the elaboration of a theory by adding a fact here, cor-

recting a discrepancy there. But no theoretical framework, what Kuhn called a "paradigm," has a monopoly on truth. A paradigm is simply a set of rules by which scientists agree to operate.

But one paradigm may replace another in a scientific revolution that forces scientists to see their world in new ways. Copernicus thus revolutionized astronomy by substituting a heliocentric for a geocentric solar system. The sixteenth century did not witness progress in astronomy as it had been but rather the radical replacement of one paradigm by another. Kuhn saw such as a scientific revolution as analogous to a shift in one's "gestalt," the pattern into which one fits the objects of the world. To adopt a new paradigm is to redefine reality.

But Kuhn did not claim that one paradigm had a better claim to truth than another. The history of science is the replacement of one theory by another with no assurance that a third will not topple the second in yet another revolution. To see the world through a different theoretical lens is no assurance that one sees the world with any greater accuracy. Thus, Kuhn introduced relativism into science: the assertion that no perspective has a greater claim to truth than another. In the process, Kuhn challenged scientists to redefine what they do. Not surprisingly some scientists rejected the notion that no paradigm has a greater claim to truth than another—a highly controversial claim. For example, evolutionary biologist and historian of biology Ernest Mayr rejects the notion that evolution has no greater claim to truth than the Genesis creation account. The theory of evolution by natural selection is not simply different from the creation account; it is superior because it better explains the origin and diversity of life.

Primary Source

"Revolutions as Changes of World View" [excerpt]

> **SYNOPSIS:** In this excerpt, Kuhn defines the work scientists do in elaborating a theory within "normal science." No theoretical framework or "paradigm" has a monopoly on truth. Rather paradigms replace one another in a series of revolutions, with no paradigm having a greater claim to objectivity than another.

Revolutions as Changes of World View

Examining the record of past research from the vantage of contemporary historiography, the historian of science may be tempted to exclaim that when paradigms change, the world itself changes with them. Led by a new paradigm, scientists adopt new instruments and look in new places. Even more important, during revolutions scientists see new and different things when looking with familiar instruments in places they have looked before. It is rather as if the professional community had been suddenly transported to another planet where familiar objects are seen in a different light and are joined by unfamiliar ones as well. Of course, nothing of quite that sort does occur: there is no geographical transplantation; outside the laboratory everyday affairs usually continue as before. Nevertheless, paradigm changes do cause scientists to see the world of their research-engagement differently. In so far as their only recourse to that world is through what they see and do, we may want to say that after a revolution scientists are responding to a different world.

It is as elementary prototypes for these transformations of the scientist's world that the familiar demonstrations of a switch in visual gestalt prove so suggestive. What were ducks in the scientist's world before the revolution are rabbits afterwards. The man who first saw the exterior of the box from above later sees its interior from below. Transformations like these, though usually more gradual and almost always irreversible, are common concomitants of scientific training. Looking at a contour map, the student sees lines on paper, the cartographer a picture of a terrain. Looking at a bubble-chamber photograph, the student sees confused and broken lines, the physicist a record of familiar subnuclear events. Only after a number of such transformations of vision does the student become an inhabitant of the scientist's world, seeing what the scientist sees and responding as the scientist does. The world that the student then enters is not, however, fixed once and for all by the nature of the environment, on the one hand, and of science, on the other. Rather, it is determined jointly by the environment and the particular normal-scientific tradition that the student has been trained to pursue. Therefore, at times of revolution, when the normal-scientific tradition changes, the scientist's perception of his environment must be re-educated— in some familiar situations he must learn to see a new gestalt. After he has done so the world of his research will seem, here and there, incommensurable with the one he had inhabited before. That is another reason why schools guided by different paradigms are always slightly at cross-purposes.

Later in the century Oresme sketched a similar analysis of the swinging stone in what now appears as the first discussion of a pendulum. His view is clearly very close to the one with which Galileo first approached the pendulum. At least in Oresme's case, and almost certainly in Galileo's as well, it was a view made possible by the transition from the orig-

Thomas Kuhn disputed the notion that science progresses toward truth by a steady accumulation of facts. He claimed that paradigms and theoretical frameworks replace one another in revolutions, none of which has any greater claim to truth than another. **PHOTOGRAPH BY STANLEY ROWIN. REPRODUCED BY PERMISSION.**

inal Aristotelian to the scholastic impetus paradigm for motion. Until that scholastic paradigm was invented, there were no pendulums, but only swinging stones, for the scientist to see. Pendulums were brought into existence by something very like a paradigm-induced-gestalt switch.

Do we, however, really need to describe what separates Galileo from Aristotle, or Lavoisier from Priestley, as a transformation of vision? Did these men really *see* different things when *looking* at the same sorts of objects? Is there any legitimate sense in which we can say that they pursued their research in different worlds? Those questions can no longer be postponed, for there is obviously another and far more usual way to describe all of the historical examples outlined above. Many readers will surely want to say that what changes with a paradigm is only the scientist's interpretation of observations that themselves are fixed once and for all by the nature of the environment and of the perceptual apparatus. On this view, Priestley and Lavoisier both saw oxygen, but they interpreted their observations differently; Aristotle and Galileo both saw pendulums, but they differed in their interpretations of what they both had seen.

Let me say at once that this very usual view of what occurs when scientists change their minds about fundamental matters can be neither all wrong nor a mere mistake. Rather it is an essential part of a philosophical paradigm initiated by Descartes and developed at the same time as Newtonian dynamics. That paradigm has served both science and philosophy well. Its exploitation, like that of dynamics itself, has been fruitful of a fundamental understanding that perhaps could not have been achieved in another way. But as the example of Newtonian dynamics also indicates, even the most striking past success provides no guarantee that crisis can be indefinitely postponed. Today research in parts of philosophy, psychology, linguistics, and even art history, all converge to suggest that the traditional paradigm is somehow askew. That failure to fit is also made increasingly apparent by the historical study of science to which most of our attention is necessarily directed here.

None of these crisis-promoting subjects has yet produced a viable alternate to the traditional epistemological paradigm, but they do begin to suggest what some of that paradigm's characteristics will be. I am, for example, acutely aware of the difficulties created by saying that when Aristotle and Galileo looked at swinging stones, the first saw constrained fall, the second a pendulum. The same difficulties are presented in an even more fundamental form by the opening sentences of this section: though the world does not change with a change of paradigm, the scientist afterward works in a different world. . . .

None of these remarks is intended to indicate that scientists do not characteristically interpret observations and data. On the contrary, Galileo interpreted observations on the pendulum, Aristotle observations on falling stones, Musschenbroek observations on a charge-filled bottle, and Franklin observations on a condenser. But each of these interpretations presupposed a paradigm. They were parts of normal science, an enterprise that, as we have already seen, aims to refine, extend, and articulate a paradigm that is already in existence. Section III provided many examples in which interpretation played a central role. Those examples typify the overwhelming majority of research. In each of them the scientist, by virtue of an accepted paradigm, knew what a datum was, what instruments might be used to retrieve it, and what concepts were relevant to its interpretation. Given a paradigm, interpretation of data is central to the enterprise that explores it.

But that interpretive enterprise—and this was the burden of the paragraph before last—can only articulate a paradigm, not correct it. Paradigms are not corrigible by normal science at all. Instead, as we have already seen, normal science ultimately leads only to the recognition of anomalies and to crises. And these are terminated, not by deliberation and interpretation, but by a relatively sudden and unstructured event like the gestalt switch. Scientists then often speak of the "scales falling from the eyes" or of the "lightning flash" that "inundates" a previously obscure puzzle, enabling its components to be seen in a new way that for the first time permits its solution. On other occasions the relevant illumination comes in sleep. No ordinary sense of the term 'interpretation' fits these flashes of intuition through which a new paradigm is born. Though such intuitions depend upon the experience, both anomalous and congruent, gained with the old paradigm, they are not logically or piecemeal linked to particular items of that experience as an interpretation would be. Instead, they gather up large portions of that experience and transform them to the rather different bundle of experience that will thereafter be linked piecemeal to the new paradigm but not to the old.

Further Resources

BOOKS

Asquith, Peter D., and Harold E. Kyburg. *Current Research in Philosophy of Science.* East Lansing, Mich.: Philosophy of Science Association, 1979.

Frank, Phillipp G. *Modern Science and Its Philosophy.* Salem, N.H.: Ayer, 1975.

Gutting, Gary, ed. *Paradigms and Revolutions: Applications and Appraisals of Thomas Kuhn's Philosophy of Science.* Notre Dame, Ind.: University of Notre Dame Press, 1980.

Kuhn, Thomas S. *The Essential Tension: Selected Studies in Scientific Tradition and Change.* Chicago: University of Chicago Press, 1977.

PERIODICALS

Cedarbaum, Daniel Goldman. "Paradigms." *Studies in History and Philosophy of Science,* April 1983, 173–213.

Eckberg, Douglas Lee, and Lester Hill. "The Paradigm Concept and Sociology: A Critical Review." *American Sociological Review,* August 1979, 925–937.

Heyl, John D. "Kuhn, Rostow and Palmer: The Problem of Purposeful Change in the 60s." *Historian,* Spring 1981, 299–313.

Kuhn, Thomas S. "The Relation between History and History of Science." *Daedalus,* Spring 1971, 271–304.

Reingold, Nathan. "Through Paradigm-Land to a Normal History of Science." *Social Studies of Science,* February 1980, 475–496.

WEBSITES

Pajares, Frank. "Thomas Kuhn." Available online at http://www.emory.edu/EDUCATION/mfp/Kuhnsnap.html; website home page: http://www.emory.edu/EDUCATION/mfp/Index.html (accessed February 7, 2003).

"Immunological Time Scale for Hominid Evolution"

Journal article

By: Vincent M. Sarich and Allan C. Wilson

Date: December 1, 1967

Source: Sarich, Vincent, and Allan Wilson. "Immunological Time Scale for Hominid Evolution." *Science* 158, December 1, 1967, 1200–03.

About the Authors: Vincent M. Sarich (1934–) was born in Chicago and was professor of physical anthropology at Stanford University from 1967 to 1981, when he joined the faculty at the University of California, Berkeley. His and Allan C. Wilson's use of DNA evidence to determine when humans and the African apes last shared a common ancestor broke new ground in paleoanthropology. He remains emeritus professor at Berkeley.

Allan Charles Wilson (1934–1991) was born in Ngaruawahia, New Zealand, and immigrated to the United States in 1955, where he served thirty-five years as professor of biochemistry at the University of California at Berkeley. He held a MacArthur Foundation Fellowship (a so-called "genius award"), was a visiting professor at Harvard University, St. Louis University, Massachusetts Institute of Technology, and universities in Israel and Kenya, and was nominated for a Nobel Prize. ∎

Introduction

British naturalist Charles Darwin considered the African apes—the two species of chimpanzee and the gorilla—humans' closest relatives, raising the question of when the African apes and humans last shared a common ancestor. That is, sometime in the past there must have been a proto-ape with two lines of descent: one leading to the African apes and one leading to humans. By definition, this proto-ape was their common ancestor.

Paleoanthropologists debated when this common ancestor lived. The influence of Darwin led many to suppose that the common ancestor had to have lived in the remote past. The mechanism of evolution, natural selection, fits an organism ever more closely to its environment. Because the environment is constant for long periods and changes only gradually, evolution is a slow process, meaning that many millions of years must have

passed to transform a protoape into a human. This view led paleoanthropologists to search for fossils of human ancestors in the remote past, possibly as long as 100 million years ago. In 1967, however, Yale University paleoanthropologist Elwyn Simons announced that he had discovered this common ancestor, *Aegyptopithecus,* in the Fayum Desert of northeastern Africa and dated it to 28 million years ago.

Significance

That year, 1967, Sarich and Wilson approached human evolution from a different perspective. They were interested not in fossils but in DNA. They understood that the common ancestor of humans and the African apes must have consisted of a single gene pool and that when the lines diverged, this gene pool must have split into two: one leading to humans and the other to the African apes. These gene pools would have become different by accumulating mutations. Sarich and Wilson measured the difference in the gene pools by sampling the differences in blood proteins. Because mutations occur at a steady rate, and because Sarich and Wilson knew the current magnitude of genetic difference between humans and the African apes, they calculated back to the time when no differences existed and only a single gene pool existed. Their calculation was 5 million years, one-sixth of the time Elwyn Simons predicted.

Their announcement in 1967 shocked paleoanthropologists, many of whom at first rejected their finding. Critics looked for errors in their method, but grudgingly they accepted Sarich and Wilson's position, settling for a date between 5 and 10 million years ago. Thus, in the 1960s, genetic evidence came to count for more than fossil evidence in determining the age of humanity.

Primary Source

"Immunological Time Scale for Hominid Evolution" [excerpt]

SYNOPSIS: In this excerpt, Sarich and Wilson assert that humans and the African apes shared a common ancestor only 5 million years ago. They arrived at this figure by measuring the differences in blood proteins as a way of measuring genetic differences between humans and the African apes. These differences could have arisen only by mutation. Because mutations occur at a steady rate, Sarich and Wilson could calculate back to the time when no differences existed, that is, to the time of the single gene pool of the common ancestor.

Abstract. *Several workers have observed that there is an extremely close immunological resemblance between the serum albumins of apes and*

Animal trainers and a chimpanzee have a meal together. It is believed that chimpanzees and humans evolved from a common ancestor roughly five million years ago. © TED STRESHINSKY/CORBIS. REPRODUCED BY PERMISSION.

man. Our studies with the quantitative micro-complement fixation method confirm this observation. To explain the closeness of the resemblance, previous workers suggested that there has been a slowing down of albumin evolution since the time of divergence of apes and man. Recent evidence, however, indicates that the albumin molecule has evolved at a steady rate. Hence, we suggest that apes and man have a more recent common ancestry than is usually supposed. Our calculations lead to the suggestion that, if man and Old World monkeys last shared a common ancestor 30 million years ago, then man and African apes shared a common ancestor 5 million years ago, that is, in the Pliocene era.

It is generally agreed that the African apes are our closest living relatives. However, the time of origin of a distinct hominid lineage has been a subject of controversy for over 100 years. . . . The absence of an adequate fossil record has forced students of hominid evolution to evaluate the phylogenetic significance of anatomical and behavioral characteristics in the living primate species in order to attempt a solution to that controversy. The nature of the problem is such, however, that no definitive answer has

yet been given. Current estimates range from a date in the late Pliocene to one in the late Oligocene or early Miocene for the origin of the hominids. This great range (4 million to 30 million years) effectively negates any meaningful discussion of the nature of our pre-Australopithecine ancestors, for the early dates bring us near to a primitive prosimian stock, while the late ones would suggest that a common ancestor for man and the African apes might well resemble a small chimpanzee.

One solution to this question lies in the measurement of the degree of genetic relationship which exists between man and his closest living relatives. As it has recently become clear that the structure of proteins closely reflects that of genes, it is to be expected that quantitative comparative studies of protein structure should aid in providing this measure of genetic relationship.

Proteins appear to evolve over time, as do the organisms of which they are a part. Thus, we may speak of the common ancestor of, for example, the human and chimpanzee serum albumin molecules, this ancestral molecule being present in the common ancestor of man and the chimpanzee. From the time that the human and chimpanzee lineages separated, their albumins have had the opportunity of evolving independently until today they are recognizably different, but homologously related, molecules. Such homologies may be studied by immunological techniques, the magnitude of the immunological cross-reaction serving as a measure of the degree of structural similarity between the two kinds of albumin. . . .

Although the primate fossil record is fragmentary, it does, in combination with the available immunological evidence, provide sufficient evidence to suggest that the lineages leading to the living hominoids and Old World monkeys split about 30 million years ago. That is, the ID of 2.3 which is the mean ID observed between the albumins of hominoids and Old World monkeys corresponds to a T value of about 30 in the above equation. If log 2.3 = k × 30, then k= 0.012. Since the mean ID between the albumins of man and the African apes is 1.13, the time of divergence of man from the African apes is log 1.13 divided by 0.012, that is, 5 million years. Proceeding similarly, we calculate that the lineage leading to the orang separated from that leading to the African apes 8 million years ago, and that the time of divergence of the gibbon and siamang lineage from that leading to the other apes and man is 10 million years. . . .

We suggest that the living apes and man descended from a small member of the widespread Miocene dryopithecines, which became uniquely successful due to the development of the locomotor-feeding adaptation known as brachiation. The adaptive success of this development and the subsequent radiation of the group possessing it may have made this group the only surviving lineage of the many apes present throughout the tropical and subtropical Miocene forests of the Old World. Possibly the African members of this radiation, in the Middle Pliocene (due perhaps to pressure from the developing Cercopithecinae), began varying degrees of adaptation to a terrestrial existence. The gorilla, chimpanzee, and man appear to be the three survivors of this later radiation. According to this hypothesis, some 3 million years are allowed for the development of bipedalism to the extent seen in the earliest fossil hominid, *Australopithecus*.

Further Resources

BOOKS

Leakey, Richard E., and Roger Lewin. *Origins: The Emergence and Evolution of Our Species and Its Possible Future.* New York: Dutton, 1977.

Lewin, Roger. *Bones of Contention.* New York: Simon and Schuster, 1987.

————. *Principles of Human Evolution: A Core Textbook.* Malden, Mass.: Blackwell Science, 1998.

PERIODICALS

Bailey, William. "Hominid Trichotomy: A Molecular Overview." *Evolutionary Anthropology,* June 1993, 100–108.

Begun, David R. "Relations among the Great Apes and Humans." *Yearbook of Physical Anthropology,* November 1994, 11–64.

Pilbeam, David. "Genetic and Morphological Records of the Hominoidea and Hominid Origins: A Synthesis." *Molecular Phylogenetic Evolution,* Autumn 1996, 155–168.

Rogers, Jeffrey. "The Phylogenetic Relationships among Homo, Pan, and Gorilla." *Journal of Human Evolution,* March 1993, 201–215.

Ruvolo, Maryellen. "Molecular Evolutionary Processes and Conflicting Gene Trees: The Hominoid Case." *American Journal of Physical Anthropology,* Summer 1994, 89–114.

WEBSITES

Smithsonian Institution. "Human Origins Program." Available online at http://www.mnh.si.edu/anthro/humanorigins (accessed February 6, 2003).

Walker, Phillip L., and Edward H. Hagen. "Human Evolution: The Fossil Evidence in 3D." Available online at http://www.anth.ucsb.edu/projects/human (accessed February 6, 2003).

"Energy Production in Stars"
Lecture

By: Hans A. Bethe

Date: December 11, 1967

Source: Bethe, H.A. "Energy Production in Stars." *Nobel Lecture,* December 11, 1967. Available online at http://www.nobel.se/physics/laureates/1967/bethe-lecture.html; website home page: http://www.nobel.se (accessed June 3, 2003).

About the Author: Hans Albrect Bethe (1906–) was born in Strassburg, Germany (now France) and earned a Ph.D. in physics from the University of Frankfurt in 1928. In 1934, he immigrated to the United States, where he became a lecturer at Cornell University. He was promoted to professor in 1937 and continued his academic career there until 1975. During World War II, he helped develop radar and served in the program to build the atomic bomb. In 1967, he won the Nobel Prize in physics. ∎

Introduction

The Greek philosopher and scientist Aristotle believed that the earth and the heavens differed. Earth was composed of substances subject to change. Water eroded rock; plants germinated and animals were born, both grew to maturity, declined in vigor, died, and decayed.

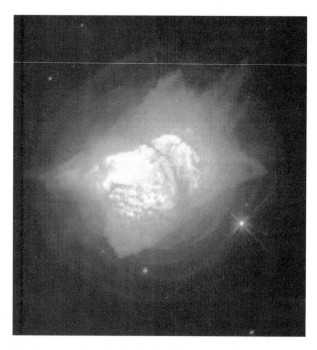

Hans Bethe won the 1967 Nobel Prize in Physics for his explanation of the life cycle of stars that culminates in nebula like this one, planetary nebula NGC 7027. A small white dwarf star at the center of this cloud of dust is all that remains of the red giant once found here. **H. BOND (STSCI) AND NASA. REPRODUCED BY PERMISSION.**

By contrast, the heavens were composed of a substance not subject to change. The stars that had lit the past would remain luminous into the eternal future. Aristotle's belief in the constancy of the heavens held during the Middle Ages, particularly during the twelfth-century revival of interest in his ideas in the new universities of Europe.

Scientists began challenging Aristotle in the seventeenth century. Italian physicist and astronomer Galileo overthrew Aristotle's notion of why objects moved. In the eighteenth century, German philosopher Immanuel Kant rejected Aristotle's notion of a static universe. The heavens were not unchanging; rather, the stars and planets had condensed from hot gases, an idea French astronomer Pierre-Simon Laplace embraced in 1796.

In the nineteenth century, scientists established that the stars are composed of the same elements as the earth. In 1814, German optician Joseph von Fraunhofer passed sunlight through a finely ground prism, discovering that it separated into a series of dark and light lines. During the 1850s, German physicist Gustav Kirchhoff discovered that the earth's elements emit the same spectrum of lines when heated, leading him to conclude that the earth and the sun were made of the same elements. Because the sun was a star, by extension all stars must be made of the same elements as those that make up the earth.

Significance

Yet none of these philosophers or scientists worked out a star's progression from birth to death. This task fell to Hans Bethe, though other scientists played a role, and his work in stellar evolution won him the 1967 Nobel Prize in physics. "Stars have a life cycle much like animals," he said in his Nobel address. "They get born, they grow, they go through a definite internal development, and finally they die, to give back the material of which they are made so that new stars may live."

In his Nobel address, Bethe focused on the decline and death of stars. As a star depletes the hydrogen in its core, it no longer has enough energy to support its mass, and the outer layers begin to collapse inward from gravity. This collapse causes a star to become hotter and more dense. This great heat then expands the star's outer layers so that it becomes a "red giant." It burns its elements quickly during this stage, fusing them together to create the heavier elements. The final collapse of a star leads to its death by explosion. In this explosion, it scatters its elements through space, where they can coalesce into new stars or planets.

Bethe's description of the later stages in a star's life explains how the universe, beginning with the hydrogen atoms that coalesced from the Big Bang, came to have the other ninety-one elements. That the earth contains iron, magnesium, sulfur, oxygen, nitrogen, carbon, and many other elements means that a dying star in the Milky Way had scattered these elements, which coalesced into Earth and the other planets in our solar system. Our solar system, then, including the sun, must have formed relatively recently during the universe's 15-billion-year existence. A day will come when the sun, like all other stars, will die, extinguishing life on Earth.

Primary Source

"Energy Production in Stars" [excerpt]

SYNOPSIS: In this excerpt from his Nobel address, Bethe described the decline and death of stars. He compared stars to animals, noting that both are born, grow to maturity, decline, and die. The death of a star scatters its elements through space, where they may coalesce into new stars and planets. In this way death leads to rebirth.

This evolution of a star was first calculated by Schwarzchild who has been followed by many others; we shall use recent calculations by Iben. When hydrogen gets depleted, not enough energy is produced near the center to sustain the pressure of the outside layers of the star. Hence gravitation will cause the center to collapse. Thereby, higher temperatures and densities are achieved. The temperature also increases farther out where there is still hydrogen left, and this region now begins to burn. After a relatively short time, a shell of H, away from the center, produces most of the energy; this shell gradually moves outward and gets progressively thinner as time goes on.

At the same time, the region of the star outside the burning shell expands. . . .

By this expansion the star develops into a red giant. Indeed, in globular clusters (which, as I mentioned, are made up of very old stars), all the more luminous stars are red giants. In the outer portion of these stars, radiative transport is no longer sufficient to carry the energy flow; therefore convection of material sets in in these outer regions. This convection can occupy as much as the outer 80% of the mass of the star; it leads to intimate mixing of the material in the convection zone.

Iben has discussed a nice observational confirmation of this convectional mixing. The star Capella is a double star, each component having a mass of about 3 solar masses, and each being a red giant. The somewhat lighter star, "Capella F" (its spectral type is F) shows noticeable amounts of Li in its spectrum, while the somewhat heavier Capella G shows at least 100 times less Li. It should be expected that G, being heavier, is farther advanced in its evolution. Iben now gives arguments that the deep-reaching convection and mixing which we just discussed, will occur just between the evolution phases F and G. By convection, material from the interior of the star will be carried to the surface; this material has been very hot and has therefore burned up its Li. Before deep convection sets in (in star F) the surface Li never sees high temperature and thus is preserved. . . .

The further developments of a massive star are more speculative. However the theory of Hoyle and collaborator is likely to be correct.

The center of the star heats up until the newly formed carbon nuclei can react with each other. This happens at a temperature of roughly 10^9 degrees. Nuclei like ^{24}Mg or ^{28}Si can be formed. There are also more complicated mechanisms in which we first have a capture reaction with emission of a gamma ray, followed by capture of this gamma ray in another nucleus which releases ^4He. This ^4He can then enter further nuclei and build up the entire chain of stable nuclei up to the most stable Fe. Not much energy is released in all of these processes.

The center of the star contracts further and gets still hotter. At very high temperatures, several milliards of degrees, thermal equilibrium is no longer strongly in favor of nuclei of the greatest binding energy. Instead, endothermic processes can take place which destroy some of the stable nuclei already formed. In the process, alpha particles, protons and even neutrons may be released. This permits the buildup of elements beyond Fe, up to the top of the periodic table. Because of the high temperatures involved all this probably goes fairly fast, perhaps in thousands of years.

During this stage, nuclear processes tend to consume rather than release energy. Therefore they no longer oppose the gravitational contraction so that contraction continues unchecked. It is believed that this will lead to an unstable situation. Just as the first contraction, at the formation of the H shell source, led to an expansion of the outer envelope of the star, a similar outward expansion is expected now. But time scales are now short, and this expansion may easily be an explosion. Hoyle *et al.* have suggested this as the mechanism for a supernova.

In a supernova explosion much of the material of the star is ejected into interstellar space. We see this, e.g., in the Crab Nebula. The ejected material probably contains the heavy elements which have been formed in the interior of the massive star. Thus heavy elements get into the interstellar gas, and can then be collected again by newly forming stars. It is believed that this is the way how stars get their heavy elements. This means that most of the stars we see, including our sun, are at least second generation stars, which have collected the debris of earlier stars which have suffered a supernova explosion.

To clinch this argument it must be shown that heavy elements cannot be produced in other ways. This has indeed been shown by Fowler. He has investigated the behavior of the enormous gas cloud involved in the original "Big Bang," and its development with time. He has shown that temperatures and densities, as functions of time, are such that heavy elements beginning with C cannot be produced. The only element which can be produced in the big bang is ^4He.

If all this is true, stars have a life cycle much like animals. They get born, they grow, they go through a definite internal development, and finally they die, to give back the material of which they are made so that new stars may live.

Further Resources

BOOKS

Berger, Melvin. *Bright Stars, Red Giants and White Dwarfs.* New York: Putnam, 1983.

Bernstein, Jeremy. *Hans Bethe: Prophet of Energy.* New York: Basic Books, 1980.

Berry, Richard. *Discover the Stars.* New York: Harmony Books, 1987.

Cooke, Donald A. *The Life and Death of Stars.* New York: Crown, 1985.

PERIODICALS

Burbridge, E. Margaret. "Synthesis of the Elements in Stars." *Review of Modern Physics,* October 1957, 22–37.

Cohen, Martin. "Do Supernovae Trigger Star Formation?" *Astronomy,* April 1982, 15–44.

Kirshner, Robert P. "Supernova: Death of a Star." *National Geographic,* May 1985, 42–50.

WEBSITES

Klein, O. "The Nobel Prize in Physics 1967." Available online at http://www.nobel.se/physics/laureates/1967/press.html; website home page: http://www.nobel.se (accessed June 3, 2003).

Nobel e-Museum. "Hans Bethe—Biography." Available online at http://www.nobel.se/physics/laureates/1967/bethe-bio.html; website home page: http://www.nobel.se (accessed June 3, 2003).

"The Earliest Apes"

Journal article, Photographs

By: Elwyn L. Simons

Date: December 1967

Source: Simons, Elwyn. "The Earliest Apes." *Scientific American* 217, no. 6, December 1967, 28–35.

About the Author: Elwyn Lavern Simons (1930–) was born in Lawrence, Kansas. He received a Ph.D. in anthropology from Princeton University in 1956 and a D.Phil. from Oxford University in 1959. He taught at Princeton, Yale University, and Duke University and was director of vertebrate paleontology at the Yale Peabody Museum in New Haven, Connecticut. ∎

Introduction

British naturalist Charles Darwin considered the African apes, which include two species of chimpanzee and the gorilla, as humans' closest relatives. This relationship focused attention on the time when the lines leading to the African apes and humans diverged. That is, paleoanthropologists wanted to know when humans and the African apes last shared a common ancestor.

Paleoanthropologists, trained in comparative anatomy, often emphasized the differences between humans and the African apes, suggesting a divergence in the remote past. Even more important was the influence of Charles Darwin. Darwin had supposed that evolution was gradual because its mechanism, natural selection, fit organisms ever more closely to their environment. Because the environment changes only gradually and in fact is stable for long periods of time, species remain stable for long periods and change only gradually. The evolution of humans from the common ancestor they shared with the African apes, an ancestor that likely was a hairy quadruped, must have taken many millions of years.

Significance

Elwyn Simons, like other paleoanthropologists, was heir to Darwin's gradualism. He concentrated his research on the Oligocene (a geological era about 30 million years ago), which he believed was the period during which the common ancestor of humans and the African apes lived. Even good scientists have a tendency to find evidence to fit their preconceptions, and Simons was no different. In the Fayum Desert of northeastern Africa, he discovered a new genus (a group of closely related species) of ape, *Aegyptopithecus,* which he dated at 28 million years ago. The Fayum had then been forest, and *Aegyptopithecus* was a nimble ape that foraged in trees. From this ape, Simons theorized, evolved three lines, one leading to the gorilla, a second leading to the two species of chimpanzee, and a third to *Australopithecus,* a biped whose postcranial skeleton resembled that of modern humans but whose brain was only a little larger than a chimpanzee's. *Australopithecus* in turn evolved into *Homo erectus,* a species of early man that arose about 2 million years ago, from which *Homo sapiens* evolved. According to Simons, *Aegyptopithecus* was thus the common ancestor of humans and the African apes.

That same year, however, molecular biologists Vincent Sarich and Allan Wilson cut his estimate by nearly five-sixths. Relying on genetics rather than the fossil record, Sarich and Wilson argued that the common ancestor was a single species with a single gene pool. When it branched into lines leading to humans and the African apes, the gene pool separated into two, with one leading to humans and the other to the African apes. These gene pools accumulated differences by mutation, which, as measured by differences in blood proteins, occurred at a steady rate. By measuring the difference between human blood proteins and those of the African apes, Sarich and Wilson could rewind the molecular clock to the time when the gene pools split. By their calculation, that split occurred only 5 million years ago.

Primary Source

"The Earliest Apes": Journal article [excerpt]

SYNOPSIS: In this excerpt, Simons announced his discovery of a new genus of ape, *Aegyptopithecus*, which he discovered in the Fayum Desert and dated to 28 million years ago. The Fayum had then been forest, and *Aegyptopithecus* had been an ape that foraged in trees. Simons believed *Aegyptopithecus* was the common ancestor of humans and the African apes. Two photographs of *Aegyptopithecus* from Simons's article are also presented.

What kind of animal gave rise to modern apes and man? The answer has been brought considerably closer by the unearthing in Egypt of the skull of an ancestral ape that dates back 28 million years

When it was that the early primates of the Old World first gave rise to the hominoid line from which the modern apes and man evolved is a question that has not had a satisfactory answer since it was first asked a century ago. Just where hominoid primates first evolved and why they evolved at all are rather more recent questions, but they too have lacked generally accepted answers. All three questions now appear to be answerable on the basis of evidence provided by fossil discoveries made during a recent series of Yale University expeditions to the Fayum region of Egypt. Our most exciting discovery, an almost complete primate cranium dating back between 26 and 28 million years, is the oldest ape skull ever found. It belongs to an individual of the newly established genus *Aegyptopithecus*. Studies of the skull, of abundant jawbones and teeth, of scarcer limb bones and of a few other skull fragments that represent this genus and five more genera of Fayum primates have added substance and precision to what was formerly a scant and hazy chapter in the record of primate evolution.

Only 60 miles southwest of Cairo, the Fayum is an area in which fertile fields gradually give way to desert badlands surrounding a large, brackish body of water called Lake Qàrùn. (The name of the region is derived from the ancient Egyptian word for lake: *pa-yom.*) The desert buttes and escarpments have been a fossil-hunter's paradise since late in the 19th century, when a few commercial collectors and professional paleontologists first explored the area. The Mediterranean coast is 120 miles away, but during Oligocene times it cut across the Fayum. There large rivers entered the sea and gradually built up layers of sand and mud that reach a total thickness of more than 600 feet. What is desert today was then a well-watered landscape in which forest was interspersed with open

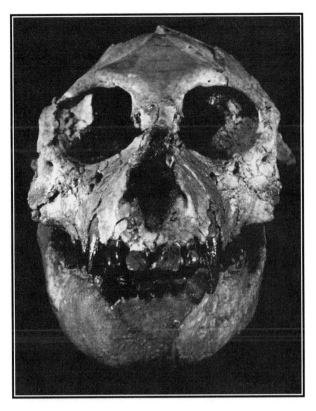

Primary Source

"The Earliest Apes:" Photograph

In 1967, Elwyn Simons discovered the fossilized skull of *Aegyptopithecus*. This photo shows the front view of the skull. The lower jaw and upper incisors are reconstructions.
PHOTO BY KELLY A. QUIN. © 2003 ELWYN L. SIMONS. REPRODUCED BY PERMISSION.

glades. Many fossilized tree trunks have been found: some are nearly 100 feet long. In trying to reconstruct the appearance of the Fayum during the Oligocene one gains the overall impression of a tropical forest along the banks of meandering rivers. . . .

With the world's oldest-known ape skull added to the rest of the fossils available for analysis, we return to the three questions raised at the beginning. As to when it was that the hominoid line leading to modern apes and man first evolved from a more generalized Old World primate, the almost inescapable answer today is during the Oligocene epoch. At least with respect to the great apes and man, the specific primate involved in the branching is *Aegyptopithecus,* although *Aeolopithecus* is perhaps a twig pointing toward the lesser apes. In turn, the primate stock from which the main branch grew could be the earlier fossil form *Propliopithecus.* An even earlier connecting link could be *Oligopithecus* of the early Oligocene,

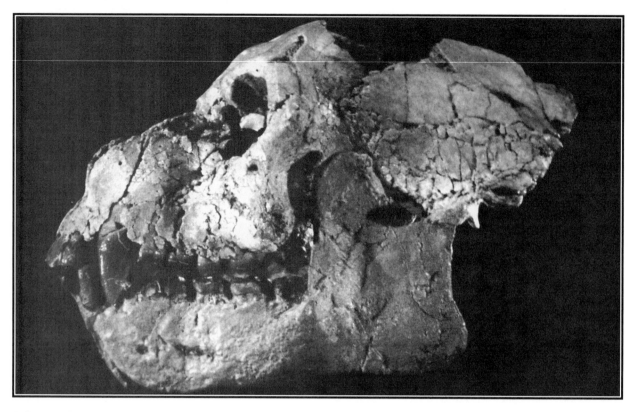

Primary Source

"The Earliest Apes:" Photograph
Side view of the skull of *Aegyptopithecus,* also called the "Dawn Ape." At 28 million years in age, it is one of the earliest known ancestors of humans and apes. PHOTO BY KELLY A. QUIN. © 2003 ELWYN L. SIMONS. REPRODUCED BY PERMISSION.

with its teeth that bear resemblances to Eocene primates as well as to most later monkeys and apes.

Obviously the second question, as to where these events took place, has already been answered. They certainly occurred in this one area of forest and glade where nameless rivers entered the sea. Presumably they were also taking place elsewhere to the west and south in Africa as boisterous populations of proto-monkeys and near-apes flourished and evolved over a span of some 12 million years. An accident of fossil preservation requires that, if we are asked, "Exactly where?" we must reply, "In the Fayum." Someday the answer may be much more wide-ranging.

It is well to remember in this connection that almost nothing is known of the Paleocene and Eocene animals of Africa, although together the two epochs comprise nearly half of the length of the Age of Mammals. Africa's fossil fauna in Oligocene and Miocene times, although better known, remain painfully scanty. The evolutionary scheme I have proposed here and the fossil genera on which it is founded

represent a rationale based on chance fossil preservation and discovery. The evidence is still susceptible to a number of alternative interpretations. Many early African primates must have existed about which we now know nothing. No one can say if some of them were more directly related to living man and the apes than any we now know.

There remains the question of why it is that hominoid primates evolved. The answer, it seems to me, is that the Oligocene primates' arboreal way of life, involving feeding on leaf buds and fruits near the end of branches, gave survival value to certain kinds of dexterity.

Further Resources

BOOKS

Leakey, Richard E., and Roger Lewin. *Origins: The Emergence and Evolution of Our Species and Its Possible Future.* New York: Dutton, 1977.

Lewin, Roger. *Bones of Contention.* New York: Simon and Schuster, 1987.

———. *Principles of Human Evolution: A Core Textbook.* Malden, Mass.: Blackwell Science, 1998.

Mayr, Ernest. *The Growth of Biological Thought: Diversity, Evolution, and Inheritance.* Cambridge, Mass.: Harvard University Press, 1982.

PERIODICALS

"Ancient Ancestor." *Time,* November 24, 1967, 62.

Begun, David R. "Relations among the Great Apes and Humans." *Yearbook of Physical Anthropology,* 72, 1994, 11–64.

Gibbons, Alice. "Sorting the Hominoid Bone Pile." *Science,* March 26, 1992, 176–177.

"Man's Earliest Known Ancestor." *Science News,* November 25, 1967, 514.

Simons, Elwyn L. "A Whole New World of Ancestors." *Evolutionary Anthropology,* July 1994, 128–139.

WEBSITES

ArchaeologyInfo. "Human Ancestry: Fossils." Available online at http://www.archaeologyinfo.com/aegypto.htm; website home page: http://www.archaeologyinfo.com/index.html (accessed February 6, 2003).

Smithsonian Institution. "Human Origins Program." Available online at http://www.mnh.si.edu/anthro/humanorigins (accessed February 6, 2003).

Walker, Phillip L., and Edward H. Hagen. "Human Evolution: The Fossil Evidence in 3D." Available online at http://www.anth.ucsb.edu/projects/human (accessed February 6, 2003).

"A Human Skeleton from Sediments of Mid-Pinedale Age in Southeastern Washington"

Journal article, illustration

By: Roald Fryxell

Date: April 1968

Source: Fryxell, Roald, et al. "A Human Skeleton from Sediments of Mid-Pinedale Age in Southeastern Washington." *American Antiquity* 33, no. 4, 1968, 511–514.

About the Author: Roald Fryxell (1934–1974), the lead author of this article, was born in Moline, Illinois, and received a Ph.D. in anthropology from the University of Idaho in 1971. He joined the faculty of Washington State University in 1962, where he served as professor of anthropology until his untimely death in an automobile accident. ∎

Introduction

Paleoanthropologists have long debated when humans arrived in the Americas. Since 1924, fossil and genetic evidence has supported British naturalist Charles Darwin's belief that humans and their ancestors originated in Africa. The earliest, the Australopithecines (bipeds with a postcranial skeleton similar to that of modern humans but a brain little bigger than that of a chimpanzee) arose more than 4 million years ago in South Africa and never left the continent. Neither did the first members of humanity's genus (a group of closely related species), *Homo habilis* and *Homo rudolfsesis* (species of early humans that made tools and had a brain about half as large as the brain of modern humans).

The first hominid to leave Africa was *Homo erectus* (a species of early humans that many paleoanthropologists believe to be the immediate ancestor of *Homo sapiens*), who migrated north to the Levant soon after his origin about 2 million years ago. From there, *Homo erectus* turned west to Europe and east to Asia, settling as far east as Indonesia. This migration suggests that *Homo erectus* built watercraft, raising the possibility that they had the technological skill to have crossed the Bering Strait from Siberia to the Americas. Yet paleoanthropologists have found their remains neither as far north as Siberia nor in the Americas. *Homo erectus* lived in tropical and temperate regions and seems never to have migrated far enough north to have crossed the Bering Strait.

Like its ancestors, *Homo sapiens* arose in Africa, perhaps between 100,000 and 200,000 years ago; the earliest fossil fragment dates to 130,000 years ago. Like *Homo erectus, Homo sapiens* migrated north out of Africa but at a slow pace. *Homo sapiens* arrived in Europe only 40,000 years ago, about when its members migrated into Australia and reached as far north as the Bering Strait.

From there, *Homo sapiens* might have crossed into the Americas, for Earth was in the grips of an ice age. Between 10,000 and 75,000 years ago, the polar caps locked up enough water in ice that the sea level fell to expose a land bridge between Siberia and the Americas. All humans had to do was walk across it.

Significance

Yet paleoanthropologists do not know when humans crossed into the Americas. Estimates of as early as 50,000 years ago are unlikely given the absence of evidence of human habitation of northeastern Siberia before 40,000 years ago. Extensive evidence of human remains in America dates only to 11,500 years ago (remains that paleoanthropolgists call the Clovis culture). This would seem to indicate that humans waited nearly 30,000 years after reaching the Bering Strait region in Asia before crossing over to North America, a delay that many find difficult to explain.

In 1968, Roald Fryxell and his associates announced the remains of a human between 11,000 and 13,000 years old. The earlier date places it within the time frame of the Clovis culture, but the later date predates the Clovis culture and may qualify it as the earliest migrant to the New World. Fryxell described the skull fragments as Mongoloid, as one would expect of a migrant from Asia. The bone fragments were broken, leading Fryxell to suspect cannibalism, a practice he believed common among the early inhabitants of the Americas.

Paleoanthropologists have identified other sites in North and South America as earlier than the Clovis culture, yet none has gained consensus. When humans arrived in America, they entered a land free from competition from other humans. In such an environment, their population should have increased rapidly, as it did around 11,500 years ago. For this reason, the majority of paleoanthropologists doubt that humans reached the Americas before 12,000 years ago, leaving the status of Fryxell's find uncertain.

Primary Source

"A Human Skeleton from Sediments of Mid-Pinedale Age in Southeastern Washington" [excerpt]: Journal article

SYNOPSIS: In this excerpt, Fryxell and his associates announced the remains of a human between 11,000 and 13,000 years old and identified it as a Mongoloid. The bone fragments were broken, leading Fryxell to suspect cannibalism.

Abstract

A living-site including human bones, bone midden, and artifacts has been discovered in sediments of mid-Pinedale age at the Marmes Rockshelter archaeological site in southeastern Washington. Radiocarbon dates, from sediments overlying the buried flood-plain surface on which these bones occur, show them to be older than 11,000 years. Geomorphic relationships suggest that the site may be younger than about 13,000 years.

■ ■ ■

Since July, 1965, staff members of the Department of Anthropology at Washington State University have been assessing the importance of charred and partially permineralized fragments of human bone exposed in sediments of 11,000–13,000 years of age at the Marmes Rockshelter archaeological site (45-FR-50) in southeastern Washington. The bones were first encountered at the base of a bulldozer trench cut for stratigraphic purposes to link sediments of the rockshelter with those of the adjacent flood plain of the Palouse River. Subsequent study at the site, primarily by Fryxell, has been conducted intermittently in both the field and the laboratory and has demonstrated that:

1. The bones (which now include nearly 50 pieces of the shattered human skull, a few pieces of rib, long bone, vertebrae, and bone from the wrist) are *in situ* in sediments comprising the surface of an abandoned flood plain of the Palouse River.

2. Bones present, in addition to those of man, include elk, deer, probably antelope and rabbit, and an unidentified species of fish. Small fragments of river mussel shell are present also.

3. Artifacts present in the limited test area now exposed include four pieces of worked bone representing one or more pointed bone implements. . . .

The skull must have belonged to a young individual, probably in its late teens or early twenties. No reliable determination of sex seems possible on the basis of the fragments unearthed so far. As could be expected on chronological grounds, all features of the skull which can be analyzed at this time reveal a fully modern (i.e., characteristic of *H. sapiens*) morphological pattern, with no traces of anything reminiscent of the earlier, more primitive (e.g., Neanderthaloid) stages of human evolution. Certain morphological details suggest that the individual was meso-, perhaps even brachy-cephalic, and that he had a broad-cheeked, flat face—a trait not surprising in what may be assumed to have been a Mongoloid population. This latter inference, however, must be considered tentative, pending the possible future recovery of other parts of the braincase, and of the facial skeleton proper.

The occurrence of these human bones with bones of animals obviously used for food raises the possibility that the human was eaten also. Definite evidence that this was the case is lacking, and the possibility that the skeletal fragments are those of a cremation burial has not been discarded. However, it should be noted that the human bones, as well as those of the animals, appear to have been cracked in the usual manner used aboriginally to extract marrow, and all bones but those of the elk have been charred. . . .

The age of the assemblage is indicated by several types of evidence:

1. The materials occur in undisturbed sediment at the base of a distinctive series of deposits, which are as follows: the weakly developed modern soil profile, formed on windblown sediment including scattered rock fragments from the nearby cliff; vol-

FACTS AND COMMENTS

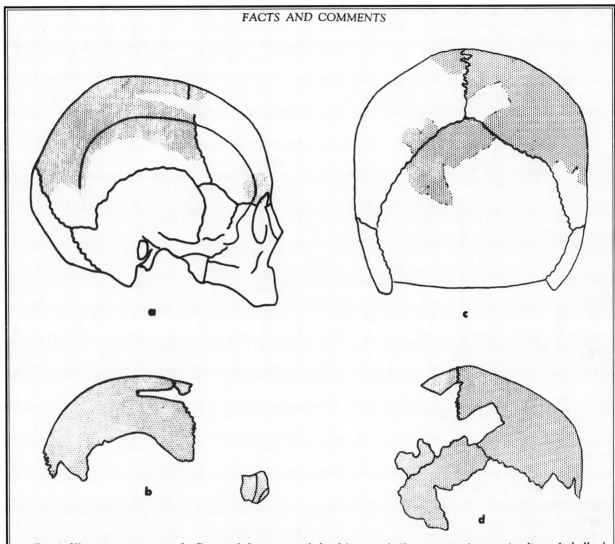

FIG. 1 [FRYXELL AND OTHERS]. Principal fragments of the Marmes skull: *a*, parietal view (outline of skull of modern Indian with analogous portions of Marmes skull shaded); *b*, actual outline of Marmes skull; *c*, occipital view (outline of skull of modern Indian with analogous portions of Marmes skull shaded); *d*, actual outline of Marmes skull.

Primary Source

"A Human Skeleton from Sediments of Mid-Pinedale Age in Southeastern Washington": Illustration
This illustration shows the skull fragments that Roald Fryxell and his colleagues believed came from the oldest human remains ever found in the Americas. REPRODUCED BY PERMISSION OF THE SOCIETY FOR AMERICAN ARCHAEOLOGY FROM AMERICAN ANTIQUITY, VOL. 33, NO. 4, 1968.

canic ash from the eruption of Mount Mazama at Crater Lake in Oregon, about 6,700 years ago; a well-developed textural and structural B-horizon representing a buried fossil soil formed on material which probably is mostly windblown in origin; coarse basalt boulders representing the toe of a now-buried talus slope which, when active, reflected a more severe frost climate than that of today; and an almost rock-free silty matrix of loess and flood-plain sediment containing a weakly defined organic horizon

which records the surface on which occupation occurred.

2. This sequence is well understood, having been studied, documented, and dated by Fryxell's research in the cave and at many other localities elsewhere in the Pacific Northwest.

3. Using the continuous exposures provided by the bulldozed cut, this sequence of sediments can be traced directly into the rockshelter itself, and thus

can be correlated with the geological and archaeological sequences exposed by Daugherty's previous excavations there.

4. Because of their continuity with the sediments in the rockshelter, sediments in the sequence outside may also be dated by radiocarbon age determinations obtained for sediments from within the shelter.

5. Three radiocarbon age determinations of 10,000–11,000 years (8800 B.C. ± 100, WSU 211; 8860 B.C. ± 275, WSU 363; 8525 B.C. ± 270, WSU 366) have been obtained from mollusk shells found at the shelter mouth in sediments which overlie those in which the midden occurs. The validity of these three dates is supported by the relationship of the samples from which they were obtained to overlying sediments from which an extensive sequence of cultural materials and radiocarbon dates have been derived. Ten radiocarbon dates, from charcoal as well as from shell, are in direct stratigraphic succession and are internally consistent in their sequence. Crosschecks are provided by the known ages of the Mazama ashfall, diagnostic projectile point types, and events of the paleoclimatic sequence reflected in the rockshelter sediments.

6. Elk bones, found associated intimately with the human bones outside the shelter occur primarily in the earliest levels of sediment within it; like some other early elk skeletons found in this region, these bones are larger than those of living representatives in the area today.

7. The sediments containing the bones appear to be the first deposited at that position in the canyon since draining of a lake which once existed there. From evidence obtained at other localities, it is known that the lake probably lasted until about 12,000–13,000 years ago, but that it was drained by at least 11,000 years ago.

8. The fragments of pointed bone shaft found with the skeleton are not incompatible with such an early date and are similar to those found at some other very early archaeological sites generally accepted to be of similar age.

Despite a century of intensive search by archaeologists, only a few discoveries have been made of even fragmentary human remains of late Pleistocene age. Not all of these finds, however, were made under circumstances in which the evidences for great age was conclusive (Irwin and Patterson 1968). The Marmes find, by fortunate coincidence, is documented by nearly six years of earlier archaeological and geological research at the site in which the discovery was made. Its potential scientific value is heightened by the direct association of midden and artifacts with the skeleton, for discovery of another archaeological site of greater than 11,000 years in age is almost as important as that of the skeletal material itself.

Further Resources

BOOKS

Dillehay, Thomas D., and David J. Meltzer, eds. *The First Americans: Search and Research.* New York: CRC, 1991.

Lewin, Roger. *In the Age of Mankind: A Smithsonian Book of Human Evolution.* Washington, D.C.: Smithsonian Books, 1988.

———. *Principles of Human Evolution: A Core Textbook.* Malden, Mass.: Blackwell Science, 1998.

PERIODICALS

Bahn, Paul G. "50,000-Year-Old Americans of Pedra Furada." *Nature,* March 11, 1993, 114–115.

Gibbons, Alice. "The People of the Americas." *Science,* September 22, 1996, 31–32.

Greenberg, Joseph. "The Settlement of the Americas." *Current Anthropology,* Spring 1986, 477–497.

Meltzer, David J. "Clocking the First Americans." *Annual Review of Anthropology* 73, 1995, 21–45.

Merriweather, Donald A. "Distribution of Four Founding Lineage Haplotypes in Native Americans Suggests a Single Wave of Migration for the New World." *American Journal of Physical Anthropology,* March 1995, 411–430.

Weiss, Kenneth M. "American Origins." *Proceedings of the National Academy of Sciences* 87, February 1994, 833–835.

WEBSITES

Parfit, Michael. "Who Were the First Americans?" *National Geographic.* Available online at http://www.nationalgeographic.com/ngm/0012/feature3/index.html; website home page: http://www.nationalgeographic.com (accessed February 7, 2003).

Apollo 11 Lunar Landing Mission

"*Apollo 11* Bootprint"
Photograph

By: Buzz Aldrin

Date: July 20, 1969

Source: Aldrin, Buzz. "*Apollo 11* Bootprint." July 20, 1969. Great Images in Nasa, National Aeronautics and Space Administration. Image no. AS11–40–5877. Available online at

Men from Earth

Autobiography

By: Buzz Aldrin and Malcolm McConnell

Date: 1989

Source: Aldrin, Buzz, and Malcolm McConnell. *Men from Earth.* New York: Bantam, 1989, 240–242.

About the Author: Edwin Eugene (Buzz) Aldrin Jr.(1930–) was born in Montclair, New Jersey, graduated from the U.S. Military Academy at West Point in 1951, and received a Ph.D. from the Massachusetts Institute of Technology in 1963. That year he became an astronaut, setting an American record for a space walk at five and a half hours in 1966. In 1969, he and Neil Armstrong became the first humans to land on the moon. In 1971, Aldrin retired from the National Aeronautics and Space Administration (NASA). ■

Introduction

The Soviet Union launched the space race in 1957 when it propelled the world's first satellite, Sputnik, into space. Congress countered in 1958 by creating NASA, the scientific agency that was to recapture America's leadership in space. But this task would not be easy, for in April 1961 the Soviet Union launched the first man, Yuri Gagarin, into orbit around earth. NASA responded on May 5, 1961, launching Navy Commander Alan Shepard Jr. into suborbital space. In February 1962, Marine Lieutenant John Glenn orbited the earth three times, besting Gagarin's single orbit.

Meanwhile on May 25, 1961, President John F. Kennedy (served 1961–1963) challenged Congress and the American people to put a man on the moon and safely return him to earth before decade's end. He framed the space race as a battle between freedom and tyranny, invoking the language of the cold war, the hostile rivalry between the United States and the Soviet Union. Yet at Vienna, Austria, in 1961 and at the United Nations in 1963 he searched for conciliation, inviting the Soviets to join the United States in a joint moon landing, but his assassination ended any chance for cooperation. The new president, Lyndon Johnson (served 1963–1969), felt he had to accomplish Kennedy's agenda in honor of his memory and pressed NASA to accelerate its efforts. In June 1965, Air Force officer Edward H. White became the first American to walk in space.

Yet not every mission succeeded. In 1967, three U.S. astronauts died in a fire and Soviet cosmonaut Vladimir

Astronaut Edwin "Buzz" Aldrin steps down from the lunar module *Eagle* to join Neil Armstrong on the moon, on July 20, 1969. Armstrong was the first man to set foot on Earth's moon, Aldrin, the second. **U.S. NATIONAL AERONAUTICS AND SPACE ADMINISTRATION.**

Primary Source

"Apollo 11 Bootprint"

SYNOPSIS: Astronaut Buzz Aldrin left this bootprint in the lunar soil so that he could then photograph it for study by soil mechanics experts. Aldrin and Armstrong spent about two hours on the surface of the moon. NASA. REPRODUCED BY PERMISSION.

M. Kamarov died during reentry into Earth's atmosphere. NASA recovered amid criticism, and in December 1968, three U.S. astronauts orbited the moon. The nation was now tantalizingly close to landing a man on the moon.

Significance

NASA launched *Apollo 11* on July 16, 1969. Aboard were Neil Armstrong, Michael Collins, and Buzz Aldrin. The command module, *Columbia,* contained the lunar module, *Eagle,* that would land on the moon. On July 20,

Armstrong and Aldrin landed on the moon. In dramatic fashion, Armstrong announced, "The *Eagle* has landed." Seven hours later he stepped on the moon, proclaiming, "That's one small step for man, one giant leap for mankind."

Aldrin joined him moments later, and the two unveiled a plaque with the words "Here Men from the Planet Earth First Set Foot Upon the Moon, July 1969, A.D., We Came in Peace for All Mankind." Knowing that more than a billion people, the largest audience in history, were watching them on television, Aldrin felt stage fright mixed with a sense of honor and duty as he and Armstrong planted a U.S. flag on the moon.

The mission did more than land Americans on the moon and beat the Soviets in the space race. It demonstrated the power of American science and technology, a power the federal government harnessed to achieve Kennedy's vision. The partnership between the federal government and science made possible the U.S. success. In the Soviet Union, the partnership between the central government and science was not even fifty years old. In the United States, in contrast, it stretched back nearly two centuries to the ideals of Thomas Jefferson, Benjamin Franklin, and George Washington.

Primary Source

Men From Earth [excerpt]

SYNOPSIS: In this excerpt, Buzz Aldrin recounted his and Neil Armstrong's landing on the moon in 1969. The two unveiled a plaque dedicating their landing to peace and all mankind and planted an American flag. On a more mundane level, Aldrin described the sensation of feeling nearly weightless as he jogged across the moon and his difficulty stopping and changing directions. Through the narration, the reader gains a sense of the historic importance of the moment.

Suiting up for the moon walk took us several hours. Our PLSS backpacks looked simple, but they were hard to put on and tricky to operate. They were truly our life-support systems, with enough oxygen, cooling water, electrical power, and radio equipment to keep us alive on the moon and in constant contact with Houston (via a relay in the LM) for four hours. On Earth, the PLSS and spacesuit combination weighted 190 pounds, but here it was only 30. Combined with my own body weight, that brought me to a total lunar-gravity weight of around 60 pounds.

Seven hours after we touched down on the moon, we depressurized the LM, and Neil opened the hatch. My job was to guide him as he backed out on his hands and knees onto the small porch. He worked slowly, trying not to jam his backpack on the hatch frame. When he reached the ladder attached to the forward landing leg, he moved down carefully.

The new capcom, Bruce McCandless, verified that we were doing everything correctly. Once Neil reached over and pulled a line to deploy the LM's television camera, Bruce said, "We're getting a picture on the TV."

"I'm at the foot of the ladder," Neil said, his voice slow and precise. "The LM footpads are only depressed in the surface about one or two inches." The surface was a very fine-grain powder. "I'm going to step off the LM now. . . ."

From my window I watched Neil move his blue lunar overshoe from the metal dish of the footpad to the powdery gray surface.

"That's one small step for . . . man, one giant leap for mankind."

∎ ∎ ∎

Lunar gravity was so springy that coming down the ladder was both pleasant and tricky. I took a practice run at getting back up to that high first step, and then I hopped down beside Neil.

"Isn't that something?" Neil asked. "Magnificent sight out here."

I turned around and looked out at a horizon that dropped steeply away in all directions. We were looking "down sun," so there was only a black void beyond the edge of the moon. For as far as I could see, pebbles, rock fragments, and small craters covered the surface. Off to the left, I could make out the rim of a larger crater. I breathed deeply, goose flesh covering my neck and face. "Beautiful, beautiful," I said. "Magnificent desolation."

Stepping out of the LM's shadow was a shock. One moment I was in total darkness, the next in the sun's hot floodlight. From the ladder I had seen all the sunlit moonscape beyond our shadow, but with no atmosphere, there was absolutely no refracted light around me. I stuck my hand out past the shadow's edge into the sun, and it was like punching through a barrier into another dimension. I moved around the legs of the LM to check for damage.

"Looks like the secondary strut has a little thermal effect on it right here, Neil," I said, pointing to some engine burn on the leg.

"Yeah," Neil said, coming over beside me. "I noticed that."

We were both in the sun again, our helmets close together. Neil leaned toward me and clapped his gloved hand on my shoulder. "Isn't it fun?" he said.

I was grinning ear to ear, even though the gold visor hid my face. Neil and I were standing together on the *moon.*

∎ ∎ ∎

As we moved about getting ready to set up our experiments, I watched the toe of my boot strike the surface. The gray dust shot out with machinelike precision, the grains landing nearly equidistant from my toe. I was fascinated by this, and for the first time *felt* what it was like to walk on the airless moon.

One of my tests was to jog away from the LM to see how maneuverable an astronaut was on the surface. I remembered what Isaac Newton had taught us two centuries before: mass and weight are not the same. I weighed only 60 pounds, but my *mass* was the same as it was on Earth. Inertia was a problem. I had to plan ahead several steps to bring myself to a stop or to turn, without falling.

But after a few jogging turns, I figured out how to move quite easily. Time was going by quickly, I realized, when Neil signaled me over to unveil the plaque. We stood beside the LM leg and Neil read the words:

"HERE MEN FROM THE PLANET EARTH

FIRST SET FOOT UPON THE MOON

JULY 1969, A. D.

WE CAME IN PEACE FOR ALL MANKIND."

One of the first things Neil did on the surface was take a sample of the lunar soil in case we had to terminate our moon walk early. Now he started working with his scoop and collection box while I set up the metal foil "window shade" of the solar wind collector. The moon was like a giant sponge that absorbed the constant "wind" of charged particles streaming outward from the sun. Scientists back on Earth would examine the collector to learn more about this phenomenon and, through it, the history of the solar system.

As we removed the flag from the equipment compartment at the base of the LM, I suddenly felt stage fright. Since childhood I'd been fascinated by explorers planting flags on strange shores. Now I was about to do the same thing, but on the most exotic shore mankind had ever reached.

Of all the jobs I had to do on the moon, the one I wanted to go the smoothest was the flag raising. Bruce had told us we were being watched by the largest television audience in history, over a billion people. Just beneath the powdery surface, the subsoil was very dense. We succeeded in pushing the flagpole in only a couple of inches. It didn't look very sturdy. But I did snap off a crisp West Point salute once we got the banner upright.

Further Resources

BOOKS

Alexander, Thomas W. *Project Apollo: Man to the Moon.* New York: Harper and Row, 1964.

Collins, Michael. *Liftoff: The Story of America's Adventure in Space.* New York: Grove, 1988.

Compton, William David. *Where No Man Has Gone Before: A History of the Apollo Lunar Exploration Missions.* Washington, D.C.: GPO, 1989.

Cooper, Henry S.F. *Apollo on the Moon.* New York: Dial, 1969.

Cox, Donald W. *The Space Race.* Philadelphia: Chilton, 1962.

Lewis, Richard S. *The Voyages of Apollo: The Exploration of the Moon.* New York: The New York Times Book Company, 1974.

Murray, Charles, and Catherine Bly Cox. *Apollo: The Race to the Moon.* New York: Simon and Schuster, 1989.

PERIODICALS

Diamond, Edwin. "Sputnik—Forty Years Ago This Month the Soviet Union Orbited a 'Man-Made Moon' Whose Derisive Chirp Persuaded Americans They'd Already Lost a Race That Had Barely Begun." *American Heritage,* June 1997.

Johnson, Nicholas L. "Apollo and Zond—Race around the Moon?" *Spaceflight,* December 1978, 403–412.

Kluger, Jeffrey. "They Asked for the Moon." *Time,* July 19, 1999, 68-71.

Oberg, James E. "Russia Meant to Win the 'Moon Race.'" *Spaceflight,* November 1975, 163–171.

WEBSITES

"The Apollo Program." Smithsonian National Air and Space Museum. Available online at http://www.nasm.edu/apollo/apollo.htm; website home page: http://www.nasm.edu (accessed April 2, 2003).

"Apollo: Thirtieth Anniversary." NASA History Office. Available online at http://history.nasa.gov/ap11ann/introduction.htm; website home page http://history.nasa.gov (accessed April 2, 2003).

John Glenn: A Memoir
Memoir

By: John Glenn

Date: 1999

Source: Glenn, John, with Nick Taylor. *John Glenn: A Memoir.* New York: Bantam, 1999, 263–265.

About the Author: John Herschel Glenn (1921–) was born in Cambridge, Ohio, joined the U.S. Marine Corps in 1943, and flew nearly 150 missions during World War II and the Korean War. In 1959, he was promoted to lieutenant colonel, and in 1962 he became the first American to orbit the Earth. He served four terms in the U.S. Senate and in 1998 became the oldest person ever to travel in space. ■

Colonel John Glenn (center) enters feet first into the Friendship 7 spacecraft, which rests atop a Saturn rocket. Glenn circled the Earth three times in the Friendship 7 on February 20, 1962, making him the first American to orbit the Earth. © BETTMANN/CORBIS. REPRODUCED BY PERMISSION.

Introduction

The space race that propelled John Glenn into orbit had its origins in the cold war, the hostile rivalry between the United States and the Soviet Union that shaped science and technology in both nations. Both had cooperated during World War II (1939–1945) against a common enemy, Nazi Germany, but after the war, the incompatibility of American capitalism and Soviet communism drove the two apart. The United States became alarmed at the Soviet occupation of Eastern Europe; the Soviets were suspicious of U.S. motives in aiding Western Europe.

During the cold war, each nation sought military superiority through scientific achievement. Each believed that the control of space would give it an edge in missile and satellite technology and that science would advance this technology. The development of the atomic bomb in 1945 gave Americans confidence in the superiority of their science and technology. This confidence collapsed in 1957 when the Soviets launched the world's first intercontinental ballistic missile and the first satellite, Sputnik. These events galvanized the United States. The next

year, Congress passed the National Defense Education Act, which funded the teaching of science, mathematics, and foreign languages in public schools. The act was a declaration that the United States would recapture leadership in science and technology. In this spirit, Congress in 1958 created the National Aeronautics and Space Administration (NASA), the scientific agency that was to recapture American leadership in the space race.

Not to be outdone, the Soviets in April 1961 launched the first man, Yuri Gagarin, into orbit around the earth. NASA responded on May 5, 1961, by launching Navy Commander Alan Shepard Jr. 116 miles into space in a flight that lasted just over fifteen minutes. Amid this rivalry, President John F. Kennedy challenged Congress and the American people on May 25, 1961, to land a man on the moon and safely return him to earth before decade's end.

Significance

As a first step toward this goal, NASA sought to catch up by sending John Glenn into three earth orbits in February 1962 (besting Gagarin's single orbit). Glenn's

Astronaut John Glenn trains at Cape Canaveral, Florida, in a Mercury spacesuit before his orbit around the earth. The Mercury spacesuit was made of an inner layer of Neoprene-coated nylon and an outer layer of aluminized nylon; the suit allowed only limited mobility. NASA. REPRODUCED BY PERMISSION.

recollection of his flight has none of the rhetoric of the Cold War, emphasizing instead the beauty of flight in space.

Glenn's flight captured the American public's imagination and was a tangible sign of what science could accomplish. Perhaps more important, it underscored the success of the partnership between science and the federal government, a partnership that had deeper roots than most Americans realized. As early as the eighteenth century, Thomas Jefferson, Benjamin Franklin, and George Washington wanted Congress to fund science in the belief that it could help farmers produce more food. Congress finally followed their advice in 1862 when it created the U.S. Department of Agriculture and the agricultural and mechanical colleges. Since then, the federal government and science have forged an ever closer relationship. During the twentieth century, scientists came to depend on federal grants to fund research. From these grants came the discovery of vitamins, the development of vitamin-fortified milk and food, and the discovery of antibiotics. Glenn's flight was an affirmation of the synergistic relationship between science and the federal government, a relationship that continues to thrive today.

Primary Source

John Glenn: A Memoir [excerpt]

SYNOPSIS: In this excerpt, John Glenn describes the beauty of seeing the sun set and rise from space. The beauty was greater than anything he had imagined and more beautiful than any sunrise or sunset he had seen from earth.

Flying backward over the Indian Ocean, I began to fly out of daylight. I was now about forty minutes into the flight, nearing the 150–mile apogee, the highest point, of my orbital track. Moving away from the sun at 17,500 miles an hour—almost eighteen times Earth's rotational speed—sped the sunset.

This was something I had been looking forward to, a sunset in space. All my life I have remembered particularly beautiful sunrises or sunsets; in the Pacific islands in World War II; the glow in the haze layer in northern China; the two thunderheads out over the Atlantic with the sun silhouetting them the morning of Gus's launch. I've mentally collected them, as an art collector remembers visits to a gallery full of Picassos, Michelangelos, or Rembrandts. Wonderful as man-made art may be, it cannot compare in my mind to sunsets and sunrises, God's masterpieces. Here on Earth we see the beautiful reds, oranges, and yellows with a luminous quality that no film can fully capture. What would it be like in space?

It was even more spectacular than I imagined, and different in that the sunlight coming through the prism of Earth's atmosphere seemed to break out the whole spectrum, not just the colors at the red end but the greens, blues, indigos, and violets at the other. It made *spectacular* an understatement for the few seconds' view. From my orbiting front porch, the setting sun that would have lingered during a long earthly twilight sank eighteen times as fast. The sun was fully round and as white as a brilliant arc light, and then it swiftly disappeared and seemed to melt into a long thin line of rainbow-brilliant radiance along the curve of the horizon.

I added my first sunset from space to my collection.

I reported to the capcom aboard the ship, the *Ocean Sentry,* in the Indian Ocean that was my fifth tracking link, "The sunset was beautiful. I still have a brilliant blue band clear across the horizon, almost covering the whole window.

"The sky above is absolutely black, completely black. I can see stars up above."

Flying on, I could see the night horizon, the roundness of the darkened Earth, and the light of the moon on the clouds below. I needed the periscope to see the moon coming up behind me. I began to search the sky for constellations.

Gordo Cooper's familiar voice came over the headset as *Friendship Seven* neared Australia. He was the capcom at the station at Muchea, on the west coast just north of Perth. "That sure was a short day," I told him.

"Say again, *Friendship Seven.*"

"That was about the shortest day I've ever run into."

"Kinda passes rapidly, huh?"

"Yes, sir."

I spotted the Pleiades, a cluster of seven stars. Gordo asked me for a blood pressure reading, and I pumped the cuff again. He told me to look for lights, and I reported, "I can see the outline of a town, and a very bright light just to the south of it." The elapsed-time clock read 4:39. It was midnight on the west coast of Australia.

"Perth and Rockingham, you're seeing there," Gordo said.

"Roger. The lights show up very well, and thank everybody for turning them on, will you?"

"We sure will, John."

The capcom at Woomera, in south-central Australia, radioed that my blood pressure was 126 over 90. I radioed back that I still felt fine, with no vision problems and no nausea or vertigo from the head movements made periodically.

The experiments continued. Over the next tracking station, on a tiny coral atoll called Canton Island, midway between Australia and Hawaii, I lifted the visor of my helmet and ate for the first time, squeezing some applesauce from a toothpastelike tube into my mouth to see if weightlessness interfered with swallowing. It didn't.

It was all so new. An hour and fourteen minutes into the flight, I was approaching day again. I didn't have time to reflect on the magnitude of my experience, only to record its components as I reeled off

the readings and performed the tests. The capcom on Canton Island helped me put it in perspective after I reported seeing through the periscope "the brilliant blue horizon coming up behind me; approaching sunrise."

"Roger, *Friendship Seven*. You are very lucky."

"You're right. Man, this is beautiful."

The sun rose as quickly as it had set. Suddenly there it was, a brilliant red in my view through the periscope. It was blinding, and I added a dark filter to the clear lens so I could watch it. Suddenly I saw around the capsule a huge field of particles that looked like tiny yellow stars. They seemed to travel with the capsule, but more slowly. There were thousands of them, like swirling fireflies. I talked into the cockpit recorder about this mysterious phenomenon as I flew out of range of Canton Island and into a dead zone before the station at Guaymas, Mexico, on the Gulf of California, picked me up. We thought we had foreseen everything, but this was entirely new. I tried to describe them again, but Guaymas seemed interested only in giving me the retro sequence time, the precise moment the capsule's retro-rockets would have to be fired in case I had to come down after one orbit.

Further Resources

BOOKS

Collins, Michael. *Liftoff: The Story of America's Adventure in Space.* New York: Grove, 1988.

Compton, William David. *Where No Man Has Gone Before: A History of the Apollo Lunar Exploration Missions.* Washington, D.C.: GPO, 1989.

Cox, Donald W. *The Space Race.* Philadelphia: Chilton, 1962.

Lewis, Richard S. *The Voyages of Apollo: The Exploration of the Moon.* New York: The New York Times Book Company, 1974.

Murray, Charles, and Catherine Bly Cox. *Apollo: The Race to the Moon.* New York: Simon and Schuster, 1989.

Wilfred, John N. *We Reach the Moon.* New York: Bantam, 1969.

PERIODICALS

Johnson, Nicholas L. "Apollo and Zond-Race around the Moon?" *Spaceflight,* December 1978, 403–412.

Oberg, James E. "Russia Meant to Win the 'Moon Race.'" *Spaceflight,* November 1975, 163–171.

12

SPORTS

WILLIAM J. THOMPSON

Entries are arranged in chronological order by date of primary source. For entries with one primary source, the entry title is the same as the primary source title. Entries with more than one primary source have an overall entry title, followed by the titles of the primary sources.

Important Events in Sports, 1960–1969

1960

- National Association for Stock Car Racing (NASCAR) Grand National tracks open at Charlotte, North Carolina, and Atlanta, Georgia.

- The New York Yankees hit a record 193 home runs during the season, winning their twenty-fifth American League pennant; they lose the series in seven games to the Pittsburgh Pirates.

- Approximately 6.5 million Americans participate in organized bowling; the top money winner among professional bowlers is Frank Clause from Old Forge, Pennsylvania, who earns over one hundred thousand dollars.

- Some $2 billion is wagered by an estimated 30 million people at American racetracks; Kelso is horse of the year, winning six consecutive stakes races and registering $293,310 in earnings.

- The second annual National Collegiate Athletic Association (NCAA) soccer championship is won by Saint Louis University, 5-2, over the University of Connecticut.

- Professional boxing is the fifth-ranked spectator sport in the United States, attracting some four million people annually to live matches.

- For the first time since 1936, the United States fails to reach the challenge round of Davis Cup tennis competition.

- On January 26, Los Angeles Rams general manager Pete Rozelle, 33, is named commissioner of the National Football League (NFL).

- From February 18 to February 28, the VIII Winter Olympics are held in Squaw Valley, California; ice-skater (and subsequent gold medal-winner) Carol Heiss is the first woman accorded the honor of reciting the Olympic oath at the opening ceremonies, which are televised live on national television.

- On March 19, Ohio State University wins the NCAA basketball championship, defeating the University of California, 75-55.

- On April 10, golfer Arnold Palmer wins the Masters Tournament; he earns seventy-one thousand dollars for the season, also finishing first in the U.S. Open on June 18.

- On May 29, Jim Beatty runs the mile in 3:58, the fastest ever by an American, in the California Relays.

- On May 30, a temporary stand collapses at the Indianapolis 500, killing two and injuring fifty. Jim Rathmann wins the race.

- On June 17, Ted Williams of the Boston Red Sox hits his five hundredth career home run against the Cleveland Indians.

- On June 20, Floyd Patterson becomes the first man to regain a world heavyweight title, knocking out Ingemar Johannson in five rounds. The fight brings revenues of over $4 million; Patterson earns $636,000, Johannson $763,000.

- From August to September, the XVII Summer Olympics are held in Rome. Soviets dominate the competition, but Americans Wilma Rudolph, Rafer Johnson, and Cassius Clay are star performers.

- On August 22, Jim Brewer of the Chicago Cubs sues Cincinnati Reds' Billy Martin for $1 million because of injuries suffered in a fight on August 4.

- On October 13, Pittsburgh Pirate Bill Mazeroski hits a home run in the bottom of the ninth in the seventh game of the World Series to beat the New York Yankees, 10-9.

- On November 29, Navy halfback Joe Bellino wins the Heisman Trophy as the outstanding college football player of the year.

- On December 26, the Philadelphia Eagles defeat the Green Bay Packers, 17-3, to win the NFL championship.

1961

- Phil Hill is the first American to win the Grand Prix driver's championship.

- The American League in professional baseball expands from eight to ten teams, adding a new team in Washington while moving the Senators and renaming them the Minnesota Twins and adding the Los Angeles Angels.

- Kelso is named horse of the year for the second year in a row, posting earnings of $425,565 and winning seven of nine races.

- On January 1, the Houston Oilers defeat the Los Angeles Chargers in the American Football League's first championship game.

- On January 2, the University of Washington defeats the University of Minnesota, 17-7, in the Rose Bowl.

- On February 15, the entire U.S. figure-skating team is killed in a plane crash while traveling to the world championships in Prague.

- On March 13, Floyd Patterson retains his heavyweight boxing championship, knocking out Ingemar Johannson in three rounds; this third meeting between the two makes their rivalry the longest series ever for the heavyweight championship.

- On March 25, favored Ohio State, featuring All-Americans Jerry Lucas and Bobby Knight, loses the NCAA basketball championship to the University of Cincinnati, 70-65; Ohio State draws 342,938 fans to its twenty-eight games that season.

- On April 16, the Chicago Black Hawks win the Stanley Cup in ice hockey, beating the Detroit Red Wings four games to two to win their first championship in twenty-three years.

• On May 6, Carry Back wins the Kentucky Derby and two weeks later the Preakness before suffering an injury in the Belmont and thus missing the Triple Crown of horse racing.

• On August 11, Warren Spahn of the Milwaukee Braves wins his three hundredth career game against the Chicago Cubs.

• On October 1, Roger Maris hits a record sixty-one home runs to break Babe Ruth's record of sixty set in 1927, but he achieves the feat in a season eight games longer than Ruth's.

• From October 4 to October 9, the New York Yankees win the World Series in five games over the Cincinnati Reds; a winning player's share is $7,979.11.

• On November 25, Boston Celtic's Bob Cousy becomes the second player in NBA history to score more than fifteen thousand points.

• On December 31, the New York Giants are humiliated, 37-0, by the Green Bay Packers in the NFL championship game.

1962

• The Ford Motor Company announces that it will begin participation in auto racing.

• Maury Wills steals 104 bases during the major-league baseball season, breaking Ty Cobb's record of 96 set in 1916.

• The professional American Basketball League (ABL) is established.

• Don Carter, with season's earnings of $49,014, is named professional bowler of the year.

• With career earnings of over $1 million, Kelso is named horse of the year for the third year in a row.

• On January 1, the University of Minnesota defeats UCLA, 21-3, in the Rose Bowl.

• On February 10, Jim Beatty becomes the first person to run the mile indoors in under 4 minutes; his time is 3:58.9. On June 8, he sets a world record for two miles with a time of 8:29.8.

• On February 24, Cleveland Browns Jim Brown wins the 1961 rushing title with 1,408 yards, his fifth consecutive rushing title.

• On March 2, Wilt Chamberlain of the Philadelphia Warriors scores one hundred points in a single game against the New York Knicks.

• On March 24, the University of Cincinnati, for the second straight year, beats Ohio State in the NCAA basketball championship.

• On April 18, the Boston Celtics win their fourth consecutive NBA title, defeating the Los Angeles Lakers in a seven-game series.

• On May 30, Rodger Ward wins the Indianapolis 500; he also wins the USAC championship for 1962.

• On June 22, Stan Musial of the St. Louis Cardinals breaks Detroit Tiger Ty Cobbs' career total base record of 5,863.

• On September 25, Sonny Liston knocks out Floyd Patterson in 2:06 of the first round to win the world heavyweight boxing championship. Patterson's purse is $1.2 million.

• On October 16, the New York Yankees win their twentieth World Series in twenty-seven attempts, beating the San Francisco Giants four games to three.

• On November 27, quarterback Terry Baker of Oregon State University wins the Heisman Trophy.

• On December 23, the Dallas Texans beat the Houston Oilers, 20-17, in sudden-death overtime to win the AFL title, for which a winning player's share is $2,261.80.

• On December 30, the Green Bay Packers beat the New York Giants in the NFL championship game, for which a winning player's share is $5,888.57.

1963

• General Motors tightens restrictions on support of automobile racing.

• Both Jack Nicklaus and Arnold Palmer win over one hundred thousand dollars; Palmer wins seven Professional Golfers' Association (PGA) tournaments; Nicklaus wins two major tournaments, including the Masters and the PGA championship.

• Kelso is named horse of the year after winning eight straight stakes races.

• On March 23, Loyola University of Chicago beats the University of Cincinnati 60-58 in overtime to win the NCAA basketball championship.

• On April 24, the Boston Celtics defeat the Los Angeles Lakers in six games to win the NBA championship for the fifth consecutive time.

• On May 30, Parnelli Jones wins the Indianapolis 500 in a controversial race after stewards fail to order him off the track because his engine is throwing oil into the paths of other racers.

• On July 30, the New York Mets snap their twenty-two game losing streak against the Los Angeles Dodgers.

• On September 25, Sonny Liston defends his world heavyweight boxing championship against Floyd Patterson with a second first-round knockout.

• On October 6, behind star pitcher Sandy Koufax, the Los Angeles Dodgers win the World Series over the New York Yankees in four games.

• On November 23, the Army-Navy football game is played on the day after the assassination of President John F. Kennedy at the request of the family. The president had planned to attend.

• In December, the University of Texas goes undefeated in college football to win the national championship. The Heisman Trophy is won by Navy quarterback Roger Staubach.

• On December 28, Chuck McKinley and Dennis Ralston lead the United States to a championship in Davis Cup against Australia.

• On December 29, the Chicago Bears beat the New York Giants for the NFL championship, 14-10.

1964

• Richard Petty sets a record average speed of 154.144 mph at the Daytona 500 and wins the Grand National NASCAR championship.

• Major-league baseball games are attended by 21,280,346 fans during the year.

• Kelso breaks the all-time winnings record in horse racing as he becomes the horse of the year for an unprecedented fifth time.

• On January 5, the San Diego Chargers beat the Boston Patriots, 51-10, in the AFL championship game.

• On January 29, the IX Winter Olympics open in Innsbruck, Austria.

• On February 25, after being fined twenty-five hundred dollars by the Miami Boxing Commission for disorderly conduct at the weigh-in, Cassius Clay beats Sonny Liston for the heavyweight boxing championship when Liston fails to answer the bell for the seventh round; after his victory Clay announces that his name is Cassius X and that he has joined the Black Muslims.

• On March 21, UCLA wins thirty games in a row and the NCAA basketball championship, defeating Duke University, 98-83, in the final game.

• On April 26, the Boston Celtics defeat the San Francisco Warriors in five games to win their sixth consecutive NBA championship.

• On May 30, A.J. Foyt, Jr., wins the Indianapolis 500, during which drivers Eddie Sachs and Dave MacDonald are killed; Foyt wins ten of twelve USAC Championship Trail races during the year.

• On June 20, Ken Venturi wins the U.S. Open, posting a thirty on the first nine of the third round; he is treated for heat exhaustion between the third and fourth rounds.

• On June 21, Jim Bunning of the Philadelphia Phillies pitches a perfect baseball game against the New York Mets.

• From October 7 to October 15, the St. Louis Cardinals beat the New York Yankees four games to three in the World Series.

• On October 10, the XVII Olympics open in Tokyo; American swimmer Don Schollander wins four of the U.S. team total of thirty gold medals.

• On October 27, driving the sixty-thousand-dollar Green Monster, driver Art Arfons breaks the land speed record, traveling 536.71 mph.

• On November 24, John Huarte, Notre Dame quarterback, is the Heisman Trophy winner.

• In December, the Universities of Alabama and Arkansas are undefeated in collegiate football, and Alabama wins the national championship.

• On December 26, the Buffalo Bills beat the Boston Patriots, 24-14, for the AFL title.

• On December 27, the Cleveland Browns beat the Baltimore Colts, 27-0, for the NFL championship.

1965

• Ned Jarrett is the NASCAR points champion.

• The Daytona Beach Continental sports car race is lengthened to twenty-four hours to rival the twenty-four-hour endurance race at Le Mans.

• On March 20, UCLA beats the University of Michigan, 91-80, to win their second consecutive NCAA basketball championship.

• On April 10, Jack Nicklaus wins the Masters by a record nine strokes.

• On April 25, the Boston Celtics win their seventh NBA title in a row, defeating the Los Angeles Lakers four games to one.

• On May 25, Muhammad Ali retains his title in a first-round knockout of Sonny Liston and on November 22, a twelfth-round knockout of Floyd Patterson.

• On May 30, Jim Clark wins the Indianapolis 500.

• From October 6 to October 14, the Los Angeles Dodgers beat the Minnesota Twins, four games to three, in the World Series.

• On November 23, Mike Garrett, University of Southern California running back, wins the Heisman Trophy.

• In December, Michigan State University is the consensus national collegiate football champion.

1966

• Chrysler announces that it will no longer support a factory racing team after the current NASCAR season; David Pearson is Grand National driving champion.

• William D. Eckert is named commissioner of baseball.

• Frank Robinson wins the Triple Crown, leading major-league baseball players in runs batted in (RBI), home runs, and batting average; he hits the longest home run ever at Baltimore Memorial Stadium—540 feet.

• Buckpasser, the first three-year-old thoroughbred ever to win $1 million, is named horse of the year.

• Chicago Blackhawks winger Bobby Hull scores a record fifty-four goals in his twentieth season as a professional hockey player.

• The NHL expands to twelve teams, awarding franchises to Los Angeles, San Francisco-Oakland, Pittsburgh, Saint Louis, Minneapolis-Saint Paul, and Philadelphia for the 1967–1968 season.

• On January 2, the Green Bay Packers beat the Cleveland Browns, 23-12, to win the NFL championship.

• On January 2, the Buffalo Bills beat the San Diego Chargers, 23-0, to win the AFL championship.

• On February 27, seventeen-year-old, three-time U.S. champion Peggy Fleming wins the world figure-skating championship in Switzerland.

• On March 19, the University of Kentucky is upset in the finals of the NCAA tournament by Texas Western College, 72-65.

• On April 11, Jack Nicklaus is the first golfer ever to win two Masters titles in succession.

- On April 28, the Boston Celtics beat the Los Angeles Lakers in seven games to win the NBA championship. Bill Russell is named coach of the Celtics; he is the first African American ever to coach a major-league team.

- On May 30, after eleven of the thirty-three cars are so damaged they cannot continue on the first lap of the Indianapolis 500, British driver Graham Hill wins the race, and Scotsman Jim Clark is second; only six cars complete the five hundred miles.

- On June 8, the AFL and NFL announce plans to merge.

- On June 20, Billy Casper beats Arnold Palmer in a playoff to win the U.S. Open golf championship.

- On July 17, nineteen-year-old Jim Ryun sets a world record of 3:51.3 in the mile, lowering the previous record by 2.3 seconds.

- From October 5 to October 9, the Baltimore Orioles sweep the World Series in four games over the Los Angeles Dodgers; after the series Dodger pitcher Sandy Koufax retires at the peak of his career.

- On November 19, before the largest television audience ever for a regularly scheduled game (30 million), the University of Michigan and Notre Dame University battle to a 10-10 tie as Notre Dame is criticized for playing a safe game at the end rather than going for a win; the two teams split the national championship.

- On November 22, quarterback Steve Spurrier of the University of Florida wins the Heisman Trophy.

1967

- Richard Petty is NASCAR points champion, winning ten straight races.

- Damascus is named horse of the year, though he finished third in the Kentucky Derby, won by Darby Dan.

- Larry Mahan wins the all-around rodeo championship with earnings of $51,966 for the year.

- The NFL expands to sixteen teams, adding the New Orleans Saints; the AFL adds the Cincinnati Bengals.

- On January 15, the Green Bay Packers beat the Kansas City Chiefs, 35-10, in the first professional football Super Bowl.

- On March 25, star center Lew Alcindor is named player of the year, and John Wooden is named coach of the year as they lead UCLA to an undefeated season and NCAA basketball championship over the University of Dayton, 79-64.

- On April 24, the Philadelphia 76ers, led by league Most Valuable Player (MVP) Wilt Chamberlain, win the NBA championship over the San Francisco Warriors in six games.

- On May 30, Andy Granatelli's STP Special turbine-powered car driven by Parnelli Jones dominates the Indianapolis 500 but drops out three laps before the finish as A.J. Foyt, Jr., wins.

- On June 20, Muhammad Ali is found guilty in federal court of draft evasion and given a five-year sentence. His boxing titles are stripped from him.

- On June 23, Jim Ryun lowers his world record in the mile to 3:51.1 and on July 8 sets a new world mark in the 1,500 meters of 3:33.1.

- From July 23 to August 6, the United States wins 225 of the 537 medals awarded to twenty-seven nations in the Pan-American games.

- From October 4 to October 12, the St. Louis Cardinals beat the Boston Red Sox in seven games to win the World Series.

- On November 28, Quarterback Gary Beban of UCLA wins the Heisman Trophy.

- In December, the University of Southern California is the consensus national collegiate football champion.

1968

- David Pearson wins the NASCAR points championship, but fellow South Carolinian Cale Yarborough wins the most money (over $130,000) during the season.

- The NBA expands to fourteen teams, adding franchises in Phoenix, Milwaukee, Seattle, and San Diego.

- The new American Basketball Association (ABA) establishes a legitimate bid for a professional league to rival the NBA.

- Larry Mahan wins the Rodeo Cowboys Association all-around championship for third time in a row.

- On January 14, the Green Bay Packers beat the Oakland Raiders 33-14 in the second Super Bowl.

- On February 10, Peggy Fleming wins an Olympic gold medal in figure skating.

- On March 23, UCLA beats the University of North Carolina, 78-55, to win the NCAA basketball championship.

- From March to April, ABC television jointly sponsors an eight-man tournament to determine the heavyweight boxing championship; Jimmy Ellis wins on April 27, but Joe Frazier, who had refused to compete because of the promotions contract required by tournament organizers, is generally acknowledged as the best of the heavyweights.

- On April 15, Bob Goalby wins the Masters golf tournament when Roberto de Vicenzo signs a scorecard that records one more stroke than he actually played; de Vicenzo would have tied had the score been kept accurately, but tournament rules stipulate that once a player signs his card, it cannot be changed for any reason.

- On May 2, the Boston Celtics, led by player-coach Bill Russell, win the NBA championship in six games.

- On May 4, Dancer's Image is disqualified as winner of the Kentucky Derby after a urine test shows signs of a painkiller. Two weeks later the horse is disqualified for obstruction after finishing third in the Preakness.

- On May 30, Bobby Unser wins the Indianapolis 500.

- On July 30, Ron Hansen of the Washington Senators makes an unassisted triple play, the first in forty-one years.

- On September 8, Billy Schumacher in *Miss Bardahl* wins the Gold Cup for hydroplane racers with speeds of up to 130 mph in straightaways.

- On September 8, tennis player Billie Jean King turns pro; she loses in the finals of the U.S. Open to Virginia Wade.

- On September 14, twenty-four-year-old Denny McLain of the Detroit Tigers wins his thirtieth game of the season. He wins the Cy Young award for finishing the season with a 31-6 record.

- From October 2 to October 10, the Detroit Tigers come from a 3 games to 1 game deficit to beat the St. Louis Cardinals in seven games to win the World Series.

- From October 14 to October 28, the XIX Olympics open. In the thin air of Mexico world-record performances are commonplace. In track and field events fourteen world records are set, nine by Americans. Al Oerter wins his fourth Olympic gold medal in the discus throw. American medal winners Tommie Smith (who set a world record in the 200-meter race) and John Carlos are stripped of their honors and suspended from the team for raising their fists in a black-power salute during the playing of the national anthem at the awards ceremony.

- On November 26, University of Southern California running back O.J. Simpson wins the Heisman Trophy.

1969

- David Pearson wins his third NASCAR points championship in four years.

- The NFL and AFL receive $34.7 million from CBS and NBC for the rights to televise professional football games.

- Arnold Palmer is forced to qualify for the U.S. Open, won by Orville Moody.

- Despite winning nine other races and beating Arts and Letters two races to one in head-to-head competition, Majestic Prince loses out to Arts and Letters in voting for the best three-year-old of the thoroughbred racing season and horse of the year.

- On January 1, Ohio State is named national collegiate football champion after beating the University of Southern California 27-16 in the Rose Bowl.

- On January 12, the New York Jets beat the Baltimore Colts, 16-7, in the third Super Bowl, becoming the first AFL team to win the championship and establishing the competitiveness of the AFL.

- On February 1, Vince Lombardi retires as coach of the Green Bay Packers.

- On February 4, Bowie Kuhn replaces William Eckert as commissioner of baseball.

- On March 22, Lew Alcindor wraps up his collegiate basketball career by leading UCLA to its third straight NCAA championship over Purdue, 92-72.

- On May 5, the Boston Celtics win the NBA championship for the tenth time in eleven years, defeating the Los Angeles Lakers in seven games.

- On May 30, Mario Andretti wins a record purse of $809,627 in the Indianapolis 500.

- From October 11 to October 16, the "Miracle" New York Mets, who had finished ninth in the National League in 1968, win the World Series over the Baltimore Orioles in five games.

Ted Williams's Farewell

My Turn At Bat: The Story of My Life

Autobiography

By: Ted Williams

Date: 1969

Source: Williams, Ted, with John Underwood. *My Turn at Bat: The Story of My Life.* New York: Simon and Schuster, 1969, 232–241.

About the Author: Ted Williams (1918–2002) was born in San Diego, California. After playing minor league ball, he was signed by the Boston Red Sox in 1938. From 1939 to 1960, interrupted by military service in World War II and Korea, Williams hit 521 home runs and compiled a .344 career batting average. After his playing career was over, Williams was a hitting instructor with the Red Sox and managed the Washington Senators and Texas Rangers.

"Our Far-flung Correspondents"

Magazine article

By: John Updike

Date: October 22, 1960

Source: Updike, John. "Our Far-flung Correspondents." *The New Yorker* 36, October 22, 1960, 109, 124, 126–129.

About the Author: John Updike (1932–) was born in Shillington, Pennsylvania. After graduating from Harvard, Updike was on the staff of the *The New Yorker*. In 1957, he began his freelance writing career, which has produced twenty novels and books of poetry, short stories, essays, and children's stories. Updike won the Pulitzer Prize twice for fiction, as well as numerous other literary awards. ■

Introduction

By 1960, the legend of baseball's Ted Williams was firmly established. The Boston Red Sox star had burst onto the scene as a brash twenty-one-year-old in 1939, followed two years later by his spectacular .406 hitting season. His military service, in World War II (1939–1945) and Korea, where he flew bombing missions, were noted both as a symbol of patriotism and the lament of lost seasons. Williams entered 1960 with 492 home runs and impressive statistics in walks, runs, runs batted in, and slugging percentage. His better-than-.340 career batting average was the best of his generation. As the 1960 season began, he was nearly forty-two years old. He had hit only .254 the previous year, the worst season of his career, but he decided to play one more season for $90,000, a pay cut of $35,000 from 1959. The season was one of ups and downs for Williams, as the aging star was nagged by persistent neck pain, but he hit his five hundredth home run early in the season and ended up batting .316. Resisting a desire for a "farewell tour" in American League cities, the Red Sox announced on September 25, 1960, that Williams would retire effective at the end of the season.

On September 28, 1960, a cold, gray, fall day at Fenway Park, the Red Sox concluded their home schedule against the Baltimore Orioles. Only 10,454 spectators attended the game. Williams was honored in ceremonies prior to the contest. The Orioles, who surprised many by contending for the American League pennant, were leading 4 to 2 in the bottom of the eighth inning. Williams had gone hitless with fly outs in two official at bats and scored a run after a walk. Jack Fisher was pitching for the Orioles, as Williams strode to the plate, swinging two bats, greeted by a standing ovation from the sparse crowd. On a one-ball, one-strike pitch from Fisher, Williams, with his classic, textbook swing, hit the ball into the nearly empty right-field stands, a 400-foot home run, his twenty-ninth of the season. As he rounded the bases, a fan raced onto the field attempting to hug Williams, but the "Splendid Splinter," head down, crossed the plate, shook the on-deck hitter's hand, and disappeared into the dugout.

Significance

After Williams went into the dugout, the game was delayed several minutes as the Fenway Park crowd, on its feet, chanted "We Want Ted," hoping he would reappear. He did not, and Williams was replaced in left field at the start of the next inning. As it turned out, the Red Sox rallied for two runs in the ninth inning to win 5-4. After the game, Williams announced his immediate retirement and that he would not play the remaining three games in New York. "Baseball has been the most wonderful thing that has ever happened to me," Williams said prior to the game, and he acknowledged "the greatest fans in America" in Boston. The refusal by Williams to tip his cap or acknowledge the cheers was in part the result of the tempestuous relationship he had with fans and the media, who were at times openly critical of his play. Williams had responded with occasional petulance, including, on one occasion, a spitting incident.

Williams' career was over, an impressive one at that. His 521 home runs stood third all time in 1960,

Ted Williams crosses the plate after hitting a home run, his 521st, on the final at bat of his career, Boston, Massachusetts, September 28, 1960. AP/WIDE WORLD PHOTOS. REPRODUCED BY PERMISSION.

along with 1,839 runs batted in, 2,019 walks, a slugging percentage of .634, an on-base percentage of .483 (still first over forty years later), and a .344 batting average. For a number of years after retirement, Williams was a Red Sox hitting instructor but primarily indulged his second love, fishing, exhibiting the same exactness and passion with rod and reel that he did in hitting a baseball. Elected to the Baseball Hall of Fame in 1966, he used his speech to argue for inclusion of Negro League stars at Cooperstown. In 1969, the struggling Washington Senators hired Williams as manager. After a winning season the first year, the Senators slipped back to mediocrity as the franchise moved to Texas in 1972. Williams resigned at year's end. In his twilight years, Williams mellowed toward fans and sportswriters and was accessible and willing to help young ballplayers. Ted Williams died at age eighty-three in July 2002.

Primary Source

My Turn at Bat: The Story of My Life [excerpt]

SYNOPSIS: In his autobiography, baseball star Ted Williams gives an account of his last season, and particularly the final game, when he hit a home run to end a memorable Hall of Fame career.

So I signed to play my last year, 1960, for $90,000, a $35,000 cut, almost 30 per cent.

I was now an old, old man as far as baseball was concerned. Forty-two in August. . . . I'd always said when you're over thirty-five you're in on a pass. But I felt good that spring. Not The Kid from San Diego any more, all full of spit and vinegar, but not old either. . . .

We came into Boston for the last series, with Baltimore, and then it got down to the last game. The team still had a doubleheader in New York that weekend, but I went to Higgins and said, "Mike, this is the last game I'm going to play. I don't want to go to New York." He said, "All right, you don't have to go." Regardless of what I had done, this was it, I'd had it, I knew it. I knew the club was thinking about youth, it hadn't been in the pennant race since 1951. I knew there was a kid named Carl Yastrzemski coming up who was going to be a hell of a player. And in all fairness I have to say that I felt that a lot of people didn't want me around any more.

Well, like the .400 season, and the World Series, and the party I missed when we won the pennant, and the picture they took with Lefty Grove when he won his three hundredth game and I wasn't there, and the letters from [John] Glenn and Dick Nixon when he was the vice president, that last game has gotten so much more important as the years go by. I wish I could remember every minute of it but I can't.

I don't remember if I arrived particularly early. I don't remember what was said in the locker room except I might have been aware of some feeling. You sense things. The players knew it was my last game. There was a headline in the paper that morning: "What Will We Do Without Ted?" I remember a guy from one of the magazines came in and I said, "What the hell are you doing here?" because I felt that gutless magazine had given me a bad time for years because I didn't show up for a banquet one time. Bud Leavitt, an old friend from the Bangor *Daily News,* was in the runway when I came out and we chatted. The photographers were crowding around. I didn't give them too much to focus on.

They had a ceremony for me at home plate. They gave me a silver bowl and a plaque. They retired my number, and the Mayor presented a $4,000 check to the Jimmy Fund for kids with cancer. I've been affiliated with the Jimmy Fund since 1947, getting a whole lot more credit than I deserve. It was just something somebody asked me to do and I did it. I went to a little field outside of Boston one night in 1947. . . .

Curt Gowdy introduced me at the ceremony as "controversial, but colorful," and called me "the greatest hitter who ever lived," which was a pleasing exaggeration. I thought about what I was going to say, but I don't know if it came out exactly right. I knew I was going to be brief. I had my hat off. I didn't tip it, I just took it off. I thanked them all, and I meant it, and I said, "Despite some of the terrible things written about me by the knights of the keyboard up there"—and I looked up at the pressbox—"and they *were* terrible things, I'd like to forget them but I can't, my stay in Boston has been the most wonderful part of my life. If someone should ask me the one place I'd want to play if I had it to do all over again, I would say Boston, for it has the greatest owner in baseball and the greatest fans in America."

I didn't take batting practice. It was one of the lousiest days you ever saw. The wind was blowing in—a dark, dreary, drizzly day, cold and threatening, a real doghouse day. And Baltimore was starting Steve Barber, a tough little sinking-ball left-hander. He never struck me out much, but he was hard to get hold of and his control was not too good.

Sure enough Barber was wilder than a March hare that day. And this is fate, it has to be. If I had had to face Barber four times that day I'd probably have gotten one good ball to hit, certainly not three. But Barber walked the first batter, walked the second, then he walked me on four straight balls. When he got behind the next batter, they pulled him out and Jack Fisher came in, another kid half my age. Fisher is a pretty good pitcher, too. He's been in the big leagues ever since. But he's a little easier to see.

The second time up I hit a fly to right center. Another day it might have gone, but the air was just too heavy. Jackie Brandt caught it easily. Then in the fifth inning I really got into one, high and deep into that gray sky, and gee, it just died. Al Pilarcik caught it against the 380 sign. I remember saying to Vic Wertz in the dugout, "If that one didn't go out, none of them will today."

I was second man up in the eighth inning. They'd turned the lights on by now. It was eerie and damp, and I had bundled up in my blue jacket in the dugout waiting for my turn to bat. Willie Tasby was up first, and I got my bat and went to the on-deck circle as soon as he moved out. This surely was going to be my last time at bat in baseball. Twenty-two years coming down to one time at bat. I remember how the fans were all up on their feet applauding when I went to the on-deck circle, and feeling the chills up my spine, and thinking how much I wanted to put one out of there—and knowing what the odds were.

The first pitch was a ball. Then, from the batter's box, it seemed to me Fisher humped up as if he were going to try to fire the ball by me. I *knew* he was going to try to pump it right past. And gee, here comes a ball I should have hit a mile, and I *missed* the son of a gun. I don't miss, *completely* miss, very often and I don't know yet how I missed that ball.

Fisher couldn't wait to throw the next one. He must have thought he threw the last one by me, and maybe he did, but all my professional life I had been a fastball hitter, and whenever I had an inkling one was coming it was that much better for me. This time I tried to be a little quicker, and I hit it a little better than the others that day. I had a little extra on it. It fought the wind, and it just kept on going into right center, toward the Red Sox bullpen, the one they put in in 1940 with the hope I'd hit a lot of homers out there. It kept going and then out.

There were only 10,454 people in Fenway Park that day, but they reacted like nothing I have ever heard. I mean they really put it on. They cheered like hell, and as I came around, the cheering grew louder and louder. I thought about tipping my hat, you damn right I did, and for a moment I was torn, but by the time I got to second base I knew I couldn't do it. Like I said, I was just fed up with that part of the act.

You can't imagine, though the warm feeling I had, for the very fact that I had done what every ballplayer would want to do on his last time up, having wanted to do it so badly, and knowing how the fans really felt, how happy they were for me. Maybe I should have let them *know* I knew, but I couldn't. It just wouldn't have been me.

I got to the dugout and went to the water cooler, then sat down, my head back against the wall, and gee, they were *still* applauding and calling my name, and players were pleading with me to go back out. "C'mon, Ted, give 'em your hat." I know they felt good for me too. Even Higgins came down and asked me to go out, and the umpire was looking over as if he expected me to. But I couldn't, and the inning ended, and Higgins sent me back out, I guess to give me another chance to acknowledge their cheers, because he had Carroll Hardy follow me to left field. When I got out there I had to turn around and run back in. From the early days I always tried to get in as fast as I could. No glad-handing, just *whhsssh*, right in. Bobby Doerr used to be that way too, like maybe he was a little embarrassed to be out there. I ran in with my head down, and the fans were all on their feet, clapping and clapping.

Celebrate? I don't remember celebrating. It was over, that's all. I was slow getting out of the clubhouse. I sat around for a while and had a beer and talked until there wasn't anybody else to talk to. Then I got dressed and sneaked out a side entrance to avoid the crowd. After that I don't remember what I did. I probably just went back to my room at the hotel, which was always a retreat for me, the place I'd gone back to so often after something bad had happened, something sure to get me in a wringer, something that started me thinking, God, here it goes again. That's when guys like Fred Corcoran and Owen Wood and Johnny Orlando would come around, to be with me for consolation when I was down. That's why they mean so much to me today.

I know I was relieved that part of it was over.

Primary Source

"Our Far-flung Correspondents" [excerpt]

SYNOPSIS: John Updike, at the time a young freelance writer, was one of 10,454 spectators at Fenway Park in Boston to witness Ted Williams's final home game with the Red Sox. He chronicles the events of the game, including Williams's home run in what turned out to be the final at bat of his career.

Fenway Park, in Boston, is a lyric little bandbox of a ballpark. Everything is painted green and seems in curiously sharp focus, like the inside of an old-fashioned peeping-type Easter egg. It was built in 1912 and rebuilt in 1934, and offers, as do most Boston artifacts, a compromise between Man's Euclidean determinations and Nature's beguiling irregularities. Its right field is one of the deepest in the American League, while its left field is the shortest; the high left-field wall, three hundred and fifteen feet from home plate along the foul line, virtually thrusts its surface at right-handed hitters. On the afternoon of Wednesday, September 28th, as I took a seat behind third base, a uniformed groundkeeper was treading the top of this wall, picking batting-practice home runs out of the screen, like a mushroom gatherer seen in Wordsworthian perspective on the verge of a cliff. The day was overcast, chill, and uninspirational. The Boston team was the worst in twenty-seven seasons. A jangling medley of incompetent youth and aging competence, the Red Sox were finishing in seventh place only because the Kansas City Athletics had locked them out of the cellar. They were scheduled to play the Baltimore Orioles, a much nimbler blend of May and December, who had been dumped from pennant contention a week before by the insatiable Yankees. I, and 10,453 others, had shown up primarily because this was the Red Sox's last home game of the season, and therefore the last time in all eternity that their regular left fielder, known to the headlines as TED, KID, SPLINTER, THUMPER, TW, and, most cloyingly, misTer Wonderful, would play in Boston. "WHAT WILL WE DO WITHOUT TED? HUB FANS ASK" ran the headline on a newspaper being read by a bulb-nosed cigar smoker a few rows away. Williams' retirement had been announced, doubted (he had been threatening retirement for years), confirmed by Tom Yawkey, the Red Sox owner, and at last widely accepted as the sad but probable truth. He was forty-two and had redeemed his abysmal season of 1959 with a—considering his advanced age—fine one. He had been giving away his gloves and bats and had grudgingly consented to a sentimental ceremony today.

these points, often observed by caricaturists, were visible in the flesh. . . .

Whenever Williams appeared at the plate—pounding the dirt from his cleats, gouging a pit in the batter's box with his left foot, wringing resin out of the bat handle with his vehement grip, switching the stick at the pitcher with an electric ferocity—it was like having a familiar Leonardo appear in a shuffle of *Saturday Evening Post* covers. This man, you realized—and here, perhaps, was the difference, greater than the difference in gifts—really intended to hit the ball. In the third inning, he hoisted a high fly to deep center. In the fifth, we thought he had it; he smacked the ball hard and high into the heart of his power zone, but the deep right field in Fenway and the heavy air and a casual east wind defeated him. The ball died. Al Pilarcik leaned his back against the big "380" painted on the right-field wall and caught it. On another day, in another park, it would have been gone. (After the game, Williams said, "I didn't think I could hit one any harder than that. The conditions weren't good.")

The afternoon grew so glowering that in the sixth inning the arc lights were turned on—always a wan sight in the daytime, like the burning headlights of a funeral procession. Aided by the gloom, Fisher was slicing through the Sox rookies, and Williams did not come to bat in the seventh. He was second up in the eighth. This was almost certainly his last time to come to the plate in Fenway Park, and instead of merely cheering, as we had at his three previous appearances, we stood, all of us—stood and applauded. Have you ever heard applause in a ballpark? Just applause—no calling, no whistling, just an ocean of handclaps, minute after minute, burst after burst, crowding and running together in continuous succession like the pushes of surf at the edge of the sand. It was a sombre and considered tumult. There was not a boo in it. It seemed to renew itself out of shifting set of memories as the kid, the Marine, the veteran of feuds and failures and injuries, the friend of children, and the enduring old pro evolved down the bright tunnel of twenty-one summers toward this moment. At last, the umpire signalled for Fisher to pitch; with the other players, he had been frozen in position. Only Williams had moved during the ovation, switching his bat impatiently, ignoring everything except his cherished task. Fisher wound up, and the applause sank into a hush. . . .

Fisher, after his unsettling wait, was wide with the first pitch. He put the second one over, and Williams swung mightily and missed. The crowd

Ted Williams bids farewell to the Fenway fans before his last game on September 28, 1960. AP/WIDE WORLD PHOTOS. REPRODUCED BY PERMISSION.

This was not necessarily his last game; the Red Sox were scheduled to travel to New York and wind up the season with three games there. . . .

Williams was third in the batting order, so he came up in the bottom of the first inning, and Steve Barber, a young pitcher who was not yet born when Williams began playing for the Red Sox, offered him four pitches, at all of which he disdained to swing, since none of them were within the strike zone. This demonstrated simultaneously that Williams' eyes were razor-sharp and that Barber's control wasn't. Shortly, the bases were full, with Williams on second. "Oh, I hope he gets held up at third! That would be wonderful," the girl beside me moaned, and, sure enough, the man at bat walked and Williams was delivered into our foreground. He struck the pose of Donatello's David, the third-base bag being Goliath's head. Fiddling with his cap, swapping small talk with the Oriole third baseman (who seemed delighted to have him drop in), swinging his arms with a sort of prancing nervousness, he looked fine—flexible, hard, and not unbecomingly substantial through the middle. The long neck, the small head, the knickers whose cuffs were worn down near his ankles—all

grunted, seeing that classic swing, so long and smooth and quick, exposed, naked in its failure. Fisher threw the third time, Williams swung again, and there it was. The ball climbed on a diagonal line into the vast volume of air over center field. From my angle, behind third base, the ball seemed less an object in flight than the tip of a towering, motionless construct, like the Eiffel Tower or the Tappan Zee Bridge. It was in the books while it was still in the sky. Brandt ran back to the deepest corner of the outfield grass; the ball descended beyond his reach and struck in the crotch where the bullpen met the wall, bounced chunkily, and, as far as I could see, vanished.

Like a feather caught in a vortex Williams ran around the square of bases at the center of our beseeching screaming. He ran as he always ran out home runs—hurriedly, unsmiling, head down, as if our praise were a storm of rain to get out of. He didn't tip his cap. Though we thumped, wept, and chanted "We want Ted" for minutes after he hid in the dugout, he did not come back. Our noise for some seconds passed beyond excitement into a kind of immense open anguish, a wailing, a cry to be saved. But immortality is nontransferable. The papers said that the other players, and even the umpires on the field, begged him to come out and acknowledge us in some way, but he never had and did not now. Gods do not answer letters.

Further Resources

BOOKS

Linn, Ed. *Hitter: The Life and Turmoils of Ted Williams*. New York: Harcourt, Brace, 1993.

Seidel, Michael. *Ted Williams: A Baseball Life*. Chicago: Contemporary Books, 1991.

PERIODICALS

Goldstein, Richard, and Robert McG. Thomas Jr. "Ted Williams, Red Sox Slugger And Last to Hit .400, Dies at 83." *The New York Times*, July 6, 2002, A1.

"Williams Hits 420-Foot Homer for Red Sox." *The New York Times*, September 29, 1960.

WEBSITES

National Baseball Hall of Fame and Museum. "Ted Williams." Available online at http://www.baseballhalloffame.org /hofers%5Fand%5Fhonorees/hofer%5Fbios/williams%5Fted .htm; website home page: http://www.baseballhalloffame .org (accessed March 4, 2003).

Roger Maris at Bat
Autobiography

By: Roger Maris and Jim Ogle

Date: 1962

Source: Maris, Roger, and Jim Ogle. *Roger Maris at Bat*. New York: Duell, Sloan and Pearce, 1962.

About the Author: Roger Maris (1934–1985) was born in Hibbing, Minnesota, and grew up in North Dakota. He signed with the Cleveland Indians in 1953 and eventually wound up with the New York Yankees in 1960. In 1961, he set the modern major league baseball mark for home runs with sixty-one and won his second consecutive American League Most Valuable Player award. After five more seasons with the Yankees, he played two seasons with the St. Louis Cardinals before retiring in 1968 to Florida, where he operated a beer distributorship. ∎

Introduction

For over thirty years, one of baseball's cherished records was Babe Ruth's sixty home runs in 1927, accomplished in a 154-game season. In 1961, with baseball's first expansion—from eight to ten teams in the American League—the schedule increased to 162 games. Still, the likelihood of Ruth's record being threatened seemed remote.

After high school, Roger Maris turned down a football scholarship to sign a baseball contract with the Cleveland Indians in 1953. Advancing through the minors, Maris joined the Indians in 1957. The next season, he was traded to the Kansas City Athletics, and following the 1959 season, to the New York Yankees. Maris, a left-handed pull hitter, was a perfect match for the short right field stands (only 296 feet from home plate) at Yankee Stadium. Beginning in 1960, he teamed with switch-hitting slugging star Mickey Mantle to become one of baseball's greatest home run hitting tandems. In 1960, Maris hit .283 with thirty-nine homers and 112 runs batted in, winning the American League's Most Valuable Player award.

Nothing, however, prepared baseball or Maris himself for the unforgettable 1961 season. He hit no home runs until the eleventh game of the season, and only nine in his first thirty-nine games. Meanwhile, Mantle had started fast in home runs and was on a pace to catch Ruth. Soon, Maris picked up the pace, and after hitting four home runs in a July 25 doubleheader at Yankee Stadium against the Chicago White Sox, he had forty home runs in ninety-six games, a pace ahead of the Ruth mark. While Maris and Mantle dueled each other and threatened the record, baseball commissioner Ford Frick, an ex-sportswriter and friend of Babe's, ruled that Ruth's mark could only be considered broken if it was done in 154 or fewer games. Soon, the edict became known as the "as-

Maris Homers Day by Day

HR No.	Game No.	Date	Opposing Pitcher and Club	Where Made
		April		
1	10	26	Foytack, Detroit (R)	Detroit
		May		
2	16	3	Ramos, Minnesota (R)	Bloomington
3	19	6	Grba, Los Angeles (R)	Los Angeles
4	28	17	Burnside, Washington (L)	New York
5	29	19	Perry, Cleveland (R)	Cleveland
6	30	20	Bell, Cleveland (R)	Cleveland
7	31	21	Estrada, Baltimore (R)	New York
8	34	24	Conley, Boston (R)	New York
9	37	28	McLish, Chicago (R)	New York
10	39	30	Conley, Boston (R)	Boston
11	39	30	Fornieles, Boston (R)	Boston
12	40	31	Muffett, Boston (R)	Boston
		June		
13	42	2	McLish, Chicago (R)	Chicago
14	43	3	Shaw, Chicago (R)	Chicago
15	44	4	Kemmerer, Chicago (R)	Chicago
16	47	6	Palmquist, Minnesota (R)	New York
17	48	7	Ramos, Minnesota (R)	New York
18	51	9	Herbert, Kansas City (R)	New York
19	54	11	Grba, Los Angeles (R)	New York
20	54	11	James, Los Angeles (R)	New York
21	56	13	Perry, Cleveland (R)	Cleveland
22	57	14	Bell, Cleveland (R)	Cleveland
23	60	17	Mossi, Detroit (L)	Detroit
24	61	18	Casale, Detroit (R)	Detroit
25	62	19	Archer, Kansas City (L)	Kansas City
26	63	20	Nuxhall, Kansas City (L)	Kansas City
27	65	22	Bass, Kansas City (R)	Kansas City
		July		
28	73	1	Sisler, Washington (R)	New York
29	74	2	Burnside, Washington (L)	New York
30	74	2	Klippstein, Washington (R)	New York
31	76	4	Lary, Detroit (R)	New York
32	77	5	Funk, Cleveland (R)	New York

[continued]

Maris Homers Day by Day [CONTINUED]

HR No.	Game No.	Date	Opposing Pitcher and Club	Where Made
		July		
33	81	9	Monbouquette, Boston (R)	Boston
34	83	13	Wynn, Chicago (R)	Chicago
35	85	15	Herbert, Chicago (R)	Chicago
36	91	21	Monbouquette, Boston (R)	Boston
37	94	25	Baumann, Chicago (L)	New York
38	94	25	Larsen, Chicago (R)	New York
39	95	25	Kemmerer, Chicago (R)	New York
40	95	25	Hacker, Chicago (R)	New York
		Aug.		
41	105	4	Pascual, Minnesota (R)	New York
42	113	11	Burnside, Washington (L)	Washington
43	114	12	Donovan, Washington (R)	Washington
44	115	13	Daniels, Washington (R)	Washington
45	116	13	Kutyna, Washington (R)	Washington
46	117	15	Pizarro, Chicago (L)	New York
47	118	16	Pierce, Chicago (L)	New York
48	118	16	Pierce, Chicago (L)	New York
49	123	20	Perry, Cleveland (R)	Cleveland
50	124	22	McBride, Los Angeles (R)	Los Angeles
51	128	26	Walker, Kansas City (R)	Kansas City
		Sept.		
52	134	2	Lary, Detroit (R)	New York
53	134	2	Aguirre, Detroit (L)	New York
54	139	6	Cheney, Washington (R)	New York
55	140	7	Stigman, Cleveland (L)	New York
56	142	9	Grant, Cleveland (R)	New York
57	150	16	Lary, Detroit (R)	Detroit
58	151	17	Fox, Detroit (R)	Detroit
59	154	20	Pappas, Baltimore (R)	Baltimore
60	158	26	Fisher, Baltimore (R)	New York
		Oct.		
61	162	1	Stallard, Boston (R)	New York

Recapitulation: 49 homers off right-handed pitchers: 12 off left-handed pitchers. (Maris bats left-handed, throws right-handed.)
Game numbers do not include a tie game played by the Yankees in 1961. It was the eighth game of the year, April 22, against Baltimore. Maris did not hit a homer in the game.

SOURCE: Table from *The New York Times*, October 2, 1961.

terisk" rule because of the possibility that sixty-one or more home runs could be hit in the 155th to 162d games, setting a new mark but not the record. The pressure on Maris was intense throughout the second half of the season. Ruth was an American icon, and Maris's assault on the hallowed record brought a stream of hate mail, insults shouted at him by fans, plus relentless questioning and resentment from the press. It got to the point where Maris could not go out in public without being harassed, and soon his hair began to fall out due to the stress.

Maris hit his fiftieth home run in his 125th game. Meanwhile, Mantle, who for years had drawn the ire of Yankee fans for not playing up to his enormous potential, had become the preferred player to break Ruth's record, but illness dropped him from contention for the mark, and he finished with fifty-four. On September 19 in Baltimore, Maris failed to top the sixty-home-run mark in 154 games. He hit his fifty-ninth on September 20 and

sixtieth in his 159th game. His ordeal ended on October 1, the final day of the regular season, as he hit his record-setting sixty-first home run off Tracy Stallard of the Boston Red Sox at Yankee Stadium. With sixty-one home runs and 142 runs batted in, Maris was the AL's Most Valuable Player again.

Significance

Maris never had another season like 1961. The next year, he hit thirty-three homers and had one hundred runs batted in, a good season for most players but not enough for his detractors. In his last four seasons with the Yankees, Maris was plagued by injuries, and in 1967, he was traded to the St. Louis Cardinals, where, not pressured by talk of the home run record, he contributed to two National League championships and a World Series title. He

Roger Maris watches his record breaking sixty-first home run travel to the right field seats at Yankee Stadium on October 1, 1961. The feat was not all joy for Maris, who received a significant amount of resentment by those who did not want to see Babe Ruth's record broken. **AP/WIDE WORLD PHOTOS. REPRODUCED BY PERMISSION.**

retired to Florida, where he ran a beer distributorship, bitter at baseball for its treatment of him in 1961. Finally, a year before his death from cancer at age fifty-one, he returned to Yankee Stadium to see old teammates, including Mantle, who was always a friend, and have his number retired.

The Maris record stood for thirty-seven years. The "asterisk" was removed from the sixty-one home runs in 1991. In 1998, in a duel reminiscent of the Mantle-Maris contest of 1961, Mark McGwire of the Cardinals hit seventy home runs to establish a new mark, and runner-up Sammy Sosa of the Chicago Cubs hit sixty-eight. Three years later, in 2001, Barry Bonds of the San Francisco Giants hit seventy-three. The recent home run marks have been shrouded in controversy as the three players involved were suspected of using druglike substances to build body mass and muscle strength; Maris had no advantage, beyond the dimensions of Yankee Stadium.

Primary Source

Roger Maris at Bat [excerpt]

SYNOPSIS: In his autobiography, New York Yankees outfielder Roger Maris gives his account of how pressure from fans and sportswriters affected him during the 1961 season, when he challenged and broke Babe Ruth's all-time home run record.

The Strain

Most of the mail was for the purpose of wishing me well and hoping that I would break the record in 154 games. This, of course, was after the Commissioner had made his ruling.

Not every letter is a boost, however, and there were some on the other side. People wrote to tell me that I was a lousy hitter and had no business hitting home runs; that I had no business to be in Babe Ruth's class and claiming to be another Babe Ruth.

Game 154

No one who saw game 154, who beheld Maris' response to the challenge, is likely soon to forget it. His play was as brave and as moving and as thrilling as a baseball player's can be. There were more reporters and photographers around him now than ever before. Newsmen swelled the Yankee party, which normally numbers 45, to 71. And this was the town where Babe Ruth was born, and the crowd had not come to cheer Maris.

The first time up, Maris shot a line drive to Earl Robinson in right field. He had overpowered Milt Pappas' pitch, but he had not gotten under the ball quite enough. Perhaps an eighth of an inch on the bat was all that kept the drive from sailing higher and farther.

In the third inning Maris took a ball, a breaking pitch inside, swung and missed, took another ball and then hit No. 59, a 390-foot line drive that all but broke a seat in the bleachers. Three more at bats and one home run to tie.

When he came up again, Dick Hall was pitching. Maris took two strikes, and cracked a liner, deep but foul, to right. Then he struck out. When Maris came to bat again in the seventh inning the players in the Yankee bullpen, behind the fence in right center, rose and walked to the fence. "Come on, Roger, baby, hit it to me," shouted Jim Coates. "If I have to go 15 rows into the stands, I'll catch that No. 60 for you."

"You know," said Whitey Ford, "I'm really nervous."

Maris took a strike, then whaled a tremendous drive to right field. Again he had overpowered the ball and again he had hit a foul. Then he lifted a long fly to right center, and there was that eighth of an inch again. An eighth of an inch lower on the bat and the long fly might have been a home run—*the* home run.

Hoyt Wilhelm was pitching in the ninth. He threw Maris a low knuckle ball, and Maris, checking his swing, fouled it back. Wilhelm threw another knuckler, and Maris moved his body but not his bat. The knuckler, veering abruptly, hit the bat and the ball rolled back to Wilhelm, who tagged Maris near first base.

"I'm just sorry I didn't go out with a real good swing," Maris said. "But that Wilhelm." He shook his head. He had overpowered pitches in four of his five times at bat and had gotten only one home run. "Like they say," he said, "you got to be lucky."

Robert Reitz, an unemployed Baltimorean, retrieved No. 59 and announced that the ball was worth $2500.

"I'd like to have it," said Maris, blunt to the end, "but I'm not looking to get rid of that kind of money for it."

The Yankees won the 154th game, 4-2, and with it clinched the American League pennant. Maris wore a gray sweater at the victory party, and someone remarked that in gray and with his crew-cut, he looked like a West Point football player. One remembered then how young he is, and how he believes in honesty as youth does.

"The big thing with you," a friend said to him, "is you tell the truth and don't go phony."

"That's all I know," Roger Maris said. "That's the only way I know how to be. That's the way I'm gonna stay."

SOURCE: Kahn, Roger. "Pursuit of No. 60: The Ordeal of Roger Maris."*Sports Illustrated.* 15, October 2, 1961. Reprinted in *Sports: The American Scene.* Robert Smith, ed. New York: McGraw-Hill, 1963, 102–115.

Those are the crackpot type of letters that you don't bother answering. Some are so vulgar that you don't even read them. You just throw them away. Yet they irk me. I have never imagined myself as a Babe Ruth, nor have I ever claimed that I am a Babe Ruth. I'm just Roger Maris, a guy trying to do the best he can. I know better than anyone that I'm no Babe Ruth and I'd certainly have a lot of nerve if I ever tried to claim that I was. . . .

. . . Some character had written a letter to the editor in which he really took me apart. He was moaning about the possibility of Ruth's record being broken, especially by a .260 hitter. He said that he would hate to see a bum like me break Ruth's great record.

What do these characters want from me? What am I supposed to do? I admire Ruth and all he stands for as much as anyone. He was the greatest, and there will never be another home-run hitter like him regardless of how many anyone ever hits. A lot of people make it sound as if I would be doing something sacrilegious if I broke the record. . . .

There were many times during the season, especially the final month, when I did feel I was ready to crack up. I felt on the verge of telling everyone to jump in the river.

There were actually times in the final weeks when I dreaded going to the park. I had to get hold of myself, remember that this was all part of the great year I was having and that I had to bear with it. No, I never actually thought of going to see a psychoanalyst, but as it got nearer the end there were times when I began to think that I would.

This was the first time that I had ever said publicly that I would be glad when the season ended. I had to keep forcing myself to stay calm. I did it by remembering that there were only a few days of the season left and kept thinking of the day the season would end. . . .

When I got up the next day, I felt sure that things would quiet down. I figured that since I hadn't hit sixty in 154 games, things would now start getting normal. I was getting worried about my falling hair and decided I would see a doctor about it.

It was then I first discovered what the home-run chase had really been doing to me. The doctor told me that there was nothing wrong with my hair or scalp. My hair was falling out because of nervous tension, strain, and being upset.

I didn't know it had been bothering me that much. The doctor warned me that it would get worse before it got better. There was a chance I would have several bald spots, but he assured me that once the strain and tension ended the hair should grow back. . . .

The Record

When I got to the park for the last game there was one thing I was certain of—this was the end. There were no more games, there could be no more excitement about the home runs. Whatever happened today would close the book. That, in itself, was a relief. I knew that this would be do or die, sink or swim, but whatever happened there was nothing I could do, so I wasn't going to worry about it.

Once again there was that air of excitement hanging over the park. Everyone looked strangely at me. I was thinking that I knew now how the monkeys in the zoo must feel. But, at least, it would all end after today. I knew that I had hit sixty. I was happy, and no matter what happened on this final day I could tell myself that I had given it my best shot.

I knew that I would have only four, perhaps five, chances to try for the sixty-first. If I didn't get it, then I just didn't. I never had a feeling that perhaps if I did hit it, people would feel that I had toppled an idol by beating Ruth. Babe had his record for 154 games, but perhaps I could get one for 162 games.

Tracy Stallard, a young right-hander, was the Boston pitcher. I knew that I wasn't going to take any walks. I was just hoping that perhaps he would be pitching trying to get me out, not to walk me. No one was going to walk me that day, I was going down swinging.

The pressure in this game, despite all it meant to me personally, was not as severe as in the 154th game. Nothing will ever equal the way I felt that day. This one, of course, was the second toughest game. I was determined to do the same as I had in the 154th . . . give it my best, go down swinging with everything I had. If I hit one, then it would be the greatest thing that ever happened to an individual. If I didn't, no one could say I didn't try.

There was a man on second when I came up in the first. I hit a long drive to left field. I found myself wishing I had pulled it. If I had and if it had gone that far to right field it would have been in the seats. At least Stallard was trying to work on me. He threw me a fast ball low on the outside corner. It so happened that I went with the pitch and didn't try to pull it.

It was 0-0 as I came up with two out in the fourth. Each time I came up there would be a stirring in the right-field stands, but otherwise it was so quiet that I almost felt the Stadium was empty. There were no cameramen on the field. They aren't allowed on the field at the Stadium. Once again it was between Stallard and me. Every eye in the Stadium was on us. Would he pitch to me again?

There was a lot of pressure on the pitcher too. He knew what was happening. His first pitch was a ball, the crowd booed. Then the second pitch was also a ball; the boos grew louder. I knew everyone was pulling for me and I dug in a little deeper. Perhaps the booing had made Stallard mad. He's a proud young man and was only doing his job.

He wound up and delivered the 2-0 pitch. It was a good fast ball, but maybe he had got it too good. I was ready and I connected. As soon as I hit it, I knew it was number sixty-one. . . . It was the only time that the number of the homer ever flashed into my mind as I hit it. Then I heard the tremendous roar from the crowd. I could see them all standing, then my mind went blank again.

I couldn't even think as I went around the bases. I couldn't tell you what crossed my mind; I don't think anything did. I was in a daze. I was all fogged out from a very, very hectic season and an extremely difficult month. It is difficult to explain how I felt or what I thought of.

I began to come to as I got to the dugout. All my teammates were there to greet me, pound my back, and congratulate me. I saw the fans standing, giving me a wonderful ovation. I didn't know what to do. I stood up on the dugout steps and waved my hat. I was afraid I was being corny and tried to get back into the dugout, but my teammates held me up on the steps and wouldn't let me get down. It began to feel as if they would never let me down.

Even as I was standing up on the steps, something inside was telling me that now I had hit more home runs than anyone in history had ever hit in a single season. I felt very proud, but also humble. I knew I hadn't done it alone. I knew I had been helped along the way. I felt that I was a very fortunate man. . . .

I was as happy as it is possible for anyone to be. I didn't care about it being in 162 games. It was the biggest home run of my life. What is the use of saying anything else? It was the greatest thrill that I have ever had or hope to have.

I was very happy for many reasons, but I was happiest because now it was all over. The pressure, the excitement, the anxiety were gone. There can be no more talk of home-run records. It is all in the book, and the book is closed.

I was tremendously happy to go past Ruth's record even if my season ran a little longer. I would have liked to have broken it in 154 games, but perhaps it is just as well that I didn't. At the time I still couldn't explain that feeling, but I believe I can now.

I believe that it is probably best that his record goes right on and that I have mine in 162 games. There is just something about Ruth and his record of sixty that seems to set it apart from other records. Mr. Ruth still has his record for 154 games, and I have mine for 162. Nothing has been ruined or shattered. He still has his record, and now I have mine. I am completely satisfied with it that way. . . .

Further Resources

BOOKS
Allen, Maury. *Roger Maris: A Man for All Seasons.* New York: D.I. Fine, 1980.

Kubek, Tony. *Sixty-One: The Team, the Record, the Men.* New York: Macmillan, 1987.

Smith, Ron. *61* The Story of Roger Maris, Mickey Mantle, and One Magical Summer.* St. Louis, Mo.: Sporting News, 2001.

PERIODICALS
Durso, Joseph. "Roger Maris Set Home Run Mark." *The New York Times,* December 16, 1985.

WEBSITES
National Baseball Hall of Fame and Museum. "Roger Maris." Available online at http://www.baseballhalloffame.org (accessed March 4, 2003).

AUDIO AND VISUAL MEDIA
"Eighth Inning: 1960–1970." *Baseball.* Walpole, N.H.: Florentine Films, 1994.

61.* Face Productions. Directed by Billy Crystal. HBO Home Video, 2001, DVD/VHS.

Roone Arledge

"It's Sport . . . It's Money . . . It's TV"

Magazine article

By: Roone Arledge with Gilbert Rogin

Date: April 25, 1966

Source: Arledge, Roone, with Gilbert Rogin. "It's Sport . . . It's Money . . . It's TV." *Sports Illustrated,* April 25, 1966, 93, 97, 98, 100, 103, 105, 106.

About the Author: Roone Arledge (1931–2002) was born in Forest Hills, New York. After graduating from Columbia University, he worked for the Dumont Network and NBC. In 1960, he went to ABC, eventually becoming vice president, then president of sports programming, producing and directing college football, *Wide World of Sports, Monday Night Football,* and several Olympic Games. In 1977, he became president of ABC News, and from 1985 to 1998, was president of the network.

"Sports All Over"

Newspaper article

By: Deane McGowen

Date: February 11, 1962

Source: McGowen, Deane. "Sports All Over." *The New York Times,* February 11, 1962. ■

Introduction

After World War II (1939–1945) and into the 1950s, sports and television were experiencing growing pains. Creativity and innovation were slow in developing, with sporting officials and sponsors exercising direct control over telecasts. In the 1960s, television was to change, primarily through one man: Roone Arledge.

Roone Arledge first made his mark at NBC, where he directed and produced children's and public affairs programs and won the first of his thirty-six Emmy Awards for a puppet show. Arledge's work at NBC caught the attention of ABC's fledgling sports division, which hired the twenty-nine-year-old in 1960 as producer for college football telecasts.

Within several years, Arledge introduced new and revolutionary concepts in sports broadcasting. He wanted to get the viewer involved in the telecast, even if, as he once said, they "didn't give a damn about sports." He created viewing experiences by putting cameras on cranes, helicopters, and blimps to get better and different angles of the stadium; handheld cameras to get close-ups of beaten and bloody players, exuberant cheerleaders, pretty coeds, eccentric fans, and hassled coaches; and long microphones to capture crowd noises and other game sounds.

In 1961, Arledge started a summer replacement sports anthology program, *Wide World of Sports,* with a former newspaper reporter, Jim McKay, as host. From that tenuous beginning, *Wide World,* with its signature lead-in, "The thrill of victory . . . and the agony of defeat," became for the next forty years a fixture on ABC, featuring sports of all kinds, from the traditional—such as auto racing, skiing, and track and field—to the unusual, such as barrel jumping, cliff diving, demolition derby, and wrist-wrestling. The show's success led to Arledge productions such as the outdoors-oriented *American Sportsman,* and enabled ABC to gain the televised rights to Summer and Winter Olympics from 1964 to 1980. Televised Olympic coverage under Arledge's production focused not only on the competition itself but an "up close and personal" look at the athletes. His most masterful Olympic coverage was in 1972 at Munich, when Arab terrorists killed eleven Israeli athletes, and he transformed sports coverage into seamless news reporting with McKay as the cool, composed anchor who informed the nation of the tragedy.

Significance

Perhaps Arledge's greatest impact on TV sports was the genesis of *Monday Night Football* in 1970. Football had never been successful on Monday nights, but NFL commissioner Pete Rozelle wanted to try again, and after CBS and NBC dismissed the idea, Arledge and ABC said yes, but with a major condition: that the network, not the league choose the announcers. This cleared the way for Arledge to put the controversial Howard Cosell on the telecast, along with Keith Jackson, folksy former Dallas Cowboy quarterback Don Meredith, and later the former New York Giant star Frank Gifford. Within a couple years, *Monday Night Football* became part of American culture and altered TV viewing habits forever.

The impact of Roone Arledge's vision of televised sports can hardly be measured. His overall impact on television, however, was far from finished. In 1977, he took over the third-place ABC news division. Over the next two decades, ABC news programs such as *World News Tonight, Nightline, 20/20, Prime Time Live,* and *This Week with David Brinkley* were begun and became successful under Arledge. By the 1990s, Arledge's control at ABC began to decline with new management, cost-cutting measures, and his increasingly poor health. Arledge retired from active management at ABC in 1998 and died in December 2002.

Primary Source

"It's Sport . . . It's Money . . . It's TV" [excerpt]

SYNOPSIS: In a *Sports Illustrated* article, Roone Arledge, executive producer at ABC sports, discusses his innovations in televising athletic events. He also assesses the television potential of most major sports, including baseball, basketball, football, golf, and hockey.

The easiest way to talk about what sport has done to television and what television has done to sport is to talk money. In 1960 it cost $50,000 to buy the rights to the Winter Olympics. In 1964 the price was $650,000, and for 1968 it's costing us $2 million. Last year the NFL completed a two-year deal with CBS that set the network back $28.2 million. For the next two years the figure is $37.6 million. In 1962 a one-minute commercial during an NFL game cost $37,000. Today it's $70,000.

But there's more to it than dollars and cents, obviously. Today there is twice as much sport on national television as there was five years ago, and the relationship has become more subtle and profound. Is television having a salutary effect on sport? Or is it taking it over, changing it and running it?

In recent years, by spending millions of dollars for the rights to sports events, television has become the biggest promoter in history, while at the same time becoming the largest source of information. This sets up a basic ethical conflict that television will have to face soon. Is it going to be strictly an entertainment medium, or is it deserving of journalistic stature? . . .

When I got into it in 1960, televising sports amounted to going out on the road, opening three or four cameras and trying not to blow any plays. They were barely documenting the game, but just the marvel of seeing a picture was enough to keep the people glued to their sets. What we set out to do was to get the audience involved emotionally. If they didn't give a damn about the game, they might still enjoy the program. We began to use cranes, blimps and helicopters to provide a better view of the stadium, the campus and the town. We developed hand-held cameras for closeups. We reran the important plays at half time so they could be analyzed. We used seven cameras, three just for environment. We asked ourselves: If you were sitting in the stadium, what would you be looking at? The coach on the sideline, the substitute quarterback warming up, the pretty girl in the next section. So our cameras wandered as your eyes would. Sound had been greatly neglected,

Roone Arledge (left) announces the hiring of Jackie Robinson as an analyst for baseball games on ABC, March 18, 1965. Arledge's *Wide World of Sports* program revolutionized sports coverage on TV. **AP/WIDE WORLD PHOTOS. REPRODUCED BY PERMISSION.**

too. All they used to do was hang a mike out the window to get the roar of the crowd. We developed the rifle-type mike. Now you can hear the thud of a football when it is punted. . . .

Baseball is a game that was designed to be played on a sunny afternoon at Wrigley Field in the 1920s, not on a 21-inch screen. It is a game of sporadic action interspersed with long lulls. Last year we tried rerunning plays in slow motion. It was redundant. On the other hand, even if nothing is happening in football, there is an aura of anticipation. The huddle is intellectually stimulating. What are they going to do next? You get a semblance of this when the manager goes out to the mound to talk to the pitcher, but how many times does it happen? And the pace and rhythm of football create an instant aura of action. Everyone in baseball *walks* everywhere. In football, even when nothing is happening, there is the appearance of action. Guys *run*.

The unique thing about baseball is that it is the only major sport where the function of the principal figure—the pitcher—is to inhibit the action. He is a defensive, anti-action kind of personage, who is,

perhaps, analogous in football not to the quarterback but to the middle line-backer. The quarterback stimulates and motivates the action. If the pitcher is doing his job well, nothing happens, which, from the standpoint of television, is deadly. . . .

Football and television have been ideal partners. They have a great affinity. The shape of the field corresponds to that of the screen. The action, although spread out, starts in a predictable portion of the field. It is a game in which action focuses on individuals. The quarterback is a meaningful focal point. The flow is natural and continuous, not like in baseball, where there is a play at third, then you cut to second, then cut to home plate. . . .

Physically, professional basketball is an excellent sport for television; it's played in a confined area and the cameras can be placed to show the agility, finesse and contact. One of the problems is a growing feeling that everything that occurs before the last 10 minutes of play is inconsequential. This is not really true unless you tune in to find out the result rather than to watch the game, or unless your sole interest is in betting. The end of the game has an intensity and a desperateness, but certainly no monopoly on great plays.

Our principal weakness is that we haven't educated the people sufficiently to the subtleties of basketball strategy, as we have done in football. However, it's not an easy game to do commentary over, because the action is constant. There is no natural break where the expert can come in, and if he tries, another basket is scored halfway through what he is saying and the subject has changed.

One of the difficulties with hockey is the relative obscurity of the players. They are almost non-people when they take their uniforms off. On the other hand, one of the reasons golfers have become such super superstars is that they don't have a uniform to take off. Hockey is probably the most exciting untapped sport—all body contact, speed, the lone goalie standing up against the onslaught. It also has a certain grandness. A player who has committed a penalty has to sit in a box in full view. It's personal, you can identify with him. Football is the only major sport where the players commit fouls anonymously. Why?

The rules of hockey are easily understood, so women like it. You are close to the players, and since they don't wear helmets you can see what they look like. It would be a perfect sport if there were one less man on each team. When you've got six players to get through, it's too damned hard to score, it's too cluttered. The plays so seldom work, there is constant frustration.

One of the problems associated with putting hockey on national television is the structure of the game. There are no time-outs or breaks to get the commercials in, and you have the two 10-minute intermissions between periods when you basically have to fill time. Hockey would best lend itself to a combination of tape and live, but when you put something on tape you lose a lot of its appeal.

Another thing is that the coverage of hockey has not been as good as it ought to be. Perhaps color will help. The puck would be easier to see, and there is something about the color of the uniforms against all that white ice. (A football, however, is harder to see in color than in black and white. I'd love to change the color of the football, but I can already hear the screams.) But the major difficulty is that hockey is so fast and the puck is so small. In automobile racing and in skiing, where you're trying to show the reality of speed, you make illusions to create reality. You can't shoot a car or a skier coming at you or going away. If you shoot a car coming at you, it looks like it's parked. That's why we shoot from a helicopter hovering directly overhead; this way, the viewer gets the feeling of the landscape going by, What we ought to be doing with hockey is slowing it down by shooting it from behind the goals.

Golf is a great game for television. First of all, it is impossible to see a tournament as well in person as on the screen and, secondly, we have taken a sport which isn't basically a head-to-head encounter, which isn't even essentially a spectator sport, and have made it so by cutting back and forth between various holes and players, so that, in effect, you've often got the three leaders in the same three-some. We've also changed the pace of the game itself to make it more exciting. For instance, you normally don't have to watch the guys walking. We've been able to take out all the lulls in golf. We know that if Nicklaus is standing over the ball we can put on a minute-and-a-half commercial, or we can cut to Chi Chi Rodriguez and then back to Nicklaus again without blowing it. You can blow golf by not knowing the sport or the players, and live television is like writing on water.

More than in any other sport, golf's heroes have been built by television. Because of the tight close-ups, you can see what they look like and watch them register every emotion. . . .

However, advertisers like golf because it appeals to a higher type than those who watch the Roller Derby or wrestling, and this kind of viewer will buy certain products, like computers. We are all influenced by our likes and dislikes, and we put things on and then rationalize. I'm ashamed to say it, but if we put on the Demolition Derby for 13 weeks the ratings would go through the roof.

Tennis is perfect for television. It is played in a small, confined area, and there are only two or four clearly defined protagonists. The camera can get close up, surround them. You can hear the sound of the ball. There is more of a hushed drama to tennis than to golf, more apparent physical agility, and it has the same blue-blood, snob appeal. . . .

With the exception of the Kentucky Derby, horse racing is not a major sport on national television. The Preakness and the Belmont are afterthoughts, and not as compelling. Almost all the interest in horse racing is in the outcome, not in the sport itself. If we had some means of flashing the results electronically, no one would watch it. There isn't any great appeal to it as a sport, because it's not promoted as such. It's like watching strangers playing roulette—it's not thrilling unless you're involved. . . .

Primary Source

"Sports All Over" [excerpt]

SYNOPSIS: *The New York Times*, in its television column, reviews favorably a new televised sports anthology show, *Wide World of Sports*, on ABC, noting the variety of athletic events covered, the performance of the host, Jim McKay, and the skill of Roone Arledge, executive producer.

A.B.C. Show Ranges Far For Ringside Viewing

The armchair sportsman, once relegated to sparse and seasonal chores (Sunday afternoon quarterbacking, Friday night prizefighting and occasional stakes racing) is fast becoming an all-round athlete with an awesome number of vicarious skills.

Through the lens and coaxial cable, sports fans have been able to see such spectator staples as basketball, football, golf, boxing and hockey as well as hitherto less exposed competitions in springboard diving, shot putting, water skiing, bobsledding and barrel jumping.

The televising of such a varied program the year round has made thousands of Americans more sports-conscious and more knowledgeable about sports.

One of the programs adding prestige to the medium is the American Broadcasting Company's "Wide World of Sports."

Now in its second year of operation under the executive production of Roone Arledge, "Wide World of Sports" will present sixteen shows during 1962, covering sporting events of national and international interest.

Schedule

Followers of this year's program already have seen, live, the American Football League All-Star game, and by video tape, the water skiing champions at Acapulco, the barrel jumping championships at Grossinger, N. Y., the Portland, Ore., invitation indoor track and field meet and the surf board championship from Hawaii.

In the coming weeks the show will present the world figure skating championships from Prague, the world Alpine skiing tournament from Chamonix, the world four-man bobsled championships from Garmisch-Partenkirchen, the St. Paul Winter Carnival, the Oxford-Cambridge crew race and the Grand National horse race from England, and the Sports Car Grand Prix from Daytona Beach.

Mr. Arledge says, "The basic concept of 'Wide World of Sports' is that we will go any place in the world to cover topline sports events. But more than that, we try to cover sports people know something about but not enough about.

"We aim to take the fan to the event, not merely bring the event into the living room or the game room. We try to put the fan in the seat in the arena or at the track or the side of road or alongside the ski jump.

"But along with presenting the action to the fan, we try to anticipate the action of the competition— what the competitors have to do and how to do it best to win."

And to provide authentic background information and technical knowhow of each sport, "Wide World of Sports" provides the viewer with an expert in the particular event as well as its regular commentator, the well-informed Jim McKay.

Further Resources

BOOKS

McKay, Jim. *The Real McKay: My Wide World of Sports.* New York: Dutton, 1998.

Rader, Benjamin G. *In Its Own Image: How Television Has Transformed Sports.* New York: Free Press, 1984.

Sugar, Bert Randolph. *The Thrill of Victory: The Inside Story of ABC Sports.* New York: Hawthorn, 1978.

PERIODICALS

Carter, Bill. "Roone Arledge, 71, A Force in TV Sports and News, Dies." *The New York Times,* December 6, 2002.

"Roone Arledge Interview." *Playboy,* October 1976.

"The Complete Concentration of Mr. Palmer"

Magazine article

By: Barry Furlong

Date: September 2, 1962

Source: Furlong, Barry. "The Complete Concentration of Mr. Palmer." *The New York Times,* September 2, 1962, 14, 43–44.

About the Author: William Barry Furlong (1927–2000) was born in Chicago, Illinois. After graduating from the Illinois Institute of Technology, he was a reporter for the *Chicago Daily News* and correspondent for *Newsweek.* He also was a freelance writer for *Harper's, Sports Illustrated, Good Housekeeping,* and *The New York Times Magazine.* In 1974, he became a staff writer for the *Washington Post.* Furlong wrote or coauthored three books.

Introduction

In the 1950s, men's golf was still perceived by many as a country club sport played by the wealthy. The advent of television lifted golf's potential as a sport for the masses. What golf needed was a player who appealed to the galleries at tournaments and television audiences watching at home—and a rival of equal or superior ability. The first was Arnold Palmer, the second, Jack Nicklaus.

Arnold Palmer learned the game from his father, a golf pro. He turned professional in 1954 after a brief but successful amateur career. After he won his first pro tournament, his career took off. Rising to prominence as television brought golf to the public in greater numbers, Palmer's "go for broke" attitude, his emotional reaction to shots, and his chain cigarette smoking on the course endeared him to spectators as a "Mr. Everyman" of sport. His loyal legion of fans, called "Arnie's Army," cheered and followed him at tournaments. Palmer won the Masters in 1958, and by the early 1960s, he was at the top of his game.

Jack Nicklaus grew up in Ohio and as a child seemed a natural golfer. Encouraged by his father, Nicklaus began playing tournaments while still in high school and won the Ohio Amateur Championship at age sixteen. At Ohio State University, he won collegiate titles as an All-

American, as well as the U.S. Amateur championship twice. Nicklaus turned professional after college in 1962.

The Nicklaus-Palmer rivalry began in 1960, when Nicklaus, at age twenty and still at Ohio State, qualified for the U.S. Open, and finished runner-up to Palmer by two strokes. Nicklaus's first professional victory in his eighteenth tournament of 1962 was a dramatic playoff win against Palmer in the U.S. Open. Palmer, however, remained on top with victories at the Masters in 1960, and the British Open in 1961. Despite losing to Nicklaus at the 1962 U.S. Open, Palmer won two other major tournaments that year: the Masters and British Open, both repeat victories.

By 1963, Nicklaus began to forge ahead in the rivalry, with victories in the Masters and PGA Championship, the latter a tournament that Palmer never won. In 1964, Palmer won his fourth and final Masters, with Nicklaus finishing tied for second. Nicklaus won back-to-back Masters in 1965 and 1966, his second and third, plus the British Open in 1966. Palmer, nearly forty years old, was no longer the champion golfer he once was and yielded dominance in the sport to the younger man, but not the adulation of the crowd. For all of Nicklaus's great skill on the course, he could not rival Palmer's crowd appeal, although over the years a devoted following developed.

Significance

For the remainder of the 1960s and 1970s, Nicklaus continued his assault on golfing history, winning the U.S. Open in 1967 and dominating the sport over the next decade. Nicklaus, whose nickname, "Golden Bear," alluded to his blond hair and large frame, transformed his image by losing weight and growing his hair longer, making him a recognizable sports figure in the seventies.

Arnold Palmer and Jack Nicklaus are two of golf's greatest players. Palmer won eighty professional championships, including seven majors: the Masters four times, the U.S. Open in 1960, and the British Open twice. By the late 1980s, Nicklaus had won eighty-nine pro championships, including a record eighteen majors: six Masters, five PGAs, four U.S. Opens, and three British Opens. Palmer, then Nicklaus, came along when the marriage between golf and television began; thus, both became recognizable athletes because of TV.

Primary Source

"The Complete Concentration of Mr. Palmer" [excerpt]

SYNOPSIS: William Barry Furlong, writing in the *New York Times Magazine,* profiles Arnold Palmer, perhaps sport's most popular performer in the early 1960s,

Jack Nicklaus helps Arnold Palmer put on the green coat, the symbol of the winner of the Masters Championship, Augusta, Georgia, April 13, 1964. Nicklaus's and Palmer's rivalry helped establish golf's large popular following. © BETTMANN/CORBIS. REPRODUCED BY PERMISSION.

by showing him in action and discussing the way he connected with his fans.

It is so complete that in a match he can look at his wife and not recognize her.

But it has helped him become top man in golf today—so Mrs. Palmer understands.

Perhaps no athlete in our time has more closely approached a fleshly apotheosis than a professional golfer named Arnold Palmer whose particular genius is one of the most envied in modern society: he doesn't let the game of golf intimidate him.

The godlike nature of this gift is reflected daily on almost any golf course where golfer after golfer can be seen in earnest imitation of the "Palmer putt" that is, in a knock-kneed stance with elbows tucked tightly into the body. On the courses, such as the Firestone Country Club in Akron, Ohio, where he competes in the television World Series of Golf next week-end, huge galleries dubbed "Arnie's Army" follow him around.

The 1963 Masters Tournament: Arnold and Augusta

I liked Arnie a lot as a person—who could not like such an appealing character? Also, having a pretty good idea of what it had taken to compile, I had appropriate respect for his record. Beyond that, however, I guess the best I can say for myself is that I looked on Arnold just the way you would expect of a blinkered youth fixated on bullheading his way to the top of the mountain. In a nutshell, once the whistle had blown, Arnold Palmer was just another player, another guy trying to go my way on a track only wide enough for one. I wanted to *win,* and then win and win and win again—every time I teed it up, now and forever. If that meant not simply beating Arnold Palmer, but also toppling a legend and throwing half the population into deep depression, well, so long as it was done fairly and squarely, fine and dandy. I respected all the tour players, but I simply did not see any supermen out there, Arnold included. I had no reservations about beating anyone else. Why, then, should I have any about beating him? . . .

In retrospect, if I had to do it all over again, I would still go as hard as I could after the same result, but with more effort to disguise the intensity or rawness of my will to win. At the age of twenty-two, it simply never oc-curred to me how apparent this was in the way I went about the game, nor that some people might interpret it as coldness of heart or bleakness of spirit. In short, although the goals I set myself probably were acceptable to everyone—maybe, even, to many of Arnie's Army—the fact is I marched toward them along too straight and narrow a path for the majority of observers to want to applaud my passage. My focus was too sharp, too inter-nalized, too locked on where I wanted to go, to recog-nize and cater to the fact that I was in the entertainment business as much as the golf-playing business. And it was this, I'm sure, that made me such a black hat to so many of the fans for so many of those early years. Sure, I was overweight and crew-cut, and, sure, I dressed like a guy painting a porch, and, sure, I had a squeaky voice and didn't laugh and joke a lot in public, and, sure, I often lacked tact and diplomacy in my public utterances. I be-lieve all of those failings might have been forgiven a young and unsophisticated individual if he had simply papered over the raw intensity of his will to win—in-cluding, particularly, trying to knock the game's best-loved idol off his throne. And the best thing I remember about it all was that, hard as I sometimes had to fight Arnold's galleries, the only way I ever had to fight him was with my golf clubs.

SOURCE: Nicklaus, Jack, with Ken Bowden. *Jack Nicklaus: My Story.* New York: Simon & Schuster, 1997.

Their dedication is as vast as their size. "They don't know anybody's here but Palmer," said Jerry Barber, the defending champion, at the Professional Golfers Association tournament in July. Some of them wear signs on their hats "Go Arnie!" Others whisper clandestine advice about how to handle an opponent: "Needle him, Arnie" or "Walk around while he's putting, Arnie." All of them worship him as the man they would like to be. . . .

Arnold Palmer's contribution to our national peace of mind is that he has shown it is possible to conquer one's self.

Now just short of his thirty-third birthday, which he will celebrate Sept. 10, Palmer goes about play-ing the game with the *élan* of a Las Vegas croupier who knows that the house odds are with him. "Palmer is the boldest player on the circuit," one golf official has said. "I guess I putt past the pin more than most anybody," Palmer has conceded. "I always like to give it a chance. Never up, never in, you know." . . .

Palmer doesn't waste time or energy wondering whether he'll make a shot; he goes immediately to the problem of how. At times, his concentration is so deep that he can look his wife, Winnie, full in the face and not recognize her. "I get the business for that every once in a while," he says.

When the problem is toughest, and the pressure is greatest, he seems to react with adrenal joy. The cigarette is pressed more purposefully between his lips and he strides about the course like a lion look-ing for raw meat. Yet somehow he never loses his human quality. Whereas Ben Hogan looked, in criti-cal moments, less like a man of woman born than a machine turned out on a lathe, Palmer looks sim-ply like a guy who enjoys spending an afternoon in the sun.

He has an astonishing capacity for regaining his concentration without irritation, once it's been in-terrupted. "I'm convinced that if, on the seventy-sec-ond hole of the Masters tournament, a little kid ran onto the putting green when Arnold was lining up a putt to win and asked for an autograph, Arnold would stop to sign it for him," says Mark McCormack, the agent, attorney, manager and all-around confidant of Palmer.

The Handshake

Much has been made of The Rivalry. Arnie versus Jack. Volumes have been written, verdicts given. My own personal take on the subject is a fairly simple and I think true reading. Jack Nicklaus was and is my greatest competition in golf, both on the course during my peak years and off it years later as our separate interests evolved in the business world. . . .

Behind the scenes of those celebrated Arnie-versus-Jack years we traveled together quite a lot, dined together, privately discussed at great depth issues of the Tour and family life, agreed philosophically on far more things than we disagreed on, and ruthlessly pounced on any opportunity to needle each other in private about beating the other at his own game. . . . We were natural adversaries, to be sure, but also clearly a good fit.

Unlike our wives, though, Jack and I never became what you might call pals off the golf course. . . . But we never failed to enjoy each other's company in a social setting, like the time I plopped a lady's wig on his head (or maybe it's the other way around; the story has been repeated so many times and so many ways, I'm beginning to forget which way it really happened) and we briefly danced together like a couple of drunken teddy bears at a tournament function, delighting everyone except the poor lady who lost her hairpiece.

The simple truth is, I like Jack and I admire him in more ways than I can probably express. But that doesn't stop me from feeling a surge of the old competitiveness—or even a stab of jealousy—when one of his companies or course design crew wins a job contract I thought we deserved. . . .

We're different men with different views, and our differing view of Mark McCormack explains a lot about us.

In July 1970, not long after his father's death, Jack assembled his own business team and decided it was time to go his own way, amicably terminating his business relationship with Mark and International Management Group. He wanted to determine his own destiny, and in retrospect I think he really needed the new mental stimulation of making his own way in the business world. Jack is, at heart, analytical, a detail man, always taking things apart to see how they run. He's also a bit of a lone wolf who prefers to do everything himself. You can see it in the way he focuses in on a golf shot, the way he appears to be scrutinizing every blade of grass for a clue when he putts. You can see it in the way he builds a golf course or runs a golf tournament, where he is master of the smallest detail. From what I've heard and even from what Jack has admitted to me, that's exactly how he runs his businesses. I, on the other hand, have always enjoyed having a number of trusted people around me and rely on them to do their jobs without too much interference from the boss. I suppose that, too, is the Pap in me. Once I trust somebody socially or in business, they have my respect and support until they prove otherwise. Jack navigates more by brain. I go more by heart. Intellect versus instinct. Jack versus Arnie. . . .

In retrospect, I see that it was clearly the right decision for him to make, and I think we've finally come full circle on that issue and others. We're closer now, in some respects, than we have ever been. We share a golden history and a thousand memories of laughter and tears. I'd feel remiss if I didn't say that. On the larger issues facing the game, for example, questions like the dominant role the equipment revolution is playing in altering the face of the game or the development of new competing tours and the formation of players' unions, it should surprise nobody that we come down in complete agreement on the side of protecting the integrity of the game, preserving the traditional values and qualities that have always made golf the most splendid and democratic pastime on earth.

Competitive golf has been the center of both our lives, and yet the differences between us—the factors that made us such intense and faithful competitors, I believe—are still as apparent as ever to anyone who wishes to take the time to look. Jack likes golf, but I don't think he actually loves and needs the game the way I still do. I try to play every day, and when I don't play—if you'll pardon the expression—I feel like a bear with a sore tail because of it.

Jack plays because he must play, and, not surprising to me, he is still capable of summoning that legendary ability to concentrate and perform that will have historians talking about his game two hundred years from now. His family and his business command more of Jack's attention than anything—and that's just the way he wants it.

My family and my business mean everything to me, too, but the third component of the mix is my need to still be out there chasing after Old Man Par, trying to make cuts and please the galleries.

Bottom line: Jack is still Jack.

And Arnie is still Arnie.

SOURCE: Palmer, Arnold, with James Dodson. *A Golfer's Life.* New York: Ballantine, 1999.

It is this quality that his fellow pros most admire and envy, for when the chips are down, this is the mystical quality which sustains Palmer. He knows he is going to win and so do his opponents. Therefore, they lose more readily out of the sheer fear of losing. "When the pressure is on, it's on you more than Palmer," says one of them. "You're sweating but he doesn't seem to feel a thing."

"So I Put a Coat on Arnie" [excerpt]

Twenty minutes before I was due to tee off I was the object of a short presentation ceremony. John Murray, who owns the Murray Biscuit Company of Augusta, had arranged with the local sheriff to have me made an honorary deputy sheriff of Richmond County. So shortly before tee-off time the sheriff presented me with my badge. I should have had Arnold Palmer locked up. . . .

. . . I ended up the round with a 73 that I felt should have been lower. On the other hand, at Augusta you always think you are playing well. The fairways are so wide it is hard to miss them, you seldom get out of play and you always feel that somehow you can get the ball around and into the hole. When you finish, it is almost always with the thought that your score should have been quite a bit lower.

There was not much to be said at this point. I was now seven shots behind Arnold and felt pretty gloomy. . . . That evening Jack Grout, my former teaching pro from Columbus who was visiting with my dad, explained what he thought had happened. Each day I had been gripping the club tighter and tighter with my right hand, an unconscious reaction, I guess, as I got more and more desperate to overtake Arnold. The result was that my right forearm and wrist had become so constricted that I was not cocking my wrists on the backswing. . . .

. . . On the practice tee I worked on keeping my right arm firm but comfortable and hit the ball very well. Of course, I had to shoot about a flat zero to catch Arnold. But he just might have a bad round. Nothing much happened on the front nine. Then I birdied 12, eagled 13, just missed a birdie on 14 and birdied 15 after one of the longest drives I have ever hit. After my tee shot left me 12 feet from the hole on 16, I felt that I had worked my way back into the tournament. "Make this putt," I told myself, "and you'll be seven under par for the tournament. Arnold is only 10 under and if you make birdies on 17 and 18 anything might happen." There is a big scoreboard at 16, and a boy had that exciting red 7 in his hand, ready to put up beside my name. Then I missed the putt. I guess it is all over, I thought. Walking up 17, I heard the yell for Arnold's birdie on 14, and I *knew* it was all over.

But depression is a luxury that an athlete cannot afford. It was not many minutes later that I was sitting, kind of numb, waiting for the presentation ceremony to begin, for the time when I would slip the green jacket over Arnold's shoulders.

SOURCE: Nicklaus, Jack. "So I Put a Coat on Arnie." *Sports Illustrated,* June 1, 1964, 52, 55–56, 58.

Nonetheless, on occasion Palmer reveals a weaker side. When, as sometimes happens, he misses a shot, he reacts with anguish. He twists has body as if tormented in mind and in soul. . . .

Of course, confidence and concentration are nice, but not enough; it is handy to have skill, too. Palmer happens to be one of the few golfers ever to have both great power in driving off the tee and the concentration to be an exceptional putter. He hones these talents. . . .

Television has made Palmer's face as familiar to sports fans as the face on the Lincoln penny. It has also given him "instant celebrity" and with it the opportunity to mine vast lodes of money. By mid-August, Palmer had won $80,198 on his golf tour; nobody will say how much he'll make outside of golf but the figure has been estimated unofficially at between $300,000 and $400,000.

He gets $3,000 as a flat fee for an exhibition on a weekday, more for week-end exhibitions—"though he doesn't like to go in for a flat fee; he'd rather play for a percentage of the gate," says Mark McCormack. He gets $6,500 a year guaranteed him by the Wilson Sporting Goods Co., plus royalties on the clubs sold under his endorsement. He gets nearly $20,000 for his syndicated golf column now distributed to "nearly 100 newspapers." He endorses shirts, slacks, shoes, socks, windbreakers, hats, golf gloves, women's clothes.

He is just opening a nationwide chain of Arnold Palmer putting greens, and when his contract runs out with Wilson in the autumn of 1963—McCormack says it's in October, a spokesman for Wilson says it's in November—he'll be free to make an arrangement for the production of clubs under his name that could make him one of the wealthiest men in sports. This vast empire wouldn't collapse if Arnold lost a tournament or two—but it is greatly nourished by victory. . . .

When he's keyed up, Palmer is all but impervious to the pressures and annoyances which bother most golfers. "When Palmer addresses an eight or a ten-foot putt, by God, he acts like he expects to sink it, which I suppose is the way you ought to think," fellow pro Dow Finsterwald has said of him.

Of course, he can sometimes hear the distracting noises in the crowd around him. It is the *one* sound—the soft snapping of a camera shutter, the tackling of a single candy wrapper, the, chirping of a lone bird—in the chapel-like silence surrounding an important shot that he finds most distracting. On the sixteenth tee of one Masters' tournament, a photographer lying on the ground shot Palmer's picture just as Palmer reached the climax of his backswing—and Palmer muffed the shot. But that was a rare enough incident so that he remembers it clearly. . . .

Through it all, Palmer remains natural and thoroughly likable. He is perfectly at ease discussing subjects other than golf. "He's the only golfer I can remember going to dinner with," says one acquaintance, "and not hearing golf. He's not just waiting for someone to drop a word that'll let him swing the talk back to golf." . . .

Only one thing seems to jar his serenity: bad feeling. "The only time he might have trouble sleeping is when he gets a nasty letter from somebody," says Winnie. The letters may be as eccentric as those from people who feel that he's "greedy" for trying to win so many tournaments or that he's setting a bad example by smoking so much. ("Really," says Winnie, "I don't think he smokes any more than a pack a day." Of course, he lights quite a few cigarettes on the course but discards them before every shot. . . .

Most people don't think that he's changed at all under the pressures of the game and of his rising fame. "He doesn't even seem to age," says one friend. His wife disagrees. "He's become more relaxed and patient and he's gotten bigger—and gotten older," says Winnie. "It used to be, when he first started out, that he was not nearly as patient with himself, with his golf game, or even with people as he is today." She paused a moment. "You'd expect it to go the other way."

Not with Arnold Palmer. The one thing that distinguishes him from his fellow human beings is the gift that made him famous: his unquenchable knowledge that he has the game of golf beaten.

Further Resources

BOOKS

Nicklaus, Jack. *The Greatest Game of All: My Life in Golf.* New York: Simon & Schuster, 1969.

Palmer, Arnold. *Go For Broke: My Philosophy of Golf.* New York: Simon & Schuster, 1973.

Sampson, Curt. *The Eternal Summer: Palmer, Nicklaus, and Hogan in 1960: Golf's Golden Year.* New York: Villard, 2000.

WEBSITES

Flatter, Ron. "Palmer Inspired Army of Followers." ESPN.com. Available online at http://www.espn.com (accessed March 24, 2003).

Vince Lombardi

Run to Daylight!
Memoir

By: Vince Lombardi, with W.C. Heinz

Date: 1963

Source: Lombardi, Vince, with W.C. Heinz. *Run to Daylight!* New York: Grosset & Dunlap, 1963; 1971, 1–2, 66–68, 160–161, 171–172, 173–174, 182–183, 184–185.

About the Author: Vince Lombardi (1913–1970) was born in Brooklyn, New York. After playing football at Fordham University, he became head coach at St. Cecilia High School in New Jersey. From 1947 to 1958, he was an assistant coach at Fordham, the U.S. Military Academy, and the New York Giants. He became head coach and general manager of the Green Bay Packers in 1959. In nine seasons at Green Bay, he won five NFL championships and the first two Super Bowls. He returned to coaching in 1969 with the Washington Redskins but died before the next season. ■

Instant Replay: The Green Bay Diary of Jerry Kramer
Diary

By: Jerry Kramer

Date: 1968

Source: Kramer, Jerry. *Instant Replay: The Green Bay Diary of Jerry Kramer.* Dick Schaap, ed. New York: Signet, 1968, 25, 26, 27, 30–31, 43, 49–50, 65, 218.

About the Author: Jerry Kramer (1936–) was born in Jordan, Montana. After playing football at the University of Idaho, he was drafted as a guard by the Green Bay Packers in 1958 and became one of the NFL's best offensive linemen. Kramer assumed the placekicking duties in 1962 and 1963. In eleven seasons, he played on five NFL championship teams, including the first two Super Bowls, and was named All-Pro four times. Kramer has written four books on his football experiences. ■

Introduction

The 1960s saw the rise of professional football to prominence and, for many, as America's favorite spectator sport. An important reason for its growth in popularity was the success of the Green Bay Packers and the dominating personality of their coach, Vince Lombardi. Lombardi's Packers symbolized professional football and sports in the 1960s, as well as having an impact on the larger culture during a decade of turbulence.

In 1959, after being passed over for several head coaching positions in the pros—which he believed was because of his Italian heritage—Lombardi became head coach and general manager of the Green Bay Packers, who had won once in twelve games the previous season.

Lombardi instituted a tough training-camp regimen and demanded the best from each player, emphasizing fundamentals of blocking and tackling. He inherited a nucleus of promising players, including quarterback Bart Starr, running back Paul Hornung, offensive linemen Forrest Gregg and Jerry Kramer, and linebacker Ray Nitschke; he also acquired defensive linemen Willie Davis and Henry Jordan in trades. The team responded to Lombardi and posted a 7-5 record in 1959, the Packers' best record in a decade. The next season, the Packers won the Western Division but lost the NFL title game to the Philadelphia Eagles. Afterward, Lombardi told his team he would not let them lose another championship game.

From that point forward, Lombardi made good on his promise. In 1961, the Packers defeated the Giants 37-0 for the title. The 1962 team was perhaps Lombardi's best, losing one game and repeating as NFL champions. Hornung's suspension for gambling in 1963 caused the Packers to fall from first place. After a subpar year in 1964, the Packers won the first of an unprecedented three consecutive NFL championships in 1965. After the AFL-NFL merger in 1966, the Packers won the first "Super Bowl." In 1967, the Packers won their third straight NFL title, defeating the Dallas Cowboys in the "Ice Bowl," when the air temperature in Green Bay was below zero, and finished off the season with a second Super Bowl victory. After the Super Bowl, Lombardi retired as Packers coach. In nine seasons, Lombardi had won five NFL titles and nine of ten playoff games.

Significance

Lombardi was restless as the Packers' general manager; signing checks and negotiating contracts was not what he did best. So in 1969, he became coach, general manager, and 5 percent owner of the Washington Redskins, another struggling franchise. In one year, Lombardi turned the team around, leading the Redskins to their first winning season since 1955. But the success was short-lived, as Lombardi developed cancer the next summer and died in September 1970.

Lombardi was a symbol of what football represented: discipline, order, and teamwork—values under assault during the late 1960s. Although quoted (he said out of context) as saying, "Winning isn't everything, it's the only thing," Lombardi was more complex than a single slogan. For example, Lombardi was ahead of his time on issues such as civil rights, assigning black and white teammates together as roommates and forbidding use of racial or ethnic slurs, both of which helped the Packers have the NFL's most racially tolerant team.

Nearly a dozen players plus Lombardi himself from the Packer years are in the Pro Football Hall of Fame. His record in ten seasons as head coach was 105 victories, thirty-five losses, and six ties. The Super Bowl trophy was renamed the Lombardi Trophy in his honor after he died. Other coaches won more games over a career, but few had Lombardi's success, nor left a lasting impact on the game of football.

Primary Source

Run to Daylight! [excerpt]

SYNOPSIS: Vince Lombardi, Green Bay Packers head coach, in a diary account, describes a typical week of preparation for a football game against almost any opponent, as he emphasized the elements of conditioning and strategy.

3:15 A.M.

I have been asleep for three hours and, suddenly, I am awake. I am wide awake, and that's the trouble with this game. Just twelve hours ago I walked off that field, and we had beaten the Bears 49 to 0. Now I should be sleeping the satisfied sleep of the contented but I am lying here awake, wide awake, seeing myself walking across that field, seeing myself searching in the crowd for George Halas but really hoping that I would not find him.

All week long there builds up inside of you a competitive animosity toward that other man, that counterpart across the field. All week long he is the symbol, the epitome, of what you must defeat and then, when it is over, when you have looked up to that man for as long as I have looked up to George Halas, you cannot help but be disturbed by a score like this. You know he brought a team in here hurt by key injuries and that this was just one of those days, but you can't apologize. You can't apologize for a score. It is up there on that board and nothing can change it now. I can just hope, lying here awake in the middle of the night, that after all those years he has had in this league—and he has had forty-two of them—these things no longer affect him as they still affect me. I can just hope that I am making more of this than he is, and now I see myself, unable to find him in the crowd and walking up that ramp and into our dressing room, now searching instead for something that will bring my own team back to earth.

"All right!" I said. "Let me have your attention. That was a good effort, a fine effort. That's the way to play this game, but remember this. You beat the Bears, but you know as well as I do that they weren't ready. They had key personnel hurt and they weren't up for this game. Those people who are coming in here next week will be up. They won again today, so they're just as undefeated as we are. They'll be coming in here to knock your teeth down your throats, so remember that. Have your fun tonight and tomorrow, but remember that."

"Right, coach!" someone behind me, maybe Fuzzy Thurston or Jerry Kramer or Ray Nitschke, shouted. "Way to talk, coach!"

Am I right and is that the way to talk, or has this become a game for madmen and am I one of them? Any day that you score seven touchdowns in this league and turn in a shutout should be a day of celebration. Even when the Bears are without Bill George, who is the key to their defense, and Willie Galimore, who is their speed, this is a major accomplishment. But where is the elation?

Once there was elation. In 1959, in the first game I ever coached here, that I ever head-coached anywhere in pro ball, we beat these Bears 9 to 6 and I can remember it clearly. I can remember them leading us into the last period and then Jimmy Taylor going in from the 5 on our 28-Weak, and Paul Hornung kicking the point, and then Hank Jordan breaking through on the blitz and nailing Ed Brown in the end zone for the safety. The year before, this team had won only one game and tied one out of twelve, so now they were carrying me off the field because a single league victory was once cause enough for celebration.

What success does to you. It is like a habit-forming drug that, in victory, saps your elation and, in defeat, deepens your despair. Once you have sampled it you are hooked, and now I lie in bed, not sleeping the sleep of the victor but wide awake, seeing the other people who are coming in next Sunday with the best defensive line in the league, with that great middle linebacker, that left defensive halfback who is as quick and agile as a cat and a quarterback who, although he is not as daring as Johnny Unitas or Y. A. Tittle or Bobby Layne, can kill you with his consistency. . . .

It began to be a part of me, this sweep, this pay-off-the-mortgage play they are now calling The Lombardi Sweep, during my days at Fordham. I was impressed playing against the Single-Wing sweep the way those Pittsburgh teams of Jock Sutherland ran it. And I was impressed again in those early days of attending coaching clinics when the Single-Wing was discussed. Today our sweep has a lot of those Sutherland qualities, the same guard-pulling techniques, the same ball-carrier cutback feature, and there's nothing spectacular about it. It's just a yard-gainer, and I've diagrammed it so many times and coached it so much and watched it evolve so often since I first put it in with the Giants eight years ago that I think I see it in my sleep.

And I can hear myself at that blackboard, over and over:

"Right end—drive that man over you in the direction of his angle. Never allow penetration to the inside or over you hard. If he penetrates inside he knocks off both our pulling guards. Your eyes and your weight should be to the inside. If he comes to the inside he takes a big gamble. If he goes to the outside you set and don't make your move until he's past your nose and then drive—drive—drive him to the sideline.

"Right tackle and fullback—you work as a unit, responsible for the left end and middle linebacker. For a sweep to be successful you can't have penetration by the defensive end. Tackle—drive the end unless he's outside you. If he's outside, slam, and set yourself up in the seal position and seal inside. Fullback—drive the first man outside your tackle, and you can't make a curved or circle approach to that man. Speed is absolutely necessary for the first guard, the onside guard, to clear. If none outside your tackle, if the tackle has taken him, seal inside for the middle linebacker.

"First guard—the onside right guard must pull hard to clear the fullback's move. Ninety-five percent of the time you will pull outside your onside end. Center—cut off that left tackle onside, because he'll have nobody over him. This is one of the two toughest blocks involved, but you must make it. Second guard—the offside left guard must pull hard, look for the hole and seal to the inside. Offside tackle—the left tackle must cut off the defensive right tackle. He'll also have nobody over him and you must pull like a guard. This is the second of the two toughest blocks, because you must take him where you find him, whether he comes across that line or whether he slides with the play. You must block him. Flanker—take the left safety man, wherever he is. Halfback—come hard until you get that ball from the quarterback. Make a little belly-out, and then wing! That's it." . . .

I walk to the center of the room, and I'm running through my mind those notes I made on that small pad. I start out by going over, for the offense, the automatics we're going to use, the plays our quarterback will call on the line when he sees that the defensive alignment will negate

Green Bay Packers quarterback Bart Starr (#15) is about to be tackled on November 22, 1962. The Packers lost their only game of the 1962 season to the Detroit Lions but went on to win the NFL championship by defeating the New York Giants. © BETTMANN/CORBIS. REPRODUCED BY PERMISSION.

what he called in the huddle, and I stress our 36 and 50.

"Now, we're going to receive," I say then, "and we've got the south goal. Remember that this club puts their speediest men as third men out from each side and they must be blocked. They must be blocked, so let's take them out of there. Let's impress them, all of them, right on that kickoff.

"I don't have to tell you," I say, "about the importance of this ball game. You know as well as I do that you're meeting today the top contender, and that no one can win it now but you. For two years these people have been on our necks, but if you beat them today you'll be making your own job easier for the rest of this year. For you to do it, though, is going to require a top effort. You know the spirit with which this other club is coming in here. You know that they think they can beat you, that they've said they will. That's why I say it's going to take a top effort.

"And now," I say, "I want you, all of you, to know this. Regardless of what happens today this is a

team of which I am proud. Regardless of the outcome today I'll still be proud of you. To win, though, you're going to have to run harder and tackle harder and block harder. It's going to take a great team effort, so let's have it! Let's go!"

Primary Source

Instant Replay: The Green Bay Diary of Jerry Kramer [excerpt]

SYNOPSIS: Jerry Kramer, Green Bay Packers offensive guard, in a season-long diary account, describes the methods, both organizational and especially psychological, of coach Vince Lombardi in training camp and during the season.

Basic Training

July 15

The whole thing is a pain in the ass. The worst part is that you're completely a captive of Lombardi and of football. It's not like you put in two hours in the morning, two in the afternoon, and two in the evening. You're required to attend breakfast at 7 A.M., ride in the bus over to the stadium, ride back in the bus, eat lunch, go over to the stadium and back again, dinner, meeting, curfew. If you're lucky, you get an hour and a half or two hours a day to do whatever you want. . . .

∎∎∎

After dinner, Lombardi conducted our first meeting of 1967, and he stressed the tremendous challenge facing the Packers this year. . . .

He lectured for a while about the importance of conditioning, about his desire to have every man in top physical shape. "Fatigue makes cowards of us all," he said, quoting his favorite source, himself. "When you're tired, you rationalize. You make excuses in your mind. You say, 'I'm too tired, I'm bushed, I can't do this, I'll loaf.' Then you're a coward." He said that when we don't use our ability to the fullest, we're not only cheating ourselves and the Green Bay Packers, we're cheating the Lord; He gave us our ability to use it to the fullest. "There are three things that are important to every man in this room," Lombardi said. "His religion, his family, and the Green Bay Packers, in that order." Vince means just what he says, but sometimes I think he gets the order confused. . . .

July 22

. . . Coach Lombardi never takes second place when it comes to Oral Roberts or any of the rest of the healers. He can just walk into a training room filled with injured players, and he'll say, "What the hell's wrong with you guys? There's nobody in here hurt." And the dressing room will clear immediately. And all the wounded will be healed. . . .

July 25

I think I'm going to live. Just one more day of two-a-days and then we settle down to normal brutality. Vince is driving us like a madman; he never lets up. It's hard to resist hating him, his ranting, his raving, his screaming, his hollering. But, damn him, he's a great coach.

I spend a lot of time thinking about him these days; I don't have much choice. I wish I could figure him out. I guess, more than anything else, he's a perfectionist, an absolute perfectionist. He demands perfection from everyone, from himself, from the other coaches, from the players, from the equipment manager, from the water boys, even from his wife. Marie Lombardi joined us at a team dinner before one game last year, and the dessert was apple pie.

Green Bay Packers coach Vince Lombardi is carried off the field with the help of Packers guard Jerry Kramer, Miami, Florida, January 14, 1968. The Packers had just defeated the Oakland Raiders 33-14 in Super Bowl II. **AP/WIDE WORLD PHOTOS. REPRODUCED BY PERMISSION.**

Marie asked the waiter if she could have a scoop of ice cream on her pie, and before the waiter could answer, Vince jumped out of his seat, red in the face, and bellowed, "When you travel with the team, and you eat with the team, you eat what the team eats."

He pays such meticulous attention to detail. He makes us execute the same plays over and over, a hundred times, two hundred times, until we do every little thing right automatically. He works to make the kickoff-return team perfect, the punt-return team perfect, the field-goal team perfect. He ignores nothing. Technique, technique, technique, over and over and over, until we feel like we're going crazy. But we win.

He seems so unfeeling at times. A few years ago, we played the 49ers in San Francisco and I got banged up something terrible. My ribs were killing me. The next day, the team doctor gave me a shot or two of novocaine, and Vince told me to shake it off. We stayed on the west coast all week, and the following weekend I played the full game against the Los Angeles Rams. When we got back to Green Bay, I went to see my own doctor and he told me that I had two broken ribs, that they had been broken for at least a week.

On Tuesday, I showed up at practice and I went up to Vince and I said, "Hey, Coach, you know I played that whole game Sunday with two broken ribs." I thought he'd pat me on the head or say, "Nice going," or something like that. Instead, he just looked at me and said, "I guess they don't hurt anymore."

Yet, in 1964, when I almost died with all my intestinal ailments, Lombardi visited me in the hospital and he told me not to worry, that the Packers would pay my salary in 1964 and 1965 even if I couldn't play and that the club would pay all my hospital bills. He does things like that. His players are his children, and he nurses them when they're sick and scolds them when they're bad and rewards them when they're good.

But his personal feelings, I suspect, end up running second to his professional feelings, which are summed up in another one of his favorite sayings. "Winning isn't everything," he tells us. "It's the only thing." . . .

Further Resources

BOOKS

Dowling Tom. *Coach: A Season with Lombardi.* New York: Norton, 1970.

Maraniss, David. *When Pride Still Mattered: A Life of Vince Lombardi.* New York: Simon and Schuster, 1999.

O'Brien, Michael. *Vince: A Personal Biography of Vince Lombardi.* New York: Morrow, 1987.

PERIODICALS

Shecter, Leonard. "The Toughest Man in Pro Football." *Esquire,* January 1968.

Wallace, William. "Vince Lombardi, Football Coach Dies." *The New York Times,* September 4, 1970.

WEBSITES

Pro Football Hall of Fame. "Vince Lombardi." Available online at http://www.profootballhof.com/players/mainpage.cfm?cont_id=100355; website home page: http://www.profootballhof.com (accessed June 3, 2003).

The New York Mets

Can't Anybody Here Play This Game?
Nonfiction work

By: Jimmy Breslin

Date: 1963

Source: Breslin, Jimmy. *Can't Anybody Here Play This Game?* New York: Viking Press, 1963. Revised ed., New York: Ballantine, 1970, 88–89, 90–93.

About the Author: Jimmy Breslin (1930–) was born in Jamaica, New York. After attending Long Island University, he worked as a sportswriter for several New York City newspapers, including the *New York Herald Tribune* and *New York Post,* before becoming a freelance journalist in 1969. He has written fourteen books, including several novels, as well as articles and columns for many newspapers and magazines.

The Perfect Game: Tom Seaver and the Mets
Autobiography

By: Tom Seaver with Dick Schaap

Date: 1970

Source: Seaver, Tom, with Dick Schaap. *The Perfect Game: Tom Seaver and the Mets.* New York: Dutton, 1970, 138–140, 154–155, 159, 161–163, 171–173.

About the Author: George Thomas Seaver (1944–) was born in Fresno, California. He was signed by the New York Mets in 1965, after an offer by the Atlanta Braves was deemed illegal. Joining the Mets in 1967, Seaver pitched for them until 1977 (and again in 1982), leading the team to a championship in 1969 and a World Series appearance in 1973. He also pitched for the Cincinnati Reds, Chicago White Sox, and Boston Red Sox, winning 311 games in his twenty-season major league career, and was elected to the Baseball Hall of Fame in 1992. Since his retirement, Seaver has worked as a broadcaster, pitching coach, and businessman. ∎

Introduction

In 1962, four years after the Brooklyn Dodgers and New York Giants moved to California, New York was awarded a National League expansion franchise, the Mets. Hired to manage the club was ex-Yankee boss Casey Stengel, who had won seven World Series in twelve seasons. The ineptitude of the Mets was apparent from the start of the season, when they lost their first nine games and quickly fell into the National League basement. The Mets finished the 1962 season with a 40-120 mark, 60½ games behind the pennant-winning Giants, giving them the worst record of any team of the twentieth century. Still, nearly a million fans showed up at the Polo Grounds that season, embracing the team as lovable losers. Over the next six seasons, the Mets finished last several times, never posting a winning record but signing many talented youngsters, including pitcher Tom Seaver.

In 1969, with former Brooklyn Dodger star Gil Hodges as manager, pitchers Seaver and Jerry Koosman, and outfielders Tommie Agee and Cleon Jones, the Mets had reason to be optimistic. But the "experts" picked them fifth, a hundred-to-one shot to win the World Series. After losing a three-game series in Houston in mid-August, the Mets's record stood at 62-51, good for second place in the National League East. They proceeded to win fourteen of their next seventeen games to end August, then won twenty-four of thirty-two games in September. The unexpected collapse of the division-leading Chicago Cubs allowed the Mets to win the East by a comfortable eight games. The team finished with one hundred victories, led by Seaver's twenty-five.

In 1969, for the first time in baseball history, each league played a championship series to determine who got into the World Series. In the National League Championship Series, the Mets swept the Western Division champion Atlanta Braves in three games. Seven years after their 120-loss season, the "Amazin'" Mets were in the World Series. However, they were given little chance against the American League representative Baltimore Orioles, winners of 109 games. But after losing the first game, the Mets won the next three. After the Orioles grabbed a 3-0 lead in game five, the Mets rallied, scoring two runs in the sixth inning, one in the seventh, and two more in the eighth, to take the Series.

Significance

When the Mets' Cleon Jones caught the final out in left field, pandemonium reigned at Shea Stadium, as fans ran onto the field, mobbed the players, and tore up the turf. The Mets, given little chance to even win their division, had accomplished the near impossible. Their victory over the heavily favored Orioles was perhaps baseball's greatest upset, and one of sports' most improbable results. The Mets' triumph occurred only nine months after the New York Jets' upset victory in Super Bowl III against another Baltimore team, the Colts. For Mets fans, who embraced the team in 1962 after the loss of the Dodgers and Giants, the World Series victory in 1969 was a dream come true.

After their magical season, the Mets seemed to develop a certain mystique, especially come playoff time. In 1973, they came from last place in August to win the Eastern Division with only eighty-two victories, and beat the favored Cincinnati Reds in the league championship—though they lost the World Series in seven games to the Oakland Athletics. Thirteen years later, in 1986, the Mets were down in game six of the World Se-

ries by two runs with two out in extra innings against the Boston Red Sox. Facing elimination, they rallied to win the game and, ultimately, the Series.

Primary Source

Can't Anybody Here Play This Game? [excerpt]

SYNOPSIS: New York newspaper journalist Jimmy Breslin spent the 1962 baseball season covering the expansion New York Mets, chronicling the team's rare ups and mostly downs, their colorful cast of characters, and their quotable manager, Casey Stengel.

The Nickel Line

The Mets opened their season on April 11, 1962, and closed it on September 30. In this time, the players did enough things wrong to convince even casual observers that there has never been a team like them. From the start, the trouble with the Mets was the fact they were not too good at playing baseball. They lost an awful lot of games by one run, which is the mark of a bad team. They also lost innumerable games by fourteen runs or so. This is the mark of a terrible team. Actually, all the Mets did was lose. They lost at home and they lost away, they lost at night and they lost in the daytime. And they lost with maneuvers that shake the imagination.

It is because of this that you do not simply use figures to say that the Mets of 1962, with 120 losses and only 40 wins, were the worst team in modern times. Instead, you investigate the matter thoroughly. Then you can say, with full authority, that the Mets were the worst team. . . .

The season, and all that went with it, went along something like this:

Opening day was to be the tenth, a night game in St. Louis. It rained, and Mrs. Payson had her two private cars hooked on to a New York-bound train and she and her party left town. Back in New York, you could watch the "Rain-Out Theatre" on television. It was presented by Rheingold. The picture was about a World War II destroyer and it starred Edward G. Robinson, Glenn Ford, and a despicable Japanese admiral. The admiral must be shipping us transistor radios today, but he sure was rough in the picture.

It came up clear the next night, and the Mets took the field against the St. Louis Cardinals. The team was dressed just as good as the Yankees. The Mets' players wore new gray flannel road uniforms which were made by MacGregor and wholesale at

New York Mets manager Casey Stengel gestures helplessly to sports writers before a game against the San Francisco Giants, June 3, 1962. The Mets went on to lose for their fifteenth time in a row. © BETTMANN/CORBIS. REPRODUCED BY PERMISSION.

$31.50. Their spikes were shined, and their sweatshirts were laundry-clean. The only difference one could see was that the Mets' jackets were blue nylon, while the Yankees wear heavier cloth jackets.

Roger Craig was the starting pitcher. In the first inning, Bill White of the Cardinals reached third base. Craig eyed him carefully. Then he started his motion to the plate. The ball dropped out of Craig's hand. The umpire ruled it a balk and waved White across the plate. The Cards led, 1-0. The Mets' season now was officially shot.

Before the night ended, the Cardinals got eleven runs. The Mets committed three errors, and the Cardinals stole three bases. Stan Musial of the Cards got three hits. This was about what he expected to do. At forty-one, Musial had spent the winter thinking of retirement. But every time he came close to calling it a career, he thought of the Mets. A man could have a pretty good year in the big leagues just by playing against the Mets alone, Musial figured. So he stayed. He was right. He damn near won the National League batting title because of the Mets' pitching.

Two days later the Mets had their home opener at the Polo Grounds. Pittsburgh was the opposition. It was a dark, wet day, but anybody who meant anything in New York was at the Polo Grounds. There were Mayor Wagner and Jim Farley, there were Bill Shea and the late Mrs. John J. McGraw, Mrs. Payson was in her box seat. Edna Stengel was on hand too. So was a man named Jack Semel. He had an umbrella and he moved over from his box seat to hold it over the heads of George Weiss and National League President Warren Giles. Jack Semel was to make history before the season ended. But right now he was just one of 12,447 spectators at the Polo Grounds. Like we said, everybody who meant anything showed up.

In the second inning, Don Hoak of the Pirates was on third and Bill Mazeroski was up with two out. Mazeroski hit a high fly into right center field. That was the third out. The moment Hoak saw the ball go harmlessly into the air, he put his head down and trotted from third to the plate. He wanted to get his glove out of the dugout. Mazeroski trotted to first. He was hoping somebody would bring his glove out of the dugout so he could go straight to his position at second base. Out in the outfield, Richie Ashburn and Gus Bell of the Mets were trotting too. Ashburn is the father of six children. Bell has seven children. They were doing this for a living. Ashburn called. He said he would make the catch. Bell did not answer. He kept waving Ashburn aside. Richie, an adult, did not argue. He stepped aside. Bell then waved himself aside. The ball hit the ground, took a bounce past them, and by the time they got it back to the infield Mazeroski was on third and Hoak was in the dugout. He had scored a run, but he did not really believe it.

The Mets fought back and by the eighth inning they had the game tied, 3-3. They also had Ray Daviault pitching. Daviault started the inning by walking Dick Groat. This is a very bad thing to do in a tight game. Never, never walk the first man up. But at least Groat was not in scoring position. Daviault took care of this. He threw a pitch that went back to the stands, and Groat moved to second. An infield out allowed Groat to reach third. Daviault then took a full windup and threw his second wild pitch. Groat scored, and the Mets lost by 4-3.

The team then lost two more games and was scheduled to play Houston in the fifth game of the season when Stengel, who said a light dew was going to turn into a hurricane, had the game postponed.

"If I was winning, I'd play five games a day because you tend to keep winning when you are win-

Major League Baseball Standings

Major League Baseball
Monday, Oct. 1, 1962

National League	**American League**
YESTERDAY'S GAMES	YESTERDAY'S GAMES
Chicago 5, New York 1	Chicago 8, New York 4
St. Louis 1, Los Angeles 0	Cleveland 4, Los Angeles 3 (1st)
San Francisco 2, Houston 1	Cleveland 6, Los Angeles 1 (2d)
Cincinnati 4, Philadelphia 0	Detroit 6, Kansas City 1
Pittsburgh 4, Milwaukee 3	Minnesota 1, Baltimore 0
	Washington 3, Boston 1 (1st)
	Boston 3, Washington 1 (2d)

Standing of the Clubs

	W	L	Pc.	GB
*Los Angeles	101	61	.623	—
*San Francisco	101	61	.623	—
Cincinnati	98	64	.605	3
Pittsburgh	93	68	.578	7½
Milwaukee	86	76	.531	15
St. Louis	84	78	.519	17
Philadelphia	81	80	.503	19½
Houston	64	96	.400	36
Chicago	59	103	.364	42
New York	40	120	.250	60

Final Standing of Clubs

	W	L	Pc.	GB
New York	96	66	.593	—
Minnesota	91	71	.562	5
Los Angeles	86	76	.531	10
Detroit	85	76	.528	10½
Chicago	85	77	.525	11
Cleveland	80	82	.494	16
Baltimore	77	85	.475	19
Boston	76	84	.475	19
Kansas City	72	90	.444	24
Washington	60	101	.373	35½

*Will play best-of-three series for championship.

SOURCE: Table from *The New York Times*, October 1, 1962.

ning," he explained. "But I had a chance to call this game, so I did. You tend to keep losing when you are losing, you know."

He was right. The Mets lost nine games before they finally got their first win of the season. During the losing streak, Stengel became a bit edgy. He sat at his desk in his office in the center-field clubhouse one night, looked down at the knots which stick out all over his old legs, and voiced a fear which he and everybody else in New York now carried in their hearts.

"The trouble is, we are in a losing streak at the wrong time," he said. "If we was losing like this in the middle of the season, nobody would notice. But we are losing at the beginning of the season and this sets up the possibility of losing 162 games, which would probably be a new record, in the National League at least." . . .

The newspapers call the Mets fans "The New Breed." This is a good name, but there is more to it than this. It goes deeper. As the Mets lost game after game, for example, you heard one line repeated in place after place all over town. It probably started in a gin mill someplace with a guy looking down at his drink and listening to somebody talk about this new team and how they lost so much. Then it got repeated, and before long you were even hearing it in places on Madison Avenue.

"I've been a Mets fan all my life."

Nearly everybody was saying it by mid-June. And nearly everybody had a good reason for saying it. You see, the Mets are losers, just like nearly everybody else in life. This is a team for the cab driver who gets held up and the guy who loses out on a promotion because he didn't maneuver himself to lunch with the boss enough. It is the team for every guy who has to get out of bed in the morning and go to work for short money on a job he does not like. And it is the team for every woman who looks up ten years later and sees her husband eating dinner in a T-shirt and wonders how the hell she ever let this guy talk her into getting married. The Yankees? Who does well enough to root for them, Laurence Rockefeller? . . .

So the Mets were a bad ball club. All right, they were the worst ball club you ever saw. So what? The important thing is they are in the National League and they are familiar. The National League, to a lot of people around New York, is something hard to describe, but important. Like the chip in the table in the living room, when you were growing up. It was

Tom Seaver of the New York Mets delivers a pitch in game four of the 1969 World Series, October 15, 1969. Seaver threw the only perfect game of the post season ever that day. © BETTMANN/CORBIS. REPRODUCED BY PERMISSION.

always there. Sometimes you can buy ten new tables over a lifetime. But the one with the chip is the one that would make you feel the best. People are that way about the National League. They are more at home looking at the box score of a game between the St. Louis Cardinals and the Philadelphia Phillies than they ever could be going over one between the Cleveland Indians and the Detroit Tigers. If they came out of Cleveland it would be different. But they are from New York, and this is National League. Now we have the Mets, and that's the way it should be. We're with familiar things again.

The Mets lose an awful lot?

Listen, mister. Think a little bit.

When was the last time you won anything out of life?

Primary Source

The Perfect Game: Tom Seaver and the Mets [excerpt]

> **SYNOPSIS:** In his autobiography, New York Mets star pitcher Tom Seaver recounts his ten-inning, com-

plete-game effort against the Baltimore Orioles in game four of the 1969 World Series.

XXIV

When I walked to the mound at Shea Stadium a few minutes before three o'clock on the afternoon of October 15, 1969, I knew precisely the position I was in. We were leading the Baltimore Orioles, 1-0, and I knew that all I had to do was retire three more batters, the heart of the order, and I'd have a World Series shutout.

I wanted that shutout as badly as I'd wanted the perfect game in July. The perfect game was for me, almost a selfish goal, but the World Series victory was only partly for me and partly for my teammates. I'd been called a leader all year, and I wanted to prove, under World Series pressure, that I was a leader.

I stood on the mound, rubbing the ball down, setting myself to deliver the first pitch of the ninth inning, and I looked over the team behind me, the team that had been laughed at and dismissed for months, the team, no longer ridiculed, that was seeking its forty-fourth victory in its last fifty-five games.

There was Jerry Grote behind the plate, tough and hungry, capable of flicking a throw that would cross the pitcher's mound only a foot above ground level and hit second base squarely on the corner.

There was Donn Clendenon at first base, a professional, stately in appearance and in manner, always a threat to hit a home run. Earlier in the year, he had announced he would quit baseball rather than accept being traded from Montreal to Houston.

There were Al Weis and Buddy Harrelson, flanking second base, two guys who, between them, didn't have enough beef for one football lineman, two guys who had whipped themselves to become big leaguers.

There was Ed Charles at third base, thirty-five years old, the easygoing "Glider," an amateur poet, in his eighteenth season of professional baseball, his ninth season in the major leagues but only his first with a first-division team.

There, in the outfield, were Cleon Jones and Tommie Agee and Ron Swoboda, three men who looked like running backs, three men who had suffered through frustrating seasons and bounced back.

Of the nine men in the field, four of us had never played for any big-league team other than the Mets, had never played, before 1969, for a team that was taken seriously. Of the nine men in the field, only three—Clendenon, Weis and Agee—had ever played, before 1969, for a team that finished in the first division. Of the nine men in the field, not one of us had ever played, before 1969, in a World Series.

I was a little surprised to see Charles still at third base and Swoboda still in right field in the ninth inning of a 1-0 game. All season long, in similar situations, Gil Hodges had brought in Wayne Garrett and Rod Gaspar, more skillful fielders. Gaspar, even though he had played far less than Jones, Agee and Swoboda, led all our outfielders in assists; he had started six double plays, more than any other outfielder in the National League.

But I didn't waste much time wondering about the defensive setup. I was a total believer. If Gil made a move, it was going to turn out right; if Gil didn't make a move, that was going to turn out right, too. If, as some people said, God was a Met fan, then Gil was His prophet. . . .

XXVI

The Orioles had the bottom third of their batting order coming up in the tenth inning, which gave me a slight edge. I needed every little advantage I could get, because physically and mentally, I was pushing myself close to my limit.

In the first nine innings, I'd thrown 135 pitches. I hadn't thrown that many pitches in one day in more than a month. It had been eighteen days since I'd pitched a complete game. In the eighteen days leading up to the fourth game of the Series, I'd pitched only twelve innings, seven against Atlanta and five against Baltimore.

Obviously, in extra innings, I was under greater mental strain than usual. I knew that if I made one large mistake, we'd have only one more time at bat to get even. I had to be more than careful.

I also had precedent going against me. Not once in the entire 1969 season had one of our starting pitchers won a game in extra innings. . . .

XXVII

For Baltimore in the bottom of the tenth inning, Billy Hunter brought in Dick Hall, a right-handed pitcher who was, at the age of thirty-nine, in his seventeenth professional season, making his first World Series appearance.

We had the bottom third of our batting order coming up to face Hall—Jerry Grote, Al Weis and, presumably, a pinch hitter for me.

Jerry Grote stepped in. . . .

Program cover for Game 5 of the 1969 World Series. THE NATIONAL BASEBALL HALL OF FAME AND MUSEUM, INC. REPRODUCED BY PERMISSION.

Gil looked down our bench for a left-handed pinch hitter to bat against Hall. He wanted someone who could bunt the runners along; obviously, he wasn't going to try me again. I thought he'd pick Ed Kranepool, a left-hander and probably the best bunter on the whole team. But, to my surprise, Gil tapped J. C. Martin.

In 1967, his sixth full season with the Chicago White Sox, J. C. batted .234. The White Sox gave up on him. They shipped him to the Mets as a throw-in to an earlier deal.

Billy Hunter called for a left-handed pitcher, Pete Richert, to replace Hall. During the regular season, Richert, ten years younger than Hall, twice a member of the American League All-Star team, had the lowest earned run average on the Baltimore pitching staff. He was making his first World Series appearance.

Gil still had one right-handed pinch hitter he could use, Duffy Dyer, but he elected to stick with J. C., even against a left-handed pitcher.

Gil, as usual, was right.

Major League Baseball Standings

Major League Baseball
Friday, Oct. 3, 1969

FINAL STANDINGS OF THE CLUBS

American League

YESTERDAY'S GAMES

Cleveland at New York (n), canceled, rain.
Minnesota 6, Chicago 5
Kansas City 6, California 2 (n)
Oakland 3, Seattle 1 (n)
Other clubs not scheduled

WEDNESDAY NIGHT

New York 4, Cleveland 3
Baltimore 2, Detroit 1 (10 inn.)
Kansas City 6, California 0 (6 inn., rain)
Seattle 4, Oakland 3
Washington 3, Boston 2

National League

YESTERDAY'S GAMES

Chicago 5, New York 3
San Diego 3, San Francisco 2
Cincinnati 8, Atlanta 3 (n)
Los Angeles 5, Houston 4 (n)
Pittsburgh 8, Montreal 2 (n)
St. Louis 3, Philadelphia 2 (n, 12 inn.)

WEDNESDAY NIGHT

Los Angeles 5, Houston 2
Pittsburgh 5, Montreal 4

Eastern Division

	W	L	Pc.	GB
Baltimore	109	53	.673	—
Detroit	90	72	.556	19
Boston	87	75	.537	22
Washington	86	76	.531	23
New York	80	81	.497	28½
Cleveland	62	99	.385	46½

Eastern Division

	W	L	Pc.	GB
New York	100	62	.617	—
Chicago	92	70	.568	8
Pittsburgh	88	74	.543	12
St. Louis	87	75	.537	13
Philadelphia	63	99	.389	37
Montreal	52	110	.321	48

Western Division

	W	L	Pc.	GB
Minnesota	97	65	.599	—
Oakland	88	74	.543	9
California	71	91	.438	26
Kansas City	69	93	.426	28
Chicago	68	94	.420	29
Seattle	64	98	.395	33

Western Division

	W	L	Pc.	GB
Atlanta	93	69	.574	—
San Francisco	90	72	.556	3
Cincinnati	89	73	.549	4
Los Angeles	85	77	.525	8
Houston	81	81	.500	12
San Diego	52	110	.321	41

SOURCE: Table from *The New York Times*, October 3, 1969.

On the first pitch, J. C. bunted, a beautiful bunt about ten feet away from home plate, toward first base. I watched the ball. I saw Richert and Elrod Hendricks move toward it, and I saw Richert pick it up, and I saw him throw toward first base.

The next thing I saw was the baseball rolling toward right field. I hadn't seen Richert's throw hit J. C. in the left wrist; I hadn't noticed that J. C. was running in fair ground where, when the ball struck him, he might have been called out for interference.

I knew right then, as soon as I spotted the loose ball, that we had won the game. I knew right then that Gaspar, an aggressive base runner, would keep going, would round third and come on home to score, that the Orioles wouldn't be able to stop him.

Then I turned my eyes and picked up Gaspar, halfway down the line between third and home, and for his last six or seven steps, all I could see was home plate and his legs, the distance between them diminishing, the winning run racing in.

Suddenly, without any conscious effort on my part, I saw my baseball life rushing through my mind. I was pitching my perfect game in the Fresno Little League, the umpire calling the key strike three on a pitch over the batter's head; I was in Wichita, Kansas, batting with the bases loaded and driving a home run more than 450 feet; I was in Shea Stadium, watching Jimmy Qualls' single fall between Cleon Jones and Tommie Agee. I was wearing a Fresno High uniform and a Southern Cal uniform and an Alaska Goldpanners uniform and a New York Mets uniform, and the characters on the field in front of me were fusing with the characters from my past. I saw men hundreds and thousands of miles away—Mike Garrett and Dick Selma and Bobby Boyd and Hank Aaron—more clearly than I saw the Orioles on the field; I felt that, in a similar way, so many people in the stands—my father, Rod Dedeaux, Nelson Burbrink, Nancy—must have been reliving some of the same scenes.

Gaspar crossed the plate, and I burst from the dugout to embrace him. I was the first man to reach Rod; I outraced Jerry Grote. I picked Rod up and gave him a big hug, and as all the emotions of victory pulsed through me, I felt strong enough to pitch another ten innings.

I didn't have to.

The New York Mets had won the fourth game of the 1969 World Series, 2-1, in ten innings.

We were ahead of the Baltimore Orioles, three games to one. One more victory, and we were the champions of the world.

Stuff it down their throats tomorrow, Jerry, I thought, with a glance at Koosman. *Let's end it right here. . . .*

Usually, after I pitched a game, I lay awake for several hours, reliving the game, trying to figure out what I had done wrong, what I would want to change.

But for once, on the night of October 15, 1969, I had no trouble falling asleep.

I didn't want to change anything that had happened. The game was beautiful. The game was perfect.

XXX

On October 16, 1969, Babe Weis hit a home run, the first he'd ever hit in Shea Stadium; Donn Clendenon hit a home run, his third of the World Series; Jerry Koosman pitched a five-hitter, and we beat the Baltimore Orioles, 5-3.

We didn't have to go back to Baltimore.

We were the champions of the world.

Further Resources

BOOKS

Cohen, Stanley. *A Magic Summer: The 1969 Mets.* San Diego: Harcourt, Brace, Jovanovich, 1988.

Durso, Joseph. *Amazing: The Miracle of the Mets.* Boston: Houghton Mifflin, 1970.

Golenbock, Peter. *Amazin': The Miraculous History of New York's Most Beloved Baseball Team.* New York: St. Martin's, 2002.

PERIODICALS

Durso, Joseph. "Mets Win 5-3, Take Series, and a Grateful City Goes Wild." *The New York Times,* October 17, 1969.

WEBSITES

National Baseball Hall of Fame and Museum. "Tom Seaver." Available online at http://www.baseballhalloffame.org /hofers%5Fand%5Fhonorees/hofer%5Fbios/seaver%5Ftom .htm; website home page: http://www.baseballhalloffame .org (accessed March 7, 2003).

Johnny Unitas

Pro Quarterback: My Own Story
Autobiography

By: Johnny Unitas and Ed Fitzgerald

Date: 1965

Source: Unitas, Johnny, and Ed Fitzgerald. *Pro Quarterback: My Own Story.* New York: Simon and Schuster, 1965, 54–63, 68–69.

About the Author: Johnny Unitas (1933–2002) was born in Pittsburgh, Pennsylvania. After playing football at the University of Louisville, he was drafted by the Pittsburgh Steelers in 1955 but cut before the season. After a year working construction jobs and playing semipro football, he signed with the Baltimore Colts in 1956. Within four years, he led the Colts to consecutive National Football League championships, in 1958 and 1959. Over seventeen seasons with the Colts, Unitas set numerous NFL passing records and was widely considered the best quarterback of all time. After a season with the San Diego Chargers, Unitas retired in 1973. In retirement, Unitas was a broadcaster and businessman.

My Story: And I'm Sticking to It
Memoir

By: Alex Hawkins

Date: 1989

Source: Hawkins, Alex. *My Story: And I'm Sticking to It.* Chapel Hill, N.C.: Algonquin Books of Chapel Hill, 1989, 75, 88–89, 98–99.

About the Author: Alex Hawkins (1937–) was born in Stringtown, West Virginia. After playing football at the University of South Carolina, he was drafted by the Green Bay Packers and later signed with the Baltimore Colts in 1959 as a wide receiver. After seven seasons with the Colts, Hawkins was selected in 1966 by the expansion Atlanta Falcons, but he returned to Baltimore the next year, then retired in 1968. Since retirement, Hawkins has been a broadcaster and businessman. ∎

Introduction

Professional football until the late 1950s was not considered "big league," because its teams were located in rust belt cities of the East and Midwest. But television and football would find each other and change the game and its hold on the American public. TV would find, almost by accident, the player who would lead football into an era of popularity: Johnny Unitas, the "Golden Arm."

Although his first pass as a Baltimore Colt was intercepted and returned for a touchdown, Unitas soon became the Colts starting quarterback. In 1958, he led Baltimore to the NFL title against the New York Giants, driving the Colts to a tying field goal late in regulation and directing his team to the winning touchdown in sudden-death overtime. The game, one of the first nationally televised professional football games, would become known as the "Greatest Game Ever Played."

After leading the Colts to a second championship in 1959, Unitas continued his heroics during the 1960s, staking a claim to being the best quarterback of his time, if not of all time. He threw twenty-five touchdown passes in 1960, but the Colts missed a third straight title. After a twenty-three-touchdown season in 1962, Unitas was named MVP and led Baltimore to the 1964 NFL title game, but lost to the Cleveland Browns. Injured in 1965, he bounced back in 1966, and in 1967 he was named the league's Most Valuable Player. An injury to his throwing hand and arm in 1968, though, would plague him for the remainder of his career.

Significance

The last few seasons of Unitas's career were bittersweet. In 1970, he led the Colts to Super Bowl V but was injured and backup Earl Morrall had to rally Baltimore to a 16-13 win over the Dallas Cowboys. In 1972, Unitas came off the bench in the last game and threw his last touchdown pass as a Colt, with the crowd cheering and a plane overhead pulling a banner reading "Unitas We Stand." Unitas played one more injury-filled season with the San Diego Chargers before retiring in 1973.

After eighteen seasons, Unitas held numerous NFL records, including 290 touchdown passes and 40,239 passing yards. Over forty years later, he still holds one of sports' greatest streaks—throwing a touchdown pass in forty-seven consecutive games from 1956 to 1960. He was named player of the decade in the 1960s and the quarterback on the NFL's fiftieth and seventy-fifth anniversary teams. He was still considered by many, even at the time of his death in September 2002, to be the greatest quarterback ever.

Primary Source

Pro Quarterback: My Own Story [excerpt]

> **SYNOPSIS:** In his autobiography, Johnny Unitas, quarterback of the Baltimore Colts, provides an insider's view of how he played the position and what he did on the field to ensure success for his team.

If you're a quarterback in the National Football League, the main thing you've got to be able to do

for your keep is throw the ball. You've got to handle it well, too, of course. You've got to know how to fake. You've got to make your hand-offs on running plays firmly and surely, so that the ball doesn't get dropped all over the backfield. You've got to know how to call the plays, unless you want to leave all of that to the coach—and no coach on the sidelines can do as good a job of calling a game as a quarterback who sees what's going on out there and knows how to take advantage of it. It helps if you can run a little, because you run away from a lot of fifteen-yard losses if you're quick on your feet and you can also (as Y. A. Tittle did for years with that bootleg play of his) run over a few touchdowns for yourself. And it isn't going to make anybody mad if you learn how to throw a good hard block. But the thing you get paid for is throwing the ball.

I grip the ball with the last two fingers of my right hand on the laces. The rest of my hand is behind the laces. If the ball is wet I move a couple more fingers right up on the laces, to get a better grip on it. The grip, of course, is the most important single factor in passing, and the manufacturers don't help us quarterbacks any with that smooth finish they put on the ball. . . .

As with everything else, you've got to practice passing all the time. We hang a net between the goal posts to stop the ball and I stand out there and throw to all of our receivers for at least half an hour every day. One of the things I practice a lot is throwing behind the receiver, making him come back for the ball. When you see one of those in a game it may look like a bad pass but it may actually be perfect. Looks don't count. It's keeping the ball away from the defender's hands and putting it into the receiver's that counts.

You've always got to think about the defender, what he can do and can't do, as well as about the receiver, what his personal likes, dislikes, and abilities are. There are a million things to consider before you put the ball up in the air. Some receivers like to have the ball come at them from left to right, some from right to left. Some are very good at catching the ball way out in front, reaching with their fingertips, and some can catch it only if you throw it right in on their chests. Some defenders search a receiver like a pickpocket going through your pockets, and some go at him like a prizefighter who has his man on the ropes and isn't going to let him get away. As much as possible, you've got to keep all of these things in mind and try to use what you know, just the way a baseball pitcher uses what he knows about all the hitters in the league—and also about all the men behind him in the field. . . .

I can throw the ball with pretty fair accuracy between fifty and sixty yards, but I seldom do throw it that far in a game. You hardly ever throw more than thirty-five or forty yards, at the most. By the time the receiver is twenty or twenty-five yards downfield, you've got to get rid of the ball. Of course, if he has run that far when you throw it, you've got to lead him with the pass another fifteen or twenty yards, so the ball may be in the air about forty yards on the average long pass. You hardly ever have time to let your man get so far downfield before you throw the ball that it goes as much as fifty yards in the air.

When I go back to throw I don't worry about the linemen coming in on me, only about what the linebackers and the secondary are doing. Once you start worrying about the linemen you're not going to be looking downfield at your receivers and at the defenders the way you should. You're not going to be doing your job, and all that means is that they're going to put somebody in there who will do it. . . .

You have to remember that sometimes, when I'm hit back there, it isn't the fault of my protection at all. It stands to reason that if you're going to hang onto the ball until the last second, the way I do, you're going to have to eat it once in a while. I like to wait until the last gasp to get it away. I get dropped a lot more that way, but I complete a lot more passes, too, and that's what I get paid for. . . .

It's exciting to see the man with the ball dodging around out there while all those monsters try to grab him, but it's not good football. It's fine for you to be able to do that when you have to, but you should never run around back there while you've still got blockers on their feet able to protect you. A roll-out is different, of course, but the quarterback who is going to have a good record of completions is the quarterback who stays inside his pocket and spends his time looking downfield instead of playing leapfrog with a bunch of blitzers. . . .

What I hope to get from my blockers is a minimum of two and a half seconds in which to get rid of the ball. If I get three seconds, I'm in pretty good shape, because my receiver has had fifteen or twenty yards in which to beat his man and break open. Also, I have had enough time to fake a pass before throwing the real one, which is important, because no matter how well you can throw the ball you aren't going to get very far unless you can fool the defense. You've got to give the defense three or four different things to worry about, not just one. If they're

Johnny Unitas poses as if throwing the football, December 5, 1965. Unitas was named player of the decade in the 1960s and the quarterback on the NFL's fiftieth and seventy-fifth anniversary teams. © BETTMANN/ CORBIS. REPRODUCED BY PERMISSION.

pretty sure they know what the receivers are going to do and what you're going to do, they can get themselves all set to pick it off. So it's up to you to make sure they can't guess accurately, or if you think they have, it's up to you to check off your play at the line of scrimmage and cross them up. . . .

If the defensive line has been giving you a bad time with a rush, one of your best weapons to fight back with is the screen pass. Your blocking is set up the same way as usual, but your men don't hold as long as they try to do on a regular pass. They will count, like maybe, a thousand-one, a thousand-two, and then they will let their man go, act like they are really beaten. The quarterback sets up at his regular passing distance at first, then, as these guys start coming in on you, you go back another ten yards gradually and then throw out to the side to one of your backs. In the meantime your linemen have got up and gone out in front of the back who is catching the ball, and if you're in luck, it's straight down the sideline for a big gain. . . .

I've always made a specialty of the long pass, the bomb, which has the same double payoff for you that the home run does in baseball. You not only get the big gain, or the score, but you also shake up the other team, you hurt their confidence, you put a lot of extra pressure on them. I will go for the long one anytime a man tells me on the way into the huddle (I don't let anybody open his mouth once we get into the huddle) that he can beat his man deep or anytime I think myself that the defensive man is playing one of our receivers extra tight and that our man probably can get behind him. . . .

Of all the bad things a quarterback can do, throwing the ball just to get rid of it is probably the worst. It's an easy habit to get into, because you don't like to take that loss of seven, eight or ten yards all the time, but you're better off doing that than throwing the ball up for grabs. Sometimes you can't help it, like when a lineman comes charging in on you with his hands up in the air and deflects the ball just enough so that it hangs up there for anybody to grab it. That's just one of those things. But a poor choice of receivers is your fault, and it can be avoided if you study your personnel and the personnel of the other team and go into the ball game knowing what patterns and what receivers are most likely to work for you, and what moves by which receivers are most likely to give you trouble.

Interceptions are the worst sin a quarterback can commit, because the main thing you have to do to win a football game is control the ball. Whenever you give the ball up it's hard to come by again, but when you give it up on an interception you're not only giving up possession but also a lot of yardage— and you can't afford to do it very often. Generally speaking, a quarterback in the National Football League is doing all right if he keeps his interceptions down below one a game for the fourteen games on the schedule. Obviously, when you throw the ball almost 300 times in a season, you're bound to get a few of them picked off. But you had better keep it down to a few. . . .

I've been lucky that in all my time in the league, I have had only one serious injury, a punctured lung and three broken ribs, which I got against the Packers in 1958. People are always asking me if it isn't dangerous playing quarterback in the NFL, if the other teams don't try to get you, but all I can say is that I've never been played dirty. Never. After all, I have been at it for a long time and not only have I, as I said, never lost a tooth, but the only game I ever missed was the one the week after I got hurt that time. I've been hit hard, been beat up a lot, but always legally. I've been hit in the face, sure, but

only with a legal shoulder or arm or helmet. I have never been punched.

I might say I don't go around punching anybody, either. I've never been in a fight on the field. I'm not big enough to be fighting anybody in this game. I'm not going to pick on somebody who's anywhere from 240 to 280, I can tell you that. Anytime they start fighting out there, I just stand around and watch. It's different in baseball, you know. Hardly anybody ever gets hurt in those baseball fights, but in football, guys are a little too big, and sometimes they get pretty heated up out there because of all that close contact work. The best thing for a guy my size to do when those big fellows get mad is just mind my own business, and that's what I do. If I keep on doing it, maybe I can stick around, calling the plays and throwing the ball, as long as Y. A. Tittle did.

Primary Source

My Story: And I'm Sticking to It [excerpt]

SYNOPSIS: In his memoir, Alex Hawkins, wide receiver and teammate of Unitas on the Baltimore Colts, provides a vivid description of Unitas as a presence on the football field. He recalls a game in 1960 against the Chicago Bears, which epitomized what made Unitas the best at quarterback.

As for John Unitas, here was a total mystery. He was from Pennsylvania, but he looked so much like a Mississippi farm hand that I looked around for a mule. He had stooped shoulders, a chicken breast, thin bowed legs, and long dangling arms with crooked, mangled fingers fastened to a pair of very large hands. . . .

John Unitas was *the* quarterback. No one ever knew or cared what John's salary called for. On his arm rested the hopes of the team. The one cardinal rule on the team was to keep Unitas healthy. To allow John to be hit was a sure one-way ticket home. Without John and his leadership the season was over. It is impossible to exaggerate the blind, unquestioning faith this team had in that man. Greatness can sometimes be measured more accurately not by what one man can do, but rather by what one man can inspire others to do. When John was on the field anything was possible. The Colts didn't just think that; they *knew* it. . . .

Out of ten years of pro football, our game with the Bears in 1960 is the one that I most remember. It is probably the one that the players on both teams remember best, because neither team recovered from the physical beating handed out that day. This particular game was the most savage contest I have ever witnessed in sports. It didn't resemble a football game so much as a dog fight. The Colts were not considered an especially physical team, but this day was different.

From the first snap of the ball until the last, it was the most bitter and brutal struggle I've ever seen. Injured players on both teams were moving onto and off the field all afternoon, getting themselves repaired, and then returning for more. Neither team would back off. At one point late in the game I looked around and every player I could see was bleeding from somewhere or other. Since I was conspicuously clean, I found myself brushing up against players, trying to get some blood on my jersey.

The Bears were in front, 20-17, and the Colts had the ball inside the Chicago forty-yard line, with just seconds remaining in the game. On third down, Unitas called a deep pattern to Lenny Moore. He told me to stay in and block. The Bears were blitzing, and Bill George managed to get hold of one of John's legs. George held him long enough for Atkins to get free and finish him off. Finishing him off was just about what Doug did. There was nothing uncalled-for about the lick he gave John; it was just the fact that Doug was so powerful.

John was slow getting up; we knew he was hurt. The trainers and doctors were running onto the field as Doug stood towering over John's limp body. Doug just stared down at him for a second, and then he spoke: "Well, kid, that's about it for you today."

John propped himself up on one hand and replied, "Not just yet it ain't." When I saw John's face I almost threw up. His nose was slashed and mangled, and his face was covered with blood. It was as if he had been hit with an ax.

Have you every noticed how deathly quiet things get when a great player goes down? A hush settled over Wrigley Field as they took John to the sideline. It seemed to take a full ten minutes to clean him up and stop the bleeding. After packing his nose full of cotton, he trotted back on the field. When he reached the huddle his nose had already swollen to twice its normal size, and both eyes were almost swollen shut. On fourth down, with no time outs and only nineteen seconds left on the clock, John called the identical deep pattern to Moore. Lenny beat his defender as Unitas uncorked a perfect thirty-nine-yard scoring strike to win it, 24-20.

It was the most dramatic finish and the damnedest spectacle I had ever seen. Things like

this don't just happen; they're caused. The man who caused this one, John Unitas, just walked off the field as if it were an everyday occurrence. No high fives, no dancing or celebrating, no fingers pointed upwards designating, "we're number one." Here was the greatest quarterback who ever played the game, walking casually off the field, having just finished a day of work. This was what he was paid to do. How often do you see that kind of dignity anywhere, anyplace?

Further Resources

BOOKS

"Johnny Unitas." In *The Pros.* Liston, Robert, ed. New York: Platt and Munk, 1968.

Schaap, Dick. "Sunday's Best." In *ESPN Sports Century.* Michael MacCambridge, ed. New York: Hyperion, 1999.

PERIODICALS

Morgan, Jon. "Colt Legend John Unitas Dead at 69." *Baltimore Sun,* September 12, 2002.

Sports Illustrated, September 23, 2002. (Issue contains several articles in tribute to Unitas).

WEBSITES

Pro Football Hall of Fame. "Johnny Unitas." Available online at http://www.profootballhof.com (accessed March 7, 2003).

Michigan State Ties Notre Dame

"An Upside-Down Game"
Magazine article

By: Dan Jenkins

Date: November 28, 1966

Source: Jenkins, Dan. "An Upside-Down Game." *Sports Illustrated,* November 28, 1966, 22–25.

About the Author: Dan Jenkins (1929–) was born in Fort Worth, Texas. After attending Texas Christian University, he wrote for the *Fort Worth Press* and the *Dallas Times-Herald.* In 1962, he joined *Sports Illustrated,* covering primarily football and golf for the next twenty-two years. After leaving *Sports Illustrated* in 1984, Jenkins wrote for a number of publications, including *Golf Digest* and *Playboy.* Jenkins has written sixteen books, including nine novels.

"No Decision"
Newspaper article

By: Arthur Daley

Date: November 20, 1966

Source: Daley, Arthur. "No Decision." *The New York Times,* November 20, 1966.

About the Author: Arthur Daley (1904–1974) was born in New York City. A baseball player at Fordham University, Daley turned to writing and was sports editor of the college newspaper. After graduation, he joined *The New York Times* in 1926, which became his lifelong job. He took over the "Sports of the *Times*" column in 1942 "until further notice," which lasted nearly thirty years until his death. Daley was a well-prepared interviewer who predicted the rise of professional basketball and football as major spectator sports. He won the Pulitzer Prize in 1956, the first sportswriter to do so, and wrote five books and numerous magazine articles. ■

Introduction

In 1966, Michigan State University and the University of Notre Dame had two of the greatest teams in college football history. Michigan State, coached by Duffy Daugherty, had won nineteen straight regular season games and were 9-0, champions of the Big Ten Conference, and ranked number two in the nation. The Spartans featured several talented players, including defensive back George Webster, defensive end Bubba Smith, and Jimmy Raye, one of the few starting African American quarterbacks in college football. The University of Notre Dame's storied football program regained prominence under coach Ara Parseghian. Notre Dame was ranked number one, with an 8-0 record, eleven All-Americans, and outstanding players such as defensive end Alan Page, running back Rocky Bleier, and quarterback Terry Hanratty. As fate would have it, the Spartans and Fighting Irish would face each other, the national championship of college football on the line. Many compared the Michigan State-Notre Dame matchup to the epic 1946 Army-Notre Dame game that ended in a scoreless tie.

Saturday, November 19, was a cold, gray day in East Lansing, Michigan. An overflow crowd of 80,011 packed Spartan Stadium, and millions watched the game on television. Spartan partisans held up signs proclaiming "Hail Mary full of grace, Notre Dame in second place" and wearing buttons saying "Kill Bubba Kill." In the first quarter, neither team scored, although Notre Dame lost Hanratty for the game with a separated shoulder. Early in the second quarter, Michigan State concluded a ten-play, seventy-three-yard drive, as Regis Cavender scored from four yards out. After Notre Dame failed to muster any offense, the Spartans drove the ball into Irish territory, leading to a field goal by Bill Kenney, Michigan State's barefoot kicker. Coley O'Brien, Notre Dame sophomore who replaced Hanratty, drove his team to a touchdown, the scoring play a thirty-four-yard pass to Bob Gladieux. The first half ended with Michigan State ahead, 10-7.

From the outset of the second half, the talented and stingy Notre Dame defense took over. The Irish had al-

lowed but four touchdowns in their first eight games. Michigan State tried every strategy, but nothing seemed to work. Fortunately for the Spartans, the Fighting Irish offense was sputtering. Near the end of the third quarter, O'Brien drove the Irish from their own twenty to the Michigan State twelve-yard line. There, Joe Azzaro, Notre Dame's placekicker came in to boot a twenty-eight-yard field goal, tying the game at the end of three quarters. The fourth quarter saw Notre Dame take control of the game. The Irish picked off Raye, taking the ball to the Spartan eighteen-yard line. But on the first three downs Notre Dame lost six yards, and Azzaro missed a forty-one-yard field goal attempt. With a minute and a half to go, Notre Dame got the ball on their thirty-yard line. Rather than risking an interception in their own territory, Notre Dame chose to run out the clock, "preserving" a 10-10 tie.

Significance

A tie game between two previously undefeated teams was bound to create controversy. But Parseghian's decision to run out the final 1:24 on the clock perplexed many and invited derision from others. The partisan Michigan State crowd booed the Irish; the Spartans players taunted Notre Dame, calling them sissies. The national press also derided Parseghian's decision, saying they "tied one for the Gipper" and parodying the Irish Victory March: "tie, tie, for old Notre Dame." Parseghian defended his decision saying, "We'd fought hard to come back and tie it up. After all that, I didn't want to risk giving it to them cheap. They get reckless and it could have cost them game. I wasn't going to do a jackass thing like that at this point."

One question remained: Who would win the national championship? Michigan State's season was over, but Notre Dame had one game remaining, against rival Southern California. The next week, shaking off the tie, the Irish routed the Trojans 54-0 to match Michigan State's 9-0-1 record. Based on the USC game, plus outscoring their opponents 362-38 in ten games, Notre Dame was crowned national college football champions. Numerous players from both teams played professional football, some with distinction, including Rocky Bleier, Bob Kuechenberg, and Alan Page from Notre Dame; and George Webster and Bubba Smith of Michigan State. Duffy Daugherty coached Michigan State until 1972, retiring with 109 wins. Ara Parseghian coached Notre Dame to another national title in 1973, but the pressure of winning at the country's premier college football program eventually took a toll, and he retired after the 1974 season with an impressive record of 95-17-4. All of Parseghian's victories at Notre Dame are remembered less than the one game he did not win or lose that cold Saturday November afternoon in 1966.

Primary Source

"An Upside-Down Game" [excerpt]

SYNOPSIS: *Sports Illustrated* writer Dan Jenkins reports and comments on the 10-10 tie between Michigan State and Notre Dame in November 1966. Jenkins questions Fighting Irish coach Ara Parseghian's decision to play for the tie rather than try for victory.

Old Notre Dame will tie over all. Sing it out, guys. That is not exactly what the march says, of course, but that is how the big game ends every time you replay it. And that is how millions of cranky college football fans will remember it. For 59 minutes in absolutely overwrought East Lansing last week the brutes of Michigan State and Notre Dame pounded each other into enough mistakes to fill Bubba Smith's uniform—enough to settle a dozen games between lesser teams—but the 10-10 tie that destiny seemed to be demanding had a strange, noble quality to it. And then it did not have that anymore. For the people who saw it under the cold, dreary clouds or on national television, suddenly all it had was this enormous emptiness for which the Irish will be forever blamed.

Forget everything that came before, all of that ferocious thudding in the line that was mostly responsible for five fumbles, four interceptions, 25 other incompletions, a total of 20 rushing plays that either lost yardage or gained none, and forget the few good plays—the big passes. Put the No. 1 team, Notre Dame, on its own 30-yard line with time for at least four passing plays to break the tie. A No. 1 team will try *something,* won't it, to stay that way?

Notre Dame did not. It just let the air out of the ball. For reasons that it will rationalize as being more valid than they perhaps were under the immense circumstances, the Irish rode out the clock. . . . Even as the Michigan State defenders taunted them and called the time-outs that the Irish should have been calling, Notre Dame ran into the line, the place where the big game was hopelessly played all afternoon. No one really expected a verdict in that last desperate moment. But they wanted someone to try. When the Irish ran into the line, the Spartans considered it a minor surrender.

"We couldn't believe it," said George Webster, State's savage rover back. "When they came up for

Notre Dame coach Ara Paraseghian (left) and Michigan State coach Duffy Daugherty leave the field after their teams played to a controversial 10-10 tie, East Lansing, Michigan, November 19, 1966. © BETTMANN/ CORBIS. REPRODUCED BY PERMISSION.

their first play we kept hollering back and forth, 'Watch the pass, watch the pass.' But they ran. We knew the next one was a pass for sure. But they ran again. We were really stunned. Then it dawned on us. They were settling for the tie."

You could see the Spartans staring at the Irish down there. They had their hands on their hips, thoroughly disdainful by now. On the Michigan State sideline, the Spartans were jeering across the field and waving their arms as if to say, "Get off the field if you've given up." And at the line of scrimmage the Michigan State defenders were talking to the Notre Dame players.

"I was saying, 'You're going for the tie, aren't you? You're going for the tie,'" said Webster. "And you know what? They wouldn't even look us in the eyes. They just turned their backs and went back to their huddle." Bubba had hollered, "Come on, you sissies," while other Spartans were yelling at Parseghian.

Notre Dame Coach Ara Parseghian made the decision to end the so-called "game of the century" that way. The players only followed instructions, some of them perhaps reluctantly. "We'd fought hard to come back and tie it up," Ara argued. "After all that, I didn't want to risk giving it to them cheap. They get reckless and it could have cost them the game. I wasn't going to do a jackass thing like that at this point."

Thus ended a game that had been slowly built up for five long weeks into the biggest collegiate

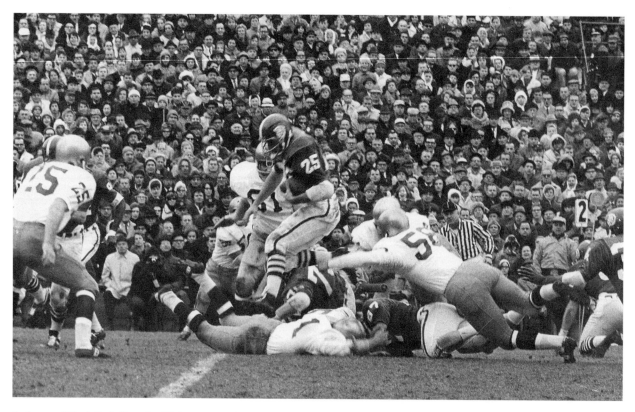

Sophomore fullback Regis Cavender (25) jumps across the goal line, scoring Michigan State's only touchdown of the game. MICHIGAN STATE UNIVERSITY SPORTS INFORMATION.

spectacle in 20 years. The last game to create such pre-kickoff frenzy was between Notre Dame and Army in 1946 at Yankee Stadium. That battle of the century was as full of as many fluky things as this one. It ended in an unsatisfactory 0-0 tie, with both teams claiming No. 1, and left thousands bewildered by the fact that such folklore characters as Johnny Lujack, Glenn Davis and Doc Blanchard had not performed the one remarkable deed that would have decided it.

So when the 1966 season is over, who will deserve to be No. 1? Duffy Daugherty thought Michigan State should be 1 and Notre Dame only 1A. He then said he would even accept a "co-championship," thinking of the Spartans' lesser voting power in the polls. . . .

Last week's game was decided a dozen punishing times, it seemed, the two national powers heaping heroics onto boners, and vice versa—as Michigan State surged to a 10-0 lead and Notre Dame struggled back to the indecisive tie that was earned but unapplauded.

The game was marked by all of the brutality that you somehow knew it would be when such gladia-

tors were to be present as Michigan State's 6-foot-7, 285-pound Bubba Smith, "the intercontinental ballistic Bubba," a creature whose defensive-end play had long ago encouraged Spartan coeds to wear buttons that said KILL, BUBBA, KILL.

Bubba killed, all right. He killed Notre Dame Quarterback Terry Hanratty early in the first quarter. When Hanratty, a sensational sophomore for eight games, slid off right tackle on a keeper, Bubba Smith whomped him in the left shoulder and separated it. He caught him just right, as they were falling. It looked as if Hanratty had been smacked by a giant swinging green door.

"That didn't help us any," Bubba said later. "It just let them put in that O'Brien who's slippery and faster and gave us more trouble. The other guy just sits there and waits, and that's what we wanted."

That is what Ara Parseghian wanted, too. Hanratty may sit and wait, but he also throws deep better than O'Brien, though Coley O'Brien threw well enough to get the tie. Ara not only would have liked to have had Hanratty but Halfback Nick Eddy and Center George Goeddeke as well. Like Hanratty, Goeddeke was valuable, one of Notre Dame's more accomplished blockers. He went out with a first-quarter ankle injury, also courtesy of Bubba. But Eddy, the best Irish ball-carrier, never even got into the game. The Grand Trunk got Eddy.

The Grand Trunk is not another name for Bubba Smith. It is the railroad train that Notre Dame rode from South Bend to East Lansing on Friday. When the train arrived, Eddy fell off the steps right onto an already injured shoulder, and sophomore Bob Gladieux was quietly told that he would start the biggest game of the 1966 season at left half.

As Notre Dame lives with the tie in the weeks and months ahead, it will never forget these injuries and the alibis they strongly suggest. But the Irish do not exactly substitute with girls from Sweet Briar, and Coley O'Brien and Bob Gladieux—the *new* Baby Bombers, somebody said—did marvelously well. "Considering everything, I thought they played super," said Parseghian. O'Brien, who must receive two insulin shots a day for diabetes, hit Gladieux with a 34-yard pass on a deep pattern straight to the goalpost. The ball barely cleared a defender's fingertips but brought Notre Dame's touchdown in the second quarter. The score narrowed the Irish deficit to 10-7 at half time.

The combination of Eddy's injury and the pressure of the game made Notre Dame an extraordinarily grim-looking group upon arrival in East Lansing. Usually loose and smiling, the Irish checked into the Jack Tar Hotel beneath a marquee that said WELCOME TO THE BIG ONE, with frozen, dedicated expressions that for some indescribable reason did not spell confidence. End Jim Seymour, the startling pass catcher and outgoing personality of earlier Saturdays, was rigid, deeply concentrating. In the game itself Seymour was double covered so well all day that he was scarcely noticeable. He had one decent chance at a pass but dropped it.

The Irish should have been happy to leave South Bend, even on the Grand Trunk, after the week of attention they got. On Monday there were dozens of reporters and photographers on hand, the number swelling each day. It was the same for the Spartans, of course. Both Parseghian and Daugherty had to hold daily press conferences and play the game over and over ahead of time. They certainly thought the game was an honor and a privilege. Parseghian said it looked like a product of Hollywood since Notre Dame was 8-0 and No. 1 and Michigan State was 9-0 and No. 2. Daugherty said it was a shame that such games come along only every few years in college football; that there could be one every year if

the NCAA would only hold a football playoff. They said they were simply going to remind their players that Saturday was going to be one of the greatest days in their lives.

The two teams were so talented and physically imposing, and had beaten their opponents so easily, that it was impossible to foretell how the game would go. It was anticipated that neither could run much but that both could strike in the air if their quarterbacks had a spare second to get the ball away. No one wanted a freak play to decide it; everyone wanted a clear winner. The last thing anyone thought about, especially the coaches, was a tie. No, that was the next to last thing. The last thing was all of the mistakes that occurred.

It seemed the two teams would never settle down and begin to look like Nos. 1 and 2 instead of Nos. 42 and 43. Of the four passes Terry Hanratty threw before he met Bubba Smith, three were atrociously off target, one a simple screen that went into the turf. The runners went nowhere, primarily because of Webster, Linebacker Charlie Thornhill, Guard Jeff Richardson and Bubba. And Notre Dame failed to get off a fourth-down punt because of a poor snapback. Michigan State countered with a fumble, a delay penalty, a clip and a penalty for interfering on a punt catch. It looked like the big intramural game at Columbia.

Primary Source

"No Decision" [excerpt]

SYNOPSIS: In his column, *New York Times* columnist Arthur Daley assesses the Michigan State–Notre Dame 10-10 tie of November 1966, dismissing any quick comparison with the 0-0 tie between the Fighting Irish and Army in 1946. Daley does not pass judgment on Notre Dame's decision to play for the tie.

East Lansing, Mich., Nov. 19—There is not a No. 2 in the National Collegiate rankings anymore. Notre Dame and Michigan must share No. 1. In a savage display of football at its primitive best, the two strongest campus teams in the land battled furiously today to a 10-10 tie under leaden skies that were laden with snow. Since neither team evinced any sign of clearcut superiority, the outcome was a fair one even though it left neither side happy.

For one half the Spartans dominated the proceedings to a considerable extent and then that smothering Irish defense wore them down to keep them from making any sort of threat. In fact, it was Notre Dame that rallied, settling for a field goal on the first play of the last quarter to bring about the deadlock.

The luck of the Irish was never too manifest, though. Terry Hanratty, the boy passing marvel, was flattened in the first quarter and removed with a shoulder separation. This misadventure seemed to let a lot of air out of the South Bend balloon. It took much huffing and puffing by Capt. Jim Lynch and the defensive platoon to blow it up again to any sort of respectable size.

The late Eddie Erdelatz said it best when he uttered his classic remark: "A tie game is as satisfactory as kissing your sister." Only the result was of an amatory nature. The game itself was as brutally and recklessly played as any roughhouse affair between the Green Bay Packers and Chicago Bears.

Not a Duplicate

"Who knows?" said the ever-smiling Duffy Daugherty in one of his pregame conversational sparring sessions. "You never can tell what might happen in a football game. This one could even develop into another of those scoreless ties like the famous 1946 Army–Notre Dame game."

The Michigan State coach was dead wrong, of course, because the points began bobbing up on the board in the second quarter but he did stir up memories of what probably was the greatest double-shutout in football history.

Frank Leahy of the Irish and Red Blaik of the cadets played everything so close to the vest in a display of super-caution that neither team moved the ball consistently. Army almost scored when Doc Blanchard rumbled into an open field but was nailed by a bone-shattering tackle by Johnny Lujack, the Notre Dame quarterback and safetyman. . . .

In view of the ferocity of the two defensive platoons, these teams extracted about as much as either deserved. The tie score must be accepted as a true balance of power.

Further Resources

BOOKS

Celizic, Mike. *The Biggest Game of All: Notre Dame, Michigan State, and the Fall of '66.* New York: Simon and Schuster, 1992.

Delsohn, Steve. *Talking Irish: The Oral History of Irish Football.* New York: Avon Books, 1998.

Gildea, William, and Christopher Jennison. *The Fighting Irish.* Edgewood Cliffs, N.J.: Prentice Hall, 1976.

PERIODICALS

"Irish Gain Standoff on Late Field Goal." *The New York Times,* November 20, 1966.

Murray, Jim. "'Tis a Pity When Irish Tie One for the Gipper." *The Los Angeles Times,* November 22, 1966.

Red Auerbach: Winning the Hard Way

Autobiography

By: Arnold Red Auerbach and Paul Sann

Date: 1966

Source: Auerbach, Arnold Red, and Paul Sann. *Red Auerbach: Winning the Hard Way.* Boston: Little, Brown, 1966, 86, 88–91, 94–95.

About the Author: Arnold "Red" Auerbach (1917–) was born in Brooklyn, New York. After graduating from George Washington University, he coached high school basketball in Washington, D.C., then coached the Washington Capitals and Tri-Cities Hawks of the Basketball Association of America before going to the Boston Celtics in 1950. Auerbach won nine NBA championships between 1957 and 1966 as Celtics coach. Retiring as coach in 1966, he remained with the Celtics as general manager and president.

Introduction

When the term "dynasty" is discussed in sports, it typifies a team that wins consecutive championships or dominates an era. In professional basketball, there is little question that the Boston Celtics of the late 1950s and 1960s—coached by Red Auerbach and his best player, Bill Russell—were a sports dynasty in the truest sense of the term.

Over his first six seasons with the Celtics, Auerbach assembled a talented team, including guards Bob Cousy and Bill Sharman, but never got to the championship round, as they lacked a dominating defensive player. After the 1956 season, Auerbach was determined to secure the rights to Bill Russell, the outstanding University of San Francisco center who had led his team to consecutive NCAA titles.

Before Russell came to the Celtics, however, he helped the United States basketball team win the gold medal at the 1956 Olympics in Melbourne, Australia. When he returned, he signed with the Celtics and immediately had an impact. In 1957, the Celtics won their first title by defeating the St. Louis Hawks in seven games. Although St. Louis got revenge the next season, the dominance of the Boston Celtics was just beginning.

In 1959, the Celtics began an amazing streak of eight consecutive championships by defeating the Minneapolis Lakers. In succession, the Celtics defeated the Hawks in 1960 and 1961; the Lakers, now relocated to Los Angeles, in 1962 and 1963; the San Francisco Warriors, with Russell's arch-rival Wilt Chamberlain, in 1964; and the Lakers again in 1965 and 1966.

After the 1966 season, Auerbach retired as coach, with a career 1,037 victories, but remained as general manager and named Russell to replace him on the bench. In 1967, Russell's first season, the Celtics streak of titles ended in the semifinals against the Philadelphia 76ers, with Chamberlain finally winning a championship over his rival. In 1968, the Celtics defeated the Lakers to regain the championship. The 1969 season saw the aging Celtics edge into the playoffs and, in a dramatic seventh game, beat the Lakers to win their eleventh title in Russell's thirteen-year career. With that last title, Russell retired in 1969.

Significance

The Celtics' success as designed by Auerbach, featured a fast-break offense, facilitated by Russell's great defensive ability to block shots, grab rebounds, and release the outlet pass up the court. In the Celtics' game plan, Russell's job was not to score points, since he had a talented group of players around him, including Cousy, Sharman, K.C. Jones (his college teammate), Sam Jones, Tom Heinsohn, Frank Ramsey, and John Havlicek. The Celtics invented the idea of the "sixth man," a key reserve; first Ramsey, then Havlicek, came off the bench to make important contributions to the game.

No team in professional sports history has approached the Boston Celtics' record of eleven championships in thirteen seasons during the Bill Russell era, and perhaps never will. But the winning tradition continued after Russell's retirement. As general manager, Auerbach built dominant championship teams in the 1970s with Havlicek, Dave Cowens, and Jo Jo White; and 1980s with Larry Bird, Robert Parrish, and Kevin McHale.

Primary Source

Red Auerbach: Winning the Hard Way [excerpt]

SYNOPSIS: In his autobiography, Red Auerbach, coach and general manager of the Boston Celtics, gives his account of how the Celtics were able to trade for the rights to University of San Francisco star Bill Russell, a move that changed the history of the Boston franchise and that of professional basketball.

Two Giants

. . . So I didn't see the new terror of the backboards in the flesh until the Dons came into Madison Square Garden for the 1955 Holiday Festival.

And I didn't go there to scout Bill Russell; he was All-American by then and way beyond my reach because the Celtics, finishing high, were going to be stuck with a late choice in the draft, as usual. I went to New York because Holy Cross was in the NIT and I wanted a good look at Tommy Heinsohn, my territorial pick, under tournament pressure. I didn't find out anything about Tommy. . . .

I did find out some things about Bill Russell, starting with the fact that the quiet genius back at GW knew exactly what he was talking about when he called me: Russell could get you the ball. I saw something else out there in the person of K.C. Jones. Reinhart had told me that he was a good little guard but didn't score enough, so I had written him off as an unlikely prospect. In the Garden, it occurred to me that the speedy K.C. was made to order for our full court press, and I felt he could learn to shoot better, too. I didn't have to worry about the little Don, though; there wasn't going to be any scramble for him in the draft. I did do some worrying about Bill Russell. Back in Boston, I began to torture the long-distance phone.

First I called Phil Woolpert, the Dons' coach. Woolpert reminded me that Bill had been a track man, too, and said he'd have no trouble fitting into anybody's fast break. . . .

Finally, I called Freddie Scolari, who had coached Baltimore before returning to the West Coast.

It was what Scolari said that floored me:

"Red, this kid can't shoot to save his ass. He can't hit the side of the basket. He's only the greatest basketball player I ever saw." . . .

Freddie said. "I'm just telling you Bill Russell is the greatest basketball player I ever saw. You want somebody to get you the ball, he'll get you the ball, but you're knocking yourself out. You haven't got a chance in the draft." . . .

I wanted to figure out a way to get the man. I could only do that if the league would let us trade for him in the draft.

Rochester was the cellar club that season, behind St. Louis, and we were headed for second place, which meant seventh pick. I couldn't imagine any club dealing Russell off, but I had to give it a shot. My first call went to Les Harrison.

Les told me he was pretty sure the Globetrotters were going after Russell. He said he couldn't compete for that kind of money, so he was going to settle for Sihugo Green of Duquesne to get some

Coach Red Auerbach and Bill Russell celebrate the Celtics's eighth straight NBA championship, Boston Massachusetts, April 28, 1966. © BETTMANN/CORBIS. REPRODUCED BY PERMISSION.

help in the backcourt. That wasn't the whole story. I found out later that Les had approached Russell, but he made the mistake of bringing along Dolly King, the ex-LIU star who had played for Rochester. Russell didn't know Dolly and didn't like the idea of an NBA owner enlisting the services of another Negro to sign him, so he set the price at $25,000 and Les went away.

Anyway, after talking to Harrison I called Ben Kerner. I knew Ben wanted Ed Macauley, who was anxious to go home to St. Louis because he had a youngster there who needed continual medical care, so I offered him the popular center for his draft pick.

Ben had a quick answer. "You got a deal," he told me.

I had the feeling that I had just pulled off the steal of the century, something like knocking over Fort Knox, but Ben is a shrewd basketball man who drives a hard bargain. He wasn't quite finished.

"There's only one little thing," he went on. "You got the rights to Cliff Hagan when he comes out of the Army, and I can use him, too. You're getting Frank Ramsey and Tommy Heinsohn and you got that

gorilla Jim Loscutoff in the corner, right? So you give me Hagan with Macauley and you get Russell and we're even up."

Now there was a nice kick in the head.

For an untested defensive specialist, I was offering Ben a high-scoring center and seven-time All-Star who would also be a natural for him at the gate. And Ben wanted the package sweetened with nothing less than the six-foot-five solid-rock Kentucky All-American, a sure-bet corner man for any NBA club even in his rookie year. Ben could have been bluffing. I had an idea he wanted Macauley so badly he might not insist on Hagan, but I couldn't take a chance on blowing the deal. . . .

I was either going to roll the dice after six years of bitter frustration or spend the rest of my life finishing high and then watching the big ones get away in that sad month of April.

I told Ben it was a deal.

Now there were a few mountains that still had to be climbed:

First, the league itself. The NBA had a rule barring the trading of first draft picks, but Kerner had told me that was nothing to worry about. He turned out to be right. The owners agreed, bless their stony hearts, that both St. Louis and Boston would be strengthened if the rule could be waived.

Next, the Globetrotters. I knew I had to go against Abe Saperstein's bankroll, and if you believed everything you read then the Trotters would have had no trouble buying themselves J. Paul Getty if he happened to be as tall as his own fortune. But Saperstein did me a favor. The newspapers were carrying Trotter price tags on Bill Russell ranging all the way up to $50,000, but when the principals sat down that torrent of gold had shrunk to a skimpy $17,000. And that was not the worst of it. Saperstein sat in the same room with the San Francisco star and did all his talking to Phil Woolpert, bartering for this piece of basketball flesh just as if the body itself wasn't in the room. This offended Russell. "Maybe I was wrong," he said later, "but I took it to mean, 'As one Great White Father to another Great White Father, this is what we'll do for this poor Negro boy.' Right or wrong, before he was finished talking, I was thinking, 'You want to talk to Woolpert, you just get Woolpert to sign a contract with you.'" So the Trotters couldn't have had Russell for a million, and that problem was out of the way.

Finally, there was the sticky matter of Bill's amateur standing. He was on the Olympic team going to Australia and we couldn't talk terms to him with-

Second Wind: The Memoirs of an Opinionated Man [excerpt]

Red would never let things get very far out of focus. He thought about winning more than I thought about eating when I was little. He ached when we didn't win; his whole body would be thrown out of whack when we lost. He didn't care about any player's statistics or reputation in the newspapers; all he thought about was the final score and who had helped put it on the board.

By design and by talent the Celtics were a team of specialists, and like a team of specialists in any field, our performance depended both on individual excellence and on how well we worked together. None of us had to strain to understand that we had to complement each other's specialties; it was simply a fact, and we all tried to figure out ways to make our combination more effective. That kind of togetherness was purely pragmatic, predicated on winning in a team sport, and it didn't have anything to do with the popular image of the Celtics as a team full of "Celtic pride,"

The Celtics played together because we all knew that it was the best way to win. Each player was as competitive as Attila the Hun, and if individual combat would have won championship, we'd have been fighting each other.

I've always thought that the main source of Celtic "togetherness" was that we were *literally* together for so long. During my thirteen-year career the Celtics made a grand total of one trade: Mel Counts for Bailey Howell. That's all.

We all knew that the game was a business and that we could be traded tomorrow, but Red did a good job of making us believe that we would stay as long as we contributed to winning, and this made us feel secure.

SOURCE: Russell, Bill, and Taylor Branch. *Second Wind: The Memoirs of an Opinionated Man.* New York: Random House, 1979, 122, 125–128.

the pivot, when to box out and when to go for the rebound, and a million and one tricks of the good big man's trade. And we talked to him about how to play the other giants in the league and how to let the pitchout go for our fast break.

There was one thing nobody had to talk to Bill Russell about, of course, and that was his fantastic sense of timing. You couldn't fake him. You could try head feints and body feints and what-have-you, but you couldn't lose the man. We knew it the first time he worked with us. And we knew it wouldn't take him long to learn what little he had to learn. I used to sit him on the bench next to me to watch Arnie out there, but I didn't have to tell him much. He had the intelligence to figure it out for himself and he was all ready to go, full time, when Arnie got hurt about a month after he joined us.

You know the rest. The new faces on that squad also included a couple of guys named Heinsohn and Ramsey, so we were 16 and 8 and leading the league by six games when Russ arrived and dispelled any doubt about where the Celtics were going for a change. He played in 48 games, averaged 20 rebounds and blocked a few shots here and there; something new had been introduced to the defense in our league. We finished with a 44-28 record, six games ahead of Syracuse, beat them in three straight in the Eastern semifinals and then took that tough seven-game series from St. Louis for our first title. It was my first taste of honey after six bitter years in Boston. We were all going to taste a lot of honey after that.

Further Resources

BOOKS
Auerbach, Arnold. *On and Off the Court.* New York: Bantam Books, 1985.

Koppett, Leonard. *24 Seconds to Shoot: An Informal History of the National Basketball Association.* New York: Macmillan, 1970.

Russell, Bill. *Go Up for Glory.* New York: Coward, McCann, 1966.

WEBSITES
Naismith Memorial Basketball Hall of Fame. "Arnold 'Red' Auerbach." Available online at http://www.hoophall.com/halloffamers/Auerbach.htm; website home page: http://www.hoophall.com (accessed March 7, 2003).

Naismith Memorial Basketball Hall of Fame. "William 'Bill' Russell." Available online at http://www.hoophall.com/halloffamers/RussellW.htm; website home page: http://www.hoophall.com (accessed March 7, 2003).

out running the risk of getting him in trouble. Silly, isn't it? . . .

There was no problem when Bill got back. We signed him for $19,500, big money back in 1956, and there was no bonus, no talk about a no-cut contract (we've never signed one) and nothing under the table. . . .

Arnie Risen, then my first-string center and winding up his career, showed Bill how to get position in

The Olympic Protests

Why?: The Biography of John Carlos

Biography

By: John Carlos with CD Jackson Jr.

Date: 2000

Source: Carlos, John, with CD Jackson Jr. *Why?: The Biography of John Carlos.* Los Angeles: Milligan, 2000, 188–190, 191, 194–195, 198–199, 200–201, 205, 206, 207.

About the Author: John Carlos (1945–) was born in New York City. He attended East Texas State University on a track scholarship, but because of racial discrimination he transferred to San Jose State, where he was a 200-meter star. He won a bronze medal at the 1968 Olympics. After his protest and suspension from the Olympics, he ran amateur track in Europe and played football in the Canadian League. In later years, he was a community activist, and high school track coach in Palm Springs, California.

"The Black Berets"

Newspaper article

By: Red Smith

Date: 1968

Source: Smith, Red. "The Black Berets." 1968. In *The Red Smith Reader.* Dave Anderson, ed. New York: Vintage, 1983, 38–39.

About the Author: Red Smith (1905–1982) was born in Green Bay, Wisconsin. After graduating from Notre Dame in 1927, Smith was a reporter and editor for various newspapers until he joined *The New York Times* in 1971, where he remained until his death. He published several collections of his columns and won numerous honors, including the Pulitzer Prize in 1976. ■

Introduction

For African Americans, gains in civil rights during the 1960s were slowed by the assassination of Martin Luther King Jr., civil unrest in American cities, and continued discrimination in many walks of life, including sports. For black athletes, it seemed time to take a stand against racism. In November 1967, Harry Edwards, a San Jose State University sociology professor, organized fifty to sixty athletes, primarily African American—including basketball star Lew Alcindor (later Kareem Abdul-Jabbar)—in a proposed boycott of the 1968 Olympics in Mexico City. Edwards' group demanded that white-ruled South Africa be permanently barred from the Olympics, International Olympic Committee president Avery Brundage resign, Muhammad Ali be reinstated as heavyweight boxing champion, and the New York Athletic Club end its whites-only policy. Among the athletes participating in the proposed boycott was San Jose State track stars Tommie Smith and John Carlos.

Both Smith and Carlos specialized in the 200-meter run (Smith also excelled at football). Smith set several world records in the event between 1965 and 1967, and each was a favorite in Mexico City. By the summer of 1968, the Olympic boycott was abandoned, and athletes were encouraged by Edwards to "protest in their own fashion." Smith and Carlos—unlike Alcindor, who boycotted—decided to compete and make a statement of their own at the Games.

After arriving in Mexico City, Smith and Carlos knew what statement they would make if either won medals. Smith asked his wife to buy a pair of black gloves. On October 16, 1968, both Carlos and Smith won their semifinal races at two hundred meters and competed two hours later in the final. After a fast start, Carlos fell to third place; after a slow start, Smith gained momentum and won the gold medal in a world record time of 19.83 seconds.

Now came the issue of how to publicly protest racism in the United States and the world. Smith pulled the gloves out of his gym bag. Carlos suggested that each man wear one glove and that that hand be raised in the air as a fist in a show of defiance and solidarity on the award stand. Smith chose the right glove and Carlos put on the left. In addition, both men wore scarves and removed their shoes, exposing black-stocking feet. Before going out to the victory stand, Carlos said to Smith, "If anyone cocks a rifle, you know the sound, be ready to move." They stood on the platform, received their medals, and when "The Star-Spangled Banner" began, Smith raised his gloved right fist and Carlos his left into the air, both with their heads bowed in prayer.

Significance

Smith's and Carlos's African American teammates were not surprised at what they did on the victory stand. Meanwhile, both athletes sought sanctuary after the medal ceremony in the Olympic Village and awaited the inevitable reaction. The U.S. Olympic Committee sternly disapproved of their action but delayed a decision, not wishing to turn Smith and Carlos into martyrs. But the International Olympic Committee, headed by Avery Brundage, threatened to expel the entire American team if Smith and Carlos were not disciplined. Two days later, on October 18, the USOC suspended the two men, ordered them to leave the Olympic Village, and revoked their credentials, meaning Smith and Carlos had to leave Mexico within forty-eight hours. Smith and Carlos returned to San Jose, heroes to some but criticized by others, including former Olympian Jesse Owens. Other African American athletes in Mexico City protested in subtler ways, with black socks or berets—removed before the anthem, however.

Tommie Smith (center) and John Carlos (right) bow their heads and raise their fists on the medal podium at the 1968 Olympic Games, Mexico City, October 16, 1968. This protest against the unequal treatment of African Americans was a milestone in Olympics history and the American civil rights movement. **AP/WIDE WORLD PHOTOS. REPRODUCED BY PERMISSION.**

In the years after the 1968 Olympics, Smith and Carlos led varied careers. Smith graduated from San Jose State and played three years as a wide receiver for the Cincinnati Bengals along with racing track profession-

ally. He was track coach and athletic director at Oberlin College before returning to California to coach track and cross country at Santa Monica College. Carlos competed in track and briefly played football in the Canadian

League before starting a varied life as a bar bouncer, then community activist, assisting in the 1984 Los Angeles Olympics. After an arrest for cocaine possession, which subsequently was cleared from his record, Carlos became a track and field coach in Palm Springs, California.

Primary Source

Why? The Biography of John Carlos [excerpt]

SYNOPSIS: In this excerpt, John Carlos, track and field athlete and winner of the bronze medal in the 1968 Olympics, recounts the protest he and fellow American Tommie Smith staged on the victory stand after receiving medals after the 200-meter race.

Opening Day

It wasn't a question about whether or not I wanted to wear the Olympic uniform: a red blazer, blue shirt, and white pants in the opening ceremony. I did not come there for a parade, so I wasn't going to get into one. My whole purpose for being there was to make a statement. Pieces of the puzzle were coming together in my mind. What I mean by the pieces of the puzzle is that I was checking out what Avery Brundage was doing, the U.S. Olympic Officials, the attitudes of the different athletes, the peoples who were poor and starving, the Mexican students that were assassinated, the number of people who paid to get into the stadium, the lack of money the athletes were given, the gold, silver, and bronze medals were not made of their material names. They were fake!

I began to reflect on my childhood vision at age seven when God showed me a stadium where people cheered for me while I stood on a platform, and suddenly without a cause known to me, they booed me. All of these things were coming together in my mind, and I knew that I was there to make a statement. So I went to Tommy Smith and I told him that I was not going to the opening ceremony, and I also explained why. He responded to what I said by saying, "If you aren't going to go, I'm not going either." I said cool! I also ran into Leon Coleman, Ron Freeman, and some more Olympians, and they were all excited, saying, "Hey Los, come on and get dressed. Aren't you going?" I said, "Naw, man, I think I'm going to pass." There was a TV room in the village; Tommy and I watched the opening ceremony with some other Olympians that had to compete the same day. The same enthusiasm that I saw expressed in the black athletes was demonstrated on the TV. In my mind I can see Ron Freeman walking into the stadium with a big smile waving to all his friends

back home when he knew that the TV cameras were on him. Then there was Randy Mattson, a big strong robust man walking, expressing joy and jubilation. Randy was a world record holder in the shot put. Wyomia Tyus, a sprinter and 4×4 hundred-meter gold medal winner was walking in proudly for a second Olympics. I gathered strength from each participant's enthusiasm, and God revealed to me that they deserved to have their dreams come true. I also felt that I would have the chance to fulfill my dream, and that was to get on that victory stand and make that statement. I was happy for them. . . .

All of the black athletes from around the world sat together in the Olympic stadium: The Jamaicans, Ghanaians, Ugandans, Kenyans, Nigerians, Americans, Puerto Ricans, Cubans, and people from the Bahamas. They were playing the steel drums, congas, and other instruments, singing and laughing and talking, enjoying themselves to the max. The smell of food permeated the area as they passed food to one another. The atmosphere was radiant, and filled with joy. The energy was so high that it was explosive. Many people looked on, never truly understanding what was going on. There was unity among blacks from around the world! . . .

Reason for the Protest

I wanted to use the protest to raise consciousness about the Olympic Games. I wanted to create a protest to tell the world that the black man and woman dominate the Olympic Games, and this particular Olympics is a black Olympics for blacks all over the world. This protest is a protest to mourn the deaths of all of the black women, men, boys, and girls that died fighting against the European kidnappers on the shores of Africa. Then to those who died in the Middle Passage along the way. Then to those who were beaten unmercifully by the slave masters, being separated from family, religion, and language.

Since 1952 reparations amount now to 3.5 billion dollars and more than 44 million acres of land have been paid to Japanese Americans, Jewish Claims on Austria, Indians, Eskimos, Japanese Canadians, Ottawas of Michigan, Chippewas, Seminoles of Florida, Sioux, Klamaths of Oregon, Alaska Natives, and German Jews. Black people have lost over 50 to one hundred million people in a span of 400 years of slavery just like the Native American Indians. Black Americans never got anything for the mistreatment of slavery by America. Somebody had to say something about the mistreatment of black people around the world. Many of the black ministers, politicians, educators, and businessmen weren't doing anything other than conforming to the status quo. They weren't talking about giving up their lives and taking a few so that their children could have it better. The black Panthers did what they could do, but they were shut down real quick. Martin and Malcolm did a great job, but they did not have a world stage until they were long dead. The Olympics gave us a world stage, and we had the opportunity to say something to it while we were being presented a medal on a victory platform. This was exciting to me. So my whole purpose was to use that world stage to represent blackness. . . .

I am free! I emphatically state that I was the most relaxed person in the stadium despite the fact that me and Tommy were facing death, ostracizing, economic death row, and a name that would spell disaster for anyone who wanted to be associated with it. I was standing there thinking about the prophetic vision of the protest that the Lord showed me when I was 7 years old. At the same time, I was reflecting back on my life, and everything that I had done up to that moment. The last thing that I thought about was the fact that out of the five billion people on the planet, Tommy, and I were selected by God to do a silent protest in front of the world. I was at peace in the middle of America's nightmare. I was ready to die!

Primary Source

"The Black Berets"

SYNOPSIS: Red Smith, syndicated columnist, writes his account of the Smith-Carlos protest a few days after the fact, when another set of athletes performs a similar, though less emphatic, symbolic protest. He does not condemn the athletes but instead criticizes U.S. and International Olympic Committee officials for creating a larger controversy than was warranted.

Mexico City, 1968

The 400-meter race was over and in the catacombs of Estadio Olimpico Doug Roby, president of the United States Olympic Committee, was telling newspapermen that he had warned America's runners against making any demonstration if they should get to the victory stand. A fanfare of trumpets interrupted him.

In stiff single file, the three black Americans marched across the track. All of them—Lee Evans,

---

George Foreman's Opinion

Mexico City, Oct. 19—George Foreman is a 19-year-old heavyweight boxer on the American Olympic team with ambitions to follow the trail to gold and glory blazed by Floyd Patterson, Cassius Clay and Joe Frazier. He also is black, and he's bigger than any of them at 218 pounds. The gesture of black power militancy by Tommie Smith and John Carlos on the victory tribunal last Wednesday left him unmoved.

"That's for college kids," he said. "They live in another world."

SOURCE: Daley, Arthur. "The Incident." *The New York Times*, October 20, 1968.

---

the winner; Larry James, second, and Ron Freeman, third—had broken the recognized world record. Rain had fallen after the finish and, although it was abating now, the runners wore the official sweatsuits of the United States team, plus unofficial black berets which may or may not have been symbolic.

Each stopped to enable John J. Garland, an American member of the International Olympic Committee, to hang the medal about his neck. Then each straightened and waved a clenched fist aloft. It wasn't quite the same gesture meaning, "We shall overcome," which Tommie Smith and John Carlos had employed on the same stand after the 200-meter final.

Lord David Burghley, the Marquis of Exeter who is president of the International Amateur Athletic Federation, shook hands with each, and they removed the berets, standing at attention facing the flagpole as the colors ascended and the band played "The Star-Spangled Banner." Smith and Carlos had refused to look at the flag, standing with heads bowed and black-gloved fists upraised.

Evans, James, and Freeman stepped down, and out from under every stuffed shirt in the Olympic organization whistled a mighty sigh of relief. The waxworks had been spared from compounding the boobery which had created the biggest, most avoidable flap in these quadrennial muscle dances since Eleanor Holm was flung off the 1936 swimming team for guzzling champagne aboard ship.

The 400-meter race was run Friday, about 48 hours after Smith and Carlos put on their act and 12 hours after the United States officials lent sig-

Offiical Reaction

Most incensed were the nine old men who form the Executive Council of the International Olympic Committee. They hail from nine different countries and are headed by Avery Brundage, their president and everybody's whipping boy, most of his condemnation undeserved. Like Brundage, they also are idealists.

The United States Olympic Committee, closer to the situation and much more aware of how sensitive it was, was inclined toward leniency. The U. S. O. C. issued a formal apology to the I. O. C., the Mexican Organizing Committee and the people of Mexico for their athletes' "discourtesy," "untypical exhibitionism" and "immature behavior."

The U. S. O. C. was inclined to take no punitive action as a way of depriving the militants of future publicity, the only objective of a protest that one member described as going over "like a leaden balloon."

But the I. O. C. was so furious over the intrusion of politics into its sacred games that it summoned Douglas Roby, the president of the U. S. O. C., to its council meeting and virtually ordered him to suspend Smith and Carlos. Thus they so dignified the protest that they blew it onto the front pages of almost every newspaper in the world.

Let one thing be understood. The Brundage role was minor. The elderly sports statesmen of eight other nations forced the issue. The Marquis of Exeter, the president of the International Amateur Athletic Federation, had bestowed the medals when the incident took place. He also had stood atop a victory pedestal 40 years ago when he was Lord David Burghley and had won the Olympic 400-meter hurdles championship.

"I will not countenance such action again," he said angrily afterward. "I'll refuse to hold a victory ceremony if any such attempt is made again."

SOURCE: Daley, Arthur. "The Incident." *The New York Times,* October 20, 1968.

nificance to their performance by firing them from the team. The simple little demonstration by Smith and Carlos had been a protest of the sort every black man in the United States had a right to make. It was intended to call attention to the inequities the Negro suffers, and without the aid of the Olympic brass might have done this in a small way.

By throwing a fit over the incident, suspending the young men and ordering them out of Mexico, the badgers multiplied the impact of the protest a hundredfold. They added dignity to the protestants and made boobies of themselves.

"One of the basic principles of the Olympic games," read the first flatulent communiqué from on high, "is that politics play no part whatsoever in them. . . . Yesterday United States athletes in a victory ceremony deliberately violated this universally accepted principle by using the occasion to advertise their domestic political views."

Not content with this confession that they can't distinguish between human rights and politics, the playground directors put their pointed heads together and came up with this gem:

"The discourtesy displayed violated the standards of sportsmanship and good manners. . . . We feel it was an isolated incident, but any further repetition of such incidents would be a willful disregard of Olympic principles and would be met with severest penalties."

The action, Roby said, was demanded by the International Olympic Committee, including Avery Brundage, president, and by the Mexican Organizing Committee. They are, as Mark Anthony observed on another occasion, all honorable men who consider children's games more sacred than human decency.

Soon after the committee acted, a bedsheet was hung from a sixthfloor window of the apartment house in Olympic Village where Carlos has been living. On it were the letters: "Down with Brundage."

There were, of course, mixed feelings on the United States team. Lee Evans was especially upset, but when asked whether he intended to run as scheduled, he would only reply, "Wait and see."

"I had no intention of running this race," he said over the air after taking the 400, "but this morning Carlos asked me to run and win."

Said Carlos: "The next man that puts a camera in my face, I'll stomp him."

Further Resources

BOOKS

Ashe, Arthur R., Jr. *A Hard Road to Glory: History of the African-American Athlete, Since 1946.* New York: Warner Books, 1988.

Edwards, Harry. *The Revolt of the Black Athlete.* New York: Free Press, 1969.

PERIODICALS

Moore, Kenny. "A Courageous Stand." *Sports Illustrated,* August 5, 1991.

———. "The Eye of the Storm." *Sports Illustrated,* August 12, 1991.

Super Bowl III

"Joe Namath: Man of Defiance Faces Biggest Challenge"

Newspaper article

By: Dave Anderson

Date: January 5, 1969

Source: Anderson, Dave. "Joe Namath: Man of Defiance Faces Biggest Challenge." *The New York Times,* January 5, 1969, sec. 5, 1.

About the Author: Dave Anderson (1929–) was born in Troy, New York. After graduating from Holy Cross in 1951, Anderson was a sports reporter for various newspapers until he joined *The New York Times,* where he became a columnist in 1971. Author of twenty-one books and dozens of magazine articles, Anderson won the Pulitzer Prize in 1981.

I Can't Wait Until Tomorrow . . . 'Cause I Get Better-Looking Every Day

Autobiography

By: Joe Namath, with Dick Schaap

Date: 1969

Source: Namath, Joe, with Dick Schaap. *I Can't Wait Until Tomorrow . . . 'Cause I Get Better-Looking Every Day.* New York: Random House, 1969, 49–50, 58–60, 62–63, 65, 66–69.

About the Author: Joe Namath (1943–) was born in Beaver Falls, Pennsylvania. After playing quarterback at the University of Alabama, he signed a $400,000 contract with the New York Jets of the American Football League. In 1968, he led the Jets to the AFL title and an upset of the Baltimore Colts in Super Bowl III. Plagued by injuries, Namath retired after twelve seasons in 1977. Since retirement, Namath has been an actor, broadcaster, and businessman.

"Upset for the Ages"

Newspaper article

By: Shirley Povich

Date: January 13, 1969

Source: Povich, Shirley. "Upset for the Ages." *Washington Post,* January 13, 1969.

About the Author: Shirley Povich (1905–1998) was born in Bar Harbor, Maine. While attending Georgetown University, he joined the *Washington Post,* where he became a sports reporter and, at age twenty-one, editor. His column ran six days a week until 1974 and periodically until his death. His career spanned seventy-five years; he covered sixty World Series, two Super Bowls, and numerous other sporting events. ■

Introduction

In 1960, the American Football League (AFL) was founded to challenge the established National Football League (NFL). By the middle 1960s, the AFL had a national television contract (with NBC), signed talented college players such as Joe Namath, and threatened an outright bidding war with the NFL. In 1966, the rival leagues negotiated a merger agreement beginning in 1970. Meanwhile the leagues would play a championship game every January. Called the "NFL-AFL Championship Game" at first, within several years the spectacle became known as the "Super Bowl." The first two Super Bowls were won handily by Vince Lombardi's Green Bay Packers of the NFL.

The New York Jets AFL team outbid the NFL's St. Louis Cardinals and signed Joe Namath for $400,000 in 1965. Namath immediately made an impact, as he became the first quarterback to pass for four thousand yards in a season. His trademark white cleats on the field and his "Broadway Joe" bachelor lifestyle off the field made him something of a celebrity. In 1968, Namath and the Jets won the AFL championship by defeating the Oakland Raiders. In the NFL that year, the Baltimore Colts advanced to the Super Bowl by compiling a 13-1 record and defeating the Cleveland Browns in the league championship. The Colts were led by quarterback Earl Morrall, who stepped in after Johnny Unitas was injured.

In the two weeks leading up to Super Bowl III, the Jets felt a growing confidence. Their coach, Weeb Eubank, who coached Baltimore to consecutive NFL titles in 1958 and 1959, knew many of the Colts personnel. Namath, with his youthful brashness, promised at one point that he "guaranteed" a Jet victory. The Colts, if not overconfident, were perhaps taking the game too much in stride. There was reason to be complacent, for the oddsmakers had made Baltimore a seventeen- to twenty-point favorite.

On January 12, 1969, Super Bowl III was played before a crowd of 75,377 at Miami's Orange Bowl and a national television audience of around 60 million. From the outset, the game went poorly for the Colts. After a scoreless first quarter, Morrall was intercepted after the Colts recovered a fumble deep in Jet territory. Starting at their own twenty yard line, Namath directed the Jets on an eighty-yard drive before Matt Snell scored on a four-yard run to give New York a 7-0 lead at halftime.

In the third quarter, a Colt fumble set up a Jets field goal, making it 10-0. With four minutes remaining in the quarter, Jet placekicker Jim Turner added another field goal, increasing the margin to 13-0. At this point, the Colts replaced the ineffective Morrall with Unitas, who also was unable to muster any offense. Early in the fourth quarter, a third Jets field goal made it 16-0. Finally, after three and a half quarters, the Colts got on the scoreboard, scoring on a one yard run by Jerry Hill. After recovering an onside kick, Unitas was directing the Colts toward another score, but the Jets defenders and Unitas's thirty-five-year-old arm kept them out of the end zone. The Jets, with Namath in charge, ran out the clock, preserving one of sports' most shocking upsets, a 16 to 7 victory over the favored Colts.

Significance

Namath, who was seventeen of twenty-eight passing for 206 yards, was named Super Bowl III Most Valuable Player, less for his statistics (he had no touchdown passes) than his masterful play calling. The twenty-five-year-old became a national celebrity as a result of his Super Bowl victory, even hosting a weekly TV talk show. Namath would never again play in a championship game or Super Bowl. Persistent injuries, especially to his knees, would reduce his effectiveness over his last nine seasons. After a final year with the Los Angeles Rams in 1977, Namath retired after thirteen seasons with 27,663 yards and 173 touchdowns.

The New York Jets' victory in Super Bowl III validated the AFL as an equal partner with the older, established NFL. For many AFL players, especially veterans from the league's early days, New York's victory was less a triumph for Joe Namath and the Jets than a victory for themselves and all those who toiled in the early years.

Primary Source

"Joe Namath: Man of Defiance Faces Biggest Challenge" [excerpt]

> **SYNOPSIS:** Sportswriter Dave Anderson interviewed New York Jets quarterback Joe Namath a week before Super Bowl III in 1969. Namath is confident of himself, his teammates, and believes that the Jets will beat the Baltimore Colts in the football game.

Joe Namath is preparing to challenge the superiority of the National Football League next Sunday in the Super Bowl game with the Baltimore Colts.

And when Joe Namath is confronted with a challenge, beware. As a $400,000 rookie he challenged the salary structure of pro football, but he proved to be a bargain. With his Fu Manchu mustache, he challenged the tonsorial tradition of American athletics, but he shaved it off for a $10,000 fee.

As the symbol of the American Football League, he is confronted with the challenge of penetrating the Colt defense.

His attitude is significant. Occasionally he presents a droopy appearance, but not now. He's alive and alert. When he saw the Jets' white uniforms, which they will wear in the Super Bowl, hanging in their lockers here, he reacted immediately.

"We're wearing the white uniforms," he shouted to his teammates. "That must mean we're the good guys."

He's anxious to face his moment of truth. But he's not awed by it or by the Colts.

"When the Colts lost to the Browns at midseason" he was saying on the Jets chartered flight last Thursday night, "they didn't get beat by any powerhouse. I'm not going to take what I read about their defense. I'm going to go with what the one-eyed monster shows me." The one-eyed monster is the projector that shows films of the Colts.

"The one-eyed monster doesn't lie," he said. "He shows it like it is." . . .

"When we won our title last Sunday, I said that Daryle Lamonica of the Raiders was a better quarterback than Earl Morrall, and now that's supposed to fire up the Colts.

"I said it and I meant it. Lamonica is better. If the Colts use newspaper clippings to get up for a game, they're in trouble. And if they're football players they know Lamonica can throw better than Morrall. I watch quarterbacks, I watch what they do.

"You put Babe Parilli with Baltimore," he continued, referring to the Jets' backup quarterback, "and Baltimore might have been better. Babe throws better than Morrall.

"There are more teams in the N.F.L. so they should have more good teams, but you put their good teams and our good teams together, or their bad teams and our bad teams together, and it's 50-50, flip a coin. And we've got better quarterbacks in our league—John Hadl, Lamonica, myself and Bob Griese."

Hadl directs the San Diego Chargers, while Griese is with the Miami Dolphins.

"I read where some N.F.L. guy joked about Lamonica and me throwing 100 passes last Sunday," he said. "We threw 97, but what's so terrible about that? How many N.F.L. teams have a quarterback who could complete many passes to their wide receivers. In our league, we throw much more to our wide receivers. . . .

"The best thrower in the N.F.L. is Sonny Jurgensen of the Redskins. I've said that if Jurgensen had been with the Packers or the Colts or the Rams the last few years, he would have won the championship for any of them. But if you put any pro quarter-back on our team, only a few would not be on third string.

"That's my opinion, and I don't care how people value my opinion. But I value it very highly, especially when I'm talking about football."

Primary Source

I Can't Wait Until Tomorrow . . . 'Cause I Get Better-Looking Every Day [excerpt]

SYNOPSIS: Joe Namath, New York Jets quarterback, recalls how he was able to lead his team to an upset victory over the Baltimore Colts in Super Bowl III, focusing on his play calling.

On the bus going to the Orange Bowl in Miami, I thought about the game, thought about specific situations. I didn't exactly daydream, but I could almost visualize certain things happening. I could see Maynard flying down the sidelines, for instance, sprinting beyond the man covering him, breaking into the clear, and I could see me lofting the ball, over the defender, into Maynard's arms, and I could see Maynard scoring. I could see the safety blitz, too. It looked beautiful to me.

In the dressing room, Jeff Snedeker, our trainer, wrapped tape all around my right knee. Then, just as he had for every game for four years, he taped a steel-and-rubber brace to the knee. Personally, I don't think the brace does anything except make it a little more difficult for me to move around, but Weeb thinks it does some good and Jeff goes along with him. I don't want to hurt their feelings.

After Jeff helped me off the table, I walked back into the locker room and listened to Weeb's pregame speech. I don't need a speech to get me up for a big game. I just half-listened. Weeb reminded a few of the guys that the Colts had gotten rid of them and that they now had a chance to get even.

I went out on the field, loose and relaxed. I just had the normal butterflies, just enough inner tension to get the adrenaline flowing good. The way I figured, I didn't have anything to worry about. It was just going to be another triumph for clean living.

The Colts kicked off to us, and on our first play from scrimmage, I called our shift, our left guard moving over between our center and our right guard. I just wanted to let the Colts know right away that we had the shift, that they were going to have to adjust their defenses to us, that we were going to act

and they'd have to react. I just wanted them to realize they weren't playing with children.

I wasn't too surprised by the way the game went. I was a little surprised how well the Colts moved the ball against our defense the first couple of times they got the ball. I watched from the sidelines and I thought, "Well, hell, maybe they're gonna score a touchdown or two." It didn't worry me. It just meant we'd have to score a few more.

I don't think we played a particularly great game, not by our standards. We played pretty much the way we'd played in our better games all year. Of course, any game's a great game when you win, but I know my own performance wasn't anything special. . . .

I can't say enough about how good our guys were in picking up the plays at the line of scrimmage. I mean, it's really a hard thing for them. When I change a play at the line, they've got to drive the play they've been thinking about from their minds and they've got to replace it with a new one and, in a few seconds, they've got to be ready for a different assignment, maybe on a different snap count, maybe in a whole different direction. Our guys didn't bust one play all day, didn't miss a single assignment as far as I could tell, never jumped offsides or anything. Two or three years earlier, if I'd tried calling all those audibles, before we really knew each other, our guys would have been flopping all over the field, getting in each other's way, missing blocks, fouling up everything. . . .

Weeb and some other people said afterward that I called a perfect game, but that's not true. I made a couple of mistakes. I threw one pass that I shouldn't have thrown. In the third quarter, on a third-down-and-long situation, I threw to Pete Lammons on a hook pattern, and Jerry Logan almost intercepted. I should never have released the ball. I was really forcing the pass. But even though I did a bad thing, I did one thing right on the play. I kept the ball outside Lammons. I saw Logan lying in the grass, wanting to go for the ball, so I threw on the far side of Lammons, away from Logan. Well, Logan lunged for the ball and touched it, but he couldn't hold it. If I'd thrown right at Lammons, Logan would have intercepted. He might even have run the ball back for a touchdown. I still don't know why I threw the ball; I should have eaten it. . . .

My only other mistake came in the fourth quarter. When we were leading, 16-0, I ran a play on the first sound. At that stage, when we were trying to use up the clock, I shouldn't have done that. It was

Bubba Smith (78) of the Baltimore Colts attempts to block a pass thrown by New York Jets quarterback Joe Namath during Super Bowl III, Miami, Florida, January 12, 1969. The Jets won the game by a score of 16 to 7. **AP/WIDE WORLD PHOTOS. REPRODUCED BY PERMISSION.**

just plain stupid on my part. But, outside of that and the pass to Lammons, I guess I've got to admit that Weeb was right.

Hell, our whole club came pretty close to being perfect, which didn't surprise me at all. That's the way we play. We don't expect to make any mistakes. Jim Hudson was practically sick after the game because he'd missed a tackle on Tom Matte when

Matte got off a long run right after our touchdown. "I had him, I had him at the line of scrimmage," Hudson said. "I was gonna kill him and I closed my eyes and I missed him. Damn." We'd just won the championship of the whole world, and Hudson was almost sick because he'd missed one tackle.

I don't want to take anything away from the Colts. Taking the world championship is enough.

They're a helluva football team. Matte's a great runner, and they hit hard, and they play clean, tough football. But, just like I'd been saying all along and everybody'd been laughing, the Jets are a great football team, too. People say Sauer and Maynard and Lammons are good, and that's not half enough to describe them. And our defense was just beyond belief. The people who came to the Super Bowl saw a great defensive team, but it wasn't the Colts. . . .

I had some night. I stayed up till the sun rose the next day. Hell, I'd been getting too much sleep all week, anyway. We were on top of the world. Number one. We were Number one. Sometimes, for no reason at all, I just broke out laughing, I felt so good.

On television that night, I watched the replay of the game. Some people were already saying that if we played the Colts again on another day, the result would be different. I watched the game on TV and I saw how conservatively I'd played, how I went for field goals instead of touchdowns, and I guess I had to agree with those people.

On another day, we would have beat Baltimore worse.

Primary Source

"Upset for the Ages" [excerpt]

SYNOPSIS: Writing the day after the New York Jets upset the Baltimore Colts in Super Bowl III, columnist Shirley Povich provides the view of most sportswriters and fans that the game was one of football's greatest upsets.

Miami, Jan. 12—Today, General Custer ambushed Sitting Bull. Men from the moon landed and sent back pictures proving the earth is flat. Russia announced it was disarming as a matter of national policy. There was another little surprise. The New York Jets kicked the bejeebers out of the Baltimore Colts in the Super Bowl. This last truly happened. Honest.

It happened because Joe Namath got protection and shredded the Baltimore defenses like a knife-thrower at work on a good day. Five minutes after the start of the second quarter, the amazing Jets had the Colts playing catch-up football, a task at which the Colts were utterly inexperienced. And in the second half, the Jets poured it on.

They had the Colts, of all teams, in a state of panic, reduced to schoolboyish trick pass plays in an attempt to get on the scoreboard. The Colts went

---

Super Bowl III Scoring and Statistics

New York Jets (16)
Ends—Sauer, Maynard, Lammons, B. Turner, Rademacher, Philbin, Biggs.
Tackles—Hill, Herman, Richardson, Walton, Rochester, Elliott, McAdams.
Guards—Talamini, Rasmussen.
Centers—Schmitt, Crane.
Linebackers—Baker, Atkinson, Grantham, Neidert.
Quarterbacks—Namath, Parilli.
Offensive Backs—Boozer, Snell, Mathis, Smolinski.
Defensive Backs—Sample, Beverly, Hudson, Baird, Christy, D'Amato, Richard, Dockery.
Kickers—J. Turner, Curley Johnson.

Baltimore Colts (7)
Ends—Orr, Richardson, Mackey, Perkins, Hawkins, Mitchell, Bubba Smith, Braase, Michaels.
Tackles—Vogel, Ball, J. Williams, Billy Ray Smith, Miller, Hilton.
Guards—Ressler, Sullivan, Cornelius Johnson.
Centers—Curry, Szymanski.
Linebackers—Curtis, Gaubatz, Shinnick, S. Williams, Porter.
Quarterbacks—Morrall, Unitas.
Offensive Backs—Matte, Hill, Brown, Pearson, Cole.
Defensive Backs—Boyd, Lyles, Logan, Volk, Stukes, Austin.
Kicker—Lee.

New York Jets	0	7	6	3	— 16
Baltimore Colts	0	0	0	7	— 7

N.Y.—Snell, 4, run (Turner, kick).
N.Y.—FG, Turner, 32.
N.Y.—FG, Turner, 30.
N.Y.—FG, Turner, 9.
Balti—Hill, 1, run (Michaels, kick).

Attendance—75,377.

Statistics of the Game

	Jets	Colts
First downs	21	18
Rushing yardage	142	143
Passing yardage	206	181
Return yardage	34	139
Passes	17–29	17–41
Interceptions by	4	0
Punts	4–39	3–44
Fumbles lost	1	1
Yards penalized	28	23

SOURCE: List and Table from "Jets Upset Colts by 16–7 for Title." *The New York Times*, January 13, 1969.

---

into the game as 17½-point favorites and barely escaped a shutout. The final score of 16-7 does not tell the degree in which the Colts lost their cool today in a football upset that belongs to the ages.

So big was the point spread that in the estimate of the oddsmakers it was tantamount to a game of solitaire for the Colts. They had everything with which to win, it seemed, before the game, but their hot hand jumped up and bit them. Toward the finish, it was the Colts depleting their own valuable timeouts in a last desperate effort to stop the merciless Jets and failing here, too. . . .

It began as if the Colts would win by 17½ points, indeed, and more, with Morrall striking John Mackey for 17 yards, Tom Matte getting ten, and Jerry Hill seven on their first three plays. And then, heavens, Lou Michaels missed a field goal from 27 yards, point-blank range for him and incredible on Baltimore television sets. The Colts got another shot at something when they recovered a George Sauer fumble on the Jets' 12, but they blew that one, too, when Randy Beverly picked off a pass by Morrall.

Now it was two awful fluffs by the Colts. In contrast were the Jets. It took them 18 minutes to get into Baltimore territory, but when they did they went all the way. Namath's calls reduced the stunting Baltimore defense to jitters. He hit with his passes and alternately called on his man Snell, who is listed from Ohio State but really is from Mt. Rushmore. Snell got the last four yards by orbiting left end, untouched.

THAT'S THE WAY it ended at the half, 7-0 Jets. Well, the Colts might not win by 19 points, but they were still favorites to win as they came out for the second half which would be theirs. But alas, after the kickoff, the Colts maintained ball-control for only one-half of one play. Tom Matte, of all great ball players, fumbled, under pressure of consecutive hits by Verlon Biggs and Bill Baird of the Jets' defense, and Ralph Baker flopped on the ball for New York.

If the Colts' defeat could be traced to one event, aside from Namath's appearance on the field at the outset, it was that dratted fumble by Matte. To what extent it drained the Colts of momentum can best be judged by later developments. Jim Turner began kicking field goals for the Jets, three of them, and the Colts were behind, 16-0.

Thus did the Jets and the racing clock take the Colts' running game away from them. Now, in the fourth quarter, there was no time for Morrall or Unitas to hand off to their running backs. The Colts' attack was stripped of most of its deception. It must be pass, pass, pass. And they might as well have invited the Jets' defense into the Baltimore huddles. . . .

At the finish, also, the Colts were missing those $15,000 paychecks that are the minimum wage payoffs for Super Bowl winners. They, too, had been intercepted by the thieving Jets, along with those four Baltimore passes the Jets stole today.

Further Resources

BOOKS

Fox, Larry. *Broadway Joe and His Super Jets.* New York: Coward and McCann, 1969.

Hanks, Stephen. *The Game That Changed Pro Football.* Secaucus, N.J.: Card Publishing Group, 1989.

Namath, Joe. *A Matter of Style.* Boston: Little, Brown, 1973.

PERIODICALS

Anderson, Dave. "Jets Upset Colts By 16-7 for Title in the Super Bowl." *The New York Times,* January 13, 1969.

Steadman, John. "Jets Upset Like David over Goliath." *Baltimore News American,* January 13, 1969.

WEBSITES

Didinger, Ray. "Joe Namath." Pro Football Hall of Fame. Available online at http://www.profootballhof.com/players/main page.cfm?cont_id=81309; website home page: http://www.profootballhof.com (accessed March 6, 2003).

Muhammad Ali and the Draft

The Greatest: My Own Story
Autobiography

By: Muhammad Ali, with Richard Durham
Date: 1975
Source: Ali, Muhammad, with Richard Durham. *The Greatest: My Own Story.* New York: Random House, 1975, 156, 165, 167–169, 172–174.
About the Author: Muhammad Ali (1942–) was born Cassius Clay in Louisville, Kentucky. Winning the Olympic Gold Medal in boxing as a light heavyweight in 1960, Clay turned professional and captured the heavyweight title in 1964. Shortly thereafter, he announced his conversion to Islam and took the name Muhammad Ali. In 1967, after being stripped of his title, Ali was convicted of draft evasion, a decision reversed by the U.S. Supreme Court in 1971. Ali regained the heavyweight title in 1974, then again in 1978, before retiring in 1981. Since retirement, Ali has battled a form of Parkinson's disease but keeps a busy schedule of personal appearances.

"The *Black Scholar* Interviews Muhammad Ali"
Interview

By: Muhammad Ali
Date: June 1970
Source: Ali, Muhammad. "The *Black Scholar* Interviews Muhammad Ali." *Black Scholar,* June 1970, 32.

Clay v. U.S.
Supreme Court decision

By: U.S. Supreme Court
Date: June 28, 1971
Source: *Clay v. United States,* 403 U.S. 698 (1971). In the *Supreme Court Reporter,* 91 S.Ct. 2068 (1971), 2068, 2073–2075. ∎

Introduction

The Vietnam War (1964–1975) was the most divisive issue of the 1960s in America, and sports was not immune. Most athletes expressed support for the war, many contributing by visiting Vietnam on United Service Organizations (USO) tours. Muhammad Ali, however, possibly singled out for induction into the armed forces, refused to serve because of his religious beliefs. By being convicted and stripped of his boxing title, Ali paid a large price for his refusal.

Cassius Clay first achieved national recognition after winning the light heavyweight gold medal at the 1960 Olympics in Rome. He turned professional afterward, supported at first by the Louisville business community. Soon, however, Clay was attracted to the beliefs of the Nation of Islam, a strict Moslem sect that advocated racial separation and disdained the mainstream civil rights movement. Among those seen with Clay was the group's best-known figure, Malcolm X. In February 1964, the brash Clay, who delighted in predicting the rounds in which he would stop opponents, unexpectedly won the heavyweight title with a sixth-round technical knockout of Sonny Liston, the reigning champion.

After defeating Liston, Clay publicly proclaimed himself a Black Muslim and announced that his name was now Muhammad Ali. In 1965 and 1966, Ali fought six title defenses, including a controversial first-round knockout rematch with Liston, a pummeling of Floyd Patterson (who persisted in calling him Clay), and several fights in Europe. Meanwhile, Selective Service had reclassified Ali 1-A, meaning that he was eligible to be drafted. He was ordered to report for induction in April 1967. Ali had already publicly stated his opposition to service because of his Islamic faith, adding that he had "no personal quarrel with those Vietcongs."

On April 28, 1967, in Houston, Texas, with press and photographers waiting outside, Ali, after taking the army physical, refused to step forward when called for induction. Barely hours after his act of defiance, his boxing license was lifted by the New York State Athletic Commission, and the heavyweight crown was declared vacant. Three months later, Ali was convicted in federal court of draft evasion and sentenced to five years in prison and a $10,000 fine. For the next four years, his lawyers appealed through the federal courts to the Supreme Court. Meanwhile, Ali was refused a boxing license in any state, and since his freedom was dependent on $5,000 bail, he could not fight outside the country. While antiwar supporters praised Ali, Middle America saw him as a traitor. Most of the sporting press was against him, with the notable exception of sportscaster Howard Cosell, who believed Ali was denied his constitutional right of due process. On June 29, 1971, just over three years after his conviction on draft evasion, the U.S. Supreme Court reversed it, ruling in an 8-0 decision that the Justice Department had misled Selective Service by advising that Muhammad Ali's conscientious objection was neither sincere nor based on religious belief.

Significance

Ironically, by the time the Supreme Court reversed Ali's draft conviction, the Vietnam War was winding down and the draft was being phased out. Ali had triumphed in the High Court but had lost over three years of his boxing career. His exile from boxing had ended in October 1970, when he defeated Jerry Quarry in Atlanta, after Georgia had issued a fight license. He then lost a fifteen-round decision to Joe Frazier, now heavyweight champion, in March 1971—a match considered the "fight of the century."

Although the loss to Frazier showed the effects of being away from the ring for three years, Ali bounced back in 1974, defeating George Foreman in Kinshasa, Zaire, to regain the heavyweight title. Four years later, after losing the crown to Leon Spinks, he won a rematch and the title. His boxing skills deteriorated rapidly after this, and soon after his last fight in 1981 the effects of years in the ring were evident as he developed a form of Parkinson's disease.

Primary Source

The Greatest: My Own Story [excerpt]

SYNOPSIS: Muhammad Ali, in his memoir, recalls his refusals to accept induction into the U.S. Army in Houston, Texas on April 28, asserting his right not to serve because of religious conviction.

The Induction

[Lt. S. Steven] Dunkley glances quickly around the room before reading his prepared statement. He's probably read it hundreds of times before, but now there is special emphasis in his voice. He tries to make sure that each word is clear: "You are about to be inducted into the Armed Forces of the United States, in the Army, the Navy, the Air Force or the Marine Corps, as indicated by the service announced following your name when called. You will take one step forward as your name and service are called and such step will constitute your induction into the Armed Forces indicated."

He pauses, and even though everyone else is watching me, it seems like he and I are the only ones in the room. . . .

The eyes of the senior officer are fixed firmly on me. A jumble of thoughts rush to my mind. . . .

Muhammad Ali (formerly Cassius Clay) outside the draft induction Center in Houston, Texas, on April 28, 1967. ABC Sports commentator Howard Cosell is at left. AP/WIDE WORLD PHOTOS. REPRODUCED BY PERMISSION.

Now I am anxious for him to call me. "Hurry up!" I say to myself. I'm looking straight into his eyes. There's a ripple of movement as some of the people in the room edge closer in anticipation.

"Cassius Clay—Army!"

The room is silent. I stand straight, unmoving. Out of the corner of my eye I see one of the white boys nodding his head at me, and thin smiles flickering across the faces of some of the blacks. It's as if they are secretly happy to see someone stand up against the power that is ordering them away from their homes and families.

The lieutenant stares at me a long while, then lowers his eyes. One of the recruits snickers and he looks up abruptly, his face beet-red, and orders all the other draftees out of the room. They shuffle out quickly, leaving me standing alone.

He calls out again: "Cassius Clay! Will you please step forward and be inducted into the Armed Forces of the United States?"

All is still. He looks around helplessly. Finally, a senior officer with a notebook full of papers walks

to the podium and confers with him a few seconds before coming over to me. He appears to be in his late forties. His hair is streaked with gray and he has a very dignified manner.

"Er, Mr. Clay . . ." he begins. Then, catching himself, "Or Mr. Ali, as you prefer to be called."

"Yes, sir?"

"Would you please follow me to my office? I would like to speak privately with you for a few minutes, if you don't mind."

It's more of an order than a request, but his voice is soft and he speaks politely. I follow him to a pale green room with pictures of Army generals on the walls. He motions me to a chair, but I prefer to stand. He pulls some papers from his notebook and suddenly drops his politeness, getting straight to the point.

"Perhaps you don't realize the gravity of the act you've just committed. Or maybe you do. But it is my duty to point out to you that if this should be your final decision, you will face criminal charges and your penalty could be five years in prison and ten thousand dollars fine. It's the same for you as it would be for any other offender in a similar case. I don't know what influenced you to act this way, but I am authorized to give you an opportunity to reconsider your position. Selective Service regulations require us to give you a second chance."

"Thank you, sir, but I don't need it."

"It is required"—he never stops talking or looking at his notes—"that you go back into the induction room, stand before the podium and receive the call again."

"Sir, why should I go back out there and waste everybody's time—"

"It's the procedure," he cuts in. "I can't tell you what to do or not to do, but we must follow procedure."

I follow him back into the room, and notice that new faces have appeared. More military personnel, a stenographer and a number of men in civilian clothes, who, I learn later, are FBI agents.

A private hands me a note. "This is from your lawyer."

It's a copy of a letter from U.S. Attorney Morton Sussman.

I am authorized to advise you that we are willing to enter into an agreement. If you will submit your client for induction, we will be willing to keep him here in the Houston area until all of your civil remedies are exhausted. Otherwise, he will be under criminal indictment.

. . .

I crumple it up and stuff it into my pocket. One of the men in civilian clothes who has been watching me now turns and walks out the door. The green-eyed officer is still standing behind the rostrum, ready to read the induction statement. This time I'm closer to him. He's less than an arm's-reach away. I can see drops of sweat on his forehead.

"Mr. Cassius Clay," he begins again, "you will please step forward and be inducted into the United States Army."

Again I don't move.

"Cassius Clay—Army," he repeats. He stands in silence, as though he expects me to make a last-minute change. Finally, with hands shaking, he gives me a form to fill out. "Would you please sign this statement and give your reasons for refusing induction?" His voice is trembling.

I sign quickly and walk out into the hallway. The captain who originally ordered me to the room comes over. "Mr. Clay," he says with a tone of respect that surprises me, "I'll escort you downstairs."

When we reach the bottom of the steps, the television cameramen who had been held up by the guards focus their lights on us, while a platoon of military police scuffle to keep them behind a rope that blocks the end of the corridor.

"Muhammad," a reporter yells, "did you take the step? Are you in the Army?"

"Can we just have a minute, Champ?" another shouts. "What did you do? Can you just tell us yes or no?"

I keep walking with the captain, who leads me to a room where my lawyers are waiting. "You are free to go now," he tells us. "You will be contacted later by the United States Attorney's office."

I step outside and a huge crowd of press people rush toward me, pushing and shoving each other and snapping away at me with their cameras. Writers from two French newspapers and one from London throw me a barrage of questions, but I feel too full to say anything. Covington gives them copies of a statement I wrote for them before I left Chicago. In it I cite my ministry and my personal convictions as reasons for refusing to take the step, adding that "I strongly object to the fact that so many newspapers have given the American public and the world the impression that I have only two alternatives in taking this stand—

either I go to jail or go into the Army. There is another alternative, and that is justice."

Primary Source

"The *Black Scholar* Interviews Muhammad Ali" [excerpt]

SYNOPSIS: Muhammad Ali, in a *Black Scholar* magazine interview, answers a question about why he refused induction into the U.S. Army in 1967 by reading a poem which he said commemorated the event.

Black Scholar: The heavyweight championship has always meant a lot to the champion's people—especially in the case of oppressed black Americans. But you have added a new dimension to the role of a champion. You fight for us both outside and inside the ring. What made you take a revolutionary stand against the war at the risk of your title in the ring and even imprisonment?

Ali: What's wrong with me going to jail for something I believe in? Boys are dying in Vietnam for something they don't believe.

I met two black soldiers a while back in an airport. They said: "Champ, it takes a lot of guts to do what you're doing." I told them: "Brothers, you just don't know. If you knew where you were going now, if you knew your chances of coming out with no arm or no eye, fighting those people in their own land, fighting Asian brothers, you got to shoot them, they never lynched you, never called you nigger, never put dogs on you, never shot your leaders. You've got to shoot your "enemies" (they call them) and as soon as you get home you won't be able to find a job. Going to jail for a few years is nothing compared to that."

We've gone too far to turn around. They've got to go on and either free me or put me in jail, because I'm going to go on just like I am, taking my stand. If I have to go to jail, if I have to die. I'm ready.

People are always asking me what I think about the draft. I wrote a little poem on it. I said:

Hell no,
I ain't going to go.
Clean out my cell
And take my tail
To jail
Without bail
Because it's better there eating,
Watching television fed
Than in Vietnam with your white folks dead.

Primary Source

Clay v. U.S. [excerpt]

SYNOPSIS: The U.S. Supreme Court, in a unanimous decision in June 1971, declared that Muhammad Ali was denied due process by the federal government in considering his refusal to serve in the Army in Vietnam for reasons of religious conviction. The excerpt gives an overview of the decision and portions of a concurrence by Justice William O. Douglas. The case was argued on April 19, 1971, and decided on June 28, 1971.

Defendant was convicted in the United States District Court for the Southern District of Texas for willful refusal to submit to induction into the armed forces. The Court of Appeals, 397 F.2d 901, affirmed. On petition for writ of certiorari, the Supreme Court, 394 U.S. 310, 89 S.Ct. 1163, 22 L.Ed.2d 297, vacated judgment and remanded. On appeal after remand, the Court of Appeals, 430 F.2d 165, affirmed and certiorari was granted. The Supreme Court held that where denial of registrant's appeal seeking conscientious objector status was based on recommendation of Department of Justice to Appeal Board that registrant did not qualify as conscientious objector in that he objected only to certain types of war in certain circumstances and objections rested on grounds primarily political and racial and he had not consistently manifested his conscientious-objector claim, and government conceded that first two grounds were not valid and the third ground erroneously advised that Board should disregard hearing officer's finding of sincerity because of circumstances and timing of registrant's claim, induction notice was grounded upon erroneous denial of conscientious objector claim and was invalid.

Reversed.

Mr. Justice Douglas and Mr. Justice Harlan filed concurring opinions.

Mr. Justice Marshall took no part in the consideration or decision of the case. . . .

Mr. Justice Douglas, concurring.

I would reverse this judgment of conviction and set the petitioner free.

In *Sicurella v. United States*, 348 U.S. 385, 75 S.Ct. 403, 99 L.Ed. 436, the wars that the applicant would fight were not "carnal" but those "in defense of Kingdom interests." *Id.,* at 389, 75 S.Ct., at 405. Since it was impossible to determine on exactly which ground the Appeal Board had based its decision, we reversed the decision sustaining the judgment of conviction. We said: "It is difficult for us to believe that the Congress had in mind this type of activity when it said the thrust of conscientious objection must go to 'participation in war in any form.'" *Id.,* at 390, 75 S.Ct., at 405.

In the present case there is no line between "carnal" war and "spiritual" or symbolic wars. Those who know the history of the Mediterranean littoral know that the *jihad* of the Moslem was a bloody war. . . .

The case of Clay is somewhat different, though analogous. While there are some bits of evidence showing conscientious objection to the Vietnam conflict, the basic objection was based on the teachings of his religion. He testified that he was

> sincere in every bit of what the Holy Qur'an and the teachings of the Honorable Elijah Muhammad tell us and it is that we are not to participate in wars on the side of nobody who—on the side of non believers, and this is a Christian country and this is not a Muslim country, and the Government and the history and the facts shows that every move toward the Honorable Elijah Muhammad is made to distort and is made to ridicule him and is made to condemn him and the Government has admitted that the police of Los Angeles were wrong about attacking and killing our brothers and sisters and they were wrong in Newark, New Jersey, and they were wrong in Louisiana, and the outright, every day oppressors and enemies are the people as a whole, the whites of this nation. So, we are not, according to the Holy Qur'an, to even as much as aid in passing a cup of water to the—even a wounded. I mean, this is in the Holy Qur'an, and as I said earlier, this is not me talking to get the draft board—or to dodge nothing. This is there before I was borned and it will be there when I'm dead but we believe in not only that part of it, but all of it.

At another point he testified:

> [T]he Holy Qur'an do teach us that we do not take part of—in any part of war unless declared by Allah himself, or unless it's an Islamic World War, or a Holy War, and it goes as far—the Holy Qur'an is talking still, and saying we are not to even as much as aid the infidels or the nonbelievers in Islam, even to as much as handing them a cup of water during battle.

> So, this is the teaching of the Holy Qur'an before I was born, and the Qur'an, we follow not only that part of it, but every part.

The Koran defines *jihad* as an injunction to the believers to war against nonbelievers:

> O ye who believe! Shall I guide you to a gainful trade which will save you from painful punishment? Believe in Allah and His Apostle and

carry on warfare (*jihad*) in the path of Allah with your possessions and your persons. That is better for you. If ye have knowledge, He will forgive your sins, and will place you in the Gardens beneath which the streams flow, and in fine houses in the Gardens of Eden: that is the great gain." M. Khadduri, War and Peace in the Law of Islam 55–56 (1955). . . .

War is not the exclusive type of *jihad*; there is action by the believer's heart, by his tongue, by his hands, as well as by the sword. War and Peace in the Law of Islam 56. As respects the military aspects it is written:

> The *jihad,* in other words, is a sanction against polytheism and must be suffered by all non-Muslims who reject Islam, or, in the case of the dhimmis (Scripturaries), refuse to pay the poll tax. The *jihad,* therefore, may be defined as the litigation between Islam and polytheism; it is also a form of punishment to be inflicted upon Islam's enemies and the renegades from the faith. Thus is Islam, as in Western Christendom, the *jihad* is the *bellum justum. Id.,* 59.

The *jihad* is the Moslem's counterpart of the "just" war as it has been known in the West. Neither Clay nor Negre should be subject to punishment because he will not renounce the "truth" of the teaching of his respective church that wars indeed may exist which are just wars in which a Moslem or Catholic has a respective duty to participate.

What Clay's testimony adds up to is that he believes only in war as sanctioned by the Koran, that is to say, a religious war against nonbelievers. All other wars are unjust.

That is a matter of belief, of conscience, of religious principle. Both Clay and Negre were "by reason of religious training and belief" conscientiously opposed to participation in war of the character proscribed by their respective religions. That belief is a matter of conscience protected by the First Amendment which Congress has no power to qualify or dilute as it did in § 6(j) of the Military Selective Service Act of 1967, 50 U.S.C.-App. § 456(j) (1964 ed., Supp. V) when it restricted the exemption to those "conscientiously opposed to participation in war in any form." For the reasons I stated in *Negre* and in *Gillette v. United States,* 401 U.S. 437, 463 and 470, 91 S.Ct. 828, 843 and 846, 28 L.Ed.2d 168, that construction puts Clay in a class honored by the First Amendment, even though those schooled in a different conception of "just" wars may find it quite irrational.

I would reverse the judgment below.

Further Resources

BOOKS

Bingham, Howard, and Max Wallace. *Muhammad Ali's Greatest Fight: Cassius Clay vs. the United States of America.* New York: M. Evans, 2000.

Hauser, Thomas. *Muhammad Ali: His Life and Times.* New York: Simon and Schuster, 1991.

Roberts, James B., and Alexander G. Skutt. *The Boxing Register: International Boxing Hall of Fame Official Record Book,* 2d ed. Ithaca, N.Y.: McBooks Press, 1999.

PERIODICALS

Lipsyte, Robert. "Clay Refuses Army Oath, Stripped of Boxing Crown." *The New York Times,* April 29, 1967.

Rosenbaum, David E. "Ali Wins Draft Case Appeal." *The New York Times,* June 30, 1971.

Wilt Chamberlain's One Hundred Point Game

Wilt

Autobiography

By: Wilt Chamberlain and David Shaw

Date: 1973

Source: Chamberlain, Wilt, and David Shaw. *Wilt: Just Like Any Other 7-Foot Black Millionaire Who Lives Next Door.* New York: Macmillan, 1973, 134–137.

About the Author: Wilt Chamberlain (1936–1999) was born in Philadelphia, Pennsylvania. At the University of Kansas, Chamberlain was an All-American basketball player, but he left college early to tour with the Harlem Globetrotters. Joining the Philadelphia Warriors in 1959, he immediately made an impact on the National Basketball Association (NBA), leading the league in scoring and rebounding numerous times. He won two NBA championships before ending his fourteen-season career with the Los Angeles Lakers in 1973.

Tall Tales

Interviews

By: Wilt Chamberlain, Harvey Pollack, Pete D'Ambrosio, Frank McGuire, Tom Meschery, Al Attles, and Richie Guerin

Date: 1992

Source: Pluto, Terry. *Tall Tales: The Glory Years of the NBA, in the Words of the Men Who Played, Coached, and Built Pro Basketball.* New York: Simon and Schuster, 1992, 219–224.

About the Author: Terry Pluto (1955–) was born in Cleveland, Ohio. After graduating from Cleveland State University, he worked as a sportswriter for various newspapers before returning to Ohio as baseball writer for the *Cleveland Plain Dealer,* then the *Akron Beacon-Journal.* Pluto has written several books, primarily on baseball and basketball. ∎

Introduction

At seven foot one, Wilt Chamberlain was an imposing presence on the court from the time he entered the NBA in 1959. Soon, he was establishing marks for scoring points, as in his third season, 1961–1962, when he averaged a never-to-be-equaled 50.4 points a game. In a December 1961 game, Chamberlain scored seventy-eight points, establishing a new league mark. Afterwards, Frank McGuire, Chamberlain's coach, commented, "He'll get 100 points someday."

On March 2, 1962, the Philadelphia Warriors played the New York Knicks in Hershey, Pennsylvania, where the Warriors played a few games each year. That day, Chamberlain drove from New York to Philadelphia and caught the team bus to Hershey. Before the game, Wilt scored big on a pinball machine in the arena lobby. When the game began, he got hot quickly, scoring twenty-three points in the first quarter—going nine for nine from the foul line—as the Warriors jumped out to an early lead. Hitting on dunks, finger rolls (a Chamberlain specialty), and even fadeaway jump shots, Chamberlain added eighteen in the second quarter for forty-one, as the Warriors led 79-68 at halftime. The announced attendance at the Hershey arena was only 4,124.

The Knicks used several players, all in vain, to try and stop Chamberlain, but he still scored twenty-eight points in the third quarter, for sixty-nine in the game. In the fourth quarter, the Knicks, in an attempt keep Chamberlain from scoring, tried to use up the full twenty-four-second clock to prevent the Warriors—and Wilt—from getting the ball. The Warriors would take the ball out of bounds and lob it high to Chamberlain up the court. Meanwhile, the crowd, aware of Chamberlain's point total (provided by the public address announcer), started chanting, "Give the ball to Wilt." With eight minutes remaining, Chamberlain broke his scoring mark of seventy-eight points. At this point, the Knicks began fouling the other Warriors players to prevent Chamberlain from scoring. The Warriors retaliated by immediately fouling Knicks so Chamberlain could get the ball back. With 1:19 left, Chamberlain dunked the ball for his ninety-seventh and ninety-eighth points, then missed three easy scoring attempts. With less than fifty seconds to play, teammate Joe Ruklick passed the ball to Chamberlain, who dunked it (although some witnesses remember it was "dropped" in) for his ninety-ninth and one hundredth points.

Significance

After Chamberlain's hundredth point, the crowd ran onto the court, and the referees ended the contest with the Warriors winning 169 to 147, which set a league mark for the most combined points in a game. Chamberlain scored his one hundred points on thirty-six of sixty-three

shots, and for Wilt, an amazing twenty-eight of thirty-two foul shots. He scored fifty-nine second-half points, including thirty-one in the fourth quarter, when teammates were passing him the ball on every play.

The 100-point game passed into sports legend. The point total has never been approached, and the seventy-eight-point game earlier that season is still second. Although just over four thousand attended the game, Chamberlain later said that at least ten thousand people over the years told him they were there. For years, Chamberlain was sensitive about the game, saying it demeaned his other accomplishments: a 30.1 career scoring average, 31,419 total points, and a 22.9 rebounding average, including fifty-five in a game against Boston and rival Bill Russell. As time passed, however, Chamberlain became more proud of the one hundred points. He won two NBA championships: with the Philadelphia 76ers in 1967 and the Los Angeles Lakers in 1972. After retirement, Chamberlain coached San Diego in the American Basketball Association, was an elite volleyball player, and even sponsored a women's track team, along with other interests. He died of a heart ailment in October 1999 at age sixty-three.

Primary Source

Wilt [excerpt]

SYNOPSIS: In his autobiography, NBA star Wilt Chamberlain remembers his 100-point game in 1962 with less fondness than teammates and sportswriters. He is more proud of other accomplishments, such as his fifty-five-rebound game against Bill Russell and the Boston Celtics.

Most basketball fans know all about that game, but hardly anyone knows about the events that led up to it. I was living in New York part-time then, and commuting to Philadelphia, and I had a date with a fine young lady in New York the night before the game. . . . I drove her back to her place in Queens, then caught an 8 A.M. train for Philadelphia—eating and talking the whole way, instead of sleeping. When I got to Philly, I met some friends who wanted to go to lunch. By the time we finished, it was almost time to catch the team bus to Hershey for the game that night.

Before I could stumble off to my room in Hershey for a few winks, I came across Eddie Gottlieb and Ike Richman, playing a pinball-type machine where you shoot a rifle at targets that light up. Ike, who later became one of the closest friends I've ever had, asked me if I was any good at the game. Naturally, I said I was. He gave me the rifle. Well, Ike and Eddie had been shooting about 300 or 400 points, and right away, I hit 900. Ike says, "Wilt, I bet you $2 you can't get 1,100." I took the bet, hit 1,125 and offered to double the bet on 1,300. Ike agreed. I hit 1,430.

What I didn't know was that Ike had already asked the doorman, who'd been there 15 or 20 years, what the highest score ever was, and he'd said 1,800. Ike was just setting me up and sucking me in—sandbagging me. When I won the second bet, he offered to bet me dinner and a good bottle of wine that I couldn't hit 1,700. I said, "Ike, I'll go you one better. The loser has to pay for the winner *and* the winner's date—and I'll get 1,800." Old Ike could barely conceal his smile. He thought he had me dead.

I got 2,040.

I guess that should've tipped me off about what to expect in the game that night. The first thing that happens is Coach McGuire comes over to me in the dressing room, and shows me two New York newspapers with quotes from some of the Knicks about how they're going to run me ragged because they "know" I'm pretty slow and don't have much stamina. Coach McGuire knows that's ridiculous, but he doesn't know I haven't had any sleep yet, so he just grins slyly and says, "Let's run 'em tonight, Wilt."

We ran, all right—and ran and ran and ran. I hit my first six jump shots from the outside, and at the end of the first quarter, we were ahead, 42-26, and I had 23 points—including nine straight free throws. At the half, I was 14 of 26 from the field and 13 of 14 from the line, and I had 41 points. The record was 78—I'd set it in December—and it looked like I had a good chance to break it. When I got 28 more points in the third quarter, the fans really started screaming. I broke the record early in the fourth quarter, and now the fans were going crazy. They were chanting "100! 100! 100!" I thought they were nuts. Whoever heard of scoring 100 points in an NBA game? But my teammates wanted me to do it, too. They started feeding me the ball even when they were wide open. The Knicks did everything they could to stop me—including holding the ball almost the full 24 seconds every time they got it late in the game. One of the Knicks, Willie Naulls, later told me their coach, Eddie Donovan, had called time out, and given them explicit orders to freeze the ball and pass up good shots so I couldn't rebound and score and embarrass them. I finally got my 100 points, on a dunk, with just 42 seconds left in the game, and the fans came pouring out of the stands and mobbed me.

Wilt Chamberlain holds a sign indicating the number of points he scored against the New York Knickerbockers on March 2, 1962. More than thirty years later, the 100-point game has not yet even been approached by another player. **AP/WIDE WORLD PHOTOS. REPRODUCED BY PERMISSION.**

There wasn't a very big crowd there that night—only 4,124—but in the 11 years since then, I'll bet I've had at least 20,000 fans tell me they saw me score the 100. I've also heard a lot of them use that game as "the ideal example of why Wilt's a loser; he got 100 points and his team lost, as usual." But we didn't lose. We won easily, 169–147.

A lot of people ask me if that 100-point game was my biggest thrill in sports. Frankly, it isn't even close to the top—for several reasons. In the first place, I've always thought field goal percentage was more important than total points; anyone can get hot and have a big game if he shoots often enough. Hell, I'm the world's worst foul-shooter, and I hit 28 of 32 free throws that night—87.5 percent. . . .

Besides, I've always thought rebounding was more important than scoring. In the NBA, a lot of guys can score. But someone has to get the ball for them first, and there's not nearly as many great rebounders as there are great scorers. That's why I'm a lot prouder of my NBA record of 55 rebounds in one game than I am of the 100 points. I'm also prouder of being the all-time NBA rebound leader than of being the all-time top scorer.

But I'd be lying if I didn't say I enjoyed scoring a lot of points. It was tremendously satisfying to the ego, and in that context, I'd have to say my greatest personal satisfaction was averaging 50.4 points a game that third year. Scoring 100 points in one game is a freak, but averaging 50 for a whole year is something else again. That's incredible consistency. I mean, no one had ever averaged over 30 until I came into the league. Fifty? That meant any time I hit 30 points in a game, it was a "bad" night; I'd have to get 70 the next night just to make up for it and stay even.

Primary Source

Tall Tales [excerpt]

SYNOPSIS: Terry Pluto, a sportswriter, collected the recollections of Philadelphia Warriors teammates and officials, New York Knicks opponents, and game officials of Wilt Chamberlain's 100-point game in Hershey, Pennsylvania on March 2, 1962. Below are parts of interviews with Harvey Pollack, the Warriors Public Relations Director; Pete D'Ambrosio, a referee; Frank McGuire, the Warriors coach; Tom Meschery and Al Attles, teammates of Chamberlain's; and Richie Guerin, a player for the Knicks.

Wilt Chamberlain: What I like best about the 100-point game is that there is no videotape or film of it. There is just a scratchy radio tape. The game is shrouded in myth and mystery, and over the years people have been able to embellish it without facts getting in the way. As I've traveled the world, I've probably had 10,000 people tell me that they saw my 100-point game at Madison Square Garden. Well, the game was in Hershey and there were about 4,000 [actually 4,124] there. But that's fine. I have memories of the game and so do they, and over the years the memories get better. It's like your first girlfriend—the picture you have in your head is always better than how she looked in real life.

Harvey Pollack: It is a mythic game because Wilt scored exactly 100, no more, no less. And the game ended after Wilt scored his 100th point even though there were 46 seconds left on the clock. Those things will never happen again.

Pete D'Ambrosio: I officiated that game with Willie Smith and there was nothing special about it.

The season was almost over. The playoff spots had been decided. The only reason it was played was because it was on the schedule. The last thing anyone expected was basketball history.

Harvey Pollack: This was supposed to be the classic NBA nonevent. Hardly any New York reporters were there. The biggest paper in Philadelphia—the *Inquirer*—didn't even send a reporter. I was the public relations man for the Philadelphia Warriors and I also was covering the game for the *Inquirer,* Associated Press and United Press International. I also was keeping the stats and my son sat next to me at courtside, keeping the running play-by-play.

. . .

Frank McGuire: Eddie Donovan was the coach of the Knicks and he is a special friend of mine. I had said earlier in the season, "Just you wait, Wilt is going to get 100 one of these nights." But that was because Wilt was the greatest offensive force this game has ever seen. Sixty, 70 points was common for him. We did not set out to get Wilt the 100.

Tom Meschery: Hershey had one of those dreary, old, dungeonlike arenas with overlapping rafters. Because the Hershey Company was there, the whole town smelled like fresh chocolate. We had trained in Hershey, so we were acquainted with the gym. Right away, I knew Wilt was in for a big night because he was making all of his free throws.

Wilt Chamberlain: To me, the 100-point game was inevitable that season. I was averaging 50 points. I had 78 in a game [three months earlier]. In high school, I once scored 90 [in 32 minutes] and shot 36-for-41. I always scored a lot, so I figured that 100 would come. But I certainly did not decide to go for it that night in Hershey. Even by halftime, I had 41 and it wasn't that big a deal. I had scored 40 in a half before.

Al Attles: Wilt just kept scoring. He had 69 after three quarters. Dave Zinkoff was doing the PA and after every basket Wilt scored in the fourth quarter, he'd announce, "That's 82 for Wilt." So everyone in the game knew the situation and it just evolved to the point where we wanted Wilt to score 100.

Wilt Chamberlain: When I got into the 80s, I heard the fans yelling for 100. I thought, "Man, these people are tough. Eighty isn't good enough. I'm tired. I've got 80 points and no one has ever scored 80." At one point, I said to Al Attles, "I got 80, what's the difference between 80 and 100?" But the guys kept feeding me the ball.

Tom Meschery: By the fourth quarter, the Knicks were waiting until the 24-second clock was about to expire before they shot. When we had the ball, they were fouling everyone except Wilt so he wouldn't get 100. So we would take the ball out-of-bounds and throw high lobs directly to Wilt near the basket. When Wilt wanted the ball, he was big enough and strong enough to go get it. Guys were hanging on his back, and he was still catching the pass and scoring. I knew it was going to happen when with about five minutes left Wilt dunked one and nearly threw two New York players into the basket with the ball, and Dave Zinkoff yelled over the PA, "Dipper Dunk for 86!"

Richie Guerin: They can complain about us fouling people, but Frank McGuire sent some subs into the game and they were fouling us immediately to get the ball back and give Wilt more chances.

Pete D'Ambrosio: The game was a real pain in the neck to call. The last three minutes of game time took about 20 minutes. The Knicks were jumping on guys just to keep the ball away from Wilt. Then New York would get the ball, and Philly would foul. . . .

Marv Albert: The irony is that Darrall Imhoff's strength as a player was his defense, but he is forever the butt of the joke that "Here's the guy who held Wilt to 100 points," even though he wasn't on the court when it happened. . . .

Harvey Pollack: Here is exactly what happened for the 100th point. Wilt took a shot and missed. It rebounded out to Joe Ruklick. Even this has been disputed, because the NBA said it was Paul Arizin, but I called them and they changed it.

Ruklick got the ball, passed it to Wilt and Wilt made a layup, not a dunk as some people reported.

The ball went through the rim with 46 seconds left, the fans rushed on the court and the game ended right there.

Frank McGuire: After he scored 100, Wilt was trying to get off the court and there were four lit-

tle kids hanging on to his shoulders and waist. It was as if he were giving them a piggyback ride.

Al Attles: After the game, Wilt was in the dressing room and he wasn't celebrating like the rest of us.

I said, "Wilt, what's the matter."

He said, "I never thought I'd take 60 shots in a game."

I said, "But you made 36—that's better than 50 percent."

He said, "But Al—63 shots, Al."

Then he just shook his head.

Frank McGuire: I do think we were more excited about the game than Wilt was. I do recall him sitting in that little locker room—it was nothing more than a high school dressing room with one long wooden bench in the middle where everyone sat. Wilt was holding the stat sheet, sweat pouring off his face, just staring at it.

Harvey Pollack: The one famous picture from that game is Wilt in the dressing room holding up a little sign that said "100." The photographers wanted something special and I just grabbed a piece of paper, wrote 100 on it, Wilt held it up and it went all over the country.

Wilt Chamberlain: The 100-point game will never be as important to me as it is to some other people. That's because I'm embarrassed by it. After I got into the 80s, I pushed for 100 and it destroyed the game because I took shots that I normally never would. I was not real fluid. I mean, 63 shots? You take that many shots on the playground and no one ever wants you on their team again. I never considered myself a gunner. I led leagues in scoring because I also led them in field goal percentage. I've had many better games than this one, games where I scored 50–60 and shot 75 percent. . . .

Richie Guerin: . . . But that game was not played as it should have been played. The second half was a travesty. I don't care what the Philly people say, I'm convinced that during the half they decided to get Wilt 100. He took nearly every shot. In the normal flow, Wilt would have scored 80–85 points, which is mind-boggling when you think about it. I'm sorry, this may be basketball history but I always felt very bad about that game. I got so sick of it that I intentionally fouled out.

Alex Hannum: I think the only guy who feels a stigma from that game is Richie Guerin. He is a combative ex-marine who never took any crap from anybody, and having Wilt score 100 against his team had to hurt. But there was no stigma against him or the Knicks. The rest of us in the league knew that Wilt was going to score 100; it just happened that night. . . .

Wilt Chamberlain: I have to admit that as the years have passed, I like the 100-point game more than I did at the time. To me, averaging 50 points in a season or being the only center in NBA history to lead the league in assists are more indicative of the kind of player I was. But the 100-point night . . . The good thing is that everyone has their stories and I can't disagree with many of them because I don't even know how I scored the last basket. It has reached fabled proportion, almost like a Paul Bunyan story, and it's nice to be a part of a fable.

Further Resources

BOOKS

Chamberlain, Wilt. *A View From Above.* New York: Villiard Books, 1991.

Libby, Bill. *Goliath: The Wilt Chamberlain Story.* New York: Dodd, Mead, 1977.

Nadel, Eric. *The Night Wilt Scored 100: Tales From Basketball's Past.* Dallas: Taylor, 1990.

PERIODICALS

"Chamberlain Scores 100 Points." *The New York Times,* March 3, 1962.

Litsky, Frank. "Wilt Chamberlain Is Dead at 63, Dominated Basketball in the 1960's." *The New York Times,* October 13, 1999.

WEBSITES

Naismith Memorial Basketball Hall of Fame. "Wilt Chamberlain." Available online at http://www.hoophall.com/hallof famers/Chamberlain.htm; website home page: http://www .hoophall.com (accessed March 5, 2003).

UCLA Basketball

Giant Steps
Autobiography

By: Kareem Abdul-Jabbar and Peter Knobler
Date: 1983

Source: Abdul-Jabbar, Kareem, and Peter Knobler. *Giant Steps.* New York: Bantam, 1983, 108–109, 144–146, 162–163.

About the Author: Kareem Abdul-Jabbar (1947–) was born Lewis Alcindor in New York City. At UCLA, Alcindor was a member of three NCAA basketball championship teams and named All-American each year. In 1969, he signed with the National Basketball Association's Milwaukee Bucks and led them to the championship in his second season. Off the court, he converted to Islam and took the name Kareem Abdul-Jabbar. Traded to the Los Angeles Lakers in 1975, he won five more NBA championships and six MVP awards. He retired in 1989 as the all-time leader in points scored and games played.

They Call Me Coach
Autobiography

By: John Wooden with Jack Tobin
Date: 1988

Source: Wooden, John, with Jack Tobin. *They Call Me Coach.* Chicago: Contemporary Books, 1988, 138, 139, 140, 142, 143, 145–148, 150–152, 154.

About the Author: John Wooden (1910–) was born in Hall, Indiana. After an All-American basketball career at Purdue University, Wooden coached high school basketball in Indiana and Kentucky, winning 84 percent of his games. He became coach at Indiana State University, then quickly switched to UCLA in 1948. Winning his first NCAA title in 1964, Wooden coached the Bruins to nine more championships through 1975, including seven straight. After his final championship, he retired with 885 total coaching victories at the college and high school levels.

"He Dared Stand Alone"
Newspaper article

By: Jim Murray
Date: April 4, 1975

Source: Murray, Jim. "He Dared Stand Alone." *Los Angeles Times,* April 4, 1975. Reprinted in Murray, Jim. *The Jim Murray Collection.* Dallas: Taylor, 1988, 141.

About the Author: Jim Murray (1919–1998) was born in Hartford, Connecticut. After graduating from Trinity College, he was a reporter for various newspapers, as well as *Time* magazine and *Sports Illustrated.* In 1961, he became a sports columnist for the *Los Angeles Times,* winning a Pulitzer Prize in 1990 and remaining there until his death. ∎

Introduction

The seeds of the UCLA basketball dynasty of the 1960s and 1970s were planted in rural Indiana and New York City. John Wooden, an Indiana native, was an All-American guard at Purdue University. After coaching high school basketball, he moved to the college ranks at Indiana State University, where, in his first season, he refused a National Association of Intercollegiate Athletics (NAIA) tournament bid because of their whites-only policy and his team had an African American player. In 1948, he was offered the coaching position at both the University of Minnesota and UCLA. When Minnesota telephoned its decision two hours late because of a snowstorm, Wooden had already reluctantly accepted the UCLA job. Although he won twenty-two games his first season, Wooden's first dozen or more years at UCLA were not altogether successful. The team played in an undersized arena, and Wooden's disciplined ways sometimes alienated talented players. By the early 1960s, changes came to UCLA. A new, larger arena was built, and better players, including promising African American players, were recruited.

In 1964, with a small and unheralded lineup, Wooden's Bruins won their first NCAA championship. After repeating as champions the next season, UCLA failed to win in 1966. But the future was bright for Wooden as he brought to UCLA a seven-foot, two-inch New York City high school legend: Lewis Alcindor. Alcindor played at Power Memorial Academy, where he dominated New York basketball. Over two hundred colleges and universities attempted to recruit him, with Wooden and UCLA winning out. After a dominant freshman year—first year players were then ineligible for the varsity—including a victory over the varsity squad, Alcindor was ready for bigger achievements.

Wooden and Alcindor were an unlikely pair: the midwestern coach with old-fashioned, disciplined ways, and the aloof, enigmatic New York youngster who embraced Islam and black activism. But they were a winning combination, unparalleled in college basketball history. As a sophomore, Alcindor led the Bruins to an undefeated season and their third title. The next season, 1967–1968, despite losing to the University of Houston in a midseason classic game at the Astrodome—before over thirty thousand spectators and the first prime-time TV audience for college basketball—Alcindor won his second championship, defeating North Carolina, after a revenge victory over Houston. As a senior, Alcindor and the Bruins roared through the regular season, then captured a third consecutive NCAA championship, easily defeating Purdue behind the big center's thirty-seven points.

Significance

In three seasons at UCLA, Alcindor was a first-team All-American three straight seasons, averaging 26.4 points a game, to go along with consecutive NCAA championships. Alcindor was one of those rare players who changed basketball, as dunking was outlawed by the NCAA at the time he arrived in college, presumably to counter his height advantage. Wooden had now coached five NCAA championships in six seasons, but

greater achievements awaited both him and his star player.

With Alcindor's graduation, Wooden's legendary status was only beginning. Now able to attract quality players to UCLA, his teams continued winning. They defeated Jacksonville in 1970 and Villanova in 1971. Wooden then recruited six-foot, eleven-inch Bill Walton, who became as dominant a player as Alcindor had been, and UCLA won championships in 1972 and 1973. UCLA's streak of seven consecutive titles ended in 1974, as the Bruins lost in the semifinals to North Carolina State. In 1975, Wooden won his final championship, defeating a Louisville team coached by his former assistant, Denny Crum. He retired after twenty-seven seasons at UCLA, compiling a 620-147 record and ten NCAA titles, an accomplishment unlikely to be topped.

Alcindor's college career made him the top choice in the 1969 professional draft by the NBA's Milwaukee Bucks and American Basketball Association's New York Nets. He chose the Bucks, signing for one million dollars. He helped the Bucks win the NBA championship his second season. In 1975, Alcindor, now Kareem Abdul-Jabbar after his conversion to Islam, was traded to the Los Angeles Lakers, where he was joined in 1979 by another college legend, Earvin "Magic" Johnson. In the 1980s, Abdul-Jabbar, who would retire as the all-time leader in points scored and games played, teamed with Johnson to lead the Lakers to five championships before his retirement in 1989.

Primary Source

Giant Steps [excerpt]

SYNOPSIS: In his autobiography, Kareem Abdul-Jabbar, formerly Lewis Alcindor, recalls how he decided, despite being a New Yorker, to go west to Los Angeles and play basketball at UCLA. He also gives his impressions of coach John Wooden.

Most of all, what UCLA offered was John Wooden. Coach Wooden's office was about the size of a walk-in closet. I was brought in, and there was this very quaint-looking midwesterner, gray hair with a part almost in the middle of his head, glasses on. I'd heard a lot about this man and his basketball wisdom, but he surely did look like he belonged in a one-room schoolhouse. He stood up, shook my hand, and invited me to sit down.

He was quiet, which was a relief because so was I. I am a great believer in my own snap judgments, and I am quick to find major fault in minor offenses, particularly in strangers who need me, but

I found myself liking Mr. Wooden right away. He was calm, in no hurry to impress me with his knowledge or his power. He could have made me cool my heels, or jumped up and been my buddy, but he clearly worked on his own terms, and I appreciated that in the first few moments we met. His suit jacket was hanging from a peg on the wall, and he was working in shirt-sleeves, casual but not far from decorum. He called me Lewis, and that decision endeared him to me even more; it was at once formal, my full name—We are gentlemen here—and respectful. I was no baby Lewie. Lewis. I liked that.

There was a plainspokenness to Mr. Wooden, a distance from cynicism that my own teenage idealism responded to, and rather than gloss over the possible conflicts that might dissuade a recruit from deciding on the school, he told me what they expected from people at UCLA.

"We expect our boys to work hard and do well with their schoolwork," he told me in his flat yet not uninviting midwestern twang, "and I know you do have good grades so that should not be a problem for you. We expect you to be at practice on time and work hard while you're there. We do not expect our boys to present any disciplinary problems, but, again, we know you're not that kind of young man, and I don't expect you will have any difficulty here at UCLA.

"You've seen the campus. Do you have any questions?"

"I like the campus very much," I told him, "and I am very impressed with UCLA's basketball program."

"That's all very good," Coach Wooden said, "but I am impressed by your grades. You could do very well here as a student, whether you were an athlete or not. That is important. We work very hard to have our boys get through and earn their degrees. I hope all my student-athletes can achieve that. It is to both our benefits; your being a good student will keep you eligible to play in our basketball program, and your degree will be of value to you for the rest of your life."

I made a point of talking with all the coaches who recruited me about topics other than basketball. These were men, one of whom might have a profound effect on the course of my life, and I wanted to be as certain as I could that, basketball aside, I did not misjudge them. Again, Coach Wooden came through as a well-read, genuinely caring man. People would always tell me that they cared about me, but I felt Mr. Wooden really meant it. I came out of his office knowing I was going to UCLA. . . .

■ ■ ■

I looked to sophomore year like real life was about to begin. The games would be for real; I'd be working with Coach Wooden; . . .

The basketball team was primed for the season. Coming off an undefeated freshman year and finally under the direct instruction of Coach Wooden himself, we expected a great deal from ourselves— the whole team—and we were ready to have fun in the process. The talent on our squad was deep and intense, but even before practice started we found we had to make some adjustments. Edgar Lacy, who had been projected as our starting forward, cracked his kneecap and would be unable to play the entire season. Mike Lynn, another upperclassman starting forward, got busted for allegedly using a stolen credit card and was banished for a year. What had promised to be a team that blended speed and power, youth and experience, was stripped of its front court and its seniors. Coach Wooden was faced with the necessity of starting four sophomores and one junior, guard Mike Warren. We had to grow up fast.

John Wooden sees basketball as a very simple game, and it is his unique talent to hone that simplicity toward perfection. His whole idea is to run with the basketball, beat the defense down the court, play good defense yourself, and get the easiest shots you can get. That's it. We drilled just the way we had drilled the year before, by the numbers, but this season what had been learned responses became natural ones. Mr. Wooden believed in supreme conditioning and unwavering fundamentals, not only knowing which plays to run and how to run them but being capable of calling up the physical and emotional stamina at the precise time you need it to win. Application is his guiding light, being tired all the time, accepting whatever pain is necessary in order to achieve your goal.

Mr. Wooden had an eye and mind that saw the game as if from above. He would drill us fiercely and expect dedication; he accepted no less. Dressed like his players in T-shirt, shorts, sweat socks and sneakers, with his jacket that read "Coach" on the back and a whistle around his neck, he would find our errors, our indecisions, and correct them. He never rode people; he treated everyone the same and displayed no favoritism, but you didn't want to make the same mistake twice. When he'd get mad he'd say, "Gracious sakes alive!" and it instilled more fear than any other coach's tirade of obscenities. "That is *not* the way to do it," he would say forcefully, the words careening around the practice gym rafters, and whoever had screwed up would stand there as if he'd been slapped.

He would blow me away sometimes when he'd leave his usual spot on the court and walk all the way up to the roof, sit in the last row and shout down instructions to a coach, who relayed them to us on the floor. It took a long time for me to realize that his comprehension of the game was so thorough that he was up there checking out the dynamics of the whole court and needed exactly that long-shot perspective to complete his study. The game flowed in his mind, and he wanted to be certain he had made it flow exactly the same in flesh and blood.

Mr. Wooden taught self-discipline and was his own best example. His awareness of what was happening in all parts of the game was very acute, but his demeanor was always contained, as if by ordering himself he was controlling all elements. His philosophy, he showed us, was that if you needed emotion to make you perform then sooner or later you'd be vulnerable, an emotional wreck, and then nonfunctional. He preferred thorough preparation over the need to rise to an occasion. Let others try to rise to a level we had already attained; we would be there to begin with. He would smile and be happy when he won, but I never saw him truly exultant; about the only overt expression he would allow himself was the tight twisting of his program, rolled not so much into a weapon as into a handle on the situation. . . .

Primary Source

They Call Me Coach [excerpt]

> **SYNOPSIS:** In his autobiography, John Wooden, UCLA basketball coach and winner of ten national championships, recalls how he outrecruited more than two hundred colleges to bring Lewis Alcindor to the Bruins and evaluates him as a player.

■ ■ ■

Lewis Ferdinand Alcindor, Jr., was, in my opinion, the finest truly big man ever to play basketball up to his time. He could do anything you asked of him, and do it almost to perfection. His tremendous physical ability, however, could not have been nearly so effective had it not been for his intelligence and exceptional emotional control. Seldom would he strike back in anger despite the fact he took more of a physical beating in his three years of basketball at UCLA than anyone I have ever seen.

Lew Alcindor (left) and John Wooden pose on the court, Louisville, Kentucky, March 22, 1969. With the help of Alcindor's 37 points, John Wooden and the UCLA Bruins won their third NCAA basketball title in a row © BETTMANN/CORBIS. REPRODUCED BY PERMISSION.

The ability to keep his emotions under control was as much responsible for our winning three successive NCAA championships in the so-called Alcindor era as anything else. He had total control of a ten to fifteen foot circle around his position on the floor. He completely intimidated opposing players merely by the threat of moving out to meet them when they were driving toward the basket.

Lewis probably could get higher in the air than any man of his size. I don't think his timing was quite so good as Bill Russell's, but it was excellent nonetheless. It's almost impossible to make an objective comparison of men who played their collegiate ball more than ten years apart. . . .

Lewis was really more like Wilt Chamberlain than Russell in all-around ability. He was more maneuverable than Wilt but not nearly so powerful. Had Wilt been surrounded by the playing cast that Russell was with the Boston Celtics, and had he had a Red Auerbach as coach, his team might well have won all those championships. Suffice it to say that Bill, Wilt, and Lewis all belong among the all-time greats. . . .

The line-up was almost a juggling act for the first thirteen games [of Alcindor's junior season]. Then came the big scene in the Astrodome, with the largest crowd ever to see a college basketball game and an even larger crowd watching on coast-to-coast television. "The Big A," as someone wrote, "versus The Big E." But it really wasn't. Alcindor was just half of himself because of his injured eye. He had been in a dark room and had not practiced in over a week. Lewis at far below par, however, was still a potent psychological force. His mere physical presence forced opponents to alter their game—both offensively and defensively.

It had not been an easy year, as most would have supposed. The internal problems of having too many standouts had confirmed my long-time conviction that if you have more than seven or eight players who could be considered starters you may be breeding discontent. All this in spite of the fact we were going along undefeated, were physically very strong, and had the best bench ever. . . .

Every one of our players was dedicated to that game. The fact that we beat North Carolina the next night for our fourth NCAA title, the second time we had two in succession, was anticlimactic, at least for the spectators. They came for the Houston affair and that's what it was. Quite an affair, and an impressive victory. One writer, I believe from the East, expressed to me later his amazement that our players didn't seem too jubilant about winning from North Carolina, 78-55.

I told him what I told my players on the bench as the clock ran down. "I don't want any out-of-control celebration. I want you to feel good, cut down the nets—but I don't want any jumping around, no dancing on the floor or acting like fools. No excessive jubilation, no spectacle." What I was really saying to them was, don't climb a mountain. And when we lost, as we did earlier that year at the Astrodome, my words of caution, "Don't hang your heads, don't bellyache, walk out with your heads high," were to remind them not to descend into the lowest valley, but to climb a steadily rising plane as they strove to reach their ultimate potential.

Just give me a group of gentlemen who play the game hard but clean, and always on an upward path. Then the championships will take care of themselves if the overall ability of the team warrants them.

■ ■ ■

By the time of Lewis Alcindor's senior season in 1968–69, it was obvious that all the glowing forecasts about him were true. My only problem was to see that the infection of success didn't set in to spoil the team's final year. . . .

We were going into the year again built around the low post offense tailored for Lewis. Shackelford was back, but now both Allen and Warren were gone from the back line. That's one place where I always planned for experience, but man's best plans often go astray, and this was an example. . . .

Lewis had reached a point where it was difficult to find even a small flaw in his game. As a sophomore and junior his timing had been a little uncertain on occasion, but now it was precise. Experience with our style and general maturity had developed this finesse and all the other necessary ones to near perfection. For a player as gifted as Lewis, it would have been simple to become blasé, to take things too easily. Not Lewis. He was a competitor, always pushing himself, always pressing to become greater. . . .

One of Lewis's greatest attributes was his ability to adapt to any situation. After the so-called Alcindor rule was passed—the outlawing of the dunk shot—some skeptics said he wouldn't be as great. They ignored his tremendous desire and determination. He worked twice as hard on banking shots off the glass, his little hook across the lane, and his turnaround jumper.

We were 29 and 1 again his senior year—88 wins and 2 defeats in three years—and while we had some fine talent to team with him, I do not believe we would have established that kind of a record without Alcindor.

Primary Source

"He Dared Stand Alone" [excerpt]

SYNOPSIS: In this *Los Angeles Times* article, Jim Murray shares his impression of legendary UCLA basketball coach John Wooden.

Don't bang the drums slowly. Don't muffle the caissons, or lead a riderless horse. Strike up the band. Let the trumpets roll. Never mind the 21-gun salute, just bring a plate of fudge. Raise your glasses in a toast if you must—but fill them with malted milk.

John Wooden is not going out as a great general or field leader. This is not Old Blood and Guts or Old Hickory, this is Mr. Chips saying goodby.

John Wooden never wanted to be thought of as a fiery leader. Life to him was a one-room schoolhouse with pictures of George Washington, Christ and a pair of crossed flags. Outside, the pumpkins ripening under a harvest moon. A pedagogue is all he ever wanted to be or remembered as. A simple country teacher.

His precepts were right off a wall motto. His idols were gentle Hoosier poets, not the purple-prose artists of the sports pages. A reserve guard stumbled out of a pregame meeting once to mumble in some shock to a frat brother, "Our game plan is by Edgar A. Guest, and our front line seems to be made up of Faith, Hope and Charity."

John Wooden, someone once said, was "the only basketball coach from the Old Testament." Others preferred to think of him as New Testament—"St. John," who walked to work across Santa Monica Bay.

His lifestyle was embodied in a cornerstone of philosophy which he called the "Pyramid of Success," which looked like a collection of Horatio Alger titles. They were real easy to follow—if you lived in a convent.

Further Resources

BOOKS

Abdul-Jabbar, Kareem. *Kareem.* New York: Warner Books, 1990.

Chapin, Dwight, and Jeff Prugh. *The Wizard of Westwood: Coach John Wooden and His UCLA Bruins.* Boston: Houghton, Mifflin, 1973.

Isaacs, Neil David. *All the Moves: A History of College Basketball,* rev. ed. New York: Harper & Row, 1984.

PERIODICALS

Kirkpatrick, Curry. "The Ball in Two Different Courts." *Sports Illustrated,* December 25, 1972, 29–33.

Smith, Gary. "Now More Than Ever, a Winner." *Sports Illustrated,* December 23 & 30, 1985, 78–94.

WEBSITES

Naismith Memorial Basketball Hall of Fame. "John Wooden." Available online at http://www.hoophall.com/halloffamers /Wooden.htm; website home page: http://www.hoophall .com (accessed March 23, 2003).

Naismith Memorial Basketball Hall of Fame. "Kareem Abdul-Jabbar." Available online at http://www.hoophall.com /halloffamers/Abdul-Jabbar.htm; website home page: http:// www.hoophall.com (accessed March 23, 2003).

Wilma

Autobiography

By: Wilma Rudolph

Date: 1977

Source: Rudolph, Wilma. *Wilma.* New York: Signet, 1977, 126–136.

About the Author: Wilma Rudolph (1940–1994) was born in Clarksville, Tennessee. At age four, her left leg was paralyzed after a bout of pneumonia and scarlet fever. After therapy, braces, and special shoes, she was able to walk normally. While in high school, Rudolph was on the 1956 U.S. Olympic track and field team, winning a bronze medal. While attending Tennessee State University, Rudolph made the 1960 Olympic team, winning three gold medals. Retiring from competition in 1962, Rudolph spent the rest of her life in various academic, business, and nonprofit endeavors. ■

Introduction

Prior to 1960, the most prominent American women's track and field athlete was Babe Didrikson, who won two gold medals at the 1932 Los Angeles Olympics, and went on to stardom in golf. Otherwise, women track and field athletes in the United States generally received little notice in the sporting press and were offered no commercial endorsements.

Wilma Rudolph grew up in rural Tennessee, one of twenty-two children in a blended family. At age four, she contracted pneumonia and scarlet fever, resulting in partial paralysis of her left leg. Once a week, Wilma's mother drove her ninety miles round trip to Nashville to receive heat and water therapy for the leg. Wilma began hobbling on the leg at age six, wore a brace at eight, and by twelve years old, she discarded her specially designed shoe. In a segregated high school, Rudolph excelled at basketball and track. Participating in summer track camp at Tennessee State University, Rudolph made the 1956 U.S. Olympic team, which competed in Melbourne, Australia. There, Rudolph failed to qualify for the 200-meter final but won a bronze medal in the 400-meter relay. She returned home and gained a track scholarship to Tennessee State.

Under the tutelage of coach Ed Temple, Rudolph made the 1960 Olympic track and field team in Rome, along with six of her Tennessee State teammates, known as the "Tigerbelles." The weather was scorching hot in Rome; the early September temperature hovered around one hundred degrees. The day before the 100-meter trials, Rudolph twisted her ankle, which became swollen and discolored. Fortunately, her ankle injury did not prevent her from tying a world record in the semifinal and winning a gold medal in the 100-meter final, timed at 11.0 seconds (a world record was disallowed because of a following wind). Two days later in the two hundred meters, after setting an Olympic record of 23.2 seconds in the qualifying heat, Rudolph won the final with a time of 24.0 seconds, slower for her due to a wet track caused by rain. Several days later, Rudolph and three Tigerbelle teammates competed in the 400-meter relay. Rudolph, running the relay's anchor leg, nearly dropped the baton

Photo finish of the women's 100-meter sprint event at the 1960 Olympic games. American Wilma Rudolph (right) won the gold in a time of 11.0 seconds. Dorothy Hyman of Great Britain was second with a time of 11.3 seconds. **AP/WIDE WORLD PHOTOS. REPRODUCED BY PERMISSION.**

on handoff but in an amazing display of speed, turned a two-yard deficit into a three-tenths-of-a-second victory over the Soviet Union team in 44.5 seconds, winning her third gold medal of the Olympics.

Significance

Wilma Rudolph returned home a national hero, even in segregated Tennessee, where the first ever integrated event in Clarksville was held: a parade in her honor, an African American woman from the South. In 1961, Rudolph won the Sullivan Award as the top American amateur athlete, male or female. For two years after the Olympics she continued racing, retiring from competition in 1962. Rudolph graduated from Tennessee State University with a degree in education. Despite her fame as an athlete, there was no money in track and field in the 1960s—especially for women—and she had to go to work for a living. Rudolph became a teacher, coached basketball and track at the grade-school and college level, served as a goodwill ambassador to western Africa, hosted a radio talk show, and served in a number of administrative positions in the public and private sectors. Later, she established the nonprofit Wilma Rudolph Foundation, dedicated to educating and inspiring underprivileged children, and was elected to the National Track and Field Hall of Fame. Wilma Rudolph died in 1994 of a brain tumor. Her achievements in 1960 set the standard for later generations of women track athletes, such as Evelyn Ashford, Florence Griffith-Joyner,

and many others. Her friend, the Olympic documentary filmmaker Bud Greenspan, called Rudolph the "female Jesse Owens," a tribute to her path-breaking achievement in Rome.

Primary Source

Wilma [excerpt]

SYNOPSIS: In her autobiography, track and field champion Wilma Rudolph recalls her experiences at the 1960 Olympic Games in Rome, along with her quest for and ultimate achievement in winning three gold medals—in the 100- and 200-meter dashes, and 400-meter team relay.

Rome

We spent a week in New York City before leaving for Rome, and during that week we were measured and outfitted with all of our Olympic uniforms and equipment. The women's track team left on an airplane with the men's rowing team, and we all arrived about two weeks before the games began. My first impression of Rome was that it was a storybook city come true: seeing the Coliseum, the catacombs, the Vatican, was like seeing pictures come to life. When we settled into the Olympic Village, Lucinda Williams was assigned as my roommate and, as things turned out, that was a very fortunate break for me. . . .

We started practicing in the afternoons as soon as we got there, because Coach Temple was all business by now. The Italian language was giving us all a lot of problems, and the U.S. Olympic Committee gave us these little books, Italian-American dictionaries, and all of us walked around Rome with them. Sometimes, when we wanted to say something to an Italian, we would just point to the right phrase. Other times, we'd have to block out almost the whole page with our hands and leave one sentence, or one paragraph showing. Eventually, we started learning key phrases ourselves, but I think the Italian people got a kick out of us. They always laughed, and seemed so jolly.

Myself, I felt loose and free, and the reason was probably because Coach Temple was there. He meant that much to me. That whole first week, we worked out under various Italian starters, who issued commands in Italian, and we had to get used to that. Then, on the last day, the man who would be the actual starter in the games came by and we went through it all with him. I listened and got the commands down pat; I wasn't going to rely solely on the sound of the gun anymore. Otherwise, the first week in Rome was pleasant and uneventful. But it would heat up.

One day, Coach Temple sat me down, and we had a very serious talk. He said that he thought my chances were very good for winning three gold medals, and then he told me about this dream he had been having. He said that for two and three nights in a row, he had dreamt that I actually did it, won three gold medals and became the first American woman in Olympic history to have done that. I felt good about that, because I knew I was running well. My practice runs were great, and the weather in Rome was perfect for me—the temperatures were in the 100s, and it felt just like it felt down in Tennessee, where I had been running in the hot weather for years. My body was used to the heat, and the hot weather actually helped put me in a good frame of mind. . . .

So finally it was Wednesday, the day before I was scheduled to run in my first race at Rome. Disaster. It was very hot that day, and we decided not to go to our assigned track to practice, since Coach Temple didn't want us to do anything more than jog a little, break a sweat, and walk out the kinks. So we went to this field right behind the Olympic Stadium; it was huge and just covered with nice green grass. The sprinklers were on, and the temperature was in the 100s again, and all of us started running

through the sprinklers to cool off a little. It was great fun, an unexpected bonus for us. Time and again, we ran through the sprinklers, jumped through the spray, and got our uniforms and ourselves soaking wet. Right near the end of the session, I jumped over this sprinkler one last time—I never even saw the hole right behind it. Well, I stepped right into the hole, turned my ankle, and heard it pop.

Everybody came running over and they pulled it out, and I was crying because the ankle hurt very badly and I thought that I had broken it and that everything was down the drain now. The trainer took one look and made this horrible face; the ankle was swollen and already it was discolored. He immediately ordered some ice, and he packed it and they carried me back to my room. There, the trainer taped it up real tight, and my foot was elevated into the air. I stayed that way until the next morning. When I got up, I didn't know what to expect. I was due to run in the afternoon in the Olympics, and here I was with a sore and swollen ankle. When I got up, I put my weight on it and, thank God, it held. I said to myself, "Thank God, it's only a sprain, I can handle that because I don't have to run any curves today, just the straightaway in the 100." . . .

When we got to the stadium, they lined us up right away in the order in which we were going to run, and then they put us through the tunnel which leads to the stadium. Coach Temple couldn't go through the tunnel, so we said goodbye there at the entrance, and I went into the tunnel alone. When I got into the tunnel with the other runners, a strange calm came over me. I was nervous in a sense, yes; but I also got a chance to take a look at the runners I would be going up against, and I felt, deep inside, that I could beat any of them. So I lay down on a bench and propped my feet up against the wall; I just lay there the whole time, waiting for them to call my name. When they did, I slowly got up and walked out into the Olympic Stadium for the first time as a participant.

The stadium was jammed; at least 80,000 people were inside it. For some reason, the Italian fans took a liking to me the very first day I arrived, and when they saw me walk out toward the track, they started cheering wildly and started chanting, "Vil-ma . . . Vil-ma . . ." I was overwhelmed by that, didn't expect it in a million years. But I decided right away to block it out of my mind. I didn't want anything to interfere with my concentration, and I was thinking, "You start smiling and waving and listening to the cheering and chanting, you're going to forget all about

Wilma Rudolph displays the three Olympic gold medals she won in 1960. © BETTMANN/CORBIS. REPRODUCED BY PERMISSION.

the real reason you're here. To win." So I put it all out of my head, and I walked slowly over to the starting blocks and took one practice start. I wasn't paying any attention to the other runners who were jumping all around and running and wasting energy. I just stayed around the starting block and waited. When the race went off, I got a good start and won easily. In the second trial heat, the same thing happened. I got off good and won without any trouble. The trial heats were conducted to whittle down the field of runners for the final on Saturday. But winning two on the first day didn't assure me of anything. I still had two more trial heats to run the next day.

That next day, I followed the same procedure. My ankle wasn't bothering me, and I actually fell asleep for a little while on the practice field. I went to sit down and rest for a bit, and my nervous reaction was to fall asleep. I won the third trial heat that day, but the fourth was the memorable one. I won it in a time of 11 seconds flat and that was a new world's record. But I didn't get it; the International Olympic Committee disallowed it because the wind velocity at my back was more than 2.2 miles an hour, it said. Now, any runner alive knows that when you're out there on the track you aren't even aware that the wind is blowing, so how could a two-mile-an-hour wind help you any? But that's what was said, and the record was not made official. That meant I lost two world records in a matter of a month because the officials disallowed them. . . .

Saturday. This was the day. The final in the women's 100 meters. The top three people, out

of six, were Jutta Heine, the tall blond girl from West Germany; Dorothy Hyman, from Great Britain, and myself. I really felt insecure about Jutta Heine all that morning. She had won all of her preliminary heats, just as I had, and she was just as tall as I was. I watched her run a heat and noticed that she had a stride just as long as I had, and, yes, she was a good runner. You knew immediately about those things; you can see it in the way runners carry themselves. But I guess I was the favorite going in; my times in the heats were :11.3 twice, and :11.4.

The tension began for all of us in the tunnel which leads out to the stadium. There was no way to get away from each other; you mingle, and you avoid looking, and you try to get yourself in a proper frame of mind. It's a little bit like a fighter before a big championship bout. Yes, you have to build up a little hatred for your opponents, and you have to psyche yourself up to instill the killer instinct. But I was not afraid or intimidated in that tunnel. I never talked, but I always looked the others straight in the eye. I knew that even if I did say something, they wouldn't be able to understand me anyway; the little English they did know would have been lost in my black southern accent. So I just kept quiet and looked them in the eyes. When we got out on the track, I followed my same routine: one practice start, then slowly walk around, with my hands on my hips, near the starting blocks. No rushing, no jumping, no running around; conserve the energy for when it really matters. I was concentrating deeply.

My start was relatively good. I came out second or third in the field, and my speed started increasing the farther I went. When I reached fifty meters, I saw that I had them all, and I was just beginning to turn it on. By seventy meters, I knew the race was mine, nobody was going to catch me. I won by five to seven yards, and Dorothy Hyman was second, and I knew then and there that Jutta Heine would not beat me. I did 11 flat again, and this time there was another mixup involving one of the officials, and the world's record was discounted. I couldn't believe that. I cried, and my coach was upset, but I was happy that I had won my first gold medal easily.

When I got back to my room, the first telegram I received was from Betty Cuthbert, the Australian runner who had won three gold medals in 1956. She was going to try for three more in 1960, but she had gotten hurt and couldn't run at all. Soon, there were so many flowers and telegrams coming into my room that the place was overrun. A lot of them were coming in from back home in Clarksville, Tennessee, and they affected me the most. . . .

The next morning, Sunday morning, I had breakfast with Coach Temple. He said to take it easy for as long as I could and, after the 200 meter race, I'd be free to do whatever I wanted in Rome. He told me to rest the ankle as long as I could because on Tuesday, in the 200-meter final, I'd be running curves for the first time since I had sprained it. Tuesday broke raining. It was miserable out there, but I felt good, no real pressure. The 200 was mine, I loved it more than anything else. A little rain meant nothing to me. In fact, before the start of the race, I was saying to myself, as a way of psyching up, "There's nobody alive who can beat you in the 200. Go get it."

The rain did slow me down a little, but I won the race easily, no problem with the ankle, no problem with the start. I really won that race a lot easier than I thought I would, against Jutta Heine and Dorothy Hyman and pretty much the same field that was in the 100. The time was 24 seconds flat, and that was like walking. I was disappointed, because I had been doing a consistent :22.9 in the 200, and 24 flat was embarrassing. Still, I said to myself that night, "That's two gold medals down and one to go."

On Friday, the 440 relay was scheduled. That was my chance to become the first American woman ever to win three Olympic gold medals. I wasn't about to blow it. The team was: Martha Hudson, running the first leg; Barbara Jones, running the second; Lucinda Williams, running the third, and me, running anchor. The teams everybody was talking about were Russia, West Germany, and Britain. Well, we wiped them all out, and we set a world's record in the process. This time, they gave us the record, no wind faults or official botch-ups. It was an easy race for us; everybody ran their best, and we won it going away.

When I broke the tape, I had my three gold medals, and the feeling of accomplishment welled up inside of me. The first American woman to win three Olympic gold medals. I knew that was something nobody could ever take away from me, ever. After the playing of "The Star-Spangled Banner," I came away from the victory stand and I was mobbed. People were jumping all over me, pushing microphones into my face, pounding my back. I couldn't believe it. Finally, the American officials grabbed me and escorted me to safety. One of them said, "Wilma, life will never be the same for you again." He was so right.

Further Resources

BOOKS

Ashe, Arthur R., Jr. *A Hard Road to Glory: A History of the African-American Athlete, Since 1946.* New York: Warner Books, 1988.

Biracree, Tom. *Wilma Rudolph.* New York: Chelsea House, 1988.

Davis, Michael. "Wilma Rudolph." In *Black American Women in Olympic Track and Field.* Jefferson, N.C.: McFarland, 1982.

PERIODICALS

Litsky, Frank. "Wilma Rudolph, Star of the 1960 Olympics, Dies." *The New York Times,* November 13, 1994.

Rhoden, William C. "The End of a Winding Road." *The New York Times,* November 19, 1994.

AUDIO AND VISUAL MEDIA

Wilma. Cappy Productions. 1977.

GENERAL RESOURCES

General

Albert, Judith Clavir, and Stewart E. Albert. *The Sixties Papers: Documents of a Rebellious Decade.* New York: Praeger, 1984.

Anderson, Terry H. *The Movement and the Sixties.* New York: Oxford University Press, 1996.

Archer, Jules. *The Incredible Sixties: The Stormy Years that Changed America.* San Diego: Harcourt, Brace, Jovanovich, 1986.

Colby, Vineta, ed. *American Culture in the Sixties.* New York: Wilson, 1964.

Gitlin, Todd. *The Sixties: Years of Hope, Days of Rage.* New York: Bantam, 1987.

Goodwin, Richard N. *Remembering America: A Voice From the Sixties.* Boston: Little, Brown, 1988.

Jamison, Andrew. *Seeds of the Sixties.* Berkeley, Calif.: University of California Press, 1994.

Margolis, John. *The Last Innocent Year: America in 1964: The Beginning of the "Sixties."* New York: William Morrow, 1999.

Miller, Jim. *Democracy in the Streets: From Port Huron to the Siege of Chicago.* New York: Simon and Schuster, 1987.

Partridge, William L. *The Hippy Ghetto: The Natural History of a Subculture.* Prospect Heights, Ill.: Waveland Press, 1985.

Singleton, Carl, and Rowena Wildin. *The Sixties in America.* Pasadena, Calif.: Salem Press, 1999.

This Fabulous Century, 1960–1970. Alexandria, Va.: Time-Life Books, 1970.

Trilling, Diana. *We Must March My Darlings: A Critical Decade.* New York: Harcourt, Brace, Jovanovich, 1997.

Viorst, Milton. *Fire in the Streets: America in the 1960s.* New York: Simon and Schuster, 1979.

Wallechinsky, David. *Midterm Report: The Class of '65: Chronicles of an American Generation.* New York: Viking, 1986.

Weiner, Rex, and Deanne Stillman. *Woodstock Census: The Nationwide Survey of the Sixties Generation.* New York: Viking, 1979.

The Arts

Ashton, Dore. *American Art Since 1945.* New York: Oxford University Press, 1982.

Bawden, Liz-Anne. *The Oxford Companion to Film.* New York: Oxford University Press, 1976.

Bell, Bernard. *The Afro-American Novel and Its Tradition.* Amherst: University of Massachusetts Press, 1987.

Belz, Carl. *The Story of Rock,* 2d ed. New York: Oxford University Press, 1972.

Berendt, Joachim Ernst. *The Jazz Book: From Ragtime to Fusion and Beyond.* Westport, Conn.: Hill, 1982.

Bordman, Gerald. *The Oxford Companion to the American Theatre.* New York: Oxford University Press, 1984.

Bradbury, Malcolm. *The Modern American Novel,* new ed. New York: Viking, 1992.

Brindle, Reginald Smith. *The New Music: The Avant-Garde Since 1945,* 2d ed. Oxford & New York: Oxford University Press, 1987.

Brooks, Elston. *I've Heard Those Songs Before, Volume II: The Weekly Top Ten Hits of the Last Six Decades.* Fort Worth, Tex.: Summit Group, 1991.

Chapie, Steve. *Rock 'n' Roll Is Here to Pay.* Chicago: Nelson-Hall, 1977.

Charters, Ann, ed. *Dictionary of Literary Biography 16: The Beats: Literary Bohemians in Postwar America.* Detroit: Bruccoli Clark/Gale Research, 1983.

Charters, Samuel B. *The Bluesmen.* New York: Oak, 1967.

Christgau, Robert. *Grown Up All Wrong:75 Great Rock and Pop Artists From Vaudeville to Techno.* Cambridge, Mass.: Harvard University Press, 1998.

Craven, Wayne. *American Art: History and Culture.* New York: Harry N. Abrams, Inc., 1994.

Curtis, Jim. *Rock Eras: Interpretations of Music and Society, 1954–1984.* Bowling Green, Ohio: Bowling Green University Popular Press, 1987.

Davis, Thadious M., and Trudier Harris, eds. *Dictionary of Literary Biography 33: Afro-American Fiction Writers After 1955.* Detroit: Bruccoli Clark/Gale Research, 1984.

Dictionary of Literary Biography 38: Afro-American Writers After 1955—Dramatists and Prose Writers. Detroit: Bruccoli Clark/Gale Research, 1985.

Ehrlich, J.W., ed. *Howl of the Censor.* San Carlos, Calif.: Nourse Publishing, 1961.

Eisen, Jonathan. *The Age of Rock: Sounds of the American Cultural Revolution—A Reader.* New York: Random House, 1969.

Eliot, Marc. *Rockonomics: The Money Behind the Music.* New York: Franklin Watts, 1989.

Ennis, Philip H. *The Seventh Stream: The Emergence of Rock'n'roll in American Popular Music.* Hanover, U.K.: Wesleyan University Press, 1992.

Enser, A.G.S. *Filmed Books and Plays, 1928–1983.* Aldershot, U.K.: Gower, 1985.

Ernst, David. *The Evolution of Electronic Music.* New York: Schirmer-Macmillan, 1977.

Ewen, David. *History of Popular Music.* New York: Barnes & Noble, 1961.

Feather, Leonard. *The Book of Jazz: A Guide to the Entire Field.* New York: Horizon, 1965.

———. *The Pleasures of Jazz.* New York: Horizon, 1976.

Fucini, Joseph J., and Susan Fucini. *Entrepreneurs: The Men and Women Behind Famous Brand Names and How They Made It.* Boston: G.K. Hall, 1985.

Gaugh, Harry F. *Willem de Kooning.* New York: Abbeville Press, 1983.

Gianetti, Louis D. *Understanding Movies.* Englewood Cliffs, N.J.: Prentice-Hall, 1987.

Goodman, Fred. *The Mansion on the Hill: Dylan, Young, Giffen, Springsteen and the Head-on Collision of Rock and Commerce.* New York: Random House, 1997.

Gordy, Berry. *To Be Loved: The Music, The Magic, The Memories of Motown.* New York: Warner Books, 1994.

Grant, Barry K., ed. *Film Genre: Theory and Criticism.* Metuchen, N.J.: Scarecrow Press, 1977.

Greiner, Donald J., ed. *Dictionary of Literary Biography 5: American Poets Since World War II,* 2 vols. Detroit: Bruccoli Clark/Gale Research, 1980.

Guilbaut, Serge. *How New York Stole the Idea of Modern Art: Abstract Expressionism, Freedom, and the Cold War,* translated by Arthur Goldhammer. Chicago: University of Chicago Press, 1983.

Guttman, Allen. *From Ritual to Record.* New York: Columbia University Press, 1978.

Haralambos, Michael. *Right On: From Blues to Soul in Black America.* New York: Da Capo, 1979.

Helterman, Jeffrey, and Richard Layman, eds. *Dictionary of Literary Biography 2: American Novelists Since World War II.* Detroit: Bruccoli Clark/Gale Research, 1978.

Hobbs, Robert Carleton, and Gail Levin. *Abstract Expressionism: The Formative Years.* Ithaca, N.Y. & New York: Herbert F. Johnson Museum of Art and Whitney Museum of American Art, 1978.

Hood, Phil, ed. *Artists of American Folk Music: The Legends of Traditional Folk, the Stars of the Sixties, the Virtuosi of New Acoustic Music.* New York: Morrow, 1986.

Houston, Penelope. *The Emergence of Film Art: The Evolution and Development of the Motion Picture as an Art, From 1900 to the Present.* New York: Norton, 1979.

Hughes, Robert. *American Visions: The Epic History of Art in America.* New York: Alfred A. Knopf, 1997.

Kael, Pauline. *5001 Nights at the Movies: A Guide From A to Z.* New York: Holt, Rinehart & Winston, 1982.

Karl, Frederick R. *American Fictions, 1940–1980: A Comprehensive History and Critical Evaluation.* New York: Harper & Row, 1983.

Kazin, Alfred. *Bright Book of Life.* Boston: Little, Brown, 1973.

Keepnews, Orrin, and Bill Grauer, Jr. *A Pictorial History of Jazz,* 2d ed. New York: Crown, 1966.

Kibler, James E., Jr., ed. *Dictionary of Literary Biography 6: American Novelists Since World War II,* Second Series. Detroit: Bruccoli Clark/Gale Research, 1980.

Koch, Lawrence O. *Yardbird Suite: A Compendium of the Music and Life of Charlie Parker.* Bowling Green, Ohio: Bowling Green University Popular Press, 1988.

Leadbitter, Mike, and Neil Slaven. *Blues Records 1943–1966.* New York: Oak, 1968.

Lindgren, Ernest. *The Art of the Film.* New York: Macmillan, 1963.

London, Herbert I. *Closing the Circle: A Cultural History of the Rock Revolution.* Chicago: Nelson-Hall, 1984.

MacNicholas, John, ed. *Dictionary of Literary Biography 7: Twentieth-Century American Dramatists.* Detroit: Bruccoli Clark/Gale Research, 1981.

Mazo, Joseph H. *Prime Movers: The Makers of Modern Dance in America.* New York: Morrow, 1977.

McDonagh, Don. *The Rise and Fall and Rise of Modern Dance,* rev. ed. Pennington, N.J.: A Cappella, 1990.

Miller, Jim, ed. *The Rolling Stone History of Rock and Roll.* New York: Rolling Stone Press/Random House, 1976.

Myron, Robert, and Abner Sundell. *Modern Art in America.* New York: Crowell-Collier, 1971.

O'Hara, Frank. *Art Chronicles, 1954–1966.* New York: George Braziller, 1975.

Payne, Charles. *American Ballet Theatre.* New York: Knopf, 1978.

Phillips, Lisa. *The American Century: Art and Culture 1950–2000.* New York: W.W. Norton & Co., 1999.

Podhoretz, Norman. *Doings and Undoings: the Fifties and After in American Writing.* New York: Farrar, Straus, 1964.

Poteet, G. Howard. *Published Radio, Television, and Film Scripts.* Troy, N.Y.: Whitston, 1975.

Reisner, Robert George. *Bird: The Legend of Charlie Parker.* New York: Da Capo Press, 1962.

Rembar, Charles. *The End of Obscenity: The Trials of Lady Chatterley, Tropic of Cancer, and Fanny Hill.* New York: Random House, 1968.

Reynolds, Nancy. *Repertory in Review.* New York: Dial, 1977.

Rosenberg, Neil V. *Bluegrass: A History.* Urbana & Chicago: University of Illinois Press, 1985.

Rosset, Barney, ed. *Evergreen Review Reader, 1957–1967: A Ten-Year Anthology.* New York: Grove, 1968.

Rotha, Paul, and Richard Griffith. *The Film Till Now.* London: Spring Books, 1967.

Sablosky, Irving. *American Music.* Chicago: University of Chicago Press, 1969.

Sandler, Irving. *American Art of the 1960s.* New York: Harper & Row, 1988.

Sanjet, Russell. *From Print to Plastic: Publishing and Promoting America's Popular Music 1900–1980.* Brooklyn, N.Y.: Institute for Studies in American Music, 1983.

Sarris, Andrew. *The American Cinema: Directors and Directions, 1949–1968.* New York: Dutton, 1968.

Southern, Eileen. *The Music of Black Americans: A History,* 2d ed. New York: Norton, 1983.

Stambler, Irwin, and Grelun Landon. *Encyclopedia of Folk, Country, and Western Music,* 2d edition. New York: St. Martin's Press, 1984.

Tanner, Tony. *City of Words: American Fiction, 1950–1970.* New York: Harper & Row, 1971.

Trowbridge, C. Robertson. *Yankee Publishing, Inc.: Fifty Years of Preserving New England's Culture While Extending Its Influence.* New York: Newcomen Society, 1986.

Ward, Brian. *Just My Soul Responding: Rhythm and Blues, Black Consciousness, and Race Relations.* Berkeley: University of California Press, 1998.

Wheeler, Daniel. *Art Since Mid-Century: 1945 to the Present.* Englewood Cliffs, N.J.: Prentice Hall / New York: Vendome, 1991.

Whitburn, Joel. *The Billboard Book of Top 40 Hits,* 5th ed. New York: Billboard Books, 1992.

Wiley, Mason, and Damien Bona. *Inside Oscar: The Unofficial History of the Academy Awards.* New York: Ballantine, 1986.

Business and the Economy

Aronowitz, Stanley. *False Promises: The Shaping of American Working-Class Consciousness.* Durham, N.C.: Duke University Press, 1992.

Breines, Wini. *Community and Organization in the New Left, 1962–1968: The Great Refusal.* New Brunswick, N.J.: Rutgers University Press, 1989.

Brooks, John. *The Autobiography of American Business.* Garden City, N.Y.: Doubleday, 1974.

Bryant, Keith L., Jr., ed. *Encyclopedia of American Business History and Biography Railroads in the Age of Regulation, 1900–1980.* Columbia, S.C.: New York: Bruccoli Clark Layman and Facts On File, 1988.

Bryant, Keith L., Jr., and Henry C. Dethloff. *A History of American Business.* Englewood Cliffs, N.J.: Prentice-Hall, 1983.

Davis, Mike. *Prisoners of the American Dream: Politics and Economy in the History of the U.S. Working Class.* London: Verso, 1986.

Dobson, John M. *A History of American Enterprise.* Englewood Cliffs, N.J.: Prentice-Hall, 1988.

Galbraith, John K. *Economic Development.* Cambridge. Mass.: Harvard University Press, 1964.

Gilder, George. *The Spirit of Enterprise.* New York: Simon & Schuster, 1984.

Gilland, Charles E., Jr., ed. *Readings in Business Responsibility.* Braintree, Mass.: D.H. Mark Publishing, 1969.

Green, James R. *The World of the Worker: Labor in Twentieth-Century America.* New York: Hill & Wang, 1980.

Halle, David. *America's Working Men: Work, Home, and Politics Among Blue-Collar Property Owners.* Chicago: University of Chicago Press, 1984.

Howe, Louise K. *Pink-Collar Workers: Inside the World of Women's Work.* New York: Avon, 1978.

Leary, William M., ed. *Encyclopedia of American Business History and Biography: The Airline Industry.* New York: Bruccoli Clark Layman and Facts On File, 1992.

Markusen, Ann R. *The Rise of the Gunbelt: The Military Remapping of Industrial America.* New York: Oxford University Press, 1991.

May, George S., ed. *Encyclopedia of American Business History and Biography: Banking and Finance, 1913–1989.* New York: Bruccoli Clark Layman and Facts On File, 1990.

Miller, Marc, ed. *Working Lives: The Southern Exposure History of Labor in the South.* New York: Pantheon Books, 1980.

Patterson, James T. *America's Struggle Against Poverty, 1900–1980.* Cambridge, Mass.: Harvard University Press, 1986.

Piven, Frances F., and Richard A. Cloward. *Poor People's Movements: Why They Succeed, How They Fail.* New York: Vintage Books, 1986.

Porter, Glenn, ed. *Encyclopedia of American Economic History: Studies of the Principal Movements and Ideas.* 3 vols. New York: Scribners, 1980.

Pusateri, Joseph C. *A History of American Business.* Arlington Heights, Ill.: Harlan Davidson, 1984.

Rae, John B. *The American Automobile: A Brief History.* Chicago: University of Chicago Press, 1965.

Ratner, Sidney, James H. Soltow, and Richard Sylla. *The Evolution of the American Economy.* New York: Basic Books, 1979.

Robinson, Archie. *George Meany and His Times: A Biography.* New York: Simon & Schuster, 1981.

Robinson, Graham. *Pictorial History of the Automobile.* New York: W. H. Smith, 1987.

Schweikart, Larry, ed. *Encyclopedia of American Business History and Biography: Banking and Finance, 1913–1989.* New York: Bruccoli Clark Layman and Facts On File, 1990.

Seely, Bruce, ed. *Encyclopedia of American Business History and Biography: Iron and Steel in the Twentieth Century.* New York: Bruccoli Clark Layman and Facts On File, 1993.

Theoharis, Athan G. *The Boss.* Philadelphia: Temple University Press, 1988.

Zieger, Robert. *American Workers, American Unions, 1920–1985.* Baltimore: Johns Hopkins University Press, 1986.

Websites

Califano, Joseph A., Jr. "What Was Really Great About the Great Society." Available online at http://www.washington monthly.com/features/1999/9910.califano.html (accessed July 7, 2003).

"Harrington, Michael (February 24, 1928–July 31, 1989)." Available online at http://people.history.ohio-state.edu/johnson1034 /H152/Harrington.htm (accessed July 7, 2003).

"Job Corps." Available online at http://www.jobcorps.org (accessed July 7, 2003).

"Lucent-Research-Telstar—A Look Back at 1962." Available online at http://www.lucent.com/minds/telstar (accessed July 7, 2003).

"Oil Development in America's Arctic, Prudhoe Bay." Available online at http://www.inforain.org/Northslope/anwr_2 .htm (accessed July 7, 2003).

"President Lyndon B. Johnson's Annual Message to the Congress on the State of the Union, January 8, 1964." Available online at http://www.lbjlib.utexas.edu/johnson/archives.hom /speeches.hom/640108.asp (accessed July 7, 2003).

"Truth in Lending Act." Available online at http://www.smart agreements.com/bltopics/Bltopi41.html (accessed July 7, 2003).

"UFW History." Available online at http://www.ufw.org/ufw .htm (accessed July 7, 2003).

"U.S. Department of Transportation (DOT)." Available online at http://www.dot.gov (accessed July 7, 2003).

"Vintage Mustang, 1965–1973." Available online at http:// www.vintage-mustang.com (accessed July 7, 2003).

Education

Aries, Philippe. *Centuries of Childhood.* New York: Knopf, 1962.

Bachman, Jerald G., Sweyzer Green, and Illona Wirtanen. *Dropping Out: Problem or Symptom?* Ann Arbor: University of Michigan Press, 1972.

Beck, Lynn G., and Joseph Murphy. *Understanding the Principalship: Metaphorical Themes, 1920s–1990s.* New York: Teachers College Press, Columbia University, 1993.

Berube, Maurice R. *American School Reform: Progressive, Equality, and Excellence Movements, 1883–1993.* Westport, Conn: Praeger, 1994.

Button, H. Warren, and Eugene F. Provenzo Jr. *History of Education and Culture in America.* Englewood Cliffs, N.J.: Prentice-Hall, 1983.

Church, Robert L., and Michael W. Sedlak. *Education in the United States: An Interpretive History.* New York: Free Press, 1976.

Cremin, Lawrence. *American Education, The Metropolitan Experience, 1876–1980.* New York: Harper & Row, 1988.

Eckberg, Douglas Lee. *Intelligence and Race: The Origins and Dimensions of the IQ Controversy.* New York: Praeger, 1979.

Eddy, John. *The Teacher and the Drug Scene.* Bloomington, Ind.: Phi Delta Kappa, 1973.

Flynn, James R. *Race, IQ, and Jensen.* Boston: Routledge, 1980.

Gould, Stephen J. *The Mismeasure of Man.* New York: Norton, 1981.

James, Thomas. *Public versus Nonpublic Education in Historical Perspective.* Stanford, Calif.: Institute for Research on Educational Finance and Governance, School of Education, Stanford University, 1982.

Kamin, Leon. *The Science and Politics of IQ.* New York: Wiley, 1974.

Karier, Clarence J. *Roots of Crisis: American Education in the Twentieth Century.* Chicago: Rand, McNally, 1973.

———. *Shaping the American Education State, 1900 to the Present.* New York: Free Press, 1975.

Knapp, Mary, and Herbert Knapp. *One Potato, Two Potato: The Secret Education of American Children.* New York: Norton, 1976.

Lazerson, Marvin, ed. *American Education in the Twentieth Century: A Documentary History.* New York: Teachers College Press, Columbia University, 1987.

Machlup, Fritz. *The Production and Distribution of Knowledge in the United States.* Princeton, N.J.: Princeton University Press, 1962.

Morgan, Harry. *Historical Perspectives on the Education of Black Children.* Westport, Conn.: Praeger, 1995.

Murphy, Majorie. *Blackboard Unions: The AFT and the NEA, 1900–1980.* Ithaca, N.Y.: Cornell University Press, 1990.

Nelkin, Dorothy. *The Creation Controversy: Science or Scripture in the Schools.* New York: Norton, 1982.

———. *Science Textbook Controversies and the Politics of Equal Time.* Cambridge, Mass.: MIT Press, 1977.

Piaget, Jean. *Play, Dreams and Imitation in Childhood.* New York: Norton, 1962.

Pride, Richard A. *The Political Use of Racial Narratives: School Desegregation in Mobile, Alabama, 1954–1997.* Urbana: University of Illinois Press, 2002.

Schramm, Wilbur, ed. *The Eighth Art.* New York: Holt, Rinehart & Winston, 1962.

Schramm, Wilbur, J. Lyle, and I. de Sola Pool. *The People Look at Educational Television.* Stanford: Stanford University Press, 1963.

Seller, Maxine Schwartz, ed. *Women Educators in the United States, 1820–1993: A Bio-Bibliographical Sourcebook.* Westport, Conn.: Greenwood Press, 1994.

Turow, Joseph. *Entertainment, Education, and the Hard Sell: Three Decades of Network Children's Television.* New York: Praeger, 1981.

Websites

"1961 Amendment to the California State Education Code." Available online at http://dynaweb.oac.cdlib.org:8088/dyna web/uchist/publid/lawlegislation/1961amendch12/@Generic _BookTextView/917 (accessed July 7, 2003).

"About Head Start." Available online at http://www.acf.hhs .gov/programs/hsb/about (accessed July 7, 2003).

"The American Experience: George Wallace: Settin' the Woods on Fire: Timeline (1952–1972)." Available online at http:// www.pbs.org/wgbh/amex/wallace (accessed July 7, 2003).

Califano, Joseph A., Jr. "What Was Really Great About the Great Society." Available online at http://www.washington monthly.com/features/1999/9910.califano.html (accessed July 7, 2003).

"Epperson v. Arkansas, 393 U.S. 97 (1968)." Available online at http://www2.law.cornell.edu/cgi-bin/foliocgi.exe/historic /query=[Group+393 (accessed July 7, 2003).

"History of Indian Education in the United States." Available online at http://www.aiefprograms.org/history_facts/history .html#1920 (accessed July 7, 2003).

"James Meredith." Available online at http://www.olemiss.edu /depts/english/ms-writers/dir/meredith_james (accessed July 7, 2003).

"Oct. 1995: Michigan Today—Vietnam Teach-in 30 Years Ago." Available online at http://www.umich.edu/newsinfo /MT/95/Oct95/mt1195.html (accessed July 7, 2003).

"U.S. Supreme Court: Engel v. Vitale, 370 U.S. 421 (1962)." Available online at http://caselaw.lp.findlaw.com/cgi-bin /getcase.pl?court=US&vol=370&invol=421 (accessed July 7, 2003).

"Vocational Education Act of 1963 (PL 88–210)." Available online at http://dana.ucc.nau.edu/mr/vte591/1963.htm (accessed July 7, 2003).

Fashion and Design

Ballard, Bettina. *In My Fashion.* New York: McKay, 1960.

Batterberry, Michael. *Mirror, Mirror: A Social History of Fashion.* New York: Holt, Rinehart & Winston, 1977.

Brown, Curtis F. *Star-Spangled Kitsch.* New York: Universe Books, 1975.

Connikie, Yvonne. *Fashions of a Decade: the 1960s.* New York and Oxford: Facts On File, 1990.

Dorner, Jane. *Fashion in the Forties and Fifties.* London: Ian Allen, 1975.

The Encyclopedia of Fashion. New York: Abrams, 1986.

Garland, Madge. *The Changing Form of Fashion.* New York: Praeger, 1970.

Howell, Georgina. *In Vogue: Six Decades of Fashion.* London: Allen Lane, 1975.

Kultermann, Udo. *Architecture in the 20th Century.* New York: Reinhold, 1993.

Mulvagh, Jane. *"Vogue" History of 20th Century Fashion.* New York: Viking, 1988.

Peacock, John. *20th Century Fashion: The Complete Sourcebook.* New York: Thames & Hudson, 1993.

Reid, Aileen. *I. M. Pei.* New York: Crescent Books, 1995.

Ryan, Mary Shaw. *Clothing: A Study in Human Behavior.* New York: Holt, Rinehart & Winston, 1966.

Stegemeyer, Anne. *Who's Who in Fashion.* New York: Fairchild, 1988.

Trahey, Jane. *Harper's Bazaar: One Hundred Years of the American Female.* New York: Random House, 1967.

Wilson, Elizabeth. *Adorned in Dreams: Fashion and Modernity.* Berkeley: University of California Press, 1987.

Wolfe, Tom. *From Bauhaus to Our House.* New York: Farrar, Straus & Giroux, 1981.

Yarwood, Doreen. *Fashion in the Western World, 1500–1990.* New York: Drama, 1992.

Government and Politics

Allison, Graham T. *Essence of Decision: Explaining the Cuban Missile Crisis.* Boston: Little, Brown, 1971.

Ambrose, Stephen E. *Eisenhower: The President.* New York: Simon & Schuster, 1984.

Bass, Jack. *Taming the Storm: The Life and Times of Judge Frank Johnson and the South's Fight Over Civil Rights.* Garden City, N.Y.: Doubleday, 1993.

Bennett, David. *The Party of Fear: From Nativist Movements to the New Right in American History.* Chapel Hill: University of North Carolina Press, 1988.

Beschloss, Michael R. *The Crisis Years: Kennedy and Khruschev, 1960–1963.* New York: Harper & Row, 1991.

———, ed. *Taking Charge: The Johnson White House Tapes, 1963–1964.* New York: Simon and Schuster, 1997.

Bickel, Alexander M. *Politics and the Warren Court.* New York: Harper & Row, 1965.

Bornet, Vaughan Davis. *The Presidency of Lyndon Johnson.* Lawrence: University Press of Kansas, 1983.

Branch, Taylor. *Parting the Waters: America in the King Years, 1954–1963.* New York: Simon & Schuster, 1988.

———. *Pillar of Fire: America in the King Years, 1963–1965.* New York: Simon and Schuster, 1998.

Caputo, Philip. *Rumor of War.* New York: Holt, Rinehart, and Winston, 1977.

Caro, Robert A. *The Years of Lyndon Johnson: Master of the Senate.* New York: Knopf, 2002.

———. *The Years of Lyndon Johnson: Means of Ascent.* New York: Knopf, 1990.

———. *The Years of Lyndon Johnson: The Path to Power.* New York: Knopf, 1982.

Carter, Daniel T. *Politics of Rage: George Wallace, the Origins of the New Conservatism, Transformation of American Politics.* New York: Simon and Schuster, 1995.

Caute, David. *The Year of the Barricades: A Journey Through 1968.* New York: Harper & Row, 1970.

Dallek, Robert. *Flawed Giant: Lyndon Johnson and his times, 1961–1973.* New York: Oxford University Press, 1998.

Evans, Sara. *Personal Politics: The Roots of Women's Liberation in the Civil Rights Movement and the New Left.* New York: Knopf, 1979.

Farber, David. *The Age of Great Dreams: America in the 1960s.* New York: Hill & Wang, 1994.

Frankel, Benjamin, ed. *The Cold War, 1945–1991: Leaders and Other Important Figures in the United States and Western Europe.* Detroit: Gale Research, 1992.

Garthoff, Raymond. *Reflections on the Cuban Missile Crisis.* Washington, D.C.: Brookings Institution, 1989.

Goodwin, Doris Kearns. *Lyndon Johnson and the American Dream.* New York: Harper & Row, 1976.

Halberstam, David. *The Best and The Brightest.* New York: Random House, 1972.

———. *The Making of a Quagmire.* New York: Random, 1965.

Hamilton, Nigel. *J.F.K.: Reckless Youth.* New York: Random House, 1992.

Hayden, Tom. *Reunion: A Memoir.* New York: Random House, 1988.

Heath, Jim F. *Decade of Disillusionment: The Kennedy-Johnson Years.* Bloomington: Indiana University Press, 1975.

Hersh, Seymour M. *The Dark Side of Camelot.* Boston: Little, Brown, 1997.

Himmelstein, Jerome. *To The Right: The Transformation of American Conservatism.* Berkeley: University of California Press, 1990.

Hodgson, Godfrey. *The World Turned Right Side Up: A History of the Conservative Ascendancy in American.* Boston: Houghton Mifflin, 1996.

Horowitz, David. *Radical Son: A Generational Odyssey.* New York: Free Press, 1997.

Kaplan, Fred. *The Wizards of Armageddon.* New York: Simon & Schuster, 1983.

Karnow, Stanley. *Vietnam: A History.* New York: Penguin, 1983.

Katz, Michael B. *The Undeserving Poor: From the War on Poverty to the War on Welfare.* New York: Pantheon, 1989.

Kennedy, Robert F. *Thirteen Days: A Memoir of the Cuban Missile Crisis.* New York: Norton, 1969.

Kissinger, Henry. *White House Years.* Boston: Little, Brown, 1979.

LaFeber, Walter. *America, Russia and the Cold War, 1945–1984.* 5th ed. New York: Knopf, 1985.

Lichtenstein, Nelson, ed. *Political Profiles: The Johnson Years.* New York: Facts on File, 1976.

———. *Political Profiles: The Kennedy Years.* New York: Facts on File, 1976.

MacNeil, Robert. *The People Machine: The Influence of Television on American Politics.* New York: Harper & Row, 1968.

Magnet, Myron. *The Dream and the Nightmare: The Sixties' Legacy to the Underclass.* New York: Bantam, 1993.

Mandelbaum, Michael. *The Nuclear Question.* New York: Cambridge University Press, 1979.

Marable, Manning. *Race, Reform and Rebellion.* Jackson: University Press of Mississippi, 1991.

Matusow, Allen J. *The Unraveling of America: A History of Liberalism in the 1960's.* New York: Harper & Row, 1984.

Miller, James. *"Democracy Is in the Streets": From Port Huron to the Siege of Chicago.* New York: Simon & Schuster, 1987.

Morris, Charles R. *A Time of Passion: America 1960–1980.* New York: Harper and Row, 1984.

Oberdorfer, Don. *Tet!* New York: Da Capo Press, 1984.

Pearson, Hugh. *Huey Newton and the Price of Black Power in America.* Reading, Mass.: Addison-Wesley, 1994.

Posner, Gerald. *Case Closed: Lee Harvey Oswald and the Assassination of JFK.* New York: Random, 1993.

Reeves, Thomas C. *A Question of Character: A Life of John F. Kennedy.* New York: Free Press, 1991.

Sale, Kirkpatrick. *SDS.* New York: Random House, 1973.

Schlesinger, Arthur, Jr. *A Thousand Days.* Boston: Houghton Mifflin, 1965.

Schwartz, Bernard, ed. *The Warren Court: A Retrospective.* New York: Oxford University Press, 1996.

Schwarz, John E. *America's Hidden Success: A Reassessment of Twenty Years of Public Policy.* New York: Norton, 1983.

Sorenson, Theodore. *Kennedy.* New York: Harper & Row, 1965.

Stern, Mark. *Calculating Visions: Kennedy, Johnson, and Civil Rights.* Brunswick, N.J.: Rutgers University Press, 1992.

Van Deburg, William L. *New Day in Babylon: The Black Power Movement and American Culture, 1965–1975.* Chicago: University of Chicago Press, 1992.

White, Theodore H. *The Making of the President 1960.* New York: Atheneum, 1961.

———. *The Making of the President 1964.* New York: Atheneum, 1965.

———. *The Making of the President 1968.* New York: Atheneum, 1969.

Wofford, Harris. *Of Kennedy and Kings: Making Sense of the Sixties.* Pittsburgh: University of Pittsburgh Press, 1980.

Law and Justice

Abraham, Henry J. *Justices, Presidents, and Senators: A History of the U.S. Supreme Court Appointments From Washington to Clinton.* New York: Rowman & Littlefield, 1999.

Chafe, William Henry, ed. *Remembering Jim Crow: African Americans Tell About Life in the Segregated South.* New York: New Press, 2001.

Clayborne, Carson, and Martin Luther King Jr. *In Struggle: SNCC and the Black Awakening of the 1960s.* Boston: Harvard University Press, 1995.

Foner, Philip, Martin Luther King Jr., and Julian Bond. *The Black Panthers Speak.* Cambridge, Mass.: Da Capo Press, 1995.

Franklin, John Hope, and Alfred A. Moss, Jr. *From Slavery to Freedom: A History of African Americans.* New York: Knopf, 2000.

Hall, Kermit L., ed. *The Oxford Companion to the Supreme Court.* New York: Oxford University Press, 1992.

Harrison, Maureen, and Steve Gilbert, eds. *Landmark Decisions of the United States Supreme Court II.* Beverly Hills, Calif.: Excellent Books, 1992.

Horwitz, Morton J. *The Warren Court and the Pursuit of Justice.* New York: Hill and Wang, 1999.

Kelly, Alfred H., Winfred A. Harbison, and Herman Belz. *The American Constitution: Its Origins and Development.* Vol. 2. 7th ed. New York: Norton, 1991.

Mikula, Mark F., and L. Mpho Mabunda, eds. *Great American Court Cases.* Farmington Hills, Mich.: Gale Group, 2000.

Palmer, Kris E., ed. *Constitutional Amendments: 1789 to the Present.* Farmington Hills, Mich.: Gale Group, 2000.

West's Encyclopedia of American Law, 2d ed. 12 vols. St. Paul, Minn.: West Publishing Co.

Websites

"The Chicago Seven Trial." Available onlinehttp://www.law .umkc.edu/faculty/projects/ftrials/Chicago7/chicago7.html; website home page: http://www.law.umkc.edu/faculty/projects /ftrials/ftrials.htm (accessed April 20, 2003).

"Mississippi Burning Trial." Available online http://www.law .umkc.edu/faculty/projects/ftrials/price&bowers/price&bowers .htm; website home page: http://www.law.umkc.edu/faculty /projects/ftrials/ftrials.htm (accessed April 20, 2003).

"The Oyez Project of Northwestern University, a U.S. Supreme Court Multimedia Database." Available online at http://www .oyez.com (accessed April 20, 2003).

"The Presidents of the United States." Available online at http://www.whitehouse.gov/history/presidents/; website home page: http://www.whitehouse.gov (accessed April 20, 2003).

"U.S. Supreme Court Opinions." Available online at http:// www.findlaw.com/casecode/supreme.html; website home page: http://www.findlaw.com (accessed March 16, 2003).

Lifestyles and Social Trends

Anderson, Terry H. *The Movement and the Sixties.* New York: Oxford University Press, 1995.

Archer, Jules. *The Incredible Sixties: The Stormy Years That Changed America.* San Diego: Harcourt Brace Jovanovich, 1986.

Bailey, Beth L. *From Front Porch to Back Seat: Courtship in Twentieth-Century America.* Baltimore: Johns Hopkins University Press, 1988.

Branch, Taylor. *Parting the Waters: America in the King Years, 1954–1963.* New York: Simon & Schuster, 1988.

———. *Pillar of Fire: America in the King Years, 1963–65.* New York: Simon & Schuster, 1998.

Bromell, Nicholas. *Tomorrow Never Knows: Rock and Psychedelics in the 1960s.* Chicago: University of Chicago Press, 2000.

Burner, David. *Making Peace With the 60s.* Princeton, N.J.: Princeton University Press, 1996.

Casale, Anthony M., and Philip Lerman. *Where Have All the Flowers Gone?: The Fall and Rise of the Woodstock Generation.* Kansas City: Andrews and McMeel, 1989.

Cavallo, Dominick. *A Fiction of the Past: The Sixties in American History.* New York: St. Martin's Press, 1999.

Chepesiuk, Ronald. *Sixties Radicals, Then and Now: Candid Conversations With Those Who Shaped the Era.* Jefferson, N.C.: McFarland & Co., 1995.

Clecak, Peter. *America's Quest For the Ideal Self: Dissent and Fulfillment in the 60s and 70s.* New York: Oxford University Press, 1983.

Dudley, William, ed. *The 1960s.* San Diego: Greenhaven Press, 2000.

Fairclough, Adam. *Better Day Coming: Blacks and Equality, 1890–2000.* New York: Viking, 2001.

Frank, Thomas. *The Conquest of Cool: Business Culture, Counterculture, and the Rise of Hip Consumerism.* Chicago: University of Chicago Press, 1997.

Gitlin, Todd. *The Sixties: Years of Hope, Days of Rage.* New York: Bantam Books, 1987.

Gitter, Michael, and Sylvie Anapol. *Do You Remember?: The Book That Takes You Back.* San Francisco: Chronicle Books, 1996.

Gregory, Ross. *Cold War America, 1946 to 1990.* New York: Facts on File, 2003.

Gross, Michael. *My Generation: Fifty Years of Sex, Drugs, Rock, Revolution, Glamour, Greed, Valor, Faith, and Silicon Chips.* New York: Cliff Street Books, 2000.

Gunnell, John A. *Sensational '60s: Wheels of Change.* Iola, Wis.: Krause Publications, 1994.

Hall, James C. *Mercy, Mercy Me: African-American Culture and the American Sixties.* New York: Oxford University Press, 2001.

Hampton, Henry, and Steven Fayer. *Voices of Freedom: An Oral History of the Civil Rights Movement From the 1950s Through the 1980s.* New York: Bantam Books, 1990.

Issel, William. *Social Change in the United States, 1945–1983.* New York: Macmillan, 1985.

Kaiser, Charles. *1968 in America: Music, Politics, Chaos, Counterculture, and the Shaping of a Generation.* New York: Weidenfeld & Nicolson, 1988.

Kallen, Stuart A., ed. *Sixties Counterculture.* San Diego, Calif.: Greenhaven Press, 2001.

Kowinski, William. *The Malling of America: An Inside Look at the Great Consumer Paradise.* New York: Morrow, 1985.

Lasch, Christopher. *The Culture of Narcissism: American Life in an Age of Diminishing Expectations.* New York: Norton, 1991.

Leuchtenburg, William E. *A Troubled Feast: American Society Since 1945.* Boston: Little, Brown, 1983.

Marty, Myron A. *Daily Life in the United States, 1960–1990: Decades of Discord.* Westport, Conn.: Greenwood Press, 1997.

McWilliams, John C. *The 1960s Cultural Revolution.* Westport, Conn.: Greenwood Press, 2000.

Salmond, John A. *"My Mind Set on Freedom": A History of the Civil Rights Movement, 1954–1968.* Chicago: Ivan R. Dee, 1997.

Sommer, Robin. *"I had one of those": Toys of Our Generation.* New York: Crescent Books, 1992.

Stern, Jane, and Michael Stern. *Sixties People.* New York: Knopf, 1990.

Wright, Lawrence. *In the New World: Growing Up With America, 1960–1984.* New York: Knopf, 1988.

Websites

"The 1960s: Primary Sources From American Popular Culture." Available online at http://www.authentichistory.com/1960s .html (accessed April 22, 2003).

"The 1969 Woodstock Festival and Concert." Available online at http://www.woodstock69.com/ (accessed April 22, 2003).

"American Cultural History, 1960–1969." Available online at http://kclibrary.nhmccd.edu/decade60.html (accessed April 22, 2003).

"The Civil Rights Era." Available online at http://memory .loc.gov/ammem/aaohtml/exhibit/aopart9.html (accessed April 22, 2003).

Media

Altschuler, Glenn C., and David I. Grossvogel. *Changing Channels: America in TV Guide.* Urbana: University of Illinois Press, 1992.

Applebaum, Irwyn. *The World According to Beaver.* New York: Bantam, 1984.

Barnouw, Erik. *Tube of Plenty: The Evolution of American Television.* 2d ed. New York: Oxford University Press, 1990.

Bartimus, Tad, et al. *War Torn: Stories of War From the Women Reporters Who Covered Vietnam.* New York: Random House, 2002.

Bodroghkozy, Aniko. *Groove Tube: Sixties Television and the Youth Rebellion.* Durham, N.C.: Duke University Press, 2001.

Collins, Jim, ed. *High-Pop: Making Culture into Popular Entertainment.* Malden, Mass.: Blackwell Publishers, 2002.

Cook, Philip S., Douglas Gomery, and Lawrence W. Lichty, eds. *The Future of News: Television-Newspapers-Wire Services-Newsmagazines.* Baltimore: Johns Hopkins University Press, 1992.

———. *The World Through a Monocle: The New Yorker at Midcentury.* Cambridge, Mass.: Harvard University Press, 1999.

Douglas, Susan J. *Listening In: Radio and the American Imagination, From Amos 'n' Andy and Edward R. Murrow to Wolfman Jack and Howard Stern.* New York: Times Books, 1999.

Draper, Robert. *Rolling Stone Magazine: The Uncensored History.* New York: Doubleday, 1990.

Erickson, Hal. *Syndicated Television: The First Forty Years, 1947–1987.* Jefferson, N.C.: McFarland, 1989.

Greenfield, Jeff. *Television: The First Fifty Years.* New York: Crescent Books, 1981.

Hallin, Daniel C. *The Uncensored War: The Media and Vietnam.* New York: Oxford University Press, 1986.

Jones, Gerard. *Honey, I'm Home: Sitcoms, Selling the American Dream.* New York: Grove Weidenfeld, 1992.

Kozol, Wendy. *Life's America: Family and Nation in Postwar Photojournalism.* Philadelphia: Temple University Press, 1994.

Landy, Elliott. *Woodstock Vision: The Spirit of a Generation.* New York: Continuum, 1994.

MacDonald, J. Fred. *One Nation Under Television: The Rise and Decline of Network TV.* New York: Pantheon Books, 1990.

McLuhan, Marshall. *The Medium Is the Massage.* New York: Random House, 1967.

Stark, Steven D. *Glued to the Set: The 60 Television Shows and Events That Made Us Who We Are Today.* New York: Free Press, 1997.

Trow, George W.S. *My Pilgrim's Progress: Media Studies, 1950–1998.* New York: Pantheon Books, 1999.

Turner, Kathleen J. *Lyndon Johnson's Dual War: Vietnam and the Press.* Chicago: University of Chicago Press, 1985.

Websites

"The Black Panther Newspaper Collection." Available online at http://www.etext.org/Politics/MIM/bpp/index.html (accessed April 22, 2003).

"Herblock's History: Political Cartoons From the Crash to the Millennium." Available online at http://www.loc.gov/rr /print/swann/herblock (accessed April 22, 2003).

"Vietnam on Film and Television." Available online at http://lists.village.virginia.edu/sixties/HTML_docs/Resources /Bibliographies/VN_on_TV_entry.html (accessed April 22, 2003).

"The Wolfman Jack Online Museum." Available online at http://www.wolfmanjack.org/ (accessed April 22, 2003).

Medicine and Health

Adler, Gerry. *Medicare 2000: 35 Years of Improving America's Health and Security.* Baltimore: Health Care Financing Administration, 2000.

Bender, Arnold E. *A Dictionary of Food and Nutrition.* New York: Oxford University Press, 1995.

The Cambridge World History of Human Disease. New York: Cambridge University Press, 1993.

Carlson, Rick J. *The End of Medicine.* New York: Wiley, 1975.

Cartwright, Frederic Fox. *Disease and History.* New York: Crowell, 1972.

Cassedy, James H. *Medicine in America: A Short History.* Baltimore: Johns Hopkins University Press, 1991.

Clark, Faith, ed. *Symposium III: The Changing Patterns of Consumption of Food.* International Congress of Food Science and Technology, Proceedings of the Congress Symposia, 1962, Vol. 5. New York: Gordon & Breach Science, 1967.

Companion Encyclopedia of the History of Medicine. London: Routledge, 1993.

Dixon, Bernard. *Beyond the Magic Bullet.* New York: Harper & Row, 1978.

Dolan, John Patrick. *Health and Society: A Documentary History of Medicine.* New York: Seabury, 1978.

Duke, Martin. *The Development of Medical Techniques and Treatments: From Leeches to Heart Surgery.* Madison, Conn.: International Universities Press, 1991.

Gizzi, Peter. *Artificial Heart.* Providence, Rhode Island: Burring Deck, 1998.

Long, Esmond R. *A History of Pathology.* New York: Dover, 1965.

Lyons, Albert S. *Medicine: An Illustrated History.* New York: Abrams, 1978.

National Institutes of Health. *Facts About Heart and Heart-Lung Transplants.* Bethesda, Md.: National Heart, Lung and Blood Institute, 1997.

Nolen, William A. *A Surgeon's World.* New York: Random House, 1972.

Nuland, Sherwin B. *Doctors: the Biography of Medicine.* New York: Knopf, 1988.

Paul, John R. *A History of Poliomyelitis.* New Haven, Conn.: Yale University Press, 1971.

Professional Guide to Diseases. 6th ed. Springhouse, Pa.: Springhouse, 1998.

Reiser, Stanley Joel. *Medicine and the Reign of Technology.* New York: Cambridge University Press, 1978.

Stephens, Trent D., and Rock Brynner. *Dark Remedy: The Impact of Thalidomide and Its Revival as a Vital Medicine.* Cambridge, Mass: Perseus Publishers, 2001.

Stevens, Rosemary. *American Medicine and the Public Interest.* New Haven, Conn.: Yale University Press, 1971.

U.S. Department of Health, Education, and Welfare. *Smoking and Health.* Washington, D.C.: GPO, 1964.

Valenstein, Elliot S. *Great and Desperate Cures.* New York: Basic, 1986.

Websites

"Arthritis Today: An Arthritis Timeline." Available online at http://www.arthritis.org/resources/arthritistoday/2000_archives/2000_01_02_TimeLine.asp (accessed April 20, 2003).

"Artificial Heart." Available online at http://inventors.about.com/library/inventors/artificialheart.htm (accessed April 20, 2003).

Califano, Joseph A., Jr. "What Was Really Great About the Great Society." Available online at http://www.washingtonmonthly.com/features/1999/9910.califano.html (accessed April 20, 2003).

"History of Heart Transplantation." Available online at http://www.heart-transplant.org/history (accessed April 20, 2003).

"The History of Medicine: 1966–Present." Available online at http://www.medhelpnet.com/medhist10.html (accessed April 20, 2003).

Johnson, Lyndon B. "President Lyndon B. Johnson's Annual Message to the Congress on the State of the Union." Available online at http://www.lbjlib.utexas.edu/johnson/archives.hom/speeches.hom/680117.asp (accessed April 20, 2003).

Johnson, Lyndon B., and Harry S. Truman. "President Lyndon B. Johnson's Remarks With President Truman at the Signing in Independence of the Medicare Bill." Available online at http://www.lbjlib.utexas.edu/johnson/archives.hom/speeches.hom/650730.asp (accessed April 20, 2003).

Levison, Robin K. "How About an Ectomorph, Mesomorph, Endomorph or Something in Between?" Available online at http://www.weightlosscontrol.com/bodytypes.htm (accessed April 20, 2003).

"Medicine and Madison Avenue—Timeline." Available online at http://scriptorium.lib.duke.edu/mma/timeline.html (accessed April 20, 2003).

"The Reports of Surgeon General: The 1964 Report on Smoking." Available online at http://www.sgreports.nlm.nih.gov/NN/Views/Exhibit/narrative/smoking.html (accessed April 20, 2003).

"Thalidomide." Available online at http://science-education.nih.gov/nihHTML/ose/snapshots/multimedia/ritn/Thalidomide (accessed April 20, 2003).

"United States Cancer Mortality From 1900 to 1992." Available online at http://www.healthsentinel.com/Vaccines/DiseaseAndRelatedData_files/she (accessed April 20, 2003).

Religion

Ammerman, Nancy T. *Bible Believers: Fundamentalists in the Modern World.* New Brunswick, N.J.: Rutgers University Press, 1987.

Beckwith, Bernham P. *The Decline of U.S. Religious Faith, 1912–1984.* Palo Alto, Calif.: B.P. Beckwith, 1985.

Bellah, Robert N., and Frederick E. Greenspahn, eds. *Uncivil Religion: Irreligious Hostility in America.* New York: Crossroads, 1987.

Brown, Charles C. *Niebuhr and His Age: Reinhold Niebuhr's Prophetic Role in the Twentieth Century.* Philadelphia: Trinity Press International, 1992.

Carroll, Jackson W. *Beyond Establishment: Protestant Identity in a Post-Protestant Age.* Louisville, Ky.: Westminster/John Knox, 1993.

Cavert, Samuel McCrea. *The American Churches in the Ecumenical Movement, 1900–1968.* New York: Association Press, 1968.

Cooney, John. *The American Pope: The Life and Times of Francis Cardinal Spellman.* New York: Times Books, 1984.

Cox, Harvey. *Turning East: The Promise and Peril of the New Orientalism.* New York: Simon & Schuster, 1977.

Dolan, Jay P. *The American Catholic Experience.* Garden City, N.Y.: Doubleday, 1985.

Eighmy, John L. *Churches in Cultural Captivity: A History of the Social Attitudes of Southern Baptists.* Knoxville: University of Tennessee Press, 1987.

Ellwood, Robert S. *The Sixties Spiritual Awakening: American Religion Moving From Modern to Post Modern.* New Brunswick, N.J.: Rutgers University Press, 1994.

Garrow, David. *Bearing the Cross: Martin Luther King Jr., and the Southern Christian Leadership Conference.* New York: Morrow, 1986.

George, Carol V. *God's Salesman: Norman Vincent Peale and the Power of Positive Thinking.* New York: Oxford University Press, 1992.

Gilkey, Langdon B. *Catholicism Confronts Modernism: A Protestant View.* New York: Seabury, 1975.

———. *Gilkey on Tillich.* New York: Crossroad, 1990.

Hunter, James Davison. *American Evangelicalism: Conservative Religion and the Quandary of Modernity.* New Brunswick, N.J.: Rutgers University Press, 1983.

Jones, Donald G., and Russell E. Richey, eds. *American Civil Religion.* San Francisco: Mellen Research University Press, 1990.

Mahan, Wayne W. *Tillich's System.* San Antonio: Trinity University Press, 1974.

Martin, Bernard. *The Existentialist Theology of Paul Tillich.* New York: Bookman Associates, 1963.

Martin, William C. *A Prophet With Honor: The Billy Graham Story.* New York: Morrow, 1991.

Marty, Martin. *Pilgrims in Their Own Land: 500 Years of Religion in America.* Boston: Houghton Mifflin, 1984.

Miller, Robert Moats. *Bishop G. Bromley Oxnam: Paladin of Liberal Protestantism.* Nashville, Tenn.: Abingdon Press, 1990.

Pauck, Wilhelm, and Marion Pauck. *Paul Tillich: His Life and Thought.* New York: Harper & Row, 1976.

Quebedeaux, Richard. *The Worldly Evangelicals.* New York: Harper & Row, 1978.

Rowley, Peter. *New Gods in America.* New York: McKay, 1971.

Shapiro, Edward S. *A Time for Healing: American Jewry since 1945.* Baltimore: Johns Hopkins University Press, 1992.

Stone, Ronald H. *Reinhold Niebuhr: Prophet to Politicians.* Nashville, Tenn.: Abingdon Press, 1972.

Wagerin, Ruth. *The Children of God: A Make-Believe Revolution?* Westport, Conn: Bergin & Garvey, 1993.

Walker, Brooks R. *Christian Fright Peddlers.* Garden City, N.Y.: Doubleday, 1964.

Wilson, Edmund. *The Dead Sea Scrolls, 1947–1969.* New York: Oxford University Press, 1969.

Zaretsky, Irving I., and Mark P. Leone, eds. *Religious Movements in Contemporary America.* Princeton, N.J.: Princeton University Press, 1974.

Science and Technology

Abshire, Gary M., ed. *The Impact of Computers on Society and Ethics: A Bibliography.* Morristown, N.J.: Creative Computing, 1980.

Belzer, Jack, Albert G. Holzman, and Allen Kent, eds. *Encyclopedia of Computer Science and Technology.* 16 vols. New York: Marcel Dekker, 1975–1981.

Bernstein, Jeremy, and Gerald Feinberg, eds. *Cosmological Constants: Papers in Modern Cosmology.* New York: Columbia University Press, 1986.

Carnegie Library of Pittsburgh, Science and Technology Department. *Science & Technology Desk Reference.* Detroit: Gale Research, 1993.

Haugelan, J. *Artificial Intelligence: The Very Idea.* Cambridge, Mass.: MIT Press, 1985.

Katz, Leslie, ed. *Fairy Tales for Computers.* Boston: Nonpareil Books, 1969.

Leakey, Richard E., and Roger Lewin. *Origins: What New Discoveries Reveal About the Emergence of Our Species and Its Possible Future.* New York: Dutton, 1977.

MacKinnon, Edward M. *Scientific Explanations and Atomic Physics.* Chicago: University of Chicago Press, 1982.

McGraw-Hill Encyclopedia of Science and Technology. 9th ed. 14 vols. New York: McGraw-Hill, 1993.

Mescowitz, Sam, ed. *The Coming of Robots.* New York: Collier, 1963.

Metropolis, N., ed. *A History of Computing in the Twentieth Century.* New York: Academic Press, 1980.

Mumford, Lewis. *The Myth of the Machine: The Pentagon of Power.* New York: Harcourt Brace Jovanovich, 1964.

Nelkin, Dorothy. *Science Textbook Controversies and the Politics of Equal Time.* Cambridge, Mass.: MIT Press, 1977.

Popper, Karl. *Realism and the Aim of Science.* Totowa, N.J.: Rowman and Littlefield, 1983.

Schichtle, Cass. *The National Space Program From the Fifties to the Eighties.* Washington, D.C.: GPO, 1983.

Silverberg, Robert, ed. *Men and Machines.* New York: Meredith Press, 1968.

Simon, Herbert Alexander. *Sciences of the Artificial.* Cambridge, Mass.: MIT Press, 1969.

Stanley, Steven M. *The New Evolutionary Timetable.* New York: Basic Books, 1981.

Trigg, George L. *Landmark Experiments in Twentieth Century Physics.* New York: Crane, Russak, 1975.

Websites

"ARS Research Timeline—Story on Green Revolution." Available online at http://www.ars.usda.gov/is/timeline/green.htm (accessed April 22, 2003).

"Bathyscaphe Trieste." Available online at http://www.wikipedia.org/wiki/Bathyscaphe_Trieste (accessed April 22, 2003).

Bethe, Hans A. "Energy Production in Stars." Available online at http://www.nobel.se/physics/laureates/1967/bethe-lecture.html (accessed April 22, 2003).

"Human Evolution: The Fossil Evidence in 3D." Available online at http://www.anth.ucsb.edu/projects/human (accessed April 22, 2003).

"The Human Origins Program at the Smithsonian Institution." Available online at http://www.mnh.si.edu/anthro/humanorigins (accessed April 22, 2003).

"NASA Apollo 11 30th Anniversary." Available online at http://history.nasa.gov/ap11ann/introduction.htm (accessed April 22, 2003).

"Peopling of the Americas." Available online at http://www.nationalgeographic.com/scw/ngm_0209_sub_popup.html (accessed April 22, 2003).

"Rachel Carson.org." Available online at http://www.rachelcarson.org (accessed April 22, 2003).

"Thomas Kuhn." Available online at http://www.emory.edu/EDUCATION/mfp/kuhnsnap.html (accessed April 22, 2003).

"William Schopf, Professor of Paleobiology & Director of IGPP CSEOL." Available online at http://www.ess.ucla.edu/faculty/schopf (accessed April 22, 2003).

Sports

Abrahams, Harold Maurice. XVII Olympiad, Rome. London: Cassell, 1960.

Allen, Maury. Roger Maris: A Man for All Seasons. New York: D. I. Fine, 1986.

Bunning, Jim. The Story of Jim Bunning. Philadelphia: Lippincott, 1965.

Burchard, S.H. Elvin Hayes. New York: Harcourt, Brace and Jovanovich, 1980.

Butler, Hal. Al Kaline and the Detroit Tigers. Chicago: Regnery, 1973.

Chamberlain, Wilt, and David Shaw. Wilt: Just Like Any Other 7-foot Black Millionaire Who Lives Next Door. New York: MacMillan, 1973.

Chapin, Dwight, and Jeff Prugh. The Wizard of Westwood: Coach John Wooden and His UCLA Bruins. Boston: Houghton Mifflin, 1973.

Cousy, Bob, and John Devaney. The Killer Instinct. New York: Random House, 1975.

Fischler, Stan. Stan Mikita; The Turbulent Career of a Hockey Superstar. New York: Cowles, 1969.

Flemming, Peggy, and Peter Kaminksy. The Long Program: Skating Toward Life's Victories. New York: Pocket, 1999.

Foyt, A.J., and William Neely. A.J. New York: Times Books, 1983.

Johnson, Patricia H., et al. A Horse Named Kelso. New York: Funk and Wagnalls, 1970.

Johnson, Rafer. The Best That I Can Be: An Autobiography. New York: Doubleday, 1998.

Knight, Bobby, and Bob Hammel. Knight: My Story. New York: Thomas Dunne, 2002.

Kram, Mark. The Ghost of Manila: The Fateful Blood Feud Between Muhammad Ali and Joe Frazier. New York: HarperCollins, 2001.

Krull, Kathleen, and David Diaz. Wilma Unlimited: How Wilma Rudolph Became the World's Fastest Woman. San Diego: Harcourt Brace, 1996.

Libby, Bill. Parnelli; A Story of Auto Racing. New York: Dutton, 1969.

Macht, Norman L. Frank Robinson. New York: Chelsea, 1991.

McCormack, Mark H. Arnie, The Evolution of a Legend. New York: Simon and Schuster, 1967.

Nicklaus, Jack, and Ken Bowden. Jack Nicklaus: My Story. New York: Simon and Schuster, 1997.

Olsen, James T., and Harold Henrikson. Muhammad Ali: "I Am the Greatest." Mankato, Minn.: Creative Education, 1974.

Palmer, Arnold, and James Dodson. A Golfer's Life. New York: Ballantine, 1999.

Parker, Robert. Carol Heiss: Olympic Queen. Garden City, N.Y.: Doubleday, 1961.

Patterson, Floyd. Victory Over Myself. New York: Scholastic, 1962.

Pepe, Phil. Kareen Abdul-Jabbar. New York: Grossett & Dunlap, 1970.

Petty, Richard, and William Neely. King Richard I: The Autobiography of America's Greatest Auto Racer. New York: MacMillan, 1986.

Rainbolt, Richard. Basketball's Big Men. Minneapolis: Lerner, 1975.

Ralbovsky, Martin. Destiny's Darlings. New York: Hawthorn Books, 1974.

Remnick, David. King of the World: Muhammad Ali and the Rise of An American Hero. New York: Random, 1998.

Riess, Steven A., ed. The American Sporting Experience. West Point, N.Y.: Leisure Press, 1984.

Ryun, Jim, and Michael R. Phillips. In Quest of Gold: The Jim Ryun Story. San Francisco: Harper and Row, 1984.

Scalzo, Joe, and Bobby Unser. The Bobby Unser Story. Garden City, N.Y.: Doubleday, 1979.

Schollander, Don, and Duke Savage. Deep Water. New York: Crown, 1971.

Shapiro, Miles, and Nathan Irvin Huggins. Bill Russell. New York: Chelsea, 1991.

Starr, Bart, and Murray Olderman. Starr: My Life in Football. New York: Morrow, 1987.

Staubach, Roger, and Frank Luksa. Time Enough to Win. Waco, Tex.: World Books, 1980.

Tosches, Nick. The Devil and Sonny Liston. Boston: Little, Brown, 2000.

West, Jerry, and Bill Libby. Mr. Clutch: The Jerry West Story. Englewood Cliffs, N.J.: Prentice-Hall, 1969.

Wills, Maury, and Mike Celizic. On the Run: The Never Dull and Always Shocking Life of Maury Wills. New York: Carroll & Graf, 1991.

Zalewski, Ted, and John Nelson. Bobby Hull: The Golden Jet. Mankato, Minn.: Creative Education, 1973.

PRIMARY SOURCE TYPE INDEX

Primary source authors appear in parentheses. Page numbers in italics indicate images, and those followed by the letter t indicate tables.

Primary source authors appear in parentheses. Page numbers in italics indicate images, and those followed by the letter *t* indicate tables.

Primary source authors appear in parentheses. Page numbers in italics indicate images, and those followed by the letter *t* indicate tables.

Primary source authors appear in parentheses. Page numbers in italics indicate images, and those followed by the letter *t* indicate tables.

GENERAL INDEX

Page numbers in bold indicate primary sources; page numbers in italic indicate images; page numbers in bold italic indicate primary source images; page numbers followed by the letter t *indicate tables. Primary sources are indexed under the entry name with the author's name in parentheses. Primary sources are also indexed by title. All primary sources can be identified by bold page locators.*

A

ABC (American Broadcasting Co.), sports broadcasting, 600–604

Abdul-Jabbar, Kareem, *657,* 655–658
  autobiography, **655–657**

Abortion, 447–449

Actresses, *38, 353*

Adams, Don, *397*

Aegyptopithecus, 568–570, *569, 570*

Aerospace industry, 111–112

AFL (American Football League), 639–640

AFL-CIO (American Federation of Labor/Congress of Industrial Organizations), 77–81

African American actors, *38*

African American athletes
  Abdul-Jabbar, Kareem, 655–658, *657*
  Ali, Muhammad, 644–649, *646*
  Chamberlain, Wilt, 649–654, *651*
  Olympic protests, 1968, 634–638, *635*
  Rudolph, Wilma, 659–663, *660, 662*
  Russell, Bill, 630–634, *632*

African American children, 139–141, *140*

African American dancers, 52–57, *53*

African American playwrights, 37, *38*

African American singers, 12–15

Aged, marketing to, 70–73, *71*

"Aggression from the North," 238–241
  paper (Rusk), **239–241**

Agnew, Spiro T., 424–428, *427*
  interview, **426–428**
  speech, **425–426**

"Agnew Tells Why He Says What He Says" (Agnew), **426–428**

Alabama, governors, *334*

Albee, Edward, 15–16, *16*
  play script, **16–18**

Albert, Marv, 653

Alcindor, Lewis. *See* Abdul-Jabbar, Kareem

Alcohol abuse, in fiction, 351–355

Aldrin, Edwin E., 422, 423–424, *575, 576–578*
  autobiography, **577–578**
  photograph, *576*

Ali, Muhammad, 644–649, *646*
  autobiography, **645–647**
  interview, **647**

All In the Family, 360

"All My Pretty Ones," 21–23
  poem (Sexton), **22–23**

Ambassadors (U.S.), *210*

American Atheists, 490

American Broadcasting Co. (ABC), sports broadcasting, 600–604

The American Dream, 15–18
  play script (Albee), **16–18**

"The American Dream" (King), **245–248**

American education, 121–126

American Federation of Labor/Congress of Industrial Organizations (AFL-CIO), 77–81

American Football League (AFL), 639–640

American Medical Association (AMA)
  journal article, **467–470**

"And Here's Johnny . . . ," 391–393
  article *(Newsweek),* **392–393**

Anderson, David
  newspaper article, **640–641**

Animism, 516

Anti-evolution statutes, 531–535

Antiwar movement
  Chicago Seven, 316–321
  Columbia University, 169–171
  Democratic convention demonstrations, Chicago, 412–416, *414*
  growth of, 374
  poetry, 42–43
  posters, *378*
  Students for a Democratic Society, 158–161, *159*
  See also Vietnam War, conscientious objectors, Draft resistance

AP (Associated Press)
  photograph, *192*

Apes, evolution of, 568–570, *569*

Apollo 11, 575–578, *575, 576*
  Manned Spacecraft Center and, 111–115
  significance of mission, 575–576

Page numbers in bold indicate primary sources; page numbers in italic indicate images;
page numbers in bold italic indicate primary source images; page numbers followed by the letter *t* indicate tables.

Page numbers in bold indicate primary sources; page numbers in italic indicate images;
page numbers in bold italic indicate primary source images; page numbers followed by the letter *t* indicate tables.

Page numbers in bold indicate primary sources; page numbers in italic indicate images; page numbers in bold italic indicate primary source images; page numbers followed by the letter *t* indicate tables.

Page numbers in bold indicate primary sources; page numbers in italic indicate images; page numbers in bold italic indicate primary source images; page numbers followed by the letter *t* indicate tables.

Page numbers in bold indicate primary sources; page numbers in italic indicate images; page numbers in bold italic indicate primary source images; page numbers followed by the letter *t* indicate tables.

Page numbers in bold indicate primary sources; page numbers in italic indicate images; page numbers in bold italic indicate primary source images; page numbers followed by the letter *t* indicate tables.

Page numbers in bold indicate primary sources; page numbers in italic indicate images;
page numbers in bold italic indicate primary source images; page numbers followed by the letter *t* indicate tables.

Page numbers in bold indicate primary sources; page numbers in italic indicate images; page numbers in bold italic indicate primary source images; page numbers followed by the letter *t* indicate tables.

Page numbers in bold indicate primary sources; page numbers in italic indicate images; page numbers in bold italic indicate primary source images; page numbers followed by the letter *t* indicate tables.

Page numbers in bold indicate primary sources; page numbers in italic indicate images;
page numbers in bold italic indicate primary source images; page numbers followed by the letter *t* indicate tables.

Page numbers in bold indicate primary sources; page numbers in italic indicate images;
page numbers in bold italic indicate primary source images; page numbers followed by the letter *t* indicate tables.

Page numbers in bold indicate primary sources; page numbers in italic indicate images; page numbers in bold italic indicate primary source images; page numbers followed by the letter *t* indicate tables.

Page numbers in bold indicate primary sources; page numbers in italic indicate images;
page numbers in bold italic indicate primary source images; page numbers followed by the letter *t* indicate tables.